ISBN 978-1-5282-5688-9
PIBN 10941739

1 MONTH OF
FREE
READING

at
www.ForgottenBooks.com

By purchasing this book you are eligible for one month membership to ForgottenBooks.com, giving you unlimited access to our entire collection of over 1,000,000 titles via our web site and mobile apps.

To claim your free month visit:
www.forgottenbooks.com/free941739

HEARING
BEFORE THE
UNITED STATES
COMMISSION ON CIVIL RIGHTS

HEARING HELD
IN
SAN FRANCISCO, CALIFORNIA
May 1–3, 1967
and
OAKLAND, CALIFORNIA
May 4–6, 1967

HEARING

BEFORE THE

UNITED STATES
COMMISSION ON CIVIL RIGHTS

———

HEARING HELD
IN
SAN FRANCISCO, CALIFORNIA
May 1–3, 1967
and
OAKLAND, CALIFORNIA
May 4–6, 1967

CR1.8:H 35/967

CONTENTS
SESSIONS

(iii)

EXHIBITS ENTERED INTO THE HEARING RECORD

*Exhibits 14, 19, 36, and 40 are individual complaints of discrimination based on race or national origin which were submitted to the Commission. These complaints have been handled through the Commission's regular complaint procedures. They are available for inspection from the commission.

UNITED STATES COMMISSION
ON CIVIL RIGHTS

MONDAY, MAY 1, 1967

The U.S. Commission on Civil Rights met at 10 a.m. in the Ceremonial Courtroom, Federal Building, Golden Gate Avenue, San Francisco, California, Eugene Patterson, Vice Chairman of the Commission, presiding.

PRESENT: Eugene Patterson, Vice Chairman; Frankie M. Freeman, Commissioner; The Reverend Theodore M. Hesburgh, C.S.C., Commissioner; Robert S. Rankin, Commissioner. Also present: William L. Taylor, Staff Director; Howard A. Glickstein, General Counsel.

PROCEEDINGS

VICE CHAIRMAN PATTERSON. This public hearing of the U.S. Commission on Civil Rights will come to order.

(Mrs. Sophie Eilperin was sworn in as Clerk. Mr. James Whelchel was sworn in as Reporter.)

VICE CHAIRMAN PATTERSON. Ladies and gentlemen, I am Eugene Patterson of Atlanta, Georgia, the Vice Chairman of the Civil Rights Commission. Our Chairman, Dr. John A. Hannah, of East Lansing, Michigan, who is President of Michigan State University, is unable to attend this opening session and will be with us tomorrow presiding in my place. I will introduce the other members of the Commission at this time.

On my immediate right is Mrs. Frankie M. Freeman of St. Louis, Missouri, who is Associate General Counsel of the St. Louis Housing and Land Clearance Authorities.

Seated next to Mrs. Freeman is Dr. Robert S. Rankin of Durham, North Carolina, Professor of Political Science at Duke University.

At my immediate left is the Reverend Theodore Hesburgh of South Bend, Indiana. Father Hesburgh is President of the University of Notre Dame.

Dean Erwin N. Griswold of Cambridge, Massachusetts, who is Dean of the Harvard University School of Law, will join us on Wednesday.

In addition to the Commissioners here present, William L. Taylor, Staff Director of the Commission, is seated next to Father Hesburgh and Howard A. Glickstein, General Counsel of the Commission, is seated at the left beside Mr. Taylor.

As the first order of business, I wish to express the Commission's appreciation to the many officials of the State of California, the counties of San Francisco, Contra Costa, Alameda, San Mateo, Marin, Sonoma, Napa, Santa Clara, and Solano and the many private organizations and citizens who have cooperated with us in the preparatory stages of this hearing.

This hearing is being held under the authority of the Civil Rights Act of 1957, as amended. As required by law, notice of the hearing was published in the Federal Register on March 29, 1967. A copy of this notice will be introduced in the record as Exhibit No. 1.

(The document referred to was marked Exhibit No. 1 and was received in evidence.)

VICE CHAIRMAN PATTERSON. The Commission on Civil Rights is an independent, bipartisan agency of the United States Government established by the Congress in 1957. Its duties are:

1. To investigate sworn allegations that citizens are being deprived of their right to vote by reason of their race, color, religion, or national origin;

2. To study and collect information concerning legal developments which constitute a denial of equal protection of the laws under the Constitution;

3. To appraise Federal laws and policies with respect to the equal protection of the laws;

4. To serve as a national clearinghouse for information with respect to denials of equal protection of the laws because of race, color, religion, or national origin; and, finally,

5. To investigate sworn allegations of vote fraud in Federal elections.

Under the law, the Commission submits reports to the President and the Congress containing its findings and its recommendations for corrective legislative or executive action.

To enable the Commission to fulfill its duties, the Congress has empowered the Commission to hold hearings and issue subpenas for the attendance of witnesses and the production of documents.

I know of no better way to explain the functions and limitations of this Commission than to quote briefly from a decision of the United States Supreme Court issued early in the Commission's life. The Court said, and I quote:

This Commission does not adjudicate; it does not hold trials or determine anyone's civil or criminal liability. It does not issue orders. Nor does it indict, punish or impose any legal sanctions. It does not make determinations depriving anyone of life, liberty or property. In short, the Commission does not and cannot take any affirmative action which will affect an individual's legal rights. The only purpose of its existence is to find facts which may subsequently be used as the basis for legal or executive action.

To carry out its legislative mandate, the Commission has held hearings in many parts of the country including Alabama, Arizona, the District of Columbia, Georgia, Illinois, Indiana, Louisiana, Massachusetts, Michigan, Mississippi, New Jersey, New York, Ohio, and Tennessee. The Commission held a hearing here in San Francisco and in Los Angeles in January 1960 on voting, housing, and education. Much of the civil rights legislation enacted in the past five years and several Presidential Executive orders reflect acceptance of findings and recommendations resulting from the Commission hearings.

Commission hearings seek to explore in one city or area the civil rights problems that are representative of problems elsewhere in the Nation. The purpose of this hearing is to collect information concerning civil rights problems in the Bay Area counties of San Francisco, Contra Costra, Alameda, San Mateo, Marin, Sonoma, Napa, Santa Clara, and Solano. This hearing in the San Francisco-Oakland Bay Area, like a hearing in Cleveland, Ohio, in April of 1966, is part of a national study of civil rights problems which the Commission is conducting in metropolitan urban centers which have significant minority group populations.

Our Bay Area hearing also inaugurates a new factfinding effort by the Commission to ascertain the status of equal opportunity for Spanish-speaking peoples throughout the country, a problem that is increasingly being brought to the attention of the Commission and other government agencies. The Commission's effort to learn more about the problems of our Spanish-speaking population will include a projected hearing, new research programs, and meetings of several of our State Advisory Committees.

At this hearing we will be concerned primarily with issues of housing and employment opportunity for Negroes, Spanish-speaking persons, and other minorities. Because the Bay Area consists of many geographical and political jurisdictions, we will have the opportunity to consider the civil rights problems of the core cities as they relate to the entire metropolitan community.

Members of the Commission staff began visiting the Bay Area several months ago and have interviewed hundreds of citizens; Federal, State, county, and municipal officials; and representatives of ethnic and civil rights organizations. Staff investigations have brought to our attention a variety of problems, but the restrictions of time allow us to hear testimony only from a limited number of witnesses on a limited number of issues. For example, we are aware that there is much concern in the Bay Area about the problem of securing equal educational opportunity for all children. But we have not made education a principal focus of this hearing because we have just concluded a major study in this field at the request of President Johnson. A report of that study entitled *Racial Isolation in the Public Schools* with recommendations for remedial action has been made to the President and the Congress.

In addition to developing a factual picture of civil rights problems involved in the issues of housing and employment, this hearing will afford the Commission the opportunity to learn about attitudes, interests and concerns of citizens which may encourage or retard meaningful solutions to civil rights problems. An understanding of the forces which tend to intensify or reduce racial isolation in our society is essential if America is to develop an open society free of racial antagonisms. Commission hearings traditionally have provided citizens and business, educational and cultural interests with a better understanding of the civil rights problems in their communities. In addition to pointing the way to Federal, State, and local remedial action, the Commission's hearings often serve to improve communications and create a better understanding between those living in the inner-city and those living outside it.

During the next 5½ days we will be hearing testimony from more than 75 witnesses, citizens who have grievances, public officials responsible for relevant government programs, and representatives of private organizations. They will provide us with information so that the facts pertaining to civil rights problems in this area can be appraised objectively and in context. The testimony we are to hear will help us and the citizens of this area to identify the barriers to equal opportunity in housing and employment. We also will learn of the steps being taken by government and the community to redress grievances and to secure equal opportunity for all citizens. As we secure information, we hope that the testimony will stimulate discussion and increase the understanding of civil rights problems among responsible community leaders and government officials.

The first three days of this hearing will be in San Francisco and the final 2½ days in Oakland. The testimony presented at each place, however, will pertain to problems in communities throughout the Bay Area.

This session of the hearing will recess at 12:50 for lunch. We will resume at 2:15 p.m. and conclude at 6 p.m. Tomorrow, we will begin at 11:30 a.m. and break at 5:30 for dinner. The Tuesday night session will begin at 7:30 and conclude at 10:30. On Wednesday we will begin in this courtroom at 9:30 a.m., recess for lunch at 12:30, resume at 2 p.m. and conclude at 6:30.

On Thursday and Friday, we will begin in the ballroom of the Oakland Auditorium at 10 Tenth Street at 9:15 a.m., recess for lunch at 12:30 p.m., resume at 1:45 p.m. and conclude at 5:30 p.m. The final session on Saturday in Oakland will begin at 9:15 a.m. and the hearing will adjourn at 12:30 p.m.

The testimony we will hear here and in Oakland will consist not only of facts and information, but also of opinion and comment about civil rights issues and problems in the Bay Area. I urge that those who follow this hearing give careful consideration to all points of view, even those points of view with which they may disagree. If there is agreement on one thing, it is that the problem of establishing equal opportunity and creating good relations among the races in the Nation's cities is of the utmost importance. This can be done only if people with differing points of view are able to approach each other with understanding and to work together toward equitable solutions to our most serious national problems.

I will now ask Commissioner Freeman to explain the Commission's rules and procedures. Mrs. Freeman.

COMMISSIONER FREEMAN. It is indeed appropriate that on Law Day our public hearing should start with a summary of the rules of procedure which are designed to insure that our proceedings are conducted in a fair and orderly manner.

At the outset I should emphasize that the observations I am about to make on the Commission's rules constitute nothing more than brief summaries of the significant provisions. The rules themselves should be consulted for a fuller understanding. Staff members will be available to answer questions which arise during the course of the hearing.

At the public hearing which begins today, almost all persons who are scheduled to appear have been subpenaed by the Commission. All testimony at the public sessions will be under oath and will be transcribed verbatim by the official reporter. Everyone who testifies, submits data or evidence is entitled to obtain a copy of the transcript on payment of costs. In addition, within 60 days after the close of the hearing, a person may ask to correct errors in the transcript of the hearing or his testimony. Such requests will be granted only to make the transcript conform to testimony as presented at the hearing.

All witnesses are entitled to be accompanied and advised by counsel. Counsel may subject his client to reasonable examination. He also may make objections on the record and argue briefly the basis for such objections.

If the Commission determines that any witness's testimony tends to defame, degrade, or incriminate any person, that person or his counsel may submit written questions which in the discretion of the Commission may be put to the witness. In addition, in such cases, the Commission may order such extension, recesses, or continuance of the public session as it deems necessary.

Under Section 102(e) of the Civil Rights Act of 1957, on which the Commission's authority to conduct these proceedings is based, the Commission may decide to receive in executive session evidence or testimony which in its judgment may tend to defame, degrade, or incriminate any person. Persons subpenaed to the public session may request that witnesses be subpenaed in their behalf. All requests for subpenas must be in writing and must be supported by a showing of the general relevance and materiality of the evidence sought.

In addition, all witnesses have the right to submit statements prepared by themselves or others for inclusion in the record provided they are submitted within the time required by the rules. Any person who has not been subpenaed may be permitted in the discretion of the Commission to submit a written statement at this public hearing. Such statements will be reviewed by the members of the Commission and made a part of the record.

Witnesses at Commission hearings are protected by the provisions of Title 18, U.S. Code, Section 1505, which make it a crime to threaten, intimidate, or injure witnesses on account of their attendance at government proceedings.

Copies of the rules which govern this hearing may be secured during any recess from a member of the Commission's staff. Persons who have been subpenaed have already been given their copies.

Finally, I should point out that these rules were drafted with the intent of insuring that Commission hearings be conducted in a fair and impartial manner. In many cases the Commission has gone significantly beyond Congressional requirements in providing safeguards for witnesses and other persons. We have done this in the belief that useful facts can be developed best in an atmosphere of calm and objectivity.

We hope that such an atmosphere will prevail at this hearing.

VICE CHAIRMAN PATTERSON. Thank you, Mrs. Freeman.

The Commission invited Governor Reagan to appear at this opening session of the hearing. His schedule secretary responded that, unfortunately, because of prior commitments during this week, he will not be able to participate, but had asked her to convey his thanks and to express his regrets at being unable to be here this morning.

We are, however, honored to have at this time the Chairman of the California State Advisory Committee to the United States Commission on Civil Rights present, and I would ask him to step forward to the witness chair at this time and say anything he would like. Bishop James A. Pike.

Be seated, if you will, Bishop Pike, and we will be very happy to hear from you.

STATEMENT OF THE RIGHT REVEREND JAMES A. PIKE, CHAIRMAN, CALIFORNIA STATE ADVISORY COMMITTEE TO THE U.S. COMMISSION ON CIVIL RIGHTS

BISHOP PIKE. Vice President, Vice Chairman, and Commissioner Patterson, my fellow priest, Commissioner Ted Hesburgh, and Commissioner Rankin, and Commissioner Freeman, Mr. Taylor, Mr. Simmons, Mr. Montez, the members of the California Committee present, the Commission's staff, witnesses, and friends.

My name for the record is the Right Reverend James A. Pike, Bishop of the Episcopal Church and staff member of the Center for the Study of Democratic Institutions in Santa Barbara.

I am very glad indeed to be here and to see this come about. I am feeling a little bit uncomfortable in the atmosphere of what seems like a judicial proceeding, being in a rather peculiar role in my own communion of Christians, kind of a bishop out on bail. I am glad I am free to be with you. I am not really nervous because the secular society has seen to it that the church can no longer burn its own officials.

On behalf of the California State Advisory Committee of this Commission, it is my pleasure to welcome the members of the Commission and of the staff to the State of California. We are extremely pleased, not just in a sentimental way, but in rather specific ways that the Commission, which held hearings here in 1960, has returned to California. I would like to read into the record, and for the benefit of our visitors, the names of our very hardworking, often to the sacrifice of their own interests and time, members of the California State Advisory Committee.

Also to show the kind of scope and coverage of our State that they represent.

I have introduced myself. I have been a member of the Committee, first appointed under the Eisenhower administration about 1959 and became Chairman about 1961 under the Kennedy administration and have continued under the Johnson administration. There is a point to that. Any newcomers to our work may not realize that this is a non-partisan Commission in its makeup from top to bottom, and we are not particularly interested in political advantages, either nationally or within a State, and while I cannot speak for all the other State Committees, I certainly can speak for the U.S. Civil Rights Commission and for our own State Committee. There has never been the slightest sign of our being other than non-partisan in the complete sense of the word.

We have certain biases. They are in favor of freedom of opportunity for all men, but that is not a political party bias.

In addition to myself, the Hon. Robert J. Drewes is our Vice Chairman and he is also Chairman of the Northern California Subcommittee. He is a municipal judge in San Francisco.

Stephen Reinhardt, Esq., is Vice Chairman of our Southern California Subcommittee, or rather Chairman of it and Vice Chairman of the State Committee. He is an attorney living in Los Angeles as Judge Drewes, indeed, lives in San Francisco.

Rabbi Morton A. Bauman, clergyman, from Tarzana, California in the San Fernando Valley.

Mr. William L. Becker, who lives in San Francisco, is director of the Human Rights Commission of San Francisco and during his time of serving on our Committee has served also as special assistant to the Governor in this general field and prior to that also was involved in the civil rights field.

Mrs. Marjorie Benedict of Berkeley is a teacher, former Republican National Committeewoman from California.

Reynaldo Carreon, Jr., M.D., is an eye specialist in Los Angeles and has a kind of hobby also of growing dates out in the Indio Desert somewhere, which he has been kind enough to supply to the members of our Committee annually, but it is not illegal, I don't think, for us to have such dates.

Bert N. Corona from Oakland is in the business of interior decoration.

The Hon. Mervyn M. Dymally, State Senator from Los Angeles.

The Reverend Donald E. Ganoung of Oakland is Director of Christians for Social Action. Father Ganoung is a priest of the Episcopal Diocese of California.

Mrs. Aileen C. Hernandez of San Francisco is a consultant and lecturer.

Dr. Harold W. Horowitz of Los Angeles is a university law professor, and from Sacramento Mrs. Carl Kuchman, housewife, and then in Los Angeles a municipal court judge, the Hon. Loren Miller, elevated to the bench since he has been on our Committee, and at one time Vice Chairman of the Committee.

Alpha L. Montgomery, Esq., an attorney in San Diego, and from San Francisco Howard N. Nemerovski, Esq., attorney at law. From Fresno Dr. Hubert Phillips, retired professor of Fresno State College.

Herman Sillas, Jr., Esq., attorney from Los Angeles, and Clinton W. White, Esq., attorney in Oakland.

We do hope that the reports and recommendations which we have forwarded over the years to the Commission have been of some help to it in preparing the present hearing, in the drafting of its reports, recommendations to the President and the Congress and perhaps for some general edification and information.

I would like to take this opportunity to describe for you and for our friends very, very briefly the highlights of our activities since your last visit.

In 1962, the Committee held open meetings in Los Angeles and in San Francisco and in Oakland on police-community relations. The hearings in Los Angeles, the great crowd in a courtroom in the State Building, perhaps the most colorful of our activities, two important public officials—this is no time to speak ill of the dead, in the case of one, and speak ill of a continuing public official in the case of another so I will not mention their names—prepared for our visit by suggesting that we had some connections with the Communist Party and also wondering why people from other parts of the State, other than Los Angeles, could invade Los Angeles to tinker with their affairs. Nevertheless, we called as witnesses many, many people, including one of these officials, and on the basis of that we issued some rather firm warnings about the situation in the ghetto there, including Central District and Watts, which we feel, on looking back on it, were quite to the point.

A church official there, embarrassed by some of the things we said, pointed out that the Chairman of the Committee did not represent the Episcopalians in Southern California, that being a separate diocese in our structure, and I answered to the A.P., no, I did not represent the Episcopalians in Southern California. I represented the Federal Government.

We saw what happened at Watts. We were polite. We didn't immediately say, "We told you so," though we had, but, rather, we waited until the McCone Commission was established in 1965 and we cooperated with the McCone Commission then investigating the Watts riot. After that Commission's publication of the report of its findings, our Southern California Subcommittee very carefully evaluated the report and prepared an analysis pointing out what we believe were deficiencies in the McCone Commission's recommendations for responding to the unmet human needs which were the underlying cause of the riots.

It is the opinion of our Committee that, as we saw it in 1962 and again in 1965, conflict between both Negroes and Mexican Americans in their relation to the police department in California continues to be a problem which should be of concern to every citizen. However, our report, which undoubtedly some of you have read, and which was distributed to every chief of police and other similar official in the State, shows that the situation is quite uneven. There are areas where very excellent relationships exist. There are areas where there are problems where very sound approaches are being taken to those problems. There are areas where there are difficulties but where obviously good intent and serious concern for them are evident. There have been some areas where we have not felt that the matter had been grasped or taken seriously enough.

Since the beginning of our activities in the State, we have also been aware that equal housing opportunities have not been a reality for members of the nonwhite races and for Spanish-speaking persons. We began our work in that field in about 1959. Since our hearings about that period, there have been certain improvements. It was a rather grim picture at that time, even in some rather surprising places.

We have attempted systematically to collect information relating to denials of equal opportunity and have supported statewide efforts to secure and retain existing fair housing laws and ordinances. We believe that the passage of the Unruh and Rumford

Acts were meaningful steps forward. The peril now before us, even though the Supreme Court of the State has held unconstitutional Proposition 14 which, by a two to one vote, struck down not only the Rumford Act but any opportunity or principal portions of it to have that kind of a fair housing law. Even though the Supreme Court struck that down, the legislature has up again the matter of its repeal now, since the people had voted as they did on the initiative measure. We are very concerned about that, obviously.

In 1964 in response to the initiation of this initiative measure supported primarily by the California Real Estate Association and local realty boards, the Committee held open meetings in Los Angeles, San Diego, and Oakland.

Facts developed that showed an increasing pattern of residential segregation and violations of law at that time, the law, after all, not having been repealed by the initiative yet. At that time we received cooperation without subpena power, which we lack as a State Committee, of almost all parties concerned except in the Oakland area where we were somewhat boycotted by the realty board, and having no subpena power we asked at that time that you or an appropriate number of you come out to our rescue and subpena these people. We were aware of your busyness and the fact that you, too, are volunteers essentially and there are other very important things which you were devoting your attention to and focusing it upon, and we were quite aware of that and we accepted with good grace your not coming, but I express that not as a complaint but to suggest that we are quite aware that we are related one to another. We feel in spirit you are back of us as we work on the home front. It would be quite natural to kind of cry out for some more imposing troops at certain points. Nevertheless, you are here now and we are very glad for that and that you are spending so much time in your hearings, a longer stretch than we, indeed, have spent in any one time, two days usually being our limit.

Based on information developed at these meetings, we concluded that although the real estate industry was critical of laws providing for equality of opportunity in housing, it had no affirmative program to increase the quality or quantity of housing available to Negroes and Mexican Americans. Subsequently we recommended the extension of the Executive order requiring nondiscrimination in federally assisted housing, that is Executive Order 11063, to cover existing housing and housing financed by savings and loan associations and other institutions whose deposits are insured by the Federal Deposit Insurance Corporation, the FDIC. The Committee also recommended that legislation be enacted to guarantee that all future Federal aid to metropolitan areas for housing and transportation be conditioned upon a community's making provision for adequate supply of low-cost housing which would be available on a nondiscriminatory basis.

In 1966, in line with the Commission's increased emphasis on problems of big city ghettos, and I must say because of my own involvement and that of other equivalent church officials, whatever calling or whatever quality of the various churches, in consideration of possible support for in the drafting of leaders in the field of community organization to come into the flatlands of West Oakland with the ecumenical church sponsorship, we all faced the gravest problem there so that we could have some public way of getting facts that could have bearings on decisions being made by dioceses, presbyteries, and so forth. I was wearing two hats at that point. One of them was called a Miter. We did hold a two-day open meeting in the flatlands of Oakland and focused on the specific problems of Negroes, Mexican Americans and Indians which, believe it or not, we have quite a lot of in increasing numbers in our less favored portions of the main metropolitan centers in this area, occasionally elsewhere, but largely in the less favored portions.

In housing, employment, welfare, police-community relations, and on part of your days over there, you can see for yourselves what is rather a distressing sight in that portion of Oakland in a State that is well advertised, particularly in large picture magazines, and whatever, as glistening beauty and progress and tidiness and modernity.

Our findings, based on the testimony at this meeting, dramatically demonstrate the fact that the gap between the standard of living between ghetto residents and the general standard of living for the white Anglo residents has very much widened. The residents appearing before the Committee vividly portrayed the debilitating effects of life in the ghetto.

Testimony was presented that indicated that the unemployment rate for Negroes was four times that of the white persons in the city of Oakland. An unusually high proportion of the population was found to be employed in low-paying menial jobs. Many persons testified to discriminatory hiring practices by public and private employers and discriminatory membership practices by trade unions. This is particularly acute and still is because of the very elaborate and expensive plan known as BART in the Bay Area, the Bay Area Rapid Transit, which will represent and already has in terms of cost and planning a very large scale and totally new transportation system for the whole Bay Area, where already it was apparent that unless something was done, that the very people whose houses and property would be torn up, or where they rent, by the emergence of BART into the scene, would be the very people not able to even be employed on the project because of the discriminatory practices of certain craft unions.

There is an organization in the area known as JOBART, taking the word "BART" and putting "J–O–B," kind of combining with it, representing many interests, church, secular or whatever, concerned that this discrimination pattern be broken down in connection with this major project.

As I say, we had testimony to show that there is a factual basis for this concern.

The enforcement of the Federal Executive order requiring equal employment opportunity on federally aided construction projects was found to be inadequate. Testimony was received indicating that State and local fair employment practices and human relations commissions were not effectively coping with problems of discrimination in employment because of insufficient funds and weak enforcement provisions in the statutes and ordinances. It is important to stress that. There are rumors about, and sometimes coming from the deprived, and one can understand why a slight paranoia can develop—sometimes we share it ourselves as a Committee. It is hard to keep our balance sometimes when we see some of these rather grave aspects of discrimination —that maybe certain Federal agencies for one reason or another really don't want to move on with these things and solve problems, but, actually, while we cannot judge motives and hearts, there is, to quote a medieval colleague, "One unto whom all hearts are open, all desires known, from whom no secrets are hid." We aren't judging motives, either positively or negatively, but there is nothing in our testimony at any point that has suggested that any Federal official, Commission, Board, Regional Representatives there had anything but complete desire to achieve the same ends that we all had, but we did see this factor over and over again of lack of sufficient funds and, therefore, lack of staffing and inadequate remedies in terms of either the provisions themselves or in terms of sanctions in order to get on with it.

Negroes and Mexican Americans in their statements before the Committee indicate a lack of confidence in the community's law enforcement, and they believe that they are not treated justly by the police. Here, too, I would like to say for the record, something known obviously by the Commissioners and by perhaps many here, we are not a court. In fact, our State Committee is less like one than your Commission, which is a quasi-judicial body in the administrative sense. Being a lawyer, and having written on administrative law, I recognize the judicial flavor and character of your hearings. We are much less of that sort of thing, of course. We are quite aware of that on law.

We would receive testimony, given freely without subpena, from persons who claimed certain injustices and even got right down to very detailed facts of events, but we never did at any point in the report or in any comment from the stage or podium, or dais or wherever we were sitting, make an adjudication in individual cases, because we had no opportunity or way of hearing both sides and cross-examination and documentary evidence and all that.

One may wonder then why we would hear one side and then the other, hear fine statements from police officers and chiefs of police one way and hear people say that this is the way it is. This is what happened to me or to my sister, or whatever.

One may wonder why we would allow such testimony to come in. Our theory all along in hearings of this type and also in terms of abuses or apparent abuses in housing was pretty much on the theory that where there is smoke there is fire. That is one thing, but, second, we felt that if in the community, particularly among a minority group, there is a strong sense that there is injustice, that in itself is a fact.

That is a fact that there is that sense of injustice, and it is an operative fact that operates in a circle as we found several times in police relations. If minority people feel that they will be treated unjustly, they act more difficult, in a more difficult way, which makes police feel more nervous around them and sometimes a little more trigger-happy, and the fact that these people know that that is the case makes them act again more hostile and the police feel less loved, or in fact, quite the reverse, somewhat hated, and you get a vicious circle operating, even if there is no factual basis at all behind any of it.

I am quite sure there is some factual basis behind some of it, but whether there was or not, we were trying to grasp a psycho-sociological phenomenon where there is this vicious circle operative and creating a great deal of difficulty in some of the communities predominantly inhabited by members of minority groups.

Now, to turn back to housing again, we found in Oakland, as we have found elsewhre, a great disparity between the need for low-cost housing and the supply of such housing. There is an inadequate supply of public housing. Urban renewal, highway and rapid transit programs and demolition, because of strict code enforcement programs were eliminating housing within the reach of the average resident at a higher rate than new construction was being made available.

When you go to Oakland, and I hope you have the tour that we went through, you will find vast areas of vacant lots, or vacant acreage in this area where for a long time things have been ripped down and nothing went ahead. It is right there in the city where at least the Federal Government or the city or whoever is holding it should turn it over to the growing of potatoes, or at least they could farm it and increase their edible income or their capacity to eat out of this, but it is blocked with fences and everything, and nobody can do anything.

A long time the land sat over there for a post office that never went there, but they ripped everything out to have a post office. Well, maybe they ought to grow flowers on it or food. I don't know. Nothing is going to happen.

Where people need housing, they need these various facilities, the old is ripped away, bad as it was and as much as it needed to be, and nothing new is put in its place. There are a combination of factors that are too complex to summarize here. But the total result is not a good thing. There is a visible scar on the landscape that tells the story, kind of sacramentally. It is an outward visible sign of the inward situation and is also a new cause of creating that which it symbolizes.

Now, many residents described alleged abuses in the administration of welfare programs. Again we weren't judging any particular case. We were simply getting what the mood was and how they were feeling about it and how it in turn made more difficult even the most well-meaning welfare program. Several persons complained of violations of privacy, humiliating procedures in establishing and maintaining eligibility, particularly with reference to the Aid to Needy Children, a problem you know of in other States. Inadequate supportive services available to aid welfare recipients. We, as a State Committee, expect to continue our explorations of problems affecting residents of the inner-city. In June we plan to hold a two-day meeting in East Los Angeles to collect information on the problems confronting approximately 75,000 Mexican American residents in that community, or portion of the city of Los Angeles.

Our preliminary investigations which have been approached with much care in advance meetings, indicate that our factfinding effort should be concerned with education, employment, public services, and again police-community relations.

We expect that the hearing that you will be holding during the next several days will contribute to greater public understanding of civil rights problems in this State and will suggest possible remedies which might be implemented by Government and private institutions, and, though it is not directly within the scope of the Commission, we have always felt that relations which might be implemented on a State, county, municipal level are not out of order, and give us leadership to work on those levels through interconnected organizations in the civil rights field or in the civic field generally to which we hope we can funnel some of these things.

Also, obviously, your very careful work based on much longer experience and the very notable membership our Committee makes up in quantity, but perhaps you have in greater quality, but with this leadership and national experience you have, and the staffing you have, we know that what you do here, the way you get at it, the procedures you follow, the kinds and types of witnesses that you have, what they say and what conclusions you draw, will be of inestimable guidance to us in our future work as we carry through on the local scene, hoping to continue to serve you, hoping to continue to serve our State and hoping to be one part of serving the whole cause of equality of opportunity for persons in this Nation and in the world.

We of the Committee believe it is essential that the Commission continue its investigative efforts and that steps be taken to disseminate fully to the community the information developed. So that speaking locally now, equality of opportunity may more and more become a real thing and not just a phrase or a homily in the Bay Area and in all of California. The Committee will lend its full support to any efforts you undertake, as I have said, and are very, very rewarded just by your coming, very much backed in our own efforts and already, even though you have hardly begun this particular important session, already very much stimulated to carry on ourselves by your coming. In fact, we are meeting this evening to begin to shape up further our next set of hearings, and we are doing that because we have thrown in an extra meeting because we have found our consciences touched and we are stimulated by the fact that we know that you are all as busy or busier than we are and have much more coverage in your volunteer work for the Government than we do. Because of that we figure that we had better meet again, too, and we will be with you in all your work, in thought, and since this is a pluralistic society, I cannot speak for every member of the Committee on this next comment, but I can say for myself certainly, and perhaps for other members of the Committee, and also in our prayers, and we hope that you have a very fine and fruitful session, and we know that you will. Thank you for this time.

VICE CHAIRMAN PATTERSON. Thank you, Bishop Pike. We are rewarded by your presence here this morning and grateful for the work that you are doing, you and your Committee.

Mr. Glickstein, would you call the first witness, please?

MR. GLICKSTEIN. Our first witness is Miss Leda Rothman, an attorney on the staff of the Commission, who will give us some background facts on the Bay Area.

(Whereupon, Miss Leda Rothman was sworn by the Vice Chairman and testified as follows:)

TESTIMONY OF MISS LEDA ROTHMAN, ATTORNEY, U.S. COMMISSION ON CIVIL RIGHTS

MISS ROTHMAN. Testimony at this hearing will focus on the Standard Metropolitan Statistical Area designated Oakland-San

Francisco which includes Alameda, Contra Costa, Marin, San Francisco, and San Mateo Counties. In 1965 the total population of these five counties was 3,020,800.

The population of San Francisco has remained relatively stable during the past 15 years compared to that of the surrounding communities; 775,357 persons lived in San Francisco in 1950, as compared to 756,900 in 1965. The composition of the population, however, has altered considerably. The nonwhite population has increased five-fold during the past 25 years. Negroes were estimated to constitute 14 percent of the population in 1965. In 1960, they were 10 percent of the total, while the Chinese-Japanese-Filipino group as a whole accounted for 7.9 percent of San Francisco's population and persons of Spanish surname for 7 percent.

Generally, minority group persons in San Francisco live in four areas—Hunters Point, the Western Addition (also known as the Fillmore), the Mission Area, and Chinatown. Hunters Point developed as a result of Negroes settling close to the shipyards during World War II. The Western Addition also was occupied by Negroes during the war, when the Japanese Americans who lived there were forced to move out.

In these areas problems of unemployment and poverty are severe. Twelve percent of the heads of families in these areas are unemployed and the others are concentrated in low occupational classifications. A Department of Labor survey of the Mission and Fillmore districts showed the unemployment rate in January 1967 in these areas to be 11 percent, compared to a rate of 4.5 percent for the entire San Francisco-Oakland Metropolitan Area. Twenty percent of those unemployed at the time of the survey in November had been out of work since July or earlier. The total subemployment rate for the area was 25 percent and the unemployment rate for teenagers was 35.7 percent.

Further, while 18 percent of the white families in San Francisco fall below the poverty level established by the State, 30 percent of the families in the Mission district, 40 percent of the families in Chinatown, 40 percent of the families in Western Addition, and 60 percent of the families in Hunters Point are below the level.

The most populous county in the Bay Area is Alameda, which is dominated by Oakland. In 1965, the population of Alameda County was 1,033,100. Oakland is a major manufacturing, trading, and shipping center, and represents the central focus of Alameda and Contra Costa Counties on the East Side of the Bay. Oakland's total population in 1965 was 385,700. Its population expanded rapidly during World War II. Between 1940 and 1945 alone, an estimated 76,000 new residents immigrated to Oakland. The shipping industry drew most of the newly arrived workers into Central and West Oakland where, because of wartime construction restrictions, they crowded into inadequate housing. Since then

Negroes have been moving eastward from their original settlements. After the war, many white families left Oakland for the suburbs and the racial composition of the city continued to change, reaching 26 percent nonwhite in 1960, and an estimated 36 percent nonwhite in 1965.

The unemployment rate for persons living in four areas designated by the Poverty Program as target areas is approximately 10.6 percent for males, 16.3 percent for females, as compared to 6.4 percent for males and 10.1 percent for females for all of Oakland. In individual target areas, the unemployment rate varies from 7 percent to 15.9 percent for males, and 8.1 percent to 21.1 percent for females.

The population of Contra Costa County was 509,900 in 1965. This was a growth in population of almost 25 percent since 1960. Richmond, the major city in the county, had an estimated population in 1966 of 78,000 persons, of whom 21,856 were Negro. Like other cities in the Bay Area, it has experienced a growth in minority population. Between 1950 and 1960 the Negro population in Richmond grew by 11 percent and the Spanish surname population, about one-third as large as the Negro population, grew by 18 percent. The total population of the city, however, decreased by 28 percent. In 1960, Richmond's population was 20 percent Negro. In 1966, it was 25 percent Negro.

Most of the population growth in the Bay Area, however, has occurred to the south of San Francisco and Oakland around the southern rim of the Bay in San Mateo, Santa Clara, and southern Alameda Counties. San Mateo County, immediately to the south of San Francisco, more than doubled in population during the 15-year period, growing from 235,659 in 1950 to 532,200 in 1965. Alameda County as a whole increased from 740,315 persons in 1950 to 1,033,100 in 1965, with virtually all the increase occurring outside of Oakland in the southern portions of the county.

The population increases in counties to the north (Contra Costa, Marin, Napa, Solano, and Sonoma) have not been as striking.

The Negro population in the Bay Area is confined primarily to the urban centers and relatively few Negroes reside in the surrounding or outlying counties. For example, in 1960 there were only 10,846 Negroes in all of San Mateo County, for the most part living in the communities of Menlo Park and East Palo Alto.

The Spanish-surname population, on the other hand, is found both in the central cities and in the suburbs. In 1960, for example, only about 35 percent of Alameda County's residents of Spanish origin resided within the city of Oakland.

Although minority group members are confined largely to the central cities, many job opportunities exist in outlying areas. Of the 1.4 million working residents of the nine-county greater Bay Area, only 43 percent now have jobs in San Francisco or Oakland.

In 1960, 11 percent of the residents of San Francisco and Oakland who worked were employed outside of these cities. This kind of reverse commuting is particularly common among nonwhites. Three times as many nonwhites commute from San Francisco to suburban jobs as come from the suburbs to San Francisco, while the number of whites who come in to work is double the number of those who commute outward. Despite the extent of commuting in the Bay Area, most people still tend to work near their homes with the result that few minority group members work in industry located in suburban communities. A 1960 survey of the nine counties showed that at least a majority of residents in each county have jobs in the community in which they live.

VICE CHAIRMAN PATTERSON. Thank you, Miss Rothman. Will Counsel proceed to call the next witness?

MR. GLICKSTEIN. The next two witnesses are Mrs. Emma Fleming and Mr. David Evers.

(Whereupon, Mrs. Emma Fleming and Mr. David Evers were sworn by the Vice Chairman and testified as follows:)

TESTIMONY OF MRS. EMMA FLEMING, SAN FRANCISCO, CALIFORNIA, AND MR. DAVID EVERS, SAN FRANCISCO, CALIFORNIA

MR. GLICKSTEIN. Would you please each state your name and address for the record? Mrs. Fleming?

MRS. FLEMING. I am Emma Fleming. I live at 838 Kansas Street, San Francisco.

MR. EVERS. David K. Evers, 2100 - 18th Street, San Francisco.

MR. GLICKSTEIN. The area that you live in is known as Potrero Hill. Is that correct?

MR. EVERS. Yes.

MR. GLICKSTEIN. Now our map isn't terribly good, but that's in the northeastern corner of San Francisco overlooking the bay. Is that correct?

MR. EVERS. Northeastern?

MR. GLICKSTEIN. Yes.

MR. EVERS. No, southeastern.

MR. GLICKSTEIN. Do you think you could show us where that is on the map?

MR. EVERS. Perhaps you could say central east, right in here.

MR. GLICKSTEIN. Mrs. Fleming, how long have you lived on Potrero Hill?

MRS. FLEMING. I have lived there all my life. Do I have to say how many years?

MR. GLICKSTEIN. No. That's all right. Mr. Evers, is your business located on Potrero Hill?

MR. EVERS. Our office is on Potrero Hill.

MR. GLICKSTEIN. And did you live on Potrero Hill at one time?

MR. EVERS. Yes.

19

MR. GLICKSTEIN. Do you live there now?

MR. EVERS. No.

MR. GLICKSTEIN. Mr. Evers, do you and Mrs. Fleming represent a neighborhood organization on the Hill?

MR. EVERS. We represent the Potrero Hill Boosters and Merchants Association.

MR. GLICKSTEIN. Will you describe the nature of that organization?

MR. EVERS. It is an organization devoted to general neighborhood improvement. We are an improvement club, to the greatest extent, although we encourage merchant activity in the organization, too.

MR. GLICKSTEIN. You are the president of the organization?

MR. EVERS. Yes, I am.

MR. GLICKSTEIN. How many members does your organization have?

MR. EVERS. Our roster consists of over 200. However, these are families. So, considering at least two or possibly more than two to a family, we estimate our membership at about 500.

MR. GLICKSTEIN. Mrs. Fleming, would you please tell us what the requirements are for joining your organization?

MRS. FLEMING. I have a copy of our bylaws. I will paraphrase them.

MR. GLICKSTEIN. Would you please paraphrase them?

MRS. FLEMING. The requirements are anybody interested in the good and improvement of the neighborhood and the only restriction, actually, usually is that they must be a resident six months.

MR. GLICKSTEIN. Do most of the members of your organization rent or own their own homes?

MRS. FLEMING. The majority own.

MR. GLICKSTEIN. And how long have most of them lived on the hill?

MRS. FLEMING. I think it would average out about 30 years.

MR. GLICKSTEIN. Thirty years or so. Mr. Evers, would you please indicate what kind of projects your organization has been involved with?

MR. EVERS. I have a list. May I refer to that?

MR. GLICKSTEIN. Certainly.

MR. EVERS. We have participated in activities such as zoning. There is a new zoning law that went into effect several years ago. We expressed our concern that the density be kept low. There was a revision to that law quite recently, which we supported. This was to further reduce the density. We have been active in such things as traffic control, I mean the need for traffic signs, stop signs, and safety of that nature. We have tried to protect the neighborhood from encroachment by freeways, with no success, from encroachment by a bridgehead that was proposed for trans-Bay crossing. Apparently we have been successful in that regard.

We strive for better transportation, better bus transportation with not too much success. We have various projects to encourage beautification. The most recent was a tree-planting ceremony that took place last Friday at the Water Department property on the Hill.

We try to encourage upkeep, maintenance, and improvements through our newspaper. We have a monthly bulletin that we put out to keep the members and other interested people informed as to what we are doing and what is happening.

Other things, some of which was before my time, the people in the organization have fought hard for a junior high which is going to be soon erected on the Hill. I understand, too, that the members were quite vocal and influential in getting our branch library on the Hill, and also attaining improvements, or I don't know whether it was improvements or a new construction of Jackson Playground which is at the base of the Hill, and things of that nature.

MR. GLICKSTEIN. I understand that on top of Potrero Hill there is a public housing project that contains about 830-some-odd units, 192 of which are temporary and are scheduled to be demolished, and houses about 4,000 people. Mrs. Fleming, do any of the public housing projects residents belong to the Boosters?

MRS. FLEMING. No, we have invited them from time to time, and some have attended our meetings, but not too often.

MR. GLICKSTEIN. Do the neighborhood residents have much contact with the people in the project?

MRS. FLEMING. Well, when there is an activity of some sort, there is, but, frankly, there doesn't seem to be too much actual give-and-take between the projects and the people in the neighborhood, and I don't know just why this is.

In the school, for instance, in the school activities we have— even in our parent-faculty group we have even made a door-to-door contact to try to encourage attendance at the meetings. This wasn't too successful.

MR. GLICKSTEIN. Children from the project go to school together with the children from the neighborhood. Is that right?

MRS. FLEMING. Oh, yes.

MR. GLICKSTEIN. Are there any Negro families in the neighborhood who do not live in the project?

MRS. FLEMING. Oh, quite a number.

MR. GLICKSTEIN. Do they belong to the Boosters?

MRS. FLEMING. We have several, yes.

MR. GLICKSTEIN. You have several?

MRS. FLEMING. In fact, one is a past vice president.

MR. GLICKSTEIN. As I mentioned earlier some of the public housing, the temporary public housing on top of the Hill, is scheduled to be demolished.

Mrs. Fleming, what position has the Boosters taken with respect to the use of the land that would be vacated when this demolition takes place?

MRS. FLEMING. We have a very firm position that this should be released for private individual building, due to the overconcentration of public housing that we have on Potrero Hill.

May I say that before the war housing was built there, there was a great deal of misunderstanding. At the time, it was during the war, the Federal Government approached the people that owned the land and these people were all of this time under the impression that when that war housing was to be returned to the city that they would have the right of first refusal. But this, sad to say, was never put in any document. This was all verbal. So now this land is up, you might say, for grabs. It will go back to the city.

I would like to point out the reason that we feel it should be for private enterprise. We will have after this war housing is demolished, we will still have the largest concentration of low-income public housing of any other district in San Francisco, outside of Hunters Point, which is a much larger area. We have about 200 acres. This is our district. We are a very small district, and of that 200 acres, 15 acres are devoted to public housing. For out of all of San Francisco I believe the percentage is—we have 15 percent of the public housing in San Francisco compared to 1.5 percent for the rest of San Francisco.

MR. GLICKSTEIN. Mr. Evers, what effect has the housing project had on property values in the neighborhood generally?

MR. EVERS. All I can do is give you a guess. I don't have any facts at my disposal. I think in the property adjacent to the project, I think that it tends to discourage people from wanting to make improvements. I think it tends to lower the values.

MR. GLICKSTEIN. Lowers the value. Now, I understand that one of the proposals for constructing housing on top of the hill is for federally subsidized housing under the 221(d)(3) program, which provides for below-market interest rates.

Could you, Mr. Evers, explain why the organization is opposed to that type of housing?

MR. EVERS. We feel that it is simply an extension of public housing or that it will be quasi-public housing. In view of the fact that it is subsidized, there has been talk about subsidizing the land, either via means of the city giving it or selling it way below market to the Redevelopment Agency. This, as I understand it, would all be implemented through the Redevelopment Agency.

So there is that subsidy. There is or there is bound to be a subsidy in property taxes. This has been the case in St. Francis Square and then, too, we have rent subsidies which we feel would tend to create more of an aspect of low-income public housing to this type of so-called moderate-priced housing that has been proposed.

MR. GLICKSTEIN. Mr. Evers, what is the attitude of most of the persons living in your neighborhood toward the persons living in the project?

MR. EVERS. Well, I don't know what you mean exactly. I don't know that there is a great attitude one way or the other. Could you be more specific?

MR. GLICKSTEIN. Are the people friendly, hostile, concerned? Do they feel threatened?

MR. EVERS. I wouldn't say friendly. I wouldn't say hostile. I think probably there is a feeling that it is a different class of people primarily because they are low-income people and concentrated and not the property owner type that at least our membership is. There is sort of a variance, a variation or a difference in social outlook, let's say.

MR. GLICKSTEIN. What are the attitudes toward Negroes in general, not just the people in the project? How do the people in the neighborhood feel about the Negroes who can afford to move into a house or are moving in?

MR. EVERS. I know of no attitude one way or the other. There are always going to be individuals that feel a certain way, but as far as a general resentment or a fear, or whatever you want to call it, of minority groups, I know of none that exists.

MR. GLICKSTEIN. Mrs. Fleming, do you think that if Negroes moved into the neighborhood in large numbers that some of the residents would be inclined to move out?

MRS. FLEMING. Well, if they moved into the neighborhood in larger numbers, we would be subject to some of this stabilization program. We would have to start being—we would be subject to one of these programs where you have to—what is it? Desegregate. Because we are very well integrated now. Not only with Negroes, with just about every race, ethnic group that you can mention. We have them all.

MR. GLICKSTEIN. When you say very well integrated, can you estimate how many Negro families are living in that neighborhood?

MRS. FLEMING. I couldn't begin to do that. I mean, I guess the school population would show that better than anything, but I couldn't begin to estimate how many families there are. I couldn't begin to estimate how many families there are either owning or renting outside of the project.

MR. GLICKSTEIN. How many Negro families do you have in your organization?

MRS. FLEMING. In our organization? At the present time I believe there are two.

MR. GLICKSTEIN. Mr. Evers, what do you believe could be done by a neighborhood group such as yours to improve conditions in the projects?

MR. EVERS. To improve conditions in the projects?

MR. GLICKSTEIN. That's right.

MR. EVERS. I imagine it is just maintaining liaison with the Housing Authority primarily, if a need for improvements within is evidenced. It is a question of voicing these facts to the Authority.

MR. GLICKSTEIN. How about the tenants in the projects? What responsibility do you think they have, if any?

MR. EVERS. I understand there is an organization in the projects. I haven't followed their activities. I can't tell you too much about them, but I understand their purpose is to effect improvements, at least in the physical plant of the project.

MR. GLICKSTEIN. Have they been very effective?

MR. EVERS. As I said, I haven't been on top of it. I understand that they have made some gains.

MR. GLICKSTEIN. I have no further questions.

VICE CHAIRMAN PATTERSON. Father Hesburgh, do you have any questions of the witnesses?

COMMISSIONER HESBURGH. This is probably a rather vague question and may not come through very well, but I will try to make it as clear as I can. Mr. Evers, could it be assumed generally that the neighborhood's total sense of community is more among the private home owners than the people in the public housing project? In other words, are there really two communities here rather than one?

MR. EVERS. I can't speak for the organization on that point, but I think there tends to be a separation of them.

COMMISSIONER HESBURGH. I wasn't thinking of your organization so much as a way of describing the community *per se*. In other words, is this really two communities?

MR. EVERS. Well, as I say, I think there is a tendency to be two communities, yes.

COMMISSIONER HESBURGH. Is there any effort to bridge that gap between the two communities?

MR. EVERS. I can't think of anything specific that has been done that I know of.

COMMISSIONER HESBURGH. What I am trying to lead towards here is would it be a good thing to have one community instead of two communities or is this humanly very difficult?

MR. EVERS. Yes, I would say.

COMMISSIONER HESBURGH. Well, I think perhaps Mrs. Fleming might like to speak to that.

MRS. FLEMING. Yes. We have tried to have communication and activities combined, but especially when—I know when my son was in grammar school we did try, and even now when there is any type of activity, we do try to participate, for instance, in bazaars. Some of our members are active, not just in the going as spectators. They actually take part in the bazaars. They had a fair about a year or so ago and quite a few of our members, not only our members donated—our merchant members donated—but many of our members went to help. This kind of stuff. But inviting them to our meetings, there is a hesitancy to come. Frankly, I don't know why. It could be the difference in interests, due to the fact that the majority of our people in our organization are home owners.

COMMISSIONER HESBURGH. Would there be an economic factor difference, too?

MRS. FLEMING. Well, no. But the economic factor would cause a little resentment, to this extent, that there are people in the projects some of them that have a higher income than the people outside of the projects.

COMMISSIONER HESBURGH. The reason for my questions, which I think I should explain to you two, I am not hostile in any sense, but simply trying to get something of the anatomy of the community and this growing out of a conviction, after seeing these situations around the country, that the community has to solve its own problems, and it can only do it if it becomes a community and it is difficult to do it if there are two distinct disparate communities instead of one.

MR. EVERS. May I make another statement along that line? We have a semi-official stand in favor of scattered public housing rather than the concentrated barracks type of public housing that is thrown into one spot. This, I feel, and I think I speak for the organization, is one of the factors that would tend to create a separate community rather than allow for an inter-relationship of the public housing residents with the other people in the community.

COMMISSIONER HESBURGH. You think that shared physical concentration geographically in one spot makes for a divergence between the two communities?

MR. EVERS. Yes.

COMMISSIONER HESBURGH. Thank you.

VICE CHAIRMAN PATTERSON. Mrs. Freeman?

COMMISSIONER FREEMAN. Mrs. Fleming and Mr. Evers, you reside in the Potrero Hills area and so do the residents of the low-income public housing units as well as those who are occupants of the temporary war residence units. I would like to know if you and the members of your association feel that by virtue of being home owners that you have a greater right there than the residents of the lower income housing units?

MRS. FLEMING. I don't believe that. I have lived there all my life. I am a native of Potrero Hill and I don't think that I have any more rights than the people in the projects. But, on the other hand, I believe I have as much. I don't know if I am saying that— if I am saying what I mean. Some of the demands recently that have been made have put the home owner in a very, very disturbing position and I don't think this is fair, and this isn't right.

COMMISSIONER FREEMAN. But the point of my question is that I believe that you as a resident are not being threatened with relocation or displacement; the persons who live there now and who are being threatened with displacement have suggested that they would prefer 221(d)(3) housing. Is this correct?

MRS. FLEMING. I don't believe the people—I don't know. I understand an informal questionnaire was circulated to the people in the Wisconsin Project. I haven't seen the results of that questionnaire. The Housing Authority has not as yet sent out an official questionnaire to the people in the Wisconsin Project. Just recently we had another war housing project that just within this past year has been demolished. Our junior high school is going on that area. As I understand it, nobody was evicted. Nobody had to move. They were given preference to move.

One thing that you must understand, the majority of the people in the war housing are over-income.

COMMISSIONER FREEMAN. This is the point that I am making. If the people who live there, they would prefer 221(d)(3), then they would be the ones who would live there. Then I am trying to understand your opposition to it since you would not be displaced by it.

MRS. FLEMING. We are not opposing 221(d)(3) because of the people that live there. We are opposing it because we will have an economic ghetto if we will have more government subsidized housing. If 221(d)(3) is the ideal solution, as it was suggested that it would be good to have 221(d)(3) adjacent to low income public housing, so as the people, as it were, graduate or become over-income for public housing, they may move into 221(d)(3), possibly with a rent supplement. This is an extension of public housing, and this is our point. We are trying to upgrade our neighborhood with all types, not just racially, economically, too; and we cannot have—and this is our main, I would say—stand. We cannot have Potrero Hill after working so hard to upgrade it, be designated as some sort of a station, way station for people that are displaced by action in other parts of the city.

COMMISSIONER FREEMAN. Well, then you consider a stigma attached to public housing?

MRS. FLEMING. No, I am sorry if I gave that impression. I didn't mean it that way. It is just an over-concentration. When you have

35 percent of your area in public housing, I think this is enough
for one district to assimilate: our churches, our Boy Scouts, these
type of services, you cannot assimilate more.

COMMISSIONER FREEMAN. Well, I didn't understand that there
was any assimilation going on, because in the Association of the
200 families only two are Negro. That is not very much assimilation.

MRS. FLEMING. This 221(d)(3) housing, we have checked into
this. The people that are displaced by Government action, for instance, redevelopment, freeways, what have you, have priority and
FHA have told us that they will furnish the tenants for these
apartments. San Francisco is in dire need of 221(d)(3) housing
to take care of all of the displaced persons from redevelopment.
Sad to state, most of them are minority people that will be displaced. This is the sad thing about redevelopment in San Francisco. So we do need—there is a crying need for 221(d)(3) to relocate these people, but our point is that it should not be on Potrero
Hill.

COMMISSIONER FREEMAN. You want it somewhere else?

MRS. FLEMING. That's right. One point in line with that: all of
eastern San Francisco, there is no public housing of any kind west
of Twin Peaks, and if San Francisco is to continue furnishing this
subsidized housing, it seems to me then some of the other parts of
San Francisco should bear some of this over-concentration, rather
than having it all in one section of San Francisco. We have, on one
hand, different agencies that are fighting segregation in the schools,
de facto segregation in the schools, ghettos, segregation in the
ghettos and things of this kind, and on the other hand, we have an
agency that wants to build some more of this type of housing, to
just multiply the problem of de facto segregation.

COMMISIONER FREEMAN. Thank you.

VICE CHAIRMAN PATTERSON. Dr. Rankin.

COMMISSIONER RANKIN. Would you be willing to accept a
reasonable amount of this type of housing on Potrero Hill, for
instance?

MRS. FLEMING. Well, our feeling is that with 15 of our precious
acres used for public housing, if this is such a good thing and a
ghetto is such a bad thing, then why not break up the ghetto and
take some of those 641 permanent housing units and convert them
to 221(d)(3) housing?

COMMISSIONER RANKIN. So your position is not against it, it's
to scatter it? Is this correct?

MRS. FLEMING. Scatter it again, not on Potrero Hill. We have
too much. If they were to break up the 641, that is another thing,
but to scatter some more housing on top of 641 housing units, this
is just too much.

COMMISSIONER RANKIN. Just one more question. Is your organization unique in San Francisco or are there others like yours? Do you happen to know about other areas in the neighborhood?

MRS. FLEMING. I don't know any area in San Francisco that has exactly the same problems that we do, but there are many organizations like us that are interested in improvement and upgrading of the neighborhood, and not worried about race. This we don't worry about. We are primarily concerned in having our district grow into the fine—we have the best climate, the best views in San Francisco, and we are—Mayor Shelley once balanced housing in San Francisco. Well, I think Potrero Hill is entitled to balanced housing, too, and I certainly think that the people that say, "Look, Ma, I want to do it myself," should have a chance.

COMMISSIONER RANKIN. Thank you.

VICE CHAIRMAN PATTERSON. I have one question, Mrs. Fleming. If the land adjacent to the existing public housing were made available for private development upon the destruction of the temporary housing, what type of housing—perhaps Mr. Evers could answer this better. What type of housing would you expect private enterprise to build there adjacent to the public housing?

MR. EVERS. Well, we figure let nature take its course. Of course, within the confines of the present zoning laws that we have, we like to encourage homes or smaller apartment house type structures. We do not favor the large multi-unit type of apartment house, although we have no specific stand against that sort of structure.

VICE CHAIRMAN PATTERSON. Thank you very much.

Any further questions? Mr. Taylor?

MR. TAYLOR. Mr. Evers, you said you were aware of the existence in the public housing projects of an organization, but I gather that you do not have much contact with that organization?

MR. EVERS. I personally haven't. I understand some of our members have visited their meetings, but I personally am not on top of it at all.

MR. TAYLOR. What would happen if your organization suggested a meeting with the residents, members of that organization, to discuss jointly what the desires of the people in the neighborhood might be?

MR. EVERS. You say what would happen if our organization suggested such a meeting?

MR. TAYLOR. Yes.

MR. EVERS. I don't know.

MR. TAYLOR. Would it be worthwhile consulting with people who live in the projects to determine what their views are about their own housing needs or about the neighborhood as a whole?

MR. EVERS. Perhaps from an informative point of view. I think they are doing a decent job with the Housing Authority, but possibly there would be something to be gained by it. I couldn't say.

MR. TAYLOR. You also said, I believe, that there are other similar organizations, organizations similar to your own throughout the city of San Francisco. Is that right?

MR. EVERS. Mrs. Fleming answered to that, but that is correct. I mean improvement clubs are quite common in San Francisco.

MR. TAYLOR. Am I correct in assuming that there might be some resistance among some of these organizations to the entry of public housing or low-income housing into their neighborhoods?

MR. EVERS. Are you asking me?

MR. TAYLOR. Either you or Mrs. Fleming.

MRS. Fleming. I think there would be.

MR. TAYLOR. If it is your belief that housing policies should be that low-income housing should be scattered throughout the city, would it be useful for your organization to discuss with similar organizations this belief and this feeling that this would be a good policy?

MRS. FLEMING. Well, I think, if I may answer this, I don't see where—I don't quite follow you, where you mean to discuss with the organization, other organizations about that this would be a good policy. I think that the housing projects, the way they are at present, is what is making people shy away from public housing, the barracks, the hundreds and hundreds of people put into one little spot. I think this is what is giving the public housing a much worse reputation than it deserves.

I would like to add something to the question, if I may, that you asked about the meeting with the organization in the housing projects. This organization, I believe, some of it gets some help from the EOC, the anti-poverty program, and it seems, since the anti-poverty program there seems to be more and more of a wall between the district and the projects. And the idea is that more and more is equal, separate but equal. Services are to be separate but equal. All these things are to be right within the confines of the project, and when they are discussed, when they discuss Potrero Hill, the residents—I mean outside the project—are referred to as the people on the other side of the Hill. We met once in connection with a community Christmas party. There had been several informal discussions to see why there is this lack of communication. There is a lack of communication. Even when we sit around the table we don't communicate, and there have been several informal hearings to try to resolve this, and out of this, this CIA, this is the improvement club in the housing project, came up with a wonderful idea to have a community Christmas party. Well, there wasn't enough time. This was, oh, maybe two weeks before our own Christmas party, and there wasn't enough time to participate as an organization, but many of our individual members did participate insofar as helping to prepare the party and all.

It ended up in a children's party, which was a huge success. It was a very fine affair and, as I understand, at a later date, when I guess they and we get around to it, we hope to have an adult get-together. There has been discussion along this line because I am sure they realize and we realize that there just is a complete lack of communication in some cases.

MR. TAYLOR. Thank you.

VICE CHAIRMAN PATTERSON. Any further questions? You are excused. Thank you very much, Mrs. Fleming and Mr. Evers.

The hearing will recess for five minutes.

VICE CHAIRMAN PATTERSON. The hearing will come to order. Will Counsel call the next witness, please?

MR. GLICKSTEIN. The next witnesses are Mrs. Carl Sundahl and Mr. Paul Sherrill.

(Whereupon, Mrs. Carl Sundahl and Mr. Paul Sherrill were sworn by the Vice Chairman and testified as follows:)

TESTIMONY OF MRS. CARL SUNDAHL, SAN FRANCISCO, CALIFORNIA AND MR. PAUL SHERRILL, SAN FRANCISCO, CALIFORNIA

MR. GLICKSTEIN. Would you each please state your name and address?

MRS. SUNDAHL. My name is Elaine Sundahl. My address is 1230 19th Street.

MR. SHERRILL. My name is Paul Sherrill and my address is 154 Texas Street.

MR. GLICKSTEIN. How long have you each lived on Potrero Hill?

MRS. SUNDAHL. I have lived on Potrero Hill off and on. The last time we moved onto Potrero Hill was six years ago and I lived there before that about 10 years ago, and at that time lived there for about two years. We did move back about five years ago, five or six years ago.

MR. GLICKSTEIN. Mr. Sherrill?

MR. SHERRILL. I have lived on Potrero Hill four years.

MR. GLICKSTEIN. Mrs. Sundahl, are you active in a neighborhood association on the Hill?

MRS. SUNDAHL. Yes, I am.

MR. GLICKSTEIN. Would you tell us the name of it and something about its size?

MRS. SUNDAHL. I am the current chairman of the Potrero Hill Residents and Home Owners Council. We are an organization of about 70 families.

MR. GLICKSTEIN. Are members primarily home owners?

MRS. SUNDAHL. We have both residents and home owners. This is why the name of our organization is the Residents and Home Owners.

MR. GLICKSTEIN. Do any of the people living in the public housing project belong to your association?

MRS. SUNDAHL. No, they do not.

MR. GLICKSTEIN. Have you made any attempt to involve the people in the project in your organization?

MRS. SUNDAHL. We have. We have had many of the residents of the project as guests at our meetings, as observers at our meetings. Our meetings are open to everybody on Potrero Hill, anybody in the city who is interested in Potrero Hill. We are very happy and very eager to have more members of our organization.

MR. GLICKSTEIN. Mr. Sherrill, what is your position with the council?

MR. SHERRILL. I am a member of the executive committee. I was chairman last year.

MR. GLICKSTEIN. What is the purpose of the council?

MR. SHERRILL. It is a neighborhood improvement association. We are concerned about housing, street lights, litter, tree planting, freeways, bridges, airport, the general run of neighborhood problems.

MR. GLICKSTEIN. We just heard some testimony about the Potrero Hill Boosters and Merchants Association. The purposes of your associations seem to be rather similar. Is that correct?

MR. SHERRILL. Yes, I would say that the two programs, two associations, were organized for more or less the same purposes, although we often have somewhat different orientation.

MR. GLICKSTEIN. How do you differ from the other group?

MR. SHERRILL. Well, one way we differ in is that our council has proposed that the Wisconsin Street Temporary Housing Project be developed for 221(d)(3) housing with the maximum rent supplements possible.

MRS. SUNDAHL. In addition, may I add something to that? We have added to our public statement, our policy statement, which was prepared after many years of discussion, this statement was prepared and has been submitted publicly to different city agencies and to the Board of Supervisors. We have added to that position along with—because of discussions with residents of the hill—we have added to that a request that a multi-service center be included in any projected plan for the use of these project lands.

MR. GLICKSTEIN. So you are in favor of 221(d)(3) housing and the multi-service center?

MRS. SUNDAHL. With the addition that the 221(d)(3) would include all rent supplements and subsidies to enable those residents of the Wisconsin Project land and any other resident on Potrero

Hill who might not be able to afford private housing, but anyone who would want to live in the 221(d)(3), who are currently residents of the Hill, we want to keep our neighbors. If they want to stay in our neighborhood, we want to keep them. We want to enable them—we want to help them to enable them in any way that we as an organization can do to help them do this.

MR. GLICKSTEIN. Aren't you concerned also that there is too much public housing, low-rent housing on the Hill, that it is not equitably distributed throughout the city?

MRS. SUNDAHL. There should be more scattered public housing throughout the city of San Francisco. With this I do agree, but I do not feel that 221(d)(3) would be additional public housing. I do not look—personally have the point of view that this is additional public housing.

MR. GLICKSTEIN. Mr. Sherrill, would you object to building another permanent public housing project on the land where the Wisconsin housing now is?

MR. SHERRILL. Yes, I think that I would consider that a bad use of the land. We have two very large projects which are perhaps too large and which perhaps because of their great size and the fact that they are a contained unit may lead to problems in the neighborhood, problems of communication between the residents of the project and people who are not residents of the project, and I think that it would be unwise to expand the public housing.

MR. GLICKSTEIN. But you don't think 221(d)(3) presents similar problems?

MR. SHERRILL. No, I do not think that it is the same thing at all.

MR. GLICKSTEIN. Mrs. Sundahl, is there much communication between your group and the Boosters, much cooperation?

MRS. SUNDAHL. There is communication insofar as we send meeting notices of our meetings to the Boosters.

MR. GLICKSTEIN. Do you find that their members come to your meetings and your members go to their meetings?

MRS. SUNDAHL. A few of the members of the Boosters do attend our Residents Council meetings. As far as our members attending the Boosters, this I am not aware of. I am sure that there have been members who have attended from time to time.

MR. GLICKSTEIN. You have attended, Mr. Sherrill.

MR. SHERRILL. I have attended the meetings.

MR. GLICKSTEIN. Mrs. Sundahl, what about communication between your group and residents of the public housing project? Is there much of that?

MRS. SUNDAHL. We have had extensive communication. We have many of our members that have attended many of the meetings of the Potrero Hill Civic Improvement Association over many years. We feel that we have good and close communication. Now I am speaking only for our group. We feel we have good and close communication. We have worked closely together on some affairs in the area. There was a party that was given at the project about two years ago. We as a group voted money to purchase some of the refreshments that were served at that affair. In addition, many of the members of our organization contributed personally to the refreshments for this particular affair.

Subsequently, there was a Christmas party that was held this last Christmas at the Potrero Hill Neighborhood House. Our organization voted and did expend our money as a contribution toward the decorations for the Christmas party. Members of our organization helped with the party, attended the party, and participated in the activities of the Christmas party. This was mainly for the children. This was all for the children.

MR. GLICKSTEIN. The previous witness said that since the Poverty Program has become active on the Hill there seems to be a greater separation between the residents of the project and the other homeowners. Have you found that to be the case?

MRS. SUNDAHL. I have not found that to be the case. I have found personally just exactly the opposite because of the fact that there is more opportunity, more availability of communication between our own group and the members of the EOC. We feel that this has opened up to us another very good channel of communication and we hope very seriously, and very sincerely we hope that we will be able to continue this and to broaden it.

MR. GLICKSTEIN. Mr. Sherrill, you mentioned that among the functions of your organization was improving neighborhood conditions, and so forth. Has your group made any attempt to work with people in the project to improve living conditions there?

MR. SHERRILL. No. I don't think we have as much as we should have. We have been in communication with them. They have a proposal of a building that they would like for a boys' club and we have written letters supporting that. This is very recent. I think that in the future we may be able to do more.

MR. GLICKSTEIN. You think it is a feasible project for a group such as yours?

MR. SHERRILL. Yes, I think so.

MR. GLICKSTEIN. Do you believe, Mr. Sherrill, that a neighborhood group such as yours can successfully integrate public housing residents into the life of the community?

MR. SHERRILL. I think it is very difficult. We have tried to. We have not succeeded, and I think that perhaps separate organizations that we have now, as long as there is some way for the various organizations to communicate, is perhaps the best we can hope for now.

MR. GLICKSTEIN. Do you think that the reasons that this is

difficult is because of the economic differences between the two groups or the racial differences? I believe that 90 percent of the residents of the public housing project are Negro. Is that not correct?

MR. SHERRILL. Yes.

MR. GLICKSTEIN. Do you believe that the racial differences or the economic differences make this difficult?

MR. SHERRILL. I think probably the economic differences and possibly it is more difficult because of the large size of the project and it is large enough to be its own community. Everything about its design makes it separate from the rest of the neighborhood.

The buildings are all laid out on a different pattern from the rest of the neighborhood. The names of some of the streets are changed. I think in physical design, the project has been designed almost purposely to make it separate from the rest of the neighborhood, and the economic barrier is great.

MR. GLICKSTEIN. Mrs. Sundahl, there was some discussion before about scattered site housing in your neighborhood. Would you be in favor of that?

MRS. SUNDAHL. What type?

MR. GLICKSTEIN. Scattered site public housing.

MRS. SUNDAHL. I would certainly be in favor of that.

MR. GLICKSTEIN. You also mention that the activities of the poverty program have not interfered with communication with persons in the project. Do you think on the whole the poverty program has been useful in your area?

MRS. SUNDAHL. I personally feel that it has been very useful.

MR. GLICKSTEIN. In what way?

MRS. SUNDAHL. In enabling people who have so far not had a voice in voicing their own problems, in discussing publicly what they would like to see done for themselves, what they would like to see done for their homes. I feel that this is an extremely important and new and valuable part of the anti-poverty program.

MR. GLICKSTEIN. Do you think that there might be some people in your neighborhood who have felt threatened as a result of this new activity and new awareness and new organization in the housing project?

MRS. SUNDAHL. I cannot speak for everyone in my neighborhood. I understand there are some people who do feel threatened by this. I think there are more people who do not feel at all threatened by it, but again this is a matter of my personal opinion.

MR. GLICKSTEIN. Thank you. I have no further questions, Mr. Chairman.

VICE CHAIRMAN PATTERSON. Father Hesburgh?

COMMISSIONER HESBURGH. Mr. Sherrill, you are an architect, aren't you?

MR. SHERRILL. Yes.

COMMISSIONER HESBURGH. Mr. Sherrill, my question is rather simple. It seems to me that public housing gets an image, let's say the public housing one sees here in San Francisco and on Potrero Hill and Hunters Point, and so forth, it gets an image of something that is rather unattractive, highly concentrated and in other parts of the country it gets a similar image, but of a different kind because it is very high-rise, bleak and concrete and very ungreen. Would you think that perhaps making use of 221(d)(3) at a different principle of both scatteration, low, attractive buildings, that this would be, first of all, financially and architecturally possible and, secondly, would it create a completely different image of public housing and perhaps get rid of some of the opposition to public housing and, thirdly, make a single community on Potrero Hill possible? I realize that these are three questions.

Let me just restate them. First, would it be possible financially, architecturally, to use 221(d)(3) as a means of recreating a different type of public housing, lower, more attractive, scattered, and, secondly, would this make inter-community relations or a single community instead of two communities more possible?

MR. SHERRILL. Yes, it certainly is financially and architecturally feasible to design an attractive 221(d)(3) project. San Francisco has one in St. Francis Square, which is very attractive. It is feasible to design attractive public housing and I think the Housing Authority is making efforts to hire more talented people, and I think some of the new projects will be quite attractive and much more favorably received by the community.

COMMISSIONER HESBURGH. I will recapitulate the other question, if you wish.

If this were done, in other words, if we have more attractive, scattered-throughout-the-community type of public housing, or even a substitute for public housing in the case of 221(d)(3), would this make a single community more possible than is possible under the present situation?

MR. SHERRILL. It might help. I really don't think I could predict what the effect will be in uniting the community. It is very hard to say.

COMMISSIONER HESBURGH. You would still have an economic difference, but possibly the proximity of the neighbors, the human contact of the neighbors, even of children might make it simpler?

MR. SHERRILL. Yes, I think that if there are—if it could be designed in such a way that there would be areas of public use that would be used by all of the community so that you would get people from the project, people from the 221(d)(3) housing, people from the private housing, using common facilities, and if this is possible, I think this would help. There are no public facilities within the project and this is one of the problems.

COMMISSIONER HESBURGH. Thank you very much.

VICE CHAIRMAN PATTERSON. Mrs. Freeman?

COMMISSIONER FREEMAN. Mrs. Sundahl and Mr. Sherrill, I was interested in the response to the question concerning communication between the residents of the council and the residents in the project, and in both instances the only communication seemed to be built around a Christmas party. I wonder the extent to which the idea of involvement and participation could be increased to the extent that on projects, such as beautification programs, and such, the extent to which either of the organizations could consider asking the residents of the project whether they would join them in this project rather than just limiting it to a Christmas party?

MRS. SUNDAHL. We have formed on Potrero Hill in the last few months, about four months ago, an organization called the Sounding Board. This is the third time in the last few years that an attempt has been made to bring representatives of the many different groups of Potrero Hill together. The Sounding Board is a group that does not take a public stand of any type, makes no public statements, but this is the place where quite successfully, I won't say with complete success, but with some success representatives of all organizations on Potrero Hill have come, have discussed mutual problems. Most of our problems are mutual problems. We have come together. We have discussed many things. The Christmas party was just one very small part of this discussion.

We have had discussions in regard to the disposition of this Wisconsin Land. We have had discussions on other problems on Potrero Hill, the transportation problem, the lack of recreation. These are problems that are common to all parts of Potrero Hill and to all organizations on Potrero Hill.

COMMISSIONER FREEMAN. That includes the Boosters Association also?

MRS. SUNDAHL. The Boosters had official representatives at the first meeting of the Sounding Board, but, as I understand, their bylaws do not permit them to participate in any other organization. They must remain autonomous. They are an autonomous group. Now I am only speaking from what I understand.

COMMISSIONER FREEMAN. I would like to ask another question about the process of becoming a member of either of these organizations. When you have been there six years, and you have been, Mr. Sherrill, there for four years, were you approached and invited to become a member?

MRS. SUNDAHL. Of which organization?

COMMISSIONER FREEMAN. Of the Homeowners Council.

MRS. SUNDAHL. Yes, I was asked to become a member of the Residents and Homeowners Council. I did become a member 10 years ago when we lived on Potrero Hill the first time and as soon as we moved back to Potrero Hill I rejoined the Potrero Hill Residents and Homeowners Council.

COMMISSIONER FREEMAN. Do you know the extent to which all the residents on Potrero Hill received such an invitation?

MRS. SUNDAHL. Our mailing list is about 150. We have mimeographed 200 to 300 announcements of every one of our meetings. These meeting announcements are posted in the public library on a bulletin board which our Residents and Homeowners Council built and donated to the library. Our meeting notices are posted in the grocery stories, in the churches, are handed out to people at different meetings. We try extensively to the best of the ability of a volunteer organization to acquaint everyone in the neighborhood. When I say "the neighborhood," I mean the entire Hill.

We try extensively to indicate in any way that we can that our meetings are open, that everyone is welcome to join our organization.

We have had many door-to-door distributions of our meeting announcements. These meeting announcements have been distributed to most parts of the Potrero Hill projects, to most parts of the residential area at one time or the other.

COMMISSIONER FREEMAN. Does that include all of the residents of the low-rent housing development?

MRS. SUNDAHL. We try to cover as many as we can. We are, though, an organization of volunteers. We try by word of mouth as well as by our mimeographed meeting notice to acquaint as many people as possible with our meetings.

COMMISSIONER FREEMAN. This is the point I am making. Could they not also be invited to become volunteers?

MRS. SUNDAHL. We would be delighted if they would. The neighbors on Potrero Hill a few months ago formed an organization called Potrero Hill Landscapers, and on this particular project everybody on the Hill was asked to come and help plant, clean up, landscape and garden a strip of land on Carolina Street that is in the middle of the street.

This is a very steep hill and this particular street is bisected by a large strip of land that was covered by rocks, grass, broken glass, cans. This has been cleaned up and has been planted. This has been worked on for the last two months. We had one weekend planting and gardening weekend where we had 75 to 80 people working both Saturday and Sunday, and I am very happy to say that our plantings are beginning to grow and this particular strip of landscaping is becoming a very important and very beautiful part of our Hill. We are very happy about this and very proud of it.

This is the second time that the residents of the Hill have come together and worked on the landscaping project. This is not just for our organization. This is for everyone, and everyone did come and help with it from all of the organizations.

VICE CHAIRMAN PATTERSON. Dr. Rankin?

COMMISSIONER RANKIN. Mrs. Sundahl, you've told us about the various subjects you've discussed. I don't think anybody has mentioned property values. Is that problem ever discussed?

MRS. SUNDAHL. Property values are a very serious problem on Potrero Hill.

COMMISSIONER RANKIN. To whom, to everybody?

MRS. SUNDAHL. To everybody. There are many people who have said that they would like to live on Potrero Hill. They come out and look for a home. They look for a piece of property. They find that it is expensive as is all of San Francisco.

COMMISSIONER RANKIN. Well, the public housing that is there now has not affected the property values of the property privately owned on Potrero Hill. Is that correct?

MRS. SUNDAHL. The only instance that I can give you is that on Carolina Street, two blocks from the Wisconsin Temporary War Housing project, there is a 25-foot lot. It does have a beautiful view. A 25-foot lot that goes back about 150 feet. There is an old house on it that I understand is being rehabilitated to a certain extent, and a young family has moved into it just recently. I understand that the owner of this 25-foot lot is asking $24,500.

COMMISSIONER RANKIN. So you would conclude that the public housing that is there now has not hurt property values?

MRS. SUNDAHL. No, I do not feel that it has.

VICE CHAIRMAN PATTERSON. Continuing that line of questioning, if privately developed housing were built adjacent to the public housing project, the permanent housing projects now on Potrero Hill, would this privately developed housing in your opinion be markedly superior to the privately owned 221 (d) (3) housing that you propose?

MR. SHERRILL. No. I think that in all likelihood that it would be inferior. We have had a lot of new building on Potrero Hill. I think that about 90 percent of it in the last few years has been built to the maximum density permitted by zoning which means three apartments per 25 by 100 foot lot. I think that density would be achieved with the 221 (d) (3) project. I think, I hope that the project might be more attractive than what we would get if the land were sold in individual parcels.

We have had a lot of new apartments on Potrero Hill. Most of them quite unattractive. Many people object to the new apartments being put up because most of them are built without the benefit of design. They are built for the maximum return and a quick resale, and I think most of them are not good buildings and that there is a possibility or a good chance that something better would result than 221 (d) (3).

VICE CHAIRMAN PATTERSON. Is it your experience that sometimes middle-income housing is built immediately adjacent to public housing projects in this city?

MR. SHERRILL. I don't know of any other cases. You mean private middle-income housing?

VICE CHAIRMAN PATTERSON. Yes.

MR. SHERRILL. There is private middle-income housing immediately adjacent to the projects on Potrero Hill.

VICE CHAIRMAN PATTERSON. Would 221 (d) (3) housing be something of a bridge in your opinion, between a public housing project and privately owned houses on the other side of it?

MR. SHERRILL. I don't think of it as a bridge, particularly.

VICE CHAIRMAN PATTERSON. I am speaking now of land factors.

MR. SHERRILL. Of land values?

VICE CHAIRMAN PATTERSON. Yes. I am simply trying to get a practical view of San Francisco and Potrero Hill in particular. We have heard testimony that indicated some fear that land values are diminished when either public housing or government subsidized housing is built in an area.

MR. SHERRILL. Well, I don't believe that to be true, and there is no way to prove it. Land values on Potrero Hill are very high. They are less high than they are in Pacific Heights. So you might say that it is public housing that has depressed them, but I don't believe public housing has lowered land values on Potrero Hill because they're very high and they're rising all the time.

VICE CHAIRMAN PATTERSON. Thank you. Mr. Taylor?

MR. TAYLOR. Mr. Sherrill, if private housing were to be built on Potrero Hill, would that housing be likely to be open to all citizens without regard to race?

MR. SHERRILL. I think probably it would. I really don't know. It would not be open to all citizens because of the cost of it. New apartments would probably rent for around $175 a month to $200 a month. It wouldn't be open to me.

MR. TAYLOR. And 221(d) (3) would be significantly less expensive than that, and would you say that there is a better likelihood that such a housing development would be integrated, more likely that that would be integrated than a private housing development?

MR. SHERRILL. Yes, I think it is much more likely.

MR. TAYLOR. Thank you.

VICE CHAIRMAN PATTERSON. Any further questions? Mrs. Sundahl, Mr. Sherrill, thank you very much for coming. You are excused. Would you call the next witness, Mr. Counsel?

MR. GLICKSTEIN. The next two witnesses are Mr. Walter Robinson and Mr. Earl Williams.

(Whereupon, Mr. Walter Robinson and Mr. Earl Williams were sworn in by the Vice Chairman and testified as follows:)

TESTIMONY OF MR. EARL WILLIAMS, SAN FRANCISCO, CALIFORNIA, AND MR. WALTER ROBINSON, SAN FRANCISCO, CALIFORNIA

MR. GLICKSTEIN. Will each of you please state your names and addresses for the record?

MR. WILLIAMS. My name is Earl Williams. I stay at 23 Waxman Way in the public housing project.

MR. ROBINSON. My name is Walter Robinson. I reside at 69 A Mirabel Street.

MR. GLICKSTEIN. Would you each please tell us what your occupation is?

MR. WILLIAMS. Community organizer for the EOC.

MR. GLICKSTEIN. "EOC" stands for Economic Opportunity Council, and it is a poverty program?

MR. WILLIAMS. Yes.

MR. ROBINSON. I am also a community organizer for the EOC.

MR. GLICKSTEIN. Mr. Robinson, would you describe the relationship between the people living in the projects and the people living on Potrero Hill in private housing?

MR. ROBINSON. Well, at the risk of refuting the statements or the attitudes of some of the previous speakers, I would have to say that the relationship is almost non-existent. I think you have two separate communities on Potrero Hill, the resident and the home-owners and the project dwellers.

MR. GLICKSTEIN. Are there problems of mutual concern to all persons living on the Hill?

MR. ROBINSON. Yes, I think there are problems of mutual concern because I think what is happening in the public housing area will certainly affect the private area.

MR. GLICKSTEIN. Have any attempts been made to work together to solve the mutual problems, the one you mentioned and others?

MR. ROBINSON. Yes, some attempts have been made to form a spirit of cooperation in solving some of the problems.

MR. GLICKSTEIN. How successful have these attempts been?

MR. ROBINSON. I am afraid they haven't been very successful. For example, recently, not too long ago, there was a project. As you probably know, the public housing sector is very much isolated from any kinds of services. There are no medical facilities, no shopping centers, no drug stores. It is an area that is completely isolated and the transportation in this area is very, very bad.

The public housing residents had expressed a need and a great desire to have some kind of medical facilities on the Hill and some doctors have been willing to come in and to buy a private house and establish a medical clinic.

At this time we discovered that two of the organizations, the two organizations that have appeared here today, were very much opposed to this idea. It seems that their main area of concern was with the rezoning and not the human need, and we were very, very disappointed that they took this attitude.

MR. GLICKSTEIN. The project would have required rezoning of some sort?

MR. ROBINSON. Yes.

MR. GLICKSTEIN. What do most of the people in the project believe should be done when the temporary housing is torn down? What do they believe should be done with that land?

MR. ROBINSON. Well, they have overwhelmingly expressed a need, first of all, for a kind of multi-service center. They dislike very much having to go up the Hill for each and every little thing they have to buy and having to rely on public transportation.

Approximately a month or a month and a half ago a little four-week old baby died in my arms. There are two doctors on the Hill and they are there by appointment only and the nearest place they can get medical attention is at the San Francisco Public General Hospital, and again transportation is very, very bad.

MR. GLICKSTEIN. What do you mean by multi-service center?

MR. ROBINSON. A place where there would be medical and dental facilities available for the residents, a place where they could buy medicines, a shopping center or a recreation area, barber shop, many of the services that you generally find within a community that are totally and completely lacking in the project area.

MR. GLICKSTEIN. And you would favor replacing the temporary war housing with this multi-service center?

MR. ROBINSON. Yes. Also there is a need for additional housing. The private housing market in San Francisco is dwindling all the time, and it is doubly hard for black people to find adequate or decent housing in the city of San Francisco.

It has been my personal experience that I have gone looking for housing, after having made initial contact over the telephone and having arrived and talked to the landlord, either the house was no longer available or the price had gone up some 20 or 30 percent, and it works a tremendous hardship on people who are black people who are seeking private housing in the city.

MR. GLICKSTEIN. Do you favor more public housing or some of the 221 (d) (3) housing?

MR. ROBINSON. Well, I am not in favor of additional public housing, but we have to face a reality here. The middle-class among black people is not growing. It is diminishing, and as I understand this 221(d)(3) housing is designed primarily for middle-class people, for near-middle-class people.

MR. GLICKSTEIN. So you think that there is a greater need for public housing which would be available?

MR. ROBINSON. I am afraid so.

MR. GLICKSTEIN. Now, you mentioned that some of the projects that people in the public housing project are interested in haven't been supported by other people on the Hill. Are there other issues that the people in the project are interested in besides the multi-service center?

MR. ROBINSON. Yes, they are interested in the conditions of public housing. This has been one of their main concerns. They feel that the houses that they are living in now are overpriced and not commensurate with the services or the lack of services. They have been in opposition to many of the policies and abuses of the San Francisco Housing Authority.

MR. GLICKSTEIN. Have the residents of the project received any support from other people on the Hill in these endeavors?

MR. ROBINSON. I think the only support that they have received has been in the latest request for an unused building, an unoccupied building, to be used as a kind of community center.

MR. GLICKSTEIN. How would you appraise the attitudes of the persons in the project toward the white majority on the Hill?

MR. ROBINSON. Well, first of all, I think that the attitude is one of mounting frustration and perhaps bitterness. They see themselves as isolated people who have to go it alone because the other people aren't really concerned about them. Their problems are uniquely their own and they feel that they are the ones that are going to have to solve their problem.

MR. GLICKSTEIN. What effect has the poverty program had on meeting the needs of the people in the project?

MR. ROBINSON. Well, it is very difficult to evaluate the effects of the poverty program on the needs of the people. I would say that on the real needs of the people the poverty program has been rather ineffectual, but I think it has served——

MR. GLICKSTEIN. When you say "real needs" do you mean on jobs, housing?

MR. ROBINSON. Yes, on jobs, housing, but I think it has given a voice to the people and has attempted with some degree of success of getting people together and having them talk about their own problems and devise possible solutions to meeting some of them.

MR. GLICKSTEIN. Mr. Williams, in your work as a community

organizer, do you see a trend toward black nationalism among the
young people in the project?

MR. WILLIAMS. No, I don't see a trend toward the black nationalism but I see a trend toward black unity.

MR. GLICKSTEIN. Black unity. How would you define that?

MR. WILLIAMS. In other words, we are not sitting back any more
and waiting on other people to dictate our lives. We are trying to
organize ourselves where we have something to say about our own
lives, and we are not going to sit back and let other organizations
dictate to us how they think our lives should be run.

MR. GLICKSTEIN. Has this trend picked up in recent years?

MR. WILLIAMS. Quite a bit, picked up quite a bit this year.

MR. GLICKSTEIN. What do you think is the reason for the trend?

MR. WILLIAMS. Well, I think—for a long time I have been
living on Potrero Hill for nine years. I think for a long time every
time something was done on the Hill it has been done by the
Boosters and the Merchants, and they don't really know what the
people are like in the projects. They go by what they hear, like this
lady brought up this morning about they have 500 members and
two blacks. If they have them, they must have gotten them this
morning.

MR. GLICKSTEIN. Do you think that this trend toward black
unity is accompanied by feelings of hostility?

MR. WILLIAMS. Well, you wouldn't know, but most people would
know that we have had hostility all our lives, and the situation on
Potrero Hill isn't helping it any.

MR. GLICKSTEIN. Do you think that the city and the persons that
hold economic power in this community are aware of the feeling of
the people on the Hill?

MR. WILLIAMS. Of course they are, but they are scared to say it.

MR. GLICKSTEIN. They are scared to say it?

MR. WILLIAMS. Yes.

MR. GLICKSTEIN. Do you think that this trend toward black
unity that you mentioned, do you think that can solve the problems
and satisfy the needs of the people?

MR. WILLIAMS. I think it is the only way to solve the problems..
When you get together and do something for yourself, and you
know what you want done, not what someone thinks you should
have, or how much of this you should have, or we don't think this
should be this way. These people don't have the right to sit up here
and say what they don't think should be on Potrero Hill. I don't
care if they have been living there 70 years. They don't have this
right.

MR. GLICKSTEIN. Do you think that there should be greater
efforts on the Hill to try to increase communication between all the
people that live on the Hill instead of trends toward separation?

MR. WILLIAMS. Well, I think the only effort we are getting right now as far creating communication is coming from the home owners and residents. Like the lady said a little while ago, that they invite everyone to their meetings, and like I say, I have been living there nine years and I never received an invitation to go to a Booster Merchants meeting yet.

MR. GLICKSTEIN. Do you think that it would be good to make an effort to improve communications?

MR. WILLIAMS. It would be good, you know, but, like I stated, I don't know how good it would be for them, for the simple reason we are not going to be dictated to any more.

MR. GLICKSTEIN. But you would be receptive to greater efforts of communication and greater attempts for all the people on the Hill to try to work out their problems?

MR. WILLIAMS. That is correct. We have tried that, and we have been trying ever since I have been there, but it is not working because you still have the selected few that is going to say what is going on, and that is the way it is supposed to be, and it is not going to be that way anymore.

MR. GLICKSTEIN. I have no further questions, Mr. Chairman.

VICE CHAIRMAN PATTERSON. Father Hesburgh?

COMMISSIONER HESBURGH. I am just wondering, in the best of all worlds, which I have to keep thinking about all the time, you don't have a good conversation unless you have a strong voice on each side. Would you agree with that, Mr. Williams?

MR. WILLIAMS. Beg pardon?

COMMISSIONER HESBURGH. You have to have a strong voice on each side of a good conversation?

MR. WILLIAMS. Well, I wouldn't say you had to have a strong voice, but I would say a strong determination.

COMMISSIONER HESBURGH. What I am thinking of is, if I read your remarks correctly, you don't want to have this conversation between whites and blacks as between superiors and inferiors. You want to have it as equal Americans. Right?

MR. WILLIAMS. That's right.

COMMISSIONER HESBURGH. So what you are doing to create a Negro community, or a black unity, as you say, could have a very positive value if coming out of it you would then be in a position to talk with a certain amount of idea, force, and vitality to the white community on the Hill. Correct?

MR. WILLIAMS. I think I would.

COMMISSIONER HESBURGH. And I get the impression, and again this is just a personal impression, but I get the impression at times looking at this around the country that people are afraid that the black unity will be a thing in itself and will create a deeper ghetto than has existed in the past. I think it would be more promising if we could look at it as a creation of a self-identity in the community and a self-consciousness even, and even a self-pride. So then, in turn, you could have a real conversation, not a phony conversation, which has so characterized past conversations. Would you agree with that?

MR. WILLIAMS. Yes.

COMMISSIONER HESBURGH. Mr. Robinson, I was curious of what your background was. Where are you from originally?

MR. ROBINSON. Where am I from originally? I am from the Midwest, Chicago.

COMMISSIONER HESBURGH. I thought I got a little of that home accent there. I was just curious. Have you been here long in California?

MR. ROBINSON. Yes.

COMMISSIONER HESBURGH. Mr. Robinson, if you really had the say completely, I mean if we could get rid of all of the structure, the establishment, the clubs and everything else, and you were to say we are going to start now and make a program for Potrero Hill in its totality with all its segments, how would you go about that?

MR. ROBINSON. Would you please repeat that?

COMMISSIONER HESBURGH. Sure. What I am thinking of, we have heard from some of the white residents on Potrero Hill. We have heard from some of the black residents on Potrero Hill. I am wondering, looking to the future, if you could say now, "This to me is an ideal of the way we would move forward on Potrero Hill to create one community that is interested in each other and one community that would be for the good of the total neighborhood there," how would you go about that? Would it be a federation of all existing forces? Would it be one single organization to which many people belonged, or how would you approach it, really?

I realize it is a difficult question I am asking you, but I am looking for a plan rather than just separate reactions off of a vacuum.

MR. ROBINSON. I would prefer to think that in any ideal situation that people of different ethnic or racial or religious backgrounds would regard the community as their community. Therefore, any problem of any resident in that community would affect every other community person.

So I would envision this kind of attitude within the community that would seek to act on the needs of individuals for the good of the community and to act jointly for the interests of the community.

COMMISSIONER HESBURGH. So what you are saying is we have to begin a conversation on the Hill between all of the parties to the Hill that live there, that are interested in it and have a stake in the neighborhood there, and to get them talking about real problems that affect everyone.

For example, this multi-service center could be everybody's center. It wouldn't have to be a black center or a white center. I think if you wind up with two of them, you again divide the community.

MR. ROBINSON. As we envision it, the service center would be open for all residents. The only thing is right now there is a greater need for this type of service for the people dwelling in the projects, because of economic reasons and because of their location.

Most of the people on the other side of the Hill, I should imagine, have their private doctors. They have their own automobiles and in cases of emergencies they can readily go to seek medical attention.

COMMISSIONER HESBURGH. But this multi-service center could be a way of uniting the community if it were, somewhat, closer to the public housing, but at the same time available to others?

MR. ROBINSON. Yes.

COMMISSIONER HESBURGH. Thank you, Mr. Robinson.

VICE CHAIRMAN PATTERSON. Mrs. Freeman?

COMMISSIONER FREEMAN. Mr. Robinson and Mr. Williams, I believe there are about 4,000 residents in the low-rent housing developments there. Is that about right?

MR. ROBINSON. I think it is slightly higher than that, Mrs. Freeman.

COMMISSIONER FREEMAN. And about how many of them are black?

MR. ROBINSON. About 5,500 or 6,000.

COMMISSIONER FREEMAN. This multi-service center that you are talking about could be provided by the San Francisco Housing Authority, could it not?

MR. ROBINSON. It has been done in other cities and I see no reason why it couldn't be provided by public housing authority in this city.

COMMISSIONER FREEMAN. I would like to know if the organization that you are talking about has made this presentation or request of the San Francisco Housing Authority.

MR. WILLIAMS. May I say something about the San Francisco Housing Authority? We can't even get them to keep our places clean, let's don't try to get them to give us something else. So I don't think they would come across with it, because we have had rats and roaches we have been crying about for the last five or six years, and they haven't even got rid of those, and that is much cheaper than a multi-service center.

MR. ROBINSON. Along these lines, if I might add, I think that it is a fairly well publicized fact that many residents in the Potrero Hill Projects are on a rent strike.

Now, they were forced to this position after repeated frustrations and meeting with the Housing Authority, trying to get very minor things changed, such as Mr. Williams mentioned, the extermination of rats and roaches, paint jobs, et cetera, and we have gotten very little cooperation from the Housing Authority. So we don't think it is feasible to even approach them on something as big as this at this time.

COMMISSIONER FREEMAN. Who owns the Wisconsin Temporary Housing Project?

MR. ROBINSON. The city, I believe.

COMMISSIONER FREEMAN. I had the opportunity to tour that area on Saturday, and it seemed to me that among those temporary housing buildings that there were a lot of vacancies. There seems to be some use that could be made, rehabilitation, or what have you, to provide the kind of facility that you are talking about. To what extent is that feasible?

MR. ROBINSON. Well, actually, I think we have another location at 1095 Wisconsin Street which is in better condition and would probably serve a better purpose than any of the temporary housing over in the Wisconsin Project site.

COMMISSIONER FREEMAN. Who owns that land?

MR. ROBINSON. The city.

COMMISSIONER FREEMAN. So that the city could provide the services?

MR. ROBINSON. Yes.

COMMISSIONER FREEMAN. The city could provide the multiservice center. I would like to know what has been done to get the city to do it.

MR. WILLIAMS. Everything except holding a gun on them. In other words, like he mentioned a few moments ago about the rent strike, anyone who has been in this area can see the shape that it is in. The shape that the houses are in, and the whole—just the whole everyday life of the people that is living in the housing projects is bad. The mayor can see this, the board of supervisors can see this, but they will not speak out on this because they might not be elected in November.

So this is the type of city government that we have here in San Francisco, a bunch of big sissies.

COMMISSIONER FREEMAN. What plans does the organization have to remedy the situation?

MR. ROBINSON. Well, recently we have had meetings with architects to study the site and to advise us on the feasibilities of our desires for this particular area. So we have started to move in this direction. Once again, that is.

VICE CHAIRMAN PATTERSON. Dr. Rankin?

COMMISSIONER RANKIN. Mr. Robinson, if it is economically feasible to have a multi-service center, you would think stores like a drug store would make money if located on the Hill? Is that correct?

MR. ROBINSON. Well, we are not that concerned about economics, Mr. Rankin. We are more concerned about need.

COMMISSIONER RANKIN. I know you are, but a store would be more concerned about being located—I am trying to find out if the zoning ordinance is keeping stores from locating there, or is it just that they feel that no money could be made by a store at that location?

MR. ROBINSON. There are businesses in the area, two small grocery stores in the area.

COMMISSIONER RANKIN. But no supermarket or anything like that?

MR. ROBINSON. No, nothing of that sort.

COMMISSIONER RANKIN. Now, do you think that would be a good location for a supermarket?

MR. ROBINSON. I think they could make money there, yes.

COMMISSIONER RANKIN. And it is not prohibited—the locating of a supermarket there is not prohibited by zoning ordinance at the present time. Is that correct?

MR. ROBINSON. I don't know what the zoning ordinance is in relation to this particular site. I know that a very short distance from there we were frustrated in our attempts to get housing rezoned in order to establish a medical clinic.

COMMISSIONER RANKIN. Well, I will agree with you it looks like a good location for a multi-service center there. I agree with you on that, and I just wonder why somebody hasn't really latched onto the opportunity.

MR. WILLIAMS. Too many groups.

VICE CHAIRMAN PATTERSON. Mr. Taylor?

MR. TAYLOR. Mr. Robinson, what are the public services that the community is lacking? I think you mentioned transportation as one. I would appreciate a little bit more detail on that and any other services the community needs.

MR. ROBINSON. I could see that there would be a need for a social welfare office, an employment office in an area where you have some 25 or 30 percent of eligible males unemployed. I should imagine that in a clinic that there should be—yes, a clinic, I imagine, you should certainly classify that as a public service. You are aware that the transportation is bad.

MR. TAYLOR. How difficult is it right now for residents to get to shopping, to the most convenient shopping place or downtown? Do the buses run frequently?

MR. ROBINSON. The buses run very infrequently and the nearest shopping center, as I know, is down in the Mission, which means that you have to come completely off the Hill and go quite a number of blocks to get into shopping areas, and most residents do have to rely on public transportation.

VICE CHAIRMAN PATTERSON. Mr. Williams, if you could achieve this black unity of which you speak, how would you apply it? How would you get things done as a result of having black unity?

MR. WILLIAMS. I think November is the answer to that. You know, as far as the voting is concerned.

VICE CHAIRMAN PATTERSON. You are speaking then primarily in terms of voting?

MR. WILLIAMS. That is correct. I notice that our assemblymen and the board of supervisors and the mayor and all of them, they are quite interested in votes in November, and since they don't want to do nothing for the poor people now, I don't think the poor people should vote for them in November, and I think if 2,000 to 3,000 adults was to change their votes, it wouldn't make that much of a difference but it might if they were all cast the same way and in the same direction for someone who they thought was going to try to help them achieve some of the goals that they would like to have in their community.

MR. ROBINSON. I would just like to comment on that, and Mr. Williams and I have discussed this at length. We would like to be able to proceed along the established democratic lines for change if this is possible, but if this is not possible, then we will have to do whatever is necessary to make these changes.

VICE CHAIRMAN PATTERSON. Does this remind you in any way, Mr. Robinson, of the way some of my own home people in the South, whites, used to talk.

MR. ROBINSON. The way they used to talk?

VICE CHAIRMAN PATTERSON. Yes, sir.

MR. ROBINSON. I am not altogether sure how people in your home town used to talk, Mr. Patterson. Could you be a bit more explicit in your question?

VICE CHAIRMAN PATTERSON. Perhaps venturing outside the democratic process on occasion. This, what I am saying, has led the South, the white South, into a long period of folly, and my question to you is, are you sure that this couldn't work the other way?

MR. ROBINSON. I am sorry. I don't wish to belabor it, but I don't fully understand what you are saying.

VICE CHAIRMAN PATTERSON. I am stating a proposition in asking the question. I am saying as a Southerner, I think that when the whites in my home region for a long period of time went outside the democratic process to achieve their wishes, this led them into many follies, and I wonder if this might not lead the Negro in the same direction.

MR. ROBINSON. I think that the black people in this country have been trying for the past 400 or so years to achieve their goals within the democratic process, and I think there is a lot of disagreement as to how well they have succeeded.

VICE CHAIRMAN PATTERSON. Thank you. Any further questions? You are excused. Thank you very much. Would you call the next witness, Mr. Glickstein?

MR. GLICKSTEIN. The next witness is Mr. Robert Jacobs.

(Whereupon, Mr. Robert Jacobs was sworn by the Vice Chairman and testified as follows:)

TESTIMONY OF MR. ROBERT C. JACOBS, PALO ALTO, CALIFORNIA

MR. GLICKSTEIN. Would you please state your name and address for the record?

MR. JACOBS. My name is Robert C. Jacobs. I used to live on Potrero Hill and had to move because of circumstances beyond my control to live in the Peninsula area. After two moves I now live in East Palo Alto at 1403 Cavanaugh Drive.

MR. GLICKSTEIN. Would you tell us what your present occupation is?

MR. JACOBS. I am project director for the Potrero Hill Manpower Project, which is an employer of the Redevelopment Research Program funded by the EOC, Economic Opportunity Council. Also I am chairman of the Potrero Hill Citizen Improvement Association, which you have heard quite a bit about.

MR. GLICKSTEIN. That is the CIA?

MR. JACOBS. Yes.

MR. GLICKSTEIN. Did you try to find a place to live on the Hill before you moved to East Palo Alto?

MR. JACOBS. Yes, I did. I had several—with the help of several of the people, the residents and home owners, they gave me several addresses and I went to try to buy a place. First I tried to lease a place.

When talking to me they would tell me that these places were for lease over the telephone. After seeing me, they hit a panic button. My very last experience I sent a white friend of mine to price a place which was priced at $22,900. I then proceeded to go and see about the place myself and it went up to $40,000.

MR. GLICKSTEIN. The property values are going up in that area.

MR. JACOBS. I discovered to my amazement for the first time that I wasn't aware of that. All my life I had been thinking that we depreciated property, and at just the sight of me it went up almost

100 percent. So we are doing quite well in this country. Quite a bit of progress has been made up to this point.

I then moved out of the project because of the money that I was making——

MR. GLICKSTEIN. Your income went up too much to permit you to live in the project?

MR. JACOBS. Yes. I could have stayed there if I was willing to pay $250 per month rent. I wasn't willing to do that because I could buy a house for less than that. I moved to Daly City, right outside the city limits, or along Mission Street. I stayed there for approximately three weeks.

MR. GLICKSTEIN. Did you have any trouble finding a place in Daly City?

MR. JACOBS. I had trouble finding a decent place in Daly City.

MR. GLICKSTEIN. Were you turned down in many places?

MR. JACOBS. Quite a few places. After finding a place for $195 a month—one of my neighbors must have been on vacation when I moved there, because when he came back and saw me, I had to resort to means that would commonly be known in the South as "acting like a nigger" because I had to promise to kill him if he came by my house again, and I realized that it isn't worth that effort. So I got out and bought me a place of my own.

MR. GLICKSTEIN. Is East Palo Alto an integrated community?

MR. JACOBS. In the particular neighborhood that I have just recently moved, there is about 60 /40 ratio in this particular neighborhood.

MR. GLICKSTEIN. What about the entire community?

MR. JACOBS. If we are going to use the entire community, there would be about 80/20, 80 percent Negroes and 20 percent white.

MR. GLICKSTEIN. Do you believe that the residents of the housing project would move if they could?

MR. JACOBS. I sure do.

MR. GLICKSTEIN. And why do you feel that?

MR. JACOBS. Because every chance one gets to economically better his condition, he gets out as quick as possible because conditions there do not warrant a person living there for the rest of his life.

MR. GLICKSTEIN. So that people there are anxious to better themselves and move out to other accommodations?

MR. JACOBS. People there are not only anxious to better themselves and move out to other accommodations, they are willing almost on any condition to move out of there. They are not there because they like it. They are there because they are victims. They have almost completely dehoused San Francisco and there is no other place for them to go but to public housing areas.

And when I sit here and hear people talk about scattered housing, I'm wondering just where they would scatter them. They have torn down every place they have lived up to this point with this new gimmick called "redevelopment," and everytime they start redevelopment into public housing all these people come and then they start screaming about concentrated ghettoes. I don't know. Maybe I am not a very intelligent person, but I keep hearing this word "ghettos," and I keep realizing, and I'm wondering don't the people realize what they are saying is, "Don't create one ghetto, but stay out of our ghettos" because ghetto doesn't just apply to black people. Ghetto applies to St. Francis Wood or any other place where you have a particular concentration of an ethnic group and what we have in our area, known as Potrero Hill, is an invisible wall. People understand that when you get to the apex of the Hill, which, as far as the blacks and the whites are concerned, is about 22nd street. When you start over that, you are out of your territory and this is the way they feel.

Now, I have sat here today and I have heard people talk about "Christmas party" and the lady asked if this was the only thing that they—we had all worked on. Well, I dreamed up the Christmas party because I felt that it was time for black people and white people to try and solve some of these problems, because I realized that another Hunters Point could come along if we didn't try to communicate with them. I realized a lack of communication could cause a lot of problems.

So I got in touch with all the organizations by telephone. I am happy to say that the Residents and Home Owners responded beautifully, and certain members of the Boosters and Merchants responded, but the organization itself responded negatively as they always do.

Now there are particular people within the organization that respond as individuals, and they go to a lot of trouble to let you know that they are responding as citizens or your neighbors, because the organization—I don't know where all these beautiful ideas came from this morning, because the Boosters have never made anybody welcome to anything on Potrero Hill. I am the very first black person that moved on that Hill, and until last year the only thing that I have ever known the Boosters to do was to do everything within their power to make us feel unwanted.

MR. GLICKSTEIN. When you say you were the first black person to move on the Hill——

MR. JACOBS. In the public housing. When they started to "integrate" the public housing area, then I moved in. Now, Mrs. Fleming has worked wonderfully with us. Yet I hear people saying they don't think there is too much of a racial problem here. When I was looking for a house, I wasn't aware that one of these Booster members was known by my wife, and my wife had been telling me for years that this one woman, if you could just let her talk long enough, you would hear her say what she has been trying to say for several years. She owns quite a bit of property over at the apex of the Hill, that divides the Negroes from the whites.

So during our friendly communication, she said that they had an eight-room flat that was empty, had been empty for quite a while, and my wife proceeded to tell her that we were looking for a place and it took my wife some 14 years to get this lady to say that "there are some good niggers. Oh, but I just cannot rent to them because all of my tenants would move out." I understand there are no tenants in there. She is living on the top floor.

MR. GLICKSTEIN. Mr. Jacobs, have you attended meetings of the Boosters and the Home Owners Association?

MR. JACOBS. I have attended meetings of the Residents and Home Owners Association.

MR. GLICKSTEIN. Do other residents of the project attend these meetings?

MR. JACOBS. Possibly my vice chairman and my secretary have.

MR. GLICKSTEIN. Why don't you think the residents of the project go to these meetings?

MR. JACOBS. After feeling unwanted over a period of years, you can't expect a person to feel like I should break my neck going now.

MR. GLICKSTEIN. You mentioned the isolation of the people in the housing project. Does this isolation have an effect, a noticeable effect, on the people living there? How would you describe that?

MR. JACOBS. First of all, it is my understanding, through quite a bit of reading and through experience that isolation has some effect on anyone. So I can't expect us to be any different. Now, as to the effect it has on the people within the area, they have tried to move out of the area. They have discovered that when they move on the other side of our public housing area that they move by the so-called "middle-class" right down in another ghetto, which would be about three or four streets, right in the heart of the industrial area.

Now, when it becomes a choice of moving out of the project into that area, you stay in the project because if you think it looks bad over there, you should go over in that area. The people there are very isolated. They are so isolated that at times, until they forced me to buy an automobile, when I had no intention because I was trying to go to school—I have—on certain occasions I have waited for something like four or five hours just to get a taxi to come four or five blocks with groceries for my family. You cannot get a taxi at night.

At one time I had sickness in my family and I tried to get a taxi. I had to pay an additional $35.00 just to get my child to the hospital, because the taxi said they couldn't find it and they didn't want to come out there. So I can imagine that the reason it would have such a tremendous amount of destruction to property out there is because they feel like they are in a cage, and I felt like I was in a cage.

I don't realize how much I felt like I was in a cage until I spent my first weekend out in a house in an area where I could move around, because the public housing area, the public housing administration hasn't done anything to make one feel like they are a part of this city.

Now, a few minutes ago I heard someone here ask what had we done to try to get the public housing area to give us this multi- — whatever kind of center they want to call it. About a year ago I personally got in touch with the San Francisco Housing Authority and wrote up a program asking for certain areas that the lady was talking about in the old buildings over there. I drew them a diagram telling them what I wanted to put in there: a nursery for the mothers, so that they could shop without having to leave their children unattended, medical center for the families, so they wouldn't have to go so far when something was wrong; and I told them I would personally go to the trouble of getting adults to be there to supervise at all times.

I was told that this can't be done. So I don't imagine that that public housing agency will be doing anything as far as this center that we want, because they frowned on that. Not only that. I got some nice architect to draw up a plan for this area they were talking about here, the 1095 Wisconsin. I was going to make that a community center. They turned that down.

Now, there are violent elements in Potrero Hill. I feel that I shouldn't be violent. I feel that I should try to talk to them, but I also realize that you need all elements in it in order to get things done. If I try all peaceful means and it can't work, then it leaves these people to get up and "raise hell." I pleaded with these people and I told them that these children need some place to work, to do their school work. They gave me an area to tutor these children for some eight or nine months. It is not there now anymore. This house that we were asking them for is sitting unattended and no one lives in it, and here we have to walk up a hill that you should need an elephant to pull most people up there, because it is very steep to get to two little insignificant stores. We have to walk down the hill to get to a doctor or we go up into the other area where they have the doctor, the drugstore and everything else that they just about need in this area, but we don't live there.

Now, I would like to feel that the people are willing to work with us, meaning the Public Housing people, and try to eliminate some of these conditions. But personally I can't because during the time as director of this program I had a survey going on. I sent out 1,000 research forms. Twenty-two percent of them went into the white area and the rest of them went into the public housing area, and out of that 22 percent something like 2 percent responded positively. The rest of them slammed doors, cursed them out, called them foul names, and one gentleman went so far as to put his hand on the lady and manhandle her, and I realized I had better pull them out.

MR. GLICKSTEIN. This was a survey to see——

MR. JACOBS. Whether there was any unemployment. I feel there should be unemployment among whites as well as unemployment among blacks. I feel the only way I could point out the critical conditions was to show whether or not there was a tremendous amount of unemployment over there as compared to the unem-. ployment over here. Yet I got no response.

MR. GLICKSTEIN. Mr. Jacobs, do you believe that theories of black nationalism or black separation are gaining followings among the residents of the project?

MR. JACOBS. I believe that the theory of black nationalism would not only gain followers in the projects, it would gain followers in any area that would perpetuate the type of condition that these people live under.

MR. GLICKSTEIN. Are you ultimately a proponent of an integrated society?

MR. JACOBS. By integration, if you mean do I believe that we all should learn to live, work together, and try to eliminate these social problems that we have, very good. Yes, I am.

MR. GLICKSTEIN. I have no further questions.

VICE CHAIRMAN PATTERSON. Father Hesburgh?

COMMISSIONER HESBURGH. Mr. Jacobs, do you think things are getting better or worse on Potrero Hill from your observations?

MR. JACOBS. I think they are getting worse.

COMMISSIONER HESBURGH. One last question: What is your educational background, Mr. Jacobs?

MR. JACOBS. I am a college graduate

COMMISSIONER HESBURGH. Where did you study?

MR. JACOBS. At the University of San Francisco, the University of California, and various other schools.

COMMISSIONER HESBURGH. Thank you, sir.

VICE CHAIRMAN PATTERSON. Mrs. Freeman?

COMMISSIONER FREEMAN. Mr. Jacobs, you have described some pretty bleak conditions where the residents have no services. You have also indicated that they have come to feel that there is nobody who is going to listen. Is this accurate?

MR. JACOBS. This is very true.

COMMISSIONER FREEMAN. What do you see as the next step?

MR. JACOBS. I feel—this is my personal opinion, that we had better, at some point or another, realize that we have human beings sitting over there that are in dire need of help, both financially, socially, and psychologically, rather than the "Negroes sitting over there needing help" because, you see, they are beginning to feel now that they are black and everything that happens to them happens because they are black.

Now, I am 39 years old. I felt this way, but I was just an individual and there was always someone around to suppress my emotions. But there is no one around to suppress their emotions anymore. You see, I bring my children in the world feeling this way and consequently I have teen-age daughters that I would not suppress because I still feel this way. They are going to have to start looking at these people as human beings, rather than Negroes, because they are tired of them doing this. They are going to have to realize that this is not just a Potrero Hill problem or a Negro problem. They are going to have to realize this is an American citizens' problem. This is an American social ill and something has to be done about it, and unless we find some effective means of communicating, breaking down these emotional walls that we have over there, we haven't seen half the problems we are going to have.

COMMISSIONER FREEMAN. Thank you.

VICE CHAIRMAN PATTERSON. Dr. Rankin?

COMMISSIONER RANKIN. Is black nationalism going to help or hurt in this project you're mentioning here, of breaking down walls?

MR. JACOBS. I can't answer that because I would have to be answering as an individual, and I have not even really questioned them. The one thing that I know that black nationalism is doing that hasn't been done prior to this time, it is establishing some kind of pride within these people where they can look at their conditions and say, as Mr. Williams said a few minutes ago, no one else has done anything for us: we are going to have to do it for ourselves.

Now, I am hoping that they don't say, "If we don't get it by working with this person, then we will have to use other means." That I don't want them to feel, as Vice Chairman Patterson was saying that we are working without the democratic process because, really, these are just words to most of us because we rather laugh when we hear it applied to us because we don't know what it means.

Now, what black nationalist groups are telling them is that, "Look, baby, nobody is going to help you but yourself, and what you had better do, you had better realize that with all the liberals in the world that you still have these conditions that you had when you met these liberals, and until you can do something about it for yourself, they will be here."

Now, how they are going to do it I don't know. I mean, I just don't know because, in the first place, I am not a person that believes in joining organizations because I can't have a person tell me how to think. I spent too much time trying to learn how to think. So I can't be bothered.

VICE CHAIRMAN PATTERSON. Mr. Taylor?

MR. TAYLOR. No questions.

VICE CHAIRMAN PATTERSON. That's all. Thank you very much, Mr. Jacobs.

VICE CHAIRMAN PATTERSON. The hearing will stand in recess until 2:15.

(Whereupon, at 12:50 p.m., the hearing recessed, to reconvene at 2:15 p.m. of the same day.)

MONDAY AFTERNOON SESSION
MAY 1, 1967

VICE CHAIRMAN PATTERSON. The hearing of the Civil Rights Commission will again come to order.

FATHER HESBURGH. Mr. Chairman, may I have the floor for a moment?

VICE CHAIRMAN PATTERSON. Father Hesburgh.

FATHER HESBURGH. Ladies and gentlemen, we don't normally have any demonstration in these hearings, but I do think we have great reason for applause at this moment.

It has just come to our knowledge that our Vice Chairman, Mr. Eugene Patterson, who, as you know, is editor of the Atlanta Constitution, has just been declared the Pultizer Prize winner for editorial writing this year. And on behalf of the staff and the members of the Commission, I would like to give him our and your best congratulations.

VICE CHAIRMAN PATTERSON. Will the General Counsel call the first witness?

MR. GLICKSTEIN. Mrs. Maxine Randolph.

(Whereupon, Mrs. Maxine Randolph was sworn by the Vice Chairman and testified as follows:)

TESTIMONY OF MRS. MAXINE B. RANDOLPH, SAN FRANCISCO, CALIFORNIA

MR. GLICKSTEIN. Mrs. Randolph, would you please state your name and your address for the record?

MRS. RANDOLPH. Maxine B. Randolph, 1686 32nd Avenue, San Francisco.

MR. GLICKSTEIN. Mrs. Randolph, what is your occupation?

MRS. RANDOLPH. My occupation is community coordinator of the OMI Project, the Oceanview, Merced Heights, Ingleside Community Stabilization and Improvement Project.

MR. GLICKSTEIN. Would you tell the Commission roughly where that area of San Francisco is?

MRS. RANDOLPH. It is in the southwest part of San Francisco, which is bordered by San Jose, Alemany Boulevard, Junipero Serra, Ocean Avenue. That is, on one side, Daly City. On the other side, the San Francisco State College, and on the other side City College. St. Francis Wood on one side, very lovely area of homes; Balboa Terrace and Monterey Heights. On the other side is Stonestown Shopping Center.

MR. GLICKSTEIN. Would you please briefly describe your responsibilities as coordinator of the OMI Project?

MRS. RANDOLPH. My responsibilities are to work directly with the committees and with the people of the community, and also to bring in those people with expertise which would help us in all of the areas in which we work, which are education, beautification, conservation, real estate and land use, community relations, intergroup relations, political education. In other words, 14 committees; some active, some not so active.

MR. GLICKSTEIN. Approximately how many people live in the OMI area?

MRS. RANDOLPH. Twenty-nine thousand.

MR. GLICKSTEIN. And what is the racial makeup of the various neighborhoods in this area?

MRS. RANDOLPH. Ocean View is about 90 percent a minority group, Negro. Merced Heights is about 50 percent—wait a minute. I have got this mixed up. Eighty percent I would say, closer to. And Ingleside Terrace is about 30 percent, or an overall 50 percent.

MR. GLICKSTEIN. Overall 50 percent?

MRS. RANDOLPH. Yes.

MR. GLICKSTEIN. What is the price range of homes in this area?

MRS. RANDOLPH. The price range is from $19,000 for a junior five to $25,000 for a two-bedroom home. It is an area of single family dwellings, and this goes from $25,000 to $38,000. In the more affluent area of Ingleside Terrace homes are upwards of $50,000 in some instances.

MR. GLICKSTEIN. Would you please tell us what the purpose of the OMI Project is?

MRS. RANDOLPH. The purpose of the project is to stabilize the project to prevent a ghetto. We say that we are working—a united community working toward a model interracial community. By that we mean that we would like to have the best schools, the most freedom for children to develop, for human beings to live creatively without fear and with human dignity.

MR. GLICKSTEIN. When was the project begun?

MRS. RANDOLPH. 1965, July.

58

MR. GLICKSTEIN. And you were aided, as I understand it, by the City Human Rights Commission?

MRS. RANDOLPH. By the Human Rights Commission and San Francisco State College. The Human Rights Commission helped to draw up the plan and assisted us in trying to find various groups in the community which would aid us. San Francisco State College has lent technical and research services to the project.

MR. GLICKSTEIN. What was the force that prompted the beginning of this project?

MRS. RANDOLPH. There are several different sources of information I have on this, but people began to be alarmed by the continuous, perhaps unethical, practices of real estate dealers in block-busting in the past, right after the war, and scare tactics used to help people or, at least, make them want—seemingly want to move.

Many of the people in the area, they are middle-and upper middle-class people, government workers, blue-collar workers, teachers, and they wanted to keep it a good community and they became alarmed by this kind of tactic.

They also became alarmed when there might be people moving in who did not have this kind of background in living in a community, and they felt that anything that they could do to help people live in a better way would be of help to the community. By this I mean that if children had been living in a ghetto most of their lives and come into a middle-class neighborhood, it was a different thing for them to have to get along with the children around them. The children around them had not been accustomed to fighting and things of this nature. That had happened a long time ago in the area, but many of these things had become better through better recreation, better schools, and more concern by the residents themselves for children. And also there was a great deal of clutter and perhaps cars left on streets. These things were signs of decay, and this is the thing that made most of the citizens aware that something was happening that they didn't want.

MR. GLICKSTEIN. Have there been any neighborhood improvement groups prior to OMI?

MRS. RANDOLPH. Yes. Merced Heights Neighborhood Improvement Association and the Ocean View-Ingleside—I mean the Ingleside-Ocean View Neighborhood Association were active. Merced Heights was extremely active and had a survey by SPUR, which helped people to understand what they wanted done and also it helped them to determine that they would stay in the community and keep it a good community.

Ingleside-Ocean View Neighborhood Improvement Association is a more recent group, but they have done the same thing. In the past there was an older group than that called the San Miguel Neighborhood Association, which is a very small area.

MR. GLICKSTEIN. In other words, your organization was attempting to prevent white people from leaving the neighborhood in large numbers. Is that correct?

MRS. RANDOLPH. Yes. Not just white people. They were attempting to prevent people leaving the neighborhood period. The kind of people that they had become accustomed to as neighbors and friends.

MR. GLICKSTEIN. Why do you feel it is important to racially stabilize the neighborhood?

MRS. RANDOLPH. Depends on what you call stabilization. The one thing that I would like to say here is that when you try to stabilize a neighborhood racially, one begins to question themselves. "Aren't we being a little presumptuous by saying that we want white people to move back into the neighborhood?" "Aren't we saying in effect that white people are better than Negro people?" And the third thing, "Are we saying, in effect, that if we want white people to move back into the neighborhood when there are homes needed for Negroes—?" These questions we have to answer first, but we know that the white people do still govern us and white people do have the big business. White people do govern our school boards, and in order to have any kind of improvements and not become a neglected and deteriorating area, we do have to have white people to help us, and this is why we are asking white people to move back. Otherwise we might be a neglected area.

MR. GLICKSTEIN. Are you in effect setting some sort of a quota?

MRS. RANDOLPH. No, definitely not. In fact, we aren't asking white people to move back. We just hope that people of all colors, pink, blue, green, or yellow, will move into our area, people who are interested in their children and their families and find it a nice place to live.

If I could have described this area, it is one of the most beautiful areas in the city. The views are fantastic.

MR. GLICKSTEIN. Do you think there is a desirable racial balance that should be maintained in a community in order for it to get the type of services that you mentioned a moment ago?

MRS. RANDOLPH. I am not going to answer that, Mr. Glickstein, because I don't know.

MR. GLICKSTEIN. But do you think there should be some white people in the community?

MRS. RANDOLPH. I think there has to be at this time until the Negro people are as effective as they can be in Government. Now they are a minority in the Government. Until they are practically equal with us, then I don't know. We don't know whether a segregated group can produce better schools. We are trying to find out.

MR. GLICKSTEIN. When a white person in the area is planning to sell his home, do you make any efforts to encourage that white person to sell his home to another white person?

MRS. RANDOLPH. We haven't done so yet, but I suppose this might be a tactic to use. This is distasteful to us to do this.

MR. GLICKSTEIN. Have you sought the assistance of the San Francisco Board of Realtors in attracting families to your area?

MRS. RANDOLPH. We have had some connection with the San Francisco Board of Realtors in the past, but more recently we have not had any contact with the Board of Realtors. We have tried—I mean we are going to.

MR. GLICKSTEIN. In what way have you wanted them to cooperate with you?

MRS. RANDOLPH. We would like the San Francisco Board of Realtors to make open housing an actuality in all of San Francisco and in all of the nine Bay Area counties, so that anyone can live wherever they want to, so that housing will be open and a person can live where he works and not have to commute. It seems to me this would solve a lot of problems.

MR. GLICKSTEIN. So you want the Board of Realtors to work with you in areas other than your own immediate community?

MRS. RANDOLPH. Yes.

MR. GLICKSTEIN. What sort of impact has the OMI Project had on the neighborhoods involved?

MRS. RANDOLPH. The impact on the area, one of the things that has happened is the recent decline in juvenile delinquency and crime, and this has been noted by Lieutenant Andriotti of our police-community relations. This has been going down for the second consecutive year, and we believe that this is probably because the people in the community do take an interest in their children and what is going on. This does not mean that all of the community knows about what is being done.

MR. GLICKSTEIN. Has the project had any impact on the racial composition of the neighborhoods involved? Have you actually managed to stabilize the community?

MRS. RANDOLPH. No. The only thing that has happened in that way has been the lack of money last year in buying homes. This helped more to stabilize the community in that way, if you are talking about racially.

MR. GLICKSTEIN. People weren't able to move out?

MRS. RANDOLPH. Right.

MR. GLICKSTEIN. Mrs. Randolph, I understand that you have a statement that you would like to submit for the record?

MRS. RANDOLPH. Yes, I have a statement that I would like to suggest as model legislation for communities to prevent the ghetto-izing of whole cities. I have several copies. I will only read in part——

MR. GLICKSTEIN. I think, Mrs. Randolph, that perhaps it would be best if you submitted this in the record and the Commission could then study it and read it. If you would like to summarize it in a minute or two, that would be perfectly all right.

MRS. RANDOLPH. The summary would be that we would like to recommend that model legislation be planned for the com-munities like ours to prevent ghettos, rather than to go in after the fact, and this would be to put all the forces available into that area in the way of schools, social services, transportation, health and welfare, that could possibly be available, and that this could be given to a municipality and through the municipality could be directed to the Human Rights Commission so that they might work with the individual communities and the community would have the third part.

No. 1, the city; No. 2, the community, and research and technical staff to help with this. But I should like to indicate here that I am not talking about another model city plan. I am talking about a plan where we would use all our private resources and funding agencies, private funding agencies and private service contractors, and that the Government would be the catalyst to get this started, because the time is very shortly coming when we will not be able to de-ghettoize a city. But we should start preventing it at once.

I should like to mention in closing that I feel that we should depart from this fragmentation and develop this plan to meet our citizens' needs, as well as to be our city's salvation.

MR. GLICKSTEIN. Mr. Chairman, may I request that Mrs. Ran-dolph's statement be introduced into the record as Exhibit No. 2?

VICE CHAIRMAN PATTERSON. So ordered.

(The document referred to was marked Exhibit No. 2 and received in evidence.)

MR. GLICKSTEIN. I have no further questions.

VICE CHAIRMAN PATTERSON. Father Hesburgh, do you have any questions of the witness?

FATHER HESBURGH. No. Thank you.

VICE CHAIRMAN PATTERSON. Mrs. Freeman?

COMMISSIONER FREEMAN. Mrs. Randolph, I note, I believe, you have five neighborhood schools within the Ocean View-Merced Heights area. Is that correct?

MRS. RANDOLPH. Yes.

COMMISSIONER FREEMAN. Will you tell us about the racial com-position of those schools? How many of them are predominantly Negro and how many are predominantly white, or do you know?

MRS. RANDOLPH. I would say that three are predominantly Negro and two are predominantly white, or I would say one is probably equal and one is predominantly white. The school program, which I have not mentioned, is one of the results of our planning.

We have a grant this year through the Unified School District for a bold and innovative program under Title III to find the ways in which children learn and to help them, and this is the composition of the schools as is. We have no preconceived ideas of what this should be at this time.

COMMISSIONER FREEMAN. Does the organization take a position with respect to whether there is damage to both Negro and white by attending segregated schools?

MRS. RANDOLPH. Yes.

COMMISSIONER FREEMAN. Has this position been communicated to the Board of Education?

MRS. RANDOLPH. Yes.

COMMISSIONER FREEMAN. Of the school district?

MRS. RANDOLPH. Yes.

COMMISSIONER FREEMAN. How long has the organization been working on the pilot program?

MRS. RANDOLPH. The pilot program?

COMMISSIONER FREEMAN. Is this a program that is geared to an elimination of racial isolation in all of the five schools?

MRS. RANDOLPH. The planning year for our elementary schools began the 31st of January, and prior to that time we had spent a year planning to get the planning grant, and now we are working in the planning year. We don't know how this will come about. We have no preconceived ideas of what will be happening at the end of the year when we ask for the actual project grant which will help to develop these schools. This year they are trying out all kinds of ideas. I cannot answer that. I am not equipped to.

COMMISSIONER FREEMAN. Is there any isolation by economic class in addition to race?

MRS. RANDOLPH. I am sure there must be, but I have not noted it. The area is predominantly middle-class, and there are a few people who are on welfare, a few who are on old age pensions and a few who have children who are on Aid to Dependent Children. This is a very small amount comparatively speaking.

We are not a poverty area, but we have a few people in our area who have poverty—I mean they would classify economically as falling in the category that has been set up by the poverty program.

COMMISSIONER FREEMAN. And these people would be Negro?

MRS. RANDOLPH. Yes.

COMMISSIONER FREEMAN. Thank you.

MRS. RANDOLPH. I won't say predominantly—I say predominantly Negro. There are also some very poor white people. As for isolation, I am not sure they are isolated completely, because many of our people work very diligently on this in the neighborhoods.

VICE CHAIRMAN PATTERSON. Mr. Taylor?

MR. TAYLOR. You said at one time, Mrs. Randolph, that you had been in touch with the organization—had been in touch with the Board of Realtors?

MRS. RANDOLPH. This is prior to my being here and I am not certain of what had been done at that time. We worked with realtors but not with the board. We worked with individual realtors.

MR. TAYLOR. Since the time that you have been involved, has the Board of Realtors been of any assistance to you in achieving the goal of opening up housing in areas other than your own?

MRS. RANDOLPH. No.

MR. TAYLOR. Do you think that it is possible for your project to be successful in the long run in maintaining a stabilized balanced neighborhood if opportunity is not open for Negroes to secure housing in other areas of the city?

MRS. RANDOLPH. It is happening now. I am going indirectly to answer your question that housing is opening up. I have one question now, is that possibly there will be a ghettoizing of another area, and I think that without the help of the San Francisco Real Estate Board that we cannot prevent people from selling a large tract of houses to people of one minority group and that we do have to have their cooperation in this to disperse people.

MR. TAYLOR. Thank you.

VICE CHAIRMAN. Any further questions? Thank you very much for coming here, Mrs. Randolph. You are excused. Will Counsel call the next witness, please?

MR. GLICKSTEIN. The next witness is Mr. Lee Diamond.

(Whereupon, MR. LEE DIAMOND, was sworn by the Vice Chairman and testified as follows:)

TESTIMONY OF MR. LEE E. DIAMOND, PACIFICIA, CALIFORNIA

MR. GLICKSTEIN. Would you please state your name and address for the record?

MR. DIAMOND. My name is Lee E. Diamond, and I live at 417 Lynbrook Drive in Pacifica.

MR. GLICKSTEIN. Are you involved with the OMI project?

MR. DIAMOND. I am.

MR. GLICKSTEIN. And what is the nature of your involvement?

MR. DIAMOND. Well, I serve on the steering committee as a delegate from the Pilgrim Men's Fellowship which is an independent organization that I belong to, and I am also presently sitting on the administrative committee.

MR. GLICKSTEIN. What results do you hope to achieve through the OMI project?

MR. DIAMOND. Well, the results that the Men's Fellowship hope will be received is that out of this project in time, we figure about five years, that this community will be the place where people of all races, creeds, and religions can live and work together in peace.

MR. GLICKSTEIN. What has been done so far to achieve that goal?

MR. DIAMOND. Well, at the present time since this project has been going, we have been working in the areas of education, beautification, housing, and recreation, the idea being that we want to create a community that would have the best education possible, the best police protection possible, the best recreational facilities possible, and the best community as far as beauty, transportation and these things are concerned.

We feel that people who are concerned about the education of their children, safety, welfare of their families would want to move into a community such as this. So we feel that one way to stabilize a community and cause it to become integrated is to create a community where people of all races would want to come and live, and this is what we mean by racial stabilization.

We feel that once people see that their children can get the best education and that this community has everything that one would want a community to have in which to live, that they would come in regardless of their race or their background.

MR. GLICKSTEIN. So in order for you to achieve your goals, in maintaining an integrated community, you do have to make all of these improvements that you just spoke of?

MR. DIAMOND. That is correct.

MR. GLICKSTEIN. Can you obtain these results if the community were to become predominantly Negro?

MR. DIAMOND. Well, my group, the Men's Fellowship, we are not opposed to the integration, but we are not necessarily for integration either. We feel that this community, through this project, is going to become the kind of community where a person can grow and develop and enjoy all of the privileges of being an American citizen, and my organization doesn't care whether the area becomes totally black or otherwise. The point being if a person comes and lives in that community they will have to come in there knowing that this is a place where every citizen has certain rights and they are going to be respected.

MR. GLICKSTEIN. Do you think that if you were able to develop the type of community you have in mind it is almost inevitable that it would be integrated?

MR. DIAMOND. We feel that integration would come based upon the makeup of the population within about five to seven years because we plan to eliminate such practices as the real estate people. We plan to eliminate such conditions like police protection where in an area where there are predominantly Negro people, these services from the police department and other governmental agencies seem to be lacking and we have plans in mind where we are going to make sure that we get, as taxpayers and as citizens, the necessary police protection that we need and the other services that all other areas of higher standards get.

MR. GLICKSTEIN. Do you feel that there is an ideal racial composition for a community?

MR. DIAMOND. An ideal racial composition, the way we feel about this, is that when people are permitted to go and come as they wish and to make their own choices, that things will settle racially based on the composition of the population.

MR. GLICKSTEIN. Do you think your neighborhood would reflect the racial composition of the entire community?

MR. DIAMOND. We do. We feel this.

MR. GLICKSTEIN. Mrs. Randolph mentioned some of the programs in the schools. In your opinion what role do the schools play in attracting and retaining white persons in the neighborhood?

MR. DIAMOND. Well, in this particular school area, in the boundaries that we have, there are only elementary schools there, and in the schools there are more Caucasian teachers, and I might add in one of the schools in particular, Ortega School, the quality of the teachers there, the quality is high. They have some of the best teachers that money can buy in this community and, of course, we intend to keep it that way.

MR. GLICKSTEIN. Do you think that it is essential or necessary that the schools be integrated in order to attract and retain white people in the area?

MR. DIAMOND. Well, I feel that in order to talk about integration as far as a school is concerned, we have to look at it in this light: white children and Negro children, if they grow up while they are young and have a chance to observe each other as individuals and as human beings, a lot of the prejudices that they receive from their parents and their loved ones would not be as severe as it is today.

Now, integration in this respect I think is good and necessary that we get to like and dislike people based upon how they relate or how we relate to them as human beings and not according to the color of their skin or their religion.

In this respect, we feel that integration is absolutely necessary, but integration as far as white and black is concerned, we are not for integration nor are we against it.

MR. GLICKSTEIN. You think you can have fine quality schools that are predominantly or entirely Negro?

MR. DIAMOND. This is what I mean when I say we are not

necessarily for integration. There is no reason in the world why a black person cannot learn to the maximum of which he is capable in a totally black school if he has the facilities and if he has the teachers that would enable him to develop fully. We feel that a black child can develop as well as a white child if in his surroundings and at his home that he does not get this superiority and inferiority thing that has been going on in the past. If we can keep him away from this inferior-superior type relationship, there is no reason why he cannot operate at his maximum capacity.

MR. GLICKSTEIN. Even in an all-Negro school?

MR. DIAMOND. Even in an all-Negro school.

MR. GLICKSTEIN. You mentioned a little while ago an experience of yourself and of your organization, predominantly Negro areas that didn't seem to get the same quality of public services as white areas. Do you think your organization is going to be able to mobilize sufficient power and influence to correct a situation of that sort?

MR. DIAMOND. Well, we are working on the plan now where we are going to get it through the avenue of—I think Mrs. Randolph mentioned that we have some kind of a political action committee set up. What we plan to do, we plan to inform the people in the community, whatever the racial composition is, as to what their rights are, what the candidates running for office stand for, what they really stand for, and then we feel that once these people become registered voters and become active citizens, then they will be able to say to the people downtown: "This is what we want." And we will get it because we have quite a number of votes out there.

MR. GLICKSTEIN. Has your organization done anything to stimulate employment or jobs in your community?

MR. DIAMOND. In the employment area, hopefully if we can continue to operate within the next two years, we plan to have in this community almost no unemployment. We are working with employers, locally, as well as throughout the city, working on jobs for every citizen in the community that wants or wishes to work.

Now recently we have an agreement with Payless Supermarkets which will become operable in September of this year, over 250 jobs are restricted to the people that live in that community, and then after they have hired all the people that wish to work and that can qualify for these jobs, then and only then will they spread out to other communities to hire and fill these 250 job vacancies.

We have been working with the merchants in the area who are helping us financially in this project and they have assured us that they will, when vacancies come up for employment, that they will come through our office and let us know about these vacancies and that they will try to create summer jobs and after-school jobs for the young people so that they will have something to do and some way to earn some money to do the things that they would like to do. So we are working on employment.

MR. GLICKSTEIN. Thank you. I have no further questions, Mr. Chairman.

VICE CHAIRMAN PATTERSON. Father Hesburgh, do you wish to question the witness?

COMMISSIONER HESBURGH. Mr. Diamond, you are an active teacher, correct?

MR. DIAMOND. Yes.

COMMISSIONER HESBURGH. You are teaching mathematics and science?

MR. DIAMOND. I am teaching science now primarily.

COMMISSIONER HESBURGH. Are you teaching in a predominantly Negro school or a predominantly white school?

MR. DIAMOND. I am teaching in a predominantly Caucasian school.

COMMISSIONER HESBURGH. Maybe you would have some help for us on a report we have just finished recently. A very difficult problem for the Commission is how you get a balanced school in neighborhoods that are 80 to 90 percent Negro at the moment.

MR. DIAMOND. This is the problem we're working on now. We feel that in order to get a balanced school racially, I think this is what you mean, that you must create a community and have in the community the necessary things that will draw people.

COMMISSIONER HESBURGH. You are getting at it from the neighborhood side of bringing more white people in?

MR. DIAMOND. Create a neighborhood that everybody would want to live in and then take the restrictions down and people flow in and out according to the population. This is a theory, but we think it is a good one.

COMMISSIONER HESBURGH. The kind of mobility that really hasn't existed in America too much up to this point?

MR. DIAMOND. No, it hasn't.

COMMISSIONER HESBURGH. Thank you.

VICE CHAIRMAN PATTERSON. Mrs. Freeman?

COMMISSIONER FREEMAN. Mr. Diamond, when you say create a neighborhood that everybody would want to live in, you are not suggesting, are you, that Negroes should accept less than white persons or should be happy with less?

MR. DIAMOND. No, I am not suggesting this. On the contrary, what I am suggesting is that—well, a good example of what I mean is we have an excellent intergroup relations situation going in our community now, in particular in the education committee. When we have our meetings and our social gatherings, we have people from the rank of Dr. Summerskill, who is the president of San

Francisco State College, and several of the professors on down to just a plain ordinary housewife and working father.

All these people communicate and socialize with one another on equal terms, on equal basis, and this is the key to the entire situation. We have created just by chance, I guess, or maybe through the desire to do something, we have created a situation where in our community we have people of all races and all backgrounds working together side by side without the inferiority-superiority type situation that has existed for so many years, and this is what I mean.

COMMISSIONER FREEMAN. What percentage of this group would be Negro?

MR. DIAMOND. I would say in the education committee it is about 40 percent Negro and about 60 percent Caucasian. In the other social gatherings that we have had, we have had a good cross-sample of different races and religions mixing together in a good atmosphere, one that really, truly tells you about the democratic principle and about America, and this is one reason why we have so much hope in this project is because we have a sample of where people can live and work together without feeling inferior to another person based upon your occupation or your race.

COMMISSIONER FREEMAN. In addition to the communication that you talked about, my question goes to the extent of actual participation and involvement.

Are you saying that the black people are free and equal participants in the decision-making process at every level of this community?

MR. DIAMOND. In our project, in all of the committees that I am familiar with, the black man is equal, has an equal voice, and in some cases has more than an equal voice than the Caucasian counterpart. The black man is free and he feels free to express his views, to participate as an equal partner, and this is unique in most cases in our society.

COMMISSIONER FREEMAN. In that community to which you are referring, is there any distinction between the services that were rendered by the city or the public authorities six years ago and those that are rendered now?

MR. DIAMOND. Well, since we have become active, we are getting much more help than normal from the city departments. We are being heard, if this is what you mean.

COMMISSIONER FREEMAN. So there had been a change or a——

MR. DIAMOND. There is an improvement.

COMMISSIONER FREEMAN. From the deterioration before the organization came into existence?

MR. DIAMOND. That is true.

COMMISSIONER FREEMAN. This is because of the change in the racial character of the neighborhood?

Mr. Diamond. No, this is because I feel that the change came about because the people in the community got together and organized.

Commissioner Freeman. I mean before they got together?

Mr. Diamond. Before they got together there was a deterioration. Maybe I didn't understand you. Before we came together and organized, the neighborhood was going down at a rapid pace.

Commissioner Freeman. As it became predominantly Negro?

Mr. Diamond. As it became predominantly Negro.

Commissioner Freeman. So they were not free and equal participants at that time?

Mr. Diamond. Before the project started, no.

Commissioner Freeman. And you are saying now they are?

Mr. Diamond. Now they are.

Commissioner Freeman. Thank you.

Vice Chairman Patterson. Dr. Rankin?

Commissioner Rankin. I am interested a little bit in your method of community action. The tax rate is the same all over San Francisco, isn't it?

Mr. Diamond. As far as I know.

Commissioner Rankin. Well, are you wanting the city to spend more money in your area than it spends in other areas? Am I correct in that?

Mr. Diamond. No. What we are saying is this, that we want everything for our community that we are entitled to as citizens and as taxpayers. What I am saying by this is that, well, let's take the rich areas, for example, where our rich people live in the city of San Francisco. They get services that other communities do not normally get. For example, they get police officers that are stationed in their communities, more or less like private officers, you might say.

Commissioner Rankin. Your criticism then is of the administration of the city functions, is that right, that it is not administered evenly, that to certain sections they give more protection than they do to others. Is that correct?

Mr. Diamond. Well, this has always been true throughout the country. The rich get the services and the poor get nothing.

Commissioner Rankin. That's a pretty broad statement, isn't it?

Mr. Diamond. I know it is pretty broad, but it is pretty true.

Commissioner Rankin. I would say in fire protection in my town everybody gets the same fire protection.

Mr. Diamond. Everybody may get fire protection, but the quality of the fire protection or the availability of the equipment is a different thing.

Commissioner Rankin. And you are saying that is not true in San Francisco?

MR. DIAMOND. Well, I don't think it is true in this country.

COMMISSIONER RANKIN. Well, I differ with you. I think in some areas—I think services are given pretty well in a nondiscriminatory fashion. I couldn't say all over the United States that all we have is discrimination. I just can't go along with you on that.

MR. DIAMOND. Ninety percent. I would settle for that.

COMMISSIONER RANKIN. Having been on the city council myself at one time, I was interested in your accusation.

VICE CHAIRMAN PATTERSON. Mr. Taylor?

MR. TAYLOR. No questions.

VICE CHAIRMAN PATTERSON. Mr. Diamond, after your experience in the OMI area, could you give any advice as to how the Potrero Hill difficulties might be solved in San Francisco?

MR. DIAMOND. Well, this project is designed and we hope that the rest of the communities in the city would follow after us and some of them are trying. Of course, their problems are a little more acute than ours because we have the colleges on either side, the junior colleges, the State College. We have a direct line to downtown. We have the freeway there. We have a view. Our community has just about everything that one would want.

We also have shopping centers on almost every side. We feel that Potrero Hill will only be able to benefit from a project such as ours if we can prove that we can make it a success. Then the thing can spread and we feel that since we are on the San Mateo County line that we can kind of, like a disease, just spread and engulf the whole city with our project one community after the other. This is the only way that they can be helped. Their problem is too severe to try to even think about working on it at the degree that we are. It is almost impossible.

VICE CHAIRMAN PATTERSON. Do you think the conditions are present to allow them to begin forming organizations similar to yours and working at it from that direction?

MR. DIAMOND. Well, I see, based upon the hearing that I listened to this morning, that they are stepping in the right direction. The only problem that they are going to have to resolve now in order to make further progress is that the Caucasian part will have to accept and recognize the Negro part on an equal basis, and I gather from the hearing this morning that the Caucasian part still at least communicate, whether they really mean this or not, communicate to the black community that we are the superior part and you are the inferior part and it is not going to work. It has to be on an equal basis or not at all.

VICE CHAIRMAN PATTERSON. Are there any further questions? Father Hesburgh?

COMMISSIONER HESBURGH. Mr. Diamond, isn't there a greater economic gulf between the white and black segments of Potrero Hill than there would be in your area?

MR. DIAMOND. There definitely is.

COMMISSIONER HESBURGH. Well, money seems to always have a direct hand. In fact, we need money ourselves. Potrero Hill has both the economic problem and the educational problem. There is no question about this. This is one reason why the Caucasians in that area are going to have to bend over a little bit more in order to get these people to feel—really feel—that they belong and they are part of the group and this takes a lot.

MR. DIAMOND. Is that part of the key of the problem?

COMMISSIONER HESBURGH. Would it be easier on Potrero Hill if you had a better educational and economic mix between the two groups?

MR. DIAMOND. I don't think that is the problem on Potrero Hill. I think the problem on Potrero Hill is the old stereotyped middle-class value system, and it has to be modified for it to work any-more. It has to be one set of rules and standards for everybody, and then those black people will go in there and work with those people and soon they will see some fruit from their labor.

COMMISSIONER HESBURGH. But the only point I am trying to make, and I don't want to belabor it, is we have been talking all morning about the lack of communication. You hear one set of witnesses say this is the situation and hear another set that says this is an entirely different situation and you hear another set that is different again. Obviously, there is not much communication going on between these sets of people, but communication gets a lot easier if you have things in common, whether it be economic status, or whether it be educational status. It becomes quite difficult if people don't talk in the same terms or don't have much in common. I mean apart from any racial consideration.

Now, it seems to me that if you tried to say why your project is working and theirs aren't working all that well, it would be interesting to find out what the difference is between the two situations.

VICE CHAIRMAN PATTERSON. Would you speak on that, Mr. Diamond? What are the factors that have enabled you to deal with some of these problems over the six years you mentioned?

MR. DIAMOND. First of all, I have to admit I don't exactly know how we got going as well as we did. I can't quite put my fingers on it except to say that I guess education is the key to this because in our project we have quite a few people, both Negro and Caucasians, that for the most part have some college, if not college degrees. This may be the key. I don't know, but I think the other part is that the people in our project, both black and white, are saying, and they are standing up in general for equal opportunity for all, regardless.

Now, in the Potrero Hill area, I realize it is kind of difficult for the Caucasians over there because they are working with a very difficult situation, but they are going to just have to say that, well, one thing that we have in common is that we all are American citizens and we are all entitled to all the benefits thereof. If they can't operate on that simple formula, they may as well just quit and go home because they are not going to get any place. And this is what we are working on over there.

We are getting some resistance now and then, but then we iron it out. We are all American citizens and we are going to work for and make sure that we all receive the benefits of being American citizens. So that is what we are really working on and this is something that we all have in common over there in general.

VICE CHAIRMAN PATTERSON. Mrs. Freeman?

COMMISSIONER FREEMAN. Mr. Diamond, there is one other dimension that I would like to pursue. That is that in Potrero Hill, part of the hostility is the opposition to the low rent housing development, and I would like to know if you would give your opinion as to what it would be if somebody would suggest to your organization that a low rent housing development be placed in the Ocean View-Merced Heights area. Would there be opposition on the part of any of this group to low rent housing tenants residing in the neighborhood?

MR. DIAMOND. Yes, there would be opposition to—I guess you might say the term "low rent." Now, here is the——

COMMISSIONER FREEMAN. Public housing I am talking about.

MR. DIAMOND. Public housing. What I think should be done if the government is going to deal with housing, and I think history in the past practices tell us that as long as you leave loopholes the realtors and everybody else is going to use them and get around these things. What needs to be done is you need to take the agencies like the FHA and let them co-sign for these people that want to better themselves as far as housing is concerned.

Now, the FHA, the way it operates now, if you are a middle-class person and if you have a good income and a steady job, and all this type of thing, then they will, you know, you can qualify for an FHA loan, so to speak, but with the people that are not quite making this $700-a-month type of thing, they can't qualify for housing through the FHA plan.

Now I know of some people, friends of mine, who live over in our area that couldn't qualify for FHA, but what they did, they borrowed $2,000 from their credit union. They got a second on their house. Then they had to make the normal down payment, and this friend of mine is paying $300 a month payment for his house. Now I went through FHA to buy a house recently and I qualified because I made enough money, and I only have to pay $150 a month for a house that is far superior to this particular house.

Now what the FHA needs to do, they need to say, "Look, we are not going to decide on whether you can qualify for a loan based upon your earning power. We are going to qualify you for a housing on FHA loan based upon how stable you are." This would say to this person that did not perhaps get the education to earn a large amount of money, or would say to this person that can only do meager mediocre type jobs, say, earn $4,000 a year, that if you want to improve yourself, if you want to get out of the ghetto-type situation, if you want your family to grow in a community where they can be proud of their parents, then this person can qualify for an FHA loan and buy this house of his choice.

So what I suggest that instead of fighting these realtors—they are going to do like they want to anyway—why don't you co-sign for these people that cannot qualify, that cannot make $700 or more a month. Co-sign for them and let them buy a home of their choice based on whether they were in jail every other day or not or whether they are on the job or not. This is something that we would accept in our community, but public housing and this type of thing, the people themselves don't want it because they are classified as being poverty-ridden and their children wear these things and then they get this feeling and then reflect this in the schools. So you are only stunting their growth.

VICE CHAIRMAN PATTERSON. Any further questions? Thank you very much, Mr. Diamond, for appearing here today. You are excused. Counsel, would you call the next witness, please?

MR. GLICKSTEIN. Mrs. Genevieve Jefferson.

(Whereupon, MRS. GENEVIEVE JEFFERSON was duly sworn by the Vice Chairman and testified as follows:)

TESTIMONY OF MRS. GENEVIEVE M. JEFFERSON, SAN FRANCISCO, CALIFORNIA

MR. GLICKSTEIN. Mrs. Jefferson, would you please state your full name and address for the record?

MRS. JEFFERSON. Genevieve M. Jefferson, 460 Ramsell Street, San Francisco.

MR. GLICKSTEIN. You live in the OMI area?

MRS. JEFFERSON. I do.

MR. GLICKSTEIN. What portion of it?

MRS. JEFFERSON. In Merced Heights.

MR. GLICKSTEIN. How long have you lived there?

MRS. JEFFERSON. Since 1952.

MR. GLICKSTEIN. What was the racial composition of the neighborhood when you first moved in?

MRS. JEFFERSON. Primarily Caucasian. Now I am talking only about Merced Heights.

MR. GLICKSTEIN. Right.

MRS. JEFFERSON. Maybe 1 or 2 percent Negro or other races, the balance Caucasian.

MR. GLICKSTEIN. And what is the approximate racial composition now?

MRS. JEFFERSON. It is very hard to estimate. I would say maybe 60, 65, 70 percent. It is anyone's guess. In the 1960 census it had gone from virtually a very small number in 1950 to about 34 percent in 1960 and has gone steadily upward.

MR. GLICKSTEIN. Now you would guess it is about 60 percent or so Negro, 60, 70 percent?

MRS. JEFFERSON. Someplace in there.

MR. GLICKSTEIN. I gather that this change was not gradual?

MRS. JEFFERSON. Well, it was not gradual. Actually there was a fairly rapid change going from almost no Negroes to roughly 34 percent Negro.

MR. GLICKSTEIN. Were your neighbors and you concerned about this change?

MRS. JEFFERSON. Well, I wasn't, but some neighbors were.

MR. GLICKSTEIN. What fears or concerns did they have?

MRS. JEFFERSON. Well, there were a number of kinds of things, I think. There were some people who clearly are prejudiced. There were some other people who were honestly puzzled. They really didn't know what was happening to their neighborhood, and these are people whose income is not too great. Their home was their greatest investment and they just weren't sure what was happening to their neighborhood and their home, and I think some of their fears were deliberately fanned by real estate dealers in their effort to secure listings for reselling.

MR. GLICKSTEIN. Were you ever contacted by real estate people during this period?

MRS. JEFFERSON. Oh, I was.

MR. GLICKSTEIN. What sort of contacts were made with you?

MRS. JEFFERSON. It is very hard to remember back that far. I guess the first impact was when a very intelligent man came by and started to chat. We were mowing the lawn and he asked if we had thought about selling our home and would we like an appraisal, and we told him firmly we weren't at all interested, and then he launched into the conversation which went something like this, "I would sure be damn mad if I were you folks with something like this happening in the neighborhood." And I was puzzled at this point. I was still pretty naive, and we exchanged conversation, and finally I said, "What do you mean? Because of Negroes moving in?" And he said, "Well, of course." So I told him that both my husband and I had been very proud of the way our neighborhood integrated without any unseemly activities, that there were no demonstrations and no unhappy events, that was just one—later——

MR. GLICKSTEIN. That person was a real estate man?

MRS. JEFFERSON. That person was what?

MR. GLICKSTEIN. That person that spoke to you on the lawn was a real estate man?

MRS. JEFFERSON. Yes. He was securing a listing and he went right on urging that we get out while we could get our money out.

Another one that I recall talked to me at some length and his approach was, "We are relocating families in this area." And I said, "What do you mean, 'relocating'? Is this an urban renewal area?" And he said, "Oh, no, no, no. We are helping families who want to get out to live in a decent place." Well, our conversation terminated shortly thereafter, but there were these kinds of ways of playing on the fears of people.

One elderly woman who was recently widowed was helped to move to a "safer" place and she didn't want to move, but her fears were just played upon.

MR. GLICKSTEIN. Where did the white families that moved out move to? Do you know?

MRS. JEFFERSON. Probably many down the Peninsula. There was a new development opening up in the Westlake area. Many of these people were—well, this was at one time occupied by quite a few city employees when people—when city employees had to live in San Francisco for residence reasons. This neighborhood was as far as you could get and still be within the county line, and I think many of these people left and may have gone to Daly City, just over the border. By that time the residence requirements were being loosened.

MR. GLICKSTEIN. What effect did the changing racial composition in your neighborhood have, particularly in the way of city services, for example?

MRS. JEFFERSON. Well, back when we were a neighborhood in transition—now, again I am talking about only Merced Heights, which is where I have been most interested. During the period when we were a neighborhood in transition, which was, oh, some place about 1961 and 1962, we began to notice little things and, as I think about them now, they were petty little things and they really don't have much significance, but the streets didn't seem to be being cleaned as often as they were previously and by this time we had a going neighborhood organization, and so we had discussions with city officials.

Another very little thing, but it still made me mad at the time, was, we were having trouble with the dogs and the city has some nice little signs they put up on telephone poles, which say "Curb Your Dog." So we wrote to the Public Works Department asking if we could have some of these as an educational device, and we got the answer that the budget did not permit, but they would keep our request on file, and when there was some money we could conceivably be considered.

Well, I first noticed one neighborhood had gotten signs and we had none, and finally the point where I noticed the second one which had gotten signs, and which was a new area which was developed after it, and I was furious, but it was this kind of thing.

MR. GLICKSTEIN. You just had a feeling——

MRS. JEFFERSON. Another thing that I think is significant that happens in this kind of situation. My neighbor came over quite upset one day. Her insurance had been cancelled. I don't know what kind of a policy she had, but I think it was something like a standard householder's policy and the man who had handled her insurance apparently had handled it ever since she was in California, and so he was very apologetic and in order to explain the reason for this he enclosed a little note from the—I don't know whether it was a broker or an insurance company or who—with whom he had placed the insurance, and the gist of it was that "We don't want to insure in that neighborhood any longer. Frankly, we don't want their business." That was the line I still remember, and it was this kind of thing that we saw happening.

MR. GLICKSTEIN. How were you able to resist moving? What prompted you to remain rather than to move?

MRS. JEFFERSON. We never had any thought of moving. We are perfectly comfortable and happy. As a matter of fact, part of the area improved after these Negroes moved in, because some of them actually maintained their homes better than some of the Caucasians who had fled.

As a matter of fact, the first ones to flee tended to be the lower middle-class, the group who were most threatened by an influx of Negroes.

MR. GLICKSTEIN. What is the present attitude of your white neighbors toward the Negro families that have moved in?

MRS. JEFFERSON. Well, I am afraid I can't speak for all of them. Probably some still have doubts in their mind, but the thing that seemed to me that happened was as people got to know one another much of the apprehension disappeared. In the first place many Caucasians had never had the privilege of knowing an intelligent or cultured Negro, and they had this stereotyped picture of what a Negro was.

Well, as we started working together in our neighborhood organization and the sole purpose of setting up our neighborhood organization was in order to work together toward our mutual objectives. As people got to know one another they found that they really weren't different, and when I really thought we had moved along—I was quite uncomfortable, since we have been talking about white and black, because some of us have almost forgotten white and black in our neighborhood association. We used to be very careful to balance our committees, so many Negroes and so many Caucasians, and then soon we just sort of forgot about this because we were just people and we selected the best people, and the balance takes care of itself.

MR. GLICKSTEIN. How have the people in your neighborhood reacted to the OMI Project?

MRS. JEFFERSON. Well, I am afraid the bulk of the neighborhood really doesn't know what is going on. I think this is the biggest weakness of the project. In the effort to get support and in fund-raising efforts, I think we have missed the boat in not doing a better job of keeping the total neighborhood informed. Originally when we started our neighborhood association we had really very good meetings, of big total membership meetings, where people came together and talked about their mutual problems.

I think in OMI we haven't yet—we have been so busy getting organized that we really haven't gotten around to involving the total neighborhood to the extent we should, and I would hope that would be our next step because the more people work together, the more they get to know one another, and this seems to me when tensions and misunderstandings disappear.

MR. GLICKSTEIN. Do you think that a project like OMI can succeed in preventing whites from leaving a neighborhood and attracting whites back to a neighborhood?

MRS. JEFFERSON. Well, I certainly think the basic idea is sound. Whether you are too little and too late I don't know. We have not had any cooperation that I know of from the real estate industry until just the last few months, and when I say the real estate industry, we now have a few realtors working with us on our real estate committee, but back during the days when the Merced Heights Neighborhood Association was attempting to secure cooperation we got nothing. What happened was, each time someone moved, this is after the original panic period, after we were relatively stabilized, and again I am talking only about Merced Heights, as individuals moved, for whatever reason, transfer for business reasons, or whatever, the only people who were brought to look at homes were members of minority races. And so we made repeated efforts to ask the individual realtors operating in the area to show the homes on an open basis, to the best qualified buyer.

At one point we sent a circular letter over our president's name to some 52 or thereabout real estate men operating in this small area. To my knowledge there was no response. I wrote a number of letters to individual realtors and I had two responses that I recall. One a visit and the other a very irate telephone call in which the man asked me if I were accusing his salesmen of block-busting, and actually I told him that I thought he was at least a

78

little overzealous in trying to secure his listings, but to my knowledge we have had relatively no cooperation.

Contacts at that time were made both with the San Francisco —I don't know which is the Board, San Francisco Board and State Commission, or vice versa. I am not sure of their names.

MR. GLICKSTEIN. Thank you. I have no further questions, Mr. Chairman.

VICE CHAIRMAN PATTERSON. Father Hesburgh, do you wish to question the witness?

COMMISSIONER HESBURGH. Mrs. Jefferson, would you say your neighborhood is fairly stabilized now?

MRS. JEFFERSON. By my standards it is compared to what it was some eight years ago, seven years ago, six years ago.

COMMISSIONER HESBURGH. Are white people shown the openings now?

MRS. JEFFERSON. Oh, no. Oh, no. I didn't mean that, but by—it is not integrated, if that is what you mean. When I say—well, it is integrated actually, but I mean we certainly are not a balanced, normal American neighborhood. We are tending to become a neighborhood of one race, which to me is not a normal American neighborhood.

COMMISSIONER HESBURGH. And the real estate people who control all the people seeing the openings only show Negroes these homes?

MRS. JEFFERSON. Well, that has certainly been true up until —so far as I know. As a matter of fact, back when there was so much turnover, and when we were asking the help of the real estate industry to—and we really laid out our objectives very carefully. We watched in the various blocks to see who was brought to look at houses, and there was never a Caucasian brought. Even worse than that, I know of two Caucasian families who tried to buy there and who were actively discouraged from buying there by being told that this was well on its way to being a Negro ghetto. These were people who were either employed at San Francisco State or doing some work on the campus. I am not sure which the situation was, but who were then steered to a more expensive home which they didn't really want to buy; but this one family, they had been renting in our area, they wanted to buy there. They were steered away from there to buy a higher-priced home with the story of, "This is about to become a ghetto."

COMMISSIONER HESBURGH. I wonder if there could be any value in your association taking on the real estate profession? In other words, in a sense they are attacking your neighborhood. They are going against the wishes of the people in the neighborhood. They are the only private group that has anything to say about this apparently in moving property. I wonder if one shouldn't resist this kind of attack and say——

MRS. JEFFERSON. I think we have tried to. We tried to both in the Neighborhood Association and now the OMI Project is attempting to do this and is attempting to do it with the help of realtors themselves, and this is what I said originally, that we do have some realtors who are working with us now on our Real Estate and Land Use Committee.

COMMISSIONER HESBURGH. Suppose everybody just said, "We will boycott the whole real estate profession if you don't go along."

MRS. JEFFERSON. We have played with that idea, too. We have talked about setting up our own cooperative listing service, but all these things take time and energy. But that idea has occurred to us.

COMMISSIONER HESBURGH. See, all the pious talk isn't going to help us if the real estate profession just goes its merry way and decides it is going to decide what neighborhoods are going to be in America. It seems to me that's essentially what's happening, at least in your neighborhood. Is that correct? Is it essentially true that your neighborhood was changed by the complete interference and connivance of the real estate profession?

MRS. JEFFERSON. That is my personal opinion.

COMMISSIONER HESBURGH. Thank you very much. That is mine, too.

VICE CHAIRMAN PATTERSON. Mrs. Freeman?

COMMISSIONER FREEMAN. Mrs. Jefferson, do you know the extent of which the sellers of property have said to the real estate broker that they would be willing to sell their property either to white or Negro persons?

MRS. JEFFERSON. I don't know whether I didn't hear you or——

COMMISSIONER FREEMAN. The person who is going to sell the property?

MRS. JEFFERSON. Would he be willing to sell through——

COMMISSIONER FREEMAN. That he would sell to either a Negro or a white person? Suppose somebody in Merced Heights today is ready to sell his property and he says to a real estate broker, "I want to sell my house to a white person." You have said earlier that the real estate broker will only bring Negroes and you would desire an integrated community. I am asking you what would the real estate broker do with that situation?

MRS. JEFFERSON. I am not sure. Isn't that illegal now? I don't know.

COMMISSIONER FREEMAN. Well, we were informed that the real estate industry opposed the Fair Housing Law because it was compulsory but that they indicated that they felt it should be voluntary and here would be a situation where the seller would say, "I want to sell it to anybody." Now, what is the role of the real estate broker here?

MRS. JEFFERSON. I think if they say, "I am happy to sell my home to anyone," the same thing will happen.

COMMISSIONER FREEMAN. So here the broker has ignored the wishes of the seller and of the community?

MRS. JEFFERSON. Well, we would only ask that they sell to whoever is interested and not prejudice a person who wants to buy there.

COMMISSIONER FREEMAN. Is the broker not licensed by the State of California?

MRS. JEFFERSON. I believe they are.

COMMISSIONER FREEMAN. Is it not possible that perhaps this might represent a conspiracy in violation of the laws? Is that something that probably you could think about?

MRS. JEFFERSON. I am afraid you are getting into questions that I am not qualified to answer, but it certainly sounds like it.

COMMISSIONER FREEMAN. I know. We're struggling for answers too, as to just how to get at it.

MRS. JEFFERSON. I think we have felt very stopped in trying to handle this problem, and this does not mean we don't want any one race. We simply, as I said before, want to be a balanced American neighborhood which is neither predominantly Caucasian or predominantly Negro or predominantly Oriental or anything else.

COMMISSIONER FREEMAN. What you are saying, there is value in a multiracial society and life together?

MRS. JEFFERSON. That is what we think.

COMMISSIONER FREEMAN. I agree with you.

VICE CHAIRMAN PATTERSON. Professor Rankin?

DR. RANKIN. No.

VICE CHAIRMAN PATTERSON. Mr. Taylor?

MR. TAYLOR. Mrs. Jefferson, do you know whether practices of the real estate brokers have been brought to the attention of the public authorities who license real estate brokers and regulate their practices?

MRS. JEFFERSON. Well, they certainly have in the past. I don't know what has been done recently.

MR. TAYLOR. Has any action been taken that you know of by the public authorities with respect to this?

MRS. JEFFERSON. I know of none.

MR. TAYLOR. Thank you.

MRS. JEFFERSON. I think—I shouldn't say that. I am sure that there—FEPC has had some actions, I assume, but I feel that, whatever has been done has been inadequate. That I can say factually.

MR. TAYLOR. Thank you.

VICE CHAIRMAN PATTERSON. Thank you very much, Mrs. Jefferson, for your testimony. You are excused. The hearing will stand in recess until 4 o'clock.

VICE CHAIRMAN PATTERSON. The Civil Rights hearing will again come to order. Would you call the next witness, Mr. Glickstein.

MR. GLICKSTEIN. Mr. Roe H. Baker.

(Whereupon, MR. ROE H. BAKER was sworn by the Vice Chairman and testified as follows:)

TESTIMONY OF MR. ROE H. BAKER, SAN FRANCISCO, CALIFORNIA

MR. GLICKSTEIN. Mr. Baker, would you please state your full name and address for the record?

MR. BAKER. Roe H. Baker, 571 Wildwood Way, San Francisco.

MR. GLICKSTEIN. What is your occupation, Mr. Baker?

MR. BAKER. Executive.

MR. GLICKSTEIN. Executive? With what company do you work for?

MR. BAKER. Westside Management Corporation.

MR. GLICKSTEIN. What is your relationship to the Serramonte Realty Company?

MR. BAKER. I am the president.

MR. GLICKSTEIN. The president of the company?

MR. BAKER. Yes.

MR. GLICKSTEIN. What is the Serramonte Realty Company?

MR. BAKER. It's a licensed real estate broker.

MR. GLICKSTEIN. Where does it operate principally?

MR. BAKER. Principally in San Mateo County.

MR. GLICKSTEIN. There is an area in Daly City known as Serramonte. What is your relationship to that?

MR. BAKER. We handle the sales for some of the owners in Serramonte.

MR. GLICKSTEIN. You handle the sales of some of the owners there?

MR. BAKER. That's correct.

MR. GLICKSTEIN. Who controls the Serramonte Realty Company?

MR. BAKER. The board of directors.

MR. GLICKSTEIN. Do you know who the principal stockholders in the Serramonte Realty Company are?

MR. BAKER. No, I don't.

MR. GLICKSTEIN. Mr. Chairman, I have a certified copy of the Articles of Incorporation of the Serramonte Realty Company that was supplied to us by the Secretary of State of the State of California, and this document indicates that Mr. Carl Gellert is the principal stockholder of this corporation.

I would like to request that this be introduced into the record as Exhibit No. 3.

VICE CHAIRMAN PATTERSON. It is so ordered.

(The document referred to was marked Exhibit No. 3 and received in evidence.)

MR. GLICKSTEIN. Do you know how many homes have been built in the Serramonte area?

MR. BAKER. Approximately 300.

MR. GLICKSTEIN. Three hundred homes?

MR. BAKER. I believe so.

MR. GLICKSTEIN. Do you know how many homes are planned for the complete development?

MR. BAKER. No, I don't.

MR. GLICKSTEIN. Do you have any idea how many people will live in the Serramonte development when it is completed?

MR. BAKER. No, I don't.

MR. GLICKSTEIN. Do you know how many people live there now?

MR. BAKER. I am estimating maybe 600.

MR. GLICKSTEIN. About 600 live there now?

MR. BAKER. That's correct.

MR. GLICKSTEIN. What is the price range of the homes in Serramonte?

MR. BAKER. I am guessing. It is roughly $22,950 to about $29,000.

MR. GLICKSTEIN. Have Negroes purchased homes in Serramonte?

MR. BAKER. I wouldn't know.

MR. GLICKSTEIN. You wouldn't know? Do you go out to the area very often?

MR. BAKER. No.

MR. GLICKSTEIN. You are usually not out there?

MR. BAKER. No.

MR. GLICKSTEIN. Did your realty company ever carry out a policy of selling Serramonte homes to whites only?

MR. BAKER. I beg your pardon? Would you repeat that?

MR. GLICKSTEIN. Did your realty company ever have a policy of selling homes to whites only?

MR. BAKER. At one time, what we do, we take listings, and at one time the law of the State of California was such that we had to follow the listing of the owner. We as a real estate firm do not— I mean we don't set policy.

MR. GLICKSTEIN. You just follow the——

MR. BAKER. The listers.

MR. GLICKSTEIN. And the policy, then, was set by the owners of the houses. Is that right?

MR. BAKER. That's correct.

MR. GLICKSTEIN. Did fair housing groups protest this policy?

MR. BAKER. Yes, they did.

MR. GLICKSTEIN. Mr. Chairman, if I may just backtrack for a moment. Mr. Baker a little while ago wasn't able to tell us how large Serramonte would be when it was completed, and we have some literature that is distributed by Serramonte that indicates that it would be one of the largest cities in San Mateo County and that it will have a population of approximately 21,000 people when the development is completed. May I request that these documents be received in evidence as Exhibit No. 4.

VICE CHAIRMAN PATTERSON. So ordered.

(The documents referred to were marked Exhibit No. 4 and received in evidence.)

MR. GLICKSTEIN. You said civil rights groups protested this?

MR. BAKER. That's correct.

MR. GLICKSTEIN. In what way did they protest?

MR. BAKER. Picketed.

MR. GLICKSTEIN. Picketed?

MR. BAKER. Right.

MR. GLICKSTEIN. Was any sort of an agreement negotiated or worked out between the civil rights groups to stop the picketing?

MR. BAKER. Our sales manager and public relations man signed an agreement with them.

MR. GLICKSTEIN. And what did the agreement provide?

MR. BAKER. You must have a copy of it. Roughly the agreement provided that the property in Serramonte be offered to anyone regardless of race, color, and creed.

MR. GLICKSTEIN. Do you consider this a binding agreement?

MR. BAKER. Our present policy is to, yes.

MR. GLICKSTEIN. Have all of your salesmen been advised of this policy?

MR. BAKER. That's correct, they have.

MR. GLICKSTEIN. And what steps have you taken, if any, to insure that your salesmen follow this policy?

MR. BAKER. If they are hungry—we don't have an awful lot of control over our salesmen. They are all independent contractors with us. They work strictly on commission. We ourselves never see a buyer. We don't know who he is, or what he is.

MR. GLICKSTEIN. But you decide who will be your independent contractors, don't you? You can select or dismiss somebody if you choose to?

MR. BAKER. Definitely, definitely. We invite them in, and if they want a contract with us they agree to, oh, sit on the model home and agree to certain things. They also have their own businesses other places.

MR. GLICKSTEIN. Have you tried to impress on these people that you have signed this agreement with civil rights organizations and you do have a nondiscrimination policy?

MR. BAKER. They are all very familiar with it.

MR. GLICKSTEIN. They are familiar with it?

MR. BAKER. That's correct.

MR. GLICKSTEIN. Has this nondiscrimination policy—and I believe this was signed approximately a year ago. Is that right?

MR. BAKER. I believe that is correct.

MR. GLICKSTEIN. Has the nondiscrimination policy affected the sale of Serramonte homes in any way?

MR. BAKER. We haven't noticed anything, no.

MR. GLICKSTEIN. You haven't noticed any?

MR. BAKER. Well, generally—wait a minute. Generally the sales of homes in Serramonte, as all over the country, you know the situation, and it has been the same in Serramonte and still is the same. So that it is—according to the papers we hope it picks up, but I wouldn't say that our policy has anything to do with that. No.

MR. GLICKSTEIN. It is a tight money policy that has affected that?

MR. BAKER. Yes.

MR. GLICKSTEIN. I believe you said about 600 homes have been sold so far?

MR. BAKER. Three hundred.

MR. GLICKSTEIN. I have no further questions, Mr. Chairman.

VICE CHAIRMAN PATTERSON. Father Hesburgh, do you have questions for the witness?

COMMISSIONER HESBURGH. Mr. Baker, this is a question from ignorance, because I don't know all that much about how this business operates, but you mentioned you work from listings. Is this listings of homes available or listings of people who want to sell homes?

MR. BAKER. No, it is from the owners. Like if you had a home and you wanted to sell it, you would go to a broker——

COMMISSIONER HESBURGH. Give him the listing.

MR. BAKER. That's right.

COMMISSIONER HESBURGH. Now, in the Serramonte Development Corporation, I take it these are new homes being sold for the first time. Is that correct?

MR. BAKER. That's correct.

COMMISSIONER HESBURGH. So there wouldn't be a listing involved here?

MR. BAKER. Well, we are not the owners of Serramonte Realty.

COMMISSIONER HESBURGH. Who would own it then, this Mr. Gellert?

MR. BAKER. No, the various corporations that actually buy land and the homes themselves. We have nothing to do with the total development.

COMMISSIONER HESBURGH. But within the total development, then, when these homes are being sold for the first time, I suppose as long as you can get someone to buy it and to pay the price, it is open for anyone to buy it. Is that correct? In other words, when these homes are being sold for the first time they are open to anyone who wants to buy them and has the money to pay for them. Is that correct?

MR. BAKER. That's correct. We are not the only real estate brokers in the area.

COMMISSIONER HESBURGH. Oh, I understand that. So, presumably, then, anybody of any race or whatever who would want to buy one of these homes and had the means of buying it, his only problem is to get a broker to sell it to him or show it to him?

MR. BAKER. Yes.

COMMISSIONER HESBURGH. So the only way this could possibly break down is if these brokers would make up their own minds as to whether they are going to show it to someone of another race?

MR. BAKER. Could possibly be, yes.

COMMISSIONER HESBURGH. Then, legally, if one were to do that, what would be the best way of correcting it? Would it be to get at the brokers?

MR. BAKER. We have a law in the State of California that the real estate broker has to service anybody that comes in regardless of race, color, or creed.

COMMISSIONER HESBURGH. I see. For any of the listings that he has?

MR. BAKER. Right, right.

COMMISSIONER HESBURGH. So that if people are upset about this, the thing to do would be to have a case against a broker?

MR. BAKER. That's correct.

COMMISSIONER HESBURGH. We have been hearing—the reason I ask this is that we have been hearing this morning about people that make arrangements over the phone and then when they show up suddenly the place isn't available or the price goes up. This would get back to the brokers, right?

MR. BAKER. One of the difficulties today is that we have been in this tight money situation and we ran into a situation where a lot of people here bought their houses but haven't been able to sell their houses. So I know that many of the owners have been unwilling to commit themselves until they know this thing is actually going to go ahead. So as a result the situation really isn't normal now.

COMMISSIONER HESBURGH. Well, we had a case this morning where a man made arrangements for a home at $20,000, and when he showed up I believe it was $40,000.

MR. BAKER. Oh, no.

COMMISSIONER HESBURGH. That sort of thing. I was just

curious who one goes to see about this sort of thing. You're an intermediate body in this whole process?

MR. BAKER. I don't think they would negotiate for a house over the phone because you want the person to see the house, because if he is going to move in there you want him to be satisfied with it.

COMMISSIONER HESBURGH. What happened exactly was he called and said, "Is there a place available?"

"Yes."

"What is the cost of it?"

"$20,000."

And: "Can I come and see it?"

"Yes." And he arrives and suddenly it is not available, in this one case we heard this morning, or in the other case the price suddenly doubled.

Would this be a matter of brokers?

MR. BAKER. They definitely don't have any authority to do anything like that with us.

FATHER HESBURGH. Good. Thank you.

VICE CHAIRMAN PATTERSON. Mrs. Freeman?

COMMISSIONER FREEMAN. Mr. Baker, you are the president of the Serramonte Realty Company?

MR. BAKER. That's correct.

COMMISSIONER FREEMAN. How large is that company? How many brokers do you have under your employ?

MR. BAKER. About 12. I believe it is, 11, 12.

COMMISSIONER FREEMAN. Do you have any Negro brokers?

MR. BAKER. No, we don't.

COMMISSIONER FREEMAN. I believe you said that you are one of the eight brokers for the sale of the—

MR. BAKER. No, I am not.

COMMISSIONER FREEMAN. Does your company have a listing contract for the sale of this property, the Serramonte Homes?

MR. BAKER. That's right.

COMMISSIONER FREEMAN. And this is property that is owned by the Gellert Corporation?

MR. BAKER. There is no Gellert Corporation.

COMMISSIONER FREEMAN. Who is also the principal stock holder in the organization of which you are president?

MR. BAKER. Well, depends on what you mean, "principal." He is a stockholder, but when you say "principal," you imply a majority or something, but he is not a majority stockholder. I mean he is not control, if that is what you mean.

COMMISSIONER FREEMAN. Well, what we would like to know is how many houses are there still to be sold?

MR. BAKER. That, as I say, depends upon the program and,

well, how many of our clients get how many lots. They don't develop the lots. They buy the lots.

COMMISSIONER FREEMAN. How many lots are there still unsold as of now?

MR. BAKER. I couldn't answer that directly, but I imagine a couple of hundred.

COMMISSIONER FREEMAN. About 200 lots, and of those 200 lots, under an agreement which you have entered into——

MR. BAKER. Excuse me. We haven't entered into any agreement on that.

COMMISSIONER FREEMAN. Those 200 lots, according to your —the Serramonte Realty Corporation, of which you are president, and which is owned by Mr. Gellert, are available to Negroes?

MR. BAKER. We are strictly brokers. We don't have those lots listed with us at all. That is what I was saying about this present situation. The owners have not been willing to go ahead and build on these lots because they have a certain investment to go into when they build, and they have sort of been holding back. Of course, we would like to get the houses so we can go ahead with the sales, but they have been holding back because of this current situation.

COMMISSIONER FREEMAN. Is there sort of an interlocking directorship here?

MR. BAKER. No interlocking directorship.

COMMISSIONER FREEMAN. The builder is also the seller in one respect?

MR. BAKER. No.

COMMISSIONER FREEMAN. And he is also the agent?

MR. BAKER. It is all separate corporations.

COMMISSIONER FREEMAN. But all going back to the same people?

MR. BAKER. Not all the same people, no.

COMMISSIONER FREEMAN. And are each of your brokers licensed by the State of California?

MR. BAKER. That's right.

COMMISSIONER FREEMAN. What steps have been taken by the Serramonte Realty Company to advise the Negro who might be interested of the availability of a lot?

MR. BAKER. Put ads in the paper. That is about all you can do.

COMMISSIONER FREEMAN. But those lots are now available to any Negro who has the money?

MR. BAKER. That's right, that's correct.

COMMISSIONER FREEMAN. What about the possibility of your company employing Negro real estate brokers?

MR. BAKER. It is highly possible. We have had these brokers that have been associated with us now for about, I would say, some as many as 25 years that right now we have more actually than we need. Unless we get more listings soon. I mean they've been pretty hungry the last six, eight months.

COMMISSIONER FREEMAN. Your brokers are hungry?

MR. BAKER. They're hungry. There haven't been many sales. You can see the newspapers, the multiple listings or any of the —I suppose the building permits would give you an indication about what is happening. Building activity has been pretty poor, and the brokers work strictly on commission. No sale, no income.

COMMISSIONER FREEMAN. Then they want to sell the lots?

MR. BAKER. That's correct.

COMMISSIONER FREEMAN. So that the more Negroes that would come in, they would be happy to have them. Is that correct?

MR. BAKER. That's correct. We just don't have the inventory now. That is what we want, but we want them to break loose with the lots.

VICE CHAIRMAN PATTERSON. Dr. Rankin?

COMMISSIONER RANKIN. Mr. Baker, you have been in this real estate business a long time, haven't you?

MR. BAKER. About 20 years.

COMMISSIONER RANKIN. Formerly did the Negroes have equal opportunity in the housing in this area, would you say?

MR. BAKER. I would say they did before there was—yes, in San Francisco they did.

COMMISSIONER RANKIN. But not outside San Francisco?

MR. BAKER. I have lived in San Francisco all my life.

COMMISSIONER RANKIN. But you would say in San Francisco for many years now, Negroes have equal opportunity for housing?

MR. BAKER. I know they did back in the old days, yes.

COMMISSIONER RANKIN. Today it is true also. Is that correct?

MR. BAKER. They have today through law, yes.

VICE CHAIRMAN PATTERSON. Mr. Taylor.

MR. TAYLOR. Mr. Baker, has there been any public sale of the stock of the Serramonte Realty Company since its incorporation or has there been any exchange of the stock? In other words, are the stockholders the same now as when the corporation was incorporated?

MR. BAKER. No, they are not.

MR. TAYLOR. Can you tell us approximately how many shares have changed hands since that time?

MR. BAKER. I couldn't without consulting the stock records.

MR. TAYLOR. I have the certificate of incorporation here, and it indicates that at the time of incorporation, or on May 17, 1966, there were somewhat more than 500 shares. Of these shares Carl Gellert held 300, Fred Gellert held 180, and then there were several parcels of 30 shares that were held in the name of various trusts, which are variously denominated Fred Gellert, Jr. Trust, Joanne Gellert Trust, Fred Gellert, Jr. Trust, Joanne Gellert Trust. Has that situation changed radically since the time of the incorporation?

MR. BAKER. Yes, it has.

MR. TAYLOR. And you cannot tell me as the president of the corporation who the principal stockholders are right now?

MR. BAKER. Not without consulting the stock records.

COMMISSIONER FREEMAN. Then you know who they are and you are just not telling?

MR. BAKER. He asked me who the principals are. I know there is something like 20 or 30 stockholders, but I couldn't tell you which one has the most.

MR. TAYLOR. Would you say the Gellerts no longer have any strong influence in your organization?

MR. BAKER. No, I wouldn't say they have. The board of directors runs this.

MR. TAYLOR. Have they sold out all of their shares?

MR. BAKER. No, they haven't.

MR. TAYLOR. A substantial part of their shares, more than half of their shares?

MR. BAKER. I couldn't tell you how many they sold, but like any corporation it is run by the board of directors. They make the decisions. That's where I get my decisions from.

MR. TAYLOR. Now, I think you said in answer to a question by Mrs. Freeman that you advertise your equal opportunity policy by putting advertisemenets in the newspaper. Is that correct?

MR. BAKER. That's correct.

MR. TAYLOR. Is there any other way in which you advertise your policy?

MR. BAKER. There is no other way we advertise generally, just in the newspaper. We have tried other means, but we have found when a person is looking for a house, basically he goes to a newspaper.

MR. TAYLOR. Mr. Chairman, I have a copy of an advertisement here which is dated April 23, 1967, in the San Francisco Examiner and Chronicle, and at the bottom of the ad, in approximately 6-point type, is the statement on An Equal Opportunity Policy. I would like to have that entered into the record, if I may.

VICE CHAIRMAN PATTERSON. It is received into the record.

(The document referred to was marked Exhibit 5 and received in evidence.)

MR. TAYLOR. Are the Examiner and the Chronicle the only newspapers in which you can conduct your advertising in?

MR. BAKER. We occasionally use newspapers in the Peninsula, but they are basically our main advertising media.

MR. TAYLOR. Have you advertised in any newspapers that are read predominantly by the Negro population of this city?

MR. BAKER. I don't know what newspapers they predominantly read, frankly.

MR. TAYLOR. Are you aware that there are newspapers that are operated by Negroes?

MR. BAKER. Strictly? No, I am not.

MR. TAYLOR. I have no further questions.

VICE CHAIRMAN PATTERSON. Father Hesburgh?

COMMISSIONER HESBURGH. I have a question which perhaps I shouldn't ask out loud of the staff, but I would like to ask it.

Since all this seems to point toward the Gellerts, why isn't one of them here instead of Mr. Baker?

MR. GLICKSTEIN. Father Hesburgh, the United States Marshals and members of our staff have been trying for the last three weeks to subpena Mr. Gellert and we have been unsuccessful in serving a subpena on him. We sent a telegram to him the other day, and if I may, I will read that into the record. The telegram was sent to his office and to his home. It says:

"The United States Commission on Civil Rights is holding hearings in San Francisco in the Federal Courthouse 450 Golden Gate Avenue, May 1st through May 3rd. Testimony concerning Serramonte Realty, Inc., Standard Building, Inc., and Suburban Realty Company, Inc., companies organized by you, will be heard on May 1st. A subpena for your appearance before the Commission has been issued. Unfortunately, you have not been available for service. The Commission is interested in hearing testimony from you concerning the development of Serramonte Tract by Suburban Realty and the sales policy of Standard Building and Serramonte Realty with respect to sales to Negro Americans. I hope that you will make yourself available for service of the subpena or appear voluntarily."

And that telegram is signed by me.

(The document referred to was marked Exhibit No. 6 and received in evidence.)

COMMISSIONER HESBURGH. Thank you.

VICE CHAIRMAN PATTERSON. Am I to understand, then, that the subpena was not served and Mr. Gellert will not appear?

MR. GLICKSTEIN. That's correct, sir.

VICE CHAIRMAN PATTERSON. Are there any further questions?

MR. GLICKSTEIN. May I ask an additional question?

VICE CHAIRMAN PATTERSON. Go ahead.

MR. GLICKSTEIN. You mentioned a little while ago, Mr. Baker, that Serramonte Realty has just carried out the instructions of the owners of the homes in selling.

MR. BAKER. That's correct.

MR. GLICKSTEIN. Is the Mangels Properties, Inc. one such company that sells homes?

MR. BAKER. Yes.

MR. GLICKSTEIN. Wildwood Park, Inc.?

MR. BAKER. That's correct.

MR. GLICKSTEIN. Forest Knolls Development Company, Inc.?

MR. BAKER. That's correct.

MR. GLICKSTEIN. And what is your relationship to each of those companies?

MR. BAKER. I believe I am on the board of each one.

MR. GLICKSTEIN. Our information indicates that you are the president of Mangels, the president of Wildwood, and the secretary of Forest Knolls. Do you know what the relationship of the Gellerts is to each of those companies?

MR. BAKER. I would still have to consult the stock records.

MR. GLICKSTEIN. Our information indicates that they are the incorporators of each of those companies.

MR. BAKER. It could possibly be.

MR. GLICKSTEIN. We a little while ago spoke about the civil rights agreement that was signed by Serramonte Realty. I would like to introduce a copy of that agreement into the record as Exhibit No. 7.

VICE CHAIRMAN PATTERSON. It is so ordered.

(The document referred to was marked Exhibit No. 7 and received in evidence).

MR. GLICKSTEIN. Mr. Baker, who are the members of the board of directors of Serramonte Realty?

MR. BAKER. I couldn't answer you that right now either.

MR. GLICKSTEIN. What is your title in the company? You are the president?

MR. BAKER. Yes.

MR. GLICKSTEIN. Who is the vice president?

MR. BAKER. I couldn't answer that.

MR. GLICKSTEIN. Who is the secretary?

MR. BAKER. I am in 40 corporations. I can't keep track of them all.

MR. GLICKSTEIN. How often does the board of directors meet?

MR. BAKER. Depending upon the business. Actually they have to meet once a year. They could meet oftener, and they do.

MR. GLICKSTEIN. When did the board last meet?

MR. BAKER. I couldn't answer you that.

MR. GLICKSTEIN. I have no further questions, Mr. Chairman.

VICE CHAIRMAN PATTERSON. Do the Commissioners have any other questions?

COMMISSIONER FREEMAN. Mr. Baker, did you say you were in 40 corporations?

MR. BAKER. Approximately, yes.

COMMISSIONER FREEMAN. Are they all real estate related?

MR. BAKER. They are not all real estate companies, no.

COMMISSIONER FREEMAN. How many of them are?

MR. BAKER. I couldn't say without the list. It is a good many of them. That is basically my specialty, real estate.

VICE CHAIRMAN PATTERSON. Thank you very much, Mr. Baker. You are excused. Would you call the next witness, Mr. Glickstein? MR. GLICKSTEIN. Mr. Sherman Eubanks.

(Whereupon, MR. SHERMAN EUBANKS was sworn by the Vice Chairman and testified as follows:)

TESTIMONY OF MR. M. SHERMAN EUBANKS, SAN FRANCISCO, CALIFORNIA

MR. GLICKSTEIN. Mr. Eubanks, would you please state your name and address for the record?

MR. EUBANKS. Yes, my name is M. Sherman Eubanks, address 660 Market Street, San Francisco.

MR. GLICKSTEIN. What is your occupation?

MR. EUBANKS. I am vice president of Crocker Land Company.

MR. GLICKSTEIN. And you are associated with the Suburban Realty Company?

MR. EUBANKS. Yes, sir, I am.

MR. GLICKSTEIN. What is your position with that company?

MR. EUBANKS. Secretary.

MR. GLICKSTEIN. Does the Suburban Realty Company develop homes on which Serramonte Homes are constructed—develop lots, I am sorry, develop lots on which Serramonte Homes are constructed?

MR. EUBANKS. Yes, they do.

MR. GLICKSTEIN. Has Suburban Realty considered requiring developers to provide assurances that homes will be sold without discrimination because of race or color?

MR. EUBANKS. Not to my knowledge, no. The subject has never come before Suburban Realty Company.

MR. GLICKSTEIN. The land on which Serramonte is located was an area, if our information is correct, that was annexed to Daly City. Is that correct?

MR. EUBANKS. Yes.

MR. GLICKSTEIN. It was formerly the Christian Ranch that Suburban Realty purchased?

MR. EUBANKS. It was primarily the Christian Ranch, yes, sir, but there were a few miscellaneous ownerships. I think the Christian Ranch contained roughly 900 or 940 acres of the approximately 1,000 that is considered Serramonte.

MR. GLICKSTEIN. And an agreement was signed to carry out this annexation. Is that correct?

MR. EUBANKS. That's correct.

MR. GLICKSTEIN. And you were one of the signatories to that agreement?

MR. EUBANKS. You mean me personally?

MR. GLICKSTEIN. Yes.

MR. EUBANKS. I really don't recall whether I was or not. I am secretary of the company and, as such, I probably did sign it. If you have it, you know better than I do.

MR. GLICKSTEIN. Mr. Chairman, I do have a copy of the agreement, and may I request that we introduce this into the record as Exhibit No. 8?

VICE CHAIRMAN PATTERSON. It is received.

(The document referred to was marked Exhibit No. 8 and received in evidence.)

MR. GLICKSTEIN. And that is signed, Mr. Eubanks, by you as secretary of Suburban Realty, and by Mr. Carl Gellert as president of Suburban Realty?

MR. EUBANKS. That sounds correct.

MR. GLICKSTEIN. Were the considerations given for the annexation agreement advantageous to both parties, to Suburban Realty as well as to Daly City?

MR. EUBANKS. I certainly think so or no agreement probably would have been signed.

MR. GLICKSTEIN. What interest did Suburban Realty have in petitioning for annexation of the tract to Daly City rather than just developing as an unincorporated entity?

MR. EUBANKS. Well, Daly City is a well established city with good government, good police and fire, and has all of the ingredients that any city should have for proper development of large subdivisions.

MR. GLICKSTEIN. Let me ask you a hypothetical question.

MR. EUBANKS. Sure.

MR. GLICKSTEIN. If Daly City had said to Suburban Realty that they would not execute the annexation agreement unless Suburban Realty agreed that all homes built on that tract would be sold without discrimination on account of race or color, would Suburban Realty have gone through with the deal?

MR. EUBANKS. I really can't answer that because that was never a consideration.

MR. GLICKSTEIN. That was never suggested to you by Daly City and the people you negotiated with?

MR. EUBANKS. Well, when you say to me, I assume you are referring to me personally?

MR. GLICKSTEIN. Within the extent of your knowledge.

MR. EUBANKS. That's right. I never heard the subject discussed.

MR. GLICKSTEIN. Does the Crocker Land Company have a policy interest in the development, construction, and leasing of Serramonte Shopping Center?

MR. EUBANKS. Crocker Land Company and the Crocker interests own 50 percent of Suburban Realty Company, and Suburban Realty Company is the owner and developer of the Serramonte Regional Shopping Center.

The Crocker part of Suburban Realty Company is primarily

responsible for the leasing and operation of the regional shopping center. Crocker's side of the Suburban Realty Company is also responsible for the keeping of the books, you might say, for Suburban Realty Company, all the accounting and that sort of thing.

MR. GLICKSTEIN. After the fair housing protests at Serramonte that Mr. Baker spoke about, did you or any officer or representative of the Crocker Land Company discuss the sales policy of Serramonte with that company?

MR. EUBANKS. No, not to my knowledge.

MR. GLICKSTEIN. Has the Crocker Land Company participated in any other real estate ventures with any Gellert Brothers organizations in the past, to your knowledge?

MR. EUBANKS. No, not in the same manner. I think—well, to go back a little bit, the Crocker Land Company, Crocker interests, have owned and still own thousands of acres around the Bay Area and in Northern California, and I think many years ago one of the Crocker companies may have sold some land in the San Francisco area. I think out in—I have forgotten the name of the area, but I would say that they have sold land to the Standard Building Company or group of companies in the past, but not for some time.

MR. GLICKSTEIN. Do you think that the interests of the Crocker Land Company in Serramonte are affected at all by the restrictive or the formerly restrictive sales policy of Serramonte Realty?

MR. EUBANKS. I don't know what you mean by "interests."

MR. GLICKSTEIN. Your financial interest, your investment. Do you think your investment is jeopardized if the development is one that restricts its sales?

MR. EUBANKS. Well, to my knowledge the sales have never been restricted. If they have, I don't have first-hand knowledge of it.

MR. GLICKSTEIN. Do you know if Suburban Realty borrowed funds to develop the Serramonte Tract?

MR. EUBANKS. If they borrowed funds?

MR. GLICKSTEIN. To develop the Serramonte Tract.

MR. EUBANKS. I think there again it depends on what you mean by "borrow." I am not prepared right now to go into the capital structure of Suburban Realty Company, but I do know that the stock was issued both to the Crocker interests and the Standard Building Company interests, which consist of a number of companies, and there have been some borrowings by Suburban Realty Company in the past, that's right, but the extent of them, I don't have the details at my fingertips.

MR. GLICKSTEIN. Were there any efforts made to have these funds insured by the Federal Housing Administration?

MR. EUBANKS. Not to my knowledge, no.

MR. GLICKSTEIN. I have no further questions, Mr. Chairman.

VICE CHAIRMAN PATTERSON. Father Hesburgh, do you have any questions?

COMMISSIONER HESBURGH. I have no questions.

VICE CHAIRMAN PATTERSON. Mrs. Freeman?

COMMISSIONER FREEMAN. Mr. Eubanks, the Crocker Land Company is the owner of the land. Is that right?

MR. EUBANKS. No, ma'am. That is not correct. Crocker Land Company and the Crocker interests own 50 percent of the stock of Suburban Realty Company and that is the company that owns the raw land on which Serramonte Subdivision is being constructed. Suburban Realty Company sells finished lots only on a wholesale basis to various builders. Among them would be the Standard Building Companies that I think one of the gentlemen referred to, the Mangels and Wildwood, and the others, and also we sold some lots recently to Alpha Homes, which is a totally unrelated builder.

COMMISSIONER FREEMAN. Your company owns the lots and, therefore, you would be the seller in this case?

MR. EUBANKS. If you are speaking of Suburban Realty Company, yes, ma'am. They own the lots and they sell them to the builders.

COMMISSIONER FREEMAN. They sell them to the builders. And where does the real estate broker come in here?

MR. EUBANKS. Well, I don't know at that point. See, we sell the lots in a finished condition to the builders. Then the builders build the homes and sell to the public, and the mechanism or means by which they are sold to the public I am not familiar with.

COMMISSIONER FREEMAN. But you are aware that you have a community or you are building a community that is totally and 100 percent white?

MR. EUBANKS. Pardon? I am sorry, Mrs. Freeman.

COMMISSIONER FREEMAN. It is all white, an all-white community, is it not?

MR. EUBANKS. Serramonte?

COMMISSIONER FREEMAN. Yes.

MR. EUBANKS. I am not aware that it is an all-white community, no.

COMMISSIONER FREEMAN. How long have you been secretary of Suburban?

MR. EUBANKS. Since its incorporation.

COMMISSIONER FREEMAN. And when was that?

MR. EUBANKS. I think in '62 or '63.

COMMISSIONER FREEMAN. And how long have they been building these homes?

MR. EUBANKS. About two years; two or three years.

COMMISSIONER FREEMAN. But you don't know about the racial composition?

MR. EUBANKS. No, I don't, because we sell the lots, we don't sell the homes. We never come in contact with any of the people that are supplying materials or the method by which the homes are sold or the buyers themselves. I personally don't know one building salesman in the—I think it is Serramonte Realty Company's staff.

COMMISSIONER FREEMAN. I believe we received some testimony that there had been protests because of denial of opportunity as far as Negroes were concerned to purchase the homes or lots. Were you familiar with the protests?

MR. EUBANKS. Only what I read in the newspapers, that's right.

COMMISSIONER FREEMAN. But you were not personally aware of what was going on?

MR. EUBANKS. That's right, Mrs. Freeman.

COMMISSIONER FREEMAN. Will you tell this Commission how you feel about Serramonte becoming an open community?

MR. EUBANKS. Well, I think, speaking for the Crocker interests, that certainly any of our developments, in any of them, we have to obey the moral and legal laws of the land, and as such it should be open to all people.

COMMISSIONER FREEMAN. Have you taken or considered taking some steps to make this known to the public?

MR. EUBANKS. No. We haven't because we are not directly involved, but I understand that the Standard Building Group has taken steps by virtue of this agreement that was discussed earlier.

COMMISSIONER FREEMAN. And are you in complete accord with the agreement?

MR. EUBANKS. I have really never read the agreement, but I understand that it says in principle that it is open to all people and we certainly subscribe to that.

COMMISSIONER FREEMAN. Thank you.

VICE CHAIRMAN PATTERSON. Dr. Rankin?

COMMISSIONER RANKIN. I am just asking for information. I get amazed at a man in 10 or 15 different real estate companies. What is the advantage of being connected with 10 or 12 real estate companies rather than just looking after one good company? I am just asking for information.

MR. EUBANKS. Well, if you are referring to Roe Baker, he will have to answer that himself.

COMMISSIONER RANKIN. Yes. I just wondered. I understand that, but I just wondered how it works out from your knowledge of the real estate business.

MR. EUBANKS. Well, I think it is more a matter of accounting and profits and that sort of thing and identity, also. From my personal standpoint, I would really prefer, and speaking again for the Crockers only, I believe in everything under one company that you—because then you only have the problem of promoting, you might say, one corporate image rather than 40 or 50 of them. So from a sales standpoint, it is much easier just having one large impressive company.

COMMISSIONER RANKIN. Then you could remember your board of directors and know what is going on?

MR. EUBANKS. That's right.

VICE CHAIRMAN PATTERSON. Mr. Taylor?

MR. TAYLOR. Mr. Eubanks, would I be correct in assuming that land is a fairly precious commodity in the San Francisco Bay Area?

MR. EUBANKS. Yes, sir, that is correct. When you say the Bay Area——

MR. TAYLOR. I mean the immediate suburban areas around San Francisco.

MR. EUBANKS. Yes, that's correct.

MR. TAYLOR. What responsibilities do you think somebody who deals in land, either buys and sells it or develops it, has to the population of the city of San Francisco at large? Do they have any responsibilities other than to conduct a good business operation?

MR. EUBANKS. I think so. I think that—and here again I am speaking for the Crocker ideas—we always have a policy in our developments that it must be something that the Crockers can be proud of, and, secondly, it must be economically feasible. Those are the two broad objectives we have in any of our developments, but beyond that we know that we have to provide a certain number of parks and playgrounds and open areas and schools and all the amenities that are good for modern day living. We never have really addressed ourselves to the question of a certain percentage of one race in any development. As a matter of fact, we are not residential developers ourselves.

In the case of Serramonte, I think this is the first time in some 40 years that our company has become involved indirectly in a residential subdivision. Most of Crocker Land Company's activities are in the area of major investments, say, Crocker Industrial Park. I don't mean to give a commercial in response, but our activities are more in the commercial and industrial field than in the residential field.

MR. TAYLOR. So you develop commercial properties for the lands that you deal with?

MR. EUBANKS. That's right.

MR. TAYLOR. Do you think that collectively the people who deal in land have some kind of responsibility to try and meet the housing needs of the total population in this area?

Mr. Eubanks. I really hadn't given that any thought, but I really don't think that any one company should undertake to solve the needs of 10,000,000 people or however many there are in the Bay Area.

Mr. Taylor. I said "collectively" rather than just——

Mr. Eubanks. Oh, yes. I think they should join hands and arms with the other big subdividers and try and provide all of the things that everybody can afford.

Mr. Taylor. One of the things that strikes me about the testimony we have been hearing is that, apart from what other effects may stem from all of this fragmentation of corporations or this diffusion of corporations, the result seems to be that nobody seems to assume any responsibility for the way property is used and for whether it is available to Negroes or whether Negroes have access to it. Do you think this is a healthy thing? I don't ask you necessarily to speak for your corporation or for anybody else but just as a citizen, do you think this is a good thing?

Mr. Eubanks. Well, I am really not—maybe I don't understand your question. Would you mind restating it, Mr. Taylor?

Mr. Taylor. Well, you purchase and sell the raw land. Someone else develops it. Someone else is responsible for marketing it and he informs us that he doesn't really market it, that he just hires independent contractors to market it, and when we go down that line nobody seems to really face the question or decision squarely about how this land should be developed, sold, and marketed and I just wondered whether you thought that was a good thing.

Mr. Eubanks. No, I think the boards of directors of the various companies that might buy the property should state their position, and as far as I know with respect to the Standard Building side of it they have stated their position and that is that it is open. I shouldn't be commenting on what they have stated, because I have never seen any agreement that they have signed or any of the information that they have given the press or anyone else, but speaking for the Crocker side again, we have never been involved in that aspect of it. So the question has never come before us.

Mr. Taylor. I have no further questions.

Vice Chairman Patterson. Mr. Eubanks, has the real estate industry as a whole in this area, either through trade associations or other groupings, attempted this collective joining of hands to do some land planning, some sales planning, to assure that the people's needs are met in this respect?

Mr. Eubanks. I don't think they have joined hands collectively in the Bay Area, but we are members of the Urban Land Institute and this is a national—really an international—primarily national though, group of men who are experienced in real estate development, and they have attempted to do something about all of the amenities that our modern civilization requires, but bringing it down into the Bay Area, I don't think there is a group in the Bay Area of owners of land and developers that have gotten together in any sort of collective form to do the kind of thing you are talking about, Mr. Patterson.

VICE CHAIRMAN PATTERSON. Do you think it would be possible to put together voluntarily such a private enterprise organization?

MR. EUBANKS. I think so, sure.

VICE CHAIRMAN PATTERSON. Could it be self-policing if a profit were available to the——

MR. EUBANKS. I believe so.

VICE CHAIRMAN PATTERSON. Any other questions?

COMMISSIONER FREEMAN. Do you believe that such an organization would take affirmative steps to include all races?

MR. EUBANKS. Yes, I believe it would.

COMMISSIONER FREEMAN. Private enterprise?

MR. EUBANKS. Yes.

COMMISSIONER FREEMAN. I am concerned here because earlier we have heard people express opposition to the subsidies and to the Federal involvement because they have said this is something that private enterprise can do, and yet then we hear testimony which indicates that private enterprise has not done it. So we find ·ourselves in a circle in which there is a need but there is no supply for a large segment of the people. What our concern is is implementation, not mere statement of policy; but how you carry it out and what are you going to do to provide the housing that we are talking about and that people need.

MR. EUBANKS. Well, I really haven't given that subject very much thought, but we in private industry like to do as much as we can on our own without involvement of governmental agencies where you are apt to get bogged down in red tape, and this has nothing to do—and this is with all due respect to the Civil Rights Commission—it has nothing to do with the racial thing at all. The involvement with governmental agencies can get bogged down in red tape.

Let me give you an example of that. In our industrial developments we possibly could go the route of public bonds, we will say, for street improvements, and this involves a local governmental agency and not the Federal Government, and rather than go through all of the red tape of getting financing with the bond route, we just put up our own private capital and put in the streets that way. This is only an example of why we prefer to do things as a private industry rather than get involved in Federal subsidies, and that sort of thing.

COMMISSIONER FREEMAN. But the effect is that you have a subdivision or a community which is white only?

MR. EUBANKS. I don't know that it is white only, Mrs. Freeman.

VICE CHAIRMAN PATTERSON. Father Hesburgh?

COMMISSIONER HESBURGH. I just want to say, Mr. Eubanks, I find your frankness refreshing, and what I really wanted to say has really come out, but let me just recapitulate briefly.

Our problem, to be equally frank with you, sir, is that somehow we look at the whole country and we know we have many Americans who are poorly housed in inadequate, unsanitary, unsafe, substandard housing, and that if this is ever going to be corrected we have to get positive programs.

Now, the Federal Government has programs, a whole list of them, and as far as we have been able to see all over the country, these haven't appreciably helped, because in many cases what the Federal Government is trying to do gets thwarted either by the Federal Government agents themselves who really don't care, or the whole real estate profession that finds 45 ways of getting around the purposes of this, or by all kinds of private conventions of one kind or another, or interlocking corporations, and nobody knows anything, nobody is responsible for anything, and as a result we find ourselves chasing shadows, and I think that the most impressive thing to me, at least listening to the whole testimony you have given, is that you are agreed that private industry could formulate some kind of a total approach to this problem, starting with the land itself, and ending with the person buying the house and having it financed properly, that would take into account somehow the social thing that we are worried about and concerned with, and the reason we are sitting here is that every person who can possibly afford it has right to decent sanitary housing at a normal, equal opportunity price, and that there will always be some people who can't even have that price and somehow we are not going to put them in the streets, but they are a very small minority of the total market. The thing that really concerns us are people who have the price of the house, have the desire for a decent, sanitary house for themselves and their youngsters, and for love or money can't get it because of all kinds of conditions about which no one knows anything and no one is responsible, and somehow we think that part of our function in each community—we have had to do this all over the country—is to try to get private enterprise or the real estate industry in its totality, from beginning to end, to be a little more forthright about what we are doing in this effort, because every time we come up with some kind of an open housing law everybody says we don't want to be regulated, we will do it by ourselves. So if there isn't any such law, then nothing happens. Our problem is, how do we make something happen, how do we somehow get our problem into the hands of those that can do something about it and be responsible for it, and I wouldn't want you to think we were picking on you, because you have been honest with us and you are pretty far from the front line of the problem. But at the same time we have somehow to get at the nub of the problem, and I think anyone sitting here can see how difficult it is to get down to who is responsible and what can be done. Excuse me for making a little speech, but I wanted to get that off my chest.

MR. EUBANKS. Yes. Well, I think that private industry could do it, but I am not sure they will, and it is not so much from the racial considerations as it is from the profit motive. We in private industry have the profit motive in mind, but it is not the overriding thing in our particular company. We are, as I say, we have two objectives: one is the profit motive and the other is a development that the Crocker people can be proud of, but we have never addressed ourselves to the questions that you pose. I am sorry I don't have a better answer than that.

COMMISSIONER HESBURGH. No. I understand.

VICE CHAIRMAN PATTERSON. Are there any further questions? Thank you, Mr. Eubanks. You are excused.

MR. EUBANKS. Thank you.

VICE CHAIRMAN PATTERSON. Will Counsel call the next witness, please?

MR. GLICKSTEIN. The next witnesses are the Hon. Bernard Lycett and Mr. Edward Frank accompanied by Mr. Albert Polonsky, Counsel.

(Whereupon, the Hon. Bernard Lycett and Mr. Edward Frank were sworn by the Vice Chairman and testified as follows:)

TESTIMONY OF THE HON. BERNARD LYCETT, MAYOR OF DALY CITY, CALIFORNIA, AND MR. EDWARD FRANK, DALY CITY, CALIFORNIA

MR. GLICKSTEIN. Mayor Lycett and Mr. Frank are accompanied by their attorney, Mr. Albert Polonsky, the City Attorney of Daly City. Gentlemen, would you please each state your name and address for the record?

MAYOR LYCETT. My name is Bernard J. Lycett. My address is 100 Fairlawn Avenue in Daly City.

MR. FRANK. My name is Edward Frank, 35 Fairview Avenue, Daly City.

MR. GLICKSTEIN. Mayor Lycett, you are the mayor of Daly City. Is that correct?

MAYOR LYCETT. Yes.

MR. GLICKSTEIN. What is your position, Mr. Frank?

MR. FRANK. I am the City Manager of Daly City.

MR. GLICKSTEIN. How long have you each held your positions?

MR. FRANK. Seven years.

MAYOR LYCETT. My position as mayor, Mr. Glickstein?

MR. GLICKSTEIN. As mayor, yes.

MAYOR LYCETT. As mayor, about three months.

MR. GLICKSTEIN. And as City Councilman?

MAYOR LYCETT. Since 1964.

MR. GLICKSTEIN. You were elected by the city council to serve as mayor?

MAYOR LYCETT. Yes, sir.

MR. GLICKSTEIN. Mr. Frank, what is the population of Daly City?

MR. FRANK. Population in 1960 was around 42,000 or 43,000. Now the estimated population is over 60,000.

MR. GLICKSTEIN. A little over 60,000?

MR. FRANK. Over 60,000.

MR. GLICKSTEIN. And what is the approximate number of Negroes living in Daly City?

MR. FRANK. We have no—the only statistics I am personally aware of came from the 1960 census and that was roughly, specifically, around 1 percent or 1½ percent, as I remember these statistics.

MR. GLICKSTEIN. Back in 1960?

MR. FRANK. That's correct.

MR. GLICKSTEIN. Do you have any feeling for whether that has grown since 1960?

MR. FRANK. I believe it has from—because of the school population, but not to any large degree that I have been able to come up with.

MR. GLICKSTEIN. You judge it from the school population. Is that correct?

MR. FRANK. That's right.

MR. GLICKSTEIN. Is the Negro population in Daly City concentrated in any particular area?

MR. FRANK. In some respects, yes, but it is pretty well scattered in my estimation.

MR. GLICKSTEIN. Are there any schools that are predominantly Negro?

MR. FRANK. Yes, I believe there are. There is one school.

MR. GLICKSTEIN. There is one school that is predominantly Negro?

MR. FRANK. Well, the high school, because that is evident. However, I think that it is divided among the elementary schools.

MAYOR LYCETT. Mr. Glickstein, I think Mr. Frank means that the school is not predominantly Negro. Is that what you're asking?

MR. GLICKSTEIN. Yes.

MAYOR LYCETT. No, it is not. The school is not predominantly Negro.

MR. GLICKSTEIN. There are no schools that are predominantly Negro?

MR. FRANK. According to the population, maybe 5 percent.

MR. GLICKSTEIN. The testimony indicates that when Serramonte is completed it will have a population of about 20,000 people. Are there any housing developments within Daly City, any other housing developments, that are this large?

MAYOR LYCETT. Are you asking me, Mr. Glickstein? I would say so.

MR. GLICKSTEIN. The copy of the annexation agreement that was entered into between Daly City and Suburban Realty has been introduced into the record.

Mr. Frank, could you tell us what factors were considered by city representatives when this agreement was drawn up?

MR. FRANK. Well, primarily factors that go into an agreement of this kind are the services that administration and policy forming groups wish to give to the people who are going to live there, and those are primarily police, fire, streets, lighting, and so forth, which is standard.

MR. GLICKSTEIN. And this is the type of services that have been agreed to in this agreement that would be provided to Serramonte by Daly City?

MR. FRANK. That is correct.

MR. GLICKSTEIN. Are there other services not specified in this agreement that the Serramonte community would be the beneficiary of as a result of the annexation?

MR. FRANK. Not that I know of.

MR. POLONSKY. Mr. Chairman, if I may interrupt, are you referring to overall city services or any special services to the Serramonte group?

MR. GLICKSTEIN. Overall city services.

MR. FRANK. Overall city services are the same in all of our —what agreements have come up.

MR. GLICKSTEIN. This agreement provides specifically for fire services and school services, but in addition to that there are the overall city services that any area that is annexed would be the beneficiary of.

MR. FRANK. That is in compliance with our Building Codes and so forth.

MR. POLONSKY. May I interrupt for a moment, Mr. Chairman? I think his interpretation of the agreement is incorrect. The agreement does not provide for fire services. It does not provide for police services. It provides for fire sites to be given to the city by the corporation which entered into the agreement and it also provides for certain other things.

VICE CHAIRMAN PATTERSON. I would feel it necessary to

admonish the counsel that if you are going to give the testimony then we will have to place you under oath.

MR. POLONSKY. I am sorry, Mr. Chairman.

VICE CHAIRMAN PATTERSON. Is it your wish to be sworn?

MR. POLONSKY. I am here only as counsel, your Honor, but I didn't want to have the misstatement made as far as the agreement. I didn't want any misapprehensions as to what the agreement provided.

VICE CHAIRMAN PATTERSON. Would you care to advise your client, then, and let him give the testimony?

MR. GLICKSTEIN. What advantages will Daly City derive, from having annexed the Serramonte tract, Mr. Frank?

MR. FRANK. Well, a general advantage would be of having a stable community, which we have, having a proper community life which goes along with the services that are given. It is a normal expansion of any community.

MR. GLICKSTEIN. Do you think that Daly City will derive substantial amounts of tax revenue from Serramonte residents?

MR. FRANK. Well, Daly City, of course, is mostly a residential community, and the tax revenues would be in the same proportion as any other annexation or any additional residential areas that might be involved.

MAYOR LYCETT. May I add to that, Mr. Glickstein? One of the added advantages to this development, of course, is the original shopping center that is going in that is quite large, and that is quite a base of our tax, sales tax in Daly City, due to the large residential area.

MR. GLICKSTEIN. So you will be deriving substantial tax benefits from the shopping center?

MAYOR LYCETT. Sales tax.

MR. GLICKSTEIN. Sales tax from the shopping center.

MR. FRANK. We only have two sources of revenue, actually. One is sales tax and the other is property tax. So we have no—less than 1 percent of any industry.

MR. GLICKSTEIN. The record indicates that May of last year there were demonstrations out at the Serramonte, protesting the white-only sales policies of Serramonte. When these demonstrations began and officials of Daly City heard of them, did Daly City take any steps to have this white-only policy reversed or to meet with the Serramonte people and discuss the problem with them?

MAYOR LYCETT. Well, Mr. Glickstein, to go back to that, we have kind of an unusual situation here. The man that is here as our counsel at that time was mayor of Daly City. So that's according to why he seems to be fitting into these questions and perhaps he should have been sworn in. However, when this did take place, there were meetings at that particular time for the people who were demonstrating in the Serramonte area. Convenient stations were made available for them, but there was no hardships imposed on them from a city standpoint. As I recall, quite a bit is being said about this, but I recall only two days being used in this area and then an agreement being reached. So, honestly, although, it seems to be blown up in this Commission while I am out there it did not seem to be that large a problem because of being settled so fast.

MR. GLICKSTEIN. Do you know if there are Negroes living in Serramonte now?

MAYOR LYCETT. Do I know if there are Negroes? I don't know myself, no.

MR. GLICKSTEIN. Do you know either, Mr. Frank? Could Daly City withhold the building permits from developers that you found discriminated on the basis of race?

VICE CHAIRMAN PATTERSON. Mr. Glickstein, if I may interrupt. If it is the wish of the witnesses, it lies within the discretion of the Commission to permit the counsel to be sworn as a witness, if you have no objection.

MR. POLONSKY. I have no objection.

(Whereupon, MR. ALBERT E. POLONSKY was sworn by the Vice Chairman and testified as follows:)

TESTIMONY OF MR. ALBERT E. POLONSKY, DALY CITY, CALIFORNIA

VICE CHAIRMAN PATTERSON. Please be seated, and would you state your name?

MR. POLONSKY. Albert E. Polonsky, 12 Fleetwood Drive, Daly City.

VICE CHAIRMAN PATTERSON. Would you like to restate the question, Mr. Glickstein, and have a new response.

MR. GLICKSTEIN. I asked whether it would be possible for the city to withhold building permits from a developer that it found was discriminating in the sale of housing.

MR. POLONSKY. In my opinion, no. At that time the city entered into the annexation agreement with the developer, the Attorney General of the State of California, Mr. Stanley Mosk, present Justice of the Supreme Court in this State, rendered an opinion that the city had no further rights in the field of housing and fair employment, and that this was solely an activity of the State.

MR. GLICKSTEIN. The city does contract, though, doesn't it?

MR. POLONSKY. In what respect?

MR. GLICKSTEIN. This annexation agreement is a form of a contract?

MR. POLONSKY. It is a contract in regards to certain items that the developer must contribute to the city before the city will accept or consider the annexation.

MR. GLICKSTEIN. Well, the annexation agreement in effect imposed many obligations on the developer. Is that correct?

MR. POLONSKY. That's correct.

MR. GLICKSTEIN. Couldn't it also have imposed an obligation on the developer not to discriminate in the sale of houses that were to be built on the tract?

MR. POLONSKY. In my opinion, legally it could not, and any such agreement would have been unenforceable by the city. There have been two decisions by the Attorney General specifically on that point, and in both decisions the Attorney General has ruled that the city can no longer handle the matter. It has been preempted by the State.

MR. GLICKSTEIN. Were those opinions dealing with annexation agreements or with fair housing statues?

MR. POLONSKY. Those agreements were dealing with whether or not a planning commission, No. 1, could go ahead and refuse to grant the variance in connection with the building upon certain property unless there was an anti-discrimination clause. The other one was asking for an interpretation of Section 35743 of the Health and Safety Code, whereby the State is declared that it is exclusively within the field of housing.

MR. GLICKSTEIN. That the State has exclusive jurisdiction within the field of housing. Mr. Frank, do you know the extent of Federal financial assistance to Daly City?

MR. FRANK. The extent?

MR. GLICKSTEIN. Yes, the source, the extent to which Federal funds for one reason or another come into Daly City?

MR. FRANK. At the present time the only extent of Federal funds has been in the area of beautification.

MR. GLICKSTEIN. Beautification.

MR. FRANK. Which has been a very nominal amount.

MR. GLICKSTEIN. Has Daly City taken advantage of any of the Federal subsidy programs that make or purport to make a contribution to solving low-income housing problems?

MR. FRANK. We are now attempting to get a Federal contribution in the way of a general plan, and our application has been in the hands of both the State and Federal bureaus.

MR. GLICKSTEIN. And it is only after this general plan is approved that you then are eligible for such things as 221(d)(3) housing and rent supplement. Is that correct?

MR. FRANK. That's correct.

MR. GLICKSTEIN. And your plan has been submitted, and it is now awaiting disposition by the Federal Government?

MR. FRANK. Waiting for money.

MR. GLICKSTEIN. Waiting for money. Mayor Lycett, do you feel that suburban communities, such as Daly City, have any responsibility toward helping the Bay Area core cities solve their racial and poverty problems?

MAYOR LYCETT. Yes, I do.

MR. GLICKSTEIN. In what way and to what extent?

MAYOR LYCETT. I don't know if I have the answer for it, Mr. Glickstein. Of course, as you know, you have been out in our community. We are a small community. We seem, as far as I can tell, to be integrating very normally out there. We don't hear of any problems. You have this particular problem where you said they demonstrated for two days, and they did. However, this seems to be the extent of our problems out there. Perhaps we should keep our fingers a little bit crossed, because it seems to be going along all right.

MR. GLICKSTEIN. Are you aware of the extent of unemployment or the lack of employment among the Negro community in your city?

MAYOR LYCETT. I am not. Are you, Ed? It would be hard due to the fact, Mr. Glickstein, that we are predominantly a residential area. In other words, when you asked about unemployment, well, then it would be necessary to delve into the records, which probably are county or State, in the area of welfare or State unemployment. I don't know where we would honestly get figures like that.

MR. GLICKSTEIN. Do you know if the Negro residents of your city work in businesses in Daly City, or do they work in San Francisco? Do you have any way of knowing that?

MAYOR LYCETT. No, I don't.

MR. GLICKSTEIN. Would you be in favor of some sort of a regional government?

MAYOR LYCETT. We smile because we are in the midst of a local situation which is called ABAG.

MR. GLICKSTEIN. That stands for Association of Bay Area Governments?

MAYOR LYCETT. Yes, and we have withdrawn from them and mistakenly people have said we have withdrawn because we are not in favor of regional government and this is not so. We have withdrawn or retreated a little bit because we have been hit with a lack of communication as to what and where we are going and we would like to know more about the plan before we give our whole-hearted support.

I don't know what kind of an answer that is to your question, but such as it is that is it. We believe in it. I am on the regional planning committee of San Mateo County and have worked for quite a while on it. I foresee various area governmental agencies that would have to be. How they are going to put them together I wouldn't know.

MR. GLICKSTEIN. How many employees does Daly City have?

MR. FRANK. About 275, Mr. Glickstein.

MR. GLICKSTEIN. Do you have any idea how many of them are Negro?

MR. FRANK. We have a number and we keep hiring them all the time. I couldn't give you the exact number.

MR. GLICKSTEIN. Do you have any idea what occupations they work in?

MR. FRANK. Well, we have had them in the custodial and engineering and streets. Of course, those are usually the services that we are involved with.

MR. GLICKSTEIN. Does Daly City enter into many construction contracts?

MR. FRANK. You mean contracts for streets or—

MR. GLICKSTEIN. Streets.

MR. FRANK. Yes. Most of our big projects are contracted out and of course, in those type of contracts we have to comply with all the laws governing such a project.

MR. GLICKSTEIN. Do you include a no-discrimination clause in your construction contracts?

MR. FRANK. I believe they are all in the advertising that goes along with the contract.

MR. GLICKSTEIN. I see. I have no further questions, Mr. Chairman.

VICE CHAIRMAN PATTERSON. Father Hesburgh?

COMMISSIONER HESBURGH. No, thanks.

VICE CHAIRMAN PATTERSON. Mrs. Freeman?

COMMISSIONER FREEMAN. Mr. Polonsky, I believe you indicated that you were the mayor at the time of the annexation agreement.

MR. POLONSKY. No, Mrs. Freeman. I became mayor two weeks before the demonstration began. I was not a member of the council nor was Mayor Lycett a member of the council at the time the annexation agreement was executed.

COMMISSIONER FREEMAN. Well, in response to a question, I believe you indicated that it was your opinion that the Attorney General would have held that Daly City did not have the power to include the open-occupancy clause in its agreement. I am trying to get more background on that.

MR. POLONSKY. Well, the Attorney General ruled in 1963, at the time that the section I quoted of the Health and Safety Code was passed, a specific question was submitted to him by a legislator and in response to that question the Attorney General ruled that the State had preempted the field of housing and fair employment and that the city had no further rights in that field.

Now, I am speaking, and it must be remembered that Daly City is a general law city and it is not a charter city, and our rights only come from the legislature.

COMMISSIONER FREEMAN. Well, I would still like to know the extent to which the proposal to include such a clause in the agreement was submitted to the Attorney General by Daly City.

MR. POLONSKY. No, this was not submitted by Daly City. Another community submitted a proposal. If I may get the book on that—it is Attorney General's opinion 63–156, which was issued on October 14, 1963, which is the same date as the agreement. The subject was discrimination. It says: "State statutes relating to employment and in housing preclude local government from enacting ordinances imposing additional restrictions in these two fields."

COMMISSIONER FREEMAN. But the enactment of an ordinance is quite different from an agreement which is an agreement of the parties to which each party says that this is what we agreed to do. Is that not correct?

MR. POLONSKY. This is correct, Mrs. Freeman, except that in this particular instance one of the parties is a municipal corporation which has only so much rights as is granted to it by the State, and in this particular field the State has said it has preempted, and any agreement that we might make or any ordinance that we may pass different from that agreement would not be binding on the other side.

COMMISSIONER FREEMAN. Is it your opinion, then, that Daly City has no powers with respect to nondiscrimination?

MR. POLONSKY. In housing and fair employment?

COMMISSIONER FREEMAN. In housing and fair employment.

MR. POLONSKY. According to my interpretation of the Health and Safety Code provisions and of the Attorney General's opinion.

COMMISSIONER FREEMAN. Prior to the annexation of Serramonte, I believe the testimony was that Negroes lived all over Daly City. Is that correct?

MR. POLONSKY. I believe that it was that they are generally about Daly City, but there are certain areas where they are more to be found than in other areas.

COMMISSIONER FREEMAN. So that where it had dispersion it now has a situation where there is segregation with respect to one area?

MR. POLONSKY. No. May I say that in certain areas you will find those of minority races. They will not be as large as in all areas, but they will be found throughout the city. They have been found previously, and they are continuing to buy homes throughout the entire city.

COMMISSIONER FREEMAN. Is not Serramonte part of the geographical boundary of Daly City now?

MR. POLONSKY. It has been since 1963.

COMMISSIONER FREEMAN. Do you know if any Negroes live in Serramonte?

MR. POLONSKY. No, I do not know of any that live in Serramonte.

COMMISSIOER FREEMAN. This is what I am saying.

MR. POLONSKY. In the Serramonte area?

COMMISSIONER FREEMAN. In the Serramonte.

MR. POLONSKY. No.

COMMISSIONER FREEMAN. So there is an island which is all-white within the city boundaries?

MR. POLONSKY. Which was discovered by us in 1966.

COMMISSIONER FREEMAN. Thank you.

VICE CHAIRMAN PATTERSON. Dr. Rankin?

COMMISSIONER RANKIN. Has the Attorney General's opinion ever been tested by a court case?

MR. POLONSKY. No, it hasn't, Mr. Rankin.

COMMISSIONER RANKIN. It could be at any time. Is that correct?

MR. POLONSKY. Well, there have been decisions. In fact, there is a constitutional provision that apparently gives you the right to discriminate in connection with the sale of property, but the Supreme Court has striken that part down insofar as the Health and Safety Code regulations which are generally known as the Hawkins Act and is part of the Unruh Civil Rights Act, and the courts have used a liberal interpretation, but the clause specifically states that the State is reserving itself these rights, and this is one of the reasons why I think it would be a futile effort to go into the State inasmuch as in this State now the courts have been finding more and more areas which are preempted by the State and taken away from a general law city.

COMMISSIONER RANKIN. Could anybody take court action?

MR. POLONSKY. Not that I know of.

COMMISSIONER FREEMAN. Is there any remedy to the discrimination that would be practiced then?

MR. POLONSKY. There is a remedy, yes. The Health and Safety Code provides a remedy. There are injunctions that can be allowed. The Unruh Civil Rights Act will provide for damages in that situation. There are a number of remedies allowed under the law for one aggrieved by any of these acts of discrimination or where there is a complaint in connection with it. And this all comes under that section of 35700 of the Health and Safety Code. It sets forth an elaborate procedure of going and on complaints bringing people in in connection with this particular aspect.

VICE CHAIRMAN PATTERSON. You say that you know of no

Negroes living in the Serramonte development? Do you know why this might be?

MR. POLONSKY. I personally do not, no. Unless it is on account of financing I don't know why because they are living in all the other areas. I don't know of any sales policy now since the agreement was entered into. At the time I was mayor is when I the first time learned of the exclusionary policy that was going on at that particular time.

VICE CHAIRMAN PATTERSON. I believe we received testimony that these houses are in the $20,000 to $29,000 category in Serramonte.

MR. POLONSKY. That's roughly correct.

VICE CHAIRMAN PATTERSON. Are Negroes in other parts of the city living in that price range?

MR. POLONSKY. Yes, they are.

VICE CHAIRMAN PATTERSON. So it might not have been financing?

MR. POLONSKY. I am sorry?

VICE CHAIRMAN PATTERSON. It might not have been financing that created their absence?

MR. POLONSKY. No, it might not have been. That is correct. There are other areas where the homes are even higher priced where they are living.

VICE CHAIRMAN PATTERSON. Mr. Frank, do you know of any Negroes living in the Serramonte development?

MR. FRANK. No, I don't.

VICE CHAIRMAN PATTERSON. Do you know why they might not be living there?

MR. FRANK. Probably along the same lines that Mr. Polonsky said. I think the finances might have the biggest bearing, although, as he also stated, I do know of some specific homes where there are minority races that are quite expensive.

VICE CHAIRMAN PATTERSON. Mayor Lycett, do you have any thoughts on this?

MAYOR LYCETT. Well, the question, if I may turn it just a little bit: does anybody know that there are not any Negroes in Serramonte? Is it a proven fact? Does your Commission know this?

VICE CHAIRMAN PATTERSON. We are dependent upon the testimony here.

MAYOR LYCETT. I don't know. I was listening to this and I don't know how familiar you people are with Daly City. Serramonte is a new development that is away on the south end tip of our town, and there is a barren area between the developed part of Daly City and where Serramonte is starting to develop. At the present time in most cases there is no need for myself to be going down to Serramonte, and I really wouldn't know. I hesitate to say that because I should know. That is why I am asking if somebody else has better knowledge than I do in that area. But I would like to go into the financial aspects of it because I believe that this is a big part of it.

Mr. Diamond, who was testifying here earlier, and I was listening to him, hit only on the FHA part of this financing, but this goes a little bit further than that. It goes into GI financing, who will qualify in the same way as the FHA, and it goes into regular conventional financing, who will make people qualify; and I believe that this is a portion of it that I would like to know what part of that is the cause. The financing part ot it. Money lenders, as far as I have known, are pretty tough people. They don't look at race or anything else. They look right at the money. And I'm a firm believer in this area.

VICE CHAIRMAN PATTERSON. Mr. Taylor?

MR. TAYLOR. Mr. Polonsky, I suspect that the legal discussion that we have been having might be of limited interest, but let me prolong it a minute or two more. I assume that you would agree that if the city itself built the housing directly it would have an obligation not to discriminate. Would you?

MR. POLONSKY. On the hypothetical situation, yes.

MR. TAYLOR. The city here is rendering valuable services, is it not? In other words, would it not cost this developer more if he had to purchase these services himself?

MR. POLONSKY. The city is obligated to render services to all residents within its territory.

MR. TAYLOR. I understand, but by the act of annexing and by providing these services, the city was rendering some valuable services to the developer, was it not?

MR. POLONSKY. No. We were not rendering any valuable services to the developer. I beg to differ with you. We would be going to render services to the citizens of that community and not to the developer. We extracted what we thought was excellent requirements from the developer in regards to park sites, regulation sites, fire house, civic center, land, all this before the State said you could do so.

MR. TAYLOR. And you do not believe that the price of the housing might have been different or that the cost to the ultimate buyer of the housing might not have been different if you had not entered into this annexation?

MR. POLONSKY. Now we are in the field of conjecture. I know of other areas in San Mateo County which have done it by special assessment districts and their houses are not substantially different than the price of the houses in Serramonte.

MR. TAYLOR. But the developer and other people concerned

must have thought they were getting something valuable by becoming——

MR. POLONSKY. In every contract both parties are certain they are getting something of value or you are not going to have an agreement.

MR. TAYLOR. Well, it is hard for me to conceive that if this contract had contained a provision that we are talking about that any court would have struck it down.

MR. POLONSKY. Well, you may be hard to conceive, but just recently we passed a hotel-motel tax provision with penalty clauses. The State has given us this right. We have just in the last three weeks received a notification of the District Courts of Appeal have said that the penalty clause is illegal and that we have no right to pass on it inasmuch as the State has preempted the field of penalty in connection with the collection of taxes. It may be hard to conceive, it is very hard for us to conceive also when the State is preempting the field and when it is not, and when you have an attorney general's opinion on these matters it is safe to go by the attorney general's provisions.

MR. TAYLOR. I think you may be construing the opinion a little more broadly than it goes but that may be neither here nor there.

Mr. Frank, you said that you had an application for a grant pending for the development of the total community plan, a 701 Plan or something of that kind.

MR. FRANK. Yes, this is what we call the 701 Program, which is for general plan of the full city of Daly City, and we have had this application on file, for, I imagine, close to five months, and first it goes to the State, which gets the allocation, but it must be approved naturally by the Federal Bureau, and the latest, I understand, is pending because of lack of funds.

MR. TAYLOR. Well, even though it hasn't been approved yet, I would suspect that perhaps you have done some thinking about what uses, about what kind of a plan you will come up with and what uses you will put Federal assistance to if you do get Federal assistance? Could you tell us anything about that?

MR. FRANK. Well, we have a planning consultant who drew up the overall proposal that would be included in the general plan, and this, I understand, must be reviewed both by the State and Federal Bureau. So I assume that they would note the general concepts that we are proposing.

MR. TAYLOR. Might it include some plans for low-income housing of various counties, low to moderate-income housing?

MR. FRANK. That I wouldn't know. I am not particularly aware of that. It might. I think all we have done so far is just comply with the requirements in order to be eligible for a grant.

114

I think the details would come later after the grant would be authorized.

MR. TAYLOR. No further questions.

VICE CHAIRMAN PATTERSON. Any further questions from the Commission? Thank you very much, gentlemen. You are excused. Mr. Glickstein, have our last witnesses arrived?

MR. GLICKSTEIN. I think, Mr. Chairman, we are 10 minutes ahead of schedule.

VICE CHAIRMAN PATTERSON. In that case we'll take a 10-minute recess.

VICE CHAIRMAN PATTERSON. The hearing will please come to order. Mr. Glickstein would you call our next witnesses?

MR. GLICKSTEIN. Our next witnesses are Mr. Cyril Magnin and Mr. Al Hicks. They are accompanied by Mr. James Murray.

(Whereupon, Mr. Cyril Magnin and Mr. Al Hicks were sworn by the Vice Chairman and testified as follows:)

TESTIMONY OF MR. CYRIL MAGNIN, SAN FRANCISCO, CALIFORNIA, AND MR. AL HICKS, SAN FRANCISCO, CALIFORNIA

MR. GLICKSTEIN. Would you each please state your name and address for the record?

MR. MAGNIN. My home address?

MR. GLICKSTEIN. Or your business address, whichever you prefer.

MR. MAGNIN. I am Cyril I. Magnin, 59 Harrison Street, San Francisco. That's my business address.

MR. HICKS. Al Hicks. 421 Montgomery Street, San Francisco.

MR. GLICKSTEIN. What is your occupation, Mr. Magnin?

MR. MAGNIN. I am president of Joseph Magnin.

MR. GLICKSTEIN. And you are active in the Chamber of Commerce?

MR. MAGNIN. I am president, also, of the Chamber of Commerce.

MR. GLICKSTEIN. You are president of the Chamber. What is your occupation, Mr. Hicks?

MR. HICKS. I am manager of the Job Development Department, San Francisco Greater Chamber of Commerce.

MR. GLICKSTEIN. If I may, Mr. Magnin, I will direct my questions to you and any question that you would like Mr. Hicks to answer, I will be happy to hear from him. How long have you been active in the Chamber of Commerce?

MR. MAGNIN. How long have I been active as president?

MR. GLICKSTEIN. How long have you been active in it and how long have you been president?

MR. MAGNIN. Three years. This is my second year as president.

MR. GLICKSTEIN. Second year as president. How many members does the San Francisco Chamber have?

MR. MAGNIN. Twenty-three hundred now.

MR. GLICKSTEIN. Does the Chamber of Commerce have an affirmative program to help minority groups?

MR. MAGNIN. Yes, we have a program in that area.

MR. GLICKSTEIN. Will you tell us what it is, please?

MR. MAGNIN. Well, we first became interested in the minority groups the early part of last year when we started our Job Fair at the Civic Auditorium here in San Francisco, where we got the major employers in the community to take space and to interview prospective people for jobs, especially among the minority and lower income groups, those that have never had an opportunity in many cases to apply for a job in a major company. And we had a large group of people visit that Fair and they were interviewed by these various companies and as a result of that I think that some of them were placed in jobs. At least they were given the opportunity to be face to face with a personnel director or manager and I think it was helpful generally.

MR. GLICKSTEIN. Why is it necessary to have something like a Job Fair to get people interested in jobs and help them find jobs?

MR. MAGNIN. Well, we thought, as I indicated, we would expose these people to personnel people, No. 1, and, second, we get our members conscious of the problem here in San Francisco and, third, generally I think it had a good effect on the public. We got a lot of publicity. In fact, Time Magazine wrote an article in a little booklet that is before you. You see that Time did a story, and I think it focused the public's interest on the problem.

MR. GLICKSTEIN. Does the Chamber have a program to attract business into San Francisco?

MR. MAGNIN. Oh, yes.

MR. GLICKSTEIN. Are you losing business in San Francisco?

MR. MAGNIN. We have been losing some industry. In turn we are gaining head office and regional office businesses that are coming to San Francisco. We are losing some blue-collar jobs, however.

MR. GLICKSTEIN. You are losing blue-collar jobs and you are gaining white-collar jobs?

MR. MAGNIN. I would guess that's it, yes.

MR. GLICKSTEIN. The new industry, then, that you are attracting does not offer substantial employment to blue-collar workers?

MR. MAGNIN. No, I think the new jobs that are created are office workers generally. We have got a program which we have been working on for the last year and a half, known as the Butch-

116

ertown Area, where we hope to put a large industrial park, and we
have just received word from Washington that the Redevelopment Agency has the money assigned to San Francisco for that
project and we should create a number of blue-collar jobs.

One of the problems has been in San Francisco that we haven't
had the area. It is a small area in square miles, I believe 44 square
miles the whole community, and up to this time I think it has
been lack of space rather than anything else that the businesses
have been leaving here.

MR. GLICKSTEIN. Why have businesses been moving out?

MR. MAGNIN. Lack of area mostly.

MR. GLICKSTEIN. Do you know if, in businesses that move out
that have large numbers of minority group employees, these
employees tend to follow the businesses?

MR. MAGNIN. I wouldn't know, but I guess a lot of them don't
but some do.

MR. GLICKSTEIN. Some do?

MR. MAGNIN. I would guess.

MR. GLICKSTEIN. Do you think most of them do?

MR. MAGNIN. Mr. Hicks feels that they generally stay put.

MR. GLICKSTEIN. They generally stay put. All right, Mr. Hicks,
why do you think that is so?

MR. HICKS. I think, No. 1, the areas in which the businesses
are moving to, there are few housing facilities for these people.
No. 2, I think that minority people normally like to be centralized
into a larger city, metropolitan area. I think they feel more at
home in a city like this and they would stay. Possibly the third
reason would be that they are not given the opportunity to go by
the employer under as favorable a condition as they think they
should have.

MR. GLICKSTEIN. I see. Mr. Magnin, what role do you think a
suburban community should play in helping to resolve the
problems of minority group persons in San Francisco?

MR. MAGNIN. Will you give me that question again?

MR. GLICKSTEIN. Do you think that the suburban communities
surrounding San Francisco have a role to play in helping to solve
the minority group problems in your city? Do you think this is
something San Francisco could do itself?

MR. MAGNIN. I think San Francisco has to do it itself. I don't
think that we can just take people and send them down to the
surrounding areas. I think they have their own problems and
have to solve them in their own way. Certainly if we work together
with the other communities in the Bay Area, it would be helpful.

MR. GLICKSTEIN. You think it would be helpful to work together? Are you in favor of some form of regional government,
or metropolitan government?

MR. MAGNIN. I would think that has to come here eventually.

MR. GLICKSTEIN. Do you have any views on what steps the Federal Government should take to deal in particular with the employment problems of minority group persons in your city?

MR. MAGNIN. Well, I don't know if it should be the Federal Government or who. I feel there are too many agencies now with jobs, looking for jobs for people, the minority people. I think there should be one area, one coordinating area, that people can go to and that the employer can go to and match the jobs with the employer. I don't object to all of these various agencies, whether more or less private or government, trying to do this, but I think we have a hard time finding the right persons at times to fit into a particular job. I think there are too many agencies trying to do the same thing. There is a great duplication of agencies.

Now, whether it should be the Federal Government or whether it should be the State or the city, I don't know, but there should be one concentrated area for the matching of jobs.

MR. GLICKSTEIN. Do you think something like the Job Fair is an effort to match people to jobs?

MR. MAGNIN. I don't think the Job Fair is—I don't think we would do it over again. I think possibly the one shot was all right, but whether we should do it again I don't know. But there should be some agency, not just one or two days a year, but continuing every business day in the year to match these people to jobs.

MR. GLICKSTEIN. Mr. Magnin, was it the riots at Hunters Point that spurred the business community to take action? Was it that that created this interest?

MR. MAGNIN. No, I think we had the Job Fair long before that. I think the Watts situation in Los Angeles gave us an indication of what could happen here, and I think the business community has been concerned with the problem. And the day after the riots in San Francisco I asked the heads of the leading corporations to come to a meeting at the Chamber Board Room and most of the major, if not all of them, were represented that day.

I said that we should find or try to place 2,000 people immediately to try to do something to help this situation. We did have a pledge of 2,000 jobs. We aren't able to fill these jobs.

MR. GLICKSTEIN. You aren't able to fill them?

MR. MAGNIN. Not all of them.

MR. GLICKSTEIN. How did you seek to fill them? Did you work with civil rights groups?

MR. MAGNIN. Worked any way we could but it was an emergency and it was a more or less—it wasn't coordinated well. It was done in a hurry and it wasn't done well.

MR. GLICKSTEIN. You wanted to fill them but you didn't have enough applicants?

MR. MAGNIN. That's right; not for the jobs that we needed to place, but if there was one central agency that we could have gone to to coordinate all these for the various agencies, if they wanted to stay in the placement business, then I think we would have had a much easier time doing that than we did.

MR. GLICKSTEIN. We've heard a lot of testimony today about housing problems in San Francisco. Has the Chamber of Commerce any housing programs, taken any position on housing projects or the development of housing in the city?

MR. MAGNIN. Of public housing?

MR. GLICKSTEIN. Of public housing, low and moderate-income housing?

MR. MAGNIN. I don't know that we have, no, but we realize and have said that housing is an important factor in this job development. There are many factors. It is education, it is housing, it is placing the right people in the right job, and finding the jobs for them.

MR. GLICKSTEIN. Thank you. I have no further questions, Mr. Chairman.

VICE CHAIRMAN PATTERSON. Father Hesburgh?

COMMISSIONER HESBURGH. I just wanted to put in the record because I didn't hear it said so far, that at this equal opportunity Job Fair, according to this booklet we have, there were 10,000 people that came to that Fair; 175 are known to have landed jobs through the Fair, and of these 48 percent were Negro, 27 percent Mexican and Spanish Americans, and 9 percent Orientals. At least this represents some positive effort that I think we would all welcome.

MR. MAGNIN. Reverend Hesburgh, I think there were more than 175.

COMMISSIONER HESBURGH. I imagine that.

MR. MAGNIN. There was no way of telling. Time Magazine said that. These were interviewed. There were little booths. Each company had their own booth and many people, I am certain, got jobs over and above the 175, as is indicated. How many more I couldn't say.

COMMISSIONER HESBURGH. In any event, will this be continued every year?

MR. MAGNIN. We don't think we will have another Job Fair. We think we have given enough exposure to it now. We think there are other areas in which we can work.

COMMISSIONER HESBURGH. I would imagine one problem is getting the employment divisions of all of the various corporations involved in this.

MR. MAGNIN. I think we have the cooperation of the business community. We did have one other Job Fair, a teenage Job Fair at Christmastime. At that time the San Francisco retail stores pledged 500 jobs to lower-income and minority groups. We had the Pacific Gas and Electric Auditorium and we invited these little high school, teen-age children to come to that auditorium.

The Department of Education agreed to give them two weeks' training in their approach to customers and their dress and so forth, and we had a group there, but out of that whole group we could only place 132 jobs. Now, we had definitely had 500 jobs pledged. These jobs were ready and willing, held open to the last minute for our group. We could only place 132, but we feel next year that we are going to have this teen-age Job Fair again and we believe we will place many more than we did this year.

COMMISSIONER HESBURGH. What was the reason for only being able to place so few?

MR. MAGNIN. Couldn't find the people.

COMMISSIONER HESBURGH. You mean they weren't qualified?

MR. MAGNIN. They didn't come.

MR. HICKS. One of the problems, Father, I think, is the fact that the method of recruitment did not meet the challenge of producing the bodies. We had at a first session, for instance, this session was embarrassing to us at the Chamber because we had 500 jobs pledged and only 60-some-odd people were involved in the thing. So the Chamber then went ahead and paid out of its budget the making up of 7,000 leaflets and they took my time and some more people's time and Murray's time on the staff to go around to radio stations, to barber shops, various places in the so-called poverty areas in San Francisco and distribute these 7,000.

Then we decided to put on a second one in order to try and increase the number, and the total number came to 132. As you know, the Chamber of Commerce is not a recruiting agency for these jobs. It is not an interviewing agency. It has to depend upon the other agencies whose business it is to do just this, and we got in to help to this extent because we found it necessary and I do have here for your consideration a copy of the letter from the Board of Education in regards to the program, and a copy of the letter from the Department of Employment, in which they say, in the last paragraph, "I believe that this project, although smaller in number than desired by the Chamber, was very successful. I would like to urge the Chamber to plan for a similar program next year. With early and careful planning this program could be even a greater success."

Our feeling is that if we are going to have those kind of jobs set aside we are going to have to produce the kind of bodies that are going to be necessary.

MR. MAGNIN. I might say, Father, that the jobs that we did place were very satisfactory people. We heard no complaints as to their ability or their conduct on the job. I am certain this year we will get the 500 jobs again and we hope we get the bodies.

COMMISSIONER HESBURGH. I just think it is so terribly important because of the enormous unemployment among teen-age groups and minority groups, to give them at least the self-confidence to know they can get a job, do a good job, be satisfactory, and look forward to something more in the future when they finish school. It also might be a great incentive to stay in school and be better qualified.

MR MAGNIN. It is, again, education in a way and not education directly, but education of these people that they can get jobs and do well, and I am certain that the 132 that worked this year will pass the word around so that next year we will be able to get a larger recruitment than we had this year.

COMMISSIONER HESBURGH. That's fine. Thank you, sir.

VICE CHAIRMAN PATTERSON. Mrs. Freeman?

COMMISSIONER FREEMAN. Mr. Magnin, of the 2,300 members of the Chamber of Commerce about how many of them would include members of firms in real estate industry?

MR. MAGNIN. How many what?

COMMISSIONER FREEMAN. Real estate industry, suburban realty company.

MR. MAGNIN. How many are in real estate?

COMMISSIONER FREEMAN. Yes. Does the Chamber of Commerce include real estate companies?

MR. MAGNIN. We include anybody in business, in any business.

COMMISSIONER FREEMAN. The Chamber of Commerce also has been in the past very aggressive with respect to those programs and policies which it endorsed, and I wonder if you have any program with respect to improving transportation. We have heard testimony that transportion for people who live in areas that are designated "poor" is very bad. Has the Chamber of Commerce taken any position with respect to that?

MR. MAGNIN. I haven't heard that complaint, Mrs. Freeman. Actually the Chamber has supported BART, which is the new subway, new transportation system that is covering the Bay Area, or most of the Bay Area. I haven't heard that the transportation is not good here in the city. Certainly if it isn't, we would like to know about it.

COMMISSIONER FREEMAN. You have not heard that the transportation to Potrero Hill is not good?

MR. MAGNIN. No. In my own company we have many employees. I will say this, that I believe that we have a high number of minorities and Negro people especially in our employ, higher than the average retail company in this area, I think, or certainly as large. I have never heard any complaints from our people regarding transportation or anybody in our company.

COMMISSIONER FREEMAN. Well, with respect to the occupancy,

the equality of opportunity in housing, has the Chamber of Commerce taken a position in support of this?

MR. MAGNIN. No, not—I don't think it has come up.

COMMISSIONER FREEMAN. No member of the Chamber of Commerce has ever brought it up?

MR. MAGNIN. Not to my knowledge. Not since I have been there. It is possible before I was there. I have only been active in Chamber work for about two and a half years now.

COMMISSIONER FREEMAN. Did any member of the Chamber of Commerce take a position with respect to Proposition 14?

MR. MAGNIN. Mr. Murray may be able to answer that. I wasn't active in the Chamber at that time.

MR. MURRAY. We were the only Chamber in California to take the stand——

VICE CHAIRMAN PATTERSON. I believe we will have to swear the witness to receive the testimony, will we not?

MR. GLICKSTEIN. Yes, Mr. Chairman.

MR. HICKS. I might answer it, if you would like.

VICE CHAIRMAN PATTERSON. Let's swear the witness.

(Whereupon, Mr. James Murray was sworn by the Vice Chairman and testified as follows:)

TESTIMONY OF MR. JAMES MURRAY,
SAN FRANCISCO, CALIFORNIA

VICE CHAIRMAN PATTERSON. What is your name and address?

MR. MURRAY. My name is James Murray, and I am the economic development manager of the San Francisco Chamber, and the San Francisco Chamber two years ago, or three years ago, went on record as the only Chamber in the State of California to be for Proposition 14, so as far as answering your question. I guess that was an issue where we did take a definite stand on the housing bill.

COMMISSIONER FREEMAN. And will you describe for the Commission the effect of this position?

MR. MURRAY. The effect? You might clarify that. I don't understand exactly what you mean.

COMMISSIONER FREEMAN. Well, what was the position? Would you explain exactly what was the position with respect to the Proposition and with respect to the Fair Housing Law of the State of California?

MR. MURRAY. We just said yes on Proposition 14. We favored that legislation.

MR. MAGNIN. I think you may have that wrong. Proposition 14, as I recall, was to the elimination of the—is that correct?

VICE CHAIRMAN PATTERSON. Yes, the vote would have been to eliminate the Rumford Act.

MR. MURRAY. Then it was a no vote.

COMMISSIONER FREEMAN. This is why I asked you if you would explain it.

MR. MURRAY. A no vote then.

VICE CHAIRMAN PATTERSON. The Chamber took the position of a "no" vote on Proposition 14?

MR. MURRAY. Of continuing the Rumford Act.

VICE CHAIRMAN PATTERSON. Of continuing the Fair Housing Act.

COMMISSIONER FREEMAN. Thank you.

VICE CHAIRMAN PATTERSON. Dr. Rankin?

COMMISSIONER RANKIN. Mr. Magnin, do you have many Negro members in your Chamber of Commerce?

MR. MAGNIN. Do we have any what?

COMMISSIONER RANKIN. Many Negro members of the Chamber of Commerce. Of the 2,300 how many of the members are Negro, approximately?

MR. MAGNIN. We have some, they tell me. I have never seen any at our meetings.

MR. HICKS. I might, in answering that, say that the way our Chamber operates, of course, is by board of directors, of which you have the people there. We do have one annual meeting a year. I do know personally that there are three that I know personally, that I have met since I have been there.

COMMISSIONER FREEMAN. Three of the 2,300?

MR. HICKS. Three that I know personally.

COMMISSIONER RANKIN. Three dues-paying members, is that it?

MR. MAGNIN. I might say that we don't bar anybody, regardless of race, creed, or color.

COMMISSIONER RANKIN. As long as he pays the dues. Of course that is the qualification. About your Fair, did you ever try one for summer jobs for students?

MR. MAGNIN. No, we haven't.

COMMISSIONER RANKIN. It is much harder for them to get jobs in the summer, I would think; much harder to find jobs for them also, but it would really be performing a service if you could do that, I would say.

MR. HICKS. Mr. Rankin, may I say that the San Francisco Chamber of Commerce, in conjunction with the Youth Opportunity Department of the California State Department of Employment, has just obtained, as a results of last week, a place located at 777 Mission Street which will serve as a summer job headquarters for students out of school during the summer. We will operate that in conjunction with the——

COMMISSIONER RANKIN. That's fine. Do you run into apprenticeship rules that hurt or hinder you from getting jobs for young people like that?

MR. HICKS. I would say that the apprenticeship rules do not prevent us from getting jobs for summer employment, but they certainly deter us in getting jobs, full-time jobs, and I would say one of the greatest hindrances toward youngsters, and especially minorities, getting jobs, I would find my experience has been so far that union restrictions in these areas has been the greatest deterrent.

COMMISSIONER RANKIN. And there is no way of changing the situation?

MR. HICKS. I think there is. I think the people when they decide to change it, will change it, and I think the legislature will reflect that change pretty soon.

VICE CHAIRMAN PATTERSON. Mr. Magnin, I am inclined to agree with you that you need a sort of clearinghouse or a traffic cop to direct you to the various agencies that are dealing and duplicating and overlapping help, some aids to the people seeking the jobs that the Government has so far provided. We certainly have encountered this in Atlanta, too, but I wonder if the Chamber of Commerce has given any thought or the city government has given any thought to establishing such a clearinghouse itself to direct the job-seeker to the various and the variety of areas that might help him find work?

MR. MAGNIN. I think we have talked about it. We haven't come up with any solution. I think that the Chamber of Commerce is not the agency or not the place for the solution to come from. I think it has to come from government. I think government has to determine where this central agency should be. That is just my personal feeling. I don't know.

MR. HICKS. We called—in my appearance before the San Francisco Human Rights Commission in January, I called upon the San Francisco Human Rights Commission to take the leadership and do just this. I am fully aware of the fact that this means he is going to step on the toes of a lot of people, but if the Human Rights Commission isn't big enough to step on these people's toes maybe we should get a new kind. I have said it before. They promised to take it under consideration and perhaps in a short while we might hear some more about it, but unless the governmental agencies are going to be big enough to step on sombody's toes and bring all these people together in some kind of a centralized operation, I think we are going to deter more and more a solution to this problem. We hope they will take that leadership.

VICE CHAIRMAN PATTERSON. But why should it be stepping on anybody's toes just to have one central place where a man looking for work or training for work would be able to go and get directions of how to get to the agency from people who know what that agency is doing? Wouldn't this be a fairly simple city function?

MR. HICKS. It is a question of procedure, I would suppose. There are a number of people, executive directors, of a number of organizations who are working in this particular field and every time you cut down his power you cut down his salary or the authority over people. So you reduce his power. I am not sure that they will be very happy in having somebody do this. I think in doing so you might be stepping on the feet.

I might add that insofar as the Chamber of Commerce is concerned in this area, we are only in here until such time as somebody fills the vacuum that needs to be filled for business. We are not here to stay at all. We are here on a very temporary basis and we are trying to put together a program that will go over peacefully and in a very orderly manner into an agency whose function will be what we hope is going to develop here and the Chamber will cooperate 100 percent and out of business we go. That is Mr. Magnin's position on that, too.

MR. MAGNIN. And we hope to be out of it by the end of this year or the end of next year at the latest.

VICE CHAIRMAN PATTERSON. It has been this Commission's experience in various hearings around the country that those cities where the business leadership takes responsibility for moving matters forward and working with government, those cities usually are best governed, it seems to me, to make my own personal generalities about it.

I was particularly impressed with your comment on the vote with respect to the Fair Housing Law. Did many Chambers of Commerce in California opt the same position that the San Francisco Chamber chose?

MR. MURRAY. None that I know of.

MR. MAGNIN. Los Angeles, I guess?

MR. MURRAY. No, they didn't.

VICE CHAIRMAN PATTERSON. This says something, it seems to me, about the business leadership in this city and I simply wanted to make that observation for the record.

MR. MAGNIN. Thank you. I believe the business leadership in this city is very enlightened and very anxious to take care of any problem that concerns the welfare of this community and the people of this community.

VICE CHAIRMAN PATTERSON. Mr. Taylor, do you have questions?

MR. TAYLOR. Yes. Mr. Magnin, I would like to explore for a moment more the question of the role of business leadership. I take it that one of the problems is that while jobs may have been made available, most of these jobs required some minimal kinds of skills. Is that correct?

MR. MAGNIN. Naturally, there has to be some skills. I don't care what the job is.

MR. TAYLOR. I wonder, though, what can be done and what is business's responsibility with respect to those who are called the hard core unemployed, those people who lack the basic education and the skills? Should business consider undertaking the basic training necessary to give these people employment?

MR. MAGNIN. Mr. Taylor, we are just working on that kind of a program which Mr. Hicks can tell you about, I believe.

MR. HICKS. Once again I think it shows the enlightened leadership of the San Francisco business community. I think perhaps we are the leading advocate of Chamber of Commerces in the United States of business cooperating with government in solving the problems where we find ourselves as we did in redevelopment with Butchertown, and once again into the recent governmental manpower development program that the President of the United States had ordered to be put together in 19 cities throughout the United States. We had our cooperative program in the hands of the Federal agencies some eight weeks ago, and we have been waiting to start the performance of the operation within the private sector community, and 1 have been told by the Labor Department that San Francisco is the leading city in the 19 cities insofar as business cooperation is concerned in this particular governmental program, and I am sure you know about it and I won't waste your time going into it, but we are going to do our part, and I assure you we won't come in last.

In answer, though, to your question that you said to Mr. Magnin about the qualifications, just for your information, for your files, too, I have brought along a complete survey for you of the jobs that you are here questioning about what business did, the number of jobs, the type of jobs, the salary range, to whom these jobs were sent to just for your own consideration. You will find that they were just really jobs I think that someone could have been found to fill.

MR. MAGNIN. I feel in that area there are too many people in government trying to do the same thing. This ought to get down to one area, two agencies, maybe one to coordinate the jobs and one for the training and placing of the jobs.

MR. TAYLOR. But you would advocate business taking on directly a greater share of the responsibilities of training and placing people?

MR. MAGNIN. I think they should, yes. That's their obligation.

MR. TAYLOR. Do most employers' businesses in this area consider a police record a disqualification for employment?

MR. MAGNIN. In some lines of businesses, and I am certain we have placed in the emergency period that time, as I recall, and even later on we placed people with police records. Is that right, Al?

MR. HICKS. That's right.

MR. TAYLOR. So you think our business is beginning to consider some of these—reconsider some of these requirements or some of these bars that they previously had to employing people with a view to providing more employment?

MR. HICKS. I might say in that regard that I have a report that was submitted to me by the San Francisco Public Community Relations Department of the San Francisco Police Department in which they say that they cannot truthfully say to what extent an arrest record is a bar to an individual's employment. There seems to be that if an employer really does not want to hire an individual who has a police record he will give some other reason for such.

Now, to what extent you see this reason he gives is affected by the fact that he has a police record nobody can say truthfully, and I would not want to quote anybody, but I do know when I asked the question specifically of some of our large employers and others, they can point to you individuals who have police records who are working. Now, how many were turned down before that have them we are still working on statistics that we hope to develop. I would say it is a program that has to be sold to the businessman like any other program and you have to get in and get your facts and get your homework done before you can tell him that he is doing something that is not for the best interests of the community and we are developing this program and we hope to have some real concrete information on it in the future.

MR. TAYLOR. How about the question of testing as a qualification for employment? Some people believe that tests are really not very realistic measures of a person's ability to perform the job and really unconsciously discriminate against people who may not have the background and orientation of people generally who take tests. Are employers considering modification of their testing requirements?

MR. HICKS. In our new program that we are developing in conjunction with the Manpower Administration, we are having what is called a central intake center and in this central intake center there will be certain kinds of tests even there that would be administered to individuals, but they will not be the kind of a test that is administered to keep a fellow from getting a job. It is to give us information as to the possibilities or non-possibility of him performing certain jobs so we will know where to put him in order to give him a better chance to better perform that type of a job, and I think that in many industries you are finding that this kind of approach to testing and examinations is being developed. They do want to know what is a person's aptitude, what is he capable of doing. This would only seem to me to be one way of protecting the employer from wasting his time and protecting the individual from being put into a situation which he cannot cope with, but I don't really believe that it is generally—the trend is getting larger. I think it is getting smaller where examinations are being used to do things that we would say are unsocial.

MR. TAYLOR. One last question, Mr. Magnin.

It is my impression that a good many people know about the Chamber of Commerce's efforts, but you find some skepticism among some people who live in the ghetto. I think maybe it is a product of years of skepticism and one of the problems that gets expressed is that people say, "These are really very low-paying jobs in some cases and they are jobs without a future and they are deadend jobs and they are not really interested in us."

Now, if that is a problem, how do you get off of this?

MR. MAGNIN. I don't think that is a problem. Of course, in that great emergency we placed any kind of jobs that we could possibly place, but generally we are looking for people at all levels. If they have the ability to do a job, and we have an opening, I am certain we can place them, but that is not, I don't think, a problem.

MR. MURRAY. As far as that last question, I think the part we were involved in was to be a placement agency as well after the riots, because our own companies and others would call up from South San Francisco or Oakland and say that "We understand that you would like to find jobs for some unemployed people," and one company specifically, Georgia Pacific in South San Francisco, called me. I would then refer them to Al or to someone else, but if Al wasn't in or if the Mayor's Job Center—if he couldn't get ahold of someone there, then I would say, "Well, if you need them badly right now, let me try myself," and I called some responsible people to send down five laborers for warehousing and the job was paying $3.50 an hour, which isn't bad. It is not the highest, but it was a good-paying job, and the man never could fill those five jobs. He only filled one of them. It took two weeks and I'll bet his name was in 10 places, 10 of these agencies.

Now, I think this again gets back to the program that Al Hicks has developed, again with Mr. Magnin. This new idea of acting as a central clearing agency where the efforts of government can be coordinated to go out and recruit more of the people who want the opportunity, but right now might have been frustrated or for one reason or another are staying home, but they are not going to the Department of Employment asking for jobs the way people used to in the 30's and 40's and 50's, and in the 30's when these departments of government were created to handle breadlines and handle people who wanted to work.

Now there has got to be some way to convince and bolster a little bit, it may be a frustrated ego, and bring these people into this central intake where business then can reach down and just kind of help them along. The point is that somehow there has to be a better recruitment from the government to bring the people in, because we can't find the people for the jobs, and this is an area that we haven't found a solution for, but we are working on this idea of short training programs specifically geared for jobs pledged, and that is all I have to say on that.

MR. HICKS. Mr. Taylor, I might go into that a little further for you, since that is more directly involved in my operation, and I want to be very fair in regards to that.

I can't say that we went around to the employer and said that you are going to hire a minority and give him $100 more than anyone else, but I have a report here which I will be happy to leave with each of you. It breaks down the jobs. For instance, there were 20 clerks' jobs. The salary was $300 to $325 a month, and it was referred to the Job Center for placement. I can't say to you that $300 to $325 is a low salary for clerks. There are nine laborers. They range from $280 to $470 a month. They were sent to the Job Center for placement.

Looking further down here, there is—they say two combination men. $525 a month. That was sent to the Employment Service. Six stockmen. The salary was open. There were six porters, $320 a month, 23 messengers, $260 to $285 a month. I can't say that these salaries are low. I can't say they are high. All we did was take the information that the employers were sent and I think the Commission should take its own time and review these statistics and come into my office and look at them if you want, because as we sent out and got replies to that letter, we asked the employer to send us back his card and this is the kind of card that they sent back to us, putting all the information down, the salary, and they signed it and told us who to get in touch with and we put here who we sent it out to.

If these people feel this is low-paying, I feel my salary is low-paying, too, for the work that I am doing, but I think you should be objective and take a look at it for yourselves and determine for yourselves if it is low or high.

MR. TAYLOR. I am not being critical, Mr. Hicks. I am just trying to explore what some of the barriers may be that prevent people from getting into jobs which they may stay with, what is keeping the unemployment rate up, and this is one problem that hasn't been expressed. Two hundred and fifty or $280 a month is less than what would generally be considered to be an adequate salary to support a family. In addition, people may have difficulty in getting to jobs, they may have transportation expenses that mount up, and the problem that has been expressed, is that we are really not creating adequate incentives, and I would assume from what you say that you agree that in some way this may be a problem and in some way we have to find ways to get at it and provide that kind of salary.

MR. HICKS. I might say in that regard all I am simply saying, that I don't think any of us think we are being paid enough, but whether or not these jobs are enough pay I don't know.

MR. MAGNIN. I want to ask Al, isn't it our purpose to find better jobs generally in the new program?

MR. HICKS. Oh, yes. One of the purposes of the new program, of course, is to weed out individuals, get them the better-paying jobs, but in the meantime, too, let's not forget, and you have to be very honest, too, as you do that you are also trying to find the better guy that fits to the better job.

It is ridiculous in talking about putting, as you spoke earlier, of a hard core individual, let's say one that dropped out of high school when he was in the eleventh grade, but mentally he dropped out when he was in the sixth grade and think you are going to give him a $600-a-month job and the employer is going to be happy and he is going to be happy. We do have to say that we are trying to get the best job that is commensurate with what he has to offer and what the employer can receive.

MR. TAYLOR. Thank you.

VICE CHAIRMAN PATTERSON. Any further questions?

MR. MAGNIN. There is just one point I want to clarify, Mr. Patterson, in connection with your question. Mr. Hicks may not agree with me.

I don't believe it is necessary to eliminate the various agencies that supply jobs, have job employment for people in their organization. I believe, however, there should be one central agency that would handle all of these jobs for these various coordinating agencies.

I know that there are many agencies, and certainly those in the private sector, like the Urban League, and organizations like that that have access to people. It may be a government agency or a super-agency wouldn't have, but if they would clear all their jobs and have a record of those jobs with a central agency, I think it would be helpful. I don't think actually they should be eliminated.

VICE CHAIRMAN PATTERSON. We do sometimes expect an awful lot of a citizen of this country, to be able to find his way through the maze of agencies and opportunities to his own particular destiny, and I certainly agree that anything we can do to simplify that course is a plus.

I appreciate very much your being here today. You are excused. The hearing will be adjourned until 11:30 a.m. in this courtroom tomorrow morning.

(Whereupon, the hearing adjourned until Tuesday, May 2, 1967, at 11:30 a.m. in the same location.)

U.S. COMMISSION ON CIVIL RIGHTS

CHAIRMAN HANNAH. The second day of this hearing of the United States Commission on Civil Rights will come to order. Mr. Glickstein, will you call the first witness?

MR. GLICKSTEIN. The first witness will be Mr. Jonathan Fleming, an attorney on the staff of the Commission, who will give the Staff Report.

(Whereupon, Mr. Jonathan Fleming was sworn by the Chairman and testified as follws:)

TESTIMONY OF MR. JONATHAN FLEMING, ATTORNEY, U.S. COMMISSION ON CIVIL RIGHTS

MR. FLEMING. In November, 1962, President John F. Kennedy signed Executive Order 11063 on Equal Opportunity in Housing. The order directed Departments and Agencies in the Federal Government to take all action necessary and appropriate to prevent discrimination in the sale, rental, or disposition of residential property, including land to be developed for residential use. The order covered all housing owned by the Government or provided by Federal financial assistance or by loans insured or guaranteed by the credit of the Federal Government. The order also directed Departments and Agencies to use their good offices, including appropriate litigation, to promote the abandonment of discriminatory practices in housing provided through Federal financial assistance or credit prior to the signing of the order.

The primary burden of implementing and enforcing the Executive order fell upon the Federal Housing Administration. This agency, now part of the Department of Housing and Urban Development, was established by Congress 33 years ago to encourage improvement in housing standards and conditions. This encouragement is offered primarily through mortgage insurance which enables lenders to finance homes and multi-family housing on liberal terms. In addition, a sound financing system is provided by the marketability of FHA mortgages and by the activities of the Federal National Mortgage Association which purchases, services, and sells mortgages insured or guaranteed by the FHA and the Veterans Administration.

In order to qualify for FHA mortgage insurance, homes must

(130)

131

be built to meet certain minimum standards and specifications and lots must meet development standards. Home builders who intend to offer homes for sale which will meet FHA mortgage insurance standards submit plans and specifications to FHA experts who advise and assist the builder. If the plans are approved FHA makes a commitment to insure mortgages on homes built in the approved tract.

FHA regulations which implement the Executive order exempt owner-occupied homes and duplexes. Thus the order covers only homes and duplexes in housing tracts for which FHA has made a commitment to insure mortgages and all multi-family housing provided by loans insured by FHA.

FHA regulations also provide for a complaint process and for sanctions against lenders and builders who discriminate in the sale or financing or rental of housing covered by the order. Sanctions include placing the offender's name on an ineligible list.

Relatively few complaints have been filed with FHA. The national total as of January 1967 is 149. In only 12 cases, however, did the person charged with discriminating prevail. Sixteen builders have been placed on the ineligible list after repeated instances of discrimination. Seven of these builders have been reinstated. The greatest number of complaints have been filed in the Washington, D.C. Metropolitan Area. The Region VI office of FHA which covers California, the Pacific Northwest States, Hawaii, and the Pacific Islands, has reported a total of 19 complaints; 10 of these complaints have come from the San Francisco Bay Area.

Since November 1962 through March 1965, the FHA in the San Francisco Bay Area Region has insured approximately 10,000 units of multi-family housing. There are three programs which will be discussed during the morning which are designed to assist private industry in providing housing for low and moderate-income families. These are Section 221(d)(3), a program under which the Commissioner of FHA is authorized to insure mortgages, including advances during construction up to the total amount of $12,500,000 for certain types of low-income and moderate-income housing.

Section 23, Leased Housing, which is authorized by the Housing Act of 1965, enables local housing authorities to lease housing from private property owners in order to provide housing for low-income people. No building may have more than 10 percent of its space leased under Section 23 except in special circumstances.

The Rent Supplement Program which is designed to provide new housing for low and moderate-income families. The usual means of construction and financing is through the 221 (d) (3) mortgage insurance program. The Federal Government agrees to underwrite the difference between the established rental and a fixed percentage of the family income that the tenant can afford for rent.

CHAIRMAN HANNAH. Any questions?

MR. GLICKSTEIN. No, Mr. Chairman.

CHAIRMAN HANNAH. You are excused. Mr. Glickstein, would you call the next witness or witnesses?

MR. GLICKSTEIN. The next witnesses are Mrs. Lucy Buchbinder and Mrs. Lois Matusek.

(Whereupon, Mrs. Lucy Buchbinder and Mrs. Lois Matusek were sworn by the Chairman and testified as follows:)

TESTIMONY OF MRS. LUCY BUCHBINDER, CASTRO VALLEY, CALIFORNIA AND MRS. LOIS MATUSEK, CONCORD, CALIFORNIA

MR. GLICKSTEIN. Would you each please state your name and address for the record?

MRS. BUCHBINDER. My name is Lucy Buchbinder. 5667 Greenridge Road, Castro Valley.

MRS. MATUSEK. My name is Lois Matusek. 5566 Michigan Boulevard, Concord, California.

MR. GLICKSTEIN. We understand that you ladies have been involved in fair housing activities. Would you please each tell us how long you have been involved in these activities.

MRS. BUCHBINDER. I have been involved for slightly over two years.

MR. GLICKSTEIN. Mrs. Matusek?

MRS. MATUSEK. I assumed the chairmanship as fair housing chairman for the Concord Citizens for Human Rights in 1965. However, I had been very active in fair housing, particularly as it related to Proposition 14 prior to that time.

MR. GLICKSTEIN. What led you to get involved in fair housing activities, Mrs. Matusek?

MRS. MATUSEK. My primary concern was the enactment of Proposition 14 in the State of California. For the benefit of the Commission, although I am sure you are quite aware of this, Proposition 14 not only nullified our State Fair Housing Act called the Rumford Act, but it also instructed the legislature that they should never again enact fair housing legislation. This created a legal void in our society that had to be filled through citizen effort to protect the rights of the minority toward social mobility.

MR. GLICKSTEIN. Mrs. Matusek, you said you were chairman of the Concord Citizens for Human Rights?

MRS. MATUSEK. I am chairman of the housing committee for that organization.

MR. GLICKSTEIN. And what organization are you associated with, Mrs. Buchbinder?

MRS. BUCHBINDER. I am chairman of the Housing Opportunities Committee of the Council for Civic Unity of the San Francisco Bay Area.

MR. GLICKSTEIN. And that organization extends throughout the Bay Area?

MRS. BUCHBINDER. It coordinates the work of 22 fair housing groups throughout the Bay Area.

MR. GLICKSTEIN. What led you to your involvement with fair housing activities?

MRS. BUCHBINDER. Also my activities on behalf of fair housing legislation during the Proposition 14 campaign.

MR. GLICKSTEIN. What do your present activities consist of?

MRS. BUCHBINDER. In addition to being chairman of the Fair Housing Council, I am also executive secretary of a local fair housing group similar to Mrs. Matusek's.

MR. GLICKSTEIN. And what type of activities do you engage in, Mrs. Matusek?

MRS. MATUSEK. My activities have been in any area in which I could find some tool or some avenue of establishing fair housing practices in our area. This would include trying to implement Federal law, trying to implement State law, after the Rumford Act was re-established, cooperating with realtors on their ethical program, negotiating with apartment house people, negotiating with industry and the military base in our area, which was required by the Civil Service or the Department of Defense to employ minority people.

We wanted to service these industries and the military base to find housing for their minority employees. I was led, wherever the demand or the need or the opportunity seemed to be, that is the way I followed.

MR. GLICKSTEIN. And you attempt to encourage persons who are selling their homes to sell them without discrimination, and do you also attempt to seek buyers for the homes?

MRS. MATUSEK. We would survey for-sale or for-rent-by-owner homes. During that period recently when the Rumford Act was not in effect, it was one of our few sources of housing at that time. As soon as possible I dropped that practice because the amount of housing that you could acquire in such a way was very limited, and I would much rather use other sources, such as the Rumford Act or a realtor agreement to open up the total market and give total mobility to any clients who might come to our area.

So far as establishing a contact with minority clients who might wish to come to our area, this was very hard, because you had to build up a feeling of trust and communicate with Negroes in the inner-city, or in the ghetto areas, who might have the economic and the psychological desire to move out to the suburbs, but had been discouraged by the reputation of our suburban area.

MR. GLICKSTEIN. But you have been in contact with minority group people attempting to encourage them to seek housing in your area?

MRS. MATUSEK. Yes. Originally we would do this by mail. We established a mailing list of any area, such as fraternal or church or civil rights groups, that we felt had a predominantly minority membership. We would also meet with minorities and visit with them and invite them out to our area.

MR. GLICKSTEIN. Mrs. Buchbinder, what have been your experiences with the Federal Housing Administration and the Veterans Administration in trying to get enforcement of the Executive order, President Kennedy's Executive order on nondiscrimination in housing?

MRS. BUCHBINDER. I have filed seven complaints to the FHA and the VA in regard to violation of the Executive order. Five of those were to the FHA and two to the VA. In only three cases was a house actually made available at the end of the proceedings to our client. In four of the cases we lost the client before the proceedings were completed.

My experiences lead me to believe that the case-by-case approach is very slow and has to be handled by people who know exactly what they are doing. It is difficult to prove discrimination. It takes a different aspect each time there is discrimination, all the way from the sales office, which refuses to show a house to a Negro buyer, to discrimination occurring weeks or months after when a client is finally told that his loan application has been turned down.

This has to be pursued carefully and consistently, and all during the proceeding the fair housing group has to give tremendous moral support to the client who during this time is exposed to constant harassment by the tract office, is asked to come many times to the tract office to sign papers. Papers are lost.

I found that the local FHA office was most cooperative in processing the complaints. However, I also had the feeling that I had to obey the rules of the game and that the rules were, No. 1, that I had to keep the client live and willing and able to buy the house, at the hearing that I was not to come with a case where I no longer had a client, and the other part of the game was that, once the house was made available, that this was the end of the case.

I never pursued a case further because, although this was never expressed to me directly, I had the feeling that this was as far as I could go, and since we were processing seven cases within seven months, almost simultaneously, I did not want to jeopardize the chances of the clients.

MR. GLICKSTEIN. Are you suggesting that it takes FHA too long to process a complaint?

MRS. BUCHBINDER. This is part of it.

MR. GLICKSTEIN. What do you think that the FHA should be doing in order to end discrimination in housing? You criticize the case-by-case method. What do you think should be done?

MRS. BUCHBINDER. I think if, first of all, that housing that is covered by the Executive order ought to be identified as such in advertising.

MR. GLICKSTEIN. And it isn't at the present time?

MRS. BUCHBINDER. At the present time it is not identified. Minority clients——

MR. GLICKSTEIN. Don't persons who—developers who have FHA coverage indicate in their ads that FHA insurance is available? Do the ads state that?

MRS. BUCHBINDER. Most of them do, though some of them do not.

MR. GLICKSTEIN. They don't say that "We are equal opportunity housing developers" or something equivalent to that?

MRS. BUCHBINDER. Right. And there is such a long history of new housing being available for whites only that unless we engage in a really vigorous, affirmative campaign to make it known that some housing is open, the minority community will not come and look.

We have had contact with close to 1,000 members of minority groups, primarily Negroes, during the past years, in my own small fair housing group, not the Council. This is just referring to my activities in my own fair housing group, and of those their visit with us to a tract office was their first experience in seeing new housing. So that I feel that housing must be identified. Whenever we have made the suggestion to HUD or to FHA we have been told that less than 20 percent of the market is covered by the Executive order and, therefore, to make developers identify their tracts as being equal opportunity tracts would be discrimination against them.

I suggest that this is a somewhat preposterous notion that we have an order covering housing and yet to advertise it as such would be to discriminate against those developers who are using publicly assisted insurance and guarantees.

MR. GLICKSTEIN. What other things do you think FHA should require besides the advertising that you just mentioned?

MRS. BUCHBINDER. I think there should be compliance inspections just as there are compliance inspections in regard to the building code of FHA.

MR. GLICKSTEIN. It is your understanding that after the FHA finds that a builder has discriminated and requires them to make a house available the FHA does not send persons around to inspect to see if the builder is continuing to refrain from discriminating?

MRS. BUCHBINDER. I would strongly suspect so, especially since I have had to issue two complaints successively against the same builder.

MR. GLICKSTEIN. Mrs. Matusek, do you also feel that the FHA has been ineffective in enforcing the Executive order and, if so, why?

MRS. MATUSEK. Yes, I feel that the FHA has been ineffective, both at the district and at the Federal level.

First, there is the interpretation of the Executive order. When I read it I thought—I am an idealist, and I thought, "This is great. This is the tool that we need." It is marvelous, because when you read the Executive order in terms of the intent it is a tremendous social document. When you get into the body of the law, there is where you run into the crux of your problem, because there is the "The director may do this or the director at his discretion will do that."

I don't know if you intend to cover it, but this was brought up at a meeting on June 6, I believe, between Mrs. Buchbinder and myself, the FHA and HUD, and at that time I asked them if the Executive order was intended to work, and they assured me that it was.

And I said, well, if this is true, then you must read the Executive order always in relation to the intent in the preamble, because if you don't you have a very, very weak ambivalent law and something that would be very difficult to administer and would allow for a tremendous margin of discretion by the agency attempting to administer it.

Besides that, the FHA, from its Washington directives, seemed to further limit the scope and intent of the Executive order.

For instance, the stipulation about the applying of sanctions. The pronouncement from Washington, if you ask them about this, is that if a developer repeats discriminatory tactics against the minority client, he shall be considered to be a repeater.

I followed this through and found out that the definition of a repeater would be two times, and so we went further into this definition of the repeater, and the opinion of the San Francisco office, which I am sure must reflect the Washington opinion, was that if a developer changed his tactics, although the ultimate result would be that he would be a discriminator against a minority client, he would not in fact be a repeater.

MR. GLICKSTEIN. Every time they use a different device it would be a new case of first instance?

MRS. MATUSEK. Yes, and it would be an opportunity, therefore, for further education of that developer by FHA. FHA primarily carries on a program of education.

Now, I contend that the FHA does the developer a tremendous disservice, because I am sure that the developer is intelligent enough to understand completely the statement that he signs on each of his contracts, that he will not discriminate, and he enters into this part of his contract voluntarily and should, therefore, in pursuance of building his tract and selling his home, should be expected to cooperate with his contractual agreement.

MR. GLICKSTEIN. Mrs. Buchbinder, do you have fairly widespread contact with builders?

MRS. BUCHBINDER. I have almost no contact with builders.

MR. GLICKSTEIN. How about you, Mrs. Matusek? Are you familiar with the attitude of builders toward the Executive order?

MRS. MATUSEK. In one instance, yes. In one instance it was a hearsay, and I would rather not—

MR. GLICKSTEIN. Let me ask both of you ladies this question. Do either of you have any way of knowing whether builders are convinced that FHA is determined to enforce the Executive order?

MRS. MATUSEK. Shall I answer that?

I think the developers, except in a few cases, now there are some, Barrett Homes is one, where the developer himself is motivated to integration. If the developer doesn't have that personal motivation, I do not think that he respects either the clause or the agency or the law.

MR. GLICKSTEIN. You don't think there are builders who are actually afraid that if they discriminate they are going to lose FHA financing?

MRS. MATUSEK. I know of none.

MR. GLICKSTEIN. Mrs. Buchbinder, the Executive order, the enforcement of the Executive order, as supervised by the President's Committee on Equal Opportunity in Housing, have you had any experience with that Committee?

MRS. BUCHBINDER. I have been asked by a staff member to sponsor a conference, and it was—this was before we really started our complaints to the Washington offices of HUD. We felt at the time that a conference is not very useful because only the people who are really on our side come to a conference, and we asked that there be a hearing rather than a conference because the Executive order does provide for the purposes of education and other purposes, hearings may be held, and we felt that our prime concern was to educate the minority community of the existence of the order.

MR. GLICKSTEIN. What do you think of the efforts of that Committee?

MRS. BUCHBINDER. Beyond this one contact, I have had no

indication that the Committee does anything in regard to the order. This is the only contact we have ever had. The only time I personally met anyone was accidentally at a conference, rather than with regard to our request for a hearing.

MR. GLICKSTEIN. I have no further questions, Mr. Chairman.

CHAIRMAN HANNAH. Mr. Taylor?

MR. TAYLOR. No.

CHAIRMAN HANNAH. Do the Commissioners have any questions? Father Hesburgh?

COMMISSIONER HESBURGH. I have a rather general question of either one of you. Do you think the Executive order in fact has changed the situation from what it was before the Executive order? In other words, do you see a difference happening once the Executive order came out? We have been a long time trying to get an Executive order, if you recall, and we finally got one and everybody was happy about it. Now has anything happened because of it? I wish each of you would take a chance in answering that if you would.

MRS. BUCHBINDER. I will start on this one.

I would say that unfortunately the Executive order has made no visible impact at all. If you go into any of the tracts in suburbia, you will see that what is happening actually is that white ghettos are growing up at a rapid rate. All you have to do is call the school district and find out whether there are any Negroes in the schools and you will find out that there are not in the suburban tracts.

COMMISSIONER HESBURGH. Since you brought up the question of tracts, Mrs. Buchbinder, we had this long, drawn-out conversation about Serramonte yesterday and no one in the whole city seems to know whether or not there are Negroes in Serramonte. Do you know if there are Negroes in Serramonte?

MRS. BUCHBINDER. I did not do any investigating. I have been told by the fair housing groups that not only are there no Negroes, but that the practices they have fought against have resumed just recently.

We had a report to our group. However, I would suggest that it would be very easy for anyone to find out on the part of the city. They would not have, as they talked about yesterday, have to walk through the tract. All they would really have to do is to call the elementary school and they would find out.

MR. GLICKSTEIN. Call the what?

MRS. BUCHBINDER. The elementary school.

COMMISSIONER HESBURGH. You have, you say, some kind of report about these practices resuming that we could have here in the Commission?

MRS. BUCHBINDER. I could certainly get one for you.

COMMISSIONER HESBURGH. I think it would be a good thing for

us to have, since it at least puts a footnote on all that conversation we listened to yesterday. Mrs. Matusek, have you seen any appreciable change since the Executive order?

MRS. MATUSEK. No, I haven't, not in my area, at all.

COMMISSIONER HESBURGH. One last question: this gets rather frustrating, you know. We pass laws. We get presidential orders. We start new divisions of government, like HUD, and nothing really seems to happen. Do you ladies have any suggestions as to something firm that might be done?

MRS. MATUSEK. I think one of the reasons that the Executive order has been not meaningful is that the FHA has insisted that the Executive order is dependent upon citizen action to work.

Now, I have really argued this with FHA. The first time it came up I was told that the policy of FHA was that they were the agency and they would only follow where the citizen pressure led them. That sounds reasonable and democratic, but I will tell you the way it works. It works like the old hound dog who is sitting by the fire and you are trying to get him to go out in the rain, and you can cajole and prod a little bit, and maybe he will just wag his tail friendly-like a couple of times, as FHA has done for us on minor things that don't matter, but you can't get that dog to get up and move unless he is motivated to do so.

This citizen action is inefficient because we are in no position to be aware of the directives that are coming out of Washington. We don't know what our district office is supposed to be doing or how it is supposed to be doing it, and it would be presumptious of us to require that these directors also report to us so that we could monitor the agency. Then, too, you might get a citizen group, such as in this area, that is very active.

Other vast areas of the United States of America may not have this citizen pressure, so that the enforcement of the Executive order would be very ineffectual and very uneven, which is not right.

The citizen action also requires this case-by-case approach, which Mrs. Buchbinder was describing to you, which is the most inefficient way of making the law work.

My further and final point is that the Executive order at no time states that it is the responsibility of the citizen to make this law effective. They do give the responsibility and the tools and the implementation to the agency, and they are the ones, I feel, who should be carrying the ball on this.

COMMISSIONER HESBURGH. So what you are suggesting is that the agency police the law as now written?

MRS. MATUSEK. Police and implement and interpret it as it was intended to be interpreted. If they can't do it, perhaps it would be a case where another agency will have to do it for them, but when you run into that problem, you run into this inter-agency ethics.

Now, we are getting a little bit of that feedback right now. The FHA did have its own intergroup relations man in their FHA office up until last fall, and the Fair Housing group, you see, go through the intergroup relations man to try to get the information that they need. This didn't seem to be working out very well because the man was an employee of the agency, and he would be put into this embarrassing position of trying to police his own agency, which obviously wouldn't work out.

So then the intergroup relations adviser was moved to HUD, and I thought, great, now maybe we will have a real breakthrough here, but it doesn't work out that way, either, because the HUD man is in even a more embarrassing position.

I can call the HUD man and ask for information and he will be put on the spot, and say, "I am awfully sorry. But I can't go over to FHA and look through their records and get this for you. You will have to call the director of the department."

So as a result we really don't have intergroup relations communication.

I called at one time in my career, called the Federal District Attorney's office. I needed an interpretation on a point of law concerning the Executive order.

Now the Attorney General is a member of the President's Committee which is supposed to help interpret and monitor the Executive Order No. 11063 but, despite that relationship, I was not even able to make an appointment with a lawyer at the Attorney General's office, because they said one agency could not monitor another, that the Executive order was under the control of FHA, and if I wanted any interpretation of the law I would have to go to FHA to get it.

COMMISSIONER HESBURGH. Thank you very much, Mrs. Matusek. I think this may be another revolution of sorts.

CHAIRMAN HANNAH. Mr. Patterson, do you have any questions?

VICE CHAIRMAN PATTERSON. One question. Mrs. Matusek, is it your opinion that the FHA has sufficient authority under the Executive order to solve this problem, if they would use it or do they need additional authority? In other words, if you pushed the old dog out in the rain, can he catch the rabbit?

MRS. MATUSEK. FHA claims that perhaps if they had more money they would be able to monitor the Executive order, more staff. I think all agencies need more money, more staff, but I swear it is motivation, and I don't know where the breakdown is. I have tried to find it and I can't.

You think, well, maybe it is in Washington and any statement that you ask of Washington, for instance, what is a repeater?

That statement, you have to have this clarified. All right. You get what I call a gung ho letter back from Washington. It is usually over the signature of Mr. Brownstein.

MR. GLICKSTEIN. Mr. Brownstein is the head of FHA, is that correct, the administrator of FHA?

MRS. MATUSEK. I believe that he is affiliated with the President's Committee, too, isn't he?

MRS. BUCHBINDER. The Deputy Comissioner.

MRS. MATUSEK. Oh, I am sorry. The Deputy Commissioner. I forgot his title, but, anyhow, he will come out with this statement, then, yes, you know, a repeater is any developer who discriminates two times.

Then you go back with factual proof on a particular developer, that he has several times been a discriminator and is still receiving tremendous subsidy from FHA, and then you get this backtrack letter.

Now this happens on the advertising, too. In this case the letter by Brownstein was sent to Senator Robert Kennedy because by now he was involved in it, and this was the statement on the advertising.

Now, according to the letter which Senator Kennedy received, you would think that the FHA was advertising these properties. When you check with the district office and with the practice in this area, which I am sure is uniform throughout the United States, but it is the only area that I can check, so I have to use it as an example, you find that the advertising doesn't apply to all the properties handled by the Executive order. It only applies to the repossessions, which I figured out, according to any statistics I could get, .1 percent of the total housing market, and besides that the advertising is not in a public journal, such as the newspaper.

In other words, your realtor who advertises these "repos" never has the equal opportunity line in his ad, and so I wrote back to Senator Kennedy and explained just exactly what Mr. Brownstein's letter meant, which is that the FHA on the 1/10 of 1 percent of the housing requires the realtor to put a poster in the window of the house that is going to be offered for sale by that realtor, which is a repossession.

If the realtor wants to, he can also put this placard in his office. He is not required to do so.

CHAIRMAN HANNAH. Mrs. Freeman?

COMMISSIONER FREEMAN. Mrs. Buchbinder and Mrs. Matusek, it seems to me that there are two sections of the order that are quite clear, and I have a question for you, but I would like to read them.

Section 101 says, of the President's order:

"I hereby direct all departments and agencies in the Executive Branch of the Federal Government insofar as their functions relate to the provision, rehabilitation or operation of housing and related facilities to take all action necessary and appropriate to prevent discrimination because of race, color, creed, or national origin."

That is very clear. Now, you have described a situation where a Federal agency has failed to comply with an order of the President, and you have also indicated that that agency is more concerned with what we say, bricks and mortar, because is it not true that the plans have to be approved with respect to building materials, etc.?

I would like to know if you in your contacts with FHA have asked them how it is that they can get the staff to assure compliance with the bricks and mortar aspect of it and not have the staff to comply with the President's order?

MRS. BUCHBINDER. We haven't put it quite that way, but we have asked that it be done.

COMMISSIONER FREEMAN. What was the answer?

MRS. BUCHINDER. We have had no direct answer to some of these questions. We usually have supplied a bill of particulars of complaints, and this particular one was not answered.

There are about three or four that usually simply are not answered. Others are answered in this way. We ask for some affirmative things. We spell them out. We do not find any response to what we have spelled out, but instead we are told, "But we do engage in affirmative action," and they list, for instance, this: in a recent letter from Mr. Brownstein to my Congressman, what is listed as affirmative action is a meeting held with Negro brokers.

Well, Negro brokers don't have anything to do with new housing. They would make no commission and, therefore, would not refer anyone to the tract offices, and this is what has happened to these suggestions, and if I may say something which relates to this indirectly. We have experiences with the enforcement of our own State laws with an agency which is not related to bricks and mortar, but is an agency whose sole purpose is to see that the law, in regard to fair employment and fair housing is enforced, and the difference between the way this agency handles complaints and the way an agency whose chief interest is in bricks and mortar handles complaints, I think, leads us to the recommendation that there ought to be an agency completely divorced from bricks and mortar and especially from the Veterans Administration, to enforce the laws of the land which relate to equal opportunities.

COMMISSIONER FREEMAN. How is the Rumford Act implemented?

MRS. BUCHBINDER. We have a Fair Employment Practices

Commission, and complaints on the Rumford Act are also channeled to the Fair Employment Practices Commission.

The procedure differs from the procedure used in FHA and VA, like night and day.

In the Fair Employment Practices Commission a consultant investigates the complaint, and if he finds there is good reason for the complaint, he then becomes the advocate of the complainant in the department and he pursues the case.

When a hearing has to be held, he does not preside at the hearing, but a hearing officer, a neutral person, presides at the hearing. In the FHA, you file the complaint and the deputy director of the FHA does all the investigating, or in the VA a loan guarantee officer does the investigating. He also decides whether or not a hearing shall be had, and then he presides at the hearing and makes the determination.

He is not a man primarily hired because of his skill in negotiations or because of any special training in human relations, nor is he a man especially dedicated to equal opportunities as the men hired in the FEPC are.

COMMISSIONER FREEMAN. Thank you.

CHAIRMAN HANNAH. Dr. Rankin?

COMMISSIONER RANKIN. I am interested in one point, Mrs. Matusek. You have dealt with Washington and the district office both, haven't you?

MRS. MATUSEK. Yes, I have.

COMMISSIONER RANKIN. Now, is policy determined by the district office? Could the district office if it wanted to implement the President's order, or would it get orders from Washington to go slow there?

I am interested in the by-play in your relationship between the two, the district office and the office in Washington.

Could one act without the other and implement the order or do you think it is Washington that is controlling?

MRS. MATUSEK. I think that the major policy interpretations of the Act and the implementation of the Act come from Washington. It must, but at the district level, the attitude of the personnel can water down even the modified nonaggressive policies of Washington to a further extent.

COMMISSIONER RANKIN. The office is dragging its heels in the district office. Is that correct? Is that your opinion?

MRS. MATUSEK. Yes, that is my feeling.

COMMISSIONER RANKIN. And, if you could get some real action from the district office, it would help. Am I correct in that?

MRS. MATUSEK. I think your motivated personnel at any level of the agency is a help.

COMMISSIONER RANKIN. And there is a lack of motivated personnel in the district office?

MRS. MATUSEK. Yes. Now, I feel perfectly free in stating this in public because the District Director of the San Francisco office three times in my presence in public declared that he was not personally motivated, that he would do what Washington told him. This was at the June 6 meeting in which the representatives from HUD and FHA were there, and this was a public statement repeated three times.

He also said that at one time, "I am sorry to be so honest with you, but this thing has been hidden under the bush for a long, long time. So please excuse me if I am honest rather than tactful."

At that same meeting, this same District Director stated that in explaining the Executive Order 11063 to the developers, a meeting was called for this purpose. He laughed, and he said, "Well, some people may say that I told the developers how to get around this order, but that's what they say."

Now, this was announced. I thought some of this would go back to Washington, the purpose of the meeting with HUD acting as a moderator between the two of us was bringing all these things out on the table, but nothing happened.

COMMISSIONER RANKIN. All right.

CHAIRMAN HANNAH. Mr. Taylor, do you have any questions?

MR. TAYLOR. No further questions.

CHAIRMAN HANNAH. Thank you very much, ladies. You are excused. Mr. Glickstein, would you call the next witness.

MR. GLICKSTEIN. Mr. Robert Snell.

(Whereupon, MR. ROBERT SNELL was sworn by the Chairman and testified as follows:)

TESTIMONY OF MR. ROBERT L. SNELL, OAKLAND, CALIFORNIA

MR. GLICKSTEIN. Mr. Snell, would you please state your full name and address for the record.

MR. SNELL. My name is Robert L. Snell, 312 - 17th Street, Oakland, California.

MR. GLICKSTEIN. What is your occupation, Mr. Snell?

MR. SNELL. I am a business manager of the Apartment House Association of Alameda County.

MR. GLICKSTEIN. What is the function of the Apartment House Association?

MR. SNELL. We are a trade organization that represents owners in management problems. We supply forms for their use in leases. We have a legal staff who they may call at any time. We have sources of purchases for them, and in general try to help them solve their problems.

Mr. GLICKSTEIN. How many members are there in the association?

Mr. SNELL. We have a few over 1,300. It varies.

Mr. GLICKSTEIN. Thirteen hundred, and how many apartment units are owned by the membership?

Mr. SNELL. I am not sure. We don't break it down. We have no reason to have that information.

Mr. GLICKSTEIN. Well, what proportion of the apartment units in Alameda County are owned by members of your association?

Mr. SNELL. Approximately 20 percent.

Mr. GLICKSTEIN. Approximately 20 percent. Does your association have Negro members?

Mr. SNELL. Yes, indeed we do.

Mr. GLICKSTEIN. What is the position of the Apartment House Association with regard to an owner's rights to refuse to rent to someone solely because of his race or color?

Mr. SNELL. Well, as you gentlemen know as well as I, we are under State law that doesn't give them the privilege to refuse them because of race, color, or creed.

Mr. GLICKSTEIN. Pardon me?

Mr. SNELL. As you know, we are under State law that forbids them to discriminate.

Mr. GLICKSTEIN. What was the association's position during the Proposition 14 controversy?

Mr. SNELL. You mean at the inception?

Mr. GLICKSTEIN. What was your position at the inception and right on the day of the balloting?

Mr. SNELL. Our association is a branch of the California Apartment House Owners Association. At that time, we took a stand in favor of Proposition 14.

Mr. GLICKSTEIN. You supported it?

Mr. SNELL. Yes.

Mr. GLICKSTEIN. Then you would think in an ideal situation, if you could change the law, an owner should have the right to refuse to sell to anybody because of his race or color?

Mr. SNELL. That is our feeling, yes.

Mr. GLICKSTEIN. Do you think that there are serious housing discrimination problems in Oakland and in Alameda County?

Mr. SNELL. To my knowledge, there are not.

Mr. GLICKSTEIN. There are not. What do you base your judgment on?

Mr. SNELL. Well, on experience that we have had over a period of time. I can't answer as to the shortage of housing for various types of people, but it seems to me that it has been rather smooth.

Mr. GLICKSTEIN. Do you think that Negroes who desire to

move into apartment houses that are owned by your members generally are able to do so?

MR. SNELL. Yes, sir.

MR. GLICKSTEIN. Do members of your association by and race?
large prefer to rent apartments in a building to members of one

MR. SNELL. We have nothing to do with the—who people should take in their building. We have not one iota of control over the type of people they take or do we try to advise them on that.

MR. GLICKSTEIN. Well, on the basis of your experience in the apartment house field and your knowledge of practices of apartment house owners, would you say that an owner of an apartment house prefers to rent apartments in his building only to members of one race?

MR. SNELL. I don't know as I am capable of answering that.

MR. GLICKSTEIN. You have no opinion on that, no basis of judgment?

MR. SNELL. No, sir.

MR. GLICKSTEIN. What is the present vacancy rate in Oakland?

MR. SNELL. It is about 9½ percent at the present time.

MR. GLICKSTEIN. Is that considered high or—

MR. SNELL. That includes all types.

MR. GLICKSTEIN. Is that considered high, 9½ percent?

MR. SNELL. That is just about normal now.

MR. GLICKSTEIN. Does your association have any program to educate apartment house owners to accept tenants of all colors?

MR. SNELL. No, we do not.

MR. GLICKSTEIN. You don't have a program. Do you think that the owners of apartment houses would be more willing to rent to any comer regardless of race or color if there were a Federal law, for example, that prohibited a person from discriminating?

MR. SNELL. You mean if there was a Federal law that said that they couldn't discriminate?

MR. GLICKSTEIN. That's right.

MR. SNELL. I am not so sure that that would solve the problem. It would probably make it mandatory on them.

MR. GLICKSTEIN. In your experience when owners are reluctant to rent to Negroes, is this something that you think is based on personal feelings or is it based on business considerations or on the desires of other tenants in the building?

MR. SNELL. I think it is an economic factor rather than on personal opinions.

MR. GLICKSTEIN. An economic factor. What is that factor?

MR. SNELL. Well, I think that the experience we have had of people being fearful their tenants have probably told them, if you do certain things, why, we will probably move out. We have heard this complaint quite a lot.

MR. GLICKSTEIN. You think the owners are concerned about how their tenants would react if they rent to Negroes?

MR. SNELL. Yes.

MR. GLICKSTEIN. Do you think that concern would be a bit lessened if there were a Federal law?

MR. SNELL. No doubt about it.

MR. GLICKSTEIN. Mr. Snell, you might have heard Mr. Fleming's description of Section 23, Leased Housing. Have members of your association in Oakland made space available under the Section 23 Program?

MR. SNELL. Yes, we have. We endorsed the program and have gone along with it since the inception.

MR. GLICKSTEIN. And what has been your experience with it? Just to clarify again what Section 23 is, this is the program under which the Public Housing Authority leases space for its tenants in regular apartment houses.

MR. SNELL. Yes.

MR. GLICKSTEIN. And the people that move into apartments under the Section 23 Program are persons who otherwise might have lived in public housing projects. Is that correct?

MR. SNELL. Yes, that's right.

MR. GLICKSTEIN. And what has been your experience under the Section 23 Program?

MR. SNELL. I believe that we have only had this in effect, as I recall, maybe a couple of months, but my information from the Oakland Housing Authority is that it is very successful.

MR. GLICKSTEIN. And have you gotten any complaints from your members about the way that the program was operating, or about the tenants that they have gotten?

MR. SNELL. Not a one.

MR. GLICKSTEIN. Do you think your tenants, your members, are by and large enthusiastic about the program? Is that going to help reduce the vacancy rate?

MR. SNELL. Yes, it has been very helpful.

MR. GLICKSTEIN. Thank you. I have no further questions.

CHAIRMAN HANNAH. Dr. Rankin?

COMMISSIONER RANKIN. Are there any large areas in the Bay Area where there are no Negroes living in a particular area, say like Redwood City or Menlo Park? Do you happen to know that?

MR. SNELL. Not on our side of the Bay, no.

COMMISSIONER RANKIN. What about the other side?

MR. SNELL. I am not acquainted with the other side. We are on the East Bay.

COMMISSIONER RANKIN. Okay. That's all.

CHAIRMAN HANNAH. Mrs. Freeman?

COMMISSIONER FREEMAN. Mr. Snell, you indicated that there are some apartment owners who have taken advantage and are participating in the Section 23 leased program?

MR. SNELL. Yes.

COMMISSIONER FREEMAN. Are there any that you know of that have tenants who are Negro who prior to their participation in the program did not have any?

MR. SNELL. I have no direct knowledge on that.

COMMISSIONER FREEMAN. Do you have any information concerning the extent of integration in the apartment houses of the owners who are members of this association?

MR. SNELL. No, no direct information. We do not do any part of management. Consequently, these things happen and we do not follow them. We have no reason to.

COMMISSIONER FREEMAN. What are some of the purposes of your association?

MR. SNELL. We have a number of purposes. We furnish managers for apartment owners. We represent them in tax matters. When I say that I mean at the local level, appearing before the council, the board of supervisors. We have contacts for their purchases. We furnish them forms, and practically any management problem they have. We accept the legal part. We have attorneys to handle that and we try to help them in their problems.

COMMISSIONER FREEMAN. Do you ever make recommendations to them about programs or policies that might improve the association or their management?

MR. SNELL. I don't know just what you mean by that. We have monthly meetings where, of course, we have speakers that are of importance to the apartment owner. We are interested in the Bay Area Transit District and many other things. So at our meetings we try to keep them informed of what is going on as far as progress is concerned, and oft-times, why, we can make savings in purchases, and so forth, which helps them financially.

COMMISSIONER FREEMAN. I was wondering about possible programs to eliminate segregation in housing.

MR. SNELL. We have had no programs on this basis.

COMMISSIONER FREEMAN. Do you think that such programs would be beneficial?

MR. SNELL. Well, I am not so sure it would be too beneficial. I think the beneficial part probably should come from the other side, from the renter rather than the owner.

COMMISSIONER FREEMAN. Which renter are you talking about, your tenants?

MR. SNELL. The tenants, yes.

COMMISSIONER FREEMAN. You then would wait for your tenants to tell you they want a Negro neighbor?

MR. SNELL. I don't mean that they would wait particularly.

My point has always been that the tenants are the ones we have to please, and if they are unhappy, why, so is the owner.

COMMISSIONER FREEMAN. Is there a minimum housing code in San Francisco?

MR. SNELL. A minimum—

COMMISSIONER FREEMAN. Minimum housing standards.

MR. SNELL. Oh, yes.

COMMISSIONER FREEMAN. Do the owners look to the tenants to determine whether they shall obey it or not?

MR. SNELL. If we what?

COMMISSIONER FREEMAN. Is this obeyed by all of the owners?

MR. SNELL. Yes, indeed.

COMMISSIONER FREEMAN. Thank you.

CHAIRMAN HANNAH. Mr. Patterson?

VICE CHAIRMAN PATTERSON. Mr. Snell, I judge from your testimony that if a tenant does not want a neighbor who is a member of a minority group, this is usually the controlling factor. Is that right? You say you try to please the tenant?

MR. SNELL. I don't exactly understand what you mean by the question.

VICE CHAIRMAN PATTERSON. Well, let me continue then. White businessmen in the South have had an interesting experience since 1964 when the public accommodations section of the Civil Rights Act of that year was passed. Before the passage of that Act, steps were attempted in many parts of the South to desegregate public accommodations, restaurants, movie houses, hotels. Many of these people who moved voluntarily lost money because they were boycotted because the wishes of the people were not for desegregation. After the passage of that Act, the matter became moot. These facilities in much of the South are now desegregated. The businessman is making more money because he has increased business and the average citizen, who may or may not have wanted desegregation, accepts it so the Negro is better off and the average white segregationist no longer has the feeling that his wishes are paramount over the law. He accepts desegregation.

Now, do you think this would extend into housing? What goes in eating establishments, hotels, would this also extend into housing if a Federal law were passed of the type that the Administration has introduced requiring open housing and enforcing it? Would the people then respond by obeying that law and making peace with it as they have on public accommodations?

MR. SNELL. I think that any law that is passed, the people will obey the law. What effect this would have, I haven't the slightest idea, but it would probably make it such that there would be less trouble.

150

VICE CHAIRMAN PATTERSON. Would you think, then, that the passage of such a law would be desirable?

MR. SNELL. Do I think it would be? You mean personally?

VICE CHAIRMAN PATTERSON. Yes.

MR. SNELL. Probably so.

COMMISSIONER PATTERSON. Thank you.

CHAIRMAN HANNAH. Father Hesburgh?

COMMISSIONER HESBURGH. Mr. Snell, I have only one question: do you think there is any chance, given the situation as you have seen it over the years, for open occupancy in the apartment houses, apart from the passage of such a law as Mr. Patterson has just discussed? In other words, do you think it is going to happen voluntarily by the good will of all the people, whatever that might be?

MR. SNELL. I think on a voluntary basis—I don't think we had any trouble a few years ago on a voluntary basis. It worked out very nicely.

COMMISSIONER HESBURGH. Every time when someone says that, however, there is always a big snicker in the courtroom, because the people who have tried to do it haven't been able to get it done.

As Mr. Patterson was just saying regarding public accommodations, when one person has to take the initiative and make the change, he is the one that can be discriminated against for making it.

In other words, his tenants can leave if they happen to be narrow minded, and it is difficult to find, sometimes, I suppose, in a given community, a whole apartment house full of understanding people. You get all sorts of a spectrum of people in a given apartment house.

It would seem to me that even from the owner's point of view, since this is clearly the intent of the way the Nation is heading, and should head, it would be in his interest to at least say everybody is going to do this. We are all going to accept the law of the land and equal opportunity, and it would just seem to me it would be so much easier to do it if everybody were doing it than to say to this or that apartment house owner, "You lead the way," and he says, "Yes, I lead the way and lose the money."

MR. SNELL. I am sure you are right.

COMMISSIONER HESBURGH. I find it hard to believe even why the apartment house owners would not want to say, "Well, if we are going this way, and this is what America is all about, let's at least all do it together rather than depend upon the good will," which I am sure is widespread in this country, but not very effective in many areas of the equality of opportunity.

CHAIRMAN HANNAH. Mr. Taylor?

MR. TAYLOR. Are you yourself an apartment house owner?

MR. SNELL. Not at the present time, no.

MR. TAYLOR. I wonder if you know what the general practice of apartment house owners is when a person applies for an apartment? Is an extensive investigation made of this person's background?

MR. SNELL. No, not extensive. There is a form that is used for most of the investigations done on the basis of their ability to pay, and then they do check where they are moving from, if they are local people but mostly it is a credit report rather than anything else.

MR. TAYLOR. So that it is perfectly conceivable that a tenant could move into a particular apartment house who might have a criminal record, or he might beat his wife, or he might beat his children, or make lots of noise in the apartment late at night?

MR. SNELL. That happens.

MR. TAYLOR. And the other tenants in the building, who are already in the building, aren't consulted generally about—they don't take a vote on whether this might be an appropriate tenant for the apartment house?

MR. SNELL. You mean when they are moving in?

MR. TAYLOR. That's right.

MR. SNELL. No, there is no vote taken.

MR. TAYLOR. I just wonder why an exception should be made in a case of people of a different race without regard to any of their personal qualities. Why should tenants desire to be so dominant in this field when they're not dominant in other areas?

MR. SNELL. I'm sure I can't speak for the tenants. I haven't had any experience along that line. The only thing is, and I think it is probably more a threat than anything else, they tell you they are going to move.

MR. TAYLOR. I wasn't asking you to speak for the tenants. I was asking you why the apartment house owners were so solicitous of the views of the tenants in this particular area and not in other areas.

MR. SNELL. I don't think they go to the tenants and ask them that. The tenants are the ones that come to them and tell them this.

MR. TAYLOR. I have no further questions.

CHAIRMAN HANNAH. Thank you very much, Mr. Snell. You are excused. Mr. Glickstein, will you call the next witnesses.

MR. GLICKSTEIN. We have a group of five witnesses, Mr. Chairman, Mr. Reed Robbins, Mr. William Kerry, Mr. Robert Atkinson, Mr. Jack Murray, and Mr. Donald Gordon.

(Whereupon, Mr. Robert Atkinson, Mr. Donald Gordon, Mr. William Kerry, Mr. Jack Murray, Mr. Reed Robbins, and Mr.

Clark Wallace were sworn by the Chairman and testified as follows:)

TESTIMONY OF MR. ROBERT ATKINSON, PIEDMONT, CALIFORNIA; MR. DONALD GORDON, SAN FRANCISCO, CALIFORNIA; MR. WILLIAM L. KERRY, SAN LEANDRO, CALIFORNIA; MR. JACK MURRAY, LAFAYETTE, CALIFORNIA; MR. REED ROBBINS, STOCKTON, CALIFORNIA; MR. CLARK WALLACE, ORINDA, CALIFORNIA

MR. GLICKSTEIN. Would each of you gentlemen please state your full name and address for the record?

MR KERRY. William L. Kerry. I reside at 1578 Graff Avenue, San Leandro, California.

MR. GLICKSTEIN. Perhaps you could also at the same time tell us what organization you represent.

MR. KERRY. I represent the Southern Alameda County Board of Realtors.

MR. GLICKSTEIN. You are the president?

MR. KERRY. Yes.

MR. ATKINSON. Robert F. Atkinson, 101 Scenic Avenue, Piedmont. I represent the Oakland Board of Realtors, president.

MR. ROBBINS. Reed Robbins, 215 North San Joaquin Street, Stockton, California. California Real Estate Association, president.

MR. GORDON. Donald Gordon. My office is at 432 Castro Street, San Francisco. I represent the San Francisco Real Estate Board as its president.

MR. MURRAY. My name is Jack Murray and I am immediate past president of the Contra Costa Board of Realtors. My home address is 707 Los Tampais Road, Lafayette, California.

MR. WALLACE. I am Clark Wallace, 2 Bryant Way, Orinda. I am Equal Rights Committee chairman, California Real Estate Association.

MR. GLICKSTEIN. I would like to start by directing questions to Mr. Robbins. Mr. Robbins, the initials for your organization, I will be using the initials CREA. Is that correct?

MR. ROBBINS. Yes.

MR. GLICKSTEIN. What is the position of CREA with respect to legislative prohibitions against discrimination in the sale or rental of housing on account of race or color?

MR. ROBBINS. Depending upon the wording, in most cases those we have experienced have had wording that we feel is very objectionable and has done more harm than good towards the aim of having a voluntary and peaceable integration.

MR. GLICKSTEIN. What wording do you think is undesirable?

MR. ROBBINS. Would you like to get into that kind of detail about the Rumford Act or Title IV? We do not believe it is proper to take away from individuals, and, of course, in individuals it shouldn't be necessary for us to specify that they come in all races and religions, but we do not feel it is proper to take away from individuals the basic freedom to contract with their property.

MR. GLICKSTEIN. You would say that it is the position of the CREA that the refusal to sell or rent because of race or color is a matter which should be left to the conscience of the individual property owner?

MR. ROBBINS. Yes.

MR. GLICKSTEIN. Aren't property owners deprived of all sorts of other rights? If a property owner, for example, wanted to erect a circus on his lawn, wouldn't that be something that the State would prevent him from doing through the zoning regulations?

MR. ROBBINS. I suspect in most areas that would be the case. Conceivably in some they could erect a circus, but we are not quite concerned with that particular right.

MR. GLICKSTEIN. Isn't that also a right of a property owner to do with his property as he pleases?

MR. ROBBINS. Not nearly that basic. I think you said "as he pleases." We were referring to renting or not renting, selling or not selling, and they are within the dictates of his conscience, and our experience has been that with this atmosphere, the masses of people in any racial or creedal orientation that you care to choose have been moving freely in the market place.

MR. GLICKSTEIN. You are, then, just concerned with the right of a property owner to sell or to rent, but not necessarily to do with his property as he pleases?

MR. ROBBINS. No, we are not concerned with protecting his right to put up a circus tent some place.

MR. GLICKSTEIN. You can see that the State should and does pass all sorts of regulations that govern the way a person can use his own property?

MR. ROBBINS. Oh, of course, and we have supported many of those that are in good conscience and are towards the good planning of a community. We have been quite active in that area.

MR. GLICKSTEIN. Some of us lawyers here have heard of something called the rule against perpetuities which prevents a property owner from tying up his property and does influence the right of a property owner to dispose of his property as he chooses. Are you also opposed to the rule against perpetuities?

MR. ROBBINS. Well, you're the lawyer. I am not. Will you tell me again what a rule of perpetuities is? I will tell you whether I am for it or not.

MR. GLICKSTEIN. I wish Dean Griswold were here today. The rule against perpetuities is a rule that goes back to common law times, which provides that a property owner cannot will his property to tie it up for generation after generation so that it cannot be disposed of on the open market. In more layman's language, it is intended to prevent dead-hand control of properties. It is intended to put property on the market after the person who originally owned it has died, rather than permit that person to tie it up from one generation to another through inheritance schemes.

MR. ROBBINS. Well, thank you for asking that question. I am not sure how that is related, but our concern is with the property rights of the living, and I don't quite understand how the question, if I understand it, relates to whether my grandfather might control what I am going to do with my property today or your grandfather controlling you in yours.

MR. GLICKSTEIN. Well, speaking of the property rights of the living, when an owner sells his house, he generally moves out of the neighborhood.

Now what difference should it make to an owner of a house who he sells it to? He probably wants to move someplace else. He wants to get his money. He wants to move out of the neighborhood. What difference does it make to the owner of a house who he sells it to? It might make a difference to the neighbors, but what difference does it make to an owner of the house?

MR. ROBBINS. I would assume that each owner might give you his own answer there. We can only speak from how different owners through voting opportunities have expressed themselves in this general area and our position has always been that the effect upon the neighbor is no business of that individual making his decision. One neighbor might have one attitude, the man next door have another attitude, and each by expressing their opinion as their conscience dictates, the end result is that the great, great majority of housing is available to all.

MR. GLICKSTEIN. But you do think that a person when he decides to whom he wants to sell his house is not so much concerned about the desires of his neighbors, but just looks to his individual conscience?

MR. ROBBINS. Oh, some might express it that way. I can't speak for all of the individual reasons for a decision as they would be made. Some would express that their neighbors, as it is, are concerned with them. You would have to ask them why they say that.

MR. GLICKSTEIN. Are Realtors in California able to accept listings from clients which instruct their Realtor not to sell to Negroes?

MR. ROBBINS. If it is done under legal circumstances.

MR. GLICKSTEIN. Under legal circumstances?

MR. ROBBINS. Yes. Under certain circumstances an owner under the Rumford Act, which is, as you know, under question at the moment, under certain circumstances the owner cannot restrict a listing. Under other circumstances, he can, a subject of inequity in itself, but the Realtor can legally take a listing from a person who is legally allowed to express a preference or an exclusion.

MR. GLICKSTEIN. Well, as I understand California law and the Code of Practices of the CREA, a Realtor is required to offer equal service to all clients without regard to race or color?

MR. ROBBINS. Very definitely.

MR. GLICKSTEIN. How can a Realtor carry out that obligation when some of his listings are restricted listings?

MR. ROBBINS. Well, again we get into the zoning kind of thing you brought up earlier. In some cases we can't sell somebody a lot that he can build a fourplex on because the zoning prohibits it. The net result is most people can buy a single family home in most areas, but they can't buy a fourplex where the zoning permits only single family. That might be a corollary, but again the net result is that hundreds of thousands of minority families have moved within this State during this 4-year period of question.

We think perhaps the atmosphere where we have taken the leadership in creating under our Equal Rights Committee has been an important factor in creating that atmosphere.

MR. GLICKSTEIN. But your Code of Practices should really be amended to read that a Realtor is required to offer equal service to all clients without regard to race or color except when he has a listing that restricts his ability to sell to a person because of race or color?

MR. ROBBINS. You have a copy of it before you, do you not?

MR. GLICKSTEIN. Right.

MR. ROBBINS. In the total copy of the Code of Practices, it does indicate that we should respect the owner's rights to make these decisions and reaffirms the fact that it should be his right to make these decisions.

MR. GLICKSTEIN. You have already referred to your voluntary equal rights in housing program. Would you describe for the Commissioners, please, the guidelines for such a program recommended by CREA to its member boards?

MR. ROBBINS. Yes. If it is permissible with you, I would like to give you a brief background and then ask Clark Wallace, our chairman, to give you the more specific areas, if that is permissible.

MR. GLICKSTEIN. Well, I think if it is brief it is permissible.

MR. ROBBINS. All right. The background will be very brief. Four years ago, in 1963, is when we did establish such a program. This was prior to the enactment of the Rumford Act. We have had two chairmen, one for two years. The man who was orig-

inal chairman is now serving on our executive committee. Clark
Wallace is our second chairman in his second term.

The Code of Practices has been adopted by every one of our
179 boards in the State, and we think is working extremely effectively. Now, on the specific areas, briefly, Clark Wallace.

MR. WALLACE. Basically, and they are a part of your kit there,
and I can't tell you which page, but they are on the back of this
little Equal Rights Speakers' Guide. You will see the three stated
purposes of our CREA Equal Rights Committee, the first being to
inform and assist members of the association in their understanding and responsibilities in giving equal service to all clients.

The second being to inform and assist member real estate boards
in their understanding of CREA policy regarding their responsibility in evaluating applicants for Realtor membership without
regard to race, color, or religion, or national origin, and the third,
to inform and assist member boards in understanding how to
meet with leaders of responsible groups and organizations for
the purpose of establishing a cooperative and harmonious relationship in the fields of property rights and other individual human
rights.

MR. GLICKSTEIN. Do you, Mr. Robbins, consider a developer or a
builder who builds several hundred houses to be sold to the public
an individual property owner who should have the right to sell
his houses as his conscience dictates?

MR. ROBBINS. Well, I will answer your question, but first, our
main area of interest is, of course, with the smaller property
owner.

There has been a great deal of discussion of whether this
stops at 100 or 500 or two or six. I will only state this, that
regardless of size, the individual should have the opportunity of
exercising his own judgment, and in the same breath I would have
to state what I have stated before. I do believe in most cases under
an atmosphere that we have helped to create that judgment is one
that ends up with the proper end result.

MR. GLICKSTEIN. We heard testimony yesterday about a development that is being put up in Daly City, Serramonte, that will
eventually house about 20,000 people, in effect, a small city.

Do you think that the developer of that project should have
the right to sell the houses as his conscience dictates?

MR. ROBBINS. Well, I see no reason to discriminate against him
from my previous statement. I don't know the gentleman or the
development. There are people here from San Francisco, if you
would like to ask them something more specific.

MR. GLICKSTEIN. Well, I am interested in the general question
of whether large developers, according to your organization,
should be able to act as their consciences dictate.

I assume that if the city of San Francisco were building a

housing project to house 20,000 people, would you say that the city should be allowed to rent those apartments as the conscience of the Housing Authority dictated?

MR. ROBBINS. We have always put the various forms of government into a different category, and in Proposition 14 we excluded any State or Federal ownerships.

MR. GLICKSTEIN. I see. So you think that governmental agencies have a responsibility to act without discrimination?

MR. ROBBINS. Well, we think they can act according to their corporate conscience, also, and as the testimony was being given as I walked into the room, an area of FHA foreclosures, for example, and in this area where the owner makes his own decision, it is our responsibility as brokers to follow through in the manner acceptable to that owner, and if all owners made a decision the city of San Francisco does make, we would be extremely happy to comply in every respect.

Most importantly, very few owners do ask for this restriction, but the privilege of knowing that they can ask for it is what gives them the guarantee of protecting this historic freedom they have had and I think want to continue having.

MR. GLICKSTEIN. Well, you have just raised a point that we are interested in—our information indicates that restricted listings carried by multiple listing services is low. In the Bay Area it is somewhat less than 2 percent, I believe. Do you think that this indicates an open market for ready and able Negro buyers?

MR. ROBBINS. Oh, yes, that among other things. That is one factor. The statewide survey we made showed that less than one-half of 1 percent were restricted.

MR. GLICKSTEIN. Less than one-half of 1 percent?

MR. ROBBINS. Yes.

MR. GLICKSTEIN. Is it a practice of some brokers to ascertain whether minority group persons will be accepted in a neighborhood before they bring such a person around to look at a house?

MR. ROBBINS. Is it or was it?

MR. GLICKSTEIN. Was it and is it?

MR. ROBBINS. All right. Presently there are restrictions on making any reference to race, the reference possibly being misunderstood as an attempt to discriminate.

Some brokers prior to this time, and often with the backing of citizens' groups who were interested in helping to introduce a minority family into a white area, for example, would agree that a certain amount of contact with the neighbors was in order, and in many cases they were willing to do this, which did take extra time and involved no pay.

In other cases the individual preferred that that not be done and in most cases they would react as their client felt would be most appropriate for them.

MR. GLICKSTEIN. Do you think as a general rule it would be desirable to do something like that?

MR. ROBBINS. I think as a general rule it should be allowable in those circumstances where the various people involved recognize it would be beneficial.

MR. GLICKSTEIN. Where the client, for example, asks that it be done?

MR. ROBBINS. Yes.

MR. GLICKSTEIN. I notice that in your equal rights handbook you discuss the Unruh Act, the Hawkins Act, the Rumford Act, Proposition 14, and the Civil Rights Act of 1964, but you do not discuss the effect of the President's Executive order on equal opportunity in housing. Is there any particular reason why that has been omitted from your handbook?

MR. ROBBINS. Only that in preparing this handbook—I think most of you have probably seen efforts made towards the aim we are attempting to accomplish, and in the development of a handbook, the wealth of material available to us was so vast that we wanted to put into this handbook the things that we felt most meaningful and that would tie together to a package to end up with saying what we wanted it to say.

There is nothing wrong with discussion of the Presidential order but like so many other things available to us, we were attempting to put out a handbook not of such voluminous nature that it would not be read.

MR. GLICKSTEIN. You were trying to advise Realtors of all of their responsibilities under appropriate laws, but don't you think a Realtor should know that if he accepted restrictive instructions that violated Federal law, the President's order, he would be violating the Code of Practices as well?

MR. ROBBINS. Well, Clark may want to answer this, but I think within the area there we have that situation covered under the Rumford Act, do we not?

MR. WALLACE. Yes. We went—in the first place, the handbook was our earliest attempt at putting together something that we could give to our membership, and consequently we realized soon after it was published that it was out of date.

At the same time, you would find that some of the information you are alluding to is now contained in our more up-to-date information, but, secondarily, the State laws generally went well beyond the Executive order and we felt that those were, therefore, the ones that our members were more keenly—not only aware of, but were more involved with and, therefore, we spent our time concentrating on those.

MR. GLICKSTEIN. In other words, it was your belief that if a member complied with the State law he would be complying with Federal law?

MR. ROBBINS. That's correct.

MR. GLICKSTEIN. Mr. Gordon, may I address some questions to you, please?

Just to refresh the recollection of the audience, you are the president of the San Francisco Board of Realtors. Is that correct?

MR. GORDON. Yes, sir. That's correct.

MR. GLICKSTEIN. In your experience, do financial institutions use different standards in determining whether whites or Negroes are qualified for home purchase loans?

MR. GORDON. You're referring, sir, to banks, savings and loan companies, as to whether they —

MR. GLICKSTEIN. Yes.

MR. GORDON. I would say no.

MR. GLICKSTEIN. They use the same standards?

MR. GORDON. Yes.

MR. GLICKSTEIN. How long have you been involved with real estate? How long have you been a Realtor?

MR. GORDON. I have been a Realtor for 20 years, sir.

MR. GLICKSTEIN. Is this the practice that you just said no to? Has that been the practice for 20 years, or do you know if the practice was ever different?

MR. GORDON. As I can recall, yes.

MR. GLICKSTEIN. It was the practice?

MR. GORDON. It is my understanding that whenever any loan application is presented to a bank or savings and loan, the information is taken and weighed on the merit or lack of merit of the application without any reference to color or creed.

MR. GLICKSTEIN. Our staff investigations have uncovered an interesting phenomenon which I am sure is well known to people in San Francisco which perhaps you could explain to us. What accounts for the fact that almost no Negroes live in the Sunset area, while Merced Heights-Ingleside area, which has comparable priced homes, has a large number of Negroes? How would you explain that?

MR. GORDON. I think primarily it could be explained as an economic situation, the fact that the Ocean View-Ingleside area is —was built at the time where homes were readily sold on FHA and G.I., and that the type of homes that were constructed by the developers at that time lent itself to the economic strata that the minority groups were in, and they were more than happy to buy in, and I think it fundamentally is an economic situation.

MR. GLICKSTEIN. You are saying that the homes in the Sunset area are much more expensive?

MR. GORDON. They are more expensive, yes.

MR. GLICKSTEIN. The testimony indicated yesterday that some of the homes in the Ingleside area, for example, cost $40,000. That sounds expensive to me.

MR. GORDON. Well, the Ingleside area that I am referring to, there is a small area, Ingleside Terrace, that does—the prices do run in this range, but the Ingleside and Ocean View area that I was referring to is removed—is contiguous but still is removed from this Ingleside Terrace.

Also I might add that the Richmond District is pretty well·integrated residential-wise and there are some homes in that area also that run from $20,000 to $35,000.

MR. GLICKSTEIN. Mr. Gordon, what is the affirmative action program of the San Francisco Board of Realtors to insure equal rights in housing?

MR. GORDON. The affirmative program is based fundamentally on the CREA activity, the fact that we permit a free flow of purchasers to buy in most any area. We try to—we make this known to our membership.

The San Francisco board has been one of the leaders in minority members. I believe it goes back to 1915 that our first Negro member was accepted on the board, and presently we have a Negro member of our board of directors and last year we had two or three minority members running as candidates for the board of directors.

MR. GLICKSTEIN. Has your affirmative action program in your judgment been effective?

MR. GORDON. Yes, I believe it has been effective and I feel that as we progress it will become more effective.

MR. GLICKSTEIN. Do you think that the activities of Realtors who are members of your organization, their activities, have succeeded in opening up new neighborhoods for Negroes that had heretofore not been open?

MR. GORDON. I do, yes.

MR. GLICKSTEIN. Mr. Atkinson, you are the president of the Oakland Board of Realtors. Is that correct?

MR. ATKINSON. That's correct.

MR. GLICKSTEIN. Does your board have an equal housing committee?

MR. ATKINSON. Yes, we do.

MR. GLICKSTEIN. Does the Committee have the responsibility of monitoring activities of Realtors which might violate the Code of Practices?

MR. ATKINSON. Yes, they would. However, we haven't had any of those cases, but most certainly in the event that something like that was called to our attention we would take immediate action.

MR. GLICKSTEIN. Thus far you haven't had any cases where a Realtor was charged with violating the Code of Practices?

MR. ATKINSON. Not to my knowledge.

MR. GLICKSTEIN. Mr. Kerry, you are the president of the Southern Alameda County Board of Realtors?

MR. KERRY. Yes, I am.

MR. GLICKSTEIN. Do you think that the supply of housing in Southern Alameda County meets the needs of employees of industries which are locating in that area?

MR. KERRY. I do, yes.

MR. GLICKSTEIN. Do you think there is an adequate supply of low to moderate-income housing?

MR. KERRY. I believe so, yes.

MR. GLICKSTEIN. There is a big flow of industry to Southern Alameda County. Isn't that correct?

MR. KERRY. Yes, very happily so.

MR. GLICKSTEIN. And the housing market is keeping up with the demands that are being made?

MR. KERRY. I believe for a while we were overbuilt. I believe that before they get started again possibly we will be in an under-supplied position.

MR. GLICKSTEIN. Mr. Murray, you are the past president of the Contra Costa County Board of Realtors?

MR. MURRAY. Correct, sir.

MR. GLICKSTEIN. Have you worked with the housing officers of local military installations to insure that military personnel are not discriminated against on the basis of race or color?

MR. MURRAY. To my knowledge we have never been contacted on that subject.

MR. GLICKSTEIN. Never been contacted?

MR. MURRAY. No.

MR. GLICKSTEIN. There are military installations though in Contra Costa County, aren't there?

MR. MURRAY. The nearest one we have is the ammunition depot in Port Chicago. That is out of our board area.

MR. GLICKSTEIN. But to your knowledge your board has never been contacted by the Federal Government military installation seeking assistance in securing housing?

MR. MURRAY. Not to my knowledge.

MR. GLICKSTEIN. I have no further questions, Mr. Chairman.

COMMISSIONER HESBURGH. I don't want to direct this to any-one in particular, but any one of you may wish to take on the problem of answering it.

Yesterday we heard about Merced Heights District where the

neighborhood had changed from white to black rather abruptly in about ten years' time. We talked to one of the ladies there who happened to be a white lady testifying and told how she was badgered continually by real estate brokers to sell her house because if she didn't she would lose money and she should feel terribly about the blacks moving into the neighborhood, et cetera.

This went on and on, and then as the neighborhood tended to stabilize somewhat, about 60 percent black, and she mentioned that they had been collaborating with San Francisco State College and that some of the faculty there who were white decided to move into this area and were talked out of it by the real estate agent who said that, "You don't want to move into that area. It is going downhill," and so forth.

I am excited and edified when I read this statement of ethics, but I don't know how I can put it together with that testimony we had yesterday.

Let me add some other testimony we had yesterday that was alluded to by our general counsel about a man who intends to build an enormous housing development in Serramonte and that this development was going to be lily white. Everybody skirts around the issue, but the fact is there are no Negroes living there as far as we can find out, and while they have come out and said that they have equal opportunity housing, you have to put on your bifocals to see it in the ad. It comes about this size as against letters like this advertising the houses.

Now, let me make one more statement and then I will put the question.

My basic statement is that we on this Commission have for 10 years been trying to do something practical to bring about equality of opportunity in this country. We find two questions that constantly thwart us. One is housing and the other is the question of education and they both go together, because as long as we create white ghettos and Negro ghettos, we are going to have white education and Negro eduation, the latter generally being inferior. At least this is what we have found in the year-long study just completed, and while we realize we can't solve the one problem by the other, neither can we divide the problems because they are inexplicably tied together and it is our belief that unless this country does solve this problem we are going to wind up with two different nations within one nation, and it is going to be to our own peril and to our own dissatisfaction as the years go on.

I must say the codes of ethics one reads do seem to be an improvement over what we were seeing 10 years ago, but the problem is that at every single hearing we have in every part of this country, San Francisco being no exception, that at every single one of these hearings the people who seem to come off worse are the real estate brokers on the way they individually —I am not talking about groups, but how they individually discriminate in both listing and persuasion and the kind of involvement they have in keeping neighborhoods white or black, or moving neighborhoods from white to black for profit, and of course the other group we are constantly hearing about is the trade unions that don't have equality of opportunity for employment.

Now, what I am asking any of you gentlemen who wishes to answer this is: granting you have a fine Code of Ethics and granting you think this should be solved by individual conscience, and I accept that if it is within a realm of the common good, but I am not sure it always is, granting those two things, how do you make sure this Code of Ethics gets into reality? What do you do when we have case after case after case in everyone of these hearings where in fact the nice words of the Code of Ethics are not carried out in practice? Do you have anybody to police that? Do you have anybody that really—has anybody in fact ever been pulled in and lost his license? Does the State get involved in seeing that what you say you are going to do you do in fact do?

And I don't like to be put off by the fact that we heard yesterday, "Well, we hire the brokers to move this property out in Serramonte and there are 10 of them and we can't police 10 people, or seven of them, or whatever, and so we can't really follow through on what each one does, what he does privately."

What I am saying is, if it isn't going to be solved privately, I will guarantee you it will be solved publicly, and I think we have had enough time to demonstrate whether or not it can be solved privately, but what I am asking is, what does the association do? What does the individual board do to move in on the individual member who just isn't convinced of this, who doesn't believe America is what we say it is and who is going his own merry way to prevent people from getting housing even though they have the money and the desire, and as we say publicly the opportunity to have it? What is done individually on this?

MR. ROBBINS. Well, Reverend, that is a good area and I say to you without any hesitation that the Code of Practices you have before you is one that the State Association is quite sincere about seeing enforced.

I think the fact that without exception every one of our local real estate boards has adopted this Code of Practices is evidence of their sincerity. We can't demand that they adopt these codes, but they did willingly, every board without exception.

Now, you made mention to testimony yesterday and the morning paper had an allusion to this testimony, and I don't know what else transpired. So I may not have the whole story. But it indicated that a real estate broker in a certain area of San Francisco had been inducing fear on the introduction of minority families, that type of thing. Let me ask you a brief question, if I may.

COMMISSIONER HESBURGH. Sure.

MR. ROBBINS. With that accusation being made against a real estate broker, did you then hear from the real estate broker?

COMMISSIONER HESBURGH. No, we did not. We heard from the lady who had been approached personally by the real estate broker, and I am sure if we had asked her she would be willing to give us the name.

She went into great detail on several encounters that she had had with real estate brokers who were going up and down the street trying to change the neighborhood quickly to put fear into people, and in fact what happened was in a matter of 10 years the neighborhood quickly changed over from being, oh, I think she told us originally 1 or 2 percent black to 60 percent black in a matter of something like 10 to 15 years. Is that correct, Bill?

MR. TAYLOR. Yes.

COMMISSIONER HESBURGH. 1950 to 1965, this happened, and then she said—and the obverse which I think really gets me, we finally get people who are willing to live in integrated neighborhoods, which is apparently true in this particular neighborhood, Merced Heights, at that point the real estate people were persuading the white people who wanted to move back into this neighborhood from coming in saying, "Well, it is —"

MR. ROBBINS. How do you know this, Reverend, from the testimony of one lady?

COMMISSIONER HESBURGH. From the testimony under oath yesterday.

MR. ROBBINS. Don't you think it would be fair to find out on the other side of that question? I don't know because I am not familiar with the example, but I think it is a good example for this reason. We do have procedures ethically within our Code of Practices and on every case that has come to our attention on the local board level or the State level we have inquired into it and conducted an investigation, and hopefully it is known in every community that we do have these facilities.

Now Mr. Gordon can answer to this in a moment, but I don't think that was reported to his board and I know it was not reported to the State. Therefore, the means that we do have to look into this has been overlooked by the very people we are able to help if they will make these reports to us.

Now this particular violation, if it is true, and again I have to be somewhat skeptical because you have heard testimony on only one side, and in the four years that we have been engaged in this very touchy area, we have heard some very strange things by some very strange people, some of which have been proven later to have been totally without truth.

Now this accusation may be perfectly valid but I think it should be treated with an analysis of the other side before we draw any inferences from that particular example.

Now, blockbusting *per se*, which is the practice that was being reported, is against State law and our association helped to write the law that made it illegal. We backed the law to make that action illegal. So if this man in fact did what he was accused of doing, he can be reported to the State for possible loss of his license, and apparently that hasn't happened, because he hasn't been reported. He can be reported to his local real estate board assuming he is a member.

Ethically we can only take care of those people who are members of our board, and fortunately almost without exception all of the leaders are members of the local boards.

This particular man, whether he is or not, I don't know, but those two procedures are available.

COMMISSIONER HESBURGH. May I ask you a question? Has any real estate broker ever lost his license because he practiced discriminatory—or was engaged in discriminatory practices?

MR. ROBBINS. Not to my knowledge, but I would not necessarily be informed. I am sure that there are no large numbers and possibly none.

MR. GORDON. Father, I think I can possibly elaborate a bit on the specifics. Approximately a year or two ago, there was some activity of one of the San Francisco Board members in this Ocean View area. The exact specifics, the exact situation I don't recall. However, it was pretty definite that there was some unethical activity that was being performed by the individual, and it was called to the attention of the Real Estate Board, and the executive vice president and the president of the board in a matter of minutes was on the phone to the member and had them in the office in a matter of hours and confronted them—the individual— with the situation, and the problem was resolved.

I wasn't in attendance, but the way it was undoubtedly presented was the fact that we have an Ethics and Professional Conduct Committee that this would have been referred to.

The individual chose to refrain or discontinue this activity and the problem was resolved.

Another situation pertaining to an apartment house development, also a member of our board, was handled in the same fashion.

COMMISSIONER HESBURGH. Is there any way it might be made known to the citizens of this community and California generally that this is an open channel?

You see, what bothers me is we hear these things individually, personally under oath all over the country, and, as I say, California is no exception.

We have heard it so much that I think one would have to be almost idiotic not to say that there isn't something happening here that is not right. Because you hear it everywhere you go and you hear it in great detail, chapter, verse and so forth.

I am sure our staff is able to follow up on some of these things, and see that the persons are bought to light and brought to your attention. But the point I am getting at is it is high time that if we take the stance that this shouldn't be done by law, that it ought to be done voluntarily, then you have got to make the voluntary work, and the only assumption I can make from the testimony yesterday or the testimony that we hear continually around the country is that it is not working in most communities and, therefore, if it doesn't work in communities voluntarily, you and I know what is going to happen because the country does stand for something, that is, it's going to happen by law.

Now I don't think we can have it both ways. You can't say we are going to make it happen voluntarily, and, therefore, we don't need a law, and if it is not working voluntarily, then we don't want a law. It is going to work one way or another, I am sure, if I sense the sense of the country right.

Now the only problem I am saying is that isn't there some way that people would know, that an individual person who runs into this—we heard at least five to 10 different aspects of this problem yesterday. I am sure our testimony will be printed and will be available to all of you.

Person after person calls up, follows up on a listing, gets an appointment, goes to see the property, he happens to be Negro, but he doesn't talk like a Negro, so they don't know it by the phone, and so immediately they say the place is not available or the price is up, or something else. Now you hear this all day long, day in and day out in these hearings. My only point is, isn't it possible to get a large ad, or something, and say "Anybody who has been discriminated against for reasons of race, religion, color, or national origin please appoint—come to Mr. X and say so with the proper evidence," and the real estate agent will be taken in and disciplined by the Association.

MR. MURRAY. Reverend, our total practice has been published in our local papers on two or three different occasions. The public should be well acquainted with this kind of thing.

COMMISSIONER HESBURGH. Well, I hope as a result of this—I don't want to prolong this because there are other Commissioners that want to talk, but I hope that as a result of this you gentlemen start hearing directly about the cases that we are constantly hearing about every time we have a hearing.

MR. GORDON. Father, if I can offer one last word in this area. The San Francisco Real Estate Board in the last three or four years has worked very closely with the Housing Division of the

Human Rights Commission in San Francisco. I am a member of the Human Rights Commission in San Francisco. We are meeting with this group, with this housing group next week. The chairman of our Board Committee and three or four representatives of the Housing Division of the Human Rights Commission, and it is very possible and we are hopeful that some positive activity and some positive approach that you are suggesting can be forthcoming from this meeting and from this joint effort, possibly.

COMMISSIONER HESBURGH. Yes. The two ladies that preceded you certainly said a lot of things that call for explanations if this Code of Ethics is in fact in practice.

CHAIRMAN HANNAH. Mr. Patterson?

VICE CHAIRMAN PATTERSON. Mr. Robbins, you mentioned I believe that all the Real Estate Boards of the State have subscribed to your Code of Ethics and I, like Father Hesburgh, am impressed by this. But as you know, there is a great problem of translating what a board genuinely wants to happen and what the individual property owner may feel he can do or wants to do, or what his customer, the man he deals with, might want to happen as an individual American.

When I was a member of the board of the Atlanta Chamber of Commerce, we took an action in 1963 as a board representing the business community urging the owners of hotels and restaurants, theaters in that city, to serve Negroes equally and to do it voluntarily because we felt it should be.

Most of the private property owners in these categories could not or would not do it. In 1964 the Civil Rights Bill with its public accommodations section was passed. My question to you is just as our board of the Chamber in Atlanta took an action, such as your boards have taken, it was unable to see it implemented. It was overtaken by a Federal law.

Do you feel that you are going to be able to make your code of ethics work on the practical level in the State of California?

MR. ROBBINS. I think there is some differences there, Mr. Patterson. The South has had some problems quite different than our problems out here. I might just as a point of clarification say we have two codes that we are speaking of. One is our basic Code of Ethics which is adopted by the National Association, quite a long time ago. Then in addition to that, we are referring to the Code of Practices which is the specific frame of reference here today. They are both important. We are proud of both of them, but the Code of Practices is the one that is covering this particular area.

I would say not only can we do it, but Reverend Hesburgh a moment ago indicated that he might have drawn a conclusion already that this isn't working in the communities. I would have to suggest that on a Commission such as yours, quite often you

168

would be hearing only from those people who have been having a problem, and for some reason haven't expressed this problem where it might have done them more good.

I would suggest to you very firmly that the history of our activities in the State with our Equal Rights Program have proven themselves now. There is four years of experience, a handful of cases, relatively speaking, aided by the forced housing type of legislation, and I think I used this figure earlier; by the most conservative statistics, you could develop 300,000 minority families moving within the State during this period presumably to locations of their choosing.

Now we do stand ready. We have issued public releases many, many times, and many of our boards have paid for ads pointing out what we are willing to do, and what we are doing, and I think in a quiet way—we don't buy a newspaper ad, for example, and say that we sold a house to a Negro at such and such an address. I don't think anybody would want us to do that, but we are doing this in such numbers that in our honest opinion we have reduced this problem to a very small problem.

There is still one remaining, and we are still here to help, and we think we have taken the leadership in providing the atmosphere that can today call it a successful program.

If we had more cooperation rather than people making statements that are not necessarily intended to lead to cooperation but working together with us I think we could lick the whole problem.

VICE CHAIRMAN PATTERSON. On this remaining problem that you say does exist, do you feel that you can assure the Commission that private property owners of this State can, acting voluntarily, end this remaining problem?

MR. ROBBINS. I think we can, yes. We cannot guarantee you this. There will still be an occasional bigot here and there, but with the atmosphere created within the State, I think the bigots are so few that they are standing in the corner talking to themselves.

VICE CHAIRMAN PATTERSON. If the testimony that we have heard does prove to be meaningful and there is a sizable problem relating to the availability of housing to minority groups, and you can't solve it voluntarily, then would you say, sure, let the Government do it?

MR. ROBBINS. Well, this would depend on what action the Government would want to take.

During the hearings on the Rumford Act, for example, in 1963, when questions that you were discussing with the previous witness here, what do you do, for example, when a Negro family moves into a white apartment house and the white occupants move out?

Mr. Rumford said, well we pass another law, make it illegal for them to move out. I would not be in favor of that kind of law.

Someone suggested you pass a law then to make it illegal for a person to refuse to buy a house because of race, religion, either the occupant, the neighbor or the man across the street, or something. I would not be in favor of that type of legislation.

We have propounded legislation in two areas so far. One is the blockbusting area where we did back this and we did put into California law for the first time legislation in this area. We do back legislation against harassment of people who do offer to rent or to sell to minority people. And harassment does take place. We don't approve of it. We believe it should be formalized.

Generally it is illegal now. We believe that the focus of the spotlight should be put in areas such as this, but on the basis of taking away the freedom of the individual, regardless of his race or religion, we would not approve of laws taking that freedom away.

VICE CHAIRMAN PATTERSON. I note in your written testimony that you feel that the taking away of that freedom would carry us along the road to abolition of private property, the goal which Karl Marx said was the basic theory of Communism.

MR. ROBBINS. No question about that, is there?

VICE CHAIRMAN PATTERSON. Do you believe that the public accommodations section of the Civil Rights Act of 1964 was wise in view of the fact that it did deprive private property owners of the free use of their property?

MR. ROBBINS. Now, the public accommodations of the hotel-motel area?

VICE CHAIRMAN PATTERSON. Yes.

MR. ROBBINS. We are fully in favor of that private accommodations area. We have it in California. We excluded it from our Proposition 14.

We believe that the transitory service is quite different than the permanency of the individual's home. The castle comes at the permanent level, not at the overnight accommodation.

VICE CHAIRMAN PATTERSON. Then you did not feel that the public accommodations section of the 1964 Civil Rights Act did carry us along the road to the abolition of private property?

MR. ROBBINS. No, sir, we in California have had that for over 50 years. Other areas, maybe such as yours, have not until recently.

VICE CHAIRMAN PATTERSON. You draw the distinction between the transitory type business and the more permanent type business, including an apartment?

MR. ROBBINS. Very definitely, a very important distinction.

VICE CHAIRMAN PATTERSON. Thank you.

CHAIRMAN HANNAH. Mrs. Freeman?

COMMISSIONER FREEMAN. Mr. Robbins, I am unable to understand what you mean by the premanency of an individual's home that he has sold.

MR. ROBBINS. The right of selling or renting, Mrs. Freeman. To use an example that might be more understandable, let's take one that we used in Stockton about the hypothetical case in an apartment unit.

We believe that there shouldn't be any question about all of us respecting the fight of the Methodist minister's widow, for example, out of respect for her departed husband's memory, to rent her apartment unit to Methodist students. Some people disagree with that. But that is a clear way of speaking of the property right that I mentioned.

There are many other reasons why a person would want to have some control over the sale of his own home. We specifically say he has no control over the neighbor's disposition of his home, but he does have on his own home, if he for his own reason wants to sell it to his own brother or somebody of his own color hair, or what have you, that should be his privilege.

COMMISSIONER FREEMAN. Will you interpret for the Commission Article V of the Code of Ethics of the National Association of Real Estate Boards which you have given us in a kit which says, "The Realtor shall not be instrumental in introducing into a neighborhood a character or property or use which would clearly be detrimental to property values in that neighborhood."

MR. ROBBINS. All right, about three pages beyond that following the Constitution and Bylaws, in the Policy and Procedure Manual, is an official interpretation of that to point out that which I will briefly state to you does not make reference to race or religion.

COMMISSIONER FREEMAN. Will you give us your interpretation?

MR. ROBBINS. Yes. It is recognized that a board cannot and could not attempt to specify in the bylaws all the qualifications for membership therein. The greater the number of restrictions placed in the bylaws, the greater the danger that the board may be accused of seeking to impose restraints upon trade.

This is about five minutes. Do you want it all?

COMMISSIONER FREEMAN. The point is that here again the seller, or the owner of property, would not be permitted to do what he wanted to do with it, if he wanted to put up a theater, if your agency considered that this was detrimental to the character of the neighborhood, and this would be in violation of his freedom to contract.

MR. ROBBINS. I am afraid I have lost you, Mrs. Freeman.

COMMISSIONER FREEMAN. Yes. If that owner wanted to sell his place to someone who wanted to put up a theater, and the Realtor determined that this was a character detrimental to the neighborhood, then you would not introduce that theater into the neighborhood.

MR. ROBBINS. There might be many other reasons why we wouldn't introduce that theater also. What you are getting at really are there any racial implications here, and I would say unequivocally no.

COMMISSIONER FREEMAN. What we are saying is that the idea of the concept of freedom to contract is really a myth.

MR. ROBBINS. I hope not.

COMMISSIONER FREEMAN. Because the property owner has to comply with the laws with respect to garbage disposal, with respect to the zoning regulations, and this is something that the Real Estate Association has accepted.

That is only in the field of human rights that the association has said that we cannot go, and I would like to ask you if you accept the National Housing Policy as declared by the Congress of the right of every American to a decent home in a suitable environment.

MR. ROBBINS. We think we have done a great deal toward that. We also have a new policy this year that hopefully time will allow us to discuss briefly. We think we have again taken leadership here that has been perhaps more significant than any other private organization and maybe more meaningful than any Government action.

COMMISSIONER FREEMAN. Did your association initiate proceedings or support the repeal of the Rumford Act?

MR. ROBBINS. We were very involved in Proposition 14 which technically was not a repeal of the Rumford Act, but we were very instrumental in backing Proposition 14.

COMMISSIONER FREEMAN. And so you are opposed to the fair housing practices?

MR. ROBBINS. We are opposed to the Rumford Act, which we call forced housing, and you call fair housing, and this may be where the difference is.

If this Act helped 100 people, and our atmosphere helped 300,000, which did the most good for minority families?

COMMISSIONER FREEMAN. Has the California Real Estate Association made the determination that every person or every family in California has equal opportunity in housing?

MR. ROBBINS. I think as I answered Mr. Patterson's question earlier, I think we have minimized the problem. We haven't been naive enough to suggest that it is completely gone, but I think our efforts have reduced it to a very workable area where any problems that come to our attention we will solve without exception.

COMMISSIONER FREEMAN. But you are opposed to laws?

MR. ROBBINS. We are opposed to improper laws, yes.

CHAIRMAN HANNAH. Mr. Rankin?

COMMISSIONER RANKIN. I have just one question.

As you know, we are a factfinding Commission here and that is why you are testifying before us so that we can understand your position and you can explain it to us. We are quite interested in your own policing methods that you use which you think have accomplished the purpose. Yet yesterday and today we have subpenaed various persons to appear and testify before this Commission, and the only person who refused to testify and who for two weeks successfully evaded the subpena was a real estate man yesterday.

MR. ROBBINS. Was he a Realtor?

COMMISSIONER RANKIN. Your definition of a Realtor, I——

MR. TAYLOR. He is a member of the San Francisco Board of Realtors.

MR. ROBBINS. A member of a constituent board subscribing to a code of ethics?

COMMISSIONER RANKIN. I am sure that the Staff Director could help me here.

MR. TAYLOR. It is Mr. Carl Gellert. He is a member of the San Francisco Board of Realtors. I wonder, since Dr. Rankin brought the matter up, whether we might enlist your—you said we are not hearing both sides of the story. Could we enlist your cooperation in this matter?

COMMISSIONER RANKIN. That was the point I was going to make.

MR. ROBBINS. I am sure if we had had some work on this earlier, we quite possibly could have prevailed upon him to come. Why he didn't, I have no idea. Our group here today has two people who came at their own expense voluntarily.

COMMISSIONER RANKIN. Well, I was just trying to show that we did try to get the information on the other side as well.

MR. ROBBINS. All right, fine.

COMMISSIONER FREEMAN. And we would like to hear from him.

CHAIRMAN HANNAH. Mr. Taylor, do you have any questions?

MR. TAYLOR. Yes, I think Mrs. Freeman was about to say that if you could—we still have some time at the hearing, and if you could secure his cooperation we will be glad to hear from him, I think.

MR. GORDON. I will follow through on this and communicate with whomever you suggest we get in touch with after our efforts as far as locating him is concerned.

MR. TAYLOR. Mr. Robbins——

MR. ROBBINS. Let't pursue that for just a moment. Who do you

want Mr. Gordon to check with on working out an appointment
for this gentleman who——

MR. TAYLOR. Well, we can speak to him after the testimony.

MR. ROBBINS. You, Mr. Taylor?

MR. TAYLOR. Yes. Mr. Robbins, you were speaking a few moments ago about these words that don't elicit a spirit of cooperation and I haven't been able to go through your whole statement,
but I did note the part that Commissioner Patterson cited, which
says that the legislation depriving a property owner of his freedom to enter into a contract with a person of his choice carries
us along the road to abolition of private property, the goal which
Karl Marx said is a basic theory of Communism.

I take it you don't mean to imply by that that if I advocate the
legislation which President Johnson submitted last year, which
would restrict the right of a property owner in this regard, that
I am either a Communist or that I am advancing the purposes
of Communism? Do you imply that?

MR. ROBBINS. Do you think we do?

MR. TAYLOR. I am asking you the question.

MR. ROBBINS. No, of course not, Mr. Taylor, of course not.

MR. TAYLOR. Well, do you think this kind of rhetoric really helps
advance the discussion?

MR. ROBBINS. Well, I think it is important. Some people forget
that these basic rights are advancing us toward this road. We
made one sentence there, and that is all. Just as a little reminder,
that if carried too far, that could be the end of this road. No one
should take objection to that.

MR. TAYLOR. Do you attach any importance at all to the right
to acquire property as a basic right?

MR. ROBBINS. Well, acquiring property within the framework
of our law of contracts, I have testified earlier that from our rather
complete observation, the problem area, the minority area, the
people have been able to acquire, and regardless of race, color,
they can acquire from anybody willing to sell, and fortunately
the market place indicates most people are willing.

MR. TAYLOR. There are, however, are there not, and I would
ask this question of anyone, large sections of the Bay Area where
Negroes and members of minority groups have not acquired housing? Is that true?

MR. ROBBINS. I don't know. I would assume there would be, depending on how you want to define the area, but I would say this:
you would have to bring to our attention the fact that a certain
minority family wants to buy there before we would accept the
fact that there is a problem.

MR. TAYLOR. If there has been a history of discrimination over
the years, do you think that it might advance things if it were

made clear in an affirmative way that minority groups which previously had not been welcome are now welcome?

MR. ROBBINS. Well, now, keep in mind, that when you say "welcome," you are speaking of a different subject than having housing being available to them in the area.

I am saying to you that housing is available to minority families in every area of this State. I am not necessarily stating that every person in that immediate neighborhood would welcome the particular family.

In most areas, most would, but if we wanted to pass a law to make everybody welcome, that would be a difficult law to pass, I think. It would be a desirable end result. Reverend Hesburgh's area, I think, is the one that has done great strides in that area and we hope that the church area work along with our private work will end up having this as an end result, but I don't see legislation possible here.

MR. TAYLOR. I don't think anybody suggested that legislation could make a person welcome in the sense that he would enjoy very good relations with his neighbor. I didn't hear that suggested, although in speaking of that, I take it—I asked Mr. Snell a few minutes ago whether apartment house owners inquired generally into the backgrounds of prospective tenants.

Now, do real estate brokers ordinarily make inquiries into the backgrounds of potential purchasers before they offer homes for sale? Do they find out whether they have a criminal record, whether they are mentally or emotionally stable, or whether they beat their wives?

MR. ROBBINS. We usually don't inquire if they beat their wives. Quite often we don't find out whether they have a criminal record or not, and we don't get a psychiatric test from them.

Our investigation, as I feel sure you do know, is more of a credit investigation, size of family, hoping to make the offerings we have in keeping with the size of the family's requirements for the nearness of schools, shopping, and that kind of thing.

Infrequently, a credit statement will show up some of these other factors, never the wife-beating factor, to my knowledge.

MR. TAYLOR. Perhaps you are saying your concern is only limited to the property owner and his right to dispose of his property, but if it is not limited to that, if it also concerns the neighbors in a new neighborhood, why aren't you concerned with these things as well?

MR. ROBBINS. Well, I specifically say that we are not concerned with the neighborhood. We are concerned with the individual property owner, and many of these make up a neighborhood, and what we are saying in this, this may be is where the point is misunderstood so often: if, for example, one man says for reasons best known to himself and unjustifiable to most of us, I don't want to sell my house to a Negro, and the man next to him having the identical house, says, I don't want to sell my house to anybody but a Negro, what is the end result? The Negro buys a house in that neighborhood. One man next door happens to have a strange viewpoint, but our approach specifically says that the neighborhood concept is not proper. The individual within that neighborhood is the one that should make his own decisions, and because of the varying backgrounds and varying motivations, the end result is, and we have proven that most properties are available to most people, and if this is the desirable end result, why take a chance on disturbing this community atmosphere of acceptance by the type of legislation that just is not acceptable by the American people.

MR. TAYLOR. Ordinarily the seller of the house doesn't know the buyer on a personal basis, does he?

MR. ROBBINS. Sometimes he does, sometimes he doesn't.

MR. TAYLOR. In the ordinary case?

MR. ROBBINS. They usually know each other casually before the transaction is completed. Very infrequently they know each other beforehand.

MR. TAYLOR. Do you think a Fair Housing Law might be improved somewhat if it made specific provision that a person could sell to a relative or to a close friend? Would that take care of your objections to it?

MR. ROBBINS. I think it could be improved somewhat if it said he could sell or rent or not sell or not rent as he chose. To answer your question, no.

MR. TAYLOR. Mr. Robbins, or any other member, I haven't had a chance to go through all this. I wonder whether you could list for me in a moment or two specific areas or neighborhoods that have been opened up as a result of your efforts, your voluntary efforts over the past year or two?

MR. ROBBINS. Well, I think we would be glad to pursue that if you think it would be productive. I don't like the phraseology of "opened up." I think that has connotations that are unacceptable. I would prefer to talk in terms of specific families who happen to be Negro who purchase houses in areas that happen to not have too many other Negroes in there.

MR. TAYLOR. How much staff do you have working on this problem?

MR. ROBBINS. Well, keep in mind we have 179 boards and within each board some boards are quite small, some are quite large. In some boards they will have a part-time secretary only. In other boards they might have a staff of 10 or 12.

MR. TAYLOR. Does each separate board make an allocation of resources from its own revenues to carry out this program?

MR. ROBBINS. I couldn't specifically state that every board has made a specific allocation of a certain sum of money.

MR. TAYLOR. Does the State Board make an allocation of money?

MR. ROBBINS. The State Real Estate Association does have a budget that has prepared the Equal Rights Kits that you see, that has prepared the handbooks that you see, that has a staff man working in the area of public relations hoping to get releases along the lines Reverend Hesburgh indicated that we should have.

It would be difficult to assess just how much cash is involved. I think it would be a substantial amount, but I find it difficult to put my finger on it.

MR. TAYLOR. Can you tell us roughly how much?

MR. ROBBINS. Well, I would hate to even guess on behalf of the various boards. I would say our own allocation is in the $40,000 to $45,000 annual area.

MR. TAYLOR. Forty to $45,000?

MR. ROBBINS. Yes.

MR. TAYLOR. And how large a portion of that would that be of your total budget?

MR. ROBBINS. Our total budget is in the $400,000 neighborhood, most of which is staff.

MR. TAYLOR. Did the State Board directly spend its own funds in this campaign against Proposition 14?

MR. ROBBINS. No, sir.

MR. TAYLOR. Did individual boards spend any money?

MR. ROBBINS. I don't know.

MR. TAYLOR. Could you estimate the size of that budget as against the size of the budget that may have gone into the feeding of Proposition 14?

MR. ROBBINS. Well, now, you asked me earlier how much money the California Real Estate Association spent, and I took a guess at it for you, and I don't have that figure exactly. I also stated that they spent no money on Proposition 14, and now you have asked me another question how much do you think was spent altogether on Proposition 14.

A lot of money was spent by a lot of volunteers, most of which were outside the board, and I have seen conflicting figures on the total. I don't know what the total is. A very large sum of money which really it shouldn't have been necessary for the public to contribute, but they did, readily. It was in the million dollar neighborhood someplace, I think.

MR. TAYLOR. I have no further questions.

CHAIRMAN HANNAH. Thank you very much, gentlemen. We are grateful for your being with us.

MR. ROBBINS. Could I offer just a few comments on our program to improve substandard housing if I keep it short?

CHAIRMAN HANNAH. Well, we are about 15 minutes behind schedule, if you will make it very short. But let me make it clear that if you will give us a written statement of whatever you think has not been adequately covered here this morning, we will include it in the record, and we will give it careful consideration.

MR. ROBBINS. Well, if you will give me 30 seconds then.

CHAIRMAN HANNAH. You take a few seconds and make what statement you want to, and then supplement it with whatever you think we should have in writing that you haven't had an opportunity to present to this body.

MR. ROBBINS. All right. The main reference in the data presented to you is a new program this year by the California Real Estate Association. It is addressing itself to eliminating substandard housing in the State of California. It does not mention the word "minority" anywhere in the program, but you can see for yourself where the net result of the effectiveness of this program would be. The conclusion is only this, which is not mentioned in the kit, that if your Commission could do something on the Federal level to keep the Federal Government from subsidizing slums, that our work would be much easier.

By this I mean a prohibition against welfare recipients spending that money in commonly accepted slum housing, making it only in housing decent, safe, and sanitary.

We think that would be a great step towards the desired end result here.

CHAIRMAN HANNAH. I appreciate that suggestion. Any others that you would care to give us in writing, we will certainly receive. Thank you very much.

CHAIRMAN HANNAH. Mr. Glickstein, are you ready?

MR. GLICKSTEIN. Yes, sir. The next witness is Mr. Jack Tuggle.

(Whereupon MR. JACK TUGGLE was sworn by the Chairman and testified as follows:)

TESTIMONY OF MR. JACK TUGGLE, SAN FRANCISCO, CALIFORNIA

MR. GLICKSTEIN. Mr. Tuggle, will you please state your name and address for the record?

MR. TUGGLE. My name is Jack Tuggle. I live at No. 2 Stantonville Court in Oakland.

MR. GLICKSTEIN. Where are you employed, Mr. Tuggle?

MR. TUGGLE. I am employed in the San Francisco Insuring Office of the Federal Housing Administration at 100 California Street, San Francisco.

MR. GLICKSTEIN. And what are your responsibilities with the FHA?

MR. TUGGLE. I am the Deputy Director of the San Francisco Insuring Office.

MR. GLICKSTEIN. Are you charged with the responsibility of carrying out the provisions of the Executive order on equal opportunity housing?

MR. TUGGLE. I am with the Director charged with this responsibility. The Director, and I am his deputy and I have the same charges that he does.

MR. GLICKSTEIN. He has delegated this responsibility to you?

MR. TUGGLE. The deputy position would automatically make me in charge with the same responsibilities with him.

MR. GLICKSTEIN. Mr. Tuggle, do you know how many new units of housing FHA has insured since 1962?

MR. TUGGLE. Not since '62· I did bring along the '66 record which was a bad year, but I did bring it along, and '65·

MR. GLICKSTEIN. You don't have the records going back to the——

MR. TUGGLE. We have them. We could get them.

MR. GLICKSTEIN. We would appreciate it if you could furnish that to us.

MR. TUGGLE. All right. I will give you a list of all insured cases —not a list, but a number.

MR. GLICKSTEIN. You do know how many were insured in '66, though?

MR. TUGGLE. Yes, sir.

MR. GLICKSTEIN. Do you know how many of the units that were insured in 1966 are occupied by Negroes?

MR. TUGGLE. I have no way of knowing, sir.

MR. GLICKSTEIN. In other words, even if we go back to 1962 and you produce those figures for us, those figures would not show which of the units are occupied by Negroes?

MR. TUGGLE. No, sir, they would not.

MR. GLICKSTEIN. In other words, the agency doesn't keep racial statistics of that sort?

MR. TUGGLE. We do not.

MR. GLICKSTEIN. Would you outline for the Commission the procedure that you follow when your office receives a complaint of discrimination in housing?

MR. TUGGLE. Well, usually when we receive a complaint in the days when we had the intergroup relations advisor, he would probably be the first to hear about it on the telephone. That is the normal procedure, and in the telephone conversation, why, he would ask the complainant to reduce his complaint to writing, if that were possible to do so, and we are charged with the responsibility of notifying our Washington headquarters within two days of the receipt of this complaint, which we do, and they set a log up on the office in the Washington headquarters to see the progress that we make in servicing the complaint.

I usually try to confer with the intergroup relations advisor or talk to the persons or parties making the complaint, either in person or on behalf of someone else.

If I can, I get on the telephone and resolve the problem right at that moment. If it is a builder, I call him, and say, "Do you know that your sales force is doing such discriminating or at least they have been charged that they are discriminating? Would you please give me a ring back before the day is over so that we can know what this is all about," and in some instances, why there is delay, and there is always the question of determining whether or not this is a legitimate complaint.

If I don't get some satisfaction that the party who is asking for a house is going to be provided with that housing within a very reasonable period of time, that the application will be accepted from him and it will be sent in for processing, then I notify— Usually try to arrange on the telephone a mutually acceptable time and I try to set up a hearing within 10 days.

Now in this hearing we advise further after the telephone in a registered letter that if they want a hearing, the time and place. We advise them, I believe, that they are entitled to counsel if they want it. If they ask, I certainly tell them. We tell them it is an informal hearing, that there won't be any formality to it. We then check to see if there is any other parties that are interested, like the Veterans Administration. If they are, we invite them to have a representative at the hearing.

We have also invited the Fair Employment Practices Commission of the State of California to have a representative at the hearing, and they have always sent someone, usually an attorney, and if there is any other parties that are interested on either behalf of the person complaining or the person complained against, who have a genuine interest in it, either as a public-spirited body or—not just as spectators, why, they are invited to be there and present.

Now, we have never had a hearing where there were more than 15 or 20 people in the room. The form of the hearing——

MR. GLICKSTEIN. You say the hearings are open to the public?

MR. TUGGLE. Well, we have never had a real question of whether or not they are open to the public. We invited those people who were interested or because they were participating to come in, and we start the hearing off usually by stating what the situation is, as we understand it from the complainant, and then we will ask the complainant to reduce to words what he is saying, and usually the person being complained against will contradict some of it and we will find that there is some areas of misunderstanding about what has transpired previously and in almost— invariably we come to a conclusion at the hearing, although a determination is not made right then, but I have in all instances, I think except one, have found that the housing would be made available to the complainant.

Now I will say that this has not been a big program although I think that effect has been rather broad. It is generally understood throughout the industry that we do this.

We have industry meetings from time to time. Myself and the Director meet with all segments of the industry. That is the realtors.

MR. GLICKSTEIN. And at these meetings that you have with the builders, how do you indicate to them what their obligations are under the Executive order?

MR. TUGGLE. We call their attention to the fact that when they made an application for mortgage insurance, or when they made an application for subdivision analysis, that they signed a statement that they would not discriminate.

MR. GLICKSTEIN. Are these statements called to the attention of the builders before they sign an application?

MR. TUGGLE. Well, they have to sign the statement and I don't see how the man could make a statement that is set out in the bottom of his acceptance of a subdivision report, and we would not proceed with our processing any further than that unless he did sign this statement, without knowing the content of it, but we repeatedly go over this with the industry as to what their obligations are under the program, under the administrative procedures of the Federal Housing Administration.

MR. GLICKSTEIN. Do you meet with builders rather frequently and discuss with them what their obligations are?

MR. TUGGLE. Well, it is not primarily for the purpose of discussing their obligations under this particular section. We meet with the industry to discuss overall industry problems.

MR. GLICKSTEIN. I see, and then——

MR. TUGGLE. This is just a part of it. It is supplemental to it. It is not the dominant subject of every meeting. If it was, I think we probably would have less interest in the meetings than we do, but, from time to time, we bring this up.

Now, in the case of brokers, I don't meet with them. I am invited to speak to them frequently and I usually make some reference to the FHA programs and what I consider to be general trends in the whole development of our real estate market here in California, and in some of the communities I have told them that although you have practically a segregated community, you are sailing into a situation in which this is going to change and you had better be ready to adjust to this.

MR. GLICKSTEIN. Mr. Tuggle, our Staff Report indicated that there had been 10 complaints under the Executive order in the

Bay Area and I believe that you indicated that all of those had been satisfactorily worked out?

MR. TUGGLE. Well, I would not say that they had all been satisfactorily worked out. They have all been resolved and we had a determination in favor of the complainant in all but one of them.

MR. GLICKSTEIN. What sanction did you impose against the builder in the nine cases?

MR. TUGGLE. We imposed, when he did what we asked him to, which was indicated, we imposed no sanctions against him.

MR. GLICKSTEIN. What you asked him to do was to make the house available to any person that complained and the builder agreed to do that?

MR. TUGGLE. Yes.

MR. GLICKSTEIN. And do you require builders that have been found to discriminate to subsequently advertise that they are an equal housing builder?

MR. TUGGLE. We do not.

MR. GLICKSTEIN. Would you consider such a requirement appropriate?

MR. TUGGLE. Would I personally consider it appropriate?

MR. GLICKSTEIN. Yes.

MR. TUGGLE. I think it might be stigmatizing that builder in picking him out as a particular target, both for people who want to discriminate and did not go to his tract because of the advertisement. It might also be that it would serve as an attraction for an excessive—when I use the word 'excessive," I mean an imbalance —I think that is a socially acceptable word now, an imbalance in his subdivision, which would not be as healthy as it should be for the whole community.

MR. GLICKSTEIN. What if you required all developers that received FHA assistance to advertise that they were equal housing developers?

MR. TUGGLE. That is a policy decision and I think as Mrs. Matusek indicated here, I am primarily one that carries out policy, and I do not set the overall general policy, like the Executive order, I would say this is the broadest level of policy, and the highest level of policy, and so my function is primarily to carry out the policy.

MR. GLICKSTEIN. You mean that policy would have to be set in Washington?

MR. TUGGLE. If there is a policy set, we will carry it out.

MR. GLICKSTEIN. And that policy would have to be set in Washington?

MR. TUGGLE. I believe it would be inappropriate for an insuring office to set policy on its own initiative.

MR. GLICKSTEIN. You mean after you heard a case involving a builder that was alleged to have discriminated, and you found that the builder discriminated, you have no discretion in deciding what sort of sanction that you would impose on that builder?

MR. TUGGLE. We do have some, but our sanctions are primarily to withdraw the benefits of the insurance program to him. That is our ultimate weapon.

MR. GLICKSTEIN. So you either have to take the ultimate step or do nothing?

MR. TUGGLE. Well, we do have the privilege of referring a case to the Attorney General's office, but that would be done at the Washington level, and it would be on a case that would be clear cut and would make a matter of law a precedent, I am sure.

MR. GLICKSTEIN. As a person who has had a great deal of experience with the Executive order, do you feel that it would be appropriate to require builders with FHA assistance to advertise that they are equal housing developers?

MR. TUGGLE. All of them?

MR. GLICKSTEIN. All of them.

MR. TUGGLE. I would like to see the whole intent of the Executive order broadened to all segments of the housing field. This is a personal statement of mine; and then it would be much easier for us to put in the implementing devices that you are suggesting.

MR. GLICKSTEIN. But assuming that the order isn't broadened, do you think—

MR. TUGGLE. Sir?

MR. GLICKSTEIN. Assuming that the order is not broadened, how do you feel about—

MR. TUGGLE. We get back to the question that has been bandied around many times before this Commission, I am sure, is the extent to which the FHA participates in the market, and in this particular office over 51 percent of the houses that are built in any one year are built with the benefit of FHA inspection and mortgage insurance or commitments.

Now, that doesn't mean they are all insured, but they are built that way, which is a very high—we maintain a rather good relationship with the industry. Nationally, I understand, it is much lower than that.

I am not as concerned with that, but I feel that anything that would tend to cause us to lose a position in the market, and the influence that we exert in the market, without having the same imperatives on other operators in the real estate field, or I shouldn't say "real estate," in the home production field, might not be as self-serving for the cause as we would like for it to be.

MR. GLICKSTEIN. Doesn't FHA impose all sorts of onerous conditions on developers that could also tend to result in a loss of business in the market? For example, FHA people that wish FHA insurance or commitments must agree that their lots be graded according to FHA specifications, building materials must meet certain FHA standards, the Fair Labor Standards Act must be complied with, FHA building standards must be met? There are all kinds of onerous restrictions that FHA imposes. Don't you think that might have an effect on—

MR. TUGGLE. I do not consider any of those to be onerous. I consider those to be minimal and what any legitimate builder would want to do to be able to deliver a product to his consumer group that would stand up and be a good product.

MR. GLICKSTEIN. But you think that requiring the builder to advertise that he is an equal opportunity builder might be onerous?

MR. TUGGLE. This would be harder to explain to some buyers than the fact that his lot was graded properly.

MR. GLICKSTEIN. What efforts does FHA make to follow up and make sure that a builder isn't continuing to discriminate, once you found that he has discriminated?

MR. TUGGLE. Well, we would be hopeful that the same source that brought the original discrimination to our attention would continue to serve as a monitor.

MR. GLICKSTEIN. You rely on individual complaints and you don't use your own staff for the monitoring purposes?

MR. TUGGLE. We do make inquiries. I can't think of a single builder which has had a hearing in which I have not informally, not asked him to give me a report, or anything like that, but I have informally checked with him to see what he is doing now and see what effect he felt was the result of having sold to a minority.

And I don't know whether it is sincere completely, but I have never had a builder who said that he felt that his program had been seriously jeopardized by having made the decision to accept and to sell to a minority.

Most of them I have—well, I think all of them have maintained a complete protestation of nondiscrimination and that this was somebody in their staff, or that they didn't understand, or that there was a misunderstanding.

One of them, I know, claimed that it was his lender who was the responsible party. In this case, we did ask the lender to let us evaluate the credit report, and the lender was willing to do that, and eventually we wound up getting the house for the complainant.

MR. GLICKSTEIN. Do you generally find that after a builder has sold to a minority person involved in your case, he then tends to sell many more houses to other members of minority groups?

MR. TUGGLE. Well, I just—because there is one builder we have had one formal hearing on and one other complaint on, I checked with him today to find out what his operations during the last year were, and he advised me that in the community of Fairfield he had sold 118 houses, and three of them had been to Negro buyers, to Negro families. Five of them had been to what we would call Asiatic families, I presume, because it is a very broad and general statement, including Filipinos, and all of the Asiatic peoples, and eight of them would be to mixed marriages.

Now, most of those mixed marriages, so there won't be any misunderstanding about what I am saying, were to soldiers who had Oriental wives.

In another tract of 160 units of sales, he had sold four properties to colored families, 11 to Orientals, and he didn't have any figures on the mixed marriages.

In another one, he had sold 87 houses, two of them to colored families, one to a Hindu who was dark skinned, and two to Oriental families, or Asiatic. When I say "Oriental," I mean Asiatic, because—now, this man probably has a broader record of selling to this particular consumer group than most because he builds in a price range which, although it seems high, it is relatively low for this area, that is, $15,000 to $18,000.

MR. GLICKSTEIN. In order to get this information, though, you had to call the builder?

MR. TUGGLE. I called him, yes, but I had talked to him previously and he told me that he was continuing to carry out a program of selling to minority buyers, and that he didn't feel that it had seriously impaired his programs in any way.

MR. GLICKSTEIN. And you feel, I believe the figures that you gave us indicate that 503 houses were sold and nine were sold to Negro families?

MR. TUGGLE. That is about right, and I would say that this is not in proportion to the population and it is not a job that I would be too proud of, but it does say that there is not, at least to my way of looking at it, there is housing available in this particular builder's three tracts during this last year.

MR. GLICKSTEIN. You don't have staff members who go out and monitor builders that have been found to discriminate? Would you feel it appropriate to send a staff member out to test a builder and see if he was discriminating?

MR. TUGGLE. I think I answered that question in our office, and I said that I would not unless he was a bona fide purchaser who wanted to send somebody out to make an inquiry about the purchase of the property.

MR. GLICKSTEIN. Would you feel it was appropriate to have members of your staff present on the site where homes are sold just to observe the activities of the brokers to make sure that members of minority groups that came to seek homes were treated fairly?

MR. TUGGLE. I don't see how that could possibly work. I mean the relationship between a salesman and his client is something that is, although it is partially open, it is partially privileged, and I don't see how we could have a man there. It would even affect the kind of sales talk that was being delivered and probably even affect the reception of that sales talk by the prospective purchaser.

I don't see how you could do that, effectively I mean. You could go through the motions of it and put on an effect of doing it, but I don't see how it could be effectively done.

MR. GLICKSTEIN. You do, though, send out staff members to see if builders are complying with FHA grading specifications and FHA building materials specifications?

MR. TUGGLE. That is very specific. If you need to, you can take an instrument and measure it.

MR. GLICKSTEIN. And you have found the method of making certain that those specifications are accurate?

MR. TUGGLE. Yes.

MR. GLICKSTEIN. Section 102 of the Housing Order, President Kennedy's Executive order on fair housing, I believe Mrs. Freeman referred to it this morning, covers housing under commitment prior to November 20, 1962, when the order was signed.

What efforts has your Department made, have you made, under Section 102 to promote the abandonment of discriminatory practices?

MR. TUGGLE. You mean by realtors, by builders, by others?

MR. GLICKSTEIN. Right.

MR. TUGGLE. Well, through the years, we have, as I say, continued to have meetings. I think that I would not want to claim credit for this for the office, but I think we have been contributory to it. When I first began to appear before realtor groups and builder groups here many years ago, there were no minorities in them. I believe most of the groups in the Bay Area now have not only white, but minority members on the board, their Board of Realtors. I am convinced that this will have a lot to do with the tone of what a Board of Realtors thinks, the mere fact that they are being monitored by a few.

Now, there are a number of Realtors—I guess the word "Realtors" is patented, but the people in the real estate business who are minorities and don't belong to a board, there are some non-minority groups or the white majority groups that don't belong, also.

I don't think that the minorities are participating in board membership to the extent that I would like to see, but there are a number of them there, and I think the mere fact that they are present and that they are monitoring what goes on in all the meetings has a very salutary effect on the conduct of that board.

The builders—we have only one or two Negro builders in the

Bay Area that I know of that build in any volume, and I don't believe that the one that I think of that builds in some volume belongs to a home builders association. I don't know whether he has made application or not. It is an interesting thought.

MR. GLICKSTEIN. Mr. Tuggle, you said that FHA does not require a builder who has been found to discriminate to advertise that he is an equal housing developer.

But how does FHA make known generally what housing is covered by the Executive order and what must be sold and rented on a nondiscriminatory basis? Do you make that known generally.

MR. TUGGLE. Yes, we do. We prepare a list of all new subdivisions and then when we issue commitments in those subdivisions we give the general description of the property, and we post it on a bulletin board in our office, and we also mail it to those people who are—or those groups who are interested in receiving that information, and if there is a change in the name of the tract, or anything like that, why, we are charged with the responsibility to see that the name change is effected and that the people who are concerned are furnished with this name change.

Now, we do not run into that problem of name changes here, but it is in our instructions. It is an academic discussion, other than the fact that—

MR. GLICKSTEIN. That is the way you treat—

MR. TUGGLE. That is new subdivisions and commitments in new subdivisions.

MR. GLICKSTEIN. How do you treat repossessed property?

MR. TUGGLE. Well, repossessed properties are—the bulk of them are handled through what we call area management brokers.

Now, the area management broker performs a number of functions for us. He takes over the property at the time of the original acquisition. He puts a sign on it that it is the property of the Federal Government. He secures it. He has the yard cleaned up and the trash hauled away.

MR. GLICKSTEIN. Excuse me. Repossessed property, just to make sure we all understand this, is a house in which FHA has insured the mortgage and the person hasn't been able to make payments and as a result FHA repossesses it?

MR. TUGGLE. The mortgage is foreclosed and that gives us the title.

MR. GLICKSTEIN. Thank you.

MR. TUGGLE. At this point we have the property analyzed by the broker to determine a repair program, we issue a repair contract. We try to bring the property into excellent condition, and up until recently we have followed a practice in this office—because we have excellent sales—of circularizing all brokers, whether they belong to a realty board or not, but if they are just a registered broker, and if they want to they can get on our list.

We have about 1,300 of them out of the San Francisco office and about 300 out of the Fresno office, and we would circularize them with the list of all the properties that were available for sale, and at the bottom of that we would have a complete statement of the equal opportunity, which is supposed to appear on all of our display advertising.

MR. GLICKSTEIN. For that type of housing there has to be display advertising?

MR. TUGGLE. No, there doesn't have to be.

MR. GLICKSTEIN. But you require that there be display advertising?

MR. TUGGLE. Well, the words "display advertising," I guess I really need some training in the advertising field, because I don't know quite what it means.

I think it either means a showcard that you have on display at the point of sale or else it means a partial cutout on a paper which would be a quarter sheet, or such matter. I think that is what our "display" means, but it may not.

MR. GLICKSTEIN. Is that what you require, though?

MR. TUGGLE. We do not require that. We haven't advertised at all as far as the agency is concerned. We are changing our policy, and we are changing it for several reasons, because we think it is a better method of marketing to start advertising, and my own thinking was that this question of the advertising has been made a cause célèbre by some people who seemed to think that we were trying to be evasive. I can assure you there was no intent for evasiveness, but if it will answer the question, each one of the ads that will appear in the column or ads in the paper will cover underneath it this nondiscriminatory language.

Now the exact size of the type I am not able to testify to, but I assume it will be equal in size to the description of the property or larger.

MR. GLICKSTEIN. Let me see if I understand what you are saying. You are going to require this for repossessed property?

MR. TUGGLE. On all of them we market.

MR. GLICKSTEIN. All the repossessed property that you market, you are going to require some indication——

MR. TUGGLE. We are not going to require it. We are going to do it ourselves and pay for it.

MR. GLICKSTEIN. And will the homes that are being sold, the homes that you have repossessed, also have signs in front of them that indicate that they are open to all persons?

MR. TUGGLE. Well, we have an FHA sign, and I tell you I haven't looked at it carefully enough to tell you whether it has that on it or not. We have another kind of display card sign that I have looked at. I think I showed you one in the office the other day, and that does have the language on it. I wouldn't want to under oath state that the traditional sign has that language on it, but I assume that it does.

MR. GLICKSTEIN. Then as I understand what you are saying, repossessed property is treated differently than new property?

MR. TUGGLE. Properties that are not owned by the Commissioner.

MR. GLICKSTEIN. That on repossessed property you do send out a list that is widely circulated among realtors indicating where the properties are and describing them? On the other hand, new FHA commitments are not advertised that extensively?

MR. TUGGLE. Well, we would be in a position of making a listing almost if we did that. You see, we are listing this with all 1,300 of these brokers, and any one of them is at liberty to sell this property. We are not at liberty to list a builder's properties because he reserves the right to list it with whatever sales organization he chooses.

We have more freedom where we own the property and are disposing of it, because we can list it with as many or as few brokers as we care to. We take a listing from any qualified broker in the State.

MR. GLICKSTEIN. Have your policies with respect to repossessed property, your policy to indicate on the notices that you send out, that it is an equal housing property and the policy that you are developing to post display cards in the homes, was this policy decided on here in the San Francisco office or was this dictated from Washington?

MR. TUGGLE. Well, most of this is Washington level thinking on how we should advertise and display.

MR. GLICKSTEIN. That did come from Washington?

MR. TUGGLE. Well, the cards, for example, that we used, the display cards that I showed you, were printed in the Government Printing Office in Washington.

MR. GLICKSTEIN. Right, but was this program devised here in the San Francisco office or did you get a directive from Washington that such a program should be instituted and carried out?

MR. TUGGLE. Well, it is a part of our whole property management disposition program which is covered in this book.

MR. GLICKSTEIN. I guess a book that long must have been printed in Washington.

MR. TUGGLE. Yes, sir. It is pretty specific instructions on how we shall——

MR. GLICKSTEIN. I have no further questions, Mr. Chairman.

CHAIRMAN HANNAH. Before we continue with the questioning, I would remind the Commissioners that we are 30 minutes behind the schedule. Are there any Commissioners that have questions?

COMMISSIONER FREEMAN. I have a question.

COMMISSIONER FREEMAN. Mr. Tuggle, you referred to FHA inspection. I wondered if you would explain to us the process of the inspection and what kind of inspections are made.

MR. TUGGLE. Well, on existing properties there would be a minimum of an appraisal which would constitute an inspection, but this would be primarily for the purpose of evaluation.

Now, on new construction, the property is—it is required of the builder that he file plans with us, and then we would have a series of inspections to determine that the property was built in accordance with those plans and specifications that were on file with us. Usually there is a foundation inspection and a framing inspection and a final inspection when the job is completed, and this would include not only the structure itself, but would include the yard area and the off-site items, which would be the streets and the utilities.

Now these inspections are signed by qualified technicians who are employed by the staff, and they can either be done on a voluntary basis or they can be called for by the builder.

COMMISSIONER FREEMAN. And these inspections are made in accordance with the rules and regulations of the——

MR. TUGGLE. In accordance with our instructions and with the minimum property standards.

COMMISSIONER FREEMAN. In response to a question concerning the number of Negroes occupying the developments covered by the Executive order, you said that you had no way of knowing which are occupied by Negroes, and I would call your attention to Section 101 of the Executive order which requires the Authority, the departments, to prevent discrimination because of race, color, or creed, and ask if you would contemplate, if you would say that this requires the agency to do the same kind of acts to assure compliance as with respect to the sidewalk or the bricks?

MR. TUGGLE. Well, it is certainly a desirable objective——

COMMISSIONER FREEMAN. Well, it is the President's order.

MR. TUGGLE. Yes, it is still desirable, but it is not as easily measured as whether or not there is one-tenth of a foot of grade on the property, because that is a physical matter and can be easily measured with the tools that we have available, whereas the other is an interpersonal matter, and I see good friends exchanging what I would take—if I didn't know them better—to be the height of insults, and yet they are still good friends.

Now, I am not saying that this is a normal relationship between people, but I am just saying you have to know the context in which a personal relationship is taking place to fully evaluate it.

COMMISSIONER FREEMAN. In terms of the number of Negroes, isn't it just as easy to count heads?

MR. TUGGLE. I would be most happy because since, oh, about 1960, we have been increasingly concerned with the problem of what kind of a job we are doing throughout the country on carrying out all of the objectives for equal opportunity, and I would like to see, if I could, but it isn't in our forms, a requirement for race.

Now, many years I was against this. Now I would like to see that put on the application forms, and then we would carry it right through our processing and it could be put in the tab machines and we could get a runout on it, and then we wouldn't have all of these implications that people like myself are trying to avoid the issue because they don't have the information available to them.

COMMISSIONER FREEMAN. But it is a fact that you have told us that you don't have the information.

MR. TUGGLE. I don't have. I can tell you about some specific subdivisions where I know something about them. I know there has been an intermix. I know there has been an honest effort, and all that sort of stuff, and I can give you some of that. I can tell you something about what we have been able to do with some of our acquired multi-family projects where we have very carefully carried out our program of trying to make the housing available to all persons. I can give you that. These are the things I have personal knowledge of. I can give you that, but I wish we did have a print-out on what we are doing in this other area.

COMMISSIONER FREEMAN. Thank you

MR. TUGGLE. It would make it much easier for me. I could answer your question and it wouldn't look like I was either stupid or evasive. I don't want to be either one.

CHAIRMAN HANNAH. Are there other questions the Commissioners would like to ask? Mr. Taylor?

MR. TAYLOR. Mr. Tuggle, you indicated earlier that you had very limited discretion in the things that you could do to enforce this order. You also pointed to the fact that FHA has a limited share of the market, or a relatively limited share. I think you said —I am quoting you, or paraphrasing you—that you have to maintain good relations with industry and that anything that would impair that relationship would not help, be self-serving, and so on.

Now, I wondered—you say you have limited discretion in one area, but do you have the discretion to determine what the potential impact of enforcing this order is on FHA's share of the market? Is that your job, or is it your job to enforce the order?

MR. TUGGLE. It is our job to enforce the order, of course. It is also our job to improve housing standards and to try to create as much housing available as possible to all persons, both new and existing.

MR. TAYLOR. But do you have the discretion to go easy in enforcing this order because you think it will diminish FHA's share of the market?

MR. TUGGLE. The question, and I think this is out of context,

Mr. Taylor, was could this office on its own initiative take and require things of the builder, like advertising that he was an equal opportunity. This could be a unilateral decision of the San Francisco Insuring Office, and we do participate in about 50 percent of the new construction.

Now, if this would reduce by half, and I don't know whether it would or wouldn't, I would be hopeful that it wouldn't reduce it by any, but if we would reduce it by some, then I would say that we would probably not be doing the job for the total community as well as we are by meeting the issues as they come forward and providing as much housing as we possibly can in this area.

Our big problem today is to try to find builders who can build within the price range of all of our consumers, because for the last 10 years the cost of producing a new unit of housing has been going up faster than the family income, and, naturally, the people in the lower income groups have suffered more than the people in the higher income groups due to this spread between the cost of producing a new unit of housing and family incomes.

This is a real problem. It is one that is going to create some housing problems for us in the future unless we are able to close this gap to where there is a better relationship between the family incomes and the cost of producing a new unit of housing.

MR. TAYLOR. Well, all I was trying to determine was whether you think you have discretion in enforcing this order to take this factor into consideration. I think you have answered my question on that. Thank you.

CHAIRMAN HANNAH. Thank you very much, Mr. Tuggle. We are grateful to you, and you are excused.

MR. TUGGLE. Thank you, sir.

CHAIRMAN HANNAH. If it is agreeable, we will have one more witness and then we will take a 10-minute break.

Call the next witness.

MR. GLICKSTEIN. Mr. Chairman, before calling the next witness, may I request that the statement of the California Real Estate Association be introduced into the record as Exhibit No. 9?

CHAIRMAN HANNAH. It is so received.

(The document referred to was marked as Exhibit No. 9 and received in evidence.)

MR. GLICKSTEIN. The next witness is Mr. Robert D. Pitts.

(Whereupon, Mr. Robert D. Pitts was sworn by the Chairman and testified as follows:)

TESTIMONY OF MR. ROBERT D. PITTS, MILL VALLEY, CALIFORNIA, REGIONAL ADMINISTRATOR, DEPARTMENT OF HOUSING AND URBAN DEVELOPMENT

MR. GLICKSTEIN. Will you please state your full name and address for the record?

MR. PITTS. My name is Robert D. Pitts. I live at 345 Montford Avenue in Mill Valley, California.

MR. GLICKSTEIN. And what is your occupation, Mr. Pitts?

MR. PITTS. I am the Regional Administrator of the Department of Housing and Urban Development.

MR. GLICKSTEIN. Mr. Pitts, do you have effective control over Federal housing activities in this area, particularly with respect to responsibilities under the Executive order on equal opportunity in housing?

MR. PITTS. It is the responsibility of the Regional Administrator to be responsible for all of the activities of the Department in the region that he supervises.

MR. GLICKSTEIN. Do you feel that you have effective control over the activities in this area that are designed to carry out the President's order on equal opportunity in housing?

MR. PITTS. The question of the effective control I think has to be related to a number of things and if I may take a moment to do so.

You probably recall that the Department of Housing and Urban Development as established now is a fairly new Department. It was organized in an effort to pull together under one head all of the activities of the Federal Government in the field of housing and urban development. The necessity for that pattern of organization grew out of the recognized fact that historically the various programs of the Federal Government in this field had come about through a spasmodic evolution of programs designed to meet certain kinds of specific emergencies. We had reached the stage in this operation where we recognized that the collection of programs passed by Congress in many succeeding years had resulted in not only conflicts between some of the programs but overlapping and some time actual competition between them.

The Department, one of its purposes, sought to pull together in an orderly fashion this historical growth of these various programs.

We are today just about a year and five months old. Within that period of time I can assure you we do not feel that we have reached the point where we have effectively and successfully offset the long evolution of the development of these programs which has occurred in many cases over 35 years.

I can assure you, however, that the Department was designed and pointed in the direction to achieve that aim.

MR. GLICKSTEIN. So whatever remnants of separatism still remain you hope will be eliminated?

MR. PITTS. Sure.

MR. GLICKSTEIN. Is it possible today that the FHA office, for example, in San Francisco is inclined to go to Washington with its problems before it comes to you?

193

MR. PITTS. The FHA operation was one of the more independent operations pulled in under the new organization. The new organization with respect to the Regional Office was patterned due to forces which need not bear here in such a way that we have a sort of quasi-responsibility over the insuring offices, a responsibility which is shared with the Zone Commissioners located in Washington, but leading directly to the Assistant Secretary who is in Washington, and together the Regional Administrator and his own Commissioner seek to develop the kind of supervision over the issuing office of FHA.

MR. GLICKSTEIN. Do you, for example, decide what the budget of the FHA office should be?

MR. PITTS. No.

MR. GLICKSTEIN. Do you have control over the employees in that office regardless of their grade?

MR. PITTS. Not in the insuring offices.

MR. GLICKSTEIN. Some higher grade, higher-paid employees are not under your jurisdiction?

MR. PITTS. That's right.

MR. GLICKSTEIN. About what grade level? Are those generally the policy-making people, would you say, that are not under your jurisdiction?

MR. PITTS. I think it would be significant to point out with respect to that question that we have an Assistant Regional Administrator for FHA whose responsibility is directly to the Regional Administrator. He is a fairly high level official, but this Assistant Regional Administrator is not connected with the local insuring offices to which you refer. His grade is about the same level as that of the director of a local insuring office.

MR. GLICKSTEIN. I see. Mr. Pitts, has your department developed an effective housing program to meet minority needs?

MR. PITTS. The answer is quite clearly no. I am quite sure that you would agree with me that nowhere in this country have we met that question adequately.

MR. GLICKSTEIN. Does the rent supplement program, for example, offer a realistic solution?

MR. PITTS. The rent supplement program certainly moved in a direction that no other program ever passed in this country did. It has been in operation for a relatively short period of time. Most of us are very hopeful that if we can sustain it long enough and get enough experience and cooperation from industry that we will be able to at least go a long ways towards solving this problem.

MR. GLICKSTEIN. Why do you think that this program will provide a realistic solution for the housing problems for minority peoples?

MR. PITTS. I should like to go back to something Mr. Tuggle said which I think is pertinent to this discussion, and that is the simple fact that for the past 20 or 25 years we have had an expanding gap between the cost of housing, particularly in urban areas, and the ability of a large number of people in those areas to pay for it.

It has become quite clear to me, certainly in the large urban centers in this area, and I am sure it is true in other areas, that this gap is likely to widen. The tremendous trend towards technology resulting in a very large—or a very large extent in a sort of stratification of job opportunities forcing a large number of former unskilled and semi-skilled people out of the market. These people are concentrated in cities. This is occurring at the same time that everybody is coming to the city and the competition for land is increasing, and the gap between the cost of housing, when you examine all of the elements that go into this cost, is increasing.

It became absolutely necessary to provide what has never before been provided in this fashion, and that is a kind of subsidy, a housing subsidy, for people who are renting in the private market. The rent supplement, geared as it is to have the Federal Government make a contribution, or a subsidy to individual rents in order to meet the cost of housing in a given community, is a first step in this direction and I think a correct one.

We only have to wait for some experience to see how well we can put it together and do it.

MR. GLICKSTEIN. Mr. Pitts, what has been the response to the Rent Supplement Program and the Section 23 Leased Housing Program in suburban areas?

MR. PITTS. The response to date has not been too good, and I think there are reasons for this.

First of all, as I indicated, it is a new program and it is geared in such a way that it seeks to develop new housing geared to 221(d)(3) program, the FHA program, in such a way to provide for bringing families into standard housing, taking into consideration what they can afford to pay and make up for the difference. Because it is new, and it introduces many new concepts in terms of the production of housing and the acquisition of housing, I think it will take some time for it really to get going, but I believe if we can survive long enough we may eliminate all the rough spots and establish a pattern of utilizing this program that it could be effective.

MR. GLICKSTEIN. Mr. Pitts, as I understand the way these programs work, suburban communities have a veto power over whether rent supplement projects built by private enterprise can be located in their communities. Do you think this is a reasonable thing to do?

MR. PITTS. I am thoroughly convinced at this stage of my understanding of this business, and certainly it has been evidenced in many instances, that if we began to give the total society the power to veto the ability of an individual to find housing anywhere, we are in trouble.

I think we would be very naive if we did not recognize the basic fact behind what we are discussing, and that is to a very large extent the housing market is still obsessed with the concept of race. The very existence of this Commission I think is indication of it.

Those of us who have been in this business for some years have been affected to the extent that we could operate because of it. We have in recent years had certain kinds of legislation, certain kinds of actions taken both at the Federal level and at State level in some cases and in certain localities which sought to adjust this kind of thing. In few instances have these acts been taken by the broadside cooperation of large segments of the general public. I am quite sure that any step wherever it has occurred, where the general public has to take action on these sort of things, until such time as we can alter that climate, I suspect that we will move very slowly

MR. GLICKSTEIN. So you think that this veto power that is given to suburban communities could really be a great roadblock in the way of——

MR. PITTS. I am convinced of it.

MR. GLICKSTEIN. I have no further questions, Mr. Chairman.

VICE CHAIRMAN PATTERSON. Father Hesburgh?

COMMISSIONER HESBURGH. No questions.

VICE CHAIRMAN PATTERSON. Mrs. Freeman?

COMMISSIONER FREEMAN. I have no questions.

VICE CHAIRMAN PATTERSON. Dr. Rankin?

Mr. Taylor?

MR. TAYLOR. Could you spell out a little bit more for me, Mr. Pitts, why FHA isn't more vigorous and effective in enforcing the housing Executive order? We have referred to a lot of testimony to lead some of us to the conclusion that it isn't very vigorous or effective at this point.

MR. PITTS. I think some of the testimony would tend to suggest some of the efforts that are being made. Let me go back again to the background of this business.

FHA, like every other Federal agency, stemmed from a society that had been largely conditioned to the thing that we are concerned about today. The nature of its personnel, if it had been any different from that of a cross-section of society, would have been most surprising. The nature of the people who put the institution together, if it had been any different from that of a cross-section of society, would have been surprising. I am not the least bit surprised that down its history some sharp questions have arisen with respect to the actions of FHA and its policies and programs in this field.

One of the things that I am equally assured of is that in recent years positive steps have been made to move away from that position. I think some of them were indicated in the actions of Mr. Tuggle.

MR. TAYLOR. But it is your feeling—or I take it that it is your feeling—that it is still too closely identified with the industry that it is supposed to be regulating, assisting as well as regulating?

MR. PITTS. Historically it has been industry-orientated and it has not been public-orientated.

MR. TAYLOR. Do you feel that Federal contract compliance efforts have been effective in the field of construction contracts, efforts to achieve equal opportunity in employment?

MR. PITTS. Here, too, we have been moving in this same climate and we have been moving at about the same slow pace growing out of the same conditions, and here, too, I think in recent years we began to move away from that. There has been some strong evidence at least in time of what the agencies are doing within the framework of their capability to do. I think that there is some strong evidence that this is true. Certainly in housing I don't think there is any question about it. With respect to the contracting with outside agencies, I think a close examination of the system which has been set up to carry out this leaves some very sharp questions as to whether or not we have reached this stage yet where we can effectively do this.

MR. TAYLOR. Are you saying that you don't believe that the Federal program is credible to contractors, that they don't believe the sanctions will be invoked?

MR. PITTS. I am saying I don't think we quite have yet either the kind of organizational pattern or the kind of steps spelled out to assure the kind of compliance that we would like to get and that is implied in the Executive order.

MR. TAYLOR. I have no further questions, Mr. Chairman, but I would like to thank Mr. Pitts because I do know that he has had to do some considerable rearranging of his schedule in order to appear here today.

MR. PITTS. Thank you.

VICE CHAIRMAN PATTERSON. Thank you very much, Mr. Pitts. You are excused. The hearing will stand in recess for 10 minutes.

CHAIRMAN HANNAH. Call the next witness, please.

MR. GLICKSTEIN. The next two witnesses are the Reverend Larry Jack Wong and Judge Harry Low.

(Whereupon, the REVEREND LARRY JACK WONG and JUDGE HARRY LOW were sworn by the Chairman and testified as follows:)

197

TESTIMONY OF JUDGE HARRY W. LOW, SAN FRANCISCO, CALIFORNIA AND THE REVEREND LARRY JACK WONG, SAN FRANCISCO, CALIFORNIA

MR. GLICKSTEIN. Would you each please state your full name and your address for the record?

JUDGE LOW. My name is Harry W. Low. My address is 104 Turquoise Way, San Francisco, California.

REV. WONG. I am Larry Jack Wong. I live at 331 Spruce.

MR. GLICKSTEIN. Would you each also please state your occupations?

JUDGE LOW. I am a judge of the municipal court for the city and county of San Francisco.

REV. WONG. I am an ordained clergyman of the United Presbyterian Church of San Francisco. Until recently I was the area director of the Chinatown-North Beach office of the San Francisco Economics Opportunities Program.

MR. GLICKSTEIN. Judge Low, would you briefly tell the Commission about the history of the Chinese in San Francisco?

JUDGE LOW. Yes. The first Chinese to arrive in California was before 1850 but there were maybe only a dozen or so before 1850. It was not until about 1852 during the period of the Gold Rush, during the period when there was extensive building of the railroads here in the West, that the need for Chinese laborers brought about a huge influx of Chinese into California and practically all of them settled here in San Francisco or in little communities throughout California. In fact, there are many little towns where there were at one time very large Chinese settlements. There are towns, such as Chinese Camp, which is known for a large settlement of Chinese.

Throughout the Mother Lode there are many areas of California where there were large settlements of Chinese.

In the 1850's and 1860's there were as many as 15,000 Chinese here in San Francisco. The population of Chinese went up and down and there was a great loss in numbers during the 1880's when there were very serious anti-Chinese pieces of legislation as well as anti-Chinese movements and many of the Chinese either went back or by natural attrition the population went down.

At the present time in San Francisco there are some 55,000–50,000 Chinese living in San Francisco and throughout the State of California, somewhere in the neighborhood of, oh, 250,000 to 300,000 Chinese, but the largest settlements are right here in the Bay Area.

MR. GLICKSTEIN. Has the Federal Government and the State of California treated Chinese immigrants differently from immigrants from other countries?

JUDGE LOW. Yes, I think historically in California there has been a little different treatment and I use that to indicate that in the past there has been considerable discrimination against Chinese.

Some of this might be illustrated in a very early case here in California called People vs. Hall, a decision that was about 1858, in which our California Supreme Court came out with a ruling that Chinese could not be witnesses in a court of law. The opinion came out with some statements that it is a race that is marked as inferior, incapable of progress, and between whom and ourselves, nature has imposed an impassable difference, and this was sort of the type of attitude that persisted during the periods through about 1900.

You may be interested to know that some of the first marks of the discriminatory legislation in schools and the area of public employment were directed against Orientals. Orientals could not work for any public corporation or for the State of California. Orientals had separate but equal schools in California. About the only cases in California were cases that arose out of the Federal courts here in the West involving discriminatory legislation against Chinese in the educational field. One of the latest separate but equal schools decisions was as late as 1902, a decision out of the Federal courts here. So that part of the legislation, State legislation, was highly discriminatory against Orientals and many of these provisions were not removed until about 1947.

In the area of Federal legislation, of course, the anti-immigration legislation was highly inflammatory and highly discriminatory against Orientals. I think that the quota up until 1963 or '64, when the immigration laws were changed, was as low as 105, 105 immigrants, from the Orient, from China in particular, as well as what we call the Asia Pacific Triangle provision which said that any Oriental, any person who had more than 50 percent of his blood identified as an Oriental, though he might have been a citizen of England or Peru or some South American country, he was still classified as an Oriental subject to the 105 quota. And I think that this was a very marked piece of Federal legislation against Orientals. Fortunately, this has been largely altered by the change in the immigration laws in the last few years.

I think an illustration of the discriminatory attitude against Orientals which might have come to the minds of many of the Commissioners here today that was the Supreme Court's decision very recently which allowed the Japanese to regain some of the confiscated money that was taken away from them when the Japanese were relocated in these "relocation centers" which the Japanese referred to as concentration camps. Some of the comments that were made during that very inflammatory period of 1942 were attributed to very leading government officials throughout the country, including our own Governor Warren, and Governor Clark of Idaho, who said that Japanese breed like rats, live like rats, and so forth. The comparison was quite a shocking display of Federal attitude.

MR. GLICKSTEIN. Reverend Wong, would you please describe for the Commissioners the Chinese community in San Francisco? For example, how many people of Chinese ancestry are here and where do they live?

REV. WONG. Yes, I would, Mr. Counsel, if I can make one comment on Judge Low's reply on the matter of immigration.

As far as the Chinese-Americans are concerned in the contemporary civil rights movement, for the Chinese-Americans, for the Orientals, when we talk about civil rights, the nub of the civil rights is centered or focused on the matter of immigration. While other citizens were fighting to gain the rights as citizens in this country, we were fighting for the rights to get in and the rights to stay. Having said this, I will proceed on to the other question.

There are approximately 30,000 Chinese-Americans living in the northeast sector of the city of San Francisco known as the Chinatown-North Beach area. Among this concentration of some 30,000, the core of Chinatown is centered around 12 blocks. The heart of it would be between California and Broadway south and north, Kearny to the east and approximately Mason to the west. There are numerous problems within this particular community. To say that it is a community is one way of saying it. To say it is a ghetto is also another way of saying it, for Chinatown is one of the earliest ghettos in San Francisco and in all of California.

This is perhaps the most misrepresented, the most overlooked, and the most neglected area in the whole of San Francisco and perhaps in the whole of the country, in that there has been a tremendous amount of myth built up regarding the Chinese in America, that they take care of their own, that there is no problem within the community, that everything is quite well, and, as a matter of fact, if you ask us today to substantiate some of the problems we would be hard put to substantiate with data. The community is so neglected that there has not been an adequate comprehensive study of the problems within that community to enable us even to argue a point, to put forth a case.

The most serious problem I would put forth is the problem of language. There are approximately 10,000 to 14,000 people in that community who are handicapped by the language facilities or the lack of the language facilities. This would get in the way of education, and very, very seriously in the area of employment.

MR. GLICKSTEIN. What does the San Francisco Unified School District do to meet this language problem?

REV. WONG. The San Francisco Unified School District has a program of adult education throughout the city and also in this particular area. However, as sincere, as hard as the Unified School has tried, they have not been meeting the problem adequately. I would say that part of the problem or the failure or the weakness within this attempt is that the Unified Schools system is some 50 years behind times in terms of approaching teaching the foreign language or teaching English as a foreign language rather than the primary language, teaching English as a second language to those of foreign-born and those with another primary language. Therefore, those who have gone through the Unified School within this system come out inadequately prepared.

JUDGE LOW. I might say that the situation is getting increasingly worse because of the recent legislation which does allow the unification of families and a liberalization of the immigration laws which is a very desirable and humanitarian act on the part of the Federal Government. The situation is compounded because we are witnessing some 3,000 to 8,000 new immigrants coming into the area, many of them settling here in San Francisco.

MR. GLICKSTEIN. Is that 3,000 to 8,000 per year?

JUDGE LOW. Per year. And this is building up. I think that the language center that has been set up in San Francisco takes only about 90 students. The public school system is very inadequate and the private sources are always going from hand to mouth and wondering whether they can maintain an existence from semester to semester and any way you add up the figures the situation is totally inadequate for the problems that are now facing the community.

MR. GLICKSTEIN. Judge Low, Reverend Wong mentioned, described the Chinatown area as a ghetto. Do you believe that there is overt discrimination in housing against Chinese-Americans?

JUDGE LOW. Yes, I would say there is. There are areas still in San Francisco where it is very difficult for a Chinese person or any Oriental person to move into. There are areas in the suburbs which were subjects of picketing just as recently as last year because they would not allow Orientals to buy.

MR. GLICKSTEIN. Where was this?

JUDGE LOW. In—

REV. WONG. Serramonte.

JUDGE LOW. Serramonte, which is about, oh—

MR. GLICKSTEIN. We have heard a little bit about Serramonte.

JUDGE LOW. Two miles south of San Francisco. I would say from a non-overt standpoint, from the silent treatment standpoint, this is much more serious.

REV. WONG. I would refuse to live in that windy area. However, discrimination in housing is much closer than that, in that on Union Street very recently, a couple of months ago, one of the directors—or coordinators—of a project within the EOC attempted to rent a place on Union Street and was told that Orientals were not welcome because they would—if they were allowed, then other minorities would be coming at the door. So this is the kind of discrimination, both overt and subtle, that the Chinese people are still suffering with in the city.

MR. GLICKSTEIN. Judge Low, is there much discrimination in the area of employment?

JUDGE LOW. I believe there is. It is a two-fold problem, one of the qualifications of those who seek employment, and also the overt discrimination against them.

The most serious problem relates to membership in some of the better unions in the city and county of San Francisco, though I think some of them are starting little programs here and there to allow a few Orientals to enter. The fact is, there are very, very few that actually are admitted to these unions, and then I am sure there are very serious examples of employers who will not and do not allow Orientals to be employed. These are not done in the manner which would allow the State FEPC to take some affirmative action but, nevertheless, you just don't see Orientals working in these places, and I am sure that there is discrimination.

MR. GLICKSTEIN. Have the unions made efforts to unionize employers in the Chinatown area?

JUDGE LOW. Yes, they have. It is a very—in fact, there is now a program to unionize a good deal of Chinatown. It has met with a little bit of difficulty and great reluctance on the part of the community to give it much support and the unionization has proceeded very, very slowly.

There is also fear that there will be a great social upset in the employment pattern in the Chinese community and so the Chinese have not really given it full support either.

MR. GLICKSTEIN. When you say there would be great social upset, what do you mean by that?

JUDGE LOW. I mean that people who are now being employed in these sewing factories and these garment shops, in the hotels and restaurants in Chinatown, may find great difficulty in finding other kinds of employment. They are subject to sort of an economic compaction right in the Chinese community. They are locked in. They can't really find employment anyplace else. So if there were a mass unionization right away, many of these people would not be able to find other kinds of employment.

MR. GLICKSTEIN. You are suggesting that if companies would unionize their wages would go up to such an extent that some of them would go out of business and people would be unemployed?

JUDGE LOW. That is part of it, plus the short-term effect upon the workers themselves, that they would not be able to find any other kind of employment in a unionized place, that they can only work where there is a "non-union" type of operation.

MR. GLICKSTEIN. Reverend Wong?

REV. WONG. Mr. Counsel, I think this is also a demonstration of a people in a community that is reluctant to accept unionization or organization or any kind of imposition of a program from a group or a company or an agency or even the State or Federal Government upon a particular community and upon a people.

The unions, as far as I know, have not really involved the community in terms of its desire to organize the Chinese community and the workers within it. They have not actually understood the problems within the community and the problems that are creating the kinds of underpaid or the kind of discrimination or the kind of problems that now exist within the community.

As early as 1964, the Greater Chinatown Community Service Organization has fought, as a matter of fact, as early as 1963, has made attempts to communicate with Mr. Mazzola, the business manager of the Plumbers Union, in an attempt to meet with him and to discuss with him the matters of the problems of unions and membership of the Chinese people within that union. We have been unable through several attempts, to even get as far as an appointment with Mr. Mazzola. To this date we have not yet met with Mr. Mazzola.

Now, in terms of the overall problems of employment, I mentioned that this is related also to language. In this particular society, the primary language is English. Many of those who come from the Orient are either handicapped or have no English facilities at all. Whether you call it skills or whether you call it training or whether you call it discrimination, I think it is all in the same bag in that people are prevented from employment opportunities because they lack the language or they lack skills or they lack the trade. But, nevertheless, the fact is they are prevented from that kind of employment opportunities and there is no provision adequate to provide for the kind of language training to enable the people to participate in the mainstream of employment opportunities.

MR. GLICKSTEIN. Reverend Wong, you were with the Poverty Program. What do you think the impact of the Poverty Program has been on the Chinese community in San Francisco?

REV. WONG. The impact of the Economic Opportunities Program is one of opening up doors and visions and perhaps made a few dreams come true, although not in the manner that we would like to have it done. Within the year and a half of the program, we have created an English Language Center, which Judge Low mentioned just briefly a while ago, in which we have attempted to supplement the efforts of the Unified school in the area of adult education.

As a matter of fact, I think in the short year and a half we have demonstrated that this particular program, using the most recent skills and material written by the center itself, is much more effective than the system that has been in operation for a number of generations.

However, we are faced with the threat of reduction of funds at every point. We are faced with innumerable kinds of problems regarding the security of that particular program and the continuation of that program, much less the expansion of that program, which is very much needed.

JUDGE LOW. I might just throw in a couple of statistics here that may be of some interest to the Commissioners on the seriousness of the poverty situation in the North Beach-Chinatown area.

Some 40 percent of the residents in that area fall within the Poverty Program classification. Is that less than $3,000, is it—

REV. WONG. The next is $4,000.

JUDGE LOW. Earning less than $4,000 a year. There are 85 percent of the men and the women who have never gone to high school in the Chinatown area. Over 58 percent of the women must work in some kind of employment in the Chinatown area and these are women over the age of 14, and they are all in the working force of some kind, either part-time or full-time.

We have a very high TB rate in San Francisco. Health problems are very serious there, inadequate facilities plus the congestion of people. We have the highest density of people in San Francisco crowded into the Chinatown area. This creates very serious health problems.

San Francisco, as some of you may know, claims the distinction of being the city with the highest suicide rate. Well, Chinatown is the area of San Francisco with the highest suicide rate in the city.

We have many other problems. The housing situation is really quite terrible in the community, that we have the highest rents for the least amount of space right there in Chinatown. This is due to the heavy demands and the lack of space.

All of these statistics kind of point out to you how much the poverty people have to do with what little they have been given to do this very monumental task.

REV. WONG. I think in addition to this it is the whole matter of the new concept in community participation, which might be called community organization, so that people would begin to participate. For the most part, the Chinese who come from Southern China, and this is the majority of the people in America, the concept of community participation is very much lacking among these people. These people have been taught and trained to be somewhat of an individualist, that they are responsible for themselves, for their immediate family and perhaps for their kin, and this is the scope of their community responsibility. They have had no experience in terms of participation in the mainstream of decision making, in terms of participation and taking part in the ongoing political structure and the political life of a community. So that for the Chinese in America, participation in this way, in this manner, is totally new. It is a new concept altogether, and so that for the Chinese in this country, we are not even able to produce the kind of organizations to put pressure on the political structure to identify the problems, and certainly to get any action on the particular problems.

So that it is a cause for real concern and disturbance, because in this particular society today there seems to be a kind of mania, a kind of an attitude that spreads around until a group of people produces a riot, the country and the political structure among its officials do not take a close look and give enough attention or to do anything about a particular problem within any kind of an area. This is demonstrated time and time again across the country, demonstrated certainly last year in Hunters Point where the Negro people have been saying all along there is a tremendous problem in Hunters Point, but no attention, no adequate attention, has been given to Hunters Point until it rioted.

This happens also in Detroit, in Rochester, and you name the cities. For the Chinese in this particular country, perhaps we will never come to a point of creating a riot or having a riot; but, nevertheless, we are very much concerned about the kind of problems that are captivating and enslaving people within a particular community, and that with or without a riot we need to have these kinds of problems attended to and solved.

MR. GLICKSTEIN. Reverend Wong, has there been much cooperation among the Chinese-American, Spanish-speaking and Negro communities in San Francisco?

REV. WONG. Generally speaking, in terms of the total community, I would say that there is a lot of room for greater activity, much more activity and a much greater amount of cooperation and intergroup relations. However, there are a number of us who have been involved in the intergroup activities with the Spanish-speaking community and with the Negro community in the city. I think this has been one of the most enlightening, one of the most exciting kind of ventures that I have had the privilege of experiencing within the city of my associations with the Negro community and with the Spanish-speaking community, as well as with other groups within the city.

MR. GLICKSTEIN. I have no further questions, Mr. Chairman.

CHAIRMAN HANNAH. I would like to ask a question or two. I am a little bit surprised by what you have to say about the degree of discrimination that continues against Orientals here. We recognize that with the considerable number of immigrants with no skill in English, that they pose a real problem. It is a little unclear to me why when you were describing the discrimination of Orientals, whether you were talking primarily about these new arrivals without skill in English or whether you meant to imply that the same situation exists with Chinese that have been in this country for generations and speak good English and have acquired the skills for which there is a demand in our society.

Would you speak a little more to that.

JUDGE LOW. Yes.

Mr. Chairman, the problem is one of the recurring or a type of treadmill type of situation where those who are born and raised and educated in a ghetto, such as Chinatown, are exposed only to Chinese students, and we have three junior highs close—at least 75 percent Oriental. We have several elementary schools that are 98 percent Oriental, Chinese, and many—several others that are well over 50 percent Oriental, where they are with Chinese practically all the time and who do not go on to a college education, who do not participate in some other outside activity that takes them out of the area.

Their facility in the English language is greatly impaired. Their exposure to the rest of the community and the ideals and the needs and accomplishments of others in the community is very, very limited, and this also limits their opportunity to rise above that.

And so we have sort of a complex problem of both the new immigrants, as well as those who have lived in this community for several generations, that they are hampered by this language problem, as well as being hampered by employment and housing and everything that goes with it, because they cannot get education, employment, and, therefore, the other good things in life that would come with better education and better employment opportunities.

CHAIRMAN HANNAH. The reason for my question, I am sure you recognize, is that in much of the country prior to World War II where certainly Orientals, Chinese, Japanese, and so on, were generally not understood by the predominant population, this was pretty well taken care of at the end of the war. I think most of our countrymen were thoroughly ashamed of the attitude that was exhibited toward the Japanese and other Orientals in California and elsewhere, and where the Chinese particularly have been dispersed, not very many in any one area, and because of a long and distinguished cultural background, the interest in education, and so on, most of us have been inclined to think that the change in attitude toward the Oriental in most of America is a demonstration of what can happen because, whether in this generation, in 20, 25 years, the Orientals are completely acceptable. There is no problem of jobs, employment, housing or anything else, but you are telling us that here that that is no longer the case or never was the case?

JUDGE LOW. I am saying that—I think what you said is right

about areas outside the concentrated segments of Chinatown here in San Francisco. That did occur, there was a rapid amount of integration and participation in almost the totally integrated society by the Chinese, and I think this is true throughout the central valley and other areas of California.

But here, right here in San Francisco, we have had this problem, and it is being compounded by the fact that there is a heavy increase in the immigration that has concentrated or aggravated the problem right here in San Francisco.

CHAIRMAN HANNAH. One of you indicated that in this—I think you referred to it as the Chinese ghetto, where the housing is very bad and people are crowded together, too little space, and poor housing facilities, who are the landlords? Who owns the housing? Are these Chinese that own the housing and take advantage of other Chinese, or are these other people?

REV. WONG. The answer to that question, Mr. Chairman, is that there are both kinds. There are those who are owned by the Chinese and there are also—there are many who are absentee landlords, but I would like to further comment on the question you asked earlier in terms of the Chinese opportunity, in terms of employment in San Francisco, as well as across the country, and I can speak to this question from personal, first-hand experience.

When I graduated from seminary, within the recruiting period a month before graduation, I was told by the recruiters that no congregation in America was quite ready to accept me as their pastor and, therefore, it would behoove me to look for a Chinese pastorate or an Indian pastorate or go into missions.

Now, this was within the structure of the church, and I have experienced this more recently in other ways. I said I was until recently the area director. I am currently unemployed and have been looking for a job and have been testing some people. I am still unemployed.

CHAIRMAN HANNAH. Let me ask you one further question and then I will desist.

You indicated that there were several thousand Chinese immigrants into this area each year?

REV. WONG. Yes. Our latest research on this, in 1966, there were approximately seven—a little over 7,000 who came into the country and approximately 45 to 50 percent of that number stayed within the Bay Area.

CHAIRMAN HANNAH. And there is no tendency for them to disperse? Once they join the Chinese community here the tendency is to stay here. Is that correct?

REV. WONG. Well, Mr. Chairman, San Francisco is Chinatown, No. 1, is the mecca for the Chinese. There are a number of reasons, that those who come without the language facilities are coming also to a new country, to a new neighborhood. They have the inclination to look for the kind of neighborhood and people that would give them the kind of security, financially, socially and otherwise, and so they look for the largest concentration of the Chinese, and look for that particular community to settle, at least for the first few years.

CHAIRMAN HANNAH. Where are these immigrants coming from, Hong Kong, Taiwan?

REV. WONG. Hong Kong and other places. Mainly Hong Kong.

CHAIRMAN HANNAH. And with no English skill when they come?

REV. WONG. Well, some of them have had some English training, but learning English from a Chinese Hong Kong-ese is like learning German from an American and try to go over to Germany and function in Germany. I have had two years of Spanish and I can't speak a word of it.

CHAIRMAN HANNAH. A very small fraction of people living in Hong Kong speak English, even though it has been part of the English colonial system for more than 100 years. Father Hesburgh?

COMMISSIONER HESBURGH. Judge Low, when we were here in 1960, the then chief of police mentioned that the Chinese community, contrary to popular myth across the country, was in fact the most law-abiding segment of San Francisco. He said he had been in charge of the homicide division for over a dozen years and hadn't had a single case of a murder, say, among the Chinese. Is that still true?

JUDGE LOW. I think that the record is very good as far as criminal acts in the Chinese community being very few. I think even at the present scale with this rapid increase of crime, this is still a proud fact of the Chinese community, that there is not much crime, but, as in other areas where the kids are becoming a little more "Americanized," there is a rise in antisocial behavior for some reason or another.

And also I think there have been other problems due to the fact that we do have this education, housing, and employment problem, particularly with the newer immigrants. Too, because you have so many working mothers, I think that 20 percent of the women who are working have children under the age of six, we are witnessing a very serious increase in juvenile delinquency in the Chinese community.

COMMISSIONER HESBURGH. I would like to ask a question of Reverend Wong if I might. Do you find that the segregation in the schools, and now we are talking of segregation among Chinese, is an impairment to their education for living in this country?

REV. WONG. I would say yes in that there are two factors at least involved in this. One is that we have long known to be possessors of a Chinatown accent, that the kind of speech, English speech, coming out of the community of students educated within that community is very distinguishable.

COMMISSIONER HESBURGH. Is there any Chinese taught in the school or is it all in English?

REV. WONG. Pardon?

COMMISSIONER HESBURGH. Is the whole course in these schools in English?

REV. WONG. In English.

COMMISSIONER HESBURGH. Is there any Chinese taught?

REV. WONG. Chinese is taught in the Chinese language schools after the regular schools, but these are privately owned schools.

COMMISSIONER HESBURGH. Do most of these Chinese youngsters know Chinese?

REV. WONG. I think there are a number of youngsters still going to the Chinese schools, but the number has been decreasing.

COMMISSIONER HESBURGH. One remark that Dr. Hannah made that might be a way out of this problem to some extent, although I realize you have your local problem here. I would guess that perhaps the largest nationality in our university teaching of the professors that don't happen to be, say, Americans, is Chinese. We have an enormous number, it seems, compared to other nationalities, teaching in the university, and I think that would be true of Michigan State.

CHAIRMAN HANNAH. It is true.

COMMISSIONER HESBURGH. Especially in science, mathematics and these areas, engineering, even in business. We have a number of Chinese professors in the business school. So I would think the opportunity for a breakthrough here is tremendous if the youngsters could take advantage of the free schooling here in the State of California.

REV. WONG. Yes, I am sure that this is perhaps so, but this is really less than a Band-aid.

COMMISSIONER HESBURGH. Yes.

REV. WONG. To the kind of problems we are talking about.

You asked the question, and I said there were two factors, at least, and the other factor is the matter earlier of the question of intergroup relationships where students or youngsters are used to associating and dealing only with one type of people. The preparation to deal with the broader community then becomes inadequate, and I say these are the two disadvantages in terms of segregated schools.

COMMISSIONER HESBURGH. Well, they are exactly the two we find with Negro segregated schools, too.

REV. WONG. That's right.

COMMISSIONER HESBURGH. It is an interesting comparison. Thank you.

CHAIRMAN HANNAH. Mr. Patterson?

VICE CHAIRMAN PATTERSON. Reverend Wong, you mentioned the difficulty of achieving unified Chinese-American political action. Does this indicate that there is an apathy among the voters, that there is little Chinese-Americans voting, or does it indicate instead that it is difficult to organize the Chinese-Americans so that they vote in their self-interest?

REV. WONG. There is no apathy in terms of the participation in voting. Even those who do not know the language well enough to do anything less than put a cross on the ballot participate in that area, but there is a serious problem in the area of organized political action where the kind of needed pressure, needed political pressure, can be brought to bear to effect decisions, to effect the dollars to be placed in the solving of problems.

VICE CHAIRMAN PATTERSON. But the vote itself is usually cast in the Chinese self-interest? Suppose that you have two candidates, one of whom is clearly a friend of the Chinese-American, and the other who is not. Would the Chinese-American community vote with some unanimity in that case?

REV. WONG. I have heard very, very few candidates who have come out on a platform that they are not friends of anybody in any political campaign.

VICE CHAIRMAN PATTERSON. Judge Low, do you have any—

JUDGE LOW. I was going to say that part of the problem in the Chinese community may be due to the philosophy of some of the Chinese themselves. I think that there is a large degree of apathy in the Chinese community on getting involved in community problems, and part of this may be the philosophy of saving face.

One doesn't admit that he has a serious housing or employment or educational problem, or the philosophy of "We take care of our own" or the philosophy of non-involvement. I think this is a difficulty in the Chinese community to do the things that Reverend Wong seemed to suggest, that maybe what we need is a big Yellow Power riot in the Chinese community to get a little more attention to some of the problems there. I say that rather facetiously, but I do think there is a degree of apathy that must be overcome internally to solve some of these problems.

CHAIRMAN HANNAH. Mrs. Freeman?

COMMISSIONER FREEMAN. Reverend Wong, I would like to suggest to you that the right to equality of opportunity is personal in an individual, and I would like to—it doesn't have to be pursued by the group.

I would like to go to the point that you made about the exclusion of the Chinese from the Plumbers Union.

This was a plumber who was qualified to pursue his trade and who was excluded from the union. The extent to which he had sought employment within a contractor who had a Government contract, a consideration was given to this, or that you would seek the remedy of the Fair Employment Law of the State of California, or the Director of Contract Compliance of the Department of Labor. Has that been done?

REV. WONG. I was speaking, Mrs. Freeman, of membership within the Plumbers Union earlier. That is, Mr. Mazzola is the business manager of the Plumbers Union, and that our community has been seeking to persuade the Plumbers Union to open up its membership to the minority people.

As far as we know, there are two members of the Chinese-American people within the Plumbers Union. Those two members were placed on there after much publicity and much protest, and they were placed on there as a personal favor to a member of the community. We do not feel that this is particularly an act of justice, an act of equal opportunity, but the matter of pursuing the problems through the proper channels, yes. We have worked with the Human Rights Commission. We have worked with the FEPC and others.

COMMISSIONER FREEMAN. You indicated that 40 percent of the residents—either you or Judge Low indicated that 40 percent of the residents—are at the poverty level. About how many of those persons would be underemployed?

REV. WONG. The only answer, Mrs. Freeman, that I could give to you is that the community, as far as employment is concerned, the primary problem is not unemployment but rather it is underemployment.

COMMISSIONER FREEMAN. That is what I mean. About how many of them are?

REV. WONG. I also said that the community is also hung up on the lack of data and the lack of research on the matter of problems. This is one of the areas where we are not able to present a substantiating data to prove the case. We have not had the resources to do that kind of study and the employment department in the State of California has not really studied that particular problem either.

COMMISSIONER FREEMAN. Recently the Department of Labor did a study of sub-employment in the San Francisco area and I wondered to what extent the Department could do such a study with respect to the Chinese community.

REV. WONG. We would welcome that kind of study or any other kind of study that would be helpful. The recent study included two areas, the Mission and the Western Addition. We didn't get in on it, in other words.

CHAIRMAN HANNAH. Dr. Rankin?

COMMISSIONER RANKIN. Judge Low, what percentage of the new immigrants fall about the poverty level, would you say?

JUDGE LOW. I would say 95 percent of them.

COMMISSIONER RANKIN. Ninety-five percent.

JUDGE LOW. Yes, the type of employment that is immediately available to these people who come in—

COMMISSIONER RANKIN. Do they come with very little money?

JUDGE LOW. With virtually no money, and are supported by a relative. Almost all of these are part of the program of uniting families. So a relative really supports them for a period.

COMMISSIONER RANKIN. Does the Chinese community as a community have any program to look after these new arrivals?

JUDGE LOW. There are several programs. There are several community centers and some of the family associations do what they can to help these people adjust to the new community, but outside of these it is very, very inadequate. The situation is quite bad. In some new kind of program, some re-examination of the situation must be made very soon.

COMMISSIONER RANKIN. Do they have the same problem in Hawaii?

JUDGE LOW. I am really not familiar with that, Mr. Rankin.

COMMISSIONER RANKIN. Reverend Wong, do you know, or do they—is the treatment different there or do they—is there less concentration?

REV. WONG. I have been in Hawaii twice, Mr. Rankin, and never gotten on shore. So I don't know anything about the problems.

JUDGE LOW. I would tend to think that most of the immigrants are coming here to San Francisco or to California rather than to Hawaii, and the figures that we have show that the vast majority of these—not the vast majority but a majority of these immigrants are coming to areas right here in the Bay Area.

COMMISSIONER RANKIN. And could I ask—it might be a personal question—you two gentlemen speak English well. You have been successful, and all that. How have you been different from the usual Chinese? What changed you or what made it possible for you to get this education and become judges and ministers?

JUDGE LOW. In my personal situation I was born and raised in a small town in Central California.

COMMISSIONER RANKIN. And that was to an advantage?

JUDGE LOW. And our family was the only Chinese family in that little community for 25 years, and I think that this, though I came to this area and adopted this area and got involved in the community in sort of a fast clip, I think that that was an invaluable thing to me, that by accident I was born and raised in a small community.

REV. WONG. I am sort of the opposite. I was born in China and came over as a youngster and grew up in Fresno, sort of an integrated community. When I decided to become a preacher I also decided that most congregations would not want to learn Chinese. So I learned English.

COMMISSIONER RANKIN. I see.

CHAIRMAN HANNAH. Mr. Taylor?

MR. TAYLOR. No questions.

CHAIRMAN HANNAH. Thank you very much, gentlemen. We appreciate your being with us. Mr. Glickstein, would you call the next witness?

MR. GLICKSTEIN. The next witness is Dr. Carlton Goodlett.

(Whereupon, Dr. Carlton Goodlett was sworn by the Chairman and testified as follows:)

TESTIMONY OF DR. CARLTON GOODLETT, SAN FRANCISCO, CALIFORNIA

MR. GLICKSTEIN. Dr. Goodlett, would you please state your full name and address for the record?

DR. GOODLETT. My name is Carlton B. Goodlett, 1360 Turk Street, San Francisco, California.

MR. GLICKSTEIN. And what is your occupation?

DR. GOODLETT. I am a registered psychologist and a physician and surgeon, holding the degrees of Ph.D. in psychology and M.D. in medicine.

MR. GLICKSTEIN. Have you held offices in any civic or business groups?

DR. GOODLETT. Well, I was for five years president of the San Francisco Branch of the NAACP and I am on the board of directors of the San Francisco Bay Area Boy Scouts; formerly on the Bay Area board of the American Red Cross and involved in a number of business activities.

MR. GLICKSTEIN. Dr. Goodlett, we understand that you were a candidate for Governor of California. What prompted you to run for Governor?

DR. GOODLETT. Well, I happened to know that Edmund G. Brown was in trouble and I felt that it was time for someone in the Democratic Party to talk sense to the people of California, and I decided to run on the basis of redefining and discussing issues that I thought would be challenging to California and to America in this part of the 20th century.

MR. GLICKSTEIN. Was your candidacy intended to achieve aims other than your election; for example, mobilizing the Negro community?

DR. GOODLETT. Well, my candidacy certainly was realistic enough to realize that I would not be elected Governor, but political campaigns exist for a number of purposes other than winning elections. They exist for the purpose of educating the electorate, and I feel that my campaign in some small measure participated in that endeavor.

MR. GLICKSTEIN. Were you appealing to the white and Negro communities?

DR. GOODLETT. Yes, I was appealing to those Californians who felt in the need more direction in politics in this State and we thought that it would be best to enroll in the efforts of the Democratic Party to achieve the same.

MR. GLICKSTEIN. Dr. Goodlett, what do you view as the principal problems and concerns of the Negro community in the Bay Area?

DR. GOODLETT. Well, the basic problems of the Negro people in the Bay Area and throughout the country is to obtain an implementation in the acts of the majority group justice and justice as an umbrella under which we can have a rule by law and not by men, personalities.

MR. GLICKSTEIN. How would you define that problem more specifically in terms of, for example, housing, education, and jobs?

DR. GOODLETT. Well, I am amazed by the fact that most public officials speak very dramatically about law and order and they demand the enforcement of the law, but I think an error is made in that we haven't created an umbrella of justice before we can demand law and order, and as long as American Negroes and other minorities are ghettoized and equal housing opportunities are denied to them, there can be no law and order in the area of housing, in equality, in the area of education, in the area of fair employment practices and even in the area of police brutality. Until we demand of every citizen the removal of injustice, we can't mouth the political cliché that there should be law and order, because there will be no law and order if we do not buttress it with justice in the land.

MR. GLICKSTEIN. You mentioned as long as Negro Americans are ghettoized. Are you in favor of programs that would disperse the Negro communities and mix up Negro families with white families?

DR. GOODLET. Well, I am in favor of a program of equal housing opportunity that gives every American the right to live where he desires, and if a man decides to live in contiguity with people of the same race or who have the same languages, this is their business. I think for political power that living in congregated areas certainly encourages representation in government, but this is a problem for the electorate to decide.

MR. GLICKSTEIN. I take it that you believe that Negroes don't live in ghetto areas out of choice?

DR. GOODLETT. I didn't get that question.

MR. GLICKSTEIN. I said I take it that you believe that Negroes don't live in ghetto areas out of choice?

DR. GOODLETT. No, they are there because of the fact that the decision-makers, along with the real estate industry, has decided that this is the place that they should live with a minimum amount of difficulty.

MR. GLICKSTEIN. In your experience is housing generally available in all parts of San Francisco to Negroes and in the Bay Area?

DR. GOODLETT. No, housing is not generally available even though we have the real estate operators claiming there is no discrimination in housing. There certainly is collusion by the lending institutions in that in some areas they will not make first mortgages to racal minorities who move outside of prescribed areas, and an individual is not able to get first mortgages or any other type of financing, and this in the main circumscribes their living mobility.

MR. GLICKSTEIN. Is it an economic problem, do you think? Are Negroes able to afford the housing that is available on an open basis?

DR. GOODLETT. Yes, there are Negroes who can afford any house that is constructed and for sale to persons of their economic class. It is a situation imposed upon them in that this housing, for reasons best known to those who operate in the industry, place certain barriers, and I think the basic difficulties must be centered around race prejudice and discrimination.

MR. GLICKSTEIN. Dr. Goodlett, I believe you are also a newspaper publisher. Is that correct?

DR. GOODLETT. Yes. I am the publisher of the only Negro newspaper in San Francisco at this time.

MR. GLICKSTEIN. Can you tell us what kinds of businesses Negroes in San Francisco generally own and operate?

DR. GOODLETT. The majority of Negro businesses are service businesses, if you would insult the name "business" to so classify them. Small cafes, small barber shops, cleaning and pressing establishments. No established businesses that in the main gross more than $150,000 unless you mention the Sun Reporter, which is the largest locally-owned business.

I might amend that by saying that the undertaking establishments represent some sizable investment of capital and the transfer of funds between the deceased's relatives and the undertaker.

MR. GLICKSTEIN. What factors impede the growth of Negro businesses in this area?

DR. GOODLETT. Well, Negro business in the main, as other forms of business, require capital and experience gained from long association in various activities dealing with commerce, and most Negro businesses are first generation businesses and, moreover, in a very competitive city, such as San Francisco, traditional businesses in which Negroes engage, such as cafes, barber shops, et cetera, are monopolized by other groups, and a Negro cafe in the main caters only to Negroes. If you cater to a poor clientele, you in the main will conduct a very poor and insecure business.

MR. GLICKSTEIN. Have any of the Federal programs that provide assistance to business, such as the programs operated by the Small Business Administration, have they been effective in stimulating the growth of Negro business?

DR. GOODLETT. Well, they have had a program which was announced with some fanfare and publicity, but in the main few Negro applicants can qualify in terms of initial capital to invest, expertise, or training in the area, and it is difficult to satisfy minimum Federal requirements.

MR. GLICKSTEIN. You think the minimum requirements are too high?

DR. GOODLETT. In the majority of instances, yes.

MR. GLICKSTEIN. What in your judgment should the Federal Government do to facilitate Negro economic development?

DR. GOODLETT. Well, I think the first thing we should do is to create a climate or a circumstance in which every American has the right to a job or a right to a guaranteed annual income. It matters not whether a man can acquire capital to go into business if his clientele in the main are persons below the poverty line, and I believe that we have to seriously commit ourselves to a society in which jobs are available for all before the Negro can get his fair share in the area of business opportunity. In the other areas that I've mentioned, before the Negro can get justice in the housing market, we have to create a social climate in which housing is available for all Americans and where the *sine qua non* of housing facilities is oversupply rather than an undersupply and before Negroes are going to get equity in the job market, we have to have a social setting in which jobs are available for everyone.

One of the tragedies happens to be that the Negro's drive for economic independence and his fair share of the housing market is occurring at a time when the blue-collar work force is decreasing very rapidly and we end up fighting our alleged friends rather than sharing in the bounty that should be every man's.

MR. GLICKSTEIN. What do you mean by "fighting your alleged friends"?

DR. GOODLETT. Organized labor. I say "alleged," because the spoken word of labor is entirely different than the deed of labor, not only in the labor union but even in political action, because some of the most repressive legislation passed recently in California could have only been placed on the statute books with the assistance of organized labor which has escaped to suburbia. I am speaking particularly of Proposition 14.

MR. GLICKSTEIN. I understand that you have on some occasions been a proponent of right to work laws. What is your position on this and why?

DR. GOODLETT. Well, first you have been misinformed. I am not a proponent yet of right to work law, but I have said that the time has come that the Negro of California should give a fair hearing to proponents of right to work, because it is obvious to me that labor for two decades has taken for granted our antagonism to right to work legislation and in our desperation for economic solvency we have to take a new look at old propositions, and we have to develop new tests for old friends. So I am in the process of testing.

MR. GLICKSTEIN. Do you think that it might occur that if right to work laws were enacted the access of Negroes to certain jobs would be increased?

DR. GOODLETT. Well, I believe that—take, for example, the following: I have in my acquaintance some Negroes who were electricians and who were plumbers in the South. They have come to California, have not been able to get work in their trades, and at the present time these men are working as janitors, making $2.10, $2.40 an hour. Well, it means very little to these former plumbers and electricians that members in these crafts in San Francisco are making $5.50 and $7 an hour. So if you would pass right to work legislation, the man who is a janitor now at $2.40 in a right to work situation might be a plumber and even though it might lower the hourly income of all plumbers, it might increase his income as much as $2.50 per hour.

So this man has an individual stake in his own economic advancement, but I would say that I believe that the time has come when organized labor must do more than give lip service to the unity of interest between racial minorities and labor, and if we are to create a society in which there is to be a guaranteed annual income for all, it must use its creative endeavor and its massive political and economic weight to create that society in the quickest time possible.

I think it is a warning to our friends that we don't want to be taken for granted any longer.

MR. GLICKSTEIN. Dr. Goodlett, getting back to Negro business, have there been any changes in the attitudes of the Negro community toward Negro businesses in recent years?

DR. GOODLETT. Well, Negroes in the main will support Negro business. I do feel that the Negro businessman has to recognize that Negroes will not pay a premium to just do business with Negroes. You have to be competitive and give no more, but no less than his competitor.

In the main the Negro businesses in San Francisco, the few stores that operate as neighborhood stores, because of the lack of capital, can only be drop-in stores and, therefore, the possibilities of them becoming large supermarkets are limited by two factors.

First, the owners have no capital to expand and they are patronized in the main by people with low economic status and it is a vicious cycle in which little can be accomplished. There is no hope or future for the businessman in this area.

MR. GLICKSTEIN. But is there a growing feeling in the Negro community that Negro businesses should be encouraged to develop?

DR. GOODLETT. Yes, this is part of the philosophy of the black power advocates, that people who reside in ghettoized areas not of their making should use even their limited economic resources to create job opportunities and to increase the economic potentials of the people who reside therein. A feeling that if the Negro were able to marshal his limited resources he would be able to command some respect in a society that is quantitative, such as ours.

MR. GLICKSTEIN. Thank you. I have no further questions, Mr. Chairman.

CHAIRMAN HANNAH. Mr. Rankin, do you have any questions? Mrs. Freeman?

COMMISSIONER FREEMAN. No.

CHAIRMAN HANNAH. Mr. Patterson?

VICE CHAIRMAN PATTERSON. No.

CHAIRMAN HANNAH. Father Hesburgh?

COMMISSIONER HESBURGH. No.

CHAIRMAN HANNAH. Mr. Taylor?

MR. TAYLOR. To what extent is automation, advancing technology, creating a problem for Negro economic development for jobs generally?

DR. GOODLETT. Well, in a society that is "cybernated" or automated, the machines are replacing the least technical workers and where you have hundreds of people who formerly operated elevators, and many people who were janitors, machines doing these types of work now, and the Negroes who have acquired jobs in this industry that are being automated are the first to be fired because they lack seniority in the main, and as we become more and more automated and "cybernated," there will be a class of people who will be underemployed and unemployed and a tremendous number of people are in the mid-passage years between 42 and 65. They are too old to compete in an automated society, but yet too young to go on social security, and this is the helpless generation in mid-passage in life. The hope is very bleak for them.

MR. TAYLOR. And this is what leads you to advocate some form of guaranteed annual income, I take it?

DR. GOODLETT. Well, this is one aspect of the social scene that leads me to advocate this.

If I am to believe that the authorities are correct in saying that by the 1980's there will be a blue-collar work force of between 12 to 14 million, at the present time there are 19 million working, that the service industries will have about 90 million people employed, that the work week will be reduced to between 18 and 24 hours, and there will be from 12 to 14½ million people permanently and totally unemployed and unemployable, this represents a crisis situation and we are going to have to use all of our intellectual resources in providing for Americans who face a hopeless tomorrow, and I am prone to believe that the majority of these people proportionately will be the racial minorities of this country and that gives me concern.

MR. TAYLOR. Thank you.

CHAIRMAN HANNAH. Thank you very much, Dr. Goodlett. We appreciate your being with us this afternoon. You are excused. Mr. Glickstein, will you call the next witness?

MR. GLICKSTEIN. The next witness is Mr. Leonard Batt.

(Whereupon, MR. LEONARD BATT was sworn by the Chairman, and testified as follows:)

TESTIMONY OF MR. LEONARD BATT, SAN FRANCISCO, CALIFORNIA

MR. GLICKSTEIN. Mr. Batt, would you please state your full name and address for the record?

MR. BATT. Yes. My name is Leonard Batt and I live at 1218 Fulton Street, San Francisco.

MR. GLICKSTEIN. What is your occupation and place of employment?

MR. BATT. I am a public accountant and an insurance broker.

MR. GLICKSTEIN. Are you associated with the San Francisco Neighborhood Co-op?

MR. BATT. Yes, I am.

MR. GLICKSTEIN. What is the nature of your association with the Co-op?

MR. BATT. I am president of the Neighborhood Co-op.

MR. GLICKSTEIN. What is the Co-op and where is it located?

MR. BATT. It is located at Third and Paul Street here in San Francisco.

MR. GLICKSTEIN. And what is it?

MR. BATT. It is a supermarket handling all merchandise, such as produce, groceries, meats, liquor, usual line of merchandise that carries on in any supermarket in the city.

MR. GLICKSTEIN. Why was this co-op organized?

MR. BATT. It was organized as an outgrowth of a general feeling on the part of some citizens in the Hunters Point, in the Bayview District, the feeling that in that area there was a gross lack of employment opportunities, there was merchandise of an inferior quality being sold at high prices, there was poor service on the part of the merchants in the area given to people who constitute the major percentage of their business.

So this group of people came together and decided that perhaps through some individual effort on their own they could be instrumental in eliminating some of the things that they felt should be done, and the best approach to it, they decided that it could be done through the process of mutual aid and self-help. So the movement was organized and it finally culminated in the supermarket as it exists today.

MR. GLICKSTEIN. Now, this market is located in the Hunters Point area. Is that right?

MR. BATT. Yes, and the Bayview District.

MR. GLICKSTEIN. And the Bayview District?

MR. BATT. Yes.

MR. GLICKSTEIN. How many shares were sold?

MR. BATT. We sold 15,000 shares at about $5 a share.

We concluded in the beginning that perhaps we needed capitalization of some $75,000 before we could start, and at the time we had finished raising this money, we had something like 1,400, 1,500 members.

MR. GLICKSTEIN. How many of the shares are owned by Negroes? Do you have any idea?

MR. BATT. I would say about 75 percent, between 75 and 80 percent.

MR. GLICKSTEIN. And are a lot of those people residents of the Hunters Point-Bayview area?

MR. BATT. Yes, a substantial portion of them are, but there is a large percentage of shareholders living outside of the district. In fact, all over San Francisco we have a representative number of shareholders.

MR. GLICKSTEIN. How many employees do you have?

MR. BATT. We have 15 employees now.

MR. GLICKSTEIN. How many of them are Negro?

MR BATT. Nine Negroes and six Caucasian. Our weekly payroll is around $2,600 a week.

MR. GLICKSTEIN. Has the store been profitable up to the present time?

MR. BATT. No, it hasn't. We opened the store in June 1965, and since that time we have not accomplished our goals, such as making a profit and being in a financial position to make refunds to the members and dividends on invested capital.

We feel that our greatest achievement has been that we have provided jobs for people as we set out to do, and we have created an opportunity there for our Negro resident manager to get training in the technical skills of management of a supermarket. We have provided an opportunity there for a Negro trainee to become a butcher and we have eliminated the high prices of inferior merchandise. So, although we are not making a profit, our effort has not been a total failure.

MR. GLICKSTEIN. Are you suggesting that these employment opportunities that you have provided would not be available in white-owned businesses in the Negro areas?

MR. BATT. I don't think so, because here, as I mentioned about the resident manager being in a position to acquire the technical skills of supermarket management, certainly such a position would not have been available in any reasonable period of time. There is a possibility that a Negro could have worked up to such a position through a number of years of employment in some establishment, but not as readily as we provided it.

MR. GLICKSTEIN. In your opinion will your business eventually be on a profitable basis?

MR. BATT. Well, we are hopeful that it will. We have now 3,000 members and we would like very much to increase our membership to something like 5,000, if that was possible. We think then we would get a total patronage and sales volume that is needed now to solve the current overhead costs.

MR. GLICKSTEIN. Have you had problems with vandalism and pilferage?

MR. BATT. Well, only to a minimum degree. I don't think we could describe it as being in excess of what usually occurs in the average business of this kind.

MR. GLICKSTEIN. Is the Co-op, Mr. Batt, regarded as a Negro business?

MR. BATT. No, it isn't. Our membership consists of both Caucasians and Negroes and some of our principal supporters are members of the Caucasian race and, of course, the cooperative movement, being a movement that embraces all nationalities and religions, creeds, we could not justly call ourselves a Co-op if we did refer to it as solely a Negro organization. That was never our purpose when we set out.

MR. GLICKSTEIN. Is it possible that the enthusiasm for your business in the Negro community would increase if you were publicized as Negro business?

MR. BATT. I have the feeling that it would not because it is well understood how our business is operated and, since its very inception, we have had Caucasians working with us at the beginning. However, the business, the entire movement was exclusively organized by Negroes and later the other races came in to help us, but we feel like there is no great economic gain that could be realized by any claim that we are an exclusively Negro operated business.

MR. GLICKSTEIN. Do you think it will be possible to establish your business on a sound economic basis as long as the rate of unemployment is as high as it is right now in the Hunters Point area?

MR. BATT. Well, the rate of unemployment certainly would affect the general prosperity of the Co-op as well as it would other lines of business because these businesses must exist on the purchasing power of the consumer. So where a condition of unemployment exists, most certainly we think our progress would be impeded and retarded.

MR. GLICKSTEIN. I have no further questions, Mr. Chairman.

CHAIRMAN HANNAH. Do the Commissioners have any questions?

COMMISSIONER FREEMAN. Mr. Batt, are there other super-markets in the Hunters Point area?

MR. BATT. Yes, there are. There are several other supermarkets in that area located, I guess, within a radius of 10 or 15 blocks away from us.

COMMISSIONER FREEMAN. With respect to the ability of the Co-op to purchase goods for sale, have you had any difficulty being competitive?

MR. BATT. No. That is one of our primary claims, that we are competitive, and we have had price surveys made between the products offered in other markets, as against those offered in the other large supermarkets, and we found that some of our products actually sell for less, and on an overall shopping tour, I am quite sure that the average shopper could shop more economically in our store than they could in other competitive markets.

COMMISSIONER FREEMAN. Are you able to advertise as much as the other supermarkets do?

MR. BATT. No. If there is a disadvantage to a cooperative enterprise, it would be its inability to compete with the mass advertising of the more prosperous market outlets. However, we seek to promote our store and our movement through member education and public information programs.

CHAIRMAN HANNAH. Any further questions? Mr. Taylor?

MR. TAYLOR. No questions.

CHAIRMAN HANNAH. Thank you very much, Mr. Batt. You are excused. Mr. Glickstein, will you call the next witness.

MR. GLICKSTEIN. Mr. Edward Becks.

(Whereupon, MR. EDWARD BECKS was sworn by the Chairman and testified as follows:)

TESTIMONY OF MR. EDWARD BECKS, EAST PALO ALTO, CALIFORNIA

MR. GLICKSTEIN. Mr. Becks, would you please state your full name and address for the record.

MR. BECKS. Edward Becks, 1173 Saratoga Avenue, East Palo Alto, California.

MR. GLICKSTEIN. And how long have you lived in East Palo Alto, Mr. Becks?

MR. BECKS. Approximately 17 years.

MR. GLICKSTEIN. What county is East Palo Alto in?

MR. BECKS. East Palo Alto is in the southeast end of San Mateo County. We could think of it that way.

MR. GLICKSTEIN. I believe we have a map here that will show the Commissioners where you reside.

MR. BECKS. On this map? The other one that you moved could probably be more easily pointed out.

East Palo Alto is here. It is in this corner here.

MR. GLICKSTEIN. Palo Alto is in Santa Clara County?

MR. BECKS. It is also in Santa Clara County, yes.

MR. GLICKSTEIN. What is your occupation, Mr. Becks?

MR. BECKS. I am a project director for an information center in East Palo Alto. It is financially under the OEO.

MR. GLICKSTEIN. And what is the function of the information center?

MR. BECKS. It is an information, referral, and service center. One primary function is to give information to refer recipients, clients, to the right agencies so that they may be properly served. Also, we do a considerable amount of work in the service area in terms of needs, et cetera.

MR. GLICKSTEIN. You mean if somebody comes in with a welfare problem you are supposed to be able to refer the person to welfare agencies? Is that the sort of thing?

MR. BECK. Refer them and argue their cases, if necessary.

MR. GLICKSTEIN. How about employment problems? Do you deal with employment problems to help people find jobs?

MR. BECKS. Also, yes.

MR. GLICKSTEIN. How many people live in East Palo Alto?

MR. BECKS. In East Palo Alto there is roughly 25,000 people.

MR. GLICKSTEIN. Is your community considered a suburban community?

MR. BECKS. Yes, a suburban ghetto, I think it is called.

MR. GLICKSTEIN. What is the racial composition of East Palo Alto?

MR. BECKS. Some of the recent proposals that have been filed have said 60/40, but it is more like 80/20.

MR. GLICKSTEIN. 80 percent Negro?

MR. BECKS. Yes.

MR. GLICKSTEIN. Has it always been a predominantly Negro community?

MR. BECKS. The East Palo Alto area is a result of an attempt to find integrated housing for the ghetto that was situated in Redwood City in the Five Points area. In the process of trying to find open housing in 1948, a number of Negro families moved to the East Palo Alto area. At that same time a number of newspapers and the real estate people, after having opened up this area, became excited. I don't know if they were excited or not but they put out the word that the whole area was going to be flooded with Negroes and those white people who were left in the area received notices in their doors saying, "You had better get out now. Colored people are coming."

MR. GLICKSTEIN. What year was this?

MR. BECKS. This was around 1950. And after having done this, also there was a concentrated effort to advertise in metropolitan Bay Area papers to draw people from Negro communities, San Francisco and Oakland.

MR. GLICKSTEIN. What is the present social and economic level of the residents of East Palo Alto?

MR. BECKS. Well, it is the lowest income area in the county, No. 1. No. 2, 32 percent are below the poverty level.

MR. GLICKSTEIN. Where do most of the residents of East Palo Alto work?

MR. BECKS. Many of the residents work in service and at one time many of them worked—

MR. GLICKSTEIN. They worked where?

MR. BECKS. In service work. At one time many of them worked in construction. Of course, you know the construction industry is low. Some of the well educated ones work at Lockheed and some of the schools in the area. There are a large number of women who work at Stanford Hospital and the Sequoia Hospital in Redwood City and the Veterans Administration Hospital.

MR. GLICKSTEIN. Do most of them work in the vicinity or do some people commute?

MR. BECKS. Many of them commute as far as San Francisco and San Jose because there is not much work in the East Palo Alto area.

MR. GLICKSTEIN. Many of them commute across the Bay?

MR. BECKS. Some of them commute across the Bay, yes.

MR. GLICKSTEIN. What are the surrounding communities? You have already mentioned Palo Alto.

MR. BECKS. Palo Alto, Menlo Park, which has a Negro section with about 6,000 members that is adjacent just north of East Palo Alto; Redwood City, Portola Valley, Woodside, San Carlos, et etera, et cetera. Those are the closest ones.

MR. GLICKSTEIN. Is East Palo Alto incorporated?

MR. BECKS. Unincorporated.

MR. GLICKSTEIN. How is it governed?

MR. BECKS. By the Board of Supervisors of San Mateo County.

MR. GLICKSTEIN. Would you say that the county government is responsive to the needs of the people in East Palo Alto?

MR. BECKS. No, they are not. It has been very difficult even for East Palo Alto to be politically influential in the area because of the serious gerrymander that exists because, even if it did not exist, in a community of over half a million, it is very difficult, say for 25,000 Negroes, to have a great deal of influence.

MR. GLICKSTEIN. Is there a differential in the type of public services that East Palo Alto receives as compared to Palo Alto and Menlo Park?

MR. BECKS. Yes, there is.

MR. GLICKSTEIN. In what respects?

MR. BECKS. In terms of police service, one; in terms of street cleaning, in terms of drainage. Right now one of the problems that we are wrestling with is what to do with the water that drains from Menlo Park into East Palo Alto and, of course, it causes serious flooding in East Palo Alto area, and we have been told this is the way it is. Gravity is sort of working against us. We find ourselves at the point where it has worked most dreadfully against us, and at this time the county is in the process of filing a proposal to HUD for a demonstration city project that would do something about streets, drainage, and upgrade the housing in the area.

MR. GLICKSTEIN. The county is filing this proposal that would affect your community?

MR. BECKS. Yes.

MR. GLICKSTEIN. Have attempts been made to incorporate East Palo Alto?

MR. BECKS. I remember three attempts. In the first attempt there was a considerable amount of progress, but a number of the industries in the area withdrew and annexed themselves to the city of Menlo Park.

MR. GLICKSTEIN. May I just clarify something: The residents of East Palo Alto in these attempts were trying to become incorporated or part of neighboring cities?

MR. BECKS. No, the attempt was to incorporate East Palo Alto and have East Palo Alto become a city, and when this process was started many of the industries on the periphery joined Menlo Park and decreased the economic base for a city.

The second time that this occurred, even more left, to the extent that Menlo Park almost surrounds East Palo Alto now. At one time it was north and west of East Palo Alto. Now it is northwest and east of East Palo Alto.

MR. GLICKSTEIN. Well, has East Palo Alto ever attempted to become annexed to Menlo Park?

MR. BECKS. The problems of annexation are difficult to this degree, that if we, the people there, decide to annex, they have to decide to annex, also, and their city council has not been agreeable up to this time to annex East Palo Alto. They have annexed those areas that were profitable for them to annex, the industry and part of the more highly developed areas or communities.

MR. GLICKSTEIN. How has the annexation of this industry in highly developed communities by Menlo Park affected East Palo Alto?

MR. BECKS. It has decreased the base and the income and has decreased the base to the extent that there is a serious question as to whether or not we could be a real city at this particular time.

MR. GLICKSTEIN. Because of the tax base?

MR. BECKS. Because of the tax base, yes.

MR. GLICKSTEIN. What in your view is the solution to the problems of obtaining better government in East Palo Alto?

MR. BECKS. Well, there are two possible solutions, I suppose, or three, within the present political structure.

One would be annexation to Menlo Park. Number two would be still incorporation, and number three would be some defining of the supervisory districts so that East Palo Alto would not only not be gerrymandered, but the weight could be felt in an election. Maybe representing a supervisor, say, from out of District No. 2, having the people only in District No. 2 vote for the supervisor rather than the whole community of a half a million people.

MR. GLICKSTEIN. At the present time supervisors are elected at large?

MR. BECKS. At large, yes, even though they pretend to represent a given district and reside in that district, actually they are elected at large.

MR. GLICKSTEIN. Is there general agreement with the views that you have just expressed?

MR. BECKS. I think the most general view in the community is that the community needs to be organized and would like to be an independent city if possible.

There is one view that I did not express, is that people have expressed the idea of joining Palo Alto. I did not express this because this is so near impossible that it is not worth mentioning. There is some territory that is being annexed by the city of Palo Alto in the county of Santa Clara that has been in limbo over 30 years, and if we are to do something to get immediate action, annexation to Palo Alto would simply throw the whole thing—

MR. GLICKSTEIN. That is more complex because Palo Alto is in a different county?

MR. BECKS. Yes, and I think it takes both counties to act on it. The city has to act on it. The people of East Palo Alto—I believe it requires something from the State legislature.

MR. GLICKSTEIN. Do the East Palo Alto residents have much contact with white people in the surrounding communities?

MR. BECKS. Well, I suppose those who work for white people do. On the other hand, it is my own feeling that the East Palo Alto area has become more and more cut off from the general community. It has become so cut off in a sense that I believe that the generation since World War II has no concept—I mean the younger generation, say, the 18, the 19 to 24, 25, has no concept of any social relationship with any people other than Negroes.

MR. GLICKSTEIN. Are the schools in East Palo Alto integrated?

MR. BECKS. The schools in East Palo Alto proper are, well, you can say neo-segregation, *de facto* desegregation, or any term you. like to use, because the desegregation occurred recently and it occurred since the Supreme Court decision.

MR. GLICKSTEIN. Have people in East Palo Alto been concerned about this problem?

MR. BECKS. It has been one of the most exciting issues in the area, I suppose. One of the things that was proposed by a commission that was established in 1964 was to phase out a high school. and send the young people to other schools so that they would have meaningful education with the idea that the present school that they are attending does not teach them to read or teach them any of the social skills that would be useful in employment.

MR. GLICKSTEIN. Has that proposal been implemented?

MR. BECKS. That proposal created some excitement. The State Board of Education thought it was a very good idea. The local Board of Education did not act on the proposal and at this point they have not. They have talked about it is a necessity, but they say that the community would not accept the idea of closing a $3½ million plant which is almost new—it is less than 10 years old—for the purpose of integrating.

MR. GLICKSTEIN. These children would be integrated into the schools?

MR. BECKS. They would be taken to five other schools. I hate to say integrated, because we have had some very poor efforts in that area in that we have another school that is about two miles from the Ravenswood High School, which is Menlo-Atherton.

MR. GLICKSTEIN. The Ravenswood—

MR. BECKS. In East Palo Alto, and then there is Menlo-Atherton, which serves the area of Menlo and Atherton and both are very high income areas.

The Bellhaven area, which is a small section of 600 Negroes, north of East Palo Alto, some of the children have been going—

MR. GLICKSTEIN. Bellhaven area is in Menlo Park?

MR. BECKS. It is within the city limits of Menlo Park. Some of these young people have been going to Menlo-Atherton and, of course, it has simply created two systems there in that the Negro students by and large are not in the classes with white students, and also even in the cafeteria there is a formation of separate lines, and I think there are two things involved, one, that the community at large and the leadership in the community has not looked upon integration as either serious or meaningful.

Two, the young people come from an area that has not allowed them to have contact with the greater community, and, therefore, have no concept of associating or making friends with any of these young people.

MR. GLICKSTEIN. Have any of the students from East Palo Alto been able to obtain an integrated education or go to predominantly white schools?

MR. BECKS. This has been done by a program called the sneakout in that we have gotten parents in other school districts to accept these children on a five-day, four-night basis as if they were their own children, and in doing this they are able to go to better schools.

At this time I would say maybe 200, 150 to 200 young people from elementary through high school are engaged in such a program.

MR. GLICKSTEIN. How are they doing?

MR. BECKS. The ones that are going seem to be doing quite well. As a matter of fact, one of the young men has just received a scholarship from several schools, I think Notre Dame is one, Claremont is the other one, and I don't remember, but they seem to be in a competitive atmosphere and they are competing.

MR. GLICKSTEIN. How do the people in your community feel about the Federal Government's commitment to school desegregation?

MR. BECKS. It is a rather interesting thing. I think many of them feel that probably the Federal Government was not serious. If it had been serious, that there would have been action taken in 1954 after the decision that in that September some efforts would have been made to shuffle the people, the school districts, the administrators, and the teachers to get an approximation of the general community operating in all the school districts. And this was probably the kind of hope that many people had, but for us in that area we have simply seen more and more segregation since the Supreme Court decision.

MR. GLICKSTEIN. You mean that people in a northern community like East Palo Alto in 1954, believed that that decision affected them?

MR. BECKS. In 1954 there was no problem of discrimination in that part of San Mateo County. In 1954, as a matter of fact, the school board bought the piece of land that Ravenswood High School is now situated on. There was some conversation about getting a school on that site to serve some of those people over there.

At that time they were talking about an area east of Bayshore that went from San Francisco to Creek to the south, to 2nd Avenue in Redwood City, cutting through Menlo Park and the city of Redwood City, but in 1957 I guess the public was duly aroused. About 4,000 of us were pretty much up in arms about the thing.

So the boundary line was modified so that it only included Menlo Park and East Palo Alto.

MR. GLICKSTEIN. I take it that you and people in your community felt that the 1954 Supreme Court decision was applicable to East Palo Alto as well as to the Southern States?

MR. BECKS. Oh, yes. We feel that it should be, yes. Not that it is, but that it should be.

MR. GLICKSTEIN. Mr. Becks, does the Black Power concept have any meaning to the people you work with?

MR. BECKS. In East Palo Alto?

MR. GLICKSTEIN. Yes.

MR. BECKS. I think the people are saying two things. They are saying that if you—you can call it Black Power, if you will, or you can call it whatever you wish, but they are saying that if we mean integration when we say it, then it seems that the powers that be should be able to do something that is positive in the direction to see that integration becomes a *fait accompli*.

Now, on the other hand, if you do not mean integration and you mean segregation, because this is what we are getting, then possibly something should be done on the other hand to see that these segregated people can control the schools and the other industries, et cetera, that exist in that segregated area.

MR. GLICKSTEIN. Do you think people are becoming more disillusioned about the likelihood of creating an integrated society?

MR. BECKS. I don't think many people in the East Palo Alto area visualize anything like an integrated society.

MR. GLICKSTEIN. I have no further questions, Mr. Chairman.

CHAIRMAN HANNAH. Father Hesburgh?

COMMISSIONER HESBURGH. Do you get any assistance from Stanford University in the study of your problems, educational tools, that sort of thing?

MR. BECKS. You say—what was the term?

COMMISSIONER HESBURGH. Some assistance.

MR. BECKS. I think the community refers to it more as to interference more than assistance, because we do get a lot of people from Stanford looking in our noses, ears, and eyes, and listening to us and tape-recording what we say, and we never see the benefit of what they do and as soon as the war on poverty came to the county we had all kinds of people from Stanford University and other areas with packaged proposals trying to get the money, and so on. In this sense, yes.

COMMISSIONER HESBURGH. One more question. Has the Poverty Program helped to galvanize or draw together the Negro leadership in your community?

MR. BECKS. It has probably helped to draw them together to some degree, because I think the community and the Negroes in San Mateo County generally have been greatly displeased with the Poverty Program in that the Negro people in the community have had very little influence on what kinds of programs they would have and who would run them.

So I think this has caused some disillusionment with the program.

COMMISSIONER HESBURGH. But it is being run to some extent, what there is of it, by the Negro community itself?

MR. BECKS. Some of it is being run by the Negro community.

COMMISSIONER FREEMAN. Mr. Becks, you indicated that San Mateo County has submitted a proposal for a model city?

MR. BECKS. Yes.

COMMISSIONER FREEMAN. And under the guidelines, there should be participation of the residents of the target area, and I wonder to what extent that you and the others that live there participated in the preparation of the proposal.

MR. BECKS. I would say very frankly we participated very little in the preparation of the proposal. There was a committee, though, that some people did participate in. It was called the Local Agency Formation Commission, and a number of people did participate in this aspect of it.

After the Commission was dismissed, the county proceeded to draw up a proposal and, of course, there have been some bad areas in the proposal that are being worked out now. I guess it was supposed to be in by noon yesterday.

COMMISSIONER FREEMAN. You are still involved in helping to work this out?

MR. BECKS. As I see the future involvement, I can't say involvement at this point, because I think the county is doing it, but the future involvement is that there will be an election and they will elect what will be called a Municipal Council, five people from the East Palo Alto area will be elected, and they will become a *de facto* city council, and the county manager will either appoint with this *de facto* city council a *de facto* city manager that will work from his office to the area of East Palo Alto.

COMMISSIONER FREEMAN. So there would, in fact, be some participation?

MR. BECKS. There would be some participation.

COMMISSIONER FREEMAN. Thank you.

COMMISSIONER RANKIN. Would annexation to Menlo Park cause property taxes to rise? What would be the additional tax?

MR. BECKS. I doubt it very seriously because we are a highly taxed area already and I doubt that adding the East Palo Alto area to Menlo Park would cause the taxes to rise. The drainage system that we got not too long ago caused our taxes to rise. The sub-station police station that we got caused our taxes to rise so that everything we do or everything that is given to us or we receive cause our taxes to rise. I don't think this act would cause them to rise any more in proportion.

COMMISSIONER RANKIN. If they are rising that way, my opinion is when you go into Menlo Park, they will rise some more. That's been my history of taxation.

CHAIRMAN HANNAH. Mr. Becks, how long have you lived in the San Francisco Bay Area?

MR. BECKS. I have lived in the San Francisco Bay Area approximately 24 years.

CHAIRMAN HANNAH. Where was your original home?

MR. BECKS. I was originally born in Texas and I came to California to help build the railroads during the war.

CHAIRMAN HANNAH. Mr. Taylor?

MR. TAYLOR. Mr. Becks, you testified to a number of efforts over the years on your part and on the part of people in East Palo Alto to become part of a larger community, to meet your problems that way.

Do the people who you deal with in East Palo Alto understand the reasons why these efforts have been frustrated? Is it possible to explain to them why these efforts have been frustrated? What is their view of it?

MR. BECKS. Well, first of all, this question of—if I could backtrack just a bit. This question of creating a dialogue seems to be almost completely out of context, because this is where we were 20 years ago, you know, trying to create this dialogue, and it seems that maybe we were more successful at this 20 years ago than we are today, and I think that many people in the community today just do not visualize any effort in connecting ourselves with the greater community as being very serious.

MR. TAYLOR. Is it possible for a community such as East Palo Alto to solve its problems entirely through its own efforts, do you think?

MR. BECKS. Well, we are doing everything we can to solve them, and I might say this, that there are two things that are said about communities like East Palo Alto. If some official agent comes into the community and he talks to two or three different people, and they express ideas or opinions that have some shades of difference, they say "You should get together," and if you move then to organize they say that there is a power struggle going on.

So it creates a very serious situation. No matter which way you go the question will be asked, can we get together? Can we solve our problems? It is very difficult, you know, considering these kind of things.

MR. TAYLOR. You're kind of in the middle, I take it, because on the one hand you are frustrated by efforts to become a part of a larger community, and on the other hand, the problem is really in solving the problem within the community?

MR. BECKS. I hope I am not in the middle and I don't feel like it.

CHAIRMAN HANNAH. Thank you very much, Mr. Becks. You are excused. We have one more witness this afternoon?

MR. GLICKSTEIN. Yes, sir. Mr. Earl Anthony.

(Whereupon, MR. EARL ANTHONY was sworn by the Chairman and testified as follows:)

TESTIMONY OF MR. EARL L. ANTHONY, SAN FRANCISCO, CALIFORNIA

MR. GLICKSTEIN. Mr. Anthony, would you please state your full name and address for the record.

MR. ANTHONY. My name is Earl L. Anthony. I live at 1061 Laguna, Apartment 23, San Francisco.

MR. GLICKSTEIN. What is your occupation, Mr. Anthony?

MR. ANTHONY. I am chairman of the Independent Action Movement.

MR. GLICKSTEIN. What is that?

MR. ANTHONY. It is a group of black organizers and political activists.

MR. GLICKSTEIN. Is it made up of a number of different organizations or are memberships given to individuals?

MR. ANTHONY. It is on individual membership, staff membership type of thing.

MR. GLICKSTEIN. Is that how you earn your living?

MR. ANTHONY. Yes, I do, and I also work part time at Potrero Hill, Potrero Hill Manpower. It's an EOC project.

MR. GLICKSTEIN. That is a poverty program?

MR. ANTHONY. Yes.

MR. GLICKSTÉIN. What are your duties there?

MR. ANTHONY. Consultant, job consultant.

MR. GLICKSTEIN. Do you help people find jobs or help them determine what training they should take or what they are qualified for?

MR. ANTHONY. We try to help them find jobs and what training—try to prepare them for the type of training or put them in the type of training they would need to prepare themselves to find jobs.

MR. GLICKSTEIN. The organization that you are chairman of,

Mr. Anthony, what are some of the activities that it has been involved in? What are its purposes?

MR. ANTHONY. Well, mainly we have been involved in activities, such as political organization in the community, the San Francisco rent strike, which is going on now.

MR. GLICKSTEIN. Where is this rent strike taking place?

MR. ANTHONY. In San Francisco, the rent strike, that is in Hunters Point, Potrero Hill and Western Addition, and we were involved in the John Muir School boycott. We organized and ran the Freedom School, and organizations such as this.

We also were responsible partly for putting on the Malcolm X Grass Roots Conference.

MR. GLICKSTEIN. What was that?

MR. ANTHONY. It was a conference that we held in February of this year to celebrate—well, actually, a memorial for the assassination of Brother Malcolm X, and we invited groups over the Bay Area, grass roots organizations, to come in to discuss the problems of the Afro-American in this country and in this area.

MR. GLICKSTEIN. What are the objectives? What are the goals of your organization? What does it seek to accomplish?

MR. ANTHONY. We hope to organize politically, economically, black people so that they can shape their own destiny within this country and make some significant change in the system.

MR. GLICKSTEIN. Do you favor the participation of white people in your activities?

MR. ANTHONY. No, we don't. We feel that white people should participate in their own areas, and that by them coming and participating in black areas, they just add to confusion and they are totally ineffective.

MR. GLICKSTEIN. Do you think that white people have a role in the civil rights movement?

MR. ANTHONY. First of all, I would like to refer to it as a human rights movement rather than a civil rights movement.

I think white people have a role in their own areas, as I said before. Rather they should, instead of participating in organizing the black community or going into the black community, which they have in the past, what they should do is organize in their own areas and fight the racism in their own areas, because this is where the major battle is, in the white communities, rather than in the black communities.

MR. GLICKSTEIN. You said, Mr. Anthony, that when white people have been involved in the human rights movement in Negro areas that it causes confusion. What do you mean by that?

MR. ANTHONY. It seems that when white people come into the movement, they bring with them a type of paternalism. It is a bad psychological type of thing for black people because they only feel that if you do anything white people have to do it instead of black people. Then white people, when they do come into the movement, are actually escaping because they are running away from the problems that are the major problems in this country and that is, organizing in their own areas and fighting racism in their own communities. I don't see why they should come in and try and tidy up somebody else's yard when they can't tidy up their own yard. I think they should take care of No. 1 first, and then let us take care of our own.

MR. GLICKSTEIN. What do you think are some of the benefits that can be achieved by the Negro community by excluding white people from the human rights movement?

MR. ANTHONY. It gives the black man a chance to really gain some type of self-pride, self-identity, and to move to organizing on a legitimate scale, which I don't believe he could if the white people are in the civil rights or in the human rights movement. Then when he organizes on this scale, he will be in a better position to move, to make some substantial changes in this system or to get his right place within this system.

MR. GLICKSTEIN. Mr. Anthony, I notice that you—I have been using the word "Negro" and you have been using the word "black." Could you tell us why you prefer that word to the word I have been using?

MR. ANTHONY. Well, "Negro" is a term. It is a type of degrading term that white people gave to the Afro-Americans. So we would rather refer to ourselves as "black" instead of "Negro," as black or as Afro-Americans. This is a thing like defining our own cultural heritage, and defining our own terms and defining our own society. "Negro" is a term given to us by the white community and it has the taint of their value system rather than our own value system.

MR. GLICKSTEIN. Is your view of the connotation that this word has generally shared by members of people you associate with or members of the black or Negro community?

MR. ANTHONY. Yes, it is. In fact, it is becoming more so increasingly, that the black community is beginning to feel this type of self-pride and self-determination and beginning to set down their own values and use their own terms, and with this they also begin to move to set up their own institutions and define how they would actually move in this country, rather than listen to the white man and find out how they should move, which has been the case in the past.

MR. GLICKSTEIN. Do you think there might be a difference in the opinion on this question depending on how old a person was?

MR. ANTHONY. No, no, I don't.

MR. GLICKSTEIN. Do you think you are speaking now for people that are your age or do you think you are speaking for a wider cross-section of people?

MR. ANTHONY. Well, I feel that any person, first of all, who is black realizes this fact. I feel that people in the younger age bracket maybe have become aware of this and maybe have moved a little quicker in this direction than people who might be a little older.

Now, of course, this is generally, I am speaking. There are exceptions to every rule, but I feel that the whole black community is moving toward this type of self-determination.

I just might say, well, maybe the younger group has moved a little quicker than the older, old generation of black people.

MR. GLICKSTEIN. Do you believe that it is realistic to assume that the black community, lacking economic and political strength, will be able to achieve the resolution of the problems that face them today?

MR. ANTHONY. First of all, I don't think the black community lacks economic or political strength. I think this is a white viewpoint, when you say the black community lacks economic or political strength. I feel that if black people are allowed to organize and allowed to move, that they have political strength and economic strength, if they can just utilize this. It is a matter of being utilized.

I think that we have been oppressed and we have been disenfranchised so we have been made to believe that we lack political and economic strength, but I believe the tools are there for black people. We do have the possibility of—take, for instance, political strength. In certain communities and in certain metropolitan cities we will be in the majority and certain communities in San Francisco, for instance, where we are in the majority; in the Bay Area, like Oakland, where we will be the majority, and so these are the tools of political strength.

So I don't think the black community lacks political strength.

MR. GLICKSTEIN. Well, you work with the Potrero Hill Manpower Project, and I imagine you are aware of the great degree of unemployment among Negro—black people—and you are aware of the problems the people have in getting training and the lack of skills. Don't you think that demonstrates a lack of economic power?

MR. ANTHONY. Well, I think that demonstrates for the last 450 years black people have been shut out of opportunities that the white man has had.

I also feel that as far as economic power goes, it is true that we have maybe—possibly we lack a certain economic status of, let's say, the white community.

However, I feel that the problem is not so much economic, how we are going to get a job, and so forth, but is how we can raise black people to feel self-pride to gain economic strength.

MR. GLICKSTEIN. But does raising someone's self-pride get him a job?

MR. ANTHONY. Yes, it does. I think it does, because this will get him out there, and they will want to take care and do the things that have to be done to get a job.

MR. GLICKSTEIN. You mean it would encourage him to seek training if he doesn't have training?

MR. ANTHONY. That's correct.

MR. GLICKSTEIN. Speaking from the point of view of a young man, what is the role of black women in the movement that you are discussing with us?

MR. ANTHONY. What is the role of black women?

No. 1, I feel that black women have to reach a position where they can encourage black men to follow the course that they have to take in these coming years, and this is a tremendous psychological—it can be a tremendous psychological force in the movement.

For instance, black women, as far as something like the draft might go, might, let's say, encourage black men to be against the draft. You know, want to stay home from Vietnam because of the implications of the war in Vietnam.

As far as culture goes, as far as training black children, they might try to raise the black children to understand Afro-American culture within this country, what the black man has really done in this 450 years here and what he did in Africa and our relationship between Africa and what is happening to Africa today, so she can bring the awareness up in black children and things of this type. This is the role of the black woman in the movement. She can support it.

MR. GLICKSTEIN. You haven't mentioned exercising political leadership or leadership of organizations. You don't think that's a proper role for women?

MR. ANTHONY. She can exercise political leadership in that if she has a mothers' club of black women, she can try to have a political education thing and bring in political education. You can often have it at whatever level.

MR. GLICKSTEIN. But you wouldn't look kindly on having a woman head your organization, would you?

MR. ANTHONY. If she was competent, I wouldn't mind.

MR. GLICKSTEIN. Mr. Anthony, do you believe there is any hope for a racially integrated society in the United States?

MR. ANTHONY. That is another thing. When you say that word, integration, that has kind of a bad overtone, because when the white community usually talks about integration, they talk about one or two people coming into the system, and that is more assimilation than integration but I feel—now we talk about racial coalitions or being on an equal terms. There could be a possibility of this. Integration, no. I don't believe in the term integration, as the way it is used now.

MR. GLICKSTEIN. What do you mean by coalition? What do you foresee that that encompasses?

MR. ANTHONY. That we meet equally on terms of, let's say, politically, socially, psychologically, economically.

MR. GLICKSTEIN. Would this also involve people, for example, going to schools together, for example, living in the same communities?

MR. ANTHONY. More so than going to schools together I would rather deal with the problem from the standpoint that it might involve that black schools are just as good as white schools. I don't think the problem is really whether a few black kids go to a white school, but whether black schools are just as good or just as competent as white schools are.

MR. GLICKSTEIN. So it is your view that black children can obtain a high quality education in an all-black school?

MR. ANTHONY. Yes, I do, because I feel that they can relate better around people that they have more common experiences with, as long as the—I think the main thing is that the quality of the school is just as good as the white school, a black school is just as good in the quality as the white school is and that hasn't been the case.

MR. GLICKSTEIN. You don't think a child that goes to a school of that sort might have some difficulties when he goes out to seek a job and confronts a white employer?

MR. ANTHONY. No, I don't, because I feel if a person is competent, if he is qualified, if he has a high self-esteem of himself, he won't face any problem when he goes out into the world to get employment.

I think that sometimes an inferiority thing is inbred from the educational system itself when we have whites and blacks going to school together. We have a type of inferiority because white teachers, they don't know how to treat black children. So they might treat black children in an inferior way. This is a subconscious. They do it subconsciously.

I also feel that if we have superior schools, or equal schools in the black community, that any teacher who comes into the black community to teach should know Afro-American history and we should have some type of school board to screen them before they come into the black community to teach black children. They should know Afro-American history, the heritage of the Afro-American people, of black people.

MR. GLICKSTEIN. Mr. Anthony, do you believe that the Federal Government can play a role in changing the racial picture in the United States?

MR. ANTHONY. Yes, I think the Federal Government can do quite a bit.

No. 1, they need to give more and more money than they have been giving to some of these federally sponsored programs, and No. 2, they should put into effect some of the laws that have been written on the books against racial injustices, all over this country, and particularly in the South.

MR. GLICKSTEIN. I have no further questions, Mr. Chairman.

CHAIRMAN HANNAH. Dr. Rankin?

COMMISSIONER RANKIN. You majored in political science, is that right?

MR. ANTHONY. Yes, I did.

COMMISSIONER RANKIN. I try to teach it also.

I was interested in your idea about voting. The Negro population is about one-tenth of the population in the United States. Isn't that correct?

MR. ANTHONY. I would say it is about 40 million, about one-eighth, I would say, between one-tenth and one-eighth.

COMMISSIONER RANKIN. Wouldn't it be bad to line up whites voting against Negroes, then? You have a Negro bloc and we have a white bloc, and when you say "We want to vote Negroes as a race," don't you think that would in the long run hurt because that would make whites say, "All right, we will vote as our race"?

MR. ANTHONY. I don't think it would hurt at all because, first of all, if we line up with any whites, we are not going to get anyplace in the first place.

COMMISSIONER RANKIN. Then how are you going to get anyplace anyway, then?

MR. ANTHONY. We can control the areas that are predominantly black.

COMMISSIONER RANKIN. Oh yes, in certain areas you can, isn't that right?

MR. ANTHONY. We haven't been doing this before, even the areas that have been predominantly black.

COMMISSIONER RANKIN. What are you going to do in the other areas?

MR. ANTHONY. In the other areas, we probably wouldn't win anyway.

COMMISSIONER RANKIN. Well, in Durham, North Carolina, where I live, the Negro population is about one-third, but we have Negroes on the city council. We have Negroes in our government, on the school board and you say they wouldn't. They do win now.

MR. ANTHONY. But, you see, this is another thing. We have

always talked about representation. I am more interested in controlling something than just being represented on something because if you have representation——

COMMISSIONER RANKIN. But do you think that 90 percent with 10 percent control—do you think that?

MR. ANTHONY. We can control certain things. I am not saying I can control the whole country. I am just saying control certain areas. That is all I am addressing myself to.

COMMISSIONER RANKIN. What areas?

MR. ANTHONY. Then, also, there might be factions in the white community that want to see some drastic, revolutionary types changes that we can probably cooperate with.

COMMISSIONER RANKIN. Then you are going to work with them? Is that correct?

MR. ANTHONY. We can have a coalition with them, yes.

CHAIRMAN HANNAH. Mrs. Freeman?

COMMISSIONER FREEMAN. Mr. Anthony, to what extent is Afro-American history included in the San Francisco schools or the Bay Area schools?

MR. ANTHONY. At San Francisco State College and Cal and San Francisco City College, they have associations like the Black Student Union, black student associations, City College, and the Afro-American Student Union at the University of California, and these organizations are primarily trying to learn about Afro-American history and Afro-American culture. They are trying to identify more closely and find out about their heritage instead of what the Western world and what the white man has told them.

Also at San Francisco State College they have a black arts program which they are trying to put into effect in May. Le Roi Jones will be heading it, he is an important playwright, and this will more or less be a black experimental college where the students will also do work in the community.

COMMISSIONER FREEMAN. Are there similar programs at the high school level?

MR. ANTHONY. There haven't been similar programs as yet at the high school level. However, several organizations have been working with high school students on Afro-American history.

COMMISSIONER FREEMAN. Thank you.

CHAIRMAN HANNAH. Mr. Patterson?

VICE CHAIRMAN PATTERSON. Mr. Anthony, isn't there some danger in your philosophy that you might repeat the mistakes made by white Americans against which we have been working for many years in establishing white self-pride through animosity toward the Negro? Isn't it implicit in what you have been saying that you would establish Negro self-pride through animosity to the white? Isn't this type of racism proven to be rather bad news in our country, what we should join in working against?

MR. ANTHONY. Actually we talk about animosity toward the whites. All we are doing is sharpening the contradictions and showing the black man what the white man is really doing to him. So he will be able to move from that position, to move more effectively. Now as far as repeating the same thing that the white man has done in this country, I don't think that we are that cruel as the white man or that barbaric but I also feel that we should move to certain positions in this country. If he is on top, we should move to at least get a big—we should try to replace him. If not replace him, to get a bigger piece of the pie or this manager system or do whatever we can to stop being oppressed by him.

VICE CHAIRMAN PATTERSON. Do you feel you can do this in a segregated society better than you can in the effort we've been making toward integration?

MR. ANTHONY. Well, see, in a segregated society—rather than what?

VICE CHAIRMAN PATTERSON. A racially segregated society you think promises the Negro more than an integrated society?

MR. ANTHONY. I feel there might be certain elements within the white society which are racial and revolutionary in their thought that there could possibly be coalitions. I mean white people who want to change the racist attitude of this country and we could probably cooperate with elements like that, that want to smash this system and put in something that is a little different or have more justice, or make it more of a democracy like it is supposed to be for all people.

CHAIRMAN HANNAH. Father Hesburgh?

COMMISSIONER HESBURGH. Mr. Anthony, I have been talking about the elements of philosophy that we have been expressing here this afternoon with some of the Negro leaders for long standing—I don't know if you consider them Negro leaders, people like Jim Farmer and Jackie Robinson and so forth,—and they seem rather violently opposed to the philosophy you put forth. Would you consider that's poor judgment on their part, or just a different point of view, or they're older or what?

MR. ANTHONY. I would consider it a different point of view.

COMMISSIONER HESBURGH. But these people have been working fairly hard for a long time. Would you just write them off?

MR. ANTHONY. No, I wouldn't just write them off. There is one thing: that when two, let's say, two black people have different points of view, then the white man usually jumps on this when he sees there is a division in ranks. However, one of the great heritages of this country is the two-party system, which is supposed to be two lines of thought. So I look at it in that perspective, as two lines of thought.

COMMISSIONER HESBURGH. You think they would each have their own following and would go at this problem in different ways or would you go at it your way and they go at it in their way?

MR. ANTHONY. I think it can be a very effective way.

COMMISSIONER HESBURGH. One of the problems I've noticed personally is a number of white youngsters who have been very much involved in the civil rights movement in the South. For example, we ran into a good amount of work done in voting in Mississippi. We had a hearing there a couple of years ago and I think it is a fair statement that we wouldn't have made the progress in Mississippi that we did make on voting which has been rather spectacular after 100 years of nothing if it were not for all the young college students that went down there, some at considerable problem, some injured, some killed, some suffering all kinds of humiliations and then suddenly it sounded to me that in your philosophy that that would all be written off like this and you would say, "We don't want you. You go home and take care of your problems." Yet that problem in Mississippi in voting wouldn't have been taken care of without the help of these white youngsters, all of whom are now written out and feel that they were kind of unappreciated for what they did. I am not saying that they should get medals for what they did or they should be given the Croix de Guerre but, at least, it seemed to me that they did something that at that point in history was very necessary to be done. They did it, I think, with good motives. I think it was enormously helpful to the Negro voter in Mississippi and hearing what you say, I just have a feeling that there is no place for this anymore.

MR. ANTHONY. Well, no. See if these people were very sincere in their efforts, like I feel that most of them probably are and probably were, what they would do then, once they had done their part and allow black people to move to the position of getting the machinery to organize for themselves. They would realize that in order for black people to organize effectively, they will have to organize themselves. Black people will have to organize, and they would be willing enough to step aside because the longer they stay in a movement like this it adds to paternalism, colonialism. If they are not willing to step aside, then we are going to always have this paternalistic type of——

COMMISSIONER HESBURGH. Most of these youngsters I am talking about, the white ones, now, were anything but paternalistic. They moved in with poor Negro families in the South, they lived with them.

241

MR. ANTHONY. Subconsciously they were probably paternalistic.

COMMISSIONER HESBURGH. That could very well be but the fact is they did a very good job and they did it out of idealism, they did it out of an idea that in this country we have to learn to live together and not have separate enclaves.

I think if we had in this country deliberately worked toward enclaves that were religiously segregated or racially segregated or nationally segregated, this is not what really the country is about. Believe me, I am not speaking against consciousness, pride, leadership, self-organization, and self-performance and all of the rest. These are all very good things for any group because it allows you to negotiate on a level basis with other people. But I think to do it as a kind of exclusive, ghetto-forming activity, I think in the long run works against that of *e pluribus unum,* you know the many one unity in this country coming out of many strong resources.

MR. ANTHONY. There, again, you have a thing where they can use this as a crutch. You take these white people who did these things in the South. If they are allowed to stay on in the human rights movement, then what they start to do is use this as a crutch rather than do what they really have to do. What they really have to do, you take a State like California with the John Birchers and the type of maniac Governor we have. What they should be doing is to be moving into the communities there and try to break up the Birchers and break up organizations of this type in the white community. And as long as they stay in the black community they feel somewhat safe because they feel like they are the Great White God who is going to lead us to wherever we have to go, where they feel that we have to go. They are never going to be able to break this crutch. So we have to take this crutch away from where they have to move over where they can do the greatest amount of good.

COMMISSIONER HESBURGH. I would say, and I'm just speaking in my own—I am enjoying this conversation, and I will stop at this point, but the thing that would bother me about what I have heard is that it seems to me that the black community, or the Negro community, whatever you call it, in this country can greatly benefit by people who are interested in the problems and can work not only with the black community, but also with the white community.

In other words, this Commission, most of our associations in a working day are with the black community, but we have to go back to Washington to fight with the white power structure to get something done. We have gotten over 75 percent of the recommendations passed into Federal law, and now we are trying to get the law carried into effect. That is one reason we are out checking on what is happening to the law.

It seems to me, if I read the white community correctly, and I can see you can read the black community better than I can, but I think I can read the white community better than you can, but if I read the white community correctly, I would say that the net result of what you are doing will be to drive away from a great movement that is beginning to show a few results, although it is a long way from home, it would be to drive away from that movement many people who are essential to success, ultimate success.

That's just a personal reason, and I respect your right to disagree with it.

MR. ANTHONY. I do disagree with that because I feel that this type of thing, this type of movement, the one that you drive away is more of a reactionary type of person and I feel that if we are to really make any changes within this system, within this country, it can't be really reactionary. It's going to be more revolutionary. What we need in this thing now is a white person who is not a liberal or reactionary but a white person who is a radical and revolutionary and then we can cooperate with them to make the only great change in the system if there is going to make any change.

COMMISSIONER HESBURGH. You are depending upon this percentage of the total percentage of the white people, because if you drive off the liberal community, if you drive off other segments who may not be liberal, but are extremely interested in human problems, all you are looking for is those in dire revolt against all the things in our society. Then I think you will be lucky if you get 2 percent of the white people. That doesn't make much of a coalition.

CHAIRMAN HANNAH. Does anyone have further questions? Thank you very much, Mr. Anthony. You are excused. We will now recess until 7:30.

(Whereupon, at 5:30 p.m., the hearing recessed until 7:30 p.m.)

TUESDAY EVENING SESSION

MAY 2, 1967

CHAIRMAN HANNAH. Ladies and gentlemen, the next witnesses to be heard will speak to the problems confronting the Mexican American and other Spanish-speaking peoples of the Bay Area. At the prior hearing of the Commission in Los Angeles in 1960 and Phoenix in '62, testimony was heard relating to the status of equal opportunity for Mexican Americans. It is our expectation that the testimony which will be received at the present hearings will contribute to the studies, investigations, and hearings on this subject which the Commission has already begun and which will be increased in the future.

As Commissioner Patterson indicated yesterday, this hearing inaugurates a new factfinding effort by the Commission to ascertain the status of equal opportunity for Spanish-speaking peoples throughout the country, an effort which will include a projected hearing, new research programs, and meetings of several of our State Advisory Committees.

The testimony to be heard this evening will be presented by a panel of four distinguished gentlemen who have for many years been concerned with the problems of the Mexican American community which in numbers is the largest ethnic minority in the State of California.

These panelists are Dr. Ernesto Galarza, author and consultant to private and public agencies; Mr. Bert Corona, State Chairman of the Mexican American Political Association; Mr. Herman Gallegos, community leader currently a consultant of the Ford Foundation; and Dr. Octavio Romano, professor of anthropology at the University of California at Berkeley.

It is our understanding that the panelists will present a broad overview of the major areas of concern to the Mexican American community, such as employment, education, urban problems, and the impact of various Federal programs in the community. In the course of subsequent sessions at these hearings here tomorrow afternoon, and later in Oakland, we shall hear further testimony from members of the Spanish-speaking American group relating in greater detail to specific issues.

Mr. Glickstein, will you call the witnesses?

(A group of approximately 15 students arose in the body of the courtroom and showed placards.)

UNIDENTIFIED SPEAKER FROM BODY OF COURTROOM. Mr. Chairman, a group of students from the Bay Area will have a very pertinent statement of great consequence to the entire hearing. We would like to read it.

CHAIRMAN HANNAH. You may show your placards and then be seated, and then we will go on with the hearing.

UNIDENTIFIED SPEAKER FROM BODY OF COURTROOM. We would like to make a statement.

CHAIRMAN HANNAH. No statement. You are out of order.

UNIDENTIFIED SPEAKER NO. 1. Let him speak.

UNIDENTIFIED SPEAKER NO. 2. Let him speak.

CHAIRMAN HANNAH. Shall we listen? How long is your statement?

244

UNIDENTIFIED SPEAKER FROM BODY OF COURTROOM. Three, two minutes at the most.

CHAIRMAN HANNAH. Proceed if it only takes only two or three minutes.

UNIDENTIFIED SPEAKER FROM BODY OF COURTROOM. Thank you.

CHAIRMAN HANNAH. The rest be seated.

(The speaker on behalf of the group was Armando Valdez.)

MR. VALDEZ. According to a report——

CHAIRMAN HANNAH. Do you wish to move to the microphone so that you can be heard?

MR. VALDEZ. Yes.

CHAIRMAN HANNAH. Just the one to the microphone. You may be seated if you want to.

MR. VALDEZ. I will stand. Thank you.

CHAIRMAN HANNAH. Okay. Go ahead.

MR. VALDEZ. According to a report issued on the U.S. Civil Rights Commission written by Nick Vaca, who worked for the Commission in the summer of 1966 and is now a graduate student at San Francisco State College, the Commission has systematically, knowingly, and insidiously practiced discrimination against the Mexican Americans and American Indians.

Nick Vaca charges that in 1966 of the 115 professional and clerical workers at the Washington, D.C. office, 52 were Negro, 62 were white Anglo, 1 was Puerto Rican, no Mexican Americans, no American Indians.

No. 2, of the six Commissioners here five are white Anglo, one is Negro. No Mexican Americans, no American Indians are or ever have been Commissioners.

No. 3, in California, Texas, New Mexico, Arizona, and Colorado, there are well over 5,000,000 Mexican Americans. This is the largest minority in each of these States. Yet only 12 of the 53 State Advisory members are Mexican Americans. This is gross exclusion.

No. 4, the four divisions of the Commission have issued 11 major publications in recent years. Not a single one of these publications deals with Mexican Americans or the American Indians.

No. 5, the Commission does not have field offices in the Southwest through which Mexican Americans can channel their legitimate grievances.

No. 6, the most diseased aspect of the Commission is their expert on Mexican American affairs who is white Anglo. He calls Mexican Americans fatalistic, mystical, and totally dominated by their religion. In this curious manner, this so-called expert lays the entire blame of the plight of the Mexican American upon the shoulders of the Mexican American, thus curtailing or eliminating the legitimate basis for grievances having to do with civil rights.

No. 7, according to Mr. Vaca, when he asked why there are no Mexican Americans on the staff, the answer the Commission members provided was that we cannot find Mexican Americans who are qualified. This is the very same statement that appalls the Commission members themselves when it is used by southern racists or by northern employers toward the Negro.

We, the Mexican Bay Area students, now ask the Commission if they can deny these charges of discriminatory practice against the Mexican Americans and American Indians. Can the Commission deny the total exclusion of Mexican Americans and American Indians? We demand, therefore, that these conditions be remedied immediately. Failure to do so would result in the continued operation in direct violation of U.S. Commission's U.S. Civil Rights Act of 1957. Thank you.

I would like to ask those of you in support of this statement to walk out with me.

CHAIRMAN HANNAH. Do you wish to leave us your statement, a copy of your statement?

MR. VALDEZ. Sure will.

CHAIRMAN HANNAH. Mr. Glickstein, will you call the witnesses?

MR. GLICKSTEIN. Will the panelists please step forward to be sworn? Dr. Galarza, Dr. Romano, Mr. Corona, and Mr. Gallegos. Is Mr. Corona here?

SPEAKER FROM COURTROOM. Mr. Chairman, Mr. Corona will be just a few minutes tardy. Mr. Corona will be here later.

(Whereupon, Dr. Ernesto Galarza, Mr. Herman Gallegos, and Dr. Octavio Romano were sworn by the Chairman and testified as follows:)

TESTIMONY OF DR. ERNESTO GALARZA, SAN JOSE, CALIFORNIA; MR. HERMAN GALLEGOS, SAN FRANCISCO, CALIFORNIA; AND DR. OCTAVIO ROMANO, OAKLAND, CALIFORNIA

MR. GLICKSTEIN. I believe each of you gentlemen has seen a copy of a Staff Report entitled: "The Spanish American Community of the San Francisco Bay Area" that was prepared by Mr. Philip Montez and Mr. Lawrence Glick of the Commission staff. Mr. Chairman, may I request that this report be introduced into the record as Exhibit No. 10.

CHAIRMAN HANNAH. It is received as Exhibit No. 10.

(The document referred to was marked Exhibit No. 10 and received in evidence.)

MR. GLICKSTEIN. Before we proceed to direct questions to you gentlemen, I think it would be helpful to the Commission if each of you would briefly comment on what you see as the principal problems facing Spanish-speaking Americans in the Bay Area in the fields of housing, employment, and education. Is there any particular preference as to who speaks first?

DR. ROMANO. I am Octavio Romano. I would like to speak in support of the students' statement on the conditions facing the Mexican American in the United States today, that the Commission has been in existence for 10 years and exhibits glaring discrepancies in representation for such a large population. It is certainly a situation that must be remedied posthaste.

I feel very sorry that it has fallen upon the shoulders of students to carry this burden, but I for one am very proud of them.

MR. GALLEGOS. My name is Herman Gallegos.

How long did you want my comments, Mr. Chairman?

CHAIRMAN HANNAH. We have set aside for the total testimony of the four of you from 7:30 until 8:50. That's an hour and 20 minutes. We would like to have you keep your statements to the minimum so we may have an opportunity to have as much in the way of questions asked by the Commissioners and the Counsel as possible.

MR. GALLEGOS. I shall make my statement very brief.

As you can see from the action which just took place, many of our people feel that the time for talking is running out and that more action is needed, and I, too, must concur with the statement of the students, regrettably. The Commission must first work at putting its own house in order if it fully expects to influence other Federal agencies to do the things that they should have been doing for many years, and I think the students have stated very eloquently the position which I share.

I also appear tonight rather hesitantly for a number of reasons. No. 1: I think that too many of our people expect too much of these hearings. I think that the expectations that those of us who are given this opportunity to make some statements will somehow be able to produce much more than finally comes from the aftermath of these hearings, and I assure my colleagues who have remained in the auditorium, and those who have left, that those of us who have assumed this responsibility to make a statement this evening do it with all the misgivings that I have stated, and I also must express my regret at the fact that the American Indians have not received more attention than they have at this hearing because in the final analysis the issue is that until the last man on the totem pole is taken care of, whether he be white, black, red, or whatever, that in the final analysis we really haven't solved the problem of helping human beings.

So that I think that while we are privileged tonight to have some time, I must assure my friends from the American Indian community that we, too, feel that as we move they must move and

that for any one group to try to move by itself is to do a disservice
to the rest of his fellowmen.

I would like to quote Senator Muskie of Maine, a recent statement which he made, because I think it is apropos to this hearing,
and I will quote him at this time:

"When our governments do not apply their laws or allocate their resources
effectively, when they do not bring the full force of their programs to bear
on social and economic problems, it is the people who suffer and it is the
Nation which loses. During the past five sessions of Congress, we have developed the most impressive package of Federal legislation since the depression
to attack poverty, ignorance, economic distress, urban blight, discrimination
and other human problems, but the success of this legislation is only as good
as the machinery which carries it to the people in the fastest, most effective
way possible."

I feel that the Commission must direct itself to this statement as
the basis by which we in the Spanish-speaking community continue to share the burdens of poverty, of low levels of education,
of disenfranchisement in terms of full political participation, in
terms of all of the problems which Mr. Montez has included in the
report, and which you can find in the multitude of volumes now
available in different places which spell out very clearly the problems of the Spanish-speaking, and I am not going to recite those
problems in any great detail except to point out that in the period
1940 to 1965, some 25 million people have left the rural areas to
the urban cities, and in spite of the massive outmigration of rural
people to the inner-city, we have not developed a coherent plan or
program or social policy which has developed to help these millions
survive or remain on the land or to prepare them for the changed
environment in the cities to which they throng.

As a consequence, we have about 1 percent of our population, that is 70 percent of our urban people, living in 1 percent
of the land, and Mexican Americans and Spanish-speaking are
no exception.

We are 84 percent urban dwellers and are increasing at a rate
faster than the Anglo population.

In the cities we find, and I can only give one very brief example,
time does not permit going through each of the areas which I
feel deserve more time, but the Spanish-speaking remain the victims of change rather than the partners in the growth and development of our great cities. In some ways the fact that no one has
a plan for rebuilding our cities means that maybe there is some
opportunity for the Spanish speaking yet to become involved in
this rebuilding, but not in the way that the big investors and land
developers try to do with the current redevelopment agency
programs.

It's the people of the Spanish-speaking communities throughout
the Southwest have been shifted and relocated and dislocated and
disjointed as a result of massive clearance programs which have

not provided for the effective means to be participants in the plans that are taking place around them.

Generally, the Spanish-speaking and other minorities remain, as I said, the victims. Nowhere do we find private foundations on any large scale or the Federal Government helping the Spanish-speaking to develop the means to be effective, that so oftentimes a standard is applied to us that the Anglo does not apply to himself, and as a consequence, our leadership is looked upon as being too middle-class or not tapped in closely enough with our community or being overidentified with the community and never are the means given to help these organizations to build political power, effective participation in the life stream of the community.

I regret to say that it appears that we have entered an area where we are prepared to spend money for riots, to offset riots or to deal with the aftermath of riots but are not doing anything to help people to build strong family life, to secure their education to which they are entitled under the law and which, administratively, by every means possible, we are entitled to in the free public education system that we have.

I sense a growing militancy within our Spanish-speaking community. If I could merely state it to you, and that something would happen, I would satisfied if my job would be done, but it is not going to happen that way. I can only recall to you very clearly the warning which one can pick up as we attempt to deal with the problems of our community.

The younger people are becoming very impatient with those of us who are somehow looked upon as leaders by the establishment, because we have been unable to bring about changes fast enough. We have been unable to deliver the kinds of goods and services which will make it possible for more talented young people to develop their full potential and capacity.

Negroes have sounded these warnings in the past and it was only until Watts and Harlem and Rochester and a few other places broke out that America began to sit up and listen. When Mexican Americans zoot suited here, were zoot suiters and were pachucos and were the victims of riots and were involved in mass disturbances throughout the Southwest, we unfortunately did so too soon or too early because we did not receive the millions of dollars that seem to come now when those kinds of things happen, but I can only appeal to you that we must move fast and deliberately because if we don't, the demonstrations will lead to greater disturbances which at that point will only be a band aid to the real problem.

I am afraid I have talked too long. I can only say that our problems deserve more time. I think these problems are far too serious to be given to discussion in only an hour and 20 minutes. I think that Mr. Montez has made a good start in his paper. I think there are some things that need to be added to it. I think that the Commission needs to make some changes immediately, including the additition of more staff, the appropriation of more time to the problems of the Spanish-speaking and the American Indians in the Southwest, that the Commission should not merely publish a report with recommendations in an attempt to do this alone. They must return within three months to meet with the community groups that have taken the time to meet with you, to review with us what you feel has been the result of all of this discussion and meeting.

If you fail to return, if you fail to come back to clarify with us as to what you regard as the priorities and what you are going to do in very tangible terms, then I say to you that you will cease to be an effective instrument and you will cease to become an effective advocate in the lives of the Spanish-speaking, American Indians, and other minorities in the Southwest.

In some respects you have already lost that opportunity, but I think you can regain it if you move deliberately and if you move fast enough. If you don't, then you have merely become another Federal agency which has continued to let the Mexican Americans down. Thank you.

CHAIRMAN HANNAH. Mr. Corona, you came late. Your colleagues have been sworn in. We would appreciate it if you would stand and raise your right hand.

(Whereupon, Mr. Bert Corona was sworn by the Chairman and testified as follows:)

TESTIMONY OF MR. BERT CORONA, OAKLAND, CALIFORNIA

CHAIRMAN HANNAH. I think, Mr. Glickstein, before you proceed with the questioning, while I don't think explanations are necessary, many of the people in the audience may not understand the role of the United States Commission on Civil Rights that was created on the recommendation of the President, by the Congress 10 years ago.

It was given a single responsibility, and that was to determine whether or not citizens of the United States were being deprived of the right to vote or to have their votes counted. Citizens of the United States were being denied their civil rights because of their race, creed, color, or national origin, and the Commission was charged with finding out what the facts were then or are now. The responsibility of making recommendations to the President and to the Congress has reference to the findings and such recommendations for immediate action as seem to be in the eyes of the Commission desirable.

Now, in the intervening 10 years the Commission has made many recommendations to the Congress and to the President. Those that called for either Congressional action or Executive action for the most part have been implemented and that's all we are about in the Bay Area this week.

In the process of holding these hearings yesterday and tomorrow and the balance of the week, tomorrow here and the last three days in Oakland, for the purpose of listening to testimony, we do not start out with predetermined conclusions. We try to get a cross-section of both sides of the issues where there are both sides, or several sides, if there are several, and then the Commission will evaluate what is presented in the way of testimony, what it receives in the way of evidence or written statements and will eventually make whatever recommendations it deems to be desirable in its eyes to the President and Congress.

Mr. Glickstein, will you proceed?

MR. GLICKSTEIN. Dr. Galarza, Mr. Corona, did either of you wish to make a statement?

MR. CORONA. Yes. Chairman Hannah, on behalf of the organization of which I have the honor of representing, the Mexican American Political Association, I would like to state a few brief facts more or less reflecting our feelings as a people, and I will just list them very briefly. It will not be an in-depth statement.

We feel that the White House Conference so greatly touted as a solution to many of the problems that have burned deeply in the breasts of the Mexican Americans for many years, we characterize it as the greatest fraud perpetrated by any President upon us, the Mexican Americans, since President Polk decided to move in and take the Southwest States from Mexico, 1847.

It was bad enough when no attention was given to us, but it is even worse when hope has been given to us and then taken away.

Federal employment. There is gross under-representation of the Mexican American in all of the agencies in the State of California. Out of 249,000 Federal positions, there are less than 10,000 Spanish surname employed. We have a higher percentage of the troops in Vietnam than we have working for the Federal Government. We want an opportunity to work and toil and serve the United States and be able to live, not just the opportunity to die for Uncle Sam. Two percent of all the Civil Service employees of all the cities, counties in the State government of California, less than two percent are Spanish surname. Yet Mexican Americans and the Spanish surname family of California constitute 12 percent of the total population.

In the area of law enforcement, thousands of our people who are continually found guilty of merely minor administrative regulations and violations have paid heavily and deeply, they and their families, because of their inability to present their side in a non-Spanish-speaking law enforcement agency or courtroom.

It is not a coincidence that one-third of the men who are to pay the final price in death row in San Quentin today are Mexican

Americans. Great miscarriages of justice are done in the sheriff's departments, in the probation departments, both juvenile and adult, because of the premeditative built-in programming, guaranteed lack of communication with the non-English-speaking Mexican American in the English agency.

Police brutality. Just to run briefly over a few cases that have occurred in the great State of California in the last 12 months. Louis Leyva, a juvenile, was killed five days ago in the city of Compton by a Compton policeman in cold blood. The inquest will take place May the 4.

In Riverside, just a little over a month ago, another juvenile, Ray Moore, was shot in the back, in cold blood, by a policeman with a high-powered .38 while he was fleeing after he had been searched and found to be unarmed and under the influence of liquor.

A week before, another Mexican American youngster in the same county was beaten to death in the police station in the city of Corona. The verdict was that he had died of vomiting. Actually, the autopsy proved that he had died of internal injuries.

In the city of Calexico, in the county below that, the Imperial County, in the year 1965 a Mexican American was shot in cold blood while crossing a field belonging to a distinguished and prominent member of the Calexico Board of Education who had drawn a bead on this Mexican crossing this field so that he wouldn't have to run around and follow the roads, taking a shortcut, with a high-powered rifle, with a high-powered telescopic sight, and the verdict in this case was justifiable homicide.

The verdict in the Corona case was justifiable homicide. The verdict in the Riverside case was justifiable homicide.

Last month a youngster in San Jose, in Santa Clara County, was again brutally beaten to death in Santa Clara County jail and the verdict again was justifiable homicide, and we wonder what the verdict will be in Compton.

In Hayward, California, just across the Bay, last year during the SAC hearings, we presented witnesses who were still bearing on themselves the evidences of very severe and brutal police beating when a Mexican baptismal party was invaded by Hayward police without a search warrant, and the participants brutally beaten. Nothing has come of this case.

We have this as a history. The whole area of law enforcement bears very heavily upon our non-English-speaking population.

We have documented facts where we have orders from the heads of government agencies, both local and State, as well as from Federal, we have documented orders from the United States Post Office in San Pedro instructing people in their agencies not to use or prohibiting them from speaking the Spanish language.

Just three weeks ago the director of the Oakland Skills Center in Oakland, Mr. Mickey, called me to tell me that there was a riot situation developing in the Oakland Skills Center, and when I questioned him about the reasons for his fears, he stated that he had been complaining to Mexicans who were using the Spanish language in the halls and they had rebuffed him when he ordered them to cease.

There is a complete absence of ample facilities in the court systems, in the booking stations of city and county police departments throughout the State of California.

In Napa County, like so many other counties, there are no interpreters in the courts, and clients have to produce their own interpreters.

In the Motor Vehicle Department which governs the daily lives of our people, there are many, many cases where because of the misunderstandings or the inability of our people to understand proper instructions, and so forth, our people lose their licenses. In the whole field of obtaining insurance, because of the liability insurance law in California, what for the typical Anglo individual might be a minor matter, to a Mexican American, who does not understand the workings of insurance companies and does not understand the full implications of his inability to obtain or the lack of his attaining of liability and collision insurance, is a grave matter leading to imprisonment, leading to the suspension of his driver's license, leading to heavy fines and leading to the deprivation of the ability to drive a car and secure proper employment.

In the post office we have had picketing of the major post offices in California by the Mexican American Political Association and six other statewide organizations in major cities in the State of California. And we can only say that the negation of affirmative action programs, the negation of a civil rights program by the post office is only equalled by this Civil Rights Commission itself, and I am going to go to that later.

We recommend as Postmaster General O'Brien recommended, too, that the postal service might better be operated by a private corporation. We say amen to that, only we say that the post office should be sold to a non-profit corporation composed of the postal unions and the minorities who work in the post office, and we believe that they could then deliver the mail faster and cheaper than is being done now.

We have had to wage a civil rights struggle against the largest employer of the United States Federal Government other than the armed forces, the United States Postal Service. A major civil rights struggle has had to be waged by the Mexican American organizations in the State of California to force the largest employer to live up to the law of the land.

In the field of education, I know it has been covered by people who are more expert than I am, I just have this to say, that the bulk of the school districts in the State of California are in the hands in the rural areas of growers and their people, or in the urban centers of conservative power structures who guarantee that the funds that they receive from Federal sources shall not be spent in the manner that the law intended those funds should be spent. They guarantee that an education that is not geared to the needs of the Spanish-speaking child is the kind of education that is given by that school district. They guarantee that the curricula, the psychology, the methodology, the whole basis of the educational system is structured for Anglo-Saxon Protestant Americans, not for Mexican Americans.

An evident proof is the fact that though 13.6 of all the students in the State are Spanish surnames, 27 percent of all the school children in this so-called special education programs in the State and these special education programs are the programs for the physically handicapped, the mentally retarded, and the emotionally disturbed are Mexican Americans.

In the field of voting rights and the obtaining of citizenship, the rights and the opportunities of Mexican Americans are grossly violated throughout the State of California. This has been so since 1888, when California ceased to be a bilingual State. Not only was the voting test in Spanish taken away, but the right to obtain citizenship in Spanish was taken away, and we feel that these two rights should be restored. There has been a continual denial, particularly in the grower-controlled counties, such as occurred in Madera County last month, and this—or in March and in April in Solano County, the denial of registration books to Mexican Americans who want to register their constituents. Protests have been lodged with this Commission and with the United States Attorney General for Civil Rights, Mr. John Doar, and we are still waiting for intervention on their behalf.

The whole question of the Immigration Service. The Mexican American views the Immigration Service, and particularly the Border Patrol, as the Gestapo is viewed by Jews in Germany. Although the Border Patrol has not burned Mexican Americans, they have deported us continually and we view the Immigration Service as merely a tool of the growers and other border and Southwest United States employers as a means, as an organ of government, to implement a cheap labor policy. This has been the story of the lives of Mexican Americans in the Southwest.

Beyond that many growers specialize in the bringing in of large families so that they can exploit them better, always using the Immigration Service to implement a policy of fear and panic is a constant factor in the lives of Mexican Americans in the Southwest.

In the rural counties where there have been efforts to organize farm workers, such as in Kern County in the past year and a half during the Delano grape strike, the District Attorney's office has consistently refused to accept citizens' complaints when they have come from farm workers, but they have been overeager to arrest on the spot farm workers that were singled out by growers who appeared on picket lines or in the ranches themselves to point out farm workers as guilty of a civil violation.

Just two weeks ago, a clipping in the Monterey in the Salinas Californian quoting the head of the Housing Authority, saying that he was for housing programs in Monterey County provided that they would produce housing in such locales where "We would not have to look at Mexican Americans."

Last week in Napa County, the Mayor of Yountville is quoted in the Napa Register, Napa County Register, stating that "If welfare and Mexicans keep increasing in the city of Yountville, we cannot have a town here."

In Blythe and Ripley, California, ample documentation exists, and in Stockton, California, documenting the plight of starvation and of shelterlessness for thousands of American citizens.

All of these things we Mexican Americans view as gross violations, not only of the rights guaranteed to us under the Constitution of the United States but also as gross violations of the treaty of Guadalupe-Hidalgo, which to us has always appeared as something that we were given for being taken over by conquest.

The Mexican American Political Association, the national CSO Community Service Organization, the oldest civil rights and community organization of Mexican Americans in the United States, the League of United Latin-American citizens and United Farm Workers and other Spanish-speaking local or regional groups met in Fresno Saturday, April 29 of 1967, and unanimously approved the charges which I have above outlined and also unanimously approved the charges filed by Attorney Rudy Ramos, the Washington, D. C., representative of the American G. I. Forum on the violation of the Civil Rights Act itself with the United States Civil Service Commission against this very United States Commission on Civil Rights, and I, as the state president of MAPA, endorse, support, and commit our organization to jointly press these charges made by our sister organization, the American G.I. Forum versus this Commission. This Commission itself is violating the law by not having a Mexican American Commissioner and by on its staff having but two Mexican Americans out of 164 employees and both hired in the last five months.

These happened to be Dr. Phillip Montez who is a temporary full-time consultant and a civil rights program assistant, Lucinda Arvizu.

In its 10 years of existence this Commission has devoted zero of its resources, personnel, and time to the Mexican American people, the country's second largest minority, who is here in this country by force of conquest, in the land of its birthright, and for the above-listed reasons I have been instructed by the leaders of these organizations in this Saturday meeting and by the State administrators of the Mexican American Political Association to appear here only under protest, under protest recognizing that this Commission is in total violation of the intent, the spirit, and the letter of all the civil rights laws themselves and that this Commission cannot possibly begin to deal seriously with its own violations of the law and its failure to concern itself with the vast problems of the Mexican American family in the United States until it sets, and it should be its next hearing, a full national hearing conducted in the Southwest with full investigations of the violations of the civil rights of the Spanish-speaking people in the United States.

For the above reasons I have been instructed by the statewide leaders of MAPA to present this statement, read it, and depart forthwith in contempt, anger, and indignation defying this Commission to hold us in contempt.

CHAIRMAN HANNAH. Anyone wish to leave? You are free to leave.

UNIDENTIFIED SPEAKER FROM BODY OF COURTROOM. Tell them we are going to picket them until they leave. We will be out there with our picket signs and tell you every day when you come in here that you people yourselves are disregarding the Civil Rights Act itself in your composition and your acts and what you are doing here. We are going to be out there every day until you change—

CHAIRMAN HANNAH. It's a free country. Proceed, Mr. Glickstein.

MR. GLICKSTEIN. Dr. Galarza, would you care to make a statement?

DR. GALARZA. Mr. Chairman, and ladies and gentlemen, lady of the Commission, gentlemen of the staff, you are perhaps the first highly-ranking body of Federal representatives on a Commission to expose yourselves to a capsule form of explanation and exposition and demonstration of what has been going on in the State of California, to my knowledge, for 50 years.

It is not for me to review or to add details to the statements that have already been made, because in the 35 or 40 years that I have lived and worked in California I have experienced in the fields of education, in housing, in farm labor organization, in relations with the police, incidents such as those that have been related to you by previous speakers.

The historic capsule that you are getting read into and spoken into the record is, however, one which, as serious and grim as it is, one which has to be set in my judgment in a still deeper focus.

I was grateful that when your staff members instructed me not to bring this evening a list of complaints or of particular grievances, but rather to take 10 minutes of your time to attempt to set forth the general background of the position of the Mexican American community in California, which gives rise to these gross violations in so many fields, and for the balance of my time this is what I am going to try to do.

You are doing an important thing here and an unusual thing for a Federal agency. You have sensed that these particular violations, sometimes they might be called crimes, committed by legal agencies happen because something equivalent has been happening to the Mexican community as a community. The Mexican community in California, as a group of people, as a distinct ethnic group, has somewhat the same history as that of the Negro community. It has put itself together in this State only within the last 50 years and it has developed neither the economic security, the educational advantages, the acceptance to build within its own structure the means to defend itself. And so Mexicans in California have been forced to wait at intervals of decades for meetings such as this one, meetings or presentations at which they can lay forth the accumulations of many, many years, of decades of mistreatment, of discrimination and of lack of opportunity.

May I stress and urge you to give much more time and thought and study to the present condition of the Mexican community in the State of California.

From 1925 to 1950, roughly speaking, well over 1,000,000 Mexicans in California were attempting to find a base to put down roots, to teach their young, to receive and deserve and exercise first-class citizenship. It was a hard struggle, and in the middle 40's, the early 50's, some of us who have seen this process thought that these communities were getting somewhere, but what happened from 1945 roughly on to the present time was that some extremely important economic changes have come about in California which have cut at the tap root which have again assaulted the stability of the Mexican community and, so to speak, kept it on the road.

Now, today in California, to give you just one illustration of what I am talking about, in California today over 80 percent of the Mexican Americans live in the large cities and some of these large cities are indicated on your map, Oakland and San Francisco, to name only two.

Now, what is happening in these cities? In the central cities of San Francisco, of San Jose, of Oakland, of Los Angeles, thousands upon thousands of Mexicans are being received every year as refugees from agriculture in which they no longer have opportunities for employment or in which such opportunities are diminishing and they go to the cities to look for work, to look for shelter, and what meets them in the cities? A brand new package of Federal programs, well-intentioned, labeled with some very impressive slogans, "The New Society," "The New Deal," "The Affluent Society," the great this and that, but the reality of the matter is that as these thousands of Mexicans crowd into already overcrowded cities, they are met with programs such as the program sponsored by the Urban Renewal Program of the Federal Government. What is taking place there is a massive assault upon those communities, those neighborhoods where Mexicans thought they had a chance to start life again, to constitute for themselves a community.

And if you gentlemen, the lady, Mrs. Freeman, want to give your appraisal of these particular grievances, in education, in police relations, in housing, and so forth, their proper perspective, I recommend that you look very intensively at what is happening to the community as a community. There is, of course, a theory that the best way to deal with the Negro and the Mexican is to boot him out of the ghetto because the ghetto is an unpleasant place to live in, anyway, and to let him look for shelter and for jobs wherever he may.

Ladies and gentlemen, the economy of California up to today has had enough flexibility and just enough of that kind of elbow room that allows some people to treat Mexicans decently, but that elbow room is disappearing, and until it is recognized that the economic pressures upon the Mexican community are producing these conditions in the central city, you are going to have more and not fewer incidents such as those that have been mentioned.

Now, Mr. Corona has suggested to you what changes Federal agencies can and must make in their hiring policies.

I want to close by suggesting to you one other thought. It has seemed to me for many years that the Federal agencies in their approach to the Mexican community have what might be described as the apple pie approach. The urban renewal people coming with their programs and they seek out within the Mexican community their part of the Mexican community to carry out their program. The Civil Rights Commission will be sending representatives into the Mexican community focusing, I hope not, but focusing entirely on civil rights. The labor people focus entirely on their Congressional statutory assignment. What is the result? A small Mexican community, or a large one, that is trying to put itself together, once more to try to become a community through which opportunity can be offered and growth and citizenship can be assured, that community is cut up into segments and so far as I can detect no agency in Washington is taking the whole view of the Mexican community and operating with a respect, a deep respect for what it is that makes a community and why a community is absolutely necessary for man, and if I were to close on one note I would say that perhaps the most promising thing that this Commission has done in its appearance here is to become aware that the framework of decent democratic living in California is not here. It is in jeopardy even more than it was 25 or 30 years ago.

Its mechanization, its cybernetics with enormous shifts in the location and investment of capital, and so on, this I think is a subject, is the frame of reference in which I want to close. Besides, of course, thanking the Commission for this opportunity to make the statement.

CHAIRMAN HANNAH. Mr. Glickstein?

MR. GLICKSTEIN. Mr. Chairman, although I have some questions, if I may I would like to reserve them until after the Commission has questioned.

CHAIRMAN HANNAH. Father Hesburgh?

COMMISSIONER HESBURGH. Mr. Galarza, first of all, I would like to mention for the record that one of our first hearings early in the Commission's life was in Phoenix, Arizona, in the first five years of our existence, if I recall correctly, and there we addressed ourselves mainly to the Mexican American community in that city and have kept some touch with them through State Advisory Committees ever since.

Several years ago we came to Los Angeles and to San Francisco and in both of these places also had discussions with the Mexican American community.

Following that we had a full-fledged study commissioned which actually was done at our University of Notre Dame on the Mexican American situation. The Commission was not completely satisfied with the study and they had another study made which also did not completely satisfy them. As a result, both of these documents became internal matters.

I would think, and I would like to get your reaction to this, that our problem with this particular problem you have so well outlined is that we find it extremely difficult to come to grips with it, to find a handle for it. In other words, in the general work of the Commission, whether it is in voting or education or employment or in housing or in public accommodations or administration of justice, while most of these programs have been somewhat stimulated by enormous involvement and pressure on the part of the Negro population of the United States, once the law is passed it applies to all minorities, because all of our laws in all of our Commission's work is related to race, religion, nationality, and origin. As a matter of fact, the some 75 percent of our recommendations have been passed into law, have been passed into law for all minorities, not for this or that minority.

Now, I am willing to concede with you that if one looks at the total work of the Commission it has somewhat responded to the pressures it has received, and the thing that I think has impeded our work or even our interest, because I have long been interested in the question that you have addressed yourself to this evening, together with your associates, is that we find it difficult to actually find the kind of leadership within the Mexican American or Spanish-speaking American community that we have found in other communities.

In other words, if you ask who are the leaders of the Negro community, immediately you can tick off a whole series of national names, whether it be Martin Luther King or James Farmer, either Carmichael or Roy Wilkins, et cetera, et cetera, whereas you bring up the normal question to anyone in the Midwest or the East, which is far from here, and this maybe is a problem of the breadth of our Nation, but if you bring it up and say who are the leaders of the Mexican American community, it is very hard to find anyone who seems to know about this.

Now, this may be ignorance on our part. I am willing to concede that, but I think what we really need from the Mexican American community is, number one, a clear identification of leadership, and I think this would help us enormously.

I will give you a chance in a second. I just want to get this off my chest before we get started.

Number two, I think we need desperately an identification of all of the associations. In other words, what is the Urban League, the NAACP? What are the comparable institutions within the Mexican American or Spanish-speaking American community?

Number three, I think we have to be able to identify the key problems, some of which you have identified, the formation of community, the problem of transition from rural to city. I think looking at the Nation as a whole there has been enormous attention to the Negro problem, because in a sense it is more visible than the Mexican American problem because it is a problem of color rather than of language basically, and I think what we need at this stage of the game, and that is why we are here, is some hard facts, some good studies, some identification of the people and the organizations with whom we might work.

The fact is, I think if you would go over all of the complaints made to the Commission over the past 10 years I would guess that perhaps less than 1 percent of our formal complaints come from the Mexican American community.

Would that be an adequate statement, Mr. Staff Director?

So we have in a sense been working in a nebulous area that we have spent some money trying to get at and we have found that our efforts haven't been very satisfactory, even to us ourselves, but I think the last thing you should think of is that we are not interested, because we are. We want very much to represent your group as well as any other minority group, but we need help because Washington is a long way from California, a long way from the Southwest, and we need help very much to identify the people and the associations and the problems, and I think as far as speaking as one member of the Commission, if we can get this kind of identification, if we could even have a list of the kinds of people qualified to work on the staff of the Commission, which we have not had, and we have looked rather hard on occasion, and if we can get this kind of identification, I think we can work much more fully. But I would think that—and this is now finally getting back after this long harangue to a question—do you think the Spanish American or Spanish American community can give us this kind of help?

DR. GALARZA. Father Hesburgh, I would first like to make this comment. Quite a number, at least I count myself among those in the Mexican American community, who have for years shied away from this concept of leadership. The Mexican community, to an outsider, has a few visible leaders, people who exercise office as president or in some other capacity of a given organization.

These are small organizations and their history is rather recent, but having spent so many years of my life in the Mexican communities, I want to assure you that there is an enormous richness of leadership. It is not absent. It is there, but it takes different forms, and when I closed with my criticism of the Federal agencies I meant to put my finger precisely upon that fact.

I think I could introduce you, sir, to 35 or 40 men and women under 35 just in my county of Santa Clara who have a commitment to the community, who have some experience, who have connections in turn, who form opinion and who command respect among the people.

The trouble is that they do not operate on the scale that you have been mentioning. They operate in what is a genuine grass roots environment. And in California we are concerned that Federal agencies reach down to that level and help us identify these people, give them support in a work which I think is very necessary and in five or 10 years, sir, you will have, I venture to say, hundreds of young people coming out as, not leaders in the old sense of the word, dressed in more or less charismatic togas, but leaders in the real sense of the word, people who live in the community, who see it face to face, day to day, who understand its needs and who are able to convey to you and persons like yourself what those needs are.

I myself am not interested in promoting a small group of a dozen Mexican Americans in California who will be handily recognized by the Civil Service Commission or the Civil Rights Commission or the Department of Labor as the leaders of the community with whom contact can immediately be made.

This I think is a very grave temptation, but it is the business of the Federal agencies to understand and I want to signal to your attention, particularly to the United States Department of Labor, for 15 years it was guilty of conniving and conspiring behind closed doors to destroy the leadership of the Mexican community in rural California, and I know of at least 50 young men and women who left the State of California, the kind of leader that you are seeking, the kind of leader in which I am addressing, they left the State of California under harassment of the joint conspiracy of the Associated Farmers of California and the United States Department of Labor.

Now, this is the thing I am talking about.

I have on more than one occasion, Father Hesburgh and Mr. Chairman, rejected the title of leader of the Mexican community. I am not. I don't aspire to it and I don't want it. I feel that the true, the genuine, the human, and the democratic concept of leadership is as I have defined it, and if the Civil Rights Commission wishes to explore with us this concept and wishes to join with us in an effort to convince every other Federal agency that it is not its business to come into California and to destroy communities but to help build them, I think you will be amazed at the existing young leadership in the Mexican American community today, and I am perfectly willing to help you identify it.

FATHER HESBURGH. Thank you, Mr. Galarza.

DR. ROMANO. I would like to concur with Dr. Galarza.

From 1839 when the first underground railroad was set up in Texas to help Negro slaves escape, this railroad was set up by Mexican Americans, Mexicans and then later Mexican Americans. From that day until the present, until the cowboy strikes in Texas, until the widespread strikes in California, there was a time in our history when Mexicans were striking in eight different states, Michigan, Illinois, Washington, California, New Mexico, Arizona, and we are still looking for leadership.

What happened, of course, when you look at other minorities, you take the Jewish people of the United States and you see the entire spectrum from extreme orthodoxy all the way to the American Council for Judaism. You look at the Negro community and you will see Roy Wilkins and Malcolm X and all of a sudden we want leaders of this population and I only say to emphatically concur with what Dr. Galarza has said, they are there.

COMMISSIONER HESBURGH. Mr. Romano, I don't want to monop-
olize this and I will stop after this.

I think I can testify here that in the past 10 years on the Commission I have spoken very often of the problems you gentlemen
have spoken of tonight and I am very deeply interested in them.
The problem that I am trying to understand is why we have had
such difficulty coming to grips with the problem. We need help
on this and we are here precisely to look for help on this. We came
here seven years ago and talked to the then existing members:
of the Mexican American community in Los Angeles and San
Francisco. We spent a whole week in the State. We published,
printed every word of their testimony, and we went back home and
heard practically nothing from then on. We have been looking
here and there for the kinds of people that could strengthen the
staff. Maybe we haven't been looking hard enough. This is not my
primary responsibility but we have spoken of this many times
on the staff. We have been concerned to come to grips with this
problem, but I just want to try and make the group understand,
I am not trying to make a debating point. I am just looking for
help and it seems to me important that as a group of 6,000,000
people, roughly, there must have to be to deal with this group
nationally, some leadership that is visible and immediate and can
be called upon, because the fact is, if you look at the Negro minority in the United States I think anybody in the room here can
tell you 10 or 12 nationally known leaders. You see them all the
time in the magazines. You hear them on the television, at the
White House talking to the President, et cetera, but the problem
is I think we need more visibility for the programs, the leader-
ships, and the associations of the Mexican Americans or the
Spanish-speaking Americans in this community, and I am only
suggesting this as one way of coming to grips with the problem.

I am as interested in coming to grips with the problem as you
are.

DR. ROMANO. And I say they are visible from the point of 19
percent casualties of Mexican Americans in Vietnam. They are
visible. We know that. They are visible to us. They are not visible
to you.

FATHER HESBURGH. That's right.

DR. ROMANO. This is the problem.

CHAIRMAN HANNAH. May I remind the Commissioners that
we have only 10 minutes left for this subject.

MR. GALLEGOS. Father Hesburgh, I would like to respond to
your question. I think the request for instant leadership frequently comes about because of the inability of communities to
look at the Mexican American community in terms of how to
attach its concern to uplift this community, because it has many
problems. We have not come up with a Marshall Plan for Mexican

Americans. We have not come up with a freedom budget for Mexican Americans, although we would believe that we would be included in that should that dream ever to become true.

We have not made those kinds of plans at this point. I would say that the Mexican American community is very busy. The Spanish-speaking community is very busy throughout the Southwest, acting to civil rights, political and so on, and so the rules are different, and part of the problem is that the Federal agencies come into our community and fail to really develop meaningful programs as Dr. Galarza indicated.

I will give you a very specific example to this point. This afternoon a gentleman from one of the Federal agencies that came in to see me wanted to recruit Spanish-speaking people to the Federal agency. He was given my name and indicated that from here he was going to Los Angeles to meet with Ralph Guzman and from there he was probably going to go to Arizona and that was going to be the extent of his visit, and I said, "What kind of program do you have in terms of not just screening those that may be interested, but what are you doing in terms of the long-run development of getting your message to schools, younger people, so we can create interest in education?"

Well, they have no budget, no money, no program, no staff, and I said, "Look, I am not about to do your work. I mean, among other things that I have to do, recruiting for you is not one of them." Although if I can get the message to someone I will. I think this is the kind of problem we are grappling with, is that Federal agencies will contact someone who is a representative of an organization and say, "Will you help us?" And I think this places a greater burden and injustice on that person and the agency, and I think we have to acquire the staff, the expertise from within and not expect it to necessarily come from outside. I think it can come from within.

FATHER HESBURGH. My only point is that one great reason that the Negro American community has gotten enormous attention and enormous support and the enormous help in the past few years is the NAACP, Urban League, et cetera, et cetera, et cetera, and unless there is some internal cohesive immediately comparable group, I can say Core and SNCC, and all the others, too, but unless there is some immediately comparable group in the Mexican American community, it is very hard to get a group to work with directly.

MR. GALLEGOS. Part of the problem is the Urban League and the NAACP have a 50 year history and our history in that kind of organization is new because we are only learning now how to militate against the influence of the Anglo pressures, and so that I think that what Dr. Galarza is perhaps referring to is the fact that within our community we have the people who can be effective. I think it is a problem of the Federal agencies not connecting themselves properly to these resources.

CHAIRMAN HANNAH. Do you have a question, Mr. Patterson?

VICE CHAIRMAN PATTERSON. No.

CHAIRMAN HANNAH. Mrs. Freeman?

DR. ROMANO. Mr. Chairman, may I make a brief statement?

CHAIRMAN HANNAH. Very brief.

DR. ROMANO. Recently there was a letter addressed to a federally funded program in this area signed by six major Mexican American organizations, plus other interested parties. It was totally ignored. The Upward Bound program geared to help minority kids into college has 40 Mexican Americans out of a total recruitment of 400. When protested, I got a reply from Dr. Frost, who was conducting that program, "This is sufficient percentage. There is nothing wrong with this."

I say the problem is not in the Mexican community. It is in the men from Washington who do not know the situation in California.

CHAIRMAN HANNAH. Mrs. Freeman?

COMMISSIONER FREEMAN. The question which I am about to address I will not address to any particular one of you.

You have been very helpful in identifying the problems of the Mexican American, and, of course, I don't have to tell you that some of them are very familiar, problems of law enforcement, discrimination in employment, education, voting rights, but I would like to ask if you would give more details about the point that you made about the Immigration Service, and how it is the tool of the growers as the means of implementing cheap labor.

As I indicated earlier, the Labor Department issued a report on San Francisco just recently in which it determined that there was a very high percentage of unemployment and underemployment, and I would like to know if you will explore this further, the extent to which the Labor Department has included in its surveys the problems of the Spanish-speaking community.

DR. GALARZA. Mrs. Freeman, I will make a very brief comment on that. It is true that the Department of Labor's studies for the last 15 or 20 years have given us some statistics and data on the flow of manpower, but particularly the supply of farm labor from across the border.

Addressing myself specifically to the question that you raised concerning the Immigration Service, I think I can answer that best by pointing out to you that American immigration policy as policy is a function of American economic policy.

Now this is a vague statement and I clarify it by adding this, that whether or not the border is open or closed, whether or not we import Braceros or don't import them, whether or not the

Border Patrol is very stringent in picking up wetbacks or whether it is very liberal in picking them up depends upon the status, the condition of production in the United States.

If industry and agriculture demand more manpower, there is a liberalization. The border isn't open, but there are big holes in it and people trickle through them by the hundreds of thousands. If the asparagus growers of San Joaquin County are in oversupply of labor, you see an enormous activity by the Border Patrol. They are just cleaning out camps day and night. If they are in short supply of labor, the Border Patrol will pick out a wetback here and a wetback there just to keep their boys informed that the Border Patrol is around and they had better work hard while they are here.

If all the details, in other words—and I am sorry that I don't have time to engage in a long conversation about this, but the details of immigration policy, of immigration enforcement, cannot be understood unless we know what the economic interests of employers in the United States happen to be at that moment, and if you know that you can practically guess whether the border is tight or whether it is loose.

Now, having laid that down as a premise, I just wanted to add this comment: I have no faith, no confidence in the Department of Labor of the United States. Its record and its history in this State is one of hostility, covert hostility, to the Mexican, and in its estimates of shortages of labor, it commits statistical crimes to sell its story to the American people.

One of the recommendations that I would urgently make upon you is that with respect to the economic rights of Mexican workers in California, you have a very close look at the history and present operation of the Farm Placement Service of California, particularly under its new chairman or new director, Mr. Talbot.

CHAIRMAN HANNAH. Before I call a brief recess, I should like to invite the gentlemen who have spoken to us this evening to expand their statements, give us anything that they have in the way of written material or care to present to us. We will keep the record open for a week or 10 days after the conclusion of this hearing and we will welcome the receipt of whatever you care to give us.

DR. ROMANO. I have a question, Mr. Chairman. In view of the allegations tonight concerning the Commission, can we expect the Commission to hold a hearing on itself?

CHAIRMAN HANNAH. Well, that the Commission will have to determine.

We will now take a recess for five minutes.

MR. GALLEGOS. Mr. Chairman, I would like to clarify one point in the San Francisco situation. We have referred primarily to

Mexican Americans, but in San Francisco, and for the record, I want it noted that we are referring to a diversity of Spanish-speaking, including Puerto Ricans and other nationality groups.

CHAIRMAN HANNAH. We understand that.

CHAIRMAN HANNAH. The hearing will come to order. Mr. Glickstein, will you call the next witness.

MR. GLICKSTEIN. The next witness is Mr. Wilfred Ussery.

(Whereupon, MR. WILFRED USSERY was sworn by the Chairman and testified as follows:)

TESTIMONY OF MR. WILFRED T. USSERY, SAN FRANCISCO, CALIFORNIA

MR. GLICKSTEIN. Will you please state your full name and address for the record.

MR. USSERY. My name is Wilfred T. Ussery. I live at 2338 Pine Street in San Francisco.

MR. GLICKSTEIN. What is your occupation?

MR. USSERY. I am currently the statewide coordinator for an all-black conference in Los Angeles, and I am affiliated with the firm of Baker Architects and Planners in San Francisco.

MR. GLICKSTEIN. Are you the coordinator for the—

MR. USSERY. Black conference in Los Angeles on May 26 through 28.

MR. GLICKSTEIN. How long have you lived in the Bay Area?

MR. USSERY. Since 1943.

MR. GLICKSTEIN. I understand you also are a member of a group called the Black Planning Committee?

MR. USSERY. Yes, sir, that is correct.

MR. GLICKSTEIN. Would you tell us what that group is, please.

MR. USSERY. That is a group of people who came together out of their common concern about the status of the black community in this country and what we recognize as present dangers to it, with the idea of planning a series of meetings and conferences to consider that question, and it is made up of people who live in San Francisco.

MR. GLICKSTEIN. When was the group formed?

MR. USSERY. Shortly after Governor Reagan was elected Governor of the State of California.

MR. GLICKSTEIN. Is that group a factor in planning the conference that you mentioned that is coming up in Los Angeles?

MR. USSERY. Most of its members constitute the Northern California component of a statewide committee. There are people in Los Angeles and in that area also involved.

MR. GLICKSTEIN. Have you held any positions with the Economic Opportunities Council in San Francisco?

MR. USSERY. Yes, until December I was the area director of the Western Addition Target Area, which is one of the five target areas in the city of San Francisco.

MR. GLICKSTEIN. Are you also associated with a national civil rights organization?

MR. USSERY. I am.

MR. GLICKSTEIN. Which one and what is your position?

MR. USSERY. The Congress on Racial Equality, and I am the national chairman.

MR. GLICKSTEIN. Mr. Ussery, Core is one of the organizations associated with the advocacy of Black Power. What does that term mean to you?

MR. USSERY. It is synonymous with black unity and it recognizes the needs for people to come together as a community, as a prerequisite for dealing in any kind of alliances, coalitions, and efforts to improve the situation that confronts our community.

MR. GLICKSTEIN. Does it mean economic or political power?

MR. USSERY. It most certainly does.

MR. GLICKSTEIN. Is it anti-white?

MR. USSERY. No, it is not anti-white in concept. However, one could expect that in the process of bringing a community together there would be a great deal of anti-white sentiment expressed, but the concept itself is not anti-white.

MR. GLICKSTEIN. Does it involve the notion of separatism?

MR. USSERY. To the degree that one must do things alone rather than always working to achieve an intergrated effort, it is synonymous with that notion. However, if one is coming together to deal and take part in a democratic process in this country, it is not inherently separatist in nature, and I think that is a very important distinction that should be made.

MR. GLICKSTEIN. Would you say it is anti-government?

MR. USSERY. Not yet. I say that because I certainly am one who feels a great deal of frustration and disenchantment with the system over a continual series of disappointments and a lack of producing or promises to a community over the last 400 years, and one is at the point now where one has questions about to what extent the system, if you can use that word, has the ability to address itself to the real dimensions of the problems in this country that are fostered and maintained by racism.

MR. GLICKSTEIN. Does the concept of Black Power involve an abandonment of the doctrine of non-violence?

MR. USSERY. It doesn't necessarily mean an abandonment of non-violence. It means that that is one of many tools for getting a job done. I don't think it at all means that.

I participated outside before I came in in a picket line whch was a non-violent picket line. I think that speaks to that point.

MR. GLICKSTEIN. What in your opinion accounts for the strong reaction among whites and among some Negroes, for the advocacy of the term "Black Power"?

MR. USSERY. Well, it is very difficult for me to try and speak for white people and, on the other hand, I am very aware of the fact that many people would like to see the black community remain infantile with respect to its sophistication for handling political institutions in this country and are very leery of any efforts that moves it further along the line of being able to make progress commensurate with its strength at the ballot box, and I think we are also the recipient of a great deal of misrepresentation by the press and many people articulating our position who are not really adherents of that particular theory. I am speaking of editorial writers, of TV commentators, of people who didn't quite understand what it was all about, and a great deal of people that the public reacted to were not really the comments that were coming from the organization who had embraced that particular philosophy.

MR. GLICKSTEIN. What has been the impact in the Bay Area of the idea of Black Power?

MR. USSERY. I think it is a much more acceptable notion now that it was six months ago or shortly after it was announced as an important policy direction of our organization as well as several others.

MR. GLICKSTEIN. Mr. Ussery, to what do you attribute the growth of Negro militancy in recent years?

MR. USSERY. If I really answer that, I have to say that it comes out of a sense of awareness that the usual kinds of tools that one has dealt with are inadequate to deal with the problem. It would also stem from recognizing that most of the definitions of the problem that we have dealt with in the past have been really quite superficial. They have not been answers or staking out of problems which really provided or would provide, even if we were successful, answers for masses of black people in this country. In order to move in that direction, it brings you into more conflict with what you have described as the system and to the real forces that run this country, and I think that really is the kind of underlying reasons for what one can regard as more militance.

I think it merely represents really that the organizations that have been in a position to supposedly speak for black people are now really beginning to identify more with the problems of the masses of black people.

MR. GLICKSTEIN. Is it necessarily inconsistent to advocate black power and integration simultaneously?

MR. USSERY. It is not at all. I had the occasion to speak in a church some two or three months ago and I used the analogy of the history of the church itself, the black church itself that I was speaking at, as a means of demonstrating what we were talking about with respect to Black Power, and that is that early in the life of this particular denomination they were an integral part of the white church. Yet the black ministers in that church saw fit at some point in time to pull away and to establish what later became the African Methodist Episcopal Church.

If you look at the various Baptist denominations in the black community, you find that their history has essentially been the same. No one has accused the National Baptist Convention of being racist or separatist. No one has accused the A.M.E. Church of being racist or separatist. The point is that they are able to operate within the total religious community on the local level or nationally and I am saying that if one as a community pulls oneself together, it is possible to use that kind of example, also politically, economically, and in other areas of life and that is what we have talked about in this philosophy and it has been totally distorted and misconstrued and so on and there are adequate examples all up and down the line to deal with this kind of point.

MR. GLICKSTEIN. But what you suggest will result in organizations being either Negro or white, will result in polarizing the races in the country.

MR. USSERY. That is correct.

MR. GLICKSTEIN. Do you think that white prejudice against Negroes and Negro prejudices against whites can ever be eradicated if racial isolation continues?

MR. USSERY. Will you please restate that question?

MR. GLICKSTEIN. Do you think that white prejudice against Negroes and Negro prejudice against whites can ever be eradicated if racial isolation continues?

MR. USSERY. I am not convinced that it can be. That is a nightmare that I live with daily, and I think that the country is headed towards a really serious confrontation on its history and the fact that it has several kinds of major commitments going on which are really in phase to bring about very serious confrontations that just have to be dealt with.

I don't see the energy in America where, instead of putting 90 cents on the dollar in developing an airliner that will cross the country in three hours, that they put 90 cents on the dollar to buy the home for a poor black person in the Fillmore or some place else, and this is the thing that you find in the area of education, where is there is not a national commitment to use the wealth of this Nation to resolve problems that everyone recognizes. You don't find it in education. You don't find it in housing. You don't find it in the area of political participation, as was exemplified by the Mexican Amerian community coming in and saying they want representation on this body.

The point that I am making is that if one really stakes out the gravity of the problem as it exists this day, in this country, relative to minority communities and how racism runs this country, I don't see the country having the energy and the wisdom to deal with that problem in light of its commitments abroad and also here at home. And I think this summer—I don't know how many more we have got—poses the awful problem of breeding through the activities that will take place.

In fact, an army of people that have to be committed to really revolutionary goals and it comes out from the kind of thing that I am talking about, that people are tired of broken promises, the May 17, 1954 Supreme Court decision, where in fact now there are more segregated schools than there were then.

Out of the income gap, black people's in relation to white people's income, it is further apart today than it was 10 years ago or—well, I don't know about 20 years ago, but at least 10 years ago, and the kind of standard indexes that you compare progress on, relative to the white community and the black community, they are not getting closer together. They are getting further apart. Yet the system's ability to deal with those problems is also, you know, diminishing.

I don't want any excuses about Black Power and Cicero and other things being excuses for not passing fair housing legislation in Congress.

That is the kind of thing that I am talking about, the fact that that can be used as an excuse is to me proof that the country does not have the ability to deal with the problem, and the fact that it does not have the ability to deal with the problem, in my mind is a series of incidents that will in fact bring about the explosion that I am speaking of.

MR. GLICKSTEIN. What you say sounds very, very pessimistic. Is there no hope at all?

MR. USSERY. I would like to say that there is hope, but I don't see any hope. I don't see any hope. I am being quite serious about this.

MR. GLICKSTEIN. Do you feel that there are any programs or activities the Federal Government could undertake in the near future that will prevent some of the things you have been speaking about?

MR. USSERY. It is a question of intent. It isn't a question of whether the Federal Government can do it. I along with many other people were invited to what was called a White House Conference To Fulfill These Rights, and it was my understanding that that weekend, or that week's affairs were for purposes of staking out a program that would in fact embrace the real dimensions of the problem and indicate to people in various Federal branches of government and so on, what kinds of ideas and what kinds of programs had to be funded in order to deal with the problem.

It is my understanding that the price tag on that was somewhere in the vicinity of $70 to $100 billion. I have heard nothing since about moving that program. And, in addition to that, one of the very controversial items that developed during that week was whether or not one can talk about when and how the Government would establish a timetable for dealing with these problems. No one wanted to do that. It was very neat to sit down and talk about we need this amount of money for housing, we need this amount of money for education or some other area, but to talk about how that money was to be spent in relation to the $30 billion a year that is being spent in Vietnam, and whether, you know, one was more important than the other or whether the country could, in fact, afford both at the same time, these were questions which the White House and, I guess it is appropriate to say that, and those who represented the White House, didn't want discussed at all.

So my total experience in terms of trying to deal with the grand answers for how you provide hope and optimism has been a very negative one, and that's what really underscores my belief that I don't think it can be really dealt with.

MR. GLICKSTEIN. Thank you. I have no further questions, Mr. Chairman.

CHAIRMAN HANNAH. Any of the Commissioners have any questions?

COMMISSIONER FREEMAN. Mr. Ussery, when you say you don't think it can be dealt with, do you mean we don't have the ability or we don't have the commitment?

MR. USSERY. I mean that the Federal establishment, and I hate to use clichés like that, I mean the people who run this country don't have the commitment to deal with problems that affect the black community in this country. That is what I really mean.

COMMISSIONER FREEMAN. Would you have any recommendations that you would make to this Commission?

MR. USSERY. Take the next plane to Washington and demand an audience with the President and tell him that this country is about to blow up. And that the repercussions from that, and I am not being dramatic about this, and that the repercussions from that, I think, have kind of Pandora Box meanings for the white and the black community, that none of us are really willing to look at now, and I am talking about a thing that I have talked about lately, about the McCarran Internal Security Act, where I am very, very convinced that if some 10 or 15 cities blow up in this country this year, this summer, that the President will in fact declare a state of internal security and that the FBI will immediately be instructed to rap on the door late at night and

272

pick up upwards of 15,000 or 20,000 people, no call to the attorney, the normal bits of due process being completely suspended, and what kind of energy that represents in terms of the division that enters into the American social fabric, and I think those kinds of things are right around the corner, and it has to do with the fact that no one really digs.

I shouldn't say "no one," but people are wise to the fact that what this country talks about as its commitment in Vietnam is a lie.

That people in Mississippi and other States and in California with respect to just simple representation on various public commissions or bodies on the city and the State level really have less involvement in the real life of a community than that person in Vietnam who is supposedly being insured of his political rights, and there are all kinds of dichotomies between how a country makes its commitments abroad and how it makes them here that are just catching up, that have caught up, and I think that it is that kind of thing which will not, you know, be permitted, that the emotions are caught up, and people's lives are caught up in this kind of lie, and I think that the chickens are really beginning to come home to roost.

I don't know what we do after the summer. These are the kinds of things that I am concerned about, and I don't have any kind of optimistic kind of program that I can suggest to you. I would like to be able to do that. It is a part of my spirit to be able to make constructive suggestions, but I don't have them, and the thing that disturbs me is that I don't think many people realize how close this country is to the blowup stage, and it might very well be that simply to communicate that would be the most important thing that you could do.

CHAIRMAN HANNAH. Any further questions?

MR. TAYLOR. Mr. Ussery, I share some of your pessimism, a good deal of your pessimism, and a good deal of your concern that no strategy or no program that is within the reach of private organiations or perhaps within the reach of this Commission is very promising at the moment for solving the problems that we have been talking about, and I would suggest that most of the approaches have been tried in one way or another, but, as you say, it is a question of commitment to them. But given the fact that what you say is that we have to have a choice among unpromising strategies, I wonder whether you feel that a strategy of separate organization, given the fact that I take it, it is your feeling there is a great deal of racism in this society, may not lead or help to lead to the repression that you are concerned about and that I am concerned about, repression by white people?

MR. USSERY. I am not sure that I understand your comment. I didn't follow you all the way on that. I am sorry.

MR. TAYLOR. What I am trying to get at is, say we have got a choice between unsatisfactory strategies. To the extent that what you are talking about is separate organization, organization which excludes direct cooperation between Negroes and whites, organization that expresses overt anti-white sentiment that isn't pinpointed, but is generalized towards whites, wouldn't this in itself, even if you feel it is just used as an excuse, wouldn't this promote the repression that you are concerned about?

MR. USSERY. That is probably true, but I don't think anything that I have endorsed or espoused, certainly anything that the organization which I represent has espoused, pushes separatism past the point of being a means of more effectively engaging in the democratic process in this country.

The question is, if we, in fact, treat it as a group, and a large part of what you are about as a body is designed to identify the problems that plague us as a community rather than as a series of really individuals, those kind of group pressures can be dealt with in a series of different ways, and I think the essence of what I am saying is that one of the problems is that of powerlessness, that one can in fact engage better in the system in making the problem that the system work, if one comes together as a community to operate politically, also to operate economically and otherwise, and that there has been the historic problem of our not being able to get as much out of the process as we are due commensurate with the numbers we have in the system in our total population because we have not been as united as we should be.

So really to argue against what we have talked about as Black Power is to say that somehow the black community in this country is better off if it does not unite, and if one wants to equate uniting with separatism, then I would say maybe that is all right, too, but I don't think the two terms are really the same at all.

MR. TAYLOR. And you would make a distinction, a strong distinction between them?

MR. USSERY. Oh, I make a distinction between the two, yes.

MR. TAYLOR. Thank you.

CHAIRMAN HANNAH. Thank you very much. We appreciate your being here. You are excused. Would you call the next witness, Mr. Glickstein.

MR. GLICKSTEIN. The next witness is Mr. Orville Luster.

(Whereupon, MR. ORVILLE LUSTER was sworn by the Chairman and testified as follows:)

TESTIMONY OF MR. ORVILLE LUSTER, SOUTH SAN FRANCISCO, CALIFORNIA

MR. GLICKSTEIN. Mr. Luster, would you please state your name and address for the record?

MR. LUSTER. My name is Orville Luster and I stay at 2545 Tipperary Street, South San Francisco.

MR. GLICKSTEIN. What is your occupation?

MR. LUSTER. I am executive director of Youth for Service.

MR. GLICKSTEIN. What is Youth for Service?

MR. LUSTER. Youth for Service is a small group agency working with teen age groups between the ages of 16 to 24 throughout San Francisco. We are sort of an interracial group. We have Negroes, Spanish, Chinese, a few Caucasians, and many other racial and ethnic groups. We do short-term weekend work projects. We also engage in a lot of other types of community activities, but the short-term work projects are the main emphasis of our program. At the present time we are also involved in one part of the Anti-Poverty Program under Title I-B, a Neighborhood Youth Program.

MR. GLICKSTEIN. When was your organization formed?

MR. LUSTER. Our organization was formed in 1957 by the American Friends Service Committee and then after that we received grants from the Rosenberg Foundation, and then in 1960 we received grants from the Ford Foundation, and then March 1, 1965 we were admitted to the United Bay Area Crusade.

MR. GLICKSTEIN. And how long have you been working with Youth for Service?

MR. LUSTER. I started in 1959.

MR. GLICKSTEIN. What type of neighborhoods do the young men you work with come from?

MR. LUSTER. Well, right now our main emphasis, our main thrust, is in what you might—I don't particularly like the word, but is the impacted or the ghetto or this type of thing. I think in San Francisco you might say the target areas. This would be Fillmore, Chinatown and Mission. These are the particular areas that we are working in now.

MR. GLICKSTEIN. How would you describe the living conditions in those neighborhoods, the type of families the young men come from?

MR. LUSTER. Are you talking about the young people that we are working with?

MR. GLICKSTEIN. Yes, sir.

MR. LUSTER. Well, a lot of the young people we are working with come from, I would say, approximately 85 percent of them are dropouts. Some come from real nice families and some come from where there is only one parent in the family, and a lot of them do not have a lot of—the income is not very high. Basically they are a good group of young people that have lacked a lot of the opportunities that the rest of the community has had.

MR. GLICKSTEIN. What kinds of problems do these young men have?

MR. LUSTER. Well, a lot of these young people have all the problems that a lot of teenagers face today. They are involved in many delinquent acts. I think the largest by the police statistics is auto theft and some burglaries, and this type of thing, that the young people are involved in.

MR. GLICKSTEIN. What other problems do they have besides involvement with the law?

MR. LUSTER. Well, I think one of the main problems is that of having an opportunity to complete school, and also to get into the real world of work with a decent job. I think this is one of the main problems that a lot of young people face, and in a city like San Francisco where you have been losing a lot of your factories, and this type of thing, since 1950, we are more of a financial center, it makes it very difficult to find the type of jobs that a lot of our young people could—which you might say the beginners' jobs, or this type of thing, the entry jobs. This makes it quite difficult.

They have been real frustrated in this particular effort. There is a move afoot now to ease some of these things, but it hasn't been to the extent that it should be. Hopefully, something will have to be rectified.

I think after last summer there was a real attempt to get a lot of jobs, but they were jobs that were not beneficial to some of the young people, whereas if they could actually move into them with the entry and beginner jobs—this was unfortunate.

MR. GLICKSTEIN. You mentioned entry and the beginners' jobs and you also mentioned decent jobs. Just what sort of jobs do the young people that you work with have in mind?

MR. LUSTER. Well, I think it would be hard to just pinpoint down because I think this is one of the problems, that a lot of people that are working with young people like this from these particular areas are sort of trying to pigeonhole them into different types of jobs. This is a job that you should have and this type of thing.

I think there is a range just like the rest of the total community. They would like possibly even to be President, if they could, but, naturally, being realistic, naturally with their skills this would not be possible, but I think that you will find that a lot of these young people have the aspirations to possibly—do any type of jobs that we will find on the job market.

Now, the main thing is trying to get them prepared for that particular market, and I feel this is what happens so many times, as far as I am concerned, with so many of the studies.

I think that a lot of us in the ghetto are being tired, we are tired of being studied all the time. I would like to see one of these days to speak before you ask what type of program. I think the type of program I would like to see developed would be where a body would write a proposal and have all the educational, all the research components, and then after you complete it and got the money, tear the proposal up and then give the money to the people, and then I know they would get it, because so many times this money never gets down to the pockets of the people you are trying to help.

We are constantly having the professional hustle off of our ghettos and we are tired of it, and I think this is where the government has wasted millions and millions of dollars and has continued to do this and the people never get this money. And the only thing we get is a tremendous amount of beautiful reports that are not even read.

So I think that if the type of program we could develop, say would be in the, say $5, $10, $15 million, write all of the components that they use to write it, tear it up and then give it to the people, and they could rectify some of their problems with some money, because when you look at the welfare subsistence, it isn't quite enough, and I think a lot of us who have decent jobs find it very difficult, and this person has to buy—has to use the same dollar that he gets, although it is a shorter dollar, to buy the same pound of butter, the same pound of coffee, and try to buy the same clothing.

So I think this is what we should do. I would be very happy to see that tried, Mr. Counsel. Maybe this Commission could help us with that, have a demonstration of actually giving the people the money for a change.

MR. GLICKSTEIN. I gather a lot of the young men you work with are unemployed?

MR. LUSTER. I would say yes, they are. I would say about 70 or 80 percent of the young people are unemployed that we work with.

MR. GLICKSTEIN. How do they subsist?

MR. LUSTER. Well, I mean, I think that this is a question that a lot of people have been asking for a long time. I have asked myself how do they subsist in their daily activities, and so forth, and I think this has been a mystery to a lot of us, how they are able to buy clothing and buy food and this type of thing.

I think, Mr. Counsel, it has been a real mystery to some of us, and possibly this is something that possibly we should have a study on. I don't know, but how are they making it——

MR. GLICKSTEIN. Are you able to shed any light at all on the mystery?

MR. LUSTER. Well, Mr. Counsel, I don't think that—I think we have some ideas and I think those ideas are about as—well, you know them about as well as I do, but how could I say that this is going on when I really couldn't pinpoint it down and say, well, I know that this is going on, but I think that this adds to the frustration, and I think that some of the young people who do get involved in some of the antisocial acts, they do this because of desperation a lot of times, and sometimes it is just for kicks, but I think that because they do not have a lot of money, sometimes they are motivated to go out and commit antisocial acts. And a lot of times it starts off with just the need for the bare necessities.

MR. GLICKSTEIN. Have you been able to help any of the young men with whom you work get regular jobs?

MR. LUSTER. Yes, we have. We have the Neighborhood Youth Corps Program which has been partially successful for us. We have, I would say, 30 percent of our young people today have jobs. I would say that one of the problems there is three problems. One, they have limited skills; secondly, it is very difficult to get them bonded, and, thirdly, they have an arrest record, and this has just compounded our problem because a lot of times the average employer will say, "Well, I can't hire this young person," and then there has always been this fear, too, of some of the young people that they really do not want to hire me, and when you've had a long history of not hiring young people with this type of background, well, it is kind of difficult to really convince them that they are going to be a part of this great American dream.

So you have a whole area here of problems that we are trying to overcome, and I think it is quite difficult.

So I think here again it goes back to the individual. You can't just lump them all together.

MR. GLICKSTEIN. What techniques do you use to encourage an unemployed young man to seek work or take a job that is offered to him?

MR. LUSTER. Well, one of the things we try to do in the Neighborhood Youth Corps and in our regular ongoing program, too, is to really give him the proper orientation and counseling that we possibly can with our workers, and then if we feel we need an extension, more professional help, we will make a proper referral, but I think one basic thing is trying to make sure that the young man we are trying to help, there is a job, and, secondly, that we can give him enough support on the job whereas he can move on up. I think it is very important to make sure it is not a dead-end job, because this is what also frustrates the young person.

I think another thing what we try to do too, is trying to help some of the parents, because in so many of our programs—that is why I would like to see some of this money given to people for a change is because very seldom you try to help the head of the household. So some of the kids find themselves making more money than their parents, and this has really created a problem, and when I say I would like to see one of these programs develop and just given it to people, I would really like to see that. I am serious about that. I would like to see what type of impact it would have on the community.

MR. GLICKSTEIN. You mentioned dead-end jobs. Do you find that when such jobs are offered to the young men you work with they refuse them or don't stay with them very long?

MR. LUSTER. Sometimes. I think that we all—our whole attitude and idea about a man's worth is where he works, what he is doing, whether it is a meaningful job, and this type of thing. Naturally, a lot of kids are not only trying to find some way of making a living, but they are trying to gain some dignity, some type of recognition, and being able to be men. I think this is particularly true of a lot of—well, the whole total community but in the minority community it is very important, to be a man, and I think that this is one of the reasons why they want this type of thing to happen. They want it to happen now.

MR. GLICKSTEIN. Mr. Luster, how do the Negro young men with whom you work feel about white people?

MR. LUSTER. Well, I think, being very truthful, I mean how could we feel that they are going to love all of the white people? I think there are some who understand the problem, but I don't think that you can expect all of the young people, or even a lot of those who are not young, to love all white people, because it is almost impossible, because sometimes we do not even love ourselves, and when you have been held down and denied certain privileges, and so forth, and opportunities, you can't love that person. You might have a certain amount of respect or a working agreement with him, but—and you keep this into what I call a manageable unit, but I think that this is a very difficult thing to expect them to love you because I don't think that—not very many of the larger communities have really been sincere in its endeavors in trying to really wrestle with this problem continuously. So you can't expect them to love you.

I think that you know the American Friends Service Committee is having their 50th Anniversary, and it says what love can do, but I wonder what would happen if our whole government, the whole inthrust, the impact would have been, trying to work out this problem with love. It would have been a wonderful thing. Maybe we would have had a real happening. I don't know. I wonder sometimes.

MR. GLICKSTEIN. Mr. Luster, do the Black Power or the Black Nationalism concepts have any appeal to the young men with whom you work?

MR. LUSTER. Some of them, yes. I think this is very natural. With any type of community you are going to have some that will be attracted by this, and I think rightly so.

We do not try to tell them what to think and do. We point out consequences. But I think this here is a natural type of thing, also, because some young people are frustrated and they also feel this is one way that they are going to solve their problem.

I think that there has been a lot of misunderstanding about the whole term "Black Power." I think that it means so many different things to the Negro as well as to the larger community, and it has been so misquoted and twisted that I think very few people could give you a decent definition of what just is Black Power, and the more and more that you listen you wonder.

I think that one of the things, as far as I am speaking just for myself, I look upon it as a development of political and economic unity to try to gain some of the better things of ife.

I think that we forget about how the Irish at one time created more hell than what any of the Black Power advocates ever thought about, and then when we go back and start thinking about what happened when we were trying to organize labor, where there were actually people who were shot down that were working in the company towns tents and the black power advocates have never been able to do this.

So I think that sometimes we forget our history and about how we have brought about change, and even the birth of our Nation.

Now, it doesn't mean that we haven't come forth and been able to do some of these things, but I think a lot of these movements would make the Black Power movement, you know, a real babe in the woods, of some of the things that really happened, and it is unfortunate that a lot of us do not read our history a little bit better, because I think that we find out that little riots we have had have been nothing to what labor had in its struggle in trying to get recognition and trying to get decent wages and all the fringe benefits.

There were a lot of people that were killed and homes bombed and everything else. So you can't expect people not to want to have some of these freedoms now, and they are going to use different methods, and I just hope that there is time. I don't know.

You have heard many, many other speakers speak to this point. So I think you can make your mind up for yourself, but I really don't know.

MR. GLICKSTEIN. Do you share the pessimism of the previous witness, whom I believe you heard?

MR. LUSTER. Well, I think that Mr. Ussery has been around and traveling over the country much more than I have. I think that some of his observations are valid. I, like I say, would not want to say whether or not this is to the extent that he has stated, but I will say this, that when you look at the 19 or 20 cities a lot of people are focusing their attention on, it must be something. Their tensions are high now. Now, whether or not there will be an eruption, only God knows.

Now there are a lot of us who would like to see a peaceful settlement to this, but, you know, really can you give a man his freedom in a peaceful way?

I mean, when you think about what is going on in Vietnam, I mean right now we are helping through war and spending billions and billions of dollars to help the South Vietnamese to get their freedom. So I am just wondering, can we—have we ever been able to give a man his freedom without some type of turmoil or some type of hostilities or eruptions? I am just wondering, can a democracy do that?

MR. GLICKSTEIN. Thank you, Mr. Luster. I have no further questions, Mr. Chairman.

CHAIRMAN HANNAH. Are there any questions that the Commissioners would like to ask Mr. Luster? Mr. Taylor?

MR. TAYLOR. No questions.

CHAIRMAN HANNAH. Thank you very much, Mr. Luster. We appreciate your being here this evening. You are excused. Mr. Glickstein, will you call the next witness?

MR. GLICKSTEIN. The next witness is Mr. James A. Richards.

(Whereupon, Mr. James A. Richards was sworn by the Chairman and testified as follows:)

TESTIMONY OF MR. JAMES A. RICHARDS
SAN FRANCISCO, CALIFORNIA

MR. GLICKSTEIN. Mr. Richards, would you please state your full name and address for the record?

MR. RICHARDS. James A. Richards, 846 Jamestown, San Francisco.

MR. GLICKSTEIN. How long have you lived in San Francisco?

MR. RICHARDS. Roughly 15 years.

MR. GLICKSTEIN. Fifteen years.

MR. RICHARDS. Yes.

MR. GLICKSTEIN. How old are you?

MR. RICHARDS. Twenty-three.

MR. GLICKSTEIN. What part of the city do you live in?

MR. RICHARDS. Bayview.

MR. GLICKSTEIN. Bayview? Is that near to the Hunters Point area?

MR. RICHARDS. Yes, it is.

MR. GLICKSTEIN. Mr. Richards, would you describe for the Commissioners the neighborhood in which you grew up. Was that the Bayview area where you grew up in?

MR. RICHARDS. Hunters Point. It was physically—well, right now, just like before, it is got old buildings up there, old war buildings, it is very torn down and it has very poor facilities. We don't have any recreational facilities, educational facilities, cultural programs, health facilities, transportation facilities, and we just—it is just all torn down houses where you can put some people back in there and create a ghetto and keep it that way, I suppose. It has been that way for years and it is still that same way.

MR. GLICKSTEIN. Most of the housing up there is public housing. Is that correct?

MR. RICHARDS. Yes.

MR. GLICKSTEIN. Were there white children in the neighborhood when you grew up?

MR. RICHARDS. Yes, for a short period of time, because when my family moved in, we were the only Negro family in this building. In the next building, about one. Something like that. Then very shortly as more Negroes began to move into the area, the whites began to move out. So that it was a very short period of time. You'd see one in a building, then one in more buildings. They were poor like us.

MR. GLICKSTEIN. Mr. Richards, what impact did growing up in this neighborhood have on your development?

MR. RICHARDS. That is a very strange thing, because you have to shift so much, because the conditions that are presented, you can't really have a stereotyped pattern to govern yourself, because our conditioning sometimes brings frustration and you are always wondering how things are going to turn out, what can you do to help things, to help yourself, and you grow up later on in life and you get in a position where you have to think of others also, just not able to go out and do anything you want, have to come under the same system, and this creates a larger problem but roughly it made me aware that I have to look at everything as a whole. As I have been looking for the cause and effect, I find a lot of things I don't like now. I think a lot of my people don't like it. And it could go a lot further than that, also.

MR. GLICKSTEIN. Could you tell us something about your family?

MR. RICHARDS. Well, my family still lives in Hunters Point and still struggling and, well, that is a matter of one generation and I can't say where the motivation could come to expect them to try to motivate themselves out of this area and try to move to a new bracket or something like this because they have been struggling now all this time and they haven't gotten any further and they feel they are out of their prime now so how can they go out and tackle the world now? They couldn't tackle it before and things are pretty rough and they aren't getting easier. I mean it is very bad but the thing is that we are all fighting, we are all fighting for the same thing and I can't just say that because my family is there that I think that they should be somewhere else. Because they are, you know, just like anyone else. I know they have problems and the condition is very frustrating for them, also.

In other words, now we are two generations we have to fight this thing together. It is sort of like an overlap. They are no longer doing for us, worrying about us. We have our own to worry about. We have our newly born and unborn that's going to have to come up under the same thing.

So that means we have the responsibility to ourselves, not only to better ourselves but try to make some kind of dent in the system so our young and unborn don't have to come up under the same thing we had to. I don't feel that it is the time now for me to sit around and see this thing going on for generation and generation. I believe there is going to be a break and it's got to break now.

MR. GLICKSTEIN. You say your family has given up hope?

MR. RICHARDS. I didn't say given up hope. I wouldn't know what it would take to motivate them. I'm quite sure they haven't given up hope but maybe the idea of growing up to a Rockefeller bracket or something like this, because when you look up and you see the middle-class bracket, the people that tend to be in the middle-class bracket, they all have more responsibility, the things they might get for some aid or something like this or another type of program that is out now, the person that is in the middle-class, they have to work and after they work they still have to pay the doctor bills and have to pay the other things and borrow money and by the time they get through paying the bills, they go to work Monday morning like this and still have $6 to make it for the next two weeks. You know you've got to constantly fight and we're about dropping back from where you just came from. So it is not just motivating to look up ahead and find the same thing waiting for you.

MR. GLICKSTEIN. Mr. Richards, were you living in the Hunters Point area during the time of the riots in 1966?

MR. RICHARDS. Yes, I was.

MR. GLICKSTEIN. Why do you think those riots took place?

MR. RICHARDS. Because the group of people are just frustrated and it is not a new thing. It was just something that happened to spark it off and it still wasn't sparked off like a lot of people tend to see it. It wasn't a major riot as a lot of people tend to see it. The reasons behind it was major, though, and they still are major and I feel that if anything that was supposed to be done, what they feel should be done, isn't even attempted, people that claim to be some of America's prominent citizens want to do so much about the problem and come by to falsify against the people and making false promises and things like this. They can't stand up under our frustration. One minute we are looking ahead and we think we see something and we turn around and again all we can see is darkness ahead. And sometimes at a time like this all they can do is strike out into the night. They don't know what they are reaching for out there.

But, as I say, it wasn't a major thing. It was just an idea to strike out at something and someone. Even if you don't do anything but break a window or a chair or something like this, you feel that you are hurting a white man or something like this because the white man is the one that is doing everything to you that causes you to have all these problems on you now.

So I just think that it is the frustration. They can't sit back and believe everything they've been told that things are going to get better because things aren't getting better. Things are getting worse and children that grew up in a poor area in this generation and getting more sophisticated of what is going on around them are going to let you know when they have to get out on the street at 14 or 15. They consider themselves to be a man and are going to take on some responsibility because he is the only man in the house and he has little brothers and sisters in the house and he sees his mother and brothers and sisters going hungry, half starving and trying to get the rent in. It is a bare house, like it is a cold feeling even to be there and you have to go out on the street and become the subject of the same thing out there. There has to be a breaking point. When you see, especially the young people that is involved in riots, and things like this, is that they see what is going on and they are not going to stand for it. I mean they are not going to stand back for another generation to take a beating from someone.

It is not, maybe all the time, physically but it is mentally because people who walk around now are dead. They just die mentally because the only thing they can see is darkness ahead, like I say.

MR. GLICKSTEIN. What role did you play in the Hunters Point riots?

MR. RICHARDS. Well, from the beginning of the riots, when the riots first began, I was observing. I was there on the scene, you know, and it was all right to me but I just knew that it wasn't going too far. I felt that at that moment, that this was just getting the frustration off—that it was going to grow larger but I didn't think at this time they were going to—just letting off steam, then, and so that was the first night. And a few shots came after the cops came out but there wasn't anyone really shaken up.

So the next day everyone was right back on the scene again and then we started—a few of us got together. A few of our friends from Hunters Point got together and we began to look at the situation the way it was standing at the time. So we thought we were going to hurt ourselves more than anything by letting the young people out. We are young, also, but I mean our younger brothers and things like that, go out and get killed, and things like this, because they wasn't ready for taking an action of this kind. So we got together and we elected some leaders and they elected me to represent us and so we tried to get a meeting with the mayor that afternoon and get him to come out but he told us that we could come down to his office and the thing was that by representing my people—they didn't want me to go down to the mayor's office. We wanted him to come out there to talk to them.

So we waited until 3 o'clock and the mayor didn't show. So we decided we would go down and we went down and tried to discuss the matter with Mayor Shelley and Chief Cahill, and before anything could become to any conclusion about what we were going to do, they said that they received a call that they said it had broken out and it was too late. So we immediately went back, the representatives from the group, and went back out to the area and it was that way. I mean they had—everything had gotten out of hand, but we had already organized ourselves to a degree where we could try to talk to them. We had a patrol like. So the cops started shooting because they said someone shot at them, and that was the worse thing of it all, because the thing was the role I was playing then was I was just a nobody because I was standing there and I couldn't do anything and see how these cops come down on their knees shooting down my brothers and sisters up there, shooting at them and shooting some down also.

They had their hands up over their heads saying they give and was running. Everyone that got shot was running because some of them that knelt down began to shoot. Everyone was running because they were just unorganized, just running, and they didn't have any guns or anything. They weren't prepared for any type of warfare but the cops did continue to shoot and I observed that. But then after that we went back downtown and began to discuss trying to negotiate with the mayor to get the police out of the area because that is the major thing and also the police brutality out in the area. We have that. And so finally he, you know, said that we could patrol, our group was named the Hunters Point Young Men for Action Council at the time we gave ourselves this name, and so we patrolled one side of Third Street on the side of Hunters Point, from Hunters Point up on the hill and they patrolled the other side of Third and the communication was so poor that we were at this meeting and it was agreed in the mayor's office about 10 o'clock that morning and the curfew was at 8 o'clock and five minutes to eight, that's when they got the message at Hunters Point that we were to be out, that they were to recognize us and to stay off the other side of Third Street. And the cop was right there and we had people that worked in the area out there like area directors of EOC that were trying and we thought that maybe it would give him some respect to call and check in and see and

285

they were still threatening us saying we had five more minutes to make it and they didn't care, they had just got the word five minutes ago and we had five more minutes to make it. So they came through and then after that we talked to the people and we got them to see the point right then, that we don't want to destroy ourselves like that, you know. If we are going to do something, we might as well do it right and make sure that the time is right and that maybe we won't benefit from it but the ones that are left behind will.

MR. GLICKSTEIN. Mr. Richards, are you attending school at this time?

MR. RICHARDS. Yes, I am.

MR. GLICKSTEIN. Why did you decide to return to school?

MR. RICHARDS. Because I know that I am dedicated to the cause to see my people gain more equal rights, to gain equality and gain human rights and this is what I plan to make my aim in life and try to achieve this goal but the thing is to be here to see it come into existence. The thing is that being sophisticated and looking at all this and knowing what's out there and what the system is doing and wanting to do something about it and knowing how technical the system is and this is the way they are keeping us down, now they are keeping us down mentally, now it's keeping us down physically because they are going to have to whip us and beat us and shoot us to keep us back in the ghettos and they don't have to come in and take food from the houses to keep us hungry. There is enough for the man, there is enough for the government, there is enough for the system. I want to get in and do what I can. I have to learn the system and that is what I am going to try and get, a formal eduation, along with looking at the world from the standpoint of my perspective of being a black man. I think that maybe I can contribute something to the cause.

MR. GLICKSTEIN. Thank you, Mr. Richards. I have no further questions, Mr. Chairman.

CHAIRMAN HANNAH. Do any of the Commissioners have questions?

CHAIRMAN HANNAH. Thank you very much, Mr. Richards. We appreciate your coming.

CHAIRMAN HANNAH. Is Mr. Gallegos in the room?

CHAIRMAN HANNAH. If he were here, I was going to hear him as he had asked, but since he is not we will forego that.

We will now recess until 9:30 tomorrow morning in this room.

(Whereupon a recess was taken at 10:30 p.m. to reconvene on Wednesday, May 3, 1967 at 9:30 a.m.)

U.S. COMMISSION ON CIVIL RIGHTS

CHAIRMAN HANNAH. Ladies and gentlemen, the hearing will come to order. I might say at the beginning that we will try to maintain a little better order today than we did yesterday. We will appreciate it if people will refrain from applause. They are going to take pictures, if they will not get up here so that they obstruct the view of the witness or upset the witness and if there are such instances, we will ask the marshals to enforce good order.

Mr. Glickstein, will you call the first witness?

MR. GLICKSTEIN. The first witness is Mr. B. R. Stokes, who is accompanied by William L. Diedrich, Counsel.

(Whereupon, Mr. B. R. Stokes was sworn by the Chairman and testified as follows:)

TESTIMONY OF MR. B. R. STOKES, ORINDA, CALIFORNIA

MR. GLICKSTEIN. Mr. Stokes, would you please state your full name and address for the record?

MR. STOKES. Yes, sir. My name is B. R. Stokes. My home address is 26 La Venida, Orinda, California.

MR. GLICKSTEIN. And what is your occupation, Mr. Stokes?

MR. STOKES. I am the general manager of the San Francisco Bay Area Rapid Transit District.

MR. GLICKSTEIN. Would you very briefly tell the Commissioners what BART is?

MR. STOKES. Yes, sir. The BART, the Bay Area Rapid Transit District, is a public agency covering three counties in the Central Bay Area created by the State legislature for the express purpose of planning and after it was approved by the voters in 1962, constructing and finally operating a regional rapid transit. system, which we hope will be the finest in the world.

MR. GLICKSTEIN. What are your duties as general manager?

MR. STOKES. I am in charge of the business affairs of the district, the chief executive officer of our public agency. I work for a board of directors which sets general policy, and it is my duty to carry out that policy and to carry out the purposes of the district.

MR. GLICKSTEIN. What is the stage of construction of BART at the present time?

MR. STOKES. At the moment we have about $350 million under

construction in the three counties. The design is about 70 percent complete. Right-of-way acquisition, about 75 percent complete. We have carried out an extensive test and demonstration program in Contra Costa County to develop new technology. This program is about complete.

We are heading into our very heavy construction activity, which we will reach the latter part of this year and next year.

MR. GLICKSTEIN. And when do you think the project will be completed?

MR. STOKES. The full completion will be in 1971 if we don't have any more bumps than we have had up to this point. We anticipate initial revenue service in the East Bay in 1969, late 1969.

MR. GLICKSTEIN. How many persons are currently employed on the BART construction?

MR. STOKES. On construction, working for contractors, at the moment, and I am going to be a bit vague about this because of all the rains we have had up until last Thursday, the construction forces had dwindled considerably. We had had rain for about 45 days straight. I believe this week probably in the neighborhood or in excess of 2,000 persons.

MR. GLICKSTEIN. And how many do you expect to be employed in the future?

MR. STOKES. We expect to reach a maximum total employment on construction projects of some 8,000 probably late this year or during 1968.

MR. GLICKSTEIN. You have 8,000 people working at one time?

MR. STOKES. Yes, sir.

MR. GLICKSTEIN. Which building and construction trade unions will furnish most of your workers?

MR. STOKES. The primary crafts will be laborers, operating engineers, teamsters, carpenters, iron workers, electricians, plumbers, and painters.

MR. GLICKSTEIN. Do you have any idea of how many workers from each of these crafts will be working when construction is at its peak?

MR. STOKES. I don't have it with me, Mr. Glickstein. However, I could provide you with a breakdown. We have made such an estimate, I believe, in times past and I could provide this for you.

MR. GLICKSTEIN. Do you have any idea what the estimate would be?

MR. STOKES. By craft?

MR. GLICKSTEIN. Yes.

MR. STOKES. No, sir, I don't recall at the moment. I could provide this for you, though.

MR. GLICKSTEIN. Do you know whether there will be hundreds of operating engineers, 20 operating engineers, 50 operating engineers?

MR. STOKES. Well, it certainly wouldn't be 20 or 50. It would be considerably more than that, but I am sorry. I just can't provide you with the specific information. We have this tabulated, our estimates made, and I could provide it for you.

MR. GLICKSTEIN. I believe I do have a copy of your estimate. Perhaps we could show it to you and it might refresh your recollection.

MR. STOKES. Yes, please. This was the chart to which I had reference.

MR. GLICKSTEIN. Would you tell us how many operating engineers that indicates would be working?

MR. STOKES. At the peak it would appear from this estimate, dated April of last year, it would appear in the range of 2,000.

MR. GLICKSTEIN. Two thousand?

MR. STOKES. Yes, sir.

MR. GLICKSTEIN. How many iron workers?

MR. STOKES. It would appear from the chart in the neighborhood of 750.

MR. GLICKSTEIN. And how many plumbers?

MR. STOKES. From this chart again it would appear in the neighborhood of 350.

MR. GLICKSTEIN. Three hundred fifty.

MR. STOKES. Yes, sir, 250 to 350.

MR. GLICKSTEIN. Mr. Stokes, who is the general contractor for BART?

MR. STOKES. I am sorry. I didn't get you.

MR. GLICKSTEIN. Who is the general contractor for BART?

MR. STOKES. There is no single general contractor, Mr. Glickstein. I think this is important to understand in this whole question.

As a public agency operating under State law, we develop a contract package and under State law that any contract that is in excess of $3,000 must be put in the form of formal specifications and advertised legally so that all interested parties may have a chance to bid, and on the prescribed date these bids are opened and we must award to the lowest responsive, responsible bidder on that particular contract.

So what I am saying is there is no general contractor.

There is a contractor for each construction package. At the moment I would say that we have probably 20 to 25 prime contractors on the various jobs and innumerable subcontractors.

MR. GLICKSTEIN. Then the prime contractors are the ones that hire the subcontractors? Is that right?

MR. STOKES. Yes, sir.

MR. GLICKSTEIN. In a smaller job the prime contractor would normally be called the general contractor. Is that right?

MR. STOKES. Yes, sir.

MR. GLICKSTEIN. How much will BART cost when it is completed, the entire cost of the project?

MR. STOKES. Our best estimate at the moment, Mr. Glickstein, and I am sure that you are aware of the fact that we have had severe money problems due to inflation and other factors. At the moment the cost appears to be in the neighborhood of $1,100 billion.

MR. GLICKSTEIN. And how much will the Federal Government contribute to the construction of BART?

MR. STOKES. At the moment they have contributed in grants under the mass transit program a total of $26 million. We have hopes that this grant program will reach $80 million, which would be something less than 10 percent of the total project.

MR. GLICKSTEIN. And which agency, which Federal agency, will this money come from?

MR. STOKES. The Department of Housing and Urban Development, through its Urban Transportation Administration branch.

MR. GLICKSTEIN. Mr. Stokes, the office of Federal Contract Compliance in the Department of Labor is the Government Agency that is supposed to insure that contracts that are carried out with Federal financial assistance are carried out without discrimination because of race, color, religion, or national origin. That is correct, isn't it?

MR. STOKES. Yes, sir.

MR. GLICKSTEIN. What has that office required of BART by way of compliance with the Executive order that the President issued requiring nondiscrimination?

MR. STOKES. Well, we are—I am very proud to talk about this particular phase of our program, Mr. Glickstein, because we have worked with the Federal Office of Contract Compliance as well as other Departments of the Federal Government since a year ago, actually June of 1966, in implementing a fair employment program for Federal grant contracts in excess of $500,000.

We met with a great number of Agency representatives in Washington in June 1966 and have had a number of meetings with these Federal Agencies since that time. We are rather proud of the fact that we were the only local public agency to participate in these meetings and, as a result of a number of meetings, both in Washington and here, a pilot program has been developed affecting all Federal Agencies and in which we are the lead agency, to put in specifics, the—really the principles and philosophy of Executive Order 11246.

Under this program the contractor on any project which receives Federal funds in excess of $500,000 must, at a pre-award conference, outline in writing to our satisfaction and to the satisfaction of the Federal Departments involved, his manner of approaching an affirmative action program, which is of some nine points, although the program does not have to be limited to those nine points. We have again taken the lead in this program, as we said we would. We have had one such pre-award conference. We have one contract underway under which the program has been instituted. We have very high hopes for it.

MR. GLICKSTEIN. At these pre-award conferences do you ask the contractor which unions he has collective bargaining agreements with?

MR. STOKES. Again, Mr. Glickstein, we have only had one of these. I personally conducted this first one, and at that time, because the program was so new, we did not.

MR. GLICKSTEIN. Do you anticipate—

MR. STOKES. However,—

MR. GLICKSTEIN. Yes?

MR. STOKES. However, in his written documents I believe this is one of the requirements that he submit in order to receive final approval on his granting, on his receipt of the contract.

MR. GLICKSTEIN. What if the contractor has a collective bargaining agreement with a union, a union that will have to work on the project, a union that is well known to have few, or no, Negro members? How is it possible in that circumstance to carry out the affirmative action program?

MR. STOKES. Well, I think one of the aspects of the Federal program is to encourage him, and through him the unions to find ways. These collective bargaining agreements do exist, and one of the points in the nine point program which has been submitted to us and which we are now working, is to encourage him, to help him find ways and means of insuring that fair employment does occur and if there are agreements that would preclude or would harm these opportunities or these chances to encourage him to find ways that these things can be removed.

MR. GLICKSTEIN. Do you have any ways in mind that you would recommend to the contractor?

MR. STOKES. If I may, Mr. Glickstein, and be a little bit diverse in my answer here, we are talking about construction employment, which is a strange breed of cat, particularly in a context here in the Bay Area and in California, which I think you must realize, and that is that construction employment, despite all the things that have been going on in this State, has been a declining activity for a good long period of time.

For instance, in March of this year there was a 9 percent decrease from March a year ago, and I saw some recent figures that in February of this year the construction employment in the State of California was the lowest of any month since February of 1962, and I say that it is important to look at this context, because, while the District is, has been, and will continue to be fully committed to doing everything in its power to insuring to the best of its ability fair employment on its contracts, and through its contractors, the fact remains that until there are new jobs created, and a great number of new jobs created, I don't think there is going to be any great increase of entry into the field, regardless of race.

I think the construction unions' problems in the past many months have been to find work for those who have been in the field for a long time and just to keep these people busy.

What I am getting at in a very roundabout way is that I think that this program that the Federal Government has instituted, which has forcibly called to the attention of anyone who may for any reason not be entirely in sympathy with the principles and philosophy of fair employment and nondiscrimination, I think all of the other programs that the District has entered into over a period of many, many months, I think all of these things have called to the attention of the contractors, I think they have brought it forcibly to the attention of any unions which may have any aspects of nondiscrimination or reluctance to embrace the full and complete tenets of fair employment. I think that it has called forcibly to their attention the fact that solutions must be found, that there is a problem, and that an atmosphere has been created which I think will pay off in great dividends once the jobs are there.

Now, when you ask me specifically what the contractors can do, I think again it has to be cooperative because I think the things you are probably referring to are in collective bargaining agreements that are strictly a matter between the unions and the contractors.

We can implore, we can plead, we can call to the attention, we can do all of these things. We can make these things stipulations in our contracts. Beyond this there is not much we can do, sir.

MR. GLICKSTEIN. If I can sum up what my interpretation of what you just said is, what you are saying, I believe, is that, although BART is heavily committed to this fair employment policy, although you are doing everything to call this policy to the attention of the contractors and the unions, and although you are doing everything to create a favorable atmosphere, as long as jobs are as unavailable as they seem to be, it is unlikely that among the 8,000, 9,000 people that BART will employ, unless there is some change in the job situation, there is not going to be very much of a change in the usual pattern of minority group employment in highly skilled trades?

MR. STOKES. I think this is a fair summary, but I must add, Mr. Glickstein, that at the moment of the 2,000 or so workers whom we estimate on our construction projects this week, we also estimate that something in excess of 30 percent of those people are members of minority groups.

MR. GLICKSTEIN. How many of them are laborers?

MR. STOKES. Sir?

MR. GLICKSTEIN. How many of those are laborers?

MR. STOKES. I would suspect that quite a large percentage are laborers, but I also know from personal experience and from personal tours that there are a great number of carpenters, cement finishers, that we have people, to the best of my knowledge, in all of the crafts in supervisory positions. In other words, as foremen or lead men, this sort of thing.

So again I am saying that I think that on our own jobs, and we take occasion to look at these things from a standpoint of visibility——

MR. GLICKSTEIN. One of the things the OFCC, the Office of Federal Contract Compliance's nine point program suggests, is that minority group contractors be utilized.

What if a minority group contractor bid on a project and the minority group contractor was non-union? Would you be able to sign a contract with such a contractor?

MR. STOKES. It would pose a very difficult problem, Mr. Glickstein. I think probably the answer is no, in view of the fact that we do have in effect a labor stabilization agreement, because we are so spread out over four counties and involving four different building and construction trades councils, and perhaps 100 different unions. I think probably that this——

MR. GLICKSTEIN. This labor stabilization agreement requires that you deal under existing collective bargaining agreements and abide by existing collective bargaining agreements. Isn't that correct?

MR. STOKES. It is not a collective bargaining agreement, but in order to insure the continued progress of the project we have entered into this as a third party. Also involved are the contractors' associations and some hundred unions.

Again the possibilities for jurisdictional disputes, this sort of thing involved in this kind of a public project, were too great not to attempt to stabilize the situation so that the progress could proceed unimpeded.

MR. GLICKSTEIN. In other words, if it appeared that the only way to have more Negroes working in some of the skilled, very skilled, trades on the job were to hire non-union Negroes, under your stabilization agreement that would be impossible?

MR. STOKES. I think the answer is yes; yes, sir. But I would like to add that we have approached this matter of minority contractors from a different viewpoint.

We have been working, for instance, recently with minority truck owners, attempting to advise them—using the Association of General Contractors as well as our own specific contractors—attempting to advise them on how they can get themselves in a position to act as truck brokers and to bid as subcontractors to some of these prime contractors. We have had discussions with two or three of these. We have worked with Mr. Hugh Taylor, Special Assistant for Manpower for the city of Oakland; with Joseph Debro, the Oakland Small Business Development Center; with the—as I said, individual contractors on our jobs, attempting to find members of minority groups who own truck rigs of one kind or another and in the business who would be interested in dirt-hauling, of which we will have a great deal.

We have had some success. A recent case, just last week, in which we have found a contractor who very possibly can put himself in a position to bid and we are pursuing this very assiduously.

So I say we have approached this matter from this standpoint. I think there is more than one way to get at this problem.

MR. GLICKSTEIN. Let me conclude by asking you a hypothetical question. If a contractor were to advise you that the likelihood of there being Negroes on the job was not very great because the union with whom he had a contract didn't have Negro members and the contractor had an exclusive hiring agreement with the union and could only hire through the agreement, would you be in a position to tell the contractor that you recognized his obligation under the collective bargaining agreement, but you also recognized his obligation under the Federal Executive order and that his obligation under the Federal Executive order supersedes his obligation under the collective bargaining agreement and, if necessary, he must violate that agreement in order to comply with the Executive order?

MR. STOKES. It is a hypothetical question because it has never arisen.

To the best of our knowledge, to this time the question has not arisen. We don't know the specific problem. You are an attorney asking a hypothetical question. I think my best answer would be may I call my own attorney here to give you another hypothetical answer from our own attorney.

I can't give you the answer, Mr. Glickstein. As I say, the problem has not faced us, has not arisen. The answer, I think, is that we require certain things on our own specifications. We require certain additional things under any project that is federally assisted. We would insist that these contract compliances—that these contract provisions be lived up to. Could I defer to Mr. Diedrich?

CHAIRMAN HANNAH. Is it agreeable?

MR. GLICKSTEIN. Yes.

MR. DIEDRICH. For the record, my name is William L. Diedrich, and I am an attorney, and my firm, Pillsbury, Madison & Sutro, is general counsel for the Bay Area Rapid Transit District.

Mr. Glickstein has asked one of those questions that I think is probably impossible to answer. The choice that you put BART to is if the Federal Government, HUD particularly, were to determine that the contractor were not complying with 11246——

MR. GLICKSTEIN. That's the Executive order?

MR. DIEDRICH. That's the Executive order.—because he felt he could not without violating the collective bargaining agreement, I fear that knowing some of the people in the office of Federal Contract Compliance, BART might be told they don't get the money. You put them, as some of my Southern friends say, between rock and a hard place.

The answer to your question, Mr. Glickstein, particularly, and this is a lawyer's answer, is that I think that you would have to do more than prove that the union had no Negro members as of the moment. You would have to prove that they were actively discriminating by whatever evidence you get by proving that people that applied for jobs through the hiring hall and had not been dispatched in the proper order, whether they were union members or not. All the necessary evidentiary material—I am not telling you anything that you don't know—that can be very difficult to obtain. I, myself, as a lawyer think that to convict or find someone at any given instance to discriminate is going to require more than a mere proof of a lily-white union.

That can be the result of history of two or three years ago, but if not, at this instant, to answer your hypothetical question.

MR. GLICKSTEIN. Thank you. I have no further questions, Mr. Chairman.

CHAIRMAN HANNAH. Any Commissioner have questions?

COMMISSIONER FREEMAN. Yes.

CHAIRMAN HANNAH. Mrs. Freeman.

COMMISSIONER FREEMAN. I would like to refer to your comments concerning—first of all, did BART have a pre-award conference prior to the award of contracts?

MR. STOKES. I assume, Mrs. Freeman, you are referring to this new Federal program?

COMMISSIONER FREEMAN. I am talking about Executive Order 11246 and where the Labor Department requires a pre-award conference. Did you have a pre-award conference with the prime contractors?

MR. STOKES. Yes, ma'am. I am sorry. I didn't quite catch the thrust of your question. The District has always had pre-award conferences with all of the contractors prior to the time that the award is actually made of the contract in which prior to the

Federal program we spelled out our own affirmative action program, our own requirements as stipulated in the specifications.

With the institution, with us as a sort of trial agency in the Bay Area, of the Federal program, yes, we did, on Washington's Birthday this year, the first of these pre-award conferences.

COMMISSIONER FREEMAN. You entered into no contract with the contractor before Washington's Birthday of this year?

MR. STOKES. No, ma'am. I am talking about the Federal program to which you are referring, the new Federal program requiring affirmative action programs in writing on projects assisted by Federal funds. This was the first to fall into the program, which was initiated last December 22.

COMMISSIONER FREEMAN. Well, under the Executive order it is the responsibility of the contracting agency to assure compliance by the contractor with the provisions of the nondiscrimination clause. Now, you have stated that you have about 20 prime contractors and you have also said that you or they have collective bargaining agreements with labor unions. Well, the order also requires that in the compliance reports that you submit you obtain from the labor union its assurances, and I would like to know what did you obtain from the labor unions before you awarded the contract?

MR. STOKES. I want to make it perfectly clear to the Commission that the District is not a contractor, has no collective bargaining agreements with any unions or with any contractors' association. We are a public agency which lets a contract to the lowest responsive, responsible bidder.

The contractor and the union between them provide the people for the jobs. The contractor himself is legally responsible for everything that happens on the job, generally speaking.

Our own contract specifications, Mrs. Freeman, in our opinion, go somewhat beyond the dictates of Executive Order 11246 and have been in effect from the very inception of our project. The new program, the Federal program, an implementation, if you please, of Executive Order 11246, this new OFCC program, which we have led the' way on in the Bay Area, the first contract in connection with that which had Federal money in it was the pre-award conference which was held last February.

But prior to that time we had had pre-award conferences on our own carrying out our own specifications and, in our opinion, our own specifications, there is no public agency certainly in the State which are more strict and more specific than we have.

COMMISSIONER FREEMAN. I would like to direct my attention to whatever program it is that has the $23 million up to $80 million.

MR. STOKES. Yes, ma'am.

COMMISSIONER FREEMAN. This is the one. Is this the program that didn't come into being until February of this year?

MR. STOKES. Yes, ma'am.

COMMISSIONER FREEMAN. Now, at that conference did you obtain from labor unions their approval of an affirmative action program?

MR. STOKES. This program, Mrs. Freeman, is directed at the contractor. The requirements are strictly from the contractor. The process is that at the pre-award conference we advise the contractor of the tenets of this program, that within a specified time after that he submits to us his affirmative action program in writing which, if we find acceptable, we transmit to our HUD representative, and from that point on it is in the hands of the Federal Government, and I assume at this time it goes through the OFCC, the EOCC, HUD itself, and goes back to Washington. But the program itself is directed at the contractor with whom we have the contract.

COMMISSIONER FREEMAN. I know this, but your attorney may advise you that Section 203(c) and (d) refers specifically to obligations of the contractor to obtain information from the labor organizations, and this is the information that I wanted to know. And then the next question with respect to this is that among the 2,000 employees that you now have, if you would submit to this Commission information concerning the number of operating engineers that are Negro, and white, the number of Spanish-speaking American, of any minority, with respect to all of the craft unions as of this period?

MR. STOKES. Is that a request, Mrs. Freeman?

COMMISSIONER FREEMAN. I think it would be helpful for us because you have indicated that all you can do is implore and plead as far as the labor union is concerned and because of the collective bargaining agreement. So we would need to have the effect of this collective bargaining agreement on the rights of the minorities to obtain employment in a public agency where $80 million is involved and $1 billion of public funds is involved.

MR. STOKES. All right. We will be glad to provide it for you.

COMMISSIONER FREEMAN. Thank you.

CHAIRMAN HANNAH. Dean Griswold?

COMMISSIONER GRISWOLD. Mr. Stokes, I assume that you would agree that your agency has some responsibility with respect to the employment of minority groups.

MR. STOKES. I think there is no question, Mr. Griswold. I think that the record will show that this concern has existed for a good long period of time.

COMMISSIONER GRISWOLD. I don't want to minimize the difficulty of your situation. Nevertheless, I get a sort of inference from your testimony that, though you accept that responsibility, there really isn't very much you can do about it, that this is a matter between the contractors and the unions and you can state requirements and you can hold sessions and you can plead and implore, but not much is going to happen about it. Is that a fair summary of what you've said?

MR. STOKES. No, I don't think it is at all, Mr. Griswold. I think there has been a great deal accomplished. Again you must realize that we are not talking about procurement; we are not talking about our employing anyone; we are not talking about our having any control or any say-so over hiring hall practices or collective bargaining agreements that have been built up over a period of time. But—

COMMISSIONER GRISWOLD. That was the essence of what I was trying to state is the summary of your testimony, that you were saying that you can urge and implore, but, after all, these things are the result of contracts which have been built over a long period of time and there really isn't anything you can do about it. Now, is that a fair summary of your testimony?

MR. STOKES. Again I will have to say no, sir. I will get into a few specifics of things we have done aside from this.

COMMISSIONER GRISWOLD. I would like to hear those and then I would like to ask you finally what you think you can do about it in the future.

MR. STOKES. All right, sir.

COMMISSIONER GRISWOLD. Because I accept in full value your testimony that you have a responsibility here and I would like to have the benefit of your experience and observation about it as to what you think you can do to carry out that responsibility.

I repeat, not minimizing the difficulties of your situation.

MR. STOKES. Yes, sir. I am glad to take a couple of minutes here to answer your question, Mr. Griswold.

The District is a public agency, as I said at the beginning of my testimony, created by the legislature for the express purpose of planning, securing approval of the voters, building and operating a rapid transit system. The Bay Area has worked for this since 1953; the legislation was set up in 1957; we had the vote of the people here in 1962; and we have a fixed budget approved by the public at this election of $792 million from property tax sources.

We are not an agency like the Federal Bureau of Public Roads, the State Division of Highways, or other agencies of this ilk which are funded all anew every year. We have a fixed budget approved by the public in this bond vote with whatever supplementary funds we can raise, which is tied to the passage of time. Our prime responsibility to the public which has voted this bond authority is to deliver the system as near like we promised it and as nearly on time as we possibly can.

There was not in that bond issue, and I would even add unfortunately perhaps, there was not in that bond issue a social cost factor. There was in that bond issue the wages of people who built it. There was in that bond issue the funds to buy the steel, to tunnel under the ground, to build aerial structures for the concrete and all the rest.

It is in this context that I say our prime responsibility is to deliver this system to the public as rapidly as possible.

Now we have accepted over a period of the past many, many months this — have accepted it very deeply the responsibility to do all we can in connection with assuring fair employment and nondiscrimination on our jobs, and again I would cite to the record which is rife with things we have done and attempted to do.

The one thing under existing laws, not our laws, but of the existing laws of this State and of this land that we cannot get into are the collective bargaining agreements that exist between the contractors and the affected unions. These laws have been built up over a period of many, many years. They have been urged, they have been supported, and they have been guided to a great degree by the Federal Government itself, to insure fair union practices and good dealings between the contractors and the unions.

This is one area that we have not gotten into and I believe we can't as a single agency get into, because, again, to do so would probably have one or two effects: either we wouldn't get bids on our contracts at all or we would be put out of business because of the size of the bids that we would get.

The point is we must award to the lowest responsive, responsible bidder. We must compete for the contractors and the union help among all of the other construction projects that are under way, not only in this State, but throughout the West and even the country, and for a time certainly in Vietnam. We have to compete and if we don't and we don't get the jobs at the prices that we are supposed to get them at, we are not fulfilling our basic obligation to the public which is to do our very best to deliver this system.

Now, you say, "Fine, and you are washing your hands of the whole thing." Well, again, I must refer you to the record that we have not washed our hands of the whole thing. We, to cite a few things, and aside again from this whole matter of dealing with the contractors through the public bidding process as required in this State, and they with the union, we have taken a great interest in the East Bay Skill Center which is a part of the Fair Employment program which the Federal Government has backed here in the Bay Area, and at the time we got interested in this Skill Center, which is basically to train disadvantaged youth and even older people for jobs, not one construction trade's business agent or official had been in this building, which is quite impressive and which struck us as certainly one of the ways it should be worked at.

As a result of our work, and you have never seen a bit of publicity about this and we have never made any great claims about what is going on, but as a result of this, practically every business agent of a craft union in the East Bay area has now been in the building, has talked with the people, and I believe I could say without fear of contradiction, unanimously support the idea of this Skill Center as a means of pre-apprenticeship training, upgrading, this sort of thing.

What are the results? Nothing so far except for the fact that we have created an understanding among these business agents and the people who are doing their best with the Skill Center that when the time comes that there are jobs that here is a ready-made opportunity to get at one of the problems, and that is to qualify some of these disadvantaged kids to compete equally with others for entry into the union.

At Bethlehem this had nothing to do with the construction contract. It is a subcontractor working with Bethlehem Shipyards here in San Francisco in connection with our Trans-Bay tube. Not a dime of Federal money in this, but working with Bethlehem on a completely private program, we recruited, helped them recruit, backed, supported, encouraged, worked with the unions involved on a training program which today I believe has trained something on the order of 200 to 250 welders for this single program. I don't have any figures for you, but I would say that the percentage of minority people probably ranges upward from 75 percent.

Similarly, on another project that has nothing to do with construction, it is a procurement contract between us and the Kaiser people up at Napa, something of the order of 350 welders have been trained, primarily members of minority groups. This was a program that was financed by the M.D.T.A., again with our encouragement, with our help, with our support, with our working with some of these other people.

I mentioned earlier that we have been working with minority contractors, attempting to advise them, to help them get themselves in a position where they can qualify to bid either as a prime or as a sub on some of these jobs as they come along, and they will come along with increasing frequency in the next few months.

I think one of the things that has been most helpful in creating a climate and this atmosphere that I talked about earlier is that at our request last year the State Fair Employment Practices Commission called at our request a meeting to bring face to face for the very first time in history in this area members of the Contractors' Associations, leaders of the construction unions, and some of the civil rights people who have been so active in trying to develop new ideas and new thoughts on this line.

We would like to think it was an historic confrontation that was called at our request, that Mr. Dellums of the State Fair Employment Practices Commission very graciously arranged the facilities for, and we think that it was the beginning of a new understanding which does exist in this Bay Area today, I insist, which does exist, and which will pay off in jobs for minority people in ever increasing quantities once the jobs are here.

We see our job right now is to get these contracts underway in an orderly process just as rapidly as we can. We think the atmosphere is here. We think that when these jobs are here that the minorities, members of the minority groups, are going to benefit and benefit greatly.

COMMISSIONER GRISWOLD. Well, thank you for that. Now, what do you think you can do in the future which will increase the opportunities for minority groups to obtain employment out of your billion dollar project? What I am trying to do now—I take what you have just told us to be a recounting of what you have done, and now what I am asking you is, is there anything more that you can do? Do you have any plans for further work along this line in the future?

MR. STOKES. Yes, sir. We have a committee working right now to see the ins and outs and the pluses and minuses in any problems that might be involved in applying the Federal formula that pertains only to federally assisted projects to all of our contracts.

We anticipate that within the next several weeks or months that we will institute these same kind of pre-award requirements of the Federal program on all of our contracts, despite the fact there is no Federal money involved.

Secondly, though, Mr. Griswold, I think that again I must get back to my basic point. We think, we honestly feel that the atmosphere for full equal opportunity employment among the construction trades exists. We think that our best shot will be to get these contracts in effect as soon as possible. We really think that the attitude here among the contractors, among the unions, if you please, is one that will pay off with these jobs.

We don't see that there is going to be any particular problem once the construction jobs exist, but until these jobs exist, until we can get over this decline, I don't think you are going to see any great result, no matter what any of us does.

COMMISSIONER GRISWOLD. Thank you, Mr. Stokes. I have only one other thing I would like to say. You emphasized earlier in your testimony that you were a public agency operating under a budget approved by the voters and that your assignment is to get the job done on time if you can and at the lowest possible cost.

MR. STOKES. Yes, sir.

COMMISSIONER GRISWOLD. And that you were obligated to award the contracts to the bidder who was qualified and made the lowest bid.

MR. STOKES. Yes, sir.

·COMMISSIONER. GRISWOLD. Is it not clear, however, that you are equally obligated to comply with some other legal provisions, some provisions which may not even have been in effect and known about when these votes were taken? For example, with respect to the $23 million to $80 million the requirements put in by the Federal Government with respect to the expenditure of Federal funds, but above and beyond that, are there not both State and Federal requirements with respect to the expenditure of the whole billion dollars, with respect to fair employment with which you must comply, and these requirements may be somewhat inconsistent with the obligation that I took you to state as your basic obligation, namely, to do the job in the cheapest possible way and get it done?

MR. STOKES. No, sir. I think that we are living up to all applicable laws, particularly the ones that we were talking about here this morning.

Our basic charge for the public is still to deliver this system, yes, sir, but we have not in any way, shape or form, and do not intend to in the future, shirk our obligations that have come into effect or that have to do with fair employment or with any other aspect of our job.

COMMISSIONER GRISWOLD. Well, let me just follow that up with one more and then I will stop.

If, on opening the bids for a particular job, you found that the lowest bidder was a contractor who you believed discriminated in employment, would you award the bid to that contractor?

MR. STOKES. He would have to certify in a compliance report prior to the award that he was not discriminatory. Unless the action could be brought forth to show that this was in error, he would not be able to bid, I assume, Mr. Diedrich?

MR. DIEDRICH. That's correct, Dean Griswold. You are back in the area of proof again. Under the Executive——

COMMISSIONER GRISWOLD. No, I didn't ask for the area of proof. I said whom you believed discriminates.

MR. DIEDRICH. Do you mean we conclude discriminates?

COMMISSIONER GRISWOLD. That's right.

MR. DIEDRICH. I agree Mr. Stokes's answer was correct. He would be disqualified.

COMMISSIONER GRISWOLD. What was Mr. Stokes' answer?

MR. DIEDRICH. That he would be disqualified.

COMMISSIONER GRISWOLD. Could Mr. Stokes give the answer?

MR. STOKES. I did, Dean Griswold, that if it could be proved that he was discriminatory, and I assume that he would be disqualified, but the case has never arisen to date.

COMMISSIONER GRISWOLD. Suppose the lowest bid came from a contractor whom you had every reason to believe was operating in the best good faith that was possible for him to operate under, but you knew that his employees came from unions that you believed discriminated. Would you award the contract to that contractor?

MR. STOKES. If he could qualify with the basic compliance report that we require and with no evidence to the contrary, yes, sir, we would award the contract.

COMMISSIONER GRISWOLD. Well, then, there really isn't very much that you can do about this problem, is there?

MR. STOKES. From the standpoint you are talking about I would have to agree with you, Dean Griswold.

COMMISSIONER GRISWOLD. Thank you.

CHAIRMAN HANNAH. Are there any questions of the Commissioners? We are getting behind our time schedule.

Other questions? Mr. Taylor?

CHAIRMAN HANNAH. Thank you. You are excused. Thank you. Mr. Glickstein, will you call the next witness?

MR. GLICKSTEIN. Mr. Al Clem and by Mr. J. R. McCray accompanied by Mr. P. H. McCarthy, Jr., counsel.

(Whereupon, Mr. Al M. Clem and Mr. J. R. McCray were sworn by the Chairman and testified as follows:)

TESTIMONY OF MR. AL M. CLEM, MILLBRAE, CALIFORNIA AND MR. J. R. McCRAY, SAN FRANCISCO, CALIFORNIA

MR. GLICKSTEIN. Mr. Clem, would you please state your full name and address for the record?

MR. CLEM. Al M. Clem, 351 Marcella Way, Millbrae, California.

MR. GLICKSTEIN. What is your occupation, Mr. Clem?

MR. CLEM. I am the business manager and chief executive officer of Local Union No. 3, Operating Engineers.

MR. GLICKSTEIN. Mr. Clem, I understand you have a very brief statement that you would like to read.

MR. CLEM. In the interest of time I have a prepared statement if, with your permission —

MR. GLICKSTEIN. That is the one-page statement?

MR. CLEM. Yes. Mr. Chairman, I am here today representing Local 3 of the Operating Engineers Union voluntarily. Before the questioning begins, I would like to state the position of Local 3 generally with regard to the problem that I assume we are here to discuss, the high unemployment rate among minority groups.

I am here to offer this Commission any information that I might have that would cast some light on this problem and to suggest some possible solutions to the problem.

If affirmative action is necessary, and I believe that it is necessary, particularly in the are of skilled employment, it must be recognized by this Commission and all others that are interested in taking affirmative action that the leadership of organized labor has a primary duty to the membership, those whose working life has been spent in the building and construction industry. This duty is not inconsistent with the solution of the problem we are here to discuss, but where proposals are offered that are designated to sacrifice the job opportunities of the working men who have spent their life in the building and construction industry, I can not acquiesce. They and no one else can expect me to.

With this in mind, we want to make it clear that we intend to cooperate in trying to alleviate the unemployment among all, including minorities. For that reason we are actively sponsoring a training for apprenticeship program which we hope the Government will adequately finance. To that end I am here today to offer what information we have available and answer such questions as you may have.

MR. GLICKSTEIN. Thank you, Mr. Clem. What is Local 3's jurisdiction?

MR. CLEM. It is Northern California, Northern Nevada, the entire State of Utah, the State of Hawaii, and the Pacific Islands.

MR. GLICKSTEIN. How many members does Local 3 have?

MR. CLEM. Approximately 32,000.

MR. GLICKSTEIN. How many journeymen and how many apprentices?

MR. CLEM. The journeymen are broken down—I don't have the exact breakdown on all of them. We have five separate charters and in some of them some workers could be considered apprentices and in others they could be considered journeymen. We organize vertically and some of them we consider journeymen and others work in factories which would fall in neither category.

MR. GLICKSTEIN. Of these 32,000 are some of those people currently enrolled in an apprenticeship program? Of the 32,000 are some of those people actively involved in an apprenticeship program right now?

MR. CLEM. Yes, sir.

MR. GLICKSTEIN. How many people do you have involved in your apprenticeship program?

MR. CLEM. Are we confining our discussion to the six Bay Area counties here?

MR. GLICKSTEIN. If you like, we can do that. Approximately how many of your 32,000 members live in the six Bay Area counties?

MR. CLEM. I don't have a breakdown on that, Counsel. I would say around, just off the top of my head, probably 9,000.

MR. GLICKSTEIN. Nine thousand. And how many people do you have in the apprenticeship program in the six counties?

MR. CLEM. Two hundred and ten of them in the program working as of this time.

MR. GLICKSTEIN. Two hundred and ten.

MR. CLEM. We have a very high unemployment situation in all of our jurisdictions, and particularly in the Bay counties.

MR. GLICKSTEIN. Mr. Clem, would you briefly tell the Commissioners what type of work operating engineers do?

MR. CLEM. Operating engineers operate earth-moving equipment, power shovels, power trains, derrick barges, survey work, and all types of paving operations and hoisting equipment.

MR. GLICKSTEIN. Mr. Clem, how many Negroes are there in your union?

MR. CLEM. I have no way of knowing, sir.

MR. GLICKSTEIN. You have no way of knowing?

MR. CLEM. No, sir.

MR. GLICKSTEIN. Mr. Clem, I suppose you are familiar with the report that just came out that was done for the San Francisco Building and Construction Trades Council by the public relations firm of Alexandro, Baccari & Associates?

MR. CLEM. I haven't had a chance to read it in its entirety, no, sir, but I have read it briefly.

MR. GLICKSTEIN. That report indicates that—I will read from it: "To assure that the survey would indeed be factual, each of the 42 participating unions composing the Council—", and your union is on the Building Trades Council, isn't it?

MR. CLEM. We are affiliated with the Building Trades Council in San Francisco.

MR. GLICKSTEIN. "—pledged full cooperation and in almost unprecedented action opened its books and records to outside probing."

Then the report at page 39 indicates the total membership of the Building and Construction Trades Council in the Bay Area is 18,334 and it indicates that of that number 3,850 persons are Negro and 3,310 bear Spanish surnames.

Now, in your efforts to cooperate in the preparation of this report, you were unable to furnish this firm with the statistics on the number of Negroes and Spanish surnames that you have?

MR. CLEM. We were unable to do so due to the fact that they are talking about 18,000 affiliates with the San Francisco Building Trades Council and we are affiliated with—we have a Building Trades Council in Oakland and one in Marin County and one in San Mateo County. We are affiliated with all of them and our people migrate back and forth and—

MR. GLICKSTEIN. So you weren't able to furnish Alexandro,

Baccari & Associates with the type of figure that they compiled here?

MR. CLEM. Not accurate figures. We wouldn't have been able to.

MR. GLICKSTEIN. So this report might not be accurate, then?

MR. CLEM. As far as we are concerned, it could or could not be accurate. For our people migrate, as I say, back from Alameda, Contra Costa into San Francisco County or in San Mateo County.

MR. GLICKSTEIN. Of your 210 apprentices do you know how many of them are Negro?

MR. CLEM. No, I don't. The apprenticeship program is in charge of a joint committee and we have the administrator here, Danny Dees, and he could answer any question that you would care to have him answer about the apprenticeship program.

MR. GLICKSTEIN. Would he know the answer to the question that I just asked?

MR. CLEM. I wouldn't know whether he would or not.

MR. GLICKSTEIN. Do the 210 apprentices meet frequently in class together?

MR. CLEM. Pardon?

MR. GLICKSTEIN. Do they attend classes together?

MR. CLEM. They could or they could not attend the same classes. As I say, we cross county lines and they could work in San Francisco and live in San Mateo County, and so they could or could not attend classes together.

MR. GLICKSTEIN. Well, I gather from what we have just been saying that one way to become a member of Local 3 is to go through the apprenticeship program. Is that correct?

MR. CLEM. That is right. We have established an apprenticeship program, hoping to upgrade the skill of the people, and this is the way they come into the industry now or generally.

The equipment is getting so large and more complex to operate and so costly the employers are cooperating with us and the unions are cooperating together to try to train skilled people to operate this complex machinery.

MR. GLICKSTEIN. Are there other ways of getting in besides the apprenticeship program?

MR. CLEM. Yes. We have a C list that the people sign, anybody can sign that wants to sign, and they are dispatched off of that if we have the rest of the people dispatched.

MR. GLICKSTEIN. The C list is made up of people who come to this area from some other part of the country, for example?

MR. CLEM. That's right.

MR. GLICKSTEIN. They would go on the C list?

MR. CLEM. If they don't have sufficient pension credits they go on the C list.

MR. GLICKSTEIN. In other words, you——

MR. CLEM. Even some of our own members go on the C list.

MR. GLICKSTEIN. You have a hiring hall that has an A list, a B list and a C list, and people are first dispatched from the A list and then from the B list and then from the C list?

MR. CLEM. In the area, that's right.

MR. GLICKSTEIN. And their eligibility for these lists depends upon their pension credits, which also depends on how long they have been employed in the area?

MR. CLEM. How long they have been employed in the industry under the collective bargaining agreement in the jurisdiction of the local union.

MR. GLICKSTEIN. I gather that the way your hiring hall operates is in conformance with Section 8(f) of the Taft-Hartley Act that you do give preference for length of service in the industry in a geographical area and with a particular employer?

MR. CLEM. It conforms with the Act, yes.

MR. GLICKSTEIN. And the effect of that provision, I guess, is to give—also to give preferential treatment to persons who have been employed in this area as operating engineers for many years and who have worked for employers in this area for many years?

MR. CLEM. We have broadened it out. As you know, the construction industry is highly mobile and people go where the jobs are and the employers are interested in getting the best help that they can, and the taxpayers, we think, are interested in also that the employers get the best help. So as work falls off in one area, our members travel.

I have heard some talk here today about this billion dollar job of BART's. Well, you members of the Commission may or may not know that there is another job in California, a project that costs in excess of a billion dollars and it is finishing up. And it is throwing a great number of our people on the out-of-work list at the present time.

We have approximately 7,500 people on the out-of-work list as of today.

MR. GLICKSTEIN. When one of your members travels——

MR. CLEM. In Northern California.

MR. GLICKSTEIN. When one of your members, for example, travels to Southern California to work, would your member then get on the C list of the local that has jurisdiction down there?

MR. CLEM. That's right; and vice versa.

MR. GLICKSTEIN. So the people that have traditionally worked in this area, for employers in this area, generally get on the A list and have preference?

MR. CLEM. The people who work in the territorial jurisdiction of Local 3 and have sufficient number of pension credits, that is correct.

MR. GLICKSTEIN. Did most of your present members become journeymen through the apprenticeship program?

MR. CLEM. No.

MR. GLICKSTEIN. Is your apprenticeship program rather new?

MR. CLEM. It has been in effect—we got it off the ground about four years ago, five years ago, and it is comparatively new, yes, in relation to other apprenticeship programs in the country.

MR. GLICKSTEIN. In the past, Mr. Clem, did Local 3 deny membership to Negroes and Orientals?

MR. CLEM. No, sir.

MR. GLICKSTEIN. Well, membership in Local 3 has always been available on an equal basis to all types of persons, all groups?

MR. CLEM. We have solicited—we have an organizing campaign now in Guam where we are trying to organize the Filipinos and Guamanians. We had an organizing campaign in the East Bay where we tried to organize the people who were employed in the Alameda Naval Air Station and the Fleet Supply Base.

Many of them were Negroes, American Mexicans, Caucasians, and so forth.

MR. GLICKSTEIN. Well, in the——

MR. CLEM. They refused to come into the union. The membership was offered to them and we were unsuccessful in securing enough authorization cards to file for recognition.

MR. GLICKSTEIN. Well, in the past, Mr. Clem, going back to 1960 and before 1960, did your union deny membership to Negroes and other minorities?

MR. CLEM. I have been a business agent since 1941 and we took everybody in the union who wanted to get in, as far as I am personally concerned. I have taken several Negroes in the union myself.

MR. GLICKSTEIN. Is it possible that when Negroes have come to the hiring hall to be referred that discrimination could have occurred there?

MR. CLEM. Not to my knowledge. We have issued strict orders. We have a hiring regulation which is nondiscriminatory. This is an understanding between our union and the contractors. The contractors do not discriminate against people by virtue of race, creed, or color, and we cannot either. That is what the hiring regulation says.

MR. GLICKSTEIN. If I may backtrack for a minute, Mr. Clem, you indicated that you don't have statistics on the number of Negro members that you have. Would it be possible for you to keep such statistics or compile such statistics?

MR. CLEM. Our records, membership records, are kept on an IBM computer, and we at this time have not been able to develop any method where we could segregate whether they were Negroes,

Indians, Greeks, or what you may have. I know one thing. There is only one or two Greeks in the union. I happen to be part Greek.

MR. GLICKSTEIN. As you probably know, the Civil Rights Act of 1964 requires that unions keep racial records, but the Equal Employment Opportunity Commission is required to publish regulations and provide forms for you to do that and the Commission hasn't done that yet. Now, when such forms are finally published, I guess then it will be possible for your union to compile these statistics?

MR. CLEM. We will do the best that we can to comply with any law that is handed down. I mean, that comes along. We have done it in the past and we intend to continue on doing it.

MR. GLICKSTEIN. Mr. Clem, what steps would the operating engineers take if Federal contractors, in order to comply with the requirements of the Executive order on fair employment, hired non-union Negro operating engineers?

MR. CLEM. Would you mind repeating the question, please?

MR. GLICKSTEIN. If a contractor was forced, because of his obligation under the provision of the Federal Executive order, to have Negroes on the job and he went outside of his agreement with you and hired non-union Negro operating engineers, what steps would your union take?

MR. CLEM. We would enforce our contract.

MR. GLICKSTEIN. Which would permit you to bring an arbitration proceeding or strike or——

MR. CLEM. No, we don't strike. Just pay the top guy on the out-of-work list.

MR. GLICKSTEIN. You would just insist that the employer discharge that man and take the top——

MR. CLEM. I didn't say that. I said he would pay the top guy on the out-of-work list.

MR. GLICKSTEIN. He would pay the top fellow on the—I see. So, in other words, the employer could keep the man on the job that he wanted to, but he would have to pay the top man on the out-of-work list?

MR. CLEM. Unless the individual went on the job through the regular channels, the same as all the rest of our members do, or if he didn't happen to be a member of the union or didn't happen to have enough pension credits, or whatever the case may be, if he could come in and sign the C list and went out in regular order of dispatching, why, we would take him in the union within eight days. That is what our contract says.

MR. GLICKSTEIN. Mr. Clem, you mentioned in your opening statement that the union does have a program or is about to launch a program that would permit more minority group people to get into the union. Would you tell the Commissioners about that program, please?

MR. CLEM. We have in Washington now a proposal to train 50 culturally disadvantaged youths. It is there as—it is a contract proposal. As you know, we run two M.D.T.A. training programs at Camp Roberts—very successfully, I might say—and we have submitted a proposal to Washington now and they are acting or trying to act on it now. I don't know what the problem is, and we told them that this was what we considered—we asked them if this would meet the criteria of the affirmative action and we was assured that it was, and so we put the program together and have submitted it to the Federal Government now, to the Labor Department for approval.

MR. GLICKSTEIN. This would be a pre-apprenticeship training program?

MR. CLEM. That is right.

MR. GLICKSTEIN. And if the young men participating in that completed the course, would they be guaranteed admission to the apprenticeship program?

MR. CLEM. They would be guaranteed, or as the same as anybody else, the right to take the aptitude test which is industry-entrance test, which is prepared by a national firm of industrial consultants, Ernst & Ernst, which we have nothing to do with. They prepare the test. The tests are sealed and they are given to everybody, and we would hope that after this training there would be no problem for these youths to get into the apprenticeship program.

MR. GLICKSTEIN. Do you think the training would prepare them to take the test and pass the test?

MR. CLEM. This is the way that the program is designed, so that they could pass the test.

I might say that, in addition to that, we have another program that we have submitted to the Labor Department to train youths in Guam to form work habits. We have no apprenticeship program in Guam. We just recently started organizing there, but it is a pitiful situation in Guam, and so we are trying to develop work habits amongst the people there.

MR. GLICKSTEIN. Mr. Clem, do you think that it would be a good idea to have more Negroes in Local 3?

MR. CLEM. I have no thoughts on the matter. If the job opportunity is there, we don't care whether they are Negroes or what they are. All we need is job opportunities and we intend to fill the jobs. We don't discriminate against any of them. If a Negro is a good operator—and we have some good operators who are Negroes; we have a great number of excellent operators who are American Mexicans. We have a great number of operators who are Filipinos. We have a great number of operators who are Japanese and Hawaiians and it doesn't make any difference to us just so long as they are qualified operating engineers that can operate the equipment. That is all we are interested in. We are interested in getting more money for our people. Maybe it is kind of a selfish motive. We know that when they are well fed and working all the time they are happy people.

Maybe they will give us a raise once in a while.

MR. GLICKSTEIN. Thank you. I have no further questions.

CHAIRMAN HANNAH. Do the Commissioners have questions?

COMMISSIONER FREEMAN. Mr. Clem, when was Local 3 organized?

MR. CLEM. Pardon me?

COMMISSIONER FREEMAN. When was Local 3 organized?

MR. CLEM. 1939.

COMMISSIONER FREEMAN. 1939. And were you an operating engineer?

MR. CLEM. Yes, ma'am.

COMMISSIONER FREEMAN. What kind of test did you take to become a member of the union?

MR. CLEM. I kept going out and seeing the boss and getting a job and getting run off all the time until I could hold one.

COMMISSIONER FREEMAN. That was all that was required of you?

MR. CLEM. That was all that was required.

COMMISSIONER FREEMAN. It is a fact that at that time—

MR. CLEM. We had no apprenticeship program at that time. I wish somebody would take us in and hold us on their lap.

COMMISSIONER FREEMAN. That union at that time required only the application for membership unless you were Negro and then you were not admitted. Isn't that correct?

MR. CLEM. No. We had Negroes in our union long before 1939.

COMMISSIONER FREEMAN. Isn't it also a fact that the apprenticeship program was not put into effect until there was some compulsion on the union to comply with the nondiscrimination provision?

MR. CLEM. That is not correct.

COMMISSIONER FREEMAN. How long is the apprenticeship program?

MR. CLEM. I said we have been active—

COMMISSIONER FREEMAN. I mean, how long does one have to serve as an apprentice?

MR. CLEM. To the best of my knowledge, it is three years.

COMMISSIONER FREEMAN. And how long will the pre-apprentice program last?

MR. CLEM. Our proposal was that we submit it to the Federal Government. I think it was six months and this is to take the hard-core unemployable and try to train them so they could enter the program.

COMMISSIONER FREEMAN. As it stands now, a person could be trained for six months and then he might become an apprentice and then he would have to serve as an apprentice for three years before he would become a journeyman?

MR. CLEM. That is correct.

COMMISSIONER FREEMAN. And this collective hiring hall requirement is permitted by the Landrum-Griffith Law. Is that right?

MR. CLEM. That's correct.

COMMISSIONER FREEMAN. Now, has it occurred to you that maybe even by the Federal law that we have an exception in behalf of craft unions that permits the very discrimination that we are objecting to?

MR. CLEM. It isn't correct, I believe, as a matter of law.

COMMISSIONER FREEMAN. Is it not true that the craft unions are the only ones that are permitted to have this preferential treatment?

MR. CLEM. No, that is not. Not as a matter of law, it is not.

COMMISSIONER FREEMAN. And what other unions are permitted to have the hiring hall?

MR. CLEM. I will refer to the attorney. He can give you probably a more intelligent answer than I can.

MR. MCCARTHY. My name is P. H. McCarthy, Jr., 518 Balboa Building, San Francisco, California, counsel for the Local 3.

The first case involving a hiring hall arose on the waterfront. The ILWU and the employers on the waterfront have maintained hiring halls, exclusive hiring halls for years. The basic principle of a hiring hall is seniority and if it is operated to cause discrimination on any basis of membership or non-membership in the union, or ra e, creed, color, sex, or national origin, it is an illegal hiring hall. c

COMMISSIONER FREEMAN. Under the law it says that the exception is to building and construction industry. That is the only exception?

MR. MCCARTHY. That exception has to do with the union shop clause under which we are permitted to require membership in eight days instead of thirty days, but has no reference to the operation of the hiring hall.

COMMISSIONER FREEMAN. And Mr. Clem indicated that if the contractor would employ a non-union worker, that the top man on his list would have to be paid under the agreement.

MR. MCCARTHY. If the man was not obtained through the hiring hall, yes.

COMMISSIONER FREEMAN. That's right.

MR. MCCARTHY. But if a non-union man was obtained through the hiring hall, and frequently is, why, then, the only obligation would be for the man to join within eight days.

COMMISSIONER FREEMAN. But there are no Negroes in the union or if there are only a handful and if he must be obtained through the hiring hall, then a Negro would never be sent out. Is that not correct?

MR. MCCARTHY. If a Negro registers on the list, he is sent out in every instance, and when that was questioned it was minutely investigated and it was found that he was treated with complete fairness.

COMMISSIONER FREEMAN. You indicated earlier, Mr. Clem, that the membership information is on the computer and that it was impossible for you to get this information. Now, the information on the computer, is that information that is given to the computer? Is it not?

MR. CLEM. That's right.

COMMISSIONER FREEMAN. And so, therefore, it is possible to obtain this information and feed it into the computer and then be able to give this Commission the information that Mr. Glickstein asked for?

MR. CLEM. Well, it has been our understanding that it was illegal to discriminate against anybody because of race, creed, color.

COMMISSIONER FREEMAN. That is correct.

MR. CLEM. So to keep out of trouble with the law we didn't ask people what they were. We ask them their name, social security number, and age, and who their dependents are, and have they ever belonged to the union before. That is all the information that we ask them when they sign an application to join the union.

COMMISSIONER FREEMAN. We would now like to know from you information concerning the membership of minority groups in the union.

MR. CLEM. I just tell you I have no way of knowing.

COMMISSIONER FREEMAN. You have no way of knowing this?

MR. CLEM. Historically, as I told you, when people make application to join the union, we ask them their name, their social security number, their age, and who their dependents are.

CHAIRMAN HANNAH. Any other questions? Father Hesburgh?

COMMISSIONER HESBURGH. The best information that I have been able to find, Mr. Clem, is that there are 30 members out of 9,000 who are Negro, and you don't have to ask him a question. You can tell a Negro by looking at him. Is that, in your judgment, an adequate statement or is it a false statement would you think?

MR. CLEM. I have no way of knowing what you are saying is right or not.

COMMISSIONER HESBURGH. What is your impression?

MR. CLEM. I think you are wrong.

COMMISSIONER HESBURGH. I see. Well, suppose that when the

new regulations come out you will be able to certify whether that is right or wrong.

MR. CLEM. We told you—we told the Commission here that we abide by all the laws and we will do the best we can to abide by any laws that come out.

COMMISSIONER HESBURGH. Well, the best information we have been able to get is that there are about 30 Negroes out of 9,000 and you think that is wrong, so that will be a matter of record and we will try to check it later. Thank you.

CHAIRMAN HANNAH. Mr. Patterson.

VICE CHAIRMAN PATTERSON. Mr. Clem, does California have a right-to-work law?

MR. CLEM. No, sir. Nevada and Utah has a right-to-work law.

VICE CHAIRMAN PATTERSON. We had a Negro witness here yesterday who suggested that many Negroes feel they are excluded from craft unions, from jobs that work under unions, and that if this couldn't be changed or wasn't changed that they might feel that a unified Negro vote might change its traditional alliance with labor and come out for the right-to-work law in order to open up jobs for Negroes. If this were done, would a right-to-work law pass in this State in your judgment?

MR. CLEM. I'd say that we operate in two States where we have right-to-work laws. I think that the gentleman who was here yesterday and wanted to get in to Local 3 all he has to do is go to Nevada and Utah and get him a job and he would get in.

We have people over here whom we have tried to get in the union. We have solicited them for membership and they turned us down. So I don't think that the right-to-work law is the solution to any job opportunities for anybody. We know that in the States where we work, where we operate where they have right-to-work laws that some unscrupulous employers tend to discriminate against everybody. They want them to work cheap. They tear down the living standards of the working people against the wishes of the scrupulous employers.

So the enacting of a right-to-work law won't change one iota whether the people get in the union or whether the minority groups are in the union or not, in my humble opinion.

VICE CHAIRMAN PATTERSON. But would it concern you if the Negroes of California began agitating for a right-to-work law in this State?

MR. CLEM. I don't think—fundamentally I think the great majority of the Negroes in California are good union people and I don't think they are going to agitate for the right-to-work law in California. I think the clear-thinking Negro or American Indian or American Mexican or Greek or Dutchman or whatever he is, people who think, I don't think they are going to advocate a right-to-work law because the record shows that where they have the right-to-work laws the conditions, the wages and the conditions do not compare in those States where we have union shops.

VICE CHAIRMAN PATTERSON. Then you are not concerned by this suggestion?

MR. CLEM. It doesn't bother me at all. I think there are so many clear-thinking of all groups that it would never pass.

VICE CHAIRMAN PATTERSON. Thank you.

CHAIRMAN HANNNH. Mr. Taylor? And then we will take a five-minute recess after you have finished any questions that you have.

MR. TAYLOR. Mr. Clem, I am just following up on Mrs. Freeman's questions. Until five years ago there was not an apprenticeship program. How long did it take to become an operating engineer during that period?

MR. CLEM. We have got people in our union that has been there for 30 years and they are not operating engineers yet.

MR. TAYLOR. But how long now—you say with the pre-apprenticeship program and an apprenticeship program it would take about three and a half years to become a journeyman?

MR. CLEM. We hope to train people in three years to become journeymen by classroom, attending classrooms and being helped by the journeymen, guided by the coordinators, helped by the administrators on the program, and with the cooperation with the employers.

MR. TAYLOR. I understand, but was that the case before the apprenticeship program was in effect or could someone become a journeyman in less time than it now takes?

MR. CLEM. Well, as I say, I never worked as an apprentice myself and I got run off a few jobs until I could get so I could hold one, and that was more or less what has happened throughout the country, and as you ladies and gentlemen may or may not know, operating engineers to a great degree are born.

MR. TAYLOR. I am sorry.

MR. CLEM. I say an operating engineer to a great degree is born. I mean, if they don't have muscle coordination, coordination of eyes, hands, and feet, they can never be operating engineers.

We have people, as I say, who have been in our union for 30 years and are not operating engineers yet.

MR. TAYLOR. Well, I am just wondering whether it wouldn't be possible to shorten the period through one means or another. In other words, is it that the job is so complex to learn or is it mainly that you are trying to limit the supply of operating engineers?

MR. CLEM. No, we are not trying to limit the supply of operating engineers. As I say, we have 7,500 of them out of work now, so we have got plenty of them.

Several apprenticeship programs are four years, so we advocated that we have a three-year program, and this is what we are trying to hold it down to. The apprenticeship program in the operating engineers is comparatively new, as I said before.

If we can make them in two years, why, I am in favor of that, as far as I am personally concerned, for they work on a wage ratio which is less than that of a journeyman until they attain journeyman's status, and we are interested in getting those wages up there where they belong.

MR. McCRAY. Excuse me, Mr. Taylor. Since Mr. Hannah swore me, I would like to say something at this point.

MR. TAYLOR. Go ahead.

MR. McCRAY. One thing regarding your question, Mr. Taylor. You are welcome to look at this book. We have a book here that over the years shows the kind of equipment operating engineers have been running. At the time Mr. Clem became a member of the operating engineers and was running a cat or whatever, things were pretty slow and everything was mechanical. Today, as a technical man can tell you, a cat will now go 25 miles an hour whereas before it went three or five. It is not mechanical. It is run on the principle of hydraulics or electronics.

The crane is a push-button affair now, no longer levers. This is one reason we had to have an apprenticeship program, because of this. Everything is faster and it is more technical.

Now, back to some other people's question about—I think you asked Mr. Clem what we would do about or what recommendation we can make for alleviating the problem of unemployment in the minority groups in the Bay Area. I have a chart I threw together and I wanted to get it in because it was a lot of work. This chart shows the number of men who are out of work in our union in the various dispatch offices in the Bay Area.

Now, the black line is 1964. Please compare that with the blue line, which is 1966. It will show that there is a considerable number of more men now than in 1966 who were out of work and in 1967 up to April 14 of this year it is extraordinarily disproportionate amount of men are out of work in the Bay Area.

That is shown by the red line way up here at the top, in case you missed it. This is a problem to solve unemployment among minority groups. We need jobs.

MR. TAYLOR. We will be glad to receive the chart. The only point I was trying to establish or ascertain was if the work were there it would not necessarily take as long as three years for people to become members if enough employment were around.

MR. CLEM. I can answer that, sir. If you are going to train a youth to become a well-rounded operating engineer, those who

can operate cats, blades, cranes, shovels, and so forth, I can say
to you in all sincerity he can not do it in three years, and this is
what we are trying to get our people to do: to have a wider range
of skills in different equipment, so that they can have more work
opportunities than they have at the present time. In fact, we are
trying to—We have a program now where we are trying to retrain
the present people who are in our union because, as Mr. McCray
tells you here, the equipment is getting so much faster and more
complex to operate.

MR. TAYLOR. I have no further questions.

CHAIRMAN HANNAH. Thank you very much, Mr. Clem and
gentlemen. We will take a 5-minute recess.

CHAIRMAN HANNAH. Mr. Glickstein, will you call the next
witness?

MR. GLICKSTEIN. The next witness is Mr. James Childers.

(Whereupon, MR. JAMES LAMAR CHILDERS was sworn by the
Chairman and testified as follows:)

TESTIMONY OF MR. JAMES LAMAR CHILDERS, ALAMEDA, CALIFORNIA

MR. GLICKSTEIN. Will you please state your full name and your
address for the record?

MR. CHILDERS. James Lamar Childers. I live at 2807 Bayview
Drive, Alameda, California.

MR. GLICKSTEIN. What is your ocupation?

MR. CHILDERS. Business representative of the Alameda County
Building & Construction Trades Council.

MR. GLICKSTEIN. And how long have you held your position?

MR. CHILDERS. I think about 15 years.

MR. GLICKSTEIN. How many unions are affiliated with the
council?

MR. CHILDERS. I guess 43 or 44.

MR. GLICKSTEIN. Forty-three or 44?

MR. CHILDERS. In that neighborhood, yes, in excess of 40.

MR. GLICKSTEIN. How many workers does the council represent?

MR. CHILDERS. Approximately 20,000.

MR. GLICKSTEIN. What function does the council perform for
its affiliated unions?

MR. CHILDERS. Oh, they elected me as sort of a spokesman for
the group. In many instances I am a coordinator and conciliator.
We organize—the council's function is to organize and enforce
contracts. We do negotiate some, engage—

MR. GLICKSTEIN. Do you negotiate some of the contracts?

MR. CHILDERS. We assist, yes.

MR. GLICKSTEIN. But, for example, the Plumbers Union is affiliated with you, their collective bargaining agreement is signed with the Plumbing Contractors' Association?

MR. CHILDERS. Right.

MR. GLICKSTEIN. You might assist in that, but you wouldn't be a signatory to the agreement?

MR. CHILDERS. No, we are not signatory to it, no.

MR. GLICKSTEIN. Mr. Childers, there have been allegations, as everybody is aware of, that there is discrimination against Negroes and Spanish-speaking Americans and other minorities and membership and apprenticeship policies of building unions. Are these allegations warranted today? Were they warranted in the past?

MR. CHILDERS. They are not warranted today. Some of them have been in the past.

MR. GLICKSTEIN. Some of them have been in the past?

MR. CHILDERS. Yes, 40 years ago, yes.

MR. GLICKSTEIN. Forty years ago?

MR. CHILDERS. Yes.

MR. GLICKSTEIN. How about four years ago?

MR. CHILDERS. No.

MR. GLICKSTEIN. Ten years ago?

MR. CHILDERS. No.

MR. GLICKSTEIN. I just would like to make something clear. Your council represents unions on the other side of the Bay. There is a San Francisco Building Trades Council also. Is that correct?

MR. CHILDERS. Very definitely, yes.

MR. GLICKSTEIN. What were the practices in the past that prevented minority group people from getting into the unions? Was it outright racial discrimination?

MR. CHILDERS. Principally no. I have actively worked as a journeyman, you know, and I have been associated with the construction industry for the last 40 years in Alameda County. So I am rather familiar with what has happened there in that period of time. Most of the craft unions in, say, 40 years ago and some of them today to a lesser extent at any rate felt that all journeymen should arrive at journeyman status through the apprenticeship training program of the particular union or a union affiliated with its international, and some of them just in the distant past—I am talking about 40 years ago or so—would not take in anybody to membership who hadn't gone through the apprenticeship training program period.

This period passed, after the passage of the Wagner Act. We inaugurated an organizing campaign in Alameda County to organize all people who worked at construction, regardless of whether they had gone through an apprenticeship training program or regardless of what color they were, where they came from or anything else. If they could hold a job as a journeyman, we wanted them in the union and we organized them and we have them today, all of them.

MR. GLICKSTEIN. How about current apprenticeship programs? Are the minority groups well represented in the current apprenticeship programs?

MR. CHILDERS. Yes, they are represented. Not as well as they would like to be, as some of their spokesmen say they would like to be. I think they are represented as well as the Negroes want to be represented.

MR. GLICKSTEIN. Mr. Childers, I know you are familiar with the Dymally Report, which is a report on apprenticeship training that was done by the staff of the Committee of the State Assembly. That report lists a number of unions in which Negro enrollment in apprenticeship programs is less than 2 percent and, among other unions, they mention the Operating Engineers. That has .77 percent Negroes, and the Plumbers have .46 Negroes, and there are seven or eight or 10 other unions mentioned in that report in the same category. Do those figures reflect present conditions?

MR. CHILDERS. I would think from my knowledge, you know, and experience that they probably do.

MR. GLICKSTEIN. Probably do. Now, you said a moment ago that you felt that the Negroes were represented in the apprenticeship program to the extent that they wanted to be.

MR. CHILDERS. Right.

MR. GLICKSTEIN. What do you mean by that?

MR. CHILDERS. Just exactly what I said, that if a Negro wants to get in the program and he is qualified, he is taken in. If he doesn't want to and doesn't make application, he is not there, you know. In the Plumbers Union in Alameda County, which I happen to have taken some interest in because of the attacks upon plumbers, I made myself familiar with this. I know that their program has been for many years a nondiscrimination program and there are very few Negroes in their program, and primarily because the Negroes who are qualified to pass the examinations do not apply.

MR. GLICKSTEIN. So you think that if the fault lies anywhere, it is with the Negroes that haven't applied in sufficient numbers to get admitted to these programs?

MR. CHILDERS. Well, out of 250, I believe, who are now on the waiting list to go to the pre-apprenticeship training school in Alameda County for the Plumbers Union, there are five Negroes.

MR. GLICKSTEIN. Does your council or unions affiliated with your council have any affirmative programs to attract or interest Negroes and other minority group members applying for apprenticeship programs?

MR. CHILDERS. We don't have any jobs. Why do we want to attract people to non-existent jobs, you know?

MR. GLICKSTEIN. So you don't at this time make any efforts?

MR. CHILDERS. No, we do not.

MR. GLICKSTEIN. When the job situation was somewhat better—

MR. CHILDERS. We are actively discouraging anybody from joining an apprenticeship program at the present time. We don't have any jobs for them, for the ones we have. Why do we want more?

MR. GLICKSTEIN. What about a year or so ago when the job situation was somewhat better? Were any attempts made to encourage minority group members to apply for apprenticeship programs?

MR. CHILDERS. There were people applying for apprenticeship programs in great numbers, you know, people, lots of people. How many Negroes there were I don't know, but in speaking with a couple of the secretaries of unions who are the first ones to be approached usually, they show me stacks of applications like this. "What am I going to do with all these? There are no jobs."

MR. GLICKSTEIN. Do you think that some of the unions have reputations for discriminating in the Negro community that are so great that Negroes are discouraged or dis-inclined to apply to those unions for apprenticeship programs or membership?

MR. CHILDERS. I don't think so.

MR. GLICKSTEIN. You don't think so. You did mention that in the past some unions have discriminated. Do you think that those unions that discriminated in the past have an affirmative obligation to take steps to overcome the effects of past discrimination?

MR. CHILDERS. I don't think that Negroes are any different from anybody else. If they want a job, they are going to go looking wherever they think they can find one. I know many Negroes, workmen and otherwise. I am associated with them daily, and they don't seem to me to be any different when they are looking for a job than anybody else, and I don't think they were discouraged at all. I think they had better opportunities someplace else and that is where they went.

MR. GLICKSTEIN. Mr. Childers, under the usual building trade agreements entered into with contractors, is the contractor bound to hire journeymen exclusively through the union hiring hall?

MR. CHILDERS. This varies. These contracts individually vary considerably, you know, from complete freedom of hiring for perhaps one group to absolutely no latitude maybe in another group. I mean there is a wide range of latitude in the individual contracts and so a general statement here would not be a true one.

MR. GLICKSTEIN. But do most of the unions affiliated with your council have some sort of referral or hiring hall system?

MR. CHILDERS. Yes, sir, they do.

MR. GLICKSTEIN. And generally to one extent or another an employer is supposed to seek employees through that hiring hall?

MR. CHILDERS. Yes.

MR. GLICKSTEIN. We have heard some discussion this morning about the responsibility of contractors to abide by the President's Executive order on equal employment opportunity. What would be the position of your council if a contractor, in order to comply with the Executive order, a contractor who had a contract with a union who had no Negro members, if that contractor were to hire non-union Negroes in order to comply with the executive order?

MR. CHILDERS. In the first place, there aren't any.

MR. GLICKSTEIN. There aren't any?

MR. CHILDERS. In Alameda County.

MR. GLICKSTEIN. There aren't any non-union Negro journeymen?

MR. CHILDERS. Right. There are none.

MR. GLICKSTEIN. What if the contractor, in order to show his good faith, decided that he would hire Negroes to train on the job in these various crafts, that if he would personally incur the expense, and set up his own apprenticeship program for training the Negroes to be plumbers or electricians or what have you, on the job?

MR. CHILDERS. Well, if he did it in accordance with the contract, it would be perfectly all right. If he did not, we would enforce the terms of the contract.

MR. GLICKSTEIN. I gather that that wouldn't be in accord with the contract?

MR. CHILDERS. Probably not.

MR. GLICKSTEIN. And when you say you would enforce the terms of the contract—

MR. CHILDERS. I mean just that.

MR. GLICKSTEIN. You might strike?

MR. CHILDERS. Right.

MR. GLICKSTEIN. Walk off the job?

MR. CHILDERS. Right.

MR. GLICKSTEIN. Do you think that unskilled persons can be taught a limited aspect of a trade, assuming that they don't have the educational background to take on full apprenticeship?

MR. CHILDERS. Yes.

MR. GLICKSTEIN. You think they could be?

MR. CHILDERS. Oh, sure.

MR. GLICKSTEIN. How would this affect the employment of journeymen?

MR. CHILDERS. We would not do it.

MR. GLICKSTEIN. Why wouldn't you do it?

MR. CHILDERS. We would be opposed to it, yes.

MR. GLICKSTEIN. Why would you be opposed to it?

MR. CHILDERS. Because we are interested in having people who are mechanics in the sense that they would be able to work at any

321

part of the trade just as nearly as possible and people with limited abilities are unemployed a good deal of the time. So that their opportunities for employment are very limited, and so they spend a good deal of their time drawing their unemployment insurance. So we would rather have people who could hold a job, you know, and do any part of their job, and so we discourage fragmentation of the jobs from this standpoint.

Now, we could easily take in a lot more people, and have a lot more members and a lot more money in the treasury probably by taking in these type of members and have them sitting on the bench half the year. But we don't think that this does the individual any good and certainly not the industry or anybody else. So we don't think it is a good idea.

Mr. GLICKSTEIN. Mr. Childers, we understand that the Building Trades Council supported several bills introduced in the California Legislature in 1966, dealing with preferential hiring in the apprenticeship admission practices. They were bills, I believe, that would have prohibited preferential hiring and preferential admission practices.

Would you state what those bills were, if you know, and why you supported them?

Mr. CHILDERS. Just offhand I don't recall.

Mr. GLICKSTEIN. You don't recall what those bills were?

Mr. CHILDERS. No, I do not.

Mr. GLICKSTEIN. We have copies of the bills here. Perhaps we can show them to you and it might refresh your recollection.

Mr. CHILDERS. It might. Do you want me to read it out loud?

Mr. GLICKSTEIN. Could you describe what the gist of the bill is?

Mr. CHILDERS. Well, let's see if I got a legislative—the Legislative Council's analysis usually is on these things. I don't see one on this particular bill here. Apparently this is the gist of the thing: it says "for an employer to hire"—section of the code, as amended, to read "It shall be unlawful—" Yes, "for an employer to hire or employ any person because of his race, religious creed, color, national origin, or ancestry, whether in order to establish or maintain any quota or proportion of employees based upon any such factor or otherwise or for an employer to discriminate in favor of or to accord preferential treatment to any person in compensation or in term—" I see. Yes.

Mr. GLICKSTEIN. Why did you support that bill?

Mr. CHILDERS. Oh, because there were groups around who were trying to impose quotas, you know, and provide preferential employment terms for Negroes, and we are in favor of nondiscrimination. We are in favor of fair employment practices. We are not in favor of discriminatory practices, whether they are for Negroes or against Negroes or for Caucasians or against Caucasians. So we supported the bill because we are in favor of fair treatment.

MR. GLICKSTEIN. Mr. Childers, I assume that you are familiar with Section 8 (f) of the Taft-Hartley Act?

MR. CHILDERS. 8 (f) ? I don't recognize it by that.

MR. GLICKSTEIN. That is the provision that deals with the building trades and provides for the eight-day union security provision, and also special provisions for hiring halls. Do you think that that provision of a Federal statute provides preferential treatment for building trades people?

MR. CHILDERS. No, I don't.

MR. GLICKSTEIN. You don't. I have no further questions.

CHAIRMAN HANNAH. Any questions from the Commissioners?

COMMISSIONER FREEMAN. Mr. Childers, you say you have been a journeyman for 40 years?

MR. CHILDERS. No, I have said I have worked here, for 40 years. I haven't been a journeyman for quite that long.

COMMISSIONER FREEMAN. In what craft are you a journeyman?

MR. CHILDERS. I am a plasterer by trade.

COMMISSIONER FREEMAN. What examination did you have to take to become a journeyman plasterer?

MR. CHILDERS. What examination did I have to take? I was sent out on the job by the business representative and along with two members of the examining board of the union, and they watched while I did plastering as they directed and this took somewhere in the neighborhood of about an hour or so and after these two members of the examining board certified that in their opinion I was qualified for journeyman status in the union, why, they accepted me.

COMMISSIONER FREEMAN. So then after about an hour you were qualified, certified as being a journeyman?

MR. CHILDERS. Right. That is what the test was.

COMMISSIONER FREEMAN. The Plasterers Union is one of the unions that has been charged with discrimination against and membership practices against Negroes, is it not?

MR. CHILDERS. Is it? No, it is not.

COMMISSIONER FREEMAN. It has not been charged with exclusion of Negroes from the union?

MR. CHILDERS. It has not been, no.

COMMISSIONER FREEMAN. You are familiar with all of the labor unions of which you are business manager and they include the Plumbers?

MR. CHILDERS. Right.

COMMISSIONER FREEMAN. Are you familiar with the charge that they exclude?

MR. CHILDERS. They have been charged, yes. It is not true.

COMMISSIONER FREEMAN. What about the Sheet Metal?

MR. CHILDERS. It is not true.

COMMISSIONER FREEMAN. The Steamfitters?

MR. CHILDERS. It is not true.

COMMISSIONER FREEMAN. The Ironworkers?

MR. CHILDERS. It is not true.

COMMISSIONER FREEMAN. The Operating Engineers?

MR. CHILDERS. It is not true.

COMMISSIONER FREEMAN. Well, is it not true that actually the membership percentages are less than 1 percent in each of those instances and that all these unions have been engaged in preferential treatment as to white persons for over 40 years?

MR. CHILDERS. No, that is not true.

COMMISSIONER FREEMAN. Thank you.

CHAIRMAN HANNAH. Any questions from the Commissioners?

COMMISSIONER HESBURGH. I think there are some figures here that ought to be read out because Commissioner Freeman said less than 1 percent. I only see one, two, three, four that are more than 1 percent but it is about a half percent and they are all less than 2 percent and more than half are less than 1 percent.

MR. CHILDERS. Aren't you reading from the Dymally Report?

MR. GLICKSTEIN. Yes, sir.

MR. CHILDERS. Whoever said that was true, that report? I know Senator Dymally and if I have ever seen a gerrymandered report, that is one. It was designed to show discrimination. I think the Senator deliberately had that thing gerrymandered to show discrimination because I don't think it is a true report.

MR. GLICKSTEIN. These statistics in the report were compiled by the State Division of Apprenticeship Standards.

MR. CHILDERS. I can compile statistics, too. You give me the book and I will come up with a different set.

MR. TAYLOR. Could you furnish us with information which would indicate the respects in which the information contained in this report is false?

MR. CHILDERS. No. Probaby not. But I know Senator Dymally. He has a program and he has an idea that he is going to prove discrimination and so he come out with a report that proves discrimination. If I were in his position, you know, I could probably prove just the opposite with the same figures.

MR. TAYLOR. Well, it would be helpful to know this because it is difficult to deal in generalizations or charges unless we know what the facts are.

MR. CHILDERS. Well, yes. O.K. So I don't have the staff that he has to come up with these kinds of reports.

MR. TAYLOR. Mr. Childers, I think you indicated that the general purpose of the council is to assert the interests and protect the interests of the constituents?

MR. CHILDERS. Right.

MR. TAYLOR. Now, I understand the council supported a bill last year to prohibit the transportation of children in order to relieve racial imbalance of schools unless the permission of the parents was first obtained. Can you tell me why the council took a public position on that bill?

MR. CHILDERS. I don't recall that we did. We did?

MR. TAYLOR. You are the secretary of the council, is that right?

MR. CHILDERS. No, I am not the secretary. I am the business representative.

MR. TAYLOR. You don't recall whether you took a position on that?

MR. CHILDERS. I don't recall, no.

MR. TAYLOR. Are you familiar with the legislation or do you yourself have a personal position on it?

MR. CHILDERS. Yes, I probably would have. I am opposed—if you want to know, I will tell you. As far as I am concerned, I am opposed to transferring, moving kids around from district to district. I don't think it is a good idea, regardless of what color they are.

MR. TAYLOR. What I am interested in knowing is what interest of the council was being asserted in taking a position?

MR. CHILDERS. I don't know. Unless we were asked to express an opinion on it by somebody or another, I don't know why we would necessarily.

MR. TAYLOR. Well, you say that you think the reputation of the council and its members is not such as would lead Negroes to think that the membership was discriminatory. Do you think taking a public position against this kind of legislation might—

MR. CHILDERS. There are many Negroes who are opposed to that. This isn't just a white and black issue.

MR. TAYLOR. I understand that. But do you think that that might in some way interfere with your position or your ability to have a reputation of being nondiscriminatory, at least among those Negroes who have some interest—

MR. CHILDERS. We try to do what is right regardless of whether it happens to suit the present climate of opinion. What we believe in, and I am not—I get paid by the council and as long as those reelect me and pay my salary, I am not too much concerned about what some other group might think, you know, really. So—and we have a number of Negroes, you know, in our council and I know what these people think because I communicate with them and they with me. They are members of the community, members of our union, and these people I listen to. Some of this other noise I don't even hear.

MR. TAYLOR. I have no further questions.

CHAIRMAN HANNAH. Any further questions? Thank you very much, Mr. Childers. You are excused. Call the next witness.

MR. GLICKSTEIN. Joseph Mazzola accompanied by Stanley Neyhart and James Duggan.

CHAIRMAN HANNAH. Mr. Mazzola, are the other gentlemen going to participate in the questioning?

MR. NEYHART. If necessary. If we are called upon.

CHAIRMAN HANNAH. Are you an attorney?

MR. NEYHART. Yes.

CHAIRMAN HANNAH. The other gentleman is not?

MR. DUGGAN. Apprentice coordinator. We were requested to be present.

CHAIRMAN HANNAH. Will all of you be sworn?

(Whereupon, Mr. Joseph Mazzola, Mr. Stanley Neyhart, and Mr. James M. Duggan were sworn by the Chairman and testified as follows:)

TESTIMONY OF MR. JOSEPH MAZZOLA, SAN FRANCISCO, CALIFORNIA, MR. STANLEY NEYHART, SAN FRANCISCO, CALIFORNIA, AND MR. JAMES M. DUGGAN, SAN FRANCISCO, CALIFORNIA

MR. GLICKSTEIN. Would each of you gentlemen please identify yourselves.

MR. MAZZOLA. Joseph Mazzola, Business Manager of the Plumbers and Pipefitters Union, Local 38.

MR. GLICKSTEIN. And what is your address?

MR. MAZZOLA. The union address?

MR. GLICKSTEIN. You can give either your home or business address.

MR. MAZZOLA. 1621 Market Street.

MR. DUGGAN. My name is James M. Duggan, apprentice coordinator of the Journeymen Plumbing Apprentice Training. The office address is 1621 Market Street, Room 202.

MR. NEYHART. Stanley Neyhart, Neyhart & Grodin, Russ Building, San Francisco. Attorney-at-law.

MR. GLICKSTEIN. Mr. Mazzola, what is Local 38's jurisdiction?

MR. MAZZOLA. Jurisdiction over the plumbing and piping industry.

MR. GLICKSTEIN. What is the geographic area that you cover?

MR. MAZZOLA. San Francisco, Marin, Sonoma, and Mendocino Counties.

MR. GLICKSTEIN. How many members does your local have?

MR. MAZZOLA. Approximately 3,000.

MR. GLICKSTEIN. Are those 3,000 journeymen or does that include the apprentices?

MR. MAZZOLA. That includes everyone in the piping industry, marine fitters, plumbers, steamfitters, appliance, utility plumbers and anyone working in the piping and plumbing trades.

MR. GLICKSTEIN. How many of those 3,000 are apprentices?

MR. MAZZOLA. Approximately 250—Correction; 262—

MR. GLICKSTEIN. Two hundred sixty-two?

MR. MAZZOLA. Well, yes, in the construction, and we have at the various yards in connection with marine there is training programs that are in conjunction with the yards themselves. So we haven't got a full count on that.

MR. GLICKSTEIN. Mr. Mazzola, how many Negroes are there in your local?

MR. MAZZOLA. Approximately 20 that we know of.

MR. GLICKSTEIN. How many Negro apprentices do you have?

MR. MAZZOLA. I believe we have three.

MR. GLICKSTEIN. Do you know how many Spanish-surname people that you have, Mexican Americans, or Spanish-speaking people?

MR. MAZZOLA. Over 200.

MR. GLICKSTEIN. Over 200. And how many Oriental people do you have?

MR. MAZZOLA. I believe we have about 16.

MR. GLICKSTEIN. Sixteen?

MR. MAZZOLA. Roughly. I'm trying to make a guess on it anyway.

MR. GLICKSTEIN. How many of the 20 Negro members that you have are in the marine aspect of the work?

MR. MAZZOLA. Probably about 12 of them.

MR. GLICKSTEIN. Twelve of the 20. How do you manage to have these figures? Do you maintain figures? Do you take a head count?

MR. MAZZOLA. Well, because your organization is constantly asking us to look them up.

MR. GLICKSTEIN. What are the procedures for admitting the plumbers as journeymen?

MR. MAZZOLA. What was that now?

MR. GLICKSTEIN. What are the procedures? How do you become a journeyman in the Plumbers Union?

MR. MAZZOLA. Well, anyone who feels they are a journeyman that comes up to the local union can register themselves on the unemployment list and also go in front of our executive board seeking the right to be able to take an examination in order to enter the union.

MR. GLICKSTEIN. That sort of procedure would be followed by somebody coming from out of the State, for example?

MR. MAZZOLA. Yes.

MR. GLICKSTEIN. Who wanted to become a member?

MR. MAZZOLA. Or anyone right here locally.

MR. GLICKSTEIN. What percentage of your 3,000 journeymen, excluding those who have come to the local from outside the Bay Area, joined through the apprenticeship route?

MR. MAZZOLA. Well, of course, in the later 20 years, since 1948, since the consolidation of all the pipe trades, our apprenticeship program, I suppose, has been the highest apprenticeship —the largest apprenticeship program—of any trades in the area. Taking into consideration the amount of journeymen, as far as the union structure is concerned, it depends on the amount of work we have in the area.

If we have conditions such as now, we don't have any journeymen coming in at all; just the apprentices are the only ones that actually enter into journeymanship. If we have any spell of employment where it might pick up, our organization is pretty well known as a union that has a pretty good reputation as a union in the way of wages and conditions, and we do get a run on us anytime from journeymen all over the Bay Area or out of the State, if the city is known to have itself some work. So it varies according to what the working conditions are, of how the work is available or not in the given area.

MR. GLICKSTEIN. Would you say that a good percentage of your members have gone through the apprenticeship route?

MR. MAZZOLA. The greater majority, yes.

MR. GLICKSTEIN. Have gone through that route. May I backtrack for a moment? You said that about 12 of your 20 Negro journeymen were marine plumbers. Is their wage scale the same as the plumbers that work on construction projects?

MR. MAZZOLA. No, it is not. The marine scale is a lesser scale.

MR. GLICKSTEIN. These people generally work in shipyards. Is that right?

MR. MAZZOLA. Shipyards and waterfront shops.

MR. GLICKSTEIN. Are they hired through the hiring hall?

MR. MAZZOLA. They are.

MR. GLICKSTEIN. How long is your apprenticeship program?

MR. MAZZOLA. It is a 5-year program.

MR. GLICKSTEIN. About how many people do you take in each year? How many people have you taken in each year in the last few years?

MR. MAZZOLA. Well, in the last year and a half we haven't taken in any. We presently have 81 apprentices in the program that are unemployed and have had an unemployment of such for the past year and a half. In fact, we had an unemployment situation prior to the last class that we had taken in a year and a half ago. We insisted pretty much so to our employers to let us have another class with the idea that it, the working conditions, the working picture was going to change and that it looked like a possible future of a greater employment, and it turned out, of course, we were wrong, and we do have this great, large existing unemployed apprenticeship amount right at the present time.

MR. GLICKSTEIN. Mr. Mazzola, you indicated that about 20 of your 3,000 members were Negro and about three of the 262 apprentices were Negro. How do you account for the fact that there are so few, the fact that there are that number and no more Negroes in your union?

MR. MAZZOLA. We haven't in all the years that I have been an officer in the union—we haven't had any actual attention in the way or interest showed by the Negro people coming on up looking to make membership in our organization.

It has been only the last couple of years that the big, you might say, the last, has been going on by various groups against our organization and making a lot of accusations and claims that are definitely not true about discriminating. If people have never shown then, of course, it just happens to be one of these things.

MR. GLICKSTEIN. Did your union ever discriminate against Negroes?

MR. MAZZOLA. Never.

MR. GLICKSTEIN. Did your international union ever have a provision in its constitution prohibiting the admission of Negro members?

MR. MAZZOLA. Never that I know of.

MR. GLICKSTEIN. Never that you know of. Under your collective bargaining agreement must the management hire plumbers exclusively through the union hiring hall?

MR. MAZZOLA. They must hire through the fair hiring hall procedure, which is a collective bargaining procedure.

MR. GLICKSTEIN. And under your agreement, if you are unable to provide a suitable person, then the contractor can hire on the open market?

MR. MAZZOLA. That's right. If for 72 hours we can't furnish a man, he can seek him anywhere and we would have to take him.

MR. GLICKSTEIN. Mr. Mazzola, we have heard some discussion this morning about the Federal Executive order that requires the contractors to follow fair hiring and employment practices. What if a plumbing contractor wanted to get a Federal contract and he was told by the Government Labor Department, the Office of Contract Compliance, that there had to be Negro plumbers on the job, that it wasn't enough just to conciliate and negotiate and to discuss, that the Government wanted results, the Government wanted to see Negroes on the job and your 20 Negro journeymen were all employed elsewhere and the contractor felt obliged to hire some non-union Negro plumbers? What would be the position of your union in such a situation?

MR. MAZZOLA. You are asking me a big, long question there.

MR. GLICKSTEIN. Do you want me to repeat it?

MR. MAZZOLA. No, I got the question, but the only thing we would do is, naturally, get in touch with our attorneys and our international to consult with them as to our procedure in the way of having full rights protected for the union and its members.

MR. GLICKSTEIN. What if a plumbing contractors' association or a particular plumbing contractor came to you and said that he was under a great deal of pressure from the Federal Government, he wasn't going to get a very big contract unless he had more Negro plumbers on the job and he wanted your cooperation and assistance to help him get the contract? What sort of advice or assistance could you give him?

MR. MAZZOLA. Well, I would tell him, even if he came to me and told me he wanted that many Irishmen or Italians, that, as far as we are concerned, we have a contract with him and we don't go by race, creed, or color and that we expect the terms of the contract naturally to be complied with.

MR. GLICKSTEIN. Then what you might be saying then is that if the Federal Government were really ever to properly and adequately enforce the Executive order in this area and require that all plumbing contractors have Negroes on the job, because of the collective bargaining agreement it might be virtually impossible to do that unless the contract is broken, the collective bargaining agreements?

MR. MAZZOLA. Well, what I am telling you in short, that we definitely would consult with our attorneys and our international as to what procedure we should be taking in the way of giving protection to our members and to the contract as a whole.

MR. GLICKSTEIN. What affirmative steps is your union taking, if any, to increase minority membership?

MR. MAZZOLA. Well, we have approximately 700 or 800 unemployed at the present time and have had them now for a couple of years. There is not much we can do in the way of giving you an answer to a question like that with a situation such as our record already is with 800 unemployed.

Not to be smart, but the question I almost want to put back to you is what do you suggest we do with the 800 we have and what kind of a recommendation could you give us to put the 800 presently that we have in our union to work?

MR. GLICKSTEIN. You have had 800 people unemployed for how long?

MR. MAZZOLA. For the last couple of years, they have run anywhere from 400 to 800 constantly unemployed.

MR. GLICKSTEIN. You asked for suggestions. Would you be in favor of dividing jobs up in such a way that they could be performed in simpler components and, therefore, you could spread the work among more people instead of requiring a plumber to know every single aspect of the industry, that you subdivided the work and had specialists? Would you be in favor of such a thing?

MR. MAZZOLA. I think that's already takes its place. Our plumbers have—an all-around plumber who has been through the apprenticeship program and trains himself is—the five years that he has is to get him so that he can have a broader scope of the overall industry and, of course, a plumber falls in the same category for a title such as an attorney or a doctor. You have doctors that specialize in all parts of the body, and we have plumbers who, some of them, are very well up on pretty much all phases of the industry, and many of them are just very limited specialty men. But in most cases by majority our plumbers are pretty well trained, at least all those who, like I have said, in the last so many years have gone through the apprenticeship program and they go through it purposely to learn all phases of the plumbing and piping industry, but when they are on the unemployment list—to get to the other part of your question—when they are sitting available for work on the unemployed list and the calls come in, the employer usually tells the dispatcher pretty much what the work is involved and pretty much what he expects this mechanic to know. In many cases he may need a special man on silver soldering, silver braze; he might be having a copper installation of complete water lines and all copper and, of course, the copper, those that are able to braze and silver solder and what not, those will take that job and all kinds of——

MR. GLICKSTEIN. Are you usually able pretty much to meet the employer's request?

MR. MAZZOLA. Pretty much, yes. This question also should be answered with the amount of men unemployed, naturally there is always—we can meet the employer's request with this amount unemployed journeymen around, you definitely can meet their request.

MR. GLICKSTEIN. Mr. Mazzola, I imagine you are familiar with an NLRB case involving your union The individual who brought the case was named Philip Havick. Are you familiar with that case?

MR. MAZZOLA. Very familiar.

MR. GLICKSTEIN. If I read that case correctly, in that situation you weren't able to supply to the contractor a qualified journeyman to suit his needs.

MR. MAZZOLA. That is one of those cases where you read it all right, but it is not true.

MR. GLICKSTEIN. That's what the trial examiner found in that case.

MR. MAZZOLA. Well, it is not true, positively not true.

MR. GLICKSTEIN. But that is what the trial examiner found and you disagree with his findings?

MR. MAZZOLA. I disagree definitely with his findings.

MR. GLICKSTEIN. And I think the trial examiner also indicated in the footnote that the out-of-work list had been exhausted.

MR. MAZZOLA. Well, would you like to hear what happened?

MR. GLICKSTEIN. I think perhaps we could submit the opinion into the record.

MR. MAZZOLA. Well, why not take a minute? The employer involved called the dispatcher for men, for a steamfitter who could take care of trouble-shooting on calls that would be more in line with boilers, steam-heating and steam boilers. The dispatcher found himself where he sent out two or three men and the employer sent them back. A man came in—no, then all of a sudden then the employer took the position that the union did not have any men, but there were still 40 to 50 unemployed men still on the list. His position was that he called and that was good enough.

We had a hearing as far as the fair hiring hall committee was concerned, both joint management and labor committee, and he was told that he definitely should call the rest of the list.

So he took his case to the NLRB and this was absolutely ignored, but by all means his place was to have exhausted the rest of the— by allowing the dispatcher to call out the other 40 men that were still on the unemployed list and, of course, this is the whole case, and where the union's position was that he did not comply with the fair hiring deal and he did not, by taking a man off the street, as far as we are concerned, he violated the contract.

MR. GLICKSTEIN. But you lost the case?

MR. MAZZOLA. Yes, we lost the case.

MR. GLICKSTEIN. And the trial examiner's decision was enforced by the NLRB and I understand the NLRB is now seeking enforcement in the courts.

MR. MAZZOLA. Well, we appealed it, yes. We have it appealed.

MR. GLICKSTEIN. May we introduce this opinion into the record as Exhibit No. 11, Mr. Chairman?

CHAIRMAN HANNAH. It will be received. Proceed.

(The document referred to was marked as Exhibit No. 11 and received in evidence.)

MR. GLICKSTEIN. Mr. Mazzola, this morning Mr. Clem described a pre-apprenticeship training program that the operating engineers are proposing. Would your union be in favor of undertaking such a pre-apprenticeship training program?

Mr. Clem indicated that the persons that would be participants in that program would be sought from the various poverty target areas in the city. He said they would be culturally deprived persons. I believe the result of it would be that the people participating in it will probably be from minority groups.

MR. MAZZOLA. Well, we have 81 at the present time unemployed who have been going to school as far back as six periods, I guess now, two and a half years, anyway, roughly, and we, to get into pre-apprenticeship training, would be more or less based on what is our future outlook in the way of employment and work opportunities for those that we might be wanting to take in.

These would all be factors. I don't think our committee—our committee had attempted, the joint committee, to put on a pre-apprenticeship training at one time and it was quite a healthy discussion between management and labor, and it was all absolutely scrapped on the basis that there was—the present record at that time was that there was too many unemployed boys, and that until we were able to give a security of employment to them, we shouldn't go into it.

So it was discussed and was thought of, and I am not saying that they would or they wouldn't, but they would have to base it definitely on the work possibilities before it would even have any merit.

MR. GLICKSTEIN. I take it that you feel that your primary responsibility and obligation is to your present members?

MR. MAZZOLA. Definitely.

MR. GLICKSTEIN. Thank you. I have no further questions.

CHAIRMAN HANNAH. Do the Commissioners have any questions? Dr. Rankin?

COMMISSIONER RANKIN. We have held hearings in the various cities and it seems that in each of the cities the members of the minority races always contend that, insofar as the Plumbers Union is concerned, there has been discrimination against that particular race.

Now the statistics have been embarrassingly small in that the number of members of the minority races in the union has really been a very small percentage of the total number. In each city the Plumbers Union's representatives of the local have denied this, have said that there has been no discrimination at all.

You have also said the same thing, that there is none. Well, then, how do we get rid of this claim that in every city we run into we have this instance where it is denied?

MR. MAZZOLA. Well, I think I can answer it. It is the same old story. I think the plumbers and steamfitters are practically on top of the pile all over the Nation, for a contract, that is, for wages and conditions. I think they have probably one of the highest rates in the working contracts and definitely I suppose that helps to draw a greater interest and attention to them. But we have about 17 registered right now, young fellows on the apprenticeship—Negroes on the apprenticeship deal, and up until the last couple of years we have never had them come around.

Now I could tell you there was a Negro contractor in here four years ago by the name of Morrison, and I brought Mr. Morrison and organized him for four Negroes and the four Negroes joined the local union, but they didn't stay with us.

Now, Mr. Morrison is still a contractor in San Francisco. He is a general contractor here in the city, and I believe he could tell you that long before this big drive went on about taking Negroes in the organization, our union already had taken in Negroes and we have taken in Japanese shops, two or three of them, and Chinese shops, and if there was a Negro shop or two right now in San Francisco, and they had Negroes in them and they were in plumbing, we would take them in. We do not go for leaving mechanics regardless of race, creed, or color, out on the street competing with our fair employers and with the journeymen that we have.

COMMISSIONER RANKIN. Well, why do they think there is discrimination against them?

MR. MAZZOLA. I believe there is a lot of people who joined in with them and helped them to get into this pitch because this is all something new, and I think after you air this thing out nationally you are going to find out that it is just not true.

We've had one Negro that was taking the examination who we wanted him to pass. A couple of business agents of the local union worked like hell to give him a hand to pass the examination, and I believe he would vouch for that.

COMMISSIONER RANKIN. The percentage of those in the union from the minority races has nothing to do with it?

MR. MAZZOLA. It has nothing to do with it. The journeyman Negro has never showed up. Evidently we haven't got the answer for it no more than professional doctors or attorneys or anyone else. We know we have a craft union and that has five years of training, two nights a week, three nights one year, and it is quite a program. They really are—I don't believe the professional world knows just what it takes to get to be a journeyman plumber. These men have quite a few courses. They have all kinds of training and the new innovations that you have today more than ever—these men take anywhere from isometric drawing and all types of systems in the way of health and safety, and to be outright mechanics in the plumbing and piping industry is much broader and much more than many people realize, and I don't believe that too many—I believe we are sort of hurt to some extent by the fact that the public and most of the professional people do not know just what it takes, what is involved in the way of teaching an apprentice to be a journeyman in the plumbing and piping industry.

COMMISSIONER FREEMAN. Mr. Mazzola, you are a plumber, are you not?

MR. MAZZOLA. I am a steamfitter.

COMMISSIONER FREEMAN. How long have you been a steamfitter?

MR. MAZZOLA. For 24 years.

COMMISSIONER FREEMAN. And how did you become a steamfitter?

MR. MAZZOLA. Well, I worked as a plumber's helper to start with. I was a laborer with one of the plumbing shops and then I went into the shipyards as a marine helper with a pipefitter and after I put three years in there I took a steamfitter's examination and in that union that is all that it required, but I did have several years of experience working as a plumber's helper which gave me my five years that enabled me to take my test, and I took my steamfitter's test.

COMMISSIONER FREEMAN. Will you tell the Commission how many plumbers are now employed on the BART project?

MR. MAZZOLA. I didn't hear the question.

COMMISSIONER FREEMAN. The Bay Area Rapid Transit.

MR. MAZZOLA. About two.

COMMISSIONER FREEMAN. About two. It is contemplated that there would be approximately 350 plumbers?

MR. MAZZOLA. Yes. I wish they would guarantee us 50 and we would say we would be happy.

COMMISSIONER FREEMAN. I would like to know, if the contractor had requested of you, of your union, any statement with respect to whether you would comply with the nondiscrimination clause. Has the contractor asked your union for any such statement?

MR. MAZZOLA. We have several hundred of them who sent them in. I have signed maybe as many as 100—150 of them.

COMMISSIONER FREEMAN. You have signed the statement, but you don't have the Negro.

MR. MAZZOLA. I have signed the statement that we would not discriminate.

COMMISSIONER FREEMAN. You signed the statement?

MR. MAZZOLA. That's right.

COMMISSIONER FREEMAN. But have you taken any steps to comply with the statement which you signed?

MR. MAZZOLA. Positively. The local union apprenticeship committee had changed their ways in the way of putting—which accepted a new ruling in which, whenever they take an apprentices, that they will notify the city, State and all agencies which normally should be notified for purposes of publicizing that there will be an opening for apprentices for an examination.

COMMISSIONER FREEMAN. At whose suggestion did the committee change its——

MR. MAZZOLA. I believe our council and our international.

COMMISSIONER FREEMAN. You have 12 marine plumbers, so that would leave about eight Negro journeymen who would be available for the BART project. Is that not correct?

MR. MAZZOLA. These men have to take their examination to be journeymen plumbers or steamfitters. Whatever the job they are working on.

COMMISSIONER FREEMAN. Who administers the examination?

MR. MAZZOLA. Well, we have a coordinator, Jim Duggan. We have a committee, joint committee of both management and labor, who are over the coordinator, the fair hiring hall procedure committee.

COMMISSIONER FREEMAN. You indicated that the pay scale is higher. Would you tell us what is the prevailing wage?

MR. MAZZOLA. Our prevailing wage, the construction rate?

COMMISSIONER FREEMAN. The steamfitters'.

MR. MAZZOLA. $6.86 an hour.

COMMISSIONER FREEMAN. $6.86 an hour. Thank you.

CHAIRMAN HANNAH. Are there any other questions?

VICE CHAIRMAN PATTERSON. One brief one, Mr. Chairman. Mr. Mazzola, a Chinese-American witness named the Reverend Wong appeared here yesterday and said that he had written a letter to you expressing his minority's interest in your union and that you had not answered his letter. Was this an oversight on your part?

MR. MAZZOLA. Well, whoever—what is his name now?

VICE CHAIRMAN PATTERSON Mr. Wong.

MR. MAZZOLA. Mr. Wong gave me a ring one time on the telephone and wanted to know if I could come out and see him and I told him, yes, I would come out and see him. And then he called me again and wanted to know if I would meet with a group such as clergymen and others who were all representatives of the various Chinatown organizations, youth organizations and what not.

When he expressed to me what this was all about as to that he wanted to have me come out and meet with him for purposes of seeing how they could bring about the putting of apprentices within the local union, at that point I told him I couldn't go out as an individual and meet with him but if he wanted to come, he could come to the Management and Labor Apprenticeship Committee any night that he would see fit.

Yes, he wrote me a letter and the papers wrote that all up, but I don't see that he had any basis for any of his statements that he —or claims that he made against our organization.

VICE CHAIRMAN PATTERSON. Did you answer his letter? That was his testimony here, that you did not answer his letter.

MR. MAZZOLA. What was that?

VICE CHAIRMAN PATTERSON. His testimony here was that you did not answer the letter.

MR. MAZZOLA. I don't know if I did or not. I usually answer all letters. I don't know. It is very possible. I would almost bet that I answered the letter, but it is very possible that I didn't.

CHAIRMAN HANNAH. Mr. Taylor?

MR. TAYLOR. Mr. Mazzola, how do the members of your union who are unemployed subsist? How do they get along during the period of unemployment?

MR. MAZZOLA. Believe me, that is the $64 question, between unemployment and right now they are very hostile and they are very, very—they are getting to the point right now—we have 187 that are off of the welfare rolls, which have been all these years covered by our local union welfare program, and we are taking steps with the insurance company at the present time to give us a retroactive guarantee of covering our men from here on in so that we would make up whatever deficit is going to be accumulated next July with the insurance company.

MR. TAYLOR. The union is paying them benefits during their period of unemployment?

MR. MAZZOLA No, no. We have no benefits. We pay our members when they are unemployed.

MR. TAYLOR. So that they are——

MR. MAZZOLA. I mentioned there that going with that question you asked me how they were getting by. I went as far as telling you that even the welfare coverage is now at a trickle.

We have 187 at the present time and every month as we go on we are picking up another 30 or 40 or 50 that are falling out of the welfare coverage, and all this makes for very—a very large, dissatisfied membership.

MR. TAYLOR. They get no benefits during their period of unemployment?

MR. MAZZOLA. No. The union dues are actually dues to pay its officers and its office staff and all its equipment in this building, its rent and all the per capitas that we pay to the various councils and internationals and what not in order to function and run the union, and that is what the union dues are for, to be a part of the labor movemet. But, no, we have no benefits.

MR. TAYLOR. What are the welfare benefits?

MR. MAZZOLA. The welfare benefits naturally are the benefits that they get when they work for employers. The employer contributes by the hour, every hour worked, and this puts them into eligibility for having welfare coverage under our group welfare plan, the union plan. But it is medical and dentistry and it is for themselves and their families to cover the medical and dentistry problems, but when they run out—they have an accredited hours system which they can accumulate all during their work period and, of course, most of them—we run better than six months of coverage after they are unemployed. Depends how the individual record is when he was employed. Some who have been steadily employed have accumulated as much as a year's steady coverage, and the others vary according to their accumulated—we have more or less a formula on the hours worked.

MR. TAYLOR. Turning back to a subject that you were asked about earlier, the Dymally Report quotes you as saying you are in favor of the system of giving preference to sons of union members in admission to apprentice programs.

MR. MAZZOLA. I personally am, but the organization through the council's salesship has asked us to get rid of that particular past practice program, which I am definitely—without any question in favor of giving the sons of the employers and the sons of the members of the local union a priority preference, but the system, I am sure as we now adopt it, it is changed.

MR. TAYLOR. Well, up until very recently a preference was given——

MR. MAZZOLA. Up to very recently, for the last 50 years, yes, they gave sons of the employers and sons of the members a priority preference, and you can just picture yourself being an employer and you being told now that you can't have your son in your industry, and that is exactly what is being pushed on them.

MR. TAYLOR. Well, you said you didn't know why a Negro might think you were discriminating. If you did until quite recently have this rule, and that very few of your members, the members of your union were Negroes, don't you think that that might give some grounds to that feeling?

MR. MAZZOLA. Well, that was only about a 50 percent deal. That is still—there was still 50 percent of all those coming in that were not sons of either the employer or the member, and I think our records could show that, if you take our total years of those who made journeymen today, I think you will find it has been a 50-50 thing. It is just that the 50 percent had a better privilege in the way of every father wants his son to be pretty much what he was. Professional people have no problem, a doctor or an attorney or anybody else, and I believe it is right that they are levying on the trades.

When the time comes when we all have lots of Negroes, I don't think anyone can say that a Negro can't have his son be a plumber. I don't think the Negroes are in any way objectable to this, because any Negro or a white man or whoever the hell he is, that's working, wherever he works, would love to have his son follow him if he can.

MR. TAYLOR. If you are a young man and your father isn't a plumber, how can you possibly get your father——

MR. MAZZOLA. Well, when they are able to qualify and get into the same opportunities—you know, I tried to be a plumber and I went up to the local union twice in 1935 and 1937, and both times I was turned down. And I was turned down in both cases because there were sons at that time of the union that were available for employment and which the business agent very clearly, made it clear to those who brought me up—I was brought up by two employers one time, by Mr. Larusso, who today is still in business, when I was a helper, a laborer; that he thought I would make a darned good plumber apprentice, and I heard the business agent say, "Look, we got plumber apprentices here that are sons of some of the boys that have been on the list for six months and we're not able to get them out yet," and I didn't get into the trade. I had to leave it and I went into everything else, and it was years later that I——. I never held it against them and I don't believe that the average person who hears that some son got a preference before them is objectable to it. I don't care if he is a Negro, Indian, white or paesano or anybody else.

MR. TAYLOR. I have no further questions.

CHAIRMAN HANNAH. Thank you very much. You are excused, sir. We will call one more witness and then we will break for lunch. Call the next witness, Mr. Glickstein.

MR. GLICKSTEIN. Mr. Morton Harris.

(Whereupon, Mr. Morton Harris was sworn by the Chairman and testified as follows:)

TESTIMONY OF MR. MORTON HARRIS, OAKLAND, CALIFORNIA

MR. GLICKSTEIN. Would you please state your full name and address for the record?

MR. HARRIS. My full name is Morton Harris. I will give you my business address. That is 1675 Seventh Street, Oakland. Mr. Glickstein, I have a prepared statement that I would like to read, if I may, which I want as part of my testimony.

MR. GLICKSTEIN. Is it very long?

MR. HARRIS. Very short. Less than two minutes.

The apathy of the American people to social and moral issues is dangerous——

MR. GLICKSTEIN. Mr. Harris, may I just interrupt you? Perhaps you could identify yourself first so that this statement will be in context. What is your occupation?

MR. HARRIS. I am the administrative officer for S. S. Silberblatt, Engineer and Building Contractor. However, our local office is in Oakland where we are building a $20 million post office.

MR. GLICKSTEIN. You are in charge of the Silberblatt operation? The Federal Post Office site in Oakland?

MR. HARRIS. Right. I might add that I was purchasing agent for the contractor that built this building.

MR. GLICKSTEIN. You were also involved in the construction of this building?

MR. HARRIS. Yes, sir.

Starting again:

The apathy of the American people to social and moral issues is dangerous. The fact is quite clear: which shows that most Americans—and that's a big most—are satisfied with the way things have been and are. This is impossible.

Today impatience, frustration and now violence are growing quickly in minority communities. These trends, if allowed to continue, can only lead to contempt of law, contempt of the public welfare, and contempt of the rights of other men.

Civil rights legislation alone cannot deal effectively with the causes of frustration. This Commission must propose broad programs designed to enable all minority groups—not just the American Negro—to achieve true equality in job opportunities, better, more extended education, decent housing, and so on.

Equally important, the President of the United States must support this far-reaching social program. For it will be his task to awaken the people to the facts of their times. In addition, he must goad the Congressmen into righting some national wrongs.

Time is fast running out for a society that refuses to adjust to the new realities of the world around it. We have reached the crisis stage in the battle for survival. Do not make the mistake of looking to State legislatures, city governments, American industry or organized labor to solve these problems or administer any affirmative action program.

This Commission on Civil Rights hearing is indeed performing an important function and you are to be commended for turning to the citizens of this community for some fresh ideas. It is my fervent prayer that the sanguine members of this august group will in all candor and honesty stimulate an entirely new human behavior concept for the world to take into account.

Thank you for the opportunity to make this statement.

MR. GLICKSTEIN. You mentioned that you are working on the Oakland Post Office. When did that job begin?

MR. HARRIS. That began about May 1, 1965.

MR. GLICKSTEIN. And when will it be completed?

MR. HARRIS. Well, at present we are behind schedule. I would say, with a little luck, about January 1, 1969.

MR. GLICKSTEIN. And you indicated it is going to cost about $20 million?

MR. HARRIS. Well, that is the construction phase of our contract. There is another phase which is about $6 million and, of course, the land costs $4 million. So you are talking of a $30 million project overall.

MR. GLICKSTEIN. Now, the Silberblatt Company is the general contractor?

MR. HARRIS. Right.

MR. GLICKSTEIN. And has the company subcontracted out the actual construction work on the post office?

MR. HARRIS. We have subcontracted all phases but the concrete work which a subsidiary company of Silberblatt is doing.

MR. GLICKSTEIN. But all other phases——

MR. HARRIS. All other phases have been subbed out.

MR. GLICKSTEIN. On the average, how many men are employed on the Oakland project?

MR. HARRIS. Well, we haven't reached our full employment cycle, so I would say at present there is about 190 men to 200 men, a little over; maybe 212.

MR. GLICKSTEIN. And how many will you have at the peak?

MR. HARRIS. Approximately 300.

MR. GLICKSTEIN. Some statistics that you have supplied to us, Mr. Harris, indicate that since the construction project began in 1965, there have been no Negro plumbers, no Negro operating engineers, no Negro sheet metal workers, no Negro ironworkers, electricians or steamfitters on the job. Is that correct?

MR. HARRIS. That is correct.

MR. GLICKSTEIN. What steps have you taken to have Negroes from all crafts work on the Post Office project?

MR. HARRIS. Well, let me say this. I haven't taken any steps for Negroes *per se*. I have taken steps for minority groups, and it seems at this meeting everybody talks about Negroes. But I want it clearly understood I talk about minority groups.

Now, the steps that S. S. Silberblatt has taken on this job, according to Executive Order 11246, we have contacted every labor union in the area and we have told them just what our contract involves, that we are bound by Executive Order 11246. We have asked them what is their position and we have asked them to give us a written statement if they conform to nondiscrimination in hiring, do they practice the precepts of the Executive Order 11246, every union in this area, and there are over 16 that I have contacted who have told me verbally that they do conform —they have gone a step further and have given me a letter so stating that they conform to all civil rights legislation, that they practice nondiscrimination, as far as race, color, or creed; that the people they will send to us will be within the terms of the Executive order.

MR. GLICKSTEIN. But so many of the unions that I have just mentioned a little while ago didn't send any Negroes to the job?

MR. HARRIS. Well, in answer to your question, they haven't sent any Negroes, that is true.

MR. GLICKSTEIN. But they all conform to the Executive order and none of them discriminates?

MR. HARRIS. That is what they have told me. I have statements in writing from them, and I may say to you gentlemen that I can't act as an investigation agency nor can I act as a lawyer and I can't make any determinations. I have to accept what these people tell me.

MR. GLICKSTEIN. Well, for example, when the contract is about to be entered into with the steamfitters, for example, and you ask them whether they conform to Executive Order 11246 and they say, "Yes, we don't discriminate." Do you then ask them how many Negro members do you have?

MR. HARRIS. Let me say this. I would have no reason to ask how many minority members they have. I did not only ask them, but I personally sent to each union a copy of Executive Order 11246 so that they would fully understand what they were talking about when they gave me a statement in writing that they do conform to this Executive order.

MR. GLICKSTEIN. But if a union conforms, tells you that they conform to the Executive order, but at the same time has no Negro members, how do you expect that there ever will be a Negro referred to work on the job by that union?

MR. HARRIS. Let me say this. I don't know whether they do have them or they don't have them. I have no way of knowing. All I can tell you is that they haven't sent any to the job.

I will go a little further and say that I have talked to a few union business representatives, talking about minorities, and they have assured me that they have them in their union, that when their name comes up on the hiring list that they will be sent to our job.

I have even asked these people is it possible that you make an exception and send some minority group members to our job. Well, this doesn't solve the problem. It is going to take—it is going to, for the moment at least in our project, show that we have a high rate of minority people working and it will again for the moment keep the contract compliance officer from bothering us too much. But these people have told me that they have certain hiring rules and regulations that they must be followed, that they don't discriminate, and in some cases they have no way of knowing who a man is. They go by a name and social security number.

So, again, I don't think it is the place of the contractor to investigate this thing and make a determination. This is a very serious matter that requires a Commission like this to look into it and make decisions.

MR. GLICKSTEIN. Mr. Harris, you are a practical business man. What you are saying is that the way the Executive order is being enforced is that you are asking unions whether they discriminate and they are sending you letters and saying, "We don't discriminate," and that is the extent of it.

Now, do you think that that Executive order is at all meaningful and can be at all effective if that is the way it is going to be enforced?

MR. HARRIS. Well, let me say this. I think you might do well to investigate just what is legally right and what isn't right under this order. That's the first thing that has to be determined. In my opinion, the Executive Order 11246, the minute the contractor will check with the union and will get a statement from that union that they don't discriminate, that our obligation has been fulfilled. That is my personal interpretation of that and I can't see where this Commission or any of your contract compliance officers who, by the way,—the one that does come to our job is a very dedicated, sincere man who does a very good job, but I don't see where they have the right to come in here and tell us that "you go out and you hire people regardless of whether they conform to" —well, whatever the race and creed is—"and bring them into the job." I don't think that this law says this. I don't think it gives us the right to do this and, as I said in my prepared statement, the Congress of the United States, if the people want it so, will pass legislation that will enforce this thing and I think that you are barking up the wrong tree when you say it is the contractor's responsibility.

I have read your report here dated February 6, memorandum to various people. I am sure you are well aware of it where it states that the contractor is the man who does all these things, and I am sure you people are very astute and intelligent gentlemen and can realize that not the contractor. This is business, and it is not his place to try and go out and try to enforce things in this society as we know it today.

MR. GLICKSTEIN. You are getting $20 million from the Federal Government, aren't you?

MR. HARRIS. That's right, and we are abiding by the laws that have been stated by the Federal Government.

MR. GLICKSTEIN. Is the government contractor required to abide by a multitude of requirements and regulations?

MR. HARRIS. Definitely, and S.S. Silberblatt abides by every one of them.

MR. GLICKSTEIN. Under your contracts if you were required to use a certain type of item in building your building, would you be satisfied if the person doing the subcontracting merely sent you a letter and said, "Yes, we use that sort of item," or wouldn't you go out and check and make sure they were using it?

MR. HARRIS. We definitely do, yes. We certainly go out and check and see if they are using that.

MR. GLICKSTEIN. And if the government regulations require that your subcontractors pay minimum wages and abide by the Davis-Bacon Act and also some other statutes, you would go out and make sure they are abiding by it?

MR. HARRIS. We would do everything we can to see that they do, and we wouldn't have anybody working for us that didn't abide by it.

MR. GLICKSTEIN. When the union tells you they are going to operate without discrimination, you don't find out how many Negroes they have in the union?

MR. HARRIS. I would say the union tells you they abide by Executive Order 11246 which we are bound by on our job, and no one has yet proven that they haven't complied with it 100 percent, and when this Commission suggests that we go in and investigate these unions and try to make these determinations, I think you make a mistake.

MR. GLICKSTEIN. Mr. Harris, when you were involved with the Federal Post Office, what was the minority group representation here in the crafts?

MR. HARRIS. In the building of this building?

MR. GLICKSTEIN. Yes, in the building of this building.

MR. HARRIS. Not the Post Office, but the Federal Court House.

MR. GLICKSTEIN. Yes.

MR. HARRIS. You could read the same list of unions and I would say that there wasn't a minority member in that same group that worked on this project, to my knowledge.

MR. GLICKSTEIN. And that is what happened here and that is what happened in Oakland, but you have no reason to suspect that these unions discriminate?

MR. HARRIS. I don't think it is a question of what I think and I suspect. I have to be guided by the law on our job, and I think it is the duty of this Commission and the duty of the Congress of the United States to pass necessary and proper legislation and that is the key, and you are overlooking that. You are trying to throw the burden to the contractor and you can't do it. Give him the tools to fight with and then he will pick it up.

MR. GLICKSTEIN. Let me ask you one final question. If the Office of Contract Compliance told you that finally it was interested in results and not just in pledges, and wanted to see Negroes on the job in each of those crafts and they didn't care how the Negroes got there, but they had to be there, would you be prepared to go outside the collective bargaining agreement and hire people off the street to meet your obligations under the Executive order?

MR. HARRIS. Well, frankly, as my own personal opinion, I think that would be in violation of our contract with the Post Office

Department, but, as I feel strongly about this matter, I certainly would recommend to our New York office that we, in keeping with whatever the law is, as our lawyers determined by their interpretation of this law, follow through, and if we felt that the Government was justified under Executive Order 11246, then we would have done this thing a long time ago. We wouldn't be sitting here now talking about hypothetical questions that you are posing. We would have done it. We feel that we have, under the law as written by the United States, the President of the United States, Executive Order 11246, that we have complied completely, and again I say to you if you want us to do something, then you give us the tools to do it with. You know and I know that if you told us tomorrow to put on Negro operating engineers, plumbers, electricians, and so on, that if the union did not,—we asked the union and they did not supply them and you forced us to go out, and I say forced us to go out and hire non-union people tomorrow, the Post Office job would be shut down.

That is a reality of life, and I am sure you know this.

MR. GLICKSTEIN. Thank you, Mr. Harris. I have no further questions.

CHAIRMAN HANNAH. Any questions from the Commissioners?

COMMISSIONER FREEMAN. Mr. Harris, your company did voluntarily enter into this contract with the Post Office, didn't it?

MR. HARRIS. Our company was one of a number that bid for this, right.

COMMISSIONER FREEMAN. So then you did agree that during the performance of the contract that you would take affirmative action to insure that employees were treated without regard to race, creed, color, or national origin? That is part of your agreement?

MR. HARRIS. We agreed to abide by the rules and regulations of our contract. One of them is Executive Order 11246. That is absolutely correct, and I say we have done this.

COMMISSIONER FREEMAN. Well, you have indicated to Mr. Glickstein that you would make inspections with respect to whether the subcontractor was giving you the proper materials or not.

Would you tell this Commission why you would consider one provision of the contract of less importance than another?

MR. HARRIS. Well, if I may correct you, we weekly give a report to the Contract Compliance Officer of the Post Office Department, which indicates how many journeymen are working on our job, the number of minority groups in each craft. We do this. So I think that you are mistaken in what you say.

COMMISSIONER FREEMAN. How many Chinese are employed in the crafts there?

MR. HARRIS. We have one Chinese employed in our project that I know of.

COMMISSIONER FREEMAN. How many Indians?

MR. HARRIS. How many American Indians? Well, now, I don't have the exact figures. We have given copies of the weekly letter to Mr. Glickstein. You have them in the file, which will tell you how many Indians we have, how many American Mexicans, how many Negroes out of the total number.

COMMISSIONER FREEMAN. And the picture would be that the number would be very small or not?

MR. HARRIS. Well, I would say that—not last week, but a few weeks ago, about 38 percent of our employees were members of minority groups.

COMMISSIONER FREEMAN. In the skilled craft unions?

MR. HARRIS. Well, this is overall.

COMMISSIONER FREEMAN. I am not talking about the laborers.

MR. HARRIS. I am talking about all of them. We take them all as a group and if you are asking me how many were electricians I would tell you zero, and the same goes for operating engineers, plumbers, steamfitters, even sheet metal workers at this time.

COMMISSIONER FREEMAN. This is true on the contract you have now and this was also true on the previous government contract?

MR. HARRIS. Well, I was with a different employer when we built this building, and that was true on this building. To my knowledge, we had no minority members.

COMMISSIONER FREEMAN. Thank you.

CHAIRMAN HANNAH. Any more questions? Mr. Taylor? Thank you very much, Mr. Harris. You are excused. We will now recess until 1:45.

(Whereupon, at 12:30 p.m., a recess was taken until 1:45 p.m.)

WEDNESDAY AFTERNOON SESSION

MAY 3, 1967

CHAIRMAN HANNAH. The hearing will come to order. Mr. Glickstein, will you call the next witness?

MR. GLICKSTEIN. Mr. Ray Dones.

(Whereupon, MR. RAYMOND DONES was sworn by the Chairman and testified as follows:)

TESTIMONY OF MR. RAYMOND DONES,
EL CERRITO, CALIFORNIA

MR. GLICKSTEIN. Mr. Dones, would you please state your full name and address for the record?

MR. DONES. My name is Raymond Dones. I live at 814 Shevlin Drive in El Cerrito.

MR. GLICKSTEIN. What is your occupation, Mr. Dones?

MR. DONES. I am an electrician.

MR. GLICKSTEIN. You are an electrician. Are you connected with any contractors' associations?

MR. DONES. Yes, sir. I am president of the General & Specialty Contractors Association at 1709 Webster Street in Oakland.

MR. GLICKSTEIN. When was this association established?

MR. DONES. This association was formed about September 26, 1966.

MR. GLICKSTEIN. Just about eight or nine months old?

MR. DONES. Yes, sir.

MR. GLICKSTEIN. What are its purposes?

MR. DONES. The purpose was to secure justice in employment and contract letting for minorities in the construction industry.

MR. GLICKSTEIN. Now, the association is made up of contractors?

MR. DONES. Yes, sir, it is.

MR. GLICKSTEIN. And you said you are an electrician. Are you also an electrical contractor or do you work with an electrical contractor?

MR. DONES. I have, since 1950, held an electrical contractor's license.

MR. GLICKSTEIN. You are a contractor as well as a journeyman electrician?

MR. DONES. Yes, sir.

MR. GLICKSTEIN. How many members does the association have?

MR. DONES. Presently we have 51 members.

MR. GLICKSTEIN. How many of the 51 are Negro?

MR. DONES. Beg pardon?

MR. GLICKSTEIN. About how many of the 51 are Negro?

MR. DONES. 40.

MR. GLICKSTEIN. And about how many are Spanish-speaking Mexican Americans?

MR. DONES. Two are Spanish-speaking.

MR. GLICKSTEIN. And how many are Oriental? Do you have any Oriental members?

MR. DONES. Yes, we have three Oriental members.

MR. GLICKSTEIN. Do you have any white members?

MR. DONES. Yes, we do.

MR. GLICKSTEIN. Why was there a need for a separate association of this sort?

MR. DONES. This formation of the association grew out of

conversations between minority contractors who felt they were victims of a conspiracy that exists in our area that prevented minorities from getting substantial employment in the construction industry.

MR. GLICKSTEIN. Are minority contractors eligible to join the general contracting associations, the ones already existing?

MR. DONES. I think so, yes.

MR. GLICKSTEIN. You would have been eligible to join the Electrical Contractors Association?

MR. DONES. I think that this is perhaps possible.

MR. GLICKSTEIN. We have heard some testimony about the membership of Negroes and Spanish-surname peoples and Orientals in the building trades. We have heard that the membership of these groups is rather low. Why aren't there more Negroes and Mexican Americans and Orientals in the building trade unions?

MR. DONES. Well, I think the building trades unions and the contractors that they work with have a pretty good arrangement going, so far as the union members and the contractor association members are concerned, and they are not about to do anything that will rock the boat.

MR. GLICKSTEIN. Are there some trucking contractors that are members of your association?

MR. DONES. Yes, there are.

MR. GLICKSTEIN. We heard some testimony this morning from a representative of BART about efforts being made to give contracts to minority group trucking contractors. Are you familiar with those efforts?

MR. DONES. I have heard a rumor that BART had approached one man with the idea that they would set him up in business as a contractor to get some of their work.

MR. GLICKSTEIN. You just heard a rumor about this. You don't know of your own knowledge?

MR. DONES. Well, I did what I could to find out who the man was and what efforts had been made to do this, and I found out that no substantial efforts had been gone through to get any contract for any minority group trucking subcontractor.

MR. GLICKSTEIN. Mr. Dones, can you estimate the number of non-union skilled construction workers in the Bay Area?

MR. DONES. No, sir, this is difficult.

MR. GLICKSTEIN. Are there many?

MR. DONES. Well, I might say that the General & Specialty Contractors Association, together with several human rights commissions and other civil rights groups are now conducting a survey to determine the exact composition of minority craftsmen in the construction industry in the six Bay Counties around the Bay Area.

MR. GLICKSTEIN. And this would indicate union and non-union people. Is that right?

MR. DONES. This is true. We have long been faced with the problem of lack of accurate figures in this field, and one method we have of compiling our own figures is to list all of the painters that we know who are minority men and then we call each one of these painters and ask them of other painters that they know. And so we can compile a list of the known painters, electricians, plumbers who are minority men, and from them we get some indication as to the problems that they are faced and the difficulties that they have experienced in becoming union members and the difficulties that they have experienced in securing employment in the construction industry.

MR. GLICKSTEIN. You have gotten some indication of the difficulties, you say?

MR. DONES. We are in the process of accumulating this information.

MR. GLICKSTEIN. Is it difficult for minority contractors to bid on State and Federal construction projects?

MR. DONES. Yes, sir, it is very difficult.

MR. GLICKSTEIN. Why is it difficult?

MR. DONES. Mainly because of the bonding requirements that are part of the contract documents that we have to comply with.

MR. GLICKSTEIN. A Federal construction contract would require that contractors be bonded. Is that correct?

MR. DONES. This is true.

MR. GLICKSTEIN. And to your knowledge, there are no Federal programs that would either subsidize the bonding or waive the bonding requirement?

MR. DONES. No, not that I know of. For instance, we are faced with the prospect of trying to bond a very small electrical job, my company was, and it was extremely difficult to find a $12,600 bond for this project. Then we have traditionally worked in the area that is known as West Oakland, where the Acorn Project is to be built.

MR. GLICKSTEIN. And the Acorn Project is a project being built on an urban renewal site?

MR. DONES. This is true, and I understand this is being done by Sproul Homes, and our company would like to bid on the electrical facet of the subcontracting work there, and we will have to post bond to the extent of the subcontract work, which is, according to some estimates, about a quarter of a million dollars.

This is an area that my company has traditionally worked in for years, until the Government, under this program, moves in and razes the houses and proposes to build a project to help minority people find good places to live, and presumably they would help them to be able to afford the rentals there.

MR. GLICKSTEIN. What you are saying is that your company had worked in the Acorn area before it was demolished by the urban renewal project and your company had worked in the family houses that are located there, and now you are trying to get a contract on the development that is going up on the urban renewal site—?

MR. DONES. This is presently true. We have one contract that we just completed within this area. It is a mortuary that was not razed, and there is a Baptist church that has not been torn down. We had traditionally—well, we have work going on there now.

MR. GLICKSTEIN. In addition to the bonding requirement, when you seek to get a contract you are required to show that you have had experience on similar jobs in the past?

MR. DONES. This is one of the requirements of the bonding company.

MR. GLICKSTEIN. So, in other words, if you had never had the experience on the jobs in the past, it is very difficult, if not impossible, to get bonded?

MR. DONES. This is true.

MR. GLICKSTEIN. Do you pay union wages to your workers?

MR. DONES. I do.

MR. GLICKSTEIN. Are they members of the union?

MR. DONES. No, they are not.

MR. GLICKSTEIN. Well, if you were to bid on a job and got the job, how would that affect your relationship with the unions?

MR. DONES. The company that I work for, and I might say that I am now an employee of this company, would bid on it and get it, and we would attempt to do it.

MR. GLICKSTEIN. Would you have to sign a collective bargaining agreement with the union?

MR. DONES. My company has, as of just about 30 days ago, signed a contract and bargaining agreement with the Local 595, the Electrical Workers Union.

MR. GLICKSTEIN. Now, if you do have this contract, why aren't your employees union members? If the company has a collective bargaining agreement, doesn't that agreement require that all employees become union members?

MR. DONES. No, this is not true. There was a reluctance on the part of the business agent, as I understand it, to sign or to have signed a building trades master agreement in this instance.

Now, our company is a small corporation and the secretary-treasurer of the corporation was authorized to sign the agreement and he was instructed to also sign the Alameda County Building Trades Council agreement by our attorney, with the idea that this would focus some attention on the requirement in the

Master Building Trades Agreement that says something like "people employed under this contract shall, within thirty days, apply for and become union membership," or something like that.

MR. GLICKSTEIN. The agreement you had with the Building Trades Council provides that, but have any of your employees applied for membership in the union yet?

MR. DONES. No, we have not.

MR. GLICKSTEIN. Mr. Dones, how effective do you think Federal contract compliance enforcement has been in the Bay Area?

MR. DONES. It has not been effective.

MR. GLICKSTEIN. It has not been effective. Do you think that the Department of Labor's new affirmative efforts policy under Executive Order 11246 will have an effect in relieving minority unemployment?

MR. DONES. As I understand the new attempts, they are still asking for voluntary compliance and there has been no show of force on the part of the Federal Government, and without this show of force that they will in fact enforce the letter and the spirit of this Executive Order 11246, there will not be any substantial compliance with it.

MR. GLICKSTEIN. What do you think the Federal Government should do to insure greater compliance? What do you mean by a show of force?

MR. DONES. I think that the contractors who have signed this agreement to do something affirmative, so far as the securing of opportunity to minority people in this area, should be required to comply with this provision the same as they would comply with the other specifications of the contract.

MR. GLICKSTEIN. How could they be forced to comply with it?

MR. DONES. I am sure that if there is the desire to involve minorities in this construction work, the legal machinery is necessary to so do. For instance, there was testimony here that there were no Negro plumbers on the post office project that is being built in Oakland. This could simply be done by subcontracting some of the work to a minority plumber that has already minority plumbers in his work force. The same is true with the painting and the electrical contracts.

There is nothing to prevent the general contractor on this job, or even one of the subcontractors on this job, to again subcontract some of the work to someone that has minorities in their present work force.

MR. GLICKSTEIN. But the minorities that you are talking about are not union members?

MR. DONES. Some are and some are not.

MR. GLICKSTEIN. Do you think it would be feasible for a contractor to bring onto the job non-union members?

MR. DONES. This is true, sir. I have been working since 1950 on jobs and I still have not a union card. So I am not a union member.

MR. GLICKSTEIN. And the union hasn't objected to your presence on the job?

MR. DONES. They have objected, but there has been no stoppage of work because of it.

MR. GLICKSTEIN. Are there Negro plumbing contractors in Oakland that have had sufficient experience to be able to work on the post office? Are there contractors that could get bonded and could get approved for a job of that sort?

MR. DONES. I don't think that there is a minority plumbing contractor who could bond the plumbing work on the post office job.

MR. GLICKSTEIN. I have no further questions.

CHAIRMAN HANNAH. Any of the Commissioners have any questions?

COMMISSIONER FREEMAN. Mr. Dones, you have indicated that you are an electrician, you are a licensed electrician. Are you required to have a license?

MR. DONES. Yes, as an electrical contractor I am required to have a license.

COMISSIONER. FREEMAN. You are licensed as an electrical contractor?

MR. DONES. Not as an electrician in this State.

COMMISSIONER FREEMAN. I am concerned about your statement that the separate organization came about because the minority contractors felt that they were victims of a conspiracy and you indicated that you were unable to get bonded on a job that required only a $12,600 bond. Is that right?

MR. DONES. Yes, ma'am.

COMMISSIONER FREEMAN. Now, this suggests that possibly that there may be some connection between the bonding companies and any unions that may be discriminatory. I wonder if you have considered bringing this matter to the attention of the Department of Justice and maybe the Department of Justice might be interested because under the Executive order the Department of Justice does have the responsibility with respect to assuring of compliance.

Have you made any contact with the Department of Justice?

MR. DONES. No, we haven't. I personally thank you for the suggestion. We will certainly pursue this. We feel that the concern of this Commission in this field is perhaps the only hope we have for redress of the legitimate grievances that we feel the minority contractors and minority craftsmen have in us here.

COMMISSIONER FREEMAN. So we have a situation where not only is the minority craft worker discriminated against, you are

saying that the minority contractor is discriminated against. He
is kept out of these jobs. Is that correct?

MR. DONES. This is true.

COMMISSIONER FREEMAN. That's all.

COMMISSIONER GRISWOLD. Mr. Dones, could you help me a little?
I don't understand whether you are an employee or an employer.

MR. DONES. Well, it will take a little time to clarify that matter
and I will have to relate to you some personal experience in order
to do so.

I became an electrician in 1943 in Denver, Colorado, and there
the city administers a journeyman's examination. So after working the trade for approximately two years I applied for and took
the city exam to become a journeyman electrician. After a period
of time I moved to California and, in trying to seek employment
as an electrician, I tried to get a job through the hiring hall that
is operated in Oakland, and I was not able to secure employment
through this referral system that they have.

I did find employment with a non-union contractor in Berkeley
and I worked for him until such time as I got a contractor's
license. Now, we worked on jobs that were union and jobs that
were non-union. In the confrontation that resulted from this
arrangement, my employer was asked to sign a referral agreement
with the union which would bind him to secure his men through
the union's referral system. He refused to do this on moral
grounds, and as a result I had to continue as best I could until
such time as I got a California State contractor's license.

Then I became eventually an employer. I and two men were
working on a job in Contra Costa County in 1958 when we had a
revealing confrontation with the union whereby they told the
person that we were working for that he would have to get the
electricians off of the job or else they would do what they could to
see that they were removed.

Now, we developed an arrangement whereby the man that I
was working for became an electrical contractor and I worked for
him and he signed as a company that he had already organized
an agreement to use the unions' referral system, which in effect
meant that they would not bother the employees that he already
had, which were myself and two other fellows, but all future
employees would have to be secured by calling the hall and taking
the fellows from the referral system.

This worked out fine for about two years, and then the union
decided that I would not be able to be an employee of this company because I was in fact a person licensed by California State
as a contractor and I was what they called a responsible, managing
employee in this arrangement. So they told him that either I

would have to not work or else they would have to discontinue this arrangement.

Now, I discontinued the association that I had with this company and organized Aladdin Electric Company, and we negotiated an agreement with 595 whereby I would not work with the tools and that the employees that I had working for me at the time would be referred out to my shop, and this pattern continued on. Whenever I needed men I would have to go to the union and get them through their referral system. And this pattern continued on for several years and none of my men were given union cards as a result of this, and no efforts were made to get them into the union.

But you must understand that the referral system that is set up in the electrical trade has five groups, and the system works to restrict minority men who have not become apprentices through the bottom of the last group. So that out of the five groups we find that most of the minority electricians are in Group 4 and 5 and they are the last hired or referred out to any electrical work.

COMMISSIONER GRISWOLD. Then you are now an electrical contractor?

MR. DONES. No, I am not. I have an electrical contractor's license, but I am employed by Aladdin Electric Corporation as their employee under a separate electrical contractor's license.

COMMISSIONER GRISWOLD. As I understand it, you are president of General & Specialty Contractors, which is an association of Negro contractors?

MR. DONES. This is true, yes, sir.

I have, under Ray Dones, California State electrical contractor's license, which I have held since 1953. Aladdin Electric Company was organized recently in order to correct some of the injustices that we see here and it was organized with a separate electrical contractor's license and it was done specifically so that I could work on the job as a journeyman.

COMMISSIONER GRISWOLD. Has that company ever bid on any government projects of any kind?

MR. DONES. It is the one that I mentioned a few minutes ago that bid on a school job in Oakland, which I understand has some Federal funding in it, and we were successful in getting this contract, and the contractor told Aladdin Electric that they would have to negotiate an agreement with the electrical union in order to work on the job.

COMMISSIONER GRISWOLD. And they didn't negotiate that agreement?

MR. DONES. They did.

COMMISSIONER GRISWOLD. Which provided for the recognition of the existing employees of the company?

MR. DONES. As workers, but not as union members.

Now, in going down to the hall to get on, to sign up for the fringe benefits, it develops that the 595 classification of our employees is Group 5, which is the last list that they have. That's what the referral man told us, which means that even though we have been working in this trade for years, still we will be the last ones referred out under an agreement.

So our only hope in this case, sir, is to stay employed under the referral that we have because if we get unemployed and go back down to the hall to be referred out, we will in fact be the last ones referred out on the job.

COMMISSIONER GRISWOLD. What I am trying to get at is how there is any possibility that minority electricians in your case, but it would apply also to plumbers and ironworkers, can ever get employment on government jobs in this area. How can that be brought about?

MR. DONES. We think that the only way it can be done is to develop the minority contractors and subcontractors to the extent that they can bid and bond and do these jobs, because they are the ones that hire the majority of the minority craftsmen here.

COMMISSIONER GRISWOLD. Would it be a help, for example, there is a Small Business Administration in Washington, if it set up a specialized bonding company which under proper limitations, but not as limited as the private companies have to do, would provide bonds for these minority contractors?

MR. DONES. That would be a tremendous help.

COMMISSIONER GRISWOLD. You regard the bond requirement as perhaps the most serious obstacle to the obtaining of jobs by minority contractors?

MR. DONES. This is true, not only for contractors, but for subcontractors, sir.

COMMISSIONER GRISWOLD. If arrangements were made so that bonds could be provided in such cases and maybe 10 minority contractors were thus able to bid on jobs, would the result be that there would be 50 minority non-union employees involved? Do you think that the local labor unions would accept that situation?

MR. DONES. I think they would unionize or ask the contractors involved to sign the referral agreement, which is the pattern that has been established by past performances.

COMMISSIONER GRISWOLD. I understand that, but would they allow the—I am now assuming 50 non-union employees of these contractors. Would they allow them to work on the job without being members of the union?

MR. DONES. Yes, sir, this is true. This, again, is the pattern that has been established by past performance.

COMMISSIONER GRISWOLD. You think they would?

MR. DONES. Yes, sir. For instance, on the job that we are working on, even though we have no union membership, we are allowed to work on the job.

COMMISSIONER GRISWOLD. So that you think that as of now the bonding requirement is really a very important factor in the picture?

MR. DONES. Yes, sir, it is.

COMMISSIONER GRISWOLD. Thank you.

CHAIRMAN HANNAH. Any other questions from Commissioners? Mr. Taylor? Thank you very much, sir. You are excused.

CHAIRMAN HANNAH. Mr. Glickstein, will you call the next witness?

MR. GLICKSTEIN. Mr. Vincent Macaluso.

(Whereupon, MR. VINCENT G. MACALUSO was sworn by the Chairman and testified as follows:)

TESTIMONY OF MR. VINCENT G. MACALUSO, WASHINGTON, D.C.

MR. GLICKSTEIN. Do you have somebody with you?

MR. MACALUSO. Yes, I have Mr. Robert Magnuson, who is the Area Coordinator for San Francisco.

CHAIRMAN HANNAH. Is he going to testify? Are you going to put questions to him?

MR. MACALUSO. I think there may be occasions when there will be some inquiries about local situations.

CHAIRMAN HANNAH. Are you willing to be sworn, sir?

MR. MAGNUSON. I am.

Whereupon, Mr. Robert Magnuson was sworn by the Chairman:)

MR. GLICKSTEIN. Mr. Macaluso, will you please state your full name and address for the record?

MR. MACALUSO. My name is Vincent G. Macaluso. My address is 1836 Park Road, N.W., Washington, D.C.

MR. GLICKSTEIN. Where are you employed?

MR. MACALUSO. I am employed in the Department of Labor by the Office of Federal Contract Compliance.

MR. GLICKSTEIN. Would you tell the Commission briefly what the Office of Federal Contract Compliance is?

MR. MACALUSO. I can do it extemporaneously or I can read a brief prepared statement, whichever you like.

MR. GLICKSTEIN. I think—

MR. MACALUSO. Maybe I can summarize that and let the statement go in the record.

MR. GLICKSTEIN. Yes, I have read your statement and I believe our questions will elicit most everything you have in the statement. If you would like to add something later on, you can certainly do that.

MR. MACALUSO. Now, your question is—?

MR. GLICKSTEIN. What is the Office of Contract Compliance?

MR. MACALUSO. The Office of Federal Contract Compliance is a subdivision within the Department of Labor which was created by the Secretary when the Department of Labor was given the responsibility or, rather its responsibility under Executive Order 11246, and this was done in the fall of 1965. One of the first things the Secretary did was to create this office to discharge his responsibilities under the order.

Now, his responsibilities are those essentially of policy guidance to the Federal contracting and administration agencies which have the primary responsibility of the implementation of the order.

MR. GLICKSTEIN. In other words, Federal agencies such as the Department of Defense or the Department of HEW that actually sign the contracts are primarily responsible for insuring compliance, and you just survey their activities. Is that correct?

MR. MACALUSO. Yes. When you say "just survey," I think perhaps there is—that isn't a complete statement of our role. Our role is one of policy guidance as I have indicated, and we also have the authority and exercise it from time to time actually to get into cases, specific cases.

MR. GLICKSTEIN. What are the ultimate sanctions under the Executive order?

MR. MACALUSO. Well, the ultimate sanction is termination of the contract. There are other sanctions. There is, in fact, quite a wide variety. When I say that; I refer to the various means which are really fairly conventional with contract administration, for one party taking remedy against another party when he feels that the other party's performance is not adequate.

In addition to that, there are remedies such as the referral of specific cases to the Department of Justice and the Equal Employment Opportunity Commission.

MR. GLICKSTEIN. These are remedies that are equally applicable to construction contracts as they are to contracts with a continuous ongoing company?

MR. MACALUSO. Yes. The only difference with construction is that construction contracts really have a broader scope than the supply contracts, and that is that in construction, the construction contracts which are covered include those which are federally assisted, and in supply contracts it is only those that have direct purchase with goods and services for the Government.

MR. GLICKSTEIN. We heard the testimony this morning that your office recently has come out with a new affirmative action program. Would you describe that, please?

MR. MACALUSO. The references I heard this morning were to what we call a pre-award order and operational plan for San Francisco, and this was in fact issued over the past winter.

The plan—well, let me take it chronologically. The order was issued about the end of the year and it essentially required all of the agencies active in contract construction in this six-county area to use it as a guideline for the affirmative action programs with certain contracts, and I will get to that in a moment. The guidelines are based on the BART agreement, with respect to the requiring of contractors and principal subcontractors to take affirmative action as a condition of their receiving the contract. Now, in the order of Mr. Sylvester in this six-county area—

MR. GLICKSTEIN. Mr. Sylvester is the Director of your Office?

MR. MACALUSO. That is correct, the Director of the Office of Federal Contract Compliance. The Federal agencies active in construction were required to use this guideline with reference to all jobs over half a million dollars in a pre-award proceeding so that they would be satisfied that the affirmative action programs of the general contractor and the principal subs for these jobs, as well as the contractors and principal subs on jobs which were not yet 25 percent complete, would have these guidelines.

Now, this order was then followed in early February by what we call an operational plan, and here we tried to give advice and guidance to the contractors—I am sorry; basically to the Federal agencies, but perhaps ultimately to the contractors, too, in how we felt these nine points could be meaningfully implemented, and we went through with what have become fairly standard reminders that it is the contractors and subcontractors that have the responsibility of designing affirmative action programs which will result in equal employment opportunity.

MR. GLICKSTEIN. Mr. Macaluso, maybe we can use a concrete example of how this program would operate.

We were told by a representative of a construction company this morning that his conception of the Executive order was that all that was necessary was to write a letter to a union and ask them whether they complied with the Executive order and if the union wrote back and said, "Yes, we do comply with the Executive order," that was sufficient and it was not necessary to inquire whether the union had any Negro members or if it referred any Negro members.

Now, what is the policy of your office now with respect to that type of position? Does the affirmative action required change that obligation?

MR. MACALUSO. No, I heard that testimony and I haven't had an opportunity to talk to that gentleman nor to talk to the Post Office officials, the contracting agency here.

I am quite confounded by his analysis.

MR. GLICKSTEIN. You think he has a greater obligation than he described?

MR. MACALUSO. I think that he is very misguided, frankly, in the statement he made, and I understand from Mr. Magnuson that there has been quite a succession of events involving the compliance of the Silberblatt Company and its major subcontractors. Mr. Magnuson has himself been involved in some of them, and this makes it quite mystifying to him also, and he can speak for himself on this if he wishes, that Mr. Harris takes this position at this point. But I would suggest that perhaps the best way for us to handle this is to get in touch with the Post Office officials and get a full record of what has transpired. I personally have had some conversations with the top officials in Equal Employment.

MR. GLICKSTEIN. Let's take a hypothetical case then if this case cannot be dealt with directly. Under the affirmative action program at the present time, is it sufficient for a contractor to obtain from the union a letter that it doesn't discriminate, and stop at that point or must the contractor do more?

MR. MACALUSO. The answer to that is no, and I have never heard anyone take that position before and I would be very happy to go further into what we consider a more appropriate description of his obligations.

MR. GLICKSTEIN. Mr. Macaluso, we were told that there were 3,000 journeymen plumbers in San Francisco, 20 of whom are Negro. If a plumbing contractor, in order to comply with the Executive order, obtained a letter from a plumbing union that it complies with the Executive order, is that enough? What more must the plumbing contractor do?

MR. MACALUSO. The answer is clearly that that is not enough. In fact, we don't consider that very meaningful, and one of the problems that we have been having is that we have been getting a lot of paper in of that kind. Part of that is inherent in some of the provisions of the——

MR. GLICKSTEIN. What more must the contractor do?

MR. MACALUSO. Well, in the San Francisco area—this is what I was getting to—in the San Francisco operational plan, and I will try to make it as brief as I can, whether he is a plumbing sub or whether he is a sub that uses some of these other higher, better paid trades, he has to propose a program which is acceptable to the Federal contracting and administering agency in concert with our office, which addresses itself meaningfully to these nine items that you have heard about.

Now, these nine items range in fact from pre-apprenticeship programs through to the use of subcontractors.

MR. GLICKSTEIN. Mr. Macaluso, you heard the testimony of the business agent of the Plumbers Union this morning I believe?

MR. MACALUSO. Yes, indeed. Mr. Mazzola.

MR. GLICKSTEIN. He indicated that he was very much opposed to any pre-apprenticeship program or to admitting any more apprentices to the Plumbers Union. Now, as a practical matter, what can a plumbing contractor in the Bay Area do to comply with the Executive order aside from getting a letter from Mr. Mazzola that he doesn't discriminate?

MR. MACALUSO. The letter from Mr. Mazzola I wouldn't think would be very material here. What we do have as Item 3, which will be the basis for the judgment that is made by the Federal contracting or administrating agency and ourselves, is actively to seek and sponsor members of minority groups for pre-apprenticeship training, to direct himself toward that objective.

MR. GLICKSTEIN. Mr. Mazzola said he was opposed to pre-apprenticeship training. He wouldn't agree to it and his union didn't want more apprentices.

MR. MACALUSO. Right. I remind you, Mr. Glickstein, that we deal with the contractors. Actually our office deals with the Federal agencies and the agencies deal with the contractor.

MR. GLICKSTEIN. If a contractor came back to you and said: "Mr. Macaluso, I have presented these nine points to the Plumbers Union, we've spoken about it for weeks, we just can't make any progress at all. It's a complete stalemate. What can I do? I have a collective bargaining agreement. I have to hire the people that Mr. Mazzola refers to me. He won't agree to Point 1; he won't agree to Point 2; he won't agree to any of the nine points. What should I do?" What would you tell him?

MR. MACALUSO. Well, there are situations that will come in to us every day. I say every day across the counry. But with respect to this particular plan, they've come in to us two or three or four times so far, and what we have to do is to look at the total proposal of the low bidder and his proposed major subs, and we have to make a judgment and that we believe is just inherent in the kind of program that we are working with here. We make a judgment as to whether or not it is acceptable.

You asked me what we do in this specific case. I think it would be impossible to make a meaningful judgment on the basis of Item 3 alone. We look at the whole package and see what was going to be done. If perhaps he took on a Negro sub under Item 9, then all of these things have to be looked at. The method of his achieving equal employment opportunity is up to him. He manages his business. What is not negotiable, what he must have is that the program gives us the assurance of getting these results of equal employment opportunity.

There is nothing novel about this, by the way, in construction. We do this across the board. It is just that quite frankly we have been considerably more successful in other industries, because special characteristics to this industry—there are resources in this industry that have made it more difficult for us, and we simply have not received results that are even nominal.

MR. GLICKSTEIN. Would your office be prepared to tell a sub-contractor that a contract will not be signed unless you can assure us conclusively that there will be minority group persons on the job, even if that requires violating your collective bargaining agreement?

MR. MACALUSO. Well, when you get to the question of if even that requires violating the collective bargaining agreement, it makes it necessary for me to clarify a point that was raised in a number of your questions this morning. And that is our position with respect to the contractor's obligations when he has a collective bargaining agreement which might interfere with his ability to perform a government contract. Now, our Executive order is not a matter of discretion with the Federal contracting and administering agency. It is necessary that when they build or when they get goods or supplies, that this be a condition of the production of this building, just as it is if it is defense hardware or any other goods or supplies.

So that if a contractor has put himself, for whatever reason, in a position so he can't perform adequately, competently, can't perform effectively, he should simply not do business with the Government. Now this is no different from any other contract clause.

MR. GLICKSTEIN. What you are saying in effect is that perhaps almost all the plumbing contractors in San Francisco are putting themselves in that position because there are just 20 Negro journeyman plumbers and it would be very difficult for all of them to be employed by these contractors to comply with these requirements?

MR. MACALUSO. No, I am not saying that, because that again makes an assumption that we are making a judgment that goes to the first part of your original question that raises this point on the dignity of collecting bargaining contracts as against the requirements of the Executive order. That is the question of what we are requiring, and I think, again, what we are requiring in San Francisco under our order and under our operational plan, does not assume the result that you are implying in your question, and that result apparently, as I infer it, is simply that there must be a Negro plumber on the job, in each job, in order for there to be compliance.

MR. GLICKSTEIN. This doesn't assume that result?

361

MR. MACALUSO. No, sir, not in the San Francisco operational plan.

MR. GLICKSTEIN. I thought that the operational plan was concerned with the results, primarily with the results, that you had stopped relying on pledges and promises, and you wanted results. And so you think the results would be satisfactory even if there were no minority group people on the job?

MR. MACALUSO. No, it is simply—it is not a question of either one or the other. It is simply a question of the fact that this operational plan and this order are based upon the nine specific points, which do not include a requirement of specific majority—minority group representation in the specific crafts. Obviously it is directed toward that objective. But I want to be very precise here in that I could not accept that. It might well be that in the specific situation —again, this is not a rigid formula. It can't be. There has to be a judgment within this particular framework. It may well be that in a given situation he couldn't follow these nine points without having three, four, or five, but I would not say to you that necessarily implies one, two—I mean that is the kind of numbers game which we do not have.

MR. GLICKSTEIN. I guess I've been playing a numbers game with you, also. I've been trying to find out how, with 3,000 journeyman plumbers in San Francisco and only 20 of them Negro—how can plumbing contractors in San Francisco comply with these nine points?

MR. MACALUSO. Well,——

MR. GLICKSTEIN. Unless these 20 men just move from job to job every other day, I can't see any other way that they can comply.

MR. MACALUSO. Well, we'd have to go through the nine points for me to indicate the kind of activity that we are looking for.

MR. GLICKSTEIN. Well, Point No. 3 indicates that the contractor shall actively seek and sponsor members of minority groups for pre-apprenticeship training. Mr. Mazzola said this morning there will be no pre-apprenticeship training in the Plumbers Union.

MR. MACALUSO. Right, and a little while ago you put an essentially similar question to me and I told you that in order to make a judgment as to whether or not we would accept or reject such a plan, we would have to look at the way in which he addressed himself to all nine points.

Now, there is one point, actually it is the last one, which has to do with subcontractors and, as a matter of fact, there is a reference to Mr. Dones' organization here. One of the sources which general contractors can work with to identify prospective bidders for subs is the General & Specialty Contractors Association. This is a non-profit corporation, minority group General & Specialty Contractors, organized to develop the building and contracting skills of its members. Now, here is another item, you see, that a contractor can address himself to in presenting this proposed affirmative action program, which is just the same kind of process that he would use in proposing how he would perform for any other specification of the contract.

MR. GLICKSTEIN. Mr. Macaluso, do you think that the Executive order as presently written will ever be able to insure that there are more minority group persons working in the building trades?

MR. MACALUSO. Well, "will ever be able to" is—

MR. GLICKSTEIN. Has any Federal construction contract ever been terminated?

MR. MACALUSO. To my knowledge, none has been terminated. Now, you realize the Federal contract administering agencies could do this or we could do this. To my knowledge, none has been terminated. This is not to say that no sanctions have been used, and this is not to say that we haven't taken some measures which are designed to bring about compliance by the use of the contractual bargaining power of the Government, and I think the really effective tools are just being forged now and have been over the last year.

I am sure you are familiar with the St. Louis—well, there have been some events in St. Louis which make us think we are on the right track. We think that we are on the right track here. We also have a program in Cleveland and it is a different program because we have made a judgment about that situation, and that is a different situation and each of these are area programs.

We believe that there is some merit to the position in the industry that the matter has to be addressed on an area basis. However, of course, our relationship with the industry is through individual contractors and so, mindful of this, we have forged these programs in which we try to indicate some standards, some frame of reference, for the area and hold the contractor accountable to figure out his own affirmative action within that framework.

MR. GLICKSTEIN. Your office was set up a year ago. Prior to that there was the President's Committee on Government Contracts?

MR. MACALUSO. Equal Employment Opportunity, that's correct.

MR. GLICKSTEIN. You have been in this business for some time now, I believe?

MR. MACALUSO. Yes, I have.

MR. GLICKSTEIN. Do you think that Government contractors are really afraid that a contract is ever going to be terminated?

MR. MACALUSO. Well, that is difficult. I feel that, certainly in generalizing about all of them. I think that there is a little more indication and awareness that the Government means business and has been, since we have started the pre-award process, since we have indicated that we are result-orientated in our requirements, and since Secretary Wirtz has put out his policy letter which was last January, and the incident that occurred in the St. Louis Arch, I feel that all these do have a cumulative effect. But I am not going to say that I think that I have been able to measure it in terms of people. I haven't, and this is very disappointing to us.

Now, you asked me before, I think, whether it can ever be. I think the only way it can ever be is with greater resources being applied, and here I have to point out again that the present program is gathering momentum. It really started only about a year ago and the staffing of the agencies is just getting underway, and in some cases this is more difficult than in non-construction, simply because of what I have described as the special characteristics of the industry, which is very obviously the fact that people are hired by the day, they have strong hiring halls, strong father-son traditions, and there is a higher unemployment level than you find in the economy as a whole. And when you add up all these factors, it makes it more difficult. In some of the Federal agencies, there is no doubt about it, there are difficult problems because, on the one hand, there are conflicting missions. Some agencies and some program managers will be involved with programs that have some of the most benevolent and important social welfare programs and they will sometimes feel there is a conflict in the good that they are trying to achieve with those and the insistence upon equal employment opportunity in construction particularly.

MR. GLICKSTEIN. Agencies with benevolent programs are more reluctant to terminate contracts?

MR. MACALUSO. I didn't say that.

MR. GLICKSTEIN. But they might be?

MR. MACALUSO. I say that is a rationalization which I just have to respect and I certainly can't accept it as a defense.

MR. GLICKSTEIN. The post office in Oakland has no Negro plumbers, operating engineers, sheet metal workers, ironworkers, electricians, steamfitters?

MR. MACALUSO. No. That is correct.

MR. GLICKSTEIN. And $20 million in Federal funds being spent there.

MR. MACALUSO. That is correct, and I would like a full statement from the Post Office on that before I can really discuss it fully with you because, as I say, I have had conversations with the Post Office officials and I can't reconcile them—that was only three weeks ago—with Mr. Harris' statement this morning. But if I may just pursue this for a moment longer. Other difficulties, particularly with construction, because, after all, they have conflicting missions, the Federal officials in other agencies have conflcting missions with other goods and supplies besides construction. But in construction, my observation is it is more difficult because there is a feeling that, after all, the contractor is in a very hard spot and we have pursued this very hard since the office of Federal Contract Compliance was established. We have done it with workshops. We have done it with policy, the 1966 proposed contract construction program in which we set forth our whole philosophy, guides for pre-award proceedings, and now with these various city areas, we are trying to meet this problem of a lack of resources, and this reorientation of philosophy.

MR. GLICKSTEIN. I have no further questions, Mr. Chairman.

CHAIRMAN HANNAH. Dean Griswold, do you have any questions?

COMMISSIONER GRISWOLD. Mr. Macaluso, I don't want to be misunderstood in this question I am going to ask you. I recognize fully that your interest is the same as ours, to try to do what we can to bring about greater equality of opportunity, and I don't want to minimize at all the difficulties in this area which have baffled almost everyone who has tried to work in it. But have the efforts of your office anywhere in the United States ever brought about the employment of one minority plumber?

MR. MACALUSO. Well, sir, these causal relations aren't always easy to establish. In terms of the ripple effect that we get from having an active affirmative action program on a construction project, I think I might point to the St. Louis situation again, in which there were—I believe these were pipefitters, but there were 10 who were taken on, on the job training program. Shortly after there was an incident at the yards in which the contractor proceeded with his affirmative action, even though there was a walkout of the AFL-CIO. That happens to be one that comes to mind because I think it was fairly dramatic.

I don't recall specifically of others. With respect to plumbers, there have been a number of situations where contractors have, as the price of getting the contract again usually, indicated that they will go out and try to bring somebody onto the job, often from a fabricating shop off the site, in order to satisfy the requirements for affirmative action.

COMMISSIONER GRISWOLD. Have the efforts of your office brought about the employment of one minority plumber in the San Francisco Bay Area?

MR. MAGNUSON. Not to my knowledge.

COMMISSIONER GRISWOLD. I don't know whether you heard the testimony of Mr. Dones this morning, which seemed to me to—I guess maybe it was this afternoon—which seemed to me to indicate that there might be some prospect of achieving this result, if it was possible, for minority contractors to get in these operations, perhaps as subcontractors or otherwise, and Mr. Dones raised the question of the bonding requirement as being a very serious obstacle to the small minority contractor.

Would you agree with what Mr. Dones said about that, that the bonding requirement is an obstacle?

MR. MACALUSO. Yes, sir. This has been my experience and I have gotten personally involved in it in at least one city, in Washington, and I would agree 100 percent. One of the items, one of the elements that we look for in affirmative action is for a general contractor to help out some of these smaller subs.

There are a number of minority group subs who have done work in residential, non-government work, and we point out to them and each area coordinator as a matter of fact—we have them operating in 22 cities—keeps a list of minority group subs, whether or not they have done government work, to try to bring them along and have the general contractor take them on as part of his affirmative action, bring them into his bag and give them the kind of support that they need.

COMMISSIONER GRISWOLD. That was what I was going to suggest to you. Sometimes the way to deal with a very difficult problem is to stop trying to hit it head on, but to try and move around it somewhat. And it would seem to me that perhaps the objective of your office could be assisted if you could find ways to make it more possible for minority contractors to get into the picture, presumably as subcontractors, although perhaps if they were successful at that they might then grow so that they could bid on bigger contracts.

MR. MACALUSO. I might point out in this connection, Dean Griswold, that the Housing and Urban Development Department had a project in New York City, 114th Street in Harlem, in which the general contractor there, H.R.H., had, I believe, as many as 30 percent of his people on the site at one time who were the employees of a whole variety of Negro subcontractors.

Now there were problems in doing this. Many of them had never had an opportunity to do this kind of work and, of course, when you are dealing with the Government, it does require more paper work. He helped them with their paper work, he helped them with their accounting, and he went bond for them in some cases. This is the kind of thing we are looking for.

COMMISSIONER GRISWOLD. Could this be done on the Oakland Post Office or in the Bay Area Rapid Transit job?

MR. MACALUSO. Well, I heard it suggested with respect to the Post Office job and I would certainly think that is one of the things that we could explore.

COMMISSIONER GRISWOLD. Thank you.

CHAIRMAN HANNAH. Mrs. Freeman?

COMISSIONER FREEMAN. Mr. Macaluso, since you have mentioned St. Louis in response to Dean Griswold's question, I would like to get a bit of clarification there because what happened in St. Louis represented the concerted efforts, not only of the Department of Labor, but of the Department of Interior and the civil rights group. With the Arch there had been the same problem of the exclusion of Negroes from the craft unions. The civil rights organizations were picketing the Arch and you may have read that somebody climbed the Arch, but the Department of Interior granted a contract, the plumbing contract, to a non-union contractor who was Negro, because of the fact that there was refusal of the plumbing union to—at least, they did not comply.

Well, after the contract was let to the Negro contractor, when he started work, four of the craft unions walked off the job and here is where the cooperation of the other forces came into effect.

The NAACP filed an action within NLRB. The Department of Justice filed suit against the unions and all of the forces working together resulted in the fact that the craft unions did return to work and some months thereafter, when faced with the fact that the Housing Authority contract would not have been awarded at all, it was at that time that the Steamfitters then announced a policy whereby they would admit Negroes to the union.

So what we are saying is that a firm policy on the part of the Department of Labor, and I'm distressed because I get the impression from you that the firmness of the policy seems to vary with the locality, a firm policy in the Department of Labor would assure compliance by the unions. I refer you specifically to Section 207 of the Executive order, which says that the Secretary of Labor shall use his best efforts directly and through contracting agencies, other interested Federal, State, and local agencies, contractors and all other available instrumentalities, to cause any labor union engaged in work under Government contracts or any agency referring workers or providing or supervising apprenticeship or training or in the course of such work to cooperate in the implementation of the purposes of this order. And my question is, has there been any instance here in the Bay Area in which the Secretary of Labor has enforced or invoked the provisions of Section 207, and I ask that in view of the testimony which we have received this morning which indicates that a contractor on at least two large Government jobs has had no Negroes employed.

MR. MACALUSO. The answer, Mrs. Freeman, with respect to Section 207 and the Secretary's actions, I think, is that the Secretary in fact regularly addresses himself to this question; the question of equal employment opportunity, particularly in construction, in regular meetings with the construction industry Joint Council which is kind of a summit group of the representatives of the larger contractor associations as well as the building trades at the national level. And, of course, this does not preclude other informal and specific communications, not all of which, I am sure, that I am familiar with.

And so that I think that the answer is there definitely is substantial implementation of Section 207.

Now, with reference to San Francisco and the specifics of San Francisco, I can't honestly say that I know anything of that.

COMMISSIONER FREEMAN. Thank you.

CHAIRMAN HANNAH. Any further questions? Father Hesburgh?

COMMISSIONER HESBURGH. Mr. Macaluso, I find it difficult to find out how you are going to get any reasonable compliance unless you have some people around with whom compliance is made possible, that is, some minority workers in the trade unions or the craft unions.

According to our information, there is about $500 million worth of federally assisted construction contracts here in the Bay Area at the same time. As I read it, that is a half a billion dollars, which amounts to a good deal of construction.

Now, all of this construction, I take it, in the normal course of events, is going to have to be done by members of the craft unions. Members of the craft unions, I think, by general admission, as I have gotten it in our hearings here, have very few members from the minority races in their present membership. To get into the membership, unless you come from another part of the country and go to the bottom of the list, normally you come in through apprenticeship. According to the study we have, which is the Dymally study, which has been questioned by some people here, but there have been no facts given against it, no counter facts, this purports to look at the number of apprentices coming into this union, which is the normal front door, and this is listed as December 1964, for these figures.

Asbestos workers, 87 apprentices, no Negroes.

Boilermakers and blacksmiths, 33 apprentices and no Negroes.

Carpet and Linoleum layers, 569 apprentices, .7 of 1 percent Negro.

Electrical trades, 2,133 apprentices, 1.69 percent Negroes.

Ironworkers (field) 422 apprentices, no Negroes.

Laborers, 459, 1.53 percent Negroes.

Operating Engineers, 259, .7 of 1 percent Negro.

Painters and Glaziers, 1,069, 1.87 percent Negro.

Pipe Trades, 2,832, .4 of 1 percent Negro.

Sheet Metal Workers, 1,381 apprentices, 1.16 percent Negroes.

Surveying, 291 apprentices, .3 of 1 percent Negro.

Telephone Installations, 55 apprentices, no Negroes.

Now, if this is the normal door into the craft unions, if you are going to look for compliance, and this is the percent of Negroes in the craft unions at the present time, this is the percent in the pipeline coming into them, and you have a half-billion dollars' worth of construction coming up, my question is how, without using mirrors, are you going to get compliance?

MR. MACALUSO. Well, Father Hesburgh, I would raise a question about your assumption, and I have heard it voiced here today, and I hear it very often in this business, that the journeyman crafts-men aren't, in fact, going to come through apprentices. I think everyone concedes it, just as a matter of fact, that the reason why less than half, or at least about half of the journeymen never went through apprenticeship is because of the expansion that came along in World War II, and right after World War II, and. I think usually these apprenticeship programs certainly aren't geared to take care of that expansion. In view of the time, the total elapsed time, for an apprenticeship, obviously in a quick expan-sion they are just not going to meet it. Training coordinators themselves will often indicate that they really are training all chiefs and no Indians, and if there is a rapid expansion, as I hope there is, this industry is in trouble, and particularly here on the West Coast.

Then I would expect that measures, such as those that were taken in World War II and right after World War II, would be taken again and I think that is appropriate and we've addressed ourselves to that in our San Francisco operational plan.

We are anticipating it. First of all, one of the things they are trying to do is to get the industry to plan ahead, some kind of manpower planning. It is not characteristic of this industry. And the next thing we are trying to do is to get them to help the minority people prepare themselves for the upgrading that we hope is going to come. We hope the opportunities are going to come, and then we want it to take place, and I might just say parenthetically that in some other cities in the country where there is a scarcity of labor, this is a program that we are pushing very hard. We are pushing it today, right now in Cleveland. So that Items 5 and 6 of these nine point programs are to improve opportunities for the upgrading of members of the construction force, and we are borrowing from some experience we have had in some of the other cities, in which we get the general contractors particularly to look among their so-called laborers and cement finishers and the lower paid people who often have related experi-ence from somewhere else and who would be the natural people to be upgraded in the case of a real expansion, and apprenticeship can't begin to take care of it.

COMMISSIONER HESBURGH. My only point is, and I don't still understand the answer, is that if, No. 1, there is a very small per-centage of Negroes and other minorities in the craft unions today, No. 2, if the normal way of getting in seems not to have very many of them in the pipe line, how in heaven's name are you going to have compliance if there aren't the people with whom to comply unless somehow there is a change of heart on the numbers coming in, either through persuasion or extra training or extra effort in this regard?

Otherwise I think this whole thing could be viewed in a very cynical way as being a paper tiger and if, in fact, you can point to project after project without a single minority Negro worker, then it is very hard to say that the President's order means anything.

If it doesn't mean anything, I think we are all wasting our time.

CHAIRMAN HANNAH. Mr. Taylor?

MR. TAYLOR. Mr. Macaluso, would you be able to do your job more effectively if this Executive order applied directly to unions?

MR. MACALUSO. Well, Mr. Taylor, I don't quite visualize how it would be. It is part of our procurement policy. I think the answer must be it depends on how it applies to unions.

MR. TAYLOR. I mean, if the obligation ran directly against unions and if sanctions could be invoked directly against unions, they might not be all of the sanctions that can be invoked against contractors, but I assume there are some sanctions that might be available against unions?

MR. MACALUSO. Well, I guess the answer would have to be categorically yes, although I would want to visualize it a little more clearly on just how it would work. Obviously the more control you have of a given situation, the more likely you are to make the necessary social changes.

MR. TAYLOR. Has that matter been given consideration, the matter of applying this order directly to unions in some manner?

MR. MACALUSO. Not to my knowledge.

MR. TAYLOR. I would like to just give you a minute or two. I think one of the problems that has come out time and again is that the order in some respects seems to lack credibility. Would I be overstating your position if I said that if—I guess I am expressing a hope more than anything else—that the test that you hope to use, the plan that you hope to use here on out, is more one of actual performance than paper compliance, that you are going to be looking at the numbers of Negroes and members of other minority groups, who are on the job, and that if there does not appear to be a number increased over what you have right now, significant numbers, then you are very seriously going to consider imposing sanctions? Or is that an over-statement of your policy?

MR. MACALUSO. No, I don't think so. I think I have tried to reflect my own judgment, which is very similar to what has been expressed by Father Hesburgh and yourself. This has been up to very recently a paper operation, to the extent that it was an operation at all.

After all, we had some form of Executive order since 1941. We didn't even really look at the construction industry until three years ago, and then it was kind of a tentative, what I shudder to characterize as a kind of an educational approach. And so the getting down to business really has been a process that was begun as a result of the approach that Mr. Sylvester has adopted in the past year. And now I am hopeful, but I am also aware that we have to prove ourselves to the industry just as the industry, I think, has to prove to the minority group communities and to demonstrate to them that things really have changed, as far as their accessibility to the better paying trades is concerned.

MR. TAYLOR. You see, there is a great deal of skepticism around. Many people believe that, while your office is trying to do a good job, that really Government as a whole, the Department of Labor, doesn't really mean business here and that really is too much subject to the influence of building trade unions and that decisions get influenced, ultimate decisions get influenced because of these influences, and I don't know how we are going to have a credible policy unless some evidence appears that contradicts this skepticism. I think that is the problem that we are up against.

VICE CHAIRMAN PATTERSON. I am not sure I heard the answer to Mrs. Freeman's question which is why can't you do over here in the Oakland Post Office what you did in St. Louis, what the Department of Interior did in St. Louis.

MR. MACALUSO. Well, sir, the Department of Interior had a pre-award procedure in St. Louis. They had an understanding with this contractor that in order for him to perform his contract, the equal opportunity aspect of his contract, he had to take on this sub, he had to take on X number of sheet metal workers and X number of electricians.

VICE CHAIRMAN PATTERSON. Don't you have this agreement under the Executive order with the contractors?

MR. MACALUSO. To my knowledge, we don't have such a specific understanding at the Oakland Post Office. Now, again, I just don't know, but I don't believe we do, and this building was begun, I think—didn't Mr. Harris say on May 1 of 1965? So that it considerably pre-dates this operation that we have here and this is just what I will have to get into. Obviously, with the situation as he described it, something has got to be done and from the way he described the situation, I don't see compliance there at all. And this is what I will have to get into.

COMMISSIONER FREEMAN. There is no compliance.

MR. MACALUSO. No. But I have other information, too, that makes me realize it is not a clear-cut picture.

CHAIRMAN HANNAH. You are excused. We appreciate your comments.

MR. GLICKSTEIN. May we introduce Mr. Macaluso's statement into the record as Exhibit No. 12?

CHAIRMAN HANNAH. It is introduced.

(The document referred to was marked as Exhibit No. 12 and received in evidence.)

UNIDENTIFIED SPEAKER FROM COURTROOM. Mr. Chairman, I have been here for the last three days and I would like to be heard, please. I have tried to get on the agenda and I can't get on the agenda. So I would like to speak, please.

CHAIRMAN HANNAH. If you will take your seat. The next time we recess I will be glad to talk to you and we will work out something if we can.

MR. GLICKSTEIN. The next witness, Mr. Chairman, is Mrs. Sophie Eilperin, a member of the staff, who will give a brief background report.

(Whereupon, Mrs. Sophie Eilperin was sworn by the Chairman and testified as follows:)

TESTIMONY OF MRS. SOPHIE EILPERIN, STAFF ATTORNEY, U.S. COMMISSION ON CIVIL RIGHTS

MRS. EILPERIN. A civil rights issue familiar to most residents of San Francisco and the Bay Area is the issue of employment by hotels and restaurants, which was the subject of conflicts between civil rights organizations and the hotel industry in 1964 and again in 1966.

In 1964 several civil rights organizations conducted picketing and sit-ins at several hotels and restaurants to protest discriminatory hiring practices. As a result, an agreement was reached between the Hotel Employers Association of San Francisco and the civil rights group which joined together as the *ad hoc* Committee to End Discrimination. The agreement was called the 1964 Civil Rights Agreement. This agreement provided that selection and promotion of employees was to be determined solely on the basis of qualifications without reference to race, that information was to be disseminated concerning the equal opportunity policy of the hotels, and that the picketing, boycotts, and demonstrations would halt. The agreement was to last for two years.

In April 1966, after the expiration of the first agreement, some of the employees at the Hilton Hotel who were Negroes had a grievance against the hotel. The Joint Executive Board of the Hotel and Restaurant Employees, the union representing these employees involved, attempted to handle the grievances. The employees, however, chose to be represented by a new coalition of civil rights groups which was being formed to press for a new civil rights agreement. The Hilton Hotel was picketed until July

19th, and civil rights leaders threatened more extensive demonstrations unless another agreement was ratified.

On July 22 the association and the civil rights groups entered into a second agreement called the 1966 Civil Rights Agreement. The agreement, which was to run for 10 years, provided, in addition to a nondiscrimination clause, that a detailed survey of employees in each job category by race would be made every 90 days by every member hotel. The agreement further listed the approximate proportions of Negro employees that the parties anticipated would be found in each employment category.

Subsequently the Joint Executive Board of the Hotel and Restaurant Employees, which was not a party to the agreement, challenged the 1966 Civil Rights Agreement in an arbitration proceeding brought against the association. The Joint Board alleged that the agreement violated the collective bargaining agreement between the unions and the association.

On November 17 the arbitration board held in favor of the unions and declared the Civil Rights Agreement void and unenforceable. The decision was based in part on the grounds that the civil rights organizations had acted as a labor organization and had executed an agreement in conflict with the union's collective bargaining agreement.

The 1966 Civil Rights Agreement, according to the arbitration board, violated the rights of employees under the union's collective bargaining agreement by providing a preference to employees of Afro-American descent. This was implied in the projected quota for such employees.

Such preferential treatment, moreover, was deemed by the arbitration board unlawful and contrary to public policy.

Finally, the arbitrator found that the agreement was void because it was procured through threat of force. A survey of the racial composition of the hotel industry work force was conducted by the industry in 1966. It showed that relatively few Negroes held positions in such job categories as waiters, waitresses, bartenders, or in office and clerical jobs, while high percentages of Negroes held housekeeping, laundry, valet, and miscellaneous culinary positions.

MR. GLICKSTEIN. Thank you, Mrs. Eilperin. The next witness is Mr. Joseph D. Sullivan accompanied by his counsel, Mr. Donald D. Connors.

(Whereupon, Mr. Joseph D. Sullivan was sworn by the Chairman and testified as follows:)

TESTIMONY OF MR. JOSEPH D. SULLIVAN, SAN FRANCISCO, CALIFORNIA

MR. GLICKSTEIN. Will you please state your full name and address for the record?

MR. SULLIVAN. Yes. Joseph D. Sullivan, 870 Market Street, San Francisco, Caifornia, and I am president of the Hotel Employers Association of San Francisco.

MR. GLICKSTEIN. And the association represents the hotel employers in the city in its negotiations with labor unions. Is that correct?

MR. SULLIVAN. That is correct.

MR. GLICKSTEIN. How many hotels does it represent?

MR. SULLIVAN. Approximately 35.

MR. GLICKSTEIN. All in the city of San Francisco?

MR. SULLIVAN. Yes.

MR. GLICKSTEIN. How many persons employed by hotels are associated with your organization?

MR. SULLIVAN. Approximately 5,000.

MR. GLICKSTEIN. Do you know the approximate racial composition of the work force?

MR. SULLIVAN. I have given the information to Mr. Bellman. May I refer to the documents there?

MR. GLICKSTEIN. Yes. Will you give Mr. Sullivan a copy of that?

MR. SULLIVAN. My recollection—I had better look at it. I don't think this information was obtained from me. I believe this was obtained from the Civil Rights—

MR. GLICKSTEIN. Human Rights Commission.

MR. SULLIVAN. Excuse me. I also gave Mr. Bellman some information on the same employment figures obtained in October of 1966 after this one was prepared.

MR. GLICKSTEIN. You have later figures than this?

MR. SULLIVAN. Mr. Bellman has the figures.

MR. GLICKSTEIN. Why don't we come back to that question?

MR. SULLIVAN. Very well.

MR. GLICKSTEIN. The figures that we have and perhaps we could just work with these for a moment as approximations, indicate that about 19.2 percent of the employees in the hotel industry are Negro, and it also indicates that the Negro employees are— there are not many of them in such categories as bartenders, office and clerical, executive, managerial, and supervisory, that most of them come in housekeeping and laundry and valet.

Why are so few Negroes employed in the hotel industry in job categories as waitresses, bartenders, bellmen, and managerial positions?

MR. SULLIVAN. Well, with respect to the first part of your question as to why the great number is in the housekeeping and services department, many of these people of the minority groups have had experience as domestics working in private homes and other institutions such as hospitals, and they were readily adaptable to this type of work and on that point I should say that since these figures were prepared, a considerable number of them proved that they were capable of doing work in the higher classifications within the framework of the housekeeping department, have been promoted. I do not have the precise figures before me. With respect to your question concerning the bartenders and the—I don't know the answer to it, frankly.

MR. GLICKSTEIN. I think the report that you have in front of you, Mr. Sullivan, indicates that there are 4,899 employees in the industry and 2,365 are Negro or members of other minority groups, and the information that you earlier provided to us indicated that there 5,300 people employed by the association, 2,961 were white and 2,339 belonged to minority groups.

MR. SULLIVAN. That is correct.

MR. GLICKSTEIN. That is correct?

MR. SULLIVAN. That is the October 1966 figure?

MR. GLICKSTEIN. Right. So the figures of persons belonging to minority groups, Negro and other minority groups, are approximately the same. The chart you have in front of you adds up to 2,365, and the figure you gave us was 2,339?

MR. SULLIVAN. Approximately the same.

MR. GLICKSTEIN. How do hotels hire workers?

MR. SULLIVAN. Well, under the terms of the collective bargaining agreement, we have with the seven unions involved in this computation here, the hotel doing the hiring will call the union for a particular type of employee, one of seven unions involved.

MR. GLICKSTEIN. You are required to call the union to—

MR. SULLIVAN. That's correct.

MR. GLICKSTEIN. You cannot hire someone off the street?

MR. SULLIVAN. Not unless the union is unable to furnish somebody.

MR. GLICKSTEIN. You must first go to the union?

MR. SULLIVAN. That's correct.

MR. GLICKSTEIN. In other words, if you wanted to hire some Negro bartenders, you would first have to go to the Bartenders Union.

MR. SULLIVAN. The agreement requires preference for employment to union members. That is right.

MR. GLICKSTEIN. Well, why has the industry been unable to recruit minority group members into some of these higher paying occupations?

MR. SULLIVAN. Well, I refer back to the comment I made in connection with the housekeeping department. You understand why these minority groups readily fitted into this particular type of work. Now the same is not true, for example, in the waiters' category, where a high degree of skill is required, particularly in a major hotel restaurant or a major street restaurant, such as a French restaurant where continental service is required. An exceptionally long period of training is required. That takes care of that, and I think that applies equally to the waitresses.

MR. GLICKSTEIN. And the bartenders?

MR. SULLIVAN. Now the bartenders, I can't tell you why there are only 11. I don't know whether this figure is still accurate today or not. These figures are almost a year old. There may be some changes on the positive side, I am not certain. But bartending is not simply mixing a Scotch and soda, either. I am informed that that requires a considerable amount of skill, not only in the physical performance of the job, but the matter of handling the cash and the checks and the things of that sort.

MR. GLICKSTEIN. Do you know if the industry has made any affirmative records to recruit Negro bartenders?

MR. SULLIVAN. The industry itself, I don't know. I have nothing to do with that. I simply handle the administration of the agreement.

MR. GLICKSTEIN. Mr. Sullivan, our Staff Report that you heard a while ago described the civil rights controversy that the hotel industry was involved in in 1964 and 1966, and that agreement was set aside by an arbitration proceeding that was brought by the union.

When you negotiated that agreement with the civil rights groups, the unions were not present. Is that correct?

MR. SULLIVAN. During 1966 July?

MR. GLICKSTEIN. Yes.

MR. SULLIVAN. No.

MR. GLICKSTEIN. The unions were not present?

MR. SULLIVAN. No.

MR. GLICKSTEIN. Is it customary to enter into agreements that involve working conditions in your industry without consulting with the union?

MR. SULLIVAN. Is it customary?

MR. GLICKSTEIN. Yes.

MR. SULLIVAN. No, it is irregular, to say the least.

MR. GLICKSTEIN. When you signed that agreement with the civil rights groups, did you have any feeling at all that it might have been illegal?

MR. SULLIVAN. Did I personally have any feeling as to its legality?

MR. GLICKSTEIN. Yes.

MR. SULLIVAN. Yes, I did.

MR. GLICKSTEIN. You thought it might not stand up? Then when the union attacked it, in the arbitration proceeding, did the Hotel Association defend it before the arbitrator?

MR. SULLIVAN. Yes, we did defend it.

MR. GLICKSTEIN. Does the Hotel Association have any training programs to bring in unskilled people?

MR. SULLIVAN. We have been working with the Mayor's Commission, Committee on Human Rights for the last several months. I say "we." The hotel industry, the restaurant industry, the club industry, all segments of the industry which employ this type of people, waiters, waitresses, bartenders, miscellaneous cooks, et cetera. That agreement is just about completed.

Some of the civil rights groups have met with us and have offered suggestions. I have been away for approximately a month. I just returned a few days ago to the office—about a week ago. But I understand it is going to be executed tomorrow morning..

MR. GLICKSTEIN. Who will finance it?

MR. SULLIVAN. That question I can't answer. Whether or not it has been determined I don't know.

MR. GLICKSTEIN. Has the hotel industry considered seeking Federal funds under any of the Federal job training programs?

MR. SULLIVAN. Yes, we have considered it, yes.

MR. GLICKSTEIN. Have you rejected it or accepted it?

MR. SULLIVAN. We rejected it originally as it was proposed to us approximately a year ago, 10 months ago. Whether or not our position is going to be changed or will change I don't know at this moment.

MR. GLICKSTEIN. Why did you reject it?

MR. SULLIVAN. Because it was our feeling, and I say my feeling representing the hotels, that the program as submitted to us was a delusion. It was not fair to the minority people. It was an alleged crash program which would tell a lot of people who were badly in need of employment, that all they had to do was take a six weeks' training course and they could qualify for any of these top jobs. And that is just not possible. We are working on what we consider a very orderly program. That is, the industry, various industry groups, and the unions, and hope that it will solve the problem we have before us.

MR. GLICKSTEIN. You felt that the Federal program that was proposed was inadequate or unrealistic.

MR. SULLIVAN. I would go a little bit further than that. I don't think it was a fair program. I think it was misrepresented to these young people who were looking for these jobs. You just can't turn out competent, highly skilled people in three to six weeks. It is just not in the cards. It would leave them at the end of six weeks with an idle promise on their hands and no work.

MR. GLICKSTEIN. I have no further questions, Mr. Chairman.

CHAIRMAN HANNAH. Do the Commissioners have any questions?

COMMISSIONER FREEMAN. Mr. Sullivan, you are president of the Hotel Employers Association. Do you have a hotel?

MR. SULLIVAN. Do I have a hotel?

COMMISSIONER FREEMAN. Yes.

MR. SULLIVAN. No, Mrs. Freeman. I should say, thank goodness.

COMMISSIONER FREEMAN. You indicated that the bartender has to have some special skills in handling money that the average minority person wouldn't have. Would you tell me how long it would take to train a person to become a bartender and handle the money the way you require?

MR. SULLIVAN. Do I know how long it would—how much time would be required?

COMMISSIONER FREEMAN. You said it. I am just trying to understand your statement. You said it required special skills in handling money in addition to making the Scotch.

MR. SULLIVAN. Making the drink?

COMMISSIONER FREEMAN. Well, making the drink.

MR. SULLIVAN. For example, taking care of a considerable number of orders where you serve a waiter or waitresses and other people at a service bar, where you are operating two cash registers, you are making drinks for the people at the front bar, and keeping track of the checks, being certain that all the money is accounted for, that your bank balances out. All of those things, in addition to making a drink.

COMMISSIONER FREEMAN. What I want to know is how long would it take a person——

MR. SULLIVAN. I don't know.

COMMISSIONER FREEMAN. But you say that the training schedule proposed was not fair.

MR. SULLIVAN. I could answer you more properly tomorrow because the schedule of the time required to complete this training will appear in this agreement we are going to execute tomorrow morning.

COMMISSIONER RANKIN. I would like to say this: that in comparison to some of the other unions that we have had testimony from, you have done fairly well as compared with them insofar as hiring minority groups.

MR. SULLIVAN. Thank you very much. We are very proud of the record, almost 50 percent.

CHAIRMAN HANNAH. Any other questions? Mr. Taylor?

MR. TAYLOR. Mr. Sullivan, I am concerned about a couple of the categories here. Following up on what Mrs. Freeman said, there seemed to be a shortage of office and clerical personnel. These Negroes and Mexican Americans or other minority groups are underrepresented in the office and clerical categories, and it would seem to me as bellmen and doormen as well as being waiters or bartenders.

Now, it seems to me that I have seen Negroes and Mexican

Americans perform these jobs in other places around the country in rather large numbers. You are not saying that these jobs are so complicated that people in this area can't perform them?

MR. SULLIVAN. No. I had specific reference to other jobs which required specialized training and skill, not bellmen and doormen obviously. But I would also point out to you that these figures are almost a year old. If you will check the number of doormen in the San Francisco hotels, you will find almost uniformly they are Negroes. As to the bellmen, I have no information since July of last year.

MR. TAYLOR. I was talking about office and clerical workers.

MR. SULLIVAN. Again, these things are a year old and if you make a personal inspection of the major hotels, I think you will find these figures will be substantially altered upward.

MR. CONNORS. The State law Mr. Taylor, forbids us to keep any kind of census based upon color or race.

MR. TAYLOR. The State law, you say?

MR. CONNORS. Yes, sir.

MR. TAYLOR. I have no further questions.

CHAIRMAN HANNAH. Thank you very much. We appreciate your being here. You are excused. Will you call the next witness?

MR. GLICKSTEIN. Mr. Joseph Belardi.

(Whereupon, Mr. Joseph L. Belardi was sworn by the Chairman and testified as follows:)

TESTIMONY OF MR. JOSEPH L. BELARDI, SAN FRANCISCO, CALIFORNIA

MR. GLICKSTEIN. Will you please state your full name and address for the record?

MR. BELARDI. Joseph L. Belardi, executive secretary of the Local Joint Board, Culinary Workers of San Francisco.

MR. GLICKSTEIN. What are your responsibilities as executive secretary of the Joint Board?

MR. BELARDI. Mine are to coordinate the work of contract negotiations and direct the work of the negotiations and also to direct the enforcement of the collective bargaining agreements.

MR. GLICKSTEIN. And how many persons are represented by the Joint Board?

MR. BELARDI. We have a president, a vice president, and a secretary, as far as officers are concerned. We have 18 delegates, three from the six locals. In the bargaining unit we have one building service, which is not part of the Joint Board, but is part of the bargaining unit.

MR. GLICKSTEIN. And what are the unions that are under your Joint Board?

MR. BELARDI. Cooks, Waiters, Waitresses, Bartenders, Hotel Service Workers, Miscellaneous Workers.

MR. GLICKSTEIN. In other words, the Joint Board acts on behalf of all of these individual unions in negotiating a contract? If a grievance comes up, does that go to the Joint Board?

MR. BELARDI. Yes, it does.

MR. GLICKSTEIN. We had some statistics—I think the list is still in front of you, Mr. Belardi—which would indicate that there isn't a very great minority group representation in such categories as waiters, waitresses, bartenders, bellmen, and in supervisory and managerial positions. How do you account for this?

MR. BELARDI. I don't know that these figures are correct.

MR. GLICKSTEIN. Well, Mr. Sullivan said that they were approximately correct although they are almost a year old.

MR. BELARDI. Well, he should know. They hire these people. Now, what are you asking me to do now?

MR. GLICKSTEIN. If you have any explanation as to why there aren't more Negro and other minority group bartenders, bellmen, people in supervisory and managerial positions, waiters?

MR. BELARDI. Well, the bartenders, I understand that they are doing pretty good to get more and more bartenders on the job. But, unfortunately, I have to agree with Mr. Sullivan that it is not a simple job to become a bartender. It does create some understanding of the job, how to handle people. It also has hard working hours. They work at night, work Saturdays and Sundays and around the clock, and a lot of people who are able to do this work shy away from it actually and go for something different that has better conditions and pays better wages. It is a skilled job. You can't put it in the category of non-skilled.

MR. GLICKSTEIN. There are Negro bartenders in San Francisco who aren't members of the union. Isn't that correct?

MR. BELARDI. Not that I know of, unless you are now talking about the non-organized areas.

MR. GLICKSTEIN. That is what I am talking about, yes.

MR. BELARDI. Oh, yes, there is.

MR. GLICKSTEIN. There are Negro bartenders in San Francisco who are not organized?

MR. BELARDI. This is correct; sure. Chinese also.

MR. GLICKSTEIN. Mr. Sullivan indicated that the hotels are required under the collective bargaining agreement to obtain employees from the union. Is that correct?

MR. BELARDI. Well, at one time this was 100 percent correct, but then they had a bill here that they call the Taft-Hartley bill that changed that somewhat around. It was my understanding, and I don't know how much of this is in practice, we ought to give them a list and they ought to choose out of that list on qualified people from the various unions, and then if they aren't able—and then they have the right to turn him down, anyone that we send—then they have the right to go on the outside and, if they do, they have to become members of the union within 30 days.

MR. GLICKSTEIN. Is it your understanding that the employers as a general rule follow the referral system?

MR. BELARDI. Well, the only way I can answer that is, let's say, as I said, the enforcement of the contract comes through my office and every once in a while we find that some of the employers do not, but I assume that the most of them do follow that system.

MR. GLICKSTEIN. If you did organize the Negro bartenders that are unorganized in this town, they would then be on the referral list and be eligible for referral to the hotels. Is that correct?

MR. BELARDI. Oh, yes, sure.

MR. GLICKSTEIN. What problems has the union had in organizing Negro—you mentioned Negro and Chinese bartenders.

MR. BELARDI. Well, we could say what problems did the union have in organizing nonorganized workers. If you study the history of our collective bargaining in the hotels, restaurants, downtown, North Beach, it was a hard, long road to hoe, believe me, and needed a lot of money, and this question of moving into Chinatown and also Fillmore becomes a real difficult job, in my opinion. The picket lines today are not what they used to be as far as unions are concerned, and at one time when I first joined the union, people did picket duty for nothing. But that is not the case anymore.

So the question of finances has become a real big problem.

MR. GLICKSTEIN. And that is one of the reasons that your organizing activities have been slowed down?

MR. BELARDI. I would say that is the key reason.

MR. GLICKSTEIN. We just heard a report on the civil rights controversy in 1964 and 1966, and Mr. Sullivan also testified about that. It was your board that brought the arbitration proceeding that set aside that agreement. Why did you do that?

MR. BELARDI. Well, it is like everything else. We feel that we have the bargaining right to represent people working in the hotels, and if you permit somebody else to come in, no matter who, to start handling your problem for you, you probably won't be around too long. So we had no other choice but to demand our rights, if it was our rights; and, if not, we would find out that we had lost these rights. We had no other choice but to go in and to make this demand from an arbitrator to tell us which was right or wrong.

MR. GLICKSTEIN. Is it fair to say that when that agreement was signed, that the union was on the spot? On the one hand, the union was in favor of improving employment opportunities to minority people and, on the other hand, the union was very anxious to protect its collective bargaining agreement and its status as exclusive bargaining agent for the employees. Would that be fair to say that you had——

MR. BELARDI. I would say that it would be fair, right. You see, our Joint Board has been against discrimination for a long time. These Negro workers that you are talking about in these other non-crafts aren't there by accident, believe me. So we know something about this question of discrimination. We deny that we discriminate at this time. We further agree that probably we are not integrated in some of the unions as much as we should be. This is a difficult problem. When we found that the arbitrator cancelled this agreement, Civil Rights Agreement of 1966, we met with the Human Rights Commission and asked all parties concerned, including all civil rights groups, to meet with us to see if we couldn't find a solution to the problem of further integrating the crafts which are not integrated, and I understand the question here is that they want no excuses, that they want black people behind some of the bars, black people in some of the dining rooms. And this is the problem that we have been trying to find the solution to, and we have been meeting with the Human Rights Commission.

We are now working, as Mr. Sullivan testified, to the finishing touches of this collective—I mean the training agreement. I hope that the training agreement that we worked out works. I am not so sure and I wouldn't want to guarantee that all you need to do is sign an agreement, go to bed, take a pill, and tomorrow morning wake up and your problem is solved. I am hopeful that the agreement that we are now working out in training does work out.

MR. GLICKSTEIN. Do you know whether, after the 1964 Civil Rights Agreement was signed, that resulted in additional minority group people being employed by the hotel industry?

MR. BELARDI. Minorities?

MR. GLICKSTEIN. Yes.

MR. BELARDI. No, I don't know that the agreement of 1964 put on one employee that the union hadn't—didn't—the largest effort did anything.

MR. GLICKSTEIN. Thank you. I have no further questions.

CHAIRMAN HANNAH. Do the Commissioners have any questions?

COMMISSIONER FREEMAN. I would like to refer again to the training program that you are talking about because you agree with Mr. Sullivan with respect to the bartenders, but you added another point, and that is that the bartender is required to know how to handle people. Are you suggesting that black people and other minorities would not know how to handle people?

MR. BELARDI. I didn't think that I left that impression. If I did, that is not the case at all. There are many black people that can handle people much easier than the white people can, but I said that to become a bartender you have to have a certain philosophy of liking people and discussing with people and to a certain extent to be a confessor, to listen to all. It is not just quite mixing drinks, collecting money, and out you go. It is not that kind of a job.

COMMISSIONER FREEMAN. Well, has your union indicated that it is open for membership to all such people?

MR. BELARDI. Maybe I didn't understand the question. What was it again?

COMMISSIONER FREEMAN. Is your union open to membership to all such people?

MR. BELARDI. Yes.

COMMISSIONER FREEMAN. There seems to be some confusion as far as the employer is concerned, or I get the impression he felt that the person had to be a member of a hiring hall, that the union had to refer the person. He had been a member and I gather from what you said that this is not required as long as the person joins the union within 30 days after having become employed?

MR. BELARDI. I don't think that our union requires anybody to join the union before they get a job, but let me clarify this. Maybe I was confused.

First, we supply the list. They select from the list. If they find that there is no one that is capable of doing the job—and don't forget the sole judgment is the employer, according to our collective bargaining agreement—then they can go on the outside and take anybody that they want and we are obligated to take them in, irrespective of race, color, religion, or otherwise, and I don't know of any that has been rejected.

Had they been rejected, in the collective bargaining agreement it provides specifically that any person that feels that he is discriminated against shall have the right to the use of the adjustment board procedure of the collective bargaining agreement, and up to this time we haven't had one case filed against any——

COMMISSIONER FREEMAN. Is the opportunity to get on that list freely available to every minority?

MR. BELARDI. Yes, I would say that every minority has an opportunity to get on the list in accordance with the agreement.

COMMISSIONER FREEMAN. With respect to every category covered by your union?

MR. BELARDI. Well, I again repeat. Maybe I don't understand the question, that my union at this time does not discriminate nor do they intend to discriminate in the future. This I say.

COMMISSIONER FREEMAN. Thank you.

CHAIRMAN HANNAH. Any other questions? Father Hesburgh?

COMMISSIONER HESBURGH. Just a brief one, Mr. Belardi. What is the best way to get in the union? Is it apprenticeship programs such as craft unions have, or is it on-the-job training?

MR. BELARDI. You see, we have several different crafts. You take the cook's craft. This is an apprenticeable trade.

Many years ago all cooks came from Europe. Even in my time I remember, in order to work at the Palace Hotel, you had not only to be European, but understand some of the French language. An American had a difficult time. So you have to have some training and that is an apprentice program.

I think that the last two people that we have in training in the hotels, as far as cooks are concerned, are Negroes. Now, the other crafts are different but, as I testified, and Mr. Sullivan testified, we have now worked out a program of on-the-job training which we are hopeful will solve the problems that we have been looking forward to solve.

COMMISSIONER HESBURGH. This is more effective, you think, than an apprentice classroom type of thing?

MR. BELARDI. No, there is a difference in comparison. This would not be effective at all in cooks because you are not going to teach a cook in 13 weeks, and the MDTA came in and tried to do just this, and all it did is what we said it would do: load people who thought they were cooks and were unable to do the job. Maybe with some of the waiters and waitresses, that sort of program would do it, but not all crafts.

COMMISSIONER HESBURGH. Thank you.

CHAIRMAN HANNAH. Any further questions? Mr. Taylor?

MR. TAYLOR. Mr. Belardi, were you saying before that there might be a problem that white people wouldn't want to tell their troubles to a Negro bartender?

MR. BELARDI. No, I didn't say that. I said generally people go have a few drinks at a bar and they want to give the bartender their problems, and so it is a little bit of different job than an ordinary just making drinks and making change.

MR. TAYLOR. I was just thinking maybe every bar ought to have a white bartender and a Negro bartender and a Mexican American bartender and an Oriental bartender, so everybody can pick the bartender of his choice.

MR. BELARDI. They can't use that many bartenders. They usually only have one or two, but I am not saying that a Negro can't be a bartender. I think he could be a good bartender.

MR. TAYLOR. Thank you.

CHAIRMAN HANNAH. Thank you very much, Mr. Belardi.

MR. BELARDI. Oh, I was told that I could leave a statement here.

CHAIRMAN HANNAH. We will put it in the record.

MR. GLICKSTEIN. Could we introduce that as Exhibit No. 13, Mr. Chairman?

CHAIRMAN HANNAH. It is received.

(The document referred to was marked Exhibit No. 13 and received in evidence.)

MR. GLICKSTEIN. The next witness is Mr. William Bradley.

(Whereupon, Mr. William Bradley was sworn by the Chairman and testified as follows:)

TESTIMONY OF MR. WILLIAM BRADLEY, SAN FRANCISCO, CALIFORNIA

MR. BRADLEY. I have a statement before the questions are asked because my organization authorized me to say something very briefly and then that really concludes whatever we have to say.

MR. GLICKSTEIN. Would you first please identify yourself for the record, Mr. Bradley, your full name and address?

MR. BRADLEY. Bill Bradley, 1686 O'Farrell, representing the Afro-American Institute.

MR. GLICKSTEIN. Would you just tell the Commissioners what the Afro-American Institute is before you make your statement?

MR. BRADLEY. The Afro-American Institute is an organization of black people dedicated to the survival of black people.

It is very clear that these hearings are a waste of time. They are an insult to black people and that you would call black people here, threaten them under legal subpena to give you evidence that you have compiled year after year that hasn't done a single black person in the United States of America a single bit of good is an insult to the entire Afro-American race.

We sit here today and we hear people laugh and giggle about reports that are clearly lies. We see white people sit up here representing both management and labor who are not only liars, but murderers, systematically starving our people to death in the hotels, the restaurants, and the unions of this city.

You, this very same Civil Rights Commission, has presided in the past over hearings in Mississippi, Alabama and other Deep Southern States where black people have testified under pain of the loss of life. Recently, I think today, they reported that in Sunflower, Mississippi, black people had an election stolen from them that they had every right legally to win, and all you have been able to do is to compile reports.

We are sitting now, you are compiling evidence while black youth are being systematically exterminated in Vietnam.

I don't think that this Commission is going to do anything about the human rights of black people or any other nonwhite people in this country. You have clearly demonstrated in the past. That is a fact, I think, that stands on the record right now. All of the legislation that you talk about enforcing, the 1954 Supreme Court decision, the President's Executive orders, Civil Rights Acts,—none of them has improved the condition of black people. Our condition has gotten worse since these bills have been passed.

I think it is very clear that these hearings are useless and that there is no real purpose for at least a representative of this organization to answer any questions from this Commission. Thank you.

CHAIRMAN HANNAH. Any comments? No? You are excused, sir, unless somebody has a question. We will now recess for 10 minutes until 4 o'clock.

CHAIRMAN HANNAH. Mr. Maxwell, the witness who is scheduled at this moment isn't here yet. You have asked for an opportunity to be heard for five minutes. If you would care to come forward, we will listen to you now.

(Whereupon, Mr. Ben Maxwell was sworn by the Chairman and testified as follows:)

TESTIMONY OF MR. BEN MAXWELL, SAN FRANCISCO, CALIFORNIA

MR. MAXWELL. I am Ben Maxwell. I am with the Welfare People for Justice Organization and I am also a candidate for mayor of the city.

I admire these people for coming here to find out the problem that we have in our city, but I feel as though that we are a city of the West in which we are supposed to lead the people and not have the people leading us.

The Commission here, I feel as though that you are doing a great thing by coming, but our leaders, our mayor, should be the one to lead us, should be the one to step out.

As a whole, you have had these people come to you and explain to you about houses, have come to you and explained to you about labor—all of these people that have come to you and have explained to you, but they have not come and told you the actual story of what is going on. The labor, they eventually avoid questions. The building material man, he is avoiding the questions. He is not actually telling you exactly what is going on. All of these people are telling you the wrong thing.

We have in our city, our ghettos; the first thing they should tell you is that the ghetto began through the white race because when the white move out, this is when they move the Negroes in. At the present time they are in the process of building homes in Daly City. Eventually they will move in and tell the whites—move into a neighborhood and put two or three Negroes in a white neighborhood and sort of panic the white and tell them they would be better off moving into this district where you have better homes, better police, better sewage facilities, and better streets. All of these things he will explain to you, but yet and still he doesn't come down and really come out and tell the actual facts about the thing.

The jobs—he discriminate in jobs. You come along and you ask him for a job. He tell you you can't—"We will hire you, O.K. We will hire you. Sit down and we will take your application." When he finish with the application, he looks it over, "Oo, this is a good application," but when you leave out of his office he tear the application up and throw it in the trash can. This has been revealed to me more than one time.

Myself, I put in an application in 1965 at the Standard Oil Company and at that particular time Standard Oil had built a new building. They did not offer to call me at no time whatsoever, and at that particular time, '65 up until '67, which is two years, with that two years' time they have had an opening for me if they wanted to give me a job. They didn't want to give me any. Not only me, but tno minority race as a whole. They suffers. They are the ones that is the least thought of, the minority race is a race of people that we don't know nothing about until we need them and that time is during the war or either political. We don't need these people during the wartime and political time if we can't use them during peacetime.

Now, as a whole, you as citizens, you come along and you say, "Well, all right. I am going to do this. I am going to write this report," but when you finish with the report up and everything, it is going to be about two years, because when you send the report back to Washington, all the other reports that you have filled in already, they have to go and sit down and go through all of these reports. And after they finish going through these report, it takes about—it is going to be about at the end of the year, and by that time our President will be in the middle of a political race for reelection. Then that is going to take about two years before you really come along and do something about it.

The best thing for you to do is to let these people know. They say give them something to work with. They already have something to work with. You give them something to work with. You give them equal employment opportunity and they didn't work with that. So the next best thing for you to do is to take their license away from them.

Anyone that is found discriminating against any minority race, their license should be revoked. It makes me feel sad when I look up and see that a minority race of people trying to do—trying to get a hold and these people are cutting them down. They cannot—they really cannot do anything for theirselves because they don't have the capital. They can't bid on these government jobs because of the capital. How are they going to bid on these jobs if they don't have the capital and enough of the equipment, the right kind of equipment? They will say, "Then you can't bid on this job," and I feel that these—many of the big wheels coming in here, in and out, they coming in and sitting up here with their lawyer. It is the same thing you got going on in Washington and all over the country.

And so I ask of you to please, when you make this report, make this report and let the people know that you really intend to do something. Don't make the report and take it and when you get it back to Washington, throw it in the trash can like the rest of these people, because, actually, I am beginning to get at the point right now where I am tired of sitting up and looking at people, looking before many people like you all and standing up, coming up, sitting in here to solve what? A minority problem. You know, I am a Negro. I admire being a Negro and I admire being a member of the minority race because for the simple reason it must be something about the minority race that you keep coming in wanting to find out why it is that they want to keep these minority people from working.

Why is it that they want to keep these minority people—they always want to have something that they say minority is lazy: they don't want to do nothing but draw welfare checks and things like this. If you would really go into the different homes and see the things that is going on, some of the minority race of people that qualifies for jobs, actually that have the diploma for jobs, and yet and still when they go to these different companies and as for the telephone company, they have got to be a certain size or either any of the other different places around here you got to be a certain size or we don't have any openings, and yet and still they have an opening. They have it advertised in the newspaper every day. "We have openings for—we need operators, telephone operators."

Now, what are you going to do about these people? The best thing for you to do is—you don't have to sit up there. The best thing for you to do is to go back to Washington and pass the law and state that anyone that is caught discriminating, their license should be revoked regardless of whther it is public or private.

We have a club here which is the Olympic Club, is supposed to be one of the best clubs. It is, but it discriminates, but our mayor belonged to it. So if our mayor belonged to a discriminating club, that means he is not for the minority race, and not only the minority race that is being discriminated against. It is some whites that is being discriminated against, but the thing about it is it is the poor white people that is being discriminated against and to a certain extent that these people—they can't get help because they living in a Negro neighborhood or something. But someone might come along and help them out and then when they do get on their feet, they rush them out of that Negro neighborhood. Thank you very much.

CHAIRMAN HANNAH. Mr. Maxwell, we are happy to have you appear before us and we have kept our commitment to you.

Is the next witness here?

MR. GLICKSTEIN. Yes, Mr. Chairman. Before we call the next witness we have had submitted to us a number of statements by various persons and groups and, if I may, I will read out the names of these persons and submit them into the record.

CHAIRMAN HANNAH. Proceed.

MR. GLICKSTEIN. We have a statement from Printers Local Union No. 4. May it be received as Exhibit No. 14?

CHAIRMAN HANNAH. Received.

(The document referred to was marked Exhibit No. 14 and received in evidence.)

MR. GLICKSTEIN. A statement from the United States Employment Service. May it be received as Exhibit No. 15?

CHAIRMAN HANNAH. Received.

(The document referred to was marked Exhibit No. 15 and received in evidence.)

MR. GLICKSTEIN. A statement from the Berkeley NAACP. May it be received as Exhibit No. 16?

CHAIRMAN HANNAH. Received.

(The document referred to was marked Exhibit No. 16 and received in evidence.)

MR. GLICKSTEIN. A report from the California State Employment Service. May it be received as Exhibit No. 17?

CHAIRMAN HANNAH. Received.

(The document referred to was marked Exhibit No. 17 and received in evidence.)

MR. GLICKSTEIN. A statement from the Hon. Terry A. Francois, member of the Board of Supervisors. May it be received as Exhibit No. 18?

CHAIRMAN HANNAH. Received.

(The document referred to was marked Exhibit No. 18 and received in evidence.)

MR. GLICKSTEIN. A complaint from Mr. Antonio Alacon. May it be received as Exhibit No. 19?

CHAIRMAN HANNAH. Received.

(The document referred to was marked Exhibit No. 19 and received in evidence.)

MR. GLICKSTEIN. A statement from Mr. Alfred C. Simmons. May it be received as Exhibit No. 20?

CHAIRMAN HANNAH. Received.

(The document referred to was marked Exhibit No. 20 and received in evidence.)

MR. GLICKSTEIN. A statement of Mr. Ricardo Callejo. May it be received as Exhibit No. 21?

CHAIRMAN HANNAH. Received.

(The document referred to was marked Exhibit No. 21 and received in evidence.)

MR. GLICKSTEIN. A statement from the California Fair Employment Practice Commission. May it be received as Exhibit No. 22?

CHAIRMAN HANNAH. Received.

(The document referred to was marked Exhibit No. 22 and received in evidence.)

MR. GLICKSTEIN. A statement from the Parents and Taxpayers Association. May it be received as Exhibit No. 23?

CHAIRMAN HANNAH. Received.

(The document referred to was marked Exhibit No. 23 and received in evidence.)

MR. GLICKSTEIN. A statement from Mr. Daniel M. Ortega. May it be received as Exhibit No. 24?

CHAIRMAN HANNAH. Received.

(The document referred to was marked Exhibit No. 24 and received in evidence.)

CHAIRMAN HANNAH. They are all received and put in the record. Will you call the next witness?

MR. GLICKSTEIN. The next witness is Mr. Rosalio Sandoval who will be accompanied by Miss Patricia Delgado, Mr. Charles Goldberg, and Mr. Gabriel Vicario. Mr. Sandoval, are you ready to testify?

MR. SANDOVAL. I haven't got the other one here.

CHAIRMAN HANNAH. Is this going to be another one of these stage productions?

MR. GLICKSTEIN. Are the three young people here who are supposed to accompany you?

MR. SANDOVAL. Yes, but I think we are early.

MR. GLICKSTEIN. We are running a little ahead of schedule. Would you please——

CHAIRMAN HANNAH. Will you raise your right hand to be sworn, sir? Are the other gentlemen going to speak, too?

MR. SANDOVAL. Well, yes.

MR. GLICKSTEIN. Where are the other two? Are they here, the other two students?

MR. SANDOVAL. Yes.

MR. GLICKSTEIN. Would they come forward?

MR. SANDOVAL. Well, they are on the way over. They are not here. I mean, they are parking the car right now. They are not here yet.

MR. GLICKSTEIN. Why don't we proceed and wait until they come in?

(Whereupon, Mr. Rosalio J. Sandoval and Mr. Charles Goldberg were sworn by the Chairman and testified as follows:)

TESTIMONY OF MR. ROSALIO J. SANDOVAL, SAN FRANCISCO, CALIFORNIA AND MR. CHARLES GOLDBERG, SAN FRANCISCO, CALIFORNIA

MR. GLICKSTEIN. Mr. Chairman, I would just like to mention that we are expecting Mayor Shelley to arrive about 4:30 and he has a very tight schedule and we agreed to interrupt whatever testimony is taking place so he could testify.

CHAIRMAN HANNAH. Would that be agreeable, Mr. Sandoval, when the mayor comes we will listen to him and excuse you and then put you back on the stand after he has come?

MR. SANDOVAL. That will be all right.

CHAIRMAN HANNAH. Fine. We will proceed with you until the mayor arrives and then we will put you back on to finish.

MR. GLICKSTEIN. Would you each please state your full name and address for the record?

MR. SANDOVAL. Let me ask a question first, please.

MR. GLICKSTEIN. Would you please identify yourself and give your name and address for the record?

MR. SANDOVAL. Yes, I will but I still feel that I would rather wait until the other two people come if you don't mind. I would like to ask this favor of you because we were supposed to appear together and I think Mr. Goldberg and the other two students would feel better if they were all here together. I am not trying to prevent us from appearing, but——

CHAIRMAN HANNAH. Is there another witness that follows Mr. Sandoval who is here?

MR. GLICKSTEIN. Will you testify, Mr. Sandoval?

MR. SANDOVAL. All right. My name is Jack Sandoval. I am director of Horizons Unlimited Project and——

MR. GOLDBERG. Charles Goldberg.

MR. GLICKSTEIN. Will you each tell the reporter your address?

MR. GOLDBERG. 98 Blackdale.

MR. GLICKSTEIN. What is your address, Mr. Sandoval?

MR. SANDOVAL. Mexican American.

MR. GLICKSTEIN. What is your address, Mr. Sandoval?

MR. SANDOVAL. Mexican American.

MR. GLICKSTEIN. Your address.

CHAIRMAN HANNAH. Your home. Where is your home?

MR. SANDOVAL. 3277 Mission Street.

MR. GLICKSTEIN. You mentioned you were director of the Horizons Unlimited Program. Would you please describe that program and tell us what its objectives are?

MR. SANDOVAL. Yes. Horizons Unlimited is a program funded by the Office of Economic Opportunity for the specific purpose of aiding potential high school dropouts to remain in high school. We offer counseling services, individual and group therapy, tutorial services, and we offer employment internship.

We also have family aid services, which was not written in the original contract, but there is a great need for it. So we also offer parental therapy, group and individual. We also develop programs between the school and students, the police department and the students, the police, the parents, and the school department. That's Horizons Unlimited basically.

It is supposed to develop leadership in the student, and it is only for a period of one year.

MR. GLICKSTEIN. How many people are participating in this program?

MR. SANDOVAL. We have 80. The contract was written so that 40 would be handled per semester, but we have 80 in all.

MR. GLICKSTEIN. Eighty in all. And what type of backgrounds are these students from?

MR. SANDOVAL. The students are all from the lower income class. They are all well within the poverty index. Most of the students come from families that are on welfare, social security, or aid to dependent children. Most of them have low grades in school, and some have police records of a juvenile delinquency nature.

MR. GLICKSTEIN. What is the racial composition of the group?

MR. SANDOVAL. The majority is Spanish-speaking surnamed people. We do have, though, Filipinos, Samoans, American Negroes, and American Indians, but the greater part is Spanish-speaking surnamed people from the Mission District.

MR. GLICKSTEIN. Are many of the students dropouts from school?

MR. SANDOVAL. The majority of the students are potential high school dropouts. We do have some dropouts, but the majority of the students are potential high school dropouts.

MR. GLICKSTEIN. Mr. Sandoval, on the basis of your experience with this program, could you tell us what kind of difficulties Spanish-speaking students experience in high school?

MR. SANDOVAL. Yes, I could, sir, and if you will allow me, I

would like to read my statement on that better that I have prepared for this particular meeting.

MR. GLICKSTEIN. Is that a short statement or——

MR. SANDOVAL. It is a statement on the problems the Spanish-
speaking youth face in trying to acquire an education.

MR. GLICKSTEIN. Would it be possible for you to summarize
it or read it?

MR. SANDOVAL. Yes, it would be possible, but I went through
a lot of trouble because I have been subpenaed to appear here
and I would like to read this.

CHAIRMAN HANNAH. Go ahead.

MR. SANDOVAL. Thank you.

Mr. Chairman, members of the Commission, I am Jack Sandoval, Project Director of Horizons Unlimited. Horizons Unlimited, a program funded by the Office of Economic Opportunity,
is designed to help potential high school dropouts to remain in
school. Through this program we offer these students counseling,
tutorship, and employment internship.

In the beginning of the program it was our assumption that by
providing employment we would help the students to remain in
school. Through recent experiences in the last several months it
has been proven that employment is not the answer and it is not
meeting the problem that leads towards causing students to drop
out. Evidence over the last several months indicates that the lack
of education is the most acute of all social evils and the one evil
that creates dropouts.

When I say the lack of education, I am referring to my topic for
today, "Quality education and educational equality for all."

Today American education is caught up in a revolution of change
and growth that has not been matched in the history of this Nation. In every State, in every city, and in nearly every town, revolution is at work in the schools and in the community. It is marked
by a new, intense interest in two concepts: quality education
and educational equality for all.

All minorities are definitely not receiving this type of quality
education, specifically the Spanish-speaking youths. For over 200
years the ugly blot of discrimination and segregation has touched
the Mexican American and all Spanish-speaking groups.

The time has come that a dramatic change in the attitudes and
the ideas of both educators and the general public is needed as
to what our schools are today, what our schools should be, and how
they should change to meet their new needs.

We all know that the Spanish-speaking people are a definite
minority in this country. We also know that the poor and disadvantaged don't learn because they are classified as minority people
for two principal reasons: (1) The Spanish-speaking people lack

income and (2) lack of a history of educational attainment within their own immediate family.

Today throughout the country programs are being written to repair these disadvantaged children and to help them deal with their handicaps, but these programs are based on the premise that poor chidren are out-of-step and need reshaping. But the fact is that the programs being created are just reinforcing the inequality of education and the humiliation of the youth. It is not the children that are out of step or need reshaping, but it is the entire institutional structure of our educational system that is out of step and needs reshaping. In other words, the present educational method and the educational programs that are being developed today through the anti-poverty funds only serve to supplement the inferior educational practices. Until we provide quality education and equality in education for all, we will not satisfy the current needs of our Spanish-speaking people.

In all respects to the educators and those concerned with better education, the teaching methods in existence today are of the equivalent of giving a man aspirin to cure cancer. Until we improve our quality of education and offer education equality to all, our society will continue to rot from within.

We all know that the children enter school with great enthusiasm and that the longer they are exposed to school, the greater the loss of enthusiasm. Why? Evidently schools have been part of the problem and not part of the solution. Therefore, the educational system is placing barriers in the way of the education for the poor. Our educational system is developing programs to emphasize failure, inadequacy, and continue to stigmatize and spoil the image of the Spanish-speaking minority. This system is the key barrier impeding the educational development of the Spanish-speaking youth.

Learning experience should give the children a sense of contribution and a feelng of anticipation about the future and a guarantee that they will have a place in it. Today this is not happening to our Spanish-speaking youth.

Therefore, because our students feel that they are NOBODY and because society gives them the impression that they are non-contributors to our American way of living, they develop an attitude of being inferior, second-class citizens, and thereby lose all sense of motivation, personal identification which leads only to "pushouts" rather than "dropouts" from the educational system and exclusion from a society that will not employ him because he failed to receive an education.

The Spanish-speaking youth is dropping out of school not because he wants to, but because of a lack of choice and lack of future. We decide that certain people cannot be educated and re-

394

fuse to educate them so they grow up uneducated. In other words, we make our initial judgment not on their individual merits and capabilities, but on his parents' educational background, income level, and we prejudge the individual because of his cultural and ethnic heritage. So what happens? We have created a role expectation within the Anglo society in which it has been taken for granted that a Spanish-speaking person cannot be educated and believing that they are not capable of doing anything, so, therefore, the Spanish-speaking youth never has the opportunity of showing what his capabilities are. It is only a matter of time before a student realizes that he has been stamped as an ILLITERATE and NON-FUNCTIONAL HUMAN BEING, thereby causing the Spanish-speaking youth to lose all sense of motivation and accepting his role identification.

We further label the student and sort him out of his heterogeneous environment into a homogeneous environment. It is only a matter of time before the student realizes that he has been separated from the "bright group" and has been placed in the "stupid group." They soon fulfill the role expected of them and they believe in the "truth" of the school's judgment of them.

Thank you.

If you notice in the last page, I had some figures about the percentages of the Spanish-speaking students enrolled in the four largest high schools in the Mission District and the junior high school, and if you will look closely at the number of counselors, you can actually see that we are being massacred and our children are not receiving proper counseling, as these students here will testify before you today.

MR. GLICKSTEIN. Dr. Hannah, I believe Mayor Shelley has arrived. Perhaps we could let the mayor testify and then recall Mr. Sandoval.

CHAIRMAN HANNAH. Mr. Sandoval, if you and the two students would take chairs at the front of the room. If it is agreeable, we will put the mayor on. He has a tight schedule, as we agreed at this time, and then we will proceed with the balance of your statement.

MR. GLICKSTEIN. The next witness, Mr. Chairman, is the mayor of the city of San Francisco, Mayor Shelley.

CHAIRMAN HANNAH Mayor Shelley, we are delighted to have you here today and we would be very much interested in any statements that you would care to make.

MAYOR SHELLEY. Thank you, Mr. Chairman, members of the Commission.

May I present the gentlemen with me, Mr. Jack Kent, Mayor's Deputy for Development in the city, and Mr. Bill Becker, the director of the city's Human Rights Commission.

Mr. Chairman, members of the Commission. I have not prepared a general statement because the information that was given me, it may have been incorrect or the way it came to me was that the general pattern was not to have just prepared statements, but more to go into the questioning from the members of the Commission.

CHAIRMAN HANNAH. Correct.

MAYOR SHELLEY. And if that is the policy, then I am prepared to at least try to answer any questions that you care to ask me.

CHAIRMAN HANNAH. We would be happy to ask you questions, sir, but if you have something that you would like—

MAYOR SHELLEY. May I just say this: I think San Francisco, like every big city, is facing very definite problems, some of which are in the civil rights field, a great many of which may not be directly what we have, over the years, referred to as civil rights, but they are all called civil rights today, and part of it is the change and the shifting in population into the large cities, the lack of adequate housing programs with which to take care of these people, particularly at prices that they can afford, and if I may be critical of some of the policies of Federal agencies, in having spent some 14 years, 14½ years as a member of Congress, and served on committees of that Congress, knowing that quite often policy legislation is drafted which holds out great hope to people in the deprived or underprivileged or uneducated or neglected groups of our society, but then when it comes to appropriating the monies to carry those promises, those policies, into execution, there is a greap gap.

One of the problems we find, for instance, in getting into rebuilding programs and renewal programs and rehabilitation programs is that to get contractors who can afford to go in under what is generally referred to as Section 221 (d) (3) of the Housing Act for moderate cost housing. They are reluctant to go in because they say, "Well, we can't assure you that we can build and provide a rent or a purchase schedule that will really afford anything for the people you are trying to accommodate."

A great many of these people are not in the category that would be qualified for low-cost public housing. They are above that, but they can't go out and get decent housing for themselves and their family in the general market. And then we hear about the rent supplement programs and we looked upon this, and I know I helped support the whole idea of rent supplements as a legislator, but now I find myself for the past three and a half years in the administrative side in a city and find that that which we established as a policy is not adequate when it comes to being financed and that the actual supplemental program doesn't seem to have enough there to really get into a program locally.

We have had, like every big city, our problems. I don't think I have to tell anybody that knows my record that I have been a supporter and a champion of the civil rights programs over 23 years in legislative capacities, 22½ years in the State legislature of the State Senate and in Congress, and I still try to follow it up in an administrative capacity here.

When we had some conflict on job opportunities in this city in early 1964, we had the cooperation of a late great man, Jim Mitchell, James Mitchell, former Secretary of Labor. I appointed a Mayor's Interim Committee on Human Rights. We realized that a mayor's committee didn't have the authority to really get into the field and move as forcefully and as adequately as the times and the situations required.

And we proposed legislation. We proposed that there be an official commission created by ordinance, enacted by the Board of Supervisors of the city and county of San Francisco, creating a Civil Rights Commission and Mr. Becker is the director of that, and I see the former director, Mr. Frank Quinn, sitting over here to my left.

There were months of hearings before the board. It was created and it has been funded. It has been working. As each of these situations developed, we have tried to meet them, but the finances and the resources of the cities, of any city, and this city is no exception, are not adequate to meet them in their entirety. We have looked and we continue to look and we will look more and we will press more to the Federal Government for support, assistance, and aid in meeting these programs of our changing times.

Very frankly, lady and gentlemen, I think we are going through a period of social revolution that must be recognized, revolution that is an effort to achieve the constitutional guarantees which all people think they are entitled to and feel they are entitled to and are entitled to.

One of the problems, and I think you will probably hear this from every mayor of every big city in the country, that we bump into is that when we go to set up programs and get Federal funds, we are told: here are our guidelines and these guidelines are written for an across-the-board application, and what may apply in one city might not apply at all in another. And I will very honestly say that as mayor of a large city, now approximately three and a half years, I am one of those who have supported and will continue to support the idea of block grants to cities with basic lines written in it simply to safeguard any misuse or misappropriation or misspending of funds, but allowing the city to write a program that will meet its own needs to a great extent.

We have bumped into a situation just recently, but I think I might just as well call it to the attention of this Commission. The

President pulled together unspent funds in several programs to set up an employment program over the next year to take effect early this summer, early in June. The basic guideline was that the prime agency or the primary contracting agency be the Anti-Poverty Council or the Economic Opportunity Council in each community. This met with resistance from both management and labor in San Francisco, who felt that they did not want to have the Economic Opportunity Council, which they felt was set up on the side, telling them how to run a program, and it was suggested that there be a joint labor-management public body set up and then use the Economic Opportunity Council to supply the support of services, but without having the right to dictate how the program should be.

The discussions and the arguments and the fight are still going on, not only here, but in other cities and in Washington right now, because the basic guidelines written in Washington was it had to go through the Economic Opportunity Council, and there are those who don't have the confidence that the Economic Opportunity Council is skilled to decide backgrounds or adaptabilities for employment, that this should be a labor-management feature of people who have worked in the field and know something about how to fit people into job slots.

I think there may be some merit to this. We are trying to work out a compromise, but again I point it out to show you that the rigid guideline that came out of Washington has created a problem that we are still unable to get around and to lose about $4½ million that could mean a year's employment, possibly, to a great many people, some of whom have never had job opportunities or any background of real work, would be the most tragic and disastrous thing that could happen, and I am determined it will not happen in San Francisco. But we are having our problems in getting around the basic rule, as created, the road block right now.

Now, there may be other things that will develop as the questions go on, Mr. Chairman. And thank you for giving me the opportunity to speak.

CHAIRMAN HANNAH. Mr. Mayor, we appreciate your being here and, in order to conserve your time, I am going to suggest that the Counsel has three or four basic questions that he might like to ask for the record, and I am sure the Commissioners may have some questions they would like to ask. Then we will go on from there.

MAYOR SHELLEY. Thank you, sir.

CHAIRMAN HANNAH. Counsel, do you have any questions you would like to ask?

MR. GLICKSTEIN. Mr. Mayor, do you believe the private sector of the economy has played an active enough role in helping to solve the problems of minority group peoples?

MAYOR SHELLEY. I think they have played an active role to some extent, but I think that the part they play can be improved upon. I don't think you can ever achieve perfection. There are some who are reluctant to get themselves involved. There are others who are perfectly willing to get involved and do so all the time. It is not adequate here in San Francisco.

MR. GLICKSTEIN. You suggested that it probably would be preferable if Federal funds were given to the city without strings attached and let the city develop its own programs and guidelines for administering those funds?

MAYOR SHELLEY. According to the local situation, the local need, yes.

MR. GLICKSTEIN. Are there any other specific Federal programs that you think are necessary to help meet the needs in your city?

MAYOR SHELLEY. Well, I think one of them is the necessity for pulling together some of the efforts of some of the Federal agencies themselves. We find some of them competing. At the present time on the situation, the last incident I mentioned here is the OEO, Office of Economic Opportunity, competing with the Department of Labor. We had meetings in my office that lasted for several hours, and we found the representatives of these two groups in competition and it left us sort of in the middle.

We find differences of agreement between HUD, FHA, the Department of Employment, the Department of Labor, branches of the Department of Labor, the Department of Employment.

We were making some headway under the efforts of Mr. Luevano, who just resigned as the regional head, or the head of the regional office here of OEO. I am pulling all of these efforts together in the Federal agencies through the Federal Executive Board, but it has sort of stopped all of a sudden.

Now, they may be going further than I am aware of at this moment, but we were making some headway. I think this is vital to the carrying out of these programs, tying together the Federal efforts so they are not competing with each other or working in divergent channels.

MR. GLICKSTEIN. Mr. Chairman, I think I would like to defer to the Commissioners at this point.

CHAIRMAN HANNAH. Vice Chairman Patterson.

VICE CHAIRMAN PATTERSON. Mr. Mayor, I am interested in your idea of block grants to cities. Isn't it true that perhaps the greatest local initiative and control over any Federal programs in the history of the Government have been those of the OEO Anti-Poverty programs?

MAYOR SHELLEY. That's right, sir.

VICE CHAIRMAN PATTERSON. Well, wouldn't this indicate, then, that the block grants, which would go just a step beyond your EOC, might also have the same problems?

MAYOR SHELLEY. No, no, because, once the OEO was set up I don't think there were enough guidelines. If they were going to do it at all, they should have set some guidelines. I think if we are going to do it all over in creating an OEO here instead of going the route of the non-profit corporation, we would have done as we did with the Human Rights Commission: set up an official city commission which would be responsible to city government, its accounting procedures, appointees by the mayor on an across-the-board representative basis of those on minority groups and everything else in the city which we have done in the Human Rights basis. But we went the other route because we thought we would go faster, and we got into problems, sort of a group that is often out by itself, and we have no right to call on them for anything. They operate by themselves.

Now, under the block grant it is certainly my thought that it would come to the city itself, who would use its existing departments and agencies to work out programs and set up citizens' committees to work with those departments and agencies in developing the programs of what was needed.

VICE CHAIRMAN PATTERSON. What about the State government? If you bypassed it with Federal block grants to cities, wouldn't the State government feel slighted?

MAYOR SHELLEY. That's too bad. I speak as the mayor of the city. I think tying the State in—I know the attitude of governors. The former Governor of this State and I argued this quite often. I haven't had a chance to argue with the present Governor. I haven't seen him since he took office.

CHAIRMAN HANNAH. Father Hesburgh, do you have any questions?

COMMISSIONER HESBURGH. Mr. Mayor, do you have a model city program projected for San Francisco?

MAYOR SHELLEY. We do not, Father.

COMMISSIONER HESBURGH. Wouldn't this give——

MAYOR SHELLEY. We served notice that we were intending to file an application. We put in over 10 months of work. Mr. Kent, as my deputy for development, conducted all the meetings. We found that first we had some problems under our city charter in regard to the requirement of city departments ceding certain of their rights to this new organization. We couldn't do that without actually a vote of the people to amend our charter, which would take a long procedure and no elections until this coming November, and I didn't want to have that kind of thing on the ballot at this time, because I am a candidate for reelection.

Now, the other thing was after 10 months of work we couldn't get an agreement amongst the neighborhood groups involved in the area proposed on the plan and the approach. Why? Because they were fearful, they were afraid; they mistrusted any agency of the Federal Government coming in even though it came in through city departments. They felt it would be beyond their reach.

Now, the model city, I know, set up a completely different approach, it called for the citizen participation, but there was complete hesitancy. Maybe Mr. Kent can supply more in detail as to some of his experiences out of that, if you would like to hear it.

COMMISSIONER HESBURGH. But as a result you won't have——

MAYOR SHELLEY. No. We then did not file our application, but we have not stopped working. We are using some city funds to continue the planning process, $70,000 of city funds, which actually could have been Federal funds, to continue the planning process, in the hope that on the next round we will have a program ready.

COMMISSIONER HESBURGH. Let me ask just one more quick one because I know the other Commissioners may have a question.

How do you feel about this general thinking one runs into all over the country today that with urbanization and the crowding in the central city and the flight of many white groups from the center of the city, it is almost impossible to face the fundamental questions of taxation, of education, of public services, except on a metropolitan, in fact, even on a regional, basis where it involves several States, like the New York-New Jersey complex?

MAYOR SHELLEY. Well, Father, I will try not to give you a jesuitical answer.

COMMISSIONER HESBURGH. Good. Not being a Jesuit, I will enjoy that.

MAYOR SHELLEY. Well, I have been educated by the Jesuits and I know what the term refers to usually, and I am proud of the education they gave me, if it sunk in at all.

I have said openly and publicly that the problem of our time and perhaps the very problem of whether or not our form of government will survive rests in the big cities of this country. Here is where the mass of people are and more coming all the time, most of them with no background of work experience for the type of work that might be available in this city. They come in from rural communities, rural backgrounds and, too, a great many of them without the educational backgrounds. Somewhere there is a gap that has to be picked up. No city can do it on its own. Therefore I think very strongly it is a national problem. This is part of the reason I suggest the block program, because I think the city has to solve its problems, but the financial aid must come from the Federal Government, and I think that unless we get down to an answer to this problem of what is the best way, this country is going to be in trouble.

COMMISSIONER HESBURGH. Do you favor the city and the suburbs joining together in a large metropolitan area to face the totality——

MAYOR SHELLEY. Yes, I have been an advocate of regional government. I recently went through some fights in what we call the Association of Bay Area Government, leading the fight for a proposal for regional government in this area, because no city is completely isolated today. All the open area between is growing up with more and more suburban development, some of which is blocked off and shut out.

One of the problems I think is very acute is in filling job opportunities. Let me first give you San Francisco's situation. San Francisco basically is not a great or a big industrial city. It has had along its history a lot of small industry, a great deal of which over the last 15 years is bit by bit moving out. Why are they moving out? Because we are only about 45, 46 square miles in our geographic area, the city and county of San Francisco, and these small industries were operating in two and three and four story loft buildings. Their handling expenses, their overhead were going up, and yet the property upon which that building was located kept increasing in value and they were on high cost property. They couldn't duplicate it or they couldn't build the type on single floor here in San Francisco, one, because the property costs were so high and, two, because there isn't that much land available. As a result, a lot of these small industries have moved down the Peninsula, across to Alameda County, Contra Costa County.

Resultantly our possibility of placing people in what I refer to generally as blue-collar work, manufacturing work, the general labor force, manual labor force, training them for skills and trades has been reduced except in the service trades, some in the building trades, because we are basically a commercial, a banking and investment city, and only twice in our history, during World Wars I and II, because of shipbuilding and related businesses did we build up a big industrial capacity.

When employment offices confine their requests for employment to the area in which the request emanates, the employer, and yet here in the big-core city is this great bulk of unemployed people, and they don't get a request, this is a break down. It is a break down in the employment service. It is a failure to take advantage of an opportunity to give people who may live in the core city an opportunity for a job that may be 20, 15, 18 miles away, a great many people who are willing and able to commute and would be glad to do it.

What the reason is I don't know, but I think it is a failure in the system to adapt itself to the problem.

COMMISSIONER HESBURGH. Thank you.

COMMISSIONER FREEMAN. Mayor Shelley, I have two questions. One concerns employment practices of the city administration itself, that is, with respect to those positions that you, as the top administrative officer, will control. Would you state what the employment pattern is with respect to the Spanish-speaking members of this community as well as Negroes?

MAYOR SHELLEY. You mean in the city government?

COMMISSIONER FREEMAN. In the city government.

MAYOR SHELLEY. In city government I don't know. We have been working along on a program. After I became mayor I sent a letter out and made a public statement of policy that the policy of the city and county of San Francisco, without any regard to what it may have been in the past, was one of employment without regard to race, creed, or color, and any job opportunities that were open, this policy would apply and should apply.

COMMISSIONER FREEMAN. Our information——

MAYOR SHELLEY. I think we have a number of nonwhite and Spanish-speaking people working in some departments, but I don't think that we have had enough of them.

Mr. Becker just tells me that generally we have about 2 percent of Spanish-speaking people employed in city government. Two percent of the 21,000 are employed.

CHAIRMAN HANNAH. If your people have any statistics, we would be interested in receiving them. Not now, but if you could send them to us, we would appreciate it. Go ahead.

MAYOR SHELLEY. We can get those for you.

COMMISSIONER FREEMAN. The other question, Mr. Mayor, some of the earlier testimony, I believe it was the first day when we were hearing testimony concerning conditions in Potrero Hill, there were persons who indicated to us that there was a need for city services for the residents of that area, that appeals had been made to the administration for, say, a multi-service center and this kind of thing, but that there had been no response. Would you care to comment on that?

MAYOR SHELLEY. Well, I don't know just exactly what services you are talking about, Mrs. Freeman.

COMMISSIONER FREEMAN. Multi-service center.

MAYOR SHELLEY. Multi-service center? There is a multi-service center being programmed. It is a State program, and now recently there is a threat to cut it out.

COMMISSIONER FREEMAN. There was also the implication that in those sections of the city that are predominantly occupied by members of the minority group that the services of the city were not adequate or were less than those in other sections where the people tended to be better off economically. Would you care to comment on that?

MAYOR SHELLEY. Well,——

COMMISSIONER FREEMAN. Garbage facilities, street-cleaning, this kind of thing.

MAYOR SHELLEY. Street-cleaning services, police services, fire services, ambulance services, because this city is a peculiar one in that we run our own emergency hospital, our own ambulance system. The employees are city employees, civil service employees. They are the same. There is no difference. I think there is one gap, and this is important, now, one that must be filled, that there has been a lag in the recreational services in these areas, but you can't solve that overnight. I say it as one who has been working on it to acquire the property for playgrounds in a given area where ground isn't open and the ground isn't available to get the money and budget ahead.

I think this is certainly one in which San Francisco has been deficient.

COMMISSIONER RANKIN. Mayor Shelley, all large cities have their problems with respect to city civil rights. Has San Francisco had any unique problems a little different from other cities?

MAYOR SHELLEY. Oh, I don't know if they are any different from other cities. I meet with some of these other mayors, and we have these mayors' conferences, and it seems we all have the same problems.

But one of the things I might as well get it out here that bothers me a little bit as an old civil rights fighter is the fracturing off of our society today into groups. I wonder if we are not all forgetting that we are looking to achieve an American basis of freedom for all people and that we are Americans and that we are weakening the possibility of getting it on that basis when we split off into nationality groups and this religious and that ethnic group and that colored group, each one working at cross purposes and demanding something on their own because really what they each want or all want is all the same thing.

Now we have had the Palace Hotel sit-ins. We had the Van Ness Automobile Row sit-ins. We had the disturbance of Hunters Point last fall, but I think some of these things are what every big city has gone through. I don't think they are any different. Maybe to us at the moment they seemed more crucial or more critical, more out of line, but when you look at what is happening——

COMMISSIONER RANKIN. Well, have you come close to solving any of them? I know you never solve them, but I wonder if there is any particular——

MAYOR SHELLEY. We have made headway, but we are not close and we will not solve them until we first find that the man can get the bread. What he needs more than anything else is jobs, jobs and job assurance, and the ability to get the job and to hold it. I think this is the basic answer to this whole problem of our society.

CHAIRMAN HANNAH. Dean Griswold?

COMMISSIONER GRISWOLD. Mayor Shelley, I must confess that I get the impression from various things I have heard here that the city government itself—and I am not speaking just to your administration; I am speaking of the past good many years—has been rather slow in recognizing the Spanish-speaking or Spanish American element in the population and, for example, has provided a rather surprisingly small number of jobs for Spanish Americans and has done very little through its school system to recognize the needs of children whose language at home is Spanish. Is that a fair statement?

MAYOR SHELLEY. Well, let me without looking or making any comment about any individual in the school system or any particular pattern. I think our whole educational system needs a whole overhauling and re-gearing towards these problems today. In fact, I tried to meet part of this situation by appointing a couple of people to the Board of Education in this city. The Board of Education under State law is autonomous and separate, but the mayor does appoint people, and then they are confirmed at the next election or refused confirmation, and I appointed two very active, intelligent, forward-looking people whom I think will help rejuvenate the attitude of the school department. Now, in regard to general employment——

MR. SANDOVAL. Mr. Chairman, the mayor is not answering Mr. Griswold's question. He is shying away from it.

CHAIRMAN HANNAH. Wait a minute, Mr. Sandoval. Will you please take your chair and for the last time, Mr. Maxwell and Mr. Sandoval, you will have an opportunity later. Mr. Maxwell has been heard.

MAYOR SHELLEY. In regard to general employment, this is a city that is run very definitely by a civil service system. There is no spoils system. I think the mayor has about four jobs outside of commissioners on Fire Commission, Police Commission, Housing Authority, and others—about four jobs he fills. Most positions or practically all of our positions are filled by examination.

Then we come to the next step. Are the requirements or the qualifications to be able to take that examination too high, and this is the great argument that we are going through now, in an effort to open up slots to people who haven't had the educational background under the requirements as they have existed for some years or who may have police records because of arrests on some misdemeanor or speeding thing or something when they were a young person that is past and forgotten now. But under our general law these things became factors.

We are working on a program of new careers trying to open up some of these fields to some of these people. It may take some change in law. Generally we haven't done enough, but we are trying to get into this field as fast as we can.

COMMISSIONER GRISWOLD. I would like to turn to another item. I recognize the problems of the cities, especially what is sometimes called the central-core city, although in some ways San Francisco is different in that respect from some others, like Philadelphia or even Boston, which are more or less completely surrounded by suburbs.

You said earlier in your statement that you thought that the only solution came from having the money supplied by the Federal Government and, as a citizen of Massachusetts, who all his life has read about the oil and gold and the scenery and the sunshine in California, I wondered a little bit why this shouldn't be the State of California that should help you solve this problem, rather than all of us back East.

MAYOR SHELLEY. Well, Mr. Griswold, I would like to ask this question: Don't you think it is a national problem?

COMMISSIONER GRISWOLD. I think it is a State problem first and a national problem. It is a problem for all of us, but I am a little concerned. After all, this is the biggest and the wealthiest State in the country. Why should you be turning to Washington to help bail you out of your problems? Why doesn't California dig into this?

MAYOR SHELLEY. Because I think your mayor, John Collins, and Jerry Cavanaugh of Detroit, have done a far better job than we've done of dipping into those Federal funds.

COMMISSIONER GRISWOLD. We are not nearly as big a State as California. We don't have a drop of oil. I never heard of an ounce of gold being taken out of Massachusetts. Maybe we need it, but I find great difficulty in thinking that you really exhausted the possibilities of impressing on the State of California, and I realize Los Angeles has similar problems, too, and you might work with them, not to mention San Diego and other places. But recognizing that this is a metropolitan problem, why shouldn't it be dealt with in California as a State problem without saying, "Oh, well, Washington will bail us out"?

MAYOR SHELLEY. Well, Mr. Griswold, I would like to nominate you to talk to the Governor and suggest that program. May I also point out, sir,——

COMMISSIONER GRISWOLD. Let me say in response to that I don't think that is a very good answer because you had another Governor for quite a while and you didn't do anything under him.

So I don't see that it turns on the personalities of the Governor. It seems to me it turns more on the conception of the responsibility of the State, and I wonder if you people in political life ought not

406

to be doing more to get this State to accept its responsibilities in this area.

MAYOR SHELLEY. You may have a point. It has not been approached that way. The approach has been directed to the city except on one or two programs.

I may also point out that California doesn't get back any portion—I mean a small portion of the taxes they pay into the Federal Government.

CHAIRMAN HANNAH. Mr. Mayor, we appreciate your being with us this afternoon. Mr. Taylor has one question and we have exhausted the time that you have allotted to us, but—

Mr. Taylor?

MR. TAYLOR. Mr. Mayor, you spoke a few minutes ago of the fragmenting of groups along ethnic or racial lines, and I wondered whether you would agree the basic reason this seems to be happening is that government as a whole is not meeting the needs and not responding fast enough to the frustrations which have been piling up over a long time, and whether the key to this question does not lie with government and with private industry in reacting a good deal faster to the need for jobs, for education.

MAYOR SHELLY. I think this is true. I think what you said is true, but also government may have to re-gear itself in order to be able to act faster.

CHAIRMAN HANNAH. Thank you very much, Mr. Mayor.

MAYOR SHELLEY. Thank you, Mr. Chairman. Thank you, members of the Commission.

CHAIRMAN HANNAH. Now, Mr. Sandoval, if you will bring your people back. I think you had some more of your students that came who were not here at the beginning.

MR. GLICKSTEIN. There are two more.

MR. SANDOVAL. They haven't been sworn.

CHAIRMAN HANNAH. Mr. Sandoval, one young man was sworn. I wonder if we could have the other two rise and raise their right hands.

(Whereupon, Miss Patricia Delgado and Mr. Gabriel Vicario were sworn by the Chairman and testified as follows:)

TESTIMONY OF MISS PATRICIA DELGADO, SAN FRANCISCO, CALIFORNIA, AND MR. GABRIEL VICARIO, SAN FRANCISCO, CALIFORNIA

CHAIRMAN HANNAH. Now, Mr. Sandoval, will you introduce the new people? You can share the microphones. They are both alive so that each of you can take two. We regret, Mr. Sandoval, the necessity of interrupting your testimony. So we would first like to have you introduce the young people who have not been introduced.

MISS DELGADO. Gentlemen of the Commission, ladies and gentlemen of the Commission. I am here to tell you about some of the problems—

MR. GLICKSTEIN. Would you just identify yourself now? Give us your name and address and we will address questions to you a little later.

MISS DELGADO. I am Pat Delgado from 1723 Palou. I am a Horizons Unlimited graduate.

MR. GLICKSTEIN. Would the young man next to you please give us his name and address?

MR. VICARIO. Gabriel Vicario, 3140 Army Street, graduate of Horizons Unlimited for Mission District.

MR. GLICKSTEIN. Mr. Sandoval, would you tell us—

CHAIRMAN HANNAH. I think the young lady has a statement that she wants to give. Is that correct?

The understanding was that we would let them do this the way they started to and then let's have the questioning. They have a program they have arranged.

MISS DELGADO. I am here to tell you about some of the problems, but first I would like all the students, all the fellow students from Horizons Unlimited that came with us, to stand. Will you please stand?

CHAIRMAN HANNAH. Members of the project? Very good. Welcome.

MISS DELGADO. They are all kind of mad today because we all spent all afternoon making signs and everything, and the police took them away. So they are kind of upset about it.

And, well, you called us here. You subpenaed us here to hear our problems, because I came here yesterday and I heard that you haven't heard our problems, you haven't seen our leaders and you don't know what our organizations are. Well, you were talking to some of the leaders last night and you are going to be talking to us today. We are leaders. Maybe we are young leaders, but we are leaders and we are going to be the future leaders, and we are tired of all of you older people trying to tell us, you know, what is good for us when who should know better but us? And I would like to say that we had a Negro boy speaking with us. He was supposed to be here on the committee, but you wanted all Latin people. But it is not all Latin people's problem. It is all minorities' problem. It is a lot of the Spanish-speaking's problem, but it has the same to do with the Negroes and the same problem. And if you want to see leaders, you see us and I could take you down to the ghettos and I could show you all the leaders of the gangs if you want to see leaders.

And if you want to hear riots and if you want to hear us making noise, you say you can't see our groups and everything, you want to see us making noise, we will have some riots for you and you can see the noise that we will make, because there are problems here.

Maybe you are looking on the outside and you are not on the inside where we are and you can't just tell by letting us talk for five or 10 minutes what our problems are. You want to hear facts, you want to hear our problems, and you want to hear all the proof of it. You didn't give us enough time to show you all the proof of it.

You come here for three days and you let us, the kids, who know the problems more because we have to live with them for the rest of our lives, you give us a half hour to talk with you, and we split it between us, and we got a few minutes. So I am going to try to tell you what some of the problems are.

O.K. You say our schools—we go to school and we all want to go to college. We want a good education and we set out for it. O.K. We try to go to school and we go to our homerooms and the first thing we do is stand and we say the pledge. The pledge says that this is a free country and everything. O.K. We go in our history class and we learn what a free country it is. Then we walk out of the school doors and it is the end of it. You go back to your crummy little house and try to get a crummy little job and all you know is that your accent is different from everybody else's and so you just can't make it.

Then the schools, if you come up from the Latin countries, they don't have any special classes for you. They will stick you in anywhere. How can you make it through if you don't understand what the teacher is talking about?

If you go into a math class and you don't know one word of English and she is trying to explain to you, what can you do about it? You just sit there and then they say the Latins don't know anything. Sure, we don't know anything in that language and you see the kids coming out of school and you will pull one out of them and you say, "What did you learn today in school?" And they will look at you like you're crazy. "What do you mean, what did I learn in school?"

Most of the Latins that I know that just came recently from their country that came here and been to school, all the stuff they know they have learned in their own country. They haven't learned here. And then the jobs you give us. The little jobs with the $1.40 an hour that you take all the taxes out of, you know. We are paying our taxes for the jobs that you give us. Then you take all the taxes back out of it.

CHAIRMAN HANNAH. May I ask the members of the class— We appreciate your enthusiasm. You have been invited. You are guests of the Commission, and if we have any more applause we are going to ask you to leave the room, because we are here for serious business.

MISS DELGADO. Well, when you're 18, if you are not a citizen or you are a citizen, you go and fight in the war. You won't let them vote. You're under 18, you can't vote. Well, if you're 18 you got to wait until you're 21 to vote. So you have no say in your government and you don't even know what you are doing in Vietnam. All you know is that when you get drafted you just go, and then you won't even give them a measly job when they're 16 or 17, but you will send them to war when they're 18 if they have an education or not, and you won't even let them finish their education, push them out of school from their education.

Then—or sometimes you give us a little program, you know, like, you know, like we are sick, you know; we have a disease and we are going to you. You're the doctor because we are telling you our problems and we are going to you with our disease, and we have a bad disease like cancer and you're our doctor, and we finally get an appointment with you like right now.

So we got this appointment with you and we tell you what is wrong with us. So you give us this little pill. We don't know what it is, you know. We go home and we take it. It is a little aspirin, you know. So we come back, you know. We have this big problem. You gave us this little pill, you know, to solve our problems, and we come back and, you know, we go out and there is a receptionist, you know. Well, it didn't help any. Well, we will be back in another seven years, you know, because that is how long it took you.

You came here seven years ago. Our problems were here seven years ago. Our leaders were here seven years ago. And you went back and it took you seven years to come back. What made you come back now after seven years? The same problems are here. You didn't do anything. I don't know if you are going to do anything now, but I am telling you what the problems are. O.K.

And another thing, we have—There is an E.O.P. program [Educational Opportunities Program] at the University of California. It is supposed to be for Spanish-speaking peoples for opportunity to go to college. It is a program for opportunity to go to college, and yet Mission High School has the most Spanish-speaking people and they won't even send one lousy person to come to Mission High School and tell us about the program. Not one lousy person, and so nobody knows about the program at the university. So what are we supposed to do? I want to go to college and I don't hear about any of these programs because they won't bother to tell us.

And so that's all I have to say and—Oh, another thing. I would say thank you, but I don't think it is a privilege to be here. I think it is a right and I think you should have came a long time ago.

MR. GLICKSTEIN. Do either of you fellows want to make a statement?

MR. VICARIO. Well, we have lots to say.

MR. GOLDBERG. Absolutely.

MR. GLICKSTEIN. I wonder if you could each tell us, tell the Commissioners, where you were born. Were each of you born in the United States?

MR. VICARIO. Well, I was born in the South.

MR. GLICKSTEIN. In what part of the United States?

MR. VICARIO. Louisiana.

MR. GLICKSTEIN. And where were your parents from?

MR. VICARIO. From the Philippines and some part of Mexico. They were born out there.

MR. GLICKSTEIN. Miss Delgado, where were you born?

MISS DELGADO. I was born in San Francisco.

MR. GLICKSTEIN. And your parents?

MISS DELGADO. Spain.

MR. GLICKSTEIN. And Mr. Goldberg, where were you born?

MR. GOLDBERG. I was born in San Francisco. My mother is from Panama and my father is from back East.

MR. GLICKSTEIN. Your father is from where?

MR. GOLDBERG. Back East.

MR. GLICKSTEIN. Did you want to make a statement, Mr. Goldberg?

MR. GOLDBERG. Yes, I will. I am going to bring up the topic today of the high school dropout and why we are having this big problem today.

In the past you people have been looked upon as the big problem, but today it is—I feel it is one of the biggest problems in this community——

And when a student enrolls in the high schools in the Mission District, you know, they tell them a bunch of stuff, you know, about the school. It is a good school, all this and that, but then, you know, it all just changes towards the student. It makes him feel that he has come in there and they are not teaching him nothing. He is getting bored and either he drops out, if he feels this way, or either he tries to stick with it. If he does, he has many problems. And another thing about—another thing about this dropout thing is that not all students are dropping out. Most of the students are being kicked out. When you turn 18 years old at my school, they kick you out. You cannot go to any other school in San Francisco except night school or a day adult school or something like this. And I feel that we are being deprived of our education. We are being—actually being cheated out of it. We are not getting the proper books and the material and things like this, and I feel that even the slop they feed us at lunchtime, that is all a part of this, too.

411

MR. GLICKSTEIN. Are there Spanish-speaking teachers at Mission High School?

MR. GOLDBERG. Very few. They are very rare.

MR. GLICKSTEIN. How about Spanish-speaking counselors?

MR. GOLDBERG. None.

MR. GLICKSTEIN. None at all?

MR. GOLDBERG. No.

MR. GLICKSTEIN. What percentage of the students in the school, would you say, are Spanish-speaking?

MR. GOLDBERG. About 30.6.

MR. GLICKSTEIN. 30.6. What year are you in high school?

MR. GOLDBERG. I am a high 11.

MR. GLICKSTEIN. Can you give any impression about what percentage of students at Mission High School drop out before they finish?

MR. GOLDBERG. Well, I will tell you like this. There is more that drop out than graduate.

MR. GLICKSTEIN. And is it largely the language problem that leads to the dropout?

MR. GOLDBERG. Yes, I feel it is the language problem and most of the students are slow in reading, in math, in other subjects, and because they are, you know, are dropping behind in subjects like this, they lose their interest in school and they lose their interest in their education, and they do not come to school.

MR. GLICKSTEIN. Are there efforts being made in the school to interest—

MR. GOLDBERG. No, there isn't.

MR. GLICKSTEIN. —interest students in going to college?

MR. GOLDBERG. No, there isn't, no.

MR. GLICKSTEIN. I have no further questions.

CHAIRMAN HANNAH. Does the other young man have something to say?

MR. VICARIO. Yes, Mr. Chairman. I have one special problem about schools.

You see, I have been going to—I am a graduate of Horizons Unlimited and from them I was sent to an architect's office to work after school for two hours, and now I am a graduate and they can't handle me any more. And so I go to the University of California Extension Building voluntarily to an architect's class, and I have a very bad problem which only myself can help. I mean, there is no one there to help me in this world anyway except myself and I have been going there voluntarily, and during the day, a few days, I was looking for a job because I need one very badly. And I have been to every Youth Opportunity Center and they can't help me because I have to be either out of school for a certain amount of time—I mean exempted—and the jobs now are working through these Youth Opportunity Centers.

So it is quite impossible for me to get a 4/4 Plan because I went down and talked to the work counselor at school and I told him about my problem. I have a 3-year-old kid and I have to support her, and he says, "Well, son, just the other day a boy came down and told me his father died and he has to support his mother and," he said, "I couldn't do nothing for him" and so he gave me the impression that who cares? I mean, you know, the guy has worse problems than yours and we can't help you.

I mean, what are we supposed to do? If it wasn't for these architects, which are Caucasian, I wouldn't be back in school now. They were ready to throw me out. The principal, I mean the dean of boys, he told me why don't I quit school and come back in September. And now I am working my ass off just to get my grades that I am. And they gave me a chance after my mother went up there and pleaded with them, and the architect's lady, the secretary there, wrote a letter to them. I have it right here. It is somewhere here. But, anyway, the people from this organization went up there and asked them to give me a chance.

I have lots of talent. They just don't give you a chance to prove it. They go by the books. They say, "Well, here, you have been absent these many days. It is a State law that you come. We can't pass you and we can't take you in." Right now the school over there where I am going, you go to class five times tardy and you get an automatic F. What kind of encouragement is that to go to class? That school is so crowded you can't walk down the halls and get to your class and to your locker on time. You go to five times late and they are ready to throw you out. They just passed that. Well, you heard our complaints.

MR. GOLDBERG. I would like each and everyone of you to come out to our school one day. I mean just to see how our school is being run. Just to see how we are getting our education and how we are being cheated out of our education.

We walk down the halls like packs of cattle. This is just how small our school is and overcrowded. We walk down the halls like packs of cattle, and then you people wonder why we have riots and fights and things like this, and you people sit up here and call us down and tell us that the younger generation is crazy and stuff like this.

I would like for you people to come out there and see what is happening. I feel that you would be amazed how we are getting our education. The people, the staff at our school are encouraging us to drop out. They tell us, you know, "If you come late to school, why not bother to come to school? Why don't you stay home and go to sleep or something like this?" And one thing I want to ask everyone of you right now, I want to ask you what is going to happen to the people that drop out? What is going to happen to the people that drop out? They go to look for a job and the people tell them, "They don't want you. They don't want you because you don't have an education. You don't have no high schol diploma." Then you look on the other side for some of them are going to feel, well, "Man, we can't make it the honest way."

So I feel that because of this and the way the schools are run in the Mission District and other districts in San Francisco, I feel that the school districts are not doing nothing but filling up prisons and gas chambers and things like this. And this is the way I feel about it.

Why should we go to school? Why should we go to school? I want one of you to tell me one reason why we should go to school.

CHAIRMAN HANNAH. I don't think this is the occasion for speeches. We are interested in your presentation. It is a pathetic presentation.

I think the audience needs to recognize as well as you young people that in this country the responsibility for education is a State and local responsibility. If what you are telling us today is an accurate picture of what is happening in the Mexican American schools in the city of San Francisco or elsewhere, it should be a matter of real concern to all of the citizens of this community. The city of San Francisco and the communities around it are responsible for the operation of the local boards of education. The kind of a school that San Francisco has at the kindergarten level through the high school is determined by the people of San Francisco, by the taxpayers, by the Board of Education. The State of California has had a lot of publicity on——

MR. GOLDBERG. Damn all that! Wait a minute. I want to hear what you are going to do about it.

CHAIRMAN HANNAH. Young man, you will give me three minutes, then we are going to adjourn this session. We are here to listen. Let me answer your question. You asked why are you looking for an education.

There is only one purpose of public education or education of any kind and that is to make it possible for young people like you to take whatever God gave them in the way of potential and encourage them to make of it something that will make it possible for you as an individual to make the best possible citizen out of yourself that you can, fit you with some skill so that you can earn a living, give you some awareness of what society is so that you may be able to carve out a life for yourself that will be interesting and satisfying to you, but this notion that an education is something that people can assure you, this is not true. An education is something that every person has to achieve for himself and once achieved it is his. Nobody can take it away from him. You can't buy it, you can't steal it, or anything of that sort.

Now, there is nothing more important in San Francisco or anywhere else in this country than that we have the best possible educational opportunity for every youngster, every color, race, religion, whatever society he may have been born into. An opportunity to make of himself everything that he can, because this is what makes America America.

A great deal of discussion takes place as to why is it that America with 7 percent of the world's population and 6 percent of the world's land area leads the world in so many directions, economically, politically, socially, educationally, militarily, and all the rest. More than any other reason it is due to the fact that the founding fathers—

Now, you look bored, and we are going to terminate your part of this hearing as soon as this is complete.

You asked a question and one of the difficulties is that somewhere along the line no one has taken the trouble to make it clear to you and other youngsters like you in San Francisco and elsewhere what this world is all about and what education is all about and all you have a right to expect is an opportunity that society should give it to you, but then it is up to you to make use of it.

Now this Commission has been the victim in the last 24 hours of some interesting side-shows. We have no responsibility whatever for determining the kind of schools that San Francisco is going to provide for its young people. We have been interested in what you have to say, what some of your colleagues have had to say. It is typical of a problem, and I think we have had all the questions that we are going to have.

Father Hesburgh can preach a better sermon than I can, but there is something wrong when we have the kind of exemplification that we have had here in the last 24 hours, and I think the people of San Francisco and Central California better be concerned about more than the school system, because I am as certain as I am that I am sitting here this afternoon that there is nothing more important to this area than the kind of an educational system, the basic philosophy of the educational system, the availability of an adequate educational system opportunity for every youngster.

All we know is what you are telling us. If what you tell us is true, and if it isn't being provided, then we have problems ahead of us.

MR. GOLDBERG. Yes, but why don't you come on out there?

MISS DELGADO. I would like to ask you something.

CHAIRMAN HANNAH. Now, we are going to have no more presentations.

MISS DELGADO. You came to listen to us and now you are leaving. See, you won't even finish listening to us.

CHAIRMAN HANNAH. We will give each of you—

MISS DELGADO. You know, we want to do something before you leave and I think Gabriel better do it now.

DEAN GRISWOLD. Mr. Chairman, it has been said that we came to listen. I think we came to learn.

If you have facts that you can tell us, I would be very much interested in having them. If all you want to tell us is that you are unhappy and you are distressed and you are uncertain and you think there are all kinds of problems and somebody ought to do something about it, I don't think it is helpful to—

MISS DELGADO. All right.

MR. GOLDBERG. What do you mean—

COMMISSIONER GRISWOLD. Just a moment, please.

MISS DELGADO. Wait a minute.

COMMISSIONER GRISWOLD. We were told a little while ago that we came out here and denounced you because you were improper, and so forth. We haven't denounced anybody. We haven't said a thing. We are just trying to learn and if you could present us with facts which will help us to learn, it could be helpful to us and to you and I think that despite the fact that the eduational system is primarily a responsibility of the city of San Francisco and the State of California, this Commission does have a responsibility with respect to any aspect of it which might involve a denial of equal protection of the laws on the ground of race or color or religion or other grounds, but I repeat, mere expressions of emotion are not helpful, are not relevant, but facts would be, and if you have facts I would be glad to hear them.

MISS DELGADO. O.K. I would like to tell you a few facts. O.K.

You are a Civil Rights Commission. O.K. So you want to know about civil rights. O.K. You come to school in the morning and you are late and the principal will come out and he will look up and down the line and he will say, "Here you are, all you Latin boys again." Emphasize on the "Latin," "All you Latin boys, always late. You don't go to church 10 minutes late. So why should you come to school late? Why don't you just go home and sleep?" That's what they say. "If you don't want to come to school, drop out and then you can sleep all you want." And if you call that encouragement, and that is a fact, O.K., you go down, somebody is—O.K.—Like Gabe here. He was getting kicked out of school but he had a legitimate reason. He was looking for a job. He has a kid to support. He is looking for a job. He goes to school, and they tell him—they tell the members of the Horizons that came with him, "The best thing you can do for this boy is get him a full-time job. That will be the best thing you could do."

A full-time job might help him now, but what happens as standards in the United States are going up and up? A full-time job, and he is a dropout? What is he going to do all his life? What's his kid going to go through?

O.K. We want better schools now, but think of the future.. What about his little boy—I mean his little girl, his little girl. His parents didn't have an education. My parents didn't have an education. My mother went to third grade. So she can't help me in school. I have to help myself. I don't have any outside help until I got with Horizons.

O.K. So they gave me some outside help. A little tutoring, a little project, you know, that you guys sent down to—that somebody gave us. I don't really know who. O.K. So do you think that he wants to drop out of school now and then have a bad job and then have his daughter have to grow up and she get a bad education, too? We want an education. We really do. We are trying to get to college. We want to learn about these things. I want to talk to my counselor and I want to tell my counselor, well, I want to be a social worker. What classes am I supposed to take? He has got a long line of kids. You get five minutes each turn to talk to your counselor. And right outside you have got a long line of kids. They all want to talk to him too. So he says, "Well, I will put you down for anything and later on when you decide what you want you come in and tell me." And so I told him I wanted to be a social worker. "What courses do I take?" Nothing; no help or anything. So we just want to, you know, there is facts. Maybe they are brought out in emotions, but the facts are behind the emotions. You show your emotions because some facts is behind it pushing the emotions out because all these things that are against you, you just get them all inside of you and, sure, they come out as emotions, but if you were here longer maybe you would listen to them and we could show you the facts.

If you would go down—you are an outsider. You can't see what is going on. You are not here living it. You are not learning one thing and going out in the world and it is a whole total different thing. It is a different thing. You learn democracy in school. You learn everything. You learn U.S. history and you go in the South and they have a whole different U.S. history. What is the truth? Who is going to tell us the truth?

We have to find it ourselves, sure, but who is lying? Where, you know, where is all this coming from? Where is the two different histories? Where is everything? We would like to know.

MR. VICARIO. Well, I would like to know if you could say—I mean—well, this is the fact, what she just said, and the South is saying that they should have won the war and we are saying that we did win and we're right. The South is saying that they are right, but they just didn't get the chance. I mean, what kind of history is that? I mean, I don't know if this is a fact, but I do hear that. You take the history course here and you go to the South and you have got to take their history course before you can graduate. I mean who is the liar? Are we or are they?

Miss DELGADO. I would like to ask you one more question or put it this way. We are over here fighting in Vietnam with our soldiers, and everything, and we are fighting for their freedom. We are trying to get them free, but are we free here? Do we have the right to set an example for another country, when we are not even free here, when just because of our color or our accent we can't go and get a job we want or get an education we want, and you are trying to set an example for other countries?

If you would set a better example here, maybe there wouldn't be so many anti-American people, because we don't have that good example. If they would see our country run well, and everybody—you know, everybody's brothers and sisters, and everything, maybe they, too, would look, oh, that is a good country. Let's be like that, but when they see us, we don't have the right to help them fight their country.

COMMISSIONER HESBURGH. Patricia, I would be glad to say something on this and I will make it very brief. If you want to see me afterwards, I will be glad to see all of you afterwards.

I have been in, I suppose, in my lifetime in 70 countries. I lived abroad a good part of my life and I come home with the conclusion that there is no country on earth like the United States. It doesn't mean it is perfect. It never has been.

When the Good Lord was born two-thirds of the world was slave, at least two-thirds, but in this country you have one great thing. I have spent a lot of time recently in Latin American, mostly in Chile, Argentina, Peru, Bolivia, San Salvador, Nicaragua, Panama, Mexico, and in all of these countries the one thing that we have that they don't have is equality of opportunity that we are constantly earning day by day, step by step, and everyone is on his own to get it.

If any of you were born in Chile, say, in Southern Chile, anywhere from Santiago hasta Puerto Montt where most of the people in Chile live, desert in the north, fjords in the south, they live in the central part, the best that you could hope for would normally be five or six years of very, very bad education. What you are getting now would look like Paradise compared to what they get there because I have been in those schools and I have seen what they have.

I have been all through Africa and there again if you get five or six years of education in most of those countries it is amazing. One-half of the children in all of Latin America have never been inside a school building in their whole life and never will be.

Now, we have got all kinds of problems here. I am not saying
this except by some comparison. You say the rest of the world
ought to look at us and I think the only thing we have in this
country is a chance for equality of opportunity that is not perfect.
It is not perfect for Negro Americans. It is not perfect for Latin
or Spanish-speaking Americans. It is not perfect in some places
for Jewish Americans. There are all kinds of exceptions to the
rule, and the only reason this group here exists, we have to move
all around the country whenever we can find time, because we have
all got about ten full-time jobs besides this one. We are doing this
in our spare time, if there is any such thing, and all we are trying
to do is look at every part of the country to find out if perhaps
there might be some way through all of the operation of the big
thing we call government, we are mainly concerned with the Federal Government, but we are also looking at the effects of local
and State government, if there is some way that they might
buttress in some way or another freedom of opportunity, but,
believe me, the best advice I can give you, Patricia and the others
of your associates here, is that freedom of opportunity is not
something you get on a platter. It is something you grind out day
by day and you have to make your own way with it, and often
you start out with it in a very bad situation and you make it
better by getting the best you can and by making more available
to other people. But especially I think it is something that has to
start inside. You have got to have a hunger for it.

When I look at the number of Spanish-speaking youngsters in
the university that I live in, I feel sick that there aren't more of
them, but we have one coming this year and she is 38 years old
and she never had a chance to go to college, but she went out and
she worked for her people for the last 20 years in Phoenix and
Tucson, Arizona, and now at age 38 she is coming back to get her
degree in law. We had to break all the rules to let her in, but Dean
Griswold said this is the thing that we ought to do, too. She is
going to come back after 20 years of serving her people and get
a degree in law and she has a youngster to support that she has
to take care of on the side because he doesn't have a father that
is around, but the important thing about this young lady is, I
think, that after 20 years of serving her people she is willing to
come back and go to school and she is going to make it and she is
going to be a great lawyer some day, but her equality of opportunity was a long, hard road and I don't think there is anybody
sitting at this table that hasn't found equality of opportunity a
long, hard road.

This man next to me won a Pulitzer Prize this week. You don't
get them with green stamps. I mean it is the top thing in your
profession if you happen to be a journalist or a newspaperman,
but he tells me he was born looking out at a swamp, and he is a

long way from that today, but he didn't get there by crying. He got there by working and grabbing at every possible way to get educated, and I would guess that everybody along this table and many people out there have one great chance to get ahead in life and that is to get educated, get educated and get more educated and to learn every day and to grab every opportunity and never to be satisfied to say that you got enough. And even though it is difficult and it is rough and it is hard and it is everything else, the day you say that the world is against me and I can't make it because things are tough, that day you are licked, but the day you say I am going to get in there and keep trying, I am going to grab the opportunity in this country which, whatever their problems, are greater than the opportunities of any country in the world, then I think you can move forward. And, believe me, that is all I would like to say, is that I hope you grab every opportunity that you have and I hope that your kids have better opportunities than you have and I hope that we keep working on creating more and more equality of opportunity. But, believe me, we got to put down our buckets where we are. We've got to start right here and if we can make it better, let's do all we can to make it better but, believe me, we have to start with what we have right now and make it better. We can't start in China. We can't start somewhere else. We've got to start right here, and, believe me, whatever the problems were, they were much worse for your mothers and fathers and much worse for your grandmothers and grandfathers and will be much better for your children, and so let's take it from there, I think.

CHAIRMAN HANNAH. We appreciate your being here and, of course, we have other witnesses yet to hear, and I should like to have you and your young people that are with you at the table and those that are out in the audience recognize that the very fact that they are participating in a project like Horizons Unlimited is encouraging and it indicates a great deal of effort on your part and on the part of others, and while we may have appeared to lose our tempers a few minutes ago, we recognize that from where you sit provocations are very real and this was an opportunity and we don't resent it at all.

MR. SANDOVAL. Well, Mr. Chairman, I feel this way, to be truthful, the students could be here all evening telling you about their problems, but if you will give me a few minutes I can briefly tell you exactly what they are facing today and what they are trying to communicate to you and we won't have to sit down there again and wait one more time. Will you allow me the privilege?

CHAIRMAN HANNAH. When you say a few minutes, if your few minutes is not more than four, I would say go ahead, but we still have what? Three more witnesses this afternoon?

MR. GLICKSTEIN. Yes, sir.

CHAIRMAN HANNAH. And a meeting of the Commission after that. So you tell us what you can in four minutes and then we are going to call the next witness.

MR. SANDOVAL. O.K. First of all, members of the Commission, what the students are trying to tell you is the fact that when the Father mentioned about the various experiences in Latin America and the other places and the philosophy he was speaking about, this is exactly what the problem is in San Francisco. Who cares about Latin America? Who cares about Africa? Our problem is right here right now.

You, yourself, Mr. Chairman, have stated earlier that we are just a Commission that is going around the country listening to problems. Now, I am not directing my attack toward you. I respect your position. I am not insulting you, but this is the problem of being a Mexican American, Spanish-speaking person.

I negotiate with the school board administrators on one level. I fight for these people in high school. I fight for them at the Board of Education. Believe me, I am a Mexican American from the day I was born. There is continuous ugly discrimination and segregation. There always has been. Nobody ever comes up to my face and tells me, "You're a dirty Mexican," but I can hear them when I walk off. I know exactly what they are thinking, but you know what the problem is? It is not our problem. It has been over 200 years. It is a problem of the Anglo society, the mono-lingual, monocultural society cannot accept, does not realize what the bicultural problem is.

Sure there is a lot of people like Robert B. Hayden and Margaret Clark and Georgia Christiansen writing books about us. To be truthful, what do they know about us? What do they know about us? You know we have a few people who write a few books, but everybody all over the United States is on this big kick about anti-poverty and about helping the poor Mexican American. But all they do is chastise him and they literally crucify him.

Robert Hayden, for example—I don't know the man, but in his stories of Spanish-speaking people in the Southwest, Dr. Manuel Guerra from USC, if you had kept up with his correspondence that David North has been mailing back and forth between these people and interested people, you can see how even a person such as Robert Hayden, who supposedly has a professional knowledge of Spanish-speaking people, is completely out of line. He is right in some respects, but monolingual, monocultural people do not understand the Spanish-speaking bicultural problem.

I will tell you this: I grew up with Anglo people in the little towns in New Mexico. Now, that Anglo person knows and under-stands the problems of Spanish-speaking people better than any-body that comes from Harvard or Notre Dame or Michigan State or Duke, or what have you. This is absolutely the truth.

I negotiate for the students over there at the Board of Education. "I have been to Latin America. I can speak in Spanish. I spoke Spanish the day I was born." This is fine, but they do not understand. This is all on a superficial level.

What we are concerned about is from the very beginning of the grass roots stages. I can't—you will never understand what I mean by our type of discrimination. It is hell to be a Spanish-speaking person, believe me, and I think it is time that everybody woke up. Even if the Commission can't do nothing about it. they can write to somebody, appeal to the President or do something, because I am one person that is up to my neck, believe me, and those people are out there, too, and the younger people today every day are calling me and coming to me, "Jack, it doesn't matter about my life or them anymore. Let's walk down that street and if anybody gets in the way we will knock them out."

CHAIRMAN HANNAH. Thank you, Mr. Sandoval. You are excused. Mr. Glickstein, will you call the next witness?

MR. GLICKSTEIN. The next witness is Mr. Arthur Padilla.

(Whereupon, MR. ARTHUR PADILLA was sworn by the Chairman and testified as follows:)

TESTIMONY OF MR. ARTHUR PADILLA, SAN FRANCISCO CALFORNIA

MR. GLICKSTEIN. Mr. Padilla, would you please state your full name and address for the record?

MR. PADILLA. I am Arthur Padilla. I live at 55 Zampa Lane, San Francisco.

MR. GLICKSTEIN. And what is your occupation, Mr. Padilla?

MR. PADILLA. I am an Equal Employment Officer with the Federal Equal Employment Opportunity Commission but I am not here in that capacity today.

MR. GLICKSTEIN. Mr. Padilla, have you been actively concerned with the school problems of Spanish-speaking, Spanish surname students?

MR. PADILLA. Yes, I have been as a member of a few of the groups that are active in the Mission District of this city where there is a very high concentration of Spanish-speaking cultural background individuals living.

MR. GLICKSTEIN. And what has been your role?

MR. PADILLA. My role has been as one of the members of a committee that is comprised of representatives from a number of organizations that are active in this Mission District, a total of 14 organizations.

I have been functioning as one of the co-chairmen of this committee and one of the persons that has participated regularly in a series of meetings we have been conducting with representatives of the Unified School District.

MR. GLICKSTEIN. Have there been organized demonstrations?

MR. PADILLA. Yes. There was one specific informational picket line demonstration which we felt was necessary in order to call attention to the needs of our community from the standpoint of education and the lack of some of the services that we feel are a problem to our community.

MR. GLICKSTEIN. How many Spanish surname, Spanish-speaking pupils are enrolled in the schools of San Francisco?

MR. PADILLA. I don't think that I have readily available the total in the number from the standpoint of numbers, but we do have some figures from—that would indicate the percentages. We have eight senior high schools, for instance.

MR. GLICKSTEIN. Eight? Pardon me?

MR. PADILLA. Eight senior high schools in San Francisco. In four of them there is a percentage total enrollment of Spanish-speaking students which exceeds 10 percent. The one in the Mission District, which you might expect, has the highest concentration and does, of course, there there are 30.6 percent of the students who are Spanish-speaking according to the figures which have been distributed by the school district itself.

In the junior high schools, I have counted six of them throughout the city that have Spanish-speaking student populations in excess of 10 percent.

Again those that are grouped around the Mission District: Everett with 22.4 percent, Horace Mann with 50.3 percent, James Denman in the peripheral area of the Mission District with 10.6 percent, James Lick with 26.9 percent and Luther Burbank with 24.6 percent.

MR. GLICKSTEIN. So there are some schools that have large concentrations of Spanish-speaking people?

MR. PADILLA. There are, and because they happen to be in what seems to be increasingly becoming a ghetto area from the standpoint of our Spanish language community and also the American Indian community, they seem to be concentrated in a specific location of the city with very little exception.

MR. GLICKSTEIN. Mr. Padilla, how many certificated and administrative personnel from the Spanish-speaking community are employed by the Board of Education?

MR. PADILLA. The San Francisco Unified School District has 1 percent of its certificated personnel who are in this category, or 67 persons.

MR. GLICKSTEIN. These statistics that you are giving us have been supplied by the School District?

MR. PADILLA. Yes, they have been. This is out of a total of 5,026 persons who are termed all certificated.

MR. GLICKSTEIN. That's 67 out of 5,026?

MR. PADILLA. That's right. These figures may be subject to revision, some error. This happens all the time people leave and some others come, and we do not have perhaps the very latest figures. The administrative and supervisory persons, for instance, in the central office total 55. Of these there are none who are Spanish-speaking. In our City College of San Francisco, which is part of our public school system, there are 16 administrative persons, of whom none is Spanish-speaking. In the City College instructors there are 323, of whom none are Spanish-speaking.

In the case of all principals and assistant principals, of a total of 243, four of them or 2 percent, are Spanish-speaking.

MR. GLICKSTEIN. How about counselors, guidance counselors?

MR. PADILLA. Insofar as counselors are concerned, of a total of 295, seven of them, or 2 percent, are Spanish-speaking.

In regard to counselors, I recall a question earlier this afternoon as to the number of counselors in Mission High School, and the answer, I believe, was that there was no Spanish-speaking counselors. This is what the question referred to, Spanish-speaking counselors; there were none in Mission High School. It is our understanding that—As a matter of fact, there is one counselor for every 751 students.

MR. GLICKSTEIN. At Mission High School?

MR. PADILLA. At Mission. This makes it almost totally impossible for them to render the type of service that a counselor should and it is one of the reasons that we approached the Board of Education in the first place with the problems that we have tried to enumerate to them on the day that we did speak to them.

MR. GLICKSTEIN. Mr. Padilla, could you tell the Commissioners what are the specific educational needs of Spanish-speaking pupils that are different from those of other pupils?

MR. PADILLA. Different. Well, certainly everybody has educational needs, and to one extent or another they are satisfied by the type of school they go to in the community.

It was said earlier that it is up to the individual to attain the education and take advantage of the opportunities available to him. To a very great extent the individuals in our ethnic-social-economic community, you might say, has a more difficult time. I think that it can be reasonably said that individuals who live in a ghetto area have a more difficult time achieving education, for a number of reasons.

It might be that the facilities are not what they are in the better-endowed areas from the standpoint of money. It might be that some of the teachers would prefer not to teach in these areas and to a certain extent there are perhaps defensible arguments to be made that some of the better teachers are not there, although we know there are very many good teachers, dedicated teachers, in some of these community schools.

In our particular community, we have a different culture that is inculcated into the young person before he even goes in the school because of the ancestry of his parents. We have a very high influx of persons coming to this country and to this country from other countries of Latin American and South America, Mexico. We can't say in San Francisco that we are only Mexican Americans. There is a very high percentage and a higher percentage perhaps of Central Americans than there are Mexican Americans.

There are also quite a few American Indians coming to live in the Mission District. Insofar as the Spanish-speaking people are concerned, with a different culture, different manner of speaking, a different language natively, they sometimes are not sufficiently prepared to cope with whatever is given to them in the way of a program by a school teacher who may be himself or herself ill-prepared to teach this child.

We feel that there is certainly, one, a lack of a comprehensive program. Not enough has been done in the past to try to meet some of the needs of our community of our students, and not only from the accepted school levels, kindergarten through twelfth grade, but also on a pre-school level basis, and also on an adult education basis.

During the course of the conversations we have been having with members of the representatives of the Unified School District, we have been up to now receiving information on programs, pilot projects, the type of policies that have been implemented in order to conduct those programs that are necessary to teach a person who is foreign born, for instance, English, Americanization classes, so called, and we find that, although this has been done in the past and the rate of this type of a program being undertaken has been accelerated with the advent of Federal monies being poured into the area—we find that some of these programs that have been instituted under the educational, the Elementary and Secondary Education Act, for instance, and under the economic opportunity programs, the monies that were first appropriated for ambitious programs have started to be cut back.

In one instance when we asked why this was the case when the need appeared to be greater, we were told that from a political standpoint the President of the United States has not asked, has not requested from Congress the monies that he could request that have been authorized by Congress. This, of course, is a political matter we must address ourselves to in the future. I would hope that this Commission might be able to put the weight of their opinion perhaps upon the President to act differently if in fact it is the President who is the one that should be taking the affirmative action.

We have programs that, although they have been implemented, we have not been able to gauge their success in many instances. We do know from the 1960 census, for instance, that in the five

Southwestern States the lowest educational achievement level has been among the so-called Spanish-surname community.

In the San Francisco-Oakland Bay Area the educational achievement level for Spanish-surnamed males has been about 9.1 years; for females, slightly over that, in contrast to 12.1 for what we call white Anglo-Caucasians.

We know that our children, our students, are not getting into colleges and universities. Very few are being put through the schools with an idea of going to colleges. We have had specific examples in some of the schools where there is a high concentration of Spanish-surnamed students, where we have gone to them asking for assistance in finding qualified students who would be eligible for free scholarships to universities, and have received no assistance to speak of. And when we had no names forthcoming—a stroll through the halls of the particular high school revealed that on a bulletin board there appeared the scholarship rolls which contained a number of Spanish-surnamed individuals, the names of a number of individuals, and an approach to these individuals indicated that, yes, they were interested in college education; they would take advantage of some scholarship if it became available, but nobody had asked them about it.

We have been told by individuals in the community that some teachers, or at least one or two counselors who have, of course, the responsibility of trying to push an individual towards achievement, have said—have been heard to say that the students in the particular district—again I am referring to Spanish-speaking people—are not interested in college. We said to the Board of Education that this was an outrageous situation and we feel it.

You heard, certainly this afternoon, and perhaps last evening —I was not present—a manifestation of the sense of urgency that is now all-pervasive in our community.

There are people that are trying to articulate to the society as a whole and to the power structure of the society that the problem is so grave now that there is very little that they can do but make some noise about it, and this is most unfortunate.

We have, as was stated, one of the best educational systems in the world and we are one of the richest Nations and we are one of the richest States in this richest Nation, and why should not the responsibility be borne by our State? Perhaps they are trying, but we have seen so little of the results that have been good.

In talking about discrimination in employment to employers, to unions, et cetera, time and time again we have been told, "Your people who come to us are not qualified." This is what started us in this role. We were trying to attack other problems in our individual community, but eventually we knew we had to attack the problem of education and we started trying to do so; and with the number of conversations that we have had so far, we are not yet at any point where we have begun to evaluate the information sufficiently to make substantive suggestions.

We know from past experience and from just the tenor of the conversations that many school administrators, school teachers, persons that have talked to us, have their own little problems to contend with. To them we are probably just another community that is agitating, and representatives from another community that is agitating, and they try to give us the type of information which they believe is going to make us happy. In some instances we have received information that has made us happy. In others we have received information which has made us most unhappy, and in many of the cases we have received information which we do not know what to do about it, and I say this as a layman because the people we are talking to are definitely the professionals, who perhaps should have some latitude for experimentation, for the development of the type of program that is going to help persons from our community that come with problems.

I mentioned the—oh, I should say that it seems to me that under the structure of organization that is our San Francisco Unified School District, this seems to be a very difficult thing to do. It seems to me, as in perhaps many structures, whether it be business or government, there seems to be quite a reticence to speak truthfully and people qualify what they say for fear perhaps of reprisal, for fear that they will be held in disfavor later on.

This I find also, this type of stifling attitude, very unfortunate. I wish there was something that could be done about this.

From the standpoint of what we are trying to do, we have offered as much as we can, to the extent that we can, whatever assistance we can render to our school district in trying to implement some of the programs to alleviate the problems.

I spoke about a comprehensive program. By this we mean from the very beginning the child centers that are needed in our area to enable parents who have to take care of children to put their children in the centers where they will be well taken care of so that they themselves, the parents, can perhaps avail themselves of educational opportunities that will enable them, if they are not now earning their own living, enable them to do so.

We want to see a higher percentage of Spanish-speaking personnel, American Indian and other minority group personnel, hired by our San Francisco Unified School District.

The pattern of employment is dismal. Any employer worth his salt, with any attempted and good, affirmative action program, can do better. We have made some suggestions. We have heard counter-proposals, denials, excuses and perhaps good reasons, but the proof of the pudding is in what the employment picture is right now, and I say it is very dismal.

We want to see Spanish-speaking individuals in there because this provides a good image for the students. It provides persons who understand the cultural background, the problems, who can communicate in Spanish. We hate to see the situation where even a good teacher, not knowing Spanish, has to cope with students who do not understand English, and they have to take the attitude that so long as the student does not make a fuss in school he will pass him with a D. Well, it is bad enough when you know English and you are graduated from high school as a functional illiterate. It is a real crime at that point, and we certainly feel it very deeply when we feel that a great proportion of the people coming from our communities are being short-changed from an educational standpoint.

We want counselors, too, and more of them. We want more teachers to make the work load in the classroom lighter. We would like to see teachers' aides to help these teachers, not only because so many of them, if they are able to recruit them as bilingual individuals, can assist the teacher, but this would also serve as a training ground for these individuals to perhaps go on into the profession later on, along the concepts of the New Careers type of program that has been receiving a great deal of publicity lately, and this to us seems to be a good idea.

We also feel that the number of classified personnel employed by the Unified School District is very little. This is somewhat of a civil service program problem and is reflective in the lack of minority group participation in jobs in government, not only on the local basis, but on the State and Federal basis as well.

MR. GLICKSTEIN. Mr. Chairman, I think Mr. Padilla has covered the points that I was going to question him about. Perhaps the Commissioners would like to ask him some questions.

CHAIRMAN HANNAH. Do the Commissioners have any questions? Father Hesburgh?

COMMISSIONER HESBURGH. Just one, Mr. Padilla. This is a personal question. I am not trying to embarrass you, but I am interested in how you came to be educated, since it is obvious that you are.

What is your personal background in education? Were you born in this city?

MR. PADILLA. My parents are Mexican. They came to this country in the early 1900's. I was born in San Francisco, did not live in a ghetto. To this extent I think perhaps I was advantaged, because I found it necessary very early in life to learn to speak English, and since Spanish was my first language, learning English later on, I unfortunately stopped developing my ability in Spanish as I started learning English.

Along with my not living in a ghetto, however, the urgency with a need to conform to the society around me came from my peers, my teachers and the society in which I was thrust. We don't think that this is necessarily healthy.

The mayor said earlier this evening that he deplores the fragmentation of our community now with various national groups, racial groups, religious groups, et cetera. I say that this is a result of the attitudes that have been imposed upon persons who are different by the Caucasian-Anglo majority. You have told the person who is different from yourself, if you are an Anglo, to change, to be American, to forget the country of your forefathers or where you might have come from. This certainly does a great deal to hurt an individual psychologically.

There have been enough studies that I am sure that most of you persons are aware of, most of the members of the Commission, that have indicated the problem and conflict that this creates in a person who is bicultural. The situation becomes most difficult when a person who is thrust into this situation starts to begin to hate himself for what he is because he should be different, and what I think is happening now in this fragmentation is a manifestation of a sense of pride in realizing that you do not have to be ashamed of what your forefathers were or what you are, and that many people now are beginning to admit that yes, they are Mexicans, yes, they are Central Americans, and have stopped feeling ashamed of it. And because of this we have banded together in a sense of identity to work on the problems which we see are pretty much unique to our community.

In my case, not only did I go through the San Francisco public schools, and I was confronted with some very good teachers, many of whom I remember with a great deal of fondness, and I was able to, after dropping out of school and joining the service in a fit of patriotic fervor, I got out of the Second World War in one piece almost and took advantage of the GI Bill. Later on I went to law school and there are many persons who could do this, too, but they have to be motivated, and I received a certain amount of motivation, but I see, unfortunately, there are so many students in our community that are not receiving this type of motivation because of various problems. Part of it is the lack of the human relations understanding of teachers and counselors, and the school administrators. This is the type of thing that we would like to alleviate.

COMMISSIONER HESBURGH. Would you say, Mr. Padilla that the greatest force militating against higher educational level in the Spanish-speaking community is lack of motivation and, secondarily, a language problem?

MR. PADILLA. It is more than that. Motivation is there in any child in the beginning. The flame of knowledge that burns in any child, it seems to me, I think it was Dr. George I. Sanchez of the University of Texas, in a study, said that in Texas schools they saw that children going into these schools seemed to be as eager to learn as the Anglo-Caucasian children, but after the third, fourth, fifth grade their achievement became less and less, so that soon they were dropping back. The problem is not only motivation that is killed, but it is also one of poverty, one of a lack of ability perhaps to finance an education. From this standpoint whatever can be done in the way of scholarships, in the way of enabling individuals to even borrow money to be paid later to finance an education, this is all to the good. But the motivation is also killed, as I said, along various levels in schools, not only in this school district, but in many areas.

And this is the type of thing that also has to be changed. A person isn't going to be motivated if he is constantly reminded that he isn't going to achieve anything because other persons such as himself did not achieve anything.

COMMISSIONER HESBURGH. Thank you.

MR. PADILLA. He isn't also going to be motivated if he thinks that he will not have an equal opportunity of employment or even buying a house where he may wish to live.

CHAIRMAN HANNAH. Thank you very much, Mr. Padilla. We appreciate your being with us. You are excused. Will you call the next witness?

MR. GLICKSTEIN. Mr. Hernandez.

(Whereupon, MR. ROGER HERNANDEZ was sworn by the Chairman and testified as follows:)

TESTIMONY OF MR. ROGER U. HERNANDEZ, SAN FRANCISCO, CALIFORNIA

MR. GLICKSTEIN. Would you please state your full name and address for the record?

MR. HERNANDEZ. Roger U. Hernandez, 1049 York Street, San Francisco.

MR. GLICKSTEIN. What is your occupation, Mr. Hernandez?

MR. HERNANDEZ. I am the executive secretary of the Catholic Council for the Spanish-Speaking in San Francisco.

MR. GLICKSTEIN. What sort of work do you do with the Catholic Council?

MR. HERNANDEZ. It is coordinate amongst the Spanish-speaking people some type of courses in catechism and liturgy as well as in social action.

MR. GLICKSTEIN. Do you come in contact with many persons who are unable to speak English?

MR. HERNANDEZ. Yes. Most of the people that I have contact are people who do not understand English, and so they come into my office and looking for some type of service, especially in the social service. They are not able to go to someplace and have this communication in agencies of the Government as well information of personal matters.

MR. GLICKSTEIN. You say people come into your office for social services. Aren't they able to go to the appropriate city and county agencies that provide social services?

MR. HERNANDEZ. The problem is that most of the people that they come as immigrant people. Maybe they are new in the country for around one year, six months, three months, even sometime they come in when they are around only 10 days in the city or the country, and they are looking for some type of information, how to start knowing the—all the technique how to live in this country.

No. 1, they come in looking for a job where they can find some jobs because I have some information of this matter, and the first thing that we are not agency to provide job, but sometime people call me up that they need some type of person and I am able to give this service, but not in the overall picture.

So what I do is to refer them to those agency who are supposed to do this job, like the Department of Employment or the Economic Opportunity Council in the Mission District, that they have more referral job than those.

MR. GLICKSTEIN. Do State and local agencies have Spanish-speaking employees who can communicate with the type of person you just spoke to us about?

MR. HERNANDEZ. My experience is that they have to go with somebody who can speak English and Spanish in order to be communicative with the agency.

MR. GLICKSTEIN. In other words, people who can't speak English that are seeking unemployment insurance or welfare benefits have difficulties in communicating with the public agencies?

MR. HERNANDEZ. I know maybe in one or two agency there is somebody who can speak Spanish, but if they go to the right window maybe they can find these people, but they don't know. So they are asking for somebody, voluntary people, to go with them to translate. I even sometime myself, I made this type of translation because the English sometime is too wider than I use it by myself.

MR. GLICKSTEIN. Do you come in contact with many people who are not American citizens?

MR. HERNANDEZ. Most of the people that I have contact, they are not Americans.

MR. GLICKSTEIN. Well, how does the lack of citizenship affect the possibility of such people obtaining employment?

MR. HERNANDEZ. It is tremendous because the only help for them is to work in the private industry.

MR. GLICKSTEIN. The only opportunity is to work in private industry?

MR. HERNANDEZ. The private industry, and in the private industry there is the big difficult of the barrier of the English language to understand, and my own experience was working in a factory, and the boss told me, "I am sorry, Roger. You have to go and learn English because I am too old to learn Spanish and I cannot understand you." And this one by that time made me to feel so low in my life. I was not so pleased with the way he told me, and this what happened to many people in my community, the lack of understanding, the lack of the way of how to talk to us, the way of the communication, is not supposed to be in the way I use this type of work, because I don't know the other ones. Too tough, you know, to speak people like all that. We do not understand the language, and so little by little we are dropping down and dropping down, and, say, well, we come into a country who are saying there is a big opportunity, but this opportunity they are not in the level of the people. They are too high. And we discovered this only after we live in 10 or 12 years in this country and then after we are able to get the communication to learning the English and start going out of the house and talk with other people different from our general speaking general conversation, talking about what happened in the overall of the country, what they are doing in Washington, what happens in Sacramento, all this type of opportunity. I believe that this is a country, that Mr. John Hannah said this is a country of opportunity, yes, but only for those who are able to see beyond the ceiling of the house.

The immigrant—this is our problem. Different culture, real deep in it. We see the ceiling of our culture. We cannot see the culture of the United States. We need time. We need programs. We need motivation to get away from the private industry and start looking in another direction and this will have to be done only through a friendship, not through making a big propagand and say we are go to the other school, and here is a beautiful building over here for you, and in big letters.

Have to be in friendship and the kind that is a human to human communication. This is the way to understand.

MR. GLICKSTEIN. One of the statements you made implied that persons who are not American citizens cannot get jobs with the city government or the State government or the county government. Is that correct?

MR. HERNANDEZ. Yes. Right now San Francisco is going to receive some grants in order to provide job, on-the-job training, the new career for the poor, and this new career for the poor is not for the Latin American who are not citizen. We will be on one side. Why? No. 1, you have to pass a test. No. 2, you have to be a citizen and this one is a big barrier for the—those who are not—those who are not able to know the—not the language, but the type of words that is using in the test.

I can do the job. I can be a janitor in the City Hall. I can be a janitor in the Post Office. I can be a janitor over here, but if I don't know the right word to answer those tests, I don't get the job and then, No. 2, I am not a citizen. So you go there for the poor, is not for the Mission, for the majority of the Mission.

You got two programs from the Government, Federal Government, working with the private contractors that they are supposed to work, put an example in the highway. This type of job is not to the man who can take a shovel to work on the highway because supposed to be an American citizen, and this one don't have any relation with the security of the country, and this one I think I would like this Commission to take notice of this in order to—You have the ears and the foot of the Congressman, the President, and bring this one down to Washington.

I understand your position. I am not angry against you. I have been hearing something about that because I recognize what is your position. The ears and the foot are our representative in Washington who are supposed to do—give some direction to our Nation, and this one is the problem that we are facing down here in San Francisco among many Mexican Americans—I mean immigrant from Mexico, immigrant from San Salvador, Nicaragua, South America.

MR. GLICKSTEIN. I have no further questions, Mr. Chairman.

CHAIRMAN HANNAH. Do any of the Commissioners have questions? Mr. Hernandez, we appreciate your being with us this afternoon. Sorry that we kept you so late.

We have one more witness. You are excused, Mr. Hernandez. Mr. Pivnick, before you come forward I want to ask you a question. You have listened to the testimony this afternoon. There have been some very critical things said about the work of the Board of Education in San Francisco. You have been subpenaed to appear this afternoon, and the Commission is willing to hear you this afternoon, although I think some of us at least would like to give you better attention than you may get this late, at the end of a bad day, and we would leave it up to you.

If you want to proceed to be heard this afternoon, we will hear you. Otherwise we will put you on the first thing tomorrow morning.

COMMISSIONER GRISWOLD. Let's hear him now because it is in Oakland tomorrow.

CHAIRMAN HANNAH. All right. Come forward.

MR. PIVNICK. I would appreciate it having the opportunity. I feel for you. Perhaps you want to stand for a minute and just relax.

(Whereupon, MR. ISADORE PIVNICK was sworn by the Chairman and testified as follows:)

TESTIMONY OF MR. ISADORE PIVNICK, SAN FRANCISCO, CALIFORNIA

MR. GLICKSTEIN. Would you please state your full name and address for the record?

MR. PIVNICK. Isadore Pivnick, 3800 Ocean Avenue, San Francisco, California.

MR. GLICKSTEIN. And where are you employed, Mr. Pivnick?

MR. PIVNICK. I am employed by the San Francisco Unified School District.

MR. GLICKSTEIN. In what position?

MR. PIVNICK. I am known as a Coordinator of Federal-State projects, which is a central office staff position.

MR. GLICKSTEIN. Are you responsible for both Federal and State grant programs?

MR. PIVNICK. Yes, I am.

MR. GLICKSTEIN. What is the extent of the Federal grant programs which the San Francisco School District has received for the current fiscal year?

MR. PIVNICK. The Title I program this school year will bring us $3 2/10 million. That is perhaps the largest single amount. May I just lump them all into one umbrella and say that from State and Federal sources we get approximately $10 million.

MR. GLICKSTEIN. Are there any Federal or State project grant funds utilized specifically for the benefit of Spanish-speaking students, including for adult education?

MR. PIVNICK. Yes, there are. I might say that these are also true for the Oriental and the Negro.

MR. GLICKSTEIN. Would you tell us about the programs that are directed at Spanish-speaking students?

MR. PIVNICK. Yes. We have programs which range from the pre-kindergarten programs clear through the adult education. We have a pilot program of roughly 80 youngsters at the Hawthorne School, which is in the center of the Mission area, which provides opportunities for three-, four-year-old youngsters.

In addition we have a State-funded program, a pilot program, which also uses Federal funds under Assembly Bill 1331, which provides for another 40 or 50 youngsters in that neighborhood.

I say that this is a pilot program because it is important that you recruit the proper staff for these schools, and this is still a difficulty.

VICE CHAIRMAN PATTERSON. 40 or 50 youngsters in what program?

MR. PIVNICK. In the preschool program, in AB-1331.

This is the program where the parent must be a welfare recipient.

We also have in these schools, in Grades 1, 2 and 3 reduced the class size to a ratio of 22 to 1 at first grade, 27 to 1, Grades 2 and 3.

We have introduced what we call a compensatory teacher in Grades 4, 5, and 6 to work with special problems of reading and special language problems at the elementary level.

We have introduced social workers, speech teachers, what we call a community teacher, to bridge the gap between the home and the school, and two of these people are Spanish-speaking.

We have introduced part-time librarian services. We have provided tutorial services after school with paid teacher help as well as Neighborhood Youth Corps students, college tutors, and tutors from the community.

We have provided aid, teachers' aides, who are serving on a voluntary basis.

MR. GLICKSTEIN. What sort of programs do you have on the high school level?

MR. PIVNICK. At the high school level we provide comparable kinds of services. We have provided special programs for youngsters who are having difficulty with reading. We recognize that these youngsters also have difficulty with math and social studies, and so we have provided special help for them there, also.

We have attempted to reduce the counseling load, but because of the curtailment of funds which you heard about earlier, this semester we had to curtail that service.

Last semester and last school year we were able to provide the community teacher, who again could bridge the gap between the home and the school—and may I say we found this especially helpful to the schools in the Mission area where many youngsters were taking time off from school rather than reporting to school. It was an opportunity—this is not an attendance worker—but it is an opportunity to talk with parents about school-related problems.

The tutorial services were provided also.

We purchased special materials and equipment which we think will serve as motivational devices for youngsters who need additional crutches.

MR. GLICKSTEIN. We heard testimony that at Mission High School the ratio of pupils to counselors is 750 to 1. Is that the ratio in other schools in other parts of the city?

MR. PIVNICK. I can't honestly attest to that high a ratio. It may be possible, and I don't know that a staff member is here that could tell us otherwise.

I would agree that universally the counselor-pupil ratio is high and in a special program which we introduced at Horace Mann and at Everett in the Mission area, junior high levels, we tried to reduce the counseling load to 50 to 1 and we would think that this would make a great deal of sense.

We also are encouraging evening counseling hours and in another instance are trying this, but not in the Mission area. We are trying it on a pilot basis.

MR. GLICKSTEIN. Is there any one administrative officer of the school district responsible for special programs for Spanish-speaking persons?

MR. PIVNICK. No. My responsibility is to be knowledgeable about all of the funds that are available to make certain that we can get as many of those funds as we can and then working through the assistant superintendents and division heads try to then create programs for the various communities.

MR. GLICKSTEIN. But there is no—the school system doesn't have a particular person whose sole responsibility is for administering programs or surveying programs that are directed at Spanish-speaking persons?

MR. PIVNICK. Not specifically the Spanish-speaking, nor for the Oriental, nor the Negro.

I might say that for five years of my life as an employee of the board my responsibility was to develop a program in 1960 for the Negro. I might say that that served as a catalyst for then introducing a $100,000 program at the local level which then gave service to the Mission area.

I have been project director for five years until recently, and now we do have a person responsible for Title I, but I still am in the innovative part of trying to develop a program to meet special needs.

MR. GLICKSTEIN. The statistics that were read before, that were supplied by the school system, indicate that less than 2 percent of the certificated personnel employed by the school system are Spanish-speaking persons.

Would you offer any comment with respect to why this number is so low?

MR. PIVNICK. I am not sure that I know the reasons why. I do know that in one of the most recent written examinations that was given for teachers in San Francisco only 13 of 389 Spanish-speaking sought to take the test.

At a recent meeting through the involvement of Mr. Padilla, our board member, our board went on record as urging our personnel director to confer with our new superintendent to seek aggressive means of recruitment for all minority groups.

It is my feeling that the future will be a brighter one for all minority groups in our city.

MR. GLICKSTEIN. At the present time does the school system actively recruit outside the city of San Francisco?

MR. PIVNICK. It has not in the past. It is my understanding that in our most recent interviews for administrative personnel this was done.

I might say also that our human relations officer is now involved in the selection and placement of all personnel in our school district and through his efforts there have been greater concern and a look-see at who it is that is being placed and where they are being placed.

MR. GLICKSTEIN. I have no further questions, Mr. Chairman.

CHAIRMAN HANNAH. Commissioners have any further questions?

VICE CHAIRMAN PATTERSON. I have one question, Mr. Chairman. We heard testimony this afternoon that a child entering the Mission School who doesn't speak English does not receive any special language instruction in English. Is this the fact?

MR. PIVNICK. There may be a degree of truth to that and perhaps it is a large degree.

I can't speak too intelligently about it, but I can say this, that we are faced today with the problem which we were faced with five years ago, when we recognized suddenly on the scene we have cultural deprivation and we said we can no longer do business as usual.

The first person we saw was the colored for those of us who were colorless, and so we began to apply no longer the Band-Aid, but a new way of doing business for the Negro. This has taken a longer transition period for many of the Spanish-speaking.

However, all along I have been a teacher in the system of San Francisco, we received youngsters who were assimilated because they were small numbers. Suddenly we are faced with a population increase of—and this is not in San Francisco, but nationally—20 percent of the people on the move every day, and when you get these large numbers of new people coming in, it does mean that we have to take a new look at the program.

This summer we are taking that new look by bringing in special teachers to look at the whole area of teaching English, as a second language for the Spanish-speaking and for the Oriental child, and it is our hope that beginning now we will make greater strides than we have in the past.

VICE CHAIRMAN PATTERSON. Well, Mr. Chairman, I would just like to observe that, coming from a region that has fallen as short as the South has in education, I am not the one to give San Francisco a lecture on the subject, but it does seem to me in the year 1967 to put a child in a schoolroom under a teacher whose language he doesn't even speak is little less than educational barbarism.

MR. PIVNICK. May I say, Mr. Patterson, that we do provide opportunity for these youngsters, who do go to a compensatory class for a portion of their day. We are looking into more—into ways of doing more for the youngsters. I am not saying that we have not done anything.

CHAIRMAN HANNAH. Father Hesburgh?

COMMISSIONER HESBURGH. I think one thing might be worth looking at.

There is a gentleman named C. C. Fries that just retired from the University of Michigan, who spent a good part of his life developing the teaching of English to people whose original language is Spanish, and he worked out this whole system mostly in Puerto Rico, with great success, and he has all of the textbooks already prepared, and I would think something like this, plus a combination perhaps of Peace Corps returnees or—California has more people in the Peace Corps than anybody I know, I think. There are many of them working in Latin and Spanish-speaking countries, and this combination of using that specially prepared book plus Peace Corps youngsters who have been used to teaching or talking Spanish in the Latin-American countries might give you a kind of combination that would be a breakthrough in this area.

MR. PIVNICK. We are looking toward the National Teacher Corps as a possibility.

We recently conducted a workshop for the teachers in our Spanish-speaking area, using Spanish-speaking members of the community, whom you have heard testimony from.

We have worked and tried to work closely, I might say, with Horizons Unlimited. We believe that they do offer something and we hope to learn from them, as well.

COMMISSIONER HESBURGH. I would think that this type of school could be run any time of the day or night and it might even be very useful to many adults who find difficulty in work because they don't really feel they control the language.

MR. PIVNICK. We have offered a program for adults for many years and still offer it, not only through local funds, but with Federal funds, NDTA funds and VEA funds.

COMMISSIONER HESBURGH. Good.

CHAIRMAN HANNAH. Mr. Taylor, do you have a question?

MR. TAYLOR. Following up on what Mr. Patterson just said, perhaps, but in the process of answering it just now, I don't know what the certification problems are, but why not just go out and find some good people who speak Spanish? Isn't it possible that they might bring a good deal more to the problem of teaching the kids than teachers who have certifications right now?

MR. PIVNICK. Well, you frame a question which would suit some of us fine, except that we do have some State laws in certification to which we must adhere. The laws have even increased the amount of time that a teacher must attend school in order to become certificated, which makes life even a little more difficult.

However, we have used aides and paid aides who are Spanish-speaking in these schools.

We are very interested in the New Careers Program. We have a training program at the City College which is a two-year program which we hope will come out with teacher aides, and I think we are attuned to the problem, and we hope to make faster strides than we have made.

I think we may be a little bit guilty, if I may say, of the same things that some other people have been. We have looked at the problem of the Negro, and thank God that we have, because as a result of looking at their problem we have now stepped out into other areas where there are comparable types of problems.

I think we are beginning to crawl a little faster, and we will soon be walking and then running, I hope.

MR. TAYLOR. One last question. We heard a few allegations this afternoon that epithets were used uncomplimentarily, racial or ethnic epithets were used by teachers or administrators in talking to pupils.

Do you have machinery which people have confidence in where this kind of complaint can be brought and would be acted upon fairly?

MR. PIVNICK. We do have the human relations officer who is charged with the responsibility of hearing such complaints, and it is our hope that these will come to his attention. It is also our hope that the members of the community will have confidence in the principal and come to him.

I have to admit, having been a principal and a teacher in schools of comparable nature, that frequently the people who have such things inflicted upon them are reluctant to come, and often we do not hear these things until they are aired before a body such as this or other bodies. I do know that when these allegations have been made before the human relations—it is my feeling, at least, that when these accusations have been made before our human relations officer, attempts have been made to get to the bottom of the problem to see what has transpired.

CHAIRMAN HANNAH. Thank you very much, Mr. Pivnick. We are grateful to you.

MR. PIVNICK. Thank you for allowing my testimony this afternoon.

CHAIRMAN HANNAH. We are now recessed to meet tomorrow morning at 9:15 at the Oakland Auditorium.

(Whereupon, at 6:30 p.m. the hearing was recessed to reconvene on Thursday, May 4, 1967, at 9:15 a.m. at the Oakland Auditorium.)

UNITED STATES COMMISSION ON CIVIL RIGHTS

The U.S. Commission on Civil Rights met at 9:15 a.m. in the Oakland Auditorium Ballroom, Oakland, California, Dr. John A. Hannah, Chairman of the Commission, presiding.

PRESENT: John A. Hannah, Chairman; Eugene Patterson, Vice Chairman; Frankie M. Freeman, Commissioner; Erwin N. Griswold, Commissioner; Robert S. Rankin, Commissioner. Also present: William L. Taylor, Staff Director; Howard A. Glickstein, General Counsel.

PROCEEDINGS

CHAIRMAN HANNAH. Ladies and gentlemen, this public hearing will come to order. Mrs. Joan P. Alexander is the reporter for this hearing. Will you please raise your right hand and be sworn?

(Whereupon, Mrs. Joan P. Alexander was sworn by the Chairman as Official Reporter.)

The Reverend Theodore Hesburgh of South Bend, Indiana, President of Notre Dame University, had to leave the city this morning on other business. He was with us during the first three days of the hearing in San Francisco.

In addition to the Commissioners, Mr. William Taylor, Staff Director of the Commission, is seated next to Mrs. Freeman, and Howard Glickstein, the Commission's General Counsel is seated to the far right beside Mr. Taylor.

This is a continuation of the hearing which began in San Francisco on Monday. This hearing is being held under the authority of the Civil Rights Act of 1957, as amended.

As required by law, notice of the hearing was published in the Federal Register on March 29, 1967. This hearing is being held under the authority of the Civil Rights Act of 1957, as amended.

The Commission on Civil Rights is an independent, bipartisan agency of the United States Government established by the Congress, and its duties are:

1. To investigate sworn allegations that citizens are being deprived of their right to vote by reason of their race, color, religion, or national origin.

2. To study and collect information concerning legal developments which constitute a denial of equal protection of the laws under the Constitution.

3. To appraise Federal laws and policies with respect to equal protection of the laws.

4. To serve as a national clearinghouse for information with respect to denials of equal protection of the laws because of race, color, religion, or national origin.

5. To investigate sworn allegations of vote fraud in Federal elections.

Under the law the Commission submits reports to the President and the Congress containing its findings and recommendations for collective legislation or executive action. To enable the Commission to fulfill its duties the Congress has empowered the Commission to hold hearings and issue subpenas for the attendance of witnesses and the production of documents.

Commission hearings seek to explore, in one city or area, the civil rights problems that are representative of problems elsewhere in the Nation. The purpose of this hearing is to collect information concerning civil rights problems in the Bay Area counties of San Francisco, Contra Costa, Alameda, San Mateo, Marin, Sonoma, Napa, Santa Clara, and Solana.

This hearing in the Oakland-San Francisco Bay Area, like a hearing in Cleveland, Ohio in April, 1966, is part of a national study of civil rights problems the Commission is conducting in metropolitan urban centers which have significant minority group populations.

Our Bay Area hearing also inaugurates a new factfinding effort by the Commission to ascertain the status of equal opportunity for Spanish-speaking people throughout the country, a problem that is increasingly being brought to the attention of the Commission and other governmental agencies.

The Commission's effort to learn more about the problems of our Spanish-speaking population will include a projected hearing, new research programs, and meetings of several of our State Advisory Committees.

At this hearing we are concerned primarily with issues of housing and employment opportunities for Negroes, Spanish-speaking Americans and other minorities. Because the Bay Area consists of many geographical and political jurisdictions we have the opportunity to consider the civil rights problems of the core cities as they relate to the entire metropolitan community.

The testimony we heard in San Francisco and the testimony we will hear here will consist not only of facts and information, but also opinion and comment about civil rights issues and problems in the Bay Area.

We urge that those following the hearing give careful consideration to all points of view, even those points of view with which they do not agree. If there is agreement on one thing it is that the problem of establishing equal opportunity and creating good relations among the races in the Nation's cities is of the utmost importance.

This can be done only if people with differing points of view are able to approach each other with understanding, and to work together toward equitable solutions to our most serious national problems.

This session of the hearing will recess at 12:40 for lunch. We will resume at 2 o'clock and conclude at about 6 o'clock.

Tomorrow we will begin at 9:15, break for lunch at about 1 o'clock, and resume at 2:15, and hopefully conclude about 5:30.

We will begin the final session of this hearing at 9:15 on Saturday, and adjourn at 12:45, but we will decide tomorrow the exact hours for this Saturday morning session.

Now, Mr. Glickstein, will you call the first witness.

MR. GLICKSTEIN. The first witnesses are Mr. Clifton Jeffers and Mr. Donald McCullum.

(Whereupon, Mr. Clifton Jeffers and Mr. Donald McCullum were sworn by the Chairman and testified as follows:)

TESTIMONY OF MR. CLIFTON JEFFERS, SAN FRANCISCO, CALIFORNIA AND MR. DONALD McCULLUM, OAKLAND, CALIFORNIA

MR. GLICKSTEIN. Will you each please state your full name and address for the record?

MR. JEFFERS. Clifton R. Jeffers, 36 Thrift Street, San Francisco.

MR. McCULLUM. Donald P. McCullum, 1615 Broadway, Oakland, California.

MR. GLICKSTEIN. Mr. Jeffers, what is your occupation?

MR. JEFFERS. I am an attorney.

MR. GLICKSTEIN. Mr. McCullum?

MR. McCULLUM. I am a lawyer.

MR. GLICKSTEIN. Mr. Jeffers, to what civil rights organizations do you belong and what offices do you hold, if any?

MR. JEFFERS. I am president of the San Francisco-Ingleside branch of the National Association for the Advancement of Colored People.

MR. GLICKSTEIN. And Mr. McCullum?

MR. McCULLUM. I am president of the Oakland branch of the National Association for the Advancement of Colored People and chairman of the West Coast Region of NAACP which comprises nine Western states.

MR. GLICKSTEIN. Mr. McCullum, over the last few days we've heard a great deal of testimony about problems affecting minority group citizens. What do you feel are the most important problems faced by Negroes in the Bay Area?

MR. McCULLUM. The most important problems facing Negroes in the Bay Area are:

1. The problem of unemployment and poverty. The lack of resources and wherewithal to participate meaningfully in a money society.

The second-most problem which embraces the one of housing and education is the attitudinal problem of the dominant society that is pervaded with racist overtones and is exemplified in the limited housing market. It is exemplified in the rigid restrictions imposed by *de facto* segregation and is exemplified by the unwillingness of governmental agencies to allow the participation of poor people and minorities at meaningful levels of government. I am attempting to restrict my remarks to Oakland.

MR. GLICKSTEIN. Mr. Jeffers, some of our previous witnesses testified about the role that Negroes must play in providing employment and dealing with some of the employment problems Mr. McCullum has commented on. What do you see as the role that the Negro community must play in this area?

MR. JEFFERS. I'm not sure that we can expect or rely upon the Negro community alone to solve the problems that the Negro citizens face. Negro citizens in San Francisco—I think this to be true in the Bay Area and perhaps across the country—face problems that were not created by the Negroes themselves, so I don't think that we can expect Negroes to solve those problems.

I think if they are going to be solved effectively we are going to have to look to governmental agencies. I think we are going to have to look for new approaches.

I'm pretty well convinced that the approaches we have used for the past 100 years have not been successful in attacking these problems, and I would submit that if this country has the resources to put a man on the moon, it certainly has the resources to effectively deal with the socio-economic problems that face the minority citizens. Unfortunately, at this time I happen to feel that the country does not have the will to address itself to these problems.

MR. GLICKSTEIN. Mr. Jeffers, we've also heard some testimony about whether or not the ghetto should be dispersed. Do you think that it's realistic to speak in terms of dispersing the ghetto, for example, in San Francisco? Can the communities where Negroes are concentrated be spread throughout the city or through certain suburban areas?

MR. JEFFERS. Under the present existing conditions, I would say no. Because the ghetto results from a number of factors, one of which is the inability of citizens who live in the ghetto areas to obtain housing of their choosing any place in the city or in the area.

So if we are going to effectively disperse ghetto areas then we are going to have to come up with some means of eliminating discrimination in housing.

MR. GLICKSTEIN. Mr. McCullum, would you comment on that from the point of view of Oakland, please?

MR. McCULLUM. Yes. Mr. General Counsel, unfortunately I do not feel that the ghetto is evil of itself. The ghetto as it is presently comprised provides an unusual opportunity for the members to be subjected to harsh and oppressive tactics by any other portion of society.

I think it is unrealistic to think that places like San Leandro, Hayward, Alameda, San Lorenzo, Orinda and Lafayette will allow Negroes to move into these areas. These are basically a white pearl necklace or noose around the city of Oakand.

Here in Oakland all of the Negroes in Alameda County, save perhaps 1 or 2 percent, live in the central city, and we are ringed by a white noose of suburbia. This is one of the gut problems of the central city, not only Oakland but San Francisco, Boston, Philadelphia, Detroit, New York, Chicago, Washington, St. Louis and so forth.

The problem of the central city is that suburbia still desires to control the central city, and at nighttime they desert it to the natives and then they return again the next morning for their own economic security.

It is my desire and my understanding that those who live in the city are the ones who should control the city, and we get to one of the basic problems that we deal with here in Oakland.

Oakland is run or ruled by Piedmont, by San Leandro, Orinda, and Lafayette. The base power of this community resides there. The problems, the needs are here in Oakland.

So we have the parasitical cities around Oakland that draw on all of the resources and at the same time they do not put anything in the central city, and we have the problems of health and welfare and crime in the central city while we have the highest type of social irresponsibility by the inhabitants of San Leandro, Piedmont, Orinda, Lafayette.

This is the problem that we are grappling with throughout America. This is the base problem in this country, the domestic problem of the problem of urbanization in the central city and the social irresponsibility of those who control and run the city and have no inputs back into the city.

MR. GLICKSTEIN. Mr. McCullum, is it economic considerations that prevent Negroes from moving into San Leandro and San Lorenzo, or do you believe it's overt discrimination?

MR. McCULLUM. Sir, the economic considerations are very, very minimal, if at all. There are any number of persons in Oakland who have attempted to buy houses in certain areas in Oakland who were limited, who were refused and turned away without any regard to the economic considerations and it apparently seems to be a concerted move by persons within the business of selling property as opposed to the individual homeowners, for apparently there is some sort of understanding that certain areas will be opened up to Negroes and other minorities and other areas will be closed and as a result there is always a constant demand for the dilapidated, secondary housing while the primary housing may be utilized for and to perpetuate the racist concept of segregation and superior needs for the dominant society.

MR. GLICKSTEIN. Mr. Jeffers, we have heard testimony that there is a high rate of unemployment among Negro youth. How have the Negro youth with whom you have come in contact reacted to their inability to obtain employment?

MR. JEFFERS. I think to a considerable extent they have developed, and are still developing attitudes which seem to say: "That if this society is such that I cannot obtain gainful employment, then I am inclined to pursue that course of action which, in my opinion, will contribute to a downfall, a deterioration, a destruction of that society that denies me the opportunity of employment."

I think we find that expressed in a number of areas in increasing numbers. We note the formation of varied and numerous black nationalist oriented organizations, and I think that is a reflection, an outgrowth of the frustration that the young people face today.

MR. GLICKSTEIN. Would you say that this attitude you've just described is something that exists among a very small minority of young people or would you say there is a significant group of people who feel that way?

MR. JEEFERS. I think there is a significant group of people who feel that way, and, unfortunately, I think the numbers are growing.

MR. GLICKSTEIN. Mr. McCullum, getting back to some of your comments about the role of the suburban communities, does the concept of metropolitan or regional government offer a solution to the problems of the Negro community?

MR. MCCULLUM. Mr. General Counsel, emphatically no. If anything, any concept of regional government will do more to return us back to slavery than some of the other recent laws that have been passed. This concerns me greatly, that once a number of events occur, the minorites come into the central city, the minorities are restricted to the central city, and political powers develop within the central city so that seven major communities within these United States can exercise considerable influence on the election of a presidential candidate.

Then we come up with the new and enlightened concept of

regional government, which again disperses a political power into some different representatives by weighted voting and the like within suburbia, which runs counter to the concept of the one man-one vote principle, and which runs counter to the concept that the majority should determine their own destinies and welfare.

I feel that many of us do not realize, and particularly even our political leaders in Oakland, the insidious concept of regional government even to their own political welfare that other agencies in Marin County and Contra Costa and Napa Counties and the other bedroom counties can wield an influence to determine how and when property must be condemned, and what resources shall be used by those who are taxed within this community. I think it's a very, very serious trend. I'm not surprised because the ingenuity of the racists in this country find all means to get around playing the game according to the rules.

MR. GLICKSTEIN. But wouldn't regional or metropolitan government of some sort break down the barriers toward Negroes moving into places like San Leandro and San Lorenzo?

MR. McCULLUM. Not at all. The very opposite. Perhaps I am not clear. The concept of regional government is not necessarily, even they use the guise that they are going to serve and solve regional problems, but the basic idea is to have all the amenities of suburbia and all the comforts associated with it, without the central city, yet at the same time to utilize and to exploit the resources of the central city without paying the price.

MR. JEEFERS. May I comment on that also, Mr. General Counsel?

MR. GLICKSTEIN. Yes.

MR. JEFFERS. I view metropolitan or regional government as perhaps a step in the direction of further depriving Negroes and other minorities of opportunities to participate meaningfully in local government. Today across the country in perhaps some 10 or more cities the Negro population is such that it represents either the majority, or it certainly represents the controlling political influence in that particular city.

Regional government would therefore deprive the Negroes of the minorities who live within the central city area of effectively exercising that political power to assure representation and meaningful action in terms of the problems that the Negroes face.

So I think that instead of perhaps providing a means of solving the problem, I think it would make the problem faced by Negroes and minorities much worse than it is because the regional government would deprive the local government of many of the powers the local governments now exercise.

I might add that in the Bay Area here under ABAG the representation is one representative from each county and one representative from each city. So we immediately find that we have a number of representatives from the white suburban community areas, and of course they have left the central city areas in part to avoid having to face the problems that the Negroes are concerned with, and the Negroes have been restricted to the central city area.

So I don't think it is realistic to expect a white suburbia to address itself to the problems faced by minorities in the regional form of government.

MR. GLICKSTEIN. Mr. Jeffers, going back to something we were discussing a while ago, you described a growing militancy among young people, Negro young people. Is that feeling also pervasive among older people, adults, people of our generation?

MR. JEFFERS. I don't think the degree of militancy is perhaps there. I do think that we find among adults a growing disenchantment with the society in which we exist, in that there seems to be a total failure at this point to effectively solve these problems and I think most people recognize that if the country really wants to solve these problems it can. And they are not just content, I believe, to continually wait and talk.

But I don't feel that the degree of militancy is there, but they just don't have the faith in the kinds of activities in which they have engaged in the past in addressing these problems.

MR. GLICKSTEIN. Mr. Jeffers, you are a representative of one of the oldest and most significant civil rights organizations in the country. How has this militancy among young people that you have described and the pessimism among older people which you have described affected the program and the attitudes of NAACP?

MR. JEFFERS. Oh, I think the NAACP fortunately has been over the years flexible enough to change with the changing attitudes of its membership, to change with the changing times as they present themselves, and I think we will find a gradual, perhaps emergence of more militancy in the organization itself.

I might point out that there are a considerable number of people associated with the association who are perhaps more militant, and maybe they might be described as more progressive in some respects than some of the old guard leadership there.

MR. GLICKSTEIN. Mr. McCullum, would you care to comment on the subject we have just been discussing?

MR. McCULLUM. I think that the NAACP—and I view it as seen from the Oakland arena—that the program of the NAACP is most adversely affected by such things as the war in Vietnam, such things as the renascent racism that has resulted in the cutbacks of the poverty-antipoverty program, the reactions that have occurred in the State of California around a statewide housing law.

I think that these are the type of programs that probably adversely affect the work of the NAACP, but I am not at all concerned about the rising tide of militancy within this country. I think that many Negroes, and perhaps even Mexican Americans, have come to the decision that if they are going to survive, and if they are not going to be the ones to be selected to go to gas ovens by some "legitimate means" then they must take necessary steps in order to protect their welfare and survival within this country because either through legislation or through emergency measures we see a disturbing trend to the isolation of individuals by reason of ethnic or cultural background for specialized activity. It disturbs me, particularly around the antipoverty program.

Great in its conception, but once it was determined that the poor people were beginning to awaken, they were beginning to involve themselves, and they were beginning to articulate their needs as they saw them within the framework of the existing law, then we begin to see a tremendous move by the League of Municipal Cities, the mayors, and the governors throughout the country to call for a cutback in this.

Poverty, the problems of the poor, are basically the problems of the minorities. We are basically talking economics, and to give you an example of the $32½ million that poured into Oakland in the last year and a half by way of Federal commitment, we have supposedly 13,500 hard core unemployed. If we divide $32½ million by 13,500 we wouldn't have a hard core unemployment problem in Oakland.

MR. GLICKSTEIN. Mr. McCullum, you said that poverty is basically a problem of the minorities. Let me ask you a question from one lawyer to another. Do you think that if the poverty programs are successful and administered properly, they are programs that are designed to assure equal protection for minority group people? Do you conceive of the poverty programs as a means of implementing the protections of the 14th amendment?

MR. McCULLUM. Yes, Mr. Counsel, I would say that the equal protection clause could easily be extended to cover legislation under the antipoverty program. I think that these persons are the ones who are *de facto* disenfranchised by reason of their economic circumstance, and it is just as real in the city of Oakland as it is in Little Rock, Arkansas that if you do not have the means, or the time for a babysitter in order to go and exercise what is a free franchise you are just as disenfranchised as if you don't have $15 to pay a poll tax.

I think it is very, very important that we understand that the poor, say, for instance, in Oakland, which has a reasonably good and viable poverty program, but which is suffering right now guerilla attacks from the city administration to cut back their authority, to cut back their participation and cut back their influence and decision-making, that this is a very disastrous trend because once the poverty program presented perhaps an opportunity and a hope for participation by these people, then once it is cut out, then you have an assurance that there is no meaningful commitment to allow them to participate in the main stream.

I'm not just talking, unfortunately, just about poor Negroes or Mexican Americans in the city of Oakland, but poor white folks as well. They are just as caught up in the problems of the poor as we are, and our problem is only one of either distinguishability or language difference.

MR. GLICKSTEIN. I have no further questions, Mr. Chairman.

CHAIRMAN HANNAH. Do the Commissioners have any questions?

COMMISSIONER FREEMAN. Yes.

CHAIRMAN HANNAH. Go ahead, Mrs. Freeman.

COMMISSIONER FREEMAN. Mr. McCullum, what percentage of the population of Oakland is Negro?

MR. McCULLUM. Depending, Mrs. Freeman, depending on who is taking the census I will say this: No less than 33 to 37 percent are Negroes of the some 384,000 to 400,000, and I have great thoughts that perhaps there are more, but it does not particularly serve some people's purpose to let them know that there are as many of us as there are here in Oakland.

COMMISSIONER FREEMAN. What about the Spanish-speaking?

MR. McCULLUM. I do not know the exact figures, but I understand that the percentage is smaller, that it is somewhere around 12 to 15 percent, and this is perhaps the most significant aspect about the city of Oakland, and that is its composition.

Oakland has a significant minority population, and yet Oakland has not moved to meet the needs of its total citizenry. Even if they want to go on, "Well, we are trying to serve the needs of most of our citizens," we would come in for some beneficial treatment.

COMMISSIONER FREEMAN. What you are saying is that the aggregate of the so-called minority would really be the majority in Oakland?

MR. McCULLUM. Yes, this is true except that we have to fight with Piedmont, San Leandro and Orinda who control us.

COMMISSIONER FREEMAN. That's my next question. You were getting to political power. Will you give us some information concerning the makeup of the local govenment, the participation of the minorities in the government at the level of appointive, elective positions, top-level positions?

MR. McCULLUM. Yes. Thank you. The city of Oakland is very peculiar. We have a city council, and until just very recently there were not any Negroes on the city council, and I might indicate that no Negroes have been elected initially to the city council. But at the times that those in power determine that it is good and proper that a Negro be placed on the city council, such occurs.

Basically, what this means is that there is little relationship between the particular needs and aspirations of the persons within that community, and the ethnic group that is on the council.

Just recently we had an election. We are caught up here in Oakland in an at-large concept which is regional government on a low-bidded scale. That is, you have to come from a certain district to be elected, but you are elected at large, and each time all that is necessary to pull out the money and the power of the press, and the same people in this community can be elected by 26,000 individuals, no matter whether 80,000 are voting or not because you vote for this man in the third district, which I don't live and have no interest in, this man in the fifth, sixth, seventh and eighth because they run at large.

This is grossly undesirable in order to bring in a meaningful representation in government.

Secondly, and particularly now, we have run into a particular problem in Oakland, and I had high hopes of Oakland with its new mayor, and with his pronounced positions of the problems of the unemployed and the poor; but the mayor has taken a position publicly with reference to the Oakland Economic Development Council that I feel is disastrous to the future of the city.

That is the attempt to emasculate the policymaking powers and the determinations that the Oakland Economic Development Council has had so far.

We started out here by making certain that the poor would participate by giving them 75 percent representation within each one of their target areas so we would be certain that they would be the ones to determine their destiny, and our mayor unfortunately has come out publicly and expressed great concern because the Oakland Economic Development Council is composed of 34 minorities out of 39 on the Council, all of which is not particularly bad, except he is factually incorrect, and there are some three or four other white people that he is apparently calling minorities who might be hurt. That is No. 1.

No. 2 is that we have endured, at least since 1960 where boards and commissions have been 110 percent white, and there has not been any question in terms of their right to govern, or their right to control and to make determinations for the benefit of all of us. It seems to me that whether the OEDC is all-black or all-white is of no moment unless these persons are not committed to the progress of all of the people within the city. I think this is one of the gut problems we are dealing with here in the city of Oakland.

COMMISSIONER FREEMAN. Mr. Jeffers, you indicated that new approaches would be needed to solve the problem. Would you give us some examples of such approaches?

MR. JEFFERS. I think for one thing the Government is going to have to take a more dynamic and progressive uncompromising role in attacking these problems. This whole problem that the minorities face is, of course, interwoven with the economics of the system under which we exist.

One of the prime areas that I think must be opened up is the area of unemployment, or the area of fair employment, rather, which of course results in a very high rate of unemployment among Negroes.

If the percentage of unemployed in this country overall was the same as that existing among Negroes to date it would be considered a national crisis. But of course it is not considered that, because in my opinion it involves Negroes.

I would like to give you an example of the kind of problem that we face in San Francisco, and which has existed for a long period of time.

The example I have in mind relates to the Golden Gate Bridge District. As of mid-1965, although there were 30 painters on the Golden Gate Bridge there was not a single Negro painter on that bridge. Up until the mid-'50's the administrators of the Golden Gate Bridge District specifically requested white-only employees when they sent out their applications for employees, but of course certain legislative and judicial actions in this State changed that.

Nevertheless, the practice continued. In mid-1965 a Negro made application for employment as a painter there, and I might add that these jobs pay approximately $1,000 per month, so they are sought after, the economics of this situation.

The Negro was denied employment, although within a week of the time he made application four or five Caucasians were employed as painters, and by virtue of their background and experience they were less qualified than the Negro.

To make a long story short, this matter then went before the FEPC, the hearing resulted in a decision that the Negro be hired. He was released again this year, you see, still pursuant to that kind of policy in an effort to return to the white-only policy that existed prior to 1965.

Now, I think Government has to take a positive hand, an uncompromising position in attacking those problems.

I might indicate another area where I think stronger action is warranted, and that is in the area of contract compliance with respect to the Federal Government.

I happen to be one of those who feel that that office has a good deal of power that can be utilized to attack and eliminate discrimination that is not being used, and I think the Federal

Government is simply going to have to take a dynamic positive role in attacking these problems.

CHAIRMAN HANNAH. Mr. Rankin.

COMMISSIONER RANKIN. What percentage of the voters in Oakland are Negro, Mr. McCullum, approximately?

MR. McCULLUM. It is my understanding that 40 percent of the voters in Oakland are Negro.

COMMISSIONER RANKIN. What type of municipal taxes do you have?

MR. McCULLUM. Real estate taxes, personal property taxes, and part of this is for the schools, the other part is for special assessment districts and the like. Are you talking about like *ad valorem* type?

COMMISSIONER RANKIN. Yes. Did you ever think of a payroll tax or an income tax? You say the people—

MR. McCULLUM. Mr. Rankin, we do not control the city, and the citizens of Oakland do not control the city.

COMMISSIONER RANKIN. Don't you think with 40 percent of the voters that 10 or 15 percent of the white voters would join with you living in the city of Oakland to have people outside join with them in paying the expenses of the city?

MR. McCULLUM. Mr. Rankin, I think that's a wonderful idea, and I am not being facetious, but a payroll tax would be getting to the very heart of what I am crying about, which is the people who come here and make the money, and take it back to suburbia, and they are the ones that have us enslaved. We are their colonies.

COMMISSIONER RANKIN. But you can vote, can't you?

MR. McCULLUM. We can vote, but you can't vote unless the issue gets on the ballot. The issue won't get on the ballot unless you have a charter change, and you can't have a charter change unless you have a charter review commission that's going to take it up, and you're not going to have a charter review commission to take it up unless the mayor appoints those that are going to bring it up, and the mayor is not going to do that.

COMMISSIONER RANKIN. You've really urged him, tried to make him do so?

MR. McCULLUM. Not with reference to income tax. We have made very many futile attempts in terms of the district representation. Another example of just that—

COMMISSIONER RANKIN. Well, you've answered my question.

MR. McCULLUM. Our school board situation is much the same way. We have our school board who just recently appointed a Negro, but our school board as represented, six out of seven all come from the monied area of the town.

COMMISSIONER RANKIN. Certainly I can recognize how unpopular such a tax would be with a large number of people who have to pay that tax, but it is worth exploring, I would think.

MR. McCULLUM. That's a very good idea.

COMISSIONER RANKIN. One other point. You spoke against regional government. As far as I can gather, you are not really against regional government *per se*. You are against the basis of representation by which the governing boards of the region are selected. Am I correct in that?

MR. McCULLUM. Again, Mr. Rankin, it came about because of the weighted voting situation, and I am only flying from the seat of my pants by experience, and that is that even if they said that regional government is going to be one man-one vote, experience has taught me otherwise and I know at this point in time in the city of Oakland there are 40 percent of the registered voters that are Negroes, and perhaps the Negroes and the white folks who are interested in the progress of Oakland can, somewhere along the line, get together.

COMMISSIONER RANKIN. But regional government itself is not bad in itself, is it?

MR. McCULLUM. No, no, regional government is not bad in itself, but in every instance that it has been sought to be applied it has adverse effects for the then existent conditions of the minorities in that community.

CHAIRMAN HANNAH. Mr. Patterson.

VICE CHAIRMAN PATTERSON. Mr. McCullum, I gather that your implication is that if white America continues on its present course that there is a possibility that Oakland and other major American cities will become predominantly Negro living in the central city inside a white noose of suburbia. Is this correct?

MR. McCULLUM. Yes, sir.

VICE CHAIRMAN PATTERSON. Would you then address yourself, look into the future, and speculate on the effect this may have on the cities of the country in political terms, and in terms of the tax base, the proliferation of suburbs, the decentralization of industry? What would you look for as a result of this?

MR. McCULLUM. I think that it was demonstrated, I guess it was what—1960—was it 1960 where some eight or nine major metropolitan areas weighted the election for Philadelphia, Boston, New York, Los Angeles, San Francisco, St. Louis, Kansas City and Atlanta.

VICE CHAIRMAN PATTERSON. Presidential election?

MR. McCULLUM. That's right, presidential election. I think that this is, one, an unhealthy trend that we have this dichotomy because the central cities are going all-black, and I might make something else clear.

That the black folks and the white folks in the community who understand what is happening are not concerned about this really. You see, the only thing that we are talking about is that we want to have the opportunity to exercise control over our destiny, and this is why I'm not concerned as much about the ghetto as a label as such, but I am concerned about the ghetto and the opportunity for invidious discrimination by reason of them being physically there.

You see, the whole of America is the central city. This is where the action is, and this is where I want to be, and this is where a large nummber of other white folks want to be, you see?

There are a lot of people who aren't hung up, because I am black and you are white. They figure that you eat three meals a day, and you bleed red, and you hurt and so forth; but there are some individuals who have nothing else to hold onto except this color difference, and this is the hang-up of America, racism, and racism is on the defensive throughout the world.

I think if we face it, if we face that we are a racist society and that I am not liked solely and exclusively because I am black and that you want to preserve your position solely and exclusively because you are white, and legislation is enacted, and rules are made, and police departments are called out in order to perpetuate the system accepted now in this world, in this time, and with the events that are going on there must be a reorienting of this concept and I'm not arguing about it.

I know about the man in Arkansas, I grew up there, and I know how he acts in Alabama, and so forth and so on, and I know how he acts in Oakland, California, and this is a basic concept that pervades our entire lives. The concept that black folks are inferior and the white folks are superior, and believe me, white people generally don't buy this. White people don't buy this.

I'm talking about white folks, and the white folks that I'm talking about know what I am talking about. They don't buy this, but we have the media, we have the police department, we have the organized establishments that do everything in order to cause it to persist, and it does not bother me. It does not bother me at all because coming up in high school I was fool enough to think that the Constitution meant what it said, and I still think that, and I think that if this country cannot endure as set forth in the Constitution it does not deserve to endure at all.

VICE CHAIRMAN PATTERSON. Presumably, if and when the 40 percent Negro vote in cities like Oakland and Atlanta becomes 55 percent and you do control say, the cities with Negro government, all-Negro if you voted as a block, could you not then change the charter of your city and enact the payroll taxes and those things?

MR. McCULLUM. Oh, yes, that is correct.

VICE CHAIRMAN PATTERSON. What other steps would you look for to result from a situation of this type?

MR. McCULLUM. Say in an all-black control. I would say at least in an all-black control it would be no worse, and the probability is it might be much better than how it has been in all-white. I might give you two or three things.

At this point the black folks in America are not hung up on money, and mainly because maybe if we had the opportunity, maybe we would. Maybe we could get corrupted, but we are not hung up on the concept that a man's measure and worth is based upon the material acquisitions that he has.

We raise your little white children up until they get 12 or 13, and wash their bottoms, and feed you and everything. We are integrated, the black people in this country are integrated. It's the white people that we are talking about that are not integrated.

They can't talk that kind of talk, they can't eat certain kinds of food, they can't do the Watusi. This is part of America.

I can speak English, and wear a Brooks Brothers suit. I can talk Latin, and I can drive an automobile, and I can do the Watusi and so on, and this is life, and this is the sterility of the type of system that is trying to be imposed upon all of us, the isolation and alienation of people.

VICE CHAIRMAN PATTERSON. Certainly this is one of the reasons we are here, in the hope we can reduce that isolation by simply finding the facts and getting them before the President and the Congress and the country.

Mr. Jeffers, do you have any thoughts on this effect in the long range on the American city of the present trend of events?

MR. JEFFERS. I think they would be beneficial.

VICE CHAIRMAN PATTERSON. Beneficial?

MR. JEFFERS. Yes, on the whole. There would be certain problems, I think perhaps it would lead, to some extent, to a continual exodus from the central city area. I think, however, once the citizens realize, those who are fleeing from the area realize that they really don't have anything to fear under a black government any more than they have to fear under a white government, then I think the problem will begin to work itself out.

But one of the problems that exists now is a failure to recognize and deal with the kinds of problems that this Commission is concerned with. With black representation in government I think we will find more meaningful efforts made to effectively solve some of the problems.

CHAIRMAN HANNAH. Are there other questions the Commissioners would like to ask? Mr. Taylor?

MR. TAYLOR. Mr. McCullum, let me just explore with you a
little further this problem of the structure of government that
may help solve the problems.

You've talked about regional government in pretty strong
terms, yet you have also said there is gross misallocation of
resources between the central city and a suburban government.

We heard also that jobs are moving out to the suburbs and
people can't get out to these jobs. That the tax base is such that
schools are better supported in the suburbs than they are in the
central city.

Now, what we are talking about here are problems of strategy
for getting at these problems. Isn't it possible that the notion of
building political power in the city, keeping a community intact
will also be a futile strategy because the control that will be
achieved over institutions won't be meaningful control? It won't
be control that will enable people to manage the affairs of the
city and to put them into the kind of shape that will afford
people decent opportunity?

MR. McCULLUM. Yes. Mr. Taylor, I think that it is basically
a political situation, and I don't mean partisan politics, but it
has to do with commitment politics.

Those people, those white folks and those black folks who feel
that a black man can adequately represent their position and
they can support him in a coalition movement in government.
It does not have to be that it always has to be a good, liberal
white man to bring the coalition together.

We must, and it has been demonstrated in some areas of the
country that maybe, too, some black man of competence can
represent their interests, and I think that it can be done. But I
don't think that in Oakland at this time—and of course we have
our own internecine fights because what it is, it's powerless
people in Oakland fighting among themselves for crumbs, and
we are misdirecting all of our activity against the wrong enemy,
if they are the enemy at all.

I'm thinking, then, in terms of the liberal whites, the poor
blacks, and the black middle-class, and the Mexican Americans,
and all of the other gradations that they use to lump together
a so-called liberal coalition. This is unfortunate because what
we are fighting about is nothing.

We don't have any power, and if power is like two sponges
rubbing against each other absolutely nothing occurs, absolutely nothing. I think that the favorable tax base—San Leandro is
a very good example.

San Leandro is a good city. San Leandro is a city that any
white person would be very happy to live in, and any black
person, if they could get into it. They have a very substantial

industrial base. They have very good schools. They don't have the problems of overcrowding.

Some of the things that occur are this: You know, if they get a big, big fire in San Leandro they will call the Oakland Fire Department. If they get a big, big police problem in San Leandro they will call the Oakland Police Department. Any of the services such as the Museum, the Symphony, Health Services and all of these are ready and waiting, which they bear no economic responsibility for, which drains what limited resources we have in Oakland and yet, at the same time, they will not even accord us the opportunity to pay the full, going price for housing there.

MR. TAYLOR. From what you say wouldn't that lead to the conclusion that what is necessary is a coalition of forces that will exercise influence on government throughout metropolitan areas, not just in the city, to achieve the things that you are concerned about? Jobs for everyone, a good education for everyone, and not limited to within the city itself.

MR. MCCULLUM. Mr. Taylor, the only thing—and everything that the members of the Commission are saying is true, except that it ain't like that. The thing is, San Leandro is not concerned about the hard core unemployed. Orinda is not concerned about *de facto* segregation. Lafayette is not concerned about the problems of the ghetto. San Lorenzo is not concerned about the high crime rate. No concern, no problem, no action.

They talk about doing something else, or having another social affair, seeing how much more money they can drag out of Oakland. These are the problems of the central city, and the only persons that are going to be able to deal with them effectively is the central city and the Federal Government.

I think the type of provincialism that exists around the central city will not make this possible. It's very good, it's beautiful, but it ain't like that.

MR. TAYLOR. Thank you.

CHAIRMAN HANNAH. Thank you very much, gentlemen. We are very grateful to you for being here this morning. You made a good contribution. You are excused. Mr. Glickstein, will you call the next witness.

MR. GLICKSTEIN. The next witness is Mr. Mark Comfort.

(Whereupon, MR. MARK COMFORT was sworn by the Chairman and testified as follows:)

TESTIMONY OF MR. MARK COMFORT, OAKLAND, CALFORNIA

CHAIRMAN HANNAH. Go ahead, Mr. Glickstein.

MR. GLICKSTEIN. Mr. Comfort, would you please state your full name and address for the record.

457

MR. COMFORT. Mark Everett Comfort, 6914 Lockwood Street, Oakland.

MR. GLICKSTEIN. Is that in East Oakland?

MR. COMFORT. Yes.

MR. GLICKSTEIN. Mr. Comfort, what is your occupation?

MR. COMFORT. Unemployed interior decorator.

MR. GLICKSTEIN. Mr. Comfort, you have worked extensively in your community with young people in various organizations. Is that correct?

MR. COMFORT. Yes, for some two years now.

MR. GLICKSTEIN. Would you tell the Commissioners what you view as the employment and housing problems faced by persons in your community.

MR. COMFORT. Well, we will start with the unemployment which always seem to be the major problems, not only here, but across the country.

Among the young black youth of the city of Oakland, and among the older blacks, but mainly the young ones, there is always the problem of finding employment.

For an example, this year you will have anywhere from between twenty and twenty-five thousand black youth on the streets of Oakland, not to speak of the Mexican, not to speak of the poor whites that live in the flatland areas that will be seeking employment, and that out of a million and some eight hundred thousand dollars that the Central Labor Council get from the Federal Government we can only place 500 people on these jobs among the youth from 16 to 21.

Last year I worked for the Central Labor Council as youth supervisor, and so a lot of jobs would be, you know, through nonprofit organizations; but the price that they paid for this War on Poverty Program is not enough for anyone to live on. $1.25 an hour, $1.30, perhaps $1.35 this year.

If they would raise the price up to $2.50 or $3 perhaps maybe we would be able to derive more through the nonprofit organizations, but it's not done this way. So I think that the unemployment problem, since the Americans are spending anywhere from $50 to $60 million a day fighting the war in Vietnam is that the problem of unemployment among the minorities will increase more heavier each year as it goes.

MR. GLICKSTEIN. How about housing problems?

MR. COMFORT. Well, the housing is the same. The Acorn Project that went through the West Oakland area, which we call the black removal, they was going to build high rise apartments down in the area. If they ever get around to doing it, the price of the apartments would cost so much that the poor people among the blacks would never be able to pay the rent anyway.

So actually if the Federal Government would think about putting in more housing units, lower-price housing units in the city of Oakland it might be able to eliminate some of the problems as far as housing. But we have so much discrimination in housing people who have the money to buy homes in different areas in Oakland can't buy anyway because of discrimination and, I guess, you know we shall see what happens, you know, on the Acorn Project. So far, nothing has happened on it yet, anyway.

MR. GLICKSTEIN. You suggested, Mr. Comfort, that there is overt discrimination in the sale of housing in the city of Oakland?

MR. COMFORT. Yes. You see, the population of the blacks in the city of Oakland is over one-third of the population, about 135,000 or 140,000 black people live in the city of Oakland, not to speak of the Mexican Americans which makes anywhere from 40,000 maybe 50,000 by now. You put that together and you have close to 200,000 minorities living in the city of Oakland, in a city of probably 386,000 people and that the great amount of discrimination in the housing for Mexican Americans and also the black Americans in the city of Oakland is very high rated not only that, through the unions also, you see. You have a whole basic phase of the unions and the contractors where you find the unions which are all really white trade unions and racist unions, on top of the fact is through your operating engineers where there is no black people, or any minorities working there.

You have the plumbers and electricians unions. You have the steel workers sometimes called "rod busters," where there are no blacks or minorities working in those. So what we have is that the man will say, "There is no qualified black people" and we have found this to be a lie because the black people come from the Southern States to the State of California and Oakland that have qualifications, but they are pushed back into a corner because of the discrimination in the unions here.

It's a damn shame because the simple reason is that in the South they were allowed to work in these jobs but not making very much money. So they came up West and up North trying to carry the same experience that they have, and the job that they do, and find they are pushed into a corner, that they have to join the labor union, and this is where they stay never having an opportunity to go ahead with their original trade.

MR. GLICKSTEIN. Mr. Comfort, on some of the things that you have just said, are you speaking from personal experience?

MR. COMFORT. For example, on this I can speak maybe because I went to school for four years in Los Angeles to become an interior decorator. I came back in 1955 and joined the union, and they wanted to push me off into the Oakland area, and I wanted to get into the Hayward local, Local 1178, because that's where all the

459

work was at that time. They said the books were closed and in 1958, you know, when I was working in the Kelly Hill area which, at that time they did not sell houses to black people either, which is heavier populated now. But in 1958 they didn't have any.

They needed painters so bad so that the contractor—I was working as a laborer—talked to his friend, which was the foreman of the painting crew, and told him that, you know, I was a painter, and I brought my papers and showed them to him.

So they gave me a piece of paper to take down to the union, and I got into the union. But it took that time, from 1955 to '58, to get in after doing four years, you know, very hard to be treated so.

MR. GLICKSTEIN. Some of the problems that you have discussed you have personally experienced?

MR. COMFORT. Yes.

MR. GLICKSTEIN. I think you indicated before that you do a lot of work with young people in your community. Would you describe to the Commissioners some of the young men and women with whom you work? What are their attitudes?

MR. COMFORT. Well, you see, coming out of a ghetto or a black community, whichever you prefer, is that it has always been a problem, and probably will continue to be one as long as the system itself is the way it is.

It's like you've heard attested to, you know, they get juvenile records. So when they get up to the age of 18 or 19 seeking employment these are used against them.

Black youth will hit the streets and start looking for jobs, and they are turned down every place they go so that eventually they get tired, you see. They just give up hope altogether, and they hit the street corners, but not because of their own will that this happens to them but because society itself has created this problem that have put them in a bag that they're in, you see.

Take last year, for instance, that the city, the schools of Oakland, had exempted 900 youths, which was walking the streets of Oakland, 90 percent of them were black.

MR. GLICKSTEIN. What do you mean by exempted?

MR. COMFORT. Meaning that if a black kid in the school system got in a fight with a kid from Oakland, a white kid, he is suspended from school and the white kid stays in. If it happens a second time the board of education would exempt him, meaning he can no longer go to school as long as he lives in the city of Oakland.

There was 900 kids that the city put out on the streets. Then, after they put them on the streets they said, "It becomes a police problem," you see? We went down to the board of education hundreds and hundreds of times with these problems. We've been to the city council and all this, and these people are so old, and

have been on there for so long that they are antiques, you see,
and they should actually be taken out of office because they don't
know what they're doing. They're messing up the whole situation
and black people don't have a chance to do anything.

Black kids come from families of eight, nine, ten. Some have
stepmothers, some have stepfathers. Some don't have no mothers
or no fathers and they are living on welfare, barely enough to
live on, and with all these problems existing, then when we walk
these lines and we bring the problems to the attention of the people, that there is a problem existing that needs to be changed, then
all of a sudden we become Communists, hoodlums and everything
else, but no one seems to want to solve the problems.

Like it's nice of you ladies and gentlemen to come down and
set up the Civil Rights Commission and the hearings, but it's
too bad you don't have the power to do anything about it.

But you put in more statistics, and that's where it goes. You
spend more money on statistics than on solving the problem.

So when things blow in the city people sit back and want to
know why, and all the time we're telling you why.

MR. GLICKSTEIN. You mentioned that a lot of the young people you work with have police records and that affects their
employment?

MR. COMFORT. Let's put it this way: Is that the companies,
perhaps, where they are going to seek employment, will use this
as an excuse, you know. That way they can get around the fact
that someone can be prejudiced, because we have a lot of racists
and unions and factories in the city of Oakland, and we might
as well face it because that's the way it is.

MR. GLICKSTEIN. Have you in any of your activities succeeded
in finding jobs for young people?

MR. COMFORT. Well, we have an organization called Youth
For Jobs, and back in 1962 we were able—well, for an example,
the—let's see, I get myself tired—the Doggie Diners told us that
we didn't have to picket Doggie Diners, because a lot of people
know it's a fact that we were able to negotiate with Doggie Diners
to start hiring minorities, and that this was during the time we
had the *ad hoc* Committee to End Discrimination. They hadn't
hired a black person since 1948 at that time to work in the Doggie
Diners, so that the agreement was signed, and that there was no
demonstration so, therefore, there was no publicity on the fact.
But since that period of time there is quite a few minorities, black
and Mexican American, which are working in Doggie Diners now.

Also the Quick Way was another Youth For Jobs that at that
time we were able to get blacks in. We only had one black person
working at that time at 21st and Telegraph, but after negotiating
with the owner of Quick Way, which there also was no publicity
on that, that we were able to negotiate the fact that since there's

a large turnover in the restaurant business anyway, that we would send them youths, and we had a number of applications filed on the Youth For Jobs at that time.

We would send a youth down, so therefore they started to hiring them. So at the present time they have quite a few black people and Mexican Americans that are working in both of those places.

And, of course, on the program last year of 1965 and '66, through the Central Labor Council I was able to shoot some couple hundred youths down to get jobs.

The point is that people will sit back and say that youth nowadays doesn't want to do anything but to hang around on the corners. They wouldn't work if you would give them a job.

This was proven to be a lie because they only had applications for 200 youths to go to work in '65 and '66, and there were some 600 showed up in a period of two days to put in an application for work. So that's $1.25 an hour—

MR. GLICKSTEIN. You only had 200 vacancies and 600 youths showed up?

MR. COMFORT. Yes, 600 showed up, but only 200 would be chosen out of that 600 which put a dent in the lie of people saying, you know, the first thing people will say when you see youths on the street corner, and they see them drinking wine and everything like that.

What people keep forgetting is that they are not there of their own choosing. They've been pushed into this corner by society and that they will rebel back any way they see is necessary.

MR. GLICKSTEIN. Mr. Comfort, has industry been moving from the Oakland area?

MR. COMFORT. Well, you take Colorado Fuel & Iron a few years ago moved out of the city of Oakland into the Southern States, which put some 1,500 people unemployed at that time. Take the Dole Pineapple, which is the cannery which employed some 2,000 people that looked forward for it each year as a part-time job. Some looked forward, for that was the only job that they had. Then, after they closed down Dole Pineapple and went back to Hawaii that put these people in the unemployment line also, and that a lot has been stated because of the taxes that are so high here that are put on the factories and through the Rapid Transit that is going through the black community and tearing out the factories, little places that were there, perhaps a lot of people that were employed there lost their jobs because these people will take this money and establish somewhere else. You take in San Leandro out of 86,000 people we only have about 12 black people, and they hired one black police officer there and couldn't even find a place for him to live in San Leandro because of discrimination.

Yet they have this deal where a factory can come into San Leandro and don't have to pay taxes on it for four years. But in

Oakland we always say that the taxes are not too high here, but industry keep moving out, believe it or not, and especially small businesses like that, that is moving out all the time.

Yet more people are becoming unemployed all the time. And yet people will go to the unemployment office and they will put out an application and, like say with the Job Fair, out of all these thousands of applications that were taken there very few of these were filled.

It was a beautiful show, you know. It looked good on paper, but as far as actually getting jobs for these people, they didn't. It's an American problem, really. It's an American problem, and I'm afraid that the monkey lies on the Federal Government's back, you see.

MR. GLICKSTEIN. What do you think the Federal Government could do to provide meaningful employment for young men?

MR. COMFORT. I think as long as the war in Vietnam continues on, I don't think they will be able to do much of anything for the young people since they're taking most of their money to fight it, and I think by the end of the year they will probably be spending $70 million a day. I think by that time the problem we're involved in will be 10 times or 20 or 40 times worse than it is now.

So I figure that if they are going to get this money for the War on Poverty Program and Youth Opportunity Programs for the ages of 16 to 21, then they should on take the situation of raising the prices of salaries for these people to at least $2 or $3 an hour. Therefore they can hire adults and supervisors, and then they can pay them a decent salary, the nonprofit organization which is here in the city of Oakland I am speaking about, and I think that the suggestion could be used across the country, is that when you go like to the port of Oakland, you know, is that the kids that were working last year, they told them they would put them in a training program this year.

What happens? This year they come back and they put them out in Livermore somewhere chopping weeds, so the kids quit because they did not fulfill the promise that they had told them the year before, you see? So therefore if the Federal Government is going to put millions of dollars into this program then they should take into consideration paying people a decent salary because they do do a man's work, because I know, because I supervised them in '65 and '66 and they will work, but not at $1.30 an hour.

Because when they take out the income tax and social security they have no money left, but yet they're still willing to work for this sum of money. There have been guys who came back from Vietnam and couldn't get work at 19 and 20 years of age, who had to go to work on this program of the Central Labor Council for this $1.30 an hour. So no one can say or hold up this old myth that they don't want to work, that they are lazy. I think that went out with the horse and buggy days.

The point is how can you work when there is no jobs, and we might as well stop fooling ourselves about it.

MR. GLICKSTEIN. I have no further questions.

CHAIRMAN HANNAH. Mrs. Freeman.

COMMISSIONER FREEMAN. Mr. Comfort, the 900 youngsters that you say were exempt, or exempt from school, did all of those youngsters want education and the school district would not make available the schools for them? Is that correct?

MR. COMFORT. Well, see, you have the Kennedy School and you have Dewey School here that some of them can go to, but they don't learn too much, but at least it's a try.

The Kennedy School was a pretty good deal for them, but it was not too much it could do to further their education that great.

What happens, a lot of these kids that were on the street went into the Job Corps where they were able to go ahead and learn enough when they came out that they could file—what's the word for it—a certificate, you know, the same as a diploma from high school.

A lot of them went into the service, and a lot of them are still walking the streets because we went down to the board of education to try and get back in the school, and they went through a whole lot of mumbo jumbo saying they would take it into consideration. The kids are still walking the streets, and that was two years ago.

COMMISSIONER FREEMAN. They're still waiting for the board of education to readmit them to school?

MR. COMFORT. Yes, because you have to request it. Then the board of education stated, "You have to have an attorney" and all of this, after the kids were sent to the reformatory for whatever the crime had to do with, fighting, whatever the problem was.

That when they came back out they were still looked on as being a criminal, therefore they are still walking the streets, like one kid named Sammy Shaw has been walking the streets for two years, and he still can't get back in school in the city of Oakland, after going down and requesting, you know, before the board of education that he had served his time, and that he wanted to continue his education in school. That was two years ago and he's still walking the streets.

COMMISSIONER FREEMAN. Thank you.

CHAIRMAN HANNAH. Any other questions? Mr. Taylor?

MR. TAYLOR. Mr. Comfort, you said that many young people are willing to take jobs even at low pay, but I understand that there are some young people who will reject a job if it only pays $1.25 or $1.50 an hour and it doesn't seem to offer much chance for advancement. Is that right?

464

MR. COMFORT. Yes, because then you are speaking of the kids 18 or 19 years old, and 20 and 21. But a kid may be 16 years old, you know, may think it's pretty good to pick up a little change like that. But still, after giving him a job and promising him something that you are not able to deliver, is that the kids, you tell them, "Well, you work this year and next year we will put you into a training program where you can further your education and learn a trade."

So the next year the kid comes back and you put him out in the field chopping weeds, and he walks off the job.

You can't blame him. Because they are not fulfilling their promise that they stated they were going to do in the first place.

MR. TAYLOR. Some people would say that a youngster should take the job even if it's very low pay, and even if the work is not very good or not very promising, simply because it's a step, and he gets a toehold, and maybe it's a step up the ladder. What is your reaction to that?

MR. COMFORT. I guess it would have to depend on the individual person. It's that the kids that came down, you know, to seek this employment through the Central Labor Council in the summer of '65 and '66 came, you know, with shoes half off their feet, and their clothes were raggedy and so forth. They figured here was a chance to make enough money to buy themselves some clothes and to get some things, maybe a raggedy old car or something they didn't have before.

The point is that was in 1966, and this year the kid perhaps may be 17 or 18 and he's looking for a little more because the price of living is so high in the country. Even at 18 years old he's going to have to at least make a decent salary to survive on, you see, and but yet there's hundreds of these kids who are willing to accept this job as it is.

Others are looking for something better, you see, because some kids can hustle that much money on the street, you see, so why should they go to work eight hours a day for $1.30 an hour, and then at the end of the week they'll take almost all of it back in income tax, social security and whatever other tax they're going to put on so he actually isn't making anything. He don't work long enough to make enough to where he can draw unemployment.

Maybe, probably he'll get a little back on the income tax return, but if he can work long enough to where he can build up unemployent, then at least that would carry him over when the jobs were ended. With $2.00, $2.50 an hour this would probably make it possible for these young people at this age to build up unemployment when they see a job close down at the end of the year.

MR. TAYLOR. Thank you.

CHAIRMAN HANNAH. Thank you very much, Mr. Comfort. We

appreciate your coming. You are excused. Mr. Glickstein, will you call the next witness?

MR. GLICKSTEIN. The next witness is Mr. Mordecai Johnson, an attorney on the staff for the Commission, who will give a brief background report.

(Whereupon, Mr. Mordecai Johnson was sworn by the Chairman and testified as follows:)

TESTIMONY OF MR. MORDECAI JOHNSON, ATTORNEY, U.S. COMMISSION ON CIVIL RIGHTS

MR. JOHNSON. Oakland residents commonly speak of the Oakland flatlands and the Oakland hills. The flatlands are predominantly nonwhite, the hills predominantly white. The flatlands consist of basically four areas—East Oakland, Fruitvale, North Oakland and West Oakland.

Extensive clearance has taken place in the Oakland flatlands in recent years. Between 1960 and 1965 about 7,000 housing units were eliminated in connection with the discontinuance of temporary public housing, code enforcement, the Acorn Redevelopment Project, and construction of a post office site in West Oakland, the Grove-Shafer Freeway and BART. Most of these units were in poverty target areas in the Oakland flatlands. Most of the clearance which already has taken place has been in West Oakland.

Approximately 37,000 persons live in West Oakland. About 9,000 are white, including 2,200 white persons of Mexican descent. In addition, there are 2,600 Negroes and 2,000 other nonwhites.

West Oakland is one of the city's oldest areas. More than 90 percent of all its housing units were built before 1939. In 1960, about two-thirds of the housing was structurally sound. If, however, those units classified as sound but lacking all or some plumbing were added to those considered deteriorated or dilapidated, almost half of the units would have been substandard.

The city's two redevelopment projects now in the execution stage—the Acorn and Oak Center Projects—are in West Oakland. The Acorn Project consisting of over 50 acres, is bounded roughly by Brush, First, Union, and Tenth Streets. Prior to clearance in the early 1960's, there were more than 4,300 persons residing in over 1,700 dwelling units. An estimated 80 percent of these persons were Negro and most of the white persons were of Mexican American background. Over 80 percent of the persons living in the project area were in substandard housing. The average family consisted of about four persons and had an income of about $4,000. About six out of eight families were renters and the average rent for a family was about $65 per month.

After relocation, the average Acorn family paid $75 a month for rent. Almost two-thirds were relocated in decent, safe, and sanitary housing. Relocation took place primarily within West Oakland, nearby North Oakland, and East Oakland. None of the displaced persons relocated to the Oakland Hills.

The Acorn Redevelopment Plan calls for industrial use, along with a small retail and commercial center, south of 8th Street and for residential development between 8th and 10th Streets. The Nimitz Freeway will serve as a buffer between the two areas. By mid-1966, new industries had created 282 new jobs in the industrial portion of the project, with an annual payroll of over $2 million. The planned residential community will consist of 34½ acres with about 900 family rental units of moderate income, racially integrated Section 221(d)(3) housing, and about 150 units for the elderly. These units will range from one to four bedrooms and rents will range from $80 to $140 per month, including utilities. The FHA has allocated about $7 million for this housing. Construction of the first 400 units is slated to begin in June, 1967.

Immediately to the north of the Acorn Project is the 56 block Oak Center Redevelopment Project. It is bounded roughly by the Nimitz Freeway, and by 18th, Brush, and 10th Streets. There are 1,098 structures within the Oak Center project area: 1,037 are residential structures. The redevelopment plan calls for conserving as many of these structures as possible.

Three other redevelopment projects are planned by the city. The 70 block, 163 acre Corridor Project, immediately east of Oak Center, will be primarily a downtown commercial venture. The $34 million Oakland Chinatown Project, immediately east of Acorn, is intended to be a "New Chinatown." It was proposed by the residents and businessmen of Oakland's Oriental section. The Peralta College Project, south of Lake Merrit, will include a downtown campus for Peralta College, high-rise dwellings, and a park.

In addition, the redevelopment agency has expressed the need for immediate attention to the blighted area immediately east of the Peralta College site in the westerly portion of East Oakland.

The redevelopment agency estimated in July, 1966 that these projects alone would displace about 8,000 families and individuals, of which about 2,400 would qualify for public housing. Oakland has relatively few units of three or more bedrooms for low-income persons. A 1966 survey of 1,000 of the city's 5,400 apartment house owners showed that of 559 vacant standard units available to low-income persons, only 38 had three or more bedrooms.

Oakland has over 1,400 units of public housing. In 1966, the city's voters approved 2,500 units for construction on a scattered site basis. In addition, the city council approved 1,100 units of scattered site leased housing under Section 23 of the Housing Act of 1937, as amended.

CHAIRMAN HANNAH. Thank you, Mr. Johnson.

Mr. Glickstein, would you call the next witnesses?

MR. GLICKSTEIN. The next witnesses are Mrs. Lillian O. Love and Mr. Ralph S. Williams.

(Whereupon, Mrs. Lillian Q. Love and Mr. Ralph S. Williams were sworn by the Chairman and testified as follows:)

TESTIMONY OF MRS. LILLIAN Q. LOVE, OAKLAND, CALIFORNIA AND MR. RALPH S. WILLIAMS, OAKLAND, CALIFORNIA

MR. GLICKSTEIN. Will you please each state your full name and address for the record?

MRS. LOVE. Mrs. Lillian Q. Love, 1223 Adeline street in Oakland.

MR. WILLIAMS. Ralph S. Williams, Sr., 3228 Magnolia Street, Oakland.

MR. GLICKSTEIN. What is your occupation, Mrs. Love?

MRS. LOVE. I'm supervisor and general assistant in the Oakland Welfare Department, Alameda County.

MR. GLICKSTEIN. How long have you lived in Oakland?

MRS. LOVE. More than 40 years.

MR. GLICKSTEIN. What is your occupation, Mr. Williams?

MR. WILLIAMS. I work for the U. S. Navy. I've worked there going on 24 years.

MR. GLICKSTEIN. How long have you lived in Oakland?

MR. WILLIAMS. Seventeen years, thereabouts.

MR. GLICKSTEIN. Mrs. Love, do you live in West Oakland?

MRS. LOVE. I live in West Oakland in the Oak Center area.

MR. GLICKSTEIN. What is the racial composition of that area?

MRS. LOVE. Majority nonwhite. I'd say approximately 95 or 90 percent.

MR. GLICKSTEIN. How many years have you lived in that area?

MRS. LOVE. For the length of time that I just told you.

MR. GLICKSTEIN. The whole period of time?

MRS. LOVE. Yes.

MR. GLICKSTEIN. Has the racial composition of that area changed over the years?

MRS. LOVE. Perceptibly. Up until World War II the area was a melting pot composed of Poles, Slavonians, Norwegians, Greeks, Italians, and the colored and others, I guess from Western Europe. It was truly a melting pot.

MR. GLICKSTEIN. It was after World War II that the changes began to take place?

MRS. LOVE. Yes. After World War II in the migration from the Southern and some Eastern States the population began to change, until now it is predominantly colored.

MR. GLICKSTEIN. Mr. Williams, you also live in West Oakland?

MR. WILLIAMS. This is true.

MR. GLICKSTEIN. And you've lived there for 17 years?

MR. WILLIAMS. Seventeen years.

468

MR. GLICKSTEIN. Would you describe the quality of the housing in your area, please.

MR. WILLIAMS. It's a mixture. You have some good houses and you have some bad houses. You have some well-kept lawns and you have some lawns that is not well kept. It's just about maybe 70-30, something like that.

MR. GLICKSTEIN. You have some inexpensive housing and some more expensive housing?

MR. WILLIAMS. Well, the way it is in West Oakland if your house is brand-new as long as you own it, particularly a Negro, it's inexpensive as long as you have it; but when it comes time for them to take your property, it's very expensive after they take it away from you.

MR. GLICKSTEIN. Mrs. Love, there have been several urban renewal projects, some of which Mr. Johnson just described in West Oakland, that have involved extensive clearance in the past. Would you tell the Commissioners something about those projects?

MRS. LOVE. I've been very interested in housing. In fact, I've been involved in it even as a teenager because my family was involved in it, having to lose three houses in the original public clearance, and this took place around 1937, '38· The Bill was passed in '36·

At that time people organized because there was a real desire not to have the area completely cleared. There was lobbying, there was some change of the law as a result of the citizens.

In spite of the fact that the area that was chosen for clearance was not as deteriorated as the authorities made people believe, the area which is known now as the Peralta Villa and the area known as Campbell Villa was completely cleared, and the people at that time—of course there was no relocation plan—the individuals residing therein had to find their own housing, and had to take the very low offers for their homes. This was in '37, '38 and '39·

Our house happened to be the last one to remain in the Peralta Villa and we stayed there two years amid acres of cleared land mainly because we were fighting in the courts and my father was determined that he would not sign for his house to go.

When we did leave it was because we were just lonely not having any neighbors around, but it certainly impressed me as to how citizens can be dealt with by authority, so I became greatly concerned.

Following that we organized the West Oakland Improvement Association which was determined to prevent further clearance. We were not completely successful. We did succeed in recalling two councilmen who were advocates of public housing because West Oakland at that time was the target. There was no talk of any other area of Oakland being used for public housing and we felt that if public housing was so good for the people of Oakland, it should be good for the rest of Oakland as well as the West Oakland area.

I might add that during that time, and I'm not talking about the time after the 1949 redevelopment law but prior, that during that time the people of Oakland were informed that there were no decent houses in the Peralta and the Campbell areas, and in order to convince the people there were houses along 3rd and 5th—some of which are still standing,—houses that were greatly deteriorated were shown to the people as the type of house in the area that was chosen for clearance.

Then, when the law was effected and the people were approving it and the council passed it, they went into the Peralta area and took what I feel was the most desirable area because it was close to what was the key system, trains, close to downtown, and they left the housing. They said it was not decent, it was not habitable, and even the houses that were chosen as being not habitable were moved to other sites in West Oakland, showing that it was fairly sound housing.

Following that the 1949 Redevelopment Act brought in a little more consideration for people. My concern has mainly been with the way citizens have been treated under urban renewal and redevelopment. There has never been, except for the last few years, any concern for what the people wanted. They were not even made aware or informed as to what was really going to happen.

There was no in-depth opportunities for people to study what was going to occur to them, and there is some of that, I think, existing in redevelopment now.

Acorn was a good example. When the surveys were made it was said that there were only five houses that were worth saving in that area.

This was not true. It was based on random surveys. It was based on information by individuals who were supposed to represent the people, and when the people became aware of exactly what was occurring at the public hearing the protests that arose at that time—and it was too late—indicated that the survey itself had not touched the people who occupied the area.

Acorn, as you know, was cleared. There was some relocation by the agency, much by the people themselves.

MR. GLICKSTEIN. Were you living in the Acorn area when it was cleared?

MRS. LOVE. I live in Oak Center. I've always lived in Oak Center and what is now the Peralta area. Living next to Acorn, what was going on was very vivid in the minds of the people and I was approached on many occasions by elderly people who said, "We must do something to prevent this from happening in our area."

I knew from the houses there, having taken a survey for the

city of Oakland in 1934, and having covered every house in the West Oakland area I knew the condition, and having lived there, I knew the condition of the majority of the homes.

I knew that there were some that were quite deteriorated. I knew there were some that were in fairly good condition, and I knew that people were not being given or allowed to get loans on their property to bring up their property to what they considered a desirable standard.

I felt that this was a disservice to people because much of this was FHA money, and yet the people in West Oakland were not being given an opportunity to use it, even if they were able to pay.

And so at the behest of many residents and working with what . was the private organization, Council of Social Planning, we decided to organize. Up to this time all of the citizen interaction with the agency was action on the basis of protest. It was reaction to what was happening. We felt that perhaps we needed a new approach, that maybe we needed to interact not on the basis of protests, but in working with the agency, in helping to bring about some change and this was the basis of our organization and has been our function since June, 1963.

We have succeeded in bringing about some change. I think it has been the pressure of the people rather than on the part of the agency itself to see that the change was brought about. It has been a step-by-step procedure. We have made gains, and then we have set-backs.

After organizing in June of '63, working closely with the agency in order to disseminate as much information as we could get to the people, getting information from the regional office, we attempted to bombard the people of Oak Center with everything that we could find about urban renewal and redevelopment. We studied the law. And then we called the agency members in, and we worked with the agency itself because we felt that a citizens group should work with a citizens group, and we could not trust the staff. We felt that they were geared for physical rehabilitation as has been redevelopment throughout the Nation up to a year or so ago.

MR. GLICKSTEIN. Your Oak Center neighborhood association was opposed to demolition of houses. Is that correct?

MRS. LOVE. We were opposed to clearance.

MR. GLICKSTEIN. To clearance?

MRS. LOVE. Yes. We knew that in any urban renewal project in Oak Center there would be some demolition, but we did not feel a random survey should clear a whole area when there were good sound houses there.

MR. GLICKSTEIN. What were you proposing as an alternative to clearance?

MRS. LOVE. We were proposing rehabilitation maximum and

this was our urgent request. We had to do our own surveys because as we went behind the surveys that were placed as official surveys we found that they were not accurate, and all of this was done with volunteer time and for a while with some staff member from the Council of Social Planning.

When new maps would come out showing that it wasn't feasible for large areas to be rehabilitated, we checked behind and we found it wasn't accurate. We found that we were told at one point that there would be a rehabilitation project, a maximum one, while the regional government was being fed information by technicians which meant that very, very few of the houses would remain, and we accused the city of lying to the people.

We did have a shake-up on the staff, and we got the present director.

We had always stressed that in the redevelopment program there should be one section set aside for dealing with people, and a section with staff members that could be concerned with the needs of people, concerned with what people wanted for their area and feeding them information. We got that about two years after our organization was formed.

We made some changes in the project, and I say this because I feel that citizens can make changes, but they have to be banded together in an organization, and the crux of the whole thing is that you are working with people who are not trained for leadership in this area, who need the Federal Government through its community relations section to make available to citizens some staff members who can speak for citizens because these are working people.

Many of them are not well educated. Many of them are not aware of the laws and regulations that would protect them, and I think that this should be a growing concern on the part of HUD, that there be somebody that can speak for people and help the people in developing their leadership.

I think there ought to be a marriage of the poverty program with the redevelopment agency in order that the neighborhood component can work toward informing people and helping to develop this leadership.

I feel that the social section of any redevelopment agency—and if they don't have one, I can see why they are in trouble. Because through our efforts, working closely with the staff after we had gotten far along, we were able to work fairly harmoniously, except when we found that things promised were not really being put into effect.

Through our efforts we have a rehabilitation project. We asked for it. In fact, we went to public hearing and we asked for it, but it was only after the result of three years of constant working, arguing, protesting, and refusing to accept some of the plans that the agency or the staff itself handed to the people.

Planners plan for what they think the people need, and often are not concerned with what the people's needs are themselves.

MR. GLICKSTEIN. Mr. Williams, are you familiar with the Acorn Project Area?

MR. WILLIAMS. To some degree, yes.

MR. GLICKSTEIN. Where did the people who were relocated as a result of clearance in that area move to?

MR. WILLIAMS. Well, to my knowledge, some went to East Oakland, Brookfield Village, Castlemont area. Some went to Berkeley, and I imagine some went to Hayward and other areas· wherever they could find a place to go.

MR. GLICKSTEIN. Do you believe that most of the people that were moved out of that area as a result of clearance will be able to move back when redevelopment is completed?

MR. WILLIAMS. No. According to the information that I received from the previous director I—not the one we have now, but just before they were changed, they were saying at that time that the houses was not being built for the people that was moved out because we specifically asked this question in a hearing one day.

No, they will not be able to move back in the area once it is rehabilitated with these high-rise apartments and these expensive, what they consider low-rent apartments. They will not be able to move back.

MR. GLICKSTEIN. The housing that is contemplated will be more expensive than the housing that was demolished?

MR. WILLIAMS. That is correct. To my knowledge at this time, I think a one-bedroom home for an elderly person it was quoted would start at maybe something like $90 a month or $80 a month, and the average one of these type of persons will be people who are retired and probably the income—they are living on a fixed income, and probably it would be something like $250 a month or maybe even $300 a month. By the time they pay the rent out of that they will not have anything else left to live on.

MR. GLICKSTEIN. We understand that attempts are going to be made to integrate the Acorn area. Do you, Mr. Williams, think that this is an important effort?

MR. WILLIAMS. Will you repeat the question?

MR. GLICKSTEIN. We understand that attempts are going to be made to integrate the housing that is being built in the Acorn area. Do you think that this is an important effort?

MR. WILLIAMS. I think it's an important effort, but I don't believe that it is going to work as they have in mind that it will work.

What they have in mind from my thinking about the matter is this: that if the majority race move in there, and what few of the minority race will move in there according to the way the rents are going to be charged, then it will be some professional person, maybe a doctor, lawyer, or some big businessman. But the average Joe that is working for a living will not be able to move in there regardless of what kind of effort is made to integrate the West Oakland Acorn Project.

MR. GLICKSTEIN. Why do you think it was decided to put up a project that would be integrated?

MR. WILLIAMS. First of all, in my mind there is a multiplicity of reasons as to why this happened that way.

No. 1, to begin with, West Oakland is the most valuable property there is in the city of Oakland due to the fact of its location.

It is geographically located as to where if you want to walk downtown you can do that for exercise. If you wanted to take a plane, you are within walking distance if you just wanted to leave home or walk to the Oakland Airport. If you want to catch a ship you can go around to the harbor and catch a ship, and these people have found that out a long time ago, and they come around, as I said before, and as long as the minority people owned this property it was valueless.

But they came along, some people had a house and two lots, and they gave them probably $12,000 as maybe the maximum. Then they took the house and the two lots, and turned right around and sold one lot for $25,000 and $30,000.

The reason why they want that property is because of its location, and this redevelopment is nothing but Negro removal, and I think this is what it's all about.

They want to move the Negroes out and what few Negroes move back when it is integrated, this is just what it will be, as I before stated.

MR. GLICKSTEIN. Do you think the area will be one that is likely to attract white people?

MR. WILLIAMS. Well, this is what they hope to do, but there are so many people that—West Oakland has been painted so badly in the minds of a lot of people that they are going to have to do a hell of a lot to change the minds of people about their attitude, about the complex makeup of West Oakland, and West Oakland is not a bad section of the city.

They are going to have to move differently from what they are. I don't think it will ever be completely integrated as they have in their minds.

Now they're talking about building new schools in West Oakland over in Project Acorn there. They're going to build a new school. This school is going to be built solely for the people that are going to move into the Acorn Project with a very few of the people from Oak Center being able to go into that school.

In building that school they're sure they are going to build it with all of the most modernistic equipment and best teachers and professors that can be found to go into this school. We feel maybe if they had some of these kind of teachers now and was interested in the presently ongoing schools in West Oakland maybe they wouldn't have any trouble integrating the schools.

But they have been painted so badly as having inferior education, and it is true that our kids generally are inferior in education in West Oakland. So if they had this kind of thing all along in the schools there they probably wouldn't have any trouble integrating Project Acorn when it's built.

MR. GLICKSTEIN. Mrs. Love, we understand you are a member of the Anti-Poverty Board, the Oakland Economic Council?

MRS. LOVE. Yes.

MR. GLICKSTEIN. And that you are also a member of the redevelopment agency. Is that correct?

MRS. LOVE. Right.

MR. GLICKSTEIN. On the basis of your experience with both of these agencies, to what extent has the priciple of citizen participation in the poverty program carried over into redevelopment?

MRS. LOVE. I don't think that there has been a close liaison between the citizen grouping in the poverty program and the redevelopment. There is an attempt now to use the poverty neighborhood group with redevelopment.

I don't think that there is enough effort being put to draw these two agencies closer together. I would feel that as we embark upon the model cities that the neighborhood component should be working toward training individuals in housing so that they can work with citizens and work with redevelopment.

MR. GLICKSTEIN. Mr. Williams, the West Oakland area currently is inhabited predominantly by Negroes. Are you in favor of programs that will disperse the Negro population throughout the city so that there should not be concentrations of people in any one area?

MR. WILLIAMS. I think Oakland has the reputation, or has the distinction somewhere of being an "All-American City" and I feel that if any of us here know the meaning of the word "All-American" then it means that people should be living all over the city as they wish and desire.

I'm not in favor of running all of the people out of West Oakland. I think a person should be able to live where he is able to live, and where he wants to live, and by so doing this I think that some of the harassment and other kind of treatments that the people in certain sections of the city are getting, and particularly ghettos in West Oakland, some of the hard things that we have to swallow that come from the agencies here, it wouldn't be that way if they were equally divided throughout the city; live where you want to live.

MR. GLICKSTEIN. So you are in favor of making efforts—

MR. WILLIAMS. Making efforts for people to live side by side, regardless of who they are, and be happy.

MR. GLICKSTEIN. Do you agree with that, Mrs. Love?

MRS. LOVE. I think people should have an opportunity to live where they want to live, but as far as I'm concerned I certainly feel there should be integration in Acorn. But I'm awfully afraid that in the effort to get integration in Acorn it might be reverse discrimination against people who are nonwhite.

I'd like to mention something about this school situation. The Oak Center Project, in its beginning, was to include the elementary school. It was to be one of the finest schools in the city of Oakland at an elementary level.

We are now right in the midst of discord with the school department because they want to put the school in Acorn, and even to offset putting it where the original location was to be.

They've talked about extending the Cole School, which is making it a laboratory school. We feel as representing citizens that the original plan should be in effect.

What they are saying is that if it's put in Oak Center it will not be integrated, and yet the school will be directly across the street from the Acorn Project so that there is no reason why the new school could not be put there, except that it appears to me that the school that will be built will be an economically segregated school in addition to possibly a racially segregated school if integration does not take any place in Acorn.

MR. GLICKSTEIN. Mr. Williams, I believe you hold a position with the Poverty Program. Is that correct?

MR. WILLIAMS. That's correct.

MR. GLICKSTEIN. Has the Poverty Program affected a citizen's ability to get adequate housing?

MR. WILLIAMS. No, it hasn't. Let me say this:

My feeling on the Poverty Program in Oakland under its present form of operation, it's the biggest gimmick to come to town since Blue Chip Stamps.

The Poverty Program has not worked in this field now. If I understand anything at all about the Poverty Program it was to motivate people, and this has not taken place in Oakland as we think it should have taken place.

As far as housing, as far as education and all this kind of thing the Poverty Program has not moved in that direction as we think it should have moved. The only person that has been motivated by the Poverty Program, unless you are a Philadelphia lawyer or a college professor, you've not gotten anything out of the Poverty Program.

Now, what we are saying here is if you talk about moving in the area of housing and moving in the area of motivating people, as the program is so designed to do, we are now saying that you should not have educated people at the top. It would be stupid to try to say, "Run a program as important as this one without having educated people at the top."

But we feel that if you got two professionals at the top, then one of these persons from any given poverty area, if these two professional people with all their literary training could not train somebody to do a job over and beyond the poverty job, then they should fire those two professional people and get somebody else to train them. If two trained minds can't train one untrained mind to some degree, then they should get rid of those.

So the Poverty Program at this time has not really reached the depths of what it was proposed to do in my way of thinking in Oakland and I would imagine in any city.

You have two classes of poor people. You have what we call the fortunate poor and the unfortunate poor, and at this time the Poverty Program has not reached the unfortunate poor man. The only persons involved to any degree is the fortunate poor.

MR. GLICKSTEIN. Thank you. I have no further questions.

CHAIRMAN HANNAH. Do the Commissioners have any questions? Thank you.

MRS. LOVE. May I add one point here? As the other speakers, I don't like the term "ghetto." I think the Federal Government, in using the term, has helped to lower the individuals who live in areas that are supposed to be disadvantaged, have helped to lower their own self-esteem. I think there needs to be some mass communication in semantics in order that individuals will not be feeling less important by being stigmatized as living in a ghetto.

I think that there seems to be an effort—and I was reading a Labor Bulletin that showed a very rundown house as indicative of all of West Oakland, and this wasn't true. I think the facts ought to come out now. I don't think that we are getting facts either at local, nor at State, nor at Federal level and if anything can be done to help raise our young people's self-esteem and help raise the esteem of the individuals who reside in areas that have been more or less neglected there should be a coordinated effort to look on one part of a city as being a part of a city and not a ghetto. I think this is real important. I think certain terminology is helping to alienate people. I think certain terminology is helping to make people feel debased, and I think it is being perpetuated at the Federal level as well as at local levels.

CHAIRMAN HANNAH. Thank you very much, Mrs. Love. We agree with you. You are excused.

Ladies and gentlemen, we are now going to take a 10-minute recess.

CHAIRMAN HANNAH. Ladies and gentlemen, the hearing will please come to order Mr. Glickstein, will you call the next witnesses?

MR. GLICKSTEIN. The next witnesses are Mr. John Williams and Mr. Eugene Wolf.

(Whereupon, Mr. John Bentley Williams and Mr. Eugene Wolf were sworn by the Chairman and testified as follows:)

TESTIMONY OF MR. JOHN BENTLEY WILLIAMS, OAKLAND, CALIFORNIA AND MR. EUGENE R. WOLF, OAKLAND, CALIFORNIA

MR. GLICKSTEIN. Would you each state your full name and address for the record?

MR. WILLIAMS. John Bentley Williams, 2207 Braemar Road, Oakland, California.

MR. WOLF. Eugene R. Wolf, 508 - 16th Street, Oakland.

MR. GLICKSTEIN. Would you tell the Commissioners your occupations?

MR. WILLIAMS. I am the executive director of the Oakland Redevelopment Agency.

MR. WOLF. I serve as community relations officer for the Oakland Redevelopment Agency.

MR. GLICKSTEIN. Mr. Williams, how long have you held your present position?

MR. WILLIAMS. For approximately two and a half years, Mr. Counselor.

MR. GLICKSTEIN. What is the present state of development of Acorn Project?

MR. WILLIAMS. As you heard earlier this morning, we are anticipating the beginning of the development of 465 new units ranging in size from one-bedroom to four-bedroom units on or about midpoint of June, 1967.

MR. GLICKSTEIN. It will be completed at that time?

MR. WILLIAMS. It will begin at that time. It will take at least a year or 18 months to complete those 465 units.

MR. GLICKSTEIN. When was the area cleared?

MR. WILLIAMS. The area was cleared, finally cleared, in the latter part of '64.

MR. GLICKSTEIN. To what do you attribute the delay from the time the area was cleared to the time of beginning construction?

MR. WILLIAMS. That's a fairly difficult question to answer, Mr. Counselor, but I will say this:

That it appears to me that some of the time that has passed was spent in the normal FHA mortgage processing, which, as I'm sure you are aware, is rather lengthy.

MR. GLICKSTEIN. You have had difficulties with FHA in getting clearance and approval to go ahead with the work on the project?

MR. WILLIAMS. I would say in part. Much of the time from the date of the award, which was February 24, 1965, until June of 1967 assuming all things going well between now and that time, that a portion of that time was absorbed in studies that were made by FHA in marketability of housing in the Oakland area.

MR. GLICKSTEIN. Isn't it possible, Mr. Williams, that FHA studies and so forth could be all completed before the area was cleared, so that after the area was cleared you could immediately begin with construction?

MR. WILLIAMS. You are asking me my professional opinion?

MR. GLICKSTEIN. Yes.

MR. WILLIAMS. The answer is yes.

MR. GLICKSTEIN. Why is it then? What defects are there in Federal law that prevent that from being done?

MR. WILLIAMS. I think first of all if we look at the total picture of housing in this country, whether it be Oakland, Cleveland, incidentally the area from which I came which is having its current problems, it would appear to me that if the commitment of the Federal Government is indeed a sincere one that certain priorities would be placed on housing demands, and that we could set up the process of expediting within these Federal agencies so that we reduce substantially the time that is required for these kinds of reviews, and at the time that the Department of Housing and Urban Development, formerly HHFA, arrives at a conclusion that an area has been designated for redevelopment and that X number of acres will be cleared on or about a certain date, that FHA should begin at that time making such market studies, doing such reviews and working with potential developers so that by the time you have supposedly adequately rehoused the families, demolished the buildings and prepared the site for construction you would have a minimum gap of maybe two or three months before you could get your groundbreaking under way.

MR. GLICKSTEIN. Will the rents and the housing to be constructed be higher than the rents that the people living in that area were paying?

MR. WILLIAMS. The answer to that is yes.

MR. GLICKSTEIN. Do you think that many of the people that were displaced by Acorn will be able to afford to move back?

MR. WILLIAMS. There will be some few that would be able to

move back based on their income. This is not a high percentage of people.

We are obligated by law, and also by our personal commitments to exercise all effort to make certain that all families that were previously living in the redevelopment area are advised of the units being built and the date upon which they become available, giving them priority in terms of entrance into these new units; but as our lives are formed, as I'm sure you are aware, people tend to move into other areas, become readjusted and very often, even those who could afford it, even if it's a quality buy of housing, would prefer to remain where they are.

MR. GLICKSTEIN. But although people that were previously there are given priority many of them would not be able to afford to move back. Is that correct?

MR. WILLIAMS. That is correct. I just answered that earlier, Mr. Counsel.

MR. GLICKSTEIN. I understand that there will not be any public housing in the Acorn area?

MR. WILLIAMS. There will not be public housing in the Acorn area, that's true. However, there is a public housing estate, as I like to call them, just immediately west of the Acorn Project area.

MR. GLICKSTEIN. The persons who have been displaced from Acorn, I assume they were eligible and were given priority into that public estate housing if they want to?

MR. WILLIAMS. Indeed, if they met the admission requirements and as we should know. At least please let me state that the national statistics reflect that when you are dealing in a redevelopment area with displacement of families, that approximately 35 to 40 percent of those families because of their incomes, qualify for low rent housing.

So as the families qualified in the Acorn area they not only went to the public housing estate immediately to the west of it, but they were given priority in other local public housing estates.

MR. GLICKSTEIN. Will there be any rent supplement housing in the Acorn area?

MR. WILLIAMS. At the moment we have not given consideration to rents supplement housing in the Acorn area. The time may come when we do.

My personal belief is that there should be some effort through the redevelopment process to deal with the whole question of social and economic mix in these areas we are carving out in these central cities so that we don't find ourselves faced with the same sorts of problems 10, 15 years from today, where we have to go back and do redevelopment all over again.

MR. GLICKSTEIN. How does the Acorn Project differ from the Oak Center Project?

MR. WILLIAMS. The Acorn Project is largely a clearance area. It is a Title I clearance program.

With the exception of the amendment in 1954 we were permitted under that plan to allow industrial expansion south of the Nimitz Freeway between roughly 5th Street and 3rd Street to give industry an opportunity to expand, and where older, dilapidated houses were cleared, lands were made available for industrial expansion and/or the opportunity for new industry to move into it.

Based on the amendment to the 1949 Housing Act, the Oak Center on the other hand, is somewhat different in that it looks at the real challenge which it has taken us a number of years to recognize, that we can't really do much about following the preamble to the 1949 Housing Act by providing a decent, safe, and sanitary living quarters for all American citizens, and that we had to indeed look at the question of saving our solid housing in the central city.

So the Oak Center area has a combination of clearance and rehabilitation, with the major emphasis on the rehabilitation program.

MR. GLICKSTEIN. Do your plans also include efforts to integrate Oak Center?

MR. WILLIAMS. They do. It would be a normal spill-over from the Acorn area to the Oak Center area to integrate that. We certainly would not want to isolate any kind of proposal for integration within a 32-acre plot of land in an area that is today substantially Negro.

MR. GLICKSTEIN. But you think that after the houses are rehabilitated some of the people that might otherwise be moving into Acorn will move into Oak Center?

MR. WILLIAMS. Yes, possibly.

MR. GLICKSTEIN. Mr. Williams, during the last few days we have heard different views on whether the goal to be set should be one of improving quality of housing in areas that are now predominantly Negro, or whether the goal should be dispersing these areas or making efforts to integrate the areas. What are your views on this issue?

MR. WILLIAMS. I'd like, if you would, Mr. Counsel, to have you please repeat that question.

MR. GLICKSTEIN. I am posing a conflict that perhaps doesn't exist, the conflict between efforts to improve the quality of housing, and only to do that, to concentrate on that in areas that are predominantly Negro, or else to extend our efforts at dispersing those areas or integrating those areas. Is that a conflict? Are those goals mutually exclusive, or can they be pursued together?

MR. WILLIAMS. It would depend on the commitment of this country in terms of what they mean by "The Great Society." It would also depend on the commitment of all of the Federal agencies that have a stake in the rebuilding of central city.

I, for one, am opposed to gilding the ghetto, which that would suggest to me.

Take the existing housing in West Oakland, for example, that if we go in and paint up and fix up and try to repair in very expensive amounts at this time the housing that exists in certain portions of West Oakland, I think this would indeed be a lost cause, and that the economic life of these structures could not be sufficiently extended to maintain the kind of standards we would like to see in the community.

On the other hand, what is the answer? It appears to me that the answer is this: that decisions must be made about the shape and form that the city should take. I think it goes without question, after all of the years that housing has been neglected in terms of basic needs like code enforcement and maintaining normal code enforcement standards for our older communities, that there is really no answer in some of our areas except but to clear.

This, incidentally, is not a situation that is peculiar to Oakland. It is peculiar to every American city in the country, where there has been some local gross neglect of ongoing code enforcement. I don't think that areas like West Oakland can be saved short of substantial clearance.

I think there are standard housing units that can be maintained and rehabilitated, but these are few. We must constantly remind ourselves, if you please, that these areas that we address ourselves to at this particular time in the growth of this country are areas that have been stomping grounds and familiar environment to all of the ethnic and racial backgrounds in this country, and these 2 by 4's and 2 by 6's are getting a little bit tired of being overloaded.

They have been neglected in terms of maintenance. People have chosen to come to this central core area of the city. Their incomes increase, the job potentials are greater, and they move on to other portions of the city, and ultimately into suburbia.

It would appear to me that if we are really going to rebuild the central city we have to look at it just like we do starting the new suburban communities of our time today.

The new city approach, which incidentally is totally supported by FHA mortgage financing, which is a little bit incongruous with the whole idea of what we do with people who live in the central city.

So it would be my conviction that we have to take a bold approach toward revitalizing the central core and that indeed will call for substantial clearance and rebuilding of that area.

MR. GLICKSTEIN. Do you think that the core cities can be

revitalized without the suburban communities playing some role?

MR. WILLIAMS. Well, I think we ought to address ourselves to the crisis of the city and the crisis in the city would in turn suggest that we no longer make it easy for suburbia to separate itself from the central core city problems.

Let me make my point clear. FHA today will certify mortgages for large tracts of land in suburbia. They will build housing for $14,000, $15,000, $16,000, with as little as $250 to $300 down payment and they make it easy for people to make the big exodus from the central city.

But when we talk about building housing for the low-moderate income people in the central city it gets to be a question of market, and I would suggest to you that maybe we need to stop the urban sprawl into suburbia.

Maybe FHA as a Federal entity can put its foot down in terms of its contribution to this kind of disease that is going to really overtake us if we are not careful, and this Bay Area is a perfect example of it.

It would be my personal suggestion that all mortgages for suburban areas be cut until we look at the certification of mortgages for the central city to build housing for low-moderate income people, to make loans available under the new housing bill, incidentally, for people to rehabilitate their existing structures when they find it economically feasible to do so, and to make these loans easily accessible to them, both through the lending institutions as well as mortgage insurance.

MR. GLICKSTEIN. Would you say that existing Federal programs are perpetuating the isolation of the races?

MR. WILLIAMS. Yes, I would.

MR. GLICKSTEIN. May I turn to Mr. Wolf, please. Mr. Wolf, how long have you held your position?

MR. WOLF. I've just been with the agency about eight months now.

MR. GLICKSTEIN. What previous experiences have you had in the area of fair housing and community relations?

MR. WOLF. Before coming to the Oakland Redevelopment Agency I served as the executive director of the Council for Civic Unity here in the Bay Area. Before that, for about eight years as the social service director for the Oakland Council of Churches. That has been how I spent my 11 years since I've been in California.

MR. GLICKSTEIN. What are your responsibilities with respect to the Acorn Project?

MR. WOLF. My assignment with the redevelopment agency is to work with the agency itself, its staff, its commissioners, and

to work with the other units such as the non-profit sponsor who
will be owning and managing the new housing in Acorn;
    To work with the builder-developer who will be building it,
to work with the other public entities in the community such
as the schools, the recreation department, the Public Housing
Authority, and other citizens' organizations to bring about the
kind of open occupancy and integrated pattern that the agency
wants to achieve in the Acorn residential complex.
    MR. GLICKSTEIN. Have you set any goal as to what an
appropriate racial composition of the project should be?
    MR. WOLF. No, we've not set any such goal.
    MR. GLICKSTEIN. What steps are you going to take to achieve
integration in the project?
    MR. WOLF. Well, I believe there are a number of factors
which relate to achieving integration in West Oakland.
    I guess anybody who has been around the Oakland scene
very long would assume on the surface that this is an impossible
task, that it is a task that will never be achieved because of the
fact that this is an area which is one of the oldest areas in the
city and they do not believe that they can revert back to a
pattern of integration.
    You can't really develop and design a plan in isolation of the
whole metropolitan scene, and I wish that our conversation here
would recognize the fact that when we are talking about Acorn
and Oak Center in one section of Oakland, we are really talking
about problems which we happen to be talking about the whole
East Bay, and the patterns of getting more diversified housing
throughout the suburban areas as well as in the central city.
So any program which the agency designs for immediate action
in terms of integrating this new development in West Oakland
is affected by the patterns and dynamics and forces that are
operating throughout the whole scene.
    If we are successful, as I believe we will be, in achieving in-
tegration in Acorn, it will be in spite of many forces and patterns
that are operating in negative fashion against our achievement
in West Oakland, and those are the things which I think the
Commission needs to give its attention to, too, if redevelopment
agencies are going to be successful in not only rebuilding older
sections of the city, but making them places where people of
all races and backgrounds will want and wish to live and be able
to live.
    MR. GLICKSTEIN. What are some of the things that the
agency intends to do in Acorn that will overcome the reputation that that section of the city has and prompt white people
to move in?
    MR. WOLF. We are convinced from our market studies, as
well as our other subjective information that there is a great

484

market need in Acorn for housing serving this income range between $5,000 and $10,500 incomes, for good, decent, new housing, whether they be Negro people, or Orientals, or Spanish-speaking, or white persons, to get new, decent housing. Rental housing in Oakland at this price range and with these rents is very difficult.

That's why you will find those who are able to get out in other areas where this housing is available, the Caucasians go to suburbia and get homes and get rentals with this kind of income background. But the minorities are restricted to only certain sections of this city.

We believe that because of the nature of the type of housing it is, the price range it is geared to serve, its physical design, its architectural design, its amenities in terms of the things that people look for when you are looking for a good house, a good rent in terms of the community amenities, in terms of the public recreation facilities that are being incorporated into this rebuilding of the area, in terms of the new school, in terms of the innovations that will take place in the learning process of that school, these are the things that we think young families look for when they look about "where should I live?"

We believe because it is a good housing buy or a good housing rent, and because it is going to have community amenities, we are not worried about finding the people who will come in and live here. They are not staking out and buying a home at this point. The are renting.

We are convinced that with this kind of housing here, with that kind of amenities, that kind of costs, we are going to have plenty people who are looking to buy or rent here, whatever their racial or ethnic background.

MR. GLICKSTEIN. What if you find when the applications for apartments start coming in that 95, 97 percent of them are from Negro families? Will you make any attempt to hold back apartments for white families, or will you just then proceed to rent the apartments on a first-come, first-served basis?

MR. WOLF. The actual management and leasing of the units will be the responsibility and the authority of the non-profit sponsor. We will be consultants and working with the non-profit sponsor, but the actual decision as to how the rental techniques will be handled will be done by them.

I would imagine that with our focus on trying to identify people of that income range of all racial and ethnic groups which we are in the process of doing now—our own staff is trying to find out where those kind of people exist today in the East Bay, so that we can be able to target in our publicity and advertising and communications to the groups that we need in order to assure an integrated pattern in the area.

If we get too many whites or too many Negroes or too many of this group so it will become a homogeneous kind of application list we can target some advertising or publicity into some other appropriate groups where we know they are who may be attracted to this kind of housing.

MR. GLICKSTEIN. When you say target the advertising, will you have some sort of control over the sponsor's rental policies, and over his technique of attracting tenants and so forth? Are you going to be involved in that or, once the houses are developed and built, will it then be turned over to the sponsor?

MR. WOLF. The non-profit sponsor will be having the responsibility of renting it, and the non-profit sponsor, having the same goal as we do, will be working in partnership to assist one another in achieving this goal. So I assume there would be no problem between their cooperation with us and ours with them since we have the same anticipated desire.

MR. WILLIAMS. May I, Mr. Counsel, just comment that we can brag, I believe, of being the first agency in the country that has a staff person working in this capacity. It was decided by our agency that we needed to watchdog the activity of the non-profit sponsor, as well as the activity of the developer-builder in this particular case, so we do not intend to let the non-profit sponsor assume the total role, but we are going to watchdog it, and we are going to provide all assistance that we can to see that these end goals are met.

MR. GLICKSTEIN. I have no further questions, Mr. Chairman.

CHAIRMAN HANNAH. Are there other questions from the Commissioners? Mrs. Freeman?

COMMISSIONER FREEMAN. Mr. Williams, how many families were displaced by the Acorn Project?

MR. WILLIAMS. Approximately 2,000 so-called relocation problems. That would constitute individuals, husband and wife, and husband, wife and children. Those were relocation responsibilities.

COMMISSIONER FREEMAN. How many of them were white?

MR. WILLIAMS. About 3 percent of them, a small number of white families. It was predominantly Negro, if not majority Negro.

COMMISSIONER FREEMAN. How many families were displaced by the Oak Center Project?

MR. WILLIAMS. We have not begun our displacement program there yet.

COMMISSIONER FREEMAN. Would you give some information about the economic level of the families that were displaced by the Acorn Project?

MR. WILLIAMS. I would guess that the family incomes in the Acorn area were not much higher than about $5,000, and for the most part were less than $4,000.

486

COMMISSIONER FREEMAN. Well, Mr. Wolf indicated that in this area there are restrictions with respect to housing available to minorities. I would like to address my question to the relocation process and ask how the relocation process operated.

What did your agency do with respect to relocating these families, all of whom had incomes less than the income that would be necessary to move back into the new housing?

MR. WILLIAMS. Well, we had a staff located at the site office in the Acorn Project Area whose full responsibility was to seek out housing that met the incomes of the families.

Let me be the first to say to you, Mrs. Freeman, that after some 15 years in the business I'm not going to sit here and tell you that. the redevelopment agency has done a fantastic job in the city of Oakland or any other American city on this question of finding adequate housing for families at this income.

However, I would say to you that we gave direct assistance in terms of finding adequate housing units that were vacant throughout the city, and tried to match them wherever possible with the incomes of the families.

A large number of families in redevelopment areas move without your direct assistance and find themselves in substandard housing, and it is generally substandard housing in areas that are probably scheduled for clearance in the future where they find rents to meet their income.

The one exception in this are the number of families that qualify for low-rent public housing. In those cases you would assume that about 35 percent of your families would find housing accommodations in public housing, either based on a program of new construction or a normal vacancy ratio of turnover each year.

There are a few exceptions of families who live in redevelopment areas who have money in the bank, or in a sack, or in a mattress, and they are awaiting the opportunity to make that first move from being a tenant to an owner.

I think in some few cases some of the families moved out of our Acorn Project and became property owners in another Negro area known as East Oakland.

COMMISSIONER FREEMAN. Did the Redevelopment Agency take any steps to make referrals to areas where Negroes had been restricted?

MR. WILLIAMS. They did, to not much avail. May I also point out, which I'm sure you must be aware of, that the section of the Housing Act labeled as 105C now has extended itself to state to all cities involved in redevelopment that they cannot convince the Federal partners that they have a feasible process for the relocation of families unless indeed they are able to refer these families to areas that heretofore were unavailable to them, so I get back to the question of enforcement.

COMMISSIONER FREEMAN. That was the next point I was going to make.

MR. WILLIAMS. I get to the question of enforcement of this regulation. I think this is the responsibility of not only the local public agency, or the so-called redevelopment agency to make certain that such referrals are made, but I also think it is the responsibility of our Federal partners to make good and sure that we do, and that if we don't our program should move no faster than we are able to adequately house families.

COMMISSIONER FREEMAN. The last question relates to the plan: there has been testimony here that the housing that is going up now in Acorn will exclude a substantial number of persons who need decent, safe, and sanitary housing.

Has any consideration been given to a modification of the plan to make available housing that would be at the reach of the means of the low-income family?

MR. WILLIAMS. For a number of years in the city of Oakland there had not been an authorization for new public housing. It wasn't until just this past election that we got approval for an additional 2,500 new units. This is to supplement the rent supplement program as well as the lease rental program under the public housing program.

We feel that maybe one of the most direct ways to provide adequate housing for the low-income family, since we cannot extend the current regulations under FHA 221(d)(3) to reach this so-called critical band between public housing and the low-moderate income families, that we ought to have a rather forceful program underway in the city where we are constructing new units to meet the demands of the large-sized families that are displaced.

There has been no recent answer in the Federal regulations which would make it possible to lower the income requirements for admission into low-moderate income housing through FHA 221(d)(3).

Maybe we need to take a look nationally at new legislation under this particular section of FHA that would suggest that we have a longer period of amortization of the mortgage and thereby be able to reach some of the lower-income families.

The other area which we will give some thought to in Oakland and in the Acorn Project, incidentally, is the section under the community facilities law which deals with housing for the elderly under Section 202. This appears to be one method through which we can achieve the end of getting low-income families into units that they can afford to rent.

CHAIRMAN HANNAH. Are there other questions from the Commissioners? Mr. Taylor?

MR. TAYLOR. What is the nature of community participation now,

Mr. Williams, in any planning that is going on to meet the future needs of the people? We heard testimony here which indicated there was a lack of community participation in the past. Has that situation improved?

MR. WILLIAMS. I should like to qualify that statement by saying I don't think that there is a total lack of participation on the part of citizens.

Let me voice my personal commitment which, if I had my druthers, I'd like to pass on to other men who sit in the same kind of warm swivel chair that I do in executing redevelopment programs, where you are affecting people.

Our society is made up, it seems to me, of a spectrum of people of all racial and ethnic backgrounds. It appears to me until the time that administrators and technicians, both at the local levels of redevelopment as well as those at the Federal levels in our various programs, are able to shake themselves from the prejudices that they hold and be sensitive to the people with whom they must deal that we are not going to really get the degree of citizens' participation that we need.

I am a very staunch believer in the process of citizens' involvement. It's a very difficult, sticky, touchy procedure. I will be the first to admit it. It's uphill most of the way.

But inasmuch as our programs are all designed presumably in the best interests of people, it would appear to me to naturally follow that in order to achieve them you have to communicate with people.

We do not have the extent of citizens' participation that we need to successfully do our total program in the city of Oakland. We are working on it at every opportunity we get through the churches, through citizens' groups, through business leadership.

The whole question of education through what we are trying to do in this rather new, hopefully quite exciting field is rather large in scale. We need to take such hearings as we have had here today. We need to do more of this on a more consistent basis so that people can better understand what some of our purposes are.

We are making every effort through our staff approach to make certain that all neighborhood associations, block clubs, community leaders, and the like are met with and talked with. We don't limit ourselves to auditoriums of 500 people. We very often reduce ourselves to living rooms of two or three people, and I think this process must continue. None of us can do it without them. I'm not about to try it.

MR. TAYLOR. Mr. Wolf, you indicated that attempts to improve the quality of education in the redevelopment area were important to a total campaign. I wonder if you can elaborate on that a little bit more.

Generally, you hear it said that you can't really achieve integrated schooling until you achieve integration in the housing area, and I take it you were suggesting that establishing good, integrated schools might be the key to establishing integrated housing. Is that what you are saying?

MR. WILLIAMS. I believe so. Your recently published report "Racial Isolation in the Public Schools" documented very well that it is not a choice between gilding the ghetto schools and integration. It is a combination of doing both.

We have had much more interest both by leadership around the country who are more willing to go along with gilding the education but not taking those steps possible and feasible to build in desegregation into the plans.

We feel that the only way you can get an excellence of education is when you do both, improve the quality in terms of teaching, the curriculum, innovation as well as an integrated student composition. Therefore, we feel that if schools in West Oakland are to be improved not only must they have these innovative services and programs in curriculum and teachers and things of that kind, but there needs to be an integration pattern developed as well.

We believe that the Acorn development will be the seedling, the beginning of a desegregation process in West Oakland even as the school district has been working for some years, to improve the quality of some of the curriculum offerings in the schools.

But the facts are that the schools still are very deficient in terms of the kind of achievement product which are coming out, and we believe that a desegregation will go a long way in being one more component in producing the kind of motivation and the kind of resource and learning process in the school and the community that will give the youngsters, whatever their race is, a better education and better achievement in West Oakland.

MR. TAYLOR. Thank you.

CHAIRMAN HANNAH. Thank you very much, gentlemen. We appreciate your being here. You are excused.

We will have one more witness before we break for lunch. Mr. Glickstein, will you call the next witness?

MR. GLICKSTEIN. Mr. Nat Frankel.

(Whereupon, MR. NAT FRANKEL was sworn by the Chairman and testified as follows:)

TESTIMONY OF MR. NAT FRANKEL, OAKLAND, CALIFORNIA

MR. GLICKSTEIN. Mr. Frankel, will you state your full name and address for the record.

MR. FRANKEL. Nat Frankel, 5410 Fernhoff Road, Oakland.

MR. GLICKSTEIN. What is your occupation, Mr. Frankel?

MR. FRANKEL. I'm a practicing attorney.

MR. GLICKSTEIN. Are you associated with the Oakland Redevelopment Agency?

MR. FRANKEL. I am.

MR. GLICKSTEIN. In what capacity?

MR. FRANKEL. Chairman of the agency.

MR. GLICKSTEIN. How long have you been chairman?

MR. FRANKEL. Since October of last year the second time. The first time was in 1962 and 1963. The chairmanship is rotated among the members of the agency.

MR. GLICKSTEIN. How long have you been a member of the agency?

MR. FRANKEL. Since the summer of 1961.

MR. GLICKSTEIN. Mr. Frankel, what do you view as the major obstacles to the development of integrated housing in the Acorn area?

MR. FRANKEL. The segregation which exists throughout the city of Oakland, elsewhere, and throughout the suburban fringe that locks in the city of Oakland. You can't integrate 25 acres of housing in a ghetto situation, and this is the problem that we've got to face and try to convince the sponsors and developers, that somehow something can be done along the lines of integration, when every conventional realtor is betting that we can't do it.

MR. GLICKSTEIN. How are you going to be able to convince them it can be done?

MR. FRANKEL. Well, we have to make an all-out effort to develop the kind of publicity and public relations that a conventional real estate developer would do in trying to rent up his project with special emphasis on those people who are known to be interested in integration, not only hopefully in their mouths, but in their daily lives, and efforts have been made in the past by Mr. Wolf of the agency to make a direct appeal to those kind of groups, church-oriented groups, young college-oriented people, and the faculties of' the various universities and colleges in the area to consider Acorn as a place to live, and to practice integration for themselves and for their children.

This is a very pious hope, I must confess, and one which not very many share my enthusiasm for.

MR. GLICKSTEIN. What sort of cooperation have you received from Federal agencies in trying to carry out this goal?

MR. FRANKEL. Well, as has been pointed out by Mr. Williams, FHA, that is supposed to be most interested in this by Federal mandate and by Executive order, unfortunately follows the conventional pattern of considering itself, and I am sure in many respects I think they are more conservative than the average banker around here in their attitude toward making loans or insuring loans, so that loans are freely available for "marketable" projects and are hard come by for those that you are trying to do a housing job for, the less than the wealthy, in areas that are already sadly blighted.

Right now, to this day we have had some questions raised in Oak Center, for example, that they are not quite ready yet to determine what the marketability is of the new housing that is going in there. The developers in Acorn were locked into a situation where FHA was dragging its feet approximately a year or year and a half ago over the issue of whether they would permit the total 450 or 460 units as the first kickdown of the first project, and it took a great deal of convincing of the FHA people locally.

MR. GLICKSTEIN. What did the FHA want? They wanted a smaller number of units?

MR. FRANKEL. They were not convinced that there was a market in the city of Oakland for housing that would rent for from $70 to $130 a month, depending on room size in the Acorn area, and therefore they wanted the developers to start with 100 units just to see whether it would work.

Well, obviously, when you are trying to make an impact in a ghetto you have to take a substantial hunk.

One of the reasons why I think Washington, D. C.'s effort was fairly successful was that they took a very large area and put in a broad spectrum of high-rise expensive housing, moderate-priced and some public housing as well as commercial, and the whole package of activities that go with a neighborhood, a substantial neighborhood.

We are just taking a very small piece as our first project, and this is what we are bucking. We think we can do it, however.

MR. GLICKSTEIN. Mr. Wolf spoke briefly about the role of schools in this effort. What do you think must be done to improve the schools?

MR. FRANKEL. Well, here again you get to the basic conflict that I think you adverted to in one of your questions of the prior witnesses. Namely, are we going to have a gilded ghetto, and if they figure that as the first step, or are we going to really try to create an integrated environment in all our core cities as well as hopefully the suburbs.

Our agency has elected to go the latter route. The first is easier. The first has a lot of support, I think, even among many of the Negro community who feel that maybe you've got to take first things first, and if you have got live in a ghetto, at least let it be a good one.

I think that is not enough. I think America is capable of far more in its efforts to improve the social and physical climate of the country. When you get to the school problem we get into a situation where right now the Acorn prospective resident will see and can see today schools which are almost 100 percent Negro in its student body, and the school department as yet in this city has shown no inclination to do any forced, shall' we say integration by way of reverse blessing, or anything of the sort.

There has been a very limited open enrollment policy started in the last year or two which has permitted Negro children to go to some of the hill area, or so-called white schools, but nothing is being done in reverse. This is one of our biggest stumbling blocks in our sales appeal, or rental appeal, to Caucasian prospective tenants in Acorn.

MR. GLICKSTEIN. Has you agency made a proposal, or do you have a proposal to integrate schools?

MR. FRANKEL. We have prepared a package in the agency which would call for a modified Princeton Plan whereof the two schools immediately north of Acorn would be the schools for the Acorn children, and that they would go from the kindergarten to the fourth grade or the third grade in the one school, and then all go to the other school. One of the problems is that the public housing project immediately adjoining the Acorn boundaries to the west is almost entirely Negro.

It has been a very difficult job for the Housing Authority, apparently, to effect integration in its public housing and this, of course, provides a nucleus of a substantial amount of Negro children built into the area already, to say nothing of the existing racial composition in Oak Center, who now feed the two schools in question.

MR. GLICKSTEIN. Do you believe that the Princeton Plan approach that you suggested would result in integration of schools?

MR. FRANKEL. Well, I don't know. This, in itself, would not be sufficient, but this, coupled with a massive effort at high-quality education in the West Oakland area, might induce Caucasians to live in an integrated environment because the opportunities for their children would be so much better than anywhere else in the city. This is what we have tried to tell the school department.

The difficulty is, as I understand it, the school department is not about to take any money away from the white schools or white areas and pump it into the West Oakland or Negro schools, and operating with a limited budget this is the fact, and there is no opportunity then to pump any large amount of monies to do any real imaginative job in the West Oakland area, which would make the schools so good that white residents, whether they lived in Acorn or not, would want the privilege of open enrollment in reverse so that they could send their kids to this unusually good school, presumably in West Oakland.

So at the moment we see nothing other than the new students

who might be coming.in to Acorn as a source of Caucasian student body in the West Oakland schools.

MR. GLICKSTEIN. You mentioned, Mr. Frankel, that public housing was by and large segregated, or predominantly Negro, at least in the Acorn area. We understand that there is a program in Oakland for low-income housing on a scattered site basis. How is that program operated?

MR. FRANKEL. As yet, Mr. Glickstein, that is a dream. It's a dream of a dedicated group of people, small in number, who, against all odds, were able to get a majority of the electorate to approve 2,500 units of new housing in the city of Oakland.

I don't believe the bulk of the people in Oakland are really too much interested yet in implementing that dream, and there has been no planning, there has been no concrete steps of any kind, even preliminary, faltering steps to implement the creation of any portion of that 2,500 units of housing.

The mayor has indicated that as far as he was concerned it was only an insurance measure to have an availability, or a source of housing available, and that he preferred to use the rent-leasing method up to its fullest capacity, or the rent subsidy before he would even embark upon the planning or building of additional units, so we have no opportunity to try scattered site housing other than the rent-leasing.method at the present time in the city of · Oakland which is proceeding as I think the director of the Public Housing Authority will tell you, rather slowly as yet.

MR. GLICKSTEIN. Mr. Frankel, there is going to be some industrial usage made in the Acorn area. Is that correct?

MR. FRANKEL. Yes, this has already been done. You see, you've got to understand that in this city you had to make the redevelopment palatable to many segments of the city that, like the rest of the country, thought redevelopment was a creation of the devil. We find now general acceptance in the city after some 10 years in which redevelopment has been underway, at least in the initial and general planning stage.

But the chief thrust, the chief interest is in industrial resuse and commercial. This .is attractive. This is marketable. You can always sell it. It brings jobs, it brings money, it increases taxes.

Housing doesn't really do much for a city, you see, particularly low-income housing, and there is a deadly fear, and it has been expressed to me by some of the members of the city council in the·past, that the increase in the introduction of additional public housing in this city will only encourage the poor or accelerate the inflow of-the poor into the city, and the poor happen to be mostly Negroes, unfortunately, in our present society.

So I am convinced that most of the people in this city are not only·not interested in public housing, they would prefer that there were no public housing, and, therefore, no poor to be housed, and that somehow if you didn't have housing, people wouldn't come.

The fact is that in our cities they come, and they come in droves, and they will continue to come, and they will continue to create worse situations in the housing level unless we take concrete steps to do something about it.

It is unfortunate that by calculated choice our first project had to be moderate-income and not low-income housing because when you start to change a ghetto into something decent you have to, in effect, change the residents somewhat, and you try to hit those, at least, who have some sort of a steady employment picture, and they have to have this in order to be able to live in Acorn at the present time.

Had we had a larger area to work on undoubtedly we could have chosen to diversify the type of housing there from an income standpoint. We didn't have that choice. In Oak Center there will be an opportunity to experiment with some of this additional scattered site housing if the city council will work with the Housing Authority to improve it. At the moment this is not happening.

MR. GLICKSTEIN. Has this industrial development in the Oak Center area relieved the unemployment situation of West Oakland residents to some extent?

MR. FRANKEL. No, it's a drop in the bucket. Sure, there have been new industry that has come in, new employment; but against the total we have something like 30 percent of the Negro males unemployed in this city. I've heard that figure and I have no reason to doubt it. The number of new industries perhaps might pick up 500, 750. It's only a beginning as far as that is concerned.

MR. GLICKSTEIN. Do you require the new industries moving in to give assurances that they will hire West Oakland residents?

MR. FRANKEL. No, except that we try to give priority to those types of industries which would employ the relatively unskilled. One of the companies happens to be an industrial laundry company that does a large volume of industrial laundry business, and they hire almost exclusively unskilled workers, so we don't ask them where they hire them from, but it is our hope that as we develop these industrial areas, this being only a very small one, I might say, that people will find it profitable and easy to live near where they work. This is a logical way to do it.

It just hasn't worked out recently because there has never been any decent housing available in the core area adjacent to commerce or industry.

MR. GLICKSTEIN. I have no further questions, Mr. Chairman.

CHAIRMAN HANNAH. Mrs. Freeman?

COMMISSIONER FREEMAN. Mr. Frankel, with respect to the industrial area that is being developed, I think it's in the Acorn Project, is that construction of industry?

MR. FRANKEL. Let me say that those industries—Acorn started out when it was first declared a redevelopment area as a very mixed combination of slum industrial, slum residential, and slum commercial. The package goes hand in hand, I might say. I'm sure it's true throughout the country that business and industry alike suffer the same blight as the residences in a slum area, so our objective was to upgrade a portion which we designated as industry.

We determined that there was an incompatibility between industry and residential as we saw it. So we cleared all the residential from an area which was to be designated as industry, and the balance of the Acorn Project then was designated as exclusively residential, and that is the direction in which we have gone.

Those industries which agreed to bring their properties up to standard and their operations up to standard and would acquire whatever land was necessary to do that we would permit to remain. Those that couldn't or wouldn't were acquired, and the property was resold to developers who would reuse immediately, that is not speculators, but who said they had a plant and they were going to put in a certain type of business or industry.

COMMISSIONER FREEMAN. You missed the point. You acquired the property and resold it to the redevelopment, and I'd like to know—

MR. FRANKEL. The redeveloper was the user. I want to make that clear. Like the redeveloper would be Ford Motor Company, the redeveloper would be Mack Truck or the laundry company.

COMMISSIONER FREEMAN. This was cleared land that was resold to a redeveloper, Ford Motor Company or whatever?

MR. FRANKEL. Right.

COMMISSIONER FREEMAN. The redevelopment agency is required to include in its purchase contract, in its sale contract, sale of the land to the redeveloper that he refrain from discrimination in the construction of any new building that went up?

MR. FRANKEL. Oh, he signs the contract all right.

COMMISSIONER FREEMAN. He signs the contract. And it is the responsibility of your agency to enforce the contract. I would like to know, with respect to the new construction that went up or is going up in the Acorn Project, the extent to which there was employment of members of minorities, Spanish-speaking, Chinese, Negroes in the construction of the new projects?

MR. FRANKEL. None, other than what the unions would permit within their established policies. We just had a go-around with the developer of Acorn yesterday at the agency meeting about this very question.

COMMISSIONER FREEMAN. The redevelopment agency did not enforce this provision of the contract then?

MR. FRANKEL. I know of no active steps while I was on the agency. If the staff did it, it was unbeknownst to me.

COMMISSIONER FREEMAN. How, when we say that a project will be cleared and it will create jobs, if the jobs that are created are not available to members of the minority groups then what really are we telling these people? "We are taking your home and you are not getting a job either."

MR. FRANKEL. I suggest to you, Mrs. Freeman, it is a job bigger than the Oakland Redevelopment Agency and has to be dealt with on an area much larger and more powerful than that of this one small agency.

COMMISSIONER FREEMAN. I suggest to you, sir, that the contract which the redevelopment agency has with the redeveloper has a clause which permits the termination of a contract.

MR. FRANKEL. Then we won't have any industry.

CHAIRMAN HANNAH. Further questions? Mr. Taylor?

MR. TAYLOR. I have no questions.

CHAIRMAN HANNAH. Thank you very much, Mr. Frankel. We appreciate your being here. You are excused, and we will now recess until 2 o'clock.

(Whereupon, a recess was taken until 2 p.m., Thursday, May 4, 1967.)

THURSDAY AFTERNOON SESSION
MAY 4, 1967

CHAIRMAN HANNAH. Ladies and gentlemen, this hearing will come to order, please. Mr. Glickstein, will you call the next witness.

MR. GLICKSTEIN. The next witness is Mr. Reginald Guichard.

(Whereupon, MR. REGINALD GUICHARD was sworn by the Chairman and testified as follows:)

TESTIMONY OF MR. REGINALD JAMES GUICHARD, OAKLAND, CALIFORNIA

MR. GLICKSTEIN. Would you please state your full name and address for the record.

MR. GUICHARD. My name is Reginald James Guichard, Jr. I live at 4153 Bale Street, Oakland. I've been a resident of Oakland all my life, for the past 49 years.

MR. GLICKSTEIN. What is your occupation, Mr. Guichard?

MR. GUICHARD. I am executive director of the Oakland Housing Authority.

MR. GLICKSTEIN. How long have you been employed by the Oakland Housing Authority?

MR. GUICHARD. Over 20 years. I have been for approximately the past three years as executive director. I have worked in all phases of the Oakland Housing Authority.

MR. GLICKSTEIN. The Housing Authority administers public housing in Oakland. Is that correct?

MR. GUICHARD. That's right.

MR. GLICKSTEIN. How many public housing needs are administered by your agency?

MR. GUICHARD. 1,422 under the conventional plan, and there is 1,100 under Section 22, the leased housing.

MR. GLICKSTEIN. Where are the projects located?

MR. GUICHARD. The projects are situated in West Oakland and East Oakland, from 8th and Campbell to 84th Avenue and G Street.

MR. GLICKSTEIN. What is the racial composition of the project?

MR. GUICHARD. It keeps changing all the time. The racial composition now, I would say, is approximately 65 percent Negro.

MR. GLICKSTEIN. Overall?

MR. GUICHARD. Overall.

MR. GLICKSTEIN. 65 percent?

MR. GUICHARD. Approximately.

MR. GLICKSTEIN. Of the public housing tenants are Negro?

MR. GUICHARD. Yes.

MR. GLICKSTEIN. How does this percentage apply, project by project? Are there some projects that are predominantly Negro, and some that are predominantly white?

MR. GUICHARD. The West Oakland projects are about 99 percent Negro, and the East Oakland projects run around, oh, 55 to 45, something like that, approximately.

MR. GLICKSTEIN. In the East Oakland projects?

MR. GUICHARD. Yes.

MR. GLICKSTEIN. Are the East Oakland projects becoming more Negro?

MR. GUICHARD. That's right.

MR. GLICKSTEIN. Does your agency have a policy with respect to integration?

MR. GUICHARD. When our agency first started the Campbell Village was totally integrated way back when it was first started, a totally integrated project.

MR. GLICKSTEIN. Your projects have been integrated from the very beginning?

MR. GUICHARD. That's right. I think that this project was one of the first ones in the United States.

MR. GLICKSTEIN. We understand, Mr. Guichard, that there is an authorization for leased public housing. Is that correct?

MR. GUICHARD. That's right. We have 1,100 units of leased housing approved broken down into these categories: 250 0-

bedrooms, 250 one's, 200 two's, 200 three's, and I can't remember this next one here.

MR. GLICKSTEIN. Overall there are going to be 1,100 units?

MR. GUICHARD. 1,100. 150 four's and 50 five's.

MR. GLICKSTEIN. We also understand you have a program for scattered sites for public housing?

MR. GUICHARD. That was our proposal at election was 2,500 units.

MR. GLICKSTEIN. Was this passed at the election last November?

MR. GUICHARD. That's right.

MR. GLICKSTEIN. How many of the units have been constructed?

MR. GUICHARD. There's none at this time.

MR. GLICKSTEIN. What is the reason no progress has been made?

MR. GUICHARD. There has been progress. First you must understand as the law says that we have to have a cooperation agreement between the Housing Authority and the city of Oakland. That is an agreement between the city and the Housing Authority stipulating certain clauses such as sewers, pavements, et cetera.

MR. GLICKSTEIN. And you haven't been able to work that out?

MR. GUICHARD. We are working it out now with the city. It is being discussed back and forth, and there are certain proposals in there that we disagree with. We have ironed them all out except one, and it will be referred back to the council.

My commission will act at their next meeting which will be May 12th. There is one problem we have to resolve.

MR. GLICKSTEIN. There was some testimony this morning that the city administration is not in favor of going ahead with scattered site public housing at this time. Is that right?

MR. GUICHARD. I do not know. All I can do is deal on facts. With regard to the Housing Authority, I do not know what is in other people's minds. As far as I am concerned, we are proceeding with the council according to the general conception.

MR. GLICKSTEIN. Is there any indication at this point where the scattered site housing will be located?

MR. GUICHARD. No, there is not now and may I make a statement on that?

As we all know, property in Oakland is very tight. This will have to be a community action for all the community. In the past it has been shown across the Nation that housing authorities have gone on their own, and we wish that there should be a survey of the whole city of Oakland to say where all types of housing ought to be, not only for one income group, but for medium, low, high, and there should be a survey so that we can know where it is and do it in a businesslike manner instead of everybody running away like water running over the dam and not knowing which way they are going.

MR. GLICKSTEIN. Will it be the policy of your agency to use a scattered site housing program to effectuate desegregation in housing?

MR. GUICHARD. That is the problem of the commission. That's what they prefer. Don't forget, we have to have financial feasibility which all over the country—which would be most three, four, five bedrooms is the need, the greatest need, and all over the United States they're having trouble getting down to financial feasibility and when I say financial feasibility I mean building it down where we can pay off the bonds in 40 years, and that is the problem that is being faced all over the Nation.

MR. GLICKSTEIN. Are you suggesting now there are some problems that are implicit in current Federal law that might make it difficult to complete or build the scattered site public housing?

MR. GUICHARD. I didn't say that. I said the cost of building is going up and we would have to get something with new ingenuities, with new building equipment, and materials, that they are using now to bring costs down or through land purchases some way.

MR. GLICKSTEIN. The present Federal law requires that there be a showing of financial feasibility. Is that right?

MR. GUICHARD. That's right.

MR. GLICKSTEIN. And you think that costs are perhaps going up so high at the present time that under present methods it might not be able to build such housing and have it financially feasible?

MR. GUICHARD. It would be hard to do. We get bulletins from the Government—in fact, one came across the desk the other day —asking any authorities in the United States that have built scattered site housing to let them know so they can tell the rest of us how to keep their costs down.

MR. GLICKSTEIN. You also mentioned you have a leased housing program under Section 23 of the Housing Act?

MR. GUICHARD. That's right. Under the leased housing section we had approval on December 9th, and we are quite proud of the leased housing section. I've brought along a chart of the city of Oakland. I will pass out and show the Commission this chart, and as of April 28th we have housed 183 families.

Now, these are houses, you can see by the chart—this is a census map of the city of Oakland. These are 183 families, and this is where those people are housed over the city of Oakland. I will give you this for your further consideration.

We are working on 309 applications from owners. We have 309. Some of them are pending, some of them are rehabs, some of them are putting people in but we have housed that many people as of that date.

MR. GLICKSTEIN. The principle of leased housing, as I understand it, is that instead of public housing authority building large projects as they have in the past, the housing authority instead will lease apartments in buildings throughout the city and make those apartments available for persons otherwise eligible for public housing?

MR. GUICHARD. That's right. We lease fair market value, and we generally get about 10 percent less than fair market value because we are standing some of the legal costs. I would like at this time to tell you as of April 28th, I'll break this down to the 183 on bedroom size: zero we have housed 4; one bedroom houses, 50; two bedrooms, 86; three bedrooms, 39; four bedrooms, 4; and five bedrooms, 0.

MR. GLICKSTEIN. I haven't had a chance to review the map you passed out to the Commissioners, but could you tell me where the leased units are located? Are many of them located in predominantly white areas?

MR. GUICHARD. Well, Oakland is, I would say, being here 49 years, predominantly integrated. They are in all areas.

MR. GLICKSTEIN. Are any of them located in the hills?

MR. GUICHARD. Now, as you know, this program is a volunteer program and we have to get the owners of property to accept this.

Now, bit by bit, week by week, owners are coming in and when they found that the program is a very good program, they are telling other property owners and more and more we are getting up. As the map shows we're in MacArthur, High Street, Fruitvale, Diamond District, North Oakland, Broadway, and Bancroft, and we are getting up there and we have to get financial feasibility, too.

MR. GLICKSTEIN. So far you haven't reached the hills?

MR. GUICHARD. No.

MR. GLICKSTEIN. Have you any feedback on how this program is succeeding, how successful it is? How have the landlords that have leased this housing reacted?

MR. GUICHARD. We haven't had any trouble from the landlords. In fact, we are getting more and more advertising from one landlord telling another by word of mouth.

MR. GLICKSTEIN. Has there been an increase in the number of white applicants in your public housing since your lease program went into effect?

MR. GUICHARD. Well, I would say they are about the same. As of May 1, 1967 we have 1,192 units, and over 90 percent of those are colored applicants.

MR. GLICKSTEIN. You indicated that of the 1,100 units that are authorized I think you said 196 have been—

MR. GUICHARD. I said 183.

MR. GLICKSTEIN. 183 have been leased already. Do you think that as time goes on this program will pick up and you will be able to go up to your authorized level?

MR. GUICHARD. We are hoping that, yes.

MR. GLICKSTEIN. Is the Authority making affirmative efforts to interest property owners in this program and to encourage them to participate?

MR. GUICHARD. We are. The Leased Housing Co-ordinator is going out and talking to ministers, going to their rectories, I'm out at night speaking. We'll speak to any organizations and clubs that want speakers to explain the situation.

The other day I talked at a real estate luncheon and explained the program, how the Government and private industry can work together, and we are talking all around, and we are getting good publicity.

In fact, more and more we are getting better publicity, and the word of mouth seems to be the best. One-third of those 183 are coming from property managements and the real estate agencies.

MR. GLICKSTEIN. We heard some testimony about the movement of industry from Oakland to the suburbs. How would you say that that process has affected the public housing tenants?

MR. GUICHARD. Well, the public housing tenants, about one-third of them I imagine in the country, have automobiles, and when industry moves out of the city and it goes to two and three zones, transportation zones, of course, then these people cannot afford the transportation to get to their jobs. So, of course, when industry moves out of any city it is going to hurt the people of the lower-income bracket.

MR. GLICKSTEIN. I have no further questions.

CHAIRMAN HANNAH. Mrs. Freeman?

COMMISSIONER FREEMAN. I have no questions.

CHAIRMAN HANNAH. Do any of the other Commissioners have questions? Mr. Taylor?

MR. TAYLOR. Did I understand you to say that the city of Oakland now was predominantly integrated?

MR. GUICHARD. I said it is pretty well integrated, yes.

MR. TAYLOR. Could you explain what you mean by that? Are there Negroes residing in the hill areas of Oakland in more than token numbers?

MR. GUICHARD. I wouldn't know what numbers, no.

MR. TAYLOR. Are there areas of the city which are predominantly or almost totally composed of minority groups?

MR. GUICHARD. Yes, that's the West Oakland area and the East Oakland area. Minority, you said.

MR. TAYLOR. Is there any difficulty in the members of minority groups obtaining housing in any areas of this city?

MR. GUICHARD. I wouldn't know. That's out of my field. Public Housing is more in the real estate section of that.

MR. TAYLOR. That's of no interest to you?

MR. GUICHARD. It is of interest to me, but we haven't had any trouble where we have integrated units. Where there is maybe eight units and we'll take two units out of these then we'll take a fourplex.

In our leased housing program we have had Chinese, Mexican American, colored, and whites all in an apartment and we haven't had any mass exits where we put a minority group into an apartment, we'll say an eight-unit building. We put one in, we haven't had any move-outs in that building. In fact, we have had property owners call us up and ask for more of our people because it seems that the ones we put in are generally better housekeepers than the ones that are living there already. We haven't had anybody move out of a unit when we have put another person in if there's other people in there.

MR. TAYLOR. You don't know of your own knowledge, whether or not it is part of your job, whether there is discrimination against Negroes or Mexican Americans in private home ownership rentals in any part of this city?

MR. GUICHARD. I do not deal with private rentals. We haven't had any on our leasing program because we follow the law and we give them the application that anybody that leases to us there is no discrimination and anybody that has leased to us that has not been a problem.

MR. TAYLOR. I thought I heard you say a few minutes ago that one explanation for the fact that leased housing had not been obtained in certain parts of the city of Oakland might be because—

MR. GUICHARD. I did not say that. I said it was a voluntary plan and that the owner has to give us the property voluntarily.

MR. TAYLOR. Do you have any idea why owners in certain areas of the city may not have given you permission to lease housing in that part of the city?

MR. GUICHARD. Well, I imagine it's too high. In some parts of the city rent is so high that we cannot get into financial feasibility. That would be one reason. I cannot tell what is in the owners' minds, no.

MR. TAYLOR. I didn't understand your answer to Mr. Glickstein's question about whether the policy of the city of Oakland Housing Authority was to secure desegregated housing with these new units that have been authorized.

MR. GUICHARD. That's the idea of the scattered site housing.

MR. TAYLOR. Well, I didn't understand. You're saying that financial conditions make it impracticable to achieve desegregation?

MR. GUICHARD. No, I didn't. I said in scattered site housing financial conditions make it hard to build scattered site housing because the cost is high to pay off the bond's indebtedness no matter who the low income people.

MR. TAYLOR. You say that 183 families have been housed under the leased housing program and, as I got your figures, 1,422 families are housed—

MR. GUICHARD. Under the conventional plan. There's something more than 1,500.

MR. TAYLOR. Could you give me any estimate as to how those units stack up against the need for low and moderate-income housing?

MR. GUICHARD. Let's get to the low-income housing. Let's not go to the moderate-income housing because we deal strictly with the low-income on our rent ratio.

We have 1,192 applicants as of May 1st. I'll leave this with you. And it breaks down to on our application 1,109 Negro applicants, 79 white, and four other. That's over 90 percent.

MR. TAYLOR. These are applicants who are not presently housed?

MR. GUICHARD. That's right.

MR. TAYLOR. Would that be the full extent of the need, do you think, or might there be other families who are living in substandard housing who cannot afford better housing?

MR. GUICHARD. No, this is just the need that we have on our waiting list. There is a greater need in Oakland because our survey has proven that you have redevelopment, you have BART and everything. But this is the actual application list we have every month to month. Now that doesn't mean that there isn't need for a lot more people to avail themselves of our services.

MR. TAYLOR. Would you say that there is a need for substantial new construction of units?

MR. GUICHARD. Yes.

MR. TAYLOR. But are you able to estimate in rough terms what the extent of that need is?

MR. GUICHARD. Not without looking at any surveys or figures, I would not be able to ascertain that at this time.

MR. TAYLOR. You have no surveys on this?

MR. GUICHARD. That is right. I can only give this list to the Commission on the Leased Housing, the breakdown on it.

MR. TAYLOR. I have no further questions.

CHAIRMAN HANNAH. Thank you very much, Mr. Guichard. You are excused. Mr. Glickstein, call your next witness.

MR. GLICKSTEIN. The next witness is Mr. Martin Sanchez. Mr. Chairman, may I request that the document that Mr. Guichard has left with us be introduced into the record as Exhibit No. 25.

CHAIRMAN HANNAH. It is accepted.

(Whereupon, the document referred to was marked Exhibit No. 25 and received in evidence.)

(Whereupon, Mr. Martin Sanchez was sworn by the Chairman and testified as follows:)

504

TESTIMONY OF MR. MARTIN SANCHEZ, OAKLAND, CALIFORNIA

MR. GLICKSTEIN. Would you please state your full name and address for the record?

MR. SANCHEZ. My name is Martin Sanchez. I live at 1250 34th Avenue in Oakland.

MR. GLICKSTEIN. What is your occupation, Mr. Sanchez?

MR. SANCHEZ. I am a coremaker in a foundry.

MR. GLICKSTEIN. Are you associated with the Poverty Program in Oakland?

MR. SANCHEZ. Yes, I am.

MR. GLICKSTEIN. What is the nature of your association?

MR. SANCHEZ. I am on one of the advisory committees, and I am a chairman of the board of directors. Now, can I read a statement here? May I read a statement?

MR. GLICKSTEIN. It is not generally our practice to hear statements. How long is your statement?

MR. SANCHEZ. It's only a little bit over a page.

CHAIRMAN HANNAH. Go ahead.

MR. SANCHEZ. I welcome the opportunity to express my views and my concern over the lack of representation for the Mexican American Spanish-speaking on your staff.

The fact that there is not one Commissioner on your group, and only two staff persons out of over 160 people demonstrates the lack of concern of your Commission for the largest minority in the State of California.

That the contribution of the Mexican American to our country has been substantial is evidenced in part by the fact that there were 17 Congressional Medal of Honor winners of Mexican American descent in World War II.

I have just completed a reading of the summary of the report by the U. S. Commission on Civil Rights entitled "Racial Isolation in the Public Schools" and not once is the word Mexican American mentioned or any other ethnic minority other than the Negro, keeping in mind that there are more Mexican American Spanish surname students in California than any other ethnic minority.

In the Post Office, the largest Government-employer in the United States is currently being picketed by the Mexican American people all over the State of California. The reason for the picketing is because of the discriminatory hiring and promotional practices. Of approximately 3,000 employees in the Oakland Post Office a recent count showed that there were only 30 to 40 Spanish surname employees. It is estimated that there are 50,000 Mexican Americans in Oakland, residing in Oakland.

The Alameda Naval Air Station is another Federal agency that is currently under attack for its discriminatory practices. Since the Federal Government, who is our parent body, is so unconcerned with our welfare and sets the example for the other levels of government to whom can we turn for positive constructive changes in attempts to improve the discriminatory conditions that exist against the Spanish surname citizens of California? If the Federal Government does not initiate a stronger attack against these discriminatory practices how can we expect the lower levels to change, the lower levels of Government, that is?

I attended last Saturday, April 29, 1967, a meeting of state-wide leaders of the Mexican American community and they, by unanimous vote, moved that I read this statement to this Commission, and then walk out in protest and indignation, and we intend to picket this hearing today.

CHAIRMAN HANNAH. Mr. Sanchez, you are under subpena. Will you resume your seat and answer any questions the Counsel wants to put to you.

MR. SANCHEZ. All right.

MR. GLICKSTEIN. Mr. Sanchez, you were telling us about your role in the Poverty Program and you are on the Spanish-speaking advisory council. Is that correct?

MR. SANCHEZ. Yes, the committee.

MR. GLICKSTEIN. How many advisory committees are there under this Poverty Program in Oakland?

MR. SANCHEZ. There are five advisory committees.

MR. GLICKSTEIN. And four of them are related to particular target areas?

MR. SANCHEZ. Yes.

MR. GLICKSTEIN. And yours is an overall advisory committee dealing with Spanish-speaking problems. Is that true?

MR. SANCHEZ. Yes.

MR. GLICKSTEIN. When did you become active in the Poverty Program in Oakland?

MR. SANCHEZ. I became active in holding office on the 1st of January of this year.

MR. GLICKSTEIN. Mr. Sanchez, would you tell the Commissioners why you feel it is necessary for the Spanish-speaking people in Oakland to have their own advisory committee as part of the Poverty Program?

MR. SANCHEZ. Yes. The other racial groups cannot give us adequate representation because of our unique problems of language and cultural differences that are foreign to the rest of the target-area people and, therefore, we understand our own problems better and we can better serve our own needs. We

know what we need, and I feel that we should represent ourselves, not someone else should represent us who has no
knowledge of our problems.

MR. GLICKSTEIN. Prior to the formation of the committee,
did the Spanish-speaking community feel that their needs were
not being met by the Poverty Program?

MR. SANCHEZ. Well, this was really before I came into the
Poverty Program. I can't speak at great length with a lot of
authority because I wasn't involved in it, so I really can't answer
that question truthfully.

MR. GLICKSTEIN. Do you feel that now that there is
a Spanish-speaking advisory committee that the needs of the
Spanish-speaking community are now being met, or at least are
being heard?

MR. SANCHEZ. Yes, we are being heard. There is room for
improvement, but we are being heard.

MR. GLICKSTEIN. Do you feel that the money and policy-
making positions within the Poverty Program are fairly distributed among different minority groups?

MR. SANCHEZ. Well, again I would hesitate to give a definite
statement on that because I haven't been involved enough to
actually be able to say.

We are being served in some areas, and there is some service
being rendered to us. Like I say, there is room for improvement,
but we are being helped.

MR. GLICKSTEIN. In addition to your being on the Spanish-
speaking advisory committee, I believe you are also that committee's representative on the parent body, the Oakland
Economic Development Council. Is that correct?

MR. SANCHEZ. Yes, I am.

MR. GLICKSTEIN. Do you feel that the voice of the Spanish-
speaking communty is being heard on the Oakland Economic
Development Council?

MR. SANCHEZ. Well, we are being heard. We have a chance
to present our problems, not always to our liking because there
are only five of us on the council of 39 total.

MR. GLICKSTEIN. Aside from the difference in language that
the Spanish-speaking community has with the Negro minority
group, do you think that the poor Negroes and the poor in the
Spanish-speaking communities have more in common than they
have dividing them?

MR. SANCHEZ. Would you repeat that question?

MR. GLICKSTEIN. Do you think that the Negro minority and
the Spanish-speaking minority have more in common than they
have dividing them?

MR. SANCHEZ. They are not divided. They have more in
common, I would say. We both have the same—we are both

discriminated against, have been in the past by the society. We have that problem. But we have to approach the solution of these problems, in my opinion, in a different manner because our problems are different to the Negro.

The Negro has an American orientation where the Spanish-speaking have the language barrier to a large extent, and we have a different culture to some extent. We haven't been entirely assimilated into the American culture of life and I might add here that we have much to contribute to the American culture.

MR. GLICKSTEIN. Thank you, Mr. Sanchez. I have no further questions, Mr. Chairman.

CHAIRMAN HANNAH. Do the Commissioners have any questions?

COMMISSIONER FREEMAN. Yes. Mr. Sanchez, are there areas in which the Negroes and the Spanish-speaking Americans work together to try to solve their problems in Oakland and the Bay Area?

MR. SANCHEZ. Well, in my contacts with the Negro and my workings with them I haven't had any real difficulties with them. Again, I want to mention that I'm new in this program. I am just now starting to get really involved, starting to familiarize myself with all the programs so I can't really make a statement in truth and say that this is the way it is.

COMMISSIONER FREEMAN. Well, we have heard testimony, and you have stated that the Mexican Americans and Negroes are discriminated against—

MR. SANCHEZ. They are.

COMMISSIONER FREEMAN. Here in the Bay Area.

MR. SANCHEZ. Yes, they are.

COMMISSIONER FREEMAN. And it seems to me that the total community effort is needed to eliminate discrimination.

MR. SANCHEZ. That's right. I repeat that again.

COMMISSIONER FREEMAN. And it certainly would not be good to build a wall between minorities, the extent of which—

MR. SANCHEZ. Who are you referring to when you say it is not good to build a wall? Who is building a wall?

COMMISSIONER FREEMAN. No, I'm not saying it is. What I am saying is that it is commendable and helpful that there be cooperation to try to get rid of discrimination.

MR. SANCHEZ. Of course, we all know that. The Spanish-speaking people understand that and we cooperate with the Negro to a very large extent, and in my dealings with the Negro it has been the same, the contacts that I've had. I haven't met with any opposition from the Negro, not any real opposition.

COMMISSIONER FREEMAN. Thank you. That is what I wanted to have clear.

CHAIRMAN HANNAH. Mr. Patterson.

VICE CHAIRMAN PATTERSON. Mr. Sanchez, could you tell me what you consider to be the greatest single problem? I know you have many problems, but the greatest single problem facing the Spanish surname minority in the Bay Area.

MR. SANCHEZ. In the Bay Area?

VICE CHAIRMAN PATTERSON. Yes.

MR. SANCHEZ. In the Bay Area, in my opinion, they're the same as they are nationally, and that is the lack of acceptance in all levels of society. From the Government, from business, from labor, the labor unions.

There are many labor unions that we don't have any representation on their apprenticeship programs here in the Bay Area and there are many businesses, factories, where our people aren't represented in the better jobs. So that is the biggest single problem we have, I would say. The bread-and-butter issues are then, in my opinion, the biggest single problem for our people because we are a low-income people.

VICE CHAIRMAN PATTERSON. Thank you.

CHAIRMAN HANNAH. Mr. Sanchez, do you have any idea as to how many immigrants are coming in from Mexico or other Spanish-speaking countries to the Bay Area each year or each month or any other period of time?

MR. SANCHEZ. Well, into the Bay Area, there are some coming in here that drift in from the farm communities, but down by the border this is another area of discontent that we have in that the border government agency, the Border Patrol, and so on, have been accused—now I don't have the facts to verify this, but I would like to mention that our people are being brought in here to alleviate a labor shortage that is caused by the striking farm workers, and I think that this is another form of—well, I don't know what the word is. I can't find the proper word for it, but it's very unjust to our farm workers who are trained to get a living wage to be subjected to this form of strike-breaking activity which the Government is a part of.

CHAIRMAN HANNAH. Mr. Sanchez, you were born in this country?

MR. SANCHEZ. I was born in Denver.

CHAIRMAN HANNAH. How much education did you have?

MR. SANCHEZ. I didn't complete the eighth grade.

CHAIRMAN HANNAH. That's all that was available to you, or your family didn't have enough money, or they were moving about the country?

MR. SANCHEZ. I had the same problems that most of us had during the depression. In Denver the discrimination was quite bad there at that time during the depression and there were other problems that we had in our family, so I quit school to go to work on a farm.

CHAIRMAN HANNAH. I would be interested in any comments you would care to make with reference to the young Mexican American or Spanish-speaking American that is born in the Bay Area and has an opportunity to go to whatever public school is available to him.

In your view, is there an adequate opportunity for them to learn English? Are they required to learn English? Do they learn English?

MR. SANCHEZ. Well, they have this problem to begin with. They come from a home that is Spanish-speaking. Spanish only is spoken in the home, and they have the disadvantage of entering a school with a language that is different from English, so right away they are handicapped. They have to learn English first. That sets them behind.

That sets them behind in their academic level, but there are also other problems along with that, psychological problems, that affect this child for the rest of his life. I think that with regard to this, our Government should take more of a sympathetic interest towards helping these people instead of adopting the attitude that, well, these Mexicans should speak English if they want to be Americans. They shouldn't take that attitude.

The attitude should be that if they are good enough to go and fight for the country regardless of what language they speak, they should be helped, they should be reached and try and work with this problem, and try to orient and assimilate them into the community. Make them socially acceptable so that we can get rid of this cycle that follows generation after generation.

CHAIRMAN HANNAH. Just one more question. I gather that what you are saying indirectly is that you feel that society or the schools or that there is a failure somewhere to make it possible for young Spanish-speaking Americans to learn English in a situation where the fact that they start out speaking Spanish, thinking in Spanish, and so on, that you feel there is a failure to take this into account and give these youngsters the opportunity and the incentive to not only learn English but get an adequate education. Is that right?

MR. SANCHEZ. Well, that's part of the problem. There are many other factors that I'm not even qualified to speak on. I'm no social expert or sociologist, but I do know our problems, and I know that this is a big problem with us. But there are other problems also such as low income and poor housing.

CHAIRMAN HANNAH. Again, this is another way of asking the same question. When you were a youngster in Denver, and you remember pretty vividly what your situation was, do you feel that the young Mexican American in the Bay Area today is as handicapped as you were a generation ago?

MR. SANCHEZ. No, no, but we don't have a depression today.

CHAIRMAN HANNAH. Aside from the depression.

MR. SANCHEZ. Given the same conditions maybe so, because things haven't really changed, to a great degree. They only appear to have been changed, and there is more talk of freedom and equal opportunity and all, but so far in my opinion it's only talk.

CHAIRMAN HANNAH. Any other questions? Mr. Taylor, do you have any questions?

MR. TAYLOR. No, I have no questions, but I would like to say to Mr. Sanchez that I appreciate his appearing here and testifying and giving information to the Commission.

CHAIRMAN HANNAH. Thank you very much, Mr. Sanchez. You are excused. Will you call the next witness?

MR. GLICKSTEIN. The next witness is Mr. Caesar Mendez.

(Whereupon, MR. CAESAR MENDEZ was sworn by the Chairman and testified as follows:)

TESTIMONY OF MR. CAESAR MENDEZ, OAKLAND, CALIFORNIA

MR. GLICKSTEIN. Mr. Mendez, would you please state your full name and address for the record?

MR. MENDEZ. My name is Caesar Flores Mendez. I live at 2020 High Street in Oakland, California.

MR. GLICKSTEIN. What is your occupation, Mr. Mendez?

MR. MENDEZ. I'm an aircraft mechanic.

MR. GLICKSTEIN. Are you also concerned or involved in activities and organizations that attempt to deal with these problems of the Spanish-speaking community?

MR. MENDEZ. At the present time I am the state secretary of the American G.I. Forum. This is the only national Mexican American war veteran organization in the United States.

I am a past state chairman of the Community Service Organization here in the State of California. This is an involvement of community affairs dealing with the Mexican American problems for the past 12 years.

MR. GLICKSTEIN. Mr. Sanchez, are you familiar with—

MR. MENDEZ. My name is Mendez.

MR. GLICKSTEIN. I'm sorry, I'm one witness behind.

MR. MENDEZ. Well, one Mexican looks like the other, don't they?

MR. GLICKSTEIN. Mr. Mendez, are you familiar with the various federally financed job-training programs?

MR. MENDEZ. I don't know what you have reference to, Mr. Glickstein.

MR. GLICKSTEIN. Do you feel that federally financed job-training programs, programs under the Poverty Program, programs under MDTA, have had an adequate impact on the Spanish-speaking community?

MR. MENDEZ. Are we generally speaking of MDTA programs or federally sponsored programs that are geared now to the Federal level, to the Bay Area, or the State of California?

MR. GLICKSTEIN. To the Bay Area.

MR. MENDEZ. Right here in the Bay Area, Oakland is considered a hot city, an explosive city. The tremendous amount of Federal money that is coming into Oakland and some of it is geared in the MDTA programs, this definitely has some impact in helping our people.

MR. GLICKSTEIN. How about on a statewide basis?

MR. MENDEZ. On a statewide basis where the Mexican American is concerned, the MDTA programs, federally financed programs have failed to reach the overall Mexican American community.

Through the local barrio and colonia throughout the San Joaquin Valley to the Mexican border there are no such stable MDTA financed programs which are geared specifically to assist, help, and train the young Mexican American in the rural area.

MR. GLICKSTEIN. Are you involved in an effort to set up programs that would meet this lack that you have just described?

MR. MENDEZ. Yes. We have been funded—the American G.I. Forum has been funded, may I say this, a subsidiary of our organization is called A Job For Progress. This is a joint venture between two of the most nationally known Mexican American organizations in the United States.

This is the LULAC, and American G.I. Forum. LULAC is a League of United Latin American Citizens and American G.I. Forum. Their sponsorship of a dual program by joint funds from the OEO and the Department of Labor have geared together to help us assist in trying to create what we have tried to pattern, after consulting with the Urban League, a skills bank and OJT and MDTA programs geared directly to the Mexican American citizens and persons throughout the five Southwest States.

MR. GLICKSTEIN. How does this program differ from the other programs the Federal Government is funding? You said it is geared specifically to the needs of Mexican Americans. What do you mean by that?

MR. MENDEZ. Well, what we have been trying to say to the overall community, to the established agencies, that the very story that has to be told is that you have failed the Mexican American and the Spanish-speaking as well as you have failed the Negro.

The Negro has learned through organizational methods to implement and create a society through which he has been able to
assist his own people through the organizational efforts of their
own race, to be able to assist in their own locals and their own
community.

We intend to do, by using the same structure and the same
methods, to be able to assist our people. We have the same goals
in mind in order to elevate a self-help program to be able to reach
down and try and create a better image to our young Mexican
Americans, a better image which now exists throughout the
United States and throughout the five Southwest States is that
we are not necessarily delegated to just be stoop labor. I don't
think that we as Mexican Americans should be relegated to a rule
of a second-class citizen or better yet, just to be used as farm
laborers.

This is the reason why we believe through organizational methods that we are going to have to deal with problems to be able to
reach to your Commission throughout the United States and with
federally assisted programs to help us establish our organizations,
put through our programs by our people, given a self-help program
and a general path in the right direction.

MR. GLICKSTEIN. Mr. Mendez, why don't you think that the
types of programs that you have just described, instead of being
operated by separate groups such as programs for Mexican Americans and programs for Negroes, be one designed to assist any
person who doesn't have the skills to get good jobs and needs
training, or who otherwise needs to be assisted in obtaining
economic security?

MR. MENDEZ. That question almost answers itself. Relative to
our position in which we are today, we are going into the 21st
Century, we as Mexican American citizens who now are only
predated by the buffalo and the Prairie Indian here in the United
States seem to have fallen in the bottom end of the economic and
educational ladder. Therefore, we have to turn to our own people
and say, "We have to show them the way."

It seems to be a way to lead and instruct to a direction of being
able to reach our people which, somehow or another, the stereo-
type agencies have failed to reach. Again we will say truthfully that
these agencies have not really tried. They have not really made an
effort to reach our people.

MR. GLICKSTEIN. The program that you described a little while
ago you said was funded by the Federal Government?

MR. MENDEZ. Yes. I would like the Commissioner, Chairman
John Hannah, to really get this, and I hope it goes into the record.

This is for the American G.I. Forum and the LULAC. This
would be a subsidiary of a joint venture, and this is called the Jobs

For Progress, Incorporated, and we call it "SER," a Spanish verb
which means "to be," and this is what we are. We want you to just
reach our plateau.

MR. GLICKSTEIN. Does SER contemplate the expansion of its
activities?

MR. MENDEZ. Yes. Our regional office is in Albuquerque, New
Mexico. We have been promised by the Federal people, the Department of Labor and OEO, that we would be able to fund four service
centers in the State of Texas and four in the State of California.

This again has disappointed many of the Mexican American top
leadership because this financial assistance has not been forthcoming. We have strived and told Washington that we direly need
these funds to put our ideas to work. We think that Washington
has turned a deaf ear to the Mexican American at this time.

We don't understand the Administration's position in this regard
for the largest minority in the Southwest States, and somehow or
another we have never got the go-ahead, the green light that these
funds are forthcoming.

As I sit here today in our latest talk with our office in Washington, D. C., and I hope this Commission has some basis on it that
we never been able to spring those funds loose to help our program.

MR. GLICKSTEIN. Mr. Mendez, will SER in addition to being a
skills bank, an agency that will direct people to jobs, also provide
training?

MR. MENDEZ. Yes. Our concept of training is identically the
same as all the rest of the training programs except it is geared
to the direction to where a self-help program in which we said the
usual programs have not been able to reach our people, and it
also is a training period for us to involve Mexican Americans in
this type of program to get that self-assurance and that poise to
be able to be and talk across the bargaining tables to management,
to business, to labor, and to the usual social services to make them
understand our particular problems as they exist today in the 20th
Century.

MR. GLICKSTEIN. Thank you. I have no further questions, Mr.
Chairman.

CHAIRMAN HANNAH. Mrs. Freeman?

COMMISSIONER FREEMAN. Mr. Mendez, with respect to the SER
project, did I understand you to say that you have a proposal for
job training for the Mexican Americans in the Bay Area that is
now pending and waiting for Federal funds? Is that correct?

MR. MENDEZ. Yes, Mrs. Freeman. This is one of the things that
we've tried to get across and spring loose. Our regional office in
Albuquerque has not been able to spring those funds loose, and
our office will be located, in which we have incorporated in the
Bay Area, and we will be operating out of San Jose, California,
but the American G.I. Forum, which is a non-veteran organization,

we have our chapters reaching as far north as into Sacramento. So, therefore, we have to have some base to operate out of, and the rest will be satellite offices, but we do hope to be able to get the funds to be able to start our program in San Jose and spring out into the regular pockets where the heavy concentration of Mexican American and Spanish-speaking are right now in the Bay Area.

That's where we are talking about the little, small communities outside of Santa Clara County. This is Alviso, DeCoto, Union City, small pockets in Hayward. Right here we have here the Fruitvale area, and then we go over across into Contra Costa County and Pittsburg, and Hayward, and Brentwood, and Oakley, and then down into, back across the way to South City, you see? These are where we have large concentrations, like in the market area in San Francisco.

COMMISSIONER FREEMAN. How many persons would be served by this project you have if it were funded?

MR. MENDEZ. Right now the statistics should now be being put in the hopper and we are trying to get this out working from the latest census figure of 1960 which, you know, are not very accurate. So, necessarily, these figures, I don't really have them at the tip of my tongue. I didn't come prepared, I'm sorry, Mrs. Freeman, but it would be in the area of sort of a 15- to 25 percent increase of the 1960 census figure as is shown for the Bay Area.

COMMISSIONER FREEMAN. Then would it substantially upgrade the condition of the Mexican American in the Bay Area if this program is put into effect in terms of planning?

MR. MENDEZ. We hope so. Mrs. Freeman, we hope that this indentation can be made. We think that naturally, like anything else, we have to have an image also, and we would like to get some guidance from our young people in saying that they can point up and be getting assistance from people who really understand their own problems and are really sympathetic and understanding to their background and their culture.

COMMISSIONER FREEMAN. It sounds like a good project.

MR. MENDEZ. We believe it is.

COMMISSIONER FREEMAN. Thank you.

CHAIRMAN HANNAH. Mr. Patterson.

VICE CHAIRMAN PATTERSON. Mr. Mendez, were you born in this country?

MR. MENDEZ. Oh, yes.

VICE CHAIRMAN PATTERSON. Did you grow up here in the Bay Area?

MR. MENDEZ. No, my mistake, like a lot of Mexicans, you know, we happened to be born in Texas.

VICE CHAIRMAN PATTERSON. Did you go to school in Texas?

MR. MENDEZ. Yes, sir, I graduated from high school in Texas.

VICE CHAIRMAN PATTERSON. We've heard testimony here in the

Bay Area that language is a major problem for the children who
go into the schools in the Bay Area. I assume that you encountered
this in your own schooling in Texas. Is that correct? A language
problem?

MR. MENDEZ. I hate to be facetious, but, you know, sometimes
when we are talking about this particular problem, and I know
my good Negro friends understand me now here in Oakland. Out
here they know me pretty well.

You see, I grew up speaking Spanish first. This is typical, no
more different than anything else. We don't commence to speak
English until we go to grade school.

Now, a guy has to be pretty sharp to "keep his cool" and be able
to make it with the rest of the kids, so this particular problem
exists right here in our own Bay Area.

Now, the reason I say that, maybe it's because there is no inflec-
tion in my voice and I do not have an accent. That is indifferent
because invariably this may be an exception to the rule.

Our experience right here in the Bay Area is that invariably
in our dropout rate, studied last year with the board of education
in Oakland, we have now exceeded a dropout factor larger than
the Negro. This should tell us one thing: one thing and one thing
only. That somehow or another that this language factor, this
basic culture has some impact on being able to obtain just our
ordinary education.

VICE CHAIRMAN PATTERSON. Well, this was going to be my
question. What proposal do you make? What would you like to see
done in the Bay Area schools to meet this language problem? Is
it a matter that addresses itself to the schools or to other agencies?
Tell me, as a practical matter, what you would like to see done
about it.

MR. MENDEZ. Well, you see, I'm not an educator. I am a civil
rights activist. No, I didn't mean that.

You see, those are educational problems, and if Dr. Phillips was
sitting here at this table—and I know I have had words with Dr.
Phillips. We have had words with Dr. Dunne. Now, if this means
anything, I mean for what it's worth, you know, there must be
something lacking in our educational system right here in my
own hometown, right here.

This is my town, Oakland, you see, and we are very concerned
about these things, and it is very important to be able to express
them to the board of education, not only solely to the Oakland
Board of Education but Alameda, Peralta; but somehow or another
still that message isn't getting through.

We have said invariably that somewhere along the line the
educational system is lacking, not only in the understanding of
the Mexican American problem because we have said this to
Dr. Phillips that his act of recruitment when we had a teacher

shortage right here in Oakland that he invariably went back into the Middle-West to recruit his teachers. In the Middle-West, and almost 18 to 25 percent of the teachers that we have here in Oakland came from the Middle-West, they didn't know any more about the Negro culture or the Mexican heritage or the Mexican culture, and they were definitely white Anglo-Saxons, and they couldn't possibly reach our people.

We are asking for them to understand, to be able to go out and we have said this: "To reach our people you are going to have to make a strenuous effort." The Negro community has said, "Go to the Negro colleges and get the Negro teachers." We have said the same thing, to go to the Southwest and pick the teachers up there from the Southwest, from the University of Texas, from the University of Mexico, University of Arizona, Texas A & R, Texas A & M, University of Colorado, so these are the things. We've said these things, but they still again seem to fall on deaf ears.

CHAIRMAN HANNAH. Mr. Mendez, I think you said that you or your organization at least thought that they had a commitment from some agency of the Federal Government to finance or encourage four offices in Texas and four in California for your SER program. Is that correct, is that what I understood you to say? But you hadn't been able to spring it loose. You thought you had a commitment and you hadn't been able to get it?

MR. MENDEZ. No, Chairman Hannah. I said we have been initially funded, seed money. This is by two joint—funding between the Department of Labor and the OEO, but this is only seed money to get our regional office in Albuquerque started.

CHAIRMAN HANNAH. You have not been able to get the programs finalized as yet?

MR. MENDEZ. Again, the white bureaucrat from Washington speaks with forked tongue. You see, they promised that and we have the original document, original contract signed by Secretary of Labor Wirtz and Sargent Shriver for OEO with full commitment to establish four service centers in Texas and four in California and one in the rest of the Southwest States.

CHAIRMAN HANNAH. All I am trying to find out from you is where you got the commitment and who has broken the commitment.

MR. MENDEZ. From the Secretary of Labor Wirtz and Sargent Shriver from OEO.

CHAIRMAN HANNAH. That's the answer I wanted. Are there other questions? Mr. Rankin?

COMMISSIONER RANKIN. Mr. Mendez, I know you are concerned about these grants, but your real concern, isn't it, insofar as the Spanish-speaking people are concerned, is your concern of the classification of second-class citizenship. What you want is first-

class citizenship for Spanish-speaking Americans. Am I correct?
Isn't that the big purpose?

MR. MENDEZ. Commissioner Rankin, I don't want it, I demand it.

COMMISSIONER RANKIN. You demand it.

MR. MENDEZ You see, this is the reason our organization got
founded and started. You know, we are American and Mexican
G.I.'s and do you understand, Commissioner, that we were born
in this country, we fought for this country, and many of them
died for this country and when one of our soldiers came back, they
wouldn't even let him be buried in their own cemetery in his own
hometown of Green Rivers, Texas. Now, if this isn't an insult,
you know.

We stop to think, "Now, what is this?" you know. But, you see,
we are the first generation of Mexican Americans to be able to
rise up and protest and say these things across this board without
the fear of reprisal, without the fear of intimidation, because at
one time, since early 1923 to 1936 do you realize over 500,000
Mexican American people have been deported back to Mexico,
and these were Mexican American citizens. We don't fear that
any more, you see.

This is the reason why we say that we do not intend to be
second-class citizens.

COMMISSIONER RANKIN. At which level of government are you
having the best success, local government, State Government or
Federal Government, or is it equally bad?

MR. MENDEZ. Choose the lesser of what evil?

COMMISSIONER RANKIN. And one last question. You've shown us
that we have a hard time, let's say, understanding you. Do you
have an equally hard time understanding us?

MR. MENDEZ. No, I think I truly understand you, sir.

COMMISSIONER RANKIN. But we can't understand you, is that
it?

MR. MENDEZ. This is true.

COMMISSIONER RANKIN. It's a one-way street, a one-way understanding. Is that correct?

MR. MENDEZ. Well, up to this point, yes.

COMMISSIONER RANKIN. But you think it can be changed?

MR. MENDEZ. Well, sir, this will leave me an opening now.

With the Chairman's permission, Mr. Hannah—I mean, I've
heard Mr. Sanchez say this, and you have to—as I say, we are
not trying to be facetious with your Commission, but you know
that we have filed a discrimination charge against this Commission. Our Washington office has done that.

CHAIRMAN HANNAH. We have had that presented once this
afternoon.

MR. MENDEZ. And we did it in San Francisco, and I guess we
are going to have to do it over here. You see, we are going to

follow a true pattern. The only thing that I can say is that I'd like to take this opportunity to file this formal complaint of discrimination.

CHAIRMAN HANNAH. We will receive it, but we've had it read once this afternoon.

MR. MENDEZ. Yes, it's all done, but I do want the audience, and I want this whole Commission to know that this is a formal complaint put across and I want the record to show, that we are at least going to be consistent, and we do hope that the Commission thinks upon these and doesn't take it too lightly, and I hope you do understand what we are trying to say.

CHAIRMAN HANNAH. I think we understand it very well. Mr. Griswold, do you have any questions?

COMMISSIONER GRISWOLD. No. No questions.

CHAIRMAN HANNAH. Any other questions. Mr. Taylor?

MR. TAYLOR. No, sir.

CHAIRMAN HANNAH. I think, Mr. Mendez, before we excuse you—and I know that you understand the nature of the Commission and we do not object at all to having you and your colleagues, since this is the first opportunity that you have had to have a Federal agency come and invite you to come and make your statements and so on, we understand fully your problem and are fully sympathetic.

I think you know also that when you refer to the Commission as a part of the Federal bureaucracy, and so on, that that is not quite accurate. I think you know the fact of the matter is that the six Commissioners are appointed by the President and confirmed by the Senate of the United States. They are not members of the bureaucracy at all.

They have full-time jobs. They give a good deal of time and effort because they have a real interest in this whole problem of civil rights as it pertains to Negroes or Spanish-speaking Americans or Indians or any other minority group. We have only one responsibility, and that is to go around the country as we are, this week here, on other occasions elsewhere in the country, and to find out whether or not it is true that American citizens are being denied their civil rights because of their color, or their race, or their religion, or other items for which they are not responsible, and then to make recommendations to the President and to the Congress to hopefully bring about a solution to some of these problems. That is what the Commission is all about.

You have been critical yesterday and today, or your colleagues have, because most of the attention in the last few years has been devoted to the problems of the Negro, and we have to admit that is true because there are many more Negroes, they have had very real problems, and of course the solutions are not yet.

We have been aware that the Mexican Americans have a problem, the American Indians have a problem, that other groups have. So we are happy to have these presentations made by you and the others who have appeared and will appear, and we intend to do what we can to at least begin to bring about a solution.

So it has been pleasant for us to have you here, and we have full recognition of what your problem is and what you are trying to accomplish. We admire you for it. You are excused, sir.

MR. MENDEZ. We appreciate your giving us this opportunity, but we were just hoping that this Commission would really act with the full authority that is delegated to it and move at a little more rapid pace, Commissioner, and this is my formal document. This is a copy of our official complaint against the Commission. We do hope that you take this into serious consideration.

CHAIRMAN HANNAH. Mr. Glickstein, will you call the next witness.

MR. GLICKSTEIN. The next witness is Dr. Norvell Smith.

(Whereupon, DR. NORVELL SMITH was sworn by the Chairman and testified as follows:)

TESTIMONY OF DR. NORVELL SMITH, OAKLAND, CALIFORNIA

MR. GLICKSTEIN. Dr. Smith, will you please state your full name and address for the record?

DR. SMITH. My name is Norvell Smith, and I am a resident of Oakland.

MR. GLICKSTEIN. Dr. Smith, what is your occupation?

DR. SMITH. I'm a bureaucrat. I am a public administrator and I'm being facetious, also. I am the director of the Department of Human Resources, which is a department of city government which, among other things, is responsible for directing the so-called war on poverty.

MR. GLICKSTEIN. How long have you been associated with the Poverty Program in Oakland?

DR. SMITH. I came to work for the city just under four years ago to direct a pilot project which was a predecessor to the war on poverty funded by the Ford Foundation in one of our four target areas. Two years ago the program was expanded under OEO to a comprehensive citywide activity.

MR. GLICKSTEIN. Would you please describe for the Commission the structure and functions of the Oakland Economic Development Council?

DR. SMITH. Yes. The OEDC is the Community Action Agency for Oakland. The present membership of 39 was formed out of an earlier nucleus of the advisory committee for the old Ford Foundation project of a dozen members who were expanded to 25 members two years ago at the outset of the OEO program, and at the same

time the Department of Human Resources was formed, which was
subsequently expanded to 40 members and then contracted to 39
as of January 1 of this year, at which time the basic structure
was changed.

As of January 1, the membership is composed of 20 elected
members from the target areas, and 19 at-large members representing the rest of the community-wide coalition which the
OEDC represents.

MR. GLICKSTEIN. How many target areas are there?

DR. SMITH. There are four geographical target areas, North
Oakland, West Oakland, Fruitvale, as we call it, and East Oakland
which has a combined population of about 140,000 to 145,000
people, about half of whom are low-income.

MR. GLICKSTEIN. And each of these target areas has an advisory
committee. Is that correct?

DR. SMITH. Yes, and as of about a year ago a fifth target area
advisory committee was formed composed of persons who are
Spanish surname who live within the entire city grouping of target
areas. We now have five groups, and four geographical areas.

MR. GLICKSTEIN. Why was the Spanish-speaking advisory committee established?

DR. SMITH. Well, I think there are two reasons. To begin with,
there was strong and aggressive action on behalf of the four or
five major organizations that operate out of Oakland, Spanish-
speaking, to have a formal representation on the OEDC. At that
time there were two at-large members of the advisory committee
who were Spanish-speaking and who also happened to be Mexican
American leaders who lived in the target areas.

I think there was recognition after the first year or year and a
half of the program that the Spanish-speaking low-income group
who were concentrated on the east side of town were having
difficulty competing with the more numerous, the more aggressive
representation in the Negro community, among the low-income
Caucasian community, and among the very great number of
middle-class leaders and social interventionists who were working
aggressively to foster the purposes of the Poverty Program.

MR. GLICKSTEIN. Were you in favor of the creation of the
Spanish-speaking advisory committee?

DR. SMITH. Yes, I've endorsed the recommendation and felt
that there was validity to it as a transitional thing and the OEDC
established the committee with the hope, and I think the understanding in the Spanish-speaking community, that this would be
a step toward building leadership and organization within the
Spanish-speaking commmunity with the hope that it would
eventually move out into the geographical areas and infiltrate

the geographical structures, that these groups would work along with other low-income groups of varied ethnic background.

MR. GLICKSTEIN. You've viewed that as a transitional device?

DR. SMITH. Yes, I did, and I think that OEDC did also. The committee has only in the last three or four, five months really come into its own. They had a serious problem of organization, and prior to January 1 of this year they didn't have their own neighborhood organization staff. There have been Spanish-speaking organizers employed by other committees, but they were not responsible to a Spanish-speaking board of directors, and I think this was one of the factors related to their inability to mobilize their resources.

I think also the fact that nine or 10 months ago the first Spanish-speaking community development program funded under OEO in the West which was started in Oakland had a lot to do with providing some cohesiveness to this movement.

MR. GLICKSTEIN. Did you have misgivings that Spanish-speaking advisory committees would become a permanent part of the program?

DR. SMITH. I wouldn't have misgivings. I would be disappointed if we had to continue with the present operation which denies the geographical areas the benefit of the ideas and concerns and contribution of the Spanish-speaking who at the moment are functioning only within their own Spanish language groups.

They have a small committee. They have not been able to develop as broad a participation as we would like or they would like, and I still have a personal feeling that they would be more effective in influencing the overall program and that their benefit would be greater when they become part of the other committees.

Now, some of the committees do have Spanish-speaking. The Fruitvale committee, which originally had a large number of Spanish-speaking representatives, has a few who still work with them, although much of the leadership in the Fruitvale area has gravitated towards the Spanish-speaking committee. The West Oakland committee has a small participation from the Puerto Rican group which has a heavy concentration in West Oakland. The Spanish-speaking, although overwhelmingly Mexican American, does include representation from many other groups, but in very small number.

MR. GLICKSTEIN. I assume that one of the reasons that there was a demand for the Spanish-speaking committee was the feeling among Spanish-speaking groups that the Poverty Program was not providing them with the benefits to which they thought they were entitled. Is that correct?

Dr. Smith. I think that was an overriding feeling, and of course it was a fact that numerically few of their people were elected to geographical committees.

In the early stages of the Fruitvale committee the first two, I think, chairmen, were Spanish-speaking, one a very strong young man who was chairman, but who left the community to take another job; and in the early stages of the development I think it was sort of assumed that the Fruitvale area would be the area of primary influence of the Spanish-speaking groups.

That was where most of the organizations were focused, and where most of the church contacts were, and this is the area where even at the present time we have concentrated our efforts to aggressively seek a Spanish-speaking staff.

Mr. Glickstein. What proportion, if you are able to guess, of the OEDC funds were allotted to programs dealing specifically with the problems of the Spanish-speaking poor?

Dr. Smith. Well, I don't think that many of our programs are not addressed to the problems of the Spanish-speaking poor. We have, as I have outlined in this brief statement, a number of very special programs that have an ethnic identity with the Spanish-speaking.

I alluded earlier to the Spanish-speaking information center that was formed about 10 months ago and which has a present budget of some $15,000 funded by OEO. We also have funded some $13,000 for a small neighborhood organization staff which is not designed to do the organization effort since they have a geographical constituency that covers the city, but to provide technical assistance to the other areas in attempting to integrate Mexican Americans and Spanish-speaking into their activities.

Just recently, a week ago, with our Ford funds—and I emphasize that we are not limited to the OEO activity in Oakland under our program. We have had over $3 million in Ford funds in the last five years. We have funded at the level of $25,000 a Spanish-speaking higher education program which is addressed to that group. Many, many of the other programs that are outlined in the summary are addressed to the poor and have aggressively attempted not only to recruit Spanish-speaking staff, but to assure participation of a representative number of Spanish-speaking in the activities of those agencies.

Certainly, the health programs, the school programs which have included concentration in Spanish-speaking target areas are good examples of that. Very large percentages of the clients of the adult minority employment project are Spanish-speaking, and the majority of those, as a matter of fact, are in the Fruitvale área which is our most productive center.

Mr. Glickstein. Am I correct in assuming, Dr. Smith, that

the basis of your hope that the Spanish-speaking advisory council should be only a transitional device is that you think it more desirable to low-income people, regardless of whether they are Spanish-speaking or Negro, to conduct a unified program rather than fragmenting their efforts? Is that correct?

DR. SMITH. I think that is true, and I think most of the enlightened Spanish-speaking leadership in Oakland that I relate to have the same feeling; but I think we all recognize that in instances such as this, and maybe even more so with reference to the fairly sizable Indian population, that it is necessary to have a special bridging activity on a transitional basis.

There is also the necessity to re-enforce the cultural image of these small minorities before they are able to develop the leadership and develop the thrust to be able to play their proportional role, and they were not playing their proportional role prior to this time, not because of any efforts on behalf of our official operation, but because of reasons that have been outlined here.

MR. GLICKSTEIN. Would you say that the forces that unite the low-income Negroes and low-income Spanish-speaking people are greater than those that divide them?

DR. SMITH. Yes, I would say that very definitely, and I would say that the Negro and Mexican American groups which in this State have always had a very close political alliance have worked very closely, as I have observed them over the last eight or 10 years in Oakland in community improvement and in social movements that have been directed toward bringing them into the so-called mainstream and helping them get their proportional share of what the economic system has to offer.

Of course, as you gentlemen and ladies know, the crux of this is the matter of integrating them into the economic system and making it possible for people who are interested and motivated and ready to work to be able to be employed and make enough money to make ends meet.

The problem in Oakland of the poor is not by any means a problem of welfare. The majority of poor people work but don't make enough money. When you combine that with the inability of major segments of the minority community to really get plugged into the system you find that the manifestations are equally applicable to Mexican Americans, and to Negroes, and also to a smaller extent to Orientals.

MR. GLICKSTEIN. What would you say was the major accomplishment of the Poverty Program with respect to the Spanish-speaking community?

DR. SMITH. Well, again, I wouldn't differentiate. I would say that the major contribution of the so-called Poverty Program—

these of the all low-income people, and equally so for the Spanish-speaking—is that we have greatly improved the system of delivering services to low-income people through decentralization, hiring low-income people, and bringing ethnic balance to the staffs of the agencies that are serving them now in a more aggressive manner.

And, secondly, that we have greatly improved the dialogue between poor and non-poor in the various ethnic groups, and I feel that the OADC represents the most significant coalition now in force in this community.

MR. GLICKSTEIN. Thank you. I have no further questions, Mr. Chairman.

CHAIRMAN HANNAH. Mrs. Freeman?

COMMISSIONER FREEMAN. Dr. Smith, I have before me your list of some of the programs that are being funded by the CAP program, and I have a question concerning some of them specifically, particularly neighborhood legal services.

This is a program which would certainly be needed, not only by the Negro, but by the Spanish-speaking persons because they are the segment of the poor that would need legal services in the field of landlord-tenant relations and of consumer credit.

So my question is the extent to which, although it is administered by the Legal Aid Societies is it not, the staff of the societies is inclusive of persons representing the Spanish-speaking community?

The question would also relate to the question of motivational counseling. We have heard testimony from some of the students yesterday that they are missing the necessary counseling. I notice that is administered by the Bay Area Urban League. Would that program include persons who are familiar with the language barrier who would be able to overcome it?

A similar question would be with respect to family counseling and home care services. Do these programs or the contractors with your agency include, as well as members of the poor, those who can overcome the language barrier?

DR. SMITH. Yes. I would start by reminding you of what I said earlier, that there has been a very conscious effort to recruit staffs for all of these programs that reflect the ethnic balance of the kind of population we are serving. As a result, as is indicated in the latter pages of this analysis, we have been able to provide professional, New Career, and clerical persons of Spanish-speaking background, most of them Mexican Americans in many of these programs.

We have not been able to recruit as many as have been sought and it is obvious, I'm sure to you, that to an extent at least as great as that in the Negro community the difficulty of finding professionally trained specialists in many of these areas such as the practice of law and public health nursing, and to a certain extent teaching and social work is an extremely difficult thing.

I doubt, for example, if there are more than a half dozen trained social workers Spanish-speaking in the East Bay Area.

I doubt seriously if there are more than a half dozen Spanish-speaking lawyers in this community. We have been unable to hold on to Spanish-speaking lawyers when we have hired them. There have been two or three, at least three lawyers Spanish-speaking employed during the past 22 or 23 months and, as of a couple weeks ago, we had lost our third Spanish-speaking lawyer in the Fruitvale area, either to private practice or to an administrative position in another, newer legal services program.

So this is the difficulty in our own department. We had an excellent young man who was a center director of the multiservice center in Fruitvale, but who left us for a promotional opportunity to become the head counselor of the Skill Center, and we were unable to replace him with another Mexican American person, although we have an Anglo who is comfortable in Spanish.

It is difficult to find professionals, particularly it is difficult to find stenographic and secretarial staffs in this group even more so than in other ethnic groups, and when they are found, because of their scarcity and their value in being bilingual it is extremely difficult to keep them unless there are many promotional opportunities within the system.

COMMISSIONER FREEMAN. Mr. Mendez spoke earlier about an MDTA training proposal. Is there any area, perhaps, in which these two can be gotten together; that the persons whom he wishes to be trained who live in the target area could be utilized in any of these programs?

DR. SMITH. I think in the clerical and technical area fields this is possible. It is not possible in the professional fields.

We are simply going to have to, through some of our specialized programs that are concentrating on the next generation, motivation and overcoming educational deficiency, hope that we can produce many more Negro, Mexican American, Indian, and other ethnically deprived young people who can be prepared to go out and exercise positions of leadership. In the immediate future I don't see the prospect. In the not too distant removed future with a lot of the impetus of our programs I think it is conceivable that we will see many, many more Mexican American and Negro professionals, technicians, and white collar workers.

The MDTA could have a bearing on the latter, too, but, as I said, and as you know as a lawyer, the difficulty in finding qualified attorneys of whatever complexion or ethnic identity is difficult in a growing area like the West.

CHAIRMAN HANNAH. Do you have any questions, Mr. Patterson?

VICE CHAIRMAN PATTERSON. No questions.

CHAIRMAN HANNAH. Any other questions? Mr. Taylor?

MR. TAYLOR. Dr. Smith, one of the Commission's concerns is in the area of public employment. As a general matter we note from the statistics that we have, that the Spanish-speaking people and, to a lesser extent, Negroes are under-represented in terms of their proportion to the total population and public employment generally in this area.

I was just looking through one of your documents here, and I was glad to note that a good many of the openings that are listed are in the area of public employment. Are you conducting a campaign to open up opportunities in the area of public employment.?

DR. SMITH. I don't think you'd call it a campaign, but it is one of our indirect activities, and certainly a basic commitment of the OEDC and our staff to expand the potential, for example, of New Careers in the public agencies, and as a public department ourselves, we feel that we have something of an inside track on influencing the leadership at least at the municipal government level, if not at the State and county level in this type of operation.

We have a structure that goes back some five years now that has been the basis of our attempt to coordinate human resources programs in Oakland, and I think as a result of the heavy involvement, for example, of the health department and of the schools in many of our programs that we indirectly have been instrumental in stimulating the expansion of careers at all levels in those agencies.

My personal feeling is that the public sector has been rather aggressive within the framework within which they work. We can't close our boundaries and simply take care of people who are here. We continue to have outsiders coming to California, as I did from South Philadelphia, looking for a better way of life.

Unless we are able to have some sort of compensatory consideration for our population we are not really making any inroads in the solution of the problem.

It isn't just jobs. It is jobs combined with the wherewithall to enable the people in Oakland to take advantage of them, because otherwise the jobs continue to go to people in the suburbs and that doesn't help us.

MR. TAYLOR. Thank you.

CHAIRMAN HANNAH. Thank you very much, Dr. Smith. We appreciate your being here. You are excused and we will now take a 10-minutes recess.

CHAIRMAN HANNAH. The hearing will come to order. Mr. Glickstein, will you call the next witnesses?

MR. GLICKSTEIN. The next witnesses are Dr. Stanley Soles and Mr. John E. Jeffrey.

(Whereupon, DR. STANLEY SOLES and MR. JOHN E. JEFFREY were sworn by the Chairman and testified as follows:)

TESTIMONY OF MR. JOHN JEFFREY, SAN FRANCISCO, CALIFORNIA AND DR. STANLEY SOLES, SAN MATEO, CALIFORNIA

MR. GLICKSTEIN. Would you each please state your name and address for the record?

MR. JEFFREY. My name is John Jeffrey. I am at 240 Golden Gate Avenue in San Francisco.

DR. SOLES. I am Stanley Soles. I live at 2044 Ticonderoga Road in San Mateo.

MR. GLICKSTEIN. Mr. Jeffrey, what is your occupation?

MR. JEFFREY. I am the executive secretary of the San Francisco City and County Employees' Union, AFL-CIO.

MR. GLICKSTEIN. Dr. Soles, what is your occupation?

DR. SOLES. I am the director of Community Action Training, a program funded by the Office of Economic Opportunity to serve training programs in the War Against Poverty for eight counties in the Bay Area.

MR. GLICKSTEIN. Dr. Soles, you have submitted a statement to the Commission which has been distributed to the Commissioners.

DR. SOLES. Yes.

MR. GLICKSTEIN. Mr. Chairman, may I request that Dr. Soles' statement be introduced into the record as Exhibit No. 26?

CHAIRMAN HANNAH. It is received.

(Whereupon the document referred to was marked Exhibit No. 26 and received in evidence.)

MR. GLICKSTEIN. I'd like to begin by directing some questions to Dr. Soles and then to Mr. Jeffrey.

DR. SOLES. May I make a correction in the statement submitted? On Page 8, the number of jobs of welfare workers in the State of California is approximately 10,000, and the number of openings would not be one for every three cases, but one for every three workers amounting to approximately 3,000 welfare aid jobs. That is Page 8.

CHAIRMAN HANNAH. The correction will be made, sir.

DR. SOLES. Thank you.

MR. GLICKSTEIN. Dr. Soles, does the program of which you are director train New Careerists?

DR. SOLES. There are some elements of New Careers patterned in the training program, but I would regard it more as a training program for non-professionals not having all of the elements of the basic nucleus program. Namely, it does not have the upgrading, it does not have the linkage with the institutions of higher education, it does not provide the certification, and, therefore, is not a career.

MR. GLICKSTEIN. Dr. Soles, the Commission has heard reference to the New Careers concept on various occasions in the last three days. Would you please briefly define for us what the New Careers concept is?

DR. SOLES. If you will, I would like to say that the New Careers concept is an outgrowth of an interpretation of three major areas. One in the economy, two in the society, and three in the culture.

In terms of its interpretations about the economy we see before us an economy in which automation is increasingly shrinking the number of job openings in the manufacturing and industrial sectors but, at the same time, there are increasing manpower needs in the human services sector and it is in this sector that the New Careers concept concentrates.

In terms of the society we see before us what Art Pearl calls a "Credential Oriented Society," a society in which in order to begin work in various fields a certification and a credential is required usually at the end of four or five years of college education. So in terms of the society, the credential society locks a number of individuals out of participating.

In terms of the culture itself the New Careers concept analyzes the dilemmas that are found between the professionals who are operating within the helping services and the poor people who are unemployed or underemployed and finds two major types of problems.

One, a service gap and, two, a communications gap. It is in this context of economy, society, and culture that the New Careers concept develops.

I would like to indicate some of the basic elements of the New Careers concept, if you will. The basic idea of the New Careers concept is a job first, and training built into the job. It is a job development and a job creation approach.

It differs from previous programs and ideas along this line by having the job to begin with, rather than a training program with no jobs at the end of the line, and by having the training built into the job and some other elements that I will mention such as upgrading, provisions for advancement, further sort of self-enhancing type jobs, jobs which really modify the self-view of individuals. These are all elements of the New Careers idea.

MR. GLICKSTEIN. Could a person employed under this program start as a non-professional or a sub-professional and work his way up to a professional capacity?

DR. SOLES. That is the basic plan of the New Careers program. At the present time, by and large, these programs are at the non-professional level and not fully operating at the career level. There is a great deal of work yet to be done to make these career programs rather than temporary non-professional jobs.

MR. GLICKSTEIN. The way it is working now people are in jobs that don't seem to have very much of a future or much of an opportunity for upgrading themselves?

DR. SOLES. Well, that depends on some things to be negotiated. I wouldn't say that they're on temporary jobs in which there is no future. They're on jobs in which the money may run out since many of the jobs, 40,000 throughout the United States, are, by and large, from the War Against Poverty funds and National Institute of Mental Health and juvenile delinquency prevention programs, Department of Labor, and other types of federally funded programs.

But the kinds of jobs they are doing, I think indicate a way in the future in which there is some possibility of permanency, providing there are a number of changes made in present practice of existing agencies and departments such as health, welfare, education, recreation and so forth in various parts of the United States. If these changes are made, these surely will be permanent jobs.

MR. GLICKSTEIN. Are most of the jobs that are currently under New Careers program or programs similar to New Careers with public agencies?

DR. SOLES. Right. The assumption underlying this effort is a job development program in areas in which there is a manpower shortage.

It would be silly to have a New Careers program tried, let's say, in the construction field right now, for example, where you have a manpower surplus. There is no effort to use this concept in such an area.

MR. GLICKSTEIN. In what type of public agencies has the New Careers program been established?

DR. SOLES. As I mentioned a moment ago in the areas of health, in the areas of education, corrections, probation, and various types of police programs—juvenile programs. In the areas of recreation, in the areas of urban renewal, in the public areas within the city such as the fire department, and in other areas.

MR. GLICKSTEIN. Is New Careers an alternative to the traditional educational process as a route to obtaining professional status?

DR. SOLES. New Careers as an educational alternative has many—well, let me say this:

New Careers has many facets, one of which is education. The implications of its change for education, I don't think have been fully realized. Although there are many elements that are old, the present educational changes that have been made in line with New Careers have been relatively limited in contrast to what is needed.

For example, you have a program, let's say of adult education in which the ideas and information from a New Careers program are related to the job that the person is learning.

One of the educational changes is to attempt to bring the information in line with the job and into the field. It consists of changes in methodology and it is a considerable change, let's say, from adult education or night-school courses.

Let me illustrate one of the points of change. You are probably familiar with the pattern, let's say, of lawyers who have attended adult education and had a part-time job, maybe as a service station attendant or something unrelated, certainly, to the legal field.

What the New Careers idea contends is that by starting with the job you make the education come to and select from those things that are relevant for doing that job so that a person coming into the field of education, for example, would get information related to his job and to his field, and as he moved into more and more complicated areas this would require changes in terms of courses, curriculum and some revolutionary aspects of it as far as I am concerned would be to bring more of the theory-oriented course work from the universities and colleges into the field and this would create new patterns of service.

I think we are seeing some of this in the work study program, we are seeing elements of this that are quite old. Antioch College has used something somewhat similar to this for many years.

New Careers is not so much a new idea as a pulling together and a new synthesis of a number of old themes, but trying to bring them to bear in terms of this manpower crisis in the human services area.

MR. GLICKSTEIN. Does the program depend upon professional employees training or helping to train the New Careerists?

DR. SOLES. Yes, it does. Along with others, the professionals are certainly an important link in having a definite say-so about the job definition of sub-professionals. This is a point that is frequently misunderstood.

The definition of sub-professional tasks, say in the field of teaching, would result from a coalition of a committee which consisted of a coalition of groups having to say which tasks are appropriate to be defined by the particular school system for sub-professional teachers.

MR. GLICKSTEIN. Do you think that New Careers can become a means of entry into employment for minority group persons and others who might be excluded because of inadequate education and lack of technical skills?

DR. SOLES. I do. I've listened to the testimony of this Commission—not of this Commission but to this Commission—for some time during the past three days and I have been impressed by the concern that has been expressed over language difficulties and, if you will permit me, I believe cultural difficulties.

As a result of this one of the things that is involved, I think, is the idea that the New Careers idea assumes that the poor people, the people who maybe have a difference in language have something positive to contribute to a job. This differs from other job training programs where the so-called attributes of low-income groups are treated as irrelevant or condescendingly as something they should be rid of.

Whereas this is treated as something that should be accepted, as something that will enable that person to perhaps better bridge in terms of service and in terms of perhaps identifying a needed type of service that the present group of professionals, not because they so intended, but in part because they may not quite have the same sort of skills in terms of dealing with an indigenous culture, so they are not able to establish rapport perhaps as easily as some of the non-professionals might.

So that this program assumes that there are assets among low-income groups. There are life styles, language patterns, and so forth that can make a positive contribution to improve the functioning and quality of service of the existing institutions right now that are presently over-crowded and the professionals themselves I think are tremendously overworked in attempting to deal with the variety of problems confronting them.

MR. GLICKSTEIN. So you think that utilizing New Careerists in welfare agencies or in a school system would have the effect of permitting the welfare agencies and the school systems to better deal with the persons that they have contact with?

DR. SOLES. Definitely. I believe that one of the difficulties right now is that there is a communication barrier, there is a lack of delivery of services, and I think it is beyond merely a question of a manpower crisis of professionals.

In other words, it is not just a shortage of professionals, but it's a breakdown of the delivery system of these various health and welfare and education services.

The testimony you have been receiving for the past few days, I think is merely symptomatic of this difficulty. For example, in the area of health, about one in 10 alcoholics is being treated. In the area of health the situation for Negroes has become increasingly worse in the past few years rather than better.

The statistics for death rate among Negro babies has changed from 75 percent, in contrast to whites, to 95 percent in contrast to whites from 1940 to 1967.

In other words, the situation as far as the delivery of service is a difficulty, and I think that we need to recognize that as being a crisis. It is a human crisis rather than merely a professional shortage so that I think that they can help define services and they can help better deliver new services.

MR. GLICKSTEIN. Do you think that the New Careers program would threaten professional employees?

DR. SOLES. I think that there are some members of the professional community, and I take perhaps, I think, an understanding view, if you will, maybe a sympathetic view, that they are operating in a condition of stress and in this condition of stress, being overworked in an institution in which they are expected to carry out fairly specialized roles, I think that they are perhaps a bit over-sensitive and overly defensive.

I believe that the people who have actually worked in programs according to the evidence from a couple of national studies cited in the papers submitted to you, these fears are unjustified. There is not an emphasis upon over-identification with the client, or a feeling of not being able to work within the authority system, or mistreating confidentiality.

There just hasn't been evidence to support these charges. There are some fears on the part of professional groups and others who are outside of programs, but within programs as I can indicate by turning to some studies along this line that the feeling on the part of teachers, for example, who have had auxiliary personnel working with them, is that they just didn't know how they could get along without the teachers' aides or without the auxiliary people afterwards. They express, rather, a kind of "I am a better teacher as a result of having an aide. It's not only that it gave me more time to plan, but also forced me to plan more specifically."

In other words, as a result of working with aides, professionals have been freed to carry out those tasks that are far more central to their role. While there well may be some teachers who identify collecting money for the milk as being a central teacher function, I rather doubt it.

MR. GLICKSTEIN. Mr. Jeffrey, you are the executive secretary of the Municipal Employees Union?

MR. JEFFREY. Yes, San Francisco City and County Employees.

MR. GLICKSTEIN. You have heard Dr. Soles' testimony and I am sure you are familiar with the New Careers concept. What is your view of the significance of New Careers to the professionals in civil service?

MR. JEFFREY. I would like to make the Commission clear as to my role as far as the New Careers is concerned. At least, I assume it would be my role.

You must understand that my union, some 2,700 members, are city and county employees who are civil service employees. They got their job by virtue of qualifying, taking a civil service test, and getting appointed therefrom and assigned to duties.

Now the bulk of our membership is clerical and professional. I would say that most of the civil service professionals in the city and county belong to our union.

I'm proud to say that as far as the racial problem is concerned we have none. We are proud of the fact that our president is a Negro. We are proud of the fact that every single staff member of the Human Rights Commission is a member of our union, and we are proud of the fact that about one-third of our members are either Negroes or members of the Chinese minority or other racial minorities.

Now we have discussed this New Careers program on a tentative basis with Dr. Soles and others, the Human Rights Commission, and, believe me, the theory of upgrading disadvantaged persons, whether it be disadvantage because of race or whatever is very appealing and we support that in general; but as far as what we've heard as to practically applying it to the public service in the city and county of San Francisco with the guidelines agreed to by all parties so far what I have heard is mostly gobbledygook and I must say that because when you talk about a person getting employment in the public service you have to start somewhere.

Now, the social service department was mentioned. The great number of welfare workers there are in the State, and the fact that social workers need help, and so on and so on. This is true. If a worker, a potential worker, has a college degree he can get a job right now, they are short of jobs, as social work trainees so that they may subsequently qualify for the civil service test and become a social worker.

The guidelines as laid down with which we agree are that New Careers or any other of these programs would not in any way take jobs that should belong to civil service employees. That is number one; or displace civil service employees; or do work which should be done by civil service employees; and when you put that much on the table then the question is where and exactly what are these people going to do, and how are they going to be upgraded?

For example, to start with, presumably most of these people would be high school dropouts. A person with a high school diploma can get a job in the city and county of San Francisco anytime, regardless of race. There is no problem. We can get him a job somewhere or other in some classification or other. So he would be presumably a high school dropout.

Now, what we have heard about so far is to take a high school dropout into, say, the social service department and train him, give him duties and responsibilities which in no way do violence to civil service for which he will get work experience and get credit, school credit presumably. And, eventually, somehow or other, he will not only get his high school diploma, but he will get his college degree, and thus qualify to become, say, a professional social worker.

Now, we'd like to see how this could be done and we are still waiting.

With respect to the other areas mentioned by Dr. Soles and others, for example the teachers' aides. Now we had a lot of preliminary discussion about what would a New Careers person do in the schools, and the first thing that was brought up is that there's a lot of clerical work done by teachers, principals, and others and they should be relieved of it, and they can learn in the process, and they will get interested in the educational system and thus study and upgrade themselves.

The only thing that is the matter with that practically as far as we are concerned is that speaking only for San Francisco, in the school system we are woefully under-staffed with regular school clerks. These are civil service personnel.

We are currently in negotiation with the board of education to double the staff. We aren't going to get the staff doubled, but we think it should be to do the job that has to be done, that should be done, and we would take a dim view of anybody coming in at a lower salary or lower classifications and doing the work that should be done by regular civil service personnel. So that the clerical aspect—and I could say more on the clerical aspect—but, anyway, the clerical aspect has been discarded and the school system in cooperation, presumably with the New Careers program, has worked out a job specification of a teachers' aide which has nothing to do with clerical work but does offer the teacher some definite aid and so on, which is acceptable to the teachers.

This we can endorse and did and do. This is fine. Now you move over to this social service department and what are you talking about, a social workers' aide? We have social worker trainees now.

The social workers are doing a great deal of clerical work from which they should be relieved. The social workers don't have time enough to do enough professional work. Case loads are excessive, the work load is increasing month by month as new programs are being added because of Medicare and everything else and all we say is show us what these people can do to be part of the New Careers service within the guidelines as mentioned and we will be happy to discuss it.

Now, we have sat down with the civil service staff and we have said the same thing. The civil service staff a month ago said to us, "We will have some concrete proposals for discussion purposes and this will be in a few weeks." That was a month ago. I spoke to Mr. George Grubb, the general manager of personnel, the other day and he said, "Well, we are not ready yet. We are working on it." And this, in my view, is the present status of New Careers.

They are working on it and personally unless they create something that doesn't now exist in the public service, the New Careers is not realistic, at least as far as civil service is concerned.

We can see a great deal of opportunity for training people to do work on civil service jobs, but that is not New Careers. We can see that the city and county can establish and should establish an apprentice system, machinists' apprentice, other apprentices and actually train people into the trade.

For example, if the brothers from the plumbers union will pardon me, one way to get plumbers—Negroes into the plumbers union is through an apprentice system run by the city to train Negro plumbers and so on. So those are our general views.

MR. GLICKSTEIN. Now that both of you gentlemen have stated your positions I'm sure that the Commissioners would like to address some questions to you.

CHAIRMAN HANNAH. Mrs. Freeman?

COMMISSIONER FREEMAN. Mr. Jeffrey, you indicated that all of the civil service employees have taken a qualifying examination. For the last three days we have been hearing testimony about unemployment and discrimination in employment, both public and private employment, both involving labor unions. Particularly were we disturbed because it appears that in public employment— I'm not sure whether it is Oakland or San Francisco—that the Spanish-speaking Americans constitute a very minimal percentage of those employed.

Now it suggests the possibility that the test itself has a cultural bias because of the language barrier. You also suggested that Negroes could become members of the plumbers union by going through an apprenticeship program of the city of Oakland.

MR. JEFFREY. City of San Francisco.

COMMISSIONER FREEMAN. I would like to hear from you how many Negro plumbers are employed by the city of San Francisco?

MR. JEFFREY. I don't know. As far as I know, I don't have any idea as to whether there are any because, you see, we don't represent the crafts and trades. We represent only the clerical and professional and related classes.

COMMISSIONER FREEMAN. The point that I am making is that we are talking about the elimination of discrimination in employment that exists against Negroes, Chinese, Spanish-speaking

Americans and others. We need a comprehensive manpower program.

Now if the only programs that are going to be suggested are those that limit employment or that limit job development, how are these people who have been the victims of discrimination in education ever going to get a chance?

MR. JEFFREY. Well, first of all, I don't know what the figures are with respect to the number of minorities who work for the city and county, but it is impressive. There are thousands of minorities that work for the city and county.

COMMISSIONER FREEMAN. In top jobs?

MR. JEFFREY. Top jobs. Our president, as I said, is a Negro. He is a clinical psychologist.

COMMISSIONER FREEMAN. That's one, but the point is that in the city of Oakland minorities constitute about half of the population.

MR. JEFFREY. True.

COMMISSIONER FREEMAN. Does the participation in the public employment market reflect the population?

MR. JEFFREY. I think it does in San Francisco, and all I can say is that any person with a minimum of a high school education, and, as you know, Negroes are going through high school every semester, and any such person—at least that certainly is my feeling, that Negroes are graduating along with everybody else. There is no reason that they can't apply and take a civil service test.

COMMISSIONER FREEMAN. Municipal employees, would that include the members of the fire department?

MR. JEFFREY. That certainly includes the fire department.

COMMISSIONER FREEMAN. I believe we have information that there are only three.

MR. JEFFREY. There are two.

COMMISSIONER FREEMAN. Two! Well, there's something wrong somewhere.

MR. JEFFREY. I would agree with you. I would agree with you. The Civil Service Commission conducts the tests for the members of the fire department. I don't have anything to do with that.

COMMISSIONER FREEMAN. Thank you.

MR. JEFFREY. It would be my opinion as an observer in that situation, and we have raised the same question that you just raised about the fact that there are only two Negro firemen working for the city and county of San Francisco, it would be my opinion that some revision in the civil service process, especially with respect to the physical qualifications should be made. Now, I know that the Human Rights Commission in San Francisco has been working on that, and I'm very hopeful that they will solve it.

This is not true in the police department, for example. It is only true in the fire department.

CHAIRMAN HANNAH. Mr. Patterson, do you have a question?

VICE CHAIRMAN PATTERSON. Do you mean that there is a higher intellectual level required to be a fireman than to be a policeman?

MR. JEFFREY. No, not at all.

VICE CHAIRMAN PATTERSON. That was the sense I got from what you said about civil service.

MR. JEFFREY. No. All I'm saying is that there are a great many more, proportionately speaking, Negroes employed as policemen than there are in the fire department.

CHAIRMAN HANNAH. Do you know how many Negro policemen there are?

MR. JEFFREY. No, but there are a considerable number. I don't know what the—see, I don't represent either policemen or firemen.

VICE CHAIRMAN PATTERSON. But do you know if policemen have to take the civil service examination?

MR. JEFFREY. Yes.

VICE CHAIRMAN PATTERSON. Do you know if it is the same examination firemen have to take?

MR. JEFFREY. No, it is not. In order to be a police officer you have to understand the criminal code and so on. In order to be a fireman you have to understand fire fighting.

COMMISSIONER RANKIN. What is the use of having good rules and regulations unless they are administered properly?

MR. JEFFREY. I have no dispute with that statement.

CHAIRMAN HANNAH. Go ahead, Mr. Patterson.

VICE CHAIRMAN PATTERSON. I'm through.

DR. SOLES. I would rather return to the central issue, as I see it, of New Careers. It seems to me in Mr. Jeffrey's statement he has brought together short-term aims and long-term aims, and I'm a little concerned that in view of the difficulties with the long-term questions that we mistake the need to form a coalition and work together on the short-term issues.

It seems to me that in some of the things you have said you do favor New Careers in the abstract, but when you get down to it you raise some question as to whether it would work.

I'd like to give you some examples of specific tasks that people do as teachers' aides which will help define some of the roles that you are saying would be competing with your clerical unit.

Let me say this: what we are talking about in New Careers are really new job creations by and large. Not so much taking over. There's no idea of taking over an existing position, but an acknowledgement of the importance of redefining some tasks, but not to redefine these tasks alone, but rather with the unions and with the professional groups.

CHAIRMAN HANNAH. Dr. Soles, if you want to give us a statement to put in the record to answer any comments that you think Mr. Jeffrey may have made that are not fair to your program we will be glad to receive them, but I don't think we want to get into an argument between the two of you.

DR. SOLES. Okay. I just think that there is a difference between the short-term goals of an entry-level position and the complexities that are involved in getting a credential for a teacher.

CHAIRMAN HANNAH. If you will put this in writing in adequate answer, we will include it in the record. Mr. Rankin, do you have any questions?

COMMISSIONER RANKIN. No.

CHAIRMAN HANNAH. Mr. Taylor?

MR. TAYLOR. Dr. Soles, I wonder if you could just in a moment define the work involved in one or two jobs in the New Career Program. Give me your idea of what best exemplifies a New Career Program.

DR. SOLES. Let me give some examples of the kinds of responsibilities of a teachers' aide, for example:

Supervising play periods, lunch yard, hallways, preparing materials for a variety of classroom projects, assisting in the personal needs of children, attending various meetings that are held, P.T.A., participating in parent conferences, operating audio-visual equipment, and in San Francisco, for example, there has been developed a teacher aide along this line with a certificate—

MR. JEFFREY. We think it's fine.

DR. SOLES. There are other types of things. I would like to give one example of a fairly large program in Detroit. I will try and be very brief, but I think it is crucial in handling the difficulty of transition and it shows the involvement by transition from subprofessional to higher levels of responsibilities.

In Detroit they started a program over a year and a half ago with about 40 teachers' aides operating at a non-professional level doing tasks that were not centrally connected with the professional function, and at the end near the summer the teachers were asked to select from those aides those who they felt had some potential, and together a group of teachers and aides attended a summer institute.

In this summer institute they examined the professional functioning of their role. As you know, Detroit is quite a union town. They were very much concerned about the professional responsibility and the defining of the role, and this was done together, and I cited a little earlier some of the experiences of people in this program.

The second semester, let's say in the fall, after the summer institute the teachers and the teachers' aides went on to carry out new types of functions at a sub-professional level with college course work brought in from Wayne State University and at the end of that period of time Detroit was willing to take on 3,000 teachers' aides moving from 40 to a much larger program.

The program dealt with a whole range of activities. They handled the training part of it by mobile training units, going out into the field setting and providing the training. I think this is an example. Too bad there aren't an awful lot of others throughout the Nation. The main difficulty now is that it is at the non-professional rather than the career level, but I think that Detroit indicates what can be done along this line and it is a collaboration rather than an exclusive task of one group.

MR. TAYLOR. Mr. Jeffrey, I know you are not an expert in all these matters and couldn't be, but I wonder if you could tell me generally whether you think that programs of education, health, and welfare are as successful as they could be in reaching residents in the slum areas?

MR. JEFFREY. I should say not. My answer is I don't think they are as successful as they could be. I should say not.

MR. TAYLOR. Well, without defining what would be involved, do you think these programs could be made more effective if people who had firsthand experience in slum areas were to work with professionals in trying to bridge the gap that may exist in communications?

MR. JEFFREY. I would think so. I would like to see specifically what the plan is, but it would seem to me that would be an excellent objective.

MR. TAYLOR. So that you are open to suggestions?

MR. JEFFREY. We are not closed to anything. We just haven't seen anything that practically is operative except the teachers' aides, which we think is great and support.

MR. TAYLOR. Sometimes programs, new ideas and new programs of this kind, take a great deal of definition, but you are not in the position of saying "We are going to squash it just because it hasn't been—"

MR. JEFFREY. Not only are we not going to squash it. We have indicated that we have met with every group that has discussed it, and we are trying ourselves to think of ways and means to bring it into being and to help the underprivileged, the minority, or whatnot into employment and into advancement and into upgrading.

One of the things that we want to blast loose out of the civil service in San Francisco, for example, is the fact that there are certain jobs that are blind alley jobs, and among those are the orderly and the porter classification which are about 98 percent Negro.

They can go up to seniority. There they stay. They stay with the city 50 years, they can't go any higher.

We think that that ceiling should be broken out of there and they should be given promotional opportunities. These are practical things that can be done without doing violence to anybody and still bringing in the possibility of upgrading and that is—and incidentally there is no such limitation in the clerical field where we have a considerable number of Negro workers who are advancing in the promotional range without any particular problems except the same problems that anybody else has, taking a promotional exam.

MR. TAYLOR. Thank you.

CHAIRMAN HANNAH. Thank you very much, gentlemen. I appreciate your being here. You are excused. Will you call the next witnesses?

MR. GLICKSTEIN. The next witnesses are Mr. Manuel Rodriguez and Mr. Charles Mitchell.

(Whereupon, Mr. Manuel Rodriguez and Mr. Charles Mitchell were sworn by the Chairman and testified as follows:)

TESTIMONY OF MR. MANUEL RODRIGUEZ, UNION CITY, CALIFORNIA AND MR. CHARLES MITCHELL, UNION CITY, CALIFORNIA

MR. GLICKSTEIN. Will you each state your full name and address for the record?

MR. RODRIGUEZ. My name is Manuel Rodriguez and I live at 33423-3rd Street in Union City.

MR. MITCHELL. My name is Charles Mitchell, my address is 33423 - 3rd Street, Union City.

MR. GLICKSTEIN. Where do each of you gentlemen work?

MR. RODRIGUEZ. We work for the Fremont-Newark-Union City Economic Opportunity Agency on a contractual basis and their head office is at 37272 Maple Street in Fremont.

MR. GLICKSTEIN. Mr. Mitchell, are you and Mr. Rodriguez involved in operating a New Careers Program?

MR. MITCHELL. Yes.

MR. GLICKSTEIN. How many people are involved in that program?

MR. MITCHELL. Roughly 15.

MR. GLICKSTEIN. How many men?

MR. MITCHELL. Four men.

MR. GLICKSTEIN. How many women?

MR. MITCHELL. Eleven women.

MR. GLICKSTEIN. How many of the 15 people are Spanish-speaking?

MR. MITCHELL. Fourteen.

MR. GLICKSTEIN. Fourteen of the 15. What jobs do they now hold?

MR. MITCHELL. A variety of jobs. Teachers' aides or assistants. Some are working as IBM operators. Some are working as counselors. One in particular is working as a counselor with the Fre-

541

mont city offices. Some are working with a survey team in Union City; librarian assistants. We have one lady that went to work as a police secretary and dispatcher.

MR. GLICKSTEIN. Mr. Rodriguez, what kind of work did the people that Mr. Mitchell just described do before they became involved in New Careers?

MR. RODRIGUEZ. Most of them were traditionally screened out people that don't have a diploma or don't have any education that would make them eligible for any kind of meaningful employment. Some of them were migrant farm workers or wives of migrant farm workers but as a rule most of them were either on some kind of State aid or county aid. For example, one of the teachers' aides couldn't speak English.

MR. GLICKSTEIN. Were many of the 15 unable to speak English?

MR. RODRIGUEZ. I think just one could not speak at all and she is one of the best teachers' aides now.

MR. GLICKSTEIN. One of the people couldn't speak English at all. Did some of the other people have difficulty with English?

MR. RODRIGUEZ. Yes. Some of them had other problems such as alcoholism or some of the other methods that people take to try to forget their poverty. I think one of them has got nine kids.

MR. GLICKSTEIN. Were any of the people illiterate?

MR. RODRIGUEZ. Well, I would say that this one that could not speak English, as far as the English language was concerned, she was completely illiterate. She couldn't read or write or speak English. Other than that they had, I think, an average of about fourth to sixth grade education.

MR. GLICKSTEIN. Mr. Mitchell, how were the applicants for this program selected?

MR. MITCHELL. It was announced on fliers that these positions were going to be open and that we were taking applications. The people that came into the office signed applications giving us all the data.

From the applications we gave the agencies the complete thing, and they were allowed to select the people that they wanted.

MR. GLICKSTEIN. You screened the applicants and the agencies made the final selections?

MR. MITCHELL. Yes.

MR. GLICKSTEIN. Mr. Rodriguez, how successful have the New Careerists and your new programs been in their new jobs? You mentioned one of the people that is a teachers' aide who has been very successful. Have the others been equally successful?

542

MR. RODRIGUEZ. Well, for example, the police aide which happens to be a female would not have qualified for that position under the standard kinds of screening out process and she is being upgraded to matron with also an upgrading in pay, and she will do actual police duties within the station itself. I understand that she is already utilized to search female prisoners and to assist in caring for the female prisoners.

MR. GLICKSTEIN. Have any of the people in the program been given permanent employment?

MR. RODRIGUEZ. I don't know. Maybe Charles can answer that better.

MR. MITCHELL. All of the people with our nucleus programs have been permanently employed.

MR. GLICKSTEIN. During the training period did you meet regularly with the trainees, Mr. Rodriguez?

MR. RODRIGUEZ. Every Friday from 1 to 5 we meet with them to give support and training which as a rule is—the kind of training that they get is identified by them. In other words, they come up and say that they need either typing skills or interview skills and then we aim the training in the direction that they identify the need.

MR. GLICKSTEIN. Did some of the people have negative attitudes toward work? Mr. Mitchell, do you want to answer that?

MR. MITCHELL. Well, the only thing that I can say that would be a truthful and factual answer would be if you had to work in a cannery for long hours, or work in the fields at stoop labor I suppose your attitude toward work would sort of be the other way, and I found that the manual type labor, most people don't want to do it, and if you give a person a chance to get a better job, what we refer to as a white collar job I'm quite sure that quite a few people would try to do their best to qualify for these type of jobs.

MR. GLICKSTEIN. Was it necessary to teach some of the people or make suggestions to some of the people in the program on how to conduct themselves on the job, such things as being punctual, things of that sort that you normally have to do when you work?

MR. MITCHELL. No, this isn't necessary. If you take a low-income grass-root poverty stricken, whatever you want to call it, a person that has been traditionally screened out of all available employment, and you give him a chance, or give her a chance to do a meaningful job you don't have to come up with things like, "Well, here in the office we start at 8 o'clock, you get off at 5. You have 45 minutes for lunch." These things aren't necessary.

No, I would feel rather out of place if I came to work at 10 o'clock and everyone has been there at 8, and I'm the only one to walk in at that time and all heads would turn in my direction. I would feel rather foolish.

So these kind of things we didn't have to worry about it. You don't have to tell a person what time to get to work. Once he finds out he will ask you what time he comes to work, what time he gets off, what time is lunch and that's it.

MR. GLICKSTEIN. Mr. Rodriguez, how would you evaluate the effect of the New Careers Program on the community in which you operate?

MR. RODRIGUEZ. Well, for one thing, I think that where it really means something to the State or the county is in the wallet. They are not having to support these people.

MR. GLICKSTEIN. You mean the people have come off welfare and other assistance programs and are now self-sufficient?

MR. RODRIGUEZ. They are now self-sufficient and they pay taxes. They are also very involved in other community activities such as M.A.P.A. or the American G. I. Forum.

They attend city council meetings. They really have taken an active interest in the community outside of their own little family circle or circle of friends.

I also think that the agencies are better off as a result of having these New Careerists. I'm pretty sure that the police department is pretty happy with the person they have. It's kind of a poor city, being a city and initially they couldn't afford to pay a person that was qualified the kind of money that this qualified person may demand somewhere else.

So in effect the employer could not compete in the open job market for the employee.

Also the teachers' aides, particularly we have a new kind of what we call a community school that we have developed along with some of our other workers out there, and a couple of weeks ago the teacher had pneumonia and she did not work for about 10 days.

A teachers' aide and another one of our community center workers maintained this basic educational class and kept it going and they were the ones that identified the need to maintain it in terms of, you know, "You have a lot of people that are now interested, and the people themselves identified what they wanted to learn, and where and if you cut it all of a sudden and keep changing the staffing patterns and all that they are going to lose interest."

So they kept it going. The poverty aspects are obvious because they are teaching something like, oh, two dozen people that can't speak, can hardly speak any English at all. They don't know anything about the A,B, C's. They don't know how to pick up a telephone and call in case of an emergency or somebody is ill.

MR. GLICKSTEIN. How do professional employees react to the New Careers program?

MR. MITCHELL. I was listening a while ago when you asked a similar question. A person that is a professional with a masters' or bachelors' degree that finds himself suddenly confronted with a non-professional worker, most professional people say that "We are in this job and we are doing a good job, the best we can under the circumstances."

And you bring a non-professional person in who has been given a chance to not only prove to himself that he can make it, but to the system also, and he is a go-getter. The person—I'm not saying that all professionals are lax at their duties, but if a person is lax and he sees this young, vibrant person doing all of his prescribed duties he does feel threatened. I would feel threatened, you would feel threatened.

Most people who have become lax in their duties would feel threatened, and for this reason you get things like "A bunch of idiots we don't want them here. They can't possibly help us. The only thing they can do is get in the way. Who is going to be in charge of this group? I don't have time for them."

But they have time to take 15, 30, 45 minute coffee breaks. I believe that if you are a public agency and you are dealing in a service a certain amount of efficiency should be maintained at all times, and if the agency isn't maintaining this efficiency rating or efficiency level it means someone is falling down on the job.

MR. GLICKSTEIN. Have the professionals that have felt threatened been reassured after the program was in operation for a while?

MR. MITCHELL. Yes. I had an evaluation meeting with one of the principals who was apprehensive about letting the New Careers into the school for no other reason than that these people didn't have teaching credentials, and one day he found himself short-handed. He had two classes and no teachers, so he had a choice to make and he made it in favor of the teacher assistant.

He put her into the classroom and she handled both classes. There wasn't any noise or fighting or throwing things. The classes ran as if there were two teachers in the classroom and he says: "You know something? She certainly surprised me. These people do have something to offer." And I find that most people that work with non-professional people for some time find out that they do have something to offer.

MR. GLICKSTEIN. Both of you gentlemen are New Careerists. Would you tell us what brought you into this program?

MR. RODRIGUEZ. Well, Charles and I are—we were members of a kind of research project that was funded under NIMH.

MR. GLICKSTEIN. NIMH?

MR. RODRIGUEZ. National Institute of Mental Health of the United States Public Health Service, Department of Health, Education, and Welfare. And they trained 18 of us New Careerists. Prior to any training at all, I think we had cost this State well over $1 million.

MR. GLICKSTEIN. You had cost the State well over $1 million?

MR. RODRIGUEZ. Collectively. See, we were all in prison. I had done the better part of 15 years, either in prison or in jail. Mr. Mitchell has done something like seven and a half years and it cost money to, you know, catch you and then convict you and then to maintain you. Most of the time that I did in prison was in San Quentin which is fairly maximum security and the cost escalates a little bit as the security escalates. Not only that, but I think that most of us cost not only the taxpayers but the people that we victimized possibly pretty close to that much money also.

Our crimes ranged all the way from narcotics addiction to bank robbery. Since being released from prison, which has been well over a year now, we have had one man go back. He robbed a loan company for $90, and one man kind of hung it up. He hasn't committed any crimes, but he is not with us. He is somewhere in Canada.

I think that most of us now are employed, and I think the minimum wages we get is about 625 bucks a month. We pay taxes. Charles and I are not only training these New Careerists, but we are currently involved in organizing the Tri-City area as per the OEO mandate and we are also developing a community school.

We are trying to bring about some kind of a health center out there because, for example, the woman that is going to have a baby has to make a round trip of something like 60 miles to go to the doctor. If she can't speak English she might not get anything done when she gets there.

We are trying to bring about some kind of a child care center. We have already started some child care as a result of some of the people in the community themselves assisting in developing this child care center after they identified this as a need. Some of us are—one of the fellows is working in New Jersey, I understand, in a New Careers kind of project where he is helping to develop new careers.

Another guy is working in New Jersey for OEO. He is a coordinator for State NYC's, I believe. Two of the guys are now in a college back East as teacher—what is that, Charles?

MR. MITCHELL. Teacher counselors.

MR. RODRIGUEZ. And one of them had two armed robbery convictions in the past, and both times there was some shooting and either somebody else or himself got shot. The second time he got shot seven times. So if you need anything to sell New Careers you can look at us.

I don't think that any of us would even, you know, steal a candy bar off of a counter now when there is nobody around. Most of us own fairly good automobiles. Some of the guys now have started buying homes.

There is a couple of the fellows that are going to get married soon. Myself, I was given—well, there was kind of a bet in the Department of Corrections that I wouldn't last 60 days outside, and according to previous curve or the previous media that was true because I went to prison, and I came out, and I was out six months the first time.

Then I went back for parole violation, and I came out and they caught me with a 357 magnum. I told them I was going duck hunting. They didn't believe me, and that time I was out 60 days, no, 90 days, so I was gradually staying out less and less time. Do you want to add something, Charles?

MR. MITCHELL. No, I don't think so. I think I'd like to say something, if I may.

I think that we have successfully demonstrated that New Careers can work. We have ex-convicts working in various positions and jobs throughout the United States, guys in colleges, guys as training directors.

We have placed one man on the President's Commission for Juvenile Delinquency, if I'm not mistaken, and all of this goes to show if a person is given a chance with some training and a meaningful job he can become very valuable to the system.

MR. GLICKSTEIN. I have no further questions, Mr. Chairman.

CHAIRMAN HANNAH. Do any of the Commissioners have any questions?

VICE CHAIRMAN PATTERSON. Mr. Chairman, I would just like to compliment these gentlemen. This is a very inspiring story you've told here today.

MR. RODRIGUEZ. I think one thing I wanted to add was in terms of resistance to New Careers. The biggest resistance I've found is the guy that has his wall papered with diplomas and all kinds of accreditations, that if he dares to admit somebody that doesn't have all that kind of accreditation may do a similar or better job than he can it's going to kind of hurt all those years he had to go to college in order to struggle and make it.

CHAIRMAN HANNAH. Well, gentlemen, we are very grateful to you. Do you have a question, Mr. Taylor?

MR. TAYLOR. I have no question. I would just like to say, Mr. Chairman, that we have been hearing some very pessimistic testimony all week, and we've been hearing a lot about people who don't care and programs that don't work. I think it is impressive and should renew our hope that we hear about some programs that do offer some real hope. Thank you.

CHAIRMAN HANNAH. We wish you well. Mr. Glickstein, do we have further witnesses?

MR. GLICKSTEIN. The next two witnesses are Mr. Alvarez and Mr. Gonzales.

CHAIRMAN HANNAH. Are they in the building?

MR. GLICKSTEIN. They are here.

(Whereupon, Mr. Salvadore Alvarez and Mr. Steven Gonzales were sworn by the Chairman and testified as follows:)

TESTIMONY OF MR. SALVADORE ALVAREZ, BERKELEY, CALIFORNIA AND MR. STEVEN GONZALES, ALBANY, CALIFORNIA

MR. GLICKSTEIN. Would each of you please state your full name and address for the record?

MR. GONZALES. Steven Gonzales, 1119H 10th Street, Albany, California.

MR. ALVAREZ. Salvadore Alvarez, 3019 Dana Street in Berkeley, California.

MR. GLICKSTEIN. Are you gentlemen involved in an organization called Quinta Sol?

MR. GONZALES. Yes.

MR. GLICKSTEIN. How many members does Quinta Sol have?

MR. ALVAREZ. Before we go on we have a statement here that we would like to present.

CHAIRMAN HANNAH. How long is the statement?

MR. ALVAREZ. It's a short statement I would like to read.

CHAIRMAN HANNAH. Go ahead.

MR. ALVAREZ. We, the members of Quinta Sol, Mexican American Student Organization at the University of California, Berkeley campus, have come here to state our strong protest against the U.S. Civil Rights Commission's pernicious policy of exclusion of Mexican Americans.

We fully support it and completely concur with the students' indictment as presented by Armando Valdez and Nick Vaca earlier this week exposing the Commission's discriminatory and exclusionary policy toward Mexican Americans.

We were subpenaed to appear before this Board in order to relate Quinta Sol's year-long protest against and demand of an investigation of the University of California's educational exclusion of Mexican Americans which has existed for the past 100 years. However, because the very agency of redress itself, the U.S. Civil Rights Commission, is the most flagrant example of the ignorance, exclusion, and oppression that Mexican Americans face, we will not conform to this masquerade, thereby granting legitimacy to the Commission and to these hearings, a legitimacy which the Commission has forfeited by its gross hypocritical actions.

MR. GLICKSTEIN. You wrote the Commission a letter requesting the right to testify, didn't you?

MR. ALVAREZ. We Mexican American students, in the militant Mexican American tradition of over 100 years know that social justice will not be granted by one's oppressor. The oppressed people must seize it through bitter conflict.

Whereas our focus now is upon the discriminatory and exclusionary policies of the University of California and the U.S. Civil Rights Commission, we, the members of Quinta Sol, will continue to expose and attack any such exploitative and oppressive practices, whether they take the form of systematic exclusion, the stupid stereotypes, or insidious paternalism. We will continue until our goal of Mexican American liberation is achieved.

CHAIRMAN HANNAH. Gentlemen, now that we have had the applause, and for the fourth time in two days we have been used for a production, Mr. Counsel, will you indicate how these gentlemen happened to be here?

MR. GLICKSTEIN. They were subpenaed, Mr. Chairman, at their request.

CHAIRMAN HANNAH. At their own request they were subpenaed?

COMMISSIONER GRISWOLD. Mr. Chairman, may I say as an educator that I regard that as a very childish statement not worthy of the students of the University of California.

VOICE FROM COURTROOM. Then how are we going to obtain a hearing on the problems of the Mexican Americans?

CHAIRMAN HANNAH. The meeting is adjourned and we do not propose to be used further by the Mexican American group for purposes like we have been today and yesterday. We will convene tomorrow morning in this room at 9:15.

(Whereupon, at 5:30 pm. the hearing was adjourned until 9:15 a.m., Friday, May 5, 1967.)

U.S. COMMISSION ON CIVIL RIGHTS

CHAIRMAN HANNAH. Ladies and gentlemen, the second session of this hearing being conducted in Oakland by the Commission on Civil Rights will come to order. Mr. Rubin, Deputy General Counsel, U.S. Commission on Civil Rights, will you call the first witness?

MR. RUBIN. The first witness is Mr. Ernest W. Henderson.

(Whereupon, Mr. Ernest W. Henderson was sworn by the Chairman and testified as follows:)

TESTIMONY OF MR. ERNEST W. HENDERSON, RICHMOND, CALIFORNIA

MR. RUBIN. Mr. Henderson, would you please state your name and address for the record?

MR. HENDERSON. My name is Ernest W. Henderson. I am at 540 29th Street in Richmond.

MR. RUBIN. What is your occupation?

MR. HENDERSON. I am planning director of the city of Richmond.

MR. RUBIN. How long have you served as planning director for Richmond?

MR. HENDERSON. About seven years.

MR. RUBIN. How long have you been with the Planning Commission?

MR. HENDERSON. Thirteen and a half years.

MR. RUBIN. Would you tell us, Mr. Henderson, in what county is the city of Richmond located?

MR. HENDERSON. Contra Costa County.

MR. RUBIN. Can you point out on this map where the area known as North Richmond is located in relation to the city of Ricmond?

MR. HENDERSON. Approximately this little uncolored area there.

MR. RUBIN. Has any part of the area known as North Richmond been annexed to the city of Richmond?

MR. HENDERSON. Yes, all of the surrounding area has been annexed so that between the older parts of the city and the recently annexed area North Richmond is completely surrounded except for a very narrow corridor in the Bay.

MR. RUBIN. But there is also an unannexed part of North Richmond, a county part. Is that correct?

MR. HENDERSON. That is correct. The North Richmond area is

(549)

a small, sort of undefined area, part of which is in the city and part of which is unincorporated.

MR. RUBIN. Could you tell from studying aerial photography of the total area where the city part ends and the county part begins?

MR. HENDERSON. Well, the aerial photo will not identify it, but of my own knowledge of the location of the boundaries I would be able to point it out to you.

MR. RUBIN. Can you tell us what the population of the unincorporated part of North Richmond is approximately?

MR. HENDERSON. At the present time, I don't know exactly, but it's about 3,700 people.

MR. RUBIN. Can you tell us the racial composition of the population?

MR. HENDERSON. It's very close to 100 percent Negro. There may be a few non-Negroes, but for all practical purposes it is 100 percent.

MR. RUBIN. Could you tell us the racial composition of the population of the city of Richmond?

MR. HENDERSON. Excuse me, let me correct that last statement. It was directed primarily at the tightly developed residential area. Part of this unincorporated area, which is generally known as North Richmond, does have a segment of florists and these are primarily Orientals, but the highly developed residential part is nearly all-Negro.

MR. RUBIN. Will you tell us the racial composition of the population of the city of Richmond itself?

MR. HENDERSON. Yes. The city of Richmond is about 30 percent Negro, 8 or 9 percent other minority groups, and the balance Caucasian.

MR. RUBIN. Mr. Henderson, in 1965, as I understand it, a petition was filed by a Mrs. Anna Johnson with the City Planning Commission to annex the unincorporated part of North Richmond to the city of Richmond and in connection with this petition the planning commission submitted a report to the city council recommending annexation of the county part of North Richmond. Is that correct?

MR. HENDERSON. That is correct.

MR. RUBIN. Mr. Chairman, I would like to introduce—is this the report, Mr. Henderson?

MR. HENDERSON. Yes, sir. That is it.

MR. RUBIN. Mr. Chairman, I would like to introduce this report into evidence as Exhibit No. 27.

CHAIRMAN HANNAH. It will be received.

(Whereupon, the document referred to was marked Exhibit No. 27 and received in evidence.)

MR. RUBIN. Were you the author of this report?

MR. HENDERSON. Yes, sir.

MR. RUBIN. Your report indicated that North Richmond would receive increased public services if it were annexed to Richmond and on Page 5 of the report you indicated that police protection was one of the services which would be most greatly increased. Would you tell us the basis for that conclusion?

MR. HENDERSON. Yes, sir. The unincorporated parts of the county receive police protection through the county sheriff's office, and the deputies that provide this service have a relatively large area to cover.

In contrast to that the incorporated parts of the city of Richmond have police protection from our own police department, and each police beat has at least one patrolman that patrols it, and this is a much more reduced area in size. Therefore, there is substantially greater police protection.

MR. RUBIN. Did your report conclude that the city of Richmond police could respond to calls more quickly than the county sheriff's department?

MR. HENDERSON. Yes, the average time of response to police calls is not to exceed about three minutes anywhere in the city.

In the county it depends upon the location of the deputy at the time of the call, if he happens to be in a remote part of his particular beat, there have been instances where it may be 20 minutes or more to be able to respond. If he happens to be right on the job, of course he may answer as quickly as a Richmond policeman.

MR. RUBIN. Could you point out to us on this map the area which is under the jurisdiction of the county sheriff's department?

MR. HENDERSON. Well, the map shows all of Contra Costa County, and he is responsible for the entire county, and for police protection. He is responsible for practically all of the unincorporated areas except those portions that do have their own community service districts which are very limited.

MR. RUBIN. So all portions which are in white would be under the jurisdiction of the county?

MR. HENDERSON. That is correct. In addition to police protection, these same deputies have other duties which carry them into the incorporated areas such as serving summons and carrying out other functions, so in some respects they cover the whole county.

MR. RUBIN. Your report also indicated that a major physical problem in the North Richmond area was poor drainage, and in the residential section storm drainage needed correction in the interests of public safety and comfort.

Do you believe that the prospects for ultimate solution of the storm drainage problem would be improved by annexation?

MR. HENDERSON. Well, I believe it will. It might also possibly be corrected eventually in the county, but the city of Richmond has entered onto a specific program of attempting to correct storm drainage throughout the city, and, therefore, I think that the chances of expediting the storm drainage would be enhanced.

MR. RUBIN. Your report also stated that annexation would open the door to more effective participation in affairs of local government. Would you tell us the basis for that conclusion?

MR. HENDERSON. Yes. The city of Richmond has nine councilmen and they are elected at large by voters throughout the city, and if this area were annexed then the voters would have an opportunity to vote on each of the nine councilmen as they are up for election.

In the county there is only one member of the board of supervisors which the people within the specific area have an opportunity to vote on.

This is a much greater opportunity to vote on the legislative body. In addition to that the city of Richmond has a number of boards and commissions that serve in various advisory capacities to the council, and the same members of the city would have the opportunity to be selected on some of these boards and commissions.

MR. RUBIN. Mr. Henderson, the 1966 annual report of the Contra Costa County Board of Supervisors states that the county population is some 531,000. Could you tell us the population of the city of Richmond?

MR. HENDERSON. Approximately 80,000.

MR. RUBIN. Would it be a fair conclusion that annexation would increase substantially the value of a person's vote in the unincorporated part of North Richmond?

MR. HENDERSON. Well, yes. As I indicated they would have a chance to vote on nine members of the city council, whereas at the present time they can only vote on one member of the board of supervisors.

MR. RUBIN. But, in addition, in the city of Richmond, since the total population is approximately one-sixth of the total population of the county, the vote, I take it, would be more diluted in the county than it would be in the city. Is that correct?

MR. HENDERSON. Well, you are saying that each person gets one vote but—

MR. RUBIN. But it counts for more in the city.

MR. HENDERSON. As far as the city council is concerned, obviously; but the people in the city of Richmond also vote for the board of supervisors at the same relative—it depends on who you are referring to and who you are voting for.

MR. RUBIN. Does your report suggest that annexation would result in other benefits to North Richmond?

MR. HENDERSON. Yes, there are some other benefits including the recreation services and improvement in the fire protection.

The county does not have recreation services. The city of Richmond does have a recreation commission and a recreation department and these services would be extended to the county. There are also other advantages. Whereas people in North Richmond now have to go to the county seat of Martinez for building permits—

MR. RUBIN. How far away is Martinez?

MR. HENDERSON. About 25 miles. These services would all be available at the City Hall, which is approximately a mile of the North Richmond area, so it would be much more convenient from this aspect. The city of Richmond also has its own library system and the residents there would be able to make full use of the library without any additional cost. I think these were the major other benefits.

MR. RUBIN. Did the city council approve the annexation proposal, consent to the circulation of the petition and resolve to submit the proposal to the registered voters residing in the unincorporated area of North Richmond?

MR. HENDERSON. Yes, sir, they did.

MR. RUBIN. Mr. Chairman, I would like to introduce the resolution of the city council submitting the proposal to an election of the qualified voters as Exhibit No. 28. I would also like to introduce into the record the section of the California Code which provides that such a resolution may not issue unless not less than one-fourth of the qualified electors residing within the area proposed for annexation sign the petition.

CHAIRMAN HANNAH. The exhibits are received.

MR. RUBIN. Mr. Henderson, under the California Code before such an election can be held, the city council must hold a protest hearing and if owners of 50 percent of the assessed value of the land in the area to be annexed protest, the annexation proceedings must be discontinued and no new annexation proceedings may be brought for one year. Mr. Chairman, I would like to introduce those sections of the California Code which contain these provisions.

CHAIRMAN HANNAH. Received as an exhibit.

(Whereupon the documents referred to were marked Exhibits No. 28 and 29 and received into evidence.)

MR. RUBIN. Was a protest hearing held, Mr. Henderson, on the proposed annexation of North Richmond?

MR. HENDERSON. Yes, it was.

MR. RUBIN. Can you tell us the result of the protest hearing?

MR. HENDERSON. The city clerk announced that in excess of 50 percent of the assessed value of the land, the owners of that assessed value had protested.

MR. RUBIN. At the time of the annexation proceedings could you tell us roughly what percentage of the assessed value of the land in North Richmond area was residential?

MR. HENDERSON. Do you mind if I look at the file here? According to the county assessor's records, about 25 percent was residential.

MR. RUBIN. Could you tell us the land use of the remainder of the assessed value?

MR. HENDERSON. About 44 percent was manufacturing and industrial. Around 10 percent was bare land, 4 percent was commercial, 4 percent was farm land, 1 percent was private institutions, and 12 percent was public.

MR. RUBIN. Absent annexation by the city of Richmond, Mr. Henderson, is there any hope that the problems of North Richmond can be solved?

MR. HENDERSON. I'm sorry.

MR. RUBIN. Absent annexation by the city of Richmond is there any hope that the problems of North Richmond can be solved?

MR. HENDERSON. Well, I presume there are. Some of the problems, of course, are being worked on by the county. There are many difficult problems to solve, and I see it is not impossible to solve them, but it is difficult.

MR. RUBIN. Is there any other area to which the county part of North Richmond could be annexed?

MR. HENDERSON. There is no practical other area because the area is completely surrounded, with the exception of about a 500 foot corridor out in the Bay.

MR. RUBIN. Was the predominantly Negro area known as Parchester Village annexed to the city of Richmond about five years ago?

MR. HENDERSON. Yes, sir, it was.

MR. RUBIN. Has the city of Richmond provided Parchester Village with any parks or playgrounds?

MR. HENDERSON. Not as yet. There is a bond issue now before the public, we vote on it next Tuesday, in which we hope to acquire parks throughout the city.

MR. RUBIN. Did the planning commission ever have a plan for improvement of drainage conditions in Richmond?

MR. HENDERSON. Not the planning commission, no, sir.

MR. RUBIN. Was there a plan?

MR. HENDERSON. Yes, sir, there is a—well, it shouldn't be called a plan. It was a study and it was a study by an engineering consulting firm for the city which would indicate how the storm drains could be handled.

MR. RUBIN. Was the city part of North Richmond included in the plan?

MR. HENDERSON. No, it was not.

MR. RUBIN. Why not?

MR. HENDERSON. I can't answer that. I don't know.

MR. RUBIN. Thank you, Mr. Henderson. I have no further questions.

CHAIRMAN HANNAH. Do the Commissioners have any questions?

COMMISSIONER RANKIN. I'd like to ask one or two questions. Is there any Federal issue involved in this annexation or is it purely local?

MR. HENDERSON. It is a purely local movement, yes, sir. It was initiated by some of the residents in the area and it was handled completely by local, city, and the county legislative bodies.

COMMISSIONER RANKIN. Then it is a demand on the part of North Richmond for certain services that it doesn't get. Is that correct?

MR. HENDERSON. Yes, sir.

COMMISSIONER RANKIN. And the city of Richmond has the services right next door. Is that correct?

MR. HENDERSON. Yes, sir.

COMMISSIONER RANKIN. Do the citizens of Richmond pay higher taxes than the people in North Richmond?

MR. HENDERSON. Yes. The tax rate in the city is higher than in the unincorporated area.

COMMISSIONER RANKIN. If these services were extended then it would mean an increase in taxation in North Richmond. Is that correct?

MR. HENDERSON. Yes, sir, that's right.

COMMISSIONER RANKIN. And the citizens there are willing to assume this extra tax?

MR. HENDERSON. Well, I can't answer that because it was never brought to a vote. There was a group who asked to be annexed, and it was never brought to a vote.

COMMISSIONER RANKIN. But they realize their situation. Is that correct?

MR. HENDERSON. I think they do. It was well discussed.

COMMISSIONER RANKIN. They cannot do it themselves. They did not get it through the county, and their only hope of getting services is through annexation. Is that the picture?

MR. HENDERSON. There may be other alternatives such as developing a special district such as a committee service district. This is done in other parts of the county. So there are probably other avenues that—

COMMISSIONER RANKIN. Has any study of efficiency been made, whether this would result in savings to the people in

North Richmond, or to the people in Richmond, or will it be expensive to both or to neither?

MR. HENDERSON. You mean the annexation?

COMMISSIONER RANKIN. Yes.

MR. HENDERSON. Yes. This report which we prepared indicated the general cost and the expected revenue to the city. It was prepared on the basis of what would be the anticipated cost of providing services, and what was to be expected in terms of revenue from the area.

COMMISSIONER RANKIN. Isn't that the crux of the matter, money rather than race?

MR. HENDERSON. Well, I think that it depends on whose viewpoint I guess you are asking this question about. As far as the city was concerned, the city was willing to annex the area and the matter of race had no official part in it. That's all I can comment on it.

COMMISSIONER RANKIN. That's all.

CHAIRMAN HANNAH. Mrs. Freeman?

COMMISSIONER FREEMAN. Mr. Henderson, North Richmond, the residential area is close to, as you said, 100 percent Negro. The result of this failure of annexation is that because they have inadequate police protection and all, or is it not correct to say that they are denied equal protection of the laws?

MR. HENDERSON. Well, I don't think I could comment on that. They certainly don't have the police protection they would have if they were in the city.

CHAIRMAN HANNAH. Any other questions by the Commissioners? Mr. Griswold, do you have any questions?

COMMISSIONER GRISWOLD. No.

CHAIRMAN HANNAH. Mr. Taylor?

MR. TAYLOR. Just one question, Mr. Henderson. You say that the issue was blocked from ever coming to a vote because a protest was filed. Do you know whether this protest was filed largely by owners of residential property or of industrial property?

MR. HENDERSON. It was announced that it was primarily by industrial.

MR. TAYLOR. Thank you.

CHAIRMAN HANNAH. Thank you very much, Mr. Henderson. You are excused, sir. Mr. Rubin, would you call the next witnesses.

MR. RUBIN. The next witnesses are Mrs. Anna M. Johnson and Mrs. Barbara McBride.

Mr. Chairman, Mrs. McBride is not here. I recommend that we proceed with questions of Mrs. Johnson.

(Whereupon, Mrs. Anna M. Johnson was affirmed by the Chairman and testified as follows:)

TESTIMONY OF MRS. ANNA M. JOHNSON,
RICHMOND, CALIFORNIA

MR. RUBIN. Would you state your name and address for the record, please?

MRS. JOHNSON. My name is Anna Mae Johnson. My address is 787-7th Street, Richmond, California.

MR. RUBIN. Mrs. Johnson, did you file a petiton in 1965 seeking to annex the unincorporated part of North Richmond to the city of Richmond?

MRS. JOHNSON. Yes, I did.

MR. RUBIN. At that time were you a resident of the county part of Richmond?

MRS. JOHNSON. No, I wasn't.

MR. RUBIN. Where were you living?

MRS. JOHNSON. At my same address, 787-7th Street, Richmond, California.

MR. RUBIN. Was that petition signed by a number of citizens of the county part of North Richmond?

MRS. JOHNSON. Yes.

MR. RUBIN. How many citizens signed the petition?

MRS. JOHNSON. Twelve or 15. I forget exactly.

MR. RUBIN. Did you subsequently obtain other signatures on the petition?

MRS. JOHNSON. Later we surveyed and got more signatures.

MR. RUBIN. Could you tell us how many roughly?

MRS. JOHNSON. About 470-something. I don't know exactly.

MR. RUBIN. Could you explain why you wanted the unincorporated area of North Richmond brought into the city of Richmond?

MRS. JOHNSON. Well, because I lived out there for 16 years, and of course at that time we had quite a lot of trouble getting police protection.

One of the main reasons I went to move from out there was because one day a man parked his car in my driveway, and I called for the sheriff so that the car could be moved, and the sheriff never did come that day, neither the next day. This was in 1956, so I moved in 1956, and then I belong to the church out there and we have quite a bit of vandalism at the church.

Sometimes we come out of the church and some of the people don't have even a wheel on their car, and they called for the police or sheriff, and it would be four or five hours before they came, sometimes 2 o'clock the next morning.

MR. RUBIN. Do you own property in the county part of North Richmond?

MRS. JOHNSON. Yes, I do.

MR. RUBIN. Was your desire to have the county part of North

Richmond annexed by the city of Richmond influenced by your interest in your property?

MRS. JOHNSON. Well, I'm interested in my property, and everybody in North Richmond that are concerned. I'm interested in the people in North Richmond also because I live out there and I know a portion of the trouble of the people out there.

MR. RUBIN. Did you feel that the value of the property would be increased with annexation?

MRS. JOHNSON. I know that the valuation of the property will be increased even the taxes and all so you could sell your property much easier if it was annexed to the city, I believe.

MR. RUBIN. Why is that?

MRS. JOHNSON. Because most people want to live in the city. There are a few who want to live in the county, but as I talked to the people, most of them want to live in the city of Richmond.

MR. RUBIN. Did you conduct a survey to determine how many residents of the unincorporated part of North Richmond were in favor of annexation?

MRS. JOHNSON. Yes, I did.

MR. RUBIN. Could you tell us what the results were?

MRS. JOHNSON. There was about 400 and something that really wanted annexation. They didn't mind the price. They knew that they couldn't get better service without paying a little bit more money.

MR. RUBIN. These were 400 home owners?

MRS. JOHNSON. Yes.

MR. RUBIN. Or tenants or—

MRS. JOHNSON. They was 400, including tenants.

MR. RUBIN. Thank you, Mrs. Johnson. I have no further questions.

CHAIRMAN HANNAH. Do the Commissioners have any questions? Mr. Patterson?

VICE CHAIRMAN PATTERSON. Have you tried to obtain these services from your county government, and if so what response have you had?

MRS. JOHNSON. Well, this one thing I haven't tried personally except I called for help over at the sheriff's office and we couldn't get it until a certain time, and of course when we went up to Martinez at one time they said they had given us their best service.

VICE CHAIRMAN PATTERSON. Do you feel these services are inadequate from the county?

MRS. JOHNSON. Yes, because a close-by city can always give you better service than a far-away city.

VICE CHAIRMAN PATTERSON. Thank you.

CHAIRMAN HANNAH. Mrs. Freeman?

COMMISSIONER FREEMAN. Mrs. Johnson, I believe this proceeding was blocked by the vote of the individuals who owned the industrial properties. About how many people did this constitute in comparison with the number of residential persons?

MRS. JOHNSON. I don't know exactly. It wasn't too many people. It was just the land value added that outnumbered the land value of the residential people.

COMMISSIONER FREEMAN. The land value, again, was a smaller number of persons because they owned a substantial portion of the land?

MRS. JOHNSON. Yes.

COMMISSIONER FREEMAN. And so they were permitted to deprive the majority of the people of their will, of exercising their will?

MRS. JOHNSON. Yes, as far as my knowledge, because it was all industrial and they own quite a bit.

COMMISSIONER FREEMAN. This was in accord with the provision of California law. Is that correct?

MRS. JOHNSON. I think so.

COMMISSIONER FREEMAN. Thank you.

CHAIRMAN HANNAH. Mr. Rankin?

COMMISSIONER RANKIN. The real injustice, then, is the California law, wouldn't you say, that does away with this one-man—one-vote principal?

MRS. JOHNSON. With the law like it is if the industrial hold like they do with more property, more land, they will always keep us people out unless they do not protest. If they don't protest I believe we can go in.

CHAIRMAN HANNAH. Mr. Griswold?

COMMISSIONER GRISWOLD. Have you tried to obtain annexation of the residential portion of North Richmond without including the industrial portion?

MRS. JOHNSON. No. I only tried the one time.

COMMISSIONER GRISWOLD. Why wouldn't it be a good idea to make that effort?

MRS. JOHNSON. Well, we hadn't thought of it too much in that way. We did at first, but under certain qualifying—a certain feeling, we thought we had to drop off.

CHAIRMAN HANNAH. Any other questions? Mr. Taylor?

MR. TAYLOR. Mrs. Johnson, do you have an opinion as to whether, if you did try what Dean Griswold just suggested, just to have the residential areas annexed and not the industrial property, do you know whether the city would be interested in doing that?

MRS. JOHNSON. I don't know whether they would or not. I really couldn't answer that.

MR. TAYLOR. Thank you.

CHAIRMAN HANNAH. If there are no further questions, Mrs. Johnson, you are excused. Thank you. Mr. Rubin, would you call the next witness?

MR. RUBIN. The next witness is Mr. William R. Brown.

(Whereupon, Mr. William R. Brown was sworn by the Chairman and testified as follows:)

TESTIMONY OF MR. WILLIAM R. BROWN, RICHMOND, CALIFORNIA

MR. RUBIN. Mr. Brown, would you please state your name and address for the record?

MR. BROWN. My name is William R. Brown. I live at 2602 Shane Drive in Richmond.

MR. RUBIN. How long have you lived in Richmond?

MR. BROWN. Since 1942.

MR. RUBIN. Do you own property?

MR. BROWN. Yes, sir.

MR. RUBIN. Where is this property located?

MR. BROWN. Some in the unincorporated portion of North Richmond, and some in the city of Richmond proper.

MR. RUBIN. Did you favor or oppose the 1965 proposal to annex North Richmond to the city of Richmond?

MR. BROWN. I opposed that effort, and the two previous efforts.

MR. RUBIN. Were you active in the opposition campaign?

MR. BROWN. Yes, sir.

MR. RUBIN. What was your role? Could you briefly explain it?

MR. BROWN. At the beginning of the campaign, I was executive director and chairman of the board of directors of the North Richmond Property Owners Association. That is the organization that handled the opposition.

MR. RUBIN. Why did you oppose the proposed annexation?

MR. BROWN. I opposed it first, because Richmond had nothing to offer the district in annexation, and, secondly, because Richmond had such a terrible reputation in dealing with its minority community, especially in the area of housing.

MR. RUBIN. Was there anything specific that the city of Richmond had done in the past which caused you to have this feeling?

MR. BROWN. Yes, sir.

MR. RUBIN. Would you tell us what that was?

MR. BROWN. It began immediately after the war period in the disposition of the temporary war housing. At that time I served on the housing committee of the Richmond Chamber of Commerce. The housing for Negro people was very bad. There was a terrific shortage of available housing. This was one of the main problems of our committee.

MR. RUBIN. That was at what time?

MR. BROWN. This was about 1945. At the same time Richmond had been planning to begin the demolition of war housing. We had admitted, the entire committee and the Chamber, that the housing shortage of the Negro people was more acute than any other group in the city.

In spite of this fact the first three houses, the first three temporary war housing declared to be torn down or disposed of were three houses, or three buildings that were occupied by Negroes.

I asked for an explanation for this. The director of housing at that time denied it. I gave him the building numbers and quoted the conversation I had had earlier that morning with Mr. Post, who was regional director of FHA, and offered to get in cars, and drive out, and show them that it was true.

At this time the housing director blew his top and made the statement that—he admitted that there were Negroes occupying houses and that "The only way we can solve this problem and many other things that is wrong with Richmond is to take a bulldozer and push all of that mess in North Richmond"—and there had been no discussion of North Richmond up to this time—"and other places where these people live in the Bay, and eventually we are going to do it in spite of William R. Brown."

I think it is interesting to note that the next day the headlines of the Independent stated that the housing director had just resigned.

This was the beginning and on down from there as they proceeded in the program to dispose of the war housing, the housing shortage was still acute, the people living in the first project coming down got themselves together, formed local voluntary organizations to do what they could to protect themselves. They selected a man who was pastor of a church in the neighborhood to lead the group and asked him to try to delay the demolition of the housing, to try to see that they had some place to go when and if it was torn down.

This organization functioned for a while, and then later in political discussions that came out it developed that this person who headed the organization was on the payroll of the city of Richmond as an expediter, to expedite the movement of the people out of the area.

A little later the Hensley Tract—

MR. RUBIN. Would you tell us, Mr. Brown, just briefly about the Hensley Tract, and what happened at that time.

MR. BROWN. Well, the Hensley Tract is a neighborhood just south of North Richmond and it was occupied by all Negro people. The city of Richmond declared that about 12 years ago as a slum district scheduled for redevelopment for industrial purposes.

Now, for between nine and 10 years they did nothing about this. They refused to issue the people permits for the improvement of their homes. They discouraged them from maintaining their homes telling them, "You can go and paint if you want to paint, but we may buy it next month, and we will tell you now if it costs you $300 for painting you won't get $300 back." So of course no one did much maintaining of their property.

After leaving the property in this condition for between nine and 10 years then they sent appraisers in—

MR. RUBIN. They did what?

MR. BROWN. Then they sent appraisers in, appraised the property and bought it, and in something like six months or a year after this date there was an article in the Independent stating that the Richmond Redevelopment Agency had a surplus of a little better than $1 million, and they were considering what to do with it, left over from money originally designated for the purpose of homes in the Hensley Tract.

MR. RUBIN. Mr. Brown, did industry support your campaign against annexation?

MR. BROWN. Yes, it did.

MR. RUBIN. Would you tell us how much financial help industry contributed to your campaign?

MR. BROWN. Oh, roughly—I can't tell you offhand, but I think it was somewhere in the neighborhood of $2,000.

MR. RUBIN. Would you say that industry was primarily responsible for the defeat of the annexation proposal?

MR. BROWN. Not at all. As a matter of fact, industry didn't even know that it was in process until I called it to their attention.

MR. RUBIN. Who cast the majority of the protest votes? Was the majority of those protesting the annexation cast by industrial owners or owners of residential property in North Richmond?

MR. BROWN. The total dollar sum might have been represented by industry, but percentagewise, it was the votes. I handled the circulation of the protest petition and we kept careful tabulations which I will offer into evidence if you want to see it at this meeting.

The total percentage of protest was between 65 and 70 percent, and the percentage of the residential area is also about 65 or 70 percent.

Now, a wrong impression may be obtained by the way the city handled this because the city clerk stopped counting. He did not count all of the protests. He counted until he had determined there was in excess of 57 percent, and then he stopped counting.

MR. RUBIN. Could you tell us whether the majority of the protesting home owners were residents?

MR. BROWN. The majority, yes.

MR. RUBIN. Would the citizens of North Richmond have benefited in any way by being annexed to the city of Richmond?

MR. BROWN. I don't think so.

MR. RUBIN. Would they have benefited from increased police protection in your opinion?

MR. BROWN. It's possible they could get an officer to answer a call a little bit earlier. On the statistics available this seems apparent, but it has not been indicated by my own personal experience of 15 years in the neighborhood.

I had a burglar in my own home, I live in Richmond, about three months ago. It took nearly a half hour to get an officer there, and my wife was afraid to go in the house.

I had three or four attempts at burglary in the laundromat that I operate. It takes me 10 minutes to drive from home to the laundromat, and most often I call an officer when my alarm goes off, and most of the time by the time I get to the laundromat the sheriff's car is there.

MR. RUBIN. You are familiar with the fact that part of the area known as North Richmond has been annexed to the city of Richmond?

MR. BROWN. Yes.

MR. RUBIN. Can you tell us whether the city has provided increased services to the city part of North Richmond?

MR. BROWN. No, sir. This was our best argument before the formation commission, as well as to the residents.

The portion of North Richmond that is in the city was annexed something like 40 years ago. This district is very largely still without curbs and gutters. It still has a street light on most corners, not on all corners. The streets are poorly maintained because it is so difficult to maintain streets without curbs and gutters.

Just less than a year after they attempted to annex, a petition was made to the city to create a special district to provide curbing and gutters for this neighborhood. The city told us if we could get out and get 109 property owners to sign the petition that they would do it. This old man, who was at that time 82 years old, got out and walked from house to house and obtained 109 signatures, carried it to the city and asked them to set up the special district and they told him they didn't have the money available, and that they wouldn't be able to do it for maybe five or six years.

However, in the unincorporated portion, by special district the community first provided street lights. They have street lights every half block in the majority of nearly all of the neighborhood.

It has curbs and gutters. Although on Mr. Henderson's report it says there is a need for curbs and gutters this district spent nearly $1/2 million by special district in 1951 and '52 to install curbs and gutters. After they had done this, then the county put in streets.

MR. RUBIN. Mr. Brown, the installation of curbs and gutters would require an expenditure would it not, from the particular residents within the special district?

MR. BROWN. Yes, sir.

MR. RUBIN. So that if the residents were too poor to pay for the curbs and gutters then that wouldn't be possible. Is that correct?

MR. BROWN. I don't believe I understood you.

MR. RUBIN. If the residents within the special district were too poor to afford the costs of curbs and gutters, it would not be possible for them to receive that kind of public service. Is that right?

MR. BROWN. I haven't seen a case yet where they took into consideration the financial ability of the residents in creating a special district. Any district that this would be proposed for now could not possibly be poorer than our district was at the time this occurred, and as a result between 35 and 50 people lost their property as a result of this.

And then I'm told that the city, through a dummy, bought in these lots, sold them back to the county and the county—this is where the county obtained the majority of the property where they put the low-rent housing that is now scattered throughout the neighborhood.

MR. RUBIN. Thank you, Mr. Brown. I have no further questions.

CHAIRMAN HANNAH. Do the Commissioners have questions of Mr. Brown? Do any of you have questions? Mr. Taylor?

MR. TAYLOR. No questions.

CHAIRMAN HANNAH. Thank you very much, Mr. Brown. You are excused. We appreciate your being with us. Mr. Rubin, may we have the next witness?

MR. RUBIN. The next witness is Mrs. Barbara McBride.

(Whereupon, Mrs. Barbara McBride was sworn by the Chairman and testified as follows:)

TESTIMONY OF MRS. BARBARA McBRIDE, RICHMOND, CALIFORNIA

MR. RUBIN. Mrs. McBride, would you please state your name and address for the record?

MRS. McBRIDE. I am Mrs. Barbara McBride. I reside at 1581 2nd Street in Richmond.

MR. RUBIN. Do you live in Richmond or in the unincorporated area of North Richmond?

MRS. MCBRIDE. I live in the unincorporated area of North Richmond.

MR. RUBIN. How long have you lived in the unincorporated area of North Richmond?

MRS. MCBRIDE. Oh, about 16 years.

MR. RUBIN. Could you tell us how many children you have?

MRS. MCBRIDE. I have four children.

MR. RUBIN. Mrs. McBride, could you tell us their ages?

MRS. MCBRIDE. Four, five, seven, and nine.

MR. RUBIN. Do you own your own home?

MRS. MCBRIDE. No, I don't.

MR. RUBIN. You are a tenant?

MRS. MCBRIDE. Yes, I am. I rent.

MR. RUBIN. Could you tell us whether there is any street gambling that you've seen in the unincorporated area of North Richmond?

MRS. MCBRIDE. Yes, there is.

MR. RUBIN. Could you tell us where that gambling takes place?

MRS. MCBRIDE. Just about the main problem where we are having problems now is at the corner of Third and Chesley.

MR. RUBIN. Is there gambling across the street?

MRS. MCBRIDE. You mean on the Richmond side?

MR. RUBIN. On the Richmond side.

MRS MCBRIDE. No.

MR. RUBIN. Would you tell us why there's gambling on the county side and not on the city side?

MRS. MCBRIDE. Well, mainly mostly because—well, this is my own feeling about it—because the Richmond side is patrolled by Richmond police more regularly than on the county side. We just have one patrol car that is on the county side that is responsible for the El Sobrante unincorporated area, the Martinez area, then it comes down through North Richmond.

So that way, if they know they can just about time it every hour or every so often when the police cars are coming around so you can gamble between those hours until you see one coming and there is just not enough intense police protection there, or someone there to patrol the area to keep this from happening.

MR. RUBIN. Can you tell us whether milk delivery service is available in North Richmond?

MRS. MCBRIDE. You mean some private companies such as Carnation. Something like home delivery?

MR. RUBIN. Yes.

MRS. MCBRIDE. No.

MR. RUBIN. Could you tell us why milk delivery service is not available?

MRS. McBRIDE. Well, we have had some robberies to occur to milkmen there. Some people use false names, then move, or when the collector comes back they don't live there, things of this type. So this way we don't get the direct service such as fresh milk or anything straight from the company itself.

MR. RUBIN. You mean because of robberies of the milk trucks?

MRS. McBRIDE. Yes.

MR. RUBIN. Do you buy your milk in the county part of North Richmond?

MRS. McBRIDE. Yes, I do, from the local drugstore—I mean—local drugstore—no, from the local grocery store there, or either I go and buy it 1½ miles away at a milk depot that they have in San Pablo.

MR. RUBIN. Why do you go there instead of buying your milk in the county?

MRS. McBRIDE. I think I like the idea of it being in a glass bottle and not a real puffy plastic container, or a cardboard container.

I feel as if I am getting freshness if I go direct to a regular milk company and get the milk there.

MR. RUBIN. Have you found that the milk in the county part of North Richmond that is sold in the stores isn't fresh?

MRS. McBRIDE. Well, I don't know whether it's fresh or not, but being a mother I always watch the containers, and if the containers are puffy on the side regardless whether it's milk or fruit drink, then I don't buy it because I know it's not going to be too long before it's sour.

MR. RUBIN. Do you have any trouble with vandalism in your area or any of the areas near where you live?

MRS. McBRIDE. Yes, we do. I am involved with the Neighborhood House, an organization in the neighborhood where we have had quite a bit of vandalism, and right now because of that we don't have any insurance on anything we have in our building, material and so forth, and there is cases of breaking in homes, things of this type.

MR. RUBIN. Has there been any destruction of property to the home in which you live?

MRS. McBRIDE. No.

MR. RUBIN. Nothing like that?

MRS. McBRIDE. No.

MR. RUBIN. Any juveniles playing in your area around your home?

MRS. McBRIDE. Well, B-B guns, broken windows, you know. Kids throw bottles in the street, this type of thing.

MR. RUBIN. Could you tell us why you think that vandalism is prevalent in your area, in the county part of North Richmond?

MRS. MCBRIDE. No, I can't really tell you that, but it's just about the same all over Richmond.

MR. RUBIN. All over both the city as well as the county?

MRS. MCBRIDE. The city as well as in North Richmond, but I really think that a lot of vandalism that happens, people have a tendency to say "Well, it's our own children." But I don't think this is true of your neighborhood children. I think this is people that come from the outside, to come from North Richmond and do what they have to do, and this leaves a stigmatism on our children and the people that live within North Richmond.

MR. RUBIN. You mean that people outside of the county part come into the county part and commit acts of vandalism?

MRS. MCBRIDE. Yes, vandalism, or if you notice in the papers, in the Independent, if there is any gambling raids that happen mostly people that are caught in the gambling raids come from other parts of the Bay Area, or the other side of the Richmond area, that are apprehended when they do have raids of this type.

MR. RUBIN. Are there many empty lots in North Richmond?

MRS. MCBRIDE. Yes, there are many empty lots.

MR. RUBIN. In the county part?

MRS. MCBRIDE. In the county part.

MR. RUBIN. Could you describe their condition?

MRS. MCBRIDE. Well, grass is waist-high, broken bottles, wood, things of this nature. They are not kept up.

MR. RUBIN. Does the county attempt to do anything about the condition of these lots?

MRS. MCBRIDE. No, I've never known them to do anything. It's just the opposite, because in the city of Richmond if you have a lot that is not taken care of, and during the summer when the grass needs burning, the city will have the grass burned and they will bill the property owner for it, and I don't know of this being done in the county, of my knowledge.

MR. RUBIN. Would you tell us whether drainage is a problem in the county part of North Richmond?

MRS. MCBRIDE. Drainage is very poor. Drainage there, oh, about a half an hour rain directly in front of my house, it comes up in the driveway, It can't get out, you know.

The kids can't get out. They just stay home from school that day if I don't have a car to take them.

MR. RUBIN. Do any industrial plants in your neighborhood contribute to this drainage problem?

MRS. MCBRIDE. As far as I know—I don't know really. I couldn't answer that truthfully. I don't know.

MR. RUBIN. Could you describe some of the problems which the drainage situation has caused to you personally?

Mrs. McBride. Oh, to me personally, I've had trouble about three years ago with Rheem Manufacturing Company who makes large septic tanks. After they make these tanks they put water within them to test them to see whether they have any leaks and so forth.

On the corner of 6th and Silver they release this water, and I live on the lower end of North Richmond and it kind of has a steady stream and it somewhat ends up kind of right in front of my door, and it goes on down the street.

It would probably run freer if we had street cleaning service, but also we do not have this either. So each gutter has to be cleaned by its own property owner or tenant or whatsoever.

It happens you can only clean up so far on your block, so the water is blocked. My little girl was three at this time, and she went out to play in the water, and she received some type of acne from it.

I took her to Kaiser for skin treatment to see if it was anything really in the water. By the time it came from Rheem to 2nd Street it had picked up all kinds of residue in the water, so there was no way of telling whether Rheem had any chemicals in their water or not, but in further looking into it we contacted the sanitation region of the health department in Richmond, and they found that it was regular tap water that is put into the water.

But I still hold it true that if Rheem had its own thing to drain the water within their own company, then this still wouldn't have happened, you know, the water coming down on us.

Mr. Rubin. Mrs. McBride, did you support the 1965 proposal to annex the unincorporated part of North Richmond to the city of Richmond?

Mrs. McBride. Did I oppose it?

Mr. Rubin. Did you support it?

Mrs. McBride. No.

Mr. Rubin. Were you in favor of the annexation proposal?

Mrs. McBride. Yes.

Mr. Rubin. Did you think that annexation would contribute to a solution of the problems that you have described here?

Mrs. McBride. Well, it might help, but I still feel as if the people in the community would still have to help get some of these things, to attend some council meetings. They can petition so far and a petition is good to some extent, but I think the property owners themselves have to really get out there and make sure that things are done for them.

Mr. Rubin. Did you actively campaign for annexation?

Mrs. McBride. Yes, I did.

Mr. Rubin. In connection with the annexation campaign did you attempt to get the support of the Rheem Company?

MRS. McBRIDE. Yes, we went to quite a few manufacturing companies and we sent letters, we visited with committees and so forth.

MR. RUBIN. Could you tell us what happened when you went to the Rheem Company?

MRS. McBRIDE. We were just turned down. They were already approached before.

MR. RUBIN. Did you cite the incident with your daughter to the Rheem Company?

MRS. McBRIDE. Yes. They also stated that they were somewhat sorry, but they felt as if her skin condition wasn't a problem of theirs, that I should have kept her out of the water.

MR. RUBIN. Thank you, Mrs. McBride. I have no further questions.

CHAIRMAN HANNAH. Do the Commissioners have any questions? Mrs. Freeman?

COMMISSIONER FREEMAN. Mrs. McBride, did I understand you to say that the Rheem Company uses the streets of North Richmond as a dumping ground?

MRS. McBRIDE. Well, they dump it out in the yard, and the water ends up, yes, in the street.

COMMISSIONER FREEMAN. And they said they had no interest in the effect of this on the residents?

MRS. McBRIDE. Well, I went as for myself. The question I asked was for myself, and they said that I should have kept my daughter out of the water.

COMMISSIONER FREEMAN. There are several manufacturing companies in North Richmond. I would like to know if you have any information concerning the number of residents in North Richmond who are employed by these companies?

MRS. McBRIDE. Oh, very—we have American Standard, but it is not directly—it's in the Hensley Tract—which makes bathtubs. I can't give you the number, but I know there are people that live in North Richmond employed there. I don't know of anyone that lives in North Richmond that is employed at Rheem Manufacturing Company who is in the unincorporated area.

COMMISSIONER FREEMAN. No resident of North Richmond is employed by the Rheem Manufacturing Company?

MRS. McBRIDE. No.

COMMISSIONER FREEMAN. Do you know of anything that the owners of these manufacturing companies have done or contributed to the benefit of the residents of North Richmond?

MRS. McBRIDE. No, I don't.

COMMISSIONER FREEMAN. Thank you.

CHAIRMAN HANNAH. Any other questions? Mr. Taylor?

MR. TAYLOR. No, sir.

CHAIRMAN HANNAH. Thank you very much, Mrs. McBride. You are excused. Mr. Rubin, will you call the next witness?

MR. RUBIN. The next witness is Mr. W. G. Kelsch.

CHAIRMAN HANNAH. Are these other gentlemen going to testify also?

MR. KELSCH. Yes, they are going to be up here with me. This is Mr. James Dempsey, and this is Mr. William D. Lyle.

(Whereupon, Mr. W. G. Kelsch, Mr. James Dempsey, and Mr. William D. Lyle were sworn by the Chairman and testified as follows:)

TESTIMONY OF MR. W. G. KELSCH, MR. JAMES DEMPSEY, AND MR. WILLIAM D. LYLE, RICHMOND, CALIFORNIA

MR. RUBIN. Mr. Kelsch and you other gentlemen, would each of you please identify yourselves for the record and state your name and addresses?

MR. KELSCH. I am Mr. W. G. Kelsch, resident plant manager, Rheem Manufacturing Company.

MR. LYLE. I am William D. Lyle, personnel director of the Richmond plant of the Rheem Manufacturing Company.

MR. DEMPSEY. I'm James Dempsey, chief accountant, Rheem Manufacturing Company, Richmond.

MR. RUBIN. Mr. Kelsch, I will direct the questions to you but if either Mr. Dempsey or Mr. Lyle can answer the question, either may do so. Could you tell us where your plant is located?

MR. KELSCH. At 801 Chesley Avenue.

MR. RUBIN. Is that in the unincorporated area of North Richmond?

MR. KELSCH. Yes. The plant actually is in the unincorporated area. The street in front of the plant is the dividing line between the city and the unincorporated area.

MR. RUBIN. How long has it been located in North Richmond?

MR. KELSCH. We moved there in 1930. Originally we were in Emeryville, and we moved from Emeryville out to that location.

MR. RUBIN. Could you tell us what kind of products you manufacture?

MR. KELSCH. All sheet steel tanks from one gallon containers up to 20,000 to 30,000 gallon tanks.

MR. RUBIN. How many employees do you have?

MR. KELSCH. At the present time, counting the office, we have something like 340.

MR. RUBIN. Could you tell us how many of those employees are Negro?

MR. KELSCH. To my best recollection, about 22 at this time.

MR. RUBIN. Can you tell us how many unskilled employees you have?

MR. KELSCH. I'm afraid I couldn't give you any definitive number on that.

MR. RUBIN. Mr. Chairman, I would like to introduce into the record as Exhibit No. 30 an Equal Employment Opportunity form which was filed by the Richmond plant of the Rheem Manufacturing Company on March 30, 1966. At that time it indicates that there was a total of 171 unskilled laborers, of whom nine were Negro.

CHAIRMAN HANNAH. It will be received.

(Whereupon, the above document was marked Exhibit No. 30 and received in evidence.)

MR. KELSCH. I would just like to mention in regard to that, that we are getting into our busy period at this time and our employment has picked up in the last couple of weeks.

MR. RUBIN. Do any of your employees live in North Richmond?

MR. KELSCH. I'm sorry, I couldn't answer that.

CHAIRMAN HANNAH. I take it you don't know, Mr. Kelsch?

MR. LYLE. I might say this, Mr. Rubin, that our employees come generally from the Richmond area. As you can see, our plant is right on the borderline. I can't answer the question directly because I don't know, but I'm sure that we have employees, some of whom live in North Richmond unincorporated area.

MR. RUBIN. That wouldn't be a high percentage of your total employees?

MR. LYLE. I wouldn't know how to answer that because I've never checked the records for that purpose.

MR. RUBIN. We've heard testimony this morning that the highly-developed residential area of the county portion of North Richmond is almost all-Negro. Is your company located in or near the highly-developed residential area?

MR. LYLE. We're in a residential area. We have homes surrounding us on one side of the plant there. Yes, we do.

MR. RUBIN. Can you tell us whether your plant has been a profitable operation over the last few years?

MR. KELSCH. I must say by good management we've been able to keep it that way. It's getting tougher every year, though, to maintain our position.

MR. RUBIN. Were you able to pay higher dividends last year than in prior years?

MR. KELSCH. I think I'll refer you to our accountant for that. I believe the record speaks for itself. Jim?

MR. DEMPSEY. The corporation as a whole, of which we are just a small part, increased their dividend last year from 30 to 35 cents per quarter I understand.

MR. RUBIN. Your company is one of the parties that protested the annexation of North Richmond in 1966. Is that correct?

MR. DEMPSEY. Yes. I'd like to correct one part of that first, though. Originally the request was made for annexation of the residential section, and we had no objection whatsoever to anything of this nature. The only reason we got into the objectionable part of it is when they wanted to include the industrial sections, and then it became a matter of the increased tax rate.

MR. RUBIN. Did industry offer an alternative annexation plan for the North Richmond area? Was there a plan offered under which only the residential portion would be taken?

MR. KELSCH. I believe that there was one offered to the city. The city turned that down. They said it would have to be all or nothing.

MR. RUBIN. Why do you think this plan was rejected?

MR. KELSCH. I couldn't tell you that.

MR. RUBIN. Do you think that the Rheem Company has any responsibility to help to solve the problems of the North Richmond community?

MR. KELSCH. Well, I think that Rheem is civic-minded from the standpoint that we are a member of the Chamber of Commerce, and that we belong to the Council of Richmond Industries. I personally am a member of the Fact Committee. This is a group headed by Mr. Charlie Bee in the city. The purpose is to place minority group members in white-collar jobs, but as far as us holding up our share, I think you'll find that we would do this, yes.

MR. RUBIN. Do you feel that the Rheem Company has a responsibility, specifically, with respect to the drainage problems of the community, the dumping of water?

MR. KELSCH. Yes. I would like to comment on that for just a minute. As I mentioned earlier, we moved there in 1930. At that time there weren't any residents in the area at all, and as the lady before me just mentioned, we do make these large tanks and they're checked for leaks, subsequently we just let the plug out and let the water run out. Originally, with no one there this was satisfactory, and I will say that since we have had complaints we have spent money now, and we have the drainage in our own yard. I don't know whether any gets out at all now, but I do know that the majority of it is diverted to a drainage system.

MR. RUBIN. The 1965 report of the Richmond Planning Commission states that the North Richmond area has a high level of unemployment. Do you believe that the Rheem Company has any responsibility to solve this problem?

MR. KELSCH. Well, I don't know how you mean this. All I can say is that our business fluctuates seasonally. We start off in

March and it runs pretty good until maybe September, and our gates are open to all qualified applicants.

As I just mentioned, in addition to the 22 Negroes we have, we have 18 Spanish, and 4 Indian people working at the plant.

MR. RUBIN. Thank you, Mr. Kelsch. I have no further questions.

CHAIRMAN HANNAH. Mrs. Freeman?

COMMISSIONER FREEMAN. Mr. Kelsch, does your company have any Government contracts?

MR. KELSCH. I can't speak for my company, but let's say our individual plant, our local plant. We don't have any at this time.

COMMISSIONER FREEMAN. Do you have any contracts with the State or any subdivision of California?

MR. KELSCH. Not to my knowledge.

COMMISSIONER FREEMAN. You are covered by Title VII of the Civil Rights Act?

MR. KELSCH. I couldn't hear you.

COMMISSIONER FREEMAN. Your company is covered by Title VII of the Civil Rights Act?

MR. KELSCH. Oh, yes.

COMMISSIONER FREEMAN. I noted in your report that the only minority group employees that you do have, even though they are less than 10 percent, are in the laboring and service categories. Would you tell us something about your recruitment practices? How do you recruit employees?

Of the officials, managers, professionals, technicians, salespersons, office, and clerical personnel you have no Negroes, and only two Spanish Americans.

MR. KELSCH. Well, I would say with regard to your question, that again the instructions we have for our personnel manager is that he should find qualified personnel, regardless of race, creed, or color.

We, at the present time, are looking for a draftsman and we would be tickled to death to get anyone.

COMMISSIONER FREEMAN. Do you think the personnel manager would care to comment on that?

MR. LYLE. Yes, I will comment on that point you are making. We use various sources for applications or applicants. We use the newspapers, we use employment agencies, we use the State Employment Service.

We call them up frequently for qualified help. We post notices on our company bulletin board that we need help of various types, and I feel that in every respect we cover the various sources that are available for help that we need.

I might say this, that we have been looking for a draftsman for several months. We've used every source at our command to get qualified people.

COMMISSIONER FREEMAN. Have you ever advertised in any of the newspapers that are oriented to the minorities, the Spanish-speaking persons or the Negro newspapers? I believe there are such in this community.

MR. LYLE. The papers we are using are the large daily papers.

COMMISSIONER FREEMAN. You don't use those other papers. Would it not be a good idea to advertise in those newspapers also?

MR. LYLE. That's something we could entertain the thought of, yes.

COMMISSIONER FREEMAN. Thank you.

CHAIRMAN HANNAH. Mr. Kelsch, you indicated that this local branch is only a small part of the total Rheem Manufacturing Company, and I must say I don't know very much about the Rheem Manufacturing Company. Where are the headquarters?

MR. KELSCH. Our corporate offices are in New York, and our division headquarters, we are in the container division, barrels and bales and things of this nature, is at Linden, New Jersey.

CHAIRMAN HANNAH. Is it a national operation?

MR. KELSCH. International.

CHAIRMAN HANNAH. Are there other plants in California besides this one?

MR. KELSCH. Yes. We have several plants in the Los Angeles area. We have another container plant in South Gate, and in Los Angeles itself we have steel mill buildings, and another large tank installation where various types of tanks are made. We also have one where we make language equipment for schools, tape recorders, things of this nature.

CHAIRMAN HANNAH. Do you have any notion as to what fraction of the total manufacturing operation the local plant is? Is it 1 percent, 5 percent, 10 percent?

MR. KELSCH. Let me ask Mr. Dempsey whether he is willing to hazard a guess.

MR. DEMPSEY. I'd say the total corporation's sales are around $135 million a year in the continental United States. The Richmond plant is around $7 million a year in sales.

CHAIRMAN HANNAH. One-twentieth.

MR. DEMPSEY. Relatively small. We'd like to expand on that a little bit.

We have 24 plants in the United States, and we have 60 plants throughout the world in foreign operations.

CHAIRMAN HANNAH. Are there any other questions?

COMMISSIONER RANKIN. I just have one question. I didn't hear very well. You said you were fulfilling your civic responsibilities by joining the Chamber of Commerce, and was there anything else? I didn't hear very well.

MR. KELSCH. I said we are also a member of the Council of Richmond Industries which is another organization industrywide. Another thing, I serve as a chairman for the Boy Scouts which covered the whole San Pablo area, which included the unincorporated area as well as the Richmond, Vallejo, and Crockett area.

COMMISSIONER RANKIN. Are you encouraged from your headquarters to participate in civic affairs and to take part?

MR. KELSCH. Yes.

COMMISSIONER RANKIN. Is this membership in the Richmond Chamber of Commerce?

MR. KELSCH. Yes, sir.

COMMISSIONER RANKIN. So your plant is in North Richmond, but you are in the Richmond Chamber of Commerce?

MR. KELSCH. That is correct.

CHAIRMAN HANNAH. Any other questions?

VICE CHAIRMAN PATTERSON. Just one. Mr. Kelsch, do you consider the California statute with respect to annexation permitting the principal property owners to veto it to be a just law?

MR. KELSCH. Well, I really hadn't given it a lot of consideration. I don't think I could give an opinion on that. In other words, if I gather what you are asking me is, is this right, that if the majority of property owners are against it that it is out, regardless whether the numbers who would want it would be greater?

VICE CHAIRMAN PATTERSON. Yes.

MR. KELSCH. I really hadn't given much thought from that standpoint.

VICE CHAIRMAN PATTERSON. Does it seem to you that this might conflict with the one man-one vote ruling of the courts?

MR. KELSCH. Well, there again I would rather not answer because I haven't given it consideration, but I can see what you are saying. Yes, it would have some confliction.

VICE CHAIRMAN PATTERSON. Do you have any knowledge of your other plants in other States operating under similar State statutes?

MR. KELSH. No, I don't.

VICE CHAIRMAN PATTERSON. Thank you.

CHAIRMAN HANAH. Mr. Taylor, do you have any questions?

MR. TAYLOR. Yes. We have heard testimony this morning, Mr. Kelsch, that there are problems of inadequate recreation facilities in the area of North Richmond, that there is a problem of inadequacies of police protection. Are you aware of any of these problems?

MR. KELSCH. I can't say that I am. I was at a Chamber of Commerce meeting the other day. I have been to one of the meetings

576

at which they have a large park program which they are trying to promote, and if I am not mistaken it would include—it was given consideration to all of the areas who need a facility at this time. But as far as I am concerned personally, I would have to say no, I am not really aware of the need as far as the area is concerned.

MR. TAYLOR. Where is your home?

MR. KELSCH. My home is in Walnut Creek.

MR. TAYLOR. Where is that?

MR. KELSCH. Twenty-four miles from the plant.

MR. TAYLOR. Did you consult with any of the citizens of North Richmond before the company took a position on the annexation question?

MR. KELSCH. No, I did not.

MR. TAYLOR. Do you think that the citizens' views as to annexation are relevant at all in the company's determination, or is it simply a financial matter, a matter of taxation?

MR. KELSCH. It's really, pure and simple, a financial matter as far as we are concerned.

MR. TAYLOR. Assuming that there are some problems in the city of North Richmond do you have any opinion as to how they may be solved if the city is not annexed to Richmond?

MR. KELSCH. I don't understand your question.

MR. TAYLOR. Assuming that there are some problems of the nature that have been described here this morning, do you have any opinion as to how these problems may be solved if North Richmond is not annexed to the city of Richmond?

MR. KELSCH. No, I don't. The only thing I could say is I heard some of the testimony this morning, and I wonder if enough of this information has been brought to the county officials' attention to get additional help on this.

MR. TAYLOR. Would you be willing to work with the citizens of North Richmond? You said the company does have some community responsibility. Would you be willing to work with the citizens of North Richmond to bring these problems to the attention of the county officials?

MR. KELSCH. I would answer in the affirmative on that if I knew exactly what you are trying to tell.

MR. TAYLOR. I have no further questions.

CHAIRMAN HANNAH. One more question. What is the land area owned by your company in acres?

MR. KELSCH. Around 15 acres.

CHAIRMAN HANNAH. Fifteen acres?

MR. KELSCH. As I said, originally when we moved out there the problem we used to have was keeping the goats and cows away from the cars. They would scratch them with their horns. There was purely no residents at all, unless some moved in.

But that is not one of our problems as far as is concerned here. Really, it is one of taxation.

CHAIRMAN HANNAH. Do any of the Commissioners have other questions? Mr. Patterson?

VICE CHAIRMAN PATTERSON. Mr. Kelsch, do I understand you correctly, then, in assuming that you would have no objection to the annexation of North Richmond to the city of Richmond if your own plant were not annexed along with it?

MR. KELSCH. You are 100 percent right.

VICE CHAIRMAN PATTERSON. You have no objection?

MR. KELSCH. Not at all.

VICE CHAIRMAN PATTERSON. So it is a financial matter with you, because you do object to paying the higher tax rate in the city of Richmond?

MR. KELSCH. Correct.

CHAIRMAN HANNAH. Further questions? Mr. Griswold?

COMMISSIONER GRISWOLD. I have one. Have any of you gentlemen made any estimate—and I recognize it could only be an estimate—as to how much that higher tax would be?

MR. KELSCH. Well, we've made an estimate, but as you say, like everything else, it is approximate. It's around $16,000 a year or so.

COMMISSIONER GRISWOLD. And that would be deductible against your Federal taxes, so that the net cost—and perhaps your State taxes—so that the net cost to you is $8,000 a year?

MR. KELSCH. I would rather ask Jim to answer that question.

COMMISSIONER GRISWOLD. Is that approximately correct?

MR. DEMPSEY. I would say closer to around $10,000 a year.

COMMISSIONER GRISWOLD. All right, call it 10. Doesn't that seem to be a relatively small contribution by your company towards a proper development of the area in which you are located?

MR. DEMPSEY. I don't think from the testimony that was presented this morning, that there is a definite question in the residents' minds as to whether or not this is proper about annexation to the city of Richmond. There is a lot of agitation against it.

COMMISSIONER GRISWOLD. Well, that may be true, but is there any way to find that out as long as your company puts in its veto?

MR. DEMPSEY. Our company is in the industrial portion of the county, and there is no reason why the industrial portion has to go in with the residential portion. They could be annexed.

COMMISSIONER GRISWOLD. No reason unless your company accepts a responsibility for the community in which it is located at what seems to me to be a rather petty cost under all the circumstances. I wonder if you've really given a serious thought to that?

MR. DEMPSEY. We have given it serious thought, and $10,000, although as you say might be petty, to us, $10,000 is a lot of money in our operation. We have to watch every $100 dollars, not necessarily just $10,000.

CHAIRMAN HANNAH. Further questions? Thank you very much, gentlemen. You are excused and we will now take a 10-minute recess.

CHAIRMAN HANNAH. The meeting will come to order. May we have quiet in the room, please. Mr. Glickstein, will you call the next witness?

MR. GLICKSTEIN. The next witness is the Hon. Milton Spinner, Mayor of Richmond.

(Whereupon, Mayor Milton Spinner was sworn by the Chairman and testified as follows:)

TESTIMONY OF THE HON. MILTON SPINNER, MAYOR OF RICHMOND, CALIFORNIA

MR. GLICKSTEIN. Mayor Spinner, would you please state your full name and address for the record?

MAYOR SPINNER. My name is Milton Michael Spinner. I live at 2835 Moyers Road, Richmond, California.

MR. GLICKSTEIN. Mayor Spinner, we have just heard some testimony about North Richmond annexation problems and perhaps we could have some of your views on the question. If North Richmond were to be annexed to Richmond, would the Richmond tax base be sufficiently enlarged so that it could extend municipal services to North Richmond?

MAYOR SPINNER. Yes. I would elaborate on this in many differerent areas, but our time would be too limited.

I would say that when the recommendation came from staff the philosophy behind it was that in the annexation we could introduce the services to the area that were needed by setting up this particular tax base.

MR. GLICKSTEIN. Would the citizens of the city of Richmond benefit from the annexation of North Richmond?

MAYOR SPINNER. I believe they definitely would. For many years the area has been a blighted area. There has been lawlessness in the area. It has been in so many ways an area that has been not responsive to what I consider the areas of good government. ·

As a result of this, we feel that as an isolated community many of these people have been living in an area of complete discomfort, and I feel that as a city we have so much to offer them in the way of police protection, in housing and other services that a city can give to an area that is completely without it.

MR. GLICKSTEIN. The city of Richmond, your city, would it benefit from the annexation?

MAYOR SPINNER. I believe it would, very much so, because I know that many of the problems of North Richmond such as the crime incidents and the other problems flow over into our city, and as a result of annexation we would be able to stop an area of lawlessness.

MR. GLICKSTEIN. There was some testimony that the city of Richmond rejected a proposal to annex only the residential portions of North Richmond. Is that correct?

MAYOR SPINNER. If that was the case it was done without my knowledge.

MR. GLICKSTEIN. Would that be a practical scheme, to annex only the residential portions of North Richmond?

MAYOR SPINNER. I much prefer the inclusion of the industrial base because the problems it would create would cause a financial drain of our present budget, and it would be difficult to administer it properly.

But if this were the only way that it could be done, I would still want to see the area included. I feel that we owe the area a very definite responsibility, and I want to see that become a realization in the very near future.

MR. GLICKSTEIN. Is there strong opposition in Richmond by white people to the annexation of North Richmond?

MAYOR SPINNER. Yes, I have felt this over a long period of time. Let's be very frank about this, and this is about the only way I could actually view this position.

That if you were to view this area, you would see many people on the streets there, some of them drinking in broad daylight, some of them acting in such capacity that they have complete disrespect for the law. In addition, you would see some of the areas that are very badly blighted.

As a result of these conditions that exist there, every single time we've tried to make an attempt at annexation there have always been a group which have sometime been very hard to identify who have opposed us.

Now, the last opposition came from over 50 percent of the assessed evaluation of the area, but behind those people, in support of those people, were a definite group who might have felt that annexation would have been a threat to their own financial security.

MR. GLICKSTEIN. These were people in the city of Richmond?

MAYOR SPINNER. Within the city of Richmond, yes.

MR. GLICKSTEIN. Mayor Spinner, if we may change the subject, our Commission has been very interested in public employment problems of racial minorities and ethnic minorities in gettng positions in public agencies, and we notice that, according to a June 1966 survey by the Richmond Human Relations Commission, only 8.3 percent of the full-time civil service employees were Negro, and I believe that the Negro population of your city is about 30 percent. How do you account for this disparity?

MAYOR SPINNER. We've been very, very badly dismayed by this situation, and I have complained, as others did, to our former city manager.

At the present time my area of disagreement has been primarily the oral review boards. Many qualified and capable Negro applicants have come before the city, and as such have been eliminated in the oral review boards.

As a result, even though we had felt that these people would be good employees and wanted to see them employed, the members of these various boards and commissions or review boards, excuse me, in this particular case, have ruled out many of the Negro applicants.

MR. GLICKSTEIN. Have the persons who were unsuccessful in getting past the oral review boards passed a written examination?

MAYOR SPINNER. Yes, in many cases they have. As a matter of fact, we were quite dismayed at this, and to prove the council's viewpoint we have at least a member of a minority on every single board and commission in the city of Richmond. Not just one, as a matter of tokenism, but we have a number of people representing different minorities within the city, and, as such, all of these people are extremely well-qualified people, and I think the record of the city in that direction is a very admirable one.

MR. GLICKSTEIN. Is the requirement for taking an oral exam a civil service requirement?

MAYOR SPINNER. Yes, it has been set up by the present civil service structure within the city whose guidance under our charter is under the direction of the personnel director and a staff and a commission which are all regulated by the city charter.

MR. GLICKSTEIN. Are steps being taken to eliminate this oral examination or to modify it in some respects?

MAYOR SPINNER. Yes. We are trying to examine the areas of where we feel the greatest of use is achieved at this particular point, and we will eventually review this and then try to do something about this.

MR. GLICKSTEIN. Are other affirmative steps being taken by the city to increase the number of minority group employees on the city payroll?

MAYOR SPINNER. Yes. We noticed—and this is purely from the council and the mayor viewpoint—we've noticed that there have been a great many administrative positions that have, for the most part, been lily-white, if I may use that expression, and primarily the janitorial staffs have been occupied with minority people.

MR. GLICKSTEIN. Are most of the Negro employees on the city staff right now with low-skill jobs?

MAYOR SPINNER. Yes, this happens to be the case. We have very recently made our wishes known, that we would like to see those people who are qualified, regardless of race, religion, or creed be given every opportunity into some of the more responsible positions.

MR. GLICKSTEIN. What sort of affirmative programs are being undertaken to carry out the wishes of the city council?

MAYOR SPINNER. The council, by statement to the personnel director, has reiterated this stand on, oh, about three or four occasions.

MR. GLICKSTEIN. Has the personnel director undertaken any affirmative recruitment campaigns or has he done anything to insure that the number of minority group people would be increased?

MAYOR SPINNER. Yes. He has at this particular point advertised within certain periodicals and other sources of information where he could reach a total group within a community.

In addition to that, he has also been advised, with the help of the Human Relations Commission, the areas that ought to be reached where he can find qualified minority people.

MR. GLICKSTEIN. He has advertised in newspapers, for example, that tend to reach minority group people?

MAYOR SPINNER. Yes. As a matter of fact, as a very specific example, I feel very recently the local Berkeley Post was one of the areas in which we insisted that there would be advertisement for all future civil service jobs in the city.

MR. GLICKSTEIN. What is the Berkeley Post?

MAYOR SPINNER. The Berkeley Post is primarily known as a Negro newspaper which also involves the Hispanic American group.

MR. GLICKSTEIN. Mayor Spinner, I believe that Richmond has an ordinance requiring that all city contracts contain a nondiscrimination clause. Is that correct?

MAYOR SPINNER. That is absolutely correct.

MR. GLICKSTEIN. Is that a new ordinance?

MAYOR SPINNER. Yes.

MR. GLICKSTEIN. Why was it felt necessary to pass such an ordinance?

MAYOR SPINNER. Well, actually, we felt there was an area of subtle discrimination. We wanted to do anything we could to prevent that from continuing on in the city of Richmond.

MR. GLICKSTEIN. Subtle discrimination by city contractors?

MAYOR SPINNER. In city's contracts, yes.

MR. GLICKSTEIN. What has been done to implement this ordinance?

MAYOR SPINNER. We have a human relations staff.

MR. GLICKSTEIN. Do you have a Human Relations Commission?

MAYOR SPINNER. Yes. As a matter of fact, I think that question could best be answered—may I use Mr. Allaire, my human relations head, as a resource person in that one area? I think he would be very well versed in that area.

MR. GLICKSTEIN. Certainly. Mr. Allaire, would you please be sworn?

(Whereupon, Mr. Jerrold Allaire was sworn by the Chairman and testified as follows:)

TESTIMONY OF MR. JERROLD ALLAIRE, RICHMOND, CALIFORNIA

CHAIRMAN HANNAH. Please be seated. You may proceed to answer the question.

MR. ALLAIRE. The ordinance that we know as the FEP and Contracts Ordinance was adopted last May and in effect says the city will not do business with a "Jim Crow" shop. The implementation of the ordinance is carried out by contract clause which accompanies all purchase orders and all bids to bid on city contracts which provides that not only will there be no discrimination, but, also, that the firms doing business with the city must enter into affirmative action agreements.

The enforcement authority is vested in the Human Relations office. Compliance reporting is required. Failure to comply with the ordinance can, if a willful violation is found, the ordinance can, in fact, be declared null and void. The ordinance has been used as a model by San Francisco in adopting its recent ordinance on the same subject and is under consideration by other communities in the State.

MR. GLICKSTEIN. What sort of affirmative action programs are contractors required to undertake?

MR. ALLAIRE. Advertisements in areas which will reach the minority community, orientation of all hiring personnel, advising them of rules that are in the ordinance, in the contract clause. The actual compliance reporting is reviewed by the staff.

MR. GLICKSTEIN. Does the city have construction contracts?

MR. ALLAIRE. Yes, it does.

MR. GLICKSTEIN. Will the city consider it a defense if a contractor indicates that he has to hire all of his employees through a union hiring hall and the union has no Negro members and that is why there are no Negroes on the job?

MR. ALLAIRE. I don't know.

MR. GLICKSTEIN. You don't know if that would be a defense?

MR. ALLAIRE. I don't know.

MR. GLICKSTEIN. Have any complaints been made under the ordinance?

MR. ALLAIRE. Not so far.

MR. GLICKSTEIN. Mayor Spinner, do you think there is a need for metropolitan regional government in the Bay Area?

MAYOR SPINNER. Yes, in many areas I do and very strongly so. I feel that our problem of smog is not being met in the area. I think our areas of water pollution are certainly not satisfactory. I think that our problems of Rapid Transit have certainly been made aware of by BART.

I think there are many areas of where we need a greater type or a metropolitan type of government which would meet the areas which cannot be met on local basis.

MR. GLICKSTEIN. Would you favor cities in the Bay Area giving up their authority to a super-government of some sort?

MAYOR SPINNER. No, I would not. I would still like to maintain this, and I think ABAG at the present time has met part of these solutions.

MR. GLICKSTEIN. That is the Association of Bay Area Governments?

MAYOR SPINNER. That is correct.

MR. GLICKSTEIN. That is a voluntary association?

MAYOR SPINNER. Yes, that is correct. I certainly feel that the local government is more responsive to the people, and I feel that if we could get a little too large we are liable to lose the principle of home rule, which I am very, very much in favor of.

I feel that I would like the government as close to the people as it possibly can be. But when it becomes a matter of meeting services in which we all have to combine I want to see a more responsive type of government on that type of basis.

MR. GLICKSTEIN. What are some of the services that you think the regional, metropolitan government should undertake? You mentioned smog control. What else?

MAYOR SPINNER. I mentioned smog control, I mentioned the case of pollution of water. I also could see the combination of services, primarily sanitary services, which is quite a problem, solid waste disposal in our area, and I could also see the areas of, oh, anywhere from combined water services, elimination services, any number of other areas which I can—

MR. GLICKSTEIN. How about schools?

MAYOR SPINNER. Schools, yes. I feel very strongly in the unification of schools in certain areas for the purpose of—

MR. GLICKSTEIN. Do you favor a metropolitan school district, for example?

MAYOR SPINNER. It would have to be up to the particular region. I would say in a city like Oakland or San Francisco, yes, I would. In an area such as Richmond and related areas I would want a unified school district.

MR. GLICKSTEIN. If there were a metropolitan school district, a school district much larger than the existing one, would that make the problem of school integration simpler?

MAYOR SPINNER. In some areas it would and in some areas it wouldn't. I certainly feel that the problem of integration is a very strong one in our particular community at the present time. I feel that because of the area being spread out and involving so many different groupings that we have had many differences of thought, but I do feel that eventually many of these problems will be overcome as the areas are settled over a period of time.

So at this particular point I could say yes, I feel very strongly for a unified school district as opposed to a metropolitan one primarily of Oakland or San Francisco; but there is an area of which I am very, very concerned specifically about the problem of integration.

MR. GLICKSTEIN. Is there public housing in Richmond?

MAYOR SPINNER. Yes.

MR. GLICKSTEIN. Is it well integrated?

MAYOR SPINNER. Yes. Let me comment on this. Not too long ago the question had come up as a result of certain actions, I think it was Core that had come before the Housing Board, and they had made certain statements as to the fact they felt that one area was all-white and the other one was all-Negro.

We became quite concerned about it, and we made demands upon the Housing Administration and told them that certainly within the province of our appointments we were going to make changes unless we saw that area integrated.

Those of you who could see the picture would see that the area has been integrated a lot better than in the past, and I haven't reviewed it very recently, but I certainly intend to in the very near future.

MR GLICKSTEIN. In other words, the housing projects that have been predominantly Negro have become less so as a result of these efforts?

MAYOR SPINNER. Yes. In some areas I would say yes. In other areas I would still want further examination.

MR. GLICKSTEIN. In housing projects that have been predominantly white, more Negroes have come to live in those?

MAYOR SPINNER. Yes, I would say so.

MR. GLICKSTEIN. Are the public housing projects in Richmond in the nature of complexes, large housing complexes?

MAYOR SPINNER. Yes. I have primarily looked for the increased public housing in Richmond because so many people have been on the housing lists.

MR. GLICKSTEIN. But is it today large complexes?

MAYOR SPINNER. No, complexes I imagine mean something like

an apartment house building. Is that what you have in mind? No, they've been primarily duplexes and houses of that nature.

MR. GLICKSTEIN. So the bulk of public housing is located in one area?

MAYOR SPINNER. Yes, primarily one section which we call Easter Hill and, of course, public housing is also the recent home which we have built for the elderly people.

MR. GLICKSTEIN. Would you favor building public housing on a scattered site basis, of scattering small units around the city rather than locating them in one particular area?

MAYOR SPINNER. I would, in some cases, yes.

MR. GLICKSTEIN. In what situation would you favor that?

MAYOR SPINNER. I would feel that there were certain areas where I wouldn't want it to become just one solid area of public housing. I would want it more or less disseminated throughout the community so that it could fit more easily into the community and not be pointed out as public housing.

MR. GLICKSTEIN. You think that would be more desirable if housing was not readily identifiable as public housing?

MAYOR SPINNER. Well, not exactly as identifiable, but as more identifiable with the community at large.

MR. GLICKSTEIN. I have no further questions.

CHAIRMAN HANNAH. Have the Commissioners any questions?

COMMISSIONER RANKIN. I have one question.

CHAIRMAN HANNAH. Mr. Rankin?

COMMISSIONER RANKIN. As mayor of the city—you are looking at an ex-councilman, and I think that a councilman who has no axe to grind and serves on the city council either ought to have his head examined or receive a medal for bravery in this day and time. But in your particular city you say that it will not increase the tax rate if you annex North Richmond, the residential and industrial areas both. Am I correct in that?

MAYOR SPINNER. Yes. This is an assumption, excuse me.

COMMISSIONER RANKIN. Yet you say some of the citizens would object. Am I correct in that because there are problems?

MAYOR SPINNER. Yes.

COMMISSIONER RANKIN. But isn't North Richmond going to be there whether it is annexed or it is not annexed?

MAYOR SPINNER. Yes, it will be there whether it will be annexed or not annexed, but the problem primarily is this:

That for years this area has been without the pale of, shall we say, the guidance of the city of Richmond As a result, there has been a great deal of lawlessness in the area. All you have to do is ride in the area and you could see some of the elements.

Now, within that framework, I cannot see where a person can

actively engage in, shall we say, activity outside the law in that area and it will not affect the city of Richmond itself.

Also, the area itself in terms of the housing, much of it is far below code of the standards we set in Richmond.

Third of all, there is a great problem of sewerage and drainage. Another problem would be the matter of curbs and streets.

What we would have to do is undertake an intelligent program of planning over a long period of time to make this part of the community. We feel primarily that with that tax base that we would offer, plus the tax base that the people would offer in that area it would not be too much of a problem financially to the city of Richmond.

As to dollars and cents right down to the nth degree I cannot give you an exact figure, but I feel that not only in terms of this area of finance, but in the finance of human resources we in the city of Richmond would be way ahead by the annexation of this area.

COMMISSIONER RANKIN. Then it is the industrial corporations that are blocking this. Is that correct?

MAYOR SPINNER. Yes, there is no question.

COMMISSIONER RANKIN. I live in a city where we have two large industrial corporations, namely American Tobacco Company and Liggett & Myers, and when I was on the council when we had a problem like this we would go to these corporations informally.

Quite frequently we didn't get all we wanted, but it was surprising how much we did get, even though it cost them a little bit, because of their feeling of responsibility for the development and welfare of the community.

I would think that the corporations in this area would have the same civic consciousness that would want to improve the area around which their plant is located. I would try the informal method. It just might work now and then.

MAYOR SPINNER. This process has been undergone for about the last two or three months. I have contacted one of the largest dissenters in the original annexation. The parties that are concerned promised me that they will do everything this time to see that the desire for annexation is not thwarted.

COMMISSIONER RANKIN. Of course, I think you have a good proposition to make, too.

MAYOR SPINNER. Thank you very much.

CHAIRMAN HANNAH. Other questions? Mr. Taylor?

MR. TAYLOR. No, sir.

CHAIRMAN HANNAH. Thank you very much, Mr. Mayor. We appreciate your being here this morning. Mr. Glickstein, will you call the next witness?

MR. GLICKSTEIN. The next witness is Mr. Jonathan Fleming, a

member of the staff of the Commission who will read a short staff report.

(Whereupon, MR. JONATHAN FLEMING was sworn by the Chairman and testified as follows:)

TESTIMONY OF MR. JONATHAN FLEMING, ATTORNEY, U.S. COMMISSION ON CIVIL RIGHTS

MR. FLEMING. In recent years the greatest industrial and residential growth in the San Francisco-Oakland Metropolitan Area has occurred in Southern Alameda County. This is the area from the Oakland city line to the Santa Clara County line.

There are approximately 185,000 jobs in Southern Alameda County; Negroes hold about 2 percent of those jobs. The unemployment rate in Southern Alameda County is less than 3 percent; in the Oakland target areas unemployment is between 15 and 20 percent.

Negroes do not live in Southern Alameda County in significant numbers. In San Leandro, which begins at the Oakland city line, there are about 25 Negro families. In Hayward in 1960, 86 Negroes lived there. In Union City, 16. In Fremont, 18. In Newark, 1. In the unincorporated areas of the county there were 1,959 Negroes living.

The Commission staff has studied employment and housing in the Tri-Cities of Alameda County because this is the area that currently is undergoing new expansion. The Tri-Cities are Fremont, Newark, and Union City. The population of the Tri-Cities is 122,000 persons as of June 1966. Nonwhites represented .2 percent of the population and persons with Spanish surnames represented about 19 percent of the population. There are 24,500 jobs in the Tri-City area, approximately 1,500 are held by Negroes. Federal contract compliance reports for 1964, the most recent year for which statistics are available, show that 19 companies are required to report; 18 of these companies employ 3,500 persons of whom only 61 are Negroes. The General Motors plant in Fremont employs about 5,200 persons of whom almost 1,000 are Negro. Public employment in the Tri-City area represents 3,500 jobs; staff investigation revealed only one Negro municipal employee in the Tri-City area.

The Commission staff has conducted a sample survey of commuting patterns among employees in certain companies in the Tri-City area. The study shows that about 75 percent of Tri-City employees reside in the Tri-City area. Negroes who work in the Tri-City area largely commute from outside this area.

The job referral practices of the California Employment Service tend to limit job opportunities in Southern Alameda County for Negroes, Mexican Americans, and other central city residents of Oakland. Local offices serve local registrants first; unfilled job orders then are forwarded to other offices in the Bay Area. However, unemployed persons may register in as many different offices as they wish and the State Employment Office suggests to job applicants who have means of transportation that they register in the Oakland, San Francisco, Hayward, and San Jose offices in the Bay Area.

The trend in the Tri-City area is toward housing which is beyond the reach of low-income families. Most home sales that Realtors handle are fairly high: of the 1,401 homes that Realtors sold in 1966, only 78 were priced below $15,000. New units that builders put up also are expensive: of the 1,542 single-family tract houses that were completed in the area during a recent one-year period, only 244 were marketed for less than $20,000.

There is a significant Federal investment in planning service funds and housing funds in the Tri-City area.

Federal Housing Administration since December 1964 has made commitments to insure 2,700 housing units in the Tri-City Area and 200 to multi-family units. The Comprehensive Urban Assistance Program of the Department of Housing and Urban Development, the so-called 701 program, has twice been the means through which each of the Tri-Cities has secured money to plan for efficient urban growth and constructive use of their land.

The California State Planning Office in Sacramento maintains quality control over plans devised with 701 funds. This function is largely a monitoring one, assuring that the plans include the three elements required in a general plan by State law—a land use component, a traffic circulation component, and supporting maps. A housing element is optional. All three cities have received significant Federal assistance in other areas.

Fremont has been able to acquire and develop some 36½ acres to serve local recreational needs with open space grants totaling $400,000. Over 25 percent of Fremont's park and recreational facilities fund for the last fiscal year was financed by the Federal Government.

Newark now intends to finance 60 acres of its proposed 86-acre park system through HUD's open space grants. The Federal contribution is expected to be somewhere around $780,000.

The East Bay Park District, which serves citizens of Alameda and Contra Costa Counties, has deposited a $56,000 HUD open space grant into a special trust fund to build up interest so that the District can purchase land for a 4,000-acre aquatic park in Fremont. As a result of flood plain improvements created by the U. S. Army Corps of Engineers, land values in the future park have gone up from $1,500 an acre to $7,500 an acre.

That is the end of my report.

MR. GLICKSTEIN. Thank you, Mr. Fleming.

CHAIRMAN HANNAH. Mr. Glickstein, will you call the next witness?

MR. GLICKSTEIN. The next witness is Mr. John Reagan.

(Whereupon, MR. JOHN REAGAN was sworn by the Chairman and testified as follows:)

TESTIMONY OF MR. JOHN REAGAN, FREMONT, CALIFORNIA

MR. GLICKSTEIN. Mr. Reagan, would you please state your full name and address for the record.

MR. REAGAN. I'm John M. Reagan. I live at 3639 Wilmington Road in Fremont.

MR. GLICKSTEIN. What is your occupation?

MR. REAGAN. I am personnel manager of the Kroehler Furniture Manufacturing Company, Fremont.

MR. GLICKSTEIN. What is the type of furniture that the Kroehler Company manufactures?

MR. REAGAN. In the Fremont plant we manufacture strictly upholstered furniture. That is, it's a full operation furniture-manufacturing plant. We grind up our own cotton, mill our own frame parts, manufacture our own spring parts, and we have 10 upholstering assembly lines.

MR. GLICKSTEIN. At what skill levels do you hire most of your employees?

MR. REAGAN. Most of the people we hire are non-skilled people. It's quite difficult for us to get skilled people in our trade because we would be competing with the custom upholstery shops which have a union scale. I think it's about $3.30 or $3.40 right now.

We have a hiring in-rate of $1.80 an hour. We put people on a 60-day trial or probationary period.

During this time they are evaluated by members of supervision, and they are given merit increases up to the basic rate, which is $2.39 an hour.

At this time they are put on what we call piecework, or an incentive pay program. They have a potential of making $2.65, $3 an hour, and over.

MR. GLICKSTEIN. Then the unskilled people that you hire receive most of their training to do your work on the job. Is that correct?

MR. REAGAN. Yes, they do.

MR. GLICKSTEIN. I understand that your plant moved from Pittsburg, California to Fremont. What were the major reasons for this move? When did it take place?

MR. REAGAN. Well, originally we had a plant in San Francisco which we closed, I believe it was in 1943. During the war it was quite difficult for the furniture manufacturers to get materials.

We had a plant in Los Angeles which we maintained doing Government work. We have plants throughout the entire United States and Canada. These are what we consider some of our smaller plants on the West Coast, the one in Inglewood, in the Los Angeles area, and the one in Fremont.

In 1950 the furniture business was such that we decided to put another plant in this area, so they went into the Pittsburg area where—it was formerly a Government building, I believe, and was strictly an assembly plant. We would ship the materials up from our Inglewood plant such as the springs, frames, covers, and so forth.

In 1956, it was decided to build a plant in the Bay Area closer to the market. Most of our dealers are in San Jose, Oakland, and San Francisco. It was not possible to enlarge the Pittsburg plant to the floor space that we required for the heavy mill machinery, spring manufacture and so forth, so people from our general office back in Naperville, Illinois near Chicago came out to the Fremont area, which was fairly new at the time and acquired the land that the Fremont plant now sits on.

We asked the people in the Pittsburg plant when we ceased operations there, we offered to move 100 percent of this work force, paying their moving expense to the Fremont area.

MR. GLICKSTEIN. What is the distance between Pittsburg and Fremont?

MR. REAGAN. It's only about 55 miles, I believe. But at the time it wasn't an easy drive. It's through the old Niles Canyon Road, Route 21 and so on. Now it's a little easier to drive. The freeways have been improved.

MR. GLICKSTEIN. Where is Pittsburg in relation to where we are now?

MR. REAGAN. Pittsburg is up in—up around Port Chicago and Antioch area, up near Bethlehem, U. S. Steel.

MR. GLICKSTEIN. In Contra Costa County?

MR. REAGAN. Yes. Like I say, we offered to move 100 percent of the work force. Now, most of these people did, we paid their moving expenses. The people that didn't move down, we paid their commute expenses for six months. I think about 70 some percent of the people did move down and relocate in Fremont.

MR. GLICKSTEIN. How many salaried and how many hourly-paid employees did you have in Pittsburg approximately?

MR. REAGAN. Oh, about, I think it was around 170.

MR. GLICKSTEIN. Of both categories, salaried and hourly?

MR. REAGAN. 150 to 170. I was transferred out here from our New York plant about three to four months prior to this plant opening.

MR. GLICKSTEIN. Do you know how many of these 170 employees were Negro or Spanish surname persons?

MR. REAGAN. About 100 of them I believe were Mexican and Portuguese.

MR. GLICKSTEIN. About 100 of the 170?

MR. REAGAN. At least. See, what our work force consisted of, at the time we opened, the State closed the Sacramento and San

Joaquin River to commercial fishing, so about all of these ex-commercial fishermen come in to work for us.

MR. GLICKSTEIN. And of that 170 how many employees were Negro?

MR. REAGAN. I believe that they had about two or three up there. Most of them were working in the steel mill.

MR. GLICKSTEIN. How many salaried and hourly-paid employees do you employ in Fremont?

MR. REAGAN. We have a total right now of about 250. We normally run about 270.

MR. GLICKSTEIN. How many of these are either Negro or Spanish surname?

MR. REAGAN. Right now we have about four or five Negro, and we probably have around, oh, I'd say maybe 50 or 60 Mexican, many Portuguese.

MR. GLICKSTEIN. Did many of the Spanish surname employees that you have with you now also work for you in Pittsburg?

MR. REAGAN. Yes.

MR. GLICKSTEIN. Were some of these employees provided with the relocation assistance you spoke of a few minutes ago?

MR. REAGAN. The supervisors we normally—that is, we move them down and pay all of their moving expenses, packing and so forth. The rest of the people in the plant, the hourly workers, we pay their moving vans and they do their own packing.

MR. GLICKSTEIN. Where do most of your present employees live?

MR. REAGAN. Well, we have some that commute from Oakland. We have still about eight or nine that commute from the Pittsburg area. Then drive back and forth every day.

Incidentally, one of our supervisors, after 17 years just about sacrificed all of his seniority. His wife refused to move down to this area, so he terminated last night. We were very sorry to see him go. He is an ex-commercial fisherman, but some of the people moved back to the Pittsburg area, but most of them that relocated down here are still there.

MR. GLICKSTEIN. Could you estimate what percentage of your 250 employees live in the Fremont area?

MR. REAGAN. What's that again?

MR. GLICKSTEIN. Could you estimate what percentage of your 250 employees live in the Fremont area?

MR. REAGAN. Oh, I'd say about 60 percent.

MR. GLICKSTEIN. Sixty percent of them. Where do most of your Negro employees live?

MR. REAGAN. I have one that lives in Berkeley, another one in Castro Valley, two in Oakland, and I had one or two were coming from Menlo Park and Redwood City, but the bridge toll was too expensive.

MR. GLICKSTEIN. Where do most of your Spanish surname employees live?

MR. REAGAN. Newark, Union City, Fremont.

MR. GLICKSTEIN. Newark and Union City are very close to Fremont, aren't they?

MR. REAGAN. Yes.

MR. GLICKSTEIN. How do your employees that do not live in the immediate area of the plant travel to work?

MR. REAGAN. They all travel by car.

MR. GLICKSTEIN. Car pools and things of that sort?

MR. REAGAN. Yes.

MR. GLICKSTEIN. Have you found that commuting of this sort leads to absenteeism or tardiness?

MR. REAGAN. No, we don't have any. In fact, I think that we probably have a greater degree of tardiness and absenteeism among our employees who probably live closer in. We find that in most cases. The people across the street are the ones that are always late.

MR. GLICKSTEIN. You don't think that having people commute from Oakland or Berkeley would present a problem?

MR. REAGAN. No. In fact, I participated in the NAACP Job Fair at McClymonds High School about a year ago and I told the people at the time that many people commute to our area and beyond us to General Motors, they are farther than we are, and that many people commute via car pools on the freeway. It's only about 23 miles, I believe it is from our plant right to here, and the Nimitz Freeway is really good. They might not have the best safety record in California, but they are convenient.

MR. GLICKSTEIN. Mr. Reagan, how does your company fill its vacant positions?

MR. REAGAN. I hire people through the Department of Employment in Hayward. I have hired people through the Committee of 1,000, which we participate in. This was people coming out of the Federal institutions where they train people in upholstery and industrial power sewing machine operators. We hire anybody that is interested in coming to work for a career after they understand our job opportunities, and so forth, and anybody that wants to come to work for us, we hire.

MR. GLICKSTEIN. Do you hire a lot of people that just come to the door?

MR. REAGAN. Yes, I do. I hire most of my work force from people coming through the door.

MR. GLICKSTEIN. Do you have many Negro applicants?

MR. REAGAN. Not too many, no.

MR. GLICKSTEIN. Why do you think that is?

MR. REAGAN. Well, I think they probably might figure it's too far to come and maybe they—the ones that do come out seem to go General Motors or Ford. Most of them, I understand that commute to General Motors or Ford have moved to the Lupinus area around there.

Mr. GLICKSTEIN. You said your starting salary is $1.80 an hour?

Mr. REAGAN. Yes.

Mr. GLICKSTEIN. Do you know if the starting salary at General Motors or Ford is higher?

Mr. REAGAN. I think it's around $3.

Mr. GLICKSTEIN. Would it help your labor market, Mr. Reagan, if there was more low and moderate-income housing available in your area?

Mr. REAGAN. I will say this: I think that probably in certain job classifications we might be able to draw, say if there was older housing. Don't forget, when we moved into the Fremont area, the population was only around 20,000. It's up around 93,000, or almost close to 100,000 right now, so naturally most of the homes are of new construction type, and new construction is in the neighborhood of around $20,000 to $28,000 dollars, in that area.

It's quite difficult for us to attract people at our starting rate that have to live in these type of housing. I post, whenever I receive in the mail, when they build new apartment houses that they are renting for $95 or $110, I'm naturally interested in posting this because some of our people are living—lots of times their wives are working. Incidentally, about 55 percent of our work force is women. Most of these women are working to supplement their husband's income and sometimes when you have this case the husband and wife pool their salaries, and we find a lot of our people are buying $25,000 houses.

But I think if we lived in an area probably and had our plant in an area where there was some older housing, where maybe there would be some cheaper rentals, like in some parts of the country—but there again, in some parts of the country where we have older housing, the apartment demand is such you will find that their rentals are just as high as new apartments. So it's—I am no housing expert. If I was, I'd get in the real estate business, I guess.

Mr. GLICKSTEIN. Has your company considered sponsoring programs to bring low or moderate-income housing into the area?

Mr REAGAN. No, we've never been approached by a program such as this.

Mr. GLICKSTEIN. I have no further questions, Mr. Chairman.

CHAIRMAN HANNAH. Do any of the Commissioners have questions of Mr. Reagan? Mrs. Freeman?

COMMISSIONER FREEMAN. Mr. Reagan, I believe you indicated that your company gave relocation assistance to its employees?

MR. REAGAN. Yes, we do.

COMMISSIONER FREEMAN. Did this relocation assistance include contacting the real estate brokers or Realtors in the neighborhood to help them find housing?

MR. REAGAN. At the time there was only a few real estate people in Fremont, and we made this information known to our people in Pittsburg, who they could contact and where some of the real estate offices were.

Many of our people came down on weekends, a lot of our people moved down about six months prior to the plant opening.

There was no definite agreement set up with any real estate people. The only agreements we had were the people that were actually doing the moving.

COMMISSIONER FREEMAN. Was this same kind of assistance in contact with the real estate industry made on behalf of Negroes also?

MR. REAGAN. Yes, everything was handled 100 percent impartially.

COMMISSIONER FREEMAN. Did the real estate industry indicate to you that there was discrimination in housing with respect to the Negroes?

MR. REAGAN. No, I've never heard it said in Fremont. That is, I never had it brought to my attention.

COMMISSIONER FREEMAN. You have no information that there is discrimination in Fremont with respect to housing of Negroes?

MR. REAGAN. No, I have no definite information. Like I say, we have the one Negro boy that lives in Oakland, a very fine employee, we've considered him for a supervision job. He is thinking of moving to Fremont, and he has been out every weekend looking and we have—another one of our inspectors is a colored boy that lives in Castro Valley, and he is thinking of moving to Fremont. I guess the taxes are going to go up in Castro Valley, so he is thinking of where he is going to locate. But in all the tracts there, there seems to be more and more colored people all the time.

COMMISSIONER FREEMAN. What I want to know is, does your company give the same assistance to its Negro employees that it does to others?

MR. REAGAN. Definitely. We are in the process right now of opening a central milling plant in Shreveport, Louisiana and we are moving many people from our Meridian, Mississippi plant to Shreveport, and we pay the same expenses for anybody.

COMMISSIONER FREEMAN. Do you assist them in finding housing?

MR. REAGAN. Like I say, we pay their moving expense. If it is a member of supervision or a key employee that we are interested in moving immediately, and if we want them—like I say, if it is a key employee that we can't find a replacement for we will move them, and if they say, "We can't sell our house" we will buy the house from them, and this is the only area where we really assist people in moving.

We pay the expenses if we request them to move, but usually almost all our people move on their own.

Sometimes in personnel—some people I have to help more than others. Some people come there every day. You have to help them with legal matters and so forth. I have to get legal counsel for them. Some people, every time they move you have to practically hire the mover for them, work with their Realtor. We are always open to help people like this.

COMMISSIONER FREEMAN. Do you have any Negroes that are considered key employees?

MR. REAGAN. Right now, yes, we do.

COMMISSIONER FREEMAN. How many?

MR. REAGAN. We have two.

COMMISSIONER FREEMAN. Thank you.

CHAIRMAN HANNAH. Other questions? Mr. Griswold?

COMMISSIONER GRISWOLD. Just as a matter of information, what other fringe benefits do you give to your employees?

MR. REAGAN. We have hospitalization, pension. They can purchase furniture at the same price we sell it to a dealer for; the normal things like retirement benefits and hospitalization and so forth.

COMMISSIONER GRISWOLD. Do they qualify for this immediately on employment?

MR. REAGAN. The only thing they don't qualify for immediately on employment, when a person is hired in, like I say, he is put on a 60-day trial period or probationary period. At the completion of his 60-day trial period he is then automatically in the union. We have a union shop.

At the first of the month after they complete 30 days of service their insurance goes into effect. This is a fringe benefit paid for by the Kroehler Manufacturing Company and it is administered through the union as a health and welfare benefit, very similar to our teamsters' insurance.

After they have been there six months they can purchase furniture, pick out a style they want and so forth.

CHAIRMAN HANNAH. Mr. Patterson, do you have any questions?

VICE CHAIRMAN PATTERSON. No, sir.

CHAIRMAN HANNAH. Mr. Reagan, the Kroehler Company operates how many places in the country?

MR. REAGAN. We have about 23 plants right now. We have our main office, which is a large plant, in Naperville, Illinois. We have two large plants in Kankakee, Illinois. We have a large plant in Binghamton, New York. We have a large case goods manufacturing company in Louisville, Kentucky, which was formerly the Mingle Furniture Company. We just acquired two case goods factories—when I am speaking about case goods, I'm talking about dining room furniture and bedroom furniture. We recently acquired two of these in the North Carolina area. We have an upholstering plant in Charlotte, North Carolina. We have an upholstering plant in Dallas, Texas. We have two lumber mills, one in Meridian, Mississippi and one in Shreveport, Louisiana. We have a cover warehouse in Xenia, Ohio and we have an upholstering plant in Xenia, Ohio. We have one in Cleveland, Ohio. I think I've missed one here.

CHAIRMAN HANNAH. That's enough. You operate nationally. Where is your national headquarters?

MR. REAGAN. We have two plants in Canada, sir.

CHAIRMAN HANNAH. Where is your national headquarters?

MR. REAGAN. In Naperville, Illinois near Chicago.

CHAIRMAN HANNAH. Mr. Taylor?

MR. TAYLOR. Mr. Reagan, let me ask you a hypothetical question. What, if during the course of a move by the company a Negro employee came to you and said, "I've worked for this company for a period of time. I'm very happy with my work. I would like to continue to work, but at the place this plant is moving there is not housing available to me and I'm facing discrimination."

What would you do to assist that employee, or would you do anything to assist that employee?

MR. REAGAN. If this is a key employee, now, are you talking about a member of supervision?

MR. TAYLOR. Supposing he's not a key employee. Supposing he's just somebody who has been with the company for a period of time and who is a good worker. I don't know what you mean necessarily by a "key employee."

MR. REAGAN. And we requested him to move?

MR. TAYLOR. No, I'm just saying, I don't know whether you have or you haven't, but this is an employee who has been with you for a period of time. He would like to go with the company, whether you requested him to or not, and he wants your assistance because he is facing discrimination in finding housing.

MR. REAGAN. Let me say this: we have an inter-plant transfer program for employees. We have a lot of employees, back East, after they've been with the company so many years they decide they want to move to California; or we might have people up here in this plant might want to move back to Dallas, Texas, or wherever they come from, Kankakee, Illinois, or want to transfer back to one of the other plants.

They will come into the personnel office and voice this desire and we will tell them that we will contact that plant, see if there are any job openings in their classifications. Many times today in almost all our plants, we don't have any problems this way because it's a similar classification, because when somebody writes me from back East and says they have a qualified upholsterer I would say, "Let me know when he is getting here" because right now we require that many skilled upholsterers. We would write the plant where this employee would like to transfer to, we would find out if they had any job opening in that classification and if they did we would give him a brief description of this man's work record and say, "He would like a transfer there" and so forth.

Then this man if he was requesting the transfer himself, we would not pay his moving expenses. He would be told that he would have to travel on his own time and pay his own moving expenses.

There again, if it is a key employee that we need, say we need a bandsawyer or we need an inspector or a cushion sewer and we ask her or him if he wants to transfer to a certain plant, here we would pay the moving expense. If he says, "Well, I'm having a problem, I can't get a house" we would probably contact that personnel department there and tell them to do everything they could to find this man a place to live, and sometimes we would probably pick up the tab.

MR. TAYLOR. I guess I'm not making myself completely clear. Let me try it a different way.

I understood you to say when your plant moved from Pittsburg to the location that you are now in you were concerned primarily with financial and economic considerations to your company, which I understand. But would you think it appropriate, do you think it appropriate, before you would move a plant from one place to another to find out whether housing is available to all of your employees who may wish to transfer, whether or not you are requesting them to transfer? Do you think that is an appropriate thing for the plant to take into consideration before it moves?

MR. REAGAN. You say we would check to see what housing is available before we make the move?

MR. TAYLOR. I'm asking you whether you think that might be an appropriate thing to do.

MR. REAGAN. I don't think we would build a plant, say 30 miles away from any housing development or naturally we would have a problem drawing a work force.

MR. TAYLOR. But you would build a plant 30 miles away from a housing development that is available to Negroes or members of other minority groups?

MR. REAGAN. I don't know of any place we have ever built a

plant—like I say, our people out of our general office make the decisions and our corporate counsel and so forth. I don't know of any plant or any example such as this. I don't know whether we have ever done anything like that. I have no record of any experience on it.

MR. TAYLOR. Does the city you move into get any benefits from the location of the plant in that city or in that area?

MR. REAGAN. I would say they get the benefit from the payroll.

MR. TAYLOR. Well, do you think that it would be too much to ask the city to make some efforts to provide housing for employees whom they wish to transfer from where they are now to where the plant is coming in? In other words, might not the city be willing to do this in order to receive the benefits it gets from having your plant in its community?

MR. REAGAN. I'd say that if a large plant—I don't know if they would do such a thing for us with only 250 employees. I would say that if we were a large plant moving in with several thousand people I imagine any efficiently run city government would probably go to work and see what they could do about providing housing for a work force that was going to be in that area.

MR. TAYLOR. I have no further questions.

CHAIRMAN HANNAH. Thank you very much, Mr. Reagan. You're excused. Call the next witness.

MR. GLICKSTEIN. The next witness is Mr. Leo F. Smith.

(Whereupon, MR. LEO F. SMITH was sworn by the Chairman and testified as follows:)

TESTIMONY OF MR. LEO F. SMITH, FREMONT, CALIFORNIA

MR. GLICKSTEIN. Would you please state your full name and address?

MR. SMITH. Leo F. Smith, 4262 Central Avenue, Apartment 115, Fremont.

MR. GLICKSTEIN. Where are you employed, Mr. Smith?

MR. SMITH. Trailmobile.

MR. GLICKSTEIN. And what is your capacity there?

MR. SMITH. Personnel manager of the Fremont plant.

MR. GLICKSTEIN. What does your company do?

MR. SMITH. Manufactures truck trailers and freight containers.

MR. GLICKSTEIN. At what skill levels do you hire most of your employees?

MR. SMITH. Generally our minimum requirement is an eighth grade education. So we hire between eighth and 12th grade.

MR. GLICKSTEIN. Your plant was located in Oakland at one time. Is that correct?

MR. SMITH. In Oakland, then Berkeley, now Fremont.

MR. GLICKSTEIN. What was the chronology of those moves?

MR. SMITH. Well, I joined the firm in 1954. They had been in Berkeley, I believe, since 1941 and had moved to Berkeley from Oakland, and I think they went there in '37 or '38·

MR. GLICKSTEIN. When did you move from Berkeley to Fremont?

MR. SMITH. In 1960.

MR. GLICKSTEIN. What was the major reason for this move?

MR. SMITH. Well, of course I wasn't in on the decision as to why the firm moved to Fremont. I do believe that the expansion required a sizable amount of land, and it wasn't possible to buy the land at an economical price in the Berkeley area where it was selling by square foot. We needed 10 times as much land as we had hope for expansion, therefore we had to move further out where land was cheaper.

MR. GLICKSTEIN. How many salaried employees and how many hourly employees did you have in Berkeley?

MR. SMITH. In 1960 just prior to the move?

MR. GLICKSTEIN. Just prior to the move, yes.

MR. SMITH. Four hundred-twenty four hourly employees and 65 salaried employees.

MR. GLICKSTEIN. And do you know how many of those persons were Negro and how many were Spanish surname?

MR. SMITH. I have no knowledge of the Spanish surname, but one year prior to the move I did conduct a survey at the request of the Berkeley office of the Department of Employment and 16 percent of our employees at that time were Negro.

MR. GLICKSTEIN. And how many salaried and how many hourly paid employees are now employed by your plant?

MR. SMITH. Well, we have 259 hourly employees on the rolls. Sad to say only 143 of them are working this morning due to lack of orders, and 55 salaried employees.

MR. GLICKSTEIN. And how many of those employees are Negro?

MR. SMITH. Eighteen of the employees are Negro.

MR. GLICKSTEIN. Eighteen of that total group?

MR. SMITH. Of the 200—well, 259 plus 55, yes.

MR. GLICKSTEIN. So, 18 out of about 310 employees are Negro?

MR. SMITH. Yes.

MR. GLICKSTEIN. And do you know how many are Spanish surnames?

MR. SMITH. Fifty-three, fifty-five because two of them are salaried.

MR. GLICKSTEIN. Did many of your Negro employees, your present Negro employees, work for you when you were in Berkeley?

MR. SMITH. Most of the present Negro employees worked for us when we were in Berkeley.

MR. GLICKSTEIN. They worked for you when you were in Berkeley?

MR. SMITH. Yes.

MR. GLICKSTEIN. Where do most of your employees live?

MR. SMITH. The majority, 10 of the 18 live in Oakland, and then they are spread out between Milpitas, San Jose, Berkeley, East Palo Alto, Hayward.

MR. GLICKSTEIN. How do most of your employees get to work? How do they travel to work?

MR. SMITH. Carpool or individual car generally.

MR. GLICKSTEIN. Do you have any geographic limits on how far you permit an employee to commute?

MR. SMITH. It depends on what our employment needs are. It is true that generally speaking we have not hired further north than Hayward, nor further south than San Jose due to, the fact that we can find people in this area who meet our employment requirements.

However, there has been a situation once or twice over the years since we have been in Fremont where we have gone further north into San Leandro, but very rarely.

MR. GLICKSTEIN. You don't come up to Oakland though?

MR. SMITH. We've never come up to Oakland since we've been in Fremont with one exception. One time we were hard-pressed to find experienced press brake operators, and we did hire one or two from Oakland only with the understanding that they move closer in, which they did. We were concerned about the commute problem on the freeway.

MR. GLICKSTEIN. I believe you said you had 18 Negro employees?

MR. SMITH. Yes.

MR. GLICKSTEIN. Where do they live, do you know?

MR. SMITH. Ten of them live in Oakland, and four of them live in Hayward. One lives in East Palo Alto, San Jose, Berkeley. That's about it.

MR. GLICKSTEIN. And the employees that live in Oakland and Berkeley are permitted to commute because they were with you before you moved?

MR. SMITH. Yes.

MR. GLICKSTEIN. So your restriction on commuting does not apply to employees that were with you in Berkeley?

MR. SMITH. That is correct.

MR. GLICKSTEIN. Do you find that commuting leads to tardiness or absenteeism?

MR. SMITH. Well, perhaps this might be a particular time to insert the story which has been told previously to the Commission representatives.

In March of '61 there was a major tie-up on the freeway system
due to an accident on the Bay Bridge. This caused many tail-end
collisions on the approaches to the bridge, and unfortunately from
our viewpoint, employees who were commuting on one of those
approaches in two cars, five in one car and four in another were
involved in tail-end collisions.

So nine people in our metal department were seriously injured,
and our metal department which is a very critical department in
our operation was handicapped for several weeks because of this.
It was at this time, coupled with the fact that right after moving
to Fremont our employment dropped from 424 to 80 employees,
that we decided that we would restrict our hiring closer to the
plant to try and eliminate the problems of absenteeism due to
freeway accidents.

MR. GLICKSTEIN. Do you think that this restriction has the
effect of limiting employment possibilities for Negroes?

MR. SMITH. I certainly think it could, yes.

MR. GLICKSTEIN. It could have that effect?

MR. SMITH. Yes, it could.

MR. GLICKSTEIN. How do you fill your vacant positions?

MR. SMITH. We list all vacancies with the department of
employment. If the department of employment is unable to meet
our requirements we do advertise.

We also fill by casual drop-ins, employee referrals, and we
notify the union, too, when we have openings on the chance that
they may be able to refer people to us.

MR. GLICKSTEIN. Do you have many Negro applicants?

MR. SMITH. Very few.

MR. GLICKSTEIN. Do you have fewer Negro applicants now than
you did when you were in Berkeley?

MR. SMITH. Oh, yes, quite a few less. I think, if my memory
serves me, we had eight Negro applicants during the first quarter
of this year.

MR. GLICKSTEIN. Your company is a government contractor.
Is that correct?

MR. SMITH. We are a division of Pullman, and Pullman does
hold government contracts. That is correct.

MR. GLICKSTEIN. So your company as Pullman Company is
responsible for complying with the nondiscrimination provision
of the Federal Executive order.

MR. SMITH. That is correct.

MR. GLICKSTEIN. I have no further questions, Mr. Chairman.

CHAIRMAN HANNAH. Mrs. Freeman?

COMMISSIONER FREEMAN. You understand, do you not, that your
company is located in an area that has racially discriminatory
housing practices, and that the effect of the policy that you have

just indicated results in the exclusion of Negroes from employment in addition to the exclusion from housing.

I would like to know if this discrimination is of concern to you and your company, and if you feel that your company has any responsibility with respect to changing the patterns of the community?

MR. SMITH. Well, I'd like to answer this question to go back for another point in the establishing of policy. Unfortunately, since our company has been located in the Fremont area we have not enjoyed the steady pattern of orders that we hoped would be accomplished when we located there. Therefore, there have been radical peaks and depths to our employment so that we have people who are laid off for considerable periods of time. It has been our experience that the further an employee lives from our plant, the less likely it is that he is going to come back when he is recalled from layoff.

I don't want to have the Commission members think that we are solely concerned just with the commute problem. It's a matter of being practical as to where you are going to get your employees to come back if they live at any great distance. I know this is not a direct response to your question.

COMMISSIONER FREEMAN. That's right, because—

MR. SMITH. But I wanted to explain this because I didn't want it understood that we were solely concerned about freeway problems.

COMMISSIONER FREEMAN. But it is still a fact that less than 1 percent of the population is Negro. Is that right?

MR. SMITH. In Fremont?

COMMISSIONER FREEMAN. Yes, sir.

MR. SMITH. I have no figures on the population in Fremont as far as percentages of minority groups.

COMMISSIONER FREEMAN. That was the other part of my question. Does your company consider that these problems of racial discrimination are any of its concern?

MR. SMITH. It certainly does.

COMMISSIONER FREEMAN. What has it done about it? Has it worked with any groups that are attempting to change the practices, to make them more democratic?

MR. SMITH. No, it has not.

MRS. FREEMAN. Thank you.

CHAIRMAN HANNAH. Mr. Griswold?

COMMISSIONER GRISWOLD. That means you have not tried in any way to provide housing. Is that correct?

MR. SMITH. We've taken no steps with respect to the housing problem.

COMMISSIONER GRISWOLD. And you plan to take no steps in the future. Is that correct?

MR. SMITH. I can't speak for what the company plans are. I know of no such plans. That does not mean that there are no such plans.

COMMISSIONER GRISWOLD. Do you think the company has the same plan for all plants, or just different plans for different plants located in different areas?

MR. SMITH. I think it is determined by plant location.

COMMISSIONER GRISWOLD. By the plant location?

MR. SMITH. Yes.

COMMISSIONER GRISWOLD. So far you've been unable to get any particular interest in housing. Is that right?

MR. SMITH. Interest in housing?

COMMISSIONER GRISWOLD. For Negroes, let's say, for your employees. That the company will go out and try to help its Negro employees get secure housing in that area.

MR. SMITH. No, there has been nothing evidenced to this day on this area.

COMMISSIONER GRISWOLD. Thank you.

CHAIRMAN HANNAH. Mr. Taylor, do you have any questions?

MR. TAYLOR. Mr. Smith, were you personally acquainted with any of the Negro employees when—where was your plant? Was it in Berkeley?

MR. SMITH. Yes.

MR. TAYLOR. Were you personally acquainted with any of them?

MR. SMITH. Yes.

MR. TAYLOR. Do you know where they are now, in what job, or if they have jobs with other companies? As I understand the statistics you gave us, at the time you were in Berkeley 16 percent of your employees were Negroes.

MR. SMITH. One year before we moved, that is the last—I only took one analysis at the request of the department, and 16 percent of those were Negroes.

MR. TAYLOR. And now about 6 percent if my arithmetic is correct?

MR. SMITH. Yes.

MR. TAYLOR. So that means that a good number of employees who were at your plant in Berkeley are no longer with the plant.

MR. SMITH. That is correct. White, Negro, any. It doesn't break down to minority groups.

MR. TAYLOR. Well, there is a substantial number of Negroes in that.

MR. SMITH. Yes.

MR. TAYLOR. I was wondering if you know where any of them are now?

Mr. Smith. Oh, certainly. We get employment inquiries from employers who like to check on background. Many inquiries have come in on employees anywhere from San Jose clear up to—into the Berkeley area.

Mr. Taylor. But you are not sure how many of them may be working or how many of them may be receiving salaries in excess of salaries they were receiving, and how many of them may be receiving salaries that are less?

Mr. Smith. Oh, no, I have no exact information on that, specific information, nothing is in my possession.

Mr. Taylor. If your company had been smaller perhaps, and you were in a closer relationship with some of these employees perhaps you would know more about what they were doing or perhaps you would be concerned about where they were now.

Mr. Smith. If our company were bigger and we had the time to spend on this, well, certainly we would have this information. But we have a situation where we—again, the cycles in employment.

I may have an assistant and a secretary one year and the next year I may only have just myself. Therefore, you can't get into keeping track of some of this information which you have just inquired about.

Mr. Taylor. You said that you don't know what your company's views are as to providing low-income housing and providing housing which would meet the needs of Negro employees so that you might have a larger number of Negroes in your work force.

Do you have any personal views on that or is that something you don't care to express?

Mr. Smith. No, I don't mind expressing my personal views. I believe that everything should be done to provide housing for all minority groups.

Mr. Taylor. Has it been a subject of discussion with the company or other officials of the company?

Mr. Smith. I attended a personnel manager's meeting in Chicago in February and at this time it was interesting to me to find that they were having great efforts expended by the company in staffing our plant in West Point, Pennsylvania. They were going to great extremes there to secure employees and bring them in and try and provide housing for them.

Mr. Taylor. Actually go out and find it?

Mr. Smith. Yes.

Mr. Taylor. Do you think that example might be extended to other areas?

Mr. Smith. Well, I frankly think, again a personal opinion, it would depend upon the company's position in adequately staffing the plant. In my own mind, if they're having great difficulty in getting people then their interests would probably be greater in providing housing. But we've never had that difficulty at the Fremont location.

MR. TAYLOR. The reason I ask some of these questions is that what you have had here in the Bay Area and a lot of other places is a series of very small—some very small, some medium sized—communities but a great many communities in one metropolitan area and one of the things that strikes me is that what happens in one community tends to be of very little concern to the other community, and perhaps there are people in your community who sit around and deplore the fact that there may be disturbances in Oakland or there may be a lot of people unemployed in Oakland but there is no meaningful communication between the communities and things that could be done, perhaps, to alleviate the situation are not done simply because people don't seem to think about it, or seem to think they have any relationship to the area. Is that a fair comment? I've only been here a short period of time.

MR. SMITH. No, in general I would certainly agree with this comment. I think that the tendency to put self-interest before community interest is predominant.

MR. TAYLOR. Thank you.

CHAIRMAN HANNAH. Thank you very much, Mr. Smith. You are excused. We will now recess for lunch, and since we are ahead of schedule, instead of convening at 2:15 let's convene at 1:45.

FRIDAY AFTERNOON SESSION
MAY 5, 1967

CHAIRMAN HANNAH. Ladies and gentlemen, the appointed hour is here. The hearing is now in session. Will you call the first witness?

MR. GLICKSTEIN. Mr. Donald F. Dillon.

(Whereupon, HON. DONALD F. DILLON was sworn by the Chairman and testified as follows:)

TESTIMONY OF HON. DONALD DILLION, RETIRED MAYOR, FREMONT, CALIFORNIA

MR. GLICKSTEIN. Would you briefly state your full name and address for the record.

MR. DILLON. Donald F. Dillon, 41932 Passo Padre Parkway, Fremont.

MR. GLICKSTEIN. What is your occupation, Mr. Dillon?

MR. DILLON. I am a grower of citrus trees in a wholesale nursery operation.

MR. GLICKSTEIN. Do you hold any public office?

MR. DILLON. Yes, at the present time I am the city councilman in the city of Fremont.

MR. GLICKSTEIN. You are a city councilman?

MR. DILLON. Right.

MR. GLICKSTEIN. Up until very recently you were mayor of the city of Fremont?

MR. DILLON. That is correct.

MR. GLICKSTEIN. For what period of time did you serve as mayor?

MR. DILLON. From August of 1965 until April of this year.

MR. GLICKSTEIN. Do you know what the population of Fremont was in 1960, approximately?

MR. DILLON. It was in the neighborhood of 40,000 I would say.

MR. GLICKSTEIN. Do you have any idea of what it is today?

MR. DILLON. It's slightly in excess of 90,000.

MR. GLICKSTEIN. You had a special census taken to compile that information. Is that correct?

MR. DILLON. Yes.

MR. GLICKSTEIN. Do you know how many Negroes live in Fremont?

MR. DILLON. No I don't of my own knowledge but I heard earlier today that it was 18 families.

MR. GLICKSTEIN. I believe that was in 1960.

MR. DILLON. I have no idea at the present moment whether it has increased or not.

MR. GLICKSTEIN. Do you have any idea how many Spanish surname people live in Fremont?

MR. DILLON. No.

MR. GLICKSTEIN. Do you know if there is a significant number or a small number?

MR. DILLON. In Fremont I would say in terms of our present population it is a relatively small number but it is a recognizable number. Percentagewise, I would be hard pressed to say.

MR. GLICKSTEIN. Would you describe to the Commission something about the economic and social characteristics of your city?

MR. DILLON. Economic and social characteristics. It is comprised pretty largely of people in the middle-income brackets. We have very few people that I would consider in the poverty area and very few people in the high-income area.

MR. GLICKSTEIN. People in the middle-income brackets?

MR. DILLON. Relatively so, yes.

MR. GLICKSTEIN. What type of industry do you have?

MR. DILLON. The most significant industry that we have is the General Motors plant. We have a branch of Borden Chemical, of Kroehler, the Heil Equipment Company, Trailmobile and so forth.

MR. GLICKSTEIN. Where is the industry coming from? Is it coming from other places in California or from other parts of the country?

MR. DILLON. General Motors was a completely new installation, a much enlarged installation now building Chevrolets, Buicks, Pontiacs, and Oldsmobiles. It previously had been, I guess, most clearly identified as the Chevrolet plant which was in Oakland and, of course, not nearly as large an operation. Borden Chemical and some of the others, I'd say, are new Eastern companies. The Can Manufacturing place is a new business created out of a co-op of fruit canners.

MR. GLICKSTEIN. Are you continuing to attract new industry?

MR. DILLON. I believe the answer to that is yes but not as rapidly as we would like and I haven't found any city in California where they think they have attracted it as rapidly as they'd like.

MR. GLICKSTEIN. Has housing for workers in the Fremont area been a factor in deciding whether to locate or not to locate there?

MR. DILLON. So far as I know this has not been a factor. We have been accused politically for some considerable time of being a bedroom community where we provide the housing for employees coming from other areas where the industries are located.

MR. GLICKSTEIN. Then the industries that came to Fremont were fairly certain that there would be housing available for their workers. Is that correct?

MR. DILLON. I can't answer as to what their knowledge or attitude about housing, per se, was. I have not discussed it with any of them nor they have not raised the question with me.

MR. GLICKSTEIN. I imagine there are officials in the city charged with the responsibility of trying to attract new industry and induce companies to come to Fremont. Is that correct?

MR. DILLON. Yes.

MR. GLICKSTEIN. And is housing a subject that those officials might talk over with industry thinking of locating in Fremont?

MR. DILLON. So far as I know this has not been a major discussion point. Availability of a work force and general wages information is available through our Chamber of Commerce, through our statistics and so forth.

MR. GLICKSTEIN. Does Fremont have a city plan?

MR. DILLON. Very decidedly.

MR. GLICKSTEIN. Does that provide sufficient opportunity to build low and moderate-income housing?

MR. DILLON. The answer to that I would have to say is this depends entirely upon the market. Our planning determines the land use and the thoroughfare plan so that we designate certain areas for commercial development, residential development, and industrial development. But as far as providing means through the plan by which this would become exclusive residential and this would become low-cost housing, *per se,* we have no techniques by which we could accomplish this.

MR. GLICKSTEIN. You don't do that under the plan?

MR. DILLON. No. The closest we would come would be to predetermine the numbers of families to an acre of ground over broad planning areas.

MR. GLICKSTEIN. Does the plan permit the construction of federally assisted housing?

MR. DILLON. There is nothing in the plan which would prohibit it.

MR. GLICKSTEIN. If there were a sponsor of a Section 221 (d) (3) project, for example, there is nothing in the plan that would prohibit that type of housing from being built?

MR. DILLON. Not that I am aware of. The only thing I can think of is if it might come in conflict in some way with say, there's a density factor. In other words, there's so many families per acre that this would be below or in excess of the densities we have prescribed and I think that even in these instances we would probably be able to accommodate them. We have what we call a planned district by which we can work with the developer in the sense of throwing off the ground rules of customary zonings and if someone comes forward with a plan of sufficient size, in excess of five acres that is comprehensive, maybe involving this mixtures of housing types, these can be accommodated. In fact, we have been criticized by some of the developers for having pressed this approach too much where we've been accused I'd say of almost insisting that in order to get something approved, you have to go into a planned district.

MR. GLICKSTEIN. As I understand the way the Federal housing program operates, for a community to be eligible to participate in those programs, it has to have a Workable Program. Does Fremont have such a program?

MR. DILLON. It must have a Workable Program? For what reason?

MR. GLICKSTEIN. It has to demonstrate to the housing authorities the nature of the plan, the manner in which housing is going to be constructed, recreation facilities, use of open spaces and so on and have that approved by the housing administration before future applications or other Federal housing programs can be accepted. Do you know if Fremont has prepared a Workable Program?

MR. DILLON. I don't know that I can answer the question and I'm not entirely certain I understand it. We have our plan, a comprehensive plan. It does account for open space and its utilization. It has been approved by the State Planning Office and it's to this fashion that we have obtained our seven grants. Now if you're talking about a program beyond that one, I'm not aware of it, of whether or not we have one.

MR. GLICKSTEIN. Has there been any resistance by Fremont residents with respect to construction of low-cost housing?

MR. DILLON. I think the answer to that would have to be yes. It depends again on what definition is given to low-cost. We had a planned district proposed which would have provided housing on a 30-acre parcel. Prices would have been in the range of about $16,000-$17,000, fairly high density, but excellent living environment. There was opposition to this proposal in the community.

MR. GLICKSTEIN. Why do you think there was such opposition?

MR. DILLON. Misunderstanding.

MR. GLICKSTEIN. In what sense?

MR. DILLON. There was a concern, I think a fear, that something devious was going on and this might tend to encourage too many, shall we say, of low-income families coming into the community.

MR. GLICKSTEIN. Did the arrival of the General Motors plant in Fremont create concern in the community that some of the workers might be moving in?

MR. DILLON. I think there was more concern about this before it came to Fremont than subsequently.

MR. GLICKSTEIN. There was more concern before the plant came in?

MR. DILLON. And apprehension.

MR. GLICKSTEIN. What were the people afraid of?

MR. DILLON. I think they were probably concerned that there would be an avalanche, so to speak, of minority groups moving into the community.

MR. GLICKSTEIN. Was anything done by the city to counteract this feeling?

MR. DILLON. Well, as an official program, no. This is the sort of thing that you hear on street corners and in stores and so forth. I came across some of this sentiment in campaigning on behalf of another candidate just ringing doorbells. The questions that were asked me, the concerns that were expressed by people led me to conclude this.

MR. GLICKSTEIN. Mr. Dillon, how many municipal workers are employed by the city of Fremont?

MR. DILLON. Oh, we've just completed a survey for this agency which has this information. I will use some of this if I may. Under date of April of this year, 315.

MR. GLICKSTEIN. Three hundred-fifteen municipal employees. Does Fremont have a residence requirement for city employees? Do you have to live in Fremont to work for the city?

MR. DILLON. There is no residence requirement.

MR. GLICKSTEIN. There is no residence requirement. Do you recruit outside of the city?

MR. DILLON. Yes.

MR. GLICKSTEIN. How many Negroes does your study show are employed by the city?

MR. DILLON. None.

MR. GLICKSTEIN. And how many Spanish surname persons?

MR. DILLON. Twenty-nine.

MR. GLICKSTEIN. In what sort of jobs are these Spanish surname persons employed?

MR. DILLON. We have seven on streets and highways, seven in the police, and 15 in fire.

I might mention that we had a planner that showed great promise, who happened to be a Negro, and he came to work as a junior planner and hadn't been with us for more than a month, if he ever actually got on the job, and he was called into active duty. He was a very promising young man and we were looking forward to having his point of view present in the community, especially in the planning department, but we are looking forward to the time he gets out again, hoping he will come back.

MR. GLICKSTEIN. You said you don't have to be a city resident to apply for a city job?

MR. DILLON. Right.

MR. GLICKSTEIN. But if a person that doesn't live in Fremont is hired is he then required to move to the city?

MR. DILLON. Our regulations are such that we do require him to live in the city. We do have a number of individuals, and I can't find my notes here right at the moment, they're probably right on top, where we have people for whom waivers have been granted in connection with residence requirements.

MR. GLICKSTEIN. Your rules do permit that?

MR. DILLON. Yes. We have at the moment 15 such employees. Eight are probationers, and rather than require them to move in before they have tenure, so to speak, they are presently on waiver.

MR. GLICKSTEIN. Would it be a ground for waiver if an employee told you that it was impossible for him to find housing in Fremont? Would that be a ground for waiver?

MR. DILLON. Conceivably it would be. I couldn't tell you the specifics. That is handled by our staff, and we have had—I have had little complaint brought to me, I would say, or so far as I know of any of the other councilmen that this authority, you might say, has been used arbitrarily or in some fashion as to discourage a person from either applying or being able to continue his employment by the city.

MR. GLICKSTEIN. Mr. Dillon, I understand that during the past year you've been chairman of the Alameda County Mayor's Conference. Is that correct?

MR. DILLON. Correct.

MR. GLICKSTEIN. Based on this experience do you think that metropolitan or regional government of some sort can be effective in solving urban and suburban housing problems?

MR. DILLON. I'm not certain whether it can solve urban and suburban housing problems. I think it can deal very effectively with many problems. It would depend entirely, of course, on the authority which was given to it.

MR. GLICKSTEIN. Would you be in favor of some super-government, or would you be in favor of the various cities in the area giving up their governing authority to a super-government of some sort?

MR. DILLON. Those are handles that I try to avoid. Super-government can be a bad thing used in that way. It depends on what visions it conjures up.

I think that a regional government is an essential thing to deal with problems which cities individually have been unable to deal with, and I think that it should serve as a means by which governments, local governments, could work together with some authority to solve regional problems.

If this is a definition of a super-government, then I am for one of those. If it is a new layer of the government which is not responsive either to the local people or to the local elected representatives, then I'm not so much in favor of it.

MR. GLICKSTEIN. One final question. The Staff Report this morning indicated that there are some 5,200 employees at General Motors and about 1,000 of them are Negro. Do you know if there have been any efforts by these Negro employees to obtain housing in Fremont?

MR. DILLON. Yes. Now these will be opinions, of course, and hearsay or information that I have received, but in talking to members of the union, official organizations so to speak, some of the workers have attempted to find housing. Some moved into Fremont with, from what I understand, not a great amount of difficulty and have since moved out again.

MR. GLICKSTEIN. Do you have any idea how many Negro workers moved into Fremont?

MR. DILLON. I do not. The figures that were prepared by a member of the union who is on our city human relations commission, Mr. John Herrera, indicates a pretty small number. There are only three presently, excuse me, this is 1964 information. He only had three out of a possible 950 Negro employees who were living in Fremont. There is no apparent explanation in this report.

MR. GLICKSTEIN. And the other Negro employees that worked for General Motors were commuting from some place?

MR. DILLON. Right.

MR. GLICKSTEIN. I have no further questions.

CHAIRMAN HANNAH. Mrs. Freeman, do you have any questions?

COMMISSIONER FREEMAN. Mr. Dillon, you indicated that the opposition of the community to the low middle-income housing was that they indicated, the residents indicated, that there might be some devious plan. Was this so-called "devious plan" because they feared that Negroes would move in?

MR. DILLON. Yes. I think the devious plan—and I have described it in this fashion because the General Motors—or not General Motors, but the United Auto Workers Union in Milpitas, you may be aware, created an integrated building, a community, a subdivision called Sunny Hills and this is quite near our southern border, you might say between Fremont and Milpitas. There were rumors afoot that this was really an unannounced effort by the United Auto Workers to create a similar housing development in Fremont.

COMMISSIONER FREEMAN. This reflects that Fremont is a community that is racist and anti-Negro, and also because you said there is such a small percentage of Spanish-speaking Americans, probably anti-minorities in other ethnic groups. Is that right?

MR. DILLON. No, I don't think you can draw that conclusion.

COMMISSIONER FREEMAN. Just anti-Negro?

MR. DILLON. No, I don't think you can necessarily draw that conclusion. It depends on who we are talking about.

We have a human relations commission, one of the first established in Alameda County. We have, as a public policy and I'd like to read it to you, that in the creation of this body adopted by the city council that the public policy of the city of Fremont is to create an environment in which all men, women, and children of the city, no matter what their race, religion, or national origin may be, may live, play, learn, and work; in harmony and in brotherhood in which each person may realize his highest potential, unhampered by discrimination based on race, religion, or national origin. This is official city policy.

COMMISSIONER FREEMAN. This is official city policy. However, there is no such practice in Fremont.

MR. DILLON. By whom?

COMMISSIONER FREEMAN. By the residents.

MR. DILLON. Well, this is an individual thing. There are those who are most sympathetic, and there are others who are not.

COMMISSIONER FREEMAN. The effect, however, is that Fremont could be accurately called an all-white community.

MR. DILLON. I think it is largely an all-white community.

COMMISSIONER FREEMAN. Thank you.

CHAIRMAN HANNAH. Do any of the Commissioners have questions? Mr. Patterson?

VICE CHAIRMAN PATTERSON. Mr. Dillon, did I understand you to say that you had no particular specific conversations with leaders of industries coming to Fremont with respect to the availability of housing for their work forces?

MR. DILLON. Not specifically, no. The concerns that have been expressed, not by the management but by the union, and again largely United Auto Workers, is their concern with transportation. We have no bus system. Workers travel from all over the place by carpool.

We are looking forward very decidedly to rapid transit which will terminate in Fremont. Here again, unfortunately, not down in our industrial zone, but this causes problems for the union, when a member of the carpool doesn't come to work or his car breaks down or one thing or another and there are four or five of those fellows who are in trouble, they're late or didn't show, and so forth. So transportation has been more of a concern as I have run into it than any other factor.

VICE CHAIRMAN PATTERSON. Doesn't it strike you as an odd practice that these leaders of the industries coming to that community would not raise specific questions about availability of housing as well as transportation? Isn't it common practice for an industry to consider this as one of the prime points for investigation in its move?

MR. DILLON. I think that housing *per se* is one part of the problem. I think they do consider the availability of a work force, and in this instance the General Motors work force, a great portion of it, was located, of course, in the southern part of Oakland, and many of those people own homes or rent places and continue to live there and to commute down to our area. This did not appear, so far as I know, as a major problem.

VICE CHAIRMAN PATTERSON. Why did General Motors move that plant from Oakland to Fremont?

MR. DILLON. One factor, they are occupying a site of about 450 acres now. This kind of space was not available for expansion at their former locations. Our planning encouraged them, I am told, by virtue of the fact we have a plan which has held up. Our industrial zones that have been thoroughly identified in the plan and they have been maintained so that there is a degree of isolation between industrial zones and the residential areas and a calculated effort to keep them from getting in one another's hair.

This kind of protection seems to be of great interest to both residents who don't want to live necessarily across the street from a manufacturing plant and the industries, we find don't care for it either, to have residents across the street. So these two factors at least have been significant.

VICE CHAIRMAN PATTERSON. One final question. You mentioned that there was fear in Fremont of an avalanche of minority groups moving in once a few did move in. That this fear tended to diminish once they became familiar with minority groups. I think this is one of the phenomena of all our lives that we are afraid of what we don't know, especially in this human area. We do tend to lose our fear.

This is certainly true of my native South, the more we know. I wonder if you would reflect from your own term in public office and your familiarity with this problem what might be done about this fear that is felt in order to diminish it more rapidly?

MR. DILLON. I wish I had a nice, neat answer to that question, sir. I don't.

VICE CHAIRMAN PATTERSON. There is no neat answer. I thought you might have a special thought on it.

MR. DILLON. I can only speak for my own personal experiences, and they have not been vast in this regard.

I am fairly active in the Congregational Church and we have a number of other churches in the Oakland area which are associated, which are Negro churches, of this faith, and we have had opportunity in this fashion to get together and to get to know each other and it's still pretty superficial relatively, but it is an essential part of it.

Our youngsters from our area are working as volunteers in some of these churches and so on and I feel we have greater strides being made by the young people in our community than some of us older ones.

VICE CHAIRMAN PATTERSON. Thank you.

CHAIRMAN HANNAH. Any other questions? Mr. Taylor?

MR. TAYLOR. Mr. Dillon, has the city of Fremont benefited in any way from the relocation of industry or the location of industry in your area?

MR. DILLON. Yes, the increase in property taxes is a benefit.

MR. TAYLOR. And I take it from what you said that the city has a continuing interest in attracting industry to the area, although it does not seem to be as easy to do this as it was in recent years. Is that right?

MR. DILLON. As easy to do where?

MR. TAYLOR. It doesn't seem as easy to attract industry as it was some time ago.

MR. DILLON. Well, you can forget the last part. It has never been easy any place.

MR. TAYLOR. Doesn't the city have a continuing interest in attracting industry?

MR. DILLON. Yes, sir.

MR. TAYLOR. Do you think that if industry did take a different position from the position it has been taking, if it did say that it was interested in having housing in the community for workers and including minority workers, and if the city joined in that interest, the leaders of the city, the officials of the city, do you think jointly you might be able to overcome whatever resistance there might be in the community to providing such housing?

MR. DILLON. I think it would become easier. I don't think it would ever be "easy."

MR. TAYLOR. But it really hasn't been tried so far. I was wondering whether leadership on the part of industry and leadership on the part of city officials might make a difference?

MR. DILLON. I think it might. Our interest has been as a city in trying to explore what in some areas are considered kind of kooky ideas. This idea of a variety of lot sizes and some thrown off the bounds.

We have established an experimental housing committee consisting of a couple of the members of the city council, a large property owner, land owner, a couple of the builders. The whole course of the inquiry to be whether or not it was possible to create low-cost housing on an experimental basis, what could be done on the part of enterprise, whether new materials, new techniques, changes in city standards, zoning requirements, the building code requirements and this sort of thing; whether we could find a way to produce a livable house, not a cheap house, but an inexpensive house. Not giving in to the desire of—I think all people have to have a place that is fit to live in in our community. They have worked with the University of California in the environmental design or environmental studies group, Ned Eicher's group, working with a Ford grant tried to get some models in these computer arrangements by which they experimented whether or not higher densities per acre, whether you could come up with lower cost housing and the premise that was started in the Cal experiment did not establish this.

Just to put more people in there did not necessarily do this, because the cost then to insure privacy and some amenities, rose on the other hand and you wound up unit costwise, it didn't achieve as much as possible. But there are groups of individuals, such as these builders, who are running a business, and they are trying to make a profit. They sell to the market just the same way a shoe manufacturer or an automobile manufacturer or anybody else tries to build a product to suit a market and still earn a profit to deal with this, and we have some fairly conscientious people who continue to work on it. Now this will still come under criticism in certain quarters.

MR. TAYLOR. There are some new programs now, are there not, which would make available rent supplements or direct subsidies to standard housing which might be constructed on an economic basis but you would be subsidizing a person who does not have adequate income. Has the city been considering that as a means of providing housing to those homes who may not have adequate income?

MR. DILLON. I think the answer to that is no. We have grown in 10 years from a city of 10,000 to a city of 90,000, and the whole thing is geared around the single-family dwelling and they are all owned by somebody. We don't have all this much stuff available to rent, so what is a rent subsidy if there aren't a lot of rentals?

Everybody more or less owns a home, you know, in connection with everybody else he owes money to, but we don't have a lot of rental housing, practically none.

By the same token, we don't have any old housing to speak of. In Niles, one of our sub-areas, there is a section where a certain number, the largest concentration of Mexican American families live and these are old houses that were built before the turn of the century, and the thing gets worse because some of these old houses are on tracts of land that have been on farms and the like, and in the course of development these are torn down, and where do these people go?

I have an employee, a Mexican American lady, first-rate person with 13 kids that lived in an old farmhouse. Well, they don't build houses for 13-kid families anymore. It's gone and she is now receiving some assistance from the county, I believe, in connection with rentals and is now actually in the process of buying a house; but it is not designed, and no house could be, to accommodate 13 kids.

MR. TAYLOR. I don't want to get into a deep discussion of the economics of building housing which would get me lost very quickly. But are high labor costs a major part of the problem of designing housing that would be within the reach of moderate-income families?

MR. DILLON. I don't know a lot about it either. I've seen some studies on this. Labor is a factor that is not tremendous. It's still a substantial figure.

Incidentally, this experimental housing committee had opened up the door, at least an inquiry, to our economic opportunity group in Union City. We have a tri-city arrangement as to whether or not they might be interested in investigating means by which homes could be built with some kind of a self-help operation. In other words, the owner or occupants could help in the construction of the thing with the thought that the talents and the ingenuity of the builders themselves might be lent to such an organization to try and build a house.

Now, this is barely off the ground, and I don't know whether it is practical or not, but these kind of inquiries at least are being made by people in our community.

MR. TAYLOR. You said your community had expanded at what seems to me to be a very rapid rate. Has that resulted in the expansion of the responsibilities of city government and the numbers of employees who are required to carry out the functions of municipal government?

MR. DILLON. Are you saying have we had to increase our number of employees by virtue of our population increase?

MR. TAYLOR. Yes.

MR. DILLON. Yes, we have. We have increased our staff. We are still—you talk to any staff person and he never has enough staff, so our police chief doesn't have enough policemen. Our fire department doesn't have enough firemen. Our building inspector doesn't have enough inspectors and nobody has enough people. So we have not kept pace the staff tells us.

The citizens, on the other hand, you know, they say, "What are all these guys doing up there?"

MR. TAYLOR. But this is an area of growing employment opportunity, not only in your community, but in other communities?

MR. DILLON. Right.

MR. TAYLOR. And if, on the other hand, we have a problem of securing employment for members of minority groups, this might be an area where, if you could get some of your problems licked, you could be providing meaningful opportunity to members of minority groups. Is that correct?

MR. DILLON. That is correct.

MR. TAYLOR. Thank you. I have no other questions.

CHAIRMAN HANNAH. Thank you very much, Mr. Dillon. We are grateful to you. Call the next witness.

MR. GLICKSTEIN. The next witness is Mr. L. A. Mitchell. He will be questioned by Mr. Rubin.

(Whereupon, MR. LEONARD A. MITCHELL was sworn by the Chairman and testified as follows:)

TESTIMONY OF MR. LEONARD A. MITCHELL, LOS ALTOS, CALIFORNIA

MR. RUBIN. Would you state your name and address for the record, please?

MR. MITCHELL. Leonard A. Mitchell, residence address 12700 Border Hill Drive, Los Altos.

MR. RUBIN. Mr. Mitchell, would you tell us where you are employed, please?

MR. MITCHELL. I am the director of industrial relations for the Lockheed Missile and Space Company in Sunnyvale. This is a group division of the Lockheed Aircraft Corporation which is headquartered in Burbank.

MR. RUBIN. How far is Sunnyvale from San Francisco?

MR. MITCHELL. Roughly 45, 50 miles.

MR. RUBIN. And from Oakland?

MR. MITCHELL. From Oakland about the same distance, maybe a little bit further.

MR. RUBIN. What kind of work is the Lockheed Missile and Space Company engaged in?

MR. MITCHELL. We are engaged principally in assistance management and in research development activities in the missiles and space systems field.

MR. RUBIN. What are your duties?

MR. MITCHELL. As director of industrial relations I'm responsible for broadly the people aspects of the operation, the recruitment, the education and training, the labor relations, negotiations of collective bargaining contracts and their administration, the industrial security aspects, the feeding, the safety, wage and salary administration. I think that covers most of my functions.

MR. RUBIN. Is your company a Government contractor?

MR. MITCHELL. Yes, it is.

MR. RUBIN. Could you tell us how much business your company does percentagewise in Government contracts?

MR. MITCHELL. Substantially all of it is on Government contract.

MR. RUBIN. Do you have any idea of the dollar volume of what the contracts would be?

MR. MITCHELL. Oh, our annual sales volume would be this year in excess of $600 million.

MR. RUBIN. Are you also a Plans for Progress employer?

MR. MITCHELL. Yes, we are.

MR. RUBIN. As a Government contractor and a Plans for Progress employer, are you under an affirmative duty to secure equal employment opportunity for minority races?

MR. MITCHELL. Very definitely.

MR. RUBIN. Could you tell us the population of Sunnyvale?

MR. MITCHELL. Roughly 90,000.

MR. RUBIN. Are there many Negroes living in Sunnyvale?

MR. MITCHELL. No, a very small number. I don't have a figure for the Negro population in Sunnyvale, but it is very small.

MR. RUBIN. Are there many Mexican Americans living there?

MR. MITCHELL. Well, very, very few Mexican Americans also in Sunnyvale.

MR. RUBIN. Are there a sizable number of Negroes or Mexican Americans living in any nearby communities?

MR. MITCHELL. Yes. The nearest community where there is any significant number of Negroes is East Palo Alto which is, oh, 10 miles, 15 miles from our facility in Sunnyvale. There is a substantial number there.

MR. RUBIN. Earlier this week we took testimony that East Palo Alto had a population roughly of 25,000, of which 80 percent were Negro. Do you have reason to dispute that?

MR. MITCHELL. I have no knowledge of it, so it is undoubtedly accurate. I just don't know. I was going to say that in San Jose there is a significant number of Mexican Americans. We don't have really up-to-date census figures, but the latest figures I have, and I think these reflect the 1960 census which is the latest available, but some studies recently indicate that the figure is in excess of it now and would indicate roughly 10 percent of the population in Santa Clara County is Mexican American.

MR. RUBIN. Do you know how many Mexican Americans there are in San Jose?

MR. MITCHELL. I don't know. The figures I have as a total for the Mexican American population in Santa Clara County is 93,000, and please understand that this may not be very accurate. It is the best figure I was able to get, but I don't have any figures that would indicate the geographical dispersion of the 93,000. Certainly, I believe most of them live in San Jose.

MR. RUBIN. Can you tell us how many employees you have at your Sunnyvale facility?

MR. MITCHELL. The count as of March 25 of this year was 24,332. When I say "Sunnyvale" I mean there our Bay Area facilities. We have a number of facilities in the Sunnyvale vicinity, not all located in Sunnyvale exactly but generally speaking in Santa Clara County.

Our research laboratory is located in Palo Alto, so the figures I give you there of 24,000 plus is the total employed in all of these facilities in what we call the Bay Area Complex.

MR. RUBIN. How many employees would you have at the Sunnyvale facility itself?

MR. MITCHELL. Well, I don't have that figure with me. I can give you an approximation. Oh, lets say roughly 22,000, but please understand when I say Sunnyvale facility I don't know— well, you were there so are aware that there is quite a complex of buildings there in the one location.

And, in fairly adjacent areas, probably 10 or 15 others, so that the total of those is really the significant figure and that would be somewhere in the neighborhood of about 24,000 more or less.

An overwhelming majority of that 24,000 would be in that general geographic area.

MR. RUBIN. Could you tell us the number of Negro employees you have?

MR. MITCHELL. As of this same date the count is 402.

MR. RUBIN. Would that be somewhere between 1 and 2 percent of the total?

MR. MITCHELL. 1.7 percent.

MR. RUBIN. And how many Spanish American employees?

MR. MITCHELL. 1,319 which is 5.4 percent. I mention, too, if it is of interest, 643 Orientals, which is 2.7 percent.

MR. RUBIN. Mr. Mitchell, your reports on equal employment opportunity to the Federal Government indicate that the percent of Spanish American employees declined from January 2, 1965 to December 24, 1966. On January 2, 1965 you had 1,035 Spanish Americans out of 23,264 employees, and on December 24, 1966, there were 984 out of 26,951. Mr. Chairman, I would like to introduce these reports into the record as Exhibit No. 31.

CHAIRMAN HANNAH. They are received.

(Whereupon the documents referred to were marked Exhibit No. 31 and received into evidence.)

MR. RUBIN. Would you comment on the reasons for the decline?

MR. MITCHELL. I can make some general explanations, yes. I can't offer any specific explanation of those temporary fluctuations. In an operation as large as ours we are having continual fluctuations up and down. Just to illustrate that, here about three or four years ago our total employment within the company was at the level of about 32,000 and we contracted within a period of about 18 months down to the level of about 22,000.

Additionally, you must understand that we are engaged, as I mentioned earlier, principally in the research and development activity. We are not, in a typical sense, a manufacturing operation.

We are engaged in the performance of literally hundreds of research and development contracts. Many of these are extremely short-term, so that they are phasing out and phasing in continually, and sometimes in a very short cycle.

The cumulative impact of this is that you have some contractions in specific areas, and these contractions are happening at the same time that in other areas you are on an extensive expansion program. So the only generalization that I can offer by way of explanation is that apparently in some of the areas in which the Mexican Americans were employed, there must have been some impact of contraction and they were affected by this.

Then, as the later figure that I mentioned here indicates that in those probably generally the same types of areas there has since been this very significant expansion. That's going on all the time.

MR. RUBIN. Has the percentage of Mexican American, Spanish American employees significantly risen during the past five years?

MR. MITCHELL. Well, the data that I have here reflects a breakdown in the Bay Area only since 1964 and the percentages there as of 1964, '65, '66 were 4.7, 4.3 and 3.8. Then this most recent figure is 5.4. So it is only this recent figure that shows an increase that happens to be a significant one.

MR. RUBIN. Can you tell me how far the community of East Palo Alto is from the Sunnyvale area?

MR. MITCHELL. In the neighborhood of 10 to 15 miles, thereabouts.

MR. RUBIN. Have you made any affirmative efforts at the East Palo Alto schools to recruit Negro employees?

MR. MITCHELL. Well, in the East Palo Alto area there is a high school, Ravenswood High School, and we are not, by the nature of our business, able to offer opportunity to people who have, generally speaking, high school backgrounds.

MR. RUBIN. Aren't more than 4,000 of your employees in the clerical-secretarial group?

MR. MITCHELL. Well, there again, I can't tell you how many we have totally in the clerical group. I can talk in some specifics about the lesser skilled clerical jobs. Broadly I can just generalize to illustrate the nature of our business by saying that 62 percent of our employees are salaried and by policy we pay on a salary basis employees who are in executive, administrative, professional capacities and exempt from fair labor standards requirements, so this illustrates the overwhelming percentage of our people that are in that kind of work.

To get back to your question, in regard to recruiting in the schools in the East Palo Alto area. As I mentioned, because we are not able to offer significant opportunities for employment to people of high school backgrounds, we have not, to my knowledge, had any contacts with Ravenswood High School except of the nature we have with high schools generally in that area, counseling, et cetera. We do have a significant amount of involvement with an organization that you may be familiar with in that area, OICW, Opportunities Industrialization Center West, which is located in East Palo Alto and which has been working now for some period of time in an effort to offer training to people who need training in order to be qualified for entry level jobs. We provided—as a matter of fact, we have two of our people on their advisory council and from the inception of the organization we have provided a substantial amount of equipment.

We trained one of their people who is to be later an instructor, by hiring him on a summertime basis, and then he went back and worked in solder training, and we still at this time have in that center solder equipment and the solder instructor is on our payroll now on a half-time basis, although he is working full time in OICW. So we have provided significant help there to the work of that organization.

MR. RUBIN. Mr. Mitchell, can you tell us approximately what percentage of the economy of the Sunnyvale area the Lockheed Missile and Space Company would account for, directly or indirectly, from salaries and wages? Subcontracts?

MR. MITCHELL. I can't give you an answer to that question. You asked that when you made the contact a few days ago. I have done some questioning in an attempt to come to a figure like this, but I haven't been able to do it.

The reason, I guess, is that so many of the people who work in the immediate area do not live in the immediate area. The contracts that are given to subcontractors, suppliers—we have a great many of those—are farmed out. The work is farmed out over sometimes quite a broad area, so I haven't been able to do it.

MR. RUBIN. Would you say it is a significant impact?

MR. MITCHELL. Yes, there's no question about that.

MR. RUBIN. Does your company recruit minority group employees from outside the Sunnyvale area?

MR. MITCHELL. Yes.

MR. RUBIN. Apart from the Ravenswood High School?

MR. MITCHELL. Are you speaking of specifically minority employees?

MR. RUBIN. Yes.

MR. MITCHELL. I'll answer yes, but I would like to enlarge a little bit on the reply.

We have used, to a limited degree, recruiting in Negro colleges this current school year that started last September. We have done recruiting at Tuskegee, Florida A&M, Texas Southern, and Tennessee A&I. We have from time to time during the past years recruited in additional schools, but the results have not been significant, and so we are contacting fewer now than we formerly did.

Partly this is because our Georgia Division located in Marietta is trying to concentrate on the schools generally in the Southeastern part of the United States and to avoid unnecessary expense and duplication of effort they're doing a bigger job than we are.

With regard to specific recruiting aimed at minority employees, we have from time to time used some of the publications in Oakland and San Francisco. If I can find them I have a list of those. I can't vouch for the current accuracy of the information. I was given this by our employment manager on this basis: that he has used recruiting advertising in these publications from time

to time—Sun Reporter, California Voice, Ravenswood Post, OICW
News, Project, and Ebony. But we do a substantial amount of
advertising in the Oakland Tribune and in the San Francisco
daily newspapers, and this advertising, of course, is aimed at
just anybody who's qualified to apply.

MR. RUBIN. When you recruit employees do you assure them
that you will be able to find suitable housing for them in the
Sunnyvale area?

MR. MITCHELL. No.

MR. RUBIN. Do you maintain a list of available housing in the
surrounding area?

MR. MITCHELL. No, we don't. We are not involved in the housing
aspects at all.

MR. RUBIN. You don't attempt to raise with public officials the
question of the availability of housing on a nondiscriminatory
basis?

MR. MITCHELL. No. I'm sure that from time to time during the
interviews with prospective employees, and we've had to do a
nationwide recruiting job in most areas because of the fact that
the types of people with the rather highly specialized backgrounds that we seek are being sought generally throughout the
country and are in short supply, so we are on a nationwide recruiting basis and unquestionably these questions frequently are raised
with respect to matters of schools, houses, churches, all of these
types of things, taxes, costs, and I think that the observation
would have been made undoubtedly by our employment people,
and accurately, that housing of a wide variety is generally
available in a wide variety of communities.

MR. RUBIN. Mr. Mitchell, what has been the experience of your
company with the employees obtained through the Opportunities
Industrialization Center West? First would you describe that
organization for us?

MR. MITCHELL. In general terms I can. It is now staffed by
professional full-time people, and has a fairly good size staff.

MR. RUBIN. Is it federally funded?

MR. MITCHELL. Federally funded substantially, yes, but not
entirely. It is funded in part by contributions from local organizations, but mostly federally funded. This director has the advantage of a council that is provided by an advisory group, which is
comprised of representatives of the various business firms generally around the area, and these, hopefully, will give him input
that will reflect what the training needs are, tying in with the
job requirements of those various employers throughout the area.

Then the OICW is attempting to offer training opportunities
to people, and again substantially in the area of people unskilled
and unemployed, aimed at giving them not any highly specialized
skill at all, but just entry level skills, and then referring them,

when they have completed the course of training, to the various employers in the area for consideration, or referring them through employment offices or through other agencies.

Pardon me, you asked, too, what our experience was with employees obtained through the Opportunities Industrial Center West?

MR. RUBIN. Yes.

MR. MITCHELL. We have had a number of people who have been trained in the OICW, and who have been referred to us for consideration, and, broadly speaking, I'm sure it is accurate to say that the people that we received from that organization have been very satisfactory.

MR. RUBIN. Could you describe your vocational improvement program to us? Could you give us the characteristics of the trainees and type of training program that they go through?

MR. MITCHELL. I'd be very happy to do that. We started this program late last year. We started out to call it the hard-core unemployed program, and we didn't like the connotation of hard-core unemployed, we felt the connotation would generally be unfavorable, so we have used a different name, the VIP, because that has a good connotation, and we have labeled it the Vocational Improvement Program.

Our objective in this program is to bring in people hopefully who have been given some preliminary training by organizations such as OICW, who have been screened by such organizations and identified as people that they would care to propose for some further training, and then to offer to these people who are first offered for consideration and then selected, some additional training, first full-time training, classroom type or shop-type training, but they go on the payroll as soon as they are referred to us from an organization such as OICW, and continue that training for a period that is intended to be I think it's four weeks.

Then following this period of classroom training, they will be referred to one of the organizations for a period of on-the-job training in an area for which they have been getting this preliminary training. They still at this point are not skilled but they have some marginal skills. And during this follow-up period of six weeks they will be assigned to a supervisor and we are going to try to stay closely in contact with them with the instructor who has been working with them during this initial period so that they will be given the benefit of just the best we are able to give in the way of training and counseling.

After they have been on the job, then for a period of six weeks we will bring them back in on a part-time basis, to the education and training organization and give them over a period of weeks about 50 hours more classroom organization instruction which will be aimed at correcting some of the deficiencies that have been identified during this period of six weeks on the job. We have just gotten started with that and at this point it is an extremely promising program.

MR. RUBIN. Are many of these employees people with arrest records?

MR. MITCHELL. Yes. When we established the program it was in line with the commitment which our president, Dan Haughton, had made to Vice President Humphrey that we were going to do something aggressive in attempting to tackle this "hardcore" unemployed program, so we are aiming at trying to bring into this program probably 75 percent of the people who are in the minority races and about 25 percent of the trainees we are expecting to select from those who have some sort of police records.

MR. RUBIN. How many employees do you have presently in the program and how many do you hope to have?

MR. MITCHELL. We have had four that completed the initial part of the training and are now going on into the on-the-job part of the training. We have added eight more. Would you be interested in a little bit of descriptive background?

MR. RUBIN. I'm afraid we don't have too much time for that. If you like, you could submit it to us or any statement that you'd like into the record.

I have no further questions.

CHAIRMAN HANNAH. We will take whatever else you may have that you want introduced into the record, sir, if you will just give it to us.

MR. MITCHELL. Thank you.

CHAIRMAN HANNAH. Mrs. Freeman, do you have a question?

COMMISSIONER FREEMAN. Yes. Mr. Mitchell, your testimony was that your company is about 100 percent Government contract?

MR. MITCHELL. Yes.

COMMISSIONER FREEMAN. Constituting a value of $600 million, and of these employees 1.7 percent are Negroes and none of them lives in the locality in which the company is located?

MR. MITCHELL. Pardon me. May I correct that, the last statement? You say none of whom—

COMMISSIONER FREEMAN. Live in the locality.

MR. MITCHELL. I can't say that because I just don't know it to that degree of exactness. Some of them may live exactly in Sunnyvale. I just don't know.

COMMISSIONER FREEMAN. I was wondering how realistic the nondiscrimination clause in employment can be as long as the company does not concern itself with the problems of housing.

Let us take a hypothetical situation and assume that there was another company in the United States that could perform the same services for the United States Government, but then it could also say that "The employees of this community will live in the community and can find a house and without being the victims of discrimination in housing." Would that possibly constitute a reason for Lockheed Company becoming concerned about the shelter of its employees?

MR. MITCHELL. No, I don't believe so. I don't believe that housing is in any sense a limiting factor on our employment and utilization of minority personnel. To understand that, of course, it is necessary to refer again to the nature of our work. We don't have many low-skilled, lesser-skilled types of jobs.

COMMISSIONER FREEMAN. I'm referring to your statement that you had gone to colleges, to the predominantly Negro colleges to recruit?

MR. MITCHELL. Yes.

COMMISSIONER FREEMAN. I don't suppose you would be recruiting low-skilled and unskilled persons from these colleges?

MR. MITCHELL. No.

COMMISSIONER FREEMAN. They would possibly be engineers. Suppose they said, "Where will I live?" What would your person say to him?

MR. MITCHELL. He would be able to say, and I'm sure he does say, that there is a big variety of places in which he can live.

COMMISSIONER FREEMAN. Except Sunnyvale?

MR. MITCHELL. No. If you got the impression that Sunnyvale is an area where a Negro can't live or doesn't live it's my fault. I didn't intend to give that impression. I'm sure there undoubtedly are Negro families and Mexican American families living there. But the question directed to me was just how many Negroes and Mexican Americans are living in Sunnyvale and I just don't know. There is only 1 percent of Negroes in Santa Clara County, but across the county line in East Palo Alto, San Mateo County, that is the nearest concentration of which I am aware of Negro personnel. But there are Negroes and Mexican Americans and other minority personnel living throughout the area.

COMMISSIONER FREEMAN. Do the white employees of Lockheed live in Santa Clara County?

MR. MITCHELL. Yes, substantially all. I was asked if I could get some figures regarding the geographical dispersement of the employees and I have that. Well, I don't find it right now. It's in the neighborhood of about 88 or 89 percent of all of our employees who live in Santa Clara County, all of our employees.

COMMISSIONER FREEMAN. So if he is white he can live in Santa Clara County?

MR. MITCHELL. Or if he is Negro or Oriental or any other race.

COMMISSIONER FREEMAN. There is no discrimination in housing in Santa Clara County?

MR. MITCHELL. Well, no, certainly I would not say that. I would
say that on an individual basis you can find almost anything, but
what I am saying is that there is a big variety of housing available, and in a big variety of locations, so in my honest judgment
it is not a limiting factor on our utilization of minority personnel.

CHAIRMAN HANNAH. Mr. Rankin?

COMMISSIONER RANKIN. I lived in Los Altos in 1940. Is it open
to Negroes to live in Los Altos now?

MR. MITCHELL. Well, I don't know how I can answer that. I
live in Los Altos, too. I happen to know that there are Negroes
living both in Los Altos and in the Los Altos Hills, and the Los
Altos Hills are across the tracks, as you know, and are supposed
to be substantially more expensive. So I couldn't say officially
one thing or the other.

I'm sure if there is any official designation it's open, but the
houses are certainly more expensive in some of those areas than
in others, and this of course presents a very limiting factor.
But a person's ability to buy a home is pretty much an individual
thing and as you know, we are fortunate in this respect, that the
Eichler Homes which have been tremendous, very large all over
in the Bay Area community, have traditionally, right from the
start, because he felt so keenly about this, been offered on the
basis of complete nondiscrimination. So there are a lot of homes
available throughout a variety of communities.

CHAIRMAN HANNAH. Dean Griswold, do you have a question?

COMMISSIONER GRISWOLD. No.

CHAIRMAN HANNAH. Mr. Patterson?

VICE CHAIRMAN PATTERSON. I believe you have 1.7 percent,
around 400 employees, who are Negro. Is this correct?

MR. MITCHELL. Yes.

VICE CHAIRMAN PATTERSON. Has race not been, or housing
opportunities not been a factor in the recruitment of these people? Have questions come to your attention about "Where will I
live?" among these people?

MR. MITCHELL. Not to me on a personal basis, nor really in my
official capacity so that I believe that this indicates that by and
large there really hasn't been a significant problem.

I'm only aware of really individual problems that have arisen
in that regard, although I would be amazed if there hasn't been
some individually.

We have among these Negroes 69 who are in salaried jobs, and
these, generally speaking, are engineers and scientists. There are
a lot of those and in other capacities, too, and I believe that they've
been able to find adequate housing. I have known of nothing to
the contrary.

VICE CHAIRMAN PATTERSON. The Government contractor, such

as Lockheed, is required to take affirmative action with respect to the employment of minority group employees, and am I correct in judging that you consider it farfetched to suggest that this would carry over into affirmative action on the part of Lockheed to concern itself with the availability of housing in the community where it is located?

MR. MITCHELL. May I answer that this way? We feel that we can make our contribution in the areas where we have both the need and the expertise, and that is in the area here of employment and educational training, and trying to introduce something in the way of added motivation that people need in order to get the extra skills they need to get jobs. So those are the areas where we are concentrating, and we haven't felt that we should get into other areas, one of which is housing.

CHAIRMAN HANNAH. Mr. Taylor?

MR. TAYLOR. On the question of training, what kinds of jobs generally are people who are in the OICW program being trained for? I don't need details; I'd simply like to get an idea.

MR. MITCHELL. Well, assembly helper, factory helper, fabrication helper—that type of thing.

MR. TAYLOR. You have had some experience with a program that trains people—where training is obtained but not directly furnished by the company. Is that right? The company itself doesn't do the on-the-job training at the beginning?

MR. MITCHELL. Not the OICW type training, right.

MR. TAYLOR. It has been suggested that perhaps we could get the job done a lot faster if we turned it over to industry and industry took the reponsibility for training people from the very beginning rather than putting all of the emphasis, or a great deal of the emphasis, on institutional training. I wonder if you have an opinion about that.

MR. MITCHELL. As a matter of fact, this is the thrust of our VIP hard-core program. We will pick up these people and put them on the payroll just as soon as they have had this preliminary which is very short, about three weeks of screening really by an organization such as OICW, or East Bay Skill Center, the Mexican American Opportunity Center, and so on.

From that point on the training will be done by Lockheed. We are hoping to do about 100 of these this year, and a couple of hundred next year, and as many as we are able to absorb. I think this is an effective way to do it.

MR. TAYLOR. Do you have any opinion whether it might be a good idea for the Government generally either to encourage or to require industry to take on this job of training employees in order to meet its obligations under the Executive order?

MR. MITCHELL. I wouldn't like to see them require it, but I

think it is being encouraged right now through MDTA. We have a number of MDTA programs and this, of course, is aimed largely at encouraging on-the-job training by companies who are engaged very heavily in this, so I think the government is very definitely doing this.

In addition, they are doing it further. We are engaged in discussions right now at both the State level and the Federal level with equal employment opportunity personnel aimed at getting a skill center established. I don't know where it would be either Santa Clara, San Jose, or Sunnyvale of the type of OICW, but meeting more nearly the needs of the people in the Santa Clara Valley area and the State government seems to be quite interested in establishing a skill center which will be financed by State funds.

MR. TAYLOR. Thank you.

CHAIRMAN HANNAH. Thank you very much, sir. We appreciate your being here. You are excused. We will now take a 10-minute recess.

CHAIRMAN HANNAH. Ladies and gentlemen, if you will resume your chairs we will proceed. Mr. Glickstein, will you call the next witness.

MR. GLICKSTEIN. The next witness is Mr. George Bradley, an attorney on the staff of the Commission who will deliver a short report.

(Whereupon, MR. GEORGE BRADLEY was sworn by the Chairman and testified as follows:)

TESTIMONY OF MR. GEORGE BRADLEY, ATTORNEY, U.S. COMMISSION ON CIVIL RIGHTS

MR. GLICKSTEIN. Mr. Bradley, will you read your statement, please.

MR. BRADLEY. The United States Naval Air Station located in Alameda, California, employs over 9,000 civilian employees. While exact figures do not exist on the number of minority group employees at the Naval Air Station, estimates are that approximately 23 percent of the employees are Negro, that 3.5 percent of the employees are Spanish American and around 5 percent are Oriental Americans. Although the percentage of Negro and Oriental Americans employed at the base greatly exceeds the percentage of those minority groups in the population of the Bay Area, the percentage of Spanish Americans employed at the base is considerably less than the percentage of that group in the Bay Area.

On February 15, 1967, and on April 1, 1967 the Naval Air Station was picketed by a group consisting largely of Negroes and

630

Mexican Americans. They were protesting alleged discrimination in promotions at the Alameda Naval Air Station.

Statistics supplied to this Commission by the Naval Air Station indicate that out of 319 blue-collar supervisors involved in direct production at the Station, 22, or less than 7 percent, are minority group employees. Of the 74 top supervisory employees, only one belongs to a minority group. There are no minority group employees among the 50 blue-collar supervisory personnel in production facilitating positions at the Station. There is only one Negro, one Spanish American and one American Indian among the 64 white-collar supervisory production facilitating positions for which blue-collar experience frequently is qualifying. Statistics compiled by the United States Civil Service Commission indicate that minority group blue-collar employees, considered as a group, earn approximately the same hourly wages as all employees. But Negro employees, considered separately, earn 92.7 percent of the average. Further, the average grade for Negro white-collar employees is 4.2 while the average grade for all employees is 6.4.

In calendar year 1966 over 2,000 new employees were hired. Although close to 40 percent of this group were minority group members, no data were available as to the income or grade level at which these individuals were hired. Minority groups received 30.8 percent of all promotions made in 1966. Minority group employees, however, received only 15 percent of the 125 promotions to supervisory levels, though they constitute over 30 percent of the total number of employees at the base.

All employees applying for specific promotions are ranked on a register by grade. An employee's grade is computed by assigning points to a written test, his experience and education, and a voucher filled out on each employee by his supervisor. The top employees on the register are considered within the "zone of selection" from which the person to be promoted is chosen. That concludes my report.

MR. GLICKSTEIN. Thank you, Mr. Bradley.

CHAIRMAN HANNAH. Will you call the next witness?

MR. GLICKSTEIN. The next witnesses are Mr. Walter Taylor and Mr. Manuel Alvarado.

(Whereupon, MR. MANUEL ALVARADO and MR. WALTER TAYLOR were sworn by the Chairman and testified as follows:)

TESTIMONY OF MR. MANUEL F. ALVARADO, ALAMEDA, CALIFORNIA AND MR. WALTER C. TAYLOR, BERKELEY, CALIFORNIA

MR. GLICKSTEIN. Would each of you please state your full name and address for the record?

MR. ALVARADO. Manuel F. Alvarado.

MR. GLICKSTEIN. What is your address?

631

MR. ALVARADO. 1618 Walnut Street in Alameda.
MR. TAYLOR. Walter C. Taylor, 2131 Ashby Avenue, Berkeley.
MR. GLICKSTEIN. Mr. Taylor, what is your occupation?
MR. TAYLOR. Presently I am a business manager for the Prince Hall Masons of California.
MR. GLICKSTEIN. Did you ever work at the Alameda Naval Air Station?
MR. TAYLOR. Twenty-five and a half years until March, 1966.
MR. GLICKSTEIN. What jobs did you hold at the Station?
MR. TAYLOR. I started off, in fact, as a laborer, and then to a helper electrician, electrician, and I think about 15 or 20 years following, a lot of years, I was an aircraft examiner electrician.
MR. GLICKSTEIN. Did you serve on any committees on the base that were apart from your usual job?
MR. TAYLOR. Yes. In January 1964 I was appointed to the Commanding Officer's Advisory Committee on Equal Employment Opportunity by Captain T. L. McCabe.
MR. GLICKSTEIN. What sort of a committee was that?
MR. TAYLOR. This committee was to look into the complaints of employees based upon race covered by, as you might know, NCPI 713, at that time which is based on race, creed, color, and national origin.
MR. GLICKSTEIN. That is a directive that prohibits discrimination based on race?
MR. TAYLOR. Right.
MR. GLICKSTEIN. What were your duties as chairman of the committee?
MR. TAYLOR. To interview employees who could substantiate their complaints based on 713.
MR. GLICKSTEIN. Was this a full-time job?
MR. TAYLOR. It was a part-time job. The committee first worked two days a week.
MR. GLICKSTEIN. During those two days you were excused from your normal duties?
MR. TAYLOR. Yes. And then the latter part of the closing two-year period on which I served, we worked pretty much full-time on some days due to the work load of the committee.
MR. GLICKSTEIN. Did you have a staff?
MR. TAYLOR. The committee was composed of originally five Negroes, two Caucasians, one Oriental and one Spanish-speaking person, and there were about six alternates of a racial mixture.
MR. GLICKSTEIN. Did you have a staff or did the members of the committee themselves investigate all complaints and reports that they received?
MR. TAYLOR. The committee's name, indicated by the mixture, was the staff.

MR. GLICKSTEIN. That was the staff?

MR. TAYLOR. Yes, support for our report work was by the technicians and the industrial relations department who typed up reports.

MR. GLICKSTEIN. The technicians of the industrial relations department did your clerical work for you?

MR. TAYLOR. Yes.

MR. GLICKSTEIN. In the course of your investigation of complaints did you discover and report cases of racial discrimination?

MR. TAYLOR. Yes, we did.

MR. GLICKSTEIN. These were cases that the committee investigated and concluded that there was racial discrimination involved?

MR. TAYLOR. Yes.

MR. GLICKSTEIN. What were the charges? Was it discrimination in hiring and promotions?

MR. TAYLOR. I might review two of them for you specifically. One was a Negro GS-3 in the supply department, and she was a clerk-typist I guess in that grade, and she came to the committee—I might say first of all that the committee worked on an informal basis. Part of our duty was to resolve the complaint by the employee, if possible, informally.

MR. GLICKSTEIN. You might in some cases meet with the employee and with the employee's supervisor and work out the situation? Is that right?

MR. TAYLOR. That's right. When a complaint was made we would talk to the employee, and if we were satisfied that the basis of his complaint was race, creed, color, or national origin, then we would accept it and based upon what he had to say then we would call in the supervisor or the other personnel involved to determine the basis of the case and make a report on the same to the commanding officer at the Station.

Now the case that I started telling you about on the Negro woman in the supply department, at the conclusion the committee, I might say, found—our report to the commanding officer was discrimination as an act or failure of action, malpractice, and collusion both in the industrial relations department and management.

At this time it was approximately around June of 1965, under Captain T. L. McCabe.

One of the last acts that Captain McCabe did, was to leave money to have this case further investigated, which came under the current Commanding Officer Captain Duncan A. Campbell. When his investigating officer investigated the findings of the committee as reported briefly, we were not permitted as an advisory committee to see the final report on the facts that we had found and turned in to his office.

MR. GLICKSTEIN. In other words, after your committe completed the investigation and drew up the report that was submitted to the captain's office, the captain's staff conducted its own investigation and came to its own conclusion. Is that correct?

MR. TAYLOR. That is correct.

MR. GLICKSTEIN. And neither supported nor rejected the study of your committee?

MR. TAYLOR. Right.

MR. GLICKSTEIN. Your committee was not the normal method for an employee at the base to process a grievance that he had. There are other methods, aren't there, for processing grievances?

MR. TAYLOR. Yes, the normal procedure which comes under 770 where there is no racial background, the normal grievance proceeding would be followed, which is termed expeditious resolution.

MR. GLICKSTEIN. If any employee had a complaint of racial discrimination and didn't want to go to your committee there are other ways that the employee could have handled that also? Isn't that correct?

MR. TAYLOR. He could go what we call the formal way. Formal grievance.

MR. GLICKSTEIN. This person you have just been talking about who wasn't promoted was a Negro?

MR. TAYLOR. Yes, this was the first one.

MR. GLICKSTEIN. Did you also have complaints regarding the Spanish surname people?

MR. TAYLOR. The cases that we handled were just about according to the racial mixture of the committee. About 50 percent of the cases were Negro, and 25 percent were Spanish-speaking persons, and the other 25 were broken down as Oriental and others, mixtures, including we had one white that had a case on discrimination based on his national origin.

MR. GLICKSTEIN. How many years were you on the committee, did you say?

MR. TAYLOR. Two years.

MR. GLICKSTEIN. And approximately how many reports did the committee file while you were on the committee in which it found there was evidence of discrimination?

MR. TAYLOR. We found two specific cases and, although we had other cases, we were able to resolve them to the satisfaction of the employee.

MR. GLICKSTEIN. In only two specific cases did you find that there had been discrimination?

MR. TAYLOR. Yes.

MR. GLICKSTEIN. And these were referred to the Commanding

Officer? Was further action taken on those cases, or any action taken on them at all?

MR. TAYLOR. In the first case we didn't know what the outcome of that was.

MR. GLICKSTEIN. You inquired about the outcome?

MR. TAYLOR. Right. We were informed that we had certain limitations, that we didn't have a right to see what the former captain had left to be investigated, and in the second instance the case was a Negro machinist who had 23 years' experience, had been on the base for 17 years, in this particular shop for seven years, and he came to the committee based upon that they were trying to rotate him out under the guise that they had read some directive that called for rotation of Negroes. It was just a guise to remove this employee from his particular job where he had been working for seven years and was a machinist instructor, qualified instructor, and had not been permitted to instruct any white employees because he was a Negro.

He had been informed by his supervisors that he was being watched because he was a Negro. This is the basis upon which we accepted his complaint.

In the opening day of the hearing the two supervisors involved, which are now called foremen, their attitude toward the committee was such that we reported it to Captain McCabe and he gave them a verbal reprimand for noncooperation.

In conclusion of the case, as we reported it to the Commanding Officer—this would be under Captain Duncan A. Campbell—his report which he signed shows how the Station avoids discrimination as an act, or failure of action. They had changed the title of the report, wrote around anything that pertains to race, and misdirected the facts and inserted information that was not true and the employee was left right out on a limb because actually what he had in his case when he complained he was set up for what was really a hidden reprisal action.

With the number of years he had and his background they put him on a machine where he was required to make production schedules. You know, the time setting of the machine, et cetera, and no employee prior to him had been required to meet production schedules on this machine.

As a matter of fact, there was none set for the machine. This was the medium that they used in setting the employee up to show that he was not qualified after all those years as a machinist.

MR. GLICKSTEIN. What you are saying then is that in the second case the report that your committee wrote was not concurred in by the captain, and the captain issued a report that came to different conclusions. Is that correct?

MR. TAYLOR. That is correct.

MR. GLICKSTEIN. Did employees on the base when you were there feel free to come before your committee?

MR. TAYLOR. I might say, Mr. Glickstein, in the beginning employees were quite suspicious. It took us about a year to establish communications, at which time we were able to talk with the employees, and a number of supervisors were very friendly toward the program of equal opportunity employment, and we resolved a number of cases which would have been grievances by talking with supervisors and the employees and then bringing them together.

MR. GLICKSTEIN. Mr. Taylor, you stated that you resigned from your position at the Naval Air Station in May of 1966?

MR. TAYLOR. I think in March.

MR. GLICKSTEIN. And you had been there for 23 years?

MR. TAYLOR. Twenty-five and a half years.

MR. GLICKSTEIN. What led to your resignation?

MR. TAYLOR. Well, frankly, I made the mistake of accepting an assignment on the committee on equal employment opportunity. And after learning how the industrial relations and management work together to deny employees equal opportunity I just decided to quit.

MR. GLICKSTEIN. You didn't feel that the committee that you were chairman of was performing a useful function?

MR. TAYLOR. Yes, I did, but we were meeting a lot of opposition in the concluding two-year period, and we determined within ourselves that we were doing more harm to the employees than good because as we tried to work with the employee and resolve his problems, we found out that we were actually harming him because once he came to the committee then he was subject, you know, to hidden reprisal from the supervisors, et cetera. So this is one of the reasons why I just called it quits.

MR. GLICKSTEIN. Were there ever instances when you heard of reprisal?

MR. TAYLOR. Yes, I have. I might cite one example.

As I stated earlier, that we had to confine ourselves to the race, creed, color, and national origin, and when we determined in the early stages of interview with the employees that it was not, then we referred it to the industrial relations department under expeditious resolution. One morning—

MR. GLICKSTEIN. Let me see if I understand you. If you were given a case and you concluded that the employee's problem was not related to race, creed, color, or national origin but might have been related to some other factor, then that case was handled by the industrial relations department?

MR. TAYLOR. Yes. One morning there was a number—about 11 employees who dropped by our office who worked on the graveyard shift. They get off at 8 o'clock in the morning, and we start to work at 7:15. After about five minutes' interview with them —and they were all Negroes—complaining about the work equipment and the reprisal actions and the attitude of the supervisor in that particular cleaning department, we called the industrial relations department in immediately, within five or 10 minutes.

As a result, two men were singled out and fired because they were temporary employees, one who had been injured that week through broken equipment, had a bad scar on his face and an injured back. He was ripped off the base without even having a chance to sign out, so this is a type of reprisal that two employees were given for just stopping by and asking a question.

MR. GLICKSTEIN. Were these instances reported to the captain?

MR. TAYLOR. Yes.

MR. GLICKSTEIN. Mr. Alvarado, would you please state your occupation.

MR. ALVARADO. Right now I am an instructor at the East Bay Skills Center.

MR. GLICKSTEIN. Under the MDTA training program?

MR. ALVARADO. That is correct.

MR. GLICKSTEIN. Since when have you been instructor there?

MR. ALVARADO. Approximately two months.

MR. GLICKSTEIN. What did you do prior to that?

MR. ALVARADO. I had been at the Naval Air Station for approximately 17 years.

MR. GLICKSTEIN. Have you resigned from your position there or are you on leave of absence?

MR. ALVARADO. No, I'm on leave of absence.

MR. GLICKSTEIN. Were you a member of any employees' groups at the Station?

MR. ALVARADO. Yes, I was a member of the Employees' Council for three years, and also a member of the policy review committee, and also a member of a committee that was brought together as a special committee to oversee what was going on as far as discrimination in hiring and upgrading and grievances at the Station.

MR. GLICKSTEIN. What is the Employees' Council?

MR. ALVARADO. This is a representation of the employee that is brought forth by a directive from the bureau in Washington. They are the representatives of the employee.

MR. GLICKSTEIN. And you said you were also in a group that considered complaints regarding racial discrimination?

MR. ALVARADO. Yes. We convened this committee because we were getting a lot of complaints.

MR. GLICKSTEIN. This committee is an unofficial committee, or was it set up by the—

MR. ALVARADO. It was a splinter of the Employees' Council. We felt that it was necessary to form a committee because we were getting a lot of complaints from the employees due to the inequities in the upgrading.

MR. GLICKSTEIN. Was your committee in competition with Mr. Taylor's committee?

MR. ALVARADO. Well, no. We were more or less working parallel to each other, but we were seeking the same aims. We convened and we started with the industrial relations department and management, asking questions as to how the people were promoted, what guidelines they were using, and they didn't want to give us any information to this effect.

They kind of were reluctant to give us this information, so we proceeded to talk to management and we wanted to know how they were promoting the aircraft instrument mechanic, electronics, which at that time we were getting most of the complaints from that area. So management sent us to IRD and IRD sent us here and there, and finally we wound up back with management.

MR. GLICKSTEIN. IRD is the Industrial Relations Division? Is that correct?

MR. ALVARADO. That is correct. So management finally sat down with us and explained that they were using a new procedure they called the job element approach. So we questioned how they did this, and they explained that they would take and evaluate an employee through procedures that involved three categories of ranking in the experience factor which meant they got either A, B, or C level.

So we questioned how they did this, and they said, "Well, it's up to the prerogative of the person that is ranking him." Which is line management often from where the promotion is going to come down. So then they stated that if he had tests or this type of experience he would fall in A category, which meant more points; and then at an intermediate level was B, which is just an average mechanic and below average would get C. So then we questioned just how they determined this.

So they told us they used the test score, the voucher, and arrived at the type of level that they would give this employee.

MR. GLICKSTEIN. The voucher is the evaluation form that the supervisor fills out evaluating an employee. Is that correct?

MR. ALVARADO. Yes, this is correct. At that time it was secret. The employee could not see what his score was.

MR. GLICKSTEIN. When was that time? At what point was that?

MR. ALVARADO. You mean—

MR. GLICKSTEIN. When was the voucher kept secret? At what time in history?

MR. ALVARADO. This was just up to about three months ago. It was just recently changed where you can see it and sign it.

MR. GLICKSTEIN. Up to that point the employee was not shown the evaluation that the supervisor had made of him?

MR. ALVARADO. No, he wasn't shown this. So then we delved into another area. They were using a supplemental form that they send the employee after he passed the test score on the test, and he was to get the supplemental form, and he was to fill in certain categories as to the type of experience and all the areas that he worked in his particular shop, but the one thing that the employees weren't told at this time was that if he failed to fill in part of this supplemental list he was automatically locked out. So this information was very important to the employee so we told them that they should print this and let the employees know because we knew that some employees were getting this information, and these were the employees that were being promoted.

MR. GLICKSTEIN. You mean this supplemental list that employees were required to fill out was a document that was considered in determining whether to promote employees. Is that right?

MR. ALVARADO. Yes.

MR. GLICKSTEIN. If part of that form was not filled out by the employee through inadvertence or for some other reason that might affect his chance of getting promoted?

MR. ALVARADO. Yes, he was locked out, which meant he was out of contention.

MR. GLICKSTEIN. He wasn't asked why he didn't fill out such and such a form?

MR. ALVARADO. No. This is another area that we asked management and IRD to print this information so all the employees would be aware of this because we knew that some of the employees were getting this information and it was a hush-hush deal. They would come over and tell certain people, "Look, you've got to do this and this, or else you won't make it." So under these conditions, these complaints we asked this information be printed and we met with a lot of opposition from IRD. We also asked them to print the ranking schedule.

MR. GLICKSTEIN. What is a ranking schedule?

MR. ALVARADO. This, like I said, is a form that states how an employee is graded, what numerical value he gets from his test.

MR. GLICKSTEIN. In other words, when there are promotions available, employees are ranked in order to determine who should be selected for the promotion?

MR. ALVARADO. That is correct.

MR. GLICKSTEIN. And they are given a numerical grade, and

they list in descending order of scores and generally the people near the top are the ones from whom the selection is made?

MR. ALVARADO. This is true.

MR. GLICKSTEIN. And the grade that the employee is given on this list is based on his score on the test on the voucher that is filled out by the supervisor, on his experience. Is that correct?

MR. ALVARADO. That is correct. So then after that—

MR. GLICKSTEIN. These lists are not posted?

MR. ALVARADO. No, they are not posted. This is another thing that we asked of management and industrial relations, to post this list, because you could be working alongside another employee, same experience, everything identical, but when you were ranked you found that this employee was maybe No. 3 on the list and you found yourself maybe No. 20, and you'd wonder what happened.

MR. GLICKSTEIN. If you went to the personnel office and asked what your score was, would you be told what your score was?

MR. ALVARADO. Yes, but they were very reluctant. The information was very reluctant in coming.

MR. GLICKSTEIN. Would you be told, for instance, that, "You are No. 20, your score is 70. The employee that works next to you is No. 3, his score is 85." Would you be told something of that sort?

MR. ALVARADO. No, you were only told what you were weak in, in order to come up a little bit higher on the register, but the information as to your ranking on the register wasn't given to you. They told you that this information would not be given to you.

MR. GLICKSTEIN. They told you what the score was, but they didn't tell you where you ranked on the register. Is that right?

MR. ALVARADO. That is true.

MR. GLICKSTEIN. So you would be told that, "Your score is 70," but you couldn't be told where you ranked on the register?

MR. ALVARADO. Well, no, they told you your score on the test, but not your numerical rating on the register.

MR. GLICKSTEIN. In other words, the score on the test was one of the factors that made up your numerical rating on the register?

MR. ALVARADO. Yes, and this related to the two other elements. Your numerical rating value determined by the ranking schedule and then the voucher. So we continued on up to IRD and tried to get them to do away with the voucher because we knew that this was detrimental, it was being used as a tool for pre-selection, and also as a tool for grooming.

MR. GLICKSTEIN. What do you mean by "pre-selection and grooming"?

MR. ALVARADO. Well, I'll state it this way. A man can be detailed to a certain area and pick up a lot of points, whereas another employee that is not detailed to this area will fall far behind in points.

MR. GLICKSTEIN. You say that if a man is detailed to a particular area he then gets a different type of experience, and on the basis of that different type of experience he gets points that are considered in promoting him. Is that correct?

MR. ALVARADO. Exceedingly so.

MR. GLICKSTEIN. So it is very valuable to a man to be detailed to a particular position. Is that correct?

MR. ALVARADO. That is correct. So we argued about the voucher, we wanted it dropped because we knew that this was being used in selection, it was being used in ranking, and it also had a numerical value with these other two elements. So we went to IRD and tried to get them to do away with the voucher.

MR. GLICKSTEIN. In other words, if two employees had the same score on the tests, if two employees had the same amount of experience they could be ranked differently because of what each of their vouchers said. Is that correct?

MR. ALVARADO. That is correct. And it was also used in selection, so actually the voucher could be used three times. It could be used three times. If the selection board deemed that it was going to be used again they would vote on it and use it again, so we knew the voucher had a tremendous importance in upgrading, so we tried to get the industrial relations to do away with it.

MR. GLICKSTEIN. Apparently you were somewhat successful in that endeavor. The voucher is still used but it is now discussed with employees. Is that correct?

MR. ALVARADO. I wouldn't call it successful because we were really heartbroken when we found out that the voucher, even though it is signed and that the employees sees it, it is still used as a tool for promoting an employee inasmuch as they can still either give you a good voucher, a high numerical voucher, or a low numerical voucher.

MR. GLICKSTEIN. But you are told what your voucher contains?

MR. ALVARADO. Yes, but you have nothing to say as far as changing it.

MR. GLICKSTEIN. But if you object to the rating you have been given, is there any recourse?

MR. ALVARADO. There's supposed to be a recourse, but when I was confronted with mine, I questioned some of the areas that I had been marked low on because I said, "I've been here 17 years, and I have a good record and my production record is good" and yet I was getting a minimum—I mean a voucher right in the center, which I thought was very unfair.

I could see that the people that belonged to the social clubs with the higher levels of supervision were getting high vouchers, and I started to question this again. So later on I questioned it in the Employees' Council meeting. This was my question to O&R Officer, Captain Miller.

MR. GLICKSTEIN. O&R stands for what?

MR. ALVARADO. Overhaul and Repair. This was before they changed it over to NARF which is another designation it has now.

MR. GLICKSTEIN. That is one of the big commands on the Station?

MR. ALVARADO. Yes, that is correct. So we asked Captain Miller if the voucher was being used the same as it was used before in ranking and also in numerical value, and also can it be used again in selection, and he concurred with this. He said that this was true, so it is still being used in the same way it was before.

MR. GLICKSTEIN. Mr. Alvarado, is there general dissatisfaction among minority group employees at the Station?

MR. ALVARADO. Yes, there is.

MR. GLICKSTEIN. How do you know this?

MR. ALVARADO. We got a lot of complaints from the minorities when I was in the Employees' Council. Almost all of them dealt with either the promotions or the grievance procedure.

MR. GLICKSTEIN. What were the complaints regarding grievance procedure?

MR. ALVARADO. Well, any time when anybody starts to grieve —I will cite one case.

This gentleman came to me and he said that in his particular shop that they were violating the promotion policy, and that they were putting people up as alternate supervisors that weren't, in effect, eligible for this position. So he questioned it and came to me and said, "What can you do about it?" So I said, "Well, I'll take it up with the Industrial Relations Department."

So the Industrial Relations Department did nothing to correct this, even though we complained quite a few times about this certain area. So he asked me if he should file a grievance, and my own experience with the grievance procedures there is quite unique, so I told him, "It's total suicide, but if you want to go ahead I'll warn you that the reprisal action will start immediately after you put in your grievance." So he said, "Okay, I'll take a chance."

So he did, all the way up through channels. And the man is now working where he started 15 years ago. I mean, the reprisals are sort of subtle in that they come slow and, well, anyway he had to quit the Naval Air Station. He just gave up and said, "I can't take it any more." He went and got a better job on the outside.

MR. GLICKSTEIN. Does your Council ever meet with the commanding officer?

MR. ALVARADO. Our Council, yes. They have a meeting—they used to have a meeting once a month, a Station-level meeting.

MR. GLICKSTEIN. What is the commanding officer's attitude toward your problems?

MR. ALVARADO. Well, generally when we would bring up something pertaining to grievances or promotions he would usually delegate the authority to some official from IRD to take the floor and either state their views or bring out the policies as they stood.

But the thing that I would like to bring out here is when Captain Campbell first took command of the Naval Air Station his very first statement was that he would stand for nothing other than equal opportunity at Naval Air Station.

At that time we had some information relating to the discriminatory practices in the upgrading. So 20 minutes after the meeting we were trying to make an appointment with Captain Campbell through his secretary, and that was two years ago. He had also stated in the meeting that his door would be open to any group or anybody that wanted to talk about or had any information relating to discriminatory practices. So 20 minutes after the meeting we were trying to get to see Captain Campbell since he said his door was open, but it closed shortly after that, and we haven't been able to meet with the captain for two years.

MR. GLICKSTEIN. Do the personnel officials at the Station make an effort to explain in detail to employees what the personnel policies are, how promotions are given, and are there efforts made to acquaint all employees with what the procedures are?

MR. ALVARADO. Well, there are efforts made. There is a lot of information that comes down, but the information that I'm talking about, the information where the loopholes are and how the policies are implemented to cause the discriminatory things that come about, this information never gets out.

We have been trying to get them to post the ranking schedules for three years, and just recently they started to do this, but I'm not sure how many of the ranking schedules they have actually posted in the personnel manual.

MR. GLICKSTEIN. I have no further questions, Mr. Chairman.

CHAIRMAN HANNAH. Do the members of the Commission have questions?

COMMISSIONER FREEMAN. I have a question that can be answered by either Mr. Taylor or Mr. Alvarado. Would you give us some information about the grades of the minorities that are employed by the Alameda Air Station? Are they in the lower grades or—well, it was stated earlier that very few are in any higher grades, but where do they tend to be concentrated?

643

MR. TAYLOR. I have an example. As a member of the Commanding Officers Advisory Committee we were permitted to sit on the selection board and I had the opportunity to review the numerical standing, and although quite a bit of emphasis was placed on education, training, et cetera, the Negro employees in the aircraft rate, aircraft examiner rate, came out very high, and if they would have picked in one area which I checked before coming today, if they had picked in one area 1, 2, 3, 4, 5, I think the first four out of seven were Negroes in this particular trade, the examination which was aircraft airframes, I believe, it shows you what we have been trying to say, Mr. Alvarado and I, that they re-ranked the new examination to pick up a man who was in the well-qualified group.

Instead of going down the list and picking them in order, they re-ranked their new examination and went down to the well-qualified group and raised a man up to the outstanding category and picked him.

Now, if you were not to pass the examination, which we call a lock-out, they would say, "Well, you didn't pass the examination, you need more education," et cetera, but they scored very well and we noticed in the selection board they talk around a minority employee, although they rank high. They talk around them and bypass them and go down and pick someone else.

And the point Mr. Alvarado brought up about the voucher, they actually use the voucher as a medium once you were ranked. If you were to rank, say, third with a low voucher when they made the selections they might change that in the outside column to be 10 or 20. This is the thing, and we notice that they all scored very well even though you are led to believe that they don't score, but they do score very well.

COMMISSIONER FREEMAN. That if they score well and if they rank high then there subsequently is a re-ranking?

MR. TAYLOR. They pass over them, if they don't want them. This is one of the very flagrant violations because if you are on these lists and ranking high it doesn't say that you are going to be selected.

COMMISSIONER FREEMAN. Did you want to say something?

MR. ALVARADO. Yes. Well, this area you are getting at is—see, management has the prerogative of selecting from the top five, and even though the minority get to the top five, they might even be No. 1 on the list, they still go around them. We have found this, and the statistics will prove it because I don't think for the past 20 years up until the time we started picketing and demonstrating against the Station two months ago, I don't think that they had ever promoted any Mexican Americans to the area of inspection or supervisory and above. In the last three months three of them have been promoted.

644

COMMISSIONER FREEMAN. That was going to be my next question, if there had been any improvement in the practice and policy of the Station.

MR. ALVARADO. Well, there hasn't been much improvement in the policy. The policy still remains the same, but they found that these three minorities—I'm talking about Mexican Americans, plus I don't know how many other Negroes, probably about three, have jumped up to supervision, I mean positions about supervisory in the last three months, since we've been demonstrating and putting the pressure on the Station.

Also, I might add that there were close to 200 journeymen promotions made in the last two or three months, and also that included quite a few minorities, and some of these had been at the Station for more than 15 years, and just all of a sudden since they started demonstrating, they were promoted.

CHAIRMAN HANNAH. Mr. Patterson?

VICE CHAIRMAN PATTERSON. Mr. Alvarado, you testified that some employees are favored through procedures which you characterized as hush-hush deals. Could you elaborate on that?

MR. ALVARADO. Well, I think I will cite a particular case. We were bringing these complaints to the captain at our meetings through the Employees' Council. One of them was that they were doing this: that some people were getting inside information on a projected promotion.

So he said we should bring him the specifics. So we did. We went to IRD and tried to get specifics, but they wouldn't give them to us, so we took it upon ourselves.

VICE CHAIRMAN PATTERSON. Excuse me. This is the type of promotions that are going to be available. Is that what you are saying?

MR. ALVARADO. Yes, projected in the near future, and we couldn't get the information from the Industrial Relations. They wouldn't give us information as to how they were ranked and things of this nature.

So we took one lead man that was just promoted, and we took 36 journeymen who were just promoted, and we reconstructed the rankings by asking them just what score they got on their tests.

From there we figured how they were ranked, and we came to the conclusion that this particular promotion that we had decided to bring before the captain, that the man that was ranked—well, actually promoted—he had a score of 70.9, and the cut-off point was 70. So this man, even though he had only been at the Station for five years managed to be ranked up in the zone of selection. Then we further—

VICE CHAIRMAN PATTERSON. This is the top five?

MR. ALVARADO. Yes. We further investigated and found that this man had been slotted into the instructor's position—this is a detail more or less—prior to this and this is how he got his excessive points to outrank people with up to 20 years of experience and with a score of 90, 96, in that area. These people were outranked due to the ranking setup and also to the voucher and et cetera.

VICE CHAIRMAN PATTERSON. How did you determine that his score was only 70.9?

MR. ALVARADO. Well, we asked him what score he had gotten on the test, and this score was printed on the paper that you would get back stating that you were on the list of eligibles. Then that would go through the ranking procedures, so I saw his score. His score was 70.9.

VICE CHAIRMAN PATTERSON. Do you know that there were five others who made better scores than that?

MR. ALVARADO. Yes. I'd say that even more than five had better scores than that that were ranked as low as No. 12 on the list.

VICE CHAIRMAN PATTERSON. You have first-hand knowledge of this from interviewing these men?

MR. ALVARADO. Yes, we categorized them as to the scores. We asked them personally. Then we took the 36 employees that were promoted to journeyman level and we found that of all the people that were ranked in the zone of selection there were very few minorities.

So then we started investigating in this area, and we tried to get information from IRD, and again they were very reluctant to come forth with the information, so we had a lot of trouble in getting this type of information.

But we found that during the course of ranking one man that was supposed to be promoted had been retired from the base prior to the time that they were promoted for six months. This indicated to us that the jackets were never opened, and they have to open the jackets to check the pertinent information that they state they have. This information is in the Form 57 in every employee's jacket, so we assumed that their jackets were never opened.

Across this man's jacket they had a label stating that he had been retired six months prior to the time of promotion. So this again was taken up by other people, and one employee released this information to the press. This employee was promoted about six months after that, but this is, of course, another form of taking the personnel that are doing their best to bring about changes in these inequities, they either promote them or they have reprisal actions or they eventually either get fired or they have to resign under pressure.

So this information we took to the captain, our O&R officer, Captain Miller, and he told us that we were delving into a very dangerous area, that he feared for us inasmuch as we might get reprisal action.

So he said he would take it from there, he would investigate further.

So the chairman of the ranking board at that time, we met with him and his opening statement as he said it was that, first of all, he says, "We, the ranking board officials, have to assume that every employee is a liar and a cheat." And this is the dialogue that the chairman of the ranking board used. So this is the information that we related to Captain Miller.

Some six months later the chairman of the ranking board was promoted. So then again we feared that the investigation had really produced no fruits as far as changes in the policy or the policies as far as promotion.

So then we again started meeting with officials of IRD, and we sent a letter to the captain stating that these inequities were going on, and the letter that the captain sent back to this particular committee at the time of looking into these inequities, his letter stated that these were serious allegations that this committee was making, but that's as far as it went, and we asked him to meet with us as quick as possible, that this matter was urgent, and this was almost two years ago and we haven't heard from him since.

VICE CHAIRMAN PATTERSON. Mr. Taylor, you've testified that two temporary employees were fired after they registered a complaint with your committee. Is that correct?

MR. TAYLOR. They didn't actually register a complaint. They came to the committee to see how to take up the matter in their shop area since they were all Negro employees, but it was not based upon their race.

VICE CHAIRMAN PATTERSON. They were fired the day after the complaint. Is that correct?

MR. TAYLOR. That's right, right off the base.

VICE CHAIRMAN PATTERSON. And you further testified that you then told the captain about this. Is that correct?

MR. TAYLOR. Yes.

VICE CHAIRMAN PATTERSON. What did the captain reply to you?

MR. TAYLOR. Nothing, no reply.

VICE CHAIRMAN PATTERSON. Did you tell him personally or did you write him a letter or what?

MR. TAYLOR. I talked with the captain personally about it, and this is the captain at O&R at that time would be Captain Kirkman. Captain Kirkman wouldn't even see the individual who was injured.

VICE CHAIRMAN PATTERSON. But he must have made some response to you when you gave him this information?

MR. TAYLOR. "Yes, thank you." And that's all there was to it. There wasn't anything done to interview the employee who was injured.

VICE CHAIRMAN PATTERSON. Thank you.

CHAIRMAN HANNAH. Questions? Mr. Taylor?

MR. TAYLOR. Mr. Alvarado, do you have an opinion about why there are not more Mexican Americans or other Spanish-speaking people employed on the base?

MR. ALVARADO. Yes, in my opinion, the work that I've done in the past three years as a councilman, my opinion is that as long as the promotion policy is as broad as it is and they use the ranking schedules the way they do and the voucher, these inequities will continue.

MR. TAYLOR. Do you know anything about the methods of recruitment used for people in various job categories?

MR. ALVARADO. You mean by that how do they select people for promotion or—

MR. TAYLOR. No, initial hiring. How do they go out and find them?

MR. ALVARADO. Well, initial hiring of course is done through news media. They advertise for certain categories of help.

MR. TAYLOR. Do they do this in ways, do you think, that would get to the Spanish—get the information around in the Spanish-speaking community, or does the information not generally reach people?

MR. ALVARADO. Well, it reaches people. It's in the newspaper, Bay Area newspapers, but I might add that when—I can cite two cases of what happens, the reason they don't get in.

One of them is I sent one gentleman, a Korean veteran approximately two years ago when they were doing quite a bit of hiring and he was turned away at the gate. They told him they had no openings, and at the same time they hired two girls just out of high school, and one of them happened to be the daughter of a gentleman in Oakland. He and his wife both worked at the Station, and she was living with them at the time, and she, I believe, is still living with her parents at this time. This is in direct violation of the Federal laws.

And I also sent another Mexican American that had eight years of documented Air Force experience in aircrafts instrument, overhaul and repair, and also electronic experience documented from the Air Force. He served 20 years with the Air Force, and he was turned away. The reason, insufficient experience.

648

MR. TAYLOR. Were you asked to seek out candidates for jobs, or did you just do this on your own?

MR. ALVARADO. I'm working with the community and this is one of the functions that we perform.

MR. TAYLOR. What I meant was were you asked by any officials at the base to seek out people?

MR. ALVARADO. Well, they made the announcements at the Station level meetings, and the O&R meetings, that there were going to be openings and if we knew of anybody that was interested in securing the job that we should send them to the gate to seek these particular jobs.

MR. TAYLOR. Was that a general announcement?

MR. ALVARADO. It was a general announcement.

MR. TAYLOR. I have no further questions.

CHAIRMAN HANNAH. Thank you very much, gentlemen. We appreciate your being with us this afternoon. Call the next witness.

MR. GLICKSTEIN. The next witnesses are Captain Duncan Campbell of the Naval Air Station, Captain Rupert Miller, and Mr. Arnold Anderson.

(Whereupon, Captain Duncan Campbell, Captain Rupert S. Miller, and Mr. Arnold Anderson were sworn by the Chairman and testified as follows:)

TESTIMONY OF CAPTAIN DUNCAN CAMPBELL, CAPTAIN RUPERT S. MILLER, NAVAL AIR STATION, ALAMEDA, CALIFORNIA, AND MR. ARNOLD O. ANDERSON, ORINDA, CALIFORNIA

MR. GLICKSTEIN. Will you please each give your name and address for the record?

CAPTAIN CAMPBELL. I'm Captain D. A. Campbell, Commanding Officer of the Naval Air Station. I live at 106 Tongue Point Road, Naval Air Station, Alameda, California.

MR. ANDERSON. I am Arnold O. Anderson. I live at 128 Appleview Road in Orinda, California.

CAPTAIN MILLER. I am Captain Rupert S. Miller, Commanding Officer of the Naval Air Rework Facility. I live at 104 San Pedro Road, Naval Air Station, Alameda.

MR. GLICKSTEIN. Will each of you also please describe your function at the Naval Air Station, the jurisdictions that you cover?

CAPTAIN CAMPBELL. I am the Commanding Officer at the Naval Air Station and responsible for all activities there.

MR. GLICKSTEIN. How does the O&R Department relate to your jurisdiction? It is now called Naval Air Repair Department?

CAPTAIN CAMPBELL. Until 1, April 1967 the O&R Department

was one of my several departments at the Naval Air Station. As of that date it became a separate command under the same officer.

MR. GLICKSTEIN. It became a separate command?

CAPTAIN CAMPBELL. Separate command under the same officer, Captain Rupert Miller, who is here beside me. Before we get into this—

MR. GLICKSTEIN. You and Captain Miller have the same level of supervision? Is that right?

CAPTAIN CAMPBELL. That is correct, since 1 April.

MR. GLICKSTEIN. Perhaps Mr. Anderson could just identify his position.

MR. ANDERSON. Yes, sir, I'm the Industrial Relations Officer at the Naval Air Station, Alameda.

MR. GLICKSTEIN. And you are responsible for industrial relations both under Captain Campbell's command and Captain Miller's command?

MR. ANDERSON. Yes. We service part of the Air Station, but we also service the Naval Air Rework Facility. I think that answers the question, does it not?

MR. GLICKSTEIN. Yes, it does.

CAPTAIN CAMPBELL. Mr. Chairman, before we get to proceeding with the questions and answers, I wonder if it's possible to make a brief statement here for the record to summarize the activity that we are—

CHAIRMAN HANNAH. How long will it take, Captain?

CAPTAIN CAMPBELL. It will be about 10 minutes.

CHAIRMAN HANNAH. Can you summarize it?

CAPTAIN CAMPBELL. This will summarize more or less the responsibilities and the programs we have had for equal opportunity.

CHAIRMAN HANNAH. We will include the entire statement in the record. If you could summarize it in under 10 minutes, we would appreciate that. We don't want to deprive you of an opportunity to say what you would like to say. We certainly will print it in the record.

MR. GLICKSTEIN. Mr. Chairman, perhaps I could suggest an alternative that after the questioning if Captain Campbell feels that some of the information he has, has not been entered into the record perhaps at that time he could—

CHAIRMAN HANNAH. Would that be agreeable?

CAPTAIN CAMPBELL. That would be agreeable, Mr. Chairman. I will provide you with statements, and I do have statements here for any others who may desire them.

CHAIRMAN HANNAH. We would like copies of them, and when the questioning is completed, if you think there are gaps we will be glad to have you present them. Proceed, Mr. Glickstein.

MR. GLICKSTEIN. I would like to address questions to individuals, but any of you may feel free to comment further, or you can refer the question to someone else.

Captain Campbell, previous witnesses mentioned some recent demonstrations at the Naval Air Station. Do you feel that this is indicative of general dissatisfaction concerning personnel problems among minority group persons at the base?

CAPTAIN CAMPBELL. No, sir, I do not. This demonstration, although widely advertised in the newspapers, expecting over 1,000 marchers and so forth, turned out to be under 50 persons, most of them press. There were not more than one or two personnel from the Naval Air Station that participated in that picket or march, and there was no support on the Station.

I might amplify that I discussed the march with the members of my Commanding Officer's Advisory Committee independently and they indicated to me there was no support on the Station whatsoever. These members, minority members that I discussed this problem with on the Station, both before, during, and after the march all indicated that they were not at all sympathetic with the program or the march.

Secondly, that these representatives came from all work levels, from the lowest paid on up to the supervisory level.

MR. GLICKSTEIN. They came from all work levels?

CAPTAIN CAMPBELL. Yes.

MR. GLICKSTEIN. What steps, Captain Campbell, has the Naval Air Station taken to insure that minority group employees are treated equally in obtaining promotions?

CAPTAIN CAMPBELL. Well, we have taken quite a wide variety of steps. One that has been mentioned is the use of the Commanding Officer's Advisory Committee. This committee, which Mr. Walter Taylor was chairman of at the time I took over the Station, was put in effect, as I recall, in January of 1964. It was in effect at the time when I took over in June of 1965.

This committee, the way I've operated it, meets weekly and any day during the week when there is a discrimination complaint. I meet formally at least once a month with the entire committee, and I bring all of my department heads with me so that they can get the briefing from the advisory committee and, more importantly, to discuss together with them ways of improving equal opportunity programs and policies on the Station.

I might give Mr. Walter Taylor a compliment. He was given a letter of commendation upon the departure of the previous Commanding Officer indicating the work that he had done, and I would like to indicate that throughout the tenure of his chairmanship he did a very fine job as chairman. He made many very fine recommendations on behalf of the committee.

Many of these were put into effect, such as the secret voucher that has been discussed. I don't think it needs any further amplification. This went into effect in 1965. I might depart here just for a moment—

MR. GLICKSTEIN. The secret voucher, you stopped using it in '65?

CAPTAIN CAMPBELL. No, we stopped having it as a secret voucher. We still have it as a rating form, an efficiency report which is discussed with the employee. The employee receives the voucher after it is made out and discusses it with his supervisor. This is required by the Station instructions, that the supervisor discuss his marking that he has given to the employee on the voucher. This is one of the major changes that was put into effect because there was a great deal of suspicion about this voucher.

I might say that there was some disagreement among various members of my staff, that is, among the various department heads as to whether we should or should not have the secret voucher or an unclassified or open voucher. You can well imagine that some supervisors are going to be reluctant to mark an individual low even though his work may not be satisfactory if he is going to face up to the man and have to point it out.

I felt, however, that the danger of any possibility of discriminatory action through the secret voucher method as has been discussed was too great, and, therefore, the benefits weighed in favor of an unclassified or open voucher.

MR. GLICKSTEIN. That voucher still is used?

CAPTAIN CAMPBELL. It is still used and it is, and I believe Mr. Anderson can confirm this, required from higher authority. I cannot see how we can do without it in the marking procedure. It is no different than in most industries.

Certainly, in the Navy we get periodic fitness reports or efficiency reports. It is true in all the services that the individual receiving mediocre grade may not agree at all with the grade he received or the student in high school may not agree with the mark that he got. The teacher is wrong and the student is right. This is correct. This is exactly the same situation here on the voucher situation.

MR. GLICKSTEIN. And if an employee is dissatisfied with his voucher, is he able to appeal that to someone above the level of his supervisor?

CAPTAIN CAMPBELL. Yes, he is. I'd like to, as far as the details of how that is handled, have it covered by Mr. Anderson, the Industrial Relations Officer or Captain Miller who has the largest number of employees dealing with the voucher.

CAPTAIN MILLER. With respect to the voucher itself, we now call it employee appraisal, the leading man, now called the foreman, discusses this with the employee after having discussed it first with his next level of supervisor, foreman No. 2. If the employee is not satisfied with the marking, he is free to carry it then up through the chain of command to the department head for discussion.

MR. GLICKSTEIN. Captain Campbell, there have been some charges made that employees that submit grievances have been penalized. Would you care to comment on that?

CAPTAIN CAMPBELL. Referring to Mr. Taylor's comments about grievance, I would like to refer to the supply clerk case that was mentioned. This case took place—the altercation took place prior to my arrival.

MR. GLICKSTEIN. This is the GS-3 female employee?

CAPTAIN CAMPBELL. Yes. The Commanding Officer's Advisory Committee on Equal Opportunity did investigate this case. It was determined by them, or reported by Mr. Taylor, that he felt that it was discrimination. It was decided that a discrimination complaint, a formal discrimination complaint should be entered in the case. When I reviewed all of the evidence there was a hearing. I reviewed all of the evidence.

MR. GLICKSTEIN. And you decided after you got the informal report to have a formal procedure?

CAPTAIN CAMPBELL. Yes, they had a formal session. Looking at both the opinions and so forth of the informal advisory committee—and I must highlight here that the Commanding Officer's Advisory Committee for Equal Opportunity is just that, an advisory committee recommendation for my action and has no official power as to the formal grievance case.

When it became formal there was a hearing and all evidence was weighed by me, and my decision in this case went counter to what was recommended by the advisory committee. I had much other advice and data to work on. I determined that where there was lack of communications between the supervisor and the employees and some administrative errors and otherwise, but there was no error in discrimination.

This case was forwarded to Washington and it is still current, so I can't go further than that.

MR. GLICKSTEIN. I understand that.

CAPTAIN CAMPBELL. The other case which was referred to as a machinist, as I recall, again it was a matter of disagreement between Mr. Taylor and myself. However, there was a formal discrimination complaint in all of the procedures in accordance with the regulations from the Civil Service Commission and from the Navy Department. It was thoroughly explored.

I recommended to higher authority that I found no discrimination. This was supported by the Secretary of the Navy and by the

Civil Service Commission that there was no discrimination in this case.

That employee stayed employed at the Station. There was no discipline involved in that case. The man has since died.

CAPTAIN MILLER. With respect to this particular complaint which derives from a rotation problem, the individual involved spent some time talking to me. I asked him what he would like to have done. He said he would like to have a list of individuals who worked in the same shop reviewed as to their history to see if they had ever been so rotated. Such a list was provided him.

Approximately 80 percent of those individuals had been so rotated. I asked him if he was satisfied with his present work station. He said he was not sure. I said, "If you are not satisfied at any time in at least one month from today, come and see me." He did so.

At the end of that month he came in and I said, "What more would you like us to do?" He said, "At the moment I have nothing more I would like done." I told the individual, "At any time that you have a further complaint you can see me directly without going through the chain of command," which is our normal procedure. He did not do so.

MR. GLICKSTEIN. Captain Campbell, did you communicate the basis for your decision in both of those cases to your advisory committee?

CAPTAIN CAMPBELL. I did, and a point of difference between primarily Mr. Taylor and myself, not the advisory committee, Mr. Taylor as an individual and myself, the point of difference was that he felt that since he did not agree with my decision that I should be required to explain and justify my decision in the matter, and I advised him and all members of the advisory committee that they were just that, an advisory committee, and that I could accept or reject their advice and not have to justify it to them.

MR. GLICKSTEIN. So you didn't justify it to them? You didn't explain it to them. You just merely announced what your decision was?

CAPTAIN CAMPBELL. I did explain it to them, but I did not go into details. They wanted a copy of the hearing report. This is privileged information and was forwarded to the Navy Department.

MR. GLICKSTEIN. When you say you explained to them, did you explain it to the extent that you said, "I have reviewed the case and I find that your conclusions are incorrect and I've come to a different conclusion," or did you go beyond that?

CAPTAIN CAMPBELL. I did tell them that I came to a different conclusion. As I say, privileged information is just that. The testimony of witnesses, as you may well know, is to be guarded, and that sort of thing.

MR. GLICKSTEIN. You were not able to tell them why, then, you came to a different conclusion?

CHAIRMAN HANNAH. I think the captain made clear this is an Advisory Committee and he did not feel obligated to explain the reasons for his disagreement to the advisory committee. I think that is an adequate answer.

CAPTAIN CAMPBELL. I would feel the same way about justifying completely to a department head or some of my staff that did not agree with me. They make the recommendations, most of them accept it if I make a decision that is counter to their views.

MR. GLICKSTEIN. Captain, a little while ago I asked you if any employees that have filed grievances have in any way been penalized as a result of that.

CAPTAIN CAMPBELL. Absolutely none to my knowledge.

MR. GLICKSTEIN. Absolutely none to your knowledge?

CAPTAIN CAMPBELL. No, sir.

MR. GLICKSTEIN. You've never heard of cases where there have been reprisals?

CAPTAIN CAMPBELL. Absolutely not. I might just come back to one point since we are speaking of the advisory committee and the service that they do render.

Over the past two years the advisory committees have looked into an average of about 20 discrimination complaints per month, and in about 90 percent of the cases on an average of one, two, or three are carried over for further examination. The others are resolved by establishing better communication between the supervisor and employee through the aegis of the two members that go out to investigate and act as sort of referees in the case to help get it understood.

In most cases it appears that it is a lack of understanding by the employee as to necessary qualifications for promotion.

Many of the complainants, I'd say at least 20 or 30 that I recall, were not even eligible for competition and wondered why they did not get promoted, or figured it was a discrimination complaint because they did not get promoted.

MR. GLICKSTEIN. Were the two cases you described to us the only cases in which your advisory committee ever found discrimination?

CAPTAIN CAMPBELL. No, I don't believe so. They were the only two cases that I recall that they particularly considered were discrimination and discriminatory. There were others that bore further investigation. I would have to check my files.

MR. GLICKSTEIN. The report that was delivered by Mr. Bradley a little while ago indicated that there are very few minority group

655

members in supervisory positions at the Naval Air Station. How would you explain that?

CAPTAIN CAMPBELL. Would you clarify the question, please?

MR. GLICKSTEIN. I said the report that was delivered, the oral report that was delivered by Mr. Bradley, indicated that there were very few minority group persons in supervisory positions at the Naval Air Station. How would you explain that?

CAPTAIN CAMPBELL. We have had a number of promotions over the past couple of years. I just really don't—you might—

MR. ANDERSON. This, of course, is a fairly difficult area which would need about a minute of background information.

CHAIRMAN HANNAH. Go ahead.

MR. ANDERSON. The median age of the employees at my command in Government service, the median year is 19½.

Some of the previous witnesses have commented on being 14 years in a job. This is not uncommon. Promotion to foreman, the leading man at first level of supervision, with one exception that I can think of in recent years averages 22 years of government employment.

To answer specifically to the question, eligibility and ranking on the registers for promotion as has been explained to you previously is determined, amongst other things, very heavily by experience.

We simply have no method nor do we have any real desire to upset this system. Consequently, we can only produce a flow up through the supervisory channels at a rate at which at least sufficient experience is accrued by the individuals to get them a consideration position on the register. We can develop and submit, if you would like, statistics which show that once considered, once these qualifications have been met, that the promotion is clearly non-biased racially. So the answer to your question is simply that the experience level of the corps of people who can be promoted is racially biased.

CAPTAIN MILLER. I wonder if I might respond to that just a bit also. In the period from the 1st of January 1965 to the 30th of April 1967, a period of some 27 or 28 months, we conducted examinations for blue-collar supervisors for 20 trades. A total of 1,173 employees applied for those jobs. Of those, 72 have been promoted, and of those 72, 13 have been minority employees.

You will notice on the list of supervisory blue-collar jobs, there are 22 minority supervisors, and 13 of those have been promoted during that period of time. I suppose in the normal course of events most of us who are not promoted—if I were not one of the 72, but one of the 1,101 who hadn't been promoted, I would have some questions about the promotion program.

If we go from first line supervisors over direct blue-collar workers to what we call production facilitating positions, these are premium jobs in the Naval Air Rework Facility. During that same period of time from the 1st of January 1965 to the 30th of April 1967 there have been 43 promotions of minority groups.

You will notice on the list, I think there are 76 serving in that capacity and 43 of those have been promoted in this last period of time. I do think it is quite important that the Commission understand that the Federal Government's position really changed from one of complaint investigating—at least this is true as far as Navy is concerned—in 1963 to one of affirmative action so what we have been trying to do is trace our progress from 1963 to today. I think we are making some real significant progress.

In 1963, after this came out, we stopped all promotions for a period of time so that we could detail some of our people who had not had significant details prior to that time to these important jobs. Then, in 1965 we began promoting again and the results are as I have just described them to you.

MR. GLICKSTEIN. Mr. Anderson, you referred to some statistics, and I believe the statistics you referred to are the statistics that were prepared under your direction for the Commission. Is that correct?

MR. ANDERSON. Yes, that is right.

MR. GLICKSTEIN. Mr. Chairman, I would like to introduce the statement of Captain Campbell and the statistics that were prepared by the Naval Air Station for us into the record as Exhibits 32 and 33.

CHAIRMAN HANNAH. They are accepted.

(Whereupon, the documents referred to were marked Exhibits No. 32 and 33 and received in evidence.)

MR. GLICKSTEIN. Would you tell the Commission what you had to do to prepare this document for us?

MR. ANDERSON. Yes. What we did was to call together about 30 or 40 of our employees and give them an indoctrination in head counting, if you will. We had an IBM runoff of all of the employees in the Naval Air Rework Facility, and then we asked these 30 employees to go out and make a head count of all of those employees and give us a racial breakdown. This was done, and then we had the figures, and this is it.

MR. GLICKSTEIN. Doesn't the Naval Air Station have a regular method of compiling and maintaining racial statistics?

MR. ANDERSON. No, we do not have. The Federal Government has changed their position on this a number of times.

Up until 1966 we used to make a head count once a year, what we call a head count. The supervisors indicated on a specially prepared form racial breakdown of employees under their jurisdiction.

In 1966 the Federal Government decided through the Civil Service Commission that this was not the proper way of doing things, that each individual working for the Federal Government should indicate by himself what his race was. This information was then sent in to Washington.

The trouble we found with it is that approximately 16 percent of the employees did not indicate, did not fill out the cards. There was no review of the card whatsoever. Each individual filled out their card designating their race and then sent that information in directly, so we found the information quite unreliable.

The Federal Government is now holding conversations with various interested people to see what the policy really ought to be, whether it ought to change or not.

I have before me the results of a meeting in the office of the Executive Director of the Civil Service Commission of the Inter-agency Advisory Group. This is the personnel directors of all of the Federal establishments and agencies in Washington, and it says, "This meeting was called to evaluate the ways used to collect the minority group data and to give suggestions on ways to further improve the methods used."

I think most personnel officials and agency heads feel that the present method is not proper and we ought to have a different method so we can tell at all times how many minority we have in various occupations.

CAPTAIN CAMPBELL. I would like to add that under present regulations we are not permitted to keep a current day-to-day count of minority employees so that it is readily available.

MR. GLICKSTEIN. Do you have to send that information to Washington?

CAPTAIN CAMPBELL. That is correct.

MR. GLICKSTEIN. So the information Mr. Anderson referred to, the questionnaire you sent out, the results went to Washington so that it was not available here?

CAPTAIN CAMPBELL. That's true. It's still not available here except the final results percentagewise.

MR. GLICKSTEIN. Would it be possible under Navy regulations for you to keep your own tabulations here? Could the regulations be changed in that respect?

CAPTAIN CAMPBELL. We expect that they will be from the comment that was just made by Mr. Anderson on the minutes of the Committee for Equal Opportunity and the Civil Service Commission.

MR. GLICKSTEIN. Do you think that would be helpful to your equal opportunity program if you had the statistics available here?

CAPTAIN CAMPBELL. We certainly think it would. We are certainly hoping that the policy of the Federal Government will be changed so we will be able to keep the statistics.

MR. GLICKSTEIN. If that were the policy then you wouldn't have had to undertake a head count. You would have just run them off on an IBM machine?

CAPTAIN CAMPBELL. That is correct.

MR. GLICKSTEIN. Captain Campbell, I understand that the Civil Service Commission recently conducted a survey of equal employment policies at the Naval Air Station and issued a report. It is my understanding that although the report did commend the Station in many respects it did also say that there were still some problems with respect to Spanish-speaking Americans.

Is the Station planning to take some steps to deal with that criticism?

CAPTAIN CAMPBELL. I would first like to identify some problems of the Spanish-speaking minority population. I think what you are referring to is that we do not have a breakdown between the various groups within the Spanish-speaking population of the minority group.

We do not have a breakdown of those that are Mexican Americans, those that are Spanish Americans and otherwise. We do hope, as we mentioned a moment ago about our surveys, that we will be able, by using automatic data, processing data, to identify Mexican Americans, Chinese Americans and others.

MR. GLICKSTEIN. Mr. Chairman, I have a copy of the Civil Service report. May that be introduced into the record as Exhibit No. 34?

CHAIRMAN HANNAH. It is received.

(Whereupon, the document referred to was marked Exhibit No. 34 and received in evidence.)

MR. GLICKSTEIN. Captain, the report, among its recommendations, states: "The problem of equal employment opportunity for the Spanish-speaking segment of the community still remains to be solved. The Station needs to survey the size and nature of this problem and work within the Station and in the community to attract, train, and promote additional numbers of Spanish-speaking persons."

Have you had a chance yet to formulate any program to meet that recommendation?

CAPTAIN CAMPBELL. No, we haven't, but I think that our equal opportunity program that presently is on the Station applies to all minority groups, to all majority and minority groups, and we will continue—we don't pretend to be perfect but we will continue to strive to improve our equal opportunity program applying to all minority groups.

MR. GLICKSTEIN. I have no further questions.

CAPTAIN CAMPBELL. Could Mr. Anderson elaborate on that last comment?

CHAIRMAN HANNAH. Go ahead.

MR. ANDERSON. We have made efforts to contact the Mexican American community. We have made contacts with the four target areas here in Oakland and then back in December and in January we were invited to come to a new organization called the Spanish-Speaking Organization, Incorporated in Oakland.

Mr. Collins of my staff and Mr. Ignacio Apodaca of our organization, that is at Naval Air Station, visited that group one evening, and went back two or three weeks later to outline to them the openings that we had and methods of applying for positions and that sort of thing. We told them at that time that we were available to come back again and discuss this matter further with them because on that second meeting they couldn't give us very much time. They were talking about the incorporation of their particular organization but we are prepared to go back and will be contacting them again to go back and talk to them about openings.

CHAIRMAN HANNAH. Gentlemen, if I understand what you are saying, I gather that you recognize that it is not only law but it is the policy of our Government now to not only see that minority group members are given fair and equitable treatment but that it is the Federal policy to see to it that they are not disadvantaged in any way. It is recognized on the part of employers that there is a responsibility to identify prospective employees and see that they are given fair opportunity; to those that are already employed, to be certain they are given not only equitable treatment but appropriate treatment to see that their skills and so on are recognized.

As I understand the answers to your questions, you recognize that this is the policy and it is your desire to proceed in that direction. Is that correct?

CAPTAIN CAMPBELL. That is correct.

CHAIRMAN HANNAH. Mrs. Freeman, do you have a question?

COMMISSIONER FREEMAN. Yes, I have. Captain Campbell, you indicated, I believe, that it is ultimately your responsibility to investigate complaints of discrimination and you have received some complaints. Was there any case in which you found discrimination?

CAPTAIN CAMPBELL. Since 1963 there have been 27 formal discrimination complaints, forwarded to Washington to the President's Advisory Commission for Equal Opportunity, the Civil Service Commission, Secretary of the Navy. All have been returned with no discrimination.

In my local formal and informal investigations on the Station

I have found no discrimination. Now there have been errors in administrative action, different ways in which we can do our job better. There have been misunderstandings, but in the final analysis there has been no discrimination *per se*.

COMMISSIONER FREEMAN. You also indicated that in many of these jobs that promotion requires certain years of experience and certain kinds of experience. Have you reviewed the personnel file under the affirmative action program which you have referred to, to determine the extent to which there may be people who have been kept at a lower level for many, many years, but who have not acquired the experience that is necessary because perhaps they were bypassed.

CAPTAIN CAMPBELL. This is true for both majority and minority groups as far as stagnation in a job. We do not promote on the tenure in a job. It is on the best qualified individual in the selection process. This is by regulation from higher authority. We have no choice in the matter.

COMMISSIONER FREEMAN. This is the point that I am making. Suppose it was a person who had the background, but who was in a rut because a supervisor did not like the Spanish American or Mexican American. How would this ever come to your attention? That's why I ask, or maybe this is Mr. Anderson's question. How often do you review the personnel folder or the Form 57 to try to cure a mistake?

MR. ANDERSON. In this regard in our affirmative action program, we do have a training program and we have also a counseling program so that we find if an individual is not passing an examination, for example, we try to find out why he has not been promoted and point out his deficiencies and make available training programs to those individuals, both after hours on the Naval Air Station and under the adult education program. Many times we find that it is a matter of formal education that is holding back an individual, so we do have this, both the counseling and the training program for these people.

Now, Captain Miller is much closer to the situation and he has had the responsibility for the majority of the workers that are involved that you are speaking of.

CAPTAIN MILLER. I'd like to describe something which may answer the question somewhat.

First of all, as recently as a year ago we have changed the experience, that is, the job content qualifications to rest more heavily on the quality of the experience rather than the length and the procedure used is the definition of elements of known ability or demonstrated ability in a certain job field.

We have what we call intermediate workers who would like to be promoted to journeyman. So we took these elements which are described as the things that must be demonstrated for promotion, and we have available to any individual who is a permanent employee of the rework facility, an intermediate worker, all he has to do is say to us, "I want to be in a rotational training program."

We will put him in a mandatory movement program from shop to shop, from job to job, a running record is kept of his performance against the elements. When he has completed this performance in all of these various areas then we say he has met the qualifications in job performance for promotion. His promotion would then of course depend on their being an existing vacancy.

This was established deliberately to take care of people who worked at one bench for a long time and never got anywhere. We also have, and this may relate to why in certain areas we have no minority group people in what we call the production control family, we have had some what we call dead-end rates.

We have a job which, after a man has performed in that job for 10 years it would be literally impossible for him to have qualified for promotion anywhere. We are changing this system.

We will arrange for people in those jobs to have training on Government time, to be selected for training so that they can work their way up the production control family.

Can I hark back to one previous question, please, which had to do with had we ever seen a case of overt discrimination?

We've never had a case of overt discrimination where we could file disciplinary charges, and I have asked for them several times.

There has been one case brought to me where the selecting official on a promotion said, "I cannot understand the action of the board." A Negro was involved. He had not been recommended for promotion.

We returned the jacket to the board and said, "Reconsider." The board came back with their original recommendation, and we withdrew from the board their right to make the recommendation, and I took it on myself.

The Negro was selected and he declined the promotion. But that's the only case that I know of.

COMMISSIONER FREEMAN. The last question relates to previous testimony in which it was stated that there was fear of reprisal, and I would like you to comment on that, and especially because of Captain Campbell's statement that at the time of the demonstration he asked the employees if they agreed with this and they all said no. If there was a fear of reprisal, then is not the no answer one to be expected?

MR. ANDERSON. I don't believe that there is a fear of reprisal. We ran some statistics on this. We find that we've had 63 formal complaints that have gone to Washington from the period of 1961 to 1967. As for reprisal, we find that 17 of those 63 have since been promoted, promoted after they filed their charges, not because of filing the charge but maybe this indicates that the better employees file the charges.

Also, we have an organization at the Naval Air Station called the Federal Employees for Equal Employment Opportunity. It's primarily a Negro organization. Since the inception of this organization in 1963 there have been 26 officers in one capacity or another and we find that nine of those officers have been promoted.

With respect to the question as to—

A Voice: Uncle Toms.

MR. ANDERSON. The question, I think, of interest is this one in the Civil Service Commission report. It says, "In general how are members of racial minority groups treated as far as promotions, training opportunities, et cetera, are concerned in your agency?" Seventy-four responded that they are given more opportunities than others of equal qualifications. One hundred fifty-six said that they were given the same opportunities, and 55 said that they were given fewer opportunities than others with equal qualifications. Fifty said, "I don't know." So more answered that they were given better opportunities than answered that they were given fewer opportunities. These were 400 chosen by the Civil Service Commission at random from our files and they received replies from 334 of them.

CHAIRMAN HANNAH. Thank you. Mr. Patterson?

VICE CHAIRMAN PATTERSON. Captain Campbell, do you have knowledge of any hidden reprisal taken against an employee who made a complaint during your tenure as Commander of the Naval Air Station?

CAPTAIN CAMPBELL. Absolutely not.

VICE CHAIRMAN PATTERSON. Do you have any knowledge of such reprisal being taken before you obtained command?

CAPTAIN CAMPBELL. No, sir.

VICE CHAIRMAN PATTERSON. Is it possible that such reprisals could be taken at a level below yours and that you might not know about it and, if so, what action would you take if you learned of it?

CAPTAIN CAMPBELL. It is possible. I've counseled all of my department heads, all of my supervisors that they must give wholehearted support to the equal opportunities program. I have invoked it in writing and in repeated oral demonstrations, indicated to all of the personnel on the base through our newspaper, in other ways, in our training sessions, reiterated that this is not only national policy, Station policy, but my personal policy and I have indicated that their fitness report as far as officers are concerned, and the vouchers as far as the civilian supervisors are concerned will be marked on the spirit in which they carry out the equal opportunity programs.

I feel confident that if there was a case of reprisals in the lower echelons that this would come to the attention of the department heads and lower supervisors.

VICE CHAIRMAN PATTERSON. Mr. Anderson, as I understood your testimony you said that you changed in the year, I believe 1963, from a policy of investigating complaints to one of affirmative action to place employees in a position for advancement.

MR. ANDERSON. That is true.

VICE CHAIRMAN PATTERSON. I note from the figures that you have more than 30 percent of your employees on the Naval Air Station from minority groups.

MR. ANDERSON. Yes.

VICE CHAIRMAN PATTERSON. But that only 7 percent of these employees are in supervisory capacities.

MR. ANDERSON. I'm not sure that is correct, but it is a lower percentage. That is certainly true.

VICE CHAIRMAN PATTERSON. Would you tell me the percentage in 1963?

MR. ANDERSON. No, I'm sorry, I can't. I can give you the number of promotions since the first of January 1965 in these better jobs. But I don't have the figures from 1963 on.

VICE CHAIRMAN PATTERSON. Do you have the figure for 1965 as to how many supervisory employees were on the Naval Air Station from minority groups at that time? Was it less?

MR. ANDERSON. I do know we have 22 now. I do know that 13 have been promoted since the first of January 1965.

VICE CHAIRMAN PATTERSON. Thirteen of 22. As I gather from 1963 to 1965 you had a moratorium of sorts on what you called promotion of men so that you could place them in details to gain experience which would lead to a promotion. Is that right?

MR. ANDERSON. That is right. Furthermore we provided that those positions since 1965. That would indicate you only had nine during this period of time. We said we would restrict it to those who had not previously had details.

The net effect of this was that many minorities were given details during that particular period of time that would build their experience.

VICE CHAIRMAN PATTERSON. But 13 of your present 22 supervisory employees from minority groups have been promoted to those positions since 1965. That would indicate you only had nine in 1965?

MR. ANDERSON. Yes.

VICE CHAIRMAN PATTERSON. This only brings us to 7 percent, leaving a disparity between the number of supervisory personnel from minority groups and the nearly one-third of your total personnel from minority groups.

MR. ANDERSON. Yes.

VICE CHAIRMAN PATTERSON. Can you assure this Commission that this 7 percent will increase as a result of the steps that you've taken since 1963?

MR. ANDERSON. I have reason to believe it will. Our record shows it is increasing. We have no reason to believe it will not continue to increase.

VICE CHAIRMAN PATTERSON. But do you have any affirmative reason to believe it will?

MR. ANDERSON. Yes, because the supervisor—rather the journeymen are now continuing to get details, credit building details, I think on a more equitable basis and many of them are taking advantage of the training that is being offered, in various methods and various ways, and I'm sure that this will continue.

VICE CHAIRMAN PATTERSON. Thank you.

CHAIRMAN HANNAH. Mr. Rankin?

COMMISSIONER RANKIN. Mr. Anderson, is this change due to any of the equal opportunity legislation or civil rights legislation?

MR. ANDERSON. I really don't know. It took place in 1963. I'm sorry I can't tell you the reason why, but it is a Navy policy and it is a Federal policy.

COMMISSIONER RANKIN. I'm just trying to find out if any employment practices have been changed at all by civil rights legislation, equal employment legislation?

MR. ANDERSON. It's possible. I suppose that in a private sector of the economy this would be particularly important. Insofar as the Federal sector is concerned, it has been governed largely, as you know, by separate Executive orders. First we had the special commission under the—directly with the President, but now it's the responsibility of the Civil Service Commission.

COMMISSIONER RANKIN. Have you ever compared your records with, say, the Memphis Naval Air Station or any of the others to see how they get along and what they are doing or how well you stack up compared with them?

MR. ANDERSON. Well, we have compared ourselves with the North Island Air Station, which is an air station of about equal size and the percentage—I'm not familiar with the percentage of Spanish-speaking or Mexican Americans, but when I checked with the industrial relations officer of that establishment a few months ago he indicated that they had I think about 10 percent of their population was Negro.

But then possibly—I don't know what the Negro population of the San Diego area is. I don't know what the situation is with respect to the naval air stations on the East Coast. Possibly Captain Miller does.

CAPTAIN MILLER. It would vary depending on the area and the size of the Station, buy Navywide the minority populations about 13 percent. We currently have about 35 percent minority that is hired on the Naval Air Station.

CHAIRMAN HANNAH. Dean Griswold?

COMMISSIONER GRISWOLD. Could you see if you can answer this question? Did these changes come about because of changes in outlook at Alameda or because of directives that came down from the Navy Department in Washington?

CAPTAIN CAMPBELL. Speaking for myself, during my tenure it is both personal, deep and personal, with me as well as directed from authority and Government policy to have equal opportunity on the Station.

I've worked extremely hard at it and my staff has as well. I think that many of the changes that came about we can thank the close cooperation between my Commanding Officer's Advisory Committee made up of minorities primarily, with three Caucasians in the membership, their hard work and efforts in trying to find solutions to many of these difficult problems.

We have adopted a great majority of their recommendations. The voucher is one. Part of our training program is another.

Another factor that I've thrown in to help the equal opportunity program is to make sure that promotions are fair and equitable, and that we select only the best qualified individual, and I have instituted a year or better ago a personal review of all promotion actions, and this is no small task when you have over 9,000 personnel employed.

The promotion board that reviews the jackets and come up with their recommendation, submit their recommendation up to the department head. The department head in person brings the jackets and the promotion board acts on the recommendations to me and explains to me or justifies his attempt to convince me that he has looked into it thoroughly and that there absolutely is no discrimination.

There have been about three cases which I have returned, one of which Captain Miller has already mentioned.

CAPTAIN MILLER. Sir, could I address myself to that? I do think there is at least one case where a directive originating in Washington has allowed us to do the kind of thing we would like to do, and that relates to the youth opportunity program which allows us to spend some money in a manner that we would like to spend it, which we would probably have been precluded from doing previously. I don't know if that is the result of legislation or not.

I think not, but it is a policy document to let us do something we would like to do.

CHAIRMAN HANNAH. Mr. Taylor?

MR. TAYLOR. Captain Campbell, you said, I believe, that there was no support from the Station whatsoever for the demonstrations, and that you did not know of personal dissatisfaction concerning the policies at the base.

I don't want to infer too much from that statement.

CAPTAIN CAMPBELL. I would like to correct you. It was not absolute, as you inferred. There was little or no support. There may have been four or five people of this kind that did participate in this demonstration you are speaking of. The total was less than 50, and the overwhelming majority were from off-station, not from on-station.

MR. TAYLOR. Are you suggesting that the previous two witnesses, Mr. Taylor and Mr. Alvarado, were speaking only for themselves?

CAPTAIN CAMPBELL. I believe so, yes.

MR. TAYLOR. Is it possible that there may be—I recognize that you've taken a good number of steps, but is it possible that there may be some dissatisfaction that you are not personally aware of?

CAPTAIN CAMPBELL. There may be some dissatisfaction. You can't please all of the people all of the time. I didn't mean that absolutely everything is sweetness and light.

We wouldn't have 20 cases to be investigated each month by my Commanding Officer's Advisory Committee on possible discrimination if there wasn't some dissatisfaction.

CAPTAIN MILLER. Of course there is dissatisfaction. Mr. Alvarado is a member of the Employees' Council under my command. He talks to me in much stronger language than he talked here today. Whether he feels he has suffered reprisal or not I do not know.

We try to proceed on the basis that any individual who says he has a problem has got a problem.

One of the things cited to you was the supplementary data promotion system and I find this to be a legitimate complaint. One of the complaints was there simply weren't enough pieces of paper to put it all on. We have directed that something be done about this, and that the information requested be printed on the form saying, "This form is necessary. Fill it out or we won't count you." So that this kind of dissatisfaction does exist. We would hope that it will not always exist, but it has, and it continues, and we try to deal with these problems as best we can.

MR. TAYLOR. I gather from some of the testimony that a part of the problem in the past has been a problem of communication and the fact that supervisors generally felt, or it was the management's position on the base, that very little information should be shared with employees. Is that correct?

667

CAPTAIN CAMPBELL. Did you mean to say that the policy on the base was that supervisors should not share information?

MR. TAYLOR. That that has been the policy in the past.

CAPTAIN CAMPBELL. Not that I know of.

MR. TAYLOR. Well, there has been testimony.

CAPTAIN CAMPBELL. There have been communication problems. Not all supervisors are outstanding leaders. There are communication problems between employees and supervisors, between seniors and juniors. Some are better leaders than others.

It is the policy of the Naval Air Station, and we have training programs to carry it out, to train supervisors to be better leaders and establish better communications and look out for their employees. There are bound to be misunderstandings and everyone is not perfect in that regard.

MR. TAYLOR. I understand, but you were saying at one time the vouchers were secret and now that policy has been changed, and I believe you said in connection with the statement you just made that supervisors are reluctant to mark a man low if they have to face up to him.

CAPTAIN CAMPBELL. Some are, yes, that's correct.

MR. TAYLOR. I take it you don't think that is a particularly good policy, that if a man is marked low perhaps the reason should be explained to him so that he can improve his performance.

CAPTAIN CAMPBELL. Exactly.

MR. TAYLOR. In this connection can employees at the base now generally obtain copies of Navy regulations governing the promotion procedures?

CAPTAIN CAMPBELL. I'd like Mr. Anderson to answer that.

MR. ANDERSON. They can certainly review them, but we just don't duplicate them, you know, for 9,000 employees. They are available for review.

MR. TAYLOR. Do you believe that making these publications available in greater numbers than they are now available might alleviate some of the concern over practices at the base?

MR. ANDERSON. I think it is important in our weekly house organ that we have articles from time to time on the promotion policy and how it works, and this is what we do.

MR. TAYLOR. So that perhaps they could be issued in summary form?

MR. ANDERSON. That's right, yes, sir.

MR. TAYLOR. Do you have any comment, Captain Campbell, on Mr. Alvarado's statement that he had sought a meeting for a period of time, I think he said two years, and was not able to obtain it.

CAPTAIN CAMPBELL. I don't recall ever having received any communication from him asking to see me.

MR. TAYLOR. I ask that question because—

CAPTAIN CAMPBELL. It certainly was not intentional on my part to freeze him out. I can tell you that. I have met with any number of the minority leaders and representatives on the base, both members of the advisory committee and others that were not members to discuss their problems and to feel the pulse of their grievances or discontent.

I might also say that I am not familiar with the committee that he kept referring to as a splinter committee of some kind. I had not heard until today that there was such a committee. It is not an official committee on the Station.

I have had a number of communications, both oral and written, with FEEO, the Federal Employees' Equal Opportunities Organization on the Station. They are a group that has been referred to here earlier.

MR. ANDERSON. May I refer you to Question 6 of the Civil Service Commission's questionnaire to employees. There were 400 questionnaires, again. The question was, "If you have a complaint what do you think would be of most help to you in settling it to your satisfaction?"

Sixteen of them said to talk it over with fellow employees. Two hundred fifty-three said to talk it over with their supervisor.

MR. TAYLOR. The problem very frequently is when a policy is adopted and even forcefully communicated to the top, the problem is to get people at the lower supervisory levels to recognize it and to feel it and to carry it out. Isn't it important when you are doing this to have sources of information other than those which are directly under you?

CAPTAIN CAMPBELL. Well, we do have sources except directly under me, and we have 40-hour training programs for supervisors, and it is a continuing program to train supervisors in getting not only equal opportunity information but promotional information and working hours and sick leave, all of these things out to their employees and it goes right down the chain of command all the way to the lowest levels of supervision.

CHAIRMAN HANNAH. Mr. Taylor, I'm sure these are good questions but I question whether or not it is desirable to ask the kind of questions that require the captain to, if he is to answer them in a popular vein, raise questions about the competence of the persons that are working for him or their having pursued the policies which he has clearly indicated are his personal policy. I don't think we should follow this line of questioning.

MR. TAYLOR. These are not intended, Mr. Chairman, as personal questions.

CHAIRMAN HANNAH. I'm sure it is not your intent.

CAPTAIN CAMPBELL. I would like to come back to the matter of whether these promotions, instructions, and so forth are published.

We have a large personnel folder like our Navy regulations for civilian employees. To publish 9,000 of these is just not possible at all. Employees wouldn't read them if you did. Most of them would be interested in 713 in detail. However, we do have, through our local newspaper which is free published once a week, opportunities listed, job openings, descriptions, where to apply, where to get the information.

We have training information, we have editorials or statements of policy written by me "the Commanding Officer says," that type of thing. We have information on our equal opportunity program. We publicize who the Commanding Officer's Advisory Committee members are. We show their pictures, the telephone number to call if they have any complaint. We have bulletin boards on promotion procedures to cover the highlights of it.

The claim has been made that my industrial relations staff is reluctant to give the information. I don't believe the claim was ever made that they refused to give information that they were eligible to provide. There is some information such as the ranking procedure that by regulation from the Civil Service Commissioner we are not permitted to divulge.

We can indicate where a person stands on his marks, his grade, but we can't divulge where everyone else who took that examination stands.

So although the industrial relations may have been slow in responding to some of these things you must remember that with 2,000 additional hirees during the past year, a 40 to 48 percent increase in tempo of operations in support of the Vietnam effort, the great degree of overtime work that we are processing there at this busy industrial air station and the staff increasing, the number on the staff has not kept pace to do all the work, and there just aren't enough hours in the day to do everything yesterday.

MR. TAYLOR. But I understand Mr. Anderson's answer to the question to be that to the extent that additional information about the procedures themselves would be helpful, to the extent that people have the grade, this is a problem. Will it at least be possible to publish these in summary form so that people can know precisely what the procedures are?

MR. ANDERSON. Yes, we use the weekly house organ for that purpose. May I make one comment if we haven't already about the promotion program. That is, on all of the promotion boards the commanding officers have invited members of his advisory committee to sit as members of the promotion board, to view the operations and report back to him.

CHAIRMAN HANNAH. Any other questions?

MR. TAYLOR. No further questions.

CHAIRMAN HANNAH. Mr. Glickstein, do you have some records that you want to include?

MR. GLICKSTEIN. Yes, Mr. Chairman. We have two statements that have been submitted to us. One is from the *ad hoc* committee for Citizens for Equal Opportunities and the other is from an individual named John Norman. May they be received in evidence as Exhibits No. 35 and 36?

CHAIRMAN HANNAH. They will be received.

(Whereupon, the documents referred to were marked Exhibits No. 35 and 36 and received in evidence.)

CHAIRMAN HANNAH. We are now in recess until 9:15 tomorrow morning. Thank you, gentlemen.

(Whereupon, the hearing was adjourned at 5:15 p.m. to reconvene the following morning at 9:15.)

U.S. COMMISSION ON CIVIL RIGHTS

CHAIRMAN HANNAH. This hearing will come to order. In accordance with the rules of the Commission, Mrs. Freeman and I are acting this morning as a specially authorized subcommittee acting on behalf of a full membership to conduct this hearing today. Mr. Glickstein, will you call the first witness?

MR. GLICKSTEIN. The first witness is The Reverend Dorel M. Londagin.

(Whereupon, The Reverend Dorel Londagin was sworn by the Chairman and testified as follows:)

TESTIMONY OF THE REVEREND DOREL LONDAGIN, SAN LEANDRO, CALIFORNIA

MR. GLICKSTEIN. Would you please state your full name and address for the record?

REV. LONDAGIN. Dorel Londagin, pastor—what is the other question?

MR. GLICKSTEIN. Your address?

REV. LONDAGIN. 1312 Fargo Avenue, San Leandro.

MR. GLICKSTEIN. What is your occupation?

REV. LONDAGIN. Pastor of the Christ Presbyterian Church.

MR. GLICKSTEIN. Would you please describe the community served by your church?

REV. LONDAGIN. It is essentially a housing area. The building program started following World War II and reached its climax between 1952 and 1956. It is essentially a bedroom community.

MR. GLICKSTEIN. How many Negroes live in the community?

REV. LONDAGIN. None in my parish.

MR. GLICKSTEIN. Your parish is located in the city of San Leandro. Is that correct?

REV. LONDAGIN. The major part of it, yes.

MR. GLICKSTEIN. And the church itself is in San Leandro?

REV. LONDAGIN. Yes.

MR. GLICKSTEIN. Do you have any idea how many Negroes live in San Leandro?

REV. LONDAGIN. Not exactly. I know it is a small number. I've never attempted to find out the exact number.

MR. GLICKSTEIN. Rev. Londagin, I wonder if you could make an observation on the fact that there is such a small number of Negroes in San Leandro, yet a few blocks away in Oakland there are many Negro families. What is your explanation for this phenomenon?

REV. LONDAGIN. I think there are many factors involved, and I know that it has always bothered me that there is such a wall that exists there. For this reason I've always tried to work for responsible integration.

My opinion is that there is a kind of an unconscious effort that has existed in the past to resist the integration of our community. How this is done I can't really say. I can't put my finger on why this is true.

MR. GLICKSTEIN. Are local citizens concerned that they are so close to a large city with such a large Negro population? '

REV. LONDAGIN. Well, there is some concern but I don't think it's enough concern. I don't think they realize the potential danger that exists in such a situation, and it is for this reason that I felt there ought to be responsible efforts to integrate to avoid any kind of a sudden influx that might disrupt and cause great tensions.

MR. GLICKSTEIN. Are city officials concerned about this problem?

REV. LONDAGIN. I recall Mayor Maltester trying to get the city council to organize or to institute a human relations commission several years ago. At that time they said there was no problem.

I have heard rumors since that they still think there is no problem, and that it's a pretty nice place, and we shouldn't get excited about human relations or poverty. Now, whether that attitude still exists with the council I don't know.

MR. GLICKSTEIN. Have you ever attended any meetings with the mayor that were designed or intended to deal with these problems.?

REV. LONDAGIN. Yes. He has attended minister alliance meetings where I have been in attendance. We have talked the problem over a number of times at informal meetings, and one distinct meeting I recall where he gathered together several industrialists, clergymen, educators, bankers, and city officials at an informal meeting to discuss our city and ways of bettering the conditions.

MR. GLICKSTEIN. Was the question of segregated housing discussed at that meeting?

REV. LONDAGIN. Yes it was, and the question was brought up about integration, what would happen if it took place and at first I sensed quite a bit of tension and fear, but as the discussion wore on it was pointed out that the Marina Fair Area and the San

Leandro Hills Area have integrated considerably and no problems have developed, and that surely it wouldn't be a problem if this occurred in the rest of the city. After that, then we began to talk about ways and means of integrating and providing housing.

One of the questions that was brought up was can industry help us at this point, and as I gathered they were dedicated to bringing in minorities into their work force but that they wanted absolutely nothing to do with an attempt to bring about integrated housing on their part, that this wasn't their prerogative.

MR. GLICKSTEIN. Was there any discussion at the meeting as to why housing appears to be segregated in San Leandro?

REV. LONDAGIN. Yes, and I don't recall how it developed, but I do recall that there was an attempt to probe out the reasons why this had not occurred, and one of the things that stood out to me was that there is a responsible attempt to be fair in many instances, but sooner or later along the way minority groups seem to be cut out. They never quite make it.

One of the questions was, "Is it the financial interests that are finally making this impossible?" and this was not pursued any further except to say that those representing the financial interests agreed that they would do all that they could to help persuade others to make it possible for minority groups to come in.

MR. GLICKSTEIN. Are you saying that there was some discussion at the meeting that perhaps one of the reasons Negroes weren't able to purchase homes in San Leandro is that they couldn't have those homes financed through financial institutions?

REV. LONDAGIN. Yes. As I say, I don't recall how the discussion came up at this point, but I do know that there was a point made of this possibility, that they were eliminated in the financial circles.

MR. GLICKSTEIN. It wasn't so much a matter of Negroes not wishing to live here, but that some of the Negroes that did wish to live here seemed to have been eliminated when they sought financing?

REV. LONDAGIN. I got the impression that the Negroes would like to live close to their place of employment, or some of them would, but this so far, by and large, is not possible or has not developed.

MR. GLICKSTEIN. Have you been active in open housing activities?

REV. LONDAGIN. Yes. I have been in the parish for 15 years and have tried to communicate my convictions about this matter of equal housing or equal opportunity, and have tried to communicate the Presbyterian Church's position, and have worked actively with various groups in trying to implement responsible integration.

MR. GLICKSTEIN. How have your church members reacted to your activities in this area?

REV. LONDAGIN. Well, at first they tolerated me, and then when the Proposition 14 issue came along, and then our attempt to bring Saul Alinsky into the Bay Area developed and when we took strong positions on certain issues a large percentage of the church membership deserted the congregation.

Those that remain now, I think for the most part have very deep conscience about this matter. At least, they are still standing by and are supporting the ministry there.

MR. GLICKSTEIN. Did you speak to the persons who left and who were opposed to your position?

REV. LONDAGIN. Yes, many times. We have been in many, many conferences together.

MR. GLICKSTEIN. What did they say their concerns were?

REV. LONDAGIN. Well, the first response, by and large, was, "Well, we like the Negroes, we have many Negro friends and we are not really against equal rights but the church has no business talking about it from the pulpit and we want to hear nothing but the gospel." The gospel, of course, meaning nothing but so-called spiritual things, and that if the church would try to convert individuals then social justice would naturally evolve.

MR. GLICKSTEIN. Did people give reasons other than that for their opposition to your stand?

REV. LONDAGIN. No, they would never admit that basically they were prejudiced. And, of course, I have no right to judge and to say that this is the basis for their hostility and their anger, but it appears to me that much of their resistance really is reflecting a deep-seated prejudice.

MR. GLICKSTEIN. Thank you. I have no further questions, Mr. Chairman.

CHAIRMAN HANNAH. Mrs. Freeman?

COMMISSIONER FREEMAN. Rev. Londagin, I would agree with you that the kind of situation that you have described reflects a deep-seated racial prejudice, and I would commend you as a minister for your efforts, because many times people refuse to recognize that what we practice should be what we preach. I would like to ask you if you would describe whether there have been houses for sale in San Leandro within the past several years, and whether there has been rental housing. What kind of housing is there in this community? Is it essentially a middle-class community?

REV. LONDAGIN. Yes. Originally the houses sold for between $9,000 and $10,000, $12,000 when they were first developed. Now they are selling for $18,500, $22,000, $22,500. We have a very small turnover in our community. Though there are houses constantly being sold, and a few are being rented.

COMMISSIONER FREEMAN. So there has been a turnover?

REV. LONDAGIN. Yes, there has been some.

COMMISSIONER FREEMAN. Do you have an opinion with respect to the role of the real estate broker or financial institution in the exclusion of Negroes from this community?

REV. LOGDAGIN. Well, my opinion is that there has been a conspiracy to keep out colored people. Now, I can't substantiate that, but this is my thinking.

COMMISSIONER FREEMAN. Yes, I asked for your opinion.

REV. LONDAGIN. For the most part there is conspiracy. I know of some who do not feel this way, but they have acquiesced under great social pressure from the community and from others in the same profession.

COMMISSIONER FREEMAN. Thank you.

CHAIRMAN HANNAH. Mr. Taylor?

MR. TAYLOR. Rev. Londagin, I understand that several months ago you attempted to aid a Negro family in finding a home in your community. Can you tell us what happened?

REV. LONDAGIN. Yes. I did what I do for any parishioner, for any family who comes into the community and seeks to settle. I go about inquiring if there is housing available. I've shown many a family houses in our community, and we had a parishioner whose house was vacant, had been rented for a couple of years and practically destroyed and he refused to allow a Realtor to rent it.

He restored it himself and then tried to rent it himself. After receiving approximately 100 inquiries about the house he still hadn't rented it, and I found out about it at this time and I asked the privilege to show it to anyone who was interested.

I attempted then to rent it. I made known to the congregation and to various organizations that I work with that the house was available, and that I would show it to anyone who came to inquire.

Well, naturally, the large percentage of those who came were colored people seeking decent housing, and I showed them—I was fair in showing it to anyone who came, regardless of color.

When it was made known that I was showing this to colored people, I received phone calls and a great deal of interest was developed, some who sympathized with my concern and some, most, who did not. We had at least three families who tried to qualify.

The rent was $160. They had to have a month's advance rent, plus a cleaning fee which was sizable, making a very large sum of money, and two families who owned other property, colored families, could not liquidate it so they had to let it go after they had made a deposit.

One, the first family we thought was going to take it, I under-

stand the wife said that the husband went to work the next day
and they told him, "Man, you don't want to go into that San Leandro area. They'll get you." This is just what the wife reported to
me. And so he backed out. We were never able to rent it to anyone, and a great deal of anger was developed in the community
and directly primarily toward me and the church. In this case I
did not involve the church in any way.

MR. TAYLOR. How was the anger toward you expressed?

REV. LONDAGIN. Phone calls, and one night there were 50 people milling around the church looking for me and I wasn't aware
that a rumor had spread in the community that there would be a
meeting at the church, so I wasn't there. I would have been had
I known of it. I only get the impression from those who observed
what was going on that some were very angry and some were
merely curious.

MR. TAYLOR. When did this occur?

REV. LONDAGIN. I found out about this house not being rented
Christmas vacation and this must have occurred then, these activities—because I had to help fix the house up. I got volunteer
members of our church, and the activities took place about the
latter part of January and the first part of February.

MR. TAYLOR. This year?

REV. LONDAGIN. This year.

MR. TAYLOR. You are on the firing line and you've been there
for some time. Do you have any observations that you have gained
from experience on how best we can deal with peoples' fears and
prejudices? What can be done to break this wall that we have
erected by isolating ourselves?

REV. LONDAGIN. Well, I wish I knew. As I said earlier, I have
been concerned for these many years and felt very guilty about our
white ghetto and our unwillingness to practice equality. My procedure has been to work with interested persons in organizations,
first of all in my own congregation and then through Echo and
Good Neighbors, and this is the way I have approached it.

Being in a housing area, I don't have much influence upon the
political or industrial or financial efforts. I haven't been able to
exert much effort there, so I have chosen to work with groups
that are sympathetic.

MR. TAYLOR. Thank you.

CHAIRMAN HANNAH. Any further questions?

MR. GLICKSTEIN. No, sir.

CHAIRMAN HANNAH. Thank you very much, sir. We appreciate your coming this morning. You are excused. Will you call
the next witness, Mr. Glickstein?

MR. GLICKSTEIN. The next witness is Mr. M. L. Sanford.

(Whereupon, Mr. M. L. Sanford was sworn by the Chairman and testified as follows:)

TESTIMONY OF MR. M. L. SANFORD, SAN LORENZO, CALIFORNIA

MR. GLICKSTEIN. Mr. Sanford, would you please state your full name and address for the record?

MR. SANFORD. My name is M. L. Sanford, secretary manager of the San Lorenzo Village Homes Association. My address is 15855 Via Del Prado, San Lorenzo.

MR. GLICKSTEIN. Would you just tell us where San Lorenzo is?

MR. SANFORD. San Lorenzo as a term has no legal definition, you might say. I look at it as being generally that area between the limits of San Leandro on the north, and Hayward on the south, Castro Valley Fire District on the east, and San Francisco Bay on the west.

MR. GLICKSTEIN. How many members does your association have?

MR. SANFORD. Our association has approximately 11,000 members, adult members, and may I add the San Lorenzo Village is where our jurisdiction lies and it is only a portion of the geographical area known as San Lorenzo.

MR. GLICKSTEIN. How long have you been executive secretary of the association?

MR. SANFORD. A little over 20 years.

MR. GLICKSTEIN. How does one become a member of the association?

MR. SANFORD. By purchase of a home in the tracts which have deed convenants covering the lots.

MR. GLICKSTEIN. I see. When you purchase a home you automatically become a member of the association?

MR. SANFORD. Technically I think it should be said that you can exercise membership privileges if you so desire, and in that sense you are a member.

MR. GLICKSTEIN. Would you please describe the history and development of San Lorenzo Village.

MR. SANFORD. San Lorenzo Village was an agricultural area in 1944. At that time the first developer bought up several hundred acres of land and built his first 1,392 homes, and later additional homes, and other developers, several of them, came in later. By 1953 or '54 practically all of the homes had been completed extended over that period of time.

MR. GLICKSTEIN. You say that when a person purchases a home one of the provisions in the deed is a provision that makes him eligible or makes him a member of the association. Is that correct?

MR. SANFORD. Yes.

MR. GLICKSTEIN. Are there other restrictions and covenants in the deed that affect the rights of a home owner?

MR. SANFORD. That affect the rights of a home owner?

MR. GLICKSTEIN. Are there restrictions, for example, on lot size and use of property?

MR. SANFORD. Yes, the minimum lot size is 5,000 square feet. There are certain restrictions in there such as if you want to add exterior improvements to the home you have to submit building plans for our approval. There are regulations on fencing, hedges, keeping of poultry, this type of thing.

MR. GLICKSTEIN. Do the deeds also contain racial and religious restrictive covenants?

MR. SANFORD. The earliest covenant, and I would say approximately half of the home lots in the village, did have the racial restriction clause in it, yes. The later tracts did not have that provision in them.

MR. GLICKSTEIN. If someone were to purchase a home from the earlier group and he looked up the deed he would find the covenant written into the deed. Is that correct?

MR. SANFORD. Yes, it would still be there, but of course not enforceable at all today.

MR. GLICKSTEIN. What explanation do you give members of the association if they ever raise questions with you about these racial and religious covenants?

MR. SANFORD. I always and consistently tell them that these, of course, are not enforceable in any sense since following the Supreme Court decisions.

MR. GLICKSTEIN. What minority groups live in San Lorenzo in significant numbers?

MR. SANFORD. Well, we have some Chinese, Japanese, Polynesian, Mexicans. We may have others, but they are not there in significant numbers.

MR. GLICKSTEIN. Are there Negroes?

MR. SANFORD. We have one Negro family that I know about. They moved in, I think about six or seven weeks ago, and I heard yesterday there was another Negro family that had moved in some time ago. I was not aware of this until yesterday.

MR. GLICKSTEIN. Was there any problem when the first Negro family moved in?

MR. SANFORD. No, none that I am aware of at all.

MR. GLICKSTEIN. Do you think there would be problems if Negro families moved in in significant numbers?

MR. SANFORD. I think that if they moved into our area in significant numbers in a concentrated area that this could involve a problem.

If they moved in and were somewhat dispersed as opposed to concentrated I do not foresee any real problems.

MR. GLICKSTEIN. Have any members of your association expressed concern to you about the prospect of Negroes moving in?

MR. SANFORD. Yes, they have. Yes, they have. If I may elaborate on that.

MR. GLICKSTEIN. Please.

MR. SANFORD. As I say, I think they fear the concentration, and number two, I think they are inclined to look at some of the worst or the most unsatisfactorily maintained areas of Oakland or Richmond or elsewhere where you have this large concentration and where the homes are not properly maintained, and I think the people fear an economic loss if this should occur.

MR. GLICKSTEIN. So the people that have spoken with you would feel that the same sort of conditions might develop in San Lorenzo that they have viewed in places like Oakland and in Richmond. Is that correct?

MR. SANFORD. Yes, this is their great fear, I think, it's the possible economic loss of this occurring. This is not the only expression I hear. I think, as a previous witness stated, there is very definitely a prejudice in our community, in our whole area.

MR. GLICKSTEIN. Does your association do anything to counteract that prejudice?

MR. SANFORD. No, we do not. My board of directors, who are elected by the people, have consistently, in all the years that I have been there, you might say, completely ignored the subject of integration. They have remained silent on the subject.

When the question arises at a meeting as it did not long ago, a lady asked, "Can I sell to a Negro?" our president responded on behalf of the members of the board by saying in effect, "We have nothing to do with the buying or selling or leasing of homes in San Lorenzo Village. This is your business."

So I would say that up to this point we have ignored the broad general question of integration in housing.

MR. GLICKSTEIN. What if a home owner would come to you and ask you whether or not it was likely that property values in San Lorenzo would deteriorate if Negroes were to move in, are you able to answer that sort of a question?

MR. SANFORD. If property values would depreciate?

MR. GLICKSTEIN. If home owners were to ask you on the basis of your experience in real estate operations if it were true that property values tend to deteriorate when Negroes move in, do you have any basis for responding to an inquiry of that sort?

MR. SANFORD. I have responded in this way: that I have told them that the law is strictly on the side of the people who wish to sell and those who wish to buy. That this is their business.

Now, I think I have agreed with some of them that a high concentration might have a bad effect upon real estate values.

MR. GLICKSTEIN. A high concentration?

MR. SANFORD. A high concentration in a given area. It has been referred to here, I think, as ghetto. I call it concentration.

MR. GLICKSTEIN. Mr. Sanford, are there fair housing groups active in San Lorenzo Village?

MR. SANFORD. Yes, there is an organization known as Echo and Good Neighbors. I am more familiar with Good Neighbors as a group that I am with the Echo group.

MR. GLICKSTEIN. That group seeks to find Negro purchasers for homes and seeks to induce sellers to sell to Negroes? Is that correct?

MR. SANFORD. That's what I understood to be the mission of the Good Neighbors Committee. In addition to that I believe their objective is to allay panic selling.

MR. GLICKSTEIN. Do you think the activities of groups such as Good Neighbors are helpful and wise?

MR. SANFORD. I think in general that this whole problem of integration must be faced sooner or later, and I have no quarrel with the methods used by Good Neighbors except in one particular. They may be right; I may be wrong.

I understand that they would arrange to find a willing seller and a willing buyer, a Negro buyer or a minority buyer, then they would go out and knock on doors and try to convince people in that neighborhood that everything was going to all right, their home values would not suffer and so forth, and then the family would move in. They would try to create a favorable environment.

My feeling was that it was a matter of timing. I felt that integration perhaps should come naturally, and that people might resent the Good Neighbors Committee taking the initiative in the matter and thus receiving a hostile reception from the committee when they went out to pacify the people. That is the only difference of opinion that exists as far as I personally am concerned.

MR. GLICKSTEIN. I see. Essentially you think that the Good Neighbor groups go too far in trying to contact people in the neighborhood, prepare them for the family that is about to move in.

MR. SANFORD. I think that due to the nature of the prejudice that does exist out there that there is considerable opposition to any group pushing too fast in the matter of integration.

MR. GLICKSTEIN. Thank you. I have no further questions, Mr. Chairman.

CHAIRMAN HANNAH. Mrs. Freeman?

COMMISSIONER FREEMAN. Mr. Sanford, is there any requirement of San Lorenzo Village Homes Association that the owner of property in the area come to you or come to the association first before he puts his home on the market?

MR. SANFORD. No, there is no such provision and no one comes to us in that regard at all.

COMMISSIONER FREEMAN. Well, is it not correct then that the most natural kind of integration would be that the home owner would just go on and sell his house to a Negro? Wouldn't that be the most natural thing?

MR. SANFORD. Yes, I would say so.

COMMISSIONER FREEMAN. Well, what is it—there have been homes for sale in San Lorenzo Village over the past several years?

MR. SANFORD. Oh, yes.

COMMISSIONER FREEMAN. As executive director of the association do you have an opinion as to why no Negro up until a few months ago has been able to buy a home?

MR. SANFORD. I can only express an opinion which is not based upon surveys or anything. My opinion is that possibly our houses may be priced in a sufficiently high bracket so as to preclude many people of the minority races from buying.

COMMISSIONER FREEMAN. What is the price of these homes?

MR. SANFORD. They'll run from, say $18,500 to $23,000, in that area.

COMMISSIONER FREEMAN. Eighteen thousand to $23,000 you think is too much for Negroes?

MR. SANFORD. I don't know. I think there are lots of them that could qualify, Mrs. Freeman, yes. But I think—I may be wrong in this, but I think that it might disqualify quite a few.

COMMISSIONER FREEMAN. Well, it would of course disqualify the poor, but there are persons who are Negro who can afford such homes.

MR. SANFORD. Definitely.

COMMISSIONER FREEMAN. You have also indicated that you believe that there would be objection to a concentration of Negroes. I would like to suggest to you, sir, that you already have a concentration of whites, and that you already have a ghetto, and the reason for the fear and the prejudice that exists in that community is because of their isolation.

That perhaps you have a responsibility as a community to try to eliminate the fear and the racial prejudice, because this is a racists' community and it is right on the bridge of Oakland, and it is bound to spill over and have some harmful effects unless the community will decide to do something about it.

Now, two Negroes who have moved there have bought the homes and I would urge you and the people who live there to look at themselves and say that they live in a ghetto and recognize that it is what it is.

CHAIRMAN HANNAH. Mr. Taylor?

MR. TAYLOR. Mr. Sanford, do you think that the practices and the attitudes of people who live in San Lorenzo Village have any relationship to feelings of discontent that the Negroes and members of other minority groups may have who live in the city of Oakland or elsewhere.

MR. SANFORD. I'm sorry. Would you repeat that.

MR. TAYLOR. Do you think that what you have described, the attitudes of some of the people who live in your community, and you have described resistance to making homes available to Negroes, do you think that has any relationship to the way Negroes and members of other minority groups may feel about things here in the Oakland area or is it entirely unrelated?

MR. SANFORD. I'm not sure, Mr. Taylor. I couldn't answer that.

MR. TAYLOR. Is there ever any discussion in your community about problems that may exist in the Oakland area or in the San Francisco area, problems of unemployment, problems of inadequate housing, racial disturbances?

MR. SANFORD. Yes, I think these things are definitely on people's minds. Very definitely.

MR. TAYLOR. Is it ever related at all to what happens in your community, or is it thought of as something entirely separate and apart?

MR. SANFORD. I think for the moment they feel somewhat isolated by it because they are removed physically from it, it being a bedroom community. But I think that certainly some people must surely feel that we are living in a dangerous situation. That these problems will have to be resolved or there will be trouble.

MR. TAYLOR. How do you think the problems can get resolved?

MR. SANFORD. I like the term that Rev. Londagin used, responsible integration, orderly integration. I think this is what should be encouraged, but you must realize that we are dealing, we think, with a preponderant population that seems to want to remain isolated for their own particular reasons, economic and otherwise, so it is quite an uphill battle for anyone who attempts to promote integration.

MR. TAYLOR. You think we need to talk about it and raise it in community meetings and discuss it in a responsible way, or is the best thing to do just to suppress it?

MR. SANFORD. I think it has to be talked about and discussed and studied and action taken. I don't think you can hide your head in the sand and expect the problem to resolve itself.

MR. TAYLOR. Thank you.

CHAIRMAN HANNAH. Any further questions, Mr. Glickstein?

MR. GLICKSTEIN. No, sir.

CHAIRMAN HANNAH. Thank you very much, Mr. Sanford. You are excused. Would you call the next witness?

MR. GLICKSTEIN. The next witness is Mr. Emil Donald Lucot.
(Whereupon, Mr. Emil Donald Lucot was sworn by the Chairman and testified as follows:)

TESTIMONY OF MR. EMIL DONALD LUCOT, OAKLAND, CALIFORNIA

MR. GLICKSTEIN. Mr. Lucot, would you please state your full name and address for the record?

MR. LUCOT. My full name and address is Emil Donald Lucot, 3021 Revere Avenue, Oakland.

MR. GLICKSTEIN. What is your occupation, Mr. Lucot?

MR. LUCOT. Banker.

MR. GLICKSTEIN. Which bank are you associated with?

MR. LUCOT. I am the assistant vice-president and manager of Wells Fargo Bank in San Leandro.

MR. GLICKSTEIN. And that branch services all of San Leandro?

MR. LUCOT. And many areas outside of San Leandro.

MR. GLICKSTEIN. What is your authority to approve or disapprove home purchase loans?

MR. LUCOT. We can approve them up to a certain amount, and over that amount they have to go to our head office for final approval.

MR. GLICKSTEIN. Up to what amount are you able to approve them?

MR. LUCOT. Up to $25,000.

MR. GLICKSTEIN. Have you ever approved a loan to a Negro to purchase a home in San Leandro?

MR. LUCOT. I don't think I can honestly answer as to whether I have approved a loan to a Negro in San Leandro, but I have approved many loans for Negroes through our office.

MR. GLICKSTEIN. Do you know where they were purchasing their homes?

MR. LUCOT. In Oakland and other areas right close to San Leandro.

MR. GLICKSTEIN. Do you know if a Negro has ever applied for a loan to purchase a home in San Leandro?

MR. LUCOT. I really can't say. I imagine we have had applications. We don't consider race or creed or religion at any time when an application comes in. It is on the merits of the application.

MR. GLICKSTEIN. On the merits of the application?

MR. LUCOT. That's right, and the collateral.

MR. GLICKSTEIN. Are you aware of any policies of developers and builders to exclude Negroes from particular tracts?

MR. LUCOT. No. In San Leandro, no.

MR. GLICKSTEIN. You have never had contacts with builders or developers who have indicated that loans should not be made to Negroes who wish to purchase homes in particular tracts?

MR. LUCOT. Never.

MR. GLICKSTEIN. How would you explain the fact that Negroes have come to you to purchase homes in Oakland, and you say that such loans have been approved, but you haven't had more Negroes who have sought loans to purchase homes in San Leandro?

MR. LUCOT. Well, when I say that I have not had an applicant we could have had because—

MR. GLICKSTEIN. You could have had?

MR. LUCOT. When the application first comes in maybe the Realtor or the builder brings it in from the tract for individual sale. We will start processing the loan as to the collateral and the credit of the buyer. We don't even see the person—if we disapprove the loan he never comes into the office. If we approve it they come in and sign the papers for the loan.

MR. GLICKSTEIN. And there is no way of telling just from an application what the race of the person is?

MR. LUCOT. So far as I know on a credit report or the application it does not designate creed or color or anything else.

MR. GLICKSTEIN. I'm sure it doesn't designate it, but isn't it possible sometimes to be able to guess from where a person lives what his race is?

MR. LUCOT. Where he lives?

MR. GLICKSTEIN. Right.

MR. LUCOT. I don't think so because we have a mixture in the area surrounding us.

MR. GLICKSTEIN. You are pretty familiar with the area. If a person had a West Oakland address, for example, is there a good possibility that he might be a Negro?

MR. LUCOT. I would say from West Oakland, but from there out I wouldn't. I mean, in the Elmhurst area and the Hill area it would be hard to determine.

MR. GLICKSTEIN. Do you think it's also possible that when a person's credit ratings are checked your employee doing that checking might be able to ascertain what the race of the applicant is?

MR. LUCOT. I don't believe so.

MR. GLICKSTEIN. You don't believe so?

MR. LUCOT. No.

MR. GLICKSTEIN. Do you think that homes in San Leandro are too expensive for Negroes to buy?

MR. LUCOT. No. In fact—you know, in San Leandro we are out of land to build tract homes, as you speak of, and it is all individual homes that are being built, and mostly in the higher priced houses right now.

But I know of a Negro that just bought one, I think it's up in the $60,000 or $75,000 class, in the last year in the Hill area. Of course, that's one case.

MR. GLICKSTEIN. In general, homes are not too expensive?

MR. LUCOT. They are from $18,000 up to $75,000 in the different areas.

MR. GLICKSTEIN. Rev. Londagin described a meeting with Mayor Maltester last December. Were you at that meeting?

MR. LUCOT. I was.

MR. GLICKSTEIN. Rev. Londagin said that one of the topics of discussion was the practices of financial institutions that deter Negroes from moving into San Leandro.

MR. LUCOT. I believe it was brought up at the meeting but nothing was ever decided there that I know of.

MR. GLICKSTEIN. What was the nature of the discussion?

MR. LUCOT. Just a general discussion. I think I did bring up that we, at our bank, did not.

MR. GLICKSTEIN. Do many Negroes use your branch for banking purposes?

MR. LUCOT. Very many.

MR. GLICKSTEIN. How many Negro employees do you have?

MR. LUCOT. Well, if you had asked me a week ago I could have told you I had one. I have three minority right there now, but no Negroes.

MR. GLICKSTEIN. No. Negroes?

MR. LUCOT. The one that we had there is in another office right now.

MR. GLICKSTEIN. What was his job?

MR. LUCOT. He was with our comptroller's department.

MR. GLICKSTEIN. I have no further questions, Mr. Chairman.

CHAIRMAN HANNAH. Mrs. Freeman?

COMMISSIONER FREEMAN. Mr. Lucot, you indicated that you have no way of knowing about the race of the applicant for the loan. Has your bank in other situations—depositors of a bank who wish to buy a home may make direct contact with the bank to find out if the bank would finance it. Are you saying that in your case that the individual does not communicate with you, that the only contact you have is with the Realtor?

MR. LUCOT. I said, as a rule, in the majority of the cases, the sales are either through Realtors or tract sales, and then you have the salesmen from the tract come in, or either the Realtor will come in and bring in the papers that they have signed at their offices.

COMMISSIONER FREEMAN. This is true, that the sale is through the Realtor, but it is the buyer who needs to make the loan, is it not?

MR. LUCOT. Yes, but they have all the information on the papers when they bring them in for us so we can order their credit report for them, so we can get the appraisal on the property, and after we get the appraisal and determine their credit report, whether their income is sufficient to service a loan then our answer is given.

COMMISSIONER FREEMAN. Your bank does not accept the application for a loan from an individual?

MR. LUCOT. Yes, we do, but I was just citing the majority of the cases, the way they come in.

COMMISSIONER FREEMAN. And you have received no applications from a Negro?

MR. LUCOT. I've received many applications from Negroes.

COMMISSIONER FREEMAN. But not for—

MR. LUCOT. I cannot specifically say San Leandro.

COMMISSIONER FREEMAN. Is your bank a national bank?

MR. LUCOT. No, State bank.

COMMISSIONER FREEMAN. Does it have public funds deposited there?

MR. LUCOT. Yes, we do.

COMMISSIONER FREEMAN. Does it have Federal funds deposited there?

MR. LUCOT. I believe so.

COMMISSIONER FREEMAN. Thank you.

CHAIRMAN HANNAH. Mr. Taylor?

MR. TAYLOR. I have no questions.

CHAIRMAN HANNAH. Do you have any questions, Mr. Glickstein?

MR. GLICKSTEIN. No, sir.

CHAIRMAN HANNAH. Thank you very much, Mr. Lucot. We appreciate your coming. Would you call the next witness?

MR. GLICKSTEIN. The next witness is the Hon. John D. Maltester.

Whereupon, the Hon. John D. Maltester was sworn by the Chairman and testified as follows:)

TESTIMONY OF THE HON. JOHN D. MALTESTER, MAYOR OF SAN LEANDRO, CALIFORNIA

MR. GLICKSTEIN. Would you please state your full name and address for the record.

MAYOR MALTESTER. It's Jack D. Maltester, 715 Woodland Avenue, San Leandro.

MR. GLICKSTEIN. What is your occupation?

MAYOR MALTESTER. Half owner in a printing business and mayor of the city of San Leandro.

MR. GLICKSTEIN. How long have you been mayor?

MAYOR MALTESTER. Since 1958.

MR. GLICKSTEIN. Are you also a member of the city council?

MAYOR MALTESTER. Yes.

MR. GLICKSTEIN. What is the population of San Leandro?

MAYOR MALTESTER. The last official population was 69,000, close to 70,000, and anticipated at this time probably closer to 75,000.

MR. GLICKSTEIN. You think it's about 75,000?

MAYOR MALTESTER. Yes.

MR. GLICKSTEIN. How many Negroes live in San Leandro?

MAYOR MALTESTER. I cannot tell you to the exact amount. I get two different reports. I would guess it's between 20 and 25, 26.

MR. GLICKSTEIN. Twenty or 25 persons or families?

MAYOR MALTESTER. Persons.

MR. GLICKSTEIN. Are Negroes employed in the industries in San Leandro.

MAYOR MALTESTER. Yes.

MR. GLICKSTEIN. Do you have any idea how many?

MAYOR MALTESTER. No, I haven't. We haven't asked for that type of a survey, although I can tell by the plants when the shifts go off duty that there are quite a few Negroes employed in our industries.

MR. GLICKSTEIN. We have some statistics, Mr. Mayor, a study we did that indicates that the companies in San Leandro employing 100 or more persons that report to the Equal Employment Opportunity Commission and that report to the office of Federal Contract Compliance, provide approximately 13,500 persons, of whom about 572 are Negroes, about 5 percent or so. Does that sound as though it might be right?

MAYOR MALTESTER. That might be right. I presume that some plants according to the type of work may employ more than others. I wouldn't question that.

MR. GLICKSTEIN. And those are companies of 100 employees or more. Companies with less than 100 employees are not included in those statistics. Are Negroes employed in stores and small businesses in San Leandro?

MAYOR MALTESTER. Yes, they are.

MR. GLICKSTEIN. How would you account for the fact that just across the border of San Leandro in Oakland there are large numbers of Negro families, and yet there are just 20 to 25 Negroes in your city?

MAYOR MALTESTER. Well, basically the question in the past has been one of prejudice. San Leandro grew from a farming community to a bedroom community for people who mainly worked in San Francisco. I guess prior to World War II there were about 20,000 people in the community.

Industry started to come in. Half of our present land area is zoned industrial. I don't think there is any question but what there was prejudice involved.

Although some of the families, Negro people who live in San Leandro, have lived there for many years. We have a very heavy Portuguese, Mexican American, Spanish people living in our community. At the present time the families that are moving in are moving in different areas of the town.

As you just heard Mr. Lucot state that the one property on the Hills at some $75,000 or $80,000. We have other families that moved into the Marina Fair and different areas which, from a personal standpoint is good for everybody, and in other words we don't get any ghetto, or where it's white or dark or anything else. It is spread throughout the community. One other thing that has, I'm sure, kept an awful lot of minority races out has been the cost of property.

MR. GLICKSTEIN. The cost of property?

MAYOR MALTESTER. The cost of property in San Leandro. I do not have facts to back this up. I get this statement from real estate people and appraisers, that the same property on one side of Durant Avenue, which is our dividing line with Oakland is worth $1,000 to $1,500 more than this property is in Oakland. The reason for that, I don't know. One has been that we have had a reduce in tax rate, and we have increased our services to the people. Beyond that I can't say, I'm just guessing.

MR. GLICKSTEIN. Do you think that the fact that two cities so close to each other, and one of them has such a large Negro population and the other has such a small one, might lead to friction of some sort?

MAYOR MALTESTER. I'm certain it will some day unless something is done. As I say, it is—I feel something is being done now, but it is being done slowly.

MR. GLICKSTEIN. Is the city concerned that racial disturbances in Oakland might affect San Leandro?

MAYOR MALTESTER. I might say as the mayor I'm concerned, yes.

MR. GLICKSTEIN. What actions or plans do you have to deal with the problem?

MAYOR MALTESTER. Well, we haven't any plans to deal with the problem. You must understand that in our community, although the mayor is directly elected by the people, we are a little different than some of the Eastern cities.

We do not have the authority as mayor, I technically do not have any more authority than any city councilman, so it is just a problem as to what you can do. We hope that we are getting, I think, more and more people in our community that realize the problem and are willing to recognize that it is there and help do something about it, but it's an awfully slow process.

MR. GLICKSTEIN. Do you have problems in your community with white racists groups?

MAYOR MALTESTER. No. In fact, the only time I knew one existed was a series of articles in a local newspaper.

MR. GLICKSTEIN. But the groups themselves you don't consider terribly significant or a force in molding opinion in the community?

MAYOR MALTESTER. No, I've checked this out with our own police department and they feel that it does not pose any problem at all in the community.

MR. GLICKSTEIN. There has been some testimony about the meeting that you held with business and religious leaders to discuss problems of racial integration in San Leandro. Have there been many such meetings?

MAYOR MALTESTER. Well, no. That was probably the largest where we've brought industry into the picture and the banks.

I have attended three or four meetings with various clergy groups and I would think that the clergy has been the most interested in the problem in the community, and probably not only the most interested but probably the most knowledgeable as to what does exist.

There have just been unofficial meetings over a cup of coffee talking about the problems as they would see one or the others that would come up.

MR. GLICKSTEIN. But in December you had a meeting which included a larger number of individuals?

MAYOR MALTESTER. That is correct. I was asked if I could get together some of the industrial people to join some of the clergy and the banks. We thought it would be a good thing to sit down and talk to them and just see what they felt.

MR. GLICKSTEIN. Has that meeting been followed up with additional similar meetings?

MAYOR MALTESTER. No, it hasn't been. It was left on the basis that see how things are going for a while and then we would get together again unofficially. When you try to get a group together like that, sometimes it takes a little time to get them together. Everybody is busy, but we undoubtedly will have other discussion. That is, if I have my way about it and they show up.

MR. GLICKSTEIN. How long have you lived in San Leandro?

MAYOR MALTESTER. I was born in San Leandro.

MR. GLICKSTEIN. On the basis of your knowledge in general, and on the basis of your experience as mayor what factors in the local real estate market do you think have kept Negroes from buying homes in San Leandro?

MAYOR MALTESTER. I don't think it is the real estate people nor the lending institutions. I think it's the people themselves. I'm quite sure that any real estate man would sell any home in San Leandro to a Negro if the seller of that home gave them the go-ahead.

There is still the fear that if one home is sold to a Negro, the whole block will be sold to Negroes and then the next block. This is a fear, I think—and I am not a historian—which grew up over many, many years which ultimately, I guess it did happen in the West Oakland area. And this, I think is the basis of fear.

I really don't—oh, there may be one or two real estate people, maybe one or two lending institutions, but I think the basic problem is with the people themselves, not only in our community but in any other community.

MR. GLICKSTEIN. But you have had some large tract developments in San Leandro where the homes were sold new by the developer.

MAYOR MALTESTER. Right.

MR. GLICKSTEIN. Not by individual sellers. Yet, those developments have turned out to be predominantly or exclusively white. Isn't that correct?

MAYOR MALTESTER. It is correct, and yet probably the largest and latest development and the last one from the land standpoint that is available now has three Negro families living in it, and the development is only five or six years old and all of the three—and one I know was sold through the developer of the tract.

MR. GLICKSTEIN. One was sold through the developer of the tract?

MAYOR MALTESTER. Definitely to the Negro.

MR. GLICKSTEIN. That is the Marina—

MAYOR MALTESTER. Marina Fair.

MR. GLICKSTEIN. That is a new area that is being developed?

MAYOR MALTESTER. Right.

MR. GLICKSTEIN. How do you account for the older tracts that were developed that were not integrated?

MAYOR MALTESTER. This, again, I cannot account for except for the fact that I think it goes back to the people themselves. I've talked to apartment house owners that the rest of their tenants have threatened to move out if they rent one apartment to a Negro family. So then who do you blame, the people or the apartment house owner?

MR. GLICKSTEIN. When Negroes have moved into San Leandro how have they been received by their neighbors?

MAYOR MALTESTER. Normally very fine. We've had one bad incident that you have undoubtedly picked up on us. This happened to be on the most expensive one we were talking about, but it had nothing to do with racial problems, just outright hoodlums, but outside of that they are well accepted.

In fact, I would think exceptionally so. The reports that I get from this Marina Fair area is that the people in the area are happy with these families. They have gone in and fixed up their homes better than they were before and joined the Home Owners Association, become active in the area. This is what I think is tending, as I say, to break down this barrier that is built up, but I don't think it will be broken down politically. It's got to be through people.

MR. GLICKSTEIN. And I gather from what has been said that you as mayor have been exercising some leadership in the direction of breaking these barriers down?

MAYOR MALTESTER. I try as much as possible, in fact maybe a little more than I am supposed to, but it has to be persuasion and on a friendly basis. Yes.

MR. GLICKSTEIN. One of the witnesses said you had proposed to the city council that a human rights commission be set up and you were unsuccessful in getting that through.

MAYOR MALTESTER. I went beyond the human relations commission. I also tacked the word responsibilities in there because this had been proposed right after President Kennedy addressed the United States Congress of Mayors in Honolulu and asked for this type of support throughout the country because I think every city has areas where the property is getting run down, and this is not always Negroes' areas. In fact, most of the time it isn't.

So we wanted not only the human relations commission aspect, we wanted some responsibilities put into it. Unfortunately, the city council decided on a five to two vote that it was not necessary, that we didn't have any problems, and I don't blame the city council because, believe me, when that proposal was put out in the press —before I made the proposal I had six votes, and when the people got through with the telephone calls I wound up with one besides my own.

MR. GLICKSTEIN. Informally, then, your fellow councilmen agreed with your position, but when they had to indicate publicly what their position was they voted differently.

MAYOR MALTESTER. That is correct.

MR. GLICKSTEIN. How many persons does your city employ?

MAYOR MALTESTER. Approximately 365.

MR. GLICKSTEIN. How many are Negroes?

MAYOR MALTESTER. One.

MR. GLICKSTEIN. And he is a—

MAYOR MALTESTER. Police officer. We did have two. We had a young lady that was a police assistant, but she decided she would rather work for the telephone company.

692

MR. GLICKSTEIN. Does the city require its employees to be residents?

MAYOR MALTESTER. Yes and no. The rule is, the civil service rule is that all employees must be residents. The civil service board has the right to suspend that rule for all examinations.

In checking our records we find it has suspended for all operations except three, they're always putting the rule to one side.

Those three operations that they have not suspended the rule for was a garbage collector, a maintenance man and the parks people, and in checking back and asking the Civil Service Commission why these three were not also allowed to not have to live in the community it is a fact that they class them in three emergency categories. I don't know, this is the answer that I got.

MR. GLICKSTEIN. Those three categories have to live in the community?

MAYOR MALTESTER. Right, and the others have to—the examinations are open. In fact, the young Negro police officer we had lived in Berkeley. Now he lives in San Leandro with his family.

MR. GLICKSTEIN. He now lives in San Leandro?

MAYOR MALTESTER. Right.

MR. GLICKSTEIN. Did he have any difficulty in finding a place to live?

MAYOR MALTESTER. I haven't talked to him. He hasn't said anything to me.

MR. GLICKSTEIN. But he did move into the city?

MAYOR MALTESTER. Yes.

MR. GLICKSTEIN. Does the city recruit employees outside the city?

MAYOR MALTESTER. Yes. This is what I was talking about on the recruitment. These are the only three that are supposed to live in the city. The rest of the recruitment comes from all over.

MR. GLICKSTEIN. And actually you make affirmative efforts to go outside of the city? You advertise outside the city?

MAYOR MALTESTER. Yes. It's advertised in all the journals, a notice is sent to the department of employment. We give it a broad advertising effect.

MR. GLICKSTEIN. Thank you. I have no further questions, Mr. Chairman.

CHAIRMAN HANNAH. Mrs. Freeman?

COMMISSIONER FREEMAN. Mayor Maltester, does your city attempt to recruit industry, large industry, to come in? Have you ever in the past attempted this?

MAYOR MALTESTER. The city as such hasn't. The Chamber of Commerce is always, of course, working to bring new industry into San Leandro, and this is where our growth assessed valuation-wise has come from, new industry over the past years.

COMMISSIONER FREEMAN. Do the majority of the persons who are employed by the industries that have come in in the past few years reside in San Leandro?

MAYOR MALTESTER. I wouldn't know. I would have to say as a guess, no. It's a pretty educated guess.

COMMISSIONER FREEMAN. Would a significant number of those that are white reside in San Leandro?

MAYOR MALTESTER. No. Again, I don't have any figures, but in my opinion no, because we have an awful lot of people that live in San Lorenzo, Hayward, Castro Valley.

I have had people tell me that even working for the city they can't live there because they can't afford it in their own city and they moved to Castro Valley.

COMMISSIONER FREEMAN. And these houses range in price from $18,000 up. Is that right?

MAYOR MALTESTER. Yes.

COMMISSIONER FREEMAN. Let me pose to you a hypothetical question that if a government agency or a government contractor indicated an interest in shelter for its employees and said to you as mayor, the leading official of the city, that, "We cannot come here because there is not a free and open housing market" what would then be your responsibility as the mayor?

MAYOR MALTESTER. Well, I would certainly want to sit down with the contractor or whoever he was and find out what the facts would be, and then sit down with our city council, so I would say that—

COMMISSIONER FREEMAN. Do you think it would make any change with respect to the—and this of course is an estimate—would the council then care enough about having a white-only ghetto to change it?

MAYOR MALTESTER. I would say that as individuals they would, and then when it got out into the newspapers I don't know where they would stand when the heat went on.

COMMISSIONER FREEMAN. I'm sorry, I didn't hear you.

MAYOR MALTESTER. I say that I am sure that as individuals the city council would be interested. I think that our city councilmen still are interested, but I would say that when the people themselves started to protest—

COMMISSIONER FREEMAN. These people, then, are so racist that they would still keep the industry out?

MAYOR MALTESTER. In my opinion if this were the issue, yes.

COMMISSIONER FREEMAN. Thank you.

CHAIRMAN HANNAH. Mr. Mayor, there are seven councilmen you say?

MAYOR MALTESTER. Six and the mayor.

CHAIRMAN HANNAH. Are you elected as mayor or as a councilman and then the councilmen elect the mayor?

MAYOR MALTESTER. I'm elected as mayor.

CHAIRMAN HANNAH. You are elected at large?

MAYOR MALTESTER. At large. Following through, we have the six councilmen who represent six districts. They have to live in the district, but they are also elected at large.

CHAIRMAN HANNAH. In your testimony this morning you've indicated that your views with reference to the presence of Negroes in your community is at variance with the views of most of the people that live in the community. When you have run for re-election has this been a handicap to you?

MAYOR MALTESTER. I couldn't say that because in the last election I didn't have any opposition, which was last year.

CHAIRMAN HANNAH. Mr. Taylor?

MR. TAYLOR. No questions.

CHAIRMAN HANNAH. Thank you very much, Mr. Mayor. We appreciate your enlightenment, and we hope that you may be able to prevail upon some of your colleagues. Having watched this development in the areas of civil rights all over the country it is as certain as anything can be that a city like San Leandro is going to move in the direction of an orderly acceptance of desirable Negroes and members of other minority groups or face, as you suspect, unhappiness and this myth that has been built up that when good citizens who happen to be black, or Mexicans or something else, move into communities, nothing really happens. There are fine people of all races and colors and religions, and somehow or other we have to get our citizens to recognize that what is important is the individual.

It is basically an educational process and if you and other enlightened leaders can follow along with the attitude that you have expressed here this morning maybe you can make progress, although it gets discouraging at times.

MAYOR MALTESTER. I hope so. I would like to thank the Commission and would like to make one statement, if I may, because I have read where the Commission has been criticized, and I would like to say that I think the most important thing that this Commission is doing is to allow the light of day to be put on some of these problems around the country, and I just hope that your job is accomplished along with the rest of us.

CHAIRMAN HANNAH. Thank you. Call your next witness.

MR. GLICKSTEIN. Mr. Chairman, I have a number of statements and exhibits that have been presented to us that I would like to have included in the record.

I have a decision of trial examiner of the National Labor Relations Board in a brief submitted to the trial examiner in connection with the labor dispute in St. Louis involving the Arch, which I would like to have included in the record in connection with some testimony we heard in San Francisco as Exhibit No. 37.

CHAIRMAN HANNAH. It is accepted in the record.

(The document referred to was marked Exhibit No. 37 and received in evidence.)

MR. GLICKSTEIN. We have a statement from the Boosters and Merchants Association from Potrero Hill that they would like to have included in the record as Exhibit No. 38.

CHAIRMAN HANNAH. It is accepted.

(The document referred to was marked Exhibit No. 38 and received as evidence.)

MR. GLICKSTEIN. A statement by Edward O. Reyes, an attorney in Oakland, that we would like to have included in the record as Exhibit No. 39.

CHAIRMAN HANNAH. It is accepted.

(The document referred to was marked Exhibit No. 39 and received in evidence.)

MR. GLICKSTEIN. And some documents submitted by Mrs. Exaphine Simpson that she would like to have included in the record as Exhibit No. 40.

CHAIRMAN HANNAH. Accepted.

(The document referred to was marked Exhibit No. 40 and received in evidence.)

CHAIRMAN HANNAH. We will now take a brief recess of not more than 10 minutes.

CHAIRMAN HANNAH. Mr. Glickstein, will you call the next witness.

MR. GLICKSTEIN. The next witness is the Hon. John J. Reading.

(Whereupon, the Hon. John H. Reading was sworn by the Chairman and testified as follows:)

TESTIMONY OF THE HON. JOHN H. READING, MAYOR OF OAKLAND, CALIFORNIA

MR. GLICKSTEIN. Mr. Mayor, would you please state your full name and address for the record.

MAYOR READING. John H. Reading, and my address is 1421 92nd Avenue, Oakland.

MR. GLICKSTEIN. How long have you been mayor of the city of Oakland?

MAYOR READING. Just one year. About one year and one month.

MR. GLICKSTEIN. Are you also a city councilman?

MAYOR READING. I was councilman for about five years.

MR. GLICKSTEIN. Prior to being mayor?

MAYOR READING. Yes.

MR. GLICKSTEIN. Mr. Mayor, the Commission has just heard some testimony regarding the cities of San Leandro and San Lorenzo. I wonder if you would like to comment on the extent that the city of Oakland can resolve problems of unemployment and housing that affect minority group citizens without the involvement of surburban communities such as San Lorenzo and San Leandro.

MAYOR READING. I would be happy to comment on that. However, Mr. Glickstein, I have a statement which I would very much like to read, and I think there have been many charges made against the city of Oakland here in the last few days, and I think it is time that we present some factual information of actually some of the projects that have been done, and perhaps some of these questions will be answered in the statement. If they aren't, I'd be happy to speak specifically to anything that you desire at the end of the statement.

CHAIRMAN HANNAH. How long is the statement, Mr. Mayor?

MAYOR READING. Probably 15 minutes. But it contains considerable factual data and I will have copies of this for you to submit for the record at the close of the statement.

CHAIRMAN HANNAH. Proceed, sir.

MR. TAYLOR. Excuse me, Mr. Mayor. You don't happen to have any additional copies handy right now, do you?

MAYOR READING. I don't. My administrative assistant was to have been here and he had additional copies. He is due at 11 o'clock so as soon as he comes in, I will give you copies which he has.

I'm very privileged and honored, and welcome the chance to appear before this Commission, particularly as a wind-up witness.

I think there have been many charges, as I say, that have been made before this Commission and I hope that I can answer some of the many questions that I know that are in your minds as a result of the testimony that has been given here previously.

I think that at this time there is an historic emphasis of our country that is acutely applicable today. Our form of cupboard government intends participation of all, but it clearly contains the parallel concept of responsibility by all.

Participation and responsibility are in policy making execution of that policy and sharing the cost of it, whether the cost is in material goods, in personal effort, or in convenience.

In the area of housing and employment, which I understand are the subjects under consideration by this Commission, participation and responsibility by all persons in the community are essential. I emphasize that this participation should be constructive and beneficial.

There is no need for exploitation of hostility or reiteration of shotgun charges against key individuals or organizations in our community. Officials of the city of Oakland have long been aware that unemployment and underemployment are the primary and tragic problems of this community.

We've had a lot of help in identifying these problems. It seems that every government entity, educational institution and active civil rights group has studied this problem so thoroughly that there are nearly as many experts in this problem as there are unemployed persons in Oakland.

It is a pleasure when we occasionally receive constructive suggestions amidst all the charges, accusations, and discouraging statistics.

A year ago, upon assuming the office of mayor, I pledged an all-out effort to organize community resources toward a solution of the employment problem. In spite of all efforts, however, it appears that we have made little dent in the over-all problem. In Oakland there are still approximately 13,000 unemployed persons, and a large unknown additional number who are barely subsisting on inadequate incomes.

To summarize the problem, it is this: lack of education, of adequate training, and in some cases, of motivation on the part of the unemployed. We also lack a sufficient number of jobs in the unskilled category to fill the total need.

Survey sheets completed at the East Bay Job Fair last fall show that lack of education was the largest single factor in the individuals inability to obtain a job, and that incidentally was based on the own individual's reason that he believed that he was unable to obtain a job. Related to this is the fact that even persons with basic education did not have the training or the ability to qualify for a given job.

On this question of motivation there is an understandable discouragement and feeling of hopelessness by persons who have been out of work most of their lives, but these persons must continue trying. Young people must stay in school, and a high school dropout who feels that working toward a diploma is of no use might have an understandable explanation, but it does not justify his giving up.

I notice, gentlemen, that my administrative assistant is here. Jim, would you come up and give copies of this statement to the members of the Commission? I will wait until this is passed out, and I'm just starting on Page 3.

Furthermore, many of the 13,000 unemployed may not really be employable. They are too old, or have a serious handicap, or may have to care for a large family, or have some other reason why they are not directly in the job market. Unemployment itself is not the only problem.

Poverty is caused just as much by inadequate incomes for persons who are underemployed. It has been stated that an Oakland family of four needs a minimum of $6,000 per year in order to live peacefully. Translated into hour wage this is approximately $3, and yet we are still arguing about a $1.40 and $1.60 minimum wage.

Employers must study their commitment to the free enterprise system. If it is valid, then it must provide incentive income to the employee. Our economy must be sound enough to pay supportive wages.

At the same time an employee must be worth such a wage through his ability to contribute to the success of the company. He must be willing to obtain the skills which will make a living wage possible.

An employer cannot merely donate weekly stipends to persons who can't pull their own weight. However, employers do have responsibility in working together with labor organizations and government to provide the necessary training. This is why I repeat that the real target of the war on poverty must be our education and economic system and the people who determine it. This calls for involvement of everyone, the poor with the rich, and the rich with the poor.

I am convinced that employment is a factor of economics much more than one of civil rights. Granted there may be areas of discrimination directly or inadvertently, and we should continue breaking barriers, urging realistic employment standards, and emphasizing full employment opportunities but in my experience, many of the unemployed are just not adequately prepared to take advantage of these opportunities. They are not equipped either in basic education or in vocational training or in some instances in their attitude towards work.

Now, many charges have been made about what is not being done in Oakland. I would like to point out that many things in fact are being done at tremendous public expense and at tremendous involvement of people working in good faith to solve these problems. So let me state some of the facts.

First, the city of Oakland has created a Manpower Commission for the purpose of coordinating the full program of recruitment, training, and placement.

We discovered that there are 29 ongoing programs in Oakland, mostly subsidized by Federal Government that have been working separately toward the same end. These programs involve millions of dollars, but because of a lack of coordination have only been partially effective. The Manpower Commission already has established a close liaison between job listing services of the California State Employment Service, the Welfare Department, the Adult Minority Employment Project, the East Bay Skill Center, the Youth Employment Center, the Bay Area Urban League, and the Opportunities Industrialization Center.

Now, for the first time a job listed with one of these agencies automatically becomes a listing with all of them and a registration by an unemployed person is similarly shared by each of these agencies, and this is just an example of the type of thing that we are trying to do on coordination.

Second, the commission, working with the Oakland Economic Development Council, has just approved a program for the use of $4,500 million under the concentrated employment program recently announced in Washington. Again, this involves coordination with public and private organizations, and I will refer to them in a few moments.

Last summer and fall the city sponsored a series of business and industry seminars to initiate discussions about employment standards and the improvement of procedures to increase employment opportunities. A majority of employers in Oakland have been very responsive to this program, and have been willing to spend time and money in cooperation with the city to solve this problem.

The city, in cooperation with the county and a number of community agencies sponsored a Job Fair which, in our estimation, was extremely successful in bringing the employment problem to the attention of the community. We were encouraged that some 600 persons obtained jobs during or after the Fair, and were surprised to discover the number of jobs that were available in the East Bay.

However, the Fair sponsors were extremely disappointed on the lack of follow-up by many persons. Employers had invited many thousands of persons to come to their facility for further interviews. Only a fraction of these persons appeared. Our efforts to discover why showed a real lack of communication, as well as motivation between the employer and the prospective employee.

The problem involves such elemental difficulties as lack of transportation or baby sitters to more difficult circumstances such as a confusion about the opportunity and a lack of faith in the fact that a job might actually be available.

In an effort to overcome these hangups a new Job Fair has been planned for next October which will involve careful screening of all employers in order to have a better understanding of what kinds of jobs will be available and a much more meaningful counseling procedure and follow-up assistance to insure that available job openings will not be missed.

Now, I frankly resent some of the charges that have been made against the city of Oakland in the last few days, both in this Commission and also in statements outside of the Commission. The truth is that we are doing a great deal, so let's be factual and let me recite some of the programs that actually are going on in Oakland, and I would refer you to Exhibit A, which is a listing of the ongoing programs that are now in existence and being followed through in Oakland.

The first of these, and in my estimation the most important, is the East Bay Skill Center, and this involves a total of about 2,400 people that are now or will be in training within the next year. However, I have to point out that we have some 3,000 that are on the waiting list on this, so it shows that there is a tremendous need and a confidence in this by the people whom it will affect, and this is being funded to the tune of about $10,900 million.

Under the Manpower Development and Training Act we have another program where we are training people on transcribing machines 50, aircraft maintenance of 100.

Under the MDTA, again, a World Airways Program where we are training or getting ready to train—now these are either people that are in training or are projected for being in training within the next year, and on this the A and E Mechanics there are 500 that will be trained under this World Airways Program.

Also under the MDTA at the Naval Air Station they are on a program now of training some 200 A and E mechanics.

Under the Home Health Aid, the Alameda County Health Department, they are training home health aides, and we have a projected 200 on that.

On the OJT training program we now have in existence about 800 people that are in this program.

The fact of the matter is that there is closer to 1,200, but this was because of employers who did not desire to take the allocation of funds for this program, so we actually have more than are listed here.

We also have the Urban League which has just been given an additional contract for 600 jobs for the development of on-the-job training with private industry.

We have the on-the-job training marketers advisory council, and this is for gas stations, the training of gas station attendants, 400 people.

On-the-job training for the division of apprenticeship standards, and this is done by the division of apprenticeship standards, and there are 2,000 that are involved or will be involved within the next year on this program.

An on-the-job training program on five different Oakland companies, another 435 people. The Opportunities Industrial Center, which I'm sure that you people are all aware of, the Philadelphia Plan which has come here and now is getting rolling and we expect probably from 200 to 300 in that within the next year.

We have the NYC Corps, the Neighborhood Youth Corps. This portion of it is run by the Central Labor Council for the development of jobs in labor, in the unions, which would be 400 people.

The NYC, which is a program under the Department of Human Resources which would be 190 people. We have another program which is under the Mexican American community development, and I don't have the number of people involved.

The Federal Government, Department of Indian Affairs, is in here with an American Indian community development, and we have about 600 people that are being brought in from the reservation. They are being trained, and they are being placed in jobs or maintained until such time as they can be placed on a job.

We have the California State Employment Service which has an active program going where people who are drawing unemployment under a special provision can continue to draw unemployment while they are in training on other jobs. This is an ongoing program.

Then, on top of that, we have the other various State and county programs which is the State Department of Adult Parolees. We have the Youth Authority, the Alameda County Probation Department has a department for developing jobs. We have the Welfare Department which has a work experience program where they have an ongoing program for people who are on welfare for job experience.

We have a Vocational Rehabilitation Service. Here, again, this is a State program, and then several other projects, but I would like to point out that if we take a look at the number of people that we have either in training now or we have potential possibility of training within the next year we are talking about almost 10,000 people. This is the massive effort that this city is doing at this point.

Now, in terms of the amount of money that is being spent on this, in terms of attempting to help—and I must say that practically all of these people are minorities.

For instance, on the Skill Center it runs about 30 percent Mexican Americans, but the balance of it is practically all Negro, and on that, in terms of the amount of money that is being spent, and most of it is Federal money, it amounts to about $22 million. $22 million that is going into this program.

Now, these are the ongoing programs that are being coordinated as much as possible through this Manpower Commission.

Previous to the time of having this Commission they were all working their separate and distinct ways. We had situations where as much as possible through this manpower commission.

businesses for job development, or if a job order, work order, came into one of these agencies there was no coordination between the three. If they didn't have a man to fill it, then the job went unfilled, so this is the attempt that we are trying to do of getting these people to work together.

All of these Federal and State agencies that are involved in this program have all agreed to work with us to follow the decisions that are made by the Manpower Commission with one exception, and that is the OEO. We've still got some problems in getting coordination there, but we are working on it and we hope that we will work it out. It was also determined that available, starting in June of this year, we will have an additional $4,500 million under the concentrated employment program for a concentrated effort in employment over and above the ongoing programs which I have just listed. The Manpower Commission and the Oakland Economic Development Council are working on this final program. Let me give you an idea of some of the programs that are under consideration on this. This is starting as of June 1 and, as I say, amounts to $4,500 million.

We have a basic education course at the Skill Center. This will expand the Skill Center over and above the figures that I gave you, and will allow about an additional 550 people, which will get us into the 3,000 applicants that we have.

We have an on-the-job training program, an additional 200 jobs which we hope to place through the Urban League.

The Neighborhood Youth Corps, 500 jobs, and here we plan on using these people for additional recreation directors, a large number of these, so that we can have a massive recreational program this summer which will be run by our city recreation department.

We have a New Careers program of some 200 people that will be in that, and this is to be placed in public, city administrative jobs, county jobs, jobs where we feel that the applicant or employee has a chance to work into a Civil Service job as a permanent position.

We also plan to use some of these funds for the Job Fair which we have planned to be in the fall. A job development program through the Oakland Small Business Development Center, another one through the Oakland Adult Minority Employment Project.

We have Litton Industries, who is coming in here with an electronics plant and they have guaranteed under this program to hire 400 people in a training production job for the training, here again, of people who are either underemployed or unemployed and don't have sufficient training to qualify for jobs. We have a basic educational pre-vocational counseling and coaching and this will be done by the OIC which will amount to some 1,600 people that we hope to be able to counsel into those jobs where they have the aptitudes to qualify for the certain job that they are going to go on and train for through these other programs.

We have a health program which will affect some 2,000 more, emergency aid another 1,000: this is run by the county and the city. A child day care through the Council of Churches, but here we are talking about another 3,750 people, potentially employed through this year's program, this $4,500 million program.

I can say frankly that our biggest problem is not in terms at this point of having sufficient training programs. Our biggest problem is where we are going to find the jobs to put all these people in when they get out and this is the thing that worries me.

I would like to note that these programs have been planned by a joint effort of business, labor, government officials, and representatives of the poor, and a total of $4,500 million will be used to involve over 3,750 persons in the on-the-job training.

In addition to these employment programs we have under discussion possible special projects for this summer, most of which were suggested by persons from the poverty areas. These are activities of an educational or recreational nature for children or young people during the summer.

Any development of this program is dependent upon funding, but we have high hopes that the money will be available. Let me very rapidly tell you some of the programs that are being planned to keep the kids off the streets this summer.

We have youth tours in which we hope to serve about 18,000, and incidentally this is one that we ran last summer which was extremely effective. This is a matter of taking kids on buses to various places of interest, whether it be to factories, or to fairs, or to educational exhibits, but it is something to keep them busy during the week.

We have planned a mobile bus program which will bring kids to centers where they will be given crafts, games, this type of thing. This was tested by Ford money last year, and it proved to be an effective program and we would like to expand it.

We have buses to pools on a swim program. We have a day camp where we hope to send 600, and a mountain camp, an additional 140.

We have a real playground need at one of our public housing authority centers, San Antonio Center, and we hope to use some of these funds to complete a playground, which is very badly needed at that public housing center.

Creative plays by children; sailing on Lake Merritt; detached workers to work with the gangs in the target areas; and we also are attempting to get the Archie Moore ABC program, which works with kids in the teens on—I don't know whether you are familiar with it or not, but it has been extremely effective in Vallejo. Archie Moore has offered to run the program for us, and it is one that we have planned that actually will reach thousands of kids in this program which he has sponsored.

In addition to those employment programs we have under discussion possible special projects—well, I'm sorry, I have explained this personally. I will go on to Page 8.

These proposals would involve over 50,000 persons for less than $100,000, and there are other tremendously significant projects underway in the city.

The Economic Development Administration is providing—and here we get into the area of where the jobs come to be filled by these people on these training programs.

The EDA has been most helpful on this in providing loans and grants to the city of Oakland and the Port of Oakland to private organizations for the purpose of adding new jobs. Funds already authorized or tentatively committed exceed $25 million.

Again, representatives of business, labor, government, and the poor are involved in committees determining many of these projects. The Redevelopment Agency of the city of Oakland has underway major rehabilitation or clearance programs, and they have been successful in reselling considerable land for industrial purposes which will help retain many existing jobs and will add new ones as the project proceeds.

In addition to this, and I am almost through, gentlemen, the city of Oakland has just submitted a request for a model city program planning grant with the Department of Housing and Urban Development. We have been encouraged to believe that this request will be accepted and that Oakland will be among the first cities to become involved in this great new experiment.

As if you are not already saturated with a listing of programs underway in Oakland, let me show you a remarkable document. I would like to have you take a look at this.

This is one which we prepared about a year ago which shows a complete digest of every Federal program that is coming into Oakland, and it amounts to 140 programs, almost all of which have some social significance here in Oakland, and it amounts to an annual Federal contribution, and this is over and above what we have talked about here, of over a $100 million. This is available to you people if you would like to go through it, but I think that it most certainly indicates that Oakland has taken advantage of every possible program that we can to solve our problems.

This does not mean that we have solved them. We've still got them, but at least we are attempting to do what we can with what is available to work with. Most of the activities relate to the well-being of our citizens in the fields of employment, of health, of urban development, and of business opportunity.

The remarkable fact is that the projects listed in this book represent Federal expenditures in this city of nearly a $100 million. It is due to the multiplicity of these programs and the almost unbelievable dispersion of these funds in too many directions that has caused me time and again to urge stronger coordination of all of these programs.

I have also urged that the agencies concerned use local, city government channels both in the policy-making process and in the implementation of these programs.

I deeply resent the constant barrage of criticism aimed at particular persons and at programs and at this city. What we need is more constructive help.

City officials are open to suggestions. We are gratified at the number of persons who are serving on committees, and are willing to spend hours of time quietly helping to solve these problems. For every headline produced by groundless charges there are a dozen unwritten stories of progress. For every militant spokesman who seeks to justify the allegiance of his followers by issuing scorching demands there is an army of patient builders constructing improvements in our city.

What we are doing, we admit, is not nearly enough, and the number of persons concerned is still far short of the need, but we are working, and we are working hard to make some progress. These are staggering figures, and they indicate a massive effort that the city charged with doing nothing is in fact doing a great deal. Possibly more per capita than any other American city. Thank you, gentlemen.

CHAIRMAN HANNAH. Mr. Glickstein?

MR. GLICKSTEIN. Mr. Mayor, have your efforts to increase the coordination among the various Federal programs met with any success?

MAYOR READING. Yes, I think we are meeting with a great deal of success. The examples which I quoted on the Manpower Commission indicate that this, as I say, was only one example of the type of thing we are trying to do.

The Skill Center, because of the fact that it has been financed by a number of Federal agencies has had really too many cooks in trying to stir the pot.

The Peralta Junior College has agreed to use the Manpower Commission as the one decision-making body for the Skill Center, and they are getting into this program. We also have been successful at the Federal level in getting a new experiment here in Oakland where a Department of HEW, HUD, Labor, and Commerce coordinating team will be working in Oakland. This is now getting set up, and we hope that here with this program we can get some close coordination with these programs within the city.

MR. GLICKSTEIN. Those four agencies are the ones that primarily sponsor the program?

MAYOR READING. This is correct. They sponsor, I'd say, probably 80 to 90 percent of the programs.

MR. GLICKSTEIN. You also said that you were concerned that after many persons, being trained into your program, finish their training you might not have jobs for them, but you mentioned that EDA was helping provide additional jobs. Do you think that there are sufficient efforts being made in that direction to provide additional jobs?

MAYOR READING. We are doing all we can. Here again this is one of the primary purposes for the Manpower Commission. It is made up of equal representation between labor, minorities, education, and business, and the business portion of it is working with local industries to maximize the opportunities.

Also, the Chad McLellan Committee is coming up here and working on an area-wide basis. We can't possibly hope to get all these people hired within the city of Oakland, *per se*, so as a result of this we are attempting to make our efforts—the General Motors plants outside the area are also included within the scope of our efforts in an effort to get more jobs.

Referring back to the industry and business seminars which I held here last year, we invited people from the whole county, in fact some people from outside the county to come here and work with us on trying to show responsibility, trying to get them to change some of their entry qualifications and get them to maximize the hiring of minorities.

MR. GLICKSTEIN. Your response takes me back to the question I asked you before you began reading your statement. Do you feel that Oakland is going to be able to solve its unemployment and under-employment problems and its housing problems without the involvement of such communities as San Leandro and San Lorenzo?

MAYOR READING. No. There is a great need here for additional public housing. We have somewhere between probably 20,000 and 25,000 families that would qualify in the poverty area. So if you would say that or accept the philosophy that everyone of these are eligible for public housing, obviously we'll never be able to do the job.

Also, by the very nature of the requirements of the Federal Government in requiring the moving of people who are displaced by redevelopment programs or by the other Government programs such as highway construction, BART construction, we are required to provide housing for these people to move, but the requirement calls that it be within the city limits itself.

So in other words, the city of Oakland which is the core city and has already been faced with the problem of the mass exodus of your middle-income is only aggravating the problem by having to assume the responsibility for all of the public housing that is rebuilt specifically for the people that live here.

I take the stand that it is a regional responsibility, particularly in terms of public housing from two standpoints.

No. 1 is that it should not be solely dependent upon Oakland to do this, but also from a standpoint of greater dispersion. Instead of creating ghettos, centers of minorities, let's move them out into other areas; so one of my recommendations for our ABAG—I don't know whether you are familiar with that association—Association for Better Government. This is a regional government. One of our recommendations for their consideration was to take on the public housing project on the theory that it is a regional problem rather than the problem of the individual city because, as I say, all you are doing is aggravating or extending the problem of a core city by requiring that the public housing be within the city limits or in close proximity to where the person is moved out by the Government activity.

MR. GLICKSTEIN. Under present law wouldn't you need the consent of the local communities in order to put up public housing or 221 (d) (3) housing?

MAYOR READING. This is correct. How else other are we going to do it unless it is accepted as a regional problem rather than an individual city problem?

MR. GLICKSTEIN. We have heard testimony that housing in many parts of Alameda County, as well as in some parts of Oakland is segregated along racial lines. Is that true?

MAYOR READING. It most certainly is true to the extent that we have areas which are practically all minorities. I do not believe it is true in terms of a planned prohibition of the minorities being able to move in any other parts of Oakland. I'm speaking of Oakland alone because in some of the outlying cities this most certainly doesn't hold true, but I don't think there is a neighborhood in Oakland that does not have Negroes represented within that neighborhood.

Now, that doesn't mean that there are not individual cases of discrimination on the part of Realtors and individual homeowners. There is no question and you and I aren't going to solve that problem here, but in terms of general acceptance in the total city I think Oakland has been extremely open in the freedom of people to move, provided they have the necessary funds or the capital or the economic background to buy homes that obviously are in middle-income and high-income areas.

MR. GLICKSTEIN. But outside of Oakland you concede there are problems?

MAYOR READING. Well, you had Mr. Maltester here before you. I think it's a sad fact that—we've heard the word "white noose." It is a fact we do have a white noose. When you get either south of the Oakland line, or when you talk about the east limits of Oakland, get over the hill into Walnut Creek and Lafayette your Negro population is fractional.

MR. GLICKSTEIN. How can you deal with this "white noose" aside from your proposal to put up more public housing?

MAYOR READING. I would like to think that maybe you people could come up with some answers. I don't have an answer on it. I wish I did.

MR. GLICKSTEIN. Do you think a Federal fair housing law would be helpful?

MAYOR READING. It most certainly would help, and I think that if there is a fair housing law that it has to be at least statewide. There has been some recommendation, some pressure to talk about an open housing law in Oakland itself, but I think that this only, here again aggravates your problem.

If you are going to do it, it has to be on a regionwide basis. Whether it is by a wide district, or whether it is statewide or whether it is Federal, doesn't make much difference, but it has to be the whole region.

MR. GLICKSTEIN. Mr. Chairman, I would like to defer to the Commission at this point and save my remaining questions.

CHAIRMAN HANNAH. Mrs. Freeman?

COMMISSIONER FREEMAN. I have no questions.

CHAIRMAN HANNAH. Mr. Taylor?

MR. TAYLOR. Mr. Mayor, we heard some testimony here concerning a program of scattered site housing, which I gather was approved by the voters last fall. Some of this testimony suggested that very little has been done since that time to actually begin work on this. Would you care to comment on that?

MAYOR READING. I most certainly do, Mr. Taylor. Here again let's look at the facts. Let's look at the facts.

I have been stated as saying—let me give you a little background here.

We already have an authorization for 1,100 units under the Rent Supplemental Program. We actually are going to get about 1,600, 1,700 because under the provision for apartment or house that is rehabilitated, it isn't included under the original allotment.

Now, the 2,500 that was passed by the voters here, and of which I led the fight in the Council to put on the ballot, of which I was the honorary chairman of the committee working for the passage of this bill, was passed. I made a statement that I looked upon this, and I have said this before when I was chairman and when it went before the Council, I looked upon this as insurance and let me explain, this word "insurance" has given a lot of people the wrong impression although I, on many occasions, have explained my stand and tried to clarify it.

In the next four to six years we are still going to have a lot of people in this town that are displaced through Government action.

Through our ongoing redevelopment program we are going to have people that are going to be displaced, and for whom we are going to have to provide some housing. Also through BART, through more highway expansion, we are going to have needs.

Now, what I said is this: that we should not go all out and build these 2,500 units at this time. Instead of that, there should be an orderly building of these based on a projection of what our needs are going to be on the people displaced and to whom we have a responsibility for providing housing.

Now, you either have to take the premise that we have need for 20,000 or 25,000 public units, or you have to take the premise that the first priority goes to those people that are displaced, and I take the stand that our first priority goes to the people that are displaced.

So I am in the process right now, and I will probably have next week—I have worked this week on a Citizens' Housing Committee which will be comprised of about 34 or 36 people. I asked for suggestions on this Citizens' Committee. I got over 125 suggestions, and we have been screening these, working it down, we're now down to about 50. By next week we will have the 34 to 36 people.

This committee is going to be charged with the responsibility of examining our needs over the next four to six years, and then, on the basis of this, come up with a phased program for the building of these 2,500 units. It is an orderly procedure. I am not against it, I know that we need it, but I am trying to do it on an orderly basis rather than succumb to the demands of some people who have suggested and demanded that we build them all as rapidly, as soon as possible. So this is my stand on this particular issue.

MR. TAYLOR. I gather, however, there is a tremendous or substantial unmet need for low-income housing that is decent, safe, and sanitary in this city, and it is a need which is not even fully reflected by the long waiting lists on public housing that exist now.

Isn't there some way—I'm not familiar with the details—that the needs can be met rapidly, and at the same time adequate provision be made to give priority to those who are displaced by renewal?

MAYOR READING. This would be up to this committee to decide if these two are compatible. In other words, on the projected needs if it can be shown, that for instance the big shortage right now is in low-cost housing with four or five bedrooms, and it could well be that this committee would come up with a recommendation, that maybe we build 200 or 300 units of four-or five bedrooms based on their projected needs over the four to six years.

Maybe it won't be as much as we anticipate, but this is the purpose for the forming of the Citizens' Committee, to determine the needs and how we should implement this program.

MR. TAYLOR. In the area of employment you have indicated that a great part of the problem is lack of skills. Are there ways that the city might consider or is considering to redefine some of the city jobs as a means for getting people who are unskilled onto a job?

MAYOR READING. You mean in the city itself?

MR. TAYLOR. Yes.

MAYOR READING. There has been considerable criticism that the very structure of the civil service system that we have prohibits or discourages minorities from being hired for the city.

I don't think that this is correct because I myself have met with the director on numerous occasions of the civil service, the personnel division. I have gone over the entrance exams that are given, and I am not a sociologist, I am not a psychologist, but I do not believe by looking at these examinations that they would be more difficult because a person was a different skin color or because of their culture or their background or their under-privileged education.

I do not believe that they are structured to work against them. It goes back to the thing that I tried to point out in my statement. That there has to be a basic education.

Secondly, on the question of restructuring some of the jobs, here again I have looked at the qualifications that are required for the jobs, and in my estimation they don't have to be overly-qualified for these particular jobs, but they do have to pass a civil service exam. But I don't feel that the civil service examinations that we have, from my observation and, as I say, as a layman, I don't feel that the examination is over-difficult for any particular job.

MR. TAYLOR. Coming back just for a minute to the housing problem, I notice the chart was passed around the other day which concerned the Leased Housing Program and it indicated that there were a good number of districts where leased housing had been obtained, but it also indicated, if I read it correctly, that there were rather large areas of Oakland, I guess the Oakland Hills, where no leased housing had been obtained. I suppose there isn't much rental housing up there?

MAYOR READING. You have to know Oakland to realize that this is undoubtedly true, but you are talking in an area where the homes run from probably a minimum of $32,000-$35,000 on up to as high as a $100,000. I don't think you can expect that this would be the type of home to be leased under the Rent Supplemental Program.

MR. TAYLOR. Is there any possibility that scattered site housing might be located in some of these areas?

MAYOR READING. No, I would doubt it because of the zoning requirements and also because of the cost of the land. I think it would be economically infeasible to build scattered site housing in this area.

On the other hand, I would like to point out that there is a large number of Negroes, professional people, doctors, attorneys, Negro businessmen who already live in the Hill area. In my own neighborhood, I happen to live in the Hill area, in my own neighborhood there are probably I'd say, probably 12 to 15 families within a 10-block radius of myself. So it is not a matter of segregation, it's a matter of economics rather—

MR. TAYLOR. It's economic segregation rather than—

MAYOR READING. This is correct, and this goes back to my old theory, that you have to get education, you have to get skills to be able to qualify for jobs that pay high income or good income.

MR. TAYLOR. Do you think that industry is really doing enough right now to meet the problems that affect the whole area on unemployment? I noticed you said that industry can't be expected to pay a man a stipend for work which is not performed, but do you think that—

MAYOR READING. By and large I think that in Oakland that most industries have made a real effort to work toward this end. Here again, you have to have people that are qualified to hold the job.

I happen to be an employer myself, and a person has to give the employer the skill necessary for him to pay a wage if he is going to continue to work. There have been some industries here in Oakland who have been outstanding in cooperation. There are others that have lagged, but, by and large, I would say that most of them have really taken an attitude of responsibility and tried to help.

In my notes here there were four or five companies that I know have done—. Let me tell you some that in my estimation and from the reports that have been given to me have really attempted to bring in as many minorities as possible: the Bank of America, Wells Fargo Bank, Alameda Naval Air Station. I understand you had someone from there the other day. The fact of the matter is that they have attempted to hire a large number of minorities and train them for jobs.

The PT&T has done a good job, Bethlehem Steel has done a good job, General Motors has done a good job, and these, of course are leading industries. Kaiser Industry has been very active in attempting to solve the problems of minorities here in Oakland.

MR. TAYLOR. But you are not suggesting that all that can be done actually is being done by business?

MAYOR READING. Businesses are just like people. They are run by the people that serve on the board of directors or in the case of individual businesses the owners, and you've got the full spectrum of attitudes.

On some you've got a completely negative attitude, on others you have a completely positive attitude. I don't think you can generalize in this situation. As I say, by and large I've found in working with industries here in Oakland that they do see the responsibility and are attempting to do something about it. The extent runs the spectrum. Some give lip service, some actually do a great deal, but it is hard to generalize on this type of thing. By and large I think they have faced up to the responsibilities. I know many of them have restructured their entry qualifications.

MR. TAYLOR. I want to make a little statement which you may or may not care to comment on, and I hope you understand it is not in any way critical, but it was stimulated by some of the things you said in your statement, and I think obviously that the criticism that is directed against public officials is sometimes justified and sometimes unjustified. Nobody likes the unjustified criticism. As a matter of fact, nobody likes the justified criticism either.

But I have been appalled by some of the testimony over the last few days on the part of public officials. Mainly they have been Federal officials. There have been times during this hearing when I've been rather ashamed to be a member of the Federal Government, to a lesser extent in some cases on the part of local officials. You spoke about lack of motivation on the part of people who don't have the skills. You spoke of not paying people a stipend unless they are doing their jobs.

I think to some extent for some reason this is applicable to some officials who are running programs. They do not seem to be sufficiently motivated to carry out the purpose of these programs, and I think that those who are in charge of supervising large public programs are sometimes faced with these problems.

Here are people who are in jobs, they are in jobs through civil service or, for one reason or another, cannot be easily moved from these jobs. But I'm wondering isn't this really a part of the problem?

MAYOR READING. I couldn't agree more wholeheartedly with you. Let me give you an example.

At the Job Fair last year which we held one of the things that we wanted to do was when potential employees, when the unemployed came into the Job Fair the first thing we wanted to do was to have a bank of some 40 tables, 40 vocational counselors who would counsel them and steer them specifically to the particular industry or job area where they felt that they would be most closely suited so that they wouldn't spin their wheels just idly going from booth to booth attempting to find a place that had need of their own particular talents.

We asked the California State Employment Service, and this was on a Saturday and a Sunday. We asked them to supply, because this was the only source that we knew for vocational counselors that were familiar with the daily needs of jobs and job applicants, to supply 40 vocational counselors on a voluntary basis to come in on Saturday and Sunday. We didn't get one single man that came in.

Now, also, I'd like to comment on your reference to my statement on motivation. I think that we have to be objective, and I hope that in my statement here that I did not give the impression that the problem was one of motivation. I think it applies to a small percentage of the people that we are trying to get jobs for.

Part of this stems from their own psychological background, and here again I go back to the basic education, need for vocational counseling, the OIC program. We've got to somehow build a motivation, build a belief, a conviction, not a hope, a conviction in their own minds that if they get an education and they try that they are going to get a job, and this is part of the motivation problem.

This is not criticism that I am leveling against minorities. I am trying to approach the job objectively. How do we get across this barrier of the hard core unemployed, the person who has been unemployed for 10 years? It is a motivational problem, but somehow we've got to approach that with a positive program to solve it.

This does not apply to the majority of Negroes or Mexican Americans. My guess is it probably applies to 10 or 15 percent, but it still is an important factor, just as the important factor is that maybe the guy didn't have carfare to get to the job, or he didn't have the belief that he could fill the skills in the job when he took it.

But to hang motivation as a red flag, which many people do, just you mention it and people think that "Gee, you are saying they won't work anyway," and this isn't true; but it is a factor in some certain cases.

MR. TAYLOR. I appreciate your statement on that very much because I think as you suggest there are some people who think generally this is just a problem of motivation.

MAYOR READING. I most certainly hope I didn't convey that impression to you, because I don't believe it.

MR. TAYLOR. And I appreciate your statement on public officials. It just seems to me that those who are placed in a position of real leadership have got to find some ways of getting around all of the little obstacles that are placed in their way of getting programs implemented. I don't really know how you do it. It is tremendously difficult.

MAYOR READING. Well, one way that we hope to do it is through this coordinating effort at the city level. We have an aggressive program. I would like to think that I am an aggressive mayor in attempting to solve these programs. We have a Manpower Commission which I picked the top people that I could get, people that I knew were motivated to a real purpose of getting something done, and we are making progress.

We are pulling these programs together. There is a cohesiveness starting to form now which we have to have if we are going to be effective. For instance, in the last year, we started out a year ago with between 13,000, 14,000 unemployed. We took a survey this spring and we found we still had the same number of unemployed.

In this time we know that we placed between 4,000 and 6,000 people that were hard core unemployed in permanent jobs, so it means that the inflow of people, either from outside the area or of people getting out of school, coming into the job market was equal to the number of people that we were able to place in permanent jobs.

So what it means is that if we are going to be more effective, if we are going to make inroads on the problem, if we are going to cut this unemployment rate that we've got to have a more effective program than we have had in the past. We do that in two ways.

One is either an expanded program which we are attempting to do, but also a more efficient program than we've been able to accomplish, and I feel that out of this coordination that we will get much greater efficiency than we have ever had, and out of it a more effective program.

MR. TAYLOR. Thank you.

CHAIRMAN HANNAH. Thank you very much, Mr. Mayor. We appreciate your being here this morning. You are excused.

Ladies and gentlemen, this public hearing of the U. S. Commission on Civil Rights is about to come to an end. We wish to express the Commission's appreciation to the many officials of California and the cities and the counties and the communities of the San Francisco-Oakland Bay Area and the many private citizens and organizations who have cooperated in holding this public hearing.

For the past five and a half days, this Commission has heard testimony concerning civil rights problems in the areas of housing and employment in the Bay Area communities. Witnesses have expressed their dissatisfactions with the progress being made in achieving equality of opportunity in our society. Mexican Americans and Chinese Americans have told us they feel that the Federal Government has not done enough to help them overcome the barriers of ethnic and cultural discrimination. Negro citizens have complained that the races are becoming increasingly isolated in our society as white residents and industry leave the cities for the suburbs, leaving the central cities populated by minorities.

In addition to facts and information, the testimony consists of opinions and comments about many aspects of our most pressing domestic issue. Some witnesses were frank and forceful in expressing their attitudes toward the Federal Government and toward this agency. We are grateful for their testimony because the right to criticize the Government is one of the basic principles of our democracy.

This hearing has shown that the problems of civil rights are becoming increasingly complex in the urban centers. The mayor of San Francisco told us that the test of the effectiveness of government rests in its ability to deal successfully with the problems in our metropolitan centers.

We believe that the testimony here and in San Francisco will prove helpful in pinpointing the problems which must be dealt with in the Bay Area. It is our hope that this hearing will prove to be helpful in improving communications between the many ethnic groups and the wide variety of industrial, educational, and cultural interests in the Bay Area. We cannot take proper remedial action until all of us understand the extent and significance of the denials of equal protection of the laws and equality of opportunity for all our citizens.

The conclusion of this hearing does not end the Commission's interest in the Bay Area. This hearing marks the beginning of an effort to learn more about the problems of the Spanish-speaking population. In addition to the projected hearing and special studies on the problems of the Spanish-speaking, several of our State Advisory Committees will hold meetings to assist us in this effort.

Following our hearing in Cleveland, Ohio last year the Commission established a Subcommittee of the Ohio State Advisory Committee and charged it with the responsibility of providing a forum through which Federal, State, and local officials and representatives of private organizations and institutions could suggest possible remedies and solutions to civil rights problems affecting the community.

The Cleveland Subcommittee was successful in stimulating action on numerous problems disclosed during the hearing in that city. Our California State Advisory Committee has indicated an interest in the establishment of a similar unit in the Bay Area, and if it is decided to proceed with plans to follow up on some of the problems disclosed at this hearing, we will assist it in any way that we can.

There have been some questions raised with reference to the role and purpose of this Commission. Most of you, or many of you, have attended several of the days' sessions, and I am not going to bore you or take your time to repeat what you already know.

This Commission was created by an act of Congress 10 years ago and charged, first of all, with the specific responsibility of finding out what the facts were in the United States in a variety of areas.

First of all, to find out whether or not it was a fact that citizens of this country were being denied the right to vote and have their votes counted because they were Negroes.

In the intervening 10 years this problem is well on its way toward solution.

The Commission was charged with the responsibility of finding out whether or not it was true that in some parts of this country the educational opportunities for young people were unequal because of their race or religion or national origin. The Commission has just completed a year's work, studying this whole problem of education more than 10 years after the Supreme Court decision.

You know, in a general way, that the Commission has found again that it is not only factual but the facts are about as they were 10 years ago. There are very large numbers of young people in America that are still denied adequate educational opportunities. What the country has got to be concerned with is better education for all people, particularly all young people, and the kind of an education that will fit young people to live in the kind of a world in which they are going to live.

It is the responsibility of our society to see to it that young citizens of all colors and races and religions have an opportunity to develop whatever God gave them in the way of potential so that they may be able to make a maximum contribution toward total society. There is no more important responsibility that rests with society. Once these young people, or older people, have developed whatever they have in potential, then there is a responsibility that rests with society to see to it that there may be jobs for them, equal opportunities for jobs, or the right kinds of jobs.

It is an obligation of our society to see to it that people who are making useful contributions to our society have the opportunity to enjoy the same advantages that most of us demand, making the same kinds of contributions. The opportunity to live in a decent house in a decent community, not in an old, second-hand house in the core of the old city just because of our race or color.

In 1967 we still have problems. Ten years ago this was the most important problem that faced the United States of America, and in 1967 it is still the most important problem. A part of the responsibility rests with the Federal Government, a part with State government, a part with local government, a part with citizens.

As we bring this meeting to a close, we can only hope that out of it may come increasing encouragement for the people of the Bay Area to recognize that this is an important problem, that it is not going to go away. Its ultimate solution requires the cooperation of Government and, beyond that, it requires the understanding of people.

Finally and fundamentally, somehow in our system, we have got to bring about the situation where people are not damned because of government and, beyond that, it requires the understanding us happen to be white, and we have not been damned all of our lives because some of our relatives, near or far off, were scoundrels. Others in our society have generally been damned and charged with every bit of undesirable behavior on the part of other people of the same color.

Well, this is a long-range problem. It takes a long-range solution. It will not go away. There is a short-range solution, there is a long-range solution, and as we bring this meeting to a close, somehow or other, if you today, tomorrow, next month, next year can contribute something to the solution of the problem, you will have served the local and the national interests.

This hearing is adjourned.

(Whereupon, at 12: 45 p.m., the hearing was adjourned.)

[EXCERPT FROM THE FEDERAL REGISTER, MARCH 29, 1967]

COMMISSION ON CIVIL RIGHTS

CALIFORNIA

Notice of Hearing

Notice is hereby given, pursuant to the provisions of the Civil Rights Act of 1957, 71 Stat. 634, as amended, that a public hearing of the U.S. Commission on Civil Rights will commence on May 1, 1967, and that an executive session, if appropriate, will be convened on April 29, 1967, to be held in the Ceremonial Courtroom in the Federal Building, Golden Gate Avenue, San Francisco, Calif., and at the Oakland Auditorium Ballroom, 10 10th Street, Oakland, Calif. to collect information concerning legal developments constituting a denial of equal protection of the laws under the Constitution because of race, color, or national origin, and in the administration of justice in the counties of San Francisco, Contra Costa, Alameda, San Mateo, Marin, Santa Clara, Sonoma, Napa, and Solano and in the State of California; to appraise the laws and policies of the Federal Government with respect to denial of equal protection of the laws under the Constitution because of race, color, or national origin, and in the administration of justice in the counties of San Francisco, Contra Costa, Alameda, San Mateo, Marin, Santa Clara, Sonoma, Napa, and Solano and in the State of California, and to disseminate information with respect to denials in the counties of San Francisco, Contra Costa, Alameda, San Mateo, Marin, Santa Clara, Sonoma, Napa, and Solano and in the State of California because of race, color or national origin in the fields of housing, employment, public facilities, education, administration of justice and related areas.

JOHN A. HANNAH,
Chairman.

MARCH 29, 1967.

[F.R. Doc. 67-3420; Filed, Mar. 28, 1967;

Exhibit No. 2

OCEAN VIEW, MERCED HEIGHTS, INGLESIDE COMMUNITY
STABILIZATION AND IMPROVEMENT PROJECT
550 HOLLOWAY AVENUE
SAN FRANCISCO, CALIFORNIA 94112

May 1, 1967

The following is testimony presented in behalf of the Ocean View,
Merced Heights, Ingleside Community Stabilization and Improvement
Project, hereinafter designated as the OMI Project.

My name is Mrs Maxine B. Randolph, Community Coordinator of the
OMI Project. I would call to your attention the history of the Project,
the Project's accomplishments, and future programs, in the attached
brochure.

The area in which the OMI Project is located is comprised of mainly
single family dwellings, which not too long ago was destined to become
a ghetto by reason of unethical real estate practices. It is a constantly
changing area of second stage housing where junior fives sell for $19,000.00
and larger homes from $25,000.00 to $38,000.00. In the Ingleside Terraces
a more affluent district in the Project Area, homes in some cases are
priced upwards of $50,000.00.

In San Francisco land is very dear because there are no more hills to
denude of trees to build homes. Peculiar to San Francisco, building
lots are parcelled in twenty five foot fronts, and lots of this dimension
are selling in the OMI Project Area from $9,000.00 to $12,000.00.

It is imperative that homes purchased through private agencies and banks,
and insured by the Federal Housing Authority, need to have definite
restrictions insofar as "closing costs" are concerned. No longer are
we dealing with an inflated real estate market, the costs are very

realistic; the need frequently for a second mortgage, and indeed even
a third mortgage makes buying a home in San Francisco an unreason-
ably precarious venture.

In 1955 the Project Area was approximately 95% Caucasian. Currently
the tri-district area is from 30% to 90% Negro; a mean in the Project
Area of approximately 50% Negro.

The Urban Planning Pamphlet is quoted: ..... "Citizens working together
toward a racially stable community sooner or later must face three
questions: (1) Why are we trying to attract white families to our area?;
(2) Doesn't this imply that they are somehow superior?; (3) Isn't this a
gratuitous insult to Negro families?. Negro families know that there is
nothing particularly desirable about white neighbors per se. They may
also feel guilty when Negroes need houses as well. The fact remains
that white citizens still control the government, big business and the
school boards. Because of this, they know from experience that all-
Negro neighborhoods are apt to suffer from a dearth of money for
schools, parks, and city services......"

This is the reason the OMI Project exists. The OMI neighbors do not
want to wait until the societal changes preclude the possibility of re-
treiving a neglected and exploited neighborhood. There is no community
until it becomes a personal thing - not until one knows another on a
person to person basis. The problems and frustrations of our modern
world will not be settled by summit conferences, but at the communal
level, the neighborhood. In a large city of changing patterns and constant moving from one city to another, one neighborhood to another, to
know one's neighbor is not the rule, but rather the unusual.

The OMI Project is an experiment in human relations. It is a test
of our maturity and ability to get along with our neighbors. Where do
human rights begin? In the neighbor's backyard, the classroom, the
shop, the factory, the office. Wherever human beings congregate is a
laboratory for human rights.

We would like to suggest that model legislation and planning be developed
to prevent the ghettoizing of whole cities as well as neighborhoods. Dr.
Louis S. Levine, Professor of Psychology on leave from Yeshiva University,
New York, as received considerable attention for a plan of national
scope in which he advocates the establishment of 400 hundred community
centers in inner cities, locally sponsored and controlled, but financed
by the Federal Government to combat the growing ghetto problem. He
suggests that the centers be allowed to establish inner-city schools
which would augment the educational facilities currently available.
There would be a choice between public schools and the financed community run private schools. He adds "the crisis is real and the time
for planning is now".

We of the Project, it should be noted, do not embrace Dr. Levine's
plan in its entirety, as we realize that "private schools" per se, are
not the answer to our problems, for reasons that are obvious.

THE OMI PLAN

We would like to recommend that both private and public funding might
better be used toward an overall plan, and that the government agencies
be the catalyst for encouraging participation by private funding agencies
and private service contractors. The legislation we propose, in general
terms would declare as its purpose to assist state and local governments

to prevent ethnic ghettos by establishing the finest social services,
education, vocational training, transportation, aged and health
services a community could provide. Civic participation by the
community would be the initial ingredient, or the community would
run the risk of losing the grant. Cultural enrichment and recreation
facilities for all ages would be an important part of the plan, because
in this enlightened age, we are supposed to have more time for leisure
and recreation.

The plan consists of: (1) a twenty four hour a day community school
and recreation center for people of all ages; (2) youth coordinating
council with small interest groups in recreation, service and work;
(3) demonstration innovative beautification planning; (4) employment
training and counseling; (5) education at a bold and innovative level;
(6) day care for children to encourage young mothers to become independent by being able to take employment and pursue education; (7)
communication systems (block or group structures); (8) creative arts;
(9) civic participation and political education.

We suggest that the Human Rights Commission in each municipality
be designated to act as the agency that would guide and develop such
projects. The Human Rights Commissions would insure the maximum,
feasible citizen participation, and collaterally, facilities for research
and technical services from schools of higher education should be made
available to such a project.

I wish to thank the Commission on Civil Rights for this opportunity
to present our ideas, and urge the urban planners and legislators to
depart from fragmentation and develop this plan to meet our citizens
needs as well as to be our cities salvation.

723

Exhibit No. 3

DEPARTMENT OF STATE

(PHOTOCOPY CERTIFICATION)

I, FRANK M. JORDAN, Secretary of State of the State of California, hereby certify:

That the photographic reproduction hereunto annexed was prepared by and in my office from the record on file of which it purports to be a copy, and that it is full, true and correct.

IN WITNESS WHEREOF, I hereunto set my hand and affix the Great Seal of the State of California this **APR 27 1967**

Secretary of State

By

Assistant Secretary of State

△ SPO

464255

FILED
In the office of the Secretary of State
of the State of California
JAN 2 1964
FRANK M. JORDAN, Secretary of State

ARTICLES OF INCORPORATION

-of-

SERRAMONTE REALTY COMPANY

KNOW ALL MEN BY THESE PRESENTS:

That we, the undersigned, residents of the United States of
America, do hereby voluntarily associate ourselves for the purpose of
incorporating a private corporation under the laws of the State of
California;

AND WE DO HEREBY CERTIFY:

First: That the name of said corporation shall be "Serramonte
Realty Company".

Second: That the purposes for which said corporation is formed
are:

(a) To conduct a general real estate business; to act as real
estate brokers, agents, operators and dealers; to conduct a general insurance business and act as insurance brokers and agents; to build and
sell buildings; to collect rents, to lease property and to manage property;
to buy, sell, mortgage, loan, hypothecate and in every manner engage in the
general real estate and insurance business.

That the specific business in which the corporation is primarily
to engage in is to act as a real estate broker.

(b) To purchase or otherwise acquire, hold, lease, sell, dispose
of and deal in real and personal property of all kinds, and in particular
land, buildings, business concerns and undertakings, mortgages, shares,
stock, debentures, securities, concessions, produce, policies, good debts
and claims, and any interest in real or personal property, and any claims
against such property, or against any person or company, and to issue in
exchange therefore the stock, bonds, or other obligations of this corpora-

725

tion, and to carry on any business, concern or undertaking so acquired, provided such business is not of the nature which can be carried on only by corporation_ organized under the banking, the insurance, the railroad and the transportation corporation laws.

(c) To acquire and hold copyrights, trademarks, licenses and patents of any sort likely to be conducive to the o jects of the company and to sell or otherwise dispose of the same.

(d) To act as agent or representative of corporations, firms and individuals and as such, to develop and extend the business interests of firms, corporations and individuals.

(e) To borrow money and to execute instruments to evidence the same a d to secure the same, and to enter into, make, perform and carry out contracts of every kind which a corporation organized under the laws of the State of California may enter into, and for lawful purposes, with any person, firm, association or corporation.

(f) In general, to carry on any other business of the same general nature in connection with the foregoing, whether investment or otherwise, and to have and to exercise all the powers conferred by the laws of the State of California upon corporations forme. thereunder.

Third: That the principal office for the t ansaction of the business of the corporation will be located in the City and County of San Francisco, State of California.

Fourth: That the total number of shares which a a corporation shall have authority to issue is two thousand five hundred (2,500) shares, and the aggregate par value of all of the shares of said corporation is twenty-five thousand (25,000) dollars, and the par value of each of said shares is ten (10) dollars.

Fifth: The number of its directors is five (5) and the names

726

and residences of those appointed to act until the first annual meeting
of stockholders or until the election and qualification of their successors
are:

Names	Residences
Roe H. Baker	San Francisco, California
Fred Gellert, Jr.	San Francisco, California
Peter J. Brusati	San Francisco, California
Theodore Hayden	San Francisco, California
Marie Simpson	San Francisco, California

Sixth: That the directors of this corporation shall not have
the power to levy assessments upon the shares or any class thereof.

In witness of these Articles of Incorporation we and each of
us, being the directors named in the foregoing Articles of Incorporation,
have hereunto subscribed our names this *13th* day of January, 1964.

727

On this _13th_ day of January, 1964, before me, Pearl M.
Maritzen, a Notary Public in and for the City and County of San Francisco,
State of California, personally appeared Roe H. Eurer, Fred Gellert, Jr.,
Peter J. Brusati, Theodore Hayden and Marie Simpson, known to me to be the
persons whose names are subscribed to the foregoing Articles of Incorporation, and who are named therein as directors of said corporation, and they
acknowledged to me that they executed the same.

IN WITNESS WHEREOF, I have hereunto set my hand and affixed my
Official Seal in the City and County of San Francisco, the day and year
last above written.

Pearl M. Maritzen, Notary Public
in and for the City and County of
San Francisco, State of California

My Commission Expires: _4-12-64_

PEARL M MARITZEN
NOTARY PUBLIC - CALIFORNIA
CITY AND COUNTY OF
SAN FRANCISCO

728

Filed bus.chg.to San Mateo County.

A 60608

FILED
MAY 20 1966

CERTIFICATE OF AMENDMENT OF ARTICLES OF
INCORPORATION OF SERRAMONTE REALTY COMPANY.

The undersigned, Roe H. Baker and Peter J. Brusati, do hereby
certify that they are respectively, and have been at all times herein mentioned, the duly elected and acting President and Secretary of Serramonte
Realty Company, a California corporation, and further that:

One: At a regular meeting of the Board of Directors of said
corporation duly held at its principal place of business at 255 Canterbury
Avenue, Daly City, County of San Mateo, State of California, at 10:00 o'clock
A. M. on the 10th day of May, 1966, at which meeting there was at all times
present and acting a quorum of the members of said Board, the following
resolution was duly adopted:

WHEREAS, it is deemed by the Board of Directors of this
corporation to be to its best interests and to the best interests
of its shareholders that its Articles of Incorporation be amended
as hereinafter provided;

NOW, THEREFORE, BE IT RESOLVED that Article Third of the
Articles of Incorporation of this corporation be amended to read
as follows:

Third: That the principal offices for the transaction of
business of the corporation will be located at 255 Canterbury
Avenue, Daly City, County of San Mateo, State of California.

RESOLVED FURTHER that the Board of Directors of this corporation hereby adopts and approves said amendment of its
Articles of Incorporation; and

RESOLVED FURTHER that the President and Secretary of this
corporation be and they hereby are authorized and directed to
procure the adoption and approval of the foregoing amendment

ALFRED E. GRAZIANI
ATTORNEY AT LAW
SAN FRANCISCO

729

by the vote or written consent of shareholders of this corporation holding at least a majority of the voting power, and thereafter to sign and verify by their oaths and to file a certificate
in the form and manner required by Section 3672 of the California
Corporations Code, and in general to do any and all things necessary
to effect said amendment in accordance wi.. said Section 3672.

Two: The number of shares of said corporation consenting to such
amendment of its Articles of Incorporation is five hundred forty (540), and
the following is a copy of the form of written consent executed by the holders
of said shares:

WRITTEN CONSENT OF SHAREHOLDERS TO AMENDMENT OF ARTICLES
OF INCORPORATION OF SERRAMONTE REALTY COMPANY.

WHEREAS, at a regular meeting of the Board of Directors of Serramonte
Realty Company, a California corporation, duly held at the principal office
for the transaction of business of said corporation at 255 Canterbury Avenue,
Daly City, California, on the 10th day of May, 1966, at which meeting a quorum
of the members of said Board was at all times present and acting, an amendment
of the Articles of Incorporation of said corporation was adopted and approved
by resolutions of said Board amending Article Third of said Articles of Incorporation to read as follows:

"Third: That the principal offices for the transaction of
business of the corporation will be located at 255 Canterbury
Avenue, Daly City, County of San Mateo, State of California."

NOW, THEREFORE, each of the undersigned shareholders of said corporation does hereby adopt, approve and consent to the foregoing amendment
of said Articles of Incorporation, and does hereby consent that Article Third
of said Articles of Incorporation be amended to read as herein set forth.

IN WITNESS WHEREOF, each of the undersigned has hereunto signed his
name and, following his name, the date of signing and the number of shares of
said corporation held by him of record on said date entitled to vote upon

-2-

730

amendments of said Articles of Incorporation of the character of the foregoing amendment.

Name	Date	No. of Shares
Carl Gellert, P. J. Brusati and Edward V. Schulhamser, Trustees of the Fred Gellert-Fred Gellert, Jr. Trust	May 12, 1966	30
Carl Gellert, P. J. Brusati and Edward V. Schulhamser, Trustees of the Fred Gellert - Joanne Gellert Trust	" "	30
Carl Gellert, P. J. Brusati and Edward V. Schulhamser, Trustees of the Gisela Gellert - Fred Gellert, Jr. Trust	" "	30
Carl Gellert, P. J. Brusati and Edward V. Schulhamser, Trustees of the Gisela Gellert - Joanne Gellert Trust	" "	30
Fred Gellert		180
Carl Gellert	" "	300

Three: The total number of shares of said corporation entitled to
vote on or or consent to the adoption of said amendment is nine hundred eleven
(911).

IN WITNESS WHEREOF, the undersigned have executed this certificate
of amendment this 12th day of May, 1966.

_____
Roe H. Baker, President of Serramonte
Realty Company

_____
Peter J. Brusati, Secretary of Serramonte Realty Company.

-3-

731

ROE H. BAKER and PETER J. BRUSATI, being first duly sworn, each for himself, deposes and says:

That Roe H. Baker is, and was at all times herein mentioned in the foregoing Certificate of Amendment, the President of Sacramento Realty Company, the California corporation therein mentioned, and Peter J. Brusati is, and was at all times mentioned therein, the Secretary of said corporation; that each has read said certificate and that the statements therein made are true of his own knowledge, and that the signatures purporting to be the signatures of said President and Secretary thereto are the genuine signatures of said President and Secretary respectively.

Subscribed and sworn to before me
this 17th day of May, 1966

Notary Public, State of California
City and County of San Francisco

My Commission Expires: 4-12-68

PEARL M. MARITZEN
NOTARY PUBLIC - CALIFORNIA
CITY AND COUNTY OF
SAN FRANCISCO

Exhibit No. 4

Serramonte:
between the city and the sea.

Serramonte offers an unmatched location, just 15 minutes from downtown San Francisco. (And scheduled new freeways will make the trip even shorter.) Men who live in Serramonte will be home, relaxing, while others are still fighting rush-hour traffic.

The community of Serramonte lies within the city limits of Daly City in San Mateo County. When Serramonte is completed, Daly City will be one of the largest cities in San Mateo County. Daly City has all the facilities of a large city such as an excellent fire department with.call box control, new modern fire fighting equipment, an efficient police department and a new City Hall.

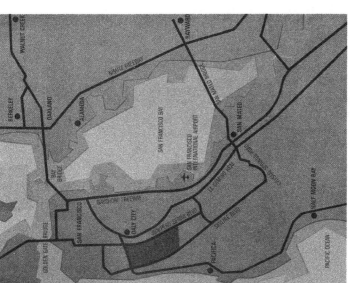

733

Exhibit No. 5

PAGE 18 REAL ESTATE   April 23, 1967
S. F. Sunday Examiner & Chronicl

A picture of a man
who **"LOVES"**
. . . his family!

So he bought them a NEW

in

can YOU get all these features?

New Clean Neighborhoods
Spacious Level Lots
New Shopping Centers
3-4 Bedrooms & 1-2 Baths
All Underground Utilities
All-Electric G.E. Kitchens
New Churches & Playgrounds
New Elementary & High Schools

ALSO "LARGEST REGIONAL SHOPPING CENTER"

PAYMENTS
LESS
THAN RENT

9 New Furnished Models

from **$23,990**

a few at only $20,950

ONLY **10%** DOWN !

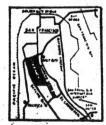

DIRECTIONS:
Go out Skyline Boulevard to
Daly City, past Pacifica turn-
off, and follow directional
signs to Hickey Blvd. or King
Drive . . . NINE model homes
for your inspection.

Interiors by NORMAN BLACK A.I.D.
of Ghirardelli Square. Equal Opportunity Housing. Furnishings by BERG'S
WOOD FURNITURE of South San
Francisco.

"BUILDING BETTER HOMES FOR 45 YEARS"

735

Exhibit No. 6

COPY OF TELEGRAM SENT TO CARL GELLERT, 44 SLOAT BLVD
FRED GELLERT, 300 GELLERT DRIVE
and at their business address: 2222 - 19th Avenue

and to <u>Albert F. Skelly</u>,Esq.
~~220 Bush~~ Street

THE UNITED STATES COMMISSION ON CIVIL RIGHTS IS HOLDING HEARINGS IN
SAN FRANCISCO AT THE FEDERAL COURT HOUSE, 450 GOLDEN GATE AVENUE,
MAY 1 - MAY 3. TESTIMONY CONCERNING SERRAMONTE REALTY, INC.,
STANDARD BUILDING COMPANY, INC., AND SUBURBAN REALTY COMPANY, INC.,
COMPANIES ORGANIZED BY YOU, WILL BE HEARD ON MAY 1. A SUBPENA FOR YOUR
APPEARANCE BEFORE THE COMMISSION HAS BEEN ISSUED. UNFORTUNATELY YOU
HAVE NOT BEEN AVAILABLE FOR SERVICE. THE COMMISSION IS INTERESTED IN
HEARING TESTIMONY FROM YOU CONCERNING THE DEVELOPMENT OF SERRAMONTE
TRACT BY SUBURBAN REALTY AND THE SALES POLICY OF STANDARD BUILDING AND
SERRAMONTE REALTY WITH RESPECT TO SALES TO NEGRO AMERICANS. I HOPE THAT
YOU WILL MAKE YOURSELF AVAILABLE FOR ~~SOME~~ SERVICE OF A SUBPENA OR APPEAR
VOLUNTARILY.

Glickstein
HOWARD A. ~~GLICKSTEIN~~
GENERAL COUNSEL

Exhibit No. 7

MEMORANDUM OF UNDERSTANDING BETWEEN THE AD HOC COMMITTEE FOR FAIR HOUSING IN

SERRAMONTE AND THE BELOW NAMED CORPORATIONS

We, Edward A. Fosdahl, General Sales Manager and Bill Cody , Public Relations Director

are authorized to make the following committments for the following corporations:

Serramonte Realty Company   Mangels Properties, Inc.
Forest Knolls Development Company   Wildwood Park, Inc.
Lawton Heights Development Company   Atlas Realty Company

1. These corporations will offer and sell any available home in the Serramonte

   tract to all persons regardless of race, color or creed upon the following

   terms; which are subject to change and any change will/be promptly reported to the

   organization in (5.) below.

> Price range: $20,950 to $23,450
> Minimum percentage down payment: 20%
> Term for loan: 25-30 years (25 available from banks; 30 from savings and
>   loan associations)
> Interest rate: 6½% (25years); 7% (30 years)
> Closing costs: approximately $600.
> Cal Vet is available
> Second loan terms: None made by Serramonte, but we offer assistance
>   in locating second loans to the extent that they are
>   available/
> Minimum monthly income without second loan 4½ to 5 times payments
> including taxes, insurance should equal income after taxes, according
> to most lenders.
> A buyer is prevented from reselling his home to anyone other than
> none of these corporations for a period of 2 years.

2. These corporations will consider offering employment as salesmen to non-Caucasians.

3. These corporations will so direct their advertising as to make it appear that

   all persons may purchase homes in the Serramonte tract and will include in their

   advertisements the statement "Equal Opportunity Housing" and will consider

   advertising in major minority newspapers in the Bay Area on the same basis as

   other advertising is considered.

4. These corporations will attempt to prevent any concentration of racial or ethnic

   ethnic groups and will take positive steps for dispersion of members of these

   groups within the Serramonte tract.

5. All complaints received shall be referred to Mr. Edward Fosdahl.

6. These corporations will make written reports quarterly to the Fair Housing

   Council of San Mateo County, P.O. Box 1532, Burlingame which disclose changes

   in the above terms, the number and locations of houses sold to each of the

   following groups: Negro, Oriental, American Indian and Mexican-American.

A G R E E M E N T

THIS AGREEMENT made and entered into at Daly City, California, the 14ᵗʰ day of October, 1983, by and between the City of Daly City, a municipal corporation, in the County of San Mateo, State of California, hereinafter referred to as Daly City, and SUBURBAN REALTY COMPANY, a California corporation, hereinafter referred to as Suburban.

R E C I T A L S:

1. There is pending before the City Council of the City of Daly City the matter of the annexation of certain uninhabited territory known as "The Christen Ranch Territory", which territory is more particularly described in Resolution No. ___3402___ of the City Council of the City of Daly City on file in the office of the City Clerk. This description therein contained is incorporated in this agreement by this reference and made a part hereof. This agreement is made in reference to said territory.

2. Suburban owns more than three-fourths of said territory and has petitioned the City of Daly City that said territory be annexed to Daly City.

3. Suburban and Daly City by this agreement desire to make necessary arrangements for the service of said territory with water and to agree between themselves as to the apportionment of and financing of the cost of improvements to and the extension of the water system of Daly City into the area.

4. Suburban desires in addition thereto to manifest its willingness to dedicate certain land to public use within said territory which said dedications are agreed to be for the benefit of the territory proposed for annexation and necessary for its proper development.

5. Suburban desires hereby to authorize when legally
permissible and in accordance with applicable law the institution
of proceedings by the City of Daly City to establish appropriate
zoning of said territory and in this connection there is attached
hereto a plat, marked Exhibit "A", which shows uses deemed by
Suburban to be consistent with accepted zoning practices and also
consistent with the orderly development of said territory.

NOW, THEREFORE, IT IS AGREED as follows:

1. No water shall in any manner at any time be stored,
distributed, transmitted or sold in said territory except by the
Water Department of the City of Daly City or such agency as may
from time to time be designated or created by Daly City for such
purpose.

2. Attached hereto and marked Exhibit "B" is a plat
entitled, "Water Schematic Christen Ranch, Drawing No. 63-D-17
prepared by the City of Daly City through its Department of Public
Works". Suburban shall construct in accordance with the specifications and requirements of the City of Daly City at its sole cost
and expense all water transmission lines and mains within the
territory proposed for annexation eight (8) inches in diameter
(inside measurement) or less. In addition thereto Suburban will
construct at its sole cost and expense the water transmission main
from the city limits of the City of Daly City if said territory is
annexed, at the southeasterly corner of said territory to the
proposed reservoir number 5-D, and in addition thereto shall
construct those transmission mains or lines to reservoir number
6-B and also to reservoir number 7-B, as shown on the attached
plat. The cost of any other water main or transmission line in
excess of eight (8) inches in diameter (inside measurement) shall
be apportioned as follows: Daly City shall bear that portion of
the cost of the line or main as the diameter of said line or main

in excess of eight (8) inches bears to the total diameter. Daly
City shall bear the cost solely of all improvements necessary
outside of the territory proposed for annexation. At the request
of Daly City, Suburban agrees to advance the cost of Daly City's
obligation hereunder and Daly City shall repay such advances in
ten (10) equal annual installments with interest at four pe-cent (4%)
per annum. The first installment shall be due on the first anniversary after Daly City has received written advice from Suburban
of any advance hereunder.

      3. Suburban shall convey to Daly City in fee simple
without charge or cost that side for a reservoir shown on the
attached plat marked Exhibit "B", which site is designated as
the site for Reservoir Number 6-B. Such site shall be of sufficient
size as to permit the construction of a reservoir with a storage
capacity of one and a half million gallons. With respect to the
reservoir site designated 5-B it is contemplated that said site
shall be of a sufficient size to provide storage capacity for ten
to sixteen million gallons. In this connection with regard to site
for Reservoir No. 5-B it is agreed that said site shall be conveyed
to the City of Daly City by Suburban in fee simple but that Daly
City shall pay to Suburban such portion of the reasonable value
of said reservoir site as relates to that portion of the storage
capacity of the reservoir itself which is in excess of the needs of
the territory proposed for annexation. The construction of reservoi
on said sites shall be at the cost and expense of Daly City but in
this connection it is agreed that Suburban shall construct said
reservoirs to the size and in accordance with the requirements of
Daly City; construction as above provided shall be commenced upon
the request of Daly City, which request shall be made no later than
five (5) years from date hereof. Daly City shall pay the cost of sa
reservoirs and its proportion of the cost of the value of the
reservoir site number 5-B in the manner following:

      Said sum shall be repaid in ten (10) equal annual

the deferred balance. The first installment shall be due and
payable with accrued interest on the first anniversary of the
completion of each reservoir and a like sum, together with interest,
shall be paid upon the same date each year following until the
principal sum plus accrued interest shall have been repaid by
Daly City.

4. Daly City, through its Water Department or other
agency, shall furnish and deliver, subject to compliance with the
terms of this agreement, water to said territory and to the owner.
and occupants thereof to the same extent and manner and at the
same rates as are available and applicable to other areas of
Daly City.

5. Suburban shall convey to Daly City in fee simple
without cost or charge to Daly City two sites for fire stations
necessary for proper fire service to the territory proposed for
'annexation. Said conveyances shall contain a reversionary clause
in the event the land conveyed is not dedicated to such use within
five (5) years from the date of the conveyance. One such site
shall be in the southerly portion of the territory and the other
in the northerly portion. In this connection it is understood that
proposals for development of the territory envision construction
to commence in the more southerly area, and further that development of the northerly area embodies the prospect of a regional
commercial area of some 75 acres or more. Consequently it is
agreed that the fire station in the southerly area shall be
immediately available and shall be approximately 100 x 150 feet
in area. It is further agreed that Suburban shall construct on a
lot immediately adjacent to said site a building otherwise suitable
as a home but with an elevated basement for the location of equipment and housing of manpower necessary for the operation of said
station. Construction of said building shall be concurrent with
the first stage of construction in the southerly portion of said

territory. Daly City shall vacate said premises not later than five years from date of occupancy. The site for the fire station in the northerly portion of the territory shall be at least 200 x 200 feet in area. Both sites must be selected by Daly City at any time prior to approval of tentative subdivision maps or development plans if the latter should be used by Suburban.

6. If requested by Daly City, Suburban shall purchase and deliver to Daly City a fire department vehicle up to the cost of $25,000.00 as may be required for the southerly fire station above mentioned. Daly City shall pay the cost of such vehicle to Suburban in five (5) equal annual installments with interest at four percent (4%) per annum, the first of said installments being due one (1) year after delivery of such vehicle, and each of the remaining installments shall be paid on each succeeding anniversary of the first install-ment until the full sum expended, plus interest, has been paid.

7. All fire alarm systems as may be required in the area shall be constructed and located by Suburban at its sole cost and expense in accordance with the applicable subdivision ordinance of the City of Daly City but in no event shall Suburban be required to install any fire alarm system beyond the limits of the territory proposed for annexation.

8. Suburban upon request of Daly City and prior to the approval of any final subdivision map within which the site or sites hereinafter referred to are to be located shall convey to Daly City in fee simple without cost or charge to Daly City the following sites for recreational use.

(a) One two acre site adjacent to or near each school site selected in the area. Daly City may at its option combine the two acre sites into one larger site should it so determine. Such conveyance shall contain a

reversionary clause unless said site or sites are dedicated
to recreational use within ten (10) years from the date of
the conveyance.

(b) In addition to the above, one site up to but
not more than six acres in area, the proposed location of which
is in the northerly portion of the territory proposed for
annexation. It is understood and agreed that this latter
site particularly may be used for governmental or recreational
purposes, and it is further agreed that said conveyance may
contain a reversionary clause in the event that said land is
not dedicated to such use by Daly City within ten (10) years
from the date of the conveyance.

It is understood and agreed particularly that the proposed conveyances specified in this paragraph are required for the proper
development of the territory proposed for annexation and the
conveyances hereunder shall benefit the said territory by providing proper recreational and governmental activities within said
territory as are required.

9. Attached to this agreement, marked Exhibit "A" and
incorporated herein by this reference, is a plat of the territory
proposed for annexation, showing proposed uses for said territory.
Said proposal has been the result of extensive study by Wilsey, Ham &
Blair, consulting engineers, and also by planning technicians, with
the objective of devising a plan for the use of said territory
consistent with economic requirements, governmental needs and
the proper and best use of said land. It is agreed that procedures
leading to the zoning of such territory in accordance with said
plan may be initiated by Daly City or by Suburban. Nothing herein
contained shall constitute approval of said plan by Daly City.
The sole purpose of this paragraph is to indicate the willingness
of Suburban that the uses proposed on the attached plan be submitted

to Daly City for the establishment of zones in accordance with the
zoning ordinance, consistent with said zoning ordinance and
subject to applicable law.

10. The terrain of the territory proposed for
annexation is such that setback requirements of Ordinance 294
of the City of Daly City (the basic zoning ordinance of the City
of Daly City) may present practical difficulties and unnecessary
hardships inconsistent with the purposes of said ordinance..
Accordingly, it is agreed that upon application for a variance
from the strict enforcement of said Ordinance 294 in connection
herewith, such application will be considered with this hardship
in mind. It is further recognized that in certain areas construction will be on one side of the street only because of terrain.
In such instances narrower street widths may be dictated because
of terrain. Lastly, fences may be constructed to the rear of
dwellings at the crest of the slope, if terrain dictates, and
not necessarily at the property line.

11. It is expressly understood and agreed that each
paragraph and covenant herein contained is made with the objective
of the orderly extension of municipal services into the territory
proposed for annexation, and further that the proposals herein
made and covenants herein made are for the benefit of the land
and the people who may occupy the same.

12. It is expressly agreed that this agreement shall
be construed as a severable agreement and that if any of the
provisions hereof shall in any way be invalid or unenforceable
such invalidity or unenforceability shall not invalidate the
whole agreement, but that in such event this agreement shall
be construed as if not containing the particular provision or
provisions held to be invalid or unenforceable and the balance
of this agreement shall be construed and enforced the same as

744

though such objectionable provision or provisions were deleted
therefrom.

13. It is agreed that the foregoing terms and agreements
are made in view of the fact that Daly City's present zoning
ordinance and proposed zoning ordinance permits construction of
single family residential homes on lots 33 x 100 feet in area.

14. This agreement shall be binding upon the heirs,
administrators, executors, successors, grantees and assigns
of the parties hereto.

Executed in duplicate the day, month and year first
above mentioned, at Daly City, California.

SUBURBAN REALTY COMPANY,
a California corporation

By _Carl Beller_
President

By _D.F. Sherman Eubanks_
Secretary

CITY OF DALY CITY, a Municipal
Corporation

By _Joseph Verduzco_
Mayor

By _Anna C. Llendorf_
City Clerk

745

RESOLUTION OF THE CITY COUNCIL OF THE CITY OF DALY CITY AUTHORIZING EXECUTION OF
AGREEMENT WITH SUBURBAN REALTY COMPANY.

RESOLVED by the City Council of the City of Daly City that it does

hereby authorize and direct the Mayor and City Clerk to execute that certain

agreement with Suburban Realty Company, a California corporation, dated

October 14, 1963.

I hereby certify the foregoing to be a true copy of a Resolution adopted by

the City Council of Daly City, California, at a regular meeting thereof held on the

_____14th___ day of _____October_____, 19_63___, by the following vote of the

members thereof:

 AYES, and in favor thereof, Councilmen:___DeBernardi, Dennis, Pacelli,___

_____St. Clair, Verducci_____

NOES, Councilmen:_____None_____

Absent, Councilmen:_____None_____

City Clerk of the City of Daly City

APPROVED:

_____JOSEPH A. VERDUCCI_____
Mayor of the City of Daly City

746

Exhibit No. 9

Testimony of

REED ROBBINS, President

California Real Estate Association

Before the

United States Commission on Civil Rights

San Francisco, California

May 2, 1967

- - - - - - - - - - - - - - -

Honorable Chairman and distinguished members of this Commission:
I am Reed Robbins, President of the California Real Estate Association.

I would like to take this opportunity to state our position concerning
legislation which addresses itself to achieving what recently has
come to be referred to as "open housing". Previously, it has been
referred to as "fair housing" or "forced housing", depending on the
point of view.

Basically, we defend the freedom of a residential property owner to
sell, lease, or rent his property to anyone of his choosing. We
believe this freedom to be among the basic freedoms of all Americans;
we believe it is worth fighting to preserve.

Since the California State Legislature passed the Rumford Act in
1963, we have become hardened to those who say America should
forsake this freedom. We reject the idea that anyone desiring residential property should have an overriding right to buy, rent or
lease that property over the owner's objections, and that the one
seeking to buy or rent should have government enforcement available
to put this new "right" into effect.

More than four and one-half milion people in California agreed to
secure to themselves their freedom of choice in the disposition of
their residential property by their vote on Proposition 14 in 1964.
We also point to the fact that whenever this question has been put
to a vote of the people in various areas of our country, they have
also voted to preserve that freedom.

We seriously state that any legislation depriving the property owner
of freedom to enter into a contract with the person of his choice
carries us along the road to abolition of private property, the goal
which Karl Marx said is the basic theory of Communism.

We have regretted to see those who advocate the destruction of such
freedom for the individual pit race against race as a weapon to
achieve their objective. This injures Americans of all races, colors,
creeds, and we believe is unworthy of those who want to take steps

toward solving the problem of providing minorities with opportunity
to improve their housing.

Concurrent with our opposition to the use of governmental force to
accomplish that purpose, we have advocated a voluntary program.
We believe that there is a vast reservoir of good will among Americans
of all economic and social levels toward anyone trying to improve
his position in society. We believe that this good will can and
is being used to give minorities opportunity to live wherever they
want and can economically afford. It needs to be encouraged strongly,
without force.

Our Association has taken several steps to encourage progress toward
that goal. Among our own members, we instituted an Equal Rights
Program just before the Rumford Act was passed by the Legislature in
1963. Because of the danger of being misunderstood, it was not
given publicity until the people had nullified the Act by their vote
in November, 1964.

At our state convention in October, 1964, our board of directors
approved a recommended code of practices which since has been
adopted by our 178 local real estate boards throughout California.
The Code sets forth the legal, ethical and moral responsibilities
of our members to give equal service to all clients regardless of

race, color, religion, national origin or ancestry.

We are submitting a copy of the Code of Practices to you today along with our testimony.

The Code of Practices specifies that the real estate broker or salesman must not make a decision concerning to whom specific residential housing shall be sold, leased or rented. Provision 1 (a) provides:

> "A Realtor should stand ready to show property to any
> member of any racial, creedal or ethnic group."

Provision 1 (b):

> "A Realtor has a legal and ethical responsibility to
> receive all offers and to communicate them to the
> property. owner. The Realtor being but an agent,
> the right of decision must be with the property
> owner."

The Code is not only an instrument to guide our members. It clarifies the position of the real estate agent in the public mind when its existence is known. It has been given publicity through the news media of the state; our local real estate boards are giving it publicity within their own committees. We will continue to

advocate widespread understanding of the Code and its practical
application.

At present, we are in the process of organizing a list of speakers
available throughout California to speak on this subject and are
urging our local boards to hold meetings with their membership and
with the public as another means of creating understanding.

Many leaders in this state, including former Governor Edmund G.
Brown, have publicly commended our Association for our Equal Rights
Program.

In March, 1966, we made a survey of all of our local boards operating
multiple listing services to see what percentage of the residential
listings they processed contained any restriction in selling to
minority group persons. The survey covered the first eleven months
of 1965. The answer came to 1,687 restricted listings out of a total
of 286,406, or approximately six-tenths of one per cent. A more
detailed analysis of the survey is included in the exhibits submitted.

This survey indicated two facts to us: First, that there is an
almost unlimited supply of housing for sale to minority group persons
in California. Second, that our Equal Rights Program, or the attitude of the people of California, or both, is contributing to the
availability of such housing.

It should be noted that this survey covered housing for sale. It
did not cover rentals. Our members do not become involved, to any
significant degree, in the rental of housing.

In other efforts to pursue our Equal Rights Program, we have worked
with many individuals and organizations that are dedicated to giving
minorities equal opportunities for housing of their choice. This
cooperation has been on a local level, through our real estate
boards, and on a state level.

A specific example of such cooperation with a local group is included
among the exhibits we are submitting here. Some of our Realtors in
the San Francisco Peninsula area held a series of meetings with
members of the Midpeninsula Citizens for Fair Housing, Palo Alto,
in late 1965 and 1966 to arrive at a mutual understanding of the
attitudes and motivations   that underlie housing transactions
involving minority group persons. They mutually sponsored a seminar
at Stanford University in February, 1966, to explore these attitudes
and motivations among a wider segment of interested people. They
are at present, under a grant from the Rosenberg Foundation, jointly
developing a film to contribute to even wider understanding.

On a state level, in January, 1965, our State President and other
appropriate leaders, met with the Division of Christian Citizenship

of the Department of Social Relations of the Episcopal Diocese
of Los Angeles in an effort to create a mutual working relationship.

Beginning in September, 1966, we have met with members of the Commission on Church and Race of the Council of Churches of Southern
California-Nevada. We submit exhibits concerning those meetings.
As an outgrowth of them, we have reminded those who feel our Code
of Practices is not being observed that we can only take action
when alleged violations are reported either to our local boards or
to our Association headquarters. We have taken action whenever
such allegations have been reported to us.

It should be remembered that our Association is a voluntary organization. Each of our 178 local real estate boards is autonomous with
its own officers, its own directors, its own machinery for disciplinary
action. Actions and recommendations of our statewide officers and
directors are essentially advisory in nature. Our ultimate disciplinary weapon, except through advice and persuasion, is to revoke
the charter of the local real estate board.

So far, we have only had to threaten such action to end inequitable
limitations on membership by one of our local boards. One case,
included in your exhibits, involved the Southwest Branch of the Los
Angeles Realty Board, which had a rule governing admission of new

members which we felt discriminated against Negroes who otherwise
were qualified. By working with the local board, we were able to
bring about a change in the rule and Negro members are now being
admitted.

In addition to our efforts to dissolve the barriers that sometimes
seem to interfere with minority group persons obtaining housing
they desire, we are this year launching a statewide program among
our members to improve substandard housing. This directly relates
to housing for minorities. Substandard housing is usually occupied
by low-income people and while there are in California many times
as many Caucasian persons below the poverty level established by
the federal government as there are other races, there still is a
sizeable number of minority persons occupying such housing.

Essentially, the program will have real estate boards at the local
level working with governmental and civic groups to bring dilapidated
housing up to an acceptable standard. Being sure there are workable
housing codes is one aim of the program. Reasonable enforcement of
those codes is another. We want communities to establish an atmosphere conducive to encourage private enterprise to provide low cost
housing for low income people. Renovation of existing housing makes
that possible, at the same time, except in extreme cases, making it
unnecessary to have a massive input of federal tax money to solve

the problem.

Gentlemen, we in the California Real Estate Association are genuinely concerned over the problem of providing decent, safe and sanitary housing for all of our people, including minority group persons. We are working as we can toward that goal. At the same time we feel strongly that the goal must be achieved without sacrificing freedom of choice for the individual property owner.

# # #

CODE OF ETHICS

NATIONAL ASSOCIATION OF REAL ESTATE BOARDS

Preamble

UNDER all is the land. Upon its wise utilization and widely allocated ownership depend the survival and growth of free institutions and of our civilization. The Realtor is the instrumentality through which the land resource of the nation reaches its highest use and through which land ownership attains its widest distribution. He is a creator of homes, a builder of cities, a developer of industries and productive farms.

Such functions impose obligations beyond those of ordinary commerce. They impose grave social responsibility and a patriotic duty to which the Realtor should dedicate himself, and for which he should be diligent in preparing himself. The Realtor, therefore, is zealous to maintain and improve the standards of his calling and shares with his fellow-Realtors a common responsibility for its integrity and honor.

In the interpretation of his obligations, he can take no safer guide than that which has been handed down through twenty centuries, embodied in the Golden Rule:

"Whatsoever ye would that men should do to you, do ye even so to them."

Accepting this standard as his own, every Realtor pledges himself to observe its spirit in all his activities and to conduct his business in accordance with the following Code of Ethics:

Part I
Relations to the Public

ARTICLE 1.
The Realtor should keep himself informed as to movements affecting real estate in his community, state, and the nation, so that he may be able to contribute to public thinking on matters of taxation, legislation, land use, city planning, and other questions affecting property interests.

ARTICLE 2.
It is the duty of the Realtor to be well informed on current market conditions in order to be in a position to advise his clients as to the fair market price.

ARTICLE 3.
It is the duty of the Realtor to protect the public against fraud, misrepresentation or unethical practices in the real estate field.

He should endeavor to eliminate in his community any practices which could be damaging to the public or to the dignity and integrity of the real estate profession. The Realtor should assist the board or commission charged with regulating the practices of brokers and salesmen in his state.

ARTICLE 4.
The Realtor should ascertain all pertinent facts concerning every property for which he accepts the agency, so that he may fulfill his obligation to avoid error, exaggeration, misrepresentation, or concealment of pertinent facts.

ARTICLE 5.
The Realtor should not be instrumental in introducing into a neighborhood a character of property or use which will clearly be detrimental to property values in that neighborhood.

ARTICLE 6.
The Realtor should not be a party to the naming of a false consideration in any document, unless it be the naming of an obviously nominal consideration.

ARTICLE 7.
The Realtor should not engage in activities that constitute the practice of law and should recommend that title be examined and legal counsel be obtained when the interest of either party requires it.

ARTICLE 8.
The Realtor should keep in a special bank account, separated from his own funds, monies coming into his possession in trust for other persons, such as escrows, trust funds, client's monies and other like items.

ARTICLE 9.
The Realtor in his advertising should be especially careful to present a true picture and should neither advertise without disclosing his name, nor permit his salesmen to use individual names or telephone numbers, unless the salesman's connection with the Realtor is obvious in the advertisement.

ARTICLE 10.
The Realtor, for the protection of all parties with whom he deals, should see that financial obligations and commitments regarding real estate transactions are in writing, expressing the exact agreement of the parties; and that copies of such agreements, at the time they are executed, are placed in the hands of all parties involved.

Part II
Relations to the Client

ARTICLE 11.
In accepting employment as an agent, the Realtor pledges himself to protect and promote the interests of the client. This obligation of absolute fidelity to the client's interest is primary, but it does not relieve the Realtor from the obligation of dealing fairly with all parties to the transaction.

ARTICLE 12.
In justice to those who place their interests in his care, the Realtor should endeavor always to be in-

formed regarding laws, proposed legislation, governmental orders, and other essential information and public policies which affect those interests.

ARTICLE 13.
Since the Realtor is representing one or another party to a transaction, he should not accept compensation from more than one party without the full knowledge of all parties to the transaction.

ARTICLE 14.
The Realtor should not acquire an interest in or buy for himself, any member of his immediate family, his firm or any member thereof, or any entity in which he has a substantial ownership interest, property listed with him, or his firm, without making the true position known to the listing owner, and in selling property owned by him, or in which he has such interest, the facts should be revealed to the purchaser.

ARTICLE 15.
The exclusive listing of property should be urged and practiced by the Realtor as a means of preventing dissension and misunderstanding and of assuring better service to the owner.

ARTICLE 16.
When acting as agent in the management of property, the Realtor should not accept any commission, rebate or profit on expenditures made for an owner, without the owner's knowledge and consent.

ARTICLE 17.
The Realtor should not undertake to make an appraisal that is outside the field of his experience unless he obtains the assistance of an authority on such types of property, or unless the facts are fully disclosed to the client. In such circumstances, the authority so engaged should be so identified and his contribution to the assignment should be clearly set forth.

ARTICLE 18.
When asked to make a formal appraisal of real property, the Realtor should not render an opinion without careful and thorough analysis and interpretation of all factors affecting the value of the property. His counsel constitutes a professional service.

The Realtor should not undertake to make an appraisal or render an opinion of value on any property where he has a present or contemplated interest unless such interest is specifically disclosed in the appraisal report. Under no circumstances should he undertake to make a formal appraisal when his employment or fee is contingent upon the amount of his appraisal.

ARTICLE 19.
The Realtor should not submit or advertise property without authority and in any offering, the price quoted should not be other than that agreed upon with the owners as the offering price.

ARTICLE 20.
In the event that more than one formal written offer on a specific property is made before the owner has accepted an offer, any other formal written offer presented to the Realtor, whether by a prospective purchaser or another broker, should be transmitted to the owner for his decision.

Part III
Relations to His Fellow-Realtor

ARTICLE 21.
The Realtor should seek no unfair advantage over his fellow-Realtors and should willingly share with them the lessons of his experience and study.

ARTICLE 22.
The Realtor should so conduct his business as to avoid controversies with his fellow-Realtors. In the event of a controversy between Realtors who are members of the same local board, such controversy should be arbitrated in accordance with regulations of their board rather than litigated.

ARTICLE 23.
Controversies between Realtors who are not members of the same local board should be submitted to an arbitration board consisting of one arbitrator chosen by each Realtor from the real estate board to which he belongs or chosen in accordance with the regulations of the respective boards. One other member, or a sufficient number of members to make an odd number, should be selected by the arbitrators thus chosen.

ARTICLE 24.
When the Realtor is charged with unethical practice, he should place all pertinent facts before the proper tribunal of the member board of which he is a member, for investigation and judgment.

ARTICLE 25.
The Realtor should not voluntarily disparage the business practice of a competitor, nor volunteer an opinion of a competitor's transaction. If his opinion is sought it should be rendered with strict professional integrity and courtesy.

ARTICLE 26.
The agency of a Realtor who holds an exclusive listing should be respected. A Realtor cooperating with a listing broker should not invite the cooperation of a third broker without the consent of the listing broker.

ARTICLE 27.
The Realtor should cooperate with other brokers on property listed by him exclusively whenever it is in the interest of the client, sharing commissions on a previously agreed basis. Negotiations concerning property listed exclusively with one broker should be carried on with the listing broker, not with the owner, except with the consent of the listing broker.

ARTICLE 28.
The Realtor should not solicit the services of an employee or salesman in the organization of a fellow-Realtor without the knowledge of the employer.

ARTICLE 29.
Signs giving notice of property for sale, rent, lease or exchange should not be placed on any property by more than one Realtor, and then only if authorized by the owner, except as the property is listed with and authorization given to more than one Realtor.

ARTICLE 30.
In the best interest of society, of his associates and of his own business, the Realtor should be loyal to the real estate board of his community and active in its work.

CONCLUSION

The term *Realtor* has come to connote competence, fair dealing and high integrity resulting from adherence to a lofty ideal of moral conduct in business relations. No inducement of profit and no instructions from clients ever can justify departure from this ideal, or from the injunctions of this Code.

The Code of Ethics was adopted in 1913. Amended at the Annual Convention in 1924, 1928, 1950, 1951, 1952, 1955, 1956, 1961, and 1962.

CONSTITUTION AND BY-LAWS

[Incorporating Amendments to and Including Jan. 8, 1966]

See Page 8, Sec. 6

CALIFORNIA REAL ESTATE ASSOCIATION
520 South Grand Avenue, Los Angeles, California 90017
Phone: (213) 628-0551

Sec. 6. No Member Board shall enforce an arbitrary numerical or other inequitable limitation on its membership; nor shall any Member Board impose any limitation upon membership because of race, color, creed or national origin.

758

See Page 11, No. 9

POLICY AND
PROCEDURE MANUAL

Governing
By-Laws and Related Activities
of Member Real Estate Boards

Published by

CALIFORNIA REAL ESTATE ASSOCIATION
520 South Grand Avenue
Los Angeles, California 90017

759

Policies and procedures covering by-laws and related activities of Member Boards of the California Real Estate Association reflect extensive study by CREA Special Counsel Moses Lasky of the San Francisco law firm, Brobeck, Phleger & Harrison.

Board officers and members are reminded that other guideposts concerning the affairs of CREA Member Boards include suggested "Rules and Regulations governing the operation of Multiple Listing Service" published by CREA. The National Association of Real Estate Boards in January 1963 published a complete review of the Realtor's Code of Ethics under the title of "Interpretations of the Code of Ethics." By-laws of the State and National Associations also govern Member Boards. Therefore, reference should also be made to both CREA and NAREB by-laws.

An Addendum to the NAREB By-laws clarifies Article 1, Section 2, relating to questions of inequitable limitations. Particular attention is directed to it.

First printing—February 1963*
Amended December 20, 1965
Amended April 6, 1966

9. Limitations on Listings.
A board should not try to regulate the type of listings its members may take. N.A.R.E.B.'s Interpretation No. 11 states that "A rule of a member board prohibiting the acceptance of open listings by members is an inequitable limitation on its membership." We advise that this is true of prohibition of acceptance of any kind of listing.

760

OFFICIAL INTERPRETATIONS
of By-laws, Article 1, Section 2 of the
NATIONAL ASSOCIATION OF REAL ESTATE BOARDS

Interpretation No. 5

"Stated qualifications for membership should be limited to those affecting integrity, competence, reputation and credit standing."

It is recognized that a board cannot—and should not attempt to—specify in its by-laws all the qualifications for membership therein. The greater the number of restrictions placed in the by-laws, the greater the danger that the board may be accused of seeking to impose restraints upon trade.

It is best for a board to provide for a continuing membership or screening committee consisting of members whose experience and judgment can be relied upon. If this committee is charged with the responsibility of investigating applicants for membership, determining the qualification, interviewing them personally, and requiring that they record their qualifications in a written form of "Application for Membership" (many boards publish and use their own forms and NAREB has such a suggested form available to boards), the governing body of the board (or the membership, as the case may be) can have much greater confidence in accepting the recommendations of such a committee rather than attempt to qualify applicants by setting forth restrictions in the by-laws.

Conditions change from time to time and it is quite possible that a restriction which may appear logical at one time will appear completely ridiculous under another set of later circumstances. If a minimum of requirements for membership is written into the by-laws, a committee can use discretion in qualifying applicants for membership. Under this circumstance, a rejected applicant need not necessarily be given reasons for his rejection, since a thorough investigation may have disclosed highly personal financial, ethical and other background that the committee would not be expected to disclose to the general membership. If, on the other hand, the applicant had met extensive requirements for membership as set forth in by-laws or published rules, he might properly demand disclosure of the reasons if he was rejected.

A membership committee should retain a record of applicants for membership and in the event that rejection of an application is recommended, a record of the basis for denial should be made, for two reasons: (1) the rejection should not be frivolous, based upon gossip or unfounded uninvestigated allegations; there should be positive reasons, and (2) there is a developing body of law sustaining the right of qualified persons to join their professional or trade associations and, therefore, a record should be made in support of any recommendation for denial of membership.

(Adopted May 11, 1965)

Interpretation No. 25

"A Board rule which prevents the participation of an Active Member, on equal terms with other Active Members, in a multiple listing service sponsored, organized, or sanctioned by the board, and which is available to Active members throughout the board's jurisdiction, is an inequitable limitation on its membership."

The question involved here related to multiple listing but it could apply to any service made available to members by a Member Board.

In developing the interpretation, care was taken to recognize that in some boards which cover a large geographic area, multiple listing or other services may be made available to members whose offices are within a partial area of the board's jurisdiction, without the same services being available to members whose offices are in other areas.

With this exception, however, it was found that if a board were to attempt to discriminate in making services available to some Active Members (Realtors), but not to other Active Members, when such services are available generally throughout the board's jurisdiction, it would be an inequitable limitation upon the membership. Thus it is not possible for a board to withhold from some Active Members services that are available to other Active Members, whether the service is organized or sponsored by the board, or otherwise under the board's ownership or authority.

Comment pertinent to the subject is quoted from *"Trade Association Law and Practice"* as follows: "The right to participate in trade association activities—the right to vote and take part in formulating association policy through meetings of the entire organization or through committees—varies among the different classes of members. Decision as to what these rights should be, like the decision on many other membership questions, is primarily a matter of policy, but it should be guided by two basic principles: The first one of equality.

Where interests and responsibilities are equal, rights should be equal. The second principle, an adjunct to the first, is that any distinction should be based on differences in classes of members, and the most extensive rights should be given members who have the most direct interest in and responsibility for association affairs."

Member Boards, therefore, may not withhold from some Active Members a service which is available to other Active Members throughout the board's jurisdiction.

CALIFORNIA REAL ESTATE ASSOCIATION

subscribes to the policy that a favorable public attitude for equal opportunity in the acquisition of housing can best be accomplished through leadership, example, education and the mutual cooperation of the real estate industry and the public.

The following is hereby stated as the Code of Practices of this Board:

1. It is the responsibility of a Realtor to offer equal service to all clients without regard to race, color, religion, or national origin in the sale, purchase, exchange, rental, or lease of real property.

    a. A Realtor should stand ready to show property to any member of any racial, creedal, or ethnic group.

    b. A Realtor has a legal and ethical responsibility to receive all offers and to communicate them to the property owner. The Realtor being but an agent, the right of decision must be with the property owner.

    c. A Realtor should exert his best efforts to conclude the transaction.

2. Realtors, individually and collectively, in performing their agency functions have no right or responsibility to determine the racial, creedal, or ethnic composition of any neighborhood or any part thereof.

    a. A Realtor shall not advise property owners to incorporate in a listing of property an exclusion of sale to any such group.

    b. A Realtor may take a listing which insists upon such exclusion, but only if it is lawfully done at the property owner's instance without any influence whatsoever by the agent.

3. Any attempt by a Realtor to solicit or procure the sale or other disposition in residential areas by conduct intended to implant fears in property owners based upon the actual or anticipated introduction of a minority group into an area shall subject the Realtor to disciplinary action. Any technique that induces panic selling is a violation of ethics and must be strongly condemned.

4. Each Realtor should feel completely free to enter into a broker-client relationship with persons of any race, creed, or ethnic group.

    a. Any conduct inhibiting said relationship is a specific violation of Article . . of the rules and regulations of this board, and shall subject the violating Realtor to disciplinary action.

California Real Estate Association
520 SOUTH GRAND AVE. • LOS ANGELES, CALIF. 90017   43 Rev. 12-66

763

California Real Estate Association
and California Real Estate Magazine

Telephone:
(Area Code 213) 628-0881

April 7, 1967

EXECUTIVE OFFICES
820 SOUTH GRAND AVE
LOS ANGELES, CALIF. 90017

TO: CREA REGIONAL VICE PRESIDENTS

Re: Equal Rights Speakers

The Equal Rights Committee, the Executive Committee, and the Board
of Directors by its approval of Clark Wallace's recommendations at
the Disneyland meeting, have agreed that we need to become more
active in pursuing our CREA Equal Rights Program.

We will soon be asking local boards to put on a program on this
subject. We want to compile a list of speakers who are knowledgeable on our Equal Rights Program and could do a good job of presenting it at a meeting of members and the general public. We
would then give this list to local boards so they could contact
speakers if they wish, inviting them to appear.

Speakers should be those who can express an impartial viewpoint
opposing forced housing by legislation, but recognizing our obligation to serve all people equally as Realtors.

Can you please suggest people in your district whom you feel will
be capable and willing to participate? We need to compile the
list by April 15, so I will appreciate receiving any suggestions
you have at once. You may use the bottom of this letter for that
purpose if you wish.

Perhaps you can work with the Equal Rights Committee District
Representative in preparing a list.

Sincerely,

Reed Robbins
RR:ll   President

764

[Sacramento Bee 3-5-65]

BROWN LAUDS CREA'S FAIR HOUSING MOVE

Governor Edmund G. Brown has praised the California Real Estate Association for making an "excellent start" in implementing its code of practice designed to provide equal opportunities in housing.

Brown met yesterday with the CREA executive committee to discuss the code which is being urged upon local member boards by the state association.

"If everyone cooperates, we can and will solve the problem of equal opportunity in buying and renting homes," said Brown.

Brown and the CREA were on opposite sides last fall in the bitterly fought campaign over Proposition 14, the constitutional amendment which nullified the Rumford Act and other state fair housing laws. Voters ultimately approved the proposition backed by the CREA and opposed by the governor.

The committee told the governor nearly all boards in California have adopted the code. Clive Graham, a real estate man and chairman of the fair employment practices commission, said an active effort to implement the code is being made by many local boards.

Brown urged other segments of the housing industry, such as apartment house owners and home builders, to adopt similar programs.

765

CALIFORNIA REAL ESTATE ASSOCIATION
NEWS SERVICE

520 SOUTH GRAND AVENUE, LOS ANGELES 90017 • PHONE 628-0551

Contact: Vern Beardsley   FOR IMMEDIATE RELEASE

March 21, 1966

CREA SURVEY REVEALS UNLIMITED
HOUSING AVAILABLE TO NEGROES

An almost unlimited supply of houses for sale is available
to Negroes and other minorities who have the financial ability
to buy them, according to a survey just released by the California Real Estate Association.

Burt Smith of Bellflower, CREA president, discussed the
survey during the Association's quarterly meeting of its board
of directors in Sacramento, ended March 19.

He said CREA queried its 176 real estate boards throughout California to learn how many houses for sale through their
multiple listing services were racially restricted by their
owners. The survey covered the first 11 months of 1965.

The answer, with 170 boards reporting, came to 1,687
listings out of a total of 286,406, or approximately six tenths
of one per cent (.589).

"This was a follow-up," Smith said, "of a sampling we took
earlier of 50 representative boards for the first 10 months of
1965. The result was almost identical. Total listings for
those 50 boards was 185,768 with 1,036 restricted, or .558
per cent. The highest rate for any one board was six per cent."

-more-

CREA SURVEY REVEALS UNLIMITED
HOUSING AVAILABLE TO NEGROES

He said the six boards not reporting on the latest survey
were small and would not "significantly alter" the finding,
representing only 1809 of a total CREA membership of 54,768 at
that date.

"Multiple listing services offer the largest pool of housing
for sale by far," he stated, "and most of them are operated by
real estate boards that are members of our association."

The survey asked these questions, with answers for the 170
boards totaled:

1. Does your board have a multiple listing service?
Yes 143, No 27.

2. Does your multiple listing service accept listings
which restrict buyers according to race, color, religion,
national origin or ancestry? Yes 73, No 70.

3. If "Yes," how many such restricted listings did your
multiple listing service handle for 1965 through November 30?
Total 1,687.

4. What was the total number of listings handled by your
multiple listing service for 1965 through November 30?
Total 286,406.

Smith pointed out that real estate agents are obligated to
show housing to any qualified buyer, the only exceptions being
those stipulated by the owner. Any violation of this obligation
makes them liable under the Unruh Act.

"There are bound to be skeptics who doubt that an owner
actually has restricted a particular piece of property," he said.

-more-

CREA SURVEY REVEALS UNLIMITED
HOUSING AVAILABLE TO NEGROES

"They can always ask to see the muliiple listing sheet, which
will state that fact when there is such a restriction. Or they
can ask the owner."

He concluded from the survey that housing for sale, "at
least that being offered through our member boards' multiple
listing services," is available to qualified Negroes and other
minorities.

"When Proposition 14 was passed," he continued, "it gave
owners of residential property freedom to choose the buyer or
renter of his property. This survey indicates, where the sale
of housing is concerned, that the owner is not using this freedom
to discriminate against buyers of another race or religion."

He added that the survey does not include rentals since they
are not a normal part of the average CREA member's business.

In other actions, the directors went on record as supporting
the federal rent subsidy program since the regulations under
FHA Section 221 (d) (3) have been rewritten to apply to low
income families only.

They also approved a resolution recommending that association members and local real estate boards support U.S.Marine
Corps Order 5710.4, known as the Marine Corps Reserve Civic
Action Program for Vietnam. The program provides food, tools
and other necessities to the South Vietnamese people through
voluntary donations forwarded to South Vietnam via the Navy and
Marine Corp's "Operation Handclasp."

#   #   #   #

768

REALTOR
CONTRACTOR
GENERAL INSURANCE

Service is Our Business

HOMES
COMMERCIAL
INDUSTRIAL

1621 EL CAMINO REAL • MOUNTAIN VIEW, CALIF. 94042 • PHONE 961-0424

December 27, 1965

Mr. Jack Pontius
520 So. Grand Avenue
California Real Estate Association
Los Angeles, California

Dear Jack:

At the first part of this year I formed a Realtors Committee for
Housing Assistance, which is composed of individual Realtors
from the following Real Estate Boards:

> Menlo Park, California
> Palo Alto, California
> Los Altos, California
> Mountain View, California and
> Sunnyvale, California.

These members reported to their Real Estate Boards of their actions,
or the actions of the committee, which are not fully approved by
each Board of Directors. We are acting solely as individuals.

The Mid-Peninsula Committe for Fair Housing which has approximately
6000 members representing the National Association of Advancement
of Colored People - CORE -, and other groups of this type, plus
leaders of the various communities and many church groups who did
raise over $100,000.00 for opposition to Proposition 14.

The Realtors Committee felt that we should meet with this group
and dicuss many common problems on housing. After several meetings
of a large group a sub-committee was appointed four Realtors and
five members from their Board of Directors to discuss in depth the
many problems we have in common.

It was decided that the sub-committee gained a great deal of
understanding and knowledge from the approximate 10 to 12 meetings
they held. This information should be dispursed to other members
of their group, other Realtors and also to the general public.

It was therefore decided to hold a Housing Seminar at Stanford
University, to which approximate 15 members of their group would
be invited, plus 15 Realtors and somewhere between 40 or 50
members of the general public.

769

Jack Pontius

Through using the Housing Seminar method it is hoped that we will be
able to get many more people enthused about helping us solve these
mutual problems. We hope then to be able to work out teams of
two to four speakers who will attend meetings of service clubs,
home-owner groups, church groups and various civic organizations
to tell our story.

It has also been suggested that the Ford Foundation might be
interested in furnishing us some money to make a movie to promote
better understanding in housing among all professions, races and
creeds. In addition the Ford Foundation might have additional money
for us to do some research in depth as to how improve human
relations between minority races and our industry.

Enclosed you will find the first group of papers as information on
a Housing Seminar to be held at Stanford University on February 12,
1966. This is the meeting at which Dave Robinson will be the key
speaker, and will also open the meeting.

The second groups of papers are the minutes of some of the meetings
held by this group. I would be glad to meet with you, Burt and
Dave at any time during the Board of Directors meeting in Los Angeles.

I hope the above meets with your approval and if you have any questions
do not hesitate to call. Would you please reproduce the above
mentioned literature and send copies to Dave Robinson and Burt Smith.

Sincerely,

Doug

DC:rs

Ecnl:

January 3, 1966
Palo Alto, California

This statement is set forth for use by Mr. Doug Couch of Los Altos
as an aid to him in his discussions with his fellow realtors to hopefully
make them aware of the need for a positive program of mutual enlightenment
and understanding.

After the resounding success of "Proposition 14" in November of 1964
in California, as a minority member I "felt" betrayed and deceived. That is,
betrayed by 16,000 million Americans in this modern day and enlightened world,
and deceived by my own naive belief that such a betrayal could not be
perpetuated in the same state within a space of twenty years.

With this as a "back-drop" you can see that the time was ripe for a
"new" approach to human or, better yet, "race" relationship. For I felt,
and I am sure many other minority members must have also, a rekindling of
almost 350 years of HATE, as opposed to what I wanted, i.e., peace,
understanding and restoration of my and every American's dream of equality
and dignity.

Thus, at the conclusion of the campaign for the "property rights" of
all Californians and "hate" of me by these same Californians, I was desperate
for a way to restore equality and dignity for all men. At about this same
time the remnants of the group formed to combat Proposition 14 (now called
"NPCFH") asked me to join them in some undetermined venture of solutions for
the reconstruction or restoration of hope for better understanding within
our own community, since the hate I felt apparently was not as strongly against
me here as perhaps it was in other parts of the state. As an old line civil
rights campaigner, this approach called for a well considered decision, for
inwardly I felt such an approach would be actionless and held little chance

for success and the participation in such a program would be "selling out". After its formation and its seeking to find meaningful programs, a "Program of Understanding" of the real estate world was initiated by MPCFH.

From this beginning has come what I loosely phrase "a mature and realistic understanding and appreciation" for certain realtors' problems, as expressed by those realtors who have shared and explored these with our group in a number of frank discussion sessions. These discussions have been aimed at distilling much of the mystery surrounding a complicated industry or profession as viewed by the realtor and the frustrations and distrust of minority members with realtors and the public at large.

In view of the foregoing, it is my considered opinion that there is still a chance for acquiring mutual understanding and appreciation for the problems of both the realtor and minority members to replace the frustrations and distrust, or better yet, hate, if we act with considered haste.

Clay Halland, Jr.
809 Richardson Ct.
Palo Alto, Calif.

STANFORD UNIVERSITY
STANFORD, CALIFORNIA

NT OF SOCIOI

January 4, 1966

Mr. Douglas Couch
Doug Couch Real Estate Inc.
1621 El Camino Real
Mountain View, California

Dear Doug:

Here is the brief account of my reactions to our weekly discussions:

The weekly seminar meetings, in addition to the information they
provided, benefitted me in several important ways. First of all, these
seminars demonstrated conclusively that it is possible to break through
the defensiveness of both fair housing partisans and realtors and thus to
discuss fundamental issues in a relatively dispassionate manner. Secondly
I gained many new insights into the causes and consequences of discrimination
in housing, particularly with regard to the all pervasive fears that
generate many of our problems. Thirdly, I came to recognize as problems,
factors that I had not previously considered such as the crucial role
financing methods play in the availability of housing. I saw
that some of the things I had previously considered as problems were not
really serious problems at all such as the attitudes the realtors themselves
held. Finally, I gained an appreciation for the position of the ethical
realtor as "the man in the middle" who is buffeted by the pressures from
those who support equal opportunity in housing and from those who are
opposed, for good reasons or bad, to integrating neighborhoods.

The initial meetings of the group spent much time in overcoming
mutual suspicion and defensiveness, defensiveness that manifested itself
either in a denial that there is any problem of discrimination in housing
or in the assertion that all problems of housing discrimination are due
to the malevolence of one group or another. It was one of the unfortunate
consequences of the Proposition 14 campaign that both sides assumed a
rigid moral stance and, in so doing, cast a moral shadow on their opposition.
This moral shadow obscured the real issues and the real problems involved
in providing equal opportunity in housing. In these weekly meetings, our
ability to avoid staunch moral stands enabled me to recognize the considerable
degree of agreement that exists between realtors and fair housing people.
For example, not only did we all agree on the undesirable social and
economic consequences of ghettos, but also agreed that we all had a stake

773

Mr. Douglas Couch
January 4, 1966
Page Two

in mitigating these problems. While we frequently differed on the details
of a specific problem or the efficacy of a particular program for meeting
a problem, there was far more consensus in defining problems and far
more desire to seek solutions than I would have imagined prior to these
sessions.

Feel free to use it in any way you see fit. Have a good trip.

Sincerely,

Bernard P. Cohen
Associate Professor of Sociology
Director, Laboratory for Social Research

MIDPENINSULA CITIZENS FOR FAIR HOUSING
Room 3, Second Floor   131 University Avenue
Palo Alto, California
323-6688

Statement for Committee on Governmental Efficiency
May 26, 1965

Midpeninsula Citizens for Fair Housing is a non-profit voluntary
organization, already 935 members strong, devoted to the purpose
of securing for all individuals, an equal opportunity to purchase
or rent property wherever they choose. (We have recently learned
that in California alone, there are some 300 groups similar to
ours.) Our main work is on the local scene, and we are gratified
with the cooperation and support we are getting from our local
Real Estate Boards, some of which have adopted anti-discriminatory
regulations for their Multiple Listing Serivces as well as in
their Code of Ethics.

Our Legal-Legislative Committee is giving careful attention to
legislation affecting Fair Housing. We have chosen to give particular
support to the Holmdahl Bill, SB #950, and its related Assembly bill,
AB #4. We wish to congratulate the CREA on its stand in support of
both these bills.

We believe it is entirely reasonable to include the suspension
or revocation of a license as a penalty for continued and wilful
violation of the existing law. Such an enactment is particularly
desirable because it is selective in its effect, and will make
it easier for professions concerned to improve the performance of
their own members; it will leave enforcement in the hands of agencies
whom the individuals trust to be reasonable and fair-minded; we
hope it will enter into the subject matter óf-examination for a
license and will thus help to educate those entering the profession.

Furthermore, this bill is an appropriate one to consider at this
time, because it does not appear to conflict with Proposition 14
or to raise other constitutional issues.

Mrs. Richard W. Lyman,
Executive Secretary, MCFH.

MIDPENINSULA CITIZENS
FOR FAIR HOUSING

and

THE COUNCIL FOR HOUSING
ASSISTANCE

together with leading midpeninsula

REALTORS

and the

DEPARTMENT OF SOCIOLOGY
OF STANFORD UNIVERSITY

sponsor a conference on:

Equal Opportunity

in

Housing:

Problems and Prospects

Saturday, February 12, 1966
8:30 A.M. to 4:30 P.M.

CUBBERLEY HALL
STANFORD UNIVERSITY

[Admission by ticket only]

NOTES

LIST OF THOSE INVITED TO PARTICIPATE

Robert Almanzan	Franklin P. Johnson
Mrs. Bella Almanzan	Roger Johnson
Charles Andrews	H. C. Kallahan
Adm E. W. Armentrout	Ryland Kelley
Robert L. Ash	Rt. Rev. Msgr. Edwin
Chester Bailey	Kennedy
Ed Becks	Larry J LaLiberte
Mike Bedwell	Mrs. James Landreth
Joseph Beh	Howard W. Lewis, Jr.
Mrs. Ida D. Berk	H. P. Little
Roscoe E. Black	Dr. Leroy Lucas
Jack Blackwell	Mrs. Jung Lyman
Richard Blakely	Bernard McCabe
Dr. Leo Blank	Paul McCloskey, Jr.
The Rev. James A. Branch	Richard Mansfield
Harry Bremond	Tony Marmon
Allan S. Brown	Mrs. Louis Mauer
Bob Brown	Mike Miles
James Burns	George Norton
H. V. Burton	Mrs Virginia Page
John Cassidy	Wesley Pomeroy
Robert Coate	H. Jackson Pontius
Ben Coe	Bill Powell
Kirke W. Comstock	James Powers
Leonard Cornell	Mrs Elizabeth Rock
James H. Crockett	Robert Rockett
Joseph Custimano	Antonio Roder
Glenn Daffern	Jesse Rodriguez
Mrs. Mary C. Davey	John Rutherford
Paul Davis	Gerard Schwartz
Mrs. Marlene De Lancie	Mrs. Fanne Stattel
Andrew Doty	Victor Shaddick
Gordon Eustice	Wesley Slade
Rick Evans	Kenneth Slater
Dr. Arthur Frank	Burton E. Smith
Irving A. Frohlich	The Rev. Carl Smith
Emmet Gatewood	Mrs. John Stern
Leland Gerber	George Stoney
Mrs. Rosemary Goodenough	Robert Swartz
Mayor Charles Gordon	Opie Tucker
Louis Green	Miss Hertha Vogelstein
Alan E. Gross	Doc Walthers
Conrad Gullixson	H. Neal Warren
Mrs. Elinor Heath	Gordon Weber
Col. Frank Higgins	Mrs. Gertrude Wilks
Douglas P. Hill	Gary Williams
Clay Holland, Jr.	Dr. Andrew W. White, Jr.
John Howard	Charles Winn
Thomas W. Howarth	Morton Wolfe
Ralph Hotkins	Eugene Wright
Leo R. Ikeda	

EQUAL OPPORTUNITY IN HOUSING: PROBLEMS AND PROSPECTS

PROGRAM

8:30 A.M. Registration
Main Vestibule, Cubberley Hall

9:00 A.M. General Session
for all conference participants
Meeting Room E-2

Speakers:

MR. DAVID ROBINSON
President, 1965
California Real Estate Association

MR. DOUG COUCH
Realtor and Chairman
Council for Housing Assistance

DR. FELIX SMITH
President
Midpeninsula Citizens for Fair Housing

Chairman:

THE REV. JOHN R. WYATT
Trinity Parish, Menlo Park

10:00 A.M. Coffee Break

At 10:30 conference participants will divide into small discussion groups according to the letter (A-C) indicated on the conference ticket. Each group will consider three major discussion topics (one in the morning, two in the afternoon).

DISCUSSION GROUP LEADERS

A—Prof. CHARLES J. MEYERS
Stanford University Law School
(meets in Room E-35)

B—Mr. PHILLIP W. SCHNEIDER
Superintendent, Whisman School District
(meets in Room E-55)

C—Dr. SAMUEL I. TAIMUTY
Physicist, Stanford Research Institute
(meets in Room E-56)

D—THE REV. GEORGE M. WILSON
First Presbyterian Church, Palo Alto
(meets in Room E-57)

E—THE REV. JOHN R. WYATT
Trinity Parish, Menlo Park
(meets in Room E-63)

F—PROF. MORRIS ZELDITCH, JR.
Stanford Department of Sociology.
(meets in Room E-61)

G—RICHARD DE LANCIE
President, URS Corporation
(meets in Room E-11)

10:30 - 12:00 DISCUSSION I:
Viewpoint—the Buyer's, the Seller's, the Realtor's, and the Neighbor's

12:00 - 1:30 LUNCHEON
Stanford Faculty Club
Stanford Hosts:
GABRIEL A. ALMOND
BERNARD P. COHEN
KENNETH CUTHBERTSON
LORENZ EITNER
RICHARD W. LYMAN
LYLE M. NELSON
ROBERT R. SEARS
JAMES P. THURBER, JR.
MORRIS ZELDITCH, JR.

1:30 - 2:30 DISCUSSION II:
Integration Economics—
Who Profits, Who Loses?

2:30 - 3:00 Coffee Break

3:00 - 4:00 DISCUSSION III:
Consequences to the Community—
Deprivation or Diversity?

4:00 - 4:30 SUMMARY SESSION
Meeting Room E-2

Evaluation form by individuals, and brief summary by the Conference Chairman on the highlights of the day.

CONFERENCE DIRECTOR: PROF. BERNARD COHEN, Department of Sociology, Stanford University

777

Midpeninsula Citizens for Fair Housing
131 University Ave., Palo Alto, Calif.
323-6688   2-25-66

(D:RECT QUOTATIONS)
SAMPLE RESPONSES TO QUESTIONS
POST-MEETING REACTION FORM
CONFERENCE ON EQUAL OPPORTUNITY IN HOUSING, FEB. 12, 1966

DID THE SESSIONS RAISE ANY NEW PROBLEMS THAT YOU PERSONALLY HAD NOT CONSIDERED BEFORE TODAY? IF SO, WHAT WERE THESE NEW PROBLEMS?

The healthy exchange of ideas and opinions served to emphasize the complexity of the whole problem of social interaction.

The "Realtor" is a nebulous term to many. The Realtor is greatly misunderstood.

The problem that few colored people are really involved in seeking integrated housing. Few can afford it.

(1) The feeling expressed by Negro discussants that the voter approval of Prop. 14 left California Negroes with little or no hope for ever bettering their lot in this state. This view seems unfortunately, though perhaps understandably, irrational. (2) The problem of whether and how to motivate minority members to seek better housing (this one previously considered but its gravity not recognized).

The problem of the identity of the realtor, how he sees himself, how he is threatened by the way others see him.

The problem the realtor has to provide open housing in the face of pressures from the "insulated" seller.

Whether the problem of integrated communities was one for the real estate people to solve or one for the members of the community to solve.

Lack of various priced housing in the area scattered throughout--not in one or two areas. Financial problems and misinformation on same of minority groups.

DID THE OTHER MEMBERS OF YOUR DISCUSSION GROUP PRESENT POINTS OF VIEW THAT YOU HAD NOT HEARD PREVIOUSLY? IF SO, WHAT WERE THESE POINTS OF VIEW? WHAT WERE YOUR FEELINGS ABOUT THEM?

Realtor activity--good sign. Fear of rejection and hostility by Negroes from whites.

I realized that I had considered the problems more from an ideological viewpoint, while here they were stated from a practical, even pragmatic point of view.

Most all points of view, if not previously directly considered, were certainly predictable and not surprising. The interest lay in observing the interaction of these points of view. I was somewhat distressed by the tendency on all sides to rationalize and to advocate one's own position rather than earnestly to consider whether it should be changed.

Impact of Negro attitude and setback from Prop. 14. Did not fully realize the Negro considered this an almost total defeat of their efforts.

Particularly regarding experimental home ownership subsidy incentive programs. Also re financing discrimination.

778

PAGE 2
DIRECT QUOTATIONS
SAMPLE RESPONSES TO QUESTIONS

Midpeninsula Citizens for Fair Housing
131 University Ave., Palo Alto, Calif.

The view that economics do create segregation by making marginal financing available
to minority groups in minority neighborhoods.

Realtors are not such bad guys.

DID THE DISCUSSIONS SUGGEST ANY PRACTICAL METHODS OF SOLVING SOME OF THE PROBLEMS
DISCUSSED?

More direct public education efforts on the "myths" of falling property values,
disintegration (of) neighborhoods because of sales to minorities.

Yes--scattered public housing.

Practical methods were not found, but a strong desire expressed itself for preparing
for the changes that are at hand.

Yes--more action and less talk! The value of informal contact between races. A
thousand small efforts may be of greater value than one big dramatic move.

Group action by realty boards to implement statements of principles; action by
other community groups to publicize and support such action.

WHAT DID YOU PERSONALLY FIND MOST WORTHWHILE IN TODAY'S CONFERENCE?

Calming fears of discussion

Listening to the _informed_ opinion of an enlightened realtor and an intelligent Negro.

The opportunity to engage in a spirited dialogue with those individuals who have, in
my mind, constituted the "foe" group.

The realization of how shallow our understanding of "community" is.

Meeting many people that are concerned and interested, and the frankness of their
statements.

Getting to know the sincere feelings of others whose political viewpoints do not
necessarily agree with mine. I wish Americans could exchange views in wonderful
sessions such as these.

The chance to hear frank discussions by minority members.

The ability to sit down and listen and discuss the problems involved.

Interchange of viewpoints changed my feelings about myths--destroyed myths.

To know that there is an honest effort being made or considered to sell and rent to
minorities by realtors.

CALIFORNIA REAL ESTATE ASSOCIATION

520 South Grand Avenue
Los Angeles, California 90017
Telephone: 628-0551

April 22, 1956

Mr. Felix T. Smith, President
Citizens for Fair Housing
Room 3, Second Floor
101 University Avenue
Palo Alto, California

Dear Mr. Smith:

Re: Request for Ford Foundation Grant

Members of the CREA Executive Committee heard a report from Douglass Couch of Palo Alto preceding our recent Directors' meeting in Sacramento.

Mr. Couch's report was most impressive and well received by the Executive Committee, all who are dedicated to the support and advancement of CREA's Equal Rights Program.

We have your letter suggesting that CREA participate in the proposed film, which could be used for the purpose of conveying to all segments of our population the sensitive facts encompassed in understanding the needs and responsibilities of all people involved, both directly and indirectly, in the vast area of housing problems.

The Executive Committee authorized me to accept your invitation that we join with you in requesting the Ford Foundation for approximately $65,000 for the development of a training film. It was the feeling of the Executive Committee that CREA should lend its wholehearted support, subject to our joint participation in the preparation of the contents of the film and our working with you in selecting the best media and individuals who are to prepare and supervise the development of such a film.

I have assured the Executive Committee that there would be no cost to the Association under such a plan. However, we will expect those appointed by me to participate jointly with your committee to make themselves available for this assignment.

We have had considerable experience ourselves in working with several Hollywood corporations in preparation of 16 millimeter color films of from 15 to 25 minutes

Mr. Felix T. Smith   -2-   April 22, 1966

duration. [We hope that this reservoir of knowledge will contribute to the progress
which we look forward to making with you in this worthwhile program.]

                    Sincerely,

                    Burt Smith, President

B:rnvs
cc Mrs. Richard Lynn
    Mr. Douglass Couch
    Mr. H. Jackson Pontius

CITIZENS FOR FAIR HOUSING
ROOM 3, SECOND FLOOR
131 UNIVERSITY AVE.
PALO ALTO, CALIF.

20 June 1966

Mr. Burton Smith
C. R. E. A.
520 South Grand Avenue
Los Angeles, Calif. 90017

Dear Mr. Smith:

You will be interested in the correspondence we have
been engaged in with the Ford Foundation. As you can
see, I believe that ours remains an important project,
even if it has to be postponed for some months. I
hope that the C. R. E. A. will also continue its
interest, since I do not think the project would be
feasible without your participation. If you have any
ideas as to where funds could be located, we would
be very happy to cooperate.

Cordially yours,

Felix T. Smith
President

FTS:ew

Encl:letter from Mr. Ylvisaker, 5-18-66
     letter to Mr. Ylvisaker, 6-17-66

782

17 June 1965

CITIZENS FOR FAIR HOUSING
ROOM 2, SECOND FLOOR
DI UNIVERSITY AVE.
PALO ALTO, CALIF.

Mr. Paul N. Ylvisaker
Director
Public Affairs Program
The Ford Foundation
477 Madison Avenue
New York, New York 10022

Dear Mr. Ylvisaker:

Thank you very much for your letter of May 13 to Mrs. Wadleigh.
What you said was not a complete surprise, since Mr. Stoney
reported essentially the same thing as a result of his conversation with you.

I believe that both Mr. Stoney and ourselves are in agreement
that the type of film we have been talking about would be
desirable even if we have to wait until early next year to
begin on it. Accordingly, I would be very happy to see you
reactivate our proposal in the fall, if there is a possibility
of funds becoming available at that time.

However, if you are really not interested and would like to be
let off the hook, we would far rather know it definitely than
maintain any illusory hopes for the future. I assume that you
recognize this as well, and therefofe I am not interpreting
your letter as a polite way of saying "no."

We have not made attempts to reach other sources of support for
this film as yet, but I presume you would not be surprised if
we should do so if any likely source proves to be interested.
Naturally, we would let you know as soon as anything definite
developed in such a direction.

I am sending copies of your letter and of this one of mine
to the California Real Estate Association for their information.

We thank you very much for your interest.

Yours very sincerely,

Felix T. Smith
President

FTS:ew

783

THE FORD FOUNDATION
477 Madison Ave.
New York, N.Y. 10022

PUBLIC AFFAIRS PROGRAM

May 18, 1966

Mrs. Elisabeth Wadleigh, Office Manager
Citizens for Fair Housing
Room 3, Second Floor
131 University Avenue
Palo Alto, California

Dear Mrs. Wadleigh:

I'm sorry to be so tardy in acknowledging your letter
of April 26. We have had a conversation with Mr. Stoney, who
spoke most persuasively for the project.

Our problem is that we've exhausted our budget for the
fiscal year, and aren't in a position to encourage or even seriously
consider the proposal. Rather than say an immediate No, we could
keep the project on our waiting list until late Fall. But this
takes away your time and gives you no promises - and we'd fully
understand if you should decide to explore more immediate sources
of financing.

I'm sorry to have to write thus.

Sincerely,

Paul N. Ylvisaker
Director

784

September 15, 1966

Mr. Felix T. Smith, President
Citizens for Fair Housing
Room 3, Second Floor
131 University Avenue
Palo Alto, California

Dear Mr. Smith:

Earlier this year we had correspondence between our
Association President Burt Smith and yourself as President
of the Mid-peninsula Citizens for Fair Housing.

Has there been any further development on the proposal
of the Ford Foundation and the development of the film which
was the subject of our previous correspondence?

We would like to keep this file active and want to be
helpful if there is any possibility.

                    Sincerely,

                    H. JACKSON PONTIUS
                    Executive Vice President

HJP:ms

cc: Mr. Douglass Couch

CITIZENS FOR FAIR HOUSING
ROOM 3, SECOND FLOOR
131 UNIVERSITY AVE.
PALO ALTO, CALIF.

5 October 1966

Mr. H. Jackson Pontius
Executive Vice President
California Real Estate Association
520 South Grand Avenue
Los Angeles, California 90017

Dear Mr. Pontius:

Thanks very much for your letter of 15 September. We are very
encouraged to know of CREA's continuing interest in this project
and we would like very much to find some way of bringing it to
fruition. As a first step, we are renewing our contacts with
the Ford Foundation, and expect fairly shortly to get some idea
of how the wind blows from that quarter. If it does not appear
encouraging, I think we should make a strong effort to find
some other source of financing.

I trust you received my message at Masonic Auditorium on
Tuesday, which I left in case you wished to know something
about our position during the CREA's current meeting. I am
sorry we were not more prompt in getting a written answer to you.

We are looking forward to continuing contacts and will keep you
informed.

Yours sincerely,

Felix T. Smith
President

FTS:ew

786

REALTOR
CONTRACTOR
GENERAL INSURANCE

DOUG COUCH INC.

Service is Our Business

HOMES
COMMERCIAL
INDUSTRIAL

1621 EL CAMINO REAL • MOUNTAIN VIEW, CALIF. 94042 • PHONE 961-0424

November 25, 1966

Mr. Burt Smith
16505 South Clark Ave.,
Bellflower, California

Dear Burt,

The Midpeninsula Citizens for Fair Housing and the
Realtors Committee for Housing Assistance have just received
a $15,000.00 grant from the Rosenberg Foundation of San
Francisco.

We plan to hold a meeting in Northern California
similar to the ones we have held in the past in Palo Alto.
Also some similar to the one held at Stanford University.

I will have a more complete plan to present to the
Executive Committee in January in San Francisco.

Sincerely,

DOUG COUCH, INC.

M. Douglass Couch

787

December 20, 1966

Mr. M. Douglass Couch
Doug Couch, Inc.
1621 El Camino Real
Mountain View, California 94042

Dear Doug:

Congratulations on your part in making it possible for
the Midpeninsula Citizens for Fair Housing and the
Realtors Committee for Housing Assistance to receive a
$15,000.00 grant from the Rosenberg Foundation of San
Francisco.

We know with your participation in planning this film
it should be a helpful tool in educating the people
concerning the problem.

CREA will be glad to assist in development of the film.
We can mail a print of the last one we produced to show
you what can be accomplished.

Cordially yours,

Burt Smith
President

BS:md

cc H. Jackson Pontius
   Felix Smith

bcc Reed Robbins

bcc Burt Smith

788

January 26, 1967

Mr. Felix T. Smith, President
Citizens for Fair Housing
Second Floor, Room 3
131 University Avenue
Palo Alto, California

Dear Mr. Smith:

Doug Couch recently made a report at our Directors'
Meeting in January on the progress of your Committee.

We will be interested in being kept informed of your
progress and in having any information which you may
have in printed form that would outline your plans in
view of the recent grant to your Committee.

Sincerely,

H. Jackson Pontius
Executive Vice President

HJP/jm

cc: Mr. Douglass Couch, Realtor, Mountain View

789

REC'D AUG 25 1966

THE COUNCIL OF CHURCHES IN SOUTHERN CALIFORNIA-NEVADA

1411 WEST OLYMPIC BOULEVARD • SUITE 501
LOS ANGELES, CALIFORNIA 90015
TELEPHONE: 388-8130

COMMISSION ON CHURCH AND RACE
JOHN M. PRATT, DIRECTOR

August 23, 1966

Mr. Jack Pontius
520 South Grand
Los Angeles, California

Sept. 7

Dear Mr. Pontius:

           The Protestant community in Southern California is deeply concerned over the problem of minority families in locating suitable housing. We are aware that this problem is creating difficulties in certain areas for employers seeking to obtain federal contracts, inasmuch as lack of housing makes it more difficult for them to employ sufficient minority personnel to meet existing federal guidelines.

           The Commission on the Church and Race believes' that it would be to the best interest of the whole Southern California real estate profession if this problem could be solved through mutual cooperation rather than through legislation. To this end we are anxious to explore the ways in which the Church can be of assistance in a forward looking and creative program, working in cooperation with the real estate profession, industrial leaders, and representatives of the minority communities.

           Accordingly, I should like to invite you to join with a small group of businessmen, realtors, and churchmen to be a guest of the Commission for a luncheon on Wednesday, September 7th, at 12:15, at the Detroit Room of the Statler Hilton. A list of those being invited is enclosed for your information.

           I hope very much that you will be able to join us on the 7th and would appreciate your letting my office know whether you can be there.

           Sincerely,

           John M. Pratt

           John M. Pratt

JMP/p

CALIFORNIA REAL ESTATE ASSOCIATION

520 South Grand Avenue
Los Angeles, California 90017
Telephone: 628-0551

March 8, 1967 *march 17 noon*

Mr. Robert Keyes, Assistant to the
   Governor for Human Rights
Governor's Office
Sacramento, California 95814

Dear Mr. Keyes:

In continuing our effort to establish communication and
create understanding between our organization and other
groups concerned with equal opportunity for housing
among minority groups, we are meeting with the Commission
on Church and Race of the Council of Churches in Southern
California-Nevada.

The meeting will be attended by our president, Reed Robbins,
myself and the southern California chairman of our Equal
Rights Committee. Others attending will be the commissions
chairman and selected representatives of major industries.
Total will be about 15 people.

We would be most pleased if you could also attend to participate in the discussion and perhaps observe what problems are considered by the group.

The meeting will be held in Conference Room 3 of the Biltmore
Hotel in Los Angeles at noon on Friday, March 17. We expect it to last no later than 3:00 p.m.

        Sincerely,

        H. Jackson Pontius
        Executive Vice President

HJP:md

bcc H. Jackson Pontius

791

THE COUNCIL OF CHURCHES IN SOUTHERN CALIFORNIA-NEVADA
1411 WEST OLYMPIC BOULEVARD . SUITE 501
LOS ANGELES, CALIFORNIA 90015
TELEPHONE 386.8130

COMMISSION ON CHURCH AND RACE
JOHN M PRATT, DIRECTOR

BISHOP GERALD KENNEDY
PRESIDENT
DR CARROLL L SHUSTER
PRESIDENT-ELECT
MRS VINCENT H COLETTA
VICE PRESIDENT
DR CLARENCE F McCALL, JR
VICE PRESIDENT
THE REV HAROLD B KEIR
SECRETARY
MR JACK L JONES
TREASURER
•
DR FORREST C. WEIR
GENERAL SECRETARY

March 10, 1967

Mr. Jack Pontius
California Real Estate Association
520 South Grand
Los Angeles, California

Dear Mr. Pontius:

On September 7th, 1966, at the Statler Hilton Hotel, a group of businessmen, realtors, and churchmen were guests of the Commission for luncheon
and conversation. The following two paragraphs of the letter of invitation
to that luncheon are included here:

"The Protestant community in Southern California is deeply concerned over
the problem of minority families in locating suitable housing. We are aware
that this problem is creating difficulties in certain areas for employers
seeking to obtain federal contracts, inasmuch as lack of housing makes it
more difficult for them to employ sufficient minority personnel to meet
existing federal guidelines.

The Commission on the Church and Race believes that it would be to the best
interest of the whole Southern California real estate profession if this problem could be solved through mutual cooperation rather than through legislation. To this end we are anxious to explore the ways in which the Church can
be of assistance in a forward looking and creative program, working in cooperation with the real estate professions, industrial leaders, and representatives
of the minority communities."

Those who attended agreed that a continuation of the conversation was desirable. The California Real Estate Association has invited the same group to be
their guest at a luncheon on Friday, March 17th, at 12 noon, in Conference
Room 3 at the Biltmore Hotel in Los Angeles. A list of those being invited
is enclosed for your information.

I hope very much that you will be able to join us on the 17th, and would appreciate your letting my office know whether you can be there.

Sincerely,

John M. Pratt

JMP/p

encl.

792

A list of participants is attached along with the names of several who were invited but could not attend. Minutes, per se, were not taken; the following summarization is intended to preserve the constructive suggestions which were made along with matters of fact which will be useful in future cooperative efforts. Most of those in attendance participated in discussion -- comments are identified only when doing so adds significance to what is said. It was agreed not to discuss legislation.

September 7, 1966 Meeting

Jack Pratt gave his impressions of the previous meeting of leaders of CREA, Church, and Industry held September 7, 1966, at the Statler Hilton. It was a gathering together of points of view of divergent groups. John Buggs had spoken on a plan to achieve housing integration which was "skip motion" whereby areas in concentric circles were skipped over in relocating minority families to avoid solidification. He had also described emotional involvements of minority families moving to white neighborhoods and reasons for some reluctance to do so. Clive Graham had indicated it ought to be the job of CREA to put fair housing committees out of business by following the CREA Code of Practices. One of the businessmen had spoken of the difficulty industry faces in hiring or retaining minority employees who have limited access to suitable housing because of race. The major purpose of the first meeting was to begin to understand each others' points of view or orientation.

Jack Pontius added to this by stating the Realtors' viewpoint which is for equal opportunity in housing without forcing from either direction. They want to assist efforts toward better attitudes and believe this is best handled through understanding and positive programs rather than legislation.

Robert Adamson added that difficulties faced by owners of multiple dwellings had also been discussed at the September meeting.

. . . .

Equal Rights Program and Handling of Violations of Code of Practices

(The "Equal Rights Speaker's Guide", an attractive blue kit, was distributed to all present at the end of the meeting.)

In discussion of common goals, it was agreed that CREA supports its Equal Rights Program and every one of its Realty Boards in California has subscribed to this (approximately 180). When CREA officers learn of violations of the Code of Practices, they talk with the local Board, dealing directly with the leaders. Additional tools for implementation are being developed.

In discussion of possibly uncooperative Boards, it was stated by President Reed Robbins, and subsequently repeated, that such cases should be reported to CREA officers since they want every Board and its members to live up to the Code of Practices. Every grievance will be adjudicated.

- 1 -

793

Training of various Boards and subsequent training of members is underway.
Constructive efforts have been going on in San Fernando Valley, including a
conference several years ago co-sponsored by the Realty Board and San Fernando
Valley Fair Housing Council.

Curt Moody stated that brokers have told him that they are afraid of reprisals
from other brokers and their own Board if they sell to Negroes and Reed Robbins
indicated he was surprised to hear this. Owners must write in their own handwriting
that they are restricting sales to non-minorities. Jack Pontius said there are
representatives from each of thirty-one districts and they wish to know of any
problems. In January, presidents were brought together for top-level training.
Any kind of retaliation is in violation of their Bylaws with the threat of CREA
taking away its charter being the means of enforcement. This is the only means
of discipline but it is effective because local Boards want their charters.

Publicity for Equal Rights Program

Jack Pratt indicated, and there was general agreement, that church people do not
know of CREA's Equal Rights Program. He suggested (1) Articles in church magazines
describing the program which would include endorsement by church leadership;
(2) Newspaper ads with endorsements by leading churchmen and politicians. A
significant public relations effort, comparable to what industry has done in
informing the general public under Plans for Progress is called for since there is
a major task in informing the public and Realtors themselves as to what CREA's
position is, namely that peaceable integration can be achieved voluntarily. His
office would be available to work with CREA's public relations staff on this or
in other ways where there is mutual agreement.

Reed Robbins indicated that statements could be incorporated such as "though we
disagree with their legislative approach, we respect their right to a different
viewpoint". Carroll Shuster thought denominational publications would use such
cooperatively produced material. Robert Adamson stated that of the 174 Boards,
some have made a public relations effort on the Equal Rights Program; they have been
for the past year in the phase of educating local Realtors to the program. There
was general agreement that the Code of Practices should be publicized by all groups.
Melvin Mould called attention to the fact that of 150,000 licensees in the state,
only 50,000 are with CREA.

Possibilities for Cooperative Efforts

1) Realtors and fair housing committees working jointly for constructive action.
2) A Publicity Committee to work with CREA Public Relations to tell of Equal Rights
Program.
3) Additional regional meetings similar to this one around a table.
4) Speakers at Real Estate meetings such as the major one last year when John Buggs sp
5) Interracial confrontations to develop understandings.
6) The Los Angeles County Human Relations Commission is ready to assist in reducing
tensions which might arise in carrying out the Code - this service seldom has
been requested by apartment owners but has been successful where used.
7) Basic study courses in Human Relations by Realtors. Two Boards have had these
but not the 170 or so others (Pico-Robertson on West Side and San Fernando are the
two - five days, two hours each in the morning.)
8) Conferences such as that in San Fernando on May 4, 1963 - The Housing Industry
and Human Relations - all day in conjunction with San Fernando Valley Fair Housing
Committee. Could explore CREA sponsorship with the Commission, CRCSC, etc.
Commission material may be copied for wider use.

- 2 -

794

<u>Fair Housing Committees</u>

Clive Graham pointed out that sometimes Human Relations groups do not know of
constructive action being taken by Realtors. If they are brought into Board
meetings, they become familiar with these. Melvin Mould spoke of the fears
generated by groups who contact homeowners by telephone to ask if they would sell
to minorities. Jack Pratt told of the Realtor in Compton who is president of the
local Human Relations Council - this has had a good effect on the Realtor image.

Walt Cobb recommended a two-hour conversation at the next meeting dealing with the
Metropolitan Fair Housing Committee and Council of Integrated Neighborhoods and
Reed Robbins asked him to drop him a line on this.

<u>Financing</u>

Jack Pratt indicated a hope that the same kind of financial backing would be given
to the Equal Rights Program as CREA had given to its legislative program. Reed
Robbins clarified the point that Realtors' dues have been about equally spent on
legislation and Equal Rights Program - the other costs of legislative effort have
been covered by gifts. Robert Hermanson reaffirmed that the Church is involved
to a major extent financially in minimizing racial prejudice, as well as personally
through the pulpit and in other ways.

Lynne Reade
March 22, 1967

795

Persons attending California Real Estate Association Luncheon Meeting
Biltmore Hotel, Los Angeles   March 17, 1967

1. Mr. Robert Adamson, Member of CREA Executive Committee

2. Mr. Vernon Beardsley, CREA Public Relations Director, Coordinator of
Equal Rights Committee

3. Dr. Walter Cobb, Consultant with Los Angeles County Commission on Human Relations

4. Mr. David S. Collins, Realtor

5. Mr. Clive Graham, CREA and FEPC

6. The Rev. Robert Hermanson, Associate Executive Secretary, Synod of California
Southern Area, United Presbyterian Church

7. Colonel Donald McClure, Consultant with CREA

8. Mr. Curt Moody, Executive Director, Community Relations Conference of
Southern California

9. Mr. Melvin L. Mould, CREA Equal Rights Committee Vice-Chairman

10. Mr. Jack Pontius, Executive Vice President, CREA

11. Mr. John M. Pratt, Executive Director, Commission on Church and Race,
Council of Churches in Southern California

12. Mrs. Lynne Reade, Coordinator of Religion and Race, Presbytery of Los Angeles,
United Presbyterian Church

13. Mr. Reed Robbins, President, CREA

14. Mr. Joseph Roos, Executive Director of Community Relations Committee of
Jewish Federation

15. Mr. Emil Seliga represented by Dr. C. Virgil Metzler, National Catholic
Conference for Interracial Justice

16. Dr. Carroll L. Shuster, Chairman, Commission on the Church and Race, Council
of Churches in Southern California

17. Dr. Forrest C. Weir, General Secretary, Council of Churches in Southern California

Invited but unable to attend this meeting:

Mr. Donald Straus, Beckman Instruments, Inc., Fullerton

Mr. Don Taffi, Electro-Optical Systems, Inc., Pasadena

Mr. Dwight Zook, Corporate Director, Personnel Services, North American
Aviation, Inc., El Segundo

CALIFORNIA REAL ESTATE ASSOCIATION
520 South Grand Avenue
Los Angeles, California   90017
Telephone: 628-0551   *April 13, 1967.*

Mr. Herbert E. Bradley, President
Santa Monica Bay District Board of Realtors
3007 Santa Monica Blvd.
Santa Monica, California 90404
Dear Mr. Bradley:

We have had a report from the Community Relations Conference of Southern California, the coordinating Fair Housing Group for the Los Angeles metropolitan area, that there have been several instances in the Santa Monica area where Negro families have not been treated equally by real estate brokers. We followed up the report on the phone by talking to Mrs. Fulkerson, 370 21st Place, in Santa Monica, chairman of the Santa Monica-Venice Fair Housing Committee.

We have asked the Community Relations Conference to notify us of any such reports so that we can take them up with our own people, if Realtors are involved. This offer was made on the grounds that only mutual understanding of the problems can ever hope to resolve such questions.

In talking to Mrs. Fulkerson, she first made it clear that her reports were not first-hand. She also felt, however, that there were enough facts to indicate that the real estate brokers involved had not acted properly. They are:

1. A 3-unit apartment owned by Messrs. Mark Faber and Grant Thompson in the Santa Monica area had been rented to white tenants. One now has a Negro living with him and the owners and tenants have been subjected to harassment for this reason by a neighboring couple who are selling their house themselves. William H. Mandel, a salesman for Harry Houston (both members of your board) phoned Mark Faber with whom he is acquainted, suggesting that the Negro should move and end this harassment. This was done quite recently, according to Mrs. Fulkerson, but the situation continues.

2. Jack Simms, a Realtor member of your board was the rental agent for a group of apartments owned by Financial Savings, with Mr. Felthoff as the contact officer. Vacancies were advertised and a particular Negro family applied several times, but one was never available, although following their visits, apartments were rented to white families. The Fair Housing Group called Mr. Felthoff who said it was not his concern, that Mr. Simms was handling rentals. Mrs. Fulkerson says she understands the apartment building has since been sold and another rental agent has it.

She indicates that, in the case of Mr. Simms, they felt there was evidence enough to take action under the Rumford Act but that the Negro family did not want to pursue the situation.

We realize that, in both cases, the allegations are difficult to prove and may even be untrue, or at least a misunderstanding may exist of the actions of their reasons. We do feel, however, that under the Code of Practices adopted by your board, the board has the obligation to investigate such complaints and to be sure members understand that they cannot make judgments on basis of race, religion or national origin where real estate sales or rentals are concerned, and that only the property owner has such a right in some cases. If the allegations are untrue, the fact that they are untrue needs to be known by the parties involved.

Sincerely,
H. JACKSON PONTIUS
Executive Vice President.

HJP:md
cc Reed Robbins
     Della M. Haskett, Executive Secretary
        Santa Monica Bay District Board of Realtors
     Clark Wallace, Chairman
        Equal Rights Committee
     Curt Moody, Community Relations Conference
        of Southern California
     John M. Pratt, Commission on the Church and Race,
        Council of Churches in Southern California
     The Rev. Robert Hermanson, United Presbyterian Church
     Vernon W. Beardsley

797

April 13, 1967

Mr. Curt Moody
Community Relations Conference
  of Southern California
2400 South Western Avenue
Los Angeles, California

Dear Mr. Moody:

We appreciated your call on April 7 reporting that
the Fair Housing Council in the Santa Monica area
feels that there have been violations of our Code
of Practices by our members in that area, where dealings with Negroes are concerned.

Carbon copies of our letters to boards following through
are enclosed.

Cordially yours,

Vernon W. Beardsley
Public Relations Director

VWB:md
enclosures

cc Reed Robbins
   H. Jackson Pontius

798

Santa Monica Bay District Board of Realtors, Inc.

1222 LINCOLN BOULEVARD
P. O BOX 856 · SANTA MONICA, CALIF 90406 · EXBROOK 3-1115

April 20, 1967

1967 OFFICERS

HERBERT E BRADLEY
PRESIDENT

CARL S SALLING
1ST VICE PRESIDENT

JACK SIMMS
2ND VICE PRESIDENT

DELLA M HESKETT
EXECUTIVE SECRETARY

CLARA L KNOSTMAN
TREASURER

1967 DIRECTORS

THOMAS F BARTON JR

ANTHONY L DITURI

UNO CARL FOGELSTROM

ROBERT D HAMILTON

GERALD HEINER

JOE HENRY

MARY MOORE

ROQUE RODRIGUEZ

ELLISON D SMITH

C CURTIS TOWLE

ASSOCIATES

MARVIN DeGROOT

RICHARD O KEEFE

Mr. H. Jackson Pontius, Executive Vice President
California Real Estate Association
520 South Grand Avenue
Los Angeles, California 90017

Re: Your letter dated April 13, 1967, concerning alleged
violations of the California Real Estate Association
Code of Practices adopted by the Santa Monica Bay
District Board of Realtors on April 1, 1965.

Dear Mr. Pontius:

On February 27, 1967, I had a luncheon meeting with Mr. Samuel
Fink, Realtor member of our board and member of the Santa Monica
Fair Housing Committee chairmanned by Mrs. Fulkerson. Mr. Fink
brought to my attention the general feeling of the Fair Housing
Committee and asked for time to make a few remarks and hold a
brief discussion with the Board of Directors of the Santa Monica
Bay District Board of Realtors, Inc. I invited him to the next
regularly scheduled Board of Directors meeting on March 9, 1967,
and he did make about a twenty-minute presentation.

Through Mr. Fink's efforts, four members representing the Board
of Realtors met at 8:00 p.m. on March 28, 1967, at Mrs. Fulkerson's
home, 370 21st Place, Santa Monica, with five members representing
the Fair Housing Committee. In attendance were: Fair Housing
Committee: Mrs. Eleanore Fulkerson, Mrs. Shirley Anderson,
Mrs. Essie Tucker, Realtor, Mr. Tom Brown, and Mr. Samuel Fink,
Realtor. Santa Monica Bay District Board of Realtors: Mr. Herbert
Bradley, President, Mrs. Della Heskett, Executive Secretary,
Mr. Roque Rodriguez, Chairman Community Relations Committee, and
Mr. Samuel Faudem, Past President (1955) and Chairman Ethics and
Arbitration Committee.

This was an exploratory meeting for the purpose of getting acquainted and finding areas of agreement. The areas of disagreement
would then need study and further discussion. Many things were
discussed in general. However, one item was discussed and explained
in great detail. The Santa Monica Bay District Board of Realtors
willingness and ability of processing reports of alleged discrimination by our members. We explained to the Fair Housing Committee
that any complaints, written by the person discriminated against,
would be reviewed by the board of directors, forwarded to the
proper committee and a hearing would be held with the complainant,
the defendant and any necessary witnesses invited to attend. The
findings of this committee would then be forwarded to the board of

"Where the Mountains Meet the Sea"

799

directors for action. An answer would be conveyed to the
complainant and the defendant, and disciplinary action taken
if deemed necessary, in no less than four (4) weeks from the
date the complaint is received by the Santa Monica Bay District
Board of Realtors, Inc. I also pointed out that I feel it is
the Fair Housing Committee's duty to the community to ascertain
that there is, in fact, discrimination and not other extenuating
circumstances.

We have not received any complaints to this date. I feel that
one of the keys to a good, workable relationship in any community
is our ability to communicate freely with our fellow man. I
thank you very much for your letter, but I am saddened to know
that we have to communicate at state levels without the opportunity
to solve our local problems in the American Democratic manner.

We have several cases of badly needed housing for families of all
races, religions and national origins. Several leading businessmen in Santa Monica, to give you one example, are looking for
housing for a family that consists of Mother, Father, and three
teenage, or young adult, children. I have had two meetings with
Deane Funk, Managing Editor of the Evening Outlook, I have made
pleas before our board of directors and our general membership
meetings. Many citizens in our community would like to have this
family live here, they have been offered housing which they have
refused. We have been unable to find housing to their satisfaction
as of now. There are other cases like this which are brought to
our attention by various churches, social clubs and fraternal
organizations and we exert every effort to serve the entire community.

I feel very strongly that the California Real Estate Association
Code of Practices has been adopted by, and incorporated into, the
by-laws of the Santa Monica Bay District Board of Realtors, Inc.,
our members have subscribed to abide by the by-laws. That is
exactly what we are doing.

Thank you for forwarding messages; any suggestions from the
California Real Estate Association will be most welcome and appreciated.

Sincerely,

Herbert E. Bradley
President

HEB:dh
Att, Copy of letter from Jack P. Simms
      Copy of letter from Harry Houston

800

Mr. H. Jackson Pontius, Executive Vice President   April 20, 1967
                                                          Page 3

cc./w. att.:   Reed Robbins
              Clark Wallace, Chairman
                  Equal Rights Committee
              Curt Moody, Community Relations Conference
                  of Southern California
              John M. Pratt, Commission on the Church and Race,
                  Council of Churches in Southern California
              The Rev. Robert Hermanson, United Presbyterian
                  Church
              Vernon W. Beardsley

April 19, 1967

Mr. Herbert E. Bradley, President
Santa Monica Bay District
Board of Realtors
1222 Lincoln Blvd.
Santa Monica, California

Dear Mr. Bradley:

A couple of years ago I sold a building at 1814 - 10th Street, Santa
Monica--a five unit, consisting of 1 2-bedroom, 3 3-bedroom and 1
4-bedroom apartments. The buyer refused to rent to children. Later
due to this policy, he lost the building. It was foreclosed by
Financial Savings & Loan of Culver City, who renovated the property
and placed it on the market for sale.

Our office obtained an "Open Listing" to sell the property. We worked
it "For Sale" only. We were not the rental agents. We began to show
the property for sale. Several weeks passed and we received a phone
call from Mr. Quinn, an administrator at Santa Monica City College,
saying that a Negro family had seen an apartment at 1814 - 10th Street
and wanted to rent it, however, Mr. Felthoff, the head of Financial
Savings & Loan had referred them to our office.

I told Mr. Quinn that we were not in the rental business and that we
had not advertised the property for rent or for sale, that we were
only concerned with the sale of the property, then referred him back
to Mr. Flethoff. I also told him that if I heard of any other rental
in this category, I would gladly let him know.

Perhaps a week later, two women from the Fair Housing Council came in
to see me. They accused me of refusing to rent the apartment to negros.
I told them that I had nothing to do with the rental of said property,
that we were only concerned with the sale. I was very close at this
point to selling the property and had a client who was going to give
me an offer. The women from the F.H.C. asked me to give them the name
of the prospective buyer which I refused to do since it might jeopardize
the sale. One of the women became very angry and left my office. The
other woman remained and we talked for about an hour.

    We did not advertise the property 'For Rent' or 'For Sale.'

    We have never met the negro family.

    We have not refused to rent the apartment to them.

In this situation, how could we possibly discriminate against them?
It seems that they are very desperate to find a case of discrimination
if this is the type of case they choose to prosecute. They have also
chosen the wrong office. I have for many years dealt with minority
groups.

Mr. Herbert E. Bradley   April 19, 1967

As to my Saleslady, Mrs. Millie Yahns, she has many friends in the
negro community. Her mother is a leader for a negro Girl Scout Troop,
#23, Marina Council.

Certainly this is a misunderstood situation, developing from a sociological problem.

I am very sorry that this situation has arisen, however, my conscience
is clear. We have not in the past, nor shall we in the future discriminate against anyone.

A Committee of the Santa Monica Bay District Board of Realtors has met
with the local Fair Housing Council, as you know, and since your announcement at the General Membership meeting of the desire of this family to
obtain housing stating the size of the family and the amount of rent they
wish to pay (not stating that they are negros) I have been endeavoring to
find housing for them.

Trusting this explanation will clear up any and all unjust charges
against me and my associates, I remain

                              Sincerely,

                              Jack P. Simms
                              Realtor

CALIFORNIA REAL ESTATE ASSOCIATION
520 South Grand Avenue
Los Angeles, California   90017
Telephone: 628-0551

April 13, 1967.

Mr. Henry G. Beaumont, President
Los Angeles Realty Board
8652 Wilshire Boulevard
Beverly Hills, California 90211

Dear Mr. Beaumont:

We have been notified by the Community Relations Conference of Southern California, the Fair Housing coordinating group for metropolitan Los Angeles, of several instances where real estate brokers or salesmen are alleged to have violated the law and our Code of Practices in their dealings with Negroes.

We have invited the Conference to report any such allegations to us so that we can take them up with the board and try to be sure that such actions are known by the board, and either found to be untrue or, if true, whatever disciplinary action they think is called for is taken. We have invited such reports as a means of protecting our members from being accused of not doing anything to try to solve such problems as exist.

The instance involving a member of your board was when a salesman for Nelson B. Nelson called on a Mrs. Farquar to list a house in the Mar Vista area. Mrs. Farquar said she made the statement that she wanted to be sure that the house was offered on a strictly open housing basis for minorities as well as others. The salesman is alleged to have evidently misunderstood, thinking she wanted to exclude Negroes, and said in effect, "Don't worry, we have no problem with handling Negro prospects." She did not list with the salesman.

This is a minor kind of complaint since she did not pursue the conversation further with the salesman, but it did leave her with the impression that the staff of Nelson B. Nelson is surreptitiously avoiding the public attitude of the Los Angeles Realty Board and Realtors of California of giving equal service to all clients.

We believe that this conversation should be called to the attention of Mr. Nelson as a warning that, if the allegation is true, he is on the verge of violating the law and the Code, and if it is not true, his salesmen should be more careful to be sure they are understood when they make any statement concerning minority clients.

Sincerely,
H. JACKSON PONTIUS
Executive Vice President.

HJF:md
cc Reed Robbins
   Earl S. Anderson, Exec. V.P.
     Los Angeles Realty Board
   Clark Wallace, Chairman
     Equal Rights Committee
   Curt Moody, Community Relations Conference
     of Southern California
   John Pratt, Commission on the Church and Race,
     Council of Churches in Southern California
   The Rev. Robert Hermanson, United Presbyterian Church
   Vernon W. Beardsley

804

REALTOR 1716 SANTA MONICA BLVD.
1716 SANTA MONICA, SANTA MONICA, CALIFORNIA, EXbrook 4-5594

April 14, 1967

Mr. Herbert E. Bradley, Realtor
3007 Santa Monica Blvd.
Santa Monica,
California

Dear Mr. Bradley:

In reference to our telephone conversation of this
date, I wish to emphasize the fact that I have never
at any time discriminated against anyone, regardless
of race, creed or national origin........whether it
be in regards to the rental or sale of property.

I have pledged myself to the Code of Ethics of the
Board of Realtors and practice according to this
Code . This applies to all those who are associated
with my office.

I trust this states my position in regards to the
matter we discussed on the telephone today.

Very truly yours,

Harry Houston

LOS ANGELES REALTY BOARD
ASSOCIATION OF REALTORS
STATLER CENTER · 900 WILSHIRE BLVD
LOS ANGELES 17, CALIFORNIA
MADISON 9-2331

April 24, 1967

Mr. Nelson B. Nelson, Jr., Realtor
11316 National Boulevard
Los Angeles, California 90064

Dear Mr. Nelson:

The California Real Estate Association has advised us that the
Community Relations Conference of Southern California, the Fair
Housing coordinating group for metropolitan Los Angeles, has
called their attention to the fact that a salesman of your firm
has possibly violated the State law and the Code of Practices
of our Board and the California Real Estate Association in his
dealings with Negroes.

The instance involved was when a salesman of your firm called
on a Mrs. Farquar to list a house in the Mar Vista area. Mrs.
Farquar said she made the statement that she wanted to be sure
that the house was offered on a strictly open housing basis for
minorities, as well as others. The salesman is alleged to have
evidently misunderstood, thinking she wanted to exclude Negroes,
and said in effect, "Don't worry, we have no problem with handling Negro prospects". She did not list with the salesman.

This is a minor kind of complaint since she did not pursue the
conversation further with the salesman, but it did leave her
with the impression that the staff of Nelson B. Nelson is surreptitiously avoiding the public attitude of the Los Angeles Realty
Board and Realtors of California of giving equal service to all
clients.

This matter is being brought to your attention as a warning that,
if the allegation is true, your firm is on the verge of violating
the law and the Code, and if it is not true, your salesmen should
be more careful to be sure they are understood when they make any
statement concerning minority clients.

For your information, we are enclosing a copy of the "Code of
Practices" of our Board, which were approved by our Board of
Directors October 12, 1965.

806

We will appreciate your submitting to us any information or comments
you have with regard to this allegation.

Sincerely yours,

EARL S. ANDERSON
Executive Vice President

ESA:s
Enclosure

bcc: Mr. H. Jackson Pontius
     Mr. Henry G. Beaumont
     B. Elliott
     R. E. Pierce

807

REC'D APR 19 1967   TELEPHONE 483-3840

Synod of California, Southern Area

THE UNITED PRESBYTERIAN CHURCH IN THE U S A

1501 WILSHIRE BOULEVARD ● LOS ANGELES, CALIFORNIA 90017

April 17, 1967

Mr. Jack Pontius
Executive Vice President
California Real Estate Association
520 South Grand Avenue
Los Angeles, California 90017

Dear Mr. Pontius:

I want simply to thank you for sending to me a copy of
your letter of April 13 to Mr. Henry B. Bomont in regard
to an alleged violation of a law in your Code. This
kind of action on your part will hastily remove false
allegations on one hand, and will, in a forthright fashion,
deal in a just manner with unworthyactions. I am happy
indeed to see your office functioning in this fashion,
and I want sincerely to commend you for it.

Cordially yours,

ROBERT F. HERMANSON
Associate Executive Secretary

RFH/imf

cc Reed Robbins
   Clark Wallace

March 4, 1966

Mr. William L. Becker
Assistant to the Governor for Human Rights
Governor's Office
Sacramento, California 95814

Dear Mr. Becker:

You earlier inquired as to our next step with regard to Kay
Murray's application in the Southwest Branch of the Los Angeles
Realty Board.

As you know, we had previously advised the Southwest Branch
of LARB that its Charter was in jeopardy if this matter were not
corrected. Following the meeting in which Kay Murray's application
was rejected, we consulted with some of the leaders of the Branch
and advised them that this matter must be corrected prior to our
March Directors' meeting.

Immediately after certification of the change in bylaws, Bob
Adamson (sponsor) with O. R. Brown (second sponsor) formally
petitioned the Board of Control of the Southwest Branch to grant
a reballot of Kay Murray's application. Mr. Adamson is confident
that the Board of Control, who had supported the bylaws change one
hundred per cent, will grant the reballot, and he is optimistic
that the application will be approved within the next two weeks.

You may recall that our first step was to convince the Southwest Branch that the old "blackball" system was inequitable. This
was changed last year to a system of a 20% vote, which we
realized was inadequate. The change which has taken place and
reflected in the Los Angeles Times news article of February 23, 1966,
enclosed, is a strong step forward.

Our next step in an effort to eliminate applicants being placed
before an uninformed body is to propose a statewide policy and
procedure whereby the membership committee will review all
applicants and, after screening the applicants, shall make their
recommendation to the Board of Directors of the Board, which shall
pass on final approval of the applicants.

Mr. William L. Becker   - 2 -   March 4, 1966

    You will recall, last year, we assured your offices that it
was not necessary to require legislation to accomplish some of the
problems before us. In our meeting with the members throughout
the State, I can assure you that we are making greater progress in
the area of human relations than has been accomplished through any
other statewide organization.

    In the event you are not aware of the recent program held at
Stanford University, we are enclosing copy of the program which
lists our last year's President, David N. Robinson, and a member
of our Equal Rights Committee, Douglass Couch. Burt Smith, our
current President, has been working with Mr. Couch in support of
this program and toward the further development of similar projects
through our CREA Equal Rights Committee Chairman, Clark Wallace of
Orinda.

                         Sincerely,

                         H. Jackson Pontius
                         Executive Vice President

HJP:lk
Enclosure
bcc - Mr. Paul N. McCarron

Realty Board Branch Lifts Racial Barrier

Votes 50 to 13 to Change By-Laws That Permit Small Minority to Bar Negroes

Barriers which had effectively prevented Negroes from becoming members of the Southwest Branch of the Los Angeles Realty Board have been removed, The Times learned Tuesday.

Members of the currently all-white branch voted 50 to 13 Monday night to change their by-laws, liberalizing a rule which had permitted a small minority to block membership by Negro realtors.

John D. South, chairman of the 550-member organization, said:

"We're now in the process of changing things. People are beginning to realize that they've got to live with these things.

"We don't have any applications by Negroes as of now, but I am sure some will be in the process soon. I think any qualified colored person who comes in here will no doubt be elected to membership."

South and his board of directors last month proposed the change in by-laws which—as a result of Monday night's vote—requires a majority of those voting at a meeting to block an application.

Old rules had permitted 20% of those voting at a meeting to bar membership.

The change is a direct result of a secret U.S. Justice Department investigation into alleged racial discrimination by the Southwest Branch and the Los Angeles Realty Board.

Justice Department investigators — working under the theory that racial discrimination is a violation of federal anti-trust laws because it restrains trade—have asked both organizations to provide detailed information on membership procedures and policies relating to the sale or rental of property to Negroes.

811

State of California

GOVERNOR'S OFFICE
SACRAMENTO 95814

EDMUND G. BROWN
GOVERNOR

March 14, 1966

Mr. H. Jackson Pontius
Executive Vice President
California Real Estate Association
520 South Grand Avenue
Los Angeles, California 90017

Dear Mr. Pontius:

Thank you very much for your letter of March 4.
It is good news indeed to know that the Southwest Branch has voted to change their bylaws.
I will certainly appreciate further news on
what happens as a result.

Thanks for keeping me informed.

Sincerely

William L. Becker
Assistant to the Governor
  for Human Rights

812

CALIFORNIA REAL ESTATE ASSOCIATION   May 1, 1967
520 South Grand Avenue
Los Angeles, California 90017

Committee to Improve Substandard Housing

A P L A N O F A C T I O N

for Local Real Estate Boards
to Improve Substandard Housing
Conditions and Prevent Neighborhood Blight

Each board should use its own judgement in applying the Plan of
Action to its city or cities. If the board feels some portions
are not applicable, apply those that are. Since these are early
steps in the program, if boards recognize areas that can be
improved, let the CREA office know of them.

A. Form a Committee to Improve Substandard Housing.

    1. Adopt a resolution to establish your acceptance of
        responsibility and desire to cooperate with local
        officials in regard to the committee's universally
        accepted goals. A sample resolution is attached.
        (Please send a copy of the resolution you adopt to
        CREA headquarters.)

    2. Issue a news release announcing your offer of help,
        and the resolution. In it give some indication of
        what your next step will be.

    3. Hold preliminary meeting with city and/or county
        officials to discuss with them the Plan of Action
        and give a copy to each with the previously adopted
        resolution. Invite their comments on either or both.
        If they might be helpful, transmit their comments and
        yours to CREA headquarters so further refinements can
        be instituted where appropriate.

B. Survey ordinances in effect in your city and county setting
    minimum housing standards and enforcement procedures. They
    should meet these requirements:

    1. If possible, all inspectors should be under one
        coordinating agency.

        (a) There should be provision for general inspectors
             to have the benefit of specialist advice and help
             if specific problems are beyond the general inspec-
             tors' knowledge (wiring, plumbing, fire, etc.).

813

        (b) Provision should be made for inspection follow-
             up, to see what action has been taken to correct
             previously noted violations of code.

        (c) Provision should exist for inspection upon com-
             plaint of all housing, including single dwellings.

2. Appeal procedure from code citations should be sufficiently protective to the property owner, but not so
overly time consuming that it could frustrate the whole
program.

3. Procedures should emphasize that inspections should be
conducive to voluntary compliance. If results do not
confirm this, major emphasis should be placed on substantive policy changes as deemed appropriate to get
the job done without force.

4. Establish procedures for demolishing condemned buildings
if owners take no remedial action within a reasonable
time following notification.

5. Establish procedures for reducing trash and weed accumu-
lation.

6. Provide for effective court enforcement of code violations.

        (a) Where the community is large enough hearings of
             code violation cases should be assigned to specific
             persons so they can become familiar with housing
             codes and enforcement procedures.

7. Regardless of income, families should not be allowed
to live in housing which is below minimum code standards.

C. Make definite recommendations to your city government.

1. For revision of your local housing codes, if they are
inadequate, out of date, or impractical.

2. For a firm, impartial, systematic and continuing enforcement policy.

3. Issue a news release containing your recommendations,
giving support to those portions of the code and procedures of which you approve.

D. Offer specific cooperation with public officials to aid them
according to local need. This can include such services as:

1. Advice in formulating a minimum housing code.

2. Housing surveys by teams or committees of the local board of Realtors.

   (a) To help identify those neighborhoods in greatest need of constructive work.

   (b) To help identify early stages of blight so protective measures can be taken.

3. Contact owners of substandard housing to enlist their cooperation on a mutual benefit basis.

4. Technical advice on the practicability of rehabilitating specific structures, perhaps with contractors and others.

5. Assist property owners in obtaining financing for rehabilitation. Get lenders together to determine what can be done to make financing available so that property owners don't turn to the federal government for assistance. (Possible pooling of risky loans.)

6. Support necessary budget appropriations where there is a need for more inspectors, neighborhood street lights, resurfacing of streets, tree planting, trash collection and similar city services.

7. Issue news releases explaining each area of cooperation and help.

E. Organize a public information campaign, stressing an atmosphere conducive to voluntary compliance by owners so that all housing can be decent, safe and sanitary and all neighborhoods can be free from blight.

   1. Issue news releases on every development in the program. Get statements from city officials, civic leaders.

   2. Enlist the support of your local newspaper publisher or publishers, and owners of radio and television stations.

   3. Get on radio and television to discuss the benefits of the program to owners, tenants and the community.

      (a) Approach program directors suggesting panels of experts made up of community leaders, a representative from your board, and a moderator to discuss the subject on the air. Suggest personal interviews.

   4. Arrange for speakers before civic clubs, church groups, and other community organizations to explain the program, its objective and benefits, and enlist their cooperation and support.

5. Use printed material supplied to you by CREA and develop
   additional material you think will be helpful. Send
   copies to CREA.

6. Get pictures of "before" and "after" rehabilitated
   housing. Furnish them to newspapers and television
   stations to demonstrate progress being made.

F. Sponsor demonstrative or supportive programs.

   1. Pick-Up, Clean-Up, Paint-Up, and Fix-Up weeks. Have
      proclaimed by mayor.

   2. Neighborhood or citywide clean up and trash removal.

      (a) Vacant lots.

      (b) Basements, attics and yards.

      (c) Junked cars.

   3. Paint house of a deserving family (10 to 20 board and
      affiliate members in a one-day project). Ask the
      Salvation Army, the local ministerial association, or
      the Department of Public Assistance to help select the
      family.

   4. Buy and rehabilitate a house as a demonstration project
      or encourage a member or affiliate to do so. Work
      closely with the inspection department at each stage
      to signify that recommended procedures are effective
      and practical.

   5. Awards to individuals or groups for efforts or results
      of efforts in helping with committee goals.

                        #   #   #

816

CALIFORNIA REAL ESTATE ASSOCIATION   May 1, 1967
520 South Grand Avenue
Los Angeles, California 90017

Committee to Improve Substandard Housing

SUGGESTED RESOLUTION

for adoption by local real estate board
Board of Directors

WHEREAS, the people of the city of _____(name)_____ can pursue
their individual goals in life adequately only when occupying housing
which meets certain minimum standards of safety, sanitation, comfort and
shelter; and

WHEREAS, the _____ Board of Realtors is concerned
that such standards be met as a means of providing the environment
necessary to our people to pursue those goals; and

WHEREAS, property values can best be maintained by prevention of
deterioration in neighborhoods; and

WHEREAS, members of the _____ Board of Realtors are,
by their professional training and ethics, in a unique position to be
helpful to local governmental officials, civic groups, and individuals
in achieving that environment; Now Therefore, Be It

RESOLVED That the _____ Board of Realtors hereby
offers its help to _(name of community official or name of city and/or
county)_ in instituting a program to effectively combat or prevent
neighborhood blight, and to improve substandard housing through consul-
tation, review of housing codes, support of reasonable enforcement, and
technical assistance to officials and property owners as needed.

Adopted by the Board of Directors
this ____ day of _____, 1967.   _____
                                              President

                                       _____
                                              Secretary

817

Exhibit No. 10

UNITED STATES COMMISSION ON CIVIL RIGHTS
WASHINGTON, D.C.

THE SPANISH-AMERICAN COMMUNITY
OF THE
SAN FRANCISCO BAY AREA

A Staff Report to the Commissioners
April 28, 1967

INTRODUCTION

*The 1960 United States Census of Population reported that 1,426,538 white persons of Spanish-surname then resided in the State of California. Almost half of this number have parents both of whom were born in the United States. Approximately 20 percent of the Spanish-surname persons in California were not born in the United States, its territories, and possessions. The Spanish-surname population in 1960 represented 9.1 percent of the total population of California, while Negroes constituted 5.6 percent of the population of California. During the decade 1950 to 1960 the Spanish-surname population in California grew by 88.1 percent compared with a 48.5 percent increase in total population for the State. The Foundation for Mexican-American Studies, Inc., of Los Angeles has indicated that the Spanish-surname population will increase in California to 2,681,891 by 1970. This projection is based on a minimal estimate.

In the San Francisco-Oakland Metropolitan Area (hereafter referred to as the Bay Area, which includes the five counties of San Francisco, San Mateo, Marin, Contra Costa, and Alameda), the 1960 Census reported there were 177,239 white persons of Spanish-surname. This figure represents 12.4 percent of the total number of Spanish-surname persons living in the State of California and it is 6.4 percent of the total population of the Bay Area.

The San Jose Metropolitan Area also will be discussed in this report. Except for Los Angeles County, Santa Clara County has the highest number of Spanish-surnamed persons of any county in the State. The San Jose area has 77,755 persons with Spanish-surnames. This is 5.5 percent of the State Spanish-surname population and 12.1 percent of that metropolitan area. The breakdown of white persons with Spanish-surnames in the two areas is shown in the following chart based on the 1960 census figures.

Rank	County	Total	Percent of Spanish Surname in Population	Native Born	Total Foreign Born	Total Born in Mexico	Total Population
1	Santa Clara	77,755	12.1	66,715	11,040	7,778	642,315
2	Alameda	67,866	7.5	57,788	10,078	5,216	908,209
3	San Fernando	51,602	7.0	35,059	16,543	6,020	740,316
4	Contra Costa	28,854	6.1	20,743	4,111	2,891	409,030
5	San Mateo	19,722	4.4	16,486	3,236	1,631	444,384
6	Marin	5,634	3.8	4,960	674	122	146,820

The sex ratios in the areas indicate that for every 100 Spanish-surnamed female in the Bay Area there are 104.8 males with Spanish surnames, whereas in the San Jose Area the ratio is 103.3 males to every 100 females. The ratio of male to female is higher than that of the general population, and is significant in evaluating the employment needs of this community.

The Spanish-speaking people in the Bay Area have a median age of 25.6

*Census Tract information—Californians of Spanish-Surname, Department of Industrial Relations, Division of Fair Employment Practices—State of California, 1964.

818

years compared to the median age of the Anglo community of 33.3 years. The San Jose Area indicates a very young Spanish-speaking population with a median age of 19.9 years compared to the Anglo group which has a 27.8 average age.

It has been estimated by persons familiar with the community that in San Francisco the Spanish-speaking population consists of about 1/3 Nicaraguans, about 1/3 El Salvadorians, slightly less than 1/3 Mexicans, and the remainder from other Latin American countries and the Caribbean. In the other counties in the Bay Area, the majority of the Spanish-speaking persons are of Mexican descent. The increase in the Spanish-speaking population over a 10-year period indicates dramatic growth for the San Francisco-Oakland Area as well as the San Jose Metropolitan Area.

	1950 Spanish-surnamed Population	1960 Spanish-surnamed Population
San Francisco-Oakland	94,683	177,239
San Jose	35,306	77,755

In the Bay Area there were 82,556 more Spanish-speaking persons in 1960 than there were in 1950 and in the San Jose Area there has been an increase of 42,449 persons.

In San Francisco, the Spanish-American population is concentrated in an area referred to locally as the "Mission District," while in Oakland more than half of the persons of Mexican origin or ancestry live in the area known as "Fruitvale" and an adjacent area known as the "Flats." Preliminary results from a 1966 sample census done by the Oakland Inter-agency Project indicates that there are 23,729 persons of Spanish surname in that city.

One of the major concerns of the Spanish-American persons in California is the fact that most surveys, reports, and other publications—both governmental and private—do not deal with Spanish Americans, despite the fact that they are the largest minority group in the State of California.

Facts and data pertaining to this ethnic group are scattered and fragmented. Available reports are of individual projects and isolated problem areas. It is believed by the community that local research by public agencies shows little awareness of Spanish-speaking people. It does not appear that local colleges and universities have done significant research on this large segment of the population. Dr. Ernesto Galarza, in his 1966 report entitled "Economic Development by Mexican Americans in Oakland, California" (Social Science Research & Development Corporation) states:

The urban districts that are most in need of renewal are precisely those with obvious economic and social handicaps. Here, it would seem, there is also the greatest need for information about the people who live in such neighborhoods. But this information is a need which has not been met. The annals of the poor, so it has been noted, are notoriously short and simple. Those of the Mexican Americans in Oakland particularly are brief. A preliminary inquiry showed only three published reports on the Mexican Americans in Oakland between 1943 and 1964. Further search may identify other sources, such as academic theses produced by students of the University of California. But thinness and obsolescence of the data suggest that Oakland knows little about the Mexican-American neighborhood targets against which the city is missing its planning artillery.

One possible reason for the absence of studies and research is the difficulty in identifying and classifying the "Spanish" minority group. Many of the people speak only Spanish and are new arrivals in this country. Others, however, speak only English and their families have been in this country for many generations. Attempts to classify the Spanish-American population have been by name and/or ancestry.

Both methods of classification have their shortcomings. The use of the term "Mexican American" to describe this population is ambiguous because all other Latins are excluded; the use of the term "Spanish surname" excludes all those who have married non-Spanish-surname persons. Another possible reason for

819

the dearth of information on Spanish Americans is that their problems and even their existence as a minority group until recently has been generally ignored.

The problems faced by Spanish-American groups in the Bay Area are similar to those they confront throughout the Southwest. These are lack of citizenship, failure of school systems to cope with cultural and language differences, difficulty in obtaining employment above menial level, prejudice on the part of the majority population toward a group viewed as foreign, and problems incidental to poverty, i.e., lack of adequate housing, poor police-community relations, and the inability of the public and private agencies to understand and properly service a bilingual and bicultural community.

In San Francisco, an additional problem faced by many persons with professional and technical training, primarily immigrants from Central and South America, is an inability to work at the level for which they are trained because they are not citizens, do not know the English language, and do not meet licensing requirements.

AREAS OF CONCERN

Education

One of the major concerns of the Spanish-American community is that the educational system is not meeting the specific needs of children from the Spanish language and cultural environment. The Spanish-surname community has the lowest median educational achievement level of any ethnic group in California. In the Bay Area, the median school years completed in 1960 by all persons 25 years old and over for the total population was 12.1 years for males and 12.2 years for females. On the other hand, the median school years completed by white persons with Spanish surnames was 9.6 years for males and 9.8 years for females. This compares unfavorably with nonwhite persons in the Bay Area. Nonwhite males have completed an average of 10.0 years and nonwhite females 10.7 years.*

In the Bay Area 15.7 percent of the Spanish-speaking people 25 years and older had less than four years of school, according to 1960 census tract data. In San Jose 25.4 percent of this population were in the category of four years or less of school. A large percentage of this ethnic population lacks the basic ability to read and write thus hindering their potential for obtaining employment.

The California State Department of Education recently (1967) has completed a study entitled "Racial and Ethnic Survey of California Public Schools." The relevant counties showed the following:

County	Number of Spanish Surname Students	Percent of Total Enrollment Spanish Surname
Santa Clara	38,182	15.52
Alameda	21,088	9.93
San Francisco	11,135	12.19
Contra Costa	8,468	6.00
San Mateo	7,190	6.10
Marin	758	1.74

According to this census, 57 percent of the Spanish-surname students in districts with more than 50,000 enrollment attend "minority schools." The Department defined a minority school as one which fails to come within 15 percent of matching the proportion of minority students in the school district as a whole.

Armando Rodriguez, chief of the Department's Bureau of Inter-group Relations who conducted the survey, commented:

In large districts, most students regardless of their racial or ethnic background attend racially imbalanced schools. It is worth noting that while Mexican-American students comprise 13.6 percent of California's public school populations, they comprise less than one percent of its college student population.

*Census Tract Information

Questions have been raised by interested citizens as to what positive action is being taken by the State colleges and universities to insure a higher enrollment of Spanish-surname students. It has been alleged that very few Spanish-surname students are aided by Federal grant and loan programs.

Educational approaches, classroom techniques, and community institutions (such as the PTA) which succeed with the middle-class Anglo child are not necessarily successful with the Spanish-speaking child. The extent of the cultural conflict between home and school is shown in an empirical study conducted in 1966 concerning the effects of the Federal Headstart Program on the Mexican American child. The research, conducted by the Foundation for Mexican-American Studies under contract with the United States Office of Economic Opportunity, showed that in 24 out of 30 attitudinal areas Headstart teachers and parents of Mexican American children displayed markedly different opinions about the education and behavior of the children. Parent and teacher had different perceptions as to the childrens' needs and expectations.

This suggests that it may be difficult for the Mexican American child placed in a monolingual setting such as the public schools provide to adjust to the new environment. The study further indicates that, with rare exception, the schools have failed to compensate for that part of the Spanish-speaking child's cultural make-up which is different from Anglo-urban.

The study indicates that many teachers do not understand these cultural differences and are not made aware of their relevance to the learning process. They tend to conclude, according to FMAS Headstart research, that "all children are alike."

Dr. Julian Samora, Professor of Sociology, University of Notre Dame, stated at the Workshop on Careers for Youth and the Mexican-American Community in January 1963:

If it is true that the schools reflect the norms and values of the community, then perhaps it is equally true that its prejudices are also reflected, through acts of commission as well as omission. Few school systems can, or do, gear their curricula to the needs of this segment of the population. Few know, empirically, what the needs are. . . .

How many teachers of American history in the Southwest begin with the Pilgrim Fathers rather than by developing the cultural and historical heritage of the area, leading to the Pilgrim Fathers? The basic question being raised is this: Is there anything about the Spanish speaking in the Southwest that is important and desirable and that could be used by the school system to bring recognition and higher status to members of that group in the eyes of their peers and the community? The answer, of course, is "yes." Do school systems take advantage of these cultural-historical experiences and contributions? Aside from a few instances, the answer, unfortunately, is "no".

It has been estimated that 50 percent of the Spanish-speaking students in California drop out of school by the eighth grade. Although no figures are available for the Bay Area, it is a fair assumption that the dropout rate in the Bay Area is considerably higher for Spanish Americans than for the rest of the population. A factor which may contribute to the high dropout rate and low educational attainment level in San Francisco is the small number of persons employed from this group in the school system.

A 1965 survey showed that in San Francisco, where Spanish-speaking persons comprise 7 percent of the population, only 45 of the 4,147 board of education professional personnel were Spanish speaking. This is .94 percent of the total. Of 229 principals and assistant principals only one was Spanish-speaking. Of 3,478 teachers in the school system only 33, or less than 1 percent, were Spanish-speaking. There were no Spanish-speaking persons in an administrative/supervisory capacity in the central office and no administrators or instructors in the junior colleges which are under control of the board of education.

In February of 1967, a group of Spanish-American persons picketed the school board office in San Francisco alleging discrimination in the employment of professional personnel and a failure of the board to develop programs to meet the unique needs of the Spanish American students. The school board promised to meet with representatives of the group to discuss their grievances. A prepared statement was presented to the board outlining their grievances and demands.

One of the major complaints of the demonstrators was that the school system was unable to cope with the language problem. They charged that little is done to help incoming students with language problems learn to speak English. Americanization classes, where students speaking foreign languages are taught English before going to a regular school, are given only to junior and high school grades. They further charged that the approach in the lower grades was to let students remain in the class and, as long as they behaved and did not disrupt the class, they were passed with a grade of "D" even though they could not speak English. They called for comprehensive educational projects to be developed in the Mission District to coordinate educational needs from preschool children through adult education. They also called for a recruitment program to hire more minority group members as teachers and to upgrade existing personnel into administrative and supervisory posts. They demanded the employment of community teachers in every school—persons who would visit the homes of students with difficulties and try to help them work out their problems. They requested, in addition, compensatory education programs in every school and a teacher's aide in every classroom of every school in the Mission District.

On March 19, 1967, a legislative conference was called by the Mexican-American Political Association in Sacramento to attempt to frame the problems of the Spanish-speaking people in California. Many in attendance were from the Bay Area and San Jose. The Education Workshop developed the following resolutions proposing:

1. That funds be made available for prekindergarten classes specifically for Mexican American children.
2. That legislation be enacted permitting classroom teaching in a language other than English.
3. That legislation be enacted to encourage teacher education for Mexican Americans.
4. That legislation be enacted providing for the employment and training of teachers' aides from the Mexican American community.
5. That funds be appropriated to provide for orientation classes in all schools having Mexican American students.
6. That any State-funded curriculum revision take into consideration the special needs of the Mexican American students.
7. That teacher training be integrated with and utilize the resources of the Mexican American community.
8. That school testing programs be revised to reflect the needs and interests of the Mexican American student.
9. That school achievement test scores be made public.
10. That racia and ethnic balance be planned and implemented in the schools. l
11. That the State higher education system recruit Mexican American and other minority students.

Language and Citizenship

While no figures are available as to the number of persons in the Bay Area who can speak only Spanish, reports range from several hundred to many thousands. There is, in addition, a much larger percentage who speak some English, but for whom Spanish remains their first language. Figures are not available, moreover, of the number of Spanish American persons in the Bay Area who are not United States citizens.

Those who are not United States citizens are unable to work for local, State, and Federal governmental agencies or government contractors. Most are able to obtain employment only in low paying, menial work. It is alleged that some employers, to maintain a source of cheap labor, exploit this inability to speak or understand English by employing Spanish-speaking supervisors who discourage Spanish-speaking employees from learning English.

Those who are unable to speak English also have serious problems in dealing with governmental agencies (which employ few Spanish-speaking per-

822

sons). Spanish American leaders say that often people who speak only Spanish are unable to obtain welfare assistance without long delays or obtain other governmental services because no one in the service office to which they must go can speak Spanish. This also leads to difficulties with police because they are unable to communicate with police when stopped. Governmental agencies, it is said, seem to take the position that it is the responsibility of the individual and not of the agency to provide interpreters, e.g., visiting social workers sometimes ask a neighborhood child to interpret for them on problems of family planning and similar problems.

Failure to obtain citizenship also excludes such persons from participating in the political process. Leaders in the community are concerned about the large numbers of such persons, because it eliminates an important potential leverage in dealing with local, State, and Federal Governments.

Employment

Closely tied to the problems of education is the concern of the Spanish American community with employment. The Spanish American community lags behind the total community in median income and consistently has a higher unemployment rate than the total community. It is, however, in a better position than nonwhites, even though it has a lower median education level than nonwhites. For example, the 1960 Census shows that in the Bay Area 4.8 percent of white males were unemployed and 5.2 percent of white females were unemployed while the unemployment rate for the Spanish surname was 7.1 percent for males and 11 percent for females. For the nonwhite, however, the unemployment rate for males was 11.3 percent and for females it was 11 percent.

In the San Jose Area the unemployment rate for the white male was 4.4 percent and for the white female, 7.6 percent. The Spanish-surname female had a 22.6 percent unemployment rate while the male had an unemployment rate of 9.3 percent. The nonwhite female had a 7.1 percent unemployment rate compared to the nonwhite male rate of 4.0 percent.

In 1959, in San Francisco, the median family income for the total population was $6,717; for the Spanish-surname group it was $5,921. This compares with the median family income for nonwhite persons of $5,305. In Alameda County, the median family income for nonwhites was $5,080 while that of the white Spanish-surname was more than $1,200 higher ($6,282). The median family income for the total population in Alameda County in 1959 was $6,766.

According to the 1960 Census, in the Bay Area close to 50 percent of all Spanish-surname employed persons 14 years old and over were involved in two industries: manufacturing (32.4 percent) and the wholesale and retail trade (17.4 percent). The percent of Spanish-surname population engaged in wholesale and retail trade was almost the same as the percentage of the total white population. But only 21.8 percent of the total white population was engaged in manufacturing. On the other hand, 14.1 percent of the white population was engaged in professional and related services while only seven percent of the Spanish-surname population was engaged in these occupations. 12.5 percent of the nonwhite population was engaged in professional and related services.

Among the factors working against the Spanish-speaking persons in the employment field are:

1. Limited education.
2. Lack of understanding of the English language.
3. Lack of United States citizenship.
4. Lack of marketable skills and the failure of programs designed to train the unskilled to read. Spanish-speaking people who lack education, citizenship, or facility with the English language.
5. Discrimination against people whose skin is dark. (In places where a fair-complexioned Mexican American may be accepted for employment, one with darker skin may be turned away.)
6. Testing procedures used by industry tend to discriminate against persons of different cultural backgrounds.

The Spanish American community is concerned with testing procedures utilized by most companies and government agencies as prerequisites to employment. They believe that such tests do not accurately measure the basic skills required to perform the job for which the test is given and, therefore, regard the tests as one of many impediments to the employment of minority group members.

For many reasons, on-the-job training programs and adult education classes are of major concern to the Spanish American community. In Oakland, for example, a diminished grant in 1966 for the federally supported East Bay Skill Center resulted in cutbacks in the length of the basic education courses. This was regarded as a serious blow to the Spanish American community. To many Spanish Americans, learning English in the basic elementary courses is of greater importance than the training programs in particular skills.

Spanish American leaders also assert that Federal agencies lack the knowledge to cope with the problems of the Spanish speaking. Disproportionately few Spanish-speaking people are employed by Government agencies. The feeling among the community leadership is that the Federal Government has done little to insist that their agencies hire Spanish-speaking people.

The Federal Government, which is supposed to help all people, is as guilty as private industry in its discriminatory hiring practices involving the Spanish-speaking people in the Bay Area. We intend to let the Federal Government know our displeasure with these practices.*

In the Bay Area, Spanish Americans are under-represented in local governmental employment as well as in Federal employment. Of 12,681 permanent employees under the jurisdiction of the San Francisco Civil Service Commission, only 319, or 1.91 percent, are Spanish-speaking. Of 1,635 uniform firemen only 23, all of whom are firemen-entrants, are Spanish-speaking. (There are 1,211 persons in the firemen-entrants' category.) Of 1,722 uniform policemen, only 22 are Spanish-speaking, of whom 19 are policemen-entrants. (There are 1,253 persons in the police-entrants' category.)

A greater percentage of Spanish American persons in the Bay Area are employed by the Federal Government than by the city of San Francisco, but Spanish Americans still are under-represented when compared with their percentage of the total population. They are concentrated, moreover, in the lower levels of both blue and white-collar categories. In contrast to the Spanish Americans, Negroes make up a larger percentage of Federal employment than their percentage of the population in the Bay Area, although they also are concentrated at the lower-level jobs.

In 1967, in a move unusual for Spanish Americans, direct action was taken to protest the employment policies of two Federal agencies, the Post Offices in San Francisco and Oakland and the Alameda Naval Air Station. They picketed the post offices protesting the lack of Spanish American employees. At the Naval Air Station, persons from Mexican American groups and Negro civil rights groups jointly picketed in protest against the promotion policy of the Station.

It is alleged by members of the Spanish American community that, of more than 10,000 persons working in Bay Area Post Offices, only 152 are Spanish American and that in both the Oakland and San Francisco offices there are no Spanish American managers. It also is alleged that during the last year the Bay Area Post Offices have hired between 3,500 and 4,000 new employees and out of that group only 26 were Spanish Americans. A common complaint in the Spanish American community is that after the Hunters Point riot in 1966 the San Francisco Post Office hired approximately 750 persons without requiring them to take the normal examination and not one of those hired was a Spanish American.

With respect to the Alameda Naval Air Station, the complaint was that minority groups were not receiving the promotions to which they are entitled.

Housing

The 1960 United States Census showed that in California more than 40

---

*Staff Interview with Bert Corona, California State Chairman of the Mexican American Political Association—April 17, 1966, Oakland, California.

percent of all-white Spanish-surname families consisted of at least five persons. The total of all-white families of more than five persons constituted less than 23 percent of the total number of white families. Large families and low income are generally reported by Spanish American spokesmen as the major factors which make it difficult for them to obtain adequate housing.

Many Spanish Americans believe that they are subjected to discrimination in housing because they are Spanish Americans, but they believe that the degree of discrimination is not of the same magnitude as that faced by Negroes. Such discrimination is said to be more prevalent with respect to rentals than to sales property. In San Leandro, for example, where virtually no Negroes live, there are more than 6,000 Spanish-surname residents. It has been reported that the darker in skin-color a Spanish American is and the greater his difficulties with the English language, the more likely he is to face housing discrimination.

The 1960 Census showed that in the Bay Area 16.6 percent of all housing units occupied by white Spanish-surname families were substandard compared to 8.9 percent of the remaining white-occupied housing units. The disparity between living conditions for Spanish-surname and other whites is even greater when the overcrowding is measured. Of the former, 16.5 percent live in overcrowded housing units while only 5.3 percent of the latter live in such units. In the San Jose Area, 29.3 percent of the Spanish-surname housing units were overcrowded compared to 6.4 percent of the Anglo housing units and 18.3 percent of those occupied by nonwhites.

The shortage of adequate housing for Spanish Americans, particularly low-income housing, appears to be the major reason Spanish American residents of the Mission District of San Francisco have united to oppose redevelopment of that area. They fear that redevelopment will result in large amounts of low-income housing being razed and that no such housing will be built to take its place. The result, they fear, is that they will be forced to move to other areas of San Francisco or even out of the city where they may not find adequate housing which they can afford. It now appears that redevelopment will soon take place, but the people of the Mission District are attempting to obtain some control over the redevelopment planning. In the Residential Segregation Study conducted at the University of California at Los Angeles (UCLA) under the Mexican-American Study Project, the city of San Jose had a segregation index of 43.0; Oakland 41.5; and San Francisco 38.1. This index indicates that the higher the number of Spanish Americans in the community, the sharper the separation between the Spanish and Anglo communities.

The following table indicates the index results in all of the cities studied in California.

Rank	City	Segregation Index
1	San Bernardino	67.9
2	Riverside	64.9
3	Los Angeles	57.4
4	Bakersfield	53.7
5	Stockton	52.6
6	Ontario	50.6
7	Fresno	49.0
8	Santa Barbara	46.5
9	San Diego	43.6
10	San Jose	43.0
11	Oakland	41.5
12	San Francisco	38.1
13	Sacramento	30.2

Organizations in Spanish-speaking Communities

Organizations in Spanish-speaking communities in the Bay Area are of four types: religious, political, social, and community organizations. Since most Spanish-speaking persons are Catholic, a significant number of organizations exist within, or are closely allied with, individual Catholic churches. The primary concern of these organizations is religious education. Allied to this primary function are social services and community improvement projects primarily designed for the benefit of members of the respective parishes. Most of these organizations are not concerned with or involved in issues affecting

825

the broader community. There are some beginning attempts by these groups to become involved in political education and civic participation.

The major organizations in Spanish-speaking communities relevant to civil rights and general community issues are political in nature. The Mexican-American Political Association (MAPA), the major organization of this type in the State, has several chapters in the Bay Area. Although membership is predominantly Mexican American, in some communities such as San Francisco, there are many other Spanish-speaking persons involved.

MAPA is primarily concerned with political issues which affect the Mexican and Spanish-speaking communities. It endorses and supports candidates for political office, conducts political education and voter registration campaigns, and some of its leaders are involved in broader civil rights campaigns in the community. It also maintains a full-time legislative representative in Sacramento. Another organization of political significance is the Mission Council on Redevelopment (MCOR). It is composed of delegates from approximately 60 groups in the Mission District of San Francisco and was formed in 1965 as a vehicle for preventing redevelopment of the Mission District without meaningful citizen participation. Although MCOR was created for mutual purposes, it has created an awareness of the results of organization structure and the importance of community organization.

Although there are few privately funded community service organizations in the Bay Area, there are many community service organizations which are funded by, and closely related to, various Office of Economic Opportunity Community Action Programs. The Community Service Organization (CSO), a national organization with chapters throughout the Southwest, receives OEO assistance in several Bay Area communities.

Many knowledgeable persons believe that many potential leaders of private organization efforts are people who now serve as board or staff members of Community Action Programs, such as the Mission Target Area of San Francisco Economic Opportunity Council and the Spanish Speaking Foundation in the Fruitvale section of Oakland.

Many Mexican American leaders allege that social service organizations such as the CSO are denied Community Chest support in many communities in the Bay Area, while organizations with similar programs receive such support.

In the San Francisco Bay Area there are many social clubs which draw their membership from persons on the basis of their national origin or ancestry. There are clubs with membership of Nicaraguans, El Salvadorians, Puerto Ricans, Costa Ricans, the South American countries, and Mexico.

Exhibit No. 11

TXD-62-66
San Francisco, Calif.

UNITED STATES OF AMERICA
BEFORE THE NATIONAL LABOR RELATIONS BOARD
DIVISION OF TRIAL EXAMINERS
WASHINGTON, D. C.

LOCAL UNION NO. 38, UNITED ASSOCIATION
OF JOURNEYMEN AND APPRENTICES OF THE
PLUMBING AND PIPE FITTING INDUSTRY OF
THE UNITED STATES AND CANADA, AFL-CIO

and   Case No. 20-CB-1297

PHILLIP HAVILL, An Individual

Barry S. Jellison, Esq., for the
  General Counsel.
Neyhart & Grodin, by Joseph R. Grodin, Esq.,
  of San Francisco, Calif., for the
  Respondent.
Robert J. Scolnik, Esq., of San Francisco,
  Calif., for the Charging Party.

Before: Paul Bisgyer, Trial Examiner.

TRIAL EXAMINER'S DECISION

Statement of the Case

      This proceeding was heard before Paul Bisgyer, the undersigned
Trial Examiner, on July 14, 15 and 16, 1965, in San Francisco, California,
on the amended complaint of the General Counsel, 1/ and the amended answer
of Local Union No. 38, United Association of Journeymen and Apprentices of
the Plumbing and Pipe Fitting Industry of the United States and Canada,
AFL-CIO, herein called the Respondent or Union. Two questions are presented
for decision -- (1) whether the Respondent, in violation of Section 8(b)(2)
and (1)(A) of the National Labor Relations Act, as amended, caused
D. I. Chadbourne, Inc., herein called the Company or Chadbourne, to discharge
Phillip Havill because he was not a member of the Union, and (2) whether
the Respondent, in violation of the same sections of the Act, operated a
contractual hiring hall in such a manner as to accord preference in job
referrals to its members. Oral argument was heard at the close of the case
and briefs were thereafter filed by the General Counsel and the Respondent
in amplification of their positions.

      Upon the entire record, 2/ and from my observation of the demeanor
of the witnesses, and with due consideration being given to the arguments
advanced by the parties, I make the following:

Findings and Conclusions

I. The business of Chadbourne

      The Company, a California corporation, is engaged in the plumbing
and heating contracting business in San Francisco, California. During 1964,

---

1/ The original charge was filed on October 29, 1964, and a copy was
    served on the Respondent the next day. An amended charge was filed,
    with a copy being similarly served on the Respondent, on May 6, 1965.
2/ The Parties' Joint Motion To Correct Transcript and General Counsel's
    Exhibits is hereby granted and the record is accordingly corrected to
    reflect the proposed changes.

827

its sales and services amounted to approximately $300,000, of which some
$29,000 was paid by various governmental agencies for work performed in
connection with national defense. During the same period, the Company
purchased materials valued at $15,000 which it received from suppliers
located outside California. I find that the Company's operations exert a
5 substantial impact on national defense.

At all material times, the Company has been a member of
Associated Plumbing, Heating and Cooling Contractors of San Francisco, Inc.,
10 herein called the Association, which is an organization comprised of various
employers engaged in the plumbing and heating contracting business. The
Association represents its employer-members in collective bargaining and
negotiated with the Respondent the agreement involved in this case. During
1964, the sales of Clausen-Patten, Inc., a member of the Association,
15 amounted to approximately $761,000. Its purchases of materials during
the same year approximated $223,900 in value, of which materials costing
in excess of $50,000 were shipped to its California establishment directly
from outside the State or were received from a California supplier who,
in turn, had received the materials from outside the State.
20
I find that the Company is engaged in commerce within the meaning
of Section 2(6) and (7) of the Act. In view of the substantial impact of
the Company's operations on national defense and its participation through
the Association in multiemployer bargaining, I find it will effectuate the
25 policies of the Act for the Board to assert jurisdiction herein.

II. The labor organization involved

The Respondent is a labor organization within the meaning of
30 Section 2(5) of the Act.

III. The alleged unfair labor practices

A. Alleged unlawful discharge of Phillip Havill
35
1. The evidence

The Company, as a member of the Association, has been party to a
collective-bargaining agreement with the Respondent. Under this agreement,
40 the Company, as well as the other contracting employers, is required to secure
qualified journeymen plumbers and pipefitters from the Union's hiring hall.
For such purposes, the Union maintains out-of-work lists for each craft.
The agreement further provides that "if the Union is unable to furnish
qualified workmen within 48 hours after an Employer calls for them, the
45 Employer shall be free to procure the workmen from any other source or
sources." (Article II, Section 7) The legality of the contractual arrangement is not questioned.

Pursuant to this agreement, Daniel I. Chadbourne, the Company's
50 president, requested Robert J. Costello, the Union's business representative
and dispatcher under the hiring hall arrangement, to send him a jobbing
plumber and pipefitter competent to service boilers. On July 27, 1964, 3/
Costello referred William Guse. Although Guse proved to be deficient in
boiler work, Chadbourne nevertheless retained him for other duties. About
55 a month later, Chadbourne informed Costello of this fact and asked for
another jobbing plumber who had the ability to service boilers. On
August 26, Costello dispatched Harold Stone who also lacked the required
boiler skills. As a result, Chadbourne, on August 28 (Friday) spoke to '

60 ———————————————————
3/ All subsequent dates refer to 1964, unless otherwise indicated.

Havill about his futile efforts to secure a competent boiler repairman from
the Union and offered the job to Havill, although Havill had never registered
on the Union's out-of-work list. 4/ It appears that Chadbourne had previously
learned of Havill's boiler experience from a customer and his conversations
5 with Havill. Havill accepted Chadbourne's offer.

In accordance with Chadbourne's instructions, Havill went to
the Union hall the following Monday afternoon, August 31, to register and
report his employment and Chadbourne's intention to send the Union written
10 notification of this fact. 5/ However, finding the dispatch office closed,
Havill spoke to Business Manager Mazzola's secretary and advised her of the
purpose of his visit. The secretary suggested that he return later to
see Costello but before doing so that he first telephone to ascertain
whether Costello was in. Havill's subsequent efforts to reach Costello
15 that afternoon were unsuccessful.

The next day, September 1, Havill managed to talk to Costello
on the telephone. After identifying himself, Havill informed Costello that
he was hired by Chadbourne and that he wanted to be cleared for the job.
20 Costello inquired about his prior employment. When Havill began to relate
his employment history, Costello interrupted him and asked what "local"
had he worked out of. In response, Havill stated, "Different locals," at
which point, Costello again interrupted and said that he was "talking
about the plumbing and pipefitting locals." 6/ Havill's negative reply
25 elicited the statement from Costello that Havill was not going to work for
Chadbourne, that he was not qualified, that he had not served an apprenticeship, and that Chadbourne could not hire whomever he wanted to. Probably at
this point, Costello alluded to the fact that Chadbourne was under contractual
obligation to utilize the Union's hiring hall to recruit tradesmen. 7/
30 Havill then remarked that Chadbourne had told him that the Union was not
sending Chadbourne qualified men and that he considered Havill qualified to
perform the boiler work he needed done. Costello denied that Chadbourne
had requested any men from the hiring hall and directed Havill to inform

35 _____
4/ Havill had been in the Company's employ at various times since the
   fall of 1963, performing work not covered by the collective-bargaining
40 contract.
   5/ In situations where an employer exercises his right to secure workmen
      from outside the hiring hall, Article II, Section 7, provides that the
      employer shall "within 48 hours of such hiring, notify the Union of
      the name, address and social security number of each workman so employed,
      and shall require each such workman to come to the office of the Union
45   for registration."
   6/ Havill so testified. According to Costello, he simply mentioned
      "locals" but not "plumbing and pipefitting locals." Considering the
      nature of their conversation, I find it very likely that Costello
      referred to "plumbing and pipefitting locals." In any event, whether
      he described the locals in those terms, it is obvious he meant local
50   unions having jurisdiction over those trades.
   7/ In the context of the interchange of remarks, I find, contrary to
      Havill's denial, that Costello mentioned the existence of the contractual
      hiring hall, as Costello testified.

Chadbourne that if he wanted men, the Union had "men sitting on the bench."
The conversation ended with Havill stating that Chadbourne had hired him
and that he was going to work the following morning and with Costello
retorting, "like hell" he was. 8/

Immediately after speaking to Costello, Havill telephoned
Chadbourne and apprised him of his experience with Costello. During their
conversation, Costello also made a call to Chadbourne which the latter
received on another telephone while Havill held on to his wire. Referring
10   to his conversation with Havill, Costello complained about Chadbourne's
intention to hire Havill, whom he characterized as a "non-union man," 9/
in disregard of Chadbourne's contractual obligation to recruit men from the
Union's hiring hall. Chadbourne responded that the Union had failed to
fill his requests for men qualified to service boilers and that therefore
15   he was hiring Havill who possessed that ability. Despite Costello's
indication that the Union would take action unless Chadbourne utilized the
hiring hall, Chadbourne expressed his determination to put Havill to work.

Thereupon, Chadbourne resumed his discussion with Havill,
20   informing him that Costello resented Havill's contemptuous attitude toward
him. Havill denied such conduct. Chadbourne then stated that he could not
afford any trouble and suggested that they drop the matter.

As indicated above, Guse and Stone, though lacking in boiler skills
25   sought by Chadbourne, were dispatched to Chadbourne. As a result,
Chadbourne communicated with Costello, expressed his disappointment over
those referrals and asked for an opportunity to interview others for the job.
On the morning of September 1, Costello dispatched Jack Baker, and on
September 3, R. W. Unger. In their interviews, Baker admitted that he had
30   not worked on boilers for 20 years and wanted to learn that phase of the
trade, and Unger conceded he had no experience in servicing boilers. For
this reason, neither was hired. The Respondent does not dispute their lack
of qualifications, but simply asserts the Union's good faith belief that
these individuals were qualified to do the required boiler work.
35

On September 3, Chadbourne called Havill and told him to report
for work the next day, which he did. In reply to Havill's inquiry whether
to return to the Union hall for clearance, Chadbourne said that it would
not be necessary but that he would send the Union a letter advising it of
40   Havill's employment. Accordingly, on the same day (September 3) 10/
Chadbourne addressed the following communication to the Union.

We have called you on numerous occasions for a qualified
workman to do our boiler and control work as we are in dire
45   need of a man for this specialized work.

_8/ Except as indicated above, the foregoing findings are based on Havill's
more convincing testimony which was not contradicted in material respects.
50   _9/ The characterization of Havill as a "non-union man" is based on
Chadbourne's testimony, which Costello contradicted. The reference to
Havill as a "non-union man" is also contained in the Union's September 22
letter, quoted infra, which Business Manager Mazzola sent to Chadbourne
after being briefed by Costello concerning Chadbourne's determination to
55   hire Havill. Moreover, Costello was not too candid when, in addition to
denying that he referred to Havill as a "non-union man," he volunteered
that he "never really knew -- /Havill's/ status." It is quite apparent
to me that not only did Mazzola derive knowledge from Costello that Havill
was not affiliated with the Respondent's parent organization, but also
60   Costello's inquiry of Havill concerning the "locals" out of which he had
worked and Havill's response, plainly reveal Costello's awareness of
Havill's "non-union status." I credit Chadbourne's above testimony.
10/ It is apparent that the letter was erroneously dated September 2, since
it mentions Unger's referral which admittedly occurred on September 3.

We put in a request August 25th and you sent Mr. Harold
Stone whom we have hired, but he has informed us he knows
nothing about boiler or controls. Since then, we called
August 28th, 31st and September 2nd requesting a workman
5 for boiler and controls. You have sent us three men and
to date you have been unable to send an experienced man
for boilers and controls.as specifically requested. This
morning you sent Mr. Unger who has been employed with a
water treatment firm and has had no background in steam
10 fitting and readily admitted this fact. We do not consider
this qualified steam fitters as requested.

Since you have been unable to furnish us with a qualified
workman, we are forced to hire a man that is familiar
15 with this type of work, and are doing so according to our
agreement as shown in Article II, Section 7, Notification
of Hiring of Unregistered Person.

Mr. Phil Havill has contacted your office and his name
20 will be appearing on our regular monthly report. He will
be employed starting September 4, 1964.

Several days after receiving this letter, Costello briefed
Joseph P. Mazzola, the Union's business manager who had previously been
25 absent from the city, about the Chadbourne situation. Costello then
telephoned Chadbourne arranged for a meeting with Mazzola concerning
Havill's employment. Apparently, there was a misunderstanding as to
the scheduled date. When Chadbourne appeared at the Union hall, Costello
told him the meeting was supposed to be held the day before and that
30 Mazzola had since left the city but assured him that he would notify
Chadbourne by mail of the rescheduled meeting date.

On September 22, Mazzola acknowledged receipt of Chadbourne's
letter
35

. . . which refers to your experience in hiring men from
Local 38. You state that you have employed Mr. Phil Havill,
a Non-Union man, as a steamfitter.

40 I am hereby serving notice that you have violated our
Agreement, and I ask that you immediately correct this
situation and get rid of all Non-Union men in your
employ.

45 We will expect you to comply with the Contract wherever the
hiring of men is concerned. We have no alternative but to
insist on this, so that we can continue to send you men as
needed, as the Contract provides. 11/

50 Mazzola's letter prompted Chadbourne to seek an immediate
appointment with him to discuss this matter. Accordingly, on September 29,
Chadbourne met with Mazzola, Costello and others in the Union hall. Mazzola
repeated his demand that Havill be discharged. Chadbourne declined to do so,
asserting that Havill possessed the experience and skills to perform the
55 boiler work he needed. Mazzola insisted that Chadbourne was in violation
of their collective-bargaining agreement by disregarding the hiring hall to
employ Havill. Chadbourne, however, countered that, notwithstanding his
many requests, the Union was unable to supply qualified men and for this
60
_____
11/ Mazzola testified that, in using the term "Non-Union man," he meant
a person who was not hired through the hiring hall.

reason, he exercised his contractual right to go outside the hiring hall
for help. It is quite clear that Chadbourne was relying on Article II,
Section 7 of the agreement which permits the employer "to procure the
workmen from any other source" he desired in the event the Union was unable
to furnish qualified workmen within 48 hours after request. Although
Mazzola verified with Costello Chadbourne's prior efforts to secure men
with boiler experience, he, nevertheless, took the position that the contract
required Chadbourne to exhaust the out-of-work list before turning to
other sources and stated that he had about 50 available men "sitting on
the bench," many of whom had experience to fill the job. In response,
Chadbourne questioned the availability of qualified men in view of the
Union's inability to fulfill his earlier requests. In the course of
the discussion, Mazzola also expressed his opposition to hiring Havill
because he was "non-union" and the employment of any "non-union help"
outside the hiring hall, asserting that otherwise it would encourage other
employers to do what Chadbourne did. The meeting closed with neither
party budging from his position. 12/

Shortly after this meeting, Chadbourne had a further discussion
with his attorney concerning the Union's demand for Havill's discharge.
His attorney offered the opinion that the hiring hall was illegal and that
if Chadbourne terminated Havill, both he and the Union would be subject to
unfair labor practice charges. The attorney therefore advised Chadbourne
to confer again with the Union before acting on the Union's demand.

About a week or so later, Chadbourne had a second meeting with
Mazzola and Costello, which others also attended. 13/ Chadbourne conveyed
his attorney's opinion, mentioned his prior involvement in unfair labor
practice charges, and expressed his desire to avoid similar charges if he
acceded to the Union's demand for Havill's termination. Chadbourne then
suggested that they solve their problem by permitting Havill to join the

---

12/ The foregoing findings are substantially based on Chadbourne's testimony which, in many respects, was not contradicted. Although Chadbourne
revealed a weakness in remembering dates of various events, the sub-
stance of his testimony had the ring of truth. Mazzola denied making
any reference to Havill's "non-union" status or to "non-union help."
Yet, only a week before, in his September 22 letter to Chadbourne,
Mazzola similarly described Havill and other persons presumed to be in
Chadbourne's employ. Moreover, Mazzola testified that Chadbourne
requested him to accept Havill in his Union as a member, which he
refused to do. According to Chadbourne, Mazzola stated at the second
meeting, later discussed, that he could not take Havill into the
Union. In light of this testimony, it seems reasonable to infer that
Chadbourne's request was prompted by Mazzola's asserted opposition
to the employment of nonunion men and in that respect corroborates
Chadbourne's testimony concerning Mazzola's "non-union" remarks. On
the other hand, I do not credit Mazzola's testimony that when he
rejected Chadbourne's proposal for Havill's membership in the Union
he (Mazzola) added that membership in the Union would not give anyone
priority in employment. Mazzola impressed me as a witness given to
exaggeration and without a reliable recollection of events. For
example, Mazzola testified that when Chadbourne spoke to the Union's
attorney on the telephone during his second meeting with Mazzola,
later discussed, Chadbourne admitted to the Union's attorney that his
own attorney agreed with the former's opinion that Chadbourne was in
violation of the hiring hall agreement in employing Havill and that
Chadbourne further stated he was not concerned about the opinion of
either attorney. This testimony was contrary to the Union attorney's
statement offered at the hearing in lieu of testimony. Another example,
is Mazzola's testimony that at the first meeting he inveighed against
Chadbourne for asking the Union for the referral of a steamfitter and
then using him for plumbing work. Costello conceded the incorrectness
of such testimony.

13/ The findings made with respect to this meeting are based on a composite
of credible testimony.

832

Union. Mazzola's response was negative but he proposed instead that
Havill register on the out-of-work list and await his turn for referral.
Admittedly, registration entailed compliance with various qualification
provisions of the contract, including passing an examination and his
5 placement into an appropriate seniority group (Article II). Chadbourne
was not amenable to this proposal because it lacked assurance that he
could retain Havill and was in disregard of his rights under the contract.
Chadbourne similarly rejected Mazzola's suggestion that Chadbourne submit
their dispute to the Joint Hiring Committee 14/ for the reason that the
10 contract explicitly gave him the right to go outside the hiring hall for
help when the Union failed to refer qualified workmen within 48 hours
after request.

During the course of this meeting, Mazzola, in Chadbourne's
15 presence, telephoned the Union's attorney. Both Mazzola and Chadbourne
took turns to speak to the Union's attorney concerning Chadbourne's right
to hire Havill under the circumstances related previously and the Union's
right to demand his discharge. The Union's attorney agreed with the
reasonableness of Mazzola's position and stated that Chadbourne was
20 obligated to exhaust the out-of-work list before employing anyone outside
the hiring hall provided the Union honestly believed there were qualified
men available. The Union's attorney also stated that on the basis of facts
given to him by Mazzola the Union's demand for Havill's discharge was not
unlawful. Chadbourne, however, replied that his attorney had given him
25 contrary advice and the Union's attorney indicated that he would discuss
the matter further with Chadbourne's attorney. 15/

On October 22, Mazzola sent Chadbourne the following letter which
the Union's attorney drafted:
30
This will renew our request that you dismiss from employment
your employee, Mr. Phil Havill, for the reason that he was
hired contrary to the provisions of our Collective Bargaining
Agreement.
35
Specifically, he was hired from outside the Hiring Hall without
first exhausting our list of available applicants for employment.

A few days later, Chadbourne discharged Havill. On October 28
40 Chadbourne handed Mazzola a communication in which he advised him that he
had terminated Havill in compliance with the Union's demand. The letter also
went on to say:

As I stated to you in our numerous discussions of this matter
45 in the past month, I do not want to get involved with a labor
dispute with your Union. I cannot afford it and I think the
cards are stacked against me.

* * * * *
50
However, I want you to know that I do not agree with the statements
in your letter. I have not violated the hiring procedure of
the union contract. Mr. Havill was hired only after the Union was
unable to supply a qualified man. When he went to the Union, he
55

14/ Article II, Section 10 of the Agreement provides for a Joint Hiring
Committee composed of an equal number of Union and employer representatives to supervise the operation of the hiring hall and to hear and
60 determine disputes. There is no evidence that the Union itself ever
submitted the propriety of its demand for Havill's discharge to this
Committee. I also credit Chadbourne's testimony, that the foregoing
proposal was made at the second and not the first meeting, as Mazzola
testified.
65 15/ Both attorneys later considered the subject between themselves. As
expected, their divergent views were based on conflicting versions
of the facts given by their respective clients.

833

was told he could not join. I told you this several
times.

I am sorry that you feel it necessary to force me to lose a
qualified employee. I am doing so only to avoid trouble, not
because it's right.

On October 29, Havill filed a charge with the Board's Regional
Office, alleging that the Union unlawfully caused his discharge. On or
about November 10, Havill, at the suggestion of a Board Agent, went to
the Union hall with the expectation of being dispatched to Chadbourne.
Upon learning that that was not the Union's intention but that he was
to undergo the contract's qualifying procedures, including taking an
examination before being dispatched in regular order, Havill left the
hall. 16/

2. Concluding findings

The General Counsel contends that the record establishes that
the Respondent caused Chadbourne to discharge Havill because Havill was
not a member of the Respondent's International Union and that it thereby
violated Section 8(b)(2) and (1)(A) of the Act. The Respondent, on the
other hand, denies that it was so motivated, justifying its action on
the ground that it in good faith believed that Chadbourne had employed
Havill outside the Union's hiring hall in complete disregard of his
contractual obligation.

From a careful evaluation of all the evidence, I am persuaded
that Havill's discharge was prompted, if not solely, then in substantial
part at least, by his lack of union membership. The Respondent's
preoccupation with Havill's nonunion status can lead to no other inference.
As found above, this attitude was clearly displayed in Business Representative Costello's inquiry of Havill when the latter unsuccessfully sought
clearance to the Chadbourne job as to what "plumbing and pipefitting
locals" he had worked out of, and Costello's utter disinterestedness in
Havill's attempted listing of his qualifying employment history; in
Costello's telephone call to Chadbourne made shortly after his conversation with Havill, complaining about his employment of a "non-union man";
in obviously advising Business Manager Mazzola that Havill was not a
Union member; and in Mazzola's subsequent letter of September 22 to
Chadbourne demanding the dismissal of Havill "a Non-Union man," 17/ which
characterization Mazzola repeated at his September 29 meeting with
Chadbourne. While it is true that Mazzola and Costello also insisted
that Chadbourne was contractually obligated to utilize the hiring hall,
this does not necessarily militate against a finding of discriminatory
motivation. If anything, it strengthens such an inference. For, it is
quite clear the the hiring hall provisions did not bar Chadbourne from
employing Havill but, on the contrary, plainly recognized his right to do so.

16/ On November 2, in accordance with Mazzola's prior request, Chadbourne
submitted to him a list of qualifications Chadbourne deemed necessary
for an applicant to possess in order to fill the job vacated by Havill.
17/ In light of all the evidence, I find, contrary to Mazzola's assertion,
that the term "Non-Union" was not used by him simply to indicate that
Havill was not hired through the hiring hall. Bricklayers, Masons and
Plasterers International Union (Park Construction Company), 150 NLRB
No. 141, cited by the Respondent, is plainly distinguishable on its
facts from the present case. There the Board found, on the basis of
the entire record, that the General Counsel failed to prove that the
union's reference to the hiring of local men meant members of the
local union rather than men living in the local area.

834

I find it difficult to believe that Mazzola and Costello were not well aware of this fact.

In unequivocal language, Article II, Section 7 provides that
5   "if the Union is unable to furnish qualified workmen within 48 hours after an Employer calls for them, the Employer shall be free to procure the workmen from any other source or sources." It is undisputed that over a period of time, by far in excess of 48 hours, Chadbourne endeavored to secure from the Union hiring hall a plumber with experience to service
10   boilers and that the Union dispatched several individuals whom Chadbourne determined, after trial or interview, were seriously lacking in the skills he needed. The Respondent does not contend that these individuals were improperly rejected or that such action was improperly inspired by a desire to circumvent the hiring hall. At most, it asserts that it in
15   good faith believed that these individuals possessed the required qualifications to perform the job and that Chadbourne was obligated to exhaust the hiring hall's out-of-work list and await 48 hours thereafter before recruiting help from other sources. 18/ However, the contract is devoid of any language which either expressly or by necessary implication places
20   such limitations on the employer's right to go outside the hiring hall where, as here, the Union fails to fill the employer's request "within 48 hours after an /e/mployer calls for" a workman. 19/ In short, the Respondent's asserted reliance upon a purported obligation of Chadbourne to utilize the Union's hiring hall does not negative the compelling
25   inference of discrimination implicit in its demands for the discharge of Havill, a "Non-Union man."

Even assuming that the Respondent entertained an honest belief that Chadbourne had breached his contractual obligation by employing
30   Havill outside the hiring hall, I find that this would not exonerate the Respondent from liability under the Act for causing Havill's discharge.

_____
18/   There is more than a faint suggestion in the record that Costello
35   had actually exhausted the out-of-work list when on August 26 he dispatched Harold Stone whom Chadbourne found was not suitable for boiler work. Costello testified that at the time of Stone's referral there were probably 55 to 60 men on the list; that he "proceeded to call down the list, explaining first the nature and type of job and
40   proceeded to exhaust the list until ---/he/ could acquire someone who would take this job referral"; and that such person was Stone who "was the only man that would take the job." After Stone proved to be unsuitable for boiler work Chadbourne hired Havill on August 28.
45   19/   It is noted that where the parties intended that the out-of-work list be exhausted specific language in the contract was used. Thus, Section 8 of Article II, entitled "Outside Contractors," provides that "it shall be a violation of this contract for any contractor having a permanent shop within the territory covered by this agreement
50   to transfer men into the area from outside that territory without first exhausting this out-of-work list maintained by the local union." (Emphasis added.)
      In view of the fact that the pertinent contract provisions are clear and unambiguous and not reasonably susceptible of a different
55   interpretation, I find no occasion for having them interpreted by the Joint Hiring Committee, as the Respondent had proposed at one of its meetings with Chadbourne. Cf. Century Papers, Inc., 155 NLRB No. 40.

835

To be sure, the Act does not outlaw nondiscriminatory hiring hall
arrangements such as that prescribed in the collective-bargaining agreement involved herein. 20/ Nor is it an unfair labor practice for a union
to seek the termination of an employee hired by an employer who bypassed
5 the union's hiring hall in contravention of his contractual obligation. 21/
However, it is quite another thing for a union to bring about the discharge of an employee hired outside the hiring hall where, as here, the
contract expressly recognizes the employer's right to do so. Such conduct
on the union's part has been held to constitute a violation of Section 8(b)(2)
10 of the Act for causing an employer to discriminate against an employee
to encourage membership in a labor organization within the meaning of
Section 8(a)(3) of the Act and a violation of Section 8(b)(1)(A) of the
Act for restraining and coercing employees in the exercise of their
statutory rights. 22/ Certainly, the Respondent's alleged good faith
15 cannot make its discharge demand lawful simply because it mistakenly
believed it was sanctioned by the hiring hall contract, which is the only
legal justification for requiring referral from the union's hiring hall.

Accordingly, I find that the Respondent, by causing Chadbourne
20 to terminate the employment of Havill for discriminatory reasons, violated
Section 8(b)(2) and (1)(A) of the Act.

B. Alleged discriminatory operation
of the hiring hall
25

As indicated in the preceding section of this Decision, the
Respondent and the Association have been for some years parties to a
collective-bargaining agreement which requires the employer members of the
Association to secure their journeymen plumbers and pipefitters exclusively
30 from the Respondent's hiring hall. 23/ In connection with the operation
of the hiring hall, Article II of the agreement contains provisions dealing
with the qualifications of journeymen plumbers and pipefitters for registration and referral; the maintenance of out-of-work lists; dispatch
35 procedures; special priority rules for the employment of a contractor's
keyman and applicants with special skills; the exemption from the hiring
hall requirement of employees of an outside contractor temporarily performing work within the area serviced by the Respondent; and priority in
referral of applicants on the basis of employment within the area covered
40 by the agreement and within neighboring areas. With respect to the order
of referral, the contract establishes the following seniority groups;

SENIORITY GROUP I shall consist of plumbers and pipefitters who
have been employed by a contractor party to this agreement for a
45 period of at least 1200 hours each year during the two years preceding their registration on the out-of-work list, in the territory
covered by this agreement or temporarily on work outside that
territory.

50 SENIORITY GROUP II shall consist of plumbers and pipe fitters who
have been employed for a period of at least 1200 hours each year
during the two years preceding their registration on the out-of-work
list, in the Greater Bay Area ---.

55 20/ Local 357, International Brotherhood of Teamsters v. N.L.R.B., 365 U.S.
667.
21/ Local 542, International Union of Operating Engineers, AFL-CIO
(Ralph A. Marino), 151 NLRB No. 55; Hoisting and Portable Engineers,
Local 302 (West Coast Steel Works), 144 NLRB 1449, 1452
60 22/ Radio Officers' Union v. N.L.R.B., 347 U.S. 17.
23/ This obligation, however, is subject to the 48-hour provision previously discussed.

SENIORITY GROUP III shall consist of all other qualified plumbers and pipe fitters.

Overall supervision of the hiring hall under the contract is vested in a Joint Hiring Committee composed of an equal number of union and employer representatives. The Committee is empowered, among other things, to promulgate all the rules and regulations it deems advisable for the proper operation of the job referral plan and to hear and determine all "grievances arising out of work registration, work referrals and the preparation of the referral registration lists."

The General Counsel concedes the validity of the hiring hall arrangement. However, the complaint alleges, and he sought to prove, that since on or about November 7, 1964, 24/ the Respondent administered the hiring hall in a manner that accorded preference in job referrals to its members. In support of this allegation, the General Counsel relies on the evidence showing the following:

a. William Helm, a member of the Union, was dispatched on different occasions from the three seniority groups, although he had never passed a written examination to qualify for journeyman status. Costello explained that Helm's was an unusual case and that, while Helm had the ability to do the work, he had difficulty passing the written part. Costello further testified that he usually dispatched Helm when he had virtually exhausted the out-of-work lists. The record also shows that there are about 1600 to 1700 members covered by the Building Trades Agreement here involved and that Helm seems to be the only one of this number who failed to qualify.

b. In placing certain members of sister locals in Seniority Group II, Costello failed to verify adequately whether the registrants possessed the required number of hours of employment to make them eligible for such classification. However, the evidence relied upon principally relates to welders and plumbers whom Costello had recruited from sister locals because of his inability at those times to fill employers' requests for such employees from the Union's available out-of-work lists. Other instances of alleged insufficient verification of eligibility pertain to individuals who, by reason of Article II, Section 8, 25/ were exempt from the referral procedures as employees of outside contractors working on a temporary job in the area. Manifestly, verification of seniority group eligibility was unnecessary in the above-indicated circumstances and registration by those employees was actually only a matter of record-keeping.

c. On occasions, Costello dispatched apprentices as helpers, even though they did not qualify for inclusion in any seniority group. However, it is clear that apprentices, although members of the Union, are not covered by, nor are they dispatched under, the referral system. At the times Costello sent them to a job it was because of the absence of the Apprentice Coordinator whose function it is to do so in conjunction with the concededly valid apprentice program which the contract also establishes.

d. Contrary to the language in the contract pertaining to Group I seniority, the Respondent permits its members to register in the Group I out-of-work list, even if they had previously left the area for

---

24/   Apparently, this date was selected because of the 6-month limitation
        period prescribed by Section 10(b) of the Act.
25/   Article II, Section 8 provides, in relevant part, that "outside
        contractors may bring into the area temporarily to perform work
        herein on each job, one plumber, one steamfitter or pipe fitter,
        one lead burner and one sprinkler fitter - - -."

837

more than 2 years. However, whether or not the Respondent's action is
justified is essentially a matter of interpretation of the phrase "temporarily
on work outside" the territory covered by the contract, as set forth in the
paragraph dealing with Group I seniority.

e. Union members were permitted to register on a higher seniority
list than that to which they were entitled. However, the record reveals
quite clearly that in many instances improper registration was due to the
loose and careless practices surrounding the signing of the out-of-work
10   lists. 26/ Indeed, the record discloses that a substantial number of
Union members eligible for Group I registration have frequently signed
Group II and III out-of-work lists. Moreover, it appears that some of
these instances of erroneous registration cited by the General Counsel
involved employees whom Costello had recruited from sister locals to fill
15   demands he could not satisfy from the Union's own lists or involved exempt
employees of outside contractors. As previously indicated, the registration
by such workmen was merely for record purposes and not for the purpose of
attaining a position on the list for future referral.

20   Evaluating the Respondent's administration of the hiring hall in
the light of all the facts and circumstances developed at the hearing, I
am not persuaded that the General Counsel has proved that the hiring hall
was operated in a discriminatory manner to the unlawful advantage of
members of the Union or sister locals. Significantly, no evidence was
25   adduced that since November 7 the Respondent has deprived any job applicant
of the right to register or referral or other rights to which he was
entitled under the hiring hall provisions because he was not a member of
the Union or a sister local. Nor is there any evidence in the record
showing any disparate treatment between union and nonunion members or that
30   union affiliation otherwise played any role in job referrals. While it is
undoubtedly true -- as the Respondent candidly admits -- that the operation
of the hiring hall leaves much to be desired, particularly in the registration and verification of seniority eligibility practices, 27/ more is
required to warrant a finding that the Respondent operated the hiring hall
35   in a manner prohibited by the Act. Indeed, the deficiencies appear to
relate to matters of peculiar concern to the Joint Hiring Committee created
by the contract to oversee the proper functioning of the hiring hall and
not to the Board whose power is restricted to the elimination of discrimination that encourages or discourages union membership, 28/ which has not
40   been established here.

As I find that the General Counsel has failed to sustain his
burden of proving that the Respondent has caused unlawful discrimination
against job applicants in the manner it operated the contractual hiring
45   hall, I find that the Respondent has not violated Section 8(b)(2) and
(1)(A) of the Act in this respect. Accordingly, I recommend dismissal of
the relevant allegations of the amended complaint.

                    IV. The effect of the unfair labor
50   practices upon commerce

The activities of the Respondent, as set forth in section III,
above, in connection with the Company's operations described in section I,
above, have a close, intimate, and substantial relation to trade, traffic,
55

26/   According to Costello, he is in charge of some 16 books in which
      job applicants register for work in the building trades covered by
      the contract involved in this case and the metal trades covered by
60   contracts with other employers.
27/   The Respondent stated at the hearing and in its brief that
      measures are being taken to rectify some of these deficiencies.
28/   Radio Officers' Union v. N.L.R.B., supra.

and commerce among the several States and tend to lead to labor disputes
burdening and obstructing commerce and its free flow.

The Remedy

Pursuant to Section 10(c) of the Act, I recommend that the
Respondent cease and desist from engaging in the unfair labor practices
found and like and related conduct and take certain affirmative action
designed to effectuate the policies of the Act.

10

To redress the discriminatory discharge of Phillip Havill, which
the Respondent has unlawfully caused, I recommend that the Union notify
the Company in writing, and furnish a copy of such notice to Havill, that
it has withdrawn its objection to Havill's employment for the job in
question in this proceeding, without prejudice to his seniority or other
rights and privileges, and that it requests such unconditional reinstatement. In addition, I recommend that the Respondent make Havill whole for
any loss of earnings he may have suffered by reason of the discrimination
against him by payment to him of a sum of money equal to that which he
normally would have earned from the date of his discharge to the date
5 days after it serves the written notice of withdrawal of objection
mentioned above. Backpay shall be computed with interest on a quarterly
basis in the manner prescribed by the Board in F. W. Woolworth Company,
90 NLRB 289, 291-294, and Isis Plumbing & Heating Co., 138 NLRB 716.
The posting of an appropriate notice is also recommended.

15

20

25

Upon the basis of the foregoing findings of fact and upon the
entire record in the case, I make the following:

30

Conclusions of Law

1. The Company is engaged in commerce within the meaning of
Section 2(6) and (7) of the Act.

35

2. The Respondent is a labor organization within the meaning
of Section 2(5) of the Act.

3. By causing the Company to discriminate against Phillip Havill
in violation of Section 8(a)(3) of the Act, the Respondent has engaged,
and is engaging, in unfair labor practices within the meaning of Section
8(b)(2) and (1)(A) of the Act.

40

4. The aforesaid unfair labor practices affect commerce within
the meaning of Section 2(6) and (7) of the Act.

45

5. The Respondent has not engaged in unfair labor practices
by reason of the manner it administered the contractual job referral system
since on or about November 7, 1964.

50

RECOMMENDED ORDER

Upon the foregoing findings of fact and conclusions of law
and upon the entire record in the case, and pursuant to Section 10(c)
of the National Labor Relations Act, as amended, it is ordered that the
Respondent, Local Union No. 38, United Association of Journeymen and
Apprentices of the Plumbing and Pipe Fitting Industry of the United States
and Canada, AFL-CIO, San Francisco, California, its officers, representatives,
agents, successors, and assigns, shall:

55

60

1. Cease and desist from:

(a) Causing or attempting to cause D. I. Chadbourne, Inc.,
to discriminate against Phillip Havill or other employees in violation of
Section 8(a)(3) of the Act by causing or attempting to cause that Company

839

TXD-62-66

to discharge them because of their nonmembership in its labor organization, except to the extent that the employees' rights in that regard may be affected by an agreement requiring membership in a labor organization as a condition of employment, as authorized by Section 8(a)(3) of the Act.

(b) In any like or related manner restraining or coercing employees of D. I. Chadbourne, Inc., in the exercise of the rights guaranteed in Section 7 of the Act.

10   2. Take the following action which is necessary to effectuate the policies of the Act.

(a) Make whole Phillip Havill for any loss of pay suffered by him by reason of the discrimination against him, as provided in
15 "The remedy" section of the Trial Examiner's Decision.

(b) Notify D. I. Chadbourne, Inc., and Phillip Havill in writing that it withdraws its objections to Havill's employment and requests the said Company to offer Havill reinstatement to his former or a substan-
20 tially equivalent position, without prejudice to his seniority or other rights and privileges previously enjoyed by him.

(c) In the event that Havill is presently serving in the Armed Forces of the United States, notify him in writing that it has no
25 objection to his employment on the ground that he is not a member of the Respondent, upon application, in accordance with the Selective Service Act and the Universal Military Training and Service Act of 1948, as amended, after discharge from the Armed Forces.

(d) Post at its meeting hall and offices, copies of the
30 notice attached hereto as an Appendix. 29/ Copies of said notice, to be furnished by the Regional Director for the Twentieth Region, shall, after being duly signed by the Respondent's representative, be posted by the Respondent immediately upon receipt thereof and maintained by it for a period of 60 consecutive days thereafter in conspicuous places, including
35 all places where notices to members are customarily posted. Reasonable steps shall be taken by the Respondent to insure that said notices are not altered, defaced, or covered by any other material.

(e) Mail to the Regional Director for the Twentieth Region
40 signed copies of the notice attached hereto as an Appendix for posting by the Company at its place of business, if it is willing to do so. Copies of said notice, to be furnished by the Regional Director, shall, after being signed by the Respondent's representative, be forthwith returned to the Regional Director for such posting.

45
(f) Notify the Regional Director for the Twentieth Region in writing within 20 days from the receipt of the Trial Examiner's Decision as to what steps the Respondent has taken to comply herewith. 30/

50 29/ In the event that these Recommendations be adopted by the Board, the words "A DECISION AND ORDER" shall be substituted for the words, "THE RECOMMENDATIONS OF A TRIAL EXAMINER" in the notice. In the further event that the Board's Order be enforced by a decree of the United States Court of Appeals, the words "A DECREE OF THE UNITED STATES
55 COURT OF APPEALS ENFORCING AN ORDER" shall be substituted for the words "A DECISION AND ORDER."
30/ In the event that these Recommendations be adopted by the Board, this provision shall be modified to read: "Notify the Regional Director for the Twentieth Region in writing within 10 days from the date of this Order as to what steps the Respondent has taken to comply herewith."

840

IT IS FURTHER ORDERED that the complaint, as amended, be and it hereby is, dismissed insofar as it alleges that the Respondent operated the contractual hiring hall in a discriminatory manner in violation of Section 8(b)(2) and (1)(A) of the Act.

Dated at Washington, D. C.

FEB 9 1966

Paul Bisgyer
Trial Examiner

841

FORM NLRB-4633
(1-65)   TXD-62-66

APPENDIX

NOTICE

TO ALL MEMBERS OF

LOCAL UNION NO. 38, UNITED ASSOCIATION OF
JOURNEYMEN AND APPRENTICES OF THE PLUMBING
AND PIPE FITTING INDUSTRY OF THE UNITED
STATES AND CANADA, AFL-CIO

PURSUANT TO

THE RECOMMENDATIONS OF A TRIAL EXAMINER OF THE

NATIONAL LABOR RELATIONS BOARD

and in order to effectuate the policies of the

NATIONAL LABOR RELATIONS ACT

we hereby notify you that:

WE WILL NOT cause or attempt to cause D. I. CHADBOURNE, INC.,
to discriminate against Phillip Havill or other employees in
violation of Section 8(a)(3) of the Act, by causing or
attempting to cause that Company to discharge them because
of their nonmembership in our labor organization, except to
the extent that the employees' rights in that regard may be
affected by an agreement requiring membership in a labor
organization as a condition of employment, as authorized by
Section 8(a)(3) of the Act.

WE WILL make whole Phillip Havill for any loss of pay he
may have suffered as a result of our discriminatory action
against him, as provided in "The remedy" section of the
Trial Examiner's Decision.

WE WILL notify D. I. CHADBOURNE, INC. and Phillip Havill
in writing that we withdraw our objections to the
employment of Havill by the said Company and that we
request the Company to offer Havill reinstatement to his
former or a substantially equivalent position, without
prejudice to his seniority or other rights and privileges
previously enjoyed by him.

LOCAL UNION NO. 38 UNITED ASSOCIATION OF
JOURNEYMEN AND APPRENTICES OF THE PLUMBING
AND PIPE FITTING INDUSTRY OF THE UNITED
STATES AND CANADA, AFL-CIO
....
(Labor Organization)

Dated .... By ....
                                          (Representative)   (Title)
NOTE: We will notify Phillip Havill, in writing, if presently serving
in the Armed Forces of the United States, that we have no objection
to his employment on the ground that he is not a member of our labor
organization, upon application, in accordance with the Selective
Service Act and the Universal Military Training and Service Act of
1948, as amended, after discharge from the Armed Forces.

This Notice must remain posted for 60 consecutive days from the date of posting, and
must not be altered, defaced, or covered by any other material.
If members have any question concerning this Notice or compliance with its provisions,
they may communicate directly with the Board's Regional Office, 13050 Federal Building,
450 Golden Gate Avenue, Box 36047, San Francisco, California (Tel. No. 556-0335).

842

D-6954
San Francisco, Calif.

... .

UNITED STATES OF AMERICA

BEFORE THE NATIONAL LABOR RELATIONS BOARD

LOCAL UNION NO 38, UNITED ASSOCIATION
OF JOURNEYMEN AND APPRENTICES OF THE
PLUMBING AND PIPE FITTING INDUSTRY OF
THE UNITED STATES AND CANADA, AFL-CIO
(O. I. Chadbourne, Inc.) 1/

and   Case No. 20-CB-1297

PHILLIP HAVILL, An Individual

DECISION AND ORDER

On February 9, 1966, Trial Examiner Paul Bisgyer issued his Decision in
the above-entitled proceeding, finding that the Respondent had engaged in certain
unfair labor practices and recommending that it cease and desist therefrom and take
certain affirmative action, as set forth in the attached Trial Examiner's Decision.
The Trial Examiner further found that the Respondent had not engaged in certain
other unfair labor practices and recommended that these allegations be dismissed.
The Respondent filed exceptions to the Trial Examiner's Decision and a supporting
brief. Thereafter, the General Counsel filed cross-exceptions and a supporting brief,
and the Charging Party and the Respondent filed reply briefs.

Pursuant to the provisions of Section 3(b) of the National Labor Relations
Act, as amended, the National Labor Relations Board has delegated its powers in
connection with this case to a three-member panel.

The Board has reviewed the rulings of the Trial Examiner made at the hearing
and finds that no prejudicial error was committed. The rulings are hereby affirmed.
The Board has considered the Trial Examiner's Decision, the exceptions, the cross-
exceptions, the briefs, and the entire record in this case, and hereby adopts the
findings, conclusions, and recommendations of the Trial Examiner, with the modif'-
cation noted below. 2/

_____
1/ The caption of this case is corrected to include the name of the Employer.
2/ In adopting the Trial Examiner's conclusion that the Respondent violated
Section 8(b)(2) and (1)(A) of the Act by causing Chadbourne to terminate the
employment of Havill for discriminatory reasons, we find it unnecessary to rely
upon the Trial Examiner's comments, in the penultimate paragraph of his Concluding
Findings, with respect to the Respondent's liability if it were assumed that the
Respondent entertained an honest belief that Chadbourne had breached its
contractual obligation by employing Havill outside the hiring hall.

160 NLRB No. 96

D-8954

ORDER

Pursuant to Section 10(c) of the National Labor Relations Act, as amended, the National Labor Relations Board hereby adopts as its Order the Recommended Order of the Trial Examiner, and orders that the Respondent, Local Union No. 38, United Association of Journeymen and Apprentices of the Plumbing and Pipe Fitting Industry of the United States and Canada, AFL-CIO, its officers, agents, and representatives, shall take the action set forth in the Trial Examiner's Recommended Order.

Dated, Washington, D. C.

Frank W. McCulloch,   Chairman

John H. Fanning,   Member

Sam Zagoria,   Member

(SEAL)   NATIONAL LABOR RELATIONS BOARD

844

Exhibit No. 12

May 1, 196?

TESTIMONY OF VINCENT G. MACALUSO
to be given before the Hearing of the U. S. Commission
on Civil Rights - May 3, 1967 - San Francisco

My name is Vincent G. Macaluso, and I live at 1836 Park Road, N. W.,

Washington, D. C. I am the Assistant Director for Construction of the Office of

Federal Contract Compliance, United States Department of Labor. The brief

statement has been reviewed by Mr. Edward C. Sylvester, Jr., Director of the

Office of Federal Contract Compliance and has his concurrence.

First I would like to describe the essential elements of the President's

Executive Order which our Office administers, and the function and authority of

our Office.

The Executive Order with which we are concerned is No. 11246, issued by

President Lyndon B. Johnson on September 24, 1965, and effective thirty days after

that date. The general subject is equal employment opportunity. Parts II and III

dealing with employment by Government contractors and subcontractors and Federally-

assisted construction contractors and subcontractors require that the Secretary of

Labor shall be responsible for the administration of these parts of the Order. Under

his authority in Part IV of the Order Secretary W. Willard Wirtz has established within

his Department, and reporting directly to him, the Office of Federal Contract Compliance.

This Office provides the policy guidance to the Federal contracting and administering

agencies in their implementation of the Order, and this Office also directly participates

in specific cases from time to time as it is authorized to do under the Order.

The Order requires that, except in the event of an exemption based upon the national interest, every contracting agency shall include in every contract and every Federal administering agency shall require as a condition for granting Federal funds for any construction contract the inclusion of a contractual provision, spelled out in the Executive Order itself, which provides not only for non-discrimination against any employee or applicant for employment because of race, creed, color or national origin, but also that the employer doing business with the Government will take "affirmative action" to insure this result.

Each Federal contracting agency, and each Federal administering agency using Federal funds for construction contracts, is primarily responsible for obtaining compliance with the rules, regulations and orders of the Secretary of Labor. They are also directed to cooperate with the Secretary of Labor and to furnish the Secretary of Labor such information and assistance as he may require in the performance of his functions under this Order.

The contractual provision which is required to be included in every contract covered by this Executive Order includes the following statement:

> "In the event of the contractor's noncompliance with the non-
> discrimination clauses of this contract or with any of such rules,
> regulations or orders, this contract may be cancelled, terminated
> or suspended in whole or in part and the contractor may be declared
> ineligible for further Government contracts in accordance with
> procedures authorized in Executive Order 11246 of September 24,
> 1965, and such other sanctions may be imposed and remedies involved

as provided in Executive Order 11246 of September 24, 1965, or by

the rules, regulations or orders of the Secretary of Labor, or as

otherwise provided by law."

The Order itself also provides that the Secretary of Labor or the appropriate Federal

contracting or administering agency may, among other things, refer cases to the

Department of Justice or the Equal Employment Opportunity Commission, or provide

that Federal agencies refrain from entering into further contracts until the contractor

has satisfied the Secretary of Labor of its compliance.

Our programs are designed to require that the contractor produce the results

of effective affirmative action, rather than simply to call upon him to put in specific

efforts that we might think appropriate. We believe that no one knows his position

better than he and that, in this matter as well as in any other aspect of management,

he should use his own imagination and ingenuity to figure out how to do the job. The

implementation of this policy has met with considerable success outside of the

construction industry. We feel it is proceeding satisfactorily, and there are in fact

many instances of dramatic results. This is not true however in contract construction.

The results there have been nominal at best.

Our programs and field operations are quite different in the contract construction

industry from other industries. This is in a large part based upon our recognition that

there are special characteristics in construction, such as that employees are hired by

the day and have strong hiring halls in most of the trades in which we are particularly

interested, unemployment in these trades is traditionally higher than average, father-son

traditions and general in-groupism are prevalent, and the better-paid building trades have failed – for whatever reasons – to have significant representation of minority groups among their members.

I would like to tell you briefly what our Office is doing about compliance in the construction industry. Soon after assuming his responsibility under the Executive Order, on January 10, 1966, Secretary of Labor Wirtz wrote the heads of all Federal contracting and administering agencies, setting forth general policy guidelines for their compliance programs. A prominent item in this letter was the extensive use of pre–award proceedings. Our Office thereupon held two–day meetings in each major geographical region of this country with the Federal agency compliance officials. An important part of these two–day meetings was a half–day session in which we discussed with these officials this Office's "1966 Proposed Contract Construction Compliance Program Under Executive Order 11246". In this document we furnished guidelines for agency construction programs, including pre–award examinations for all projects exceeding $100,000 in total construction costs. We also provided a recommended form which would structure the pre–award examination to assure that the real needs for affirmative action would be explored and would be dealt with meaningfully before the contract was signed.

Another integral part of our construction program is the use of Area Coordinators. This is a cooperative program of Federal agencies predominant in Federally–involved contract construction, and there are now fifteen Area Coordinators who serve in twenty–two areas identified by the largest city in their area. Their main function is to provide the service of assisting the agencies to carry out the agencies' responsibilities to require their contractors to achieve compliance. The primary responsibility for compliance with this provision of the contract, as with any other provision of the contract, continues to remain with the Federal or contracting agency involved in the contract.

The Coordinators address themselves to general area problems, in the construction industry and to coordinating the compliance activities of the Federal agencies in their attempt to see that the Federal Government has a uniform area approach.

In view of the inability of the Federal contracting and administering agencies to provide adequate staffing to do the whole job at one time with the intensity required, we have selected a succession of particular city areas upon which to concentrate, in order to use our resources most effectively. Our present plans are to proceed to other cities as quickly as our resources allow. Our selection of one before another does not imply a judgment that the problems in the construction industry are significantly worse there, but rather usually that the Federal involvement, and perhaps the expectation of greater Federal construction involvement, warrants closer attention. We have given this closer attention to three cities so far, and in all three our Office has required pre-award understandings, including acceptable affirmative action commitments, on all significantly large Federally-involved construction jobs. A year ago this program was established in St. Louis. This past winter we got underway in San Francisco and Cleveland.

I will be glad to discuss our Operational Plan for San Fran cisco. This Plan contains a specific set of nine items, ranging from pre-apprenticeship to the encouragement of sub-contractors with minority group identification, which construction contractors and sub-contractors in the Bay Area must cover adequately in designing their affirmative action programs, as a condition of getting a Federally-involved contract. These nine items with which the contractor must deal effectively in his affirmative action program were

849

first among the equal employment opportunity provisions in a grant agreement
between Bay Area Rapid Transit (BART) and the United States Department of Housing
and Urban Development. BART felt, and we heartily agreed, that the most effective
way for it to implement its program was to have the same program required as a
condition for the spending of Federal construction money throughout the six-county
area here in San Francisco Bay Area. Mr. Sylvester or I try to participate personally
in each significant event in the development of this program. The Operational Plan
went into effect in early February. There have been less than half a dozen contracts
covered by the Plan since that time. All of these have met the requirements of the
Plan.

This is the end of my opening statement. I would of course be happy to discuss
the matter further with you if you wish.

850

Exhibit No. 13

TO THE UNITED STATES COMMISSION ON CIVIL RIGHTS:

> STATEMENT OF JOSEPH BELARDI ON BEHALF OF SAN
> FRANCISCO LOCAL JOINT EXECUTIVE BOARD OF
> CULINARY WORKERS, BARTENDERS, AND CLUB SERVICE
> WORKERS OF THE HOTEL AND RESTAURANT EMPLOYEES
> AND BARTENDERS INTERNATIONAL UNION (AFL-CIO).

I am the Executive Secretary of the San Francisco
Local Joint Executive Board of Culinary Workers, Bartenders and
Club Service Workers of the Hotel and Restaurant Employees and
Bartenders International Union (AFL-CIO). Said Joint Board
represents some 25,000 San Franciscans (over half of whom it is
estimated are of minority race), and is composed of the following
six local unions of the Hotel and Restaurant Employees and
Bartenders International Union: Waiters and Dairy Lunchmen's
Union, Local No. 30; Bartenders Union, Local No. 4I; Cooks,
Pastry Cooks and Assistants Union, Local No. 44; Waitresses
Union, Local No. 48; Miscellaneous Culinary Employees Union,
Local No. 110; and Hotel, Motel & Club Service Workers Union,
Local No. 283.

The Local Joint Board negotiates and enforces collective bargaining agreements for said six Local Unions, and, where
applicable, for a seventh Union: Apartment, Motel, Hotel, and
Elevator Operators Union, Local 14, of Building Service Employees
International Union.

In addition to voluntarily appearing before said
Commission in San Francisco, at its request, to answer whatever
questions may be asked, it is my desire to submit this background
statement to assist the Commission. Superficial and uninformed
criticism of the recent arbitration award handed down under our
collective bargaining agreement, which award set aside the so-
called "1966 San Francisco Civil Rights Agreement",has resulted

851

in a widespread, distorted view of today's conditions in our
industry in San Francisco.

At the outset, let me say that the Joint Board and
the Unions represented by it have an earnest desire to do everything within their power to insure that there will be no discrimination in San Francisco in our industry. Specifically, we are
taking affirmative action to encourage the employment of more
negroes and other minorities. It is our belief that we, together
with management and under the auspices of the San Francisco Human
Rights Commission, are now already embarked on a meaningful approach
to a workable solution to complete integration of our industry. We
are now fully and irrevocably committed to getting this job done.

The immediate problem, of course, is to get jobs in our
industry for more negroes. Our Local Unions do not discriminate at
this time against negroes or any other minorities, and I assure
you that our Local Unions will not discriminate in the future.

The lack of any existing discrimination by our Locals
is borne out by reference to the NLRB, to the State FEPC, to our
International Union's record, and to our collective bargaining
agreement. Moreover, there now exists a climate of public opinion
and public awareness which we feel is perfectly suited to accom-
plishing the final giant step in our march towards our goal of
complete integration in our industry in our City.

This favorable climate has resulted in large measure
from the aforesaid Arbitration Award and from the resulting
community and industry realization that civil rights problems
can be, and must be, resolved within the framework of the law
and of existing non-discriminatory collective bargaining agreements.

At the time of the Arbitration Award, to present the
true facts to the public and to publicly pledge our intention to
affirmatively work towards ridding our industry of any and all

852

discrimination, our Unions went to the expense of running a
full page ad in the local papers. The words contained in this
ad were not propaganda. To us, they were words to live by, and
we submit that we have done so! The "ad" truthfully sets forth
the background of the Arbitration Award and states our pledge
for affirmative action. The "ad" is equally representative of
our Unions' position today. Therefore, I have attached a copy
of it hereto as Appendix A and request that it be read and
considered as an integral part of this statement.

As pledged in the "ad", our Unions set forth on a
program of affirmative action. After publication of the "ad"
we were invited by the San Francisco Human Rights Commission to
try to find, under its auspices, ways and means of solving the
problem of further integration. We were more than willing to
utilize the offices of the Commission to aid us in finding ways
and means to accomplish our stated objective. However, we first
insisted that the Commission recognize the integrity of our nondiscriminatory collective bargaining agreement. After several
meetings the Commission agreed to do so.

It was our further position that all Employer groups
in our industry in our City should meet with us and with the
Human Rights Commission and that invitations to all Civil Rights
groups who were interested in furthering integration should be
sent out. It was and is our firm belief that the soundest approach
to the problem must of necessity include all interested parties
if a prompt, meaningful and binding solution is to result. Delay
and disappointment naturally followed when after repeated invitations
the major civil rights groups declined to participate in the meetings
called by the Commission. However, we have insisted on carrying on
towards our stated goal, and, with this in mind, we have continued
to meet with the Employer groups under the auspices of the Commission

We have had good meetings, and I sincerely think that
more progress has been made in the last 30 days towards laying
a foundation for solving the problem of integration in our industry
than has been made in the last several years.

Proof of our progress is evidenced by this recent
release from the San Francisco Human Rights Commission:

> A proposed training program in the hotel, motel and
> restaurant industries of San Francisco was agreed upon
> in substance by both labor and management representa-
> tives, at a meeting on March 22, 1967, announced Director
> William Becker of the San Francisco Human Rights
> Commission. The training proposal is the product of
> intensive work done by an industry team, the State
> Division of Apprenticeship Standards and the San
> Francisco School Board.
> "The proposal is noteworthy," said Mr. Becker, "because
> it includes training in job categories covered by all
> of the unions in the Culinary Joint Board. It does not
> now call for the use of any federal funds, and it will
> require brief pre-job training to be provided by the
> San Francisco Unified School District. I want to add",
> Director Becker continued, "that the industry is now
> sharing the proposal with the Bay Area Urban League and the
> five Economic Opportunity Council Area Boards so they can
> suggest changes which the labor-management committee will
> consider before finalizing the proposal."
> The Working Committee also repeated its call for the
> expansion of the various hotel and restaurant training
> programs now regularly conducted by the school system
> in order to provide more entry opportunities for minorities.

. .

Additionally, through the San Francisco Labor Council
the Joint Board and the Local Unions it represents are now
committed to an all-out drive to organize our City's "Chinatown"
and thereby raise up the standards and opportunities of these
minority race employees -- long oppressed by non-union employers.

In summary, the Joint Board and the Local Unions it
represents pledge that we will do all in our power to insure full
integration in our industry in our City. We will keep this pledge!
If the employers cooperate and keep their pledge and if the civil
rights groups lend their good works within the framework of our
lawful, non-discriminatory collective bargaining agreement integration will be accomplished!

Respectfully submitted,

854

JOBS and HOTELS
"A Rational and Orderly Way
To Better Understanding"

WE'RE AGAINST LOW WAGES.

We're also against long hours and sweatshop conditions and employers who push their employees around.

That's our job. Our union was organized—and it exists today—to defend its members against economic exploitation.

The law recognizes us as the sole collective bargaining representative of all San Francisco hotel employees whose jobs fall, in our bargaining unit.

That same law requires us to represent all such employees fairly—all of them, mind you, without regard to race or creed or color or national origin or sex. And without regard to whether they belong to our union.

That's not hard. With us, non-discrimination is a matter of principle and practice as well as law. Why not? We probably represent more members of more minority groups than any organization in town.

The chief tool on our job is our Union contract.

It spells out in detail our wages and working conditions and fringe benefits. It protects our seniority, our right to have our complaints heard and adjusted. It is our Constitution and Declaration of Independence and Bill of Rights rolled up into one. Without it, we would be helpless.

This is the only way we know to keep from being forced to haul luggage or pick up dirty dishes or tend bar or wait on tables for 50 cents an hour—and tips, if any.

WHERE IT STARTED

In the spring of 1964, the Sheraton Palace Hotel was the scene of a massive sit-in. Out of it came the 1964 civil rights agreement, underscoring the equal opportunity employment policy in the city's hotels.

Please note two points about that agreement: 1. Union representatives

took part in writing it. And, 2. It plainly respected the existing Union contracts in the hotels and deliberately avoided conflict with them

Two years later, certain civil rights groups raised the question of renewing the agreement. They used a manufactured dispute involving some maids and the Hilton Hotel as their leverage. Out of it came the 1966 civil rights agreement.

This was different. When certain civil rights leaders were reminded of the Union contracts, they replied, "We don't give a damn about the Union and the collective bargaining agreement." Then they turned around and negotiated a collective bargaining agreement of their own that was in violent conflict with the Union contract.

On July 26, we formally complained that the Hotel Employers had violated their contract with us by negotiating and signing this agreement with these civil rights groups.

Our complaint was submitted to an arbitration board with Robert E. Burns, a prominent attorney and an experienced arbitrator, as impartial

855

chairman On November 17, he
handed down his Award.
Then the roof fell in
The fastest lips in the West hied
from the hip without pausing to look
at any facts. Their comment was uninformed, prejudiced loaded with
self-interest and misinformation 'We
were clobbered

In good conscience and fair play,
it is time to consider these basic
points

1. The Union contract is a necessary and desirable instrument for
preventing economic exploitation
and improving living standards.

2 The Union has a moral and legal
duty to maintain the integrity of its
contract

3. The Union has a concurrent
duty, both moral and legal, to administer its contracts without discrimination or favor

The Burns Arbitration Award is no
obstacle to fair employment or equal
opportunity Actually, along with the
Union's proposal (see below), it
points an orderly and rational way to
better understanding

LEGAL DUTIES VIOLATED

The Burns Award found the 1966
civil rights agreement unlawful, because

1 The law requires the employer
to bargain collectively only with the
chosen representative of his employees. It also requires him not to
bargain with any other employee
representative. The hotel employers
violated these duties.

2 The civil rights groups acted as
a "labor organization," as defined by
the law and the courts. The Award
says "The civil rights group had no
right to represent . . . the employees
of the hotels with respect to terms or
conditions of employment since the
union was the authorized bargaining
representative."

AGAINST PUBLIC POLICY

Further, the Burns Award held the
1966 civil rights agreement void and
unenforceable.

Its purpose and effect unlawfully
require discrimination in favor of
Afro-Americans and against those
who do not belong to some minority
group. The Award says this is
against public policy of the United
States and State of California . . . and
contrary to the statutes made and
provided to prevent discrimination
in employment."

POINTS OF CONFLICT

Finally, the Award found that the
1966 civil rights agreement is in di-

rect conflict at several crucial points
with the Union contract

1 Seniority rights in the contract,
the Award says, give an employee "a
preferred claim to present and future
work in the industry . . . provides
security to the employee as he ex-
pends his working years. Seniority is
a goal most employees seek through
their collective bargaining." These
rights are vested by law in the employees, the Award says, neither the
union nor the employers nor any
third party can legally disturb them

2 The contract provides for binding arbitration of grievances. The
civil rights agreement also provides
for arbitration The Award finds,
however, that the civil rights agreement commits to an arbiter questions which "inevitably" affect the
Union contract and the rights of the
employees, but without allowing the
Union or its members proper or legal
representation.

ANOTHER QUESTION

Nevertheless, questions of real or alleged discrimination hang on The
Burns Award makes these findings

1 The Union contract requires the
hotels to apply to the Union for
available qualified employees But,
within specified limits, the hotels
reserve the final decision on the
"suitability and competence" of employees They retain the "right to
choose from among all applicants
and, within those limits, "to reject
any job applicant referred by the
Union" Thus, the contract puts
responsibility for job discrimination
on the employer who has the power
to hire and fire.

2 The contract requires the Union
to pick applicants for referral on a
nondiscriminatory basis. Beyond
this, the Award notes, "the Union
has the clear, legal duty to represent
fairly all of the employees . . ." including "the obligation of the Union
to abstain from racial discrimination.";

3 Any person, the Award underscores, who believes the hiring provisions have not been properly applied, may appeal — without cost to
him — to an impartial arbitration
board

4 The Award declares further:
"The union has the obligation by
law and under its contract with the
hotels not to discriminate against
any person, minority or other group.
The union fully performed its obligations under the collective bar-
reement "

5. Particularly in the Hilton Hotel dispute with a number of its maids. The Award states, "There was no discrimination against Negroes or any minority race or against any person by the Hilton Hotel, the association, or the unions. There is nothing in the record which in any-way indicates any such discrimination. To the contrary, the record established that the union promptly and successfully represented the complaining maids at the Hilton Hotel in their grievances."

6. The Award finds that the maids quit their jobs and picketed the Hilton Hotel, refusing to return to work "even though they were repeatedly requested to do so" by the Union business agent. The Award adds: "The maids violated their obligations under the collective bargaining agreement by engaging in a work stoppage, picketing, and refusing to utilize the grievance procedures of the collective bargaining agreement..."

STRANGE BEDFELLOWS

The advocates of "right to work" laws and the compulsory open shop have been quick to denounce the Union. They are strange recruits to the cause of equal opportunity and civil rights.

The Chamber of Commerce and the Federated Employers fought fair employment legislation – in San Francisco and in Sacramento. We have fair employment laws now largely because the union movement insisted on having them.

The labor movement has fought for more jobs, for better housing, for greater educational opportunity. It has made its own proposals for affirmative action to expand job and housing opportunities. But the men with money are suddenly struck dumb.

Civil rights spokesmen who join these strange bedfellows in their anti-union cause serve their followers badly. Any Southern worker can testify to the results of "right to work" laws – Negro workers in the South can testify even more eloquently.

They create no jobs, these right-to-work laws; they only cut the pay, stretch the hours, and wreck job conditions.

Minority group workers and labor belong in close alliance, not in armed camps.

We do not pretend to know all the answers to the knotty questions of civil rights. Nor do we righteously claim that we, alone, are without sin. We are human and fallible; that's why we make this proposal:

We welcome the recognition that our collective bargaining contracts are vital, living documents, an important and necessary part of economic life.

We pledge our continued efforts to administer our contracts without discrimination and to work toward expanded opportunity and higher living standards for San Franciscans of whatever racial, religious, or ethnic background.

We stand ready to meet with the Human Rights Commission, with the responsible representatives of civil rights groups and minority communities, and with our employers, to discuss, to explore, to help where we can in resolving mutual problems.

Exhibit No. 14*

INDIVIDUAL COMPLAINT

858

Exhibit No. 15
Report From U.S. Employment Service

FUNCTIONS AND RESPONSIBILITIES OF THE REGIONAL OFFICE OF THE BUREAU
OF EMPLOYMENT SECURITY WITH RESPECT TO EQUAL EMPLOYMENT OPPORTUNITIES
AND OTHER PHASES OF NON-DISCRIMINATION CAN BE DIVIDED INTO TWO MAJOR
CATEGORIES: (1) THE BUREAU OF EMPLOYMENT SECURITY IS RESPONSIBLE TO
SEE THAT STATE EMPLOYMENT SECURITY AGENCIES ADHERE TO ALL PROVISIONS OF
THE CIVIL RIGHTS ACT INSOFAR AS INTERNAL PERSONNEL PRACTICES ARE CONCERNED.
THIS HAS TO DO WITH HIRING PRACTICES, TRAINING PROGRAMS, AND PROMOTIONAL
POLICIES, AS THESE ALL INVOLVE EQUITABLE STAFFING OF THE STATE AGENCY
ITSELF; (2) AS A PUBLIC AGENCY OFFERING EMPLOYMENT SERVICES TO
INDIVIDUALS AND TO EMPLOYERS, THE EMPLOYMENT SECURITY AGENCY HAS A
RESPONSIBILITY TO PROMOTE EQUAL EMPLOYMENT POLICIES ON THE PART OF
EMPLOYERS AND TO ASSIST APPLICANTS IN OBTAINING APPROPRIATE EMPLOYMENT
BASED ON QUALIFICATIONS, AND WITHOUT REGARD TO THEIR STATUS WITH RESPECT
TO RACE, COLOR OR SEX.

THE SAN FRANCISCO REGIONAL OFFICE HAS TRADITIONALLY WORKED CLOSELY WITH
STATE AGENCIES ON BOTH CATEGORIES OF EQUAL EMPLOYMENT OPPORTUNITY
DESCRIBED ABOVE. SUCH ACTIVITY HAS BEEN IN RESPONSE TO LONG STANDING
BUREAU POLICY REGARDING NON-DISCRIMINATION.

(1) THE REGIONAL OFFICE HAS BEEN CONTINUALLY AWARE OF ITS REQUIREMENTS OF
MANNING THE REGIONAL OFFICE ORGANIZATION UNDER THE EQUAL OPPORTUNITY PRIN-
CIPLE. AT PRESENT THERE ARE ON THE STAFF 20, OR 40% OF PROFESSIONALS OF

PREPARED BY: GLENN E. BROCKWAY, REGIONAL ADMINISTRATOR, BUREAU
                    OF EMPLOYMENT SECURITY, U. S. DEPARTMENT OF LABOR,
                    REGION X, SAN FRANCISCO

SUBMITTED TO: UNITED STATES COMMISSION ON CIVIL RIGHTS

AT: COMMISSION HEARING, SAN FRANCISCO, CALIFORNIA

DATE: MAY 1, 1967

859

MINORITY EXTRACTION AND 6, OR 27.3% NON-PROFESSIONALS.

IN 1965 THE NATIONAL OFFICE OF THE BUREAU REQUESTED THAT WE LOAN A FULL
TIME STAFF MEMBER TO FOLLOW UP ON COMPLAINTS RECEIVED BY THE EQUAL
EMPLOYMENT OPPORTUNITY COMMISSION, OR BY THE DEPARTMENT OF LABOR, OF
ALLEGED DISCRIMINATION IN EMPLOYMENT WHERE STATE EMPLOYMENT SERVICES
WERE INVOLVED. THIS WAS DONE, AND WAS CONSISTENT WITH RESPONSIBILITIES
SET FORTH IN TITLE VI OF THE CIVIL RIGHTS ACT OF 1964. THIS REGIONAL
OFFICE EMPLOYEE IS UNDER NATIONAL OFFICE DIRECTION AND CONTROL, AND IS
NOT RESPONSIBLE TO ANY REGIONAL OFFICE, THUS ASSURING IMPARTIALITY IN
FACT GATHERING AND RECOMMENDATIONS FOR ACTION. THIS IS AN ON GOING
ACTIVITY, BASED ON COMPLAINTS OR CONTINUOUS INSPECTIONS OF LOCAL OFFICES.

REPRESENTATIVES FROM THE OFFICE OF THE SECRETARY AND THE NATIONAL OFFICE
OF THE BUREAU DISCUSS THE RESULTS OF THESE INVESTIGATIONS WITH THE
REGIONAL OFFICE AND THE STATES, AND REQUEST THAT A COURSE OF ACTION BE
TAKEN TO CORRECT ANY DEFICIENCIES FOUND. THESE REQUESTS ARE IN WRITING,
AS ARE CHARGES AND FINDINGS.

THE REGIONAL OFFICE REQUESTS PERIODIC REPORTS OF STATE EMPLOYMENT SERVICE
STAFFING PATTERNS TO DETERMINE ETHNIC COMPOSITION BY OCCUPATION AND
RESPONSIBILITY LEVEL. WE PROVIDE GUIDANCE AND ASSISTANCE TO STATES TO
PROMOTE ADEQUATE HIRING AND PROMOTIONAL PRACTICES, AND REQUEST REMEDIAL
ACTION WHERE SHORTCOMINGS ARE FOUND.

THE REGIONAL OFFICE HAS INITIATED BI-REGIONAL AND REGIONAL TRAINING

PROGRAMS TO PROMOTE ENLIGHTENED STATE ADMINISTRATIVE AND PERSONNEL
PRACTICES. STATE AGENCIES HAVE IN TURN HELD TRAINING SESSIONS TO
FURTHER DISSEMINATE THIS INFORMATION WITHIN THEIR AGENCIES.

THE REGIONAL OFFICE AND THE STATE EMPLOYMENT SERVICE RECENTLY CONDUCTED
A HOUSEHOLD SURVEY IN TWO POVERTY AREAS OF SAN FRANCISCO. THIS WAS
THE FIRST SURVEY OF ITS KIND AND PROVIDED IMPORTANT STATISTICS WITH
RESPECT TO EMPLOYMENT, SUB-EMPLOYMENT AND UNEMPLOYMENT AMONG MINORITIES.

(2) THE SECOND CATEGORY OF EQUAL EMPLOYMENT POLICY MAY BE DESCRIBED AS
EXTERNAL, AS OPPOSED TO THE INTERNAL ACTIVITIES ENGAGED IN TO ASSURE
APPROPRIATE EMPLOYMENT PRACTICES IN PERSONNEL PERFORMANCE AND PROCEDURES
OF THE STATE AGENCY.

SINCE THE LATE 1940'S THE REGIONAL CHIEF OF THE EMPLOYMENT SERVICE (NOW
REGIONAL DIRECTOR) HAS ENCOURAGED STATE AGENCIES TO ADOPT AFFIRMATIVE
POLICIES TOWARD EMPLOYERS AND APPLICANTS TO ASSURE MAXIMUM MANPOWER
UTILIZATION THROUGH CONSIDERATION OF QUALIFICATIONS RATHER THAN NON-
OCCUPATIONAL REQUIREMENTS. SERVICE TO MINORITIES HAS BEEN ONE OF OUR
MAJOR SPECIAL WORKER PROGRAMS, ALONG WITH SERVICES TO YOUTH, OLDER WORKERS,
HANDICAPPED AND VETERANS.

AS SOCIAL AND ECONOMIC CONDITIONS HAVE CHANGED, AND AS ATTITUDES HAVE
BECOME INCREASINGLY ENLIGHTENED, ADDITIONAL EMPHASIS HAS BEEN PLACED ON
MORE DIRECT AND SPECIFIC SERVICES TO SPECIAL WORKERS, INCLUDING MINORITIES.
THE REGIONAL OFFICE HAS ALSO RESPONDED TO BUREAU POLICY RESULTING FROM
LEGISLATION. WITH THIS INCREASED EMPHASIS, IT WAS NECESSARY FOR THE
REGIONAL OFFICE TO EXPAND STAFF TIME ALLOCATED TO THESE SERVICES. IN

861

1961 A FULL TIME STAFF MEMBER WAS ASSIGNED TO THE REGIONAL U. S. EMPLOY-
MENT SERVICE TO SPONSOR SPECIAL WORKER PROGRAMS OF STATE AGENCIES IN
THIS REGION. THE SPECIAL WORKER REPRESENTATIVE CONCENTRATED ON REVIEW
AND EVALUATION OF STATE AGENCY POLICIES AND ACTIVITIES AS THEY RELATED
TO MINORITIES, AND OTHERS. CONTINUING VISITS HAVE BEEN MADE TO STATE,
CENTRAL AND LOCAL OFFICES, AND DISCUSSIONS HELD WITH ADMINISTRATIVE AND
OPERATING STAFF AT ALL LEVELS OF THE STATE AGENCY ORGANIZATION. WHERE
SHORTCOMINGS WERE FOUND, EITHER IN ATTITUDE OR PRACTICES, THESE WERE
BROUGHT TO THE ATTENTION OF APPROPRIATE ADMINISTRATORS AND PERSONNEL AT
BOTH THE LOCAL AND STATE LEVEL. FOLLOW-UP PROGRAMS WERE DEVELOPED TO
ASSURE THAT PROPER STEPS WERE TAKEN TO ASSURE COMPLIANCE WITH BUREAU
POLICY. WHEN PROBLEMS OCCURRED, WHICH THEY DID IN SUCH AREAS AS LACK
OF QUALIFICATIONS BY MINORITIES, LACK OF ACCEPTANCE BY EMPLOYERS, AND
POOR SOCIAL ATTITUDES ON THE PART OF SOME EMPLOYEES, GUIDANCE AND ASSIST-
ANCE WERE PROVIDED TO THE STATES TO HELP THEM IN OVERCOMING THESE
PROBLEMS. TO OUR KNOWLEDGE NO COMPLAINTS HAVE BEEN FILED UNDER TITLE VII
OF THE CIVIL RIGHTS ACT OF 1964 AGAINST THE CALIFORNIA STATE EMPLOYMENT
SERVICE.

LOCAL OFFICE EVALUATIONS ARE CONTINUOUSLY CONDUCTED TO ASSESS THE QUALITY
OF SERVICES BEING PROVIDED TO APPLICANTS. APPLICATIONS, COUNSELING
RECORDS AND REFERRALS ARE EXAMINED, AS WERE ACTIONS TAKEN BY EMPLOYERS
IN RESPONSE TO REFERRALS OF MINORITIES. WHERE REAL OR STATISTICAL
INEQUITIES ARE OBSERVED, THESE ARE REPORTED TO STATE OFFICIALS WITH A
REQUEST THAT REMEDIAL ACTION BE TAKEN. FOLLOW-UP IS PROVIDED EITHER
BY LATER REVIEW OR BY ANALYSIS OF SUBSEQUENT REPORTS FROM STATE AGENCIES.

862

AN IMPORTANT RESPONSIBILITY OF THE REGIONAL OFFICE IS THE ADMINISTRATION
OF THE MANPOWER DEVELOPMENT AND TRAINING ACT OF 1962. A STEADY INCREASE
IN MINORITY INVOLVEMENT IN TRAINING PROJECTS HAS OCCURRED SINCE THE
INCEPTION OF THE PROGRAM. IN REGION X ALMOST 90% OF INDIVIDUALS
CURRENTLY IN TRAINING ARE MEMBERS OF MINORITY GROUPS. OUR MANPOWER
DEVELOPMENT AND UTILIZATION DIVISION, THROUGH CONTACT WITH STATE EMPLOY-
MENT SERVICE AGENCIES AND OTHER ORGANIZATIONS, ASSURES THAT TRAINING
OPPORTUNITIES ARE RESERVED TO THE MAXIMUM EXTENT POSSIBLE FOR DISADVANTAGED
PERSONS, INCLUDING MINORITIES.

THE REGIONAL OFFICE WAS INSTRUMENTAL IN CALIFORNIA, ARIZONA AND NEVADA
IN PERSUADING THESE STATES TO ASSIGN A FULL TIME INDIVIDUAL TO THE
CENTRAL OFFICE STAFF TO SUPERVISE SERVICES TO MINORITIES (CALIFORNIA
NOW HAS TWO STATE MINORITY SPECIALISTS). IN ADDITION, CALIFORNIA
HAS A FULL TIME MINORITY SPECIALIST IN EACH OF ITS FOUR ADMINISTRATIVE
AREAS, AND AT LEAST ONE PERSON IN EACH LOCAL OFFICE HAS FULL RESPONSI-
BILITY FOR EMPLOYMENT SERVICES TO MINORITIES WITHIN THAT OFFICE'S JURIS-
DICTION. STATE, AREA AND LOCAL MINORITY SPECIALISTS SPEND A SIGNIFICANT
PORTION OF THEIR TIME WORKING WITH EMPLOYERS TO REDUCE EMPLOYMENT BARRIERS,
MAINTAINING CONTACT WITH MINORITY GROUP ORGANIZATIONS TO KEEP THEM ADVISED
OF EMPLOYMENT SERVICE PROGRAMS AND MEETING WITH OTHER AGENCIES AND THE
GENERAL PUBLIC TO APPRISE THE COMMUNITY OF THE IMPORTANCE OF EQUAL
EMPLOYMENT OPPORTUNITIES.

DUE TO SOCIAL AND ECONOMIC CONDITIONS, THE ETHNIC COMPOSITION OF THE
AGRICULTURAL WORK FORCE IN THE SOUTHWEST IS HEAVILY MEXICAN-AMERICAN.

TO SURMOUNT A SERIOUS LANGUAGE BARRIER, AND TO PROMOTE MORE EFFECTIVE
INTERVIEWING RELATIONSHIPS, THE REGIONAL OFFICE HAS ENCOURAGED STATE
EMPLOYMENT SERVICE AGENCIES TO HIRE A LARGE NUMBER OF MEXICAN-AMERICAN
INTERVIEWERS AND COUNSELORS IN THEIR FARM LABOR RECRUITMENT PROGRAMS.

OVER A PERIOD OF SEVERAL YEARS, THE REGIONAL ADMINISTRATOR, ASSISTANT
REGIONAL ADMINISTRATOR, REGIONAL USES DIRECTOR, AND THE CHIEF OF
SPECIAL WORKER SERVICES HAVE MADE PUBLIC APPEARANCES THROUGHOUT THE
REGION WHERE THEY HAVE SPOKEN TO ALL TYPES OF GROUPS AND ORGANIZATIONS
ON THE SUBJECT OF EQUAL EMPLOYMENT.

ALTHOUGH A GREAT DEAL HAS YET TO BE DONE IN PROVIDING TRUE EQUAL
EMPLOYMENT OPPORTUNITY TO ALL CITIZENS, OUR REVIEW OF THIS PROGRAM
OVER A PERIOD OF 10 YEARS REVEALS THAT SUBSTANTIAL PROGRESS HAS BEEN
MADE IN REGION X. WE HAVE SEEN IMPORTANT CHANGES AND IMPROVEMENTS IN
THE ATTITUDES OF STATE EMPLOYMENT SERVICE PERSONNEL. THERE HAS BEEN
INCREASINGLY EFFECTIVE ADMINISTRATION OF EQUAL EMPLOYMENT POLICIES.
EMPLOYERS HAVE SIGNIFICANTLY MODIFIED THEIR HIRING PRACTICES TO CONFORM
TO MORE ENLIGHTENED STANDARDS SOUGHT BY THE BUREAU. THE MINORITY COMMUNITY
ITSELF, THOUGH NOT YET SATISFIED, HAS ADMITTED THROUGH ITS LEADERSHIP
THAT IMPORTANT GAINS HAVE BEEN MADE IN THIS REGION. ON SEVERAL OCCASIONS
LOCAL AND STATE MINORITY ORGANIZATIONS HAVE PRESENTED OFFICIAL RECOGNITION
TO STATE ADMINISTRATORS AND LOCAL PERSONNEL FOR LEADERSHIP THEY HAVE
DEMONSTRATED IN FOSTERING EQUAL EMPLOYMENT OPPORTUNITIES. REGIONAL
PERSONNEL HAVE ALSO BEEN COMMENDED FOR THEIR EFFORTS.

864

Exhibit No. 16

POSITION STATEMENT
on
FEDERAL CONTRACT COMPLIANCE

The following position is based ón a study of Executive Order #11246, dated Tuesday, September 28, 1965; Rules and Regulations of the President's Committee on Equal Employment Opportunity, effective July 22, 1961, as amended September 7, 1963; and a Memorandum from Edward C. Sylvester Jr., Director of the Office of Federal Contract Compliance, Department of Labor, to Heads of all Agencies, Subject: San Francisco Bay Area Construction Contracts.

A. Major Weaknesses of Compliance Program

    1. The non-diserimination provision of the Executive Order which refers to "affirmative action" is so vague that it cannot be used as it is written as the basis for assuring equal employment opportunities.

    2. This vagueness is particularly alarming because it is only when a contractor fails to comply with the non-discrimination provisions of his contract that the Secretary of Labor or the appropriate federal contracting agency can impose those sanctions which would compel the contractor to take positive steps to assure equal employment opportunity.

    3. It is essential that the non-discrimination provisions of the Order be modified to ensure that the minimally acceptable criteria for "affirmative action" be clearly stated. Apparently, no effort was made to establish criteria in the construction field until the December 22nd Memorandum from the Director of the Office of Federal Contract Compliance, Department of Labor.

    4. Although the December 22nd Memorandum is a step in the right direction, it has two major weaknesses. First of all, the criteria established are not strong enough. Secondly, since it is not an order but merely a request, it has no enforcement power over the agencies to which it is directed.

    5. Apparently, no rules and regulations have been published by the Secretary of Labor since Executive Order #11246 was signed.

B. Specific Recommendations for Improvement

    1. The Secretary of Labor should devise rules and regulations which supercede the old rules and regulations of the President's Committee that will clarify the non-discrimination provisions of the Order, and incorporate the ideas enumerated below.

    2. In light of the ethnic composition of the current unemployed work force, the history of racial prejudice and discrimination in this country and the present government's avowed aims of correcting past and present injustices, w we submit that two fundamentally important aspects of the "equal employment opportunity" concept be recognized:

        a. Each employer must ensure that his recruiting and screening policies and practices neither systematically exclude nor significantly diminish the chances that the following persons or groups of persons be

865

considered for employment at all occupational levels: (1) members of any particular ethnic or other group in the geographical area that has a history of not being equitably represented in the work force, and (2) individuals of whatever group who are capable of performing the job.

b. Each employer must make special provisions to ensure that members of certain groups that have been historically denied a fair chance of obtaining employment (e.g., ethnic minority groups) will be preferentially selected for journeyman and training positions in those occupations where minority group representation is significantly lower than the representation of minority group persons in the population.

3. The existence of an acceptable affirmative action plan must be one of the preconditions for the awarding of a contract.

4. The following should be added to the list of minimal criteria for an "acceptable" affirmative action plan:

a. Minority group persons must be employed in all occupations of the work force to, an extent which is not significantly lower than their representation in the surrounding community or larger geographical area, whichever is higher.

b. When the minority group persons are represented in an occupation to a degree which is significantly less than their representation in the surrounding community or larger geographical area, the employer must give evidence of persistent and prolonged efforts to increase the number of minority group employees. He must be able to clearly enumerate whatever specific obstacles have prevented him from hiring minority group persons in that occupation.

c. Prime contractors must notify unions with which they have collective bargaining agreements, and must insist that their subcontractors in turn notify the unions with which they have agreements, that the contractors are bound by the provisions of Executive Order #11246, that the union must cooperate with the contractor in reaching the objectives of the contractor's affirmative action plan, and that if union policies or practices interfere with the contractor's execution of his plan, the union will be considered an obstacle to the contractor's fulfilling his obligations under the Order, and the union will, therefore, be subject to referral to the Department of Justice per Section 209(a)(2) of the Order.

5. The purpose of pre-award conference must be to ascertain whether the contractor is able to execute an affirmative action plan which is acceptable. The contract must not be awarded if the affirmative action plan is judged to be not acceptable or if the contractor is unable to give clear evidence of the manner in which he intends to execute his plan.

6. Representation from the minority community at pre-award conferences is essential. Preference should be given to Civil Rights groups as representatives of the minority community.

866

POSITION STATEMENT: FEDERAL CONTRACT COMPLIANCE

7. Reports which detail the racial composition of the work force in all occupations must be submitted to the appropriate contracting agency at least on a weekly basis.

8. These reports must be reviewed regularly by the agency as one way of evaluating the effectiveness of the contractor's affirmative action program.

9. All records and correspondence related to compliance with Executive Order #11246 must be a matter of public record, and copies must be made available upon request.

10. A regular method must be devised by the agency to periodically determine whether the data reported by the contractors is correct.

11. The Secretary of Labor and the appropriate contracting agency must notify all unions that they should actively participate with contractors in carrying out acceptable affirmative action plans, and that if their policies or practices prevent the contractor from fulfilling his obligations, the union will be referred to the Department of Justice per Section 209(a)(2) of the Order.

12. To the extent that union policy prohibits the contractor from fulfilling the obligations of his affirmative action plan, the Secretary of Labor and/or the appropriate contracting agency, must stand ready to refer the union to the Department of Justice as provided in Section 209(a)(2) of the Order.

13. When the Department of Justice receives a referral from the Secretary of Labor or from a federal contracting agency which indicates that a labor union has been obstructing a contractor in his efforts to carry out an acceptable affirmative action plan, the Department of Justice must stand ready to prosecute.

Prepared by:

COMMITTEE ON GOVERNMENT CONTRACT COMPLIANCE
BERKELEY BRANCH N.A.A.C.P.
LaVerda Allen
William B. Woodson, Ph.D.
Co-Chairmen

Excerpts from Executive Order 11246

SEC. 202. Except in contracts exempted in accordance with Section 204 of this Order, all Government contracting agencies shall include in every Government cont~act hereafter entered into the following provisions:

"During the performance of this contract, the contractor agrees as follows:

"(1) The contractor will not discriminate against any employee or applicant for employment because of race, creed, color, or national origin. The contractor will take affirmative action to ensure that applicants are employed, and that employees are treated during employment, without regard to their race, creed, color, or national origin. Such action shall include, but not be limited to the following: employment, upgrading, demotion, or transfer; recruitment or recruitment advertising layoff or termination; rates of pay or other forms of compensation; and selection for training, including apprenticeship. The contractor agrees to post in conspicuous places, available to employees and applicants for employment, notices to be provided by the contracting officer setting forth the provisions of this nondiscrimination clause.

* * *

SEC. 209. (a) In accordance with such rules, regulations, or orders as the Secretary of Labor may issue or adopt, the Secretary or the appropriate contracting agency may:

* * *

(2) Recommend to the Department of Justice that, in cases in which there is substantial or material violation or the threat of substantial or material violation of the contractual provisions set forth in Section 202 of this Order, appropriate proceedings be brought to enforce those provisions, including the enjoining, within the limitations of applicable law, of organizations, individuals, or groups who prevent directly or indirectly, or seek to prevent directly or indirectly, compliance with the provisions of this Order.

* * *

868

Exhibit No. 17

745 Franklin Street, Room 302
San Francisco, California 94102

April 28 1967

Mr. Howard Glickstein
U. S. Civil Rights Commission
Maurice Western Hotel
761 Post Street
San Francisco California 94109

Dear Mr. Glickstein:

Enclosed is the statement I have prepared in response to the
request of Mr. Glen Brockway to Mr. Peter Weinberger on
April 13, 1967. This portion is in response to the second
part of the request, covering the Department's activities in
the Oakland and San Francisco areas in behalf of ethnic
minorities.

I will be available to answer any questions you may wish to
raise.

Yours very truly,

Marc W. Johnson
Area Manpower Administrator

BM:eb

REPORT TO UNITED STATES CIVIL RIGHTS COMMISSION

BY

MARC W. JOHNSON
AREA MANPOWER ADMINISTRATOR

CALIFORNIA DEPARTMENT OF EMPLOYMENT

SERVICES FOR ETHNIC MINORITIES

OAKLAND - SAN FRANCISCO AREA

May 1, 1967

Services for Ethnic Minorities - Oakland-San Francisco Area

I have been requested to submit a description of the activities of the
Department of Employment in promoting and assuring equal employment for
minority groups in my administrative area. Since this particular phase of
our total program has received special emphasis in recent years, and is a
program in which we are all most vitally concerned personally, I am happy
to do so.

In the Bay Area, both in San Francisco and the East Bay, poverty pockets have
been identified where unemployment rates, especially for ethnic minorities, far
exceed the overall rate. A substantial portion of the middle class population,
and much of our metropolitan industrial establishments are moving to the suburbs
while the disadvantaged remain in greater numbers in the cities. In San Francisco,
five poverty pockets, or "Target Areas" have been identified: Hunters Point-
Bayview, Western Addition, Mission, Chinatown-North Beach, and the Central City.
The ethnic characteristics of these neighborhoods vary, but the ghetto conditions
are present.

In San Francisco, 25% of the population are of racial, religious, and ethnic
minority backgrounds: Negroes, Spanish-speaking, Oriental, and American Indians,
as reported in the recent annual report of the San Francisco Human Rights Commission. In the target areas, the problem of employment status figures prominently.
According to the latest figures available, while 18% of the white families in San
Francisco fall below the poverty line established by the state, over 30% of the
families in the Mission District fall below that line, 40% of the families in
Chinatown, 40% of the families in Western Addition, and 60% of the families in
Hunters Point. 12% of the heads of families in these areas are unemployed, and
the others are concentrated in low occupational classifications.

In the East Bay, severe problems have been identified in Oakland; almost two
thirds of the population in the four identified target areas are non-whites
(Negro and other). Of the total population of Oakland, about 36% were found to
be Negro and other non-white ethnic groups. Almost 75% of these ethnic minorities
reside in the target areas.

The unemployment rate for target areas residents is approximately 10.6% for males,
16.3% for women, compared to 6.4% and 10.1% respectively for all of Oakland.
In individual target areas, the unemployment rate varies from 7.0% to 15.9% for
males, 8.1% to 20.1% for females. These figures were derived from an abstract
of the preliminary tabulations from a sample census prepared for the Department of
Employment by the Survey Research Center, University of California in 1966, a copy
of which I am attaching for your further information. The survey covers in detail
social and economic characteristics of the population of Oakland. (Exhibit 1)

As early as 1947, a Minority Employment Advisory Committee was established in
Coastal Area. This group is composed of local citizens representing various
employers, unions, educational, religious, civic, and civil rights groups. Its
function is to advise us on minority group employment problems. This Committee is
still active and forms an important adjunct to our program. The structure of the
committee has varied from time to time, depending on our needs and community
response.

At the present time, two studies are under way, at the suggestion of the committee.
One study, being carried out in conjunction with the California State Personnel
Board, will list State jobs for which unskilled and semi-skilled applicants could
qualify. It is planned that these job openings which the State is having difficulty
in filling can be brought to the attention of employed minorities seeking these
types of jobs. The State "hiring freeze" has temporarily halted this project,
but it will continue as soon as conditions will allow. A second study is being

conducted by the Area Research and Statistics section on referrals and placements by ethnic group in various local offices, to provide concrete information
on which to base recommendations for future activities. By identifying our
problem areas, and the techniques and methods used to bring about effective
minority placement activities in the successful operations, the total operation
can be strengthened.

In 1963, the first Youth Opportunities Center in the nation was opened, providing
outreach services to a disadvantaged area - Hunters Point in San Francisco. It
was the first such center where the public employment service was the dominant
agency, and has served as a prototype for others in various parts of the country.
Agencies participating in addition to the Employment Service were the Bayview
Neighborhood Center, Hunters Point Boys Club, Langley-Porter Neuropsychiatric
Institute, and San Francisco Housing Authority, Public Welfare Department,
Police Department and the Unified School District, as well as UC School of
Criminology, and Youth for Service - providing a variety of services. It was
discovered that the most intense problem of the youngsters in this area was not
finding jobs for them but in making them employable. Years of ghetto living,
malnutrition, poor housing, insufficient education, and the pervading air of
defeat had left scars too deep to be removed by the simple process of referral
to a job. To assist these people effectively, it would be necessary to deal
with the total person and assist him to solve many problems before placement in
itself would be a permanent solution. Innovations in terms of intensive counseling,
group counseling, use of consultant services, and many other approaches were
attempted here.

As the values of these approaches became apparent, and the success of reaching
the target group by locating in the neighborhood became apparent, plans were made
for YOC branches in other localities and other target areas in San Francisco.
In preparation for the expansion and development of other YOC branch locations,
special training for outreach personnel was conducted. In addition to sociologists
from the academic community to provide the historical and sociological background
for understanding problems of ethnic and poverty groups, indigenous leaders from
the "grass roots" provided frank expressions of the feelings of the potential
client group, to promote a deeper understanding on the part of staff members for
the problems faced by this group. Sensitivity training was also provided, in
order to assist staff members deal more effectively with the applicant group.
By 1966 YOC branches were opened in the Mission, in Western Addition, and interviewers stationed in North Beach-Chinatown, in addition to the Central YOC, which
had been in existence for several years.

A review of the most recent registration statistics from the YOC's indicate that
the outreach offices are reaching the ethnic groups that do not habitually come
into the centrally located offices.

The Central YOC including the Chinatown out-station registered 1114 whites during
March 1967, 314 Negroes, 105 Spanish surnamed, and 233 others. The Mission Branch,
located in a Spanish-speaking neighborhood, registered 93 whites, 33 Negroes,
16 Spanish surnamed, and 5 others. Western Addition YOC, in a predominantly
Negro neighborhood, registered 29 whites, 72 Negroes, and 2 other; Hunters Point,
in a predominantly Negro neighborhood registered 3 whites, 58 Negroes, and 1
Spanish surnamed. These figures indicate that an appropriately higher percentage
of an ethnic group registers in the outreach than could normally be expected in
a downtown office. I am attaching charts with these figures. (Exhibit 2)

872

In attempting to provide effective outreach service, it became apparent that
a different type of person was necessary on the staff to establish communication
with the indigenous community. A new civil service classification was established
for "Employment Community Worker", the primary qualification being the ability
to relate to the target community. Indigenous personnel were chosen for these
jobs, and great flexibility was allowed in assigning job duties. These people
were to move about in the community, to "reach out" to the pool hall, street
corner, or wherever youth gathered, to acquaint them with services available
through the YOC, and speaking the language of the ghetto, persuade them to avail
themselves of these services. The position was written into the promotional
pattern of career jobs, so that the chance for advancement would be available
to the Employment Community Worker. The incumbents are more than proving their
worth in serving as the liaison between professional staff and the client. An
equally important phase of the assignment, unforeseen at the time of its inception,
is the support to the applicant in the job seeking situation and follow-through
when employment begins. This personal attention may often be the critical factor
in attaining or retaining employment.

In 1963, representatives of the San Francisco chapter of the NAACP called upon
the Department of Employment for assistance in the employment problems of Negroes.
A registry or Skill Survey was planned whereby Negroes could indicate the desire
and qualifications for employment, or for better employment. The registration
was accomplished by volunteer workers from many community organizations. 2276
persons registered. In addition to job referrals and placements for a portion
of these applicants, important data was collected pointing to the need for
training and upgrading, and for out reach services. Many of the registrants were
individuals in need of services but who would not come into our offices to register.
This project made it clear that the Department must go out into the deprived
community and seek those in need of employment counseling, motivational services,
training and job placement.

Outreach services for adults in the identified target areas were developed in
the Adult Opportunity Centers, established in late 1965 in target neighborhoods.
In these new offices many new techniques were tried. Job Workshops help to
prepare the individual to make an effective job search; tutoring programs have
helped to prepare applicants to pass Civil Service Examinations and to become
more employable. Special training programs, in addition to the MDTA financed
programs have supplied needed skills to trainees in such fields as typing and
key-punch operation. Assistance in obtaining a driver's license, required for
many jobs, is provided.

Outreach service is also provided through the State Service Center, where an
Employment Service component joins with other agencies in providing "one-stop"
service.

Following the August 1966 disturbances in Hunters Point, when the Chamber of
Commerce and San Francisco employers rallied to provide jobs for youth, the
Employment Service staffed a Job Center through which these job orders were
funnelled.

Studies over the past few years indicate the enrollments in MDTA classes in San
Francisco have consistently included 60-70% ethnic minorities. I am attaching
the latest report showing personal characteristics including racial data for
trainees enrolled in institutional MDTA classes in San Francisco for the year
ending June 30, 1966. Almost 64% of the enrollees were ethnic minorities.
Current and upcoming programs have been designed for the disadvantaged, so it
is anticipated that this ratio will continue.   (Exhibit 3)

In the East Bay, as in San Francisco, poverty pockets identified as target areas indicated the need for outreach services. In 1963, a group of employers in Oakland, concerned with the high unemployment and welfare costs, especially among members of the Negro community, sought a means of reaching into the Negro community and making offers of employment to those with identified unused skills. After contacting other groups without success, they approached the Department of Employment for advice and possible assistance. The need for training and upgrading of the minorities was identified as a critical problem.

The result of considerable consultations among the employer group, leaders of the minority community, and Department representatives was an application for special funds to finance a project to bring into gainful employment hard-core, long-term unemployed members of the minority labor force, with particular emphasis on the head of household. It was designated as an "Experimental and Demonstration Project" with funds being granted on the basis that there was no similar activity being conducted anywhere in the United States. Offices were opened in West Oakland and East Oakland, in the heart of the Negro ghettos. A third and fourth office was opened later in the Fruitvale area, where emphasis is placed on the Mexican-American and other Spanish-speaking groups, and in North Oakland, also a predominantly Negro district. These are housed in the premises of the Neighborhood Service Centers, facilities of the Oakland Economic Development Council, the CAP in Oakland. Shared job orders were received through the regular Employment Service office and applicants registered. However, most of the job orders required skills which did not exist among any of the applicants registered with the project; most of the minority applicants were not qualified and could not be referred to openings without intensive training. The proposal for the East Bay Skills Center was the suggested response to this critical need.

The Skills Center is unique in housing the training in a separate geographical location in an atmosphere quite different from the regular school situation where so many of the trainees were unsuccessful. The original plans included basic education, to bring trainees to a level where they would be ready and able to absorb vocational training, and pre-vocational exposure to a variety of occupational areas in order to enable trainees to identify aptitudes and interests.

Following these phases, trainees were to be referred to specific vocational training for the duration of their courses. Subsequently, funding shortages forced the elimination of the pre-vocational phase of the plan, and severely curtailed the basic education available. An exception to this has been allowed for a recent input of 190 underachievers and mono-lingual Spanish-speaking trainees. Recruitment has been concentrated on the disadvantaged, ethnic minorities, head of household. I am including an attachment which shows the personal characteristics of trainees for several different inputs. 77% of the trainee population is Negro. (Exhibit 4)

In Fiscal Year 1967, slots have been approved for 1000 adults and 400 youth. Over 60% of these slots will be filled from Oakland target areas. Other trainees are referred from Berkeley, Hayward, Richmond, Pittsburg, Vallejo, and Napa. The length of time trainees are in these programs varies, in general, from 20 to 49 weeks, depending upon the level of the occupational training, with the average being about 35 to 40 weeks.

Peralta Junior College District acts as the training facility, choosing instructors for their ability to work with the disadvantaged.

The first class graduated from the Skills Center in January of this year, and subsequent graduations are occurring throughout this year. Placement is planned through a special Job Development unit at the Skills Center and through the referring offices.

In 1965 the Youth Section of the regular Employment Service was separated to become a Youth Opportunity Center for Alameda County (excluding Hayward). As facilities became available, outreach branches were established in West Oakland, East Oakland, and Berkeley. The accompanying registration statistics for March 1967 indicate the ethnic composition of the applicant load handled by these branches.

During the 12-month period ending November 30, 1966, the Department of Employment in Alameda County accomplished 39,410 placements.

These estimated percentages by race based are on Oct-Nov 1966 survey:

White	- 61.0%
Negro	- 31.4%
Mex-Am	- 5.6%
Other non-whites	2.0%

52% of the total Alameda County placements were made in Oakland offices, or 20,414.

Estimated percentage by race of these placements are:

White	- 45.5%
Negro	- 44.7%
Mex-Am	7.2%
Other non-whites	2.6%

Group counseling, job clinics, training in test techniques and skill brush-up have been some resources developed by YOC staff.

Many other agencies are involved in projects in the Oakland area, designed to alleviate the problems of unemployment and underemployment. One of these, supported by private funding is O. I. C. Oakland, where occupational training is provided. Here, the Department has offered assistance as needed, as we are providing for the OIC West project in Palo Alto by stationing an interviewer in the facility and referring applicants when appropriate.

Bordering Oakland and Alameda County, critical poverty areas have been identified in Richmond and Southern Alameda County.

875

In North Richmond (a ghetto which is 98% Negro), there has been a community
organisation called Neighborhood House for well over five years; this organisation concerns itself with the needs of the underprivileged, culturally deprived
and delinquent youth. Although few, if any of these youth were ready for
employment at the inception of the program, the Employment Service was one of
the early participants offering counseling (often on street corners), motivational
services, and placement and job development when the applicant is finally ready
for a tentative approach to a work situation. Our interviewers have been out-
stationed here for several years, providing outreach counseling and upgrading
services to the youth of the area. At the present time, funding for the
Neighborhood House is terminating, but a proposal has been submitted requesting
financing for the assumption of this project by the Employment Service. Outreach
services are also provided in San Pablo and the Iron Triangle areas, in addition
to the Richmond Service Center in the blighted downtown area.

In Southern Alameda County, where the unemployment rate is approximately 12%,
and a significant percentage of the population (about 12%) are Spanish-speaking
monolinguals, scattered poverty pockets entrap an almost invisible disadvantaged
group. Outreach services were particularly essential in this almost-rural area
where lack of transportation intensified the problem of isolation. In January
1966, outreach services were initiated here, with the opening of a neighborhood
CSES office in the Spanish-speaking ghetto of Union City, a branch of the
Hayward local office. Lack of staff in sufficient numbers to provide adequate
outreach was augmented by the use of CSES trained Community Aides from CAA (local CA
agency) for work at the grassroots level. At the present time both youth and
adult disadvantaged are being served on a case-holding basis in Hayward, Union
City, Livermore, and Fremont.

I would like to comment briefly on several programs in which all or several of
our Employment Service offices participate.

Our participation in Job Corps Recruitment provides a major resource for our
YOC counselors and interviewers. Job Corps is designed for the disadvantaged
youth, providing him with occupational training in a setting where he can learn
to adjust his behavior problems as well. Oakland, San Francisco, and Vallejo
YOC's have a full-time Job Corps Placement specialist who is concerned with the
job development and placement of Job Corps graduates. Neighborhood Youth Corps
projects have been developed in most of our local office areas. Our recruitment
and screening for these has enabled us to refer many disadvantaged and ethnic
minority youths to situations where they can become oriented to the "world of work."

Last summer we received Federal financing for a Summer Youth Demonstration Project
(TIDE) which was carried out in three of our YOC's, including San Francisco and
Oakland. The project enabled us to put some youth on our payroll for summer
jobs. These youngsters were utilized in clerical assignments, and for community
relations, contacting employers for job development and publicising the program.
In addition, daily group sessions provided other youngsters with orientation to
vocational areas, employer requirements, employment tests, community facilities.
For both groups, emphasis was placed on the severely disadvantaged, and ethnic
minorities. In addition to benefits received by the participants, both monetarily
and in experience, this program provided a means of demonstrating to the minority
community our desire to relate by accepting these individuals in positions behind
our counters.

876

A state-wide agreement with Urban League was recently signed, confirming cooperative arrangements between that group and our agency. We work closely with them, especially in connection with OJT training programs, job development, and referral services. Office space for their interviewers has been provided to Urban League in some of our local offices.

In each local office area, cooperation with other local agencies is developed, and MDTA advisory committees made up of representatives of the local community provide the local office manager with advise on proposed projects.

It is hoped that this information will be useful to your committee. Additional details can be furnished if you request.

attach

877

Preliminary Tabulations From
The 701 Sample Census of Oakland

CHARACTERISTICS OF THE POPULATION OF OAKLAND, CALIFORNIA 1966

Prepared For

The Department of Employment
State of California

By

The Survey Research Center
University of California, Berkeley

December 2, 1966

William L. Nicholls II, Study Director

878

CONTENTS

879

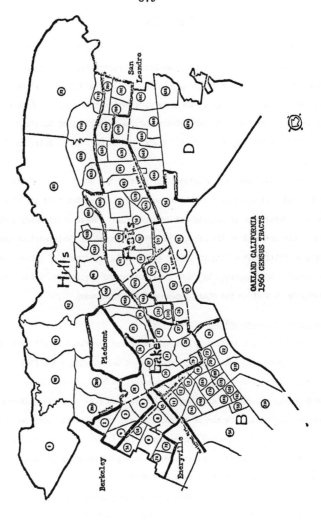

FIGURE 1

REPORTING AREAS OF 701 SAMPLE CENSUS OF OAKLAND

OAKLAND CALIFORNIA
1960 CENSUS TRACTS

Introduction

This report presents preliminary results from the 701 Sample Census of Oakland. It consists of a set of tabulations describing selected social and economic characteristics of the population residing in households within the City of Oakland, California. The data were obtained by personal interviews conducted by the Survey Research Center of the University of California at a sample of 2,643 households during the months of May, June, July, and August of 1966.

This sample census constitutes one part of the 701 Project of the City of Oakland. It was made possible by an Urban Planning Grant to the City from the U.S. Department of Housing and Urban Affairs. These preliminary tabulations were prepared at the request of the Department of Employment of the State of California acting on behalf of the U.S. Department of Labor. Their preparation was supported by funds provided by the Department of Labor and administered through the State Department of Employment.

Population Coverage and Reporting Areas

The population covered by the sample census consisted of all persons residing in housing units, except those noted below, within the City of Oakland. Persons residing in group quarters, such as institutions, hospitals, dormitories, and rooming and boarding houses with more than five tenants, were not included. The sample census also excluded persons whose usual residence was a hotel or similar accommodation for transients and those residing in housing units within structures which were predominantly group quarters, such as a manager's apartment in a dormitory.

The tabulations present results for seven geographical areas of Oakland. These are defined by Oakland's 1960 census tracts in Figure 1 on page ii..

881

The areas designated A, B, C, and D are the four target areas of Oakland's
anti-poverty program under the Economic Opportunity Act. They are known
locally as the North Oakland, West Oakland, Fruitvale, and East Oakland
Target Areas, respectively. The remainder of the city has been divided into
three areas labeled the Hills, Flats, and Lake. These have been named for
prominant features of their terrain. In the tabulations, the first four
areas are referred to collectively as the Target Areas, the last three as
Other Areas.

Description of Tables

There are five basic tables. The first three describe social and economic characteristics of the total population, the Negro population, and the
Mexican American population, respectively. The fourth presents a simultaneous
breakdown of employment status by age and sex. The fifth itemizes components
which entered into the employment status estimates and presents the results
of an additional probe on looking for work.

In Tables 1 and 2, information on the same item is arranged over two
succeeding pages. The first page presents the totals for Oakland, for the
Target Areas, and for Other Areas. The second page presents information for
the separate reporting areas. In Table 2, only four of these areas are included, since the numbers of sampled Negroes in the remaining three were
insufficient to support meaningful figures.

Why the Tabulations Are Called Preliminary

When the State Department of Employment requested these tabulations,
most of the information contained in them had not yet been coded and prepared
for electronic data processing. The Survey Research Center accepted the commission of preparing the tabulations with the understanding that they would

be recognized as preliminary and might differ slightly from the final results. The tabulations should be regarded as preliminary in three respects.

First, since it was not possible to process the full interview schedules in the time available, only those items required for the preliminary tabula-tions were coded and checked for inconsistencies. When the full interviews are processed at a later date, some responses may be reclassified through cross-checking against more complete data.

Second, to complete the processing in the time available, it was necessary to circumvent some coding problems by classifying ambiguous or difficult to interpret responses to "no answer." For example, the educational attainment of persons receiving their education in foreign countries was coded "no answer" if the interviewer had recorded the details of this education but had failed to determine its American equivalent in years of school completed. Similarly, household income was coded "no answer" where ambiguities or inconsistencies were encountered in the income figures which could not quickly be resolved.

Third, some revisions may be made for the final tabulations in the weights utilized to adjust for disproportionate sampling and non-response. While the revised weights should have little effect on percentages obtained from the figures in this report, estimated population totals, especially for the population outside the target areas, may differ in the final tabulations.

Population Characteristics*

Race and Color

The three major race categories distinguished in this report are white, Negro, and other races. Among persons of "other races" are American Indians,

---

* The definitions of population characteristics presented here have been liberally borrowed from U.S. Census publications.

Japanese, Chinese, Filipinos, Koreans, Asian Indians, and Malayans. Negroes and persons of "other races" taken together constitute "nonwhite" persons. Persons of Mexican birth or descent who are not definitely of Indian or other nonwhite race are classified as white. Race was determined in the 701 Sample Census primarily by interviewer observation.

Mexican Descent

Mexican descent was determined by a pair of questions which asked: (a) "Could you tell me what country your family came from (originally)?" and (b) "IF MARRIED: How about your husband's family? What country did they come from originally?" Mexican American descent as determined by the 701 Sample Census should not be taken as the equivalent of Spanish surname as reported in the 1960 U.S. Census.

Age

The age classification is based on the age of the person in completed years as of May 1, 1966, as determined from the reply to a question on month and year of birth.

Years of School Completed

The data on years of school completed were derived from the answers to two questions: (a) "What is the highest grade (or year) of regular school he has ever attended?" and (b) "Did he finish this grade (or year)?" Persons were to answer No to the second question if they were attending school, had completed only part of a grade before they dropped out, or failed to pass the last grade attended. Educational attainment was determined at the time of the interview.

884

Employment Status

The three questions used to determine employment status were taken from the 1960 U.S. Census and were asked for the calendar week prior to the date of interview. Since the greater part of the interviews were completed during late May, June, July, and the first week of August, the employment statistics reported here refer primarily to the first three of these months.

Employed persons comprise all civilians 14 years old and over who were either (a) "at work"--those who did any work for pay or profit, or worked without pay for 15 hours or more in a family business; or (b) were "with a job, but not at work"--those who did not work and were not looking for work but had a job or business from which they were temporarily absent because of bad weather, industrial dispute, vacation, illness, or other personal reasons.

Persons were classified as unemployed if they were 14 years old and over and not "at work" but looking for work or waiting to be called back to a job from which they had been laid off or furloughed. In conformity with U.S. Census practice, a person was considered as looking for work not only if he actually tried to find work in the week before the interview but also if the information was volunteered, in response to the standard Census questions, that he had made such efforts recently (i.e., within the past 60 days) and was awaiting the results of these efforts.

The "civilian labor force" includes all persons classified as employed or unemployed as described above. The "labor force" also includes members of the Armed Forces (persons on active duty with the United States Army, Air Force, Navy, Marine Corps, or Coast Guard). Persons "not in the labor force" comprise all those 14 years old and over who are not classified as members of the labor force.

885

The standard Census questions on employment status, which are reproduced
as used here at the end of this report, were followed by an additional probe
which read: "Was he looking for work at any time in the past 60 days?"
Persons for whom a Yes answer was received have not been classified as unemployed in Tables 1 through 4 but are separately shown in Table 5. While
some of the Yes answers may represent persons who were no longer interested
in finding work, others may represent instances where the time reference of
the standard Census question was misunderstood.

Household Characteristics

The few items of information pertaining to the housing unit or household
have been incorporated in the tables on social and economic characteristics
of the population to avoid a confusing proliferation of table numbers.

Housing Units

A house, an apartment, or other group of rooms, or a single room is
regarded as a housing unit when it is occupied or intended for occupancy as
separate living quarters, that is when the occupants do not live and eat with
any other persons in the structure and there is either (1) direct access from
the outside or through a common hall or (2) a kitchen or cooking equipment
for the exclusive use of the occupants of the unit.

Although a hotel room is counted as a housing unit by the Census if it
is the usual residence for the person living there or if he has no usual
residence elsewhere, such units were not included in the 701 Sample Census
and are not tabulated in Tables 1, 2, and 3. The estimates presented in
these tables also exclude housing units in structures which were predominantly
group quarters, such as a manager's apartment in a dormitory.

Occupied Housing Units

A housing unit is "occupied' if it was the usual place of residence for the person or group of persons living in it when the interviewer first called. Included are units occupied by persons who were only temporarily absent, for example, on vacation.

Household and Household Head

A household consists of all the persons who occupy a housing unit. The head of the household is the member reported as the head by the household respondent. However, if a married woman, living with her husband is reported as the head, her husband is classified as the head for the purposes of the tabulations.

Household Income

The income statistics relate to the 1965 calendar year. Information on income was requested separately for each person 14 years old and over in the household, and separate questions were asked to determine the wage and salary income, self-employment income, and other income of each. The questions used to elicit this information are reproduced at the end of this report. Definitions of the three types of income were those of the 1960 U.S. Census. The household income is the algebraic sum of the amounts received by all income recipients in the household. Although the time period covered by the income statistics is 1965 and the composition of the households refers to the time of the interview, for more of the households, the income reported was received by persons who were members of the household throughout the period.

Income is rarely reported as a household characteristic, and the figures presented here should not be confused with the more common family and/or

887

individual income figures. A household may consist of a single individual, a family, two or more unrelated individuals, or a combination of a family (or families) and unrelated persons. However, since most households are comprised either of single individuals living alone or of single families, the figures are perhaps best read as an approximation of combined family and individual income estimates. While family and individual income estin⸱ ⸱es will be presented in the final report, they could not be placed in convenient form in time for these preliminary tabulations.

Sampling and Estimation Methods

All tabulations are population estimates based on a sample of approximately 1 in 50 of Oakland's households. A disproportionately stratified, area probability sample was employed, using city blocks as the primary sampling units and housing units as the second stage. Sampling ratios were set to yield approximately 400 occupied housing units per reporting area. Given the smaller size of Areas A, B, C, and D relative to the remainder of the city, the effect was to oversample the city's target areas. Actual sample sizes and response rates per areas are presented in Tables A and C respectively.

The population estimates presented in the main body of tables were obtained by weighting the sample results for disproportionate sampling and for non-response. Although the estimates have not been rounded, their last two digits should be regarded as meaningless. A population estimate of 13,133 should be read, for example, merely as 13,100.

Since the statistics in this report are based on a sample, they are subject to sampling variability. Some indication of the extent of this variability can be gained by consulting the approximate standard errors presented for selected estimates in Table B. The standard error is a measure of how

888

close the sample estimate is likely to be to the same estimate if it were made from a complete count, using the same schedules, instructions, and interviewers. The probability is roughly .68 (or about two chances out of three) that the sampling process would produce an estimate differing in either direction by less than one stand error from the results of a complete count. The probability is about .95 that this difference would be less than twice the standard error. These standard errors do not reflect, however, the effect of non-response, miscoding, or other non-sampling biases and errors.

889

Table 1.

SOCIAL AND ECONOMIC CHARACTERISTICS OF THE POPULATION OF OAKLAND, BY AREA OF CITY

Subject	Total Oakland	Target Areas	Other Areas.
RACE			
Total Population............	365,127	142,057	223,069
White........................	234,576	48,295	186,281
Negro........................	110,125	86,090	24,035
Other non-white..............	20,425	7,673	12,753
White persons of Mexican descent..	17,866	10,727	7,139
AGE			
Male.........................	170,584	67,240	103,344
Under 10 years...................	33,243	17,395	15,848
10 to 19 years...................	28,259	12,555	15,705
20 to 29 years...................	22,954	7,889	15,065
30 to 39 years...................	18,460	6,881	11,578
40 to 49 years...................	19,660	6,862	12,798
50 to 59 years...................	20,806	6,705	14,101
60 to 69 years...................	16,329	5,136	11,193
70 to 79 years...................	8,178	2,596	5,582
80 years and over................	2,695	1,222	1,474
Under 6 years	19,842	10,656	9,186
18 years and over................	113,807	38,998	74,810
21 years and over................	107,469	36,599	70,871
65 years and over................	17,631	6,071	11,561
Female.......................	194,542	74,817	119,725
Under 10 years...................	32,348	17,257	15,091
10 to 19 years...................	31,614	12,843	18,771
20 to 29 years...................	26,814	9,916	16,899
30 to 39 years...................	18,983	7,640	11,343
40 to 49 years...................	24,892	8,902	15,990
50 to 59 years...................	24,548	7,458	17,091
60 to 69 years...................	19,211	5,593	13,618
70 to 79 years...................	11,706	3,834	7,872
80 years and over................	4,427	1,376	3,051
Under 6 years....................	19,115	10,334	8,781
18 years and over................	136,753	46,773	89,980
21 years and over................	127,588	43,857	83,731
65 years and over................	25,381	8,261	17,120

Table 1--Continued

SOCIAL AND ECONOMIC CHARACTERISTICS OF THE POPULATION OF OAKLAND, BY AREA OF CITY

Subject	A	B	C	D	Hills	Flats	Lake
RACE							
Total Population....	23,997	37,177	42,046	38,838	89,477	83,979	49,613
White.....................	5,641	8,822	'24,451	9,380	78,815	64,808	42,658
Negr......................	17,358	26,346	13,921	28,465	7,319	13,809	2,907
Other non-white..........	997	2,009	3,673	993	3,343	5,362	4,048
White persons of							
Mexican descent.........	357	2,233	5,694	2,442	1,522	4,656	962
AGE							
Male...............	11,624	17,382	19,788	18,447	43,004	38,150	22,190
Under 10 years...........	2,237	4,295	4,499	6,364	6,771	5,969	3,108
10 to 19 years...........	1,844	3,309	3,712	3,690	7,704	5,690	2,311
20 to 29 years...........	1,401	1,676	2,894	1,919	4,570	5,341	5,153
30 to 39 years...........	1,222	1,355	2,280	2,025	4,463	4,403	2,712
40 to 49 years...........	1,259	1,901	2,110	1,593	6,416	4,231	2,151
50 to 59 years...........	1,647	1,922	1,606	1,530	6,525	4,873	2,703
60 to 69 years...........	1,075	1,801	1,499	762	4,223	4,896	2,074
70 to 79 years...........	693	776	728	399	1,787	2,452	1,343
80 years and over........	248	348	461	165	544	295	635
Under 6 years............	1,411	2,314	2,817	4,115	3,725	3,508	1,953
18 years and over........	7,712	10,047	12,173	9,067	29,301	27,621	17,440
21 years and over........	7,288	9,699	11,273	8,339	28,140	26,147	16,585
65 years and over........	1,311	2,151	1,765	843	3,520	4,840	3,201
Female...............	12,373	19,795	22,258	20,391	46,473	45,829	27,423
Under 10 years...........	2,037	3,943	5,207	6,071	6,406	6,195	2,491
10 to 19 years...........	1,731	3,146	3,655	4,311	8,262	8,003	2,506
20 to 29 years...........	1,660	2,019	3,345	2,892·	4,948	5,679	6,272
30 to 39 years...........	1,270	1,935	2,246	2,189	4,362	4,210	2,771
40 to 49 years..........	1,670	2,800	2,541	1,891	8,066	5,358	2,565
50 to 59 years...........	1,594	2,248	2,084	1,532	7,376	6,229	3,486
60 to 69 years...........	1,147	2,054	1,575	818	4,228	6,432	2,958
70 to 79 years...........	896	1,166	1,248	524	2,193	2,486	3,192
80 years and over........	370	484	359	164	632	1,238	1,182
Under 6 years............	1,090	2,321	3,135	3,789	3,417	3,796	1,568
18 years and over........	8,938	13,208	14,002	10,624	33,395	33,449	23,136
21 years and over........	8,526	12,551	13,148	9,632	31,139	30,839	21,753
65 years and over........	1,841	2,777	2,472	1,171	4,266	6,926	5,928

Table 1--Continued

SOCIAL AND ECONOMIC CHARACTERISTICS OF THE POPULATION OF OAKLAND, BY AREA OF CITY

Subject	Total Oakland	Target Areas	Other Areas
AGE NON-WHITE			
Male........................	61,442	43,708	17,734
Under 10 years....................	16,728	13,055	3,673
10 to 19 years....................	13,099	9,010	4,089
20 to 29 years....................	7,263	4,589	2,674
30 to 39 years....................	6,131	4,756	1,374
40 to 49 years....................	7,500	4,844	2,655
50 to 59 years....................	5,398	3,826	1,571
60 to 69 years....................	4,189	2,584	1,604
70 to 79 years....................	905	813	92
80 years and over.................	230	230	-
Under 6 years....................	9,957	7,744	2,213
18 years and over.................	33,082	22,523	10,559
21 years and over.................	31,121	21,339	9,782
65 years and over.................	2,494	2,064	430
Female......................	69,108	50,054	19,054
Under 10 years....................	16,456	12,915	3,541
10 to 19 years....................	14,548	10,213	4,335
20 to 29 years....................	9,509	6,944	2,565
30 to 39 years....................	7,976	5,400	2,576
40 to 49 years....................	8,757	5,989	2,768
50 to 59 years....................	6,210	4,190	2,020
60 to 69 years....................	3,984	2,814	1,170
70 to 79 years....................	1,240	1,162	78
80 years and over.................	428	428	-
Under 6 years....................	9,540	7,727	1,813
18 years and over.................	40,294	28,621	11,674
21 years and over.................	37,200	26,359	10,842
65 years and over.................	3,266	2,801	466

- Represents zero.

Table 1--Continued

SOCIAL AND ECONOMIC CHARACTERISTICS OF THE POPULATION OF OAKLAND, BY AREA OF CITY

Subject	A	B	C	D	Hills	Flats	Lake
AGE							
NON-WHITE							
Male....................	8,503	13,146	8,001	14,059	a	a	a
Under 10 years..................	1,975	3,618	2,230	5,231	a	a	a
10 to 19 years..................	1,612	2,749	1,581	3,068	a	a	a
20 to 29 years..................	943	1,076	1,303	1,267	a	a	a
30 to 39 years..................	930	1,199	1,084	1,542	a	a	a.
40 to 49 years..................	1,072	1,574	932	1,266	a	a	a
50 to 59 years..................	924	1,324	504	1,075	a	a	a
60 to 69 years..................	689	1,171	302	422	a	a	a
70 to 79 years..................	241	341	64	166	a	a	a
80 years and over..............	116	93		21	a	a	a
Under 6 years..................	1,214	1,828	1,304	3,398	a	a	a
18 years and over..............	5,027	6,973	4,276	6,249	a	a	a
21 years and over..............	4,867	6,700	4,067	5,707	a	a	a
65 years and over..............	516	1,119	153	277	a	a	a
Female....................	9,853	15,209	9,594	15,399	a	a	a
Under 10 years..................	1,993	3,296	2,786	4,841	a	a	a
10 to 19 years..................	1,650	2,725	2,147	3,692	a	a	a
20 to 29 years..................	1,429	1,668	1,671	2,176	a	a	a
30 to 39 years..................	1,115	1,591	988	1,706	a	a	a
40 to 49 years..................	1,346	2,203	1,024	1,416	a	a	a
50 to 59 years..................	1,042	1,571	587	991	a	a	a
60 to 69 years..................	712	1,421	263	418	a	a	a
70 to 79 years..................	417	534	91	121	a	a	a
80 years and over..............	150	201	37	40	a	a	a
Under 6 years..................	1,090	1,802	1,750	3,085	a	a	a
18 years and over..............	6,513	9,672	5,047	7,390	a	a	a
21 years and over..............	6,132	9,079	4,558	6,590	a	a	a
65 years and over	865	1,375	187	374	a	a	a

a. Estimate not presented when sample size less than 100.

- Represents zero.

893

Table 1--Continued

SOCIAL AND ECONOMIC CHARACTERISTICS OF THE POPULATION OF OAKLAND, BY AREA OF CITY

Subject	Total Oakland	Target Areas	Other Areas
YEARS OF SCHOOL COMPLETED			
Persons 25 years old and over..	211,605	72,883	138,722
No school years completed..........	2,913	1,705	1,208
Elementary: 1 to 4 years..........	8,647	5,751	2,895
5 to 7 years..........	15,809	9,186	6,623
8 years..............	20,582	9,145	11,437
High School: 1 to 3 years..........	40,095	17,475	22,620
4 years..............	62,358	18,634	43,725
College: 1 to 3 years..........	30,419	6,508	23,911
4 years or more.......	25,539	2,672	22,867
No Answer........................	5,244	1,808	3,436
EMPLOYMENT STATUS			
Male			
Total, 14 years old and over...	123,864	43,947	79,917
Labor force........................	96,681	32,045	64,638
Percent of total............	78.1%	72.9%	80.9%
Civilian labor force.............	94,376	31,234	63,142
Employed......................	88,354	27,924	60,430
Unemployed....................	6,021	3,310	2,712
Percent of civilian labor force....................	6.4%	10.6%	4.3%
Not in labor force..................	27,182	11,903	15,279
Female			
Total, 14 years old and over...	149,037	51,584	97,456
Labor force........................	69,327	24,172	45,155
Percent of total............	46.5%	46.9%	46.3%
Employed......................	62,337	20,254	42,084
Unemployed....................	6,990	3,918	3,072
Percent of civilian labor force....................	10.1%	16.3%	6.8%
Not in labor force..................	79,712	27,412	52,300

Table 1--Continued

SOCIAL AND ECONOMIC CHARACTERISTICS OF THE POPULATION OF OAKLAND, BY AREA OF CITY

Subject	A	B					
YEARS OF SCHOOL COMPLETED							
Persons 25 years old and over..	14,534	20,404	21,764				
School years completed...........	294	677					
Elementary: 1 to 4 years..........	1,314	2,225	1,057	1,145			
5 + 7 years..........	2,006	2,923	2,363	1,814	1,904		
8 years...............	1,538	2,836	2,443	2,328	3,448		
High School: 1 to 3 years..........	3,105	5,348	4,925	4,098	6,662		
4 years...............	3,934	3,703	6,824	4,173	18,099		
College: 1 to 3 years..........	1,396	1,209	2,289	1,614	9,155	8,017	
4 years or more.......	592	701	1,093	287	14,481	2,592	
Not reported...............	277	783	372	377		1,517	
EMPLOYMENT STATUS							
Male							
Total, 14 years old and over...	8,533	11,174	13,875	10,366			
In labor force......................	6,233	7,518	10,261	8,033		23,501	14,83
Percent of total............	73.0%	67.3%	74.0%	77.5%		80.6%	81.2
Civilian labor force..............	6,164	7,376	9,833	7,861	25,985	22,322	14,83
Employed.....................	5,731	6,201	8,900	7,093	25,405	21,202	13,82
Unemployed......................	434	1,175	933			1,120	1,01
Percent of civilian labor force........................	7.0%	15.9%	9.5%	9.8%		5.0%	6.8
Not in labor force...................	2,300	3,656	3,614	2,333	6,169	5,671	3,439
Female							
Total, 14 years old and over...	9,625	14,462	15,371	12,126	36,869	36,620	23,961
In labor force......................	4,702	6,753	7,384	5,282		16,228	2
Percent of total............	48.9%	46.7%	48.0%	43.6%		44.3%	5
Employed.....................	4,373	5,624	6,039	4,218	14,995	14,944	2
Unemployed.....................	381	1,129	1,344	1,064	1,004	1,284	
Percent civilian labor force........................	8.1%	16.9%	18.2%	20.1%			
Not in labor force...................	4,872	7,709	7,988	6,844	20,870	20,392	1

Table 1--Continued

SOCIAL AND ECONOMIC CHARACTERISTICS OF THE POPULATION OF OAKLAND, BY AREA OF CITY

Subject	Total Oakland	Target Areas	Other Areas
All occupied housing units	134,824	47,720	87,104
RACE OF HOUSEHOLD HEAD			
White............................	97,623	29,061	77,563
Negro............................	31,507	25,539	5,968
Other non-white..................	5,694	2,120	3,573
White of Mexican descent.........	4,386	2,539	1,847
NUMBER OF PERSONS			
1 person.........................	34,367	12,955	21,412
2 persons........................	46,984	12,833	34,152
3 persons........................	20,529	6,969	13,560
4 persons........................	12,465	4,989	7,476
5 persons........................	9,201	3,944	5,257
6 persons........................	5,316	2,758	2,558
7 persons........................	2,879	1,371	1,508
8 persons........................	1,477	832	644
9 persons or more................	1,606	1,069	537
HOUSEHOLD INCOME IN 1965			
Under $1,000.....................	2,786	1,041	1,745
$1,000 to $1,999.................	9,478	5,683	3,795
$2,000 to $2,999.................	9,167	4,705	4,462
$3,000 to $3,999.................	9,910	4,438	5,472
$4,000 to $4,999.................	8,861	3,870	4,991
$5,000 to $5,999.................	10,181	4,293	5,888
$6,000 to $7,999.................	19,155	7,430	11,725
$8,000 to $9,999.................	12,471	4,364	8,107
$10,000 to $14,999...............	20,407	3,624	16,783
$15,000 to $24,999...............	7,688	1,005	6,683
$25,000 and over.................	1,770	85	1,686
No answer........................	22,951	7,183	15,768

Table 1--Continued

SOCIAL AND ECONOMIC CHARACTERISTICS OF THE POPULATION OF OAKLAND, BY AREA OF CITY

Subject	A	B	C	D	Hills	Flats	Lake
All occupied housing units	9,078	14,082	14,449	10,111	29,223	33,180	24,702
RACE OF HOUSEHOLD HEAD							
White......................	3,060	4,242	9,582	3,176	27,117	27,775	22,672
Negro......................	5,781	9,177	3,848	6,733	1,412	3,818	738
Other non-white...........	237	662	1,019	202	694	1,587	1,292
White of Mexican descent..	107	653	1,263	516	392	1,107	349
NUMBER OF PERSONS							
1 person..................	2,377	5,030	4,086	1,462	2,990	7,954	10,468
2 persons.................	3,057	3,888	3,798	2,091	11,623	13,574	8,955
3 persons.................	1,464	1,746	1,974	1,785	5,677	5,443	2,440
4 persons.................	947	1,011	1,689	1,342	3,566	2,463	1,448
5 persons.................	539	1,025	1,060	1,319	2,816	1,585	856
6 persons.................	346	628	1,097	688	1,465	825	268
7 persons.................	205	121	433	613	465	884	159
8 persons.................	83	223	171	356	217	320	108
9 persons or more.........	61	410	142	455	404	133	
HOUSEHOLD INCOME IN 1965							
Under $1,000..............	307	174	338	222	522	489	734
$1,000 to $1,999..........	852	2,847	1,307	677	243	2,216	1,337
$2,000 to $2,999..........	851	1,776	1,264	814	951	2,145	1,366
$3,000 to $3,999..........	641	1,464	1,316	1,017	1,150	1,929	2,393
$4,000 to $4,999..........	707	1,526	939	698	895	1,696	2,401
$5,000 to $5,999..........	693	1,169	1,557	873	955	2,831	2,103
$6,000 to $7,999..........	1,559	1,567	2,195	2,110	2,933	5,888	2,903
$8,000 to $9,999..........	775	670	1,630	1,290	2,230	3,331	2,546
$10,000 to $14,999........	770	539	1,368	947	7,436	5,670	3,678
$15,000 to $24,999........	176	251	480	98	4,395	1,274	1,014
$25,000 and over..........	20	-	65	-	1,157	73	455
No answer.................	1,728	2,099	1,989	1,367	6,356	5,640	3,772

- Represents zero.

Table 2.

SOCIAL AND ECONOMIC CHARACTERISTICS OF THE NEGRO POPULATION OF OAKLAND, BY AREA

Subject	Total Oakland	Target Areas	Other Areas
AGE			
Male......................	51,183	40,210	10,973
Under 10 years................	14,593	12,055	2,538
10 to 19 years................	10,880	8,338	2,542
20 to 29 years................	5,695	4,286	1,410
30 to 39 years................	5,224	4,236	989
40 to 49 years................	5,974	4,447	1,527
50 to 59 years................	4,600	3,435	1,165
60 to 69 years................	3,147	2,401	746
70 to 79 years................	840	783	57
80 years and over.............	230	230	-
Under 6 years.................	8,471	7,097	1,374
18 years and over.............	26,932	20,678	6,254
21 years and over.............	25,369	19,585	5,784
65 years and over.............	2,354	1,959	395
Female....................	58,942	45,880	13,062
Under 10 years................	14,511	11,889	2,622
10 to 19 years................	12,515	9,391	3,125
20 to 29 years................	8,023	6,202	1,821
30 to 39 years................	6,477	4,824	1,654
40 to 49 years................	7,489	5,437	2,053
50 to 59 years................	4,748	3,941	807
60 to 69 years................	3,625	2,645	980
70 to 79 years................	1,162	1,162	-
80 years and over.............	391	391	-
Under 6 years.................	8,258	7,026	1,232
18 years and over.............	33,836	26,198	7,638
21 years and over.............	31,142	24,033	7,109
65 years and over.............	3,151	2,764	387

Represents zero.

898

Table 2--Continued

SOCIAL AND ECONOMIC CHARACTERISTICS OF THE NEGRO POPULATION OF OAKLAND, BY AREA

Subject	A	B	C	D
AGE				
Male...................	7,965	12,227	6,424	13,593
Under 10 years..............	1,837	3,386	1,735	5,097
10 to 19 years..............	1,504	2,621	1,244	2,969
20 to 29 years..............	866	1,076	1,093	1,251
30 to 39 years..............	911	1,055	781	1,488
40 to 49 years..............	964	1,415	842	1,226
50 to 59 years..............	899	1,149	362	1,025
60 to 69 years.............:	627	1,121	302	350
70 to 79 years..............	241	312	64	166
80 years and over..........	116	93		21
Under 6 years..............	1,100	1,671	1,016	3,311
18 years and over..........	4,736	6,414	3,532	5,998
21 years and over..........	4,576	6,141	3,394	5,475
65 years and over..........	516	1,039	153	252
Female.................	9,392	14,119	7,498	14,872
Under 10 years..............	1,888	2,951	2,285	4,764
10 to 19 years..............	1,545	2,565	1,797	3,484
20 to 29 years..............	1,306	1,597	1,196	2,103
30 to 39 years..............	1,065	1,375	758	1,626
40 to 49 years..............	1,293	2,057	711	1,375
50 to 59 years..............	1,017	1,498	459	966
60 to 69 years..............	712	1,341	200	392
70 to 79 years..............	417	534	91	121
80 years and over	150	201		40
Under 6 years..............	1,039	1,589	1,366	3,033
18 years and over..........	6,208	9,087	3,777	6,590
21 years and over..........	5,880	8,494	3,312	6,347
65 years and over..........	865	1,375	150	374

Represents zero.

Table 2--Continued

SOCIAL AND ECONOMIC CHARACTERISTICS OF THE NEGRO POPULATION OF OAKLAND, BY AREA

Subject	Total Oakland	Target Areas	Other Areas
YEARS OF SCHOOL COMPLETED			
Persons 25 years old and over...	50,459	39,366	11,093
No school years completed............	544	469	75
Elementary: 1 to 4 years...........	3,459	3,307	152
5 to 7 years...........	5,960	4,836	1,124
8 years................	5,069	4,185	884
High School: 1 to 3 years...........	14,298	11,287	3,011
4 years................	12,060	9,782	2,278
College: 1 to 3 years...........	6,122	3,755	2,367
4 years or more........	1,777	871	909
No Answer..........................	1,170	874	296
EMPLOYMENT STATUS			
Male			
Total, 14 years old and over....	30,864	23,945	6,919 c
Labor force.........................	24,334	18,578	5,765
Percent of total..............	78.8%	77.6%	b
Civilian labor force..............	23,827	18,171	5,656
Employed......................	21,113	15,858	5,256
Unemployed....................	2,714	2,313	400
Percent of civilian labor force....	11.4%	12.7%	b
Not in labor force..................	6,530	5,367	1,164
Female			
Total, 14 years old and over....	38,299	29,579	8,720
Labor force.........................	20,729	15,510	5,218
Percent of total..............	54.1%	52.4%	59.8%
Employed......................	17,637	12,822	4,815
Unemployed....................	3,028	2,624	403
Percent civilian labor force....	14.6%	17.0%	b
Not in labor force..................	17,571	14,070	3,501

b. Rate not presented when sample base less than 100.

c. Estimates based on sample size less than 100. Presented to permit calculation of employment statistics for both sexes combined.

900

Table 2--Continued

SOCIAL AND ECONOMIC CHARACTERISTICS OF THE NEGRO POPULATION OF OAKLAND, BY AREA

Subject	A	B	C	D
YEARS OF SCHOOL COMPLETED				
Persons 25 years old and over...	9,550	13,316	5,789	10,711
No school years completed............	82	242	85	60
Elementary: 1 to 4 years...........	741	1,659	265	642
5 to 7 years...........	1,541	1,807	485	1,003
8 years...............	929	1,668	406	1,181
High School: 1 to 3 years...........	2,518	3,904	1,881	2,983
4 years...............	2,295	2,433	1,923	3,131
College: 1 to 3 years...........	1,021	766	659	1,310
4 years or more........	242	300	84	245
No Answer...........................	182	537		156
EMPLOYMENT STATUS				
Male				
Total, 14 years old and over....	5,398	7,368	4,218	6,960
Labor force.........................	4,252	5,235	3,409	5,682
Percent of total.............	83.4%	71.1%	80.8%	81.6%
Civilian labor force..............	4,206	5,136	3,255	5,574
Employed.........................	3,821	4,311	2,697	5,030
Unemployed.............:...:.....	386	825	558	545
Percent of civilian labor force.....................	9.2%	16.1%	b	9.8%
Not in labor force..................	1,147	1,120	680	1,278
Female				
Total, 14 years old and over....	6,843	10,005	4,325	8,406
Labor force.........................	3,647	5,249	2,491	4,123
Percent of total.............	53.3%	52.5%	57.6%	49.0%
Employed.........................	3,389	4,198	1,944	3,290
Unemployed.'.....................	257	987	547	833
Percent civilian labor force.....................	7.6%	19.0%	b	20.2%
Not in labor force..................	3,197	4,757	1,834	4,283

b. Rate not presented when sample base less than 100.

901

Table 2--Continued

SOCIAL AND ECONOMIC CHARACTERISTICS OF THE NEGRO POPULATION OF OAKLAND, BY AREA

Subject	Total Oakland	Target Areas	Other Areas
All occupied housing units...	31,507	25,539	5,968
NUMBER OF PERSONS			
1 person.........................	5,366	5,133	a
2 persons........................	8,236	6,391	a
3 persons........................	4,932	4,006	a
4 persons........................	4,044	3,225	a
5 persons........................	3,590	2,607	a
6 persons........................	2,170	1,727	a
7 persons........................	1,453	969	a
8 persons........................	710	612	a
9 persons or more...............	1,007	868	a
HOUSEHOLD INCOME IN 1965			
Under $1,000.....................	222	222	a
$1,000 to $1,999.................	2,953	2,872	a
$2,000 to $2,999.................	2,485	2,278	a
$3,000 to $3,999.................	2,461	2,143	a
$4,000 to $4,999.................	2,485	2,349	a
$5,000 to $5,999.................	2,906	2,548	a
$6,000 to $7,999.................	5,533	4,591	a
$8,000 to $9,999.................	2,885	2,410	a
$10,000 to $14,999...............	4,028	2,036	a
$15,000 to $24,999...............	729	300	a
$25,000 and over.................	66	-	a
No answer........................	4,755	3,790	a

a. Estimates not presented when sample size less than 100.

Represents zero.

Table 2--Continued

SOCIAL AND ECONOMIC CHARACTERISTICS OF THE NEGRO POPULATION OF OAKLAND, BY AREA

Subject	A	B	C	D
All occupied housing units.....	5,781	9,177	3,848	6,733
NUMBER OF PERSONS				
1 person................................	1,103	2,783	573	674
2 persons...............................	1,891	2,507	853	1,140
3 persons...............................	910	1,201	767	1,120
4 persons...............................	768	901	507	1,049
5 persons...............................	489	796	310	1,012
6 persons...............................	293	398	415	617
7 persons...............................	177	121	220	451
8 persons...............................	83	113	140	277
9 persons or more......................	61	357	64	385
HOUSEHOLD INCOME IN 1965				
Under $1,000..........................	101	39	25	56
$1,000 to $1,999.....................	445	1,744	327	356
$2,000 to $2,999.....................	414	1,140	237	487
$3,000 to $3,999.....................	332	923	375	513
$4,000 to $4,999.....................	550	1,054	180	566
$5,000 to $5,999.....................	600	908	516	523
$6,000 to $7,999.....................	1,116	1,026	763	1,687
$8,000 to $9,999.....................	569	435	562	844
$10,000 to $14,999...................	508	427	440	662
$15,000 to $24,999...................	152	83	27	38
$25,000 and over.....................	-	-	-	-
No answer............................	993	1,400	396	1,001

Represents zero.

903

Table 3.

SOCIAL AND ECONOMIC CHARACTERISTICS OF THE WHITE POPULATION OF MEXICAN DESCENT
OF OAKLAND, BY AREA

Subject	Total Oakland	Target Areas	Other Areas
AGE			
Male...................	9,073	5,146	a
Under 10 years..................	2,647	1,790	a
10 to 19 years..................	1,757	1,036	a
20 to 29 years..................	1,222	619	a
30 to 39 years..................	1,573	806	a
40 to 49 years..................	724	334	a
50 to 59 years..................	471	224	a
60 to 69 years..................	571	229	a
70 to 79 years..................	31	31	a
80 years and over..............	76	76	a
Under 6 years..................	1,689	1,225	a
18 years and over..............	4,929	2,414	a
21 years and over..............	4,671	2,321	a
65 years and over..............	352	137	a
Female...................	8,794	5,581	a
Under 10 years..................	3,222	2,210	a
10 to 19 years..................	1,602	1,100	a
20 to 29 years..................	1,191	744	a
30 to 39 years..................	1,306	692	a
40 to 49 years..................	662	287	a
50 to 59 years..................	397	332	a
60 to 69 years..................	368	169	a
70 to 79 years..................	14	14	a
80 years and over..............	33	33	a
Under 6 years..................	2,092	1,423	a
18 years and over..............	4,044	2,346	a
21 years and over..............	3,798	2,161	a
65 years and over..............	141	141	a

a. Estimates not presented when sample size less than 100.

904

Table 3--Continued

SOCIAL AND ECONOMIC CHARACTERISTICS OF THE WHITE POPULATION OF MEXICAN DESCENT
OF OAKLAND, BY AREA

Subject	Total Oakland	Target Areas	Other Areas
YEARS OF SCHOOL COMPLETED			
Persons 25 years old and over..	7,551	3,895	a
No school years completed...........	530	386	a
Elementary: 1 to 4 years...........	1,089	662	a
5 to 7 years..........	1,319	877	a
8 years..............	634	414	a
High School: 1 to 3 years...........	1,432	651	a
4 years..............	1,482	545	a
College: 1 to 3 years..........	507	82	a
4 years or more.......	136	-	a
No Answer...........................	421	278	a
EMPLOYMENT STATUS			
Male			
Total, 14 years old and over...	5,708	2,921	a
Labor force.........................	4,560	2,163	a
Percent of total.............	79.9%	b	a
Civilian labor force..............	4,511	2,114	a
Employed......................	4,156	1,820	a
Unemployed....................	355	294	a
Percent of civilian labor force....................	7.9%	b	a
Not in labor force.................	1,149	759	a
Female			
Total, 14 years old and over...	4,682	2,782 c	a
Labor force.........................	1,751	865	a
Percent of total.............	37.4%	b	a
Employed......................	1,485	715	a
Unemployed....................	266	150	a
Percent civilian labor force....................	a	b	a
Not in labor force.................	2,931	1,917	a

a. Estimates not presented when sample size less than 100.
b. Rate not presented when sample base less than 100.
c. Estimates based on sample size less than 100. Presented to permit calculation of employment statistics for both sexes combined.
- Represents zero.

Table 3--Continued

SOCIAL AND ECONOMIC CHARACTERISTICS OF THE WHITE POPULATION OF MEXICAN DESCENT
OF OAKLAND, BY AREA

Subject	Total Oakland	Target Areas	Other Areas
All occupied housing units...	4,386	a	a
NUMBER OF PERSONS			
1 person.........................	518	a	a
2 persons........................	523	a	a
3 persons........................	671	a	a
4 persons........................	768	a	a
5 persons........................	964	a	a
6 persons........................	510	a	a
7 persons........................	229	a	a
8 persons........................	74	a	`a
9 persons or more...............	129	a	a
HOUSEHOLD INCOME IN 1965			
Under $1,000.....................	28	a	a
$1,000 to $1,999.................	302	a	a
$2,000 to $2,999.................	449	a	a
$3,000 to $3,999.................	576	a	a
$4,000 to $4,999.................	373	a	a
$5,000 to $5,999.................	313	a	a
$6,000 to $7,999.................	890	a	a
$8,000 to $9,999.................	583	a	a
$10,000 to $14,999..............	216	a	a
$15,000 to $24,999..............	49	a	a
$25,000 and over................	-	a	a
No answer.......................	608		

a. Estimates not presented when sample size less than 100

906

Table 4

EMPLOYMENT STATUS OF POPULATION BY SEX, AGE, AND AREA OF OAKLAND

Employment Status	Total Oakland	Target Areas	Other Areas
MALE			
Total, 14 to 19 years old··············	14,782	6,657	8,126
In labor force····························	6,797	2,948	3,849
Percent of total··················	46.0%	44.3%	47.4%
Civilian labor force··················	6,720	2,948	3,772
Employed··························	4,861	1,915	2,946
Unemployed························	1,859	1,033	826
Percent of civilian labor force··	27.7%	35.0%	b
Not in labor force····················	7,986	3,709	4,277
Total, 20 to 24 years old··············	12,464	3,716	8,749
In labor force····························	11,739	3,532	8,207
Percent of total··················	87.8%	95.1%	93.8%
Civilian labor force··················	10,302	3,225	7,077
Employed··························	9,285	2,734	6,551
Unemployed························	1,017	491	526
Percent of civilian labor force··	9.9%	(15.2%)a	b
Not in labor force····················	725	184	542
Total, 25 to 34 years old··············	20,085	7,801	12,284
In labor force····························	19,086	7,317	11,770
Percent of total··················	95.0%	93.8%	95.8%
Civilian labor force··················	18,681	6,991	11,691
Employed··························	17,557	6,225	11,332
Unemployed························	1,125	766	359
Percent of civilian labor force··	6.0%	11.0%	3.7%
Not in labor force····················	999	485	515
Total, 35 to 44 years old··············	18,065	6,601	11,465
In labor force····························	17,348	5,980	11,368
Percent of total··················	96.0%	90.6%	99.1%
Civilian labor force··················	17,040	5,882	11,158
Employed··························	16,239	5,591	10,648
Unemployed························	800	290	510
Percent of civilian labor force··	4.7%	4.9%	4.6%
Not in labor force····················	717	621	97

a. Sample base 93, rate shown to illustrate trend.

b. Rate not presented when sample base less than 100.

907

Table 4--Continued

EMPLOYMENT STATUS OF POPULATION BY SEX, AGE, AND AREA OF OAKLAND

Employment Status	Total Oakland	Target Areas	Other Areas
MALE--Continued			
Total, 45 to 64 years old..............	40,836	13,103	27,733
In labor force..............................	37,799	11,602	26,196
Percent of total..................	92.6%	88.5%	94.5%
Civilian labor force...................	37,717	11,522	26,196
Employed.............................	36,564	10,859	25,704
Unemployed.........................	1,153	662	491
Percent of civilian labor force..	3.6%	5.8%	1.9%
Not in labor force..........................	3,039	1,502	1,537
Total, 65 years old and over..........	17,631	6,071	11,561
In labor force..............................	3,915	666	3,249
Percent of total..................	22.2%	11.0%	28.1%
Civilian labor force...................	3,915	666	3,249
Employed.............................	3,848	599	3,249
Unemployed.........................	68	68	-
Percent of civilian labor force..	b	b	b
Not in labor force..........................	13,716	5,404	8,312
FEMALE			
Total, 14 to 19 years old..............	18,459	6,867	11,539
In labor force..............................	7,311	2,201	5,110
Percent of total..................	39.6%	32.0%	44.1%
Employed.............................	4,766	1,112	3,712
Unemployed.........................	2,486	1,088	1,398
Percent of civilian labor force.....	34.3%	b	b
Not in labor force..........................	11,149	4,666	6,483
Total, 20 to 24 years old..............	15,592	5,409	10,183
In labor force..............................	9,540	3,211	6,336
Percent of total..................	61.2%	59.4%	62.2%
Employed.............................	8,452	2,547	5,931
Unemployed.........................	1,069	664	405
Percent of civilian labor force.....	11.2%	b	b
Not in labor force..........................	6,046	2,198	3,848

b. Rate not presented when sample base less than 100

Represents zero.

908

Table 4--Continued

EMPLOYMENT STATUS OF POPULATION BY SEX, AGE, AND AREA OF OAKLAND

Employment Status	Total Oakland	Target Areas	Other Areas
FEMALE--Continued			
Total, 25 to 34 years old..............	21,252	8,452	12,800
In labor force.............................	12,790	4,836	7,954
Percent of total.................	60.2%	57.2%	62.1%
Employed...............................	11,710	4,152	7,590
Unemployed.............................	1,047	684	364
Percent of civilian labor force......	8.2%	14.2%	b
Not in labor force.........................	8,463	3,616	4,847
Total, 35 to 44 years old..............	21,462	8,525	12,936
In labor force.............................	12,003	4,974	7,029
Percent of total.................	55.9%	58.3%	54.3%
Employed...............................	10,992	4,182	6,810
Unemployed.............................	1,011	792	219
Percent of civilian labor force......	8.4%	15.9%	b
Not in labor force.........................	9,459	3,552	5,907
Total, 45 to 64 years old..............	46,893	14,070	32,823
In labor force.............................	25,034	8,037	16,997
Percent of total.................	53.4%	57.1%	51.8%
Employed..............................	23,770	7,347	16,423
Unemployed.............................	1,264	691	574
Percent of civilian labor force......	5.0%	8.6%	3.4%
Not in labor force.........................	21,859	6,033	15,826
Total, 65 years old and over..........	25,381	8,261	17,120
In labor force.............................	2,644	914	1,731
Percent of total.................	10.4%	11.1%	10.1%
Employed...............................	2,532	914	1,618
Unemployed.............................	113	-	113
Percent of civilian labor force......	b	b	b
Not in labor force.........................	22,737	7,347	15,389

b. Rate not presented when sample base less than 100.

- Represents zero.

909

Table 5

COMPONENTS OF EMPLOYMENT STATUS ESTIMATES BY SEX

COMPONENTS AND SEX	Total Oakland	Target Areas	Other Areas
BOTH SEXES			
Total, 14 years old and over········	272,903	95,531	177,372
Labor force[a]······························	166,008	56,215	109,793
Member of armed forces···················	2,422	926	1,496
Civilian labor force·····················	163,586	55,289	108,297
Employed·································	150,575	48,062	102,514
Unemployed·······························	13,011	7,227	5,783
Looking for work······················	11,320	6,299	5,021
On layoff, not looking for work·····	1,691	928	762
Not in labor force·····················	106,895	39,315	67,579
Looked for work in past 60 days[b]·······	2,037	905	1,131
Did not look for work in past 60 days···	104,858	38,410	66,448
Standard unemployment rate[c]···········	8.0%	13.1%	5.3%
Alternate unemployment rate[d]··········	9.1%	14.5%	6.3%
MALE			
Total, 14 years old and over········	123,864	43,947	79,917
Labor force[a]······························	96,682	32,045	64,638
Member of armed forces···················	2,306	811	1,496
Civilian labor force·····················	94,376	31,234	63,142
Employed·································	88,354	27,924	60,430
Unemployed·······························	6,021	3,310	2,712
Looking for work·····················	5,284	2,873	2,412
On layoff, not looking for work·····	737	437	300
Not in labor force·····················	27,182	11,903	15,279
Looked for work in past 60 days[b]·······	735	270	465
Did not look for work in past 60 days···	26,447	11,633	14,814
Standard unemployment rate[c]···········	6.4%	10.6%	4.3%
Alternate unemployment rate[d]··········	7.1%	11.4%	5.0%

a. Labor force as determined by standard U.S. Census questions.

b. Persons who were not reported looking for work by standard Census questions but who were described as looking for work in the past 60 days in response to an additional probe.

c. Percent of civilian labor force unemployed by standard Census definitions.

d. Percent of civilian labor force unemployed when persons found looking for work in the past 60 days by the additional probe are added to the unemployed and to the civilian labor force.

910

Table 5--Continued

COMPONENTS OF EMPLOYMENT STATUS ESTIMATES BY SEX

COMPONENTS AND SEX	Total Oakland	Target Areas	Other Areas
FEMALE			
Total 14 years old and over.........	149,037	51,584	97,456
Labor force[a].............................	69,327	24,172	45,155
Member of armed forces..................	116	116	-
Civilian labor force.....................	69,211	24,056	45,155
Employed...............................	62,221	20,138	42,084
Unemployed.............................	6,990	3,918	3,072
Looking for work....................	6,037	3,426	2,610
On layoff, not looking for work.....	953	492	462
Not in labor force.......................	79,712	27,412	52,300
Looked for work in past 60 days[b]........	1,301	636	666
Did not look for work in past 60 days...	78,411	26,776	51,634
Standard unemployment rate[c]...........	10.1%	16.3%	6.8%
Alternate unemployment rate[d]..........	11.8%	18.4%	8.2%

a. Labor force as determined by standard U.S. Census questions.

b. Persons who were not reported looking for work by standard Census questions but who were described as looking for work in the past 60 days in response to an additional probe.

c. Percent of civilian labor force unemployed by standard Census definitions.

d. Percent of civilian labor force unemployed when persons found looking for work in the past 60 days by the additional probe are added to the unemployed and to the civilian labor force.

- Represents zero.

911

Table A

SAMPLE SIZE FOR SELECTED SEGMENTS OF THE POPULATION, BY AREA

Segment of Population	Total Oakland	Target Areas	Other Areas
TOTAL SAMPLE			
Sample of households.............	2,623	1,508	1,115
Sample of persons................	7,546	4,627	2,919
Male...........................	3,535	2,175	1,360
14 years old and over........	2,452	1,403	1,049
In civilian labor force....	1,834	1,003	831
Female..........................	4,011	2,452	1,559
14 years old and over........	2,922	1,659	1,263
In civilian labor force....	1,342	764	578
Persons 25 years old and over..	4,127	2,326	1,801
NEGRO SAMPLE			
Sample of households.............	912	838	74
Sample of persons................	3,209	2,908	301
Male...........................	1,492	1,352	140
14 years old and over........	879	792	87
In civilian labor force....	672	601	71
Female..........................	1,717	1,556	161
14 years old and over........	1,094	988	106
In civilian labor force....	570	502	62
Persons 25 years old and over..	1,435	1,297	138
MEXICAN AMERICAN SAMPLE			
Sample of households.............	108	81	27
Sample of persons................	450	348	102
Male...........................	220	166	54
14 years old and over........	135	96	39
In civilian labor force....	105	72	33
Female..........................	230	182	48
14 years old and over........	116	88	28
In civilian labor force....	40	27	13
Persons 25 years old and over..	178	126	52

Table A--Continued

SAMPLE SIZE FOR SELECTED SEGMENTS OF THE POPULATION, BY AREA

Segment of Population	A	B	C	D	Hills	Flats	Lake
TOTAL SAMPLE							
Sample of households............	343	346	407	412	438	347	330
Sample of persons................	901	906	1,234	1,586	1,329	916	674
Male.........................	431	424	571	749	639	414	307
14 years old and over........	312	274	395	422	488	309	252
In civilian labor force....	226	178	279	320	389	237	205
Female.......................	470	482	663	837	690	502	367
14 years old and over........	361	352	446	500	548	395	320
In civilian labor force....	177	159	202	226	244	165	169
Persons 25 years old and over..	544	500	623	659	821	546	434
NEGRO SAMPLE							
Sample of households............	224	223	110	281	20	44	10
Sample of persons................	664	646	417	1,181	106	158	37
Male.........................	304	299	188	561	54	68	18
14 years old and over........	204	178	120	290	33	41	13
In civilian labor force....	159	122	89	231	24	37	10
Female.......................	360	347	229	620	52	90	19
14 years old and over........	259	243	132	354	31	60	15
In civilian labor force....	140	119	71	178	16	35	11
Persons 25 years old and over..	366	325	160	446	48	75	15

APPROXIMATE STANDARD ERRORS OF SELECTED ESTIMATES

Estimate	Total Oakland	Target Areas	Other Areas	A	B	C	D	Hills	Flats	Lake
Estimated number of persons...	365,127	142,057	223,069	23,997	37,177	42,046	38,838	89,477	83,979	49,613
Standard error...	8,350	3,670	7,490	925	2,190	2,180	1,740	3,160	6,390	2,310
Estimated percent Negro...	30.2%	60.6%	10.8%	72.3%	70.9%	33.1%	73.3%	8.2%	16.4%	5.9%
Standard error...	1.1%	1.5%	1.2%	2.3%	2.6%	2.3%	1.9%	1.5%	3.2%	2.0%
TOTAL										
Estimated labor force participation rate[a]	60.8%	58.8%	61.9%	60.5%	55.7%	60.3%	59.2%	61.0%	60.4%	65.7%
Standard error...	1.0%	1.1%	1.4%	2.3%	2.6%	2.3%	1.9%	1.5%	3.2%	2.0%
Estimated unemployment rate[b]	8.0%	13.1%	5.3%	7.5%	16.4%	13.2%	13.9%	3.8%	6.2%	6.5%
Standard error...	0.6%	0.9%	0.7%	1.4%	2.0%	1.8%	1.8%	0.8%	1.5%	1.4%
MEN										
Estimated labor force participation rate[a]	78.1%	72.9%	80.9%	73.0%	67.3%	74.0%	77.5%	81.0%	80.6%	81.2%
Standard error...	1.1%	1.4%	1.5%	2.5%	3.0%	2.7%	2.4%	1.8%	3.3%	2.7%
Estimated unemployment rate[b]	6.4%	10.6%	4.3%	7.0%	15.9%	9.5%	9.8%	2.2%	5.0%	6.8%
Standard error...	0.6%	1.2%	0.7%	1.8%	2.6%	2.5%	1.9%	0.7%	1.4%	2.0%
WOMEN										
Estimated labor force participation rate[a]	46.5%	46.9%	46.3%	48.9%	46.7%	48.0%	43.6%	43.4%	44.3%	53.9%
Standard error...	1.3%	1.6%	1.8%	3.3%	3.2%	3.1%	2.5%	2.4%	3.7%	3.1%
Estimated unemployment rate[b]	10.1%	16.3%	6.8%	8.1%	16.9%	18.2%	20.1%	6.3%	7.9%	6.1%
Standard error...	1.0%	1.5%	1.2%	1.9%	2.8%	3.6%	2.8%	1.8%	2.5%	1.8%

a. Percent of persons 14 years old and over in the labor force.
b. Percent of civilian labor force unemployed.

TABLE C

SURVEY RESPONSE RATE BY AREA

	Total Oakland	Target Areas	Other Areas	A	B	C	Flats	Lake
Total housing units sampled......	3,434	2,009	1,475	457	492	547	447	505
Vacant units................	259	170	89	32	58	48	37	37
Occupied units..............	3,225	1,839	1,336	425	434	499	410	469
Interviews completed........	2,623	1,508	1,115	343	346	407	347	330
Percent of occupied units.	81.3%	82.0%	80.1%	80.7%	79.7%	81.6%	84.6%	70.4%

A1. What was the highest grade (or year) of regular school PERSON has ever attended?

Grade: K 1 2 3 4 5 6 7 8   High: 1 2 3 4
College: 1 2 3 4 5 6+   ☐ No School
Also: (SKIP TO A6)

A2. Did PERSON finish this grade (or year)?
1. Yes   2. No

A8. Did PERSON work at any time last week?
(INCLUDE PART-TIME WORK SUCH AS SATURDAY JOB OR DELIVERING PAPERS, BUT NOT OWN HOUSEWORK)
1. Yes (CHECK W BOX   2. No (ASK A9)
AND SKIP TO A14)

A9. Was PERSON looking for work, or on layoff from a job?

CHECK BOXES AND SKIP TO A12

1. Yes, looking   3. No (ASK A10)
for work (LW)
2. Yes, layoff (LYO)

A10. Even though PERSON did not work last week, does ... have a job ... usually work(s) at?
1. Yes (CHECK JNW BOX   2. No (ASK A11)
AND SKIP TO A12)

A11. Was PERSON looking for work at any time in the past 60 days?

1. Yes, looking (CHECK   2. No (CHECK OTH
LW BOX AND ASK A12)   BOX, ASK A12)

Re e

A34. (To sum up) How many weeks did PERSON work
in 1965, either full-time or part-time? (We want
to count paid vacation, paid sick leave, and
military service as weeks worked.)

        0. None (SKIP TO A36)

    1. 13 weeks or less   4. 40-47 weeks
    2. 14-26 weeks   5. 48-49 weeks
    3. 27-39 weeks   6. 50-52 weeks

A35. How much did PERSON earn in 1965 in wages
and salary from all jobs? (That's before taxes
and other deductions and including commissions
and tips.)

        $ _____.00

        ☐ Take home only

☐ None   ☐ No idea

A36. Did PERSON earn any money OR (How much did
PERSON earn) in 1965 working in his own business
(professional practice, partnership, or farm)?
(I need the net income after business expenses.)

        $ _____.00

        ☐ Loss

☐ None   ☐ No idea

A37a. Last year, in 1965, did PERSON receive any
income from: (CODE ALL THAT APPLY)

    1. Rent, interest, or dividends?

    2. Social security, pensions, or veteran's
       payments?

    3. Unemployment insurance?

    4. Public assistance or welfare payments?

    5. Anything else--like annuities, regular
       contributions from persons not living
       in the household, alimony, etc.?
       (SPECIFY _____)
       ☐ None of these

b. IF ANY: How much in total did PERSON
receive from these sources in 1965?

        $ _____.00

A38. Total for This Person:
   (ADD FROM ABOVE) $ _____.00

917

Exhibit 2

NEW APPLICATIONS   -   RACIAL CHARACTERISTICS   -   March 1967

Local Office	Total	White	Negro	Mex-Amer	Other
503 - S.F. Prof & Coml	2349	1866	266	103	114
504 - S.F. Ind & Serv	2442	1348	541	317	236
431 - S.F. YOC Central Chinatown	1766	1114	314	105	233
442 - Hunters Pt Branch YOC	62	3	58	1	0
440 - Mission Branch YOC	199	93	33	68	5
441 - Western Addition YOC	103	29	72	0	2
504 - S.F. Adult - all branches	478	70	154	110	144
533 - S.F. Service Center	84	12	66	2	4
507 - Oakland ES	2358	1492	663	116	87
432 - Oakland YOC Central	880	495	265	59	61
445 - Berkeley Branch YOC	273	180	76	8	9
443 - East Oakland Branch YOC	232	51	147	30	4
444 - West Oakland Branch YOC	102	3	97	2	0
568 - Oakland Adult - all branches	999	120	689	175	15
034 - Hayward	1532	1318	33	139	42
446 - Hayward YOC	798	718	14	59	7
035 - Richmond	845	565	216	44	20
032 - Berkeley	775	413	296	35	31

918

Exhibit 3

California Department of Employment
Coastal Area   March 1967
Research and Statistics

Table I
Number of Persons Completing Institutional Training and Obtaining Employment
San Francisco County
Classes Ending April 1, 1965 through March 31, 1966

Occupation	Total No. Enrolled	No. Completed Courses	Percent Completing Course[1]	Number of Trainees Obtaining Jobs Total[2]	Training Related	Non-Training Related
Total	869	505	58.1	251	199	52
Professional	27	21	77.8	7	6	1
Nurse, Registered	27	21	77.8	7	6	1
Semi-Professional	32	15	46.9	10	10	0
Licensed Voc. Nurse	32	15	46.9	10	10	0
Clerical	513	289	56.3	158	144	14
Insurance Rate Clerk	24	14	58.3	11	11	0
Duplicating Machine Opr.	35	21	60.0	7	4	3
Clerk-Typist	293	148	50.5	68	60	8
Stenographer	143	94	65.7	66	63	3
Telephone Operator	18	12	66.7	6	6	0
Agricultural	44	23	52.3	14	1	13
Groundskeeper & Gardener	44	23	52.3	14	1	13
Skilled	132	93	70.5	27	11	16
Welder	42	32	76.2	11	3	8
Carpenter	23	21	91.3	6	1	5
Painter	27	18	66.7	1	1	0
Dry Cleaner	14	9	64.3	3	3	0
Office Mach. Serviceman	26	13	50.0	6	3	3
Semiskilled	121	64	52.9	35	27	8
Taxi Driver	40	27	67.5	14	14	0
Plant Wireman	62	25	40.3	15	10	5
Coin Mach. Serviceman	19	12	63.2	6	3	3

[1] Percent of total number enrolled.
[2] Total number of trainees who completed course and obtained jobs.

919

California Department of Employment
Coastal Area   March 1967
Research and Statistics

Table II

Racial Composition of Institutional MDTA Classes
San Francisco County
July 1, 1965 through June 30, 1966

Occupation	Total No. Enrolled	Number of Trainees by Race				
		White	Negro	Mexican-American	Other Non White	Unknown
Total Enrollment	1069	388	482	160	38	1
Professional	14	13	0	1	0	0
Nurse, Registered	14	13	0	1	0	0
Semi-Professional	89	62	7	13	7	0
Draftsman	86	60	7	12	7	0
Radio Dispatcher	1	1	0	0	0	0
Embalmer	1	1	0	0	0	0
Programmer	1	0	0	1	0	0
Clerical	618	189	300	111	17	1
Clerk, General	82	18	53	11	0	0
Clerk, Room	1	1	0	0	0	0
Insurance Rate Clerk	24	2	19	1	2	0
Office Boy	24	2	16	2	4	0
Duplicating Mach. Opr.	16	15	0	1	0	0
Clerk-Typist	341	100	143	90	8	0
Stenographer	71	45	18	5	2	1
Telephone Operator	59	6	51	1	1	0
Service	1	1	0	0	0	0
Cook	1	1	0	0	0	0
Agricultural	15	12	1	2	0	0
Groundskeeper/Gardener	15	12	1	2	0	0
Skilled	133	72	39	18	4	0
Welder	45	30	8	7	0	0
Carpenter	27	23	3	1	0	0
Dry Cleaner	46	13	22	8	3	0
Auto Mechanic	3	2	0	1	0	0
Diesel Mechanic	1	1	0	0	0	0
Office Mach. Serviceman	9	1	6	1	1	0
TV and Radio Technician	2	2	0	0	0	0
Semiskilled	56	14	38	1	3	0
Taxi Driver	24	5	17	1	1	0
Plant Wireman & Frameman	32	9	21	0	2	0
Pre-Vocational Occupations	143	25	97	14		

California Department of Employment
Coastal Area
Research and Statistics

March 1967

Table III
Number of Institutional MDTA Trainees
Enrolled by Age
July 1, 1965 through June 30, 1965
San Francisco County

Occupation	Total No. Enrolled	Age of Trainees				
		Under 19 yrs.	19 to 21 yrs.	22 to 34 yrs.	35 to 44 yrs.	45 yrs. & over
Total Enrollment	1069	178	332	257	163	139
Professional	14	0	0	0	9	5
Nurse, Registered	14	0	0	0	9	5
Semi-Professional	89	1	13	56	16	3
Draftsman	86	1	13	55	14	3
Radio Dispatcher	1	0	0	0	1	0
Embalmer	1	0	0	0	1	0
Programmer	1	0	0	1	0	0
Clerical	618	116	211	125	100	66
Clerk, General	82	19	47	9	3	4
Clerk, Room	1	0	0	0	0	1
Insurance Rate Clerk	24	0	10	0	14	0
Office Boy	24	9	15	0	0	0
Duplicating Mach. Opr.	16	8	8	0	0	0
Clerk-Typist	341	48	85	97	69	42
Stenographer	71	10	9	19	14	19
Telephone Operator	59	22	37	0	0	0
Service	1	0	0	0	0	1
Cook	1	0	0	0	0	1
Agricultural	15	0	0	2	4	9
Groundskeeper/Gardener	15	0	0	2	4	9
Skilled	133	5	7	40	29	52
Welder	45	0	0	8	12	25
Carpenter	27	0	0	9	3	15
Dry Cleaner	46	0	2	20	13	11
Auto Mechanic	3	0	0	3	0	0
Diesel Mechanic	1	0	0	0	0	0
Office Mach. Serviceman	9	4	5	0	0	0
TV and Radio Technician	2	0	0	0	1	1
Semiskilled	56	15	18	16	4	3
Taxi Driver	24	0	1	16	4	3
Plant Wireman & Frameman	32	15	17	0	0	0
Pre-Vocational Occupations	143	41	83	18	1	0

California Department of Employment
Coastal Area
Research and Statistics

March 1967

Table IV
Number of Institutional MDTA Trainees
by Years of Schooling
San Francisco County
July 1, 1965 through June 30, 1966

Occupation	Total No. Enrolled	Years of Schooling				
		Under 8 yrs.	8 yrs.	9-11 yrs.	12 yrs.	Over 12 yrs.
Total Enrollment	1069	4	30	308	515	212
Professional	14	0	0	0	0	14
Nurse, Registered	14	0	0	0	0	14
Semi-Professional	89	0	0	1	32	56
Draftsman	86	0	0	1	32	53
Radio Dispatcher	1	0	0	0	0	1
Embalmer	1	0	0	0	0	1
Programmer	1	0	0	0	0	1
Clerical	618	0	3	187	313	115
Clerk, General	82	0	1	38	41	2
Clerk, Room	1	0	0	1	0	0
Insurance Rate Clerk	24	0	0	2	20	2
Office Boy	24	0	1	10	13	0
Duplicating Mach. Opr.	16	0	0	6	8	2
Clerk-Typist	341	0	1	77	187	76
Stenographer	71	0	0	19	19	33
Telephone Operator	59	0	0	34	25	0
Service	1	1	0	0	0	0
Cook	1	1	0	0	0	0
Agricultural	15	0	2	6	3	4
Groundskeeper/Gardener	15	0	2	6	3	4
Skilled	133	3	20	50	48	12
Welder	45	2	9	25	7	2
Carpenter	27	1	4	6	12	4
Dry Cleaner	46	0	6	14	21	5
Auto Mechanic	3	0	1	2	0	0
Diesel Mechanic	1	0	0	1	0	0
Office Mach. Serviceman	9	0	0	2	7	0
TV and Radio Technician	2	0	0	0	1	1
Semiskilled	56	0	4	16	30	6
Taxi Driver	24	0	3	5	12	4
Plant Wireman & Frameman	32	0	1	11	18	2
Pre-Vocational Occupations	143	1		48	89	5

California Department of Employment
Coastal Area
Research and Statistics

March 1967

Table V
Number of Institutional MDTA Trainees
Enrolled by Years in the Labor Force
San Francisco County
July 1, 1965 through June 30, 1966

Occupation	Total No. Enrolled	Years in the Labor Force		
		Under 3 yrs.	3 to 10 yrs.	Over 10 yrs
Total Enrollment	1069	538	295	236
Professional	14	1	9	4
Nurse, Registered	14	1	9	4
Semi-Professional	89	16	50	23
Draftsman	86	16	50	20
Radio Dispatcher	1	0	0	1
Embalmer	1	0	0	1
Programmer	1	0	0	1
Clerical	618	361	181	76
Clerk, General	82	49	21	12
Clerk, Room	1	0	0	1
Insurance Rate Clerk	24	24	0	0
Office Boy	24	21	3	0
Duplicating Mach. Opr.	16	14	2	0
Clerk-Typist	341	172	123	46
Stenographer	71	24	30	17
Telephone Operator	59	57	2	0
Service	1	0	0	1
Cook	1	0	0	1
Agricultural	15	0	2	13
Groundskeeper/Gardener	15	0	2	13
Skilled	133	16	19	98
Welder	45	0	5	40
Carpenter	27	0	5	22
Dry Cleaner	46	7	8	31
Auto Mechanic	3	0	0	3
Diesel Mechanic	1	1	0	0
Office Mach. Serviceman	9	8	1	0
TV and Radio Technician	2	0	0	2
Semiskilled	56	28	11	17
Taxi Driver	24	0	7	17
Plant Wireman & Frameman	32	28	4	0
Pre-Vocational Occupations	143	116	23	4

California Department of Employment
Coastal Area
Research and Statistics

March 1967

Table VI
Number of Institutional MDTA Trainees Enrolled by
Family Status and by U.I. Claimant Status
San Francisco County
July 1, 1965 through June 30, 1966

Occupation	Total No. Enrolled	Family Head	UI Claimants
Total Enrollment	1069	451	202
Professional	14	1	0
Nurse, Registered	14	1	0
Semi-Professional	89	46	36
Draftsman	86	43	36
Radio Dispatcher	1	1	0
Embalmer	1	1	0
Programmer	1	1	0
Clerical	618	236	92
Clerk, General	82	29	11
Clerk, Room	1	1	0
Insurance Rate Clerk	24	4	0
Office Boy	24	3	0
Duplicating Mach. Opr.	16	3	0
Clerk-Typist	341	162	50
Stenographer	71	21	31
Telephone Operator	59	13	0
Service	1	1	0
Cook	1	1	0
Agricultural	15	9	0
Groundskeeper/Gardener	15	9	0
Skilled	133	90	54
Welder	45	35	18
Carpenter	27	24	18
Dry Cleaner	46	22	17
Auto Mechanic	3	3	1
Diesel Mechanic	1	1	0
Office Mach. Serviceman	9	3	0
TV and Radio Technician	2	2	0
Semiskilled	56	27	11
Taxi Driver	24	20	10
Plant Wireman & Frameman	32	7	1
Pre-Vocational Occupations	143	41	0

EAST DAY SKILLS CENTER

Characteristics of 129 Trainees in Group III **

August 8, 1966

1. **SEX**

   <u>Male</u>   <u>Female</u>

   97 3/4%   2½%

2. **AGE**

   <u>Below 20</u>   <u>20-25</u>   <u>26-30</u>   <u>31-40</u>   <u>41-50</u>   <u>51-60</u>

   3 3/4%   21 3/4%   17 3/4%   31½%   18 3/4%   6 3

   <u>61 & over</u>

   0

3. **HEAD OF HOUSEHOLD**

   <u>Yes</u>   <u>No</u>

   86 3/4%   13½%

4. **NUMBER OF DEPENDENTS**

   <u>0-2</u>   <u>3-5</u> *

   45%   55%

   *Of these, 37 or approximately 28½% of the total 129 have 5 or more dependents.

5. **HIGHEST GRADE COMPLETED**

   <u>0-4</u>   <u>5-7</u>   <u>8-9</u>   <u>10 & above</u>

   17 3/4%   21 3/4%   31%   29½%

6. **PUBLIC ASSISTANCE RECIPIENT**

   <u>Yes</u>   <u>No</u>

   31%   69%

7. **WEEKS UNEMPLOYED***

   <u>Less than 5</u>   <u>5-14</u>   <u>15-26</u>   <u>27-52</u>   <u>52 & over</u>

   16½%   22½%   13 3/4%   15½%   13½%

   *Some of these persons were underemployed or employed part time upon entering the Skills Center. Approximately 18 3/4% of the total 129 can be included in this group.

8. **SPANISH--PRIMARY LANGUAGE**

   17%

9. **UNEMPLOYMENT INSURANCE CLAIMS REQUESTS ON FILE**

   18 3/4%

EAST BAY SKILLS CENTER

Characteristics of Trainees Entering on January 9 (Based on 204)

March 1, 1967

1. Sex: Male 94% (97 1/2%)* Female 6% (2 1/2%)

2. Age: Below 20 37% (3 1/4%) Note: 4% out of 204 are below 18.

    20-25 37% (21%); 26-30 11% (18 3/4%); 31-40 13% (27 3/4%);

    41-50 2% (21 1/2%); 51-60 0% (7 1/4%); 61 and over 0% (1/2%).

3. Head of Household: Yes 46% (80 1/2%); No 54% (19 1/2%).

4. Number of Dependents: 0 55% 1-2 19%; 3-5 and over 26%.

    (0-2 52 3/4%; 3-5 47 1/4%).

5. Highest Grade Completed: 0-4 0% (6 1/2%); 5-7 2% (16 1/2%);

    8-9 13% (24 1/2%); 10-11 49%; 12 33%; college 3%.

    (Note: In the April, 1966 group only one was from college,
    57 1/2% had completed 10th or above, but 90% of that group had
    gone no further than the 10th grade.)

6. Public Assistance Recipient: Yes 12% (27%); No 88% (73%)

7. Weeks Unemployed: Less than 5 31% (27%); 5-14 33% (23 3/4%);

    15-26 14% (21 1/2%); 27-52 13% (15 1/4%); 52 & over 9% (12 1/2%)

8. Spanish Primary Language: Unknown (24 1/2%).

9. Unemployment Insurance Claims Requests on File: 15% (25%)

10. Veteran: Yes 24% (unknown); No 76%

*All those figures in parentheses are percentages pertaining to the first
400 trainees who entered the Skills Center in April, 1966.

EAST BAY SKILLS CENTER

Characteristics of Trainees Entering on February 14, 1967

March 22, 1967

1. Sex: Male 86%   Female 14%

2. Age: Below 30   20-25   25-30   31-40   41-50   51-60   Over 60
        18%   29%   20%   19%   13%   1%   0

3. Dependents: 0   1-2   3-5 and over
               31% 36%   33%

4. Highest grade: 0-4   5-7   8-9   10-11   12   College
                   .5%   2%   14%   48%   28.5% 7%

5. Public assistance: yes   no
                       27%   73%

6. Unemployment claims on file: yes   no
                                 21%   79%

7. Weeks unemployed: Less than 5   5-14   15-26   27-52   52 and over
                      19%   31%   15%   11%   15%

   Never employed   Underemployed
   .5%   8.5%

8. Veteran: yes   no
             31%   69%

EAST BAY SKILLS CENTER

Characteristics of Trainees Entering on November 28, 1966

March. 22, 1967

1. Sex: Male   49%   Female   51%

2. Age: Below 20.   20-25
           *49%   51%

3. Head of Household: yes   No.
                            32.5%   67.5%

4. Number of Dependents: 0-2   3-5
                            96.6%   3.4%

5. Highest Grade Completed: 0-4   5-7.   8-9   10 and over
                              0   .5%   17%   87.4%

6. Public assistance: yes   no
                            19%   81%

7. Weeks unemployed: Less than 5   5-14   15-26   27-52   52 and over
                            27%   26%   13%   12%   22%

*This figure includes a significant number of trainees who are age 18, several who are 17, and one 16. This group is 19% of the total input and 39.5% of the "below 20" figure.

928

East Bay Skills Center

Characteristics of First 400 Trainees

April 27, 1966

1. SEX

Male	Female
97½%	2½%

2. AGE

Below 20	20-25	26-30	31-40	41-50	51-60	61 & Over
3½%	21%	18 3/4%	27 3/4%	21½%	7½%	½%

3. HEAD OF HOUSEHOLD

Yes	No
80½%	19½%

4. NUMBER OF DEPENDENTS

0-2	3-5
52 3/4%	*47½%

*Of these,90 or Approximately 22½% of the total 400 have 5 or more dependents.

5. HIGHEST GRADE COMPLETED

0-4	5-7	8-9	10 & above
6½%	16½%	24½%	52¾%

6. PUBLIC ASSISTANCE RECIPIENT

Yes	No
27%	73%

7. WEEKS UNEMPLOYED

Less than 5	5-14	15-26	27-52	52 &Over
*27%	23 3/4%	21½%	15½%	12½%

* Some of these persons were underemployed or employed part time upon entering the Skills Center. Approximately 10% of the total 400 can be included in this group.

8. SPANISH-PRIMARY LANGUAGE

24½%

9. UNEMPLOYMENT INSURANCE CLAIMS REQUESTS ON FILE

25%

Exhibit No. 18

San Francisco   May 1, 1967

<u>Statement of Hon. Terry A. Francois, member of the Board of Supervisors, City and County of San Francisco, prepared for submission to the United States Commission on Civil Rights</u>

SCHOOL INTEGRATION: THEN WHAT?

As a Negro long identified with the Civil Rights struggle, and as a City and County official attempting to deal realistically with San Francisco's racial problems, I have become extremely stimulated by the possibilities of the Multi-Culture Program, a daring new plan calculated to attack the very roots of racial and ethnic hostilities in our cities.

This program, currently being developed with particular reference to the San Francisco Bay Area, would effect <u>radical</u> changes in our whole approach to integrated education and has clear and important implications for <u>every</u> major American city.

The Multi-Culture Project developed from the concern that increased integration and other such advances, although necessary, are <u>insufficient</u> to reverse the tide of mounting racial tensions.

In the schools where our citizens are molded, it has generally been assumed that proximity of different groups to one another will <u>automatically</u> result in intergroup understanding. And yet, we know that very often it does not, and may actually reinforce bigotries.

At present, children can and do go through 12 or more years of typical schooling (whether in segregated or integrated classes) and come out totally unlearned in intergroup relations — in either information or attitudes.

Their learnings cannot be left to chance. They require intentional teaching; yet the teachers who want to provide this have no training and almost no resources to call on. Indeed, those who attempt such teaching must <u>deviate</u> from the school program in order to do so!

Another common assumption of public education has been that the most useful way in which to realize the American dream is to assimilate all minority groups, and to do this by <u>ignoring</u> or <u>minimizing</u> cultural differences.

This unrealistic approach has, contrary to its intended purpose, deepened feelings of alienation among minority youth, and produced both majority and minority youngsters who have inadequate understandings of themselves and of others.

A child <u>knows</u> if he is different in the national origin of his parents, their religious affiliation, or the color of their skin. If he is taught, explicitly or implicitly, that the less said about this aspect of his identification the better, he will have low self-esteem, feelings of unworthiness, bitterness and cynicism—creating <u>personal pain and social problems</u> not intended by <u>the American dream.</u>

At a time when physical integration is an ever-increasing fact, we must plan those changes in the outlook of our schools and similar institutions which are indicated by heterogeneous communities.

930

For example, just as the schools provide affective and cognitive learnings relevant to
the child's identity as a "Californian" and as a "San Franciscan," so might the schools
provide similar learnings for those other important aspects of his identity.

The specific hypotheses of the project have very important implications. They are that:

1) It is possible to devise a school program which gives children an intensive and extensive knowledge of their racial or ethnic identification in such a way as to enhance
the effectiveness and the breadth of their general education, and to foster their
feelings of self-worth, of belonging, of having a stake in the American future, — as
well as the concomitant feelings of social responsibility and of compassion toward
others.

2) This program can greatly enhance the children's understanding and appreciation of
American groups other than their own.

3) Children experiencing such a program will tend to be strongly committed to American
ideals of democratic reciprocity among people of diverse backgrounds.

There is no such Multi-Culture program on a large scale in existence. Yet, every
sociologist, psychologist, anthropologist, or similar expert interviewed by members of
the Multi-Culture Institute Board of Trustees has called this a need of major priority.

The initial demonstration will be a full program in which the school day of participating
children, representing several different ethnic groups (both of the more "arrived," and
the less "arrived" categories), will consist of the following:

1) Integrated classes for an excellent program of general studies (e.g. English, arithmetic);

2) Separated classes for each ethnic group to have an extensive and intensive study of
the language and culture of its group;

3) Combined classes in which each group will, in a sense, teach the others about its
own group.

The program will be designed to further positive group identification without creating
feelings of isolation or alienation; to show children that having a particular ethnic
identification does not mean they are "better" or "worse" than other children who are
unique in their own ways.

It will also seek to impart an appreciation of the beauty of diverseness, which must not
be distorted into barriers against intellectual and social communication. Thus, one
major objective will be cultivation of delight in sharing of group cultures with one
another.

Jewish children celebrating the Passover seder with its theme of the end of Hebrew
slavery would be hosts for that occasion to all other students at the school. The
celebration would not only demonstrate a facet of Jewish life; it would be a springboard
for a general consideration of the universal human desire for freedom and dignity. In
a parallel way, the same theme might well be expressed by Negro children in the context
of milestones in the Negro's search for the same goals.

The objectives of the ethnic classes can be summed up as follows:

1) enjoyable experiences with the group identification; a "good feeling" about being
part of that group;

931

2) a realistic grasp of the group's common past and present, and of its potential for contributing to society as a whole;

3) development of creative tools for further self-definition and exploration of one's past;

4) cultivation of the habit of evaluating individuals on their own merits, rather than prejudging them as members of "natural" groups (i.e. the various groups and associations they were "born into");

5) a sense of belief in the overriding humanity which unites all mankind, regardless of differences.

In an era of great emphasis on integration, this program proposes intentionally to separate children at certain periods of time, in order to allow them adequate time to talk among themselves, to learn about themselves, and to examine their relationship to others.

Shocking as this may be to some, it is precisely what the older children are already doing on their own initiative in ever-increasing numbers throughout the country. The tragedy is that they are doing it with little or no involvement of the schools, and thus without the information and mature thinking that well-prepared teachers could bring to the groups.

We must face realities now. Our efforts to end de facto school segregation, at least in the north, are meeting with increasing success. But what happens if we end our efforts here — will we have achieved a real integration? The children are segregated on the very buses that carry the all white or all Negro children to their "integrated" school. And in a natural way, these children who have not learned to place a positive value on either their own differentness or that of others, maintain a most effective segregation within the school building, within the classrooms where we have placed them in supposed proximity.

The middle-class parents are watching with great concern to see if the standards of their children's middle class schools will suffer from the influx of ghetto children. We who have imposed bussing upon them have promised that they will not. But what will actually happen when these "different" children bring their feelings of shame, alienation, futility, and rootlessness with them to the shiny school building? Can integration make good its promises without major changes in the orientation, not only of schools, but of all our institutions that deal with people of diverse groups?

The Multi-Culture Project has been harshly criticized by some, on the grounds that it is a considerable departure from present practice. Yet, the results we are getting from present practice would indicate that nothing short of a considerable departure will do.

Statement of
Supervisor Terry A. Francois
Member of the San Francisco Board of Supervisors

Prepared for Submission to the
United States Commission on Civil Rights

May 3, 1967

CIVIL RIGHTS AND URBAN RENEWAL

Attitude of Civil Rights Groups Toward Renewal

Attitudes on the part of civil rights groups toward urban renewal appears to
have gone through three phases.

1. At the end of World War II civil rights groups shared the general
   enthusiasm for the elimination of slums and the rebuilding of
   attractive communities combined with a vigorous program to attain
   the national goal of "a decent home and a decent neighborhood for
   every family". The persistence of discriminatory practices, the
   magnitude of the relocation needs, and the complexities of inter-
   related physical and social problems were all grossly underestimated.

2. As a reaction toward many redevelopment projects which, in an unfortunate number of cases throughout the United States, did displace
   minority group families from slum areas and rebuilt cleared land with
   luxury apartments, there was a strong reaction against urban redevelopment as "Negro removal".

   Most of these projects had their inception before the Housing Act of
   1954 which allowed and encouraged the rehabilitation of existing
   residential properties as an integral part of the renewal effort.
   Other than a limited provision for public housing—for which large
   scale disenchantment had already set in—there were no mechanisms for
   financing the construction for any additional housing resources for
   families of low and moderate income.

3. In recent years with growing sophistication on the part of civil rights
   groups there has been emphasis on the evaluation of each proposed renewal
   program on its own merit. There is recognition that urban renewal is a
   tool of government which can be used to perpetuate or even create evil
   conditions but at the same time is a tool which, when used imaginatively,
   can be of great benefit to the community and particularly to minority groups
   within the community. In its publication, entitled "The Urban Renewal
   Program and NAACP Guidelines to Integration", the NAACP stated succinctly
   that "urban renewal should be planned and executed to advance racial and

933

economic diversification" and that "urban renewal must be used as a
program to serve the whole community and improve the environment and
all of the people who reside in it." In recent years civil rights
groups have taken a more active part in the analysis and debate of
proposed renewal programs. The NAACP legal defense fund stopped the
use of Federal urban renewal monies in a city in Tennessee on the
basis that the plan was not designed to serve the whole community and
would not improve the lot of all the people who resided in the city.
On the other hand, the Fort Lauderdale NAACP is an active proponent of
a large-scale rehabilitation-renewal program designed to upgrade the
worst section of the Negro area of that city.

Needed Safeguards for Minority Group Members

During the past year in San Francisco I had an opportunity to participate in the
formulation of a statement of policy to guide renewal planning in the Inner Mission
District in San Francisco. Although the Board of Supervisors, acting under strong
right wing pressures, did not allow planning to proceed, I believe these safeguards are meaningful and have wider application.

The key elements in this policy statement may be summarized as follows:

1. The detailed planning for the neighborhood must be done primarily in
   a neighborhood office in order to be readily available to the affected
   citizens and subject to their continuing review.

2. The planning staff must fully engage the community in the planning
   process and reports, plans, models should be specifically designed
   to promote its understanding and participation. Regular written
   reports should be made by the planning staff to the general public
   and to the local City Council or Board of Supervisors. There must
   be an adequate time period for the public to study and examine the
   completed plan before public hearings are undertaken.

3. Renewal plans must emphasize social objectives including improvement
   of housing, job opportunities, improvement of schools, cultural and
   recreational facilities. If at all possible, renewal plans should
   increase the net housing supply at prices the residents can afford
   and, if this is not part of the renewal program, there should be
   specific justification as to reasons.

4. Relocation guarantees including the right of appeal to Housing Appeal
   Boards must be made an integral part of every renewal program.

5. One mechanism for assuring citizen participation warranting careful
   consideration is the appointment of a committee representing all of
   the elements and organizations in the affected neighborhood by the
   Mayor to guide the development of the plan and act in the manner of
   a neighborhood planning commission.

If such protections are available to the minority groups, they should not hesitate
to support urban renewal (and other public programs such as model cities, federally
assisted code enforcement) designed to improve the cities of America. Moreover,
the civil rights organizations should actively search out opportunities to make

use of these new improvement tools and support and encourage their utilization
in the community.

Tools Available for Neighborhood Improvement

In recent years, particularly in the Housing Acts of 1965 and 1966, the Congress
of the United States, responding to the valid criticisms of earlier programs, has
provided a series of new tools which have significant potential. These include:

1. rent supplements

2. scattered site public housing

3. leased private units for public housing (Section 23 for short-term
    and Section 10(c) which provides for long-term leasing)

4. moderate priced private housing (Section 221(d)(3))

5. housing for the elderly (Sections 202 and 231)

6. low interest loans for rehabilitation (Section 312)

7. rehabilitation grants up to $1500 for hardship cases (Section 115)

8. improved counseling services on rehabilitation and

9. improved relocation assistance for residents and businessmen.

The moderate priced private housing program, the senior citizen housing program
and the rent supplement program apply to rehabilitated as well as new units.

Recommendations

Please recognize that my comments on renewal stem from a background of ten years
of opposition to the inequities of renewal programs. Long before the current
rash of Alinsky trainees discovered that renewal programs served as an ideal
mechanism for community organization (regardless of the merits or demerits of the
proposed program) I was active in opposition to improperly prepared renewal efforts
(during the years 1958, 1959 and 1960). Those of us active in the movement have
seen great advances in the civil rights law, great advances "on paper". Now we
are disillusioned that these "paper" advances have meant so little to our people.
I have come to the conclusion that when a local church, taking advantage of the
new legislation, sponsors a program of moderate priced private housing, either
in the construction or rehabilitation, this is a real and tangible benefit to
the total community. The church then designates, say one-third of these units,
for very low income families who, with rent supplements, will be able to live
in the middle income development on an anonymous basis. In San Francisco and
in many other communities with imaginative efforts, these units can be reasonably
integrated. I have come to believe that this kind of brick and mortar progress
should not be neglected and while fully recognized that these programs don't go

far enough, we should take advantage of every program available.

Thus I urge upon the Civil Rights Commission two key directions of effort. First, the Civil Rights Commission should encourage all communities to utilize the tools of urban renewal, model cities, and code enforcement as a positive force to increase the supply of low and moderate income housing and to advance racial and economic diversification. Secondly, I urge the Civil Rights Commission to use its influence with fellow agencies of the Federal government to ease the administrative barriers which are preventing the new programs to be utilized as Congress expected them to be used. Specifically I make the following suggestions:

1. That in high cost areas—such as San Francisco—the cost of construction be realistically taken into account and adjusted so as to ease the unit cost limitation and allow needed programs to accelerate.

2. Provide that rent supplements for moderate income housing shall be available under the low interest rate procedure (sub-market rate interest) as a standard procedure rather than as potential program.

3. Ease the financing of moderate income housing through permission of the inclusion of a greater percentage of development integrated with such development, the income which can be authorized to help support the maximum integration. In addition, a five percent vacancy factor should be allowed for computing gross incomes to support maximum integration (the great demand for low and moderate income housing means that the vacancy rate will always be lower than the 10 to 15 percent factor usually considered prudent in luxury housing).

4. The term of loans for moderate income housing should be extended from the present 40 years to a 50-year term to reduce the monthly payments required.

Review will indicate many other areas of potential advance.

Some of these improvements may require legislation but the Civil Rights Commission can provide a real service by urging the Department of Housing and Urban Development, including FHA, to utilize its administrative discretion to the utmost in forwarding these programs.

936

References

National Association for the Advancement of Colored People.
Annual Convention Resolutions, 1953, 1956, 1961, 1965, 1966.

National Association for the Advancement of Colored People.
The Urban Renewal Program and NAACP Guidelines to Integration. (undated)

National Committee Against Discrimination in Housing.
Trends in Housing Volume XI Number 4. April 1967.

The New York Times, April 9, 1967
Fort Lauderdale Negroes Bitter over Rejection of Renewal Plan.

San Francisco Board of Supervisors. Proposed Resolution File No. 148-67-2.
To Further and Safeguard the Interests of the Present Residents, Businessmen,
Property Owners, and Organizations and To Insure Citizen Participation in
Planning.

937

Exhibit No. 19*

INDIVIDUAL COMPLAINT

Exhibit No. 20

STATEMENT TO THE U.S. COMMISSION ON CIVIL RIGHTS

Jobs in our schools constitute a large share of the economic power within a community. In this state fifty seven percent of the tax dollar goes into educational needs. Any segment of the community that is denied participation in the opportunities made possible by this vast outlay of tax money will be poor indeed.

The racial minority community is denied its fair share of jobs as teachers, counselors, administrators, and as supervisors in the several categories. In our local schools this policy is effective from kindergarten to college; in federal programs the same policy is evident from Head Start to Upward Bound.

The extent to which racial minority teachers are denied the dignity, respect, and opportunity to work as teachers, counselors, and other status positions to an equal or greater extent will all children be denied quality education.

The children of our schools are basicly honest; they are impatient with grown-ups who show arrogance toward other children based upon race. When they see unfair practices operating at the hands of our schools the children tend to reject the total educational program.

To perpetuate injustice in education there must be continuous scapegoating in order to justify things being as they are. There are those sincere people who believe that racial minority children are inherently inferior. In one area the Spanish and Mexican children were assigned subservient roles to caucasian children, "because that's the role their parents play in real life".

Wherever laws are broken, wherever rights of men and women are violated for whatever reason with the permission of a community be it expressed or implied, chaos will be the ultimate results. Because of the total obsession of education with racism that denies the racial minority community's needs and expose its children to great hurt, we have lost sight of our moral values and sense of fair-play. We are so engrossed in the tasks of putting out fires of various assortments, quieting rumors of all shades, and pretending that all is well that we are losing great potential simply because we refuse to face up to our folly.

A recent survey conducted by the University of California of its 27000 students disclosed that there were only 235 Negroes. Of this number only 29 were from San Francisco and only 5 of these entered U.C. directly from high

939

schools in San Francisco . There were three from Lowell High and two from
Balboa High School. Seventeen transferred from San Francisco State College
and eight from S.F. City College to make the total twenty-nine.
Oakland had a total of twenty seven, Berkeley had eleven; and Richmond had
seven. Now if this represents the best we can do for Negro children under our
present educational programming and planning, we should stop and question the
whole system. Our schools, ofcourse, imply that our children are inferior
deprived and otherwise handicapped. This could be true with a reasonable
fraction of any group, but it is hard to convince the community that only
29 Negro students in San Francisco, 27 Negro students in Oakland, and 11 in
Berkeley who qualify academically for admission to The University of California
at Berkeley over a four or five year period.
Our schools continue to tell us that Negro teachers are hard to find; yet
Negro teachers dominate the substitute teachers' list. They just do not get
the jobs when they become available.
We are convinced that neither progress nor peace can come to this community
unless and until our schools can become less arrogant toward - and more
respectful of - the racial minority community generally, and the Negro
community particularly.

                    Alfred C. Simmons

940

Exhibit No. 21

asociación politica de habla/apellido español

spanish speaking/surnamed political association, inc.

625 MARKET STREET · SAN FRANCISCO, CALIFORNIA 94105   (415) 986-4653

Founders (Fundadores)
RICARDO A. CALLEJO
SAL CORDOVA
WALDO VELASQUEZ

May 1, 1967

To The Members of the United States Civil Rights Commission

Re: Meetings in San Francisco, May 1, 2 and 3, 1967

Gentlemen:

Enclosed for your consideration are the following items.

    1. My letter of February 16 to the Commissioner of Internal Revenue.

    2. Copy of the Commissioner's letter of April 20 in answer to my letter.

    3. Copy of my letter of May 1st.to the Commissioner.

The above matters should serve to delineate our position before your Committee.

In addition to the above I should like to call your attention to the following facts. We had apprised Mr.Glick, of your office, of our activities concerning the rights of the Spanish speaking/surnamed people and had fully expected to appear before your Committee. Mr. Glick informed us this morning that we had not been included on the agenda.

I had the pleasure of meeting Mr. David Rubin, Deputy General Counsel of your Commission,who informed me that under Section 702.10 we could appear at the discretion of the Commission. We, hereby, request that you exercise that discretion so as to permit us to be heard. We also request that the matters, herein-above contained be made part of the record and that we be provided with a copy of the Agenda of your hearings, matter which we requested this morning and which was denied "not available to the public", which makes us wonder.

Yours truly,

Ricardo A. Callejo
Legal Counsel

RAC:mbg

Asociación política de habla/apellido español

Spanish speaking/surnamed political association, inc.

February 16, 1967

SAN FRANCISCO, CALIFORNIA 94110   (415) ███-████

███████ Service
██████, D.C.   Re: The right of Spanish speaking TAX
                                   people to equal protection of/law

On behalf of this new national political Association I
██████ to refer to the above captioned and our concern with
the following questions:

1. Why doesn't the IRS have income tax
████ and information printed in Spanish in areas known to have
██████ █████████ populations?

2. What are the legal factors involved
█████████ of tax particularly why is no interest paid on
██ refund when it is due just as interest is charged on tax
███ ██████████?

3. How can a small taxpayer appeal or
██████ the equal benefit of the tax law if he has been deprived
of the equal chance or opportunity to overcome language difference?

4. In what sense can the Statute of
Limitations be said to have run out against a person or group
which denied or which education opportunity nullifies the language
basis upon which ignorance of the law is said to not be an excuse?

5. When a tax appeal concerning a
████ and ██ █████ suffering from inadequate or complete lack of
██ if no administrator or interpreter is provided, how can the
accused be entitled to said to test the truth of the matter if there
is no actual attempt the party in interest said in his native
tongue but only the English translation of the interpreter?

6. With specific reference to Spanish,
which was the native language of the Southwest and remains the
██████ tongue of 10 million Americans, which was guaranteed by
Treaty(Guadalupe Hidalgo),by Constitution(both Federal-incorporated
by reference in the Treaty, and State-see First California Constitution of 1849,Art.11,Sec.21,guaranteeing Spanish as an official
language forever and illegally repealed in 1879),there should be
some administrative procedure for filing a grievance to suit the
██████ circumstances of the language difference.

The above questions are propounded as a forerunner of
our intent to file either an administrative action or a suit. Therefore as a courtesy to you and in the hope of administrative remedy
we request a prompt reply indicating Statutes and pertinent law
and administrative decisions or policies concerning these questions.

We hope to be in Washington, D.C., by March 7th to meet
with a member of your staff to pursue this matter. We should appreciate your designation of a subordinate for the purpose.

Sincerely yours,

Ricardo A. Callejo
Legal Counsel

RicCembe
cc: Senator Magnuson
cc: Senator Kuchel

942

U. S. TREASURY DEPARTMENT

 Commissioner of Internal Revenue

WASHINGTON 25, D. C.

APR 2 5 1967

RECEIVED MAY 1 1967

Dear Mr. Callejo:

This is in response to your letter of February 16, 1967, in which you raised several questions relating to the administration of the internal revenue laws as regards Spanish-speaking individuals. I regret to say I never received the original of your letter. It was brought to my attention by our District Director, San Francisco, Joseph Cullen, who sent me a copy on March 20.

We recognize that individuals who are not familiar with the English language encounter additional difficulties in attempting to comply with the requirements of the Internal Revenue Code. We further recognize that the fair and efficient administration of the internal revenue laws requires that we take effective action to assist such individuals in satisfying these requirements.

We have, in the past, given consideration to your suggestion that forms and instruction booklets be made available in languages other than English, but have found substantial practical difficulties which preclude such a course of action. One of these is the various linguistic backgrounds of taxpayers. In addition to the Spanish-s ' ' communit there are subst.. he United States. Moreover, foreign language returns wo d cause substantial problems in the Revenue Service's processing and audit activities.

Because of these problems, we do not believe that foreign language tax forms and instruction booklets are a feasible method of providing assistance to non-English speaking taxpayers. At the present time, the Revenue Service does have in operation several programs to acquaint these individuals

Mr. Ricardo A. Callejo

with the requirements of the Internal Revenue Code and to
assist them in meeting these requirements. In conjunction
with foreign language newspapers and radio and television
stations, the Revenue Service is engaged in an intensive
public information program. In major cities, bilingual Tax
Assistors are available to help these individuals in preparing
their returns, and Revenue Service personnel have participated
in meetings of foreign language business groups. Of course,
the Revenue Service has encountered some difficulty in
recruiting employees who have the necessary qualifications,
but we do actively seek such individuals. We believe that
these programs represent a more effective and more efficient
means of assisting these taxpayers.

In your letter you asked why no interest is paid on tax
which is withheld from wages. In requiring that tax be currently
withheld and paid over the Internal Revenue Code imposes a
current liability and there is in no sense a borrowing by the
Government which would give rise to an interest obligation.

You referred, in your letter, to the problem of determining
on appeal the truthfulness of testimony in cases in which the
witness speaks little or no English and the record consists of a
translator's interpretation of the witness's testimony. We
recognize the problem of preserving the subtleties of the
original language in translating from one language to another.
In view of the fact that the record of a trial must be in a
form that an appellate court can understand, we do not see any
alternative to the present system. Moreover, under our system
of jurisprudence, questions such as the weight to be attached
to testimony and the credibility of a witness are generally not
subject to review upon appeal. However, if a translator's
interpretations are inaccurate, it would appear that, during
the course of a trial, a party could object to such inaccuracies
and, in a proper case, raise the question on appeal.

You also raised the question of the result of an individual's being deprived of equal educational opportunities
upon his ability to understand the tax laws and take advantage
of the beneficial provisions thereof. As you indicate in your

letter, the source of the difficulties of such an individual
is the fact that he has not received an adequate education.
Moreover, it would appear that the problem is much broader
than the difficulty in understanding the internal revenue laws
and taking advantage of the beneficial provisions thereof. The
problem extends to the full and meaningful participation in all
aspects of community life.

It is believed that the solution to the problems of unequal
economic opportunity is most likely to be found in improved
educational opportunities. While the administration of general
educational programs is obviously not within the province of
the Revenue Service, as noted above, the Revenue Service is
currently engaged in a number of limited educational and assistance programs to aid such individuals in understanding and
complying with the tax laws. Of course, these programs are
being constantly evaluated for effectiveness. We would welcome
any suggestions for improving these programs. The Federal
Government has engaged in a variety of programs in the last
several years to increase educational opportunities. As these
programs mature, I believe we can expect all Americans to become
increasingly familiar with English including those of our fellow
citizens who, up to now, may have been deprived of opportunity
to become conversant in this language.

Sincerely,

Commissioner

Mr. Ricardo A. Callejo
Spanish Speaking/Surnamed
  Political Association, Inc.
625 Market Street
San Francisco, California 94105

945

asociación política de habla/apellido español

spanish speaking/surnamed political association, inc.

625 MARKET STREET · SAN FRANCISCO, CALIFORNIA 94105   (415) 986-4653

Founders (Fundadores)   May 1, 1967

RICARDO A. CALLEJO
SAL CORDOVA   Sheldon S. Cohen, Esq.
WALDO VELASQUEZ   Commissioner
                   Internal Revenue Service
                   Washington, D. C.

Re: Right of the Spanish Speaking people to Equal Protection of
             Tax Law.

Dear Commissioner Cohen:

          Thank you for your letter of April 25, in response to my
letter of February 16 concerning the above captioned and certain
specific questions.

          Aside from the fact that the Federal Constitution is written
in English, there is no statement therein stating that the rights
referred to can only be granted or otherwise enjoyed in English
only. During the isolationistic period the suppression of other
languages and cultures has brought us to the sorry situation we
now face of being a mono-lingual country in a multi-lingual, multi-
cultural world in which Democracy must compete with other governmental forms for the support of great masses of people. These
masses are not likely to learn English, both because of its difficulty and because of its colonial association. These masses of
people look to see how Democracy works in the United States. As of
now the last barrier to equal protection of the laws and due
process of law is language.

          My own view, which I also express on behalf of the members
of this new National Political Association, is that we must become
a multi-lingual, multi-cultural country at the earliest possible
moment.

          For all that is to follow let us distinguish between what is
expedient and practical (in the immediate sense) and what is lawful
and just (in the immediate and long term sense).

          1. Spanish, UNLIKE, Chinese, German, Slavic, etc., was spoken
in all of the Southwest BEFORE English and was GUARANTEED by Treaty
(Guadalupe-Hidalgo, 1848), U.S. Constitution, State Constitutions
(See California Constitution of 1849) as an official language,
along with English, as a means of insuring the political and civil
rights of the Spanish speaking people in the conquered territory

ASOCIACION POLITICA DE
HABLA/APELLIDO ESPANOL
SPANISH SPEAKING/SURNAMED
POLITICAL ASS'N., INC.
625 MARKET ST.
SAN FRANCISCO, CALIF. 94105

To:Sneldon S. Cohen, Esq.

of the Southwest. The same was true of Puerto Rico under the
Treaty with Spain (1898).

2. Nevertheless, we agree in principle that language,
any language, should NOT be an obstacle to the fulfillment
of Human rights, Consitutional rights, and the corresponding
responsibilities.

3. Priority should be given to Spanish because of the
aforementioned legal and historical factors as well as the
large numbers of Spanish speaking people, who as a consequence
of the suppression of these rights, suffer second class
citizenship.

4. San Francisco tax information has just begun in
Spanish radio but includes a directive to "bring your own
interpreter if you do not know English well..." Clearly this
will not meet the need to develop a bilingual and then a
multilingual service consistent with needs of taxpayers.
On what ground can the discrimination in favor of English
speaking taxpayers be based - certainly NOT on the United States
Constitution!

5. Please indicate the legal basis upon which Internal
Revenue Service "imposes a current liability" upon taxpayers
through withholding so as to avoid an interest obligation.

6. There is no legal basis that I know of for saying
an Appellate Court can only be conducted in English or that a
bi-lingual transcript could NOT be used as it is indeed used
in every Treaty or International area of Government - if we
can do it in the United Nations and at International Conferences,
we certainly ought to be able to do it in the United States.

7. Federal Taxation is used for ALL Governmental services,
including guarantees under the Civil Rights Acts that States
shall use such funds, as well as the Federal Government, without discrimination based on arbitrary or unreasonable denials
or impairments of equal protection and due process of law.
Denial of equal protection in education has given rise to the
inability of many Spanish speaking people to know English.
Until recently the English only rule in the schools, contrary
to guaranteed rights, forced Spanish speaking children out of
school, so that the denial has been compounded and forced
Spanish speaking people into second class citizenship.

947

ASOCIACION POLITICA DE
HABLA/APELLIDO ESPANOL
SPANISH SPEAKING/SURNAMED
POLITICAL ASS'N., INC.
625 MARKET ST.
SAN FRANC'SCO, CALIF. 94105

To: Sheldon S. Cohen, Esq.

      Therefore, in thinking about the above, let us remember
that the survival of DEMOCRACY and its fulfillment at home
depends on a just and reasonable solution to the fulfillment
of rights and responsibilities through the positive use of
language rather than its continued rejection.
Bi-lingual and Multi-lingual people must be used in Government
to stimulate these vital steps.
I should like to meet with you to discuss these and related
matters at the earliest possible moment.

                                      Sincerely,

                                      Ricardo A. Callejo
                                      Legal Counsel
                                      S.S./S. P. A.

Copies sent to:

The Honorable Senators:
Thomas H. Kuchel, Esq.
Warren Magnuson, Esq.
Eugene McCarthy, Esq.

ABC:mbg.

948

Exhibit No. 22

State of California

FAIR EMPLOYMENT PRACTICE COMMISSION

Statement presented to the United States Commission on Civil Rights, meeting in San Francisco, California, May 1, 1967, by Pier A. Gherini, Chairman, California Fair Employment Practice Commission

As background to your commission hearings in the San Francisco Bay Area, I would like to offer a brief description of the activities of the California Fair Employment Practice Commission, which is the single agency officially established in this state to deal with discrimination in employment and housing based on race, color, creed, national origin or ancestry. I do not propose to comment on the strengths or weaknesses of the state's equal opportunity laws as they relate to the needs of California's minority citizens, nor to offer very much detail, but I do think it will be of interest to you to know broadly of FEPC programs in jobs and housing.

The California Fair Employment Practice Commission was created by the state legislature in 1959 to deal with problems of employment discrimination. In 1963, the legislature added administration of the state's Fair Housing Law to the Commission's responsibilities. Generally, the major activity of FEPC is based on receiving, investigating, and resolving complaints through conciliation, and only rarely resorting to formal proceedings of hearing and enforcement. This complaint process has been supplemented generally with information and education endeavors. FEPC is also empowered to initiate

949

investigations of apparently unlawful practices, but may not go
beyond persuasion and conciliation in efforts to remedy such violations. In the last several years, like similar agencies in
other states, we have undertaken "affirmative actions" with employers, unions or others willing to consult with us concerning
possible improvements in their work force or membership as to
utilization of minority manpower. As budget and staff permit, we
are most anxious to increase such efforts.

Let me very briefly review our case complaint experience,
especially in Northern California, the area of primary concern
to your hearings.

Between September 1959, when the FEP Act took effect, and
March 31, 1967, a total of 5661 employment cases were docketed.
About 2800 of these were in Northern California, the majority
centered in the Bay Area. In about 2100 of these cases a determination was reached on the question of discrimination, and well
over 800 such cases were closed with corrective action taken on
the part of the respondent.

It should be pointed out that there are constructive consequences that frequently go beyond the corrective action taken in
settlement of an individual complaint. For example, an employer
may look more closely at his job policies and modify them, whether
or not FEPC investigation revealed grounds supporting the original
complaint. Such cooperative compliance, clearly part of the intent of the FEP Act, is sought wherever possible by FEPC.

A most fruitful supplement to individual case handling is
the compliance activity resulting from affirmative action programs. Cooperation in the programs has come from a wide variety
of the state's leading employers -- large industries, banks,
major utilities, firms in trade and commerce, educational institutions, government agencies, federal defense agencies, labor
organizations and others. In all such affirmative programs, the
voluntary cooperation of the employer is the key to the success
of the project. There is no supposition that the FEP law has
been violated; employer participation is offered willingly. Out
of such cooperative endeavors have come scores, even hundreds of
jobs for minority workers, particularly in those large firms
which are building new facilities and making new hires, or in
plants that are relocating to new areas. A guideline to the kind
of procedure FEPC recommends to employers participating in
affirmative programs is found in the FEPC booklet "Promoting
Equal Job Opportunity."

A further and far-reaching aspect of an affirmative approach
to minority employment opportunity is shown in FEPC's concern with
job testing and the potential of that screening procedure to offer
a discriminatory barrier. One of six FEPC advisory committees,
the Technical Advisory Committee on Testing, which is composed of
high-level testing and personnel experts from industry, universities and public agencies, has accomplished pioneer work in this
area, with impact not only on California employers, but nationally
as well. Continuing such affirmative efforts as these is of vital

951

concern to FEPC, and we shall work toward increasing our effectiveness through expansion of these and similar positive programs.

Now to housing: Since the state Fair Housing Act took
effect in September 1963, until March 31, 1967, FEPC received a
statewide total of 498 complaints of discrimination in housing.
During eighteen months of this period, a constitutional amendment -- since declared unconstitutional by the California
Supreme Court -- reduced the average of housing cases received
to about 5 per month. About 270 of the total cases have been
in Northern California, all but a few in the San Francisco Bay
Area. In those cases in which a determination on the question
of discrimination was made, nearly two-thirds resulted in corrective action taken by the respondent.

The achievement of equal opportunity under the Fair Housing
Law has been hampered by the cloud of controversy and argument
which surround the law. Some broad affirmative approaches have
been attempted by FEPC nonetheless, including frequent public
reports on the administration of the law, guidelines to realtors,
and periodic contact for informational purposes with the 190
volunteer fair housing groups across the state.

Affirmative work beyond the case complaint procedure has
also included the successful attempt to persuade a large tract
builder in the Bay Area to publicly declare an equal opportunity
policy in home sales, where before minorities had been openly
excluded. Additionally, FEPC has established a Housing Advisory
Committee, composed of leaders from real estate, banking,

mortgage lending, contracting and home building industries, together with individuals familiar with the needs of the minority
community. Only recently formed, this committee has agreed
upon the necessity for equal opportunity in housing and is working out ways to advance it through the various industry associations represented by its members. The potential for meaningful
affirmative achievement by this committee is very good.

It would of course be possible to go into a great deal more
detail on FEPC activities, both past and present, but that is
not my purpose at this time. A considerable amount of FEPC
printed material spells out these and other programs. It is
available to your commission at your request.

It has been seven years since FEPC was established to help
further the goals of equal opportunity for all California citizens. In that time we have made a start on a big job. But much
remains to be done. I am sure that the testimony you hear during
your stay in the Bay Area will explore in depth those areas, with
the result, I am hopeful, of shedding more light on problems
which have been too long neglected or misunderstood.

953

Exhibit No. 23

PAT

PARENTS AND TAXPAYERS
Post Office Box ~~387~~ 1754   San Francisco, California 94101

TO THE

UNITED STATES COMMISSION ON CIVIL RIGHTS

IT IS WELL KNOWN IN SAN FRANCISCO THAT
PARENTS AND TAXPAYERS HAS TAKEN A FIRM STAND
AGAINST "FORCED BUSSING" OF SCHOOL CHILDREN,
AND ALL THE OTHER SCHEMES OF MANIPULATING
CHILDREN TO ACHIEVE RACIAL BALANCE.
WHY WAS OUR ORGANIZATION NOT CONTACTED BY
YOUR COMMISSION? THIS IS A REAL EXAMPLE OF
DISCRIMINATION.

THANK YOU,

Maurine Koltugin

Maurine Koltugin,
Education Chairman

888 Chestnut Street
San Francisco 94133
PRospect 5 1071

What is P.A.T.?

P.A.T. is an organization of Parents and Taxpayers in San Francisco dedicated to the preservation of the Neighborhood School. Its membership is non-sectarian, non-partisan.

We believe that everyone, whatever his race, religion or creed, must be accorded his God-given right to dignity and respect and the right to legal and social justice. We conceive it to be God's plan and the American belief that children are not wards of the State but are the' responsibility of their parents and, as such, must remain under their control.

We are organized to protect the welfare of our children. We oppose the involuntary mass transportation of young children from their family neighborhood to another area to correct what is in reality a social problem and not an educational deficiency problem.

We affirm it to be the duty of the parents to assure that their children are reared and educated in familiar surroundings and receive a proper and adequate education. If our children are permitted to leave the family neighborhood, where we cannot control their environment or where certain conditions are beyond our reach, then good education and the molding of character is impossible.

We object to the hardship, inconvenience and danger incident to their being forced to travel about the city instead of walking to their neighborhood school, returning home for lunch and being near to us if sickness or accident occur.

We object to the early start and late return which will interfere or even curtail their after school religious instruction and their cultural enrichment programs, their daylight hours of healthful play and participation in scouting and other church and community programs.

We object to the tremendous expense such a program will entail and its utilization of the scarce education dollar for purposes other than better education.

We object further, as taxpayers, to assuming these extra costs as part of our already too-heavy tax burden.

We feel that if there are disadvantages in education between various schools they can and must be solved without the abandonment of the Neighborhood School. Voluntary Transfer could be permitted, under proper conditions, to parents dis-satisfied with the school to which their child has been assigned. But should this inconceivable condition exist, then we offer our full cooperation towards improving that or any other school in every area of our city.

We consider forcible transfers and the distribution of children on the basis of race, religion or creed to be contrary to the heritage of our democratic form of government, in violation of existing laws and a withdrawal of the rights and privileges of parents.

We hold our individual freedoms in too high an esteem to permit their arbitrary withdrawal.

We hereby serve notice upon those who would deprive us of these freedoms that we will use all legal means to preserve them and furthermore we will resort to other meaningful actions, including the power of the vote, to ensure and maintain our rights as free men.

Preserve Our Neighborhood Schools * Attend Our Meetings * Join Now * Support Our Cause

955

April 27, 1967

U.S. Commission on Civil Rights.
@ Maurice Hotel Rm. 1401
761 Post Street
San Francisco Calif.

Attention Mr. Glick.

Gentlemen:

Since I am not able to appear before your honorable body in person,
I would like to submit the following statements:

A person once said: "Everybody is equal, but there are some who
are more equal." Think about it while I introduce myself.

My name is Daniel M. Arteaga, better known as Dan Arteaga. My
address is 156 Curry Street, Richmond, Calif. 94801.

I was born in Mexico, and by the grace of God and the Congress
of the United States I became a citizen of this Country.

Because of previous national influence, I once had the idea that
everybody was against me, and more so the United States. Eventually
with the assistance and advise from some of my friends I came to
the conclusion that I was more prejudist than those surrounding
me. It was at this point that my intire life took a turn for the
better. I began to take a closer interest in public and personal
affairs with a keen interest on what has been my motive throughout
my life, that is: human rights and dignity.

It is interesting to know that I was first inducted into a Labor
Organization when I was thirteen years old. Ironically enough,
that was where I experienced my first taste of discrimination,
meaning that whereas I was compelled to pay full union dues and
to attend every union meeting and every rally under the threat
of expulsion or fine, I had no voice or vote in its affairs.

Without trying to impress your mind in any respect, and for the
purpose of qualifications , and reasons to address your honorable
body, I would like to mention some of the activities in which
I have been engaged in the past.

Throughout the last thirty years of my working life I have been
engaged in many social, civic, and labor organizations. Although
I am not speaking on behalf of any of them, I will mention the
following: Member of a Painters Union. Delegate from the same
to a District Council of Painters. Building Trades Council.
Committee and Council on Apprenticeship. Ceveral onventions.
The Central Labor Council of ontra Costa ounty, and from this
body I have been a delegate and alternate delegate to the Equal
Opportunity ouncil of the same ounty. I also have been a member
of the American G.I. Forum. The Human Relations ommission in

U.S. Commission on Civil Rights.

Richmond, Calif. The Council of Spanish Speaking Organizations.
A Director in a private recidential Corporation and some other
organizations dealing primerly with human individuals, their
rights, their problems. etc. etc.

Having in mind my personal experience as a poor born child, the
lack of education and skill, and the barrier of the English
language suffered by me at one time, I certainly can appreciate
the value of, and the intention of the Civil Rights Act and its
sponsores along with what has been accomplished so far in this
field.

The abolishment of discrimination, if such can be done and the
enjoyment of personal civil rights granted to the individual by
the Almighty creator since the beginning of the creation has been
and will continue to be, the thorn in the side of humanity by
the simple reason of humanity itself.

Discrimination as defined by the dictionary means: "The act of
distinguish: the act of making or, observing a difference,...."
My concept of discrimination is "The abuse or suppression of
human rights and dignity by means of physical, social, educational, wealth, and/or political force." Discrimination is exer-
cized not only by the denial of a productive job and a place to
live, but also by a suppression of advancement in dignity and
social position. On the other hand, a call toward responsibility and the adherence to public laws may be construed as an act
of discrimination.

The Civil Rights Act if I understand it correctly, is aimed to
protect the rights of every citizen and individual in this
United States without favoring any particular group or person.
This is no so. I repeat: The Civil Rights act has not been
applied or enforced on an equal basis.

I appreciate the fact that through the Civil Rights Act, a lot
has been accomplished; I appreciate the fact that many of our
fellowmen and brothers in the Negro community have been able
to obtain jobs, to support their families and to enjoy some of
the privileges to which they are entitled to; I appreciate the
fact that the door of opportunity, being educated and to take
a place in society, has been opened to them. To join a Labor
organization, to serve in public offices, and to feel as an
equal in opportunity and obligation as I have experienced the
expression of hundreds of my Negro friends and fellow-workers
who communicate with me and enjoy this valuable experience.
However, this does not mean that the Civil Rights Act has
worked or accomplished the intention for which it was enacted.
The Commission and Congress should be aware that while the
Act has not accomplished the advancement of many individuals,
the peacefull co-existence and harmony amongst the citizentry,
at the same time a group of opportunitists has been arised to
disturb and too obstruct the aims of the Act throughout the
Nation.

957

U.S. Commission on Civil Rights.

The Commission shoul be aware of the fact that whereas the
Negro community.. has been advanced and protected in many respects,
this has been done in many instances at the expense of other
groups and individuals. In the field of employment and promotion other people have been exposed to the impact and consequences
primerly mentioning the Mexican-American society, and the Spanish-
speaking people. In the area of Los Angeles, as well as in Arizona and New Mexico, the slogan among the Mexican people is:
I could have a better job if I was a Negro." In the SF. Bay Area
where the impact is not as critical as it is L.A.; still it is
the general consensus of opinion that in matters of employment,
the Negro is favored versus the Mexican. Once I asked a friend
who is working in the Public Employment Office if this was true.
He answered: "This is correct."

Gentlemen: I am not suggesting by any means that the opportunity
should be deminished, or that some privileges should be taken
away from the Negro and given to the Mexican. No by all means,
as a firm beliver that we all are created by God, and as a
supporter of human rights, I ask you to continue in your efforts
to improve the conditions of the Negro and all the so called
minority races; but not at the expense of the Mexicn or anyone
else for that matter. I want you to be aware that this preferential attitude on the part of Covermental Officials for political reasons; and of the employers because of preasure and
retaliation from Government and some irresponsible groups, is
causing a tremendous feeling of resentment against the Government
and the Negro community with a detrimental effect toward the
Nation as a whole. I am positive that neither you or the Govern
ment want this to hapen. This is discrimination by political
force.

In the field of education primerly in public elementary schools,
it is well known that some of the youths are taking the opportunity of the preferential attitude shown to the Negro by the
teachers and principals either voluntarly or by preasure, causing
internal strife among the pupils, discrimination against the
Whites and resentment against the authorities.

The language barrier is another type of disadvantage and discrimination. The Spanish speaking community has this added
obstacle. I do not advocate that our people should remain
ignorant of the National language, but should admit that this
exist and should seek the means to remedy the situation.
It is well known that the barriers of a formal education have
been removed to accomodate some of the Negro people; the same
should be offered to the Mexican-American.

Finally, I'd like to mention one pertinent case where the Federal Government and public funds are involved.

958

U.S. Commission on Civil Rights.

The Equal Opportunity Council of Contra Costa County where I am
a delegate, representing Labor, is divided into fourty groups
covered by one-hundred Directors. Out of these fourty groups,
twenty of them supposedly come from "thePoor", and the rest
from associated groups.
Twentyfive groups are dominated by the Negro community. Two
are representing a Labor Union (one person) and another person
Labor in the County as a whole. Ten other groups from the County
and other miscellaneous Organizations, some of which are partial
to the Negro, and three groups are from the Mexican American
community. As you can see, this figure is extremly out of proportion, obviouslt showing discrimination against the Mexican
since these two groups are the predominant minority population
in the County.

Another example of discrimination in this Council is the fact
that out of one hundred delegates composing the Council, no
more that ten, and certainly five of them take control of the
Council's meetings by rude behaviour, lack of adherence to
parlamentary procedure, abuse against the past Chairman (who
was a Mexican-American) and a total disregard to the rights
of other Directors especially when those speaking are Mexicans
and if they dissent from the position of the Negro. All of these
leading to a delay of pertinent issues which would be taken
care of after most of the Directorshave left the floor at late
hours of the night.

I had the disgusting experience of observing on several occasions
how the Chairman was abused by some of the Directors from the
floor because he would not yield to presure in breaking the
Council's rules. This Gentleman has since resigned from such
position in the Council.

In regard to the distribution of money, it is obvious that the
predominat groups would act just to their pleasure.

In regard to the interpretation and translation of the language,
it should be noted that whereas the official interpreter may have
ex number of points to his credit in this field; in many cases
such experience is too high or inadequate to cope with the
poor comprehensive ability of the poor educated Mexican, causing
therefore a disadvantage to the subject.

Gentlemen: this in short are some of the observations and objections from this party. There will be some who may want to discred-
it my testimony because of personal obligations to a group, or
because of political expediency. The only obligation that I have
is to the public, to the protection of those who would remain
silent, and to my councience. It is essential that these things
be brought to your attention. I suggest that it is your duty to
see to it that the Civil Rights Act be applied on an equal basis
if the same would ever accomplish the intention for which it
was enacted. Thak you for your attention.

Daniel M. Arteaga
156 Curry Street
Richmond, Calif.

OUSING AUTHORITY OF THE CITY OF OAKLAND CALIFORNIA

ADMINISTRATIVE OFFICE
935 UNION STREET
832 3202

LEASE STATUS
April 26, 1967

	O BR	1 BR	2 BR	3 BR	4 BR	5 BR	TOTAL
Total Housed	4	50	86	39	4	0	183
* Total Ready for Leasing	6	15	21	4	1	0	47
Pending Leases	6	22	41	8	2	0	79
TOTAL:							309

REHABILITATED

	O BR	1 BR	2 BR	3 BR	4 BR	5 BR	TOTAL
Total Housed	2	27	42	26	4	0	101
* Total Ready for Leasing	3	10	15	4	1	0	33
Pending Leases	5	11	32	8	2	0	58
TOTAL:							192

21 White
162 Negro

STATUS OF WAITING LIST TENANT SELECTION DEPARTMENT AS OF May 1, 1967—TOTAL 1192

ELIGIBLE 910
APPARENT. 282
ELIG. 1192

ELIGIBLE FAMILIES		0 BRS (0)	1 BRS (43)	2 BRS (20)	3 BRS (37)	4 BRS (17)	5 BRS (5)	TOTAL (122/21/0)
BROKEN FAMILIES WOMEN	N	23	104	189	195	48	13	572
	W	2	7	12	8	2	1	32
	O	0	0	2	0	0	0	0
BROKEN FAMILIES MEN	N	9	11	3	0	0	0	23
	W	0	0	0	0	0	0	0
	O	0	0	0	0	0	0	0
SINGLE WOMEN	N	0	63	36	24	3	4	132
	W	0	1	3	2	0	0	4
	O	0	0	0	2	0	0	2
TOTAL ELIGIBLE	N	32	221	248	256	70	22	849
	W	2	12	20	13	6	4	57
	O	0	0	2	2	0	0	4
APPARENTLY ELIGIBLE FAMILIES	N	0	21	16	20	6	4	67
	W	0	0	2	4	2	0	8
	O	0	0	0	0	0	0	0
BROKEN FAMILIES WOMEN	N	13	27	53	46	9	9	157
	W	0	3	7	4	0	0	14
	O	0	0	0	0	0	0	0
BROKEN FAMILIES MEN	N	8	2	4	0	0	0	14
	W	0	0	0	0	0	0	0
	O	0	0	0	0	0	0	0
SINGLE WOMEN	N	0	8	8	4	1	1	22
	W	0	0	0	0	0	0	0
	O	0	0	0	0	0	0	0
APPARENTLY ELIGIBLE TOTAL	N	21	58	81	70	16	14	260
	W	0	3	9	8	2	0	22
	O	0	0	0	0	0	0	0
RECAP	N	53	279	329	326	86	36	1109
	W	2	15	29	21	8	4	79
	O	0	0	2	2	0	0	4

STATUS OF SENIOR CITIZEN WAITING LIST IN TENANT SELECTION AS OF May 1, 1967.

	0 BRS			1 BRS			TOTAL		
	N	W	O	N	W	O	N	W	O
ELIGIBLE COUPLES	0	0	0	2	0	0	2	0	0
BROKEN FAMILIES WOMEN	23	2	0	1	0	0	24	2	0
BROKEN FAMILIES MEN	9	0	0	1	0	0	10	0	0
TOTAL ELIGIBLE	32	0	0	4	2	0	36	4	0
APPARENTLY ELIGIBLE COUPLES	0	0	0	0	0	0	0	0	0
BROKEN FAMILIES WOMEN	13	0	0	2	0	0	15	0	0
BROKEN FAMILIES MEN	8	0	0	1	0	0	9	0	0
TOTAL APPARENTLY ELIGIBLE	21	0	0	3	0	0	24	0	0
RECAP	53	2	0	7	2	0	60	4	0

ELIGIBLE . . . . : 40
APPARENTLY ELIGIBLE . . . : 24

TOTAL 64

THE 64 SENIOR CITIZENS HAVE BEEN INCLUDED IN THE TOTAL COUNT OF 1192

962

"NON-PROFESSIONALS MOVE TOWARD NEW CAREERS - 1967"

by

Dr. Stanley Soles*

In the last five years throughout the United States, there have been various programs utilizing non-professionals in jobs in the human services. This paper presents a statement of the meaning of New Careers, the basic elements in New Career Programs, New Careers as a method of job development, the extent of New Careers, and a summary of a survey on evaluation of the relative progress in the New Careers Movement by mid-1967.

What are New Careers?

New Careers refers to programs that combine new and old ideas into a new synthesis. New Careers refers to a method of job development and a series of programs that link training to the job with opportunity for advancement and further training built in. Assumptions are made about our economy, society, and culture.

In terms of the economy in an age of automation, we find that some sectors in production and agriculture are shrinking in the job market; while in the helping fields and human services, there are predicted expanded manpower needs. For example, between 1960-1975, given the expanded population, a 65% increase in professional and allied occupations is needed to handle existing programs without taking into account expansion of services. In education alone, 5 to 7 million more teachers are needed in the next ten years. For other fields, estimates for new jobs are: health, 1,200,000; welfare, 700,000; protective services, 350,000; recreation and conservation, 1,300,000.[1] All studies indicate the need for more staff expansion to meet the demand for needed services more than existing or increases in professional schools are going to be able to produce.

As to the unemployed, minorities are still hardest hit. Figures show that minorities are 3 times the national figures for whites. Unemployment in 1960 Census for poverty-impacted areas of San Francisco is, for example: Western Addition 9% (11-1966)2 Chinatown 7% , Hunter's Point 8% , Mission 8% . The unemployment rate picture of teenagers is even more drastic; e.g., Negro teenagers 35.7% . Expansion in human services is likely, and automation is not as likely to cut into the human service fields as other parts of the economy.

---

* Director, Regional Community Action Training; Chairman, New Careers Planning Committee, San Francisco; Associate Professor, San Francisco State College (on leave)

Statement prepared to submit to U.S. Civil Rights Commission Hearings, San Francisco-Oakland, May 1-6, 1967.

[1] National Commission on Technology Automation & Economic Progress, 1966.

Unemployment in the areas of San Francisco, 1967, Department of Labor

963

In terms of our society, the avenues to qualify for jobs have increasingly emphasized specialized education. We have what Art Pearl calls a "Credential Society,"[3] which, in effect, locks out many people with potential for some community services unless they complete the present route through college and professional school to a credential.

In practice, the professionals find an increase in demand for services. Frequently, the professional is overworked and carries out many duties that are not central to his professional role, and tasks that could be carried out by others with less training and thereby free the professional to do a better job. In terms of the work setting, professionals find themselves parts of large formal organizations with bureaucratic elements that define their roles in more specialized terms, whether it be medical doctor, nurse, teacher, social worker, or police officer.

In terms of culture, we find that there exists both gaps of service between professionals and low-income clients and gaps of communication between the styles of life and communication patterns of the professional and the low-income client. The gap of services and communication is not intended by the poor or by the professional practitioners involved. But it does exist.

The teachers, social workers, nurses, police, and others are dedicated to their jobs; but the models within which they are operating do not enable them to effectively "reach out" from the existing formal organizational structure into the life experiences of the low-income clients. Teachers have made efforts to deal with "culturally-disadvantaged" persons, but we are a long way from having basic teaching materials, decent class size, and the special skills.

In terms of the poor persons themselves, made up of low-income persons and minorities, they are not a single homogeneous group. There are older persons permanently out of the labor force on limited, fixed low income; the handicapped and those unable to work as well as others on welfare for child support. Ther' are the underemployed and unemployed. Each poor person requires a different program for chance and change.

The New Careers plan does not harbor romantic illusions of the poor endowed with some mystical magic. It recognizes the fact that many poor persons do not come to the clinic for medical attention or for welfare or unemployment services, or that they do not participate in the PTA. Some poor persons in San Francisco have special language problems, with English as a second language--their native language being Chinese or Spanish or another. Many of these low-income persons are not yet citizens, excluded even more from many employment opportunities.

[3] Arthur Pearl and Frank Riessman, New Careers for the Poor (Free Press, 1965).

964

Many of the poor persons have the ability to communicate with other poor persons. They have a style, the language and manner that may enable them to establish rapport in instances where some professionals are not able to get through to the clients. *[4]

In the above brief analysis of economy, society, and culture, New Careers programs offer the poor a chance for jobs with training built in. These jobs are mainly in the human services field of the public and private non-profit sector. The New Careers approach is a proposed solution to the present crisis of Manpower. It provides for utilization of low-income persons in productive self-enhancing ways in those sectors of the economy in which there is an expanding job market and manpower shortage.

Basic Elements of New Careers as Programs

New Careers programs are underway in a number of parts of the United States. At the present time, it is more a non-professional movement than New Careers Movement as an effort to meet a number of goals. It has a number of phases and stages that combine a series of basic elements.

First, the basic idea of New Careers is providing jobs first, with training built in. These jobs are entry level jobs, but the approach differs from the usual pre-job training programs or training programs for some non-existent jobs or soon-to-be automated jobs.

Second, New Careers Programs propose jobs with a future. This means not merely the entry level menial jobs, but training for possible advancement through a series of graded steps--a ladder for possible advancement in line with performance and additional study.

Third, New Careers proposes meaningful jobs with dignity and that are life changing, that may break a poverty cycle.   Evidence shows that non-professionals see their tasks as more than just another job, but see some hope for future careers and get basic satisfaction from work.[5] The problems of poverty are not just no jobs, but the culture of poverty that surrounds individuals' sense of helplessness, futility, and immediacy. New Careers offers to put some of his knowledge to use in constructive ways. For minorities, the stigma of discrimination and prejudice has left its mark and compounds the job problems. New Careers offers a possibility of choice, or an alternative to a career is a job with a future.

Fourth, New Careers as a program implies training built into the job with supervision and in-service training a definite part of the job. There are many implications: In the apprentice system, each one learns from the more experienced by starting with training and the job. Information for training can be selected in line with experience and the job and action.

[4] Anselm L. Strauss, "Medical Ghettos," Trans-action, May, 1967.

[5] Yankelovich

965

Fifth, New Careers provides an opportunity for advancement in graded steps
that must be built into the career path. Basic job training can lead to
advancement and further training for those who, by performance and qualification,
may advance. At this time, career patterns do not now exist by this route
except in a few programs. This does not mean that every aide or non-professional
must accept the position, or strive for advancement, or will eventually become
a fully-qualified professional in the same sense as present professionals. It
does mean that a long-term goal for New Careers is an alternative route and a
choice should be possible.

Sixth, in terms of educational changes by bringing the training to the job,
the field site, relating the theory to practice, benefits for the function of
the institutions are made on the spot. By providing for non-professionals to
become qualified for carrying out sub-professional functions with appropriate
training may mean new certificates and credentials that do not now exist.
Night school and in-service training could become expanded and job related.
One distinctive feature of the New Careers Program is that it seeks to make
training related to the job. Many night schools/have students part-time jobs; but few,
if any, of the part-time jobs are related to the career goals of the education.
Few law students work on part-time law-connected jobs, or future teachers with
youth in tutorial programs, except recently through work-study programs.

New Careers as a Method of Job Development

New Careers is not only a series of programs but a method of job development. As a method of job development, New Careers is relevant to a situation
of expanding job market and manpower shortage. It is not advocated for old
careers or situations for manpower surplus. It differs from other programs by
its acceptance of the positive attributes of the low-income culture rather than
liabilities. One of the present difficulties of the delivery system of helping
services is the fact that low-income groups do not get the services to which
they are entitled. Some New Careers programs have provided a bridging function
in helping to identify needed service gaps, and in defining possible jobs to
carry out and meet the service needs. These have been efforts by non-
professionals at job creation, and these new service-linked jobs themselves
have been filled by non-professionals and auxiliary personnel.

The New Careers approach seeks to use low-income persons in filling the
communication gap, as well as the service gap, between the poor and community
services. Many examples of types of New Careers, non-professional aides'
jobs have been developed. For example, some are descriptive of their
bridging function by the title: Police Community Aide, School Community Aide,
Neighborhood Health Aide, Caseworker Aide.

The effect is two-way, as gaps of needs for service are being met and new
services carried out, new quality of service results. The standards of
services are likely to improve over the present ones in which overworked
professionals attempt to carry out too many activities with all too little
help. Many of the tasks they are required to carry out are not central to the
major tasks; some of the tasks are actually extraneous to carrying out the
central job.

Non-Professional Move Toward New Careers - 1967

A new work unit is formed as a professional works with a non-professional. If training is provided and an opportunity for sub-professional tasks to develop, then the professionals are involved in any developing definition of sub-professional jobs for the auxiliary personnel. This emergence to definition of new jobs is done in coalition with relevant professional and union groups. Job definitions are not designed to take away existing jobs, but to create new ones.

The new work unit of professional and non-professional has the potential of enhancing a new professional role even more and to not only provide for utilization of trained manpower, but to provide better quality of service as well. Most initial resistance on the part of professional and union groups has been highest as outsiders because after working with non-professionals a short time, most professionals have stated that "they couldn't get along without them". [6]

What Progress Has Been Made in the New Careers Movement?

A number of studies have been made of the progress to date for the non-professionals in human services. There are over 50,000 new non-professionals hired in various programs throughout the United States, most of them through anti-poverty legislation. These reports of projects are in such fields as Education, Health, Welfare, Corrections, or the work of New Careers Demonstration projects for a series of agencies.

The evidence reported is drawn from Yankelovich, Inc., Study of Non-Professionals in Community Action Programs in nine cities, dealing with 5,000 non-professionals; along with Banks Street Study of Auxiliary Personnel in Education in 15 Cities; and other studies from Contra Costa County Community Services Series on New Careers and New Careers Development Project (Sacramento, California); and New Careers for the Poor by Arthur Pearl and Frank Riessman.

Administrative Structures and New Career Models

The existing models of New Career programs have different administrative structures in different cities, with some advantages and disadvantages to each. Most of the money for non-professionals is presently from the Federal Government. The major types of administrative structures are as follows:

1. A non-profit corporation receives federal money, runs its own program with some private agencies, and cooperates with city and federal authorities (New Haven, St. Louis, Chicago, Syracuse, Atlanta, Newark)

2. Civil Service recruitment and selection, in cooperation with city anti-poverty effort, program sub-contracted to private agencies. Jobs are Civil Service. (Detroit)

---

[6] Evidence from Yankelovich, Banks Street, and New Careers for Non-Professionals in Education by J. R. Hartley, California CAP 896-1, 1965.

967

Non-Professional Move Toward New Careers

3. Pittsburgh is decentralized so that all programs are handled through non-governmental agencies.

4. Separate organization to recruit and select, but staff place in private agencies as soon as possible. (Los Angeles, NAAP)

5. San Francisco has a small central office with maximum authority for target areas to build out-reach functions into community organization. Outside training resource provides services to augment staff development programs.

6. Demonstration-type programs of Contra Costa County and Sacramento, California, develop non-professional positions across the board for a series of agencies.

These administrative structures exist in various parts of the country. The pattern of programs for non-professionals falls into three main categories:

First, there is the Medical model approach, in which some non-professional and sub-professional jobs are defined but leave the existing professional roles untouched.

A second model is what Art Pearl calls a "Plantation" model, in that jobs for the poor are provided and then no training to develop the necessary skills is provided. This situation is a self-fulfilling prophecy. It reinforces some of the skepticism of professionals about the lack of abilities of poor people to learn to do a job and reinforces the feelings and mistreatment of the poor.

A third model would be the New Careers model that would include non-professional jobs at the entry level with training built in, sub-professional jobs carved out of existing professional positions in terms of relevant and needed services with the collaboration of the professionals in defining tasks and appropriate training, supervision, and reorientation of professionals working with non-professionals. Some of these new jobs would be based upon identification of gaps of existing services and defining new job descriptions around them. The first two models are more numerous than the third model.

The New Careers model has the long-range goal of bringing about a number of social changes in terms of revitalizing the professional and reorganizing the field of human services--education, health, welfare, social welfare, corrections, and other areas. At the present stage, however, there has been no sizeable development of careers; emphasis has been upon non-professionals providing that. Yankelovich, in a study of 5,000 non-professionals in nine cities, and Bank Street College of Education's study of 15 education projects found that sub-professionals can be employed effectively in bridging the gap, reaching the poor and helping the poor utilize services.

Non-Professional Move Toward New Careers

In contrast to some of the fears predicted by professionals, both Yankelovich and Bank Street found the non-professionals gave evidence of high morale and saw their work as more than just another job, but some hope of a future career. Generally speaking, they have been well accepted by the professionals with whom they work. More difficulty was found with those who are outside the program than other professional staff members.

According to the Yankelovich survey, evidence indicated that there have not been significant difficulties with issues such as confidentiality, authority, over-identification with client or agency as was anticipated.

Some evidence was reported to indicate that the experience with job and training has modified the self-view of non-professionals; they now have greater confidence in their ability, based upon their successful job experiences.

Dangers and Difficulties of the Non-Professional Movement in Not Becoming New Careers

While there has been some progress in defining entry-level jobs for non-professionals, legislation has been passed to establish funds for some 30,000 more New Career-type positions (Scheuer, Economic Opportunity Act II, 205e). We still have, for the most part, temporary jobs on entry level jobs, few new jobs, and many old positions. We do not have career developments at the present at the present time, except in very few locations in the nation.

All is not without problems in the Non-Professional Movement. For one thing, in a New Careers program, one does not negotiate all the issues once at the beginning and then merely carry out a program. Settlement of career issues takes local, state and federal efforts. Issues are under continual examination and modification. The commitment to get non-professionals at entry level jobs with training on government funds is not as difficult as getting commitments to place non-professionals on eventual permanent status of local budget.

There is pessimistically the danger that a program will never become a career and that training will cease, upgrading will not be possible, and changes in educational routing not brought about.

The extent of possible New Careers placement in Human Services has not really be applied in many local areas. The City of San Francisco, through the New Careers Task Force, in December sought to estimate how many non-professionals could be absorbed if federal funds were available. Estimates were made without detailed study of new services figures from the departments as follows:

Non-Professional Move Toward New Careers

Survey of Mayor's Task Force on New Careers in San Francisco

Health Departments	750
City Schools	1100
Welfare-Social Service	625
Public Protection	235
Recreation	125
Urban Renewal Housing	100
Fire	20
	2955

To extrapolate figures from a number of units, one may estimate the number of positions possible for given categories through the State of California. Brief estimates in the fields of health, education, welfare and public protection are as follows:

In Health, there are some 200 units. If each unit took between 3-10, that would mean between 600 - 1,000 jobs.

In education, there are 91,000 elementary school classrooms and 34,000 secondary ones. If each room had one teacher aide, that would total 125,000 teacher aides for California.

There are presently 10,000 welfare workers in the state. If there were one welfare aide for every three workers, that would mean 3,000 jobs.

There are over 630 public protection units; if each unit had 5 aides, that would mean 3,150 jobs for various public protection aides.

Non-professional jobs have been developed in such areas as indicated by the job title as follows:

Psychiatric technician, school community aide, child care aide, homemaker aide, rehabilitation worker aide, police community relations aide, public health aide, recreation aide, research aide, program development aide, probation aide.

Money for developing these jobs into careers comes from the Federal Government under provision of the Scheuer Amendment to the Economic Opportunity Act, revised in 1966.

In carrying out the program for non-professionals in public employment, survey findings reveal some difficulties in recruitment, selection, supervision, upgrading, and training. These comments are presented in the next sections.

Non-Professional Move Toward New Careers

Recruitment

Generally, recruitment has been by word of mouth--individuals in programs telling others. The Yankelovich survey found most of the aides were female. Further examination showed it possible to successfully recruit males. Community Action personnel in various anti-poverty programs could be involved in recruitment in an effort to seek out unemployed males and hard-core poor. 3/4 of the 5,000 non-professionals in the Yankelovich survey had completed high school, yet the Department of Labor found 48% of the unemployed in San Francisco did not graduate from high school.

In recruitment, there is the danger of building up false hopes in the promise of a "career" and only getting an entry level job. Present recruitment in programs is unplanned--not a systematic part of non-professional jobs. It is important to show how entry level is the first step and the way out of poverty, but not imply an "instant" professional career.

Selection

Recruitment and selection have gone together in programs. Frequently, pre-service orientation has been eclipsed. Criteria for selection should be related to the clear objectives of the program. Non-professionals to engage in providing services may not be the same as those to engage in promoting social change. Criteria to maintain commitment to bring about social shange, end poverty may be lost if the non-professional is outnumbered in the agency setting by professionals.

Techniques of selection have included a panel of professionals and non-professionals, group interviews, even peer ratings when possible. In programs with large numbers of applicants, interviewers were overwhelmed. Prior clear criteria are all the more important.

Supervision

Lack of time and personnel for the supervisory responsibility has been the usual complaint. The fact that administrative structures are divided--Community Action Agency, local government or agencies, and outside training resources-- has made accountability difficult. In schools, teachers supervise; but in some settings, principals used non-professionals (aides) in a pool to be sent to trouble spots. The lack of clear-cut tasks has resulted in vague ideas of the job to be done. The suggestion of the Director of Non-Professionals for central tasks of coordination has some merit, but operationally, it puts a person in a line position working with staff from various units. This splits the loyalties of the non-professionals.

[7] Sub-Employment in the Slums of San Francisco

971

Upgrading

Criteria for performance evaluation and procedures for review and conferences are common in this program. Programs vary, some have made little progress and have one entry level salary. Other programs, such as New Haven, have developed a scheme for allowing non-professionals in to supervisory roles without educational requirements, but performance rating. Survey evidence called for performance criteria and the authority to enforce regulations to deal with unsatisfactory performances.

Training

Evidence from surveys show that training is highly important and of much interest in details of training. There is general satisfaction, yet there are demands for more and better training. Studies revealed a tendency to view training as providing "instant" skill development and as a panacea of all the problems of the functioning of the agency or operation.

The goals of training, linked with the goals of the Community Action Agencies or departments, deal with elements of social change. Responsibility and sanction for training are unclear. Authority for training is unclear, and the responsibility is shifted from personnel or staff director as a part of staff development to outside training resources.

Time for training is at a premium. When placed on the job first, training is frequently postponed due to action on the job. The limitation of the number of trainers who were trained and available to conduct training has produced some gaps in actual training and supervision. This runs the danger of what Arthur Pearl calls the "Plantation Model"--i.e., jobs without training.

Placement of non-professionals in field placement has not been easy. Training and supervision of staff assigned to agencies is a collaborative task. Time for professional reorientation of supervisors and the non-professionals in ongoing seminars and supervisor conferences needs to be guarded; otherwise, more time on the job consumes scheduled time for training.

In terms of training orientation, an initial inservice may be provided; but the continual need for additional training and time to do it was found to be a problem. Programs that offer an advanced work at junior colleges for two or more years may or may not lead to a certificate or credential. Transfer from a two-year college to a four-year college may place the non-professional in a position of starting all over. Little actual change in the pattern of pre-professional training within the colleges has occurred. Efforts to bring some college course with appropriate systematically organized theory into the field site, are still in the planning stages in most areas and are moving rather slowly. The Newark, New Jersey New Careers Program, with Fairleigh Dickinson University, is an exception.

Education and Accreditation and Certification

The utilization of various educational institutions is only beginning. Adult education, junior college, and four-year colleges are needed. New course patterns, off-campus field work, with theory brought to the job. New courses for professionals are all needed. Certificates and new credentials for various levels of training and development will require changes in laws and requirements.

The linkage and articulation between the adult schools, junior colleges, and four-year college cirriculum and credit has yet to be worked out. Legal restrictions and college requirements may be obstacles that imaginative and innovative trainers and programs will have to overcome. General education requirements for a Bachelor's degree expand the number and range of course work needed from the vocational emphasis of the non-professional course sequence.

Training Trainers

In the light of the shortage of sufficient numbers of qualified trainers, a number of efforts are being made to train trainers, including training professionals and aides and conducting training of trainers institutes.

Summary

The New Careers idea and program is a series way of dealing with the manpower crisis and the credential society and to provide needed human services. At the present, non-professionals are employed in human services positions on government funds from anti-poverty programs. The long-term goals of New Careers require that further development be made in terms of securing placement, upgrading, supervision, training, certification, and permanent funding. The implementation of New Careers ideas into action is a program of change and innovation. It is bound to encounter clashes of interests.

The long-term goals of revitalizing and reorganizing the human services hold the promise of improving the quality of human services and providing an alternative route for development and education of persons in our society.

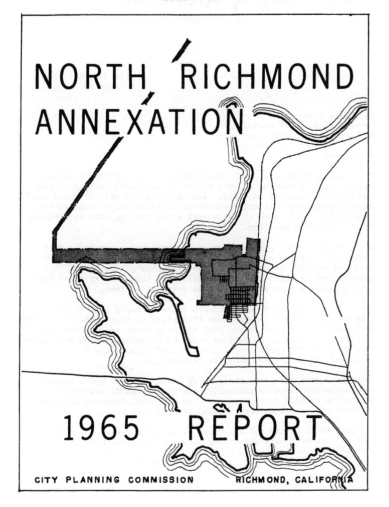

NORTH RICHMOND ANNEXATION

1965 REPORT

CITY PLANNING COMMISSION   RICHMOND, CALIFORNIA

974

OFFICE OF THE
NNING DIRECTOR

City of Richmond

CALIFORNIA

TELEPHONE 232-1212
EXTENSION 425

file 348.No.Rich.
October 19, 1965

Honorable Mayor and
Members of the City Council
Richmond, California

Gentlemen:

The Planning Commission has considered the attached report and conducted a public hearing on this matter at a special meeting of the
Commission on October 14, 1965. This hearing was well attended and
many persons spoke setting forth their position for or against the
annexation of this area and gave very clear and specific reasons for
their particular position.

Those residents who are in favor of the annexation generally feel
that such an action will provide the mechanism for improving their
area and solving many of the problems that now plague them. They
realize that annexing to the city will cost them more in taxes but
that this extra expense will be well worth it to them.

There were a number of residents who spoke strongly against annexation and described the conditions that exist in that portion of North
Richmond that has been in the city for many years as evidence that
little improvement in conditions could be expected through annexation.
They claimed that these property owners had been paying the increased
taxes but not receiving commensurate benefits.

There were also spokesmen for several industries who spoke against
the annexation claiming generally that industries do not need
recreation or park facilities and that municipal services would not
be worth the increased cost imposed through city taxes.

The Commission considered all these facts and opinions and then voted
4 to 2 (3 members were absent) to recommend that the City Council
proceed with the annexation action.

Honorable Mayor and
<u>Members of the City Council</u>   <u>Page 2</u>   <u>October 19, 1965</u>

The majority of the Commission was of the opinion that since this
area is effectively surrounded by the City of Richmond there is no
reasonable alternative to the eventual annexation of this area.
Since this is the case then the most desirable course is to commence
immediately to set the wheels in motion toward improvement of the
North Richmond area.

The Commission feels that those who favor annexation and even those
residents who spoke against annexation would be willing cooperators
in joint efforts to improve conditions there.

The Commission recognized that the present and potential industrial
development in the area proposed to be annexed will help substantially
in balancing the costs of services and improvements.

                          Respectfully submitted,

                          Frank Calton

EWH:mm   FRANK CALTON, Chairman
Attach. - Report

cc: City Manager
    City Attorney

976

October 4, 1965

file   348 No. Rich

Mr. Frank Calton, Chairman
Richmond City Planning Commission
City Hall
Richmond, California

Dear Chairman Calton:

    I am transmitting to the Planning Commission
and the interested public the 1965 Report Pertaining to
Annexation of the North Richmond Area. This report contains the factual data that the Planning Department has
been able to assemble on this subject.

    It is recommended that the City Planning
Commission call a special meeting for Thursday, October 14,
1965 in the Council Chambers in City Hall, to conduct a
public hearing on this subject in line with the request of
the City Council. This public hearing will give every
interested party an opportunity to present his views
pertaining to the advisability of this annexation and broad-
en the background for the Planning Commission in making its
recommendation to the City Council.

    Ample copies of this report have been printed
to make them available to every interested party. They
may be obtained at the Planning Department in City Hall.

      Respectfully submitted,

      Ernest W. Henderson
      Planning Director

EWH:mc

cc: Planning Commissioners

TABLE OF CONTENTS

Page

Plng. 2005

978

DESCRIPTION OF NORTH RICHMOND AREA

The location of the North Richmond Area is shown on the cover of this report. It lies immediately west of the City of San Pablo from the Southern Pacific Railroad tracks to Garden Tract Road and extends from Gertrude and Chesley to approximately one-fourth mile north of Parr Boulevard. It also includes a long narrow corridor extending west across the tideflats and the Bay hooking around past Point Pinole to the city limits of Pinole.

Within this area are a total of approximately 1,480 acres:

State-owned water and tideland area	540 acres
Privately-owned tideland	80 acres
Upland	860 acres
Total	1,480 acres

EXISTING CONDITIONS

Population.--It is estimated that the population of this area in 1965 was approximately 3,700 persons in about 1,030 families. The majority of the population is Negro although there is a substantial number of Japanese and white families in Voting Precinct #5 which consists of the area north of Wildcat Creek. Average family size is estimated to be about 3.7 persons per family.

In July, 1965 there were 1,284 registered voters. Although the bulk of the registered voters live south of Wildcat Creek there were 53 registered voters in Precinct #5.

General Problems of the Area.--The major physical problems evident throughout this area are: Poor drainage conditions, inadequate and poorly located thoroughfares--particularly for heavy trucking, poor condition of street paving and a high percentage of residential structures which are old and in poor structural condition.

The major other problems are an inadequate level of police protection, inadequate recreation facilities and major social problems such as high level of unemployment, high rates of school drop-outs, inadequate financing available for home improvement, etc., which have generally existed in segregated Negro communities.

Residential Section.--There are approximately 800 privately-owned and 226 publicly-owned housing units (dwellings or apartments) in the unincorporated portion of North Richmond. Approximately 30% or a total of 290 privately-owned housing units are in poor structural condition.

979

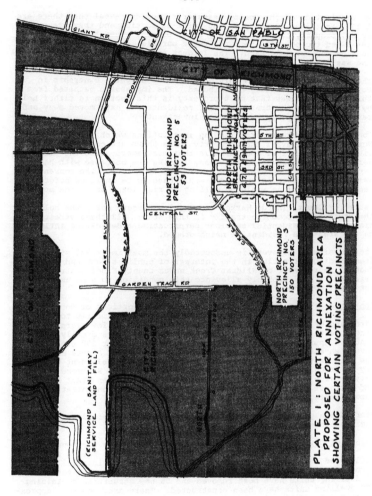

PLATE 1: NORTH RICHMOND AREA PROPOSED FOR ANNEXATION SHOWING CERTAIN VOTING PRECINCTS

980

An examination of the County Assessor's records reveal that there are
1,151 parcels of property in the built-up portion and they are owned
by 847 property owners. Seventy-eight percent owned a single parcel,
14% owned two parcels, 5% owned three parcels, the remaining 3% held
four or more parcels each. The largest number of parcels held by anyone was nine.

The conclusion drawn from this data is that property ownership in
North Richmond is widely distributed. The impression gathered from
the tax records was that most property in this section is either held
by residents of the area or former residents who have moved away and
retain their property as a modest investment.

Conversations with several lending institutions which are active in
North Richmond reveal that property loans there are considered poor
risks. The principal complaint is that mortgagers abuse the property and then default on the loan, leaving the morgagee with heavy
expense to put the property into saleable condition. The consensus
was that confidence in this area would have to be improved before
lending institutions would be willing to risk loans on a wide scale.

Castro, Filbert, Third, Market and Chesley Streets carry the bulk of
the truck and automobile traffic in this area. All these streets
traverse the residential sections perpetuating a depressing influence
on the area as a residential neighborhood.

Storm drainage, however, is undoubtedly the most important single
item needing correction in the interest of public safety and comfort.
Channel improvement of Wildcat Creek under County Flood Control District No. 7 will probably alleviate this condition to some extent,
but local systems will remain an urgent requirement.

Non-Residential Section.--The non-residential portions of North Richmond have been devoted primarily to truck
gardening or other agricultural uses until the past few years. In
recent years conversion of land to industrial use has greatly accelerated. Approximately eight new industries with over 200 employees
have been established along Parr Boulevard, Goodrick Avenue and in
the area west of Third Street. There is a major development consisting of greenhouses centered around Brookside Drive. Richmond Sanitary Service is located in the corridor west of Garden Tract Road
and north of West Gertrude Avenue there is a great concentration of
auto wrecking yards.

Storm drainage and adequate roads are the two major problems confronting these areas.

Trends of Development.--According to information from the County
Building Department there has been a substan-
tial trend toward improvement in the condition of residential housing
structures in recent years. During the last three years a total of
81 dwelling units have been removed and 56 new structures containing
109 dwelling units have been constructed. There are, however, approximately 217 additional residential structures that are in very poor
structural condition.

981

Since 1960, there has been a population increase of approximately 530
persons in this area. A substantial number of vacant lots exist
which make it possible for this population to increase substantially
in the future.

Nine or ten new industrial buildings have been constructed in this
area in the past few years indicating a definite trend which has ever
evidence of continuing in the future.

It is estimated that there are 1,200 persons employed in the industri
al and commercial establishments in this area. This number can be
expected to increase at least 500 more in the next ten years.

The increases in population and employment will result in increased
traffic on the thoroughfares serving this area.

CHANGES IN GOVERNMENTAL AND UTILITY SERVICES IF AREA IS ANNEXED

Services That Will Not Be Affected By Annexation.--Many of the current services in
this area will not be effected directly as a result of annexation.
The following governmental services will not be effected:

> Schools including elementary, junior high, high
> school and junior college
> East Bay Water District services
> Sanitary Sewer District services
> Transit District services
> Hospital District services
> Flood Control services under the County Flood Control
> District

The public housing will continue to be operated by the Housing Authority of Contra Costa County and there will be no change in rents or
policies as a result of annexation.

There will be no change in the following privately operated utilities
either in service or rates:

> Pacific Gas and Electric Company electrical or gas service
> Pacific Telephone and Telegraph Company telephone service
> Richmond Sanitary Service refuse pick up

Services That Will Be Affected By Annexation.--In the event of annexation, the North Rich-
mond area will be withdrawn from two special districts which now levy
taxes. These are a special street lighting district and the San Pabl
Fire Protection District. After annexation the City of Richmond will
pay for the cost of operating the street lights and will either provide fire protection with its existing Fire Department employees and
equipment or contract with San Pablo Fire Protection District to continue the existing protection.

Fire protection by the City of Richmond will be somewhat more adequate than has been available to this area in the past due to the greater depth of fire companies and manpower available in the Richmond Fire Department.

Present response distances for the North Richmond area as a whole are practically the same from the closest Richmond Fire Station as from the present San Pablo station. When Richmond's Station #2 is relocated, as planned, these distances will be reduced by more than one-half mile.

The City of Richmond enjoys a better fire protection rating than the San Pablo Fire Protection District. Therefore, fire insurance rates will be reduced somewhat after annexation.

Police protection is one of the services that will be most greatly increased by annexation. Richmond police have been able to respond to calls in the City within three or four minutes. This level of service is a considerable improvement over what the County Sheriff's Deputies have normally been able to provide because of the large area beyond North Richmond which they must cover. The Chief of Police anticipates that the North Richmond area would be organized as one police beat with a two-man patrol in a car on duty 24 hours a day.

Recreation services are now provided by the City of San Pablo Recreation Department and the Richmond Schools. Presently recreation is being provided adequately in some areas. No park facilities other than those associated with Verde School are available. In the event of annexation the City of Richmond Recreation and Parks Department will assume responsibility for the public recreation in this area. It is estimated that there are approximately 1,500 children 14 years of age and under. Of this number about 800 are of elementary school age. The Recreation and Parks Director estimates that three recreation leaders would be provided to conduct the recreation program. This would include operation of the Verde School recreation program.

The City of Richmond Recreation and Park standards call for a total of 7.8 acres of neighborhood recreation space and 4.7 acres of recreation space for a district facility. It is anticipated that this park space could be acquired and developed if the forthcoming Recreation and Parks bond issue is successfully passed, and this area is annexed prior to the bond issue action.

Public works services now provided by the Public Works Department of Contra Costa County would be taken over by the City Public Works Department. Street sweeping service will also be added on the same basis as other similar parts of the City. Streets that are fully paved and have curbs and gutters are swept about every 30 days. There is a substantial backlog of capital improvements that need to be financed and installed in this area. They include curbs and gutters, side-strip paving, resurfacing and reconstruction of streets and storm drainage. Curbs, gutters and side-strip paving must be paid for by the property owners. The other items will be paid for and installed by the City as funds become available.

983

Gas tax funds are utilized to make necessary improvements on the
City's Select Street System. Approximately three miles of existing
streets, consisting of Market, Filbert, Parr, Brookside and Fifth
Streets would qualify for inclusion in the Select System. It is anticipated that the City would receive approximately $25,000 per year
in gas tax funds. However, it is estimated that in the first seven
years there would need to be an expenditure of $459,000 on resurfac-
ing and reconstruction of streets throughout the area. Actual replacement of some of the street work would be dependent on the property owners' willingness or ability to install concrete curbs and
gutters and side-strip paving at the same time or upon the finding
of other means of financing these improvements.

Storm drainage improvements for areas outside the Wildcat Creek District #7 are estimated to cost approximately $200,000. The present
financing program now being worked out by the City may be able to
provide a means of paying for these improvements.

Building permits and related inspection services as well as inspections pertaining to enforcement of the Housing Code are currently
handled by the County Building Inspector in Martinez. After annexation all such permits and inspections would be issued and conducted
by the Building Regulations Division at City Hall in Richmond. The
Building Codes and Housing Codes adopted by the City and County are
very nearly the same.

Planning and Zoning.--In the event of annexation the Richmond City
Planning Commission and the Richmond City Plan-
ning Department would assume responsibility for preparing long-range
plans for this area and administering the Zoning Ordinance. The
Richmond General Plan which was adopted in September, 1964, includes
the North Richmond area and proposes to retain the present residential area as residential. The non-residential area is proposed to
be devoted to the two classes of industrial, i.e., special industrial
and general industrial. It also proposes the North Richmond Bypass --
a new major thoroughfare connecting Castro Street with Parr Boulevard
along the western edge of the residential area -- to remove all the
industrial and most of the automobile traffic from Filbert Street.

The General Plan anticipates the preparation and subsequent adoption
of local area or neighborhood plans as part of the General Plan as is
being done for the Santa Fe and Pullman Neighborhoods in cooperation
with the local neighborhood councils. After annexation, it would be
expected that a similar planning program would be undertaken for
North Richmond at an early date.

The Richmond Zoning Ordinance provides that areas annexed will automatically be zoned to the City zoning classification nearest to that
existing in the County. As the ordinance now stands annexation
would make little difference in zoning regulations in most areas.
However, at present the Richmond ordinance does not have a zone comparable to the Heavy Agricultural Zone adopted by the County to provide for the special needs of the greenhouse industry. Adoption of

such a zone patterned after the County's zone has been under preliminary discussion with representatives of the greenhouse industry in
Richmond. It is anticipated that such a zone will be adopted by the
City of Richmond prior to the time a vote could be taken pertaining
to annexation.

Library Services.--All property inside the City of Richmond pays a
                    reduced tax rate for General County Services since
the City has its own library system. Services of the Richmond Library
and Bookmobile would be extended to and open to residents of this
area in the event of annexation. A number of services are provided
by the Richmond Library which are either not available through the
County Library Branches or which are inconvenient to use because of
distances from the neighborhood. This includes loaning privileges
to obtain films and a large selection of 33-1/3 rpm records of
classical music, etc. The Richmond Library service also includes an
excellent children's librarian and boys' and girls' library section
at the 4th and Nevin Branch as well as the Civic Center Library, both
of which are readily available to all neighborhood areas including
North Richmond.

Sanitation Services.--Public health and sanitation inspections now
                      provided by the County would be performed by
the City Health Department in the event of annexation.

A number of other general governmental services would be provided at
the conveniently located City Hall rather than at the County Building in Martinez. Of particular not is the Richmond Human Relations
Commission and the services available to Neighborhood Councils. Although the North Richmond Neighborhood Council has participated in
the Richmond Neighborhood Council Program the services of the Neighborhood Organization Consultant have been somewhat restricted in
neighborhoods not entirely within the City. Annexation would make
these services as fully available to North Richmond as to any other
of the neighborhoods.

The City of Richmond has a variety of boards and commissions which
assist and advise the City Council by studying and administering various aspects of problems incidental to urban growth and development.
Of particular importance to the North Richmond area is the Industrial
Development Commission which has as its primary responsibility the
promoting of industrial growth and development in the industrial
areas. Also of great importance is the Chamber of Commerce which is
partially supported by the City and which is particularly active in
efforts to attract and locate new industries on available sites in
the City. There is also the Recreation and Parks Commission, the
Library Commission and the Planning Commission, plus the Housing
Appeals Board.

HOW ANNEXATION WILL AFFECT RESIDENTS AND PROPERTY OWNERS

Annexation will provide easy access to the bulk of local government
administration by having these activities based at City Hall,

Richmond, rather than in Martinez. This will simplify the task of obtaining information about many important government functions. It will also save many trips to Martinez each year.

Annexation will also open the door to more effective participation in the affairs of local government. All registered voters will be able to vote on all nine Councilmen rather than just the one County Supervisor who lives in the local area.

The large variety of official boards and commissions which are made up of average citizens after appointment by the Mayor offer substantial opportunity for residents of the City to be appointed to one of these important posts and thereby actively participate in the affairs of local government.

Changes in Costs and Taxes.--The greater volume of municipal services provided by the City does involve increased cost to the property owner and citizen as well as some savings. The additional cost to the City of providing normal and necessary services to the North Richmond area are itemized in Table I. Annual revenue estimated to be received by the City from this area is shown on Table II. How these changes in cost will affect the property owner are itemized in Table III, "Changes in Tax Rate Due to Annexation." While some of the taxes now collected by the County will be eliminated by annexation there will be some increase in the overall tax rate paid by the property owner. The amount of the increase will vary according to the local needs as determined by the City Council from year to year.

Fire insurance rates will be reduced somewhat as a result of the better rating enjoyed by the City of Richmond.

HOW ANNEXATION WILL AFFECT THE CITY OF RICHMOND

Cost to the City to Extend Services to Area.--Table I itemizes the various types of anticipated costs to provide appropriate services to this area as reported by the department heads.

The Chief of Police reports that this annexation will require creation of a new police beat which will require nine additional patrolmen plus equipment.

The Superintendent of Building Regulations reports that this additional work load will require additional inspectors and secretarial help.

The Director of Recreation and Parks reports that to provide recreation services will require employment of three part-time recreation personnel plus additional park maintenance personnel after new parks are provided.

986

Other Departments believe that their services can be extended without requiring additional personnel. However, the Assessor reports that although the addition of an additional 1,000 parcels to the assessment rolls in and of itself would not require additional personnel the 3,526 other parcels that have been added by past annexation since 1953 without any additional personnel plus the new parcels would require an appraiser and at lease one clerk if the office staff is to remain effective and efficient in operation.

<u>Additional Revenues for City as Result of Annexation</u>.--Table II itemizes the various sources and amounts of revenue that can be expected in the event of annexation.

The Fire Chief reports that this annexation will have the effect of reducing the overall per capita cost of fire protection to the remainder of the City inasmuch as fire protection can be extended to this area without additional personnel or equipment over what is already in existence or required for present City areas.

<u>How Capital Improvements May Be Financed</u>.--The City is now establishing a special program for correcting the storm drainage problem by earmarking a portion of the tax rate for that purpose and also by applying for Federal Grants which may total 50% of the costs.

Park land acquisition and development is an integral part of the proposal for a Park and Recreation Master Plan, "Resources for Leisure," and the proposed bond issue intended to finance it. Acquisition and development of the proposed parks in North Richmond along with other parks throughout the City will depend upon successful passage of the park bond issue if annexation occurs previous to action on the bond issue.

State gas tax revenue received by the City as a result of this annexation cannot finance all the necessary road improvements on local streets. Therefore, either other revenue must be utilized or the street improvement program must be stretched out over a long period of years.

HOW ANNEXATION WILL AFFECT OTHER GOVERNMENTAL AGENCIES

The only other governmental agencies that will be affected substantially by this annexation will be the County and the San Pablo Fire District.

The County will be relieved by reducing the services it must provide and yet its tax revenue will not be reduced correspondingly. Therefore, this annexation will be beneficial to it.

The San Pablo Fire District will lose approximately $6,000,000 of its tax base without reducing its need in terms of men and equipment. It appears that this annexation will be somewhat disadvantageous to the Fire District.

TABLE I
ESTIMATED COSTS OF SERVICES

Function	Annual Costs	Capital Costs	Remarks
. Police	$ 81,460	$	A new police beat is recommended. Two-man patrol cars are recommended for at least one year. Cost of above service plus new cars included in this estimate.
2. Fire	-0-	-0-	Area can be served with existing men and equipment.
3. Assessor- Tax Collector	500	2,500	Prorated annual operating cost plus cost of initial setup of records.
4. Library	1,800		Includes two bookmobile stops.
5. Finance	5,980		Prorated on population.
6. Personnel	-0-	-0-	
7. Health	2,500		Prorated cost of Dept. cost.
8. Planning and Zoning	1,500		Prorated costs of present operations which would be extended to this area.
9. General Administration	-0-	-0-	
10. City Clerk	250		Cost of Biennial Elections
11. Legal	-0-	-0-	
12. Public Works A) Street lighting B) Street signs C) Mapping, Surveys, etc. D) General Overhead E) Storm Drainage Improvement	4,700 2,000 1,000	 2,000 200,000	

988

TABLE I, Cont'd.
ESTIMATED COSTS OF SERVICES

Function	Annual Costs	Capital Costs	Remarks
12. Public Works, Cont.			
F) Streets			
1) Reconstruction			
Total	$441,000		
1st year		137,000	
3rd year		205,000	
5th year		99,000	
2) Resurfacing	18,300		
1st year		900	
3rd year		5,200	
5th year		10,500	
7th year		1,700	
3) Curb Returns	9,000		
13. Building Regulations and Conservation	12,243		
14. Recreation and Parks			
A) Maintenance and Leadership	24,768		Cost of recreation leadership and
B) Supplies	2,500		parks maintenance
C) Recreation Space	512,500		personnel
Neighborhood Park Land		195,000	Capital costs could be covered in pro-
Neighborhood Park Development		124,800	posed city-wide
District Park (land)		117,500	park bond issue providing annexa-
District Park (development)		75,200	tion occurs previous to action on the bond issue.

TOTAL ANNUAL COSTS $141,201

TOTAL CAPITAL COSTS $1,185,300

TABLE II

ESTIMATED ANNUAL REVENUE

ASSESSED VALUATIONS

A. Residential Property South of Wildcat Creek

Land	$ 281,340
Improvements	1,067,030
Personal Property	68,720
Sub-total	$1,417,090
Exemptions	91,480
Total Taxable	$1,325,610

B. Non-Residential Property

Land	$ 872,220
Improvements	2,871,990
Personal Property	1,117,090
Sub-total	$4,861,300
Exemptions	2,200
Total Taxable	$4,859,100

TOTAL TAXABLE ASSESSED VALUATION	$6,184,710

Taxes at $2.30/$100 Assessed Valuation	$ 142,000*	
Special Revenues (Business Licenses,etc.)	6,100	
Estimated Sales Tax	3,000	
Zoning Fees	200	
Building Fees	16,500	
Payment in lieu of taxes from Contra Costa County Public Housing Authority	2,800	
Subventions		
1965 rate for motor vehicle in lieu funds	$ 4.38	
1965 rate for gasoline tax	6.80	
Subvention rate, per capita	$11.18	
Times estimated population 3,700 =		$ 41,300**

TOTAL ESTIMATED ANNUAL REVENUES	$ 211,900

---

*A portion of this revenue is to be earmarked for storm drainage.
**$25,000 of this revenue must be used on Select City Streets.

990

TABLE III

CHANGES IN TAX RATE DUE TO ANNEXATION

Note: Total tax rates change each year as a result of many factors.
Significant recent changes occurred because of unification of
the School Districts, fluctuations in the transit district's
tax rates and creation of the Wildcat Creek Flood Control Zone.
None of the above tax rates will be affected by annexation.

LISTED BELOW ARE THE ONLY TAX RATES THAT WILL BE DIRECTLY AFFECTED
BY ANNEXATION:

Taxing Jurisdiction	1965-66 Tax Rate in the County	1965-66 Tax Rate if Annexed to Richmond
San Pablo Fire Protection District	.690	-
Street Lighting District L 36	.103	-
Contra Costa County	2.322	2.175*
Total Tax Rate of Above Jurisdictions	3.115	2.175
City of Richmond Tax Rate (Provides municipal services including fire protection, street lighting and library services)	-	2.300
Total Tax Rate Affected by Annexation	3.115**	4.475**
		-3.115
TOTAL INCREASE IN TAX RATE DUE TO ANNEXATION		1.360***

---

*County tax rate will be reduced because City has its own
library system.
**Total tax rate paid will also include taxes levied which are
not affected by annexation.
***The increase in taxes will be offset to some extent through
savings on fire insurance costs.

BALANCE OF COSTS AND REVENUES:

Annual Estimated Revenue from Table II   ; 211,900

Annual Estimated Costs from Table I   141,201

    Annual Net Revenue to Apply Toward
    Capital Improvement Costs   ⸗ 70,699

    (Approximately $6,000 of this revenue is earmarked
    for storm drainage, and $25,000 must be used on
    Select City Street System.)

Total Estimated Capital Improvement Costs $1,185,300

The Major Capital Improvements Include:

    Storm Drainage $ 200,000

    Street Reconstruction   441,000

    Park Acquisition and
    Development   512,500

                      $1,153,500

992

GENERAL CONSIDERATIONS

During the time that this annexation is being considered by the property owners and voters in the area the City of Richmond should take
the following actions to insure that undesirable circumstances will
not develop or to make, without delay, all possible provision for
making necessary improvements.

A. The City should amend its Zoning Ordinance to include a new zone
   patterned after the County's Heavy Agricultural Zone to accommodate the greenhouse industries.

B. Continue its efforts to obtain all possible Federal assistance
   being made available through the 1965 Housing Act for installing
   public improvements such as street paving, curbs, gutters, etc.,
   as well as home improvement grants and other assistance for low
   income families.

C. Continue its efforts to complete its Community Renewal Program
   with special emphasis on the North Richmond area to work out the
   most effective and acceptable means of obtaining the desired
   improvements and upgrade the area with the least disruption to
   the lives and financial condition of the residents involved.

D. Institute special studies on how to solve and finance the storm
   drainage problems outside of Wildcat Creek Zone #7.

10/1/65

993

APPENDIX

STEPS IN ANNEXATION PROCEEDINGS

(Each step must be favorably completed or
Proceedings will be halted)

Steps	Minimum or Maximum Time Period Allowed
1. Planning Commission makes its report to the City Council.	
2. City Council grants its informal consent and directs various departments of the City to assist in the annexation proceedings.	
3. Annexation proposal must be filed with the Local Agency Formation Commission.	
4. Local Agency Formation Commission makes its report and grants approval of annexation.	Within 60 days after being filed
5. Formal petitions must be circulated and signed by one-fourth of the registered voters in the area to be annexed.	
6. City Council must adopt a Resolution of Intention to annex the area.	
7. City Council must hold a public hearing to hear protests against the annexation. Further proceedings shall not be taken if written protest is made by public and private owners of one-half of the assessed value of land, exclusive of improvements thereon.	In not less than 15 nor more than 40 days after adoption of Resolution
8. City Council must adopt a resolution declaring whether or not a majority protest was made.	Within 30 days after close of protest hearing.
9. City Council must call a special election to be held.	Between 45 and 75 days after protest hearing. Election must be between 60 and 115 days after step 6, Adoption of Reso. of Intention.
10. City Clerk reports results of election to Secretary of State.	Action must be completed within one year after approval of Local Agency Formation Commission.

994

Exhibit No. 28   *agenda* 3/21

RESOLUTION NO._____   *approved*

RESOLUTION OF THE COUNCIL OF THE CITY OF RICHMOND DECLARING ITS
INTENTION TO CALL A SPECIAL ANNEXATION ELECTION, AND FIXING A TIME
AND PLACE FOR PROTESTS BY PROPERTY OWNERS.

BE IT RESOLVED by the Council of the City of Richmond:

1. That it is the intention of the City Council of the City
of Richmond to call a special election to be held in certain inhabited territory contiguous to said City, proposed to be annexed
thereto, for the purpose of submitting to the qualified electors
residing in said territory the question of whether or not said
territory shall be annexed to the City of Richmond, and the property
in the territory subjected to taxation after annexation equally
with property within the City of Richmond to pay the bonded indebtedness of the City of Richmond outstanding or authorized, at the
date of the first publication of the notice of election, for the
acquisition, construction or completion of municipal improvements.

2. That said territory hereby is designated and identified
as "North Richmond", and is more particularly described in
Exhibit "A" attached hereto, and by this reference made a part
hereof as though fully set forth at this point.

3. Notice is hereby given that on the 11th day of April, 1966,
at the hour of 8:00 o'clock p.m., in the Council Chamber of the
City Hall, City of Richmond, California, any person owning real
property within said territory so proposed to be annexed and having
any objection to the proposed annexation may appear before said
City Council and show cause why such territory should not be
annexed. Such protest must be in writing and shall state the name
or names of the owner or owners of the property affected by such
annexation and the location and area of such property in general
terms. If it be found that protest is not made by public and
private owners equal to one-half of the value of the territory

further proceedings shall be taken in accordance with the law for the holding of such special election.

4. That the City Clerk shall certify to the adoption of this resolution and cause the same to be published in THE INDEPENDENT once a week for the two weeks prior to the hearing.

I certify that the foregoing resolution was adopted by the Council of the City of Richmond at a regular meeting thereof on March 21, 1966, by the following vote:

Ayes: Unanimous

Noes:

Absent:

_____

Clerk of the City of Richmond

Approved:

_____

Mayor

Approved as to form:

_____

City Attorney

996

EXHIBIT A

Beginning at a point on the boundary of the City of Richmond
as established by annexation to the City of Richmond by Ordinance
No. 1398 adopted May 11, 1953 and certified by the Secretary of the
State of California May 12, 1953, said point being the intersection
of the eastern right of way line of the Southern Pacific Railroad
Company with the southern line of Chesley Avenue (formerly Road No.
25) as shown on the "Map of the San Pablo Rancho accompanying and
forming a part of the Final Report of the Referees in Partition"
filed in the office of the Recorder of Contra Costa County, California, March 1, 1894 in Map Rack No. 2; thence

along the boundary of the City of Richmond as established by
annexation to the City of Richmond by Ordinance No. 817 adopted
August 7, 1939 and certified by said Secretary of State of the
State of California, August 10, 1939 as follows:

Westerly along said southern line of Chesley Avenue to its
intersection with the center line of York Street as shown on the
"Map of Wall's Second Addition to the City of Richmond," filed in
the office of said Recorder on March 4, 1912 in Book 6 at page 140;
thence

southerly along said center line of York Street 100 feet to the
intersection with the easterly extension of the northern line of
Lot 15, Block 206 of said Map of Wall's Second Addition to the
City of Richmond; thence

westerly along said extension of said northern line 25 feet to
the northeast corner of said Lot 15; thence

continuing easterly along said northern line of Lot 15 and the
northern lines of Lots 19 and 20 of said Block 206 to the northwestern corner of said Lot 20; thence

southerly along the western line of said Lot 20 and the
southern extension of said line to the center line of Gertrude
Avenue as shown on said Map of Wall's Second Addition; thence

easterly along said center line of said Gertrude Avenue to the
intersection with the center line of said York Street; thence

southerly along said center line of said York Street to a
point on the northern boundary of the City of Richmond as established by the annexation of 1905 and certified by said Secretary of
State of the State of California, December 26, 1905, said point
being on the north boundary line of the "Map of the Andrade Gularte
Tract," filed in the office of said Recorder on July 27, 1912 in
Book 7 at page 175; thence

easterly along said northern boundary to the point of beginning
of the description of that parcel annexed to the City of Richmond by
Ordinance No. 1307 adopted June 6, 1949 and certified by said
Secretary of State of the State of California, June 10, 1949, said
point being on the exterior boundary of said Map of the San Pablo
Rancho between Stations 13 and 14; thence

along the boundary of the City of Richmond as established by said Ordinance No. 1307 as follows:

North 11° 45' East, 33.93 feet to said Station 13; thence

North 60° 34' East, 201.26 feet to Station 12 of said San Pablo Rancho; thence

North 13° 02' East, 999.78 feet to Station 11 of said San Pablo Rancho; thence

North 54° East, 224.40 feet to Station 10 of said San Pablo Rancho; thence

North 1° 45' West, 93.18 feet to a point on the northern line of Gertrude Avenue as described in the deed from East Bay Water Company to the City of Richmond recorded April 30, 1923 in Volume 431 of deeds at page 346 in the office of said recorder; thence

westerly along said northern line of Gertrude Avenue to the south-eastern corner of that parcel annexed to the City of Richmond by Ordinance No. 1703 adopted March 20, 1961 and certified by said Secretary of State of the State of California, March 24, 1961, said corner being the southeastern corner of a tract of land described as Parcel Two in the deed from Harold Booth to The Standard Oil Company of California, recorded January 22, 1960 in Volume 3541 of Official Records at page 231 in the office of said Recorder; thence

along the boundary of the City of Richmond as established by said Ordinance No. 1703 as follows:

northerly 854.07 feet along the western line of said parcel (3541 OR 231) to the southern line of that parcel described in the deed from John H. McCosker and Marian D. McCosker to John H. McCosker, Inc. recorded May 16, 1949 in Volume 1387 of Official Records at page 519 in the office of said Recorder; thence

easterly along said southern line to the southeast corner of said parcel (1387 OR 519); thence

northerly along the eastern line of said parcel (1387 OR 519) to the northeastern corner of said parcel; thence

westerly along the northern line of said parcel 72.22 feet; thenc

leaving said northern line, North in a direct line to a point on the eastern line of a road designated as County Road 6A, said point being the intersection with the eastern extension of the southern line of that parcel described in the deed from Theresa M. Ratto to The Standard Oil Company of California recorded June 16, 1960 in Volume 3641 of Official Records at page 435 in the office of said Recorder; thence

Exhibit A - contd

westerly along said extension of said southern line 30 feet
to the southeast corner of said parcel (3641 OR 435), said corner
being on the western line of said County Road 6A; thence

northerly along said western line of County Road 6A to the
southeast corner of that parcel described in the deed from Onorato
Chiozza to the San Pablo Sanitary District, recorded July 17, 1953
in Volume 2162 of Official Records at page 85 in the office of said
Recorder; thence

westerly and northerly along the southern and western lines
respectively of said parcel (2162 OR 85) to the northeast corner
of Lot 4, Section 2, Township 1 North, Range 5 West, Mount Diablo
Base and Meridian; thence

westerly along the northern line of said Lot 4, 660 feet to
the northwest corner of said Lot 4, said corner being on the
northern boundary of the City of Richmond as established by said
annexation of 1905; thence

along said northern boundary as follows:

West along the northern lines of Lots 5, 6, 7 and 8 of said
Section 2, to the northeast corner of Lot 1, Section 3, of said
Township 1 North, Range 5 West; thence

continuing West along the northern lines of Lots 1, 2, 3, 4
and 5 of said Section 3 to the northwest corner of said Section 3;
thence

continuing West to the intersection with the common boundary
between Marin County and Contra Costa County; thence

northerly and northeasterly along said common boundary to the
intersection with the southwestern boundary of the City of Pinole;
thence

southeasterly along said City of Pinole boundary to the most
northern corner of that parcel annexed to the City of Richmond by
Ordinance No. 72 N. S. adopted November 2, 1964 and certified by
said Secretary of State of the State of California, November 6,
1964; thence

southwesterly along the northwestern boundary of said annexed
parcel to the most northern corner of that parcel annexed to the
City of Richmond by Ordinance No. 1568 adopted December 16, 1957
and certified by said Secretary of State of the State of California, December 18, 1957; thence

along the boundary of the City of Richmond as established by
said Ordinance No. 1568 as follows:

Exhibit A - contd

southwesterly and southerly parallel with and 300 feet distant southeasterly and easterly respectively from said common boundary between Marin County and Contra Costa County to the intersection with the westerly extension of the southern line of Lot 19, Section 34, Township 2 North, Range 5 West, Mount Diablo Base and Meridian; thence

easterly along said westerly extension to the southwest corner of said Lot 19; thence

continuing easterly along the southern line of said Lot 19 and the southern line of Lots 18 and 17 of said Section 34 to the southwest corner of Lot 24 of Section 35 of said Township 2 North, Range 5 West; thence

continuing easterly along the southern line of said Lot 24 and the southern lines of Lots 23, 22, 21, 20, 19, 18 and 17 respectively to the most westerly corner of that certain parcel described in the deed from Howard L. Biel, et al, to R. A. Taliaferro, dated February 25, 1952 and recorded April 17, 1952 in Volume 1920 of Official Records at page 91, in the office of said recorder; thence

In a generally northeasterly direction along the western boundary of said parcel (1920 OR 91) to the most westerly corner of that certain parcel described in the deed from Vivian E. Goodale, et al, to Parr-Richmond Terminal Corporation dated March 27, 1945 and recorded in Volume 816 of Official Records at page 170, in the office of said recorder; thence

easterly along the southern line of said parcel (816 OR 170) to the eastern line of that certain parcel described in the resolution by Contra Costa County Board of Supervisors dated November 27, 1953 and recorded January 4, 1954 in Volume 2248 of Official Records at page 571, in the office of said recorder said eastern line being the eastern line of a county road known as Goodrick Avenue; thence

southerly along the eastern line of said Goodrick Avenue (2248 OR 571) to the northern line of that certain parcel described in the resolution by the Contra Costa County Board of Supervisors dated February 24, 1951 and recorded September 24, 1951 in Volume 1826 of Official Records at page 463, in the office of said recorde said northern line being the northern line of a county road known as Parr Boulevard; thence

easterly along the northern line of said Parr Boulevard (1826 OR 463) to the western line of that certain parcel described in the deed from Parr-Richmond Terminal Corporation to Rheem Manufacturing Company dated December 13, 1946 and recorded in Volume 969 of Official Records at page 395; thence

northerly and easterly along the western and northern lines respectively of said parcel (969 OR 395) to the western line of the Southern Pacific Railroad Company right of way; thence

1000

easterly, traversing the said right of way of the said Southern Pacific Railroad, along the easterly extension of the north line of said parcel (969 OR 395) to a point on the western line of that parcel annexed to the City of Richmond by said Ordinance No. 1398, said line being the eastern line of said Southern Pacific Railroad Company right of way; thence

along the boundary of the City of Richmond as established by said Ordinance No. 1398 as follows:

South 4° 00' West along said eastern right of way line to the intersection with the north line of Raod 20 as shown on said Map of the San Pablo Rancho; thence

westerly along said northern line of Road 20, 25 feet, more or less, to the eastern line of said Southern Pacific Railroad Company right of way; thence

southerly along said eastern line to the center line of Wildcat Creek as shown on said Map of the San Pablo Rancho; thence

southeasterly along said center line of Wildcat Creek to the eastern right of way line of said Southern Pacific Railroad Company; thence

southerly along said eastern right of way to a point on the north line of Lot 197 of said San Pablo Rancho; thence

westerly along the north line of said Lot 197, 100 feet, more or less, to a point on the eastern right of way line of said Southern Pacific Railroad Company; thence

southerly along said eastern right of way line to the Point of Beginning.

WTW-DP/vg
11.15.65
Dwg. 20-D-1173

1001

§ 35116. Election in territory proposed to be annexed: Resolution of intention: Effect of insufficiency of petition. Upon receiving a petition signed by not less than one-fourth of the qualified electors residing within the territory, as shown by the county registration of voters, containing a description of the new territory proposed to be annexed and asking that the territory be annexed, the city legislative body shall without delay pass a resolution of intention to call a special election and of its intention to submit the question of annexation to the electors residing in the territory and of its intention to submit the question to the electors of the city if such election is required pursuant to Section 35122. The city clerk and the county officer having charge of the registration of voters shall, within two weeks, check the petition and certify the sufficiency thereof. If the clerk's certificate shows the petition to be insufficient, a supplemental petition bearing additional signatures may be filed within 10 days of the date of the certificate of insufficiency. The clerk and the county officer having charge of the registration of voters shall, within 10 days after the supplemental petition is filed, examine it and certify the sufficiency thereof. If the petition is not signed by the requisite number of electors, the legislative body is without jurisdiction to proceed further, and all prior proceedings, including such petition, shall be null and void.

LEGISLATIVE HISTORY

1. Added by Stats 1949 ch 79 § 1 p 118. Based on Stats 1913 ch 312 § 2 1st, 10th sents p 588, as amended by Stats 1933 ch 227 § 1 p 733, without substantial change.

2. Amended by Stats 1953 ch 1125 § 1 p 2618, adding the second sentence.

3. Amended by Stats 1955 ch 1163 § 1 p 2155, (1) omitting "giving at least 50 days notice thereof" after "call a special election" in the first sentence; and (2) adding the third, fourth and fifth sentences.

3. Amended by Stats 1961 ch 2168 § 2 p 4490, adding "and of its intention to submit the question to the electors of the city if such election is required pursuant to Section 35122" at the end of the first sentence.

NOTES OF DECISIONS

A cotenant is authorized to sign a protest against an annexation which would subject the tenants' property to municipal taxation. Morin v San Jose (1952) 109 CA2d 268, 240 P2d 688.

Protests against an annexation under this article need not be executed with any particular formality, and, in the absence of a challenge, are effective notwithstanding one tenant signs his cotenants' names thereto without disclosing authority to do so. Morin v San Jose (1952) 109 CA2d 268, 240 P2d 688.

The phrase "At any time not later than the hour set for hearing objections," means at any time not later than the closing hour; it does not mean after the closing hour for hearing protests has been fixed by resolution of city council. Foth v Long Beach (1954) 125 CA2d 520, 270 P2d 868.

A person may own property within territory proposed to be annexed to a city without the fact of ownership being of record, and city attorney erroneously advised counsel that a non-record owner could not protest. Foth v Long Beach (1954) 125 CA2d 520, 270 P2d 868.

A protest against annexation of territory to a city is not premature and invalid if signed prior to adoption of resolution by city council fixing a date for annexation election, since the election is only one step in effecting an annexation. Foth v Long Beach (1954) 125 CA2d 520, 270 P2d 868.

Appellate court will not disturb trial court's decision that city's purported annexation of certain area was ineffective where evidence sustains finding that city council acted arbitrarily, unfairly in protest hearing, and that proceedings for annexation sought to include area which was subject to valid, pending proceedings under Uninhabited Territory Act of 1939 for annexation to different city. Hubbell v Los Angeles (1956) 142 CA2d 1, 297 P2d 724.

Prior to enactment of § 35012, specifically permitting city councils in annexation proceedings to accept requests for withdrawal of protests to proposed annexation, city council did not have implied power to accept such withdrawals under this section, since, if protest withdrawals were permitted up to very adjournment of annexation hearing, organized opposition to annexation would face uncertainty until last moment as to whether their protests had been fruitful or futile, while proponents of annexation would be encouraged during same time to importune individual protesting land owners to change their minds, and since, when Legislature has wanted to grant authorization to cities to permit protest withdrawal in other instances it has done so expressly, as in § 35012, which indicates creation of new right rather than clarification of right already held by cities. Cockerill v Redding (1961) 198 CA2d 108, 17 Cal Rptr 754.

§ 35121. Hearing of protest: When further proceedings not to be taken. At the time set for hearing protests, or to which the hearing may have been continued, the city legislative body shall hear and pass upon all protests so made:

(a) If privately owned property and no publicly owned property is proposed to be annexed, further proceedings shall not be taken if protest is made by private owners of one-half of the value of the territory proposed to be annexed. The value given such property for protest purposes shall be that shown on the last equalized assessment roll if the property is not exempt from taxation. If the property is exempt from taxation, its value for protest purposes shall be determined by the county assessor in the same amount as he would assess such property if it were not exempt from taxation.

(b) If privately owned property and publicly owned property are proposed to be annexed in the same proceeding, further proceedings shall not be taken if protest is made by public and private owners of one-half of the value of the territory. The value given privately owned property shall be determined pursuant to subdivision (a) of this section. The value given publicly owned property for protest purposes shall be determined by the county assessor in the same manner as is provided in subdivision (a) of this section for privately owned property, exempt from taxation.

(c) The value for protest purposes to be given property held in joint tenancy or tenancy in common shall be determined by the legislative body in proportion to the proportionate interest of the protestant in such property.

(d) As used in this article, "value of the territory" means the value of the land, exclusive of improvements thereon.

(e) When property is subject to a written recorded agreement to buy, the purchaser under the agreement may protest and the seller may not even though he is shown as the owner on the last equalized assessment role.

Determinations of the value of publicly owned property, or private-owned property exempt from taxation by the county assessor for protest purposes shall be obtained from the assessor by the protestant and submitted to the legislative body with the written protest.

LEGISLATIVE HISTORY

1. Added by Stats 1949 ch 79 § 1 p 118, the section then reading: "At the time set for hearing protests the city legislative body shall hear and pass upon all protests so made. If it finds that protest is made by the owners of a majority of separate parcels of property within the territory, no further proceedings for the annexation of any of the territory shall be taken for one year after the finding." Based on:

(a) Stats 1913 ch 312 § 2 8th sent p 588, as amended by Stats 1933 ch 227 § 1 p 733, without substantial change.

(b) Stats 1913 ch 312 § 2a, as added by Stats 1947 ch 1250 § 1 p 2761, without substantial change.

2. Amended by Stats 1955 ch 702 § 2 p 1188.

3. Amended by Stats 1955 ch 1948 § 2 p 3579, amending the section to read: "At the time set for hearing protests, or to which the hearing may have been continued, the city legislative body shall hear and pass upon all protests so made. If it finds that protest is made by the owners of one-half of the value of the territory proposed to be annexed as shown by the last equalized assessment roll, or if protest is made by public and private owners equal to one-half of the value of the territory, further proceedings shall not be taken. The value to be given publicly owned property for protest purposes shall be

If protests are made by petition, the petition shall contain the same information required of individual protests, and there shall be attached to the petition an affidavit made by a voter or owner of property within the territory described in the petition, or an agent of either such owner or voter. The affidavit shall state that the affiant circulated that particular paper, saw written the signatures appended thereto; that he resides at .... ; and that according to the best information and belief of affiant:

(a) Each is the genuine signature of the person whose name it purports to be.

(b) The signer is an owner or duly authorized agent of the owner of property within the territory.

The city shall, on request and without charge, provide forms of protest petitions and the affidavit required by this section to owners of property within the territory. [Amended by Stats 1963 ch 889 § 1.]

1. Deleted: "there are insufficient protests"
2. Deleted: "10-day"

§ 35121. Hearing of protest: When further proceedings not to be taken.

11 UCLA LR 46 (standard to determine sufficiency of protest).

§ 35121.1. Hearing of protest: Resolution declaring whether majority protest made: Limitation on further proceedings.

The city legislative body shall find and declare by resolution adopted at the hearing or within [1] *30 days after the closing of the* hearing on protests whether or not a majority protest has been made. If it does not adopt such a resolution within such period, it shall be deemed to have adopted on the [2] *30th* day a resolution that a majority protest has been made.

If a resolution finding and declaring that a majority protest is made is adopted or deemed adopted, no further proceedings for the annexation of any of the same territory to the city shall be taken for one year after the date of the adoption of the resolution *except upon the petition or consent of all property owners of the territory proposed to be annexed.* [Amended by Stats 1963 ch 1894 § 1; Stats 1965 ch 1603 § 1.]

1. Deleted: "10"
2. Deleted: "10th"

§ 35121.6. Same: Resubmission of changed boundaries to local agency formation commission: Amendment of boundary description.

If the legislative body of the city makes any changes in the boundaries in accordance with the provisions of Section 35121.5, it shall resubmit the boundaries as changed to the [1] *local agency formation commission pursuant to Government Code Section 54790* for report as to definiteness and certainty. Upon receipt of the report the city legislative body may, if necessary, amend the boundary description to make the boundary description definite and certain. [Amended by Stats 1965 ch 587 § 6.]

1. Deleted: "county boundary commission"
See note to § 34303.5.

1005

Exhibit No. 30

Standard Form 100 (Revised)
JANUARY 1967
APPROVED BOB-124-R002.1
100-104

JOINT REPORTING COMMITTEE
- Equal Employment Opportunity Commission
- Office of Federal Contract Compliance
- Plans for Progress Program

**EQUAL EMPLOYMENT OPPORTUNITY
EMPLOYEE INFORMATION REPORT EEO-1**

IMPORTANT - Read the attached instructions carefully before preparing this report. The form contains references to sections in the instructions. Before March 31, submit all reports in duplicate to: Joint Reporting Committee, Federal Depot, 1203 East 10th St., Jeffersonville, Indiana, 47130. If after reading the instructions you find that you are subject to the requirements for reporting employment data, complete the form as instructed and file with the Joint Reporting Committee. If you find that you are not subject to the reporting requirements, return the form, completing only sections A, B and C.

If the reporting unit is part of a multi-establishment company, send your reports to company headquarters for forwarding to the Joint Reporting Committee. Individual unit reports of a multi-establishment company must not be sent directly by the individual establishments to the Jeffersonville address. Establishments with less than 50 employees, and establishments in certain industries regardless of size, are to be combined at company headquarters in accordance with instructions, section 8e, f and g.

See instructions	Section A – COMPANY IDENTIFICATION (To be answered by all respondents)				OFFICE USE ONLY
	1. Reporting unit for which this report is filed. (If a combined report covering two or more units please so indicate and identify the area covered by the combined report.)				
8, 9a(1)	a. Name of reporting unit				a.
	Address (Number and street) Robart Manufacturing Company, Richmond Plant		State	ZIP code	
11j, 11m	801 Chesley Ave. Richmond	Contra Costa	California	94604	b.
	b. Employer Identification No.		c. Reporting Unit No. (Insert if the unit is a part of a multi-establishment company)		c.
9a(2), 11b, 11m	2. Principal office or headquarters of company (Answer only if the reporting unit is part of a multi-establishment company)				
	a. Name of principal office or headquarters	b. Employer Identification No. (If different from number listed in 1b above)			
	Robart Manufacturing Company	County	State	ZIP code	
	400 Park Ave. New York		New York	10022	
9a(3), 11j, 11u	3. Parent or affiliated company (Answer only if your company is a separate corporate entity owned or controlled by, or affiliated with another employer.)				
	a. Name of parent or affiliated company	b. Employer Identification No.			
	Address (Number and street)	City or town	County	State	ZIP code

	Section B – EMPLOYERS WHO ARE REQUIRED TO FILE (To be answered by all single establishment employers and on the consolidated report of all multi-establishment employers)	
5, 9b	**NOTE:** These questions apply to the entire company and not to any individual establishment. If the answer is "Yes" to questions 1, 2, 3 or 4, you are required to complete all questions on this form unless otherwise instructed. If your answer is "No" to all these questions, mark the box for Item 5, complete section G and return the form. If you have answered "Yes" to either of questions 1-4 but contend that you are not covered by the reporting requirements, return the form with a statement in section F indicating specifically why you claim to be exempt.	
11c(1),	1 ☐ Yes 2 ☐ No	1. Does the entire company have at least 100 employees in the payroll period for which you are reporting?
5b, 11c(3), 11f, 12	1 ☐ Yes 2 ☐ No	2. Does the company or any of its divisions or establishments: a. Have a prime contract, a first-tier subcontract, or a purchase order with any agency of the Federal Government or a Federal or Federally-assisted construction contract or subcontract at any tier; and b. Have at least one such contract or order amounting to $50,000 or more, or serve as a depository of Federal Government funds in any amount; and c. Have at least 50 employees in the payroll period for which you are reporting? NOTE: The answer to question 3 is "YES" only if a, b and c are all true.
3c, 11c(2)	1 ☐ Yes 2 ☐ No	4. Is the company a member of the national Plans for Progress program (a voluntary organization through which it has signed a pledge with the Vice-President of the United States to carry out the principles of equal employment opportunity)? IF A MEMBER ONLY OF A STATE OR LOCAL GROUP USING THE NAME "PLANS FOR PROGRESS," ANSWER "NO."
5	1 ☐	5. Company does not meet filing requirements set forth in questions 1-4 (If marked, complete section G and return to the Joint Reporting Committee)

	Section C – REPORTING UNIT INFORMATION		
9c, 11k, 11l	1. Indicate by marking in the appropriate box the unit for which this copy of the form is submitted (MARK ONLY ONE OF BOXES (a) THROUGH (j).)		
8a, 11p	SINGLE ESTABLISHMENT UNIT 1 ☐ (a) Employer has no more than one establishment		
11q, 8b	MULTI-ESTABLISHMENT EMPLOYER 2 ☐ (b) Consolidated Report (Filing of a consolidated report for the entire company is required)		
8c, 11n	INDIVIDUAL REPORTING UNIT OF MULTI-ESTABLISHMENT EMPLOYER 3 ☐ (c) Principal or headquarters office (A separate report is required in all cases)		
8d	4 ☐ (d) Individual establishment with 50 or more employees at one location only (Separate report required unless special rules apply)		
8e–8i 11o, 11v	COMBINED REPORTING UNIT OF MULTI-ESTABLISHMENT EMPLOYER – The following types of reports must include the attachments described in the instructions. Note that (e), (f) and (g) apply to all establishments in the Retail Trade, Wholesale Trade, Finance, Insurance, Real Estate, and Service Industries as well as establishments with less than 50 employees in other industries.)		
8e, 8f, 16	5 ☐ (e) Combined unit of two or more establishments located at same city	9 ☐ (i) Combined reporting unit of establishments located in two or more States with permission from the Joint Reporting Committee to report in this manner
8e, 8f, 15	6 ☐ (f) Combined unit of two or more establishments located in the same Standard Metropolitan Statistical Area	0 ☐ (j) Other – Explain
8e, 8f, 15	7 ☐ (g) Combined unit of two or more establishments within the same State outside of Standard Metropolitan Statistical Areas	
8g, 8i	8 ☐ (h) Combined "small establishment report" of units located in two or more States and qualifying for special reporting method. (List showing employment figures by occupation and State must be attached as instructed.)	
9c(2)	2. If this reporting unit is an individual establishment ((a), (c) or (d) above) a. Is its location the same as that reported last year? 1 ☐ Yes 2 ☐ No	b. Is the major activity at this unit the same as that reported last year? 1 ☐ Yes 2 ☐ No 3 ☐ No report last year	OFFICE USE d.
11r	3. What is the major activity of this reporting unit? (Be specific, i.e., manufacturing steel castings, retail grocer, wholesale plumbing supplies, title insurance, etc. Include the type of product or type of service provided. "Manufacturing," "Wholesale," "Retail," "Processing," "Sales," etc., are not sufficient.		e.
	Answer only if this is the consolidated report of a multi-establishment employer 4. How many separate reports are you submitting? .... _____ reports		f.

1006

Section D – FOR FEDERAL GOVERNMENT CONTRACTORS AND FEDERALLY ASSISTED CONSTRUCTION CONTRACTORS ONLY

This section must be filled out by all single establishment employers and on the consolidated report of all multi-establishment employers who answered "Yes" to section B, question 3. All other employers should proceed to section E.

1. Is the employer – Mark one only

1 ☐ A prime contractor of the Federal Government?

2 ☐ A first-tier subcontractor of the Federal Government?

3 ☐ A Federal or Federally-assisted construction contractor or subcontractor at any tier?

2. Is the equal employment opportunity clause included in all your contracts subject to Executive Order 11246?

1 ☐ Yes   2 ☐ No

3. Have you informed your subcontractors of their responsibilities under Executive Order 11246?

1 ☐ Yes   2 ☐ No

4. Compliance Agency – Note: A Compliance Agency is the Federal Government agency responsible for the employer's compliance with Executive Order 11246. (It is NOT the prime contractor, a State or local governmental body or the Joint Reporting Committee.)

a. If the employer has been informed that a particular Federal Government agency has been named as his Compliance Agency, what is that Compliance Agency? _____

b. If the employer is a prime contractor for nonconstruction contracts of the Federal Government, with which Federal Government agency does the employer have the largest dollar volume of contracts? _____

c. If the employer is a first-tier subcontractor for nonconstruction contracts of the Federal Government –
(1) What is his prime contractor with which he has the largest dollar volume of subcontracts? .... _____

(2) What is that prime contractor's Compliance Agency? .... _____

d. If the employer is a Federal Government construction contractor or subcontractor or is a Federally-assisted construction contractor or subcontractor, from what Federal Government agency does the employer receive the largest dollar volume of contracts and assistance? .... _____

OFFICE USE ONLY

g.

h.

i.

j.

K.

Section E – EMPLOYMENT DATA

Please note that these data may be obtained by visual survey or post-employment records. Neither visual surveys nor post-employment records are prohibited by any Federal, State or local law. All specified data are required to be filled in by law.

1. How was information as to race or ethnic group in section E5 obtained?
1 ☐ Visual Survey   3 ☐ Other – Specify _____ Personal con-
2 ☒ Employment Record

2. Dates of payroll period used – data at the reporting unit during only one payroll period in December, January or February. Multi-establishment employers need not use the same payroll period for all units.

3. Date of last report submitted for this reporting unit   March 30, 1966

4. Are there any employee facilities (i.e., drinking fountains, rest rooms, recreational areas, lunchrooms, etc.) at this reporting unit which are provided for employees on a racially separate basis?
1 ☐ Yes
2 ☐ No

5. Employment at this reporting unit – Report all permanent, temporary, or part-time employees unless specifically excluded as set forth in section I1f of the instructions. Enter the appropriate figures on all lines and in all columns. Blank spaces will be considered as zeros.
(See section 9e of the instructions on how to fill out this table, and section 10 for a description of the columns 1, 2 and 3, include all employees in the reporting unit, not merely those in minority groups.)

Job categories	ALL EMPLOYEES			MINORITY GROUP EMPLOYEES							
				Male				Female			
	Total (Col. 2+3)	Male	Female	Negro	Oriental	American Indian	Spanish American	Negro	Oriental	American Indian	Spanish American
	(1)	(2)	(3)	(4)	(5)	(6)	(7)	(8)	(9)	(10)	(11)
Officials and managers											
Professionals	31	31				2					
Technicians	16	15	1								
Sales workers	4	4									
Office and clerical	8		8								
Craftsmen (Skilled)	26	5	21								
Operatives (Semi-skilled)	50	50		1							
Laborers (Unskilled)	171	167	4	9		2	15				
Service workers	7	7									
TOTAL	313	287	26	11		4	18				
Total employment from previous report (if any)	269						15				
Apprentices											
On-the-job trainees — White collar											
Production											

(The data below shall also be included in the figures for the appropriate occupational categories above)

1 See explanation of "minority group identification" in section 9 of the instructions.   2 Report only employees enrolled in formal on-the-job training programs.

Section F – REMARKS

Use this item to give any identification data appearing on last report which differs from that given above, explain major changes in employment, changes in composition of reporting units, and other pertinent information.

Section G – SIGNATURE AND IDENTIFICATION (To be answered by all respondents)

Name (Signature) William D. Lyle	Address (Number and street)	Date March 15, 1967
Name (Type or print)	City 801 Chesley Ave.	County
Title William D. Lyle	State Richmond ZIP Contra Costa California 94804	Area code 41. Number 234 7 Extension 114 312 / Telephone

WILLFULLY FALSE STATEMENTS ON THIS REPORT ARE PUNISHABLE BY LAW, U.S. CODE, TITLE 18, SECTION 1001
See section 2 of instructions for penalties for failure to file

1007

Exhibit No. 31

Standard Form 100 (Revised)
JANUARY 1967
APPROVED BOB-124-R002.1
100-104

<table>
<tr><td colspan="2">JOINT REPORTING COMMITTEE
• Equal Employment Opportunity Commission
• Office of Federal Contract Compliance
• Plans for Progress Program</td><td>EQUAL EMPLOYMENT OPPORTUNITY
EMPLOYEE INFORMATION REPORT EEO-1</td></tr>
</table>

IMPORTANT — Read the attached instructions carefully before preparing this report. The form contains references to sections in the instructions. Before March 31, submit all reports in duplicate to: Joint Reporting Committee, Federal Depot, 1201 East 10th St., Jeffersonville, Indiana, 47130. If after reading the instructions you find that you are not subject to the requirements for reporting employment data, complete the form as instructed and file with the Joint Reporting Committee. If you find that you are not subject to the reporting requirements, return the form, completing only sections A, B and C.

If the reporting unit is part of a multi-establishment company, send your reports to company headquarters for forwarding to the Joint Reporting Committee. Individual unit reports of a multi-establishment company must not be sent directly by the individual establishments to the Jeffersonville address. Establishments with less than 50 employees, and establishments in certain industries regardless of size, are to be combined at company headquarters in accordance with instructions, section 8e, f and g.

Section A – COMPANY IDENTIFICATION
(To be answered by all respondents)

					OFFICE USE ONLY
8, 9a(1)	1. Reporting unit for which this report is filed. *(If a combined report covering two or more units please so indicate and identify the area covered by the combined report.)*				
	a. Name of reporting unit **Consolidated Report**				a.
	Address (Number and street) **P. O. Box 504**	City or town **Sunnyvale**	County **Santa Clara**	State **California**	ZIP code **94088**	b.
11j, 11m	b. Employer Identification No. 9 5 0 9 4 1 8 8 0			c. Reporting Unit No. *(Insert if the unit is a part of a multi-establishment company)*		c.
	2. Principal office or headquarters of company *(Answer only if the reporting unit is part of a multi-establishment company)*					
9a(2), 11n, 11m	a. Name of principal office or headquarters **Lockheed Missiles & Space Company**		b. Employer Identification No. *(If different from number listed in 1b above)* 9 5 0 9 4 1 8 8 0			
	Address (Number and street) **P. O. Box 504**	City or town **Sunnyvale**	County **Santa Clara**	State **California**	ZIP code **94088**	
	3. Parent or affiliated company *(Answer only if your company is a separate corporate entity owned or controlled by, or affiliated with another employer.)*					
9a(3), 11j, 11u	a. Name of parent or affiliated company **Lockheed Aircraft Corporation**		b. Employer Identification No. 9 5 0 9 4 1 8 8 0			
	Address (Number and street) **P. O. Box 551**	City or town **Burbank**	County **Los Angeles**	State **California**	ZIP code **91503**	

Section B – EMPLOYERS WHO ARE REQUIRED TO FILE
(To be answered by all single establishment employers and on the consolidated report of all multi-establishment employers)

NOTE: These questions apply to the entire company and not to any individual establishment. If the answer is "Yes" to questions 1, 2, 3 or 4, you are required to complete all questions on this form unless otherwise instructed. If your answer is "No" to all these questions, mark the box for item 5, complete section C and return the form. If you have answered "Yes" to either of questions 1-4 but contend that you are not covered by the reporting requirements, return the form with a statement in section F indicating specifically why you are exempt.

11f(1), 11f	☑ Yes ☐ No	1. Does the entire company have at least 100 employees in the payroll period for which you are reporting?
5a, 9b	☐ Yes ☑ No	2. If your answer is "No," is your company affiliated through common ownership and/or centralized management, with other entities in an enterprise with a total employment of 100 or more?
5b, 11e(3), 11f, 12	☑ Yes ☐ No	3. Does the company or any of its divisions or establishments: a. Have a prime contract, a first-tier subcontract, or a purchase order with any agency of the Federal Government or a Federal or Federally-assisted construction contract or subcontract at any tier; and b. Have at least one such contract or order amounting to $50,000 or more, or serve as a depository of Federal Government funds in any amount; and c. Have at least 50 employees in the payroll period for which you are reporting? **NOTE:** The answer to question 3 is "YES" only if a, b and c are all true.
5c, 11e(2)	☑ Yes ☐ No	4. Is the company a member of the national Plans for Progress program (a voluntary organization through which it has signed a pledge with the Vice-President of the United States to carry out the principles of equal employment opportunity)? IF A MEMBER ONLY OF A STATE OR LOCAL GROUP USING THE NAME "PLANS FOR PROGRESS," ANSWER "NO."
5	☐	5. Company does not meet filing requirements set forth in questions 1-4 *(If marked, complete section G and return to the Joint Reporting Committee)*

Section C – REPORTING UNIT INFORMATION

9c, 11k, 11l	1. Indicate by marking in the appropriate box the unit for which this copy of the form is submitted *(MARK ONLY ONE OF BOXES (a) THROUGH (j).)*	
8a, 11p	SINGLE ESTABLISHMENT UNIT 1 ☐ (a) Employer has no more than one establishment	
11g, 8b	MULTI-ESTABLISHMENT EMPLOYER 2 ☑ (b) Consolidated Report *(Filing of a consolidated report for the entire company is required)*	
8c, 11n	INDIVIDUAL REPORTING UNIT OF MULTI-ESTABLISHMENT EMPLOYER 3 ☐ (c) Principal or headquarters office *(A separate report is required in all cases)*	
8d	4 ☐ (d) Individual establishment with 50 or more employees at one location only *(Separate report required unless special rules apply)*	
8e–8i, 11o, 11w	COMBINED REPORTING UNIT OF MULTI-ESTABLISHMENT EMPLOYER — The following types of reports must include the attachments described in the instructions: Note that (e), (f) and (g) apply to all establishments in the Retail Trade, Wholesale Trade, Finance, Insurance, Real Estate, and Service industries as well as establishments with less than 50 employees in other industries.	
8e, 8f, 16	5 ☐ (e) Combined unit of two or more establishments located at same city	9 ☐ (i) Combined reporting unit of establishments located in two or more States with permission from the Joint Reporting Committee to report in this manner
8e, 8f, 15	6 ☐ (f) Combined unit of two or more establishments located in the same Standard Metropolitan Statistical Area	0 ☐ (j) Other – Explain
8e, 8f, 15	7 ☐ (g) Combined unit of two or more establishments located within the same State outside of Standard Metropolitan Statistical Area	
8g, 8i	8 ☐ (h) Combined "small establishments report" of units located in two or more States and qualifying for special reporting method *(List showing employment figures by occupation and State must be attached as instructed.)*	
9c(2)	2. If this reporting unit is an individual establishment *((a), (c) or (d) above)* a. Is its location the same as that reported last year? 1 ☐ Yes 2 ☐ No 3 ☐ No report last year	b. Is the major activity at this unit the same as that reported last year? 1 ☑ Yes 2 ☐ No 3 ☐ No report last year	OFFICE USE d.
11r	3. What is the major activity at this reporting unit? (Be specific, i.e., manufacturing steel castings, retail grocer, wholesale plumbing supplies, title insurance, etc. include the type of product or type of service provided. "Manufacturing," "Wholesale," "Retail," "Processing," "Sales," etc., are not sufficient. **Aerospace Research & Development**		e.
	Answer only if this is the consolidated report of a multi-establishment employer		
	4. How many separate reports are you submitting? .... _____ reports		f.

1008

Section D - FOR FEDERAL GOVERNMENT CONTRACTORS AND FEDERALLY ASSISTED CONSTRUCTION CONTRACTORS ONLY

This section must be filled out by all single establishment employers and on the consolidated report of all multi-establishment employers who answered "Yes" to section II, question 3. All other employers should proceed to section E.

1. Is the employer - Mark one only

1 [X] A prime contractor of the Federal Government?

2 [ ] A first-tier subcontractor of the Federal Government?

3 [ ] A Federal or Federally-assisted construction contractor or subcontractor at any tier?

2. Is the equal employment opportunity clause included in all your contracts subject to Executive Order 11246? 1 [X] Yes 2 [ ] No

3. Have you informed your subcontractors of their responsibilities under Executive Order 11246? 1 [X] Yes 2 [ ] No

4. Compliance Agency - Note: A Compliance Agency is the Federal Government agency responsible for the employer's compliance with Executive Order 11246. (It is NOT the prime contractor, a State or local governmental body or the Joint Reporting Committee.)

a. If the employer has been informed that a particular Federal Government agency has been named as his Compliance Agency, what is that agency?   Department of Defense

b. If the employer is a prime contractor for nonconstruction contracts of the Federal Government, with which Federal Government agency does the employer have the largest dollar volume of contracts?   Department of the Navy

c. If the employer is a first-tier subcontractor for nonconstruction contracts of the Federal Government -
(1) What is his prime contractor with which he has the largest dollar volume of subcontracts?
(2) What is that prime contractor's Compliance Agency?

d. If the employer is a Federal Government construction contractor or subcontractor or is a Federally-assisted construction contractor or subcontractor, from what Federal Government agency does the employer receive the largest dollar volume of contracts and assistance?

OFFICE USE ONLY

Section E - EMPLOYMENT DATA

Please note that these data may be obtained by visual survey or post-employment records. Neither visual surveys nor post-employment records are prohibited by any Federal, State or local law. All specified data are required to be filled in by law.

1. How was information as to race or ethnic group in section E5 obtained? 1 [ ] Visual Survey 2 [ ] Other - Specify 3 [X] Employment Record

2. Dates of payroll period used - You should gather and report employment data at the reporting unit during only one payroll period in December, January or February. Multi-establishment employers need not use the same payroll period for all units.   As of 12-24-66

3. Date of last report submitted for this reporting unit   As of 1-1-66

4. Are there any employee facilities (i.e., drinking fountains, rest rooms, recreational areas, lunchrooms, etc.) at this reporting unit which are provided for employees on a racially separate basis? 1 [ ] Yes 2 [X] No

5. Employment at this reporting unit - Report all permanent, temporary, or part-time employees unless specifically excluded as set forth in section II of the instructions. Enter the appropriate figures on all lines and in all columns. Blank spaces will be considered as zeros. (See section 9 of the instructions on how to fill out this table, and section 10 for a description of the job categories.) In columns 1, 2 and 3, include all employees in the reporting unit, not merely those in minority groups

Job categories	Total (Col. 2+3)	Male	Female	Male Negro	Male Oriental	Male American Indian	Male Spanish American	Female Negro	Female Oriental	Female American Indian	Female Spanish American
	(1)	(2)	(3)	(4)	(5)	(6)	(7)	(8)	(9)	(10)	(11)
Officials and managers	1519	1505	14	5	15		24				
Professionals	14467	13991	476	88	469		319	5	11		10
Technicians	1958	1741	217	35	91	3	73	1	7		3
Sales workers											
Office and clerical	4190	1400	2790	45	18	1	90	28	64	1	132
Craftsmen (Skilled)	3633	3314	319	60	66	1	207	7	1		17
Operatives (Semiskilled)	691	423	268	42	15		56	29	2		24
Laborers (Unskilled)	115	115		14	6		7				
Service workers	378	364	14	29	32		40	1			2
TOTAL	26951	22853	4098	318	712	5	796	71	85	1	188
Total employment from previous report (if any)	23351	19812	3539	244	543		776	42	70		185

(The data below shall also be included in the figures for the appropriate occupational categories above)

Apprentices											
On-the-job trainees	White collar										
	Production										

1 See explanation of "minority group identification" in section 9 of the instructions. 2 Report only employees enrolled in formal on-the-job training program.

Section F - REMARKS

Use this item to give any identification data appearing on last report which differs from that given above, explain major changes in employment, changes in composition of reporting units, and other pertinent information.

Section G - SIGNATURE AND IDENTIFICATION (To be answered by all respondents)

Name (Signature)

Name (Type or print)   L. A. Mitchell

Title   Manager of Industrial Relations

Address (Number and street)   1111 Lockheed Way

City   Sunnyvale

County   Santa Clara

State   California

ZIP code   94088

Date

Area code   408   Number   743-0835   Extension

WILLFULLY FALSE STATEMENTS ON THIS REPORT ARE PUNISHABLE BY LAW, U.S. CODE, TITLE 18, SECTION 1001
See section 2 of instructions for penalties for failure to file

PART II—EMPLOYMENT STATISTICS

7. EMPLOYMENT BY RACE, OCCUPATION, AND SEX										7a. DATES OF PAYROLL PERIOD

As of January 2, 1965

OCCUPATIONS (See Item 6) of the Instructions)	MALE EMPLOYEES					FEMALE EMPLOYEES					TOTAL ALL EMPLOYEES
	TOTAL MALES	MINORITY GROUPS				TOTAL FEMALES	MINORITY GROUPS				
		NEGRO	* ORIENTAL	* AMERI- CAN INDIAN	SPANISH AMERI- CAN		NEGRO	* ORIENTAL	* AMERI- CAN INDIAN	SPANISH AMERI- CAN	
OFFICIALS AND MANAGERS	1312	2	10		21	12	0	0		0	1324
PROFESSIONALS	11443	66	275		311	358	4	9		14	11801
TECHNICIANS	1319	16	103		72	183	2	4		3	1502
SALES WORKERS	0	0	0		0	0	0	0		0	0
OFFICE AND CLERICAL	2370	29	13		87	2454	13	47		164	4824
CRAFTSMEN (SKILLED)	3212	67	30		214	232	4	0		15	3624
OPERATIVES (SEMI-SKILLED)	404	36	9		53	296	11	2		23	790
LABORERS (UNSKILLED)	76	2	9		13	1	0	0		0	77
SERVICE WORKERS	322	10	20		40	0	0	0		0	322
TOTAL	19703	223	187		911	3756	39	62		224	23264
TOTAL EMPLOYMENT FROM PREVIOUS REPORT (If any)	25012	319	532		1046	4591	50	63		319	30143
8. Figures for the following classifications shall also be included in appropriate category above the "Total" line.											
APPRENTICES											
ON-THE-JOB TRAINEES— PRODUCTION											
ON-THE-JOB TRAINEES— WHITE COLLAR											

*To be reported where such group constitutes an identifiable factor in the local labor market. (For Spanish American see 2g of the instructions.)

9 REMARKS (Explain major changes in employment, changes in composition of reporting units, and other pertinent information)

It will be noted that there was a total reduction in force of 6879 employees. Minority employees were involved in these reductions, resulting in the following changes in the ratios of minority employees to total workforce:

	Ratios as reflected on last-9 report	Ratios as reflected on this report	% Increase/Decrease
Negro	1.22	1.15	5.7% decrease
Oriental	1.97	2.23	12.8% increase
Spanish/American	4.50	4.15	1.1% decrease

10a. DATE REPORT SUBMITTED	10b. SIGNATURE AND TITLE OF AUTHORIZED REPRESENTATIVE	10c. ADDRESS
1-13-65	L. A. Mitchell Manager of Industrial Relations	Sunnyvale, California 91036

Willfully false statements on this Report are punishable by law (U S Code Title 18, Section 1001)

1010

Exhibit No. 32

STATEMENT OF CAPTAIN D. A. CAMPBELL, COMMANDING OFFICER, NAVAL AIR
STATION, ALAMEDA, TO THE UNITED STATES COMMISSION ON CIVIL RIGHTS,
MEETING IN OAKLAND, CALIFORNIA, ON 5 MAY 1967

Mister Chairman:

I am pleased to have this opportunity to report the progress the

Naval Air Station has made over the past 4 years in providing

opportunities for the employment and promotion of members of minor-

ity groups. I believe that the Equal Employment Program of the Air

Station is unsurpassed among employers, both public and private,

in the East Bay Area.

In 1963, an Equal Employment Opportunity Evaluation Team appointed

by the Secretary of the Navy, visited, among other activities, the

Alameda Naval Air Station. The Team met with the Commanding Officer,

his Department Heads, the Masters and Foremen employed at the Air

Station, officers of the National Association of Supervisors, and

the Naval Civilian Administrative Association, the members of the

Federal Employees for Equal Opportunity and the Naval Air Station

Study Group on Equal Employment Opportunity as well as with minor-

ity group leaders and representatives in the community. The team

emphasized the need to do everything possible within rules and

regulations to promote minority group members into jobs above

journeyman level. Supervisors were informed that assignments to

temporary details, temporary promotions and selection for training

must be made on an equitable basis so as to include minority group

members, particularly Negroes. The responsibility of supervisors

in carrying out the spirit and intent of the Navy's Equal Employment

Opportunity Program was particularly emphasized. The Team also

listened to complaints of alleged inequities which minority group

members had experienced in the past and the frustrations they felt

Prior to the Team's visit, my predecessor in command of the Naval

Air Station had appointed an Equal Employment Opportunity Study

Group. This Study Group was to determine whether or not an

Advisory Committee on Equal Employment Opportunity should be

established at the Naval Air Station. As a result of the recom-

mendations of the Study Group and the Secretary's Evaluation Team,

the Commanding Officer's Advisory Committee on Equal Employment

Opportunity was established on 28 January 1964.

This Committee was established as an advisory body to investigate

informal complaints of discrimination for the Commanding Officer,

to help establish communications between employees and their

supervisors thereby alleviating misunderstandings, and through its

recommendations and advisory opinions to assist the Commanding

Officer in developing sound equal employment policies in accord-

ance with established regulations and with a view toward preventing

discrimination.

On 11 March 1964, a moratorium on the filling of all supervisory

and production facilitating rates was declared. This was done to

allow minority group members a better opportunity to become quali-

fied and compete for promotions to supervisory positions. Over

2,000 employees participated in tests in connection with this

program. In addition, during the 15 months following the inaugera-

tion of this program, details to temporary higher level assignments

leading to qualification for promotion were equitably distributed

among all employees. Preference was given to eligible minority group

employees who had not previously been detailed to such assignments.

In 1964, as a result of contact with the Bureau of Indian Affairs,

8 American Indians were tested and hired by the Naval Air Station.

Six are still employed as Helper Generals and 2 have moved into

The files of the Urban League of Oakland were made available to
the Air Station and from these files many applicants were referred
to the Air Station, tested, and successfully placed in Accounting
Technician and Payroll Clerk positions.

During 1964 also, tests were administered to 100 job applicants
from the Richmond Vocational Rehabilitation Center of the Contra
Costa Welfare Department. Of the 9 applicants who passed the test,
all were placed on the rolls of this Activity.

On 18 June 1965, I assumed command of the Naval Air Station. It
was during 1965 that the Air Station first inaugerated the Summer
Youth Oppor'.unity Program by employing 137 young people. In the
fall of 1965, we employed 172 other youngsters in the Back-to-
Schcol Program, a year-around program designed to assist educationally and economically disadvantaged children in continuance of their
schooling while employed on a part-time basis. Of this latter
group, 54 were Caucasian, 97 Negroes, 15 Spanish Americans and
6 Orientals.

Applicants for employment at the Naval Air Station were actively
sought and recruited through and with the assistance of the
President of the Mexican-American Political Association, the
Brookfield Association of East Oakland and the Camp Parks Job
Corps Center as well as the various East Bay Chapters of the NAACP.

In order to eliminate any possibility of discrimination within the
Station's Merit Promotion Program, I instituted a system whereby
I personally review with the Department Head concerned all
selection board actions.

Selection action was taken during 1965 and 1966 which led to the
promotion of 157 employees to the journeyman level in the skilled
aircraft trades. This number included 40 Negroes, 9 Orientals
and 4 Spanish-Americans. In addition, during the past two years
minority group employees, for the first time, have been promoted
to or employed in positions typified by the following:

    Production Controlman

    Inspector, Auto Repair

    Electrical Engineer, GS-12

    Numerically Controlled Machine Tool Mechanic

    Supervisory Cost Accountant, GS-11

    Computer Aid (Scheduler), GS-9

    Supervisory Personnel Staffing Specialist, GS-9

    Personnel Staffing and Employee Relations Specialist, GS-9

    Assistant Planner and Estimator (Machinist)

    Foreman Metalsmith

    Foreman Airframes Mechanic

    Foreman Aircraft Engine Mechanic

    Foreman Aircraft Painter

A look at statistics or at unusual individual cases when considering
achievements made in promotions for minority group employees to
supervisory level positions may be misleading and seem to indicate
that little has been accomplished over the past few years. But
you must consider that only a few years ago members of minority
groups were not even in positions which would qualify them for
further promotions to the supervisory level. By comparing this
with the increasing number of minority group employees who are now
in journeyman level positions and knocking at the door for promotion to supervisory positions, I submit that the progress has been

Since January 1965, 1173 employees have competed for blue collar
supervisory positions. Of 513 eligible, 72 were finally selected.
Thirteen were from minority groups.

1966 was a busy year as the Equal Employment Opportunity Program
moved into high gear. Naval Air Station representatives visited
the four branch offices of the Oakland Adult Minority Project
which are located in predominantly Negro and Mexican-American
communities in Oakland. One hundred people were tested for
clerical and Helper General positions and all 17 who passed the
tests were employed by the Naval Air Station. During other visits,
the then-new Worker-Trainee position was explained to interested
persons. As a result, 45 Worker-Trainees were employed. The East
Bay Skills Center in Oakland was visited several times during the
year. Tests were administered to 195 applicants and all 83 who
passed the tests were employed.

Early in 1966, following a 3-day disturbance at an East Oakland
high school, a Naval Air Station representative visited this
school to obtain the names of drop-outs in the area who could be
tested for vacancies existing at the Naval Air Station. Twelve
youths were tested for the occupations of Helper General, 4 were
employed. Seven local organizations were contacted under the
Neighborhood Youth Corps Project. Four Youth Corps enrollees are
presently employed on the Station and efforts are continuing to
find sponsorship so that additional youths can be employed.

The Naval Air Station participated in a Job Fair held in the
Exposition Building in Oakland on 19-20 February 1966. During
the Job Fair, Naval Air Station employees manned a booth for two
full days furnishing information and employment applications for
vacant positions at the Air Station.

A job rotation program was established in 1966 to provide better
opportunities for employees to advance to the journeyman level.
Particular emphasis was placed on minority group employees. Five
hundered eighty employees have taken advantage of this program.

One hundred eighty eight are minority group employees. Forty-
three percent of all minority group employees who are eligible
for the program have taken advantage of the opportunity for such
training.

During the last eight months of 1966, an accelerated counseling
program was provided to low-skilled employees in the Supply
Department with a view toward skills upgrading. Two hundred
forty-three employees, primarily minority group employees, were
counseled during this period by trained staff specialists. They
assisted each individual in recognizing his own shortcomings,
concentrating heavily in the method and manner of taking written
examinations. The employees were made aware of after-hours
training courses designed for their own self-help which were
available on the Air Station as well as through community adult
education programs. Other employees with good educational background and work achievement records were encouraged to take full
advantage of the Air Station's promotional plan by competing in
examinations.

During 1966, Mr. Wilmont Sweeney, Berkeley Councilman, a well-known
attorney and a leader in the Civil Rights movement, addressed
all Naval Air Station officers and supervisors as part of a supervisory training program on board the Station, emphasizing education and ideas for positive corrective approaches to the total
equal employment program.

Numerous local conferences on employment of minorities and other
e·"al opportunity programs were attended by key Air Station
officials during 1966 as well as the years preceding. During the
Conference on Employment of Minorities in the West, presented by
the National Urban League in San Francisco, the Naval Air Station
representation was greater than that of all other Federal activities
in the Bay Area.

I meet monthly with my key department heads and my Advisory Committee on Equal Employment Opportunity. This gives the Committee an
opportunity to provide the top Air Station management officials
and me with frequent reports of their activities and to have a
full and free interchange of ideas.

During 1966, the second consecutive Summer Youth Opportunity
Program was held on the Naval Air Station. Two hundred sixty-nine
youngsters were hired; a figure not exceeded by any other Naval
installation in the entire nation that year--63 were Caucasian,
158 Negroes, 40 Spanish-Americans and 8 Orientals. In the Back-to-
School Program, which continued through 1966, 161 young people were
employed; 40 Caucasian, 105 Negroes, 15 Spanish-Americans and '1
Oriental.

It is still too early to assess our accomplishments during 1967.
However, Naval Air Station officials have met with representatives
from the Alameda County Welfare Department, the Oakland Mayor's
Manpower Commission, the Oakland Skills Center, the Opportunities
Industrialization Center, Oakland, 22 counsellors from high schools
in the Bay Area, and many others to explain employment opportunities
and solicit employment applications.

A large scale testing program is currently underway in an effort
to bring 250 additional apprentices into the Worker-Trainee program.
Applicants are being sought from areas heavily populated by minority

Plans are currently being made to expand the Summer Youth Opportunity Program to accommodate about 400 youngsters during the summer of 1967.

Tours and lectures are being provided for Junior High School students with a view towards their future employment at the Naval Air Station.

An expanded program of supervisory training sessions is also underway. On 10 March 1967, in furtherance of this program, I wrote personal letters to each Naval Air Station supervisor stressing the importance of the Equal Opportunity Program.

Since March 1963, 27 formal discrimination complaints have been filed by employees of the Naval Air Station. In all 27 cases, a finding "no discrimination" has been upheld by the Secretary of the Navy.

In June 1963, the Naval Air Station employed 7,607 persons; 2,469 (or about 32 ½ %) were from minority groups.

In June 1965, the Naval Air Station employed 7,563 persons; 2,417 (or about 32 %) were from minority groups.

In April 1967, the Naval Air Station employed 9,847 persons. By extrapolation from a recent census conducted at the Naval Air Rework Facility, Alameda, it would appear that there are now about 3,430 (or about 35 %) minority group employees at the Naval Air Station.

The Naval Air Station has frequently been commended for its outstanding Equal Employment Opportunity Program by both local and national leaders. The U. S. Civil Service Commission recently

for its fine progress and accomplishments. I have attached a copy
of the Civil Service Commission's report to this statement for your
information.

The programs I have outlined are only highlights in a continuing
agressive Equal Employment Opportunity Program being carried out
at Naval Air Station, Alameda. My concern with efforts to achieve
Equal Opportunity affirmative action goals is deep and personal.
It will continue to be. Past accomplishments are not as important
as those things yet to be done. Although there is still, and
there always will be, room for improvement in our program, I am
firmly convinced that the Naval Air Station has a progressive
program. By continuing to work closely with the leaders in the
East Bay Community as well as with my own staff, we can and will
accomplish even more.

A personal message from the Commanding Officer

To all Supervisors

Subject   Support of the Equal Employment Opportunity Program

1. I would like to discuss with you our affirmative action program for equal employment opportunity. Your complete support of our efforts to achieve equal employment opportunity here at Alameda is sincerely appreciated. As you know, this program is demanded by the concept of the brotherhood of man found in all religions and by our democratic concepts of equal justice and equal opportunity.

2. Apart from its moral justification, there are practical realities that give urgency to our efforts. Recent civil rights gains resulting from direct action campaigns have awakened expectations that even more can be accomplished. This has given rise to an impatience for results which are felt to be long overdue. In addition, the increased draft calls have reawakened in minority groups the feeling that if they are called upon to risk their lives or the lives of their sons or husbands on far-off battlefields, then there is no excuse for a lack of fair treatment at home. The fact that the proportion of Negroes being killed in combat in Viet Nam is greater than the proportion of Caucasians reinforces this feeling.

3. In view of these moral imperatives and practical realities, we must increase our efforts to treat all of our employees solely on the basis of their job performance, conduct, knowledge, skill, and aptitude. I cannot tolerate discriminatory treatment of any kind or degree.

4. I urge you to go beyond a mere absence of discrimination to provide positive assistance to your minority employees to enable them to acquire the type of education and experience that they need to develop their talents. There are many after-hours courses available at the Station, in local colleges, and in adult education programs run by local school boards that would help employees develop their job skills and their ability to pass promotion tests. Also you should rotate your employees around the shop or office to the extent feasible, and in accordance with regulations, so that they might obtain the widest possible range of developmental experience.

5. By taking these positive steps, you will be demonstrating your commitment to national policy and to the religious and democratic principles that have made our nation great.

D. A. CAMPBELL

1020

JEFFERY COHELAN
7TH DISTRICT, CALIFORNIA

COMMITTEE ON
APPROPRIATIONS

ADMINISTRATIVE ASSISTANT:
PETER V. CLUTE

FIELD REPRESENTATIVES:
MR. AND MRS. ROY LEMON
LATHAM SQUARE BUILDING
OAKLAND, CALIFORNIA 94612

Congress of the United States
House of Representatives
Washington, D.C. 20515

April 18, 1967

Captain D. A. Campbell
Commanding Officer
U. S. Naval Air Station
Alameda, California 94501

Dear Captain Campbell:

Thank you for sending me a copy of the April 8 issue of the Alameda County Weekender.

Your record on equal employment quite clearly speaks for itself, but I want to commend you again on the efforts you are making.

With kindest regards.

Sincerely yours,

Jeffery Cohelan

Member of Congress

Exhibit No. 33

DIRECT PRODUCTION

NON-SUPERVISORY BLUE-COLLAR

Wage Level	Current Wage Range	Amer. Indian	Negro	Oriental American	Spanish American	All Others	Total
Patternmaker	4.50-488					6	6
16	4.41-477						
15	4.22-4.58						
14	4.04-4.38					33	33
13	3.86-4.18	1	17	19	4	73	114
12	3.68-3.98		31	26	10	168	235
11	3.49-3.79	7	426	227	182	1762	2604
10	3.39-3.67		47	?	11	99	160
9	3.28-3.56		18	4	6	26	52
8	3.18-3.44	5	279	26	45	519	874
7	3.06-3.32		168	13	12	111	304
	2.96-3.20	2	·234	14	8	94	352
	2.85-3.09	4	295	20	45	477	841
	2.81-3.05		?				?
	2.78-3.02		/				/
	2.75-2.97		8				12
	2.69-2.91						
Apprentice	2.37-3.32	2	32	21	8	151	214
Worker Trainee	1.82-1.89		7			?	10
		21	1571	372	331	3525	5820

DATE CENSUS TAKEN: APR 24 1967

DIRECT PRODUCTION

SUPERVISORY BLUE-COLLAR

Wage Level	Current Wage Range *	Amer. Indian	Negro	Oriental American	Spanish American	All Others	Total
Superintendent II.	14,352 **					5	5
Superinten. I.	12,209.60**					16	16
General Fore- man II	5.41-5.87					3	3
	4.88-5.28					1	1
General Fore- man I.							
14	5.44-590						
13	5.26-5.70						
12	5.08-5.50					⁴	⁷
11	4.90-5.30					37	37
10	4.97-5.19					4	4
6	4.36-4.72						2
Foreman							
14	4.92-5.32					2	2
13	4.73-5.13					1	1
12	4.55-4.93					18	18
11	4.37-4.73	1	6	1	2	173	183
10	4.26-4.62				1	9	10
9	4.16-4.50					2	2
8	4.05-4.39						
7	3.94-4.26						2
	3.83-4.15					5	12

1023

SUPERVISORY BLUE-COLLAR

Wage Level	Current Wage Range *	Amer. Indian	Negro	Oriental American	Spanish American	All Others	Total
Leaders							
¬	3.48-3.78						
	3.38-3.66						

SUMMARIES

Superintendent II						⊃	⊃
Superintendent I						16	16
General Foreman II						4	4
General Foreman I			ı			48	49
Foreman		1	16	1	3	219	240
Leader						5	5
		1	17	1	3	297	319

* Varies at each level of supervision below Superintendent I depending upon wage of rating(s) supervised.

** Fixed annual salary is prescribed for this level.

DATE CENSUS TAKEN: ___APR 2 4 1967___

PRODUCTION FACILITATING

NON-SUPERVISORY BLUE-COLLAR

Rating	Current Wage Range*	Amer. Indian	Negro	American Oriental	Spanish American	All Others	Total
Planner & Est.	4.37-4.73			5	1	108	114
Asst. P&E	4.10-4.44						
	3.92-4.25					4	
Progressman	4.37-4.73						
A/C Examiner	4.23-4.59						
	4.05-4.39	1	3	5	-	65	76
Prod.Control-man	4.23-4.59			4		5	9
	4.05-4.39	1	2	2		35	43
Asst. Prod. Controlman	3.96-4.28		3	2		4	9
	3.77-4.09		1	2		51	56
Inspectors	4.23-4.59	1	2	5			16
	4.14-4.48					1	1
	4.05-4.39		.		4	119	132
	3.77-4.09		9		^	18	30
	3.46-3.74					1	1
Shop Planner	3.92-4.24					/	7
Maint.Sched.	4.20-4.54					1	1

*Varies for most of these ratings depending on the trade speciality required.

DATE CENSUS TAKEN: APR 2 4 1967

1025

PRODUCTION FACILITATING

SUPERVISORY BLUE-COLLAR

Wage Level	Current Wage Range*	Amer. Indian	Negro	American Oriental	Spanish American	All Others	Total
Supvy P&E	4.90-5.30					20	20
Supvy Prog.	4.90-5.30						
Senior Supvy A/C Exam.	5.41-5.87						
Supvy A/C Ex.	4.90-5.30						
Senior Supvy Inspectors	5.60-6.06						
Senior Supvy A/C Inspec.	5.41-5.87						
Supvy A/C Electron.Sys.	5.08-5.50						
Supvy A/C Inspec.	4.90-5.30					10	10
Assoc.Supvy A/C Insp.	4.37-4.73					8	8

* Varies for most of those depending on the levels of ratings supervised.

DATE CENSUS TAKEN:_____**APR 24 1967**_____

PRODUCTION FACILITATING

NON-SUPERVISORY SELECTED* WHITE-COLLAR

Type of Work	Grade Level	Current Salary Range	Amer. Indian	Negro	American Oriental	Spanish American	All Other	Total
Production Controllers	GS-12	10,927-14,338						
Quality Cont.Spec.	GS-11	9,221-12,056						
	GS-9	7,696-.10,045					28	31
Operations Analysis	GS-9	7,696-10,045				1	45	50
Indus. Engr. Technicians	GS-11	9,221-12,056					✓	✓
	GS-9	7,696-10,045		4		1	27	39
	GS-7	6,451 8,360				1	8	15

* Selected to include only those white collar Production Facilitating positions for which Blue-Collar experience frequently is qualifying.

DATE CENSUS TAKEN: APR 24 1967

PRODUCTION FACILI: 'TING

SUPERVISORY SELECTED* WHITE-COLLAR

Type of Work	Grade Level	Current Salary Range	Amer. Indian	Negro	American Oriental	Spanish American	All Other	Total
Production Controllers	GS-14	15,106-19,813						
	GS-13	12,073-16,905						
	GS-12	10,927-14,338					13	14
	GS-11	9,221-12,056					16	16
	GS-9	7,696-10,045						
Quality Cont.Spec	GS-14	15,106-19,813						
	GS-13	12,073-16,905						
	GS-12	10,927-14,338					4	4
Operations Analysis	GS-13	12,873-16,905						
	GS-12	10,927-14,338						
	GS-11	9,221-12,056					0	0

Type of Work	Grade Level	Current Salary Range	Amer. Indian	Negro	American Oriental	Spanish American	All Other	Total
Ind.Engr. Technicians	GS-13	12,873-16,905						
	GS-12	10,927-14,338					4	4
	GS-11	9,221-12,056						

* Selected to include only those white collar Production Facilitating positions for which Blue-Collar experience frequently is qualifying.

DATE CENSUS TAKEN: _____APR 24 1967_____

1029

Exhibit No. 34

U.S. CIVIL SERVICE COMMISSION
SAN FRANCISCO REGION

REPORT OF SPECIAL INQUIRY

U.S. NAVAL AIR STATION

ALAMEDA, CALIFORNIA

DATES OF INSPECTION: March 6 - 17, 21, 1967

Inspector: John A. Tworek

1030

1031

EQUAL EMPLOYMENT OPPORTUNITY FOR MINORITY GROUPS

Introduction, Summary and Recommendations

This inquiry was conducted as part of a review of progress being made
in the East Bay area in contributing to national goals of equal employment for minority groups. Factfinding was accomplished through interviews with various management, supervisory, and Industrial Relations
Department representatives; Personnel Questionnaires distributed to
400 employees of which 334 were completed and returned; a group interview
of 21 employees (the names of these employees as well as of those to
whom Personnel Questionnaires were distributed, were selected at random);
several individual employee interviews; a meeting with officials of
Federal Employees for Equal Opportunity, an employee organization which,
essentially, represents minority group employees; participation in a
weekly meeting of the Captain's Advisory Committee for Equal Employment
Opportunity (COACEEO); interviews with various minority group organization
representatives in the community (see attached list); reviews of personnel
folders, Station issuances, and promotion, training, complaint, appeal,
and grievance records.

Summary

Our review shows that the Commanding Officer of the Naval Air Station
has demonstrated by word, letter, and action that he strongly endorses
the equal employment opportunity program. This is evidenced by his
personal participation in the EEO training program for all supervisors
early in 1966, periodic meetings with minority group organization representatives, personal review of all recommendations for promotion,
monthly meetings in which he, Department Heads, and COACEEO members
get together for the purpose of discussing problems in the EEO area and
the corrective action required; periodic letters to all supervisors on
behalf of the EEO program, etc.

Just how the Commanding Officer's leadership role in EEO matters and publi
relations Station contacts with minority group organizations will
be affected as the result of the change effective April 1, 1967, of
the former Overhaul and Repair Department*(with approximately 86% of
the Station's employees) to a Command status of its own had not been deter
mined at the time of our review. The continuance of a single contact
point for EEO matters and but one Advisory Committee on Equal Employment Opportunity would be highly desirable not only from the standpoint
of avoiding duplication but because of the communications problems
that more than one contact point would create for community and minority
group organizations.

*Now the Naval Air Rework Facility

Although the attitudes and actions in support of the EEO program of
supervisors and management officials other than the Commanding Officer
do not stand out in as sharp a relief as his do, employment figures
showing the percentage of minority group applicants being hired, trained
and promoted, personnel questionnaire responses, etc., evidence a positively oriented program of recruitment, training, and promotion. Minority
group organizations are being advised that jobs are available and that
minority group applicants are actively being sought. Employment opportunities and training are being provided for minority groups and the
disadvantaged through summer jobs, year round part-time employment,
the Apprentice program and the Worker Trainee program - Worker-Trainee
is a specially created position which permits the hiring of applicants
without any requirement of experience or written test.

A number of minority group organization representatives stated that
the Naval Air Station has made substantial progress in recruitment of
minority groups, especially the disadvantaged. Minority group organization representatives were, however, critical of the Station's promotion
program. Although we found that rating, ranking, and selection for
promotion were being accomplished equitably and that the number of minority
group employee promotions is roughly proportionate to the number of
minority group employees on the rolls, the lack of data on their occupational and organizational distribution makes it difficult to measure
progress being made in making promotion opportunities available to such
employees. The wide variations of opinion among Station employees as
well as among minority group organization representatives about how
well the promotion program is working indicates that data on occupational
and organizational distribution are needed so that problem areas, trends
and training needs can be identified and required action can be initiated.
(We understand that the Station is in the process of collecting this
kind of information for the U.S. Commission on Civil Rights representatives who are to begin hearings in Oakland, California on May 1, 1967.) The
lack of any discernible progress in the lot of Negro Classification
Act employees needs further study and action. As indicated in our report,
the average grade of these employees advanced only .3% from June 1963
to June 1966 as compared to .5% for the average employee.

Action needs to be taken to improve service to the job seeking public.
Applicants should be able to get service reasonably promptly and at
any time during the work day. Since Station offices and shops are
spread out over an extensive area in wnich a newcomer can easily get
lost we suggest that a Station map be prepared for visitors unfamiliar
with the Station who are being referred for job interview, medical
examination, etc.

1033

Some staffing problems in the Industrial Relations Department are
indicated. Station, including IRD, staffing ratios were being looked
into by a Navy Manpower Validation Team during our review.

Although the Station has been publicizing the steps it has been taking
on behalf of achieving equal employment opportunity and its efforts have
been given publicity in the community by local newspapers, particularly
by the Alameda Times-Star, there is a need for more emphasis (with
supporting statistical data) on telling employees and the general public
about the Station's accomplishments in developing and promoting minority
group employees. There is considerable evidence that the public,
minority group organization representatives and Station employees form
some of their judgments after hearing employee versions or actions without benefit of all of the facts.

The following list summarizes some of the major affirmative actions to
promote equal employment opportunity which have been taken at the Naval
Air Station since our last review of the program early in 1964:

(1) All managers and supervisors were given training to provide them
with a better understanding of the EEO program and of their obligation
to assist all employees in their self development. The training consisted
of lectures by the Commanding Officer and a Negro member of the Berkeley
City Council. This was followed by a second training session which
consisted of conference sessions of small groups of managers and supervisors with Department Heads or their Deputies acting as conference
leaders. The second session emphasized each participant's responsibility
for good communications, knowledge of each subordinate's job aspirations,
and employee counseling.

(2) The Commanding Officer periodically writes a letter to all supervisors (the last such was dated March 10, 1967) to stimulate their
interest and to emphasize the need for continuing efforts on behalf of
the EEO program.

(3) A multiracial committee (Commanding Officer's Advisory Committee
on Equal Employment Opportunity) has been established to assist the Commanding
Officer in discharging his responsibilities for the EEO program. The Committee has proved to be an effective instrument for the expeditious resolution of informal complaints of discrimination. The Committee meets once
a week to review action that has been taken on individual complaint
cases, to recommend corrective action and make suggestions concerning
the overall program. Once a month the Committee meets with the Commanding

Officer and Department Heads. This meeting not only operates to keep
top management informed of the status of the EEO program but also
serves as a continuing reminder to the Station of management's active
interest in and support of the program.

(4) Beginning in March 1964, all promotions to first level blue-collar
supervisory positions and production facilitating positions such as
Shop Planner, Progressman etc., were suspended for a 15 to 18 month
period and a temporary assignment system was implemented to give as
many employees as possible an opportunity to upgrade their experience
for such positions. The system provided preference in temporary assignment to employees who had never had assignments to the positions involved.

(5) The confidential evaluation form previously used in ranking employees
for promotion has been discontinued and replaced by an evaluation form
which is discussed with the employee concerned.

(6) All recommendations for promotion are personally reviewed by the
Commanding Officer to assure that nominees are the best qualified candidates available and that racial discrimination is not a factor in promotions.

(7) A rotational training program has been established and is in
operation for aircraft mechanics at the intermediate pay level in four
aircraft trades which virtually assures their promotion to journeyman
status upon the successful completion of their training.

(8) The Station has been providing employment opportunities for disadvantaged youth. Current plans call for hiring 400 or more disadvantaged
youths for the coming summer. As the result of its contacts with high
schools, community and minority group organizations, the Station has
motivated more minority youths to compete in the apprentice examination.
As a result there has been a substantial increase in the Station's
minority group apprentice population during the past two years.

(9) Station representatives are exploring with the Economic Development
Administration and the California Department of Employment the possibility of using Station facilities to train as aircraft mechanics
approximately 400 disadvantaged youths, primarily from hard core
unemployment areas.

(10) A representative of the Commission's Regional Office in San Francisco
is working with Station representatives on the development of a career
advancement program which will provide an opportunity for employees
without trade backgrounds to progress to higher paying jobs in production facilitating work.

(11) The Station Supply Department has initiated a career counselling program. Individual interviews are being conducted with all employees. Several hundred had been completed at the time of our review.

Recommendations

Although the Station has made substantial progress toward meeting national equal employment opportunity goals, much remains to be done. We recommend for the attention of Station management action of the following kinds:

1. Continue and intensify indoctrination and exposure of all managers and supervisors to the concepts of the EEO program so that they will better implement national, departmental and Station policy.

2. Obtain and maintain adequate statistical information to help in identifying and analyzing problems of minority group employment.

3. Look for creative ways to improve relationships with minority groups.

4. The problem of equal employment opportunity for the Spanish speaking segment of the community still remains to be solved. The Station needs to survey the size and nature of this problem and work within the Station and in the community to attract, train and promote additional numbers of Spanish speaking persons.

5. Improve the physical appearance of the Employment Office and keep it open to the public during regular working hours.

6. Determine whether the delays in obtaining service from IRD that were reported by operating officials are also reflected in inadequate service to employees and in inadequate attention to minority group problems and if so allot additional resources to provide adequate service.

7. Give employees a periodic report on the racial distribution of employees by occupation and organization and on promotions.

1036

Statistical Data

Although some statistical data on the racial mix of the Station's employees are available it is inadequate as information which would show the progress being made in providing equal employment opportunity. Because of the large percentage (16.6%) of Station employees who chose not to disclose their racial identity in the voluntary census conducted last June, the print out report furnished in October 1966 by the Navy Department's Office of Civilian Manpower Management was considered as of dubious or little value. A recent inquiry to OCMM asked whether they could furnish occupational and organizational distributions in addition to the minority group employee distributions by Classification Act grades and wage-board pay levels which had been provided. OCMM indicated that because of other commitments it would be unable to furnish additional data until about September 1967, and that it was planning to request authority from the Civil Service Commission for the use of some system other than the voluntary census for collecting minority group employee statistics in the future.

Available data show that Station strength in March 1967 was just over 9,000 employees, up about 1,000 from March 1966. Breakdowns by ethnic groups which were obtained through employee surveys in 1963, 1965 and 1966 are included below for comparative purposes.

As of	Total Employ-ees	CATEGORY AND PERCENTAGE				
		Negro	Spanish-American	American Indian	Oriental American	Unidentified
6-30-63	7697	1756(22.8)	426 (5.5)	14 (.001)	402 (5.2)	None
6-30-65	7565	1733(22.9)	246 (3.2)	12 (.001)	428 (5.6)	None
6-30-66	7992	1666(20.8)	286 (3.5)	83 (.01)	389 (4.8)	1334 (16.6)

It is probable that the group of 1,334 unidentified employees shown for 1966 contains a substantial number of minority group employees, in view of the fact that over a third of the more than 2,000 persons hired in calendar year 1966 were minority group members. Short of a head count of all employees, it is not possible to determine how many of the unidentified are minority group members.

The 1965 figures for Spanish-American employees do not cover all Spanish speaking employees because the 1965 survey instructions asked only for employment data about the Mexican and Puerto Rican segments of the Spanish-American population.

1037

Recruitment

Hiring has been accelerated during the last year or two because of increased demands for services and supplies in support of Vietnam operations. The Station expects to add over a 1,000 employees to its rolls in the next 15 months. This includes replacements for approximately 300 military personnel in Fiscal Year 1968. Turnover in calendar year 1966 exceeded 1,000 employees, while as shown below, accessions exceeded the 2,000 mark:

Total Accessions	Negro	%	Span. Amer.	%	Amer. Indian	%	Orien. Amer.	%	Total Minor Group	%
2080	702	33.7	89	4.2	7	.3	26	1.2	824	39.6

At the time of our review, the Station had over 200 vacancies, primarily in wage-board positions in which there is a shortage of qualified applicants. Plans were being made for visiting the Los Angeles area during April in an attempt to recruit some aircraft mechanics out of that area.

Primary use is made of civil service registers for filling entrance and journeyman level positions. In the absence of eligibles on registers or applicants in the Station's applicant file, job orders are placed with the California Department of Employment. Representatives of the Station advise minority group organizations that jobs are available and that minority group applicants are actively being sought. Station representatives have visited a number of minority group organizations in the evening hours to discuss employment opportunities and provide information about jobs.

Use is made of paid newspaper advertising. In addition, Station vacancies are listed in the bulletin "JOBS" distributed by the Navy's Regional Office of Civilian Manpower in San Francisco to some 150 Federal agencies. at various locations throughout the United States. While it is highly desirable to publicize shortage category positions throughout as wide a geographical area as possible, we question the advisability of nation-wide publicity for some of the job opportunities now listed in "JOBS," particularly those for positions at grades GS-2 and 3 (e.g., card punch operator positions), or for temporary part-time appointments. It is noted that use is not being made of the San Francisco Interagency Board "Job Opportunity Bulletin" for publicizing vacancies. Inasmuch as the Bulletin is given widespread publicity in the San Francisco Bay Area and Central California, it would be a much more effective recruiting vehicle for low level as well as for intermediate and journeyman level jobs than one which seeks to draw applicants from great distances.

1038

Action is being taken to provide employment opportunities and training
for minority groups and the disadvantaged. Station representatives participated in the Oakland Job Fair last September, an event designed to
bring employers and minority group applicants together. Station representatives working with the Economic Development Administration and the
California Department of Employment are currently exploring the possibility
of using the Station to provide aircraft maintenance and repair training
to up to 400 persons from hard core unemployment areas.

Of 347 Youth Opportunity Campaign trainees hired in 1966, 269 were
minority group members, predominantly Negro. Along with the trainees
the Station hired two Negro high school teachers to serve as counsellors
for the trainees. The most promising youths, 124 in number, were retained
at the end of the summer and are still working part-time while continuing
their schooling. Among those retained were 59 Negroes, 29 Spanish-
Americans and 5 Oriental Americans.

A group of 15 high school teachers were recently hosted at the Station
incident to plans for hiring about 400 or more disadvantaged youths
during the coming summer.

Another step in the direction of providing jobs and training for the
disadvantaged was the employment last fall of 45 "worker trainees."
The persons appointed were selected as the result of the Worker Trainee
examination in which applicants were ranked on the basis of ability and
potential without any experience or written test requirement. Present
indications are that a substantial number of those appointed will be
promoted to higher level jobs upon the completion of their one year
training period.

Written tests for stenographers and typists are conducted periodically
at local high schools.

During 1966 the apprentice examination was held at the Job Corps Center
at Pleasanton in addition to conducting it at the Alameda High School.
Only a handful of the Job Corps Center trainees, five, acquired eligible
ratings. When their names were eventually reached for selection, the
Station went so far as to locate suitable housing for the trainees, but
all five declined employment in order to return to their home areas
back East. The apprentice examination was also held at McClymonds
High School, a predominantly Negro school in Oakland.

The Station's overall experience with apprentice eligibles appointed
in 1966 was disappointing. A number had to be dropped from the program
because of scholastic deficiencies, primarily inability to do arithmetic or algebra problems. In the 1966 examination, apprentice applicants were able to satisfy the algebra portion of the written test by

1039

presenting evidence of the successful completion of a high school algebra course. Some of the otherwise eligible applicants who had "successfully" passed their algebra courses with grades of "D" and were appointed were subsequently found to be unable to do relatively simple arithmetic problems. A new apprentice examination announcement to be issued by the San Francisco Interagency Board in the very near future will prescribe an algebra test for all competitors. The new examination will utilize a less demanding written test than that prescribed in Test 179, the current apprentice written test, as the latter is considered too tough for the job's requirements.

Of the 289 apprentices hired between February 1965 and February 1967, 78 (26.9%) were minority group members. Negroes filled 44 apprentice jobs (15.2%), a substantially higher number than the 16 which were filled by Negroes during the preceding two year period.

A random sampling of certificates of eligibles issued during the past year to the Station by the former 12th Naval District Board of U.S. Civil Service Examiners and the San Francisco Interagency Board shows no evidence of discrimination in making selections. The certificates reflected a consistently high rate of selections, better than 90%, with only an occasional recourse to the appointing officer's statutory prerogative to nonselect under the "Rule of Three," e.g.:

Certificate Number	Issue Date	Position and Pay Level	Eligibles Available	Selections
SF-1-1369	1-4-66	Apprentice	41	39
SF-1-1383	1-11-66	Aircraft Metal Worker W-8	46	43
SF-1-1400	1-12-66	Helper General W-5	91	84
SF-1-1562	3-16-66	Aircraft Metal Worker W-8	21	18
SF-1-168	6-24-66	Aircraft Metal Worker W-8	9	8
FR 5652	10-6-66	Aircraft Electrical Worker W-8	7	6
FR 5656	10-7-66	Aircraft Metal Worker W-8	8	7
FR 11849	1-27-67	Aircraft Electrician W-11	12	12

It should be emphasized that typically, large numbers of minority group members apply for lower level positions.

1040

Physical Facilities - Service to the Public

The Employment Office and the Employment Processing and Records Branch
Office were displaced last fall by a higher priority tenant from the
space they had occupied at the Station. Both offices are temporarily
housed in two separate buildings at the former Civil Defense Training
Center in Alameda, about two miles from the Station's Main Gate. Space
in the building in which the Employment Office is located is inadequately
heated by portable electric heaters; lighting is sub-standard; the
bulletin board is located in a dimly lighted passageway about three feet
wide; and both the passageway and the bulletin board are in need of
painting. Because of lack of staff the Employment Office is only open
to the public from 8:00 to 12:00 in the mornings, there is only one
telephone and it rings almost constantly. Although applicants are
treated courteously and the quality of the information and counseling
dispensed by the staff of two is good, some individuals have to wait
for service for 30 minutes or longer because of the number of applicants
and the volume of telephone traffic. A prominently located bulletin
board for posting positions for which applications are being accepted,
plus a rack for blank applications, would facilitate service for those
interested only in information about immediate employment and examination prospects. In view of the President's concern about improving
service to the public every effort should be made to obtain sufficient
staff to man the Employment Office at least 8 hours a day, to provide
adequate telephone equipment and service, and to improve the appearance
of the office.

Inasmuch as the Employment Office is not supplied with the Basic Federal
Personnel Manual, Navy Civilian Personnel Instructions or the Station's
Civilian Personnel Manual, clerical personnel must obtain answers to
questions which require recourse to these publications by telephoning
the Employment Office Supervisor located in the adjacent building. As
the Employment Office apparently will remain at its present location
for some time to come, it would be highly advisable to supply it with
the Basic FPM, NCPI and other issuances the staff need to answer inquiries
promptly and properly.

It was noted that applicants were being referred to the Post Office
Board in Oakland for written examination without prior clearance with
the Board, and that in some cases they could not be tested because the
Board had other commitments or did not have test material for the examination involved. Hereafter, advance arrangements will be made so that
applicants will not be inconvenienced.

Promotions and Temporary Assignments to Higher Grade Duties

Employees and employee organizations as well as department heads are
consulted in the development of major revisions of the Station's Merit
Promotion Plan. The plan has been revised on one or more occasions
during the last several years to put into effect employee and employee
organization suggestions relating to temporary assignment to experience-
building positions, other assignments, rotation of Alternate Shop Supervisor, rating schedules, ranking procedures, and so forth. The latest
revision, which is to be issued in the near future, is the result of
the new performance evaluation procedure which became effective in January 1967 for ranking candidates for promotion. Under the new procedure,
supervisors are required to evaluate employee performance annually on
a special form which replaces the "secret" vouchers hitherto used in
ranking candidates. The new procedure requires each supervisor to discuss his evaluation with the employee concerned pointing up the employee's
strengths and deficiencies, or training needs, and exploring with the
employee possible ways for him to improve his performance.

Promotion opportunities are publicized in the Station's weekly newspaper The Carrier, and when advisable (because of the grade, pay level,
dearth of well-qualified candidates on the Station, etc.) throughout
the Naval District or an even broader area. Extensive use is made of
subject matter experts in ranking candidates. Recommendations for selection are made by a Promotion Board consisting of from three to five
employees designated by the selecting official (Commanding Officer,
department head, etc.). No promotion can be effected until it has been
reviewed by the department head with the Commanding Officer. The purpose
of this review is to provide additional assurance that there has been
no discrimination and that the person selected is the best qualified.

A review of promotion records shows that rating, ranking, and selection
for promotion is being accomplished consistent with the Promotion Plan
and pertinent qualification standards and rating schedules. It is
noted, however, that the promotion records do not contain Promotion
Board summary recommendations. Whenever these have been prepared they
should, of course, be retained with the promotion records. It was
also noted that all temporary promotions are not documented, as required
by the promotion plan, to show why it was necessary to place any time
limit on a given promotion action. Apparently some temporary promotions
are being made to provide a "probationary period" or to protect the reten-
tion rights of employees already holding positions in the same competitive
level. This was discussed with the Commanding Officer who asked the
IRO to look into the matter and to take whatever corrective action was
necessary.

The Station's Promotion Plan provides that all candidates may review the approved ranking procedure or rating schedule for the vacant position. We agree that candidates should on request be able to review the applicable rating schedule and ranking procedure, but are concerned that these are being duplicated and distributed as part of the Station's Instructions on Promotions. Rating schedules contain information which is intended primarily for use by rating and ranking officials. While their contents may be discussed with candidates who wish to know why they were rated as they were, rating schedules should to all intents and purposes be treated as is written test material.

Measurement of the progress being made in providing promotion opportunities for minority group employees is hampered by the lack of data on occupational distribution by ethnic groups.

As will be seen from the following tables, the average grade of minority group employees occupying wage-board positions is much closer to the average grade and pay rate of all wage-board employees than is the average grade of minority group Classification Act employees to the average grade of all Classification Act employees. The average pay rate of Negro wage-board employees is slowly creeping upward while the average grade of Negro Classification Act employees increased but .3 of a grade from 1963 to 1966 as compared with .5 for all Classification Act employees. It should, however, be pointed out that it is not actually possible to make precise comparisons between the averages for 1963, 1965 and 1966, because of the large number of employees (1334) who were not identified as to race in the 1966 census.

Average Grade (Classification Act Employees)

As of	All Employees	% of Avg.	Negro	% of Avg.	*Span Amer	% of Avg.	Amer Indian	% of Avg.	Orien Amer	% of Avg.
6-3-63	5.9	100	3.9	66.1	5.2	88.1	6.5	100	7.5	127
6-30-65	6.5	100	4.2	64.6	5.3	81.5	11.0	169	7.1	109
6-30-66	6.4	100	4.2	65.5	6.4	100	6.0	93.7	7.6	118.7

Average Hourly Rate (Wage-Board Employees)

As of	All Employees	% of Avg.	Negro	% of Avg.	*Span Amer	% of Avg.	Amer Indian	% of Avg.	Orien Amer	% of Avg.
6-30-63	$3.26	100	$2.99	91.1	$3.22	98.7	$3.09	91.7	$3.25	99.6
6-30-65	$3.51	100	$3.24	92.3	$3.40	96.8	$3.26	92.8	$3.55	101.1
6-30-66	$3.56	100	$3.30	92.7	$3.53	99.1	$3.51	98.5	$3.57	100.2

*The 1965 figures for Spanish-American employees do not include all Spanish speaking employees because the 1965 survey instructions asked only for employment data about the Mexican and Puerto Rican segments of the Spanish-American population.

The 873 promotion actions taken in calendar year 1966 were distributed by racial groups as follows:

Total	Negro	%	Spanish-American	%	American Indian	%	Oriental American	%	Total Minority Group	%
873	187	21.4	35	4.0	1	.001	46	5.2	269	30.8

Minority group employees received 18 (of whom 13 were Negroes) of the 125 promotions to supervisory positions.

Current data on the number and distribution of minority group supervisors is not available. A head count as of June 30, 1965 showed the following with respect to the total number of Wage-Board supervisors and Negro Wage-Board supervisors:

Rating	Total	Negro
Master	6	0
Foreman	14	0
Chief Quarterman	5	0
Quarterman	65	2
Leadingman	245	10
Head	19	4
Supv. Planner & Estimator	19	0
Supv. Progressman	1	0
Supv. A/C Examiner	7	0

Figures for the period July 1 to December 31, 1965 are not available. During calendar 1966, one Negro was promoted to Head and nine to Leadingman positions. Management's explanation for the relatively small number of minority group employee promotions to supervisory positions is that such employees come within reach for selection on promotion rosters less frequently than Caucasians and that this is due to a combination of factors such as: minority group employees did not have the opportunity in the past they have now of acquiring experience; they do not do as well as Caucasians in written tests and oral interviews because of their educational level; Caucasian competitors for wage-board supervisory positions generally have more years of higher level experience and more years of service, for example, in one department, the last employee selected for promotion as Leadingman had 14 years of service while the ones before him had 15, 19 and more years. The situation which the Station is working hard to correct is generally a legacy from the past when a positive program of anti-discrimination was not pursued aggressively. In our judgment, as the present efforts to improve the skills and work experience of Negroes and other minority group employees bear fruit, the Station will be taking long strides forward toward equal employment opportunity.

1044

Breakthrough (first-time) placements of minority group members during the past two year period occurred in positions such as:

Production Controlman	Numerically Controlled Machine Tool Mechanic
Leadingman Transportation	Instructor
Aircraft Examiner	Supervisory Cost Accountant GS-11
Inspector, Electrical Systems	Computer Aid (Scheduler) GS-9
Inspector, Auto Repair	Supervisory Personnel Staffing Specialist GS-9
Plane Captain	Personnel Staffing and Employee Relations Specialist GS-9
Electrical Engineer GS-12	Employee Relations Specialist GS-9
Counsellor GS-9	Management Technician GS-7
Industrial Engineering Technician GS-11	

Employee responses to the Commission's Personnel Questionnaire indicated that most employees know where to find out about the Station's promotion system. They also show a wide variance of opinion about the operation of the program which ranges from confidence in its integrity to a belief that all promotions are rigged. As the largest employer in the East Bay, the Station presents the most visible target and provides the largest number of employee incidents with which minor group organizations can find fault. As is the case with on-Station opinion, off-Station opinion ranges widely from the view that minority group employees do not get their share of promotions to the view that they get more than their share. In answering the following question in our Personnel Questionnaire, "In general, how are members of racial minority groups treated as far as promotions, training opportunities, etc., are concerned in your agency?" 74 employees (22.1%) indicated they believe minority groups are given more opportunities while 55 (16.4%) believe minority groups are given fewer opportunities; 156 (46.7%) indicated that minority groups are given the same opportunities as others and 49 (14.6%) said "I don't know."

It is noted that from time to time the Station has had to respond to inquiries or allegations that it is not doing enough or is doing too much for minority group employees. A periodic "report" to employees and the community via the Station paper and local publications would do much to set the record straight and dispel some of the beliefs now held.

1045

Criticisms Presented by the Federal Employees for Equal Opportunity
Organization and CSC Findings

One of the most active employee organizations on behalf of minority group
employees is the organization called Federal Employees for Equal Opportunity. The number of employees belonging to FEEO is not known to Station
officials but whatever the number, it was not large enough to qualify for
formal recognition. The organization has had informal recognition since
its request for representation was approved in February 1964. FEEO maintains that it is concerned with equal opportunity for all employees without
regard to race, nationality, etc.

During our representative's meeting with FEEO representatives, the latter
made a number of allegations as follows: (1) that there is only token
implementation of equal employment at Alameda Naval Air Station; (2) that
reprisal action is taken against employees who submit grievances; (3)
that Caucasians are selected for most training assignments; (4) that employees are not advised of their rights to have a representative at
hearings; (5) that employees' statements are distorted and used against
them; (6) that supervisory levels cover up for and support one another
no matter what; (7) that employees in the recently instituted rotational
training program for Aircraft Mechanics are not receiving training in all
aspects of a given job element; (8) that FEEO is not always able to get
requested information from management or the Industrial Relations Department; (9) that management's policy with respect to rehire of former
employees separated for cause is negative; (10) that qualification standards and rating procedures are changed from one promotion examination to
the next to assure the promotion of prepicked candidates, etc.

(1) Our findings with respect to recruiting efforts, percentage of minori
group employees being hired, promoted and trained show that there is a
substantial effort being made at the Station to achieve EEO program objectives (as evidenced in the figures cited earlier relating to promotion
and in-hires). While much remains to be done, what has been done represents, in our view, more than token implementation.

(2) The allegation that reprisal action is taken against employees who
submit complaints is not supported by the facts. A review of actions
taken in the case of the 63 employees who filed formal complaints of
discrimination between 1961 and 1967 shows (see table) that complaints
appear to have little or no effect on selections for promotion, awards, et

	No. actions taken prior to filing complaint	No. actions taken after filing complaint
Promotions	20	17
Awards	5	7
Temporary assignment to higher level duties	9	20
Disciplinary actions	3	-

Information obtained as the result of our personnel questionnaires likewise does not support the allegation that reprisal action is taken against employees who file complaints. Of the 334 employees who answered the question "If you had a complaint, what do you think would be of most help to you in settling it to your satisfaction?", 253 (75%) checked "Talking it over with my supervisor," 40 (11.9%) answered "Talking it over with some one in the Personnel or Administrative Office," 14 (4.1%) answered "Turning in a formal complaint without discussing it with anyone," while only seven or eight (about 2%) indicated that it was useless or hopeless to file a complaint.

(3) As far as could be ascertained, minority group employees received a reasonably proportionate share of the training assignments that are available; minority group Youth Opportunity Campaign trainees outnumber Caucasians; a substantially increasing number of minority group employees are being entered in the apprentice training program; all employees who volunteered for training under the newly instituted rotation training program for Aircraft Mechanic have been rotated into positions with new duties; employees are being selected for detail to supervisory positions on an objective basis (e.g., written test scores), and preference in details is given to employees who have not had previous details, etc.

(4) Our review of the several appeal cases processed during the past year showed that employees are advised of their right to have a representative at hearings.

(5 & 6) The FEEO group did not offer any specific illustrations of distorted use made of employee statements or of supervisor cover up and support of other supervisors.

(7) The rotational program for Aircraft Mechanics was initiated last November. The number of days training in each of several job elements depends on the element involved and can range from 3 to 24 months. Our representative was advised by one FEEO official that he would be furnished the names of employees in the rotation program who are not getting training in all aspects of a given job element. To date such information has not been provided nor any other information furnished which would permit a further review of this charge. The variation in the number of training days devoted to each job element may partly explain the FEEO impression that trainees are treated differently.

(8) With respect to the charge that FEEO is not always able to get information from management or the Industrial Relations Department, management believes that sometimes the explanations it provides are regarded as inadequate solely because they run counter to what is desired. According to management, minority group representatives are sometimes not in possession of all of the facts, or are unable to properly evaluate them because they do not have the expertise or an adequate frame of reference. IRD staffing deficiencies may also be partially responsible for the problem. Some operating officials complained to our representative about delays in getting service from the Industrial Relations

Department. For fear their remarks might be construed as implying ineptitude on the part of the IRD, some of these officials tempered their comments with the observation that IRD had been operating without sufficient staff for some time and that it has had an unusually heavy workload. A member of a Navy Manpower Validation Team which was making a review of the Station's staffing and manpower utilization programs participated in our representative's closing discussion with the Industrial Relations Officer and his staff and was able to get first hand information about some IRD staffing problems mentioned in this report.

FEEO representatives appear to be suspicious and skeptical of management's intentions and willingness to help. One representative stated he was unable to get information about the duties of a Worker-Trainee (since supplied by this office) but had not bothered to ask IRD because based on past experience he believed it was useless to ask that office for information. There is need for IRD to look for communications problem areas and take whatever steps are necessary to correct them.

(9) FEEO officials believe that management's attitude relative to rehiring former employees separated for cause is negative and is not in harmony with policies and procedures now in effect for the consideration for employment of persons with criminal records. FEEO's point is well taken. Applicants with discharge records should be given the treatment described in FPM Letter No. 731-2 that is, such persons should "... receive, on an individual basis mature and sophisticated decisions, taking into consideration the social and humane need for their rehabilitation as well as the requirements of the positions for which they apply."

(10) Aside from a number of changes in qualification standards which were either directed or initiated by the Civil Service Commission, we found only one qualification standards change which the Station had initiated. It involved the position of Maintenanceman in the Public Works Department which is concerned with plumbing and electrical work. The Civil Service Commission's standard for Maintenanceman positions is a general standard designed to cover Maintenanceman jobs in a variety of trade duty combinations, e.g., Painter and Carpenter, Carpenter and Cement Finisher, Plumber and Electrician, etc. It was proper of the Station to limit qualifying experience to plumbing and electrical work rather than utilizing the Commission's general standard as the latter allows applicants to qualify on the basis of experience in any combination of two building trades.

NAS Alameda has been dramatically in the limelight in the past few months. This was highlighted by two public demonstrations organized by Mr. John D. Burrell, a former Station employee. Mr. Burrell had been removed from the position of Airframe Worker (Pay level 8) effective December 15, 1966 on the charge of conduct unbecoming a Government employee. This charge was based on Mr. Burrell's conduct and attitude, e.g., failure to perform assigned work, threatening his supervisors, threatening to blow up the Air Station, etc. Mr. Burrell has appealed his removal through Navy channels. Final action has not yet been taken on his appeal.

On February 9, 1967, the Oakland Tribune (clipping enclosed) stated
that James C. Dixon, Chairman, Labor-Industry Committee, NAACP, Oakland,
California, "... was withholding endorsement of the proposed march
pending negotiations with base officials being conducted by an ad hoc
committee of several organizations." The February 16, 1967, edition of
the Alameda Times-Star (clipping enclosed) stated "In a pre-march press
conference ... James C. Dixon ... all expressed support to Burrell's
move." The article did not state when the pre-march press conference
took place. Station representatives have advised us that the February
15, 1967, article is in error, as NAACP did not participate in
Mr. Burrell's demonstrations or actually support his cause.

The second demonstration, reportedly with about 30 adult participants
was not given any newspaper publicity.

Mr. Burrell's reported support (Alameda Times-Star, February 16, 1967)
by the Secretary of the American GI Forum apparently represents the
latter's personal support rather than that of Forum members. In this
connection, see the attached copy of a letter addressed to the Commanding
Officer of the Alameda Naval Air Station on February 24, 1967, by the
Fremont Chapter of the American GI Forum. This letter repudiates any
actions taken on behalf of Fremont Chapter employee-members. Allegedly,
the Fremont Chapter represents most of the Mexican-American employees at
the Station.

1049

<u>IMPROVING COMMUNICATIONS WITH THE PUBLIC</u>

A military Public Affairs Officer and his staff maintain liaison with the local community on Station activities. Local newspapers have been very cooperative in publicizing the Station's recruiting needs and the efforts being made to promote equal employment opportunity. The Alameda Times-Star, San Leandro Morning News and Fremont-Newark News Register devoted 12 pages of their Alameda County Weekender newspaper insert on April 8, 1967, to news articles and photographs dealing with Station employment which emphasized the Station's equal employment opportunity program.

A copy of the outgoing correspondence originating in the Naval Air Rework Facility at the Station goes to the Commanding Officer of the Facility as one means of assuring that responses not only conform with policy but are clear and understandable.

A representative of the Industrial Relations Department participated in the training course on Improving Communications with the Public and the Communications Workshop both of which were conducted by the Commission's Regional Office early in 1966.

Other efforts designed to improve communications included the following training courses given in calendar 1966:

Title	No. Participants
Supervisory Development Communication	42
Written Communications	69
Telephone Courtesy	24

1050

STANDARDS OF ETHICS AND CONDUCT

The Station Instruction on Standards of Conduct was revised in December 1966 to incorporate the latest Department of Defense Directive on this subject. In accordance with the Department's Directive, the Station identified employees whose duties and responsibilities are such as to require the filing of a "Confidential Statement of Employment and Financial Interests" and obtained such statements from them.

The Training Division's indoctrination course for new employees includes coverage of the standards of conduct. Department Heads are responsible for bringing the standards to employee attention semi-annually. This is generally accomplished through staff meetings. A semi-annual reminder to employees is also included in the Station newspaper.

A notice on the Code of Ethics for Government Service is kept posted on Station bulletin boards at all times.

1051

AMERICAN GI FORUM OF THE U.S.
NATIONAL VETERANS FAMILY ORGANIZATION

Attachment 1

FREMONT CHAPTER

Post Office Box 11
Fremont, California

February 24, 1967

Captain D. A. Campbell
Commanding Officer
U. S. Naval Air Station
Alameda, California

Dear Sir:

The American G.I. Forum is a veterans family organization
dedicated to the improvement of the Social, Economic and
Political conditions of the Mexican-American community
through education. As such the Fremont Chapter of the G.I.
Forum deplores and repudiates any actions taken, present or
past, by irresponsible persons on behalf of the Fremont Chapter.

The majority of membership in this chapter is employed at this
installation and have not now or ever sought representation
by leaders in unjust demonstrations.

Please rest assured that whenever conditions warrant action,
the American G.I. Forum, Fremont Chapter, will act on behalf
of its membership in its own name. We stand on our merit and
our own ideals.

To further clarify our position on this matter we are asking
that we be granted an opportunity to meet with you or your
representative at your earliest convenience.

I shall appreciate a prompt reply from you in regard to the
above request.

Respectfully,

Demetrio Reyes
Chairman

"EDUCATION IS OUR FREEDOM AND FREEDOM SHOULD BE EVERYBODY'S BUSINESS"

MINORITY GROUP ORGANIZATIONS CONTACTED DURING SURVEY

American GI Forum, Oakland

Mexican American Political Association, Oakland

Spanish Speaking Information Center, Oakland

Spanish Speaking Neighborhood Organization Project, Oakland

United Council of Spanish Speaking Organizations, Richmond

Richmond Neighborhood House, Richmond

Urban League, Oakland

National Association for the Advancement of Colored People,
   Alameda

National Association for the Advancement of Colored People,
   Oakland

Federal Employees for Equal Employment, NAS Alameda

Oakland American Indian Association, Oakland

Intertribal Friendship House, Oakland

United Bay Area Council of Indian Affairs, Oakland

Chinese Citizens Alliance, Oakland

Japanese Americans Citizens League, Berkeley

1053

Attachment 3

Berkeley Gazette, Jan. 13, 1967

PROTEST IS DELAYED

A demonstration protesting alleged discrimination at the Alameda Naval Air Base has been postponed from today until Feb. 15, to allow time for more negotiations, one of its organizers said.

Rev. John D. Burrell of Oakland said the demonstration was called to protest "discrimination in the upgrading of Negroes" employed at the base.

He said most Negroes are "denied promotion" with very few established in the highest paying jobs on the base. He also charged the "janitorial shop is 100 per cent Negro, and they are being asked to work Saturdays and Sundays with no overtime."

Rev. Burrell said he and another Negro employe of the base were "fired" for "talking about the race problem." He is now fulltime pastor of a church in Oakland.

He said a chapter of the NAACP is engaged in talks with the base officials, with the demonstration called off until Feb. 15.

Oakland Tribune, Feb. 9, 1967

Protest

CIVIL RIGHTS PARADE SET FOR FEB. 15

Several civil rights organizations yesterday announced plans for a Feb. 15 parade to protest what spokesmen called "discriminatory racial practice" at Alameda Naval Air Station.

The Rev. John Burrell, chairman of the Citizens Committee for Equal Opportunity, said the groups were protesting practices in promotions, not hiring.

Rev. Burrell sat beside King L. H. Narcisse, founder of the Mount Zion Spiritual Temple, at a press conference in the temple dining hall.

Others at King Narcisse's table on a red-carpeted platform were civil rights activist Mark Comfort; Cesar Mendez, state secretary of the American GI Forum, a Mexican-American group and James Dixon, chairman of the Oakland NAACP Industrial Labor Committee.

Dixon said the NAACP was withholding endorsement of the proposed march pending negotiations with base officials being conducted by an ad hoc committee of several organizations.

The Navy has continually denied charges of discrimination.

The protest leaders said the march would proceed three miles from the naval station main gate.

San Francisco Chronicle, Feb. 16, 1967

DEMONSTRATION AT AIR BASE

About 35 demonstrators marched to the gates of the Alameda Naval Air Station yesterday to protest alleged discrimination in the assignment and promotion of Negro civilian workers.

They demonstrated without incident, and said they would ask for a Government investigation in the name of the Citizens for Equal Opportunity. Previous inquiries have rebuffed the charges.

1054

Attachment 4

Alameda Times Star, Thursday, February 9, 1967

DEMONSTRATION MARCH PLANNED
NEAR AIR STATION WEDNESDAY

If there is no critical change in the plans of several combined "inter-racial" agencies before February 15, Alameda will have one of the largest "demonstration marches" in its hostory.

John Burrell, founder of the Naval Air Station Federal Employees for Equal Opportunity organization, and a former worker at the Station, has requested a permit from the City to hold a parade next Wednesday, with a 3:00 p.m. start at the Station's main gate.

The reason for the parade is contained in a brochure distributed yesterday by the "Mexican-American" element that has joined forces with Burrell, along with others.

It reads: "Alameda Naval Air Station has, in 26 history packed years, grown from a small Tidewater facility to one of the largest and most complete Naval Air Stations in the world; except for one thing—its employment practices. Its employment practices have made little history toward the equal opportunities of minority groups among its 8000 civilian employees. We don't say that Mexican-Americans, Negroes, American-Indians, Orientals, etc., have been refused (as a rule) employment. When we do say, however, is that we are tired of running into that well known dead end street."

The brochure continues with a statement that the "racial groups" form the lower part of the economic ladder, and that although they rank high on experience, they are denied opportunity to join the top ranks.

The parade will run from the Main Gate of the station, as far as Webster Street, and back again.

In a pre-march meeting held yesterday at the Mount Zion Spiritual Temple, 1480 14th Street, Oakland, Burrell explained his plans—and introduced leaders of organizations that have pledged support.

In the hall of King L. H. Narcisse, spiritual leader of many Negroes in the West Oakland section, he announced: This is a problem of twenty years at the Naval Air Station—we have finally gotten together to do something.

He was backed by King Narcisse who followed with: "I don't think the structure of Black Power is hate—it is that the black people want to be recognized." He then asked that the demonstration be peaceful and invoked a "prayer for peace."

James C. Dixon, Chairman of the labor group of the NAACP for the Oakland area also pledged support. "The only way NAACP and Mexican-Americans can participate, is to look at the entire job picture at NAS. Why can't people get the jobs at upper levels."

Dixon was followed by Cesar Mendez, the powerful State Secretary of the nationwide 40,000 member G. I. Forum, and by Mark Comfort, President of Oakland's Direct Action Committee.

A spokesman for the Mexican-American element said: "We are in conjunction with the Negro community, and are concerned as much as the Negroes. Negotiations have not proceeded as desired and we have tried for changes in procedure at the Station, but it has been in vain."

Burrell said that he anticipated "one thousand marchers," and added that the protest would not end with the parade.

He said that a token force of "a few" would maintain vigil at the Station main gate from dawn to dusk: "Until the negotiations within the gates are completed."

1055

Attachment 5

[Alameda Times Star, February 10, 1967]

NAVAL AIR STATION ANSWERS
CHARGE OF 'DISCRIMINATION'

Captain D. A. Campbell, Commanding Officer, NAS Alameda, met for lunch Wednesday with Donald P. McCullum, President, Oakland Branch NAACP, and James Dixon, Chairman, Labor-Industry Committee, Oakland branch, NAACP and discussed equal employment opportunity.

At the meeting Capt. Campbell gave McCullum a letter outlining Equal Employment Opportunity at NAS Alameda which is quoted in part.

"I am interested in the concern that your organization and the others represented have displayed regarding the Equal Employment Opportunity Program at the Naval Air Station, Alameda. It is my belief that our fundamental goals are mutual and that any exchange concerning more effective methods of achieving a greater degree of affirmative action regarding the program would be most useful."

In an enclosure to the letter a resume of affirmative action steps taken by NAS Alameda was outlined in question and answer form.

"What is the overall employment picture?

—Minority group employees comprise approximately 26 per cent of the total work force; of these, approximately 22 per cent are Negroes.

"What has been done to improve the effectiveness of the Station's Promotion Program?

—Elimination of confidential evaluation system used in promotion program and replacement with an evaluation completed periodically by the supervisor and discussed with the employee.

—Personal review of all promotion recommendations by the Commanding Officer.

—Participation (by members of the Commanding Officers Advisory Committee on Equal Employment) as observers in Promotion Board procedures.

—Study of written tests to eliminate any questions reflecting "cultural bias."

"What are the fundamental principles of the Equal Employment Opportunity Program at Naval Air Station Alameda?

—Insuring that the application . . . of the principles of good personal management and administration is in no way based on race, color, creed, or national origin.

—Making special efforts, within the confines of legal, effective, and feasible personnel management practices, to compensate for opportunities denied individuals because of discriminatory practices in society.

—To achieve relations with the surrounding community that will develop more effective achievement of program goals.

To what extent does the Station participate in the Youth Opportunity Campaign?

—Summer hiring in 1966 totaled 269.

—Approximately 59 per cent of these were Negroes, 15 per cent were Mexicans, 3 per cent Orientals, and 23 per cent Caucasians.

What are some future plans concerning the EEO program?

—A survey of employees in lower level positions for the purpose of identifying feasable efforts to provide career development programs.

—Schedule of visits to the station by individuals in the community who are invited in efforts related to the EEO Program.

—Exploring with representatives of the Economic Development Administration and the California Department of Employment the possibilities of using the Station to provide aircraft maintenance and repair training to up to 400 persons from hard core unemployment areas."

Officials at NAS Alameda have expressed deep concern over claims of discrimination and are ready to meet at the conference table at any time. The Commanding Officer Advisory Committee on Equal Employment Opportunity processes complaints of discrimination from all people.

1056

Attachment 6

[Alameda Times Star, Thursday, February 16, 1967]

NAS — ALAMEDA APPARENTLY VINDICATED BY MARCH
ONE THOUSAND MARCH FAILS TO MATERIALIZE

The "demonstration march" of 3:00 p.m. yesterday afternoon, set to highlight alleged discrimination in hiring and promotional procedures at the Naval Air Station, Alameda, and scheduled to proceed from the East Gate of the Station to Webster Street along Atlantic Avenue, was held—and went "Pfizzz."

John Burrell, founder and head of the "Federal Employe for Equal Opportunity" organization, had secured a City permit to hold the parade, and had mustered the strength of several "minority" groups to back what he called the answer "to the problem of twenty years at the Naval Air Station."

In a pre-march press conference, King L. H. Narcisse, a spiritual leader of many Negroes in the West Oakland section, James C. Dixon, Chairman of the labor group of the NAACP for the Oakland area, Caesar Mendez, State Secretary of the nationwide 40,000 member G. I. Forum, and Mark Comfort, President of the Oakland Direct Action Committee, all expressed support to Burrell's move.

The number of demonstrators expected at the march was set at 1,000 plus, with a future vigil to be maintained at the East Gate every morning and every afternoon until "negotiations within the gates are completed."

Command at the Station answered with statistics: Minority group employees comprise approximately 26 per cent of the total work force; of these, approximately 22 per cent are Negroes."

The Station added that during the Youth Opportunity Campaign of 1966, 269 youngsters were hired: 59 per cent Negro; 15 per cent Mexican; three per cent Oriental, and 23 per cent Caucasian.

The stage was set for the demonstration.

At 3:00 p.m., kickoff time, there were thirty demonstrators—less than the standby police force, newsmen, and cameramen present.

At 3:30 p.m., there were about three dozen demonstrators, and the change of shift was just in evidence at the gate of the Station.

Hundreds of workers, both negro and white, walked and drove past the demonstrators, both going to work, and coming from work. They ignored the gathering.

The march finally began at about 4:00 p.m. A head count by both newsmen and police put the tally at "forty-two."

Statement From Navy

The demonstration against the Naval Air Station organized by John D. Burrell apparently was a dismal failure indicating the NAS Alameda equal employment opportunity is a good one.

Mr. Burrell, who was removed from the Air Station for not meeting basic standards of employee conduct obtained almost no support for himself or his associates.

The Citizens Committee for Equal Opportunity is a title chosen by Burrell and does not represent any organized group or recognized activity.

Captain Duncan A. Campbell, Commanding Officer of the Naval Air Station, stated yesterday that the small turnout for the "protest march" led by Burrell indicates that employees of the Air Station, as well as citizens in the community, strongly support his quiet efforts in furthering a vigorous affirmative action equal employment program at NAS Alameda.

Captain Campbell, who considers the demonstration unjustified, is planning to get on with constructive efforts to continue the achievements for an equal employment program that is one of the most successful anywhere. He is confident that he has support from station employees and from the community.

Press Release - February 14, 1967

AD HOC COMMITTEE FOR CITIZENS FOR EQUAL OPPORTUNITIES

WHY WE DEMONSTRATE

The Alameda Naval Air Station, in its past history, has made giant strides in it growth as a facility for overhaul and repair of aircraft and other components.

But in contrast, the promotion and hiring practices leave a lot to be desired.

The merit promotional system, as it stands today, and the way it is implemented is a disgrace to our citizens and our country -- a country that was founded on freedom, equality and justice for all.

The minorities, especially the Mexican-American, Negro and the Whites in the lower part of the economic ladder have been discriminated against time and again because of the apathy of the Industrial Relations Department towards the employee

Their promotion policy is so full of loop holes and deviations, that management has the prerogative of making or breaking any employee it so desires.

The tools used along with these guidelines are as follows:

(1) The ranking procedures; they are so broad and complex, that a grade or score between two employees with the same amount of experience can vary as much as 20 points. (That makes the difference between being kept in contention, locked-out or not making the zone of selection).

(2) Along with the ranking schedules, a supervisory evaluation form is used. This evaluation form, up to last month, was a secret document. There has been a minor change in that the employee will now read and sign this document, but it will still have the same effect. This document can be used in selection as well as ranking.

(3) Along with the above, there is also grooming and pre-selection. This is done very effectively by special assignment, loan, detail or temporary appointment.

The truth of the matter is, that if a well-liked employee or member of the "clan" takes a test for promotion and passes the point of cut off, which often is drawn in pencil, along with the ranking procedure, the voucher and the other mechanics used, there is very little doubt as to who is going to get that promotion when it comes to selection.

Their greivance procedures are virtually non-existant, therefore, the minorities must put up with these sub-standard conditions; for, if they come forth and expos the truth, they subject themselves to reprisal and intimidation.

We work the pits, the cleaning shops and the dirty menial jobs while we go to school nights to attain higher levels of education -- some of us have even attained college degrees. Yet, at NAS we still remain "status quo" maintaining our loyalty to our jobs in defense of our Country.

Nevertheless, the crude fact still remains -- that as long as the deck is stacked against us, there is no other avenue. Therefore, the 15th of February is "D" day for all minorities. We will march on NAS and peacefully demonstrate to let the public know the conditions under which we have suffered for years.

We will endeavor to meet with Capt. D. A. Campbell and again attempt to come to a just and fair solution concerning hiring practices, promotion policies and grievance procedures, otherwise, we are prepared to be in Washington by the 15th of March.

We do not want the standards lowered or changed. This is not the reason why the above mentioned minorities don't get upgraded. There are enough qualified people in these catagories who are well qualified and in the zone of selection, but

1058

Exhibit No. 36*

INDIVIDUAL COMPLAINT

*This complaint was submitted to the Commission and has been handled through the Commission's regular complaint procedures. It is available for inspection at the Commission's office, Washington, D.C.

1059

Exhibit No. 37

UNITED STATES OF AMERICA
BEFORE THE NATIONAL LABOR RELATIONS BOARD
FOURTEENTH REGION

INTERNATIONAL BROTHERHOOD OF ELECTRICAL
WORKERS, LOCAL 1, AFL-CIO
(E. Smith Plumbing Company)

PIPEFITTERS LOCAL 562, UNITED ASSOCIATION
OF JOURNEYMEN AND APPRENTICES OF THE
PLUMBING AND PIPEFITTING INDUSTRY OF THE
UNITED STATES AND CANADA, AFL-CIO

LOCAL 36, SHEET METAL WORKERS' INTERNATIONAL
ASSOCIATION, AFL-CIO

BUILDING AND CONSTRUCTION TRADES COUNCIL
OF ST. LOUIS, AFL-CIO

LOCAL 42, LABORERS' INTERNATIONAL UNION
OF NORTH AMERICA, AFL-CIO   Cases Nos. 14-CC-348
                                                        14-CC-349
          and   14-CC-350
                                                        14-CC-352
ROBERT F. HOEL, an Individual   14-CC-358

          and   Case No.   14-CC-357

NATIONAL ASSOCIATION FOR THE ADVANCEMENT
OF COLORED PEOPLE

BUILDING AND CONSTRUCTION TRADES COUNCIL
OF ST. LOUIS, AFL-CIO
(E. Smith Plumbing Company)

          and   Case No.: 14-CC-359

CONGRESS OF INDEPENDENT UNIONS, LOCAL
NO. 99

BRIEF TO THE TRIAL EXAMINER

Background

The complaint alleges that the Respondents violated Section

8(b)(4)(i)(ii)(B) of the Act.

This case arises out of the concerted efforts of the Council,

Respondent Unions who were Council members, and their agents to force

the National Park Service, an agency of the United States Government, and

Hoel-Steffen Construction Company, a general contractor, to cease doing

business with E. Smith Plumbing Company. All of the Respondents are

affiliated with the AFL-CIO, but Smith's employees are not but instead work wit   emp oyees o...

Arch, which policy was given wide publicity. The result was that the
employees of various contractors and subcontractors, who hire members
the Respondent Unions, refused to perform any services at the Arch project where Smith's employees were working on a subcontract let by Hoel-
Steffen.

Jurisdiction

The General Counsel relies upon the Board's rules for secondary
boycott cases, which permits consideration for jurisdictional purposes
not only of the primary employer's operations, i.e., Smith's, but "also
the operation of any secondary employers to the extent that they are
affected by the conduct above." 1/ Here, it is plain that the Board's
standards are met. St. Louis Sheet Metal Company, a subcontractor, alone
brought over $50,000 in duct work to the project in Missouri directly
from Ohio. In addition, it has purchased a compressor for $52,000
from a supplier in Minnesota, which compressor will be shipped directly
to the Arch jobsite in M.ssouri.

Facts

Around the middle of November 1965 a meeting was held by
Superintendent of Parks Leroy Brown to discuss why the government hadn't
let the contract for the Interim Visitors' Center for the Arch jobsite.
(TR 40) Attending this meeting, among others, were W. W. Zenfell, the
Supervisory Park Engineer of the National Park Service; Robert Hoel,
president of Hoel-Steffen; and Joseph Cousin, executive secretary-
treasurer of the Building and Construction Trades Counci. (TR 41) At
this meeting it was suggested that the plumbing work be subcontracted to
an employer who hired CIU members. Mr. Cousin was asked if the AFL-CIO
employees represented by unions that were members of the Council would
work with the CIU employees. Mr. Cousin's reply was that the AFL-CIO

1/ International Brotherhood of Teamsters, etc. (McAllister Transfer,
Inc.), 110 NLRB 1769; Local 25, International Brotherhood of
Electrical Workers (A. C. Electric), 148 NLRB 1560.

employees definitely would not work with the CIU employees. (TR 41-46
and 169) On December 21, 1965, Mr. Zenfell went to see Mr. Cousin. On
this occasion Mr. Cousin asked Mr. Zenfell to talk to Superintendent of
Parks Brown, who is also the contracting officer for the Parks Service
on the Arch project, to persuade Brown to remove E. Smith Plumbing from
the Arch job. At this time Cousin reminded Zenfell that he had said
earlier that the AFL-CIO building trades would not work with the CIU
employees. (TR 171-172) The Council held a meeting on December 21,
1965. All of the Respondents were present. After a discussion of the
Arch project, Respondents' representatives agreed unanimously that the
policy of the affiliated local unions was that they would not work on
a job that wasn't manned one hundred percent by AFL-CIO employees.
(General Counsel's Exhibits 3 and 7) Again, on January 14, the Council's
members voted unanimously to stand on their action taken on December 21
regarding the Arch. (General Counsel's Exhibit 5)

In the meantime a number of things had been happening. During
the day of December 21, Joseph Cousin had asked Mr. Zenfell to talk to
Brown about removing Smith from the Arch job, as stated above. The
policy adopted by the Council on December 21 had been reduced to writing
on December 27, 1965 (General Counsel's Exhibit 3), and a copy was sent
to Hoel-Steffen and to the National Park Service. (TR 136) Arthur Hunn,
president of the Council, had given wide publicity to the Council's
statement of policy through newspaper interviews, appearances on television, and statements on the radio. (TR 136-137 and 217) Members of
the various respondent unions who had been asked to work on the Arch
project had refused because of the presence of Smith's CIU employees.
(TR 194-198) Hoel-Steffen had ordered the subcontractors to man the
job. The St. Louis Sheet Metal Company sent its employees, who were
members of Respondent Local 36, to the job; Lorraine Engineering sent
its employees, who were members of Respondent Local 562, to the job;

CIU employees were working. (TR 194-198) The business representative of Respondent Laborers Local 42 had gone to the jobsite and instructed Willie West, an employee of Hoel-Steffen, to not perform any services and leave the jobsite. (TR 178-182) Moreover, Respondent Local 36 had mailed instructions to its members who were scheduled to work at the jobsite informing them that it was the Union's policy not to work with CIU employees on the Arch job. (TR 150-152; General Counsel's Exhibit 11)

As a result of the refusal of the electricians to work, the lights in the underground Visitor's Center were not turned on and so the carpenters did not work and were sent home by Hoel-Steffen, and the whole job was shut down and remained shut down until after February 7, 1966, when the Federal District Court enjoined the Respondents from continuing their activities (TR 201), at which time the Respondents informed their members that they were revoking the policy they had announced in the December 27 statement. (See General Counsel's Exhibit 10.)

In brief summary, the employees of the various subcontractors had been informed by the Respondents, either by TV, radio, letters, or personal contact, that it was their union's policy that they as members of AFL-CIO unions should not work on the Arch jobsite where Smith's CIU employees were working, and it is clear that this inducement had its intended effect.

Analysis

The Illegal Object

That the object of the Respondents was to cause the Park Service, an agency of the U.S. Government, and Hoel-Steffen to cease doing business with E. Smith Plumbing Company is clear. Early in November, Mr. Cousin of the Council had warned Hoel-Steffen and the Park Service that the AFL-CIO crafts wouldn't work with members of the CIU. This warning was adopted and reiterated and a statement of policy adopted by representatives of Respondent Unions acting in concert through their Trade

1063

would have E. Smith Plumbing Company removed from the Arch job.

Respondents Violated Section 8(b)(4)(ii)(B)
of the Act by Threatening, Coercing, and
Restraining Hoel-Steffen and the Park Service

In November 1965, Mr. Cousin, at a meeting where representatives of Hoel-Steffen and the Park Service were present, threatened that the building trades unions would not work on the Arch jobsite if there were CIU members working there. This threat was ratified by respondent members of the Council by their unanimous action on December 21, 1965, which action was communicated to both Hoel-Steffen and the National Park Service by sending each of them a copy of the statement of policy (General Counsel' Exhibit 3). Further restraint and coercion are to be found in the actions of the Laborers' business agent who ordered Hoel-Steffen employee Willie West to quit work and leave the job and in the refusal of all of the subcontractors' employees to work at the jobsite.

It is undenied that Respondent Unions furnished employees to the various employers upon request (TR 205, 213, 220 and 221) and it is further undenied that the job could not be completed on schedule withou the services of AFL-CIO craftsmen. (TR 75) The actions of the Respondent Unions in causing their members to withhold their services from the Arch jobsite because E. Smith Plumbing Company was on the job violates 8(b)(4) (ii)(B) of the Act. See Local 5, United Association of Journeymen, etc. (Arthur Venneri Company), 137 NLRB 828; Columbus Bldg. & Construction Trades Council (The Kroger Co.), 149 NLRB 1224.

Respondents Violated Section 8(b)(4)(i)(B)
by Inducing Employees to Refuse to Perform
Services at the Arch Jobsite

After the Respondent's firmed up their decision not to work at the Arch jobsite with Smith's CIU employees on December 21, both Joseph Cousin, president of the Trades Council, and Arthur Hunn, its executive secretary, gave wide publicity to the decision by their statements to the press, appearances on television, and statements on the radio. The only acceptable explanation for this publicity is that

the job. However, some of the Respondents feared that even this publicity
might not reach all of their members and so the Sheet Metal Workers sent
a letter to its members who were scheduled to work at the Arch, instructing
them further on the policy and John Shehane, business representative of
Respondent Laborers Union, actually went out to the jobsite and instructed
Willie West that he must leave if E. Smith employees came on the job.

Conclusion

In conclusion, Counsel for the General Counsel contends that
the evidence is clear that the Respondents, acting in concert, induced
and encouraged employees of the contractors and various subcontractors to
refuse to work at the Arch jobsite and threatened, coerced and restrained
an agency of the Federal Government and Hoel-Steffen Construction Company
where in each case an object was to force the Government and Hoel-Steffen
to cease doing business with E. Smith Plumbing Company in violation of
Section 8(b)(4)(i)(ii)(B) of the Act and that, therefore, an order should
be issued requiring the Respondents to cease engaging in, inducing or
encouraging any individual employed by Hoel-Steffen Construction Company
or any other person engaged in commerce, or in an industry affecting
commerce, to engage in a strike or a refusal in the course of his employment to use, manufacture, process, transport, or otherwise handle or
work on any goods, articles, materials, or commodities, or perform
any services, or threatening, coercing, or restraining an agency of the
U.S. Government, Hoel-Steffen Construction Company, or any other person
engaged in commerce or in an industry affecting commerce, where in
either case an object thereof is to force or require an agency of the
U.S. Government or Hoel-Steffen Construction Company, or any other person,
to cease doing busines with E. Smith Plumbing Company, or any other
employer or persons because such employer or person does not hire

ployees who are members of an AFL-CIO Union. 2/

Dated at Saint Louis, Missouri, this 14th day of June, 1966.

/s/ John S. Stevens
_____
John S. Stevens
Counsel for General Counsel
Fourteenth Region
National Labor Relations Board
Suite 1040, Boatmen's Bank Building
314 North Broadway
Saint Louis, Missouri 63102

_____
/ The broad order is necessary because of the demonstrated proclivity
of the AFL-CIO unions involved to engage in secondary boycott activities to force employers or persons to cease doing business with
persons whose employees do not belong to an AFL-CIO affiliated union.
For example, consider cases 14-CC-371, 14-CC-375, 14-CC-380 and
14-CC-381 involving Zeni-McKinney Williams Corporation, which cases
were heard by this same Trial Examiner on May 16-18, 1966, and
which cases involve a similar attempt of AFL-CIO unions to force an
employer to cease doing business with a non-AFL-CIO employer, in
which situation Local 562 of the Pipefitters and Local 1, IBEW are
also involved. See Local 202, Teamsters (United States Trucking
Corporation), 146 NLRB 956, which authorizes such broad order in
the circumstances of this case.

CERTIFICATE OF SERVICE

I hereby certify that I have this day caused to be served

by certified mail, return receipt requested, a copy of the attached

Brief to the Trial Examiner upon the following parties:

William Bartley, Esquire
Bartley, Siegel & Bartley
130 South Bemiston   (Cert. 459883)
Clayton, Missouri 63105

Robert F. Hoel
d/b/a Hoel-Steffen Construction Co.
4547 Green Park   (Cert. 459884)
St. Louis, Missouri 63123

E. Smith Plumbing Co.
5225 Maple   (Cert. 459885)
Saint Louis, Missouri 63113

Schuchat, Cook & Werner
Attorneys at Law
705 Olive Street   (Cert. 459886)
Saint Louis, Missouri 63101

Harry Craig, Esquire
Wiley. Craig, Armbruster & Wilburn
7 North 7th Street   (Cert. 459887)
Saint Louis, Missouri 63102

Harold Gruenberg, Esquire
Gruenberg, Schobel and Souders
905 Chemical Building
721 Olive Street   (Cert. 459888)
Saint Louis, Missouri 63102

N.A.A.C.P
Attn: Mrs. Ina Boon, Adminir. Sec.
3529 Franklin Avenue (Cert. 459889)
Saint Louis, Missouri 63106

C.I.U., Local 99
Attn: Clark Libhart, Bus. Repr.
6505 Delmar Boulevard (Cert. 459890)
Saint Louis, Missouri 63130

Regular Mail

Building & Const. Trades Council
  of St. Louis, AFL-CIO
275 Union Boulevard
Saint Louis, Missouri

Int'l. Bro. of Electrical Workers,
  Local 1, AFL-CIO
5850 Elizabeth Avenue
Saint Louis, Missouri 63110

Pipefitters, Local 562, AFL-CIO
1242 Pierce
Saint Louis, Missouri

Local 36, Sheet Metal Workers Int'l.
  Association, AFL-CIO
310 S. Ewing
Saint Louis, Missouri 63103

Sachs Electric Company
P. O. Box 96
5540 West Park Avenue
Saint Louis, Missouri 63166

St. Louis Sheet Metal Company
2731 Hamilton Avenue
Saint Louis, Missouri 63112

Loraine Engineering Company
716 Walsh Street
Saint Louis, Missouri 63111

Midwest Contractors Association
1512 Pendleton
Saint Louis, Missouri 63113

Local 42, Laborers' International
Union of North America, AFL-CIO
3700 Enright Avenue
Saint Louis, Missouri 63108

Dated at Saint Louis, Missouri this 14th day of June, 1966.

/s/ Joseph H. Solien
_____
Joseph H. Solien, Regional Attorney
Fourteenth Region
National Labor Relations Board
1040 Boatmen's Bank Building
314 North Broadway

1067

Exhibit No. 38

POTRERO BOOSTERS AND MERCHANTS ASSOCIATION

MEETS LAST MONDAY OF EVERY MONTH
AT
POTRERO BRANCH LIBRARY
SAN FRANCISCO

PRESIDENT

February 26th, 1965

ADDRESS REPLY TO

Mrs.Victor Fleming

838 Kansas St.
San Francisco,
Calif. 94107

San Francisco Planning Commission,
100 Larkin St.,
San Francisco, Calif. 94102

RE: DISPOSITION OF SURPLUS SCHOOL PROPERTY ON POTRERO HILL.

Gentlemen:

Despite claims of proponents of "moderate-priced" housing under FHA
221 (d)(3) to the contrary, such housing is government controlled, and
not private housing. FHA Bulletin #221, revised August 1963, states
"All housing financed under the program must operate in accordance with
regulations as to rentals, charges, methods of operation and occupancy
requirements set forth by the FHA Commissioner." The Bulletin further
states that preference shall be given to displaced families. A phone
call to the FHA confirmed that under the latter, the FHA can and will,
if necessary, provide tenants for such housing. Furthermore, the new
Housing Program, as outlined by Mayor Shelley, calls for rent subsidies
to help low income families obtain better housing. When such a plan is
effected, low-income families will be moved into "moderate-priced" housing. Hence, such housing will become government controlled low-income
public housing.

As to the effect on the Potrero Hill neighborhood of additional social-
ized housing, whether "moderate-income" or "low-income", we would like
to point out the following:

1. There currently exists on the Hill a total of 933 low-income public
    housing units. This constitutes approximately 12% of the total pub-
    lic housing in San Francisco.

2. According to the Housing Authority's estimate, there are about 4500
    residents in public housing on Potrero Hill. This constitutes ap-
    proximately 30% of the total population of the Hill.

3. Based on the data supplied by the Land-Use Survey, published by the
    City Planning Department, October 1964, Potrero Hill has a net area
    of little over 200 acres. 15% of this acreage is devoted to public
    housing. This compares with a city-wide average of only 1.5%; giv-
    ing Potrero Hill ten times the city average.

Potrero Boosters & Merchants Association

In addition to the above statistics, we should also like to point out that Potrero Hill is basically a middle-income area. The incomes of most residents are well within the ceilings established by the FHA for "moderate-income" housing ($7,500 to $11,450), and yet these residents are capable and willing to own or rent totally private housing free of government control or subsidy. Furthermore, since tax-forgiveness is a basic part of the "moderate-income" housing program, remaining taxpayers will have to share the burden of increased taxes to support such a program. This burden will be felt most by self-sustaining middle-income families. The logical approach is to place surplus property on the tax rolls in order to provide citizens some relief from the high degree of taxation we have today.

Despite the economic level of an area, the residents should have the opportunity of self-determination. If an area is overburdened with government controlled low or/and "moderate" income housing, any possibility of self-determination and upgrading will be destroyed, creating an economic ghetto. Such a situation is contrary to the aims of all social planners, who strive to create an economic cross-section within an area in order to establish a healthy community.

Potrero Hill is one of the last areas in San Francisco offering the opportunity to develop attributes of urban living, and this Hill well promises to be a fine area comprised of residents in all income categories.

The above mentioned facts should make it patently clear, that the community of Potrero Hill, consisting of self-sustaining middle-income and private and public low-income housing, would suffer a severe housing imbalance by the addition of any more government controlled housing, whether low or "moderate", which will not achieve Mayor Shelley's objective of balanced housing.

Therefore, for the above reasons, we urgently request that the Potrero Hill surplus school property (and any other city-owned property on this Hill that may be declared surplus) should be turned over to the Director of Property, for unrestricted sale for private development, under R-3.

The Boosters further propose that the property in question be divided into single lots in order that individuals may have an opportunity to purchase a portion of said property.

Your favorable consideration of our viewpoint, will be greatly appreciated.

Yours truly,

POTRERO BOOSTERS & MERCHANTS ASSN.

—————— President ————————

————— 1st Vice-President —————

CC: Mayor John S. Shelley   Mr. Harry Ross, Controller
    Board of Supervisors   Mr. Philip Rezos, Director of Prop.
    Mr. Thomas J. Mellon, C.O.A.   Arthur D. Little Co.
    Board of Education   Central Council of Civic Clubs

1069

Exhibit No. 39

EDWARD O. REYES
Attorney at Law
1419 Broadway, Suite 229
Oakland, California 94612

FOR THE CIVIL RIGHTS COMMISSION HEARING
MAY, 1967, AT OAKLAND, CALIFORNIA

THE UNEQUAL PROTECTION OF THE LAW
AS IT APPLIES TO THE SPANISH-SPEAKING PEOPLE

As a practicing attorney in the Bay Area and legal adviser
to the Community Service Organization and the G. I. Forum, I deal
with many Spanish-speaking people, both Mexican-Americans and
Puerto Ricans. I will limit my remarks to the impact that the law
has upon them. From the very moment that a police officer or any
other law enforcement agent apprehends or starts to investigate a
suspect who happens to be a Spanish-speaking individual, that individual is already one or two steps down from the other citizen.

Usually the investigating or arresting officer does not speak
Spanish; therefore, it follows that the individual suspect is deprived of the equal protection of the laws. Most police officers
instruct the individual who has been stopped or arrested: (1) that
he has a right to remain silent; (2) that he is entitled to have
an attorney represent him at all stages of the proceedings; (3)
that if he does not have money to hire a lawyer, one will be
appointed for him; and (4) that if he does say something, it may
be used against him during a trial of the matter under investigation. But if the accused or the individual apprehended does not
speak English, if he cannot understand the officer's instructions,
he does not have afforded to him those rights guaranteed to him
under the United States Constitution. Few police officers or investigators in metropolitan areas speak Spanish, even in those
areas where the Spanish-speaking group may be the largest minority.

If the individual has in fact been arrested or taken down to

headquarters for questioning, he is afforded no better relief.
Generally no one is available who is capable of functioning as an
adequate interpreter; there is no one who is unbiased, or who is
properly trained to interpret from English to Spanish and back
to English. Even Alameda County, which has over one million
inhabitants, has no uniform system for obtaining interpreters.
The California Government Code provides for interpreters to be
part of the Court Clerk system in counties which have over one
million inhabitants. At no additional cost to the County, a uniform Civil Service system could be installed, so that interpreters
would be on hand daily, available when needed for the orderly
execution of the judicial process.

Unfortunately, when a defendant does not speak English, he may
be compelled to await the arrival of an interpreter, or he may be
required to waste an additional day so that the interpreter can be
notified to be present in Court when the defendant is present.
This causes economic loss to the defendant. Until the interpreter
is obtained, the defendant may not even know what he is accused of,
or what may be done to get out on bail or on his own recognizance,
or how to contact friends, relatives, or employers on the outside.

In the very fortunate event that the county has a Public
Defender System to represent those who are too poor to hire their
own attorneys, there will be no deputy who speaks Spanish, or who
can communicate with the defendant through an interpreter sufficiently to prepare a proper investigation or defense of the case.
Such inadequate representation is virtually a violation of the
Sixth and Fourteenth Amendments of the United States Constitution,
guaranteeing due process--including representation by counsel--to
the accused. To those trained in the law, it is apparent that
proper communication is necessary between the defendant and his
attorney. Anything short of this is a farce and a travesty of
justice to the unfortunate accused.

1071

No judge of any Justice Court, Municipal Court, or Superior
Court located in the nine counties surrounding the San Francisco
Bay, speaks Spanish. This is no criticism of the judges themselves, but it is a sharp criticism of the system which does not
take into account the special problems of the Spanish-speaking
people. All the justice is not accomplished by the Courts in
open session; many rules of procedure by which the Courts operate
are agreed upon in judges' conferences, where no one speaks on
or is cognizant of the problems of the Spanish-speaking people.
How can these judges represent or speak for all of the community?
They don't understand the man, his problems, or his culture.

In the trial of a case--unless a jury is selected, at additional cost to the defendant in regard to attorneys' fees and
lost time from his job--a plea of not guilty is, before most
Judges, merely a "slow plea of guilty." Judges are prone--as
are juries--to mistrust someone who has to speak through an interpreter. The trial takes twice as long, and the Court may be impatient to go on with the rest of the heavy calendar. A trial
through an interpreter is like "shaking hands with justice with
a glove on." It is pretty close to justice, but not close enough.

If the defendant is found guilty by the Court or convicted by
a jury, then he must go through a probation department interview,
in the event that he may be eligible for probation. The same
problem that the defendant had when he was first stopped begins
all over again. The probation officer does not speak Spanish, or,
if by chance he does, he is overworked beyond description. If he
is any good, he has graduated from the probation department to
other, more lucrative jobs where the pressure is not so oppressive.

From beginning to end, because of his language barrier, his
natural timidity, and, as one writer said, his "edifice complex,"
the accused does not receive the equal protection of the law.
Our system continues to demand that unskilled workers be brought

into this country for work in the fields and in the factories at
low salaries. Therefore, it is an obligation of the community
to see that the people who perform these services are served themselves in these many law enforcement agencies, from the Police
Department through the Probation Department, in the language that
best affords communication between those serving and those served.

-oOo-

1073

Exhibit No. 40*

INDIVIDUAL COMPLAINT

*This complaint was submitted to the Commission and has been handled through the Commission's regular complaint procedure. It is available for inspection at the Commission's office, Washington, D.C.

1074

Exhibit No. 41

BART LABOR AGREEMENT

THIS AGREEMENT, made and entered into this __8th__ day
of ___April___, 1965, by and between the San Francisco Bay
Area Rapid Transit District, acting by and through its duly authorized
agent, Parsons Brinckerhoff-Tudor-Bechtel, and the International and
Local Unions signatory hereto, all of which (except the International
Brotherhood of Teamsters, Chauffeurs, Warehousemen and Helpers of
America) are affiliated with the Building and Construction Trades
Department of the AFL-CIO,

WITNESSETH:

WHEREAS, the successful completion of the San Francisco
Bay Area Rapid Transit District System is of the utmost importance
to the general public in the San Francisco Bay Area; and

WHEREAS, during the construction of the BART project,
large and varied segments of population will be directly and
indirectly involved; and

WHEREAS, the work to be done will require maximum cooperation from the many groups who will be involved; and

WHEREAS, large numbers of skilled and unskilled workmen
will be required in the performance of the construction work, and
the parties recognize that in all likelihood the majority of such
skilled and unskilled craftsmen will be represented by unions affiliated with the Building and Construction Trades Department of the
AFL-CIO or by the International Brotherhood of Teamsters, Chauffeurs,
Warehousemen and Helpers of America and employed by contractors who
are signatory to agreements with said labor organizations; and

WHEREAS, it is recognized that on a project of this magnitude, spreading over an area with multiple labor contracts and
employer associations, conflicts of interest could delay or disrupt
orderly completion of the project; and

WHEREAS, the parties recognize that it is to their mutual
interest to avoid strikes and other work stoppages on this project

1075

to the maximum extent possible, and to facilitate the orderly performance of the work, so as to reduce the cost to the public by improving
the efficienty of the operation,

NOW, THEREFORE, IT IS AGREED by the parties hereto as
follows:

Section 1. Definitions

(a) As used herein, the term "BART" means the San Francisco
Bay Area Rapid Transit District.

(b) As used herein, the term "BART project" means the
construction of the BART system.

(c) As used herein, the term "Unions" means the International and Local Unions signatory hereto, all of which (except the
International Brotherhood of Teamsters, Chauffeurs, Warehousemen and
Helpers of America and its signatory constituent locals) are affiliated
with the Building and Construction Trades Department of the AFL-CIO;
the term "Union" means any one of the Unions.

(d) As used herein, the term "Employers" means those
employers who, during the term of this Agreement, are or become signatory to or bound by any collective bargaining agreement, covering
construction work with any Union, which agreement is applicable
within the geographical area in which such Employer is to perform or
performs construction work on the BART project; the term "Employer"
means any such employer.

(e) As used herein, the term "Employer Association" means
any organization, association, council, corporation or other group
of Employers, or including Employers, which, to any degree, has or
exercises collective bargaining authority for and on behalf of any
Employer within the geographical area covered by the BART project.

(f) As used herein, the term "PBTB" means Parsons
Brinckerhoff-Tudor-Bechtel, a joint venture, as agent for BART.

(g) As used herein, the term "construction work" means

1076

the construction of facilities and works to be performed under
contracts let by BART and which are within the construction
jurisdiction of the Unions as recognized by the Building & Construction
Trades Department of the AFL-CIO or, in the case of the International
Brotherhood of Teamsters, Chaufferus, Warehousemen and Helpers of
America, as recognized by the Building & Construction Trades Department of the AFL-CIO when such union was a member thereof.

Section 2. Intention of the Parties
        The purpose of this agreement is to establish and maintain
harmonious labor relations on the BART project, and to preclude, to
the maximum extent possible, strikes, lockouts, and delays in the
prosecution of the work on said project.

Section 3. Scope of Agreement
        (a) This agreement shall apply to all construction work
performed on the BART project by employees represented by any Union
and employed by any Employer under the terms of a collective bargaining agreement with such Union, including, without limitation, all
additions, extensions, changes and extra work in connection therewith.
        (b) This agreement is not intended to, and does not,
cover all or any part of the operation of the BART system.
        (c) This agreement shall apply only to those employees
covered by any collective bargaining agreement referred to in
Section 1(d).

Section 4. Effect of Agreement
        (a) By executing this agreement, Unions agree to be
bound by each and all of the provisions herein. By accepting any
award of construction work, either as contractor or subcontractor (of
any level or tier), on any part of the jobsite of the BART project,
each employer who is or thereafter becomes an Employer agrees (as of
the time he is or becomes an Employer) (i) to be bound by each and

Every provision of this agreement, (ii) to execute, either personally
or through a duly authorized agent (in the form set forth in either
Exhibit A or Exhibit B hereto) its agreement to that effect, and
(iii) to require that any Employer which is a subcontractor to it
agree in writing (in the form set forth in either Exhibit A or Exhibit
B hereto) to be bound by the terms of this agreement.

(b)   This agreement is not intended to supersede existing
collective bargaining agreements already in existence or hereafter
executed between any Employer performing work on the BART project
and any Union, except to the extent the provisions hereof are inconsistent therewith.

(c)   Except as specifically provided in Section 6, this
agreement shall not affect territorial jurisdiction as between the
various Unions. Such territorial jurisdiction is recognized to be
as defined by Unions.

(d)   This agreement shall not apply to any operations of
PBTB or any of its constituent firms, or to the operations of any
employer other than on the BART project. None of the provisions of
this agreement shall affect or modify any existing or future agreements on other work in the area.

Section 5. No Strikes, Lockouts or Other Work Stoppages

(a)` ` During the duration of the BART project, or the term
of this agreement, whichever is the lesser, Unions agree (i) that
there will be no strikes, slowdowns, partial strikes, picketing, or
other work stoppages, or actions inducing or encouraging work
stoppages, of any kind or nature whatsoever, directed at or against
any Employer by any Union, and (ii) that no Union will honor any
picket line directed at or against any Employer by any other union
or unions. Each Employer agrees that, during the duration of the
BART project, or the term of this agreement, whichever is the lesser,
there will be no lockouts directed at or against any Union.

1078

(b) (i) Paragraph (a) of this Section 5 shall not apply to a Union or an Employer which is party to or bound by a collective bargaining agreement covering any part of the geographical area covered by the BART project during the period from the termination or opening of such collective bargaining agreement to the execution of a successor or amended collective bargaining agreement, and clause (ii) of said paragraph (a) shall not apply to any Union during such period with respect to such an Employer.

(ii) Paragraph (a) of this Section 5 shall not apply to any action or conduct by a Union against any Employer who has failed or refused either (a) to pay the fringe benefits provided for in the applicable collective bargaining agreement, or (b) to adhere to the provisions of such collective bargaining agreement with respect to the hiring of men; provided, however, that such action or donduct by a Union is specifically authorized by the applicable collective bargaining agreement of such Union, and provided, further, that the Union, before taking any such action or conduct, give written notice to PBTB forty-eight (48) hours in advance thereof stating the reason or reasons for the intended action or conduct and the Employer against whom such action or conduct is to be directed.

(c) In the event of any interruption of work on the BART project, the responsible officers or agents of the Union or Unions involved and of the Employer or Employers involved shall, in cooperation with BART and PBTB, promptly take all steps as are necessary or appropriate to remedy such interruption and will spare no effort in this regard until work has fully resumed.

Section 6. Movement of Men

When an Employer is awarded a specific contract that extends over more than one geographical jurisdiction of any Union it is agreed that the Employer shall request a conference with the local unions within whose geographical jurisdiction the work will be per-

formed before the work in question starts. At such conference the
estimated manpower to be needed will be stated by the Employer and
an agreement shall be reached as to the supply and movement of men
on such work. In the event of a failure to reach an agreement,
either the Employer or one of the local unions may appeal to the
International Union having jurisdiction for a decision. The Unions
and Employer mutually agree that men will be supplied and may be
moved in accordance with the terms of such agreement or decision
without delay to the progress of the work.

Section 7. Jurisdictional Disputes

(a) Jurisdictional disputes will be settled in accordance with the procedural rules of the National Joint Board for the
Settlement of Jurisdictional Disputes or any successor body thereto
which is set up by or recognized by the Building and Construction
Trades Department.

(b) PBTB shall, to the extent possible, coordinate work
assignments made by Employers on the BART project so that such
assignments will be both uniform and consistent with the various
jurisdictional agreements entered into between Unions and with the
jurisdictional awards of the Building and Construction Trades
Department.

Section 8. Grievance and Arbitration Procedures

In the event of any disputes or grievances of any kind or
nature whatsoever between any Union and any Employer, other than
jurisdictional disputes, such disputes or grievances shall be settled
in accordance with the grievance and arbitration procedures provided
for in the appropriate collective bargaining agreement. If such
agreement does not contain provisions for settlement of disputes by
grievance or arbitration, or if either party refuses or fails to
follow the grievance and arbitration procedures which are set

forth in such agreement, then any dispute arising between any Union
and any Employer operating under any such agreement shall be settled
in accordance with the following procedure:

Step 1: Upon receipt of written notification from
any Union or Employer of a dispute which is, for the
reasons hereinabove stated, unresolved, PBTB shall,
within a period not to exceed five (5) working days,
make an effort to settle the dispute between the appropriate Employer representative and the appropriate Union
representative.

Step 2: If, within said five (5) working days,
the dispute has not been resolved, the parties to such
dispute shall select an arbitrator to hear and determine
the same. If such parties cannot agree upon an arbitrator within three (3) working days following said five (5)
day period, or if such parties mutually desire, PBTB
shall request the Federal Mediation and Conciliation
Service to present a list of five recommended arbitrators.
PBTB shall then arrange for the Union and the Employer
involved alternately to strike names from said list
until a single name remains, who shall be the arbitrator
designated to hear the dispute.

The parties involved shall promptly submit the dispute to final and binding arbitration before said
arbitrator. The expenses of said arbitration shall be
borne equally by the Union and Employer involved.

Section 9. Project Labor Relations Committee

The parties hereto, together with representatives of
Employers and Employer Associations performing work on the BART
project, will form a permanent BART Project Labor Relations Committee

1081

for the purpose of considering specific labor relations problems
which may arise on the BART project, achieving prompt, peaceful and
mutually satisfactory solutions to such problems, recommending such
amendments or supplements to this agreement as may be necessary and
appropriate, and otherwise acting to promote harmonious labor relations on the BART project.

Section 10. Term of Agreement

This agreement shall become effective upon the date first
above written and shall continue in full force and effect to and
including December 31, 1970, or to the completion date of the BART
project, whichever comes first; provided, however, that any party
hereto may reopen this agreement as of October 1, 1966, upon giving
written notice of its desire to reopen to all other parties hereto
no less than sixty (60) days prior to October 1, 1966.

IN WITNESS WHEREOF, the parties hereto have executed this
agreement the day and year first above written.

SAN FRANCISCO BAY AREA RAPID TRANSIT DISTRICT
BY: PARSONS BRINCKERHOFF-TUDOR-BECHTEL, Its Agent

By _W. O. Legg_

F. W. Morrison

Agreement Adopted April 8, 1965

1082

AGREEMENT TO BE BOUND

The undersigned, as a contractor or subcontractor on the San Francisco Bay Area Rapid Transit District project, for and in consideration of the award to him of a contract to perform work on said project, and in further consideration of the mutual promises made in the "BART Labor Agreement", hereby:

(1)   Accepts and agrees to be bound by the terms and conditions of the "BART Labor Agreement", together with any and all amendments and supplements thereto;

(2)   Certifies that he has no commitments or agreements which would preclude his full and complete compliance with the terms and conditions of said agreement;

(3)   Agrees to secure from any Employer (as defined in said agreement) which is a subcontractor (of any tier) to him a duly executed Agreement To Be Bound in form identical to this document or to Exhibit B attached to said agreement.

Dated: _____

_____

By_____

EXHIBIT A

1083

AGREEMENT TO BE BOUND

The undersigned, an Employer Association as defined in the "BART Labor Agreement", as agent by and for those of its members listed below, for and in consideration of the award to one or more of such members of a contract to perform work on the BART project, and in further consideration of the mutual promises made in the "BART Labor Agreement", hereby:

(1) Warrants that it has the authority to execute this Agreement To Be Bound for and on behalf of its members listed below;

(2) For and on behalf of its members listed below, accepts and agrees to be bound by the terms and conditions of the "BART Labor Agreement", together with any amendments and supplements thereto;

(3) Certifies that none of its members has any commitments or agreements which would preclude their full and complete compliance with the terms and conditions of said agreement;

(4) For and on behalf of its members listed below, agrees that each of such members as may be awarded work on the BART project shall secure from any Employer (as defined in said agreement) which is a subcontractor (of any tier) to him a duly executed Agreement To Be Bound in form identical to this document or to Exhibit A attached to said agreement.

Dated _____

_____

By_____

Members Covered:

EXHIBIT B

Exhibit No. 42

BART ETHNIC COUNT ON-SITE
WORK FORCE

Count conducted between
May 12 - 18, 1967

	Journey-men	Neg.	Span.	Orien.	Amer. Ind.	Fore-men	Neg.	Span.	Orien.	Amer. Ind.	Appren.	Neg.	Span.	Orien.	Amer. Ind.	Total
Carpenter Pile Driver	314	39	14	0	2	75	0	1	0	0	13	1	4	0	0	402
Engineer Surveyor	230	3	13	2	2	28	0	6	0	0	1	0	0	0	0	259
Ironworker	45	0	13	0	0	10	0	1	0	0	3	0	0	0	0	58
Teamster	65	8	6	0	0	3	0	0	0	0	0	0	0	0	0	68
Cement Fin.	19	12	1	0	0	4	3	0	0	0	0	0	0	0	0	23
Laborer	492	236	86	1	7	41	7	3	0	2	0	0	0	0	0	533
Electrician	38	0	0	0	0	7	0	0	0	0	0	0	0	0	0	45
Plumber	2	0	0	0	0	1	0	0	0	0	0	0	0	0	0	3
TOTAL	1205	298	133	3	11	169	10	11	0	2	17	1	4	0	0	1391

Spanish and Oriental surnames are to be secured from the payroll when available; when not available, general foreman will be questioned.
Negroes are to be counted by visual methods.
Foremen and general foreman are to be reported in the same manner as journeymen; apprentices are to be reported in the same manner as journeymen.

	Neg.	Span.	Orien.	Amer. Ind.
On Site Office Force	1	1	7	0

Total office empls.   178

A.

Association of Bay Area Governments (ABAG), 107, 401, 445, 583, 708
Acorn Project, 348, 458, 465 ff.
Afro-American History and Culture, 234, 237, 239
Afro-American Institute, 384
Alameda County Building and Construction Trades Council, 317 ff.
Alameda County, Tri-City Area (Fremont, Newark, Union City), 587 ff.
  Board of Realtors, 162
  Commission Study of, 587
  Employment, 587
  Housing Discrimination, 594, 608 ff.
  Industry, 587, 590, 599 ff.
  Job Opportunities, 587 ff.
  Population, 17, 587
Allaire, Jerrold, 582
Alvarado, Manuel, 630
Alvarez, Salvadore, 547
American G.I. Forum, 510 ff.
Anderson, Arnold O., 648
Anthony, Earl, 232
Apartment House Association of Alameda County, 145
Atkinson, Robert F., 152

B.

Baker, Roe H., 81
Bay Area Rapid Transit (BART), 287 ff.
  Construction Activity, 287, 288
  Construction Costs, 287
  Employment Roll, 288
  Hiring Practices, 11, 287 ff., 334 ff.
  Relationship to Unions, 288
  Union Management, 288 ff.
  Work Forces Agreement, 288, 290 ff.
Batt, Leonard, 219
Becks, Edward, 222
Belardi, Joseph L., 378
Black Nationalism, 54 ff., 279
Black Planning Committee, 267
Black Power, 229, 268 ff., 274, 279, 280
Block-Busting, 165, 169
Bradley, George, 629
Bradley, William, 384
Brown, William, 560
Buchbinder, Lucy, 132

C.

California Real Estate Association (CREA), 10, 152 ff.
  Code of Practices, 155, 158, 163
  Equal Rights in Housing Program, 155 ff.
California State Advisory Committee, 6
California Fair Employment Practice Commission, 179, 201, 299, 300
Campbell, Captain Duncan A., 648
Catholic Council for the Spanish-Speaking, 429
Central Labor Council, 457 ff.
Childers, James, 316
Chinese Community, 197 ff.
  Attitude, 210
  Community Service Organization, 202
  Education, 199, 205, 208
  Employment, 201 ff.
  Health, 203
  History, 197 ff.
  Housing, 200, 203, 206
  Immigration, 200, 206, ff.
  Language problem, 199, 200, 202
  Population, 197, 199
  Unions, Exclusion from, 201 ff.
Christian Ranch, 92
Civil Rights Act of 1964, 149, 158, 308
  Whites' Role, 232, 233, 240
Clem, Al M., 302
Closing Statement, John A. Hannah, Chairman, 714
Comfort, Mark, 456
Community Action Training (CAT), 519, 527
Concord Citizens for Human Rights, 132
Connors, Donald D., 372
Contra Costa Board of Realtors, 63, 161
Corona, Bert, 243, 249
Council for Civil Unity, 133
Crocker Land Company, 92

D.

Daly City, 50, 93, 101
  Annexation Agreement with Suburban Realty, 93, 103
  Employment, 108 ff.
  Federal Subsidy Programs, 106
  Housing, 106, 112 ff.
  Minority Housing, 109 ff.
  Municipal Services, 103

1088

O.

Oakland
Citizens Housing Committee 709
Economic Development Council, 449, 474, 506, 519 ff., 699
Education, 459
Employment, 17, 444, 451, 457 ff., 494, 698 ff., 710
Enrichment Programs, 703
Exodus of Industry, 461
Housing Authority, 496
Housing Patterns, 706 ff.
Manpower Commission, 698 ff.
Political Structure, 448 ff.
Population, 16, 448, 451, 458, 465
Post Office Project, 339 ff.
Poverty Program, 475 ff., 504 ff.
Public Housing, 457 ff., 466, 468 ff.
Redevelopment Agency, 477 ff., 490 ff.
Relocation, 75, 465 ff.
Spanish - Speaking Community Development Program, 521
Suburbs, 443
Welfare, 467 ff.
Oakland Board of Realtors, 160
Oceanview, Racial Composition, 57
Oak Center Project, 465 ff.
Office of Federal Contract Compliance (OFCC), 355 ff.
Bonding for Minority Contractors, 348
Contractor Discrimination, 216, 289 ff., 347 ff.
Union Discrimination, 289 ff.
Olympic Club, 387
OMI Project (Oceanview, Merced Heights, Ingleside Community Stabilization and Improvement Project) 56 ff.
Attitude of Residents, 76 ff.
Economic Condition, 62
Effectiveness, 59 ff.
Employment, 66 ff.
Housing, 60, 78 ff.
Public Services, 68 ff.
Purpose, 57
Racial Composition, 74
Schools, 61 ff.
Open Housing, 132 ff.
CREA Position, 152 ff.
Effect of Possible Federal Law, 146
Proposition 14 (See Fair Housing Laws) 10, 122, 132, 171, 215
Opening Statements:
Eugene Patterson, Vice Chairman, 1
John A. Hannah, Chairman, 439

Opportunities Industrialization Center (OIC), 621, 623, 624, 628, 699, 713

P.

Padilla, Arthur, 421
Pike, The Rt. Rev. James A., 6
Pilgrim Men's Fellowship, 63
Pitts, Dr. Robert, 192
Pivnick, Isadore, 433
Polonsky, Albert, 103
Potrero Hill, 18 ff.
Public Housing, 20 ff.
Racial Composition, 20, 22
Potrero Hill Boosters and Merchants Association, 19
Racial Composition, 22, 23
Potrero Hill Citizen Improvement Assocation, 49
Potrero Hill Manpower Project, 49
Potrero Hill Residents and Home Owners Council, 29 ff.
Racial Composition, 52
Poverty
Bay Area, 16 ff.
As Equal Protection Argument, 447
Oakland, 17
Program Targets, 17
San Francisco, 16
Proposition 14 (See Fair Housing Laws) 10, 121, 122, 132, 171, 215
Pullman Company, 601

Q.

Quinta Sol, 547

R.

Randolph, Maxine, 56
Reading, Hon. John H., 695
Reagan, John M., 589
Redevelopment Research Program, 49
Relocating, 75
Rent Strike, San Francisco, 232
Rheem Manufacturing Company, 570 ff.
Hiring Practices, 573
Racial Composition of Employees, 573
Richards, James A., 280
Richmond, 549 ff.
Annexation of North Richmond, 549 ff.
Antidiscrimination Ordinance, 582
Berkeley Post, 581
Construction Contracts, 582
Employment, 580 ff.
Gambling, 565
Hensley Tract, 561 ff.
Human Relations Commission, 582 ff.

T.

Taylor, Walter C., 630
Trailmobile Manufacturing Company, 598 ff.
  Employee Personnel, 599
  Minority Personnel Housing, 600
  Number of Minority Employees, 601
  Recruitment Procedures, 601
Transportation, 48, 120
  BART, 286 ff.
Tuggle, Jack, 177

U.

Unions
  Apprentices, 305 ff., 319 ff., 327, 332, 367, 508
  Construction Workers, 311
  Culinary Workers of San Francisco, 378 ff.
  Discrimination, 318 ff., 337 ff., 374, 458 ff.
  Executive Order 11246, 329, 320, 341
  Hiring Halls, 307 ff., 312, 319, 327
  Ironworkers Union, 323
  Operating Engineers, 302, 308, 314, 318, 323
  Negro Membership, 307
  Training Program, 309, 314
  Plasterers Union, 322
  Plumbers Union, 318, 325, 330
  Steamfitters Union, 323
  Sheetmetal Union, 323
  Wage Rates, 335
  Welfare Benefits, 336
U.S. Naval Air Station, Alameda, 629 ff.
  Advisory Committee on Equal Employment, 631 ff., 650, 666

Civil Service Commission Report, 668
Employees' Council, 636
Employment of Minorities, 629 ff., 647, 655 ff., 663 ff.
Federal Employees' Equal Opportunities Organization, 636, 668
Industrial Relations Division, 637
Overhaul and Repair Department, 641, 648
Picketing and Demonstrations, 629, 650, 661
Promotions, 643, 651, 655, 660 ff.
Unruh Civil Rights Act, 110
Urban Problems, 395 ff.
Ussery, Wilfred T. 266

V.

Valdez, Armando, 244
Vaca, Nick C., 244
Vicario, Gabriel, 406

W.

Wallace, Clark, 152
Welfare People for Justice, 385
West Oakland, 465
  Acorn Project, 465 ff.
  Oak Center Project, 465 ff.
  Population, 465
  Racial Composition, 465
Williams, Earl, 39
Williams, John Bentley, 477
Williams, Ralph S., 467
Wolf, Eugene R., 477
Wong, Rev. Larry Jack, 197

Y.

Youth for Jobs, 460
Youth for Service, 274

☆ U. S. GOVERNMENT PRINTING OFFICE · 1967 O - 268-012

Lightning Source UK Ltd.
Milton Keynes UK
UKHW021827301218
334694UK00011B/691/P

9 781528 256889